003079
010082

The Bedford Anthology of
World Literature
The Middle Period, 100 C.E.–1450

D1370283

Book 2

The Bedford Anthology of
World Literature

The Middle Period, 100 C.E.–1450

EDITED BY

Paul Davis

Gary Harrison

David M. Johnson

Patricia Clark Smith

John F. Crawford

THE UNIVERSITY OF NEW MEXICO

BEDFORD / ST. MARTIN'S   Boston ♦ New York

For Bedford/St. Martin's

Executive Editor: Alanya Harter
Associate Developmental Editor: Joshua Levy
Production Editor: Paula Carroll
Senior Production Supervisor: Nancy Myers
Marketing Manager: Jenna Bookin Barry
Editorial Assistant: Jeffrey Voccola
Production Assistant: Kerri Cardone
Copyeditor: Melissa Cook
Map Coordinator: Tina Samaha
Text and Cover Design: Anna George
Cover Art: Persian Garden, fifteenth century, Persian School. Bibliothèque Nationale, Paris,
    France. © Ford / Bridgeman Art Library
Composition: Stratford Publishing Services, Inc.
Printing and Binding: R. R. Donnelley & Sons Company

President: Joan E. Feinberg
Editorial Director: Denise B. Wydra
Editor in Chief: Karen S. Henry
Director of Marketing: Karen Melton
Director of Editing, Design, and Production: Marcia Cohen
Managing Editor: Elizabeth M. Schaaf

Library of Congress Control Number: 2002112262

Copyright © 2004 by Bedford / St. Martin's

All rights reserved. No part of this book may be reproduced, stored in a retrieval system, or transmitted in any form or by any means, electronic, mechanical, photocopying, recording, or otherwise, except as may be expressly permitted by the applicable copyright statutes or in writing by the Publisher.

Manufactured in the United States of America.

8   7   6
f   e   d   c

For information, write: Bedford / St. Martin's, 75 Arlington Street, Boston, MA 02116
(617-399-4000)

ISBN: 0–312–24872–5

Acknowledgments

Dante Alighieri, "Inferno" from *The Divine Comedy,* translated by Robert Hollander and Jean Hollander. Copyright © 2002 by Robert Hollander and Jean Hollander. Reprinted with the permission of Anchor Books, a division of Random House, Inc.

Acknowledgments and copyrights are continued at the back of the book on pages 1213–17, which constitute an extension of the copyright page. It is a violation of the law to reproduce these selections by any means whatsoever without the written permission of the copyright holder.

PREFACE

☙ *The Bedford Anthology of World Literature* has a story behind it. In 1985, a group of us received a grant from the National Endowment for the Humanities. Our task: to develop and team teach a new kind of literature course—one that drew from the rich literary traditions of Asia, India, the Middle East, and the Americas as well as from the masterpieces of the Western world. We learned so much from that experience—from our students and from each other—that we applied those lessons to an anthology published in 1995, *Western Literature in a World Context.*

In that first edition of our anthology, our goal was to add works that truly represented *world* literature to the list of Western classics and to place great literary works in their historical and cultural contexts. We've kept that focus in the newly titled *Bedford Anthology*—but we've also drastically reshaped, redesigned, and reimagined it to make it the book you hold today. We talked to hundreds of instructors and students in an effort to identify and confirm what they considered challenging about the world literature course. The design and content of these pages represent our attempt to meet these challenges.

The study and teaching of world literature have changed significantly in the past twenty to thirty years. Formerly, most world literature courses consisted of masterpieces of Western literature, while the literary traditions of Asia, Africa, and Latin America were virtually ignored. The movement to broaden the canon to more accurately represent our world—and to better represent oral and marginalized traditions in the West—has greatly increased the number of texts taught in world literature courses today. Although the specifics remain controversial, nearly all teachers of literature are committed to the ongoing revaluation and expansion of the canon.

The last few decades have also seen instructors reconsidering the traditional methods of teaching world literature. In the past, most world literature courses were designed along formalistic or generic principles. But the expanded canon has complicated both of these approaches. There are no developed criteria for defining masterworks in such formerly ignored genres as letters and diaries or for unfamiliar forms from non-Western cultures, and we are frequently reminded that traditional approaches sometimes impose inappropriate Eurocentric perspectives on such works. As content and methodology for the course have been evolving, recent critical theory has reawakened interest in literature's historical and cultural contexts. All of these factors have both complicated and enriched the study of world literature. With this multivolume literature anthology, we don't claim to be presenting the definitive new canon of world literature or the last word on how to teach it. We have, however, tried to open new perspectives and possibilities for both students and teachers.

One anthology — six individual books. *The Bedford Anthology of World Literature* is now split into six separate books that correspond to the six time periods most commonly taught. These books are available in two packages: Books 1–3 and Books 4–6. Our motivation for changing the packaging is twofold and grows out of the extensive market research we did before shaping the development plan for the book. In our research, instructors from around the country confirmed that students just don't want to cart around a 2,500-page book — who would? Many also said that they focus on ancient literatures in the first semester of the course and on the twentieth

The Bedford Anthology of World Literature has been dynamically reimagined, redesigned, and restructured. We've added a second color, four hundred images, three hundred pronunciation guides, forty maps, six comparative time lines — and much more.

Portuguese Caravels Leaving to Explore the World, 1775   *The eighteenth century was a time of unprecedented global communication — political, social, economic, and literary. These painted blue tiles are found on the walls of the town of Paco de Arcos, near Lisbon, Portugal. (The Art Archive / Dagli Orti.)*

The Eighteenth Century

1650 - 1800

century in the second semester. In addition, many instructors teach an introduction to world literature that is tailored specifically to the needs of their students and their institution and thus want a text that can be adapted to *many* courses.

We believe that the extensive changes we've made to *The Bedford Anthology of World Literature* — breaking the anthology into six books rather than only two, creating a new two-color design, increasing the trim size, and adding maps, illustrations, numerous pedagogical features, an expanded instructor's manual, and a new companion Web site — will make the formidable task of teaching and taking a world literature course both manageable and pleasurable.

An expanded canon for the twenty-first century. In each of the six books of *The Bedford Anthology,* you'll find a superb collection of complete longer works, plays, prose, and poems — the best literature available in English or English translation. Five of the books are organized geographically and then by author in order of birth date. The exception to this rule is Book 6, which, reflecting our increasingly global identities, is organized by author without larger geographical groupings.

Aphra Behn's Oroonoko *is one of the texts we include in its entirety — highlighting important issues of race, gender, and slavery in the eighteenth century.*

☙ APHRA BEHN
1640–1689

Aphra Behn.
Engraving from
*Histories and
Novels, 1696.*
*This is the earliest
surviving image
of Behn. (The
Huntington Library,
San Marino, CA)*

Poet, playwright, and novelist Aphra Behn was one of the most prolific writers of her time. During a period in England when women were strongly discouraged from seeking literary recognition, she not only managed to earn a living as a professional writer but also directly engaged such traditionally "masculine" themes as political corruption, sexual politics, and social reform. In *Oroonoko* (1688), she openly addresses the complexities of rulership, sexual desire, and social injustice. Though her talent as a writer earned her much popularity and praise, the supposed presumptuousness and boldness of her work resulted in vicious attacks on her moral integrity. Associating her entrance into the public sphere of print and stage with prostitution, the satirist Robert Gould labeled her a vile "Punk¹ and Poetesse." Largely because of this stigma of indecency, publishers and scholars ignored Behn's work for years after her death. Only recently has she returned to center stage as a great literary talent, a major contributor to the development of the early English NOVEL, and a revolutionary figure in the tradition of women's writing in English.

Mystery, Travel, and Espionage. It is difficult to pin down the facts of Behn's early life. According to many sources, she was born near Canterbury to Bartholomew Johnson, a barber, and Elizabeth Denham. Her surprisingly advanced education and language skills (she was learned in Latin and French), which would have been unusual for a barber's daughter, might be attributed to a close association with the well-to-do family of Colonel Colepeper and to frequent exposure to Huguenot² and Dutch immigrants in Canterbury. Some recent scholarship, however, claims she was born in Kent and the daughter of John and Amy Amis or Amies. This would make her a possible relation, through her father, of Francis, Lord Willoughby of Parham, who at one time held a position for the British government in the West Indies. We know that in 1663 Behn traveled to the West Indies with her family after her father was named lieutenant-general of the colony of Surinam.³ Though the stay in Surinam only lasted two months (her father died on the voyage), this experience influenced the writing of her most famous narrative work, *Oroonoko.*

The circumstances surrounding the adoption of Aphra Behn's last name are even more cloudy than those of her birth. Though there is no extant marriage record, scholars speculate that after the trip to Surinam, Behn wed a London merchant or seaman of Dutch or German descent. If

---

¹ **punk:** Prostitute.

² **Huguenots:** French Protestants who were members of the Reformed Church established in France by John Calvin circa 1555. Because of religious persecution, they fled to other countries in the sixteenth and seventeenth centuries.

³ **Surinam:** A British sugar colony on the South American coast below Venezuela.

she married, she and her husband were together for only a short time before either he died or the two parted ways to live separate lives. More interesting is the suggestion that Behn imagined a spouse for herself so that she could gain the respectable title of widow. Several critics comment that, assuming Behn's maiden name was Johnson, taking the last name Behn creates an intriguing allusion to the famous seventeenth-century playwright Ben (Behn) Jonson.

The creation of a fictional husband may well seem like a bold act for a woman of the seventeenth century, but Behn was not one to shy away from taking chances or embarking on daring adventures. In 1666, for example, she served as a spy for Charles II (r. 1660–85) in the Anglo-Dutch War.⁴ Recruited by her associate Thomas Killigrew, she was charged with convincing one William Scot to be a double agent, reporting on expatriots, and providing information on Dutch military plans. Her foray into espionage was largely ignored — what information she provided to the English crown was largely ignored, and she was never repaid for her expenses. Deep in debt and forced to borrow money for the cost of her return to England, it is likely that she spent some time in debtor's prison in 1688.

Writing Politics and the Politics of Writing. Aphra Behn lived through a period of monumental political unrest and social change. In 1642, two years after her birth, England became embroiled in a bloody civil war over religious authority, class privileges, and economic practices, among other issues. Charles I (r. 1625–49) was brought to trial and executed in 1649. Despite the promise of a new kind of governance, the ensuing rule of Oliver Cromwell⁵ — under whom Britain was called the "Commonwealth," then the "Protectorate" — proved only that a citizen given the power to govern may be more ineffective and tyrannical than a monarch. The period known as the Restoration, beginning in 1660 with the restoration of Charles II as king of England, saw a newfound celebration of, and freedom in, the arts but did not provide long-term political stability. Charles's successor, James II (r. 1685–88), was quickly ousted and sent into exile, primarily because he was a professed Roman Catholic. In what is called the "Glorious Revolution" of 1688,⁶ the Dutch Protestant William of Orange and his wife Mary came to power.

As shown by her service as a spy for Charles II, Behn was dedicated to the preservation of the monarchy and to the system of aristocratic rule. Much of her work is informed by this sociopolitical agenda. In texts

---

⁴ **Anglo-Dutch War:** Battles between the British and the Dutch for control of the seas and trade routes (1652–84).

⁵ **Oliver Cromwell** (1599–1658): A soldier, politician, and staunch Puritan who attacked the bishops of the Church of England and advocated widespread political and religious reform. He came to power as "Lord Protector" of England (1653–58) shortly after the execution of Charles I.

⁶ **Glorious Revolution:** The birth of a son to the Catholic James II led prominent statesmen in England to invite Dutchman William of Orange and his wife, Mary, to assume the throne. William arrived in 1688, promised to protect the Protestant faith and the liberties of the English, and took the throne without opposition. James II, denounced by Parliament, fled to France.

www For links to more information about Behn and a quiz on *Oroonoko,* see *World Literature Online* at bedfordstmartins.com/worldlit.

We've tried to assemble a broad selection of the world's literatures. We've updated our selection of European texts; we have also included American writers who have had significant contact with world culture and who have influenced or defined who we are as Americans. And of course we have added many works from non-Western traditions, both frequently anthologized pieces and works unique to this anthology, including texts from Mesopotamia, Egypt, Israel, India, Persia, China, Japan, Arab countries of the Middle East, Africa, native America, Latin America, and the Caribbean.

Over thirty-five complete, longer works. These include Homer's *Odyssey* and *The Epic of Gilgamesh* in Book 1, Dante's *Inferno* and Kalidasa's *Śhakuntala* in Book 2, Marlowe's *Doctor Faustus* and Shakespeare's *The Tempest* in Book 3, Bashō's *The Narrow Road through the Backcountry* in Book 4, Dostoevsky's *Notes from Underground* in Book 5, and Achebe's *Things Fall Apart* in Book 6.

When a work is too long to be produced in its entirety, we've presented carefully edited selections from it; examples include the Rig Veda, *Ramayana, Mahabharata,* Qur'an, *The Thousand and One Nights, The Song of Roland,* Sei Shonagon's *Pillow Book,* Lady Murasaki's *Tale of Genji,* Cervantes's *Don Quixote,* Swift's *Gulliver's Travels,* Equiano's *Interesting Narrative,* Benjamin Franklin's *Autobiography,* Chikamatsu's *The Love Suicides at Amijima,* and Cao Xueqin's *The Story of the Stone.* In most cases the excerpts are not fragments but substantial selections wherein the structure and themes of the whole work are evident. The anthology also contains a generous selection of prose writing — short stories, letters, and essays.

Several hundred lyric poems. *The Bedford Anthology* includes the work of such fine poets as Sappho, Bhartrhari, Nezahualcoyotl, Petrarch, Kakinomoto Hitomaro, Rumi, Li Bai, Heine, Mirabai, Ramprasad, Baudelaire, Dickinson, Ghalib, Akhmatova, Neruda, Rich, and Walcott. Unique *In the Tradition* clusters collect poems that share a tradition or theme: poetry about love in Books 1, 2, and 3, Tang dynasty poetry in Book 2, Indian devotional poetry in Book 3, and poetry on war in Book 6.

∾ RAMPRASAD SEN
1718–1775

The intensely religious village life of India produced not only storytellers — whose primary purpose was transmitting the stories of gods, goddesses, heroes, and heroines — but also poets who expressed ordinary

BAHK-tee

people's spiritual longing for God. Emotional worship or surrender to God in Hinduism is called *bhakti,* a term that has its origins in the Upanishads. Bhakti became a religious movement in India during the religious reforms of the eighth, ninth, and tenth centuries. A particular version of

SHAHK-tee, KAH-lee
RAHM-pruh-sahd

bhakti was devoted to feminine divinity; in India there had been a long history of worshiping the greatgoddess **Shakti** — also known as **Kali** and Durga — but a resurgence of her worship, led by the poet **Ramprasad** Sen, took place in Bengal during the eighteenth century. Like medieval Christian poets devoted to the Virgin Mother, Bengal poets of this time favored the feminine dimension of God, which seemed to invite a personal relationship, an opportunity for conversation, and expressions of sadness and longing.

Ramprasad's poems, primarily songs to Kali, were extremely popular at the end of the eighteenth century when Bengal was in a time of darkness and despair. The region had been under Muslim rule for about five hundred years when the British defeated the Mughal army in the Battle of Plassey in 1757. Robber barons controlled large parts of Bengal, and Kali was their patron deity. Regional kings promoted Kali worship by supporting court poets who composed and sang songs to the goddess. The songs became part of an extremely precarious village life. Bengal is a region of

www   For links to more information about Ramprasad and a quiz on his poetry, see *World Literature Online* at bedfordstmartins .com/worldlit.

extremes, feast or famine, due to unpredictable rains. Some years bring little rain or droughts, while others have heavy rain and flooding. Occasionally there are years when just the right amount of rain falls at the appropriate times; these times are thought to be blessed by Kali.

Ramprasad's simple lyricism and familiar images touched a broad range of listeners; his songs appealed to scholars and peasants alike. His poetic skills influenced succeeding generations of Indian poets. Rabindranath Tagore,[4] the most famous Bengali writer of the late nineteenth cen-

[1] **Shakti:** Shakti is the collective name for the consort of Shiva who has several names. **Shakti** is the feminine dynamic energy by which God creates, preserves, and dissolves the world. **Kali** is usually portrayed as terrifying: blue-black, three-eyed, and four-armed, with a necklace of human heads and a girdle of severed hands. **Durga,** "the unfathomable one," is one of the oldest versions of the Great Mother: fair complexioned and riding a lion, she releases humans from rebirth with her touch.
[2] **Bengal:** A region in the northeast Indian peninsula, now divided between India and Bangladesh.
[3] **Battle of Plassey:** Plassey is a village in West Bengal state where the British defeated the Bengal army in 1757, leading to Britain's control of northeast India.
[4] **Rabindranath Tagore** (1861–1941): A native of Bengal anxious to preserve the cultural richness of traditional village life while at the same time bridging the philosophical and literary gap between East and West. (See Book 5.)

612

Literature in context. In addition to individual authors presented in chronological order, *The Bedford Anthology* features two types of cross-cultural literary groupings. In the more than thirty *In the World* clusters, five to six in each book, writings around a single theme—such as the history of religions, science, love, human rights, women's rights, colonialism, the meeting of East and West, imperialism, and existentialism—and from different countries and cultural traditions are presented side by side, helping students understand that people of every culture have had their public gods, heroes, and revolutions, their private loves, lives, and losses. Titles include "Changing Gods: From Religion to Philosophy," in Book 1; "Muslim and Christian at War," in Book 2; "Humanism, Learning, and Education" in Book 3; "Love, Marriage, and the Education of Women," in Book 4; "Emancipation," in Book 5; and "Imagining Africa," in Book 6. The second type of grouping, *In the Tradition,* presents poetry on love in Books 1, 2, and 3 and literature on war and American multiculturalism in Book 6. These clusters gather together such widely disparate figures as Hammurabi, Heraclitus, Marcus Aurelius, Li Bai, Ibn Battuta, Marco Polo, Joan of Arc, Galileo, Bartolomé de las Casas, Mary Wollstonecraft, Mary Astell, Shen Fu, Karl Marx, Elizabeth Cady Stanton, Swami Vivekananda, Aimé Césaire, and Bharati Mukherjee.

In the World *clusters bring together texts from different literary traditions and help students make thematic connections and comparisons.*

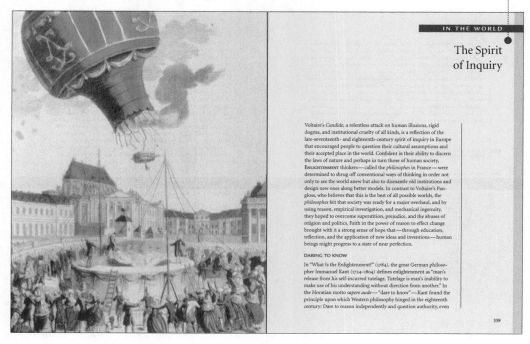

IN THE WORLD

The Spirit
of Inquiry

Voltaire's *Candide,* a relentless attack on human illusions, rigid dogma, and institutional cruelty of all kinds, is a reflection of the late-seventeenth- and eighteenth-century spirit of inquiry in Europe that encouraged people to question their cultural assumptions and their accepted place in the world. Confident in their ability to discern the laws of nature and perhaps in turn those of human society, ENLIGHTENMENT thinkers—called the *philosophes* in France—were determined to shrug off conventional ways of thinking in order not only to see the world anew but also to dismantle old institutions and design new ones along better models. In contrast to Voltaire's Pangloss, who believes that this is the best of all possible worlds, the *philosophes* felt that society was ready for a major overhaul, and by using reason, empirical investigation, and mechanical ingenuity, they hoped to overcome superstition, prejudice, and the abuses of religion and politics. Faith in the power of reason to effect change brought with it a strong sense of hope that—through education, reflection, and the application of new ideas and inventions—human beings might progress to a state of near perfection.

DARING TO KNOW

In "What Is the Enlightenment?" (1784), the great German philosopher Immanuel Kant (1724–1804) defines enlightenment as "man's release from his self-incurred tutelage. Tutelage is man's inability to make use of his understanding without direction from another." In the Horatian motto *sapere aude*—"dare to know"—Kant found the principle upon which Western philosophy hinged in the eighteenth century: Dare to reason independently and question authority, even

339

Helping students and teachers navigate the wide world of literature. The hundreds of instructors we talked to before embarking on *The Bedford Anthology* shared with us their concerns about teaching an introduction to world literature course, no matter what their individual agendas were. One concern was the sheer difficulty for students of reading literature that not only spans the period from the beginning of recorded literatures to the present but also hails from vastly different cultures and historical moments. Another was the fact that no one instructor is an expert in *all* of world literature. We've put together *The Bedford Anthology of World Literature* with these factors in mind and hope that the help we offer both around and with the selected texts goes a long way toward bringing clarity to the abundance and variety of world writings.

Helping students understand the where and when of the literature in the anthology. Each book of *The Bedford Anthology* opens with an extended overview of its time period as well as with a **comparative time line** that lists what happened, where, and when in three overarching categories: history and politics; literature; and science, culture, and technology. An interactive version of each time line serves as the portal to the online support offered on our Book Companion Site. In addition,

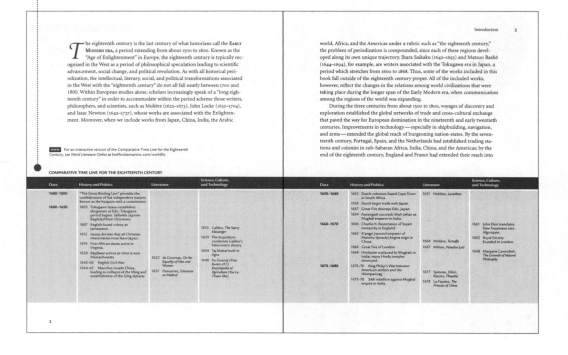

"Time and Place" boxes in the introductions to the different geographical group-ings of writers further orient students in the era and culture connected with the lit-erature they're reading by spotlighting something interesting and specific about a certain place and time.

Maps included throughout the anthology show students where in the world various literatures came from. Besides the maps that open each geographical section and show countries in relation to the larger world at a given time in history, we've supplied maps that illustrate the shifting of national boundaries; industrial growth; the effects of conquest, conquerors, and colonialism; and the travels of Odysseus, Ibn Battuta, and Bashō.

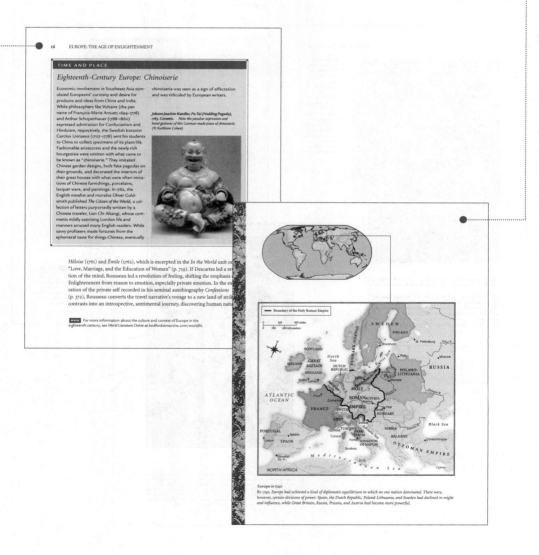

16   EUROPE: THE AGE OF ENLIGHTENMENT

TIME AND PLACE

Eighteenth-Century Europe: Chinoiserie

Economic involvement in Southeast Asia stim-ulated Europeans' curiosity and desire for products and ideas from China and India. While philosophers like Voltaire (the pen name of François-Marie Arouet; 1694–1778) and Arthur Schopenhauer (1788–1860) expressed admiration for Confucianism and Hinduism, respectively, the Swedish botanist Carolus Linnaeus (1707–1778) sent his students to China to collect specimens of its plant life. Fashionable aristocrats and the newly rich bourgeoisie were smitten with what came to be known as "chinoiserie." They imitated Chinese garden designs, built fake pagodas on their grounds, and decorated the interiors of their great houses with what were often imita-tions of Chinese furnishings, porcelains, lacquer ware, and paintings. In 1762, the English novelist and moralist Oliver Gold-smith published *The Citizen of the World*, a col-lection of letters purportedly written by a Chinese traveler, Lien Chi Altangi, whose com-ments mildly satirizing London life and manners amused many English readers. While savvy profiteers made fortunes from the ephemeral taste for things Chinese, eventually chinoiserie was seen as a sign of affectation and was ridiculed by European writers.

Johann Joachim Kandler, Pu-Tai (Nodding Pagoda), 1765. Ceramic. Note the peculiar expression and hand gestures of this German-made piece of chinoiserie. (© Kathleen Cohen)

Héloise (1761) and *Émile* (1762), which is excerpted in the *In the World* unit on "Love, Marriage, and the Education of Women" (p. 719). If Descartes led a revo-lution of the mind, Rousseau led a revolution of feeling, shifting the emphasis of the Enlightenment from reason to emotion, especially private emotion. In the explo-ration of the private self recorded in his seminal autobiography *Confessions* (p. 372), Rousseau converts the travel narrative's voyage to a new land of striking contrasts into an introspective, sentimental journey, discovering human natu

www   For more information about the culture and context of Europe in the eighteenth century, see *World Literature Online* at bedfordstmartins.com/worldlit.

—— Boundary of the Holy Roman Empire

SWEDEN

FINLAND

SCOTLAND
North
Sea
IRELAND   GREAT
BRITAIN   DENMARK-NORWAY
ENGLAND
DUTCH
REPUBLIC   POLAND-
LITHUANIA   RUSSIA

ATLANTIC
OCEAN   HOLY
ROMAN AUSTRIA
FRANCE   SWITZ. EMPIRE
SAVOY   HUNGARY
Black Sea
GENOA TUSCANY
PORTUGAL   PAPAL
STATES   SERBIA
SPAIN   KINGDOM   BALKANS
OF NAPLES   OTTOMAN EMPIRE
Sardinia
NORTH AFRICA   M e d i t e r r a n e a n   S e a   Cyprus

*Europe in 1740
By 1740, Europe had achieved a kind of diplomatic equilibrium in which no one nation dominated. There were, however, certain divisions of power: Spain, the Dutch Republic, Poland-Lithuania, and Sweden had declined in might and influence, while Great Britain, Russia, Prussia, and Austria had become more powerful.*

The anthology's many illustrations—art, photographs, frontispieces, cartoons, and cultural artifacts—are meant to bring immediacy to literature that might otherwise feel spatially and temporally remote. A few examples are a photo of the Acropolis today juxtaposed with an artist's rendering of what it looked like newly built, a sketch of the first seven circles of Dante's hell, a scene from Hogarth's *Marriage à la Mode*, the ad Harriet Jacobs's owner ran for her capture and return, an editorial cartoon mocking Darwin's evolutionary theories, and a woodcut depicting Japanese boats setting out to greet Commodore Perry's warship in their harbor.

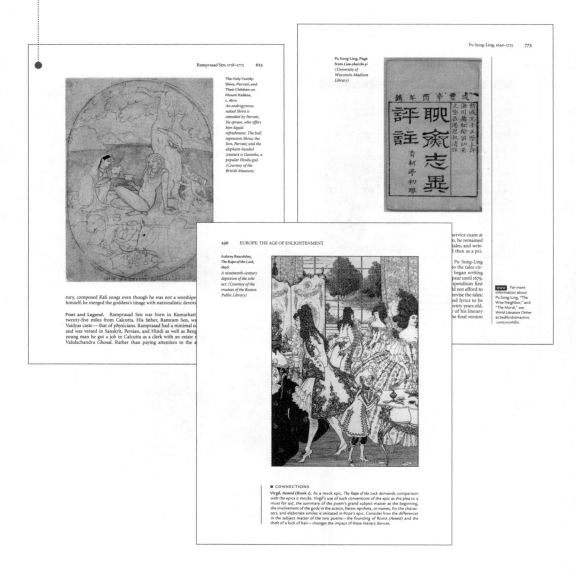

Ramprasaad Sen, 1718–1775   613

The Holy Family: Shiva, Parvati, and Their Children on Mount Kailasa, c. 1800
An androgynous, naked Shiva is attended by Parvati, his spouse, who offers him liquid refreshment. The bull represents Shiva; the lion, Parvati; and the elephant-headed creature is Ganesha, a popular Hindu god. (Courtesy of the British Museum)

tury, composed Kali songs even though he was not a worship... himself; he merged the goddess's image with nationalistic devoti...

Poet and Legend. Ramprasad Sen was born in Kumarhatt... twenty-five miles from Calcutta. His father, Ramram Sen, wa... Vaidyas caste—that of physicians. Ramprasad had a minimal e... and was versed in Sanskrit, Persian, and Hindi as well as Beng... young man he got a job in Calcutta as a clerk with an estate ... Valulachandra Ghosal. Rather than paying attention to the a...

Pu Song-Ling, 1640–1715   773

Pu Song-Ling, Page from *Liao-zhai zhi-yi* (University of Wisconsin–Madison Library)

service exam at ... n, he remained ... tales, and writ... I then as a pri-

Pu Song-Ling ... to the tales cir... A nineteenth-... pear until 1679, ... npendium first ... d not afford to ... revise the tales; ... nd lyrics to be ... venty years old, ... f his literary ... he final version

www For more information about Pu Song-Ling, "The Wise Neighbor," and "The Mural," see *World Literature Online* at bedfordstmartins .com/worldlit.

236   EUROPE: THE AGE OF ENLIGHTENMENT

Aubrey Beardsley, *The Rape of the Lock*, 1896
A nineteenth-century depiction of the title act. (Courtesy of the trustees of the Boston Public Library)

■ CONNECTIONS

Virgil, *Aeneid* (Book 1). As a mock epic, *The Rape of the Lock* demands comparison with the epics it mocks. Virgil's use of such conventions of the epic as the plea to a muse for aid, the summary of the poem's grand subject matter at the beginning, the involvement of the gods in the action, heroic epithets, or names, for the characters, and elaborate similes is imitated in Pope's epic. Consider how the differences in the subject matter of the two poems—the founding of Rome (*Aeneid*) and the theft of a lock of hair—changes the impact of these literary devices.

Practical and accessible editorial apparatus helps students understand what they read. Each author in the anthology is introduced by an informative and accessible literary and biographical discussion. The selections themselves are complemented with generous footnotes, marginal notes, cross-references, and critical quotations. Phonetic pronunciation guides are supplied in the margins of introductory material and before the selections for unfamiliar character and place names. Providing help with literary and historical vocabulary, bold-faced key terms throughout the text refer students to the comprehensive glossary at the end of each book.

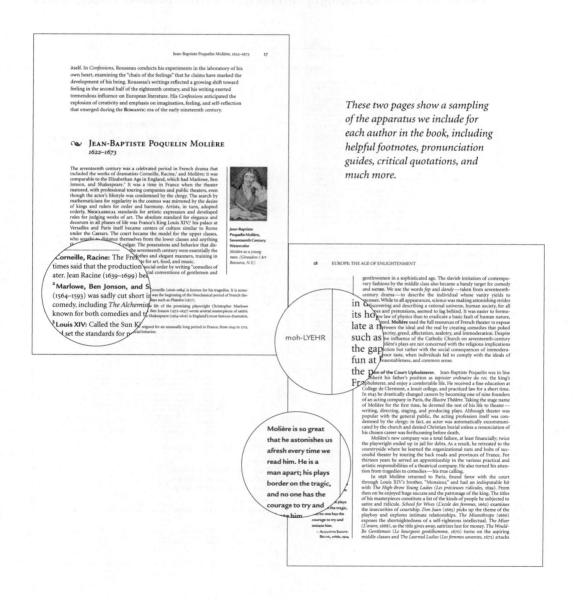

These two pages show a sampling of the apparatus we include for each author in the book, including helpful footnotes, pronunciation guides, critical quotations, and much more.

Jean-Baptiste Poquelin Molière, 1622–1673   17

itself. In *Confessions*, Rousseau conducts his experiments in the laboratory of his own heart, examining the "chain of the feelings" that he claims have marked the development of his being. Rousseau's writings reflected a growing shift toward feeling in the second half of the eighteenth century, and his writing exerted tremendous influence on European literature. His *Confessions* anticipated the explosion of creativity and emphasis on imagination, feeling, and self-reflection that emerged during the ROMANTIC era of the early nineteenth century.

JEAN-BAPTISTE POQUELIN MOLIÈRE
1622–1673

The seventeenth century was a celebrated period in French drama that included the works of dramatists Corneille, Racine,[1] and Molière; it was comparable to the Elizabethan Age in England, which had Marlowe, Ben Jonson, and Shakespeare.[2] It was a time in France when the theater matured, with professional touring companies and public theaters, even though the actor's lifestyle was condemned by the clergy. The search by mathematicians for regularity in the cosmos was mirrored by the desire of kings and rulers for order and harmony. Artists, in turn, adopted orderly, NEOCLASSICAL standards for artistic expression and developed rules for judging works of art. The absolute standard for elegance and decorum in all phases of life was France's King Louis XIV;[3] his palace at Versailles and Paris itself became centers of culture similar to Rome under the Caesars. The court became the model for the upper classes, who sought to distance themselves from the lower classes and anything ... vulgar. The possessions and behavior that dis- ... the seventeenth century were essentially the ... othes and elegant manners, training in the ... for art, food, and music. ... ocial order by writing "comedies of ... ial conventions of gentlemen and

Jean-Baptiste Poquelin Molière, Seventeenth Century. Watercolor Molière as a young man. (Giraudon / Art Resource, N.Y.)

Corneille, Racine: The Fre ... times said that the production ... ater. Jean Racine (1639–1699) be ...

[2] **Marlowe, Ben Jonson, and S** ... (1564–1593) was sadly cut short i ... comedy, including *The Alchemist* ... known for both comedies and t ...

[3] **Louis XIV:** Called the Sun K ... d set the standards for ...

Corneille (1606–1684) is known for his tragedies. It is some-
...was the beginning of the Neoclassical period of French the-
plays such as *Phaedra* (1677).
...life of the promising playwright Christopher Marlowe
...Ben Jonson (1572–1637) wrote several masterpieces of satiric
...Shakespeare (1564–1616) is England's most famous dramatist,
...reigned for an unusually long period in France, from 1643 to 1715,
...ocial behavior.

moh-LYEHR

Molière is so great that he astonishes us afresh every time we read him. He is a man apart; his plays border on the tragic, and no one has the courage to try and ... imitate him.
— AUGUSTIN SAINTE-BEUVE, critic, 1914

18   EUROPE: THE AGE OF ENLIGHTENMENT

gentlewomen in a sophisticated age. The slavish imitation of contemporary fashions by the middle class also became a handy target for comedy and SATIRE. We use the words *fop* and *dandy*—taken from seventeenth-century drama—to describe the individual whose vanity yields to ... cesses. While to all appearances, science was making astonishing strides in ... iscovering and describing a rational universe, human society, for all ... pes and pretensions, seemed to lag behind. It was easier to formu- late a n... w law of physics than to eradicate a basic fault of human nature, such as ... eed. Molière used the full resources of French theater to expose ... etween the ideal and the real by creating comedies that poked ... the gap ... ocrisy, greed, affectation, zealotry, and immoderation. Despite ... we influence of the Catholic Church on seventeenth-century ... fun at ... lière's plays are not concerned with the religious implications ... ection but rather with the social consequences of immodera- the p... oor taste, when individuals fail to comply with the ideals of Fr...apholsterer ... easonableness, and common sense.

...on of the Court Upholsterer. Jean-Baptiste Poquelin was in line ... inherit his father's position as *tapissier ordinaire du roi*, the king's ... upholsterer, and enjoy a comfortable life. He received a fine education at College de Clermont, a Jesuit college, and practiced law for a short time. In 1643 he drastically changed careers by becoming one of nine founders of an acting company in Paris, the *Illustre Théâtre*. Taking the stage name of Molière for the first time, he devoted the rest of his life to theater— writing, directing, staging, and producing plays. Although theater was popular with the general public, the acting profession itself was condemned by the clergy; in fact, an actor was automatically excommunicated by the church and denied Christian burial unless a renunciation of his chosen career was forthcoming before death.

Molière's new company was a total failure, at least financially; twice the playwright ended up in jail for debts. As a result, he retreated to the countryside where he learned the organizational nuts and bolts of successful theater by touring the back roads and provinces of France. For thirteen years he served an apprenticeship in the various practical and artistic responsibilities of a theatrical company. He also turned his attention from tragedies to comedies—his true calling.

In 1658 Molière returned to Paris, found favor with the court through Louis XIV's brother, "Monsieur," and had an indisputable hit with *The High-Brow Young Ladies* (*Les précieuses ridicules*, 1659). From then on he enjoyed huge success and the patronage of the king. The titles of his masterpieces constitute a list of the kinds of people he subjected to satire and ridicule. *School for Wives* (*L'ecole des femmes*, 1662) examines the insecurities of courtship. *Don Juan* (1665) picks up the theme of the playboy and explores intimate relationships. *The Misanthrope* (1666) exposes the shortsightedness of a self-righteous intellectual. *The Miser* (*L'avare*, 1668), as the title gives away, satirizes lust for money. *The Would-Be Gentleman* (*Le bourgeois gentilhomme*, 1670) turns on the aspiring middle classes and *The Learned Ladies* (*Les femmes savantes*, 1672) attacks

These terms cover the generic conventions of fiction, poetry, and drama; historical forms such as epic, epigram, and myth; and relevant historical periods such as the European Enlightenment or the Edo period in Japan.

Making connections among works from different times and places. At the end of each author introduction are two catalysts for further thought and discussion. **Questions** in the Connections apparatus tie together Western and world texts, both those within a single book and selections from other centuries, making the six books more of a unit and aiding in their interplay. **Further Research bibliographies**

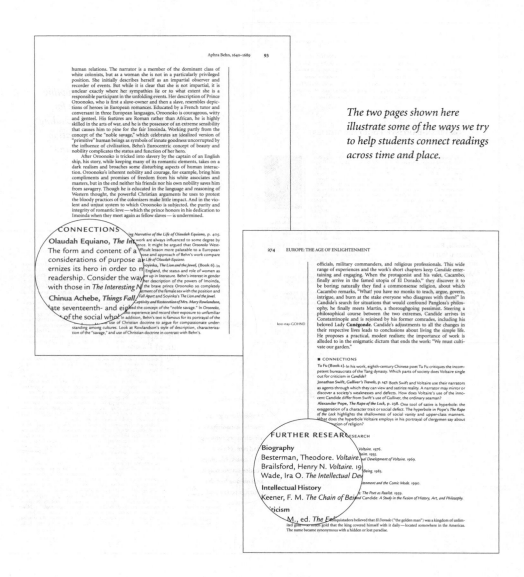

The two pages shown here illustrate some of the ways we try to help students connect readings across time and place.

provide sources for students who want to read more critical, biographical, or historical information about an author or a work.

Print and online ancillaries further support the anthology's material. Two instructor's manuals, *Resources for Teaching THE BEDFORD ANTHOLOGY OF WORLD LITERATURE,* accompany Books 1–3 and Books 4–6 (one for each package), providing additional information about the anthology's texts and the authors, suggestions for discussion and writing prompts in the classroom and beyond, and additional connections among texts in the six books.

We are especially enthusiastic about our integrated Book Companion Site, *World Literature Online,* which provides a wealth of content and information that only the interactive medium of the Web can offer. **Web links** throughout the anthology direct

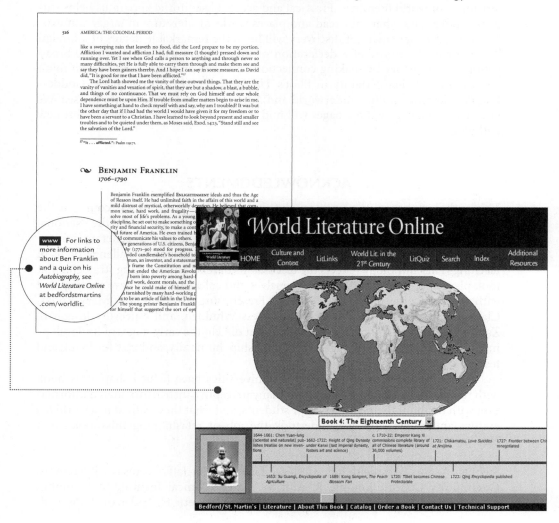

students to additional content on the Web site, where interactive illustrated time lines and maps serve as portals to more information about countries, texts, and authors. Culture and Context overviews offer additional historical background and annotated research links that students can follow to learn more on their own. Illustrated World Literature in the Twenty-First Century discussions trace the enduring presence in contemporary culture of the most frequently taught texts in world literature courses. Maps from the book are available online. Quizzes in LitQuiz offer an easy way for instructors to assess students' reading and comprehension. And LitLinks — annotated research links — provide a way for students to learn more about individual authors.

This wide variety of supplementary materials, as well as the broad spectrum of literary texts, offers teachers choices for navigating the familiar and the unfamiliar territories of world literature. Practical and accessible editorial apparatus helps students understand what they read and places works of literature in larger contexts. For some, the excitement of discovery will lie in the remarkable details of a foreign setting or in the music of a declaration of love. Others will delight in the broad panorama of history by making connections between an early cosmological myth and the loss of that certainty in Eliot's *The Waste Land* or between the Goddess Inanna's descent into the underworld and Adrienne Rich's descent into the sea. We hope all who navigate these pages will find something that thrills them in this new anthology.

ACKNOWLEDGMENTS

This anthology began in a team-taught, multicultural "great books" course at the University of New Mexico, initially developed with a grant from the National Endowment for the Humanities. The grant gave us ample time to generate the curriculum for the course, and it also supported the luxury and challenge of team teaching. This anthology reflects the discussions of texts and teaching strategies that took place over many years among ourselves and colleagues who have participated with us in teaching the course — Cheryl Fresch, Virginia Hampton, Mary Rooks, Claire Waters, Richard K. Waters, Mary Bess Whidden, and especially Joseph B. Zavadil, who began this anthology with us but died in the early stages of its development. Joe's spirit — his courage, wit, scholarship, humanity, and zest for living and teaching — endures in this book.

Reviewers from many colleges and universities have helped shape this book with their advice and suggestions. And many perceptive instructors shared information with us about their courses, their students, and what they wanted in a world literature anthology when we undertook the job of refashioning this book's first edition. We thank them all:

Stephen Adams, Westfield State College; Tamara Agha-Jaffar, Kansas City, Kansas, Community College; Johnnie R. Aldrich, State Technical Institute at Memphis; Allison Alison, Southeastern Community College; Jannette H. Anderson, Snow College; Kit Andrews, Western Oregon University; Joan Angelis, Woodbury University; Shirley Ariker, Empire State College; Sister Elena F. Arminio, College of Saint Elizabeth; Rose Lee Bancroft, Alice Lloyd College; John Bartle, Hamilton College; Amy M. Bawcom, University of Mary Hardin-Baylor; M. Susan Beck, University of Wisconsin-River Falls; Frank Beesley, Dalton State College; Peter Benson, Farleigh Dickinson University; Michael Bielmeier, Silver Lake College; Dale B. Billingsley, University of Louisville; Mark Bingham, Union University; Stephen Black, Dyersburg State Community College; Neil Blackadder, Knox College; Tyler Blake, MidAmerica Nazarene University; Gene Blanton, Jacksonville State University; James Boswell Jr., Harrisburg Area Community College; Lisa S. Bovelli, Itasca Community College; Lois Bragg, Gallaudet University; Kristin Ruth Brate, Arizona Western College; Marie Brenner, Bethel College; Linda Brown, Coastal Georgia Community College; Keith Callis, Crichton College; Charles P. Campbell, New Mexico Tech.; Zuoya Cao, Lincoln University; William Carpenter, College of Maine Atlantic; May Charles, Wheeling Jesuit College; R. J. Clougherty, Tennessee Technical College; Helen Connell, Barry University; Lynn Conroy, Seton Hill College; Sue Coody, Weatherford College; Thomas A. Copeland, Youngstown State University; Peter Cortland, Quinnipiac University; R. Costomiris, Georgia Southern University; H. J. Coughlin, Eastern Connecticut State University; Marc D. Cyr, Georgia Southern University; Sarah Dangelantonio, Franklin Pierce College; James Davis, Troy State University; Barbara Dicey, Wallace College; Wilfred O. Dietrich, Blinn College; Michael Dinielli, Chaffey College; Matt Djos, Mesa State College; Marjorie Dobbin, Brewton-Parker College; Brian L. Dose, Martin Luther College; Dawn Duncan, Concordia College; Bernie Earley, Tompkins-Cortland Community College; Sarah M. Eichelman, Walters State Community College; Robert H. Ellison, East Texas Baptist University; Joshua D. Esty, Harvard University; Robert J. Ewald, University of Findlay; Shirley Felt, Southern California College; Lois Ferrer, CSU Dominguez Hills; Patricia Fite, University of the Incarnate Word; Sr. Agnes Fleck, St. Scholastica College; Robert Fliessner, Central State University; M. L. Flynn, South Dakota State University; Keith Foster, Arkansas State University; John C. Freeman, El Paso Community College; Doris Gardenshire, Trinity Valley Community College; Susan Gardner, University of North Carolina-Charlotte; Jerry D. Gibbens, Williams Baptist College; Susan Gilbert, Meredith College; Diana Glyer, Azusa Pacific University; Irene Gnarra, Kean University; R. C. Goetter, Glouster Community College; Nancy Goldfarb, Western Kentucky University; Martha Goodman, Central Virginia Community College; Lyman Grant, Austin Community College; Hazel Greenberg, San Jacinto College South; Janet Grose, Union University; Sharon Growney-Seals, Ouachita Technical College; Rachel Hadas, Rutgers University; Laura Hammons, East Central Community College; Carmen Hardin, University of Louisville; Darren Harris-Fain, Shawnee State University; Patricia B. Heaman, Wilkes University; Charles Heglan, University of South Florida; Dennis E. Hensley, Taylor University; Kathleen M. Herndon, Weber State University; Betty Higdon, Reedley College; David Hoegberg, Indiana University; Diane Long Hoeveler, Marquette University; Tyler Hoffman, Rutgers University; Lynn Hoggard, Midwestern State University; Greg Horn, Southwest Virginia Community College; Roger Horn, Charles County Community

College; Malinda Jay-Bartels, Gulf Coast Community College; Mell Johnson, Wallace State Community College; Kathryn Joyce, Santa Barbara City College; Steven Joyce, Ohio State University-Mansfield; Ronald A. T. Judy, University of Pittsburgh; Alan Kaufman, Bergen Community College; Tim Kelley, Northwest-Shoals Community College; Shoshanna Knapp, Virginia Technical College; Jim Knox, Roane State Community College; Mary Kraus, Bob Jones University; F. Kuzman, Bethel College; Kate Kysa, Anoka-Ramsey Community College; Linda L. Labin, Husson College; Barbara Laman, Dickinson State University; R. Scott Lamascus, Georgia-Southwestern State University; Sandi S. Landis, St. Johns River Community College; Ben Larson, York College; Craig Larson, Trinidad State Junior College; Linda M. Lawrence, Georgia Military College; Simon Lewis, C. of Charleston; Gary L. Litt, Moorhead State University; H. W. Lutrin, Borough of Manhattan Community College; Dennis Lynch, Elgin Community College; Donald H. Mager, Johnson C. Smith University; Barbara Manrique, California State University; W. E. Mason, Mid-Continent College; Judith Matsunobu, Atlantic Community College; Noel Mawer, Edward Waters College; Patrick McDarby, St. John's University; Judy B. McInnis, University of Delaware; Becky McLaughlin, University of Southern Alabama; Edward E. Mehok, Notre Dame College of Ohio; Patricia Menhart, Broward Community College; Arthur McA. Miller, New College of Florida; Mark James Morreale, Marist College; Toni Morris, University of Indianapolis; Philip Mosley, Penn State–Worthington; George Mower, Community College of Alleghany County; L. Carl Nadeau, University of St. Francis; Walter Nelson, Red Rocks Community College; Steven Neuwirth, Western Connecticut State University; Carol H. Oliver, St. Louis College of Pharmacy; Richard Orr, York Technical College; Geoffrey Orth, Longwood College; Ramenga M. Osotsi, James Madison University; Bonnie Pavlis, Riverside Community College; Craig Payne, Indian Hills College; Leialoha Perkins, University of Hawaii; Ralph Perrico, Mercyhurst College; Charles W. Pollard, Calvin College; Michael Popkin, Touro College; Victoria Poulakis, Northern Virginia Community College; Alan Powers, Bristol Community College; Andrew B. Preslar, Lamar University; Evan Radcliffe, Villanova University; Belle Randall, Cornish College of the Arts; Elaine Razzano, Lyndon State College; Lucia N. Robinson, Okaloosa-Walton Community College; John Rooks, Morris College; William T. Ross, University of South Florida; Andrew Rubenfeld, Stevens Institute of Technology; Elizabeth S. Ruleman, Tennessee Wesleyan College; Olena H. Saciuk, Inter-American University; Mary Lynn Saul, Worcester State College; MaryJane Schenck, University of Tampa; Kevin Schilbrack, Wesleyan College; Deborah Schlacks, University of Wisconsin; Michael Schroeder, Savannah State University; Helen Scott, Wilkes University; Asha Sen, University of Wisconsin; Mary Sheldon, Washburn University; Lisa Shoemaker, State Technical Community College; Jack Shreve, Allegany College of Maryland; Meg Simonton, Albertson College; Susan Sink, Joliet Junior College; Henry Sloss, Anne Arundel Community College; T. Sluberski, Concordia University; Betty Smith, The Criswell College; Jane Bouman Smith, Winthrop University; John Somerville, Hillsdale College; Claudia Stanger, Fullerton College; Patrick Sullivan, Manchester Community-Technical College; Joan S. Swartz, Baptist

Bible College of PA; Leah Swartz, Maryville University; Sister Renita Tadych, Silver Lake College; Janet Tarbuck, Kennebee Valley Technical College; Gina Teel, Southeast Arkansas College; Daniel Thurber, Concordia University; John Paul Vincent, Asbury College; Paul Vita, Morningside College; Tim Walsh, Otera Junior College; Julia Watson, Ohio State University; Patricia J. Webb, Maysville Community College; Lynne Weller, John Wood Community College; Roger West, Trident Technical College; Katherine Wikoff, Milwaukee School of Engineering; Evelyn M. Wilson, Tarrant County College; Carmen Wong, John Lyle Community College; Paul D. Wood, Paducah Community College; Fay Wright, North Idaho College; and finally, Pamela G. Xanthopoulos, Jackson State Community College.

We also want to thank a special group of reviewers who looked in depth at the manuscript for each book, offering us targeted advice about its strengths and weaknesses:

Cora Agatucci, Central Oregon Community College; Michael Austin, Shepherd College; Maryam Barrie, Washtenaw Community College; John Bartle, Hamilton College; Jeffry Berry, Adrian College; Lois Bragg, Gallaudet University; Ron Carter, Rappahannock Community College; Robin Clouser, Ursinus College; Eugene R. Cunnar, New Mexico State University; Karen Dahr, Ellsworth Community College; Kristine Daines, Arizona State University; Sarah Dangelantonio, Franklin Pierce College; Jim Doan, Nova SE University; Melora Giardetti, Simpson College; Audley Hall, North West Arkansas Community College; Dean Hall, Kansas State University; Wail Hassan, Illinois State University; Joris Heise, Sinclair Community College; Diane Long Hoeveler, Marquette University; Glenn Hopp, Howard Payne University; Mickey Jackson, Golden West College; Feroza Jussawalla, University of New Mexico; Linda Karch, Norwich University; David Karnos, Montana State University; William Laskowski, Jamestown College; Pat Lonchar, University of the Incarnate Word; Donald Mager, The Mott University; Judy B. McInnis, University of Delaware; Becky McLaughlin, University of South Alabama; Tony J. Morris, University of Indianapolis; Deborah Schlacks, University of Wisconsin; James Snowden, Cedarville University; David T. Stout, Luzerne County Community College; Arline Thorn, West Virginia State College; Ann Volin, University of Kansas; Mary Wack, Washington State University; Jayne A. Widmayer, Boise State University; and William Woods, Wichita State University.

No anthology of this size comes into being without critical and supportive friends and advisors. Our thanks go to the Department of English at the University of New Mexico (UNM); its chair, Scott Sanders, who encouraged and supported our work; and Margaret Shinn and the office staff, who provided administrative and technical assistance. Among our colleagues at UNM, we particularly want to thank Gail Baker, Helen Damico, Reed Dasenbrock, Patrick Gallacher, Feroza Jussawalla, Michelle LeBeau, Richard Melzer, Mary Power, Diana Robin, and Hugh Witemeyer. Several graduate students also helped with this project: Jana Giles contributed the final section on American multicultural literature; Mary Rooks wrote the sections on Aphra Behn and Wole Soyinka and served heroically as our assistant, record keeper, all-purpose editor, and consultant.

We have benefited from the knowledge and suggestions of those who have corrected our misunderstandings, illuminated topics and cultures with which we were unfamiliar, critiqued our work, and suggested ways to enrich the anthology: Paula Gunn Allen, Reynold Bean, Richard Bodner, Machiko Bomberger, Robert Dankoff, Kate Davis, Robert Hanning, Arthur Johnson, Dennis Jones, James Mischke, Harlan Nelson, Barrett Price, Clayton Rich, Julia Stein, Manjeet Tangri, William Witherup, Diane Wolkstein, and William Woods.

Resources for Teaching THE BEDFORD ANTHOLOGY OF WORLD LITERATURE was expertly developed, edited, and assembled by Mary Rooks, assisted by Julia Berrisford. Along with Mary, Shari Evans, Gabriel Gryffyn, Rick Mott, Susan Reese, Kenneth Kitchell, Randall Colaizzi, Bainard Cowan, William Flesch, Fidel Fajardo-Acosta, Yigal Levin, and John Phillips each wrote a section of the manual. The manual itself was a large and challenging endeavor; we are grateful to its authors for their enthusiasm and hard work.

A six-volume anthology is an undertaking that calls for a courageous, imaginative, and supportive publisher. Chuck Christensen, Joan Feinberg, Karen Henry, and Steve Scipione at Bedford/St. Martin's possess these qualities; we especially appreciate their confidence in our ability to carry out this task. Our editor, Alanya Harter, and her associate, Joshua Levy, have guided the project throughout, keeping us on track with a vision of the whole when we were discouraged and keeping the day-to-day work moving forward. In particular, they helped us to reconceptualize the anthology's format and content. Without their suggestions, unacknowledged contributions, and guidance, this anthology would not be what it is today. They were assisted by many others who undertook particular tasks: The brilliant design was conceived by Anna George; Genevieve Hamilton helped to manage the art program, and together with Julia Berrisford she managed the final stages of development. Martha Friedman served as photo researcher, and Tina Samaha was design consultant and map coordinator. Jeff Voccola acted as editorial assistant, taking on many tasks, including the onerous ones of pasting up and numbering the manuscript. Ben Fortson expertly and efficiently supplied the pronunciation guides. Harriet Wald tirelessly and imaginatively oversaw the content and production of the Web site, an enormous task; she was helped along the way by Coleen O'Hanley, Chad Crume, and Dave Batty. Jenna Bookin Barry enthusiastically developed and coordinated the marketing plan, especially challenging when six books publish over a span of six months.

We were blessed with a superb production team who took the book from manuscript to final pages. For Books 4 and 6, we owe special thanks to Senior Production Editor Karen Baart, whose dedication and eye for detail made the project better in every way. Stasia Zomkowski efficiently served as production editor for Books 3 and 5, Ara Salibian for Book 1, and Paula Carroll for Book 2; they were ably assisted by Courtney Jossart, Kerri Cardone, and Tina Lai. Melissa Cook's careful and thoughtful copyediting helped to give consistency and clarity to the different voices that contributed to the manuscript. Managing Editor Elizabeth Schaaf oversaw the whole process and Senior Production Supervisor Nancy Myers realized our final vision of design and content in beautifully bound and printed books.

Most of all, we thank our families, especially Mary Davis, Marlys Harrison, and Mona Johnson, for their advice, stamina, and patience during the past three years while this book has occupied so much of our time and theirs.

Paul Davis
Gary Harrison
David M. Johnson
Patricia Clark Smith
John F. Crawford

A NOTE ON TRANSLATION

Some translators of literary works into English tended to sacrifice form for literal meaning, while others subordinated literal meaning to the artistry of the original work. With the increasing number of translations of world literature available by a range of translators, it has become possible to select versions that are clear and accessible as well as literally and aesthetically faithful to the original. Thus our choice of Robert Fitzgerald's *Iliad* and *Odyssey,* Horace Gregory's poems by Catullus, Mary Barnard's poems by Sappho, Theodore Morrison's *Canterbury Tales,* Edward Seidensticker's *Tale of Genji,* and Willa and Edwin Muir's *The Metamorphosis,* among others.

There are those who question whether poetry can ever be adequately translated from one language and culture into another; our concern, however, is not with what might be lost in a translation but with what is gained. The best translations do not merely duplicate a work but re-create it in a new idiom. Coleman Barks's poems of Rumi, Stephen Mitchell's poems of Rilke, Miguel León-Portilla's translations of Nahuatl poetry, and David Hinton's poems of the Tang dynasty are in a way outstanding English poems in their own right. And William Kelly Simpson's love poems of ancient Egypt, Robert and Jean Hollander's *Inferno,* Richard Wilbur's *Tartuffe,* W. S. Merwin's poems of Ghalib, Judith Hemschemeyer's poems of Anna Akhmatova, and Robert Bly's poems of Pablo Neruda are examples of translations done by major poets whose renderings are now an important part of their own body of work. Michael Swanton's prose translation of *Beowulf* renders this challenging work with consummate accuracy and fidelity to the text.

Barbara Stoler Miller's translation of the Bhagavad Gita and Donald Keene's translation of Chikamatsu's *Love Suicides at Amijima* communicate the complexity of a literary work. Richard Bodner's contemporary translation of Bashō's *The Narrow Road through the Backcountry,* especially commissioned, does justice to both the prose and the resonant haiku in that work. David Luke's excellent translation of *Death in Venice* pays tribute to Thomas Mann's original German and is at the same time very readable.

More is said about the translations in this book in the notes for individual works.

About the Editors

Paul Davis (Ph.D., University of Wisconsin), professor emeritus of English at the University of New Mexico, has been the recipient of several teaching awards and academic honors, including that of Master Teacher. He has taught courses since 1962 in composition, rhetoric, and nineteenth-century literature and has written and edited many scholarly books, including *The Penguin Dickens Companion* (1999), *Dickens A to Z* (1998), and *The Life and Times of Ebeneezer Scrooge* (1990). He has also written numerous scholarly and popular articles on solar energy and Victorian book illustration.

Gary Harrison (Ph.D., Stanford University), professor and director of undergraduate studies at the University of New Mexico, has won numerous fellowships and awards for scholarship and teaching. He has taught courses in world literature, British Romanticism, and literary theory at the University of New Mexico since 1987. Harrison's publications include a critical study on William Wordsworth, *Wordsworth's Vagrant Muse: Poetry, Poverty and Power* (1994); and many articles on the literature and culture of the early nineteenth century.

David M. Johnson (Ph.D., University of Connecticut), professor emeritus of English at the University of New Mexico, has taught courses in world literature, mythology, the Bible as literature, philosophy and literature, and creative writing since 1965. He has written, edited, and contributed to numerous scholarly books and collections of poetry, including *Fire in the Fields* (1996) and *Lord of the Dawn: The Legend of Quetzalcoatl* (1987). He has also published scholarly articles, poetry, and translations of Nahuatl myths.

Patricia Clark Smith (Ph.D., Yale University), professor emerita of English at the University of New Mexico, has taught courses in world literature, creative writing, American literature, and Native American literature since 1971. Her many publications include a collection of poetry, *Changing Your Story* (1991); the biography *As Long as the Rivers Flow* (1996); and *On the Trail of Elder Brother* (2000).

John F. Crawford (Ph.D., Columbia University), associate professor of English at the University of New Mexico–Valencia, has taught medieval, world, and other literature courses since 1965 at a number of institutions, including California Institute of Technology, Herbert Lehman College of CUNY, and, most recently, the University of New Mexico. The publisher of West End Press, Crawford has also edited *This Is About Vision: Interviews with Southwestern Writers* (1990) and written articles on multicultural women poets of the Southwest.

Pronunciation Key

This key applies to the pronunciation guides that appear in the margins and before most selections in *The Bedford Anthology of World Literature*. The syllable receiving the main stress is CAPITALIZED.

a	mat, alabaster, laugh	MAT, AL-uh-bas-tur, LAF
ah	mama, Americana, Congo	MAH-mah, uh-meh-rih-KAH-nuh, KAHNG-goh
ar	cartoon, Harvard	kar-TOON, HAR-vurd
aw	saw, raucous	SAW, RAW-kus
ay (or a)	may, Abraham, shake	MAY, AY-bruh-ham, SHAKE
b	bet	BET
ch	church, matchstick	CHURCH, MACH-stik
d	desk	DESK
e	Edward, melted	ED-wurd, MEL-tid
ee	meet, ream, petite	MEET, REEM, puh-TEET
eh	cherub, derriere	CHEH-rub, DEH-ree-ehr
f	final	FIGH-nul
g	got, giddy	GAHT, GIH-dee
h	happenstance	HAP-un-stans
i	mit, Ipswich, impression	MIT, IP-swich, im-PRESH-un
igh (or i)	eyesore, right, Anglophile	IGH-sore, RITE, ANG-gloh-file
ih	Philippines	FIH-luh-peenz
j	judgment	JUJ-mint
k	kitten	KIT-tun
l	light, allocate	LITE, AL-oh-kate
m	ramrod	RAM-rahd
n	ran	RAN
ng	rang, thinker	RANG, THING-ker
oh (or o)	open, owned, lonesome	OH-pun, OHND, LONE-sum
ong	wrong, bonkers	RONG, BONG-kurz
oo	moot, mute, super	MOOT, MYOOT, SOO-pur
ow	loud, dowager, how	LOWD, DOW-uh-jur, HOW
oy	boy, boil, oiler	BOY, BOYL, OY-lur
p	pet	PET
r	right, wretched	RITE, RECH-id
s	see, citizen	SEE, SIH-tuh-zun
sh	shingle	SHING-gul
t	test	TEST
th	thin	THIN
th	this, whether	*TH*IS, WEH-*th*ur
u	until, sumptuous, lovely	un-TIL, SUMP-choo-us, LUV-lee
uh	about, vacation, suddenly	uh-BOWT, vuh-KAY-shun, SUH-dun-lee
ur	fur, bird, term, beggar	FUR, BURD, TURM, BEG-ur
v	vacuum	VAK-yoo-um
w	western	WES-turn
y	yesterday	YES-tur-day
z	zero, loser	ZEE-roh, LOO-zur
zh	treasure	TREH-zhur

When a name is given two pronunciations, usually the first is the most familiar pronunciation in English and the second is a more exact rendering of the native pronunciation.

In the pronunciations of French names, nasalized vowels are indicated by adding "ng" after the vowel.

Japanese words have no strong stress accent, so the syllables marked as stressed are so given only for the convenience of English speakers.

CONTENTS

❧ CHINA: From the Collapse of the Han Dynasty to the Mongol Invasions 295

❧ ARABIA AND PERSIA: The World of Islam *355*

◥ JAPAN: Birth of a Culture *1011*

SEI SHONAGON [c. 966–1017]   *1059*

MURASAKI SHIKIBU, LADY MURASAKI [c. 973–1030]   *1086*

THE TALE OF THE HEIKE [1371]   *1148*

The Bedford Anthology of
World Literature
The Middle Period, 100 C.E.–1450

Camel Caravan, fourteenth century *This detail from a fourteenth-century Catalan atlas shows a group of Westerners en route to Cathay (the name by which north China was known at the time) crossing the Ural Mountains of central Russia. The Middle Period was a time of increasing exploration and travel between the East and West. (Bridgeman Art Library)*

*T*he term MIDDLE PERIO is a historical label that means something different for each world civzation to which it is applied. The European Middle
Ages refers to a periobetween the end of the Roman era in the fourth
century C.E. and the RENAISSAE, which began in Italy in the thirteenth century
and spread north through Eupe in the fourteenth and fifteenth centuries. The
Middle Period in China begavith the collapse of the Han dynasty in 200 C.E. and
ended with the fall of China the Mongol invaders in the thirteenth century.
Within this period the Tang dasty, which lasted from the seventh to the ninth
century, marked the highest int of Chinese civilization. Japan came under extensive Chinese influence in thighth century but soon built its own national culture
through a process of absorpn and synthesis. The height of the Japanese achievement during this time occud during the Heian dynasty (794–1185), followed by a
literary revival during the l:Kamakura and early Muromachi periods (fourteenth and fifteenth centur). The Islamic world originated with Muhammad in

www For an interactive version of the Conrative Tine Line for the Middle Period,
see *World Literature Online* at bedfordstmartimom/worllit.

COMPARATIVE TIME LINE FOR THE MILE PERIOD

Date	History and Politics	Literature	Science, Culture, and Technology
1–400	c. 30 Death of Jesus 47 Paul begins preachin	65–70 Gospel of Mark 85–90 Gospel of Matthew 100–250 Tamil poetry in southern India 130 Gospel of John 200–300 Sanskrit confirmed as literary language of India.	
	265–420 Chin dynasty (Qa) 306–337 Reign of EmperConstare 313 Edict of Milan: Rom tolerati of religions c. 330 Capital of Romarnpire ms to Constantinople. 320–550 Gupta dynastynorther India		c. 300 Widespread use of paper in China
		365–427 Tao Qian, Chinese poet	350 Buddhism flourished in China.
	376–415 Reign of Changupta I 395 Permanent divisiorf Easter Western Roman Epire	c. 415 Kalidasa, *Shakuntala*	

Arabia in the seventh century; its leaders dominated Near Eastern, Middle Eastern, North African, Spanish, and northern Indian politics until the fourteenth century. Its greatest period of literary vitality occurred during the height of the Abbasid dynasty in Baghdad (750–c. 950) and under the last Umayyad dynasty in Cordova (tenth and eleventh centuries). In India, the highest civilization in this period existed in the northern capitals during the Gupta Empire (c. 350–550). During this time, Indian literature was recorded in the court language, SANSKRIT, except in the resistant Tamil culture to the south.

Despite the problems of assigning a historical label to sometimes radically different parts of the world, this anthology uses the term Middle Period (and sometimes the adjective *medieval*) to designate a span of fourteen hundred years that saw the emergence of Christianity and Islam from the Near East; the rise of Christian society in Europe; the spread of Islamic authority across North Africa and Spain, the Near and Middle East, and part of the Far East; the rule of the Tang dynasty in China and the Heian dynasty in Japan; and the Gupta period in India. At different times during these fourteen hundred years, each of the major civilizations of the world built capital cities of great wealth and influence, among which were Constantinople in Asia Minor; Baghdad in ancient Mesopotamia; Cordova in

Date	History and Politics	Literature	Science, Culture, and Technology
400–625		c. 400　St. Augustine, *The Confessions*	
		c. 405　St. Jerome, Latin Vulgate Bible	
	410　Visigoths sack Rome.		
	420–588　China split into northern and southern dynasties.		425　University of Constantinople founded.
	481–511　Rule of King Clovis the Frank		c. 450　Buddhist monastery, university founded in Nalanda, India
		c. 500　Literary revival in south China	537　Hagia Sophia Cathedral built in Constantinople.
	552　Buddhism introduced in Japan.	500–600　Era of traditional Arab oral poetry: Arab *qasidah*, Persian heroic epic	
	571　Birth of Muhammad		570　Invention of abacus
	581–618　Sui dynasty reunifies China.		
	590–604　Pope Gregory the Great		
	600–800　Time of heaviest Chinese influence in Japan	600–700　Bhakti movement in southern India	
	c. 610　Muhammad's visions begin.		
	618–907　Tang dynasty: revival of the arts and culture		
	623　Muslim conquest of Arabia begins.		

Andalusia (Spain); Ch'ang-an in China; Heian (Kyoto) in Japan; and the twin capitals of Ujayyini and Taamralipti in India. Trade routes connecting Europe, the Near East, the Middle East, and the Far East were developed, resulting in a sharing and exchange of cultures as well as goods. For example, the collection of popular stories known as the *Arabian Nights* in the thirteenth and fourteenth centuries reflected aspects of all regions. Major disruptions of these cultures occurred in the thirteenth century caused by the Mongol invasions of China, the Near East, and Europe; and in the middle of the fourteenth century, when the Black Death — or bubonic plague — and succeeding epidemics broke out in Europe, the Middle East, North Africa, and China. Historians mark the end of the Middle Period in the fifteenth century, during a time of development of new secular states in Europe and the expansion of the Ottoman empire in the Near East.

THE EXPANSION OF CULTURES

The spread of world religion provided some of the original impetus for the expansion of medieval cultures. Classical Buddhism traveled from India to China by the third century and to Japan by the sixth. Christianity was adopted by the Roman Empire in the fourth century, established an Eastern stronghold in Constantinople

Date	History and Politics	Literature	Science, Culture, and Technology
625–725	629–645 Chinese Buddhist Hsuan-tsang visits India.		
	632 Death of Muhammad		
	633–656 Islamic conquests to east, west, and south		
		c. 653 Composition of *The Qur'an*	
	661 Founding of Umayyad dynasty in Damascus		
		fl. 680–700 Kakinomoto Hitomaro, greatest Japanese court poet	691 Completion of the Dome of the Rock, Jerusalem
		c. 700 Tang poets: Wang Wei (699–761), Li Bai (701–762), Du Fu (712–770)	c. 700 Invention of gunpowder in China
			Frankish metallurgy (decorated swords)
	710 Conquest of Andalusia (Spain)	Transcription of Arabic odes, including *Mu'allaqah* of Imru' al-Quays	
	710–784 Nara period in Japan.		710–784 Capital at Nara; first great Japanese cultural period
	711 Arab incursion into Sind province in western India		
		712 *Record of Ancient Matters*	712–756 Construction of Chinese capital at Chang-an begins
	712–756 Reign of Hsuan-tsung in China		

in the fourth and fifth centuries, and spread across Europe from the fifth to eighth centuries. The religion of Islam, born in the spiritual and political turmoil of Arabia in the seventh century, spread in a hundred years across the Middle East, North Africa, and the southern fringe of Europe.

In some instances, such as when Japan came under Chinese influence in the eighth century, new cultures and religions were established in imitation of other societies. In others, such as with the Muslim territories, new cultures were spread first by conquest and later by influence. Travel and trade created new relationships between Europe and the Middle East and between India and China. Eventually, trade routes, such as the "Silk Road" that ran between the Middle East and China, became the principal means of exchanging both material goods and cultural traditions throughout the entire region.

The fortunes of various medieval civilizations were changed rapidly by religious, political, and cultural forces. Despite its adoption of Christianity, the Roman Empire fell into decline, with Germanic troops increasingly filling the ranks of its legions until finally the entire civilization crumbled. Remnants of the empire mingled for several hundred years (fourth to sixth centuries) with foreign invaders with rival claims to authority. Christianity itself splintered in two; the Western

Date	History and Politics	Literature	Science, Culture, and Technology
725–800	732 Farthest extension of Islamic conquests in Europe; Charles Martel, founder of Carolingian dynasty, defeats Arabs at Tours.	732 The Venerable Bede, *Ecclesiastical History of the English People*	
	750 Founding of Abbasid dynasty in Baghdad	750 Beginning of the great age of Islamic literature	750 Construction of the city of Baghdad
	755 Revolt of An Lushan weakens Tang rule.	Ibn Ishaq, *Biography of the Prophet*	
	756 Founding of separate Umayyad caliphate in Andalusia	759 *Man'yoshu,* anthology of historical poetry published in Japan	
	768-814 Charlemagne, King of the Franks; named Holy Roman Emperor in 800	762 New Eastern capital of Islam established in Baghdad	768-814 Carolingian Renaissance (cultural revival) in Europe
		772-846 Bo Juyi, Chinese poet	783 Paper made in Baghdad
	786-809 Rule of Harun al-Rashid in Baghdad		786-809 Innovations in music, science, and the arts in Arabia and Persia

church stayed in Rome, spreading the gospel in Europe through conversion missions, while the Eastern church established itself in Constantinople as part of the Byzantine empire. Soon after the death of the prophet Muhammad in 632, Muslim armies came forth out of Arabia. Within a hundred years they established their authority in North Africa and Spain and from the Middle East to Asia Minor. Christian Crusaders who attempted to dislodge the Muslims from the Holy Land in the twelfth and thirteenth centuries were eventually driven back, succeeding only in slowly regaining Spain for Christian Europe from the eleventh to the fifteenth centuries. Meanwhile, in the thirteenth century, both eastern Europe and the Muslim territories were threatened by an onslaught of Mongols from China, but the invaders ultimately fell short in their drive for conquest after which their strength rapidly diminished. Western and Middle Eastern trade with Asia, begun well before the Mongol invasions, continued. Although the bubonic plague decimated the world's population by as much as a third in the mid fourteenth century, the expansion and development of the world's cultures continued.

"THE WORLD" IN THE MIDDLE PERIOD

Despite whatever knowledge they had acquired through historic migration, accidental voyages, and organized expeditions, educated Europeans, Asians, and North

Date	History and Politics	Literature	Science, Culture, and Technology
725–800 (cont.)	794–1185 Heian period in Japan		794–1185 Capital moves to Heian (Kyoto). Second great Japanese cultural period
800–900			c. 800–c. 850 Consolidation of system of Japanese writing
		830 Einhard, *Life of Charlemagne*	c. 830 Invention of algebra by al-Khwarizmi, Arab mathematician
	843 Carolingian empire divided (development of feudalism)		
900–950	907 End of Tang dynasty; period of local rule	c. 900 *Beowulf* composed.	c. 900 Muslims introduce cotton and silk industry in Andalusia.
	912–961 Rule of an-Nasir li-Din Allah in Andalusia	905 *Kokinshu*, anthology of courtly poetry published in Japan.	912–961 Construction of the city of Cordova, with its university library
	c. 950 Decline of the Abbasids; Persians rule Baghdad.		

Africans of the Middle Period had no systematic understanding of the true dimensions of the world and the makeup of its inhabitants. (Icelanders, it is true, had sailed to the edges of Newfoundland in the fourteenth century, but their attempts at colonization along the coastline eventually failed.) Even some of the known areas of the world, such as sub-Saharan Africa and northern Russia, were isolated by weather and forbidding geographical features. The *mappai mundi*, or world maps, of the period, frequently painted on hide or inscribed on vellum, convey both the era's curiosity about the world and its limited geographical knowledge.

Within the known medieval world of Europe, North Africa, the Near East, and the Far East, travel and military expeditions provided considerable knowledge of faraway lands and to some extent facilitated the sharing of cultures. The animosity between Muslim and Christian societies did not preclude their maintaining trade relations, with the result that cultural contact existed between the Middle East and Europe as well as between the Middle East and the rest of the Near East as early as the eighth century. The Vikings of Scandinavia traveled across Russia to the Middle East in the same period. The two highly developed societies of China and India engaged in commerce with each other early in the Middle Period. Themes of the "Orient" existed everywhere by the end of the period, when India and China were well connected to the Near East and Europe by trade. In the Middle Period,

Date	History and Politics	Literature	Science, Culture, and Technology
950–1000 (cont.)	960–1279 Sung dynasty reunifies China.		
		980–1037 Ibn Sina (Avicenna), philosopher	
		994–1064 Ibn Hazm, Cordova poet and philosopher	
1000–1100	c. 1000 Leif Ericson visits North America	1000–1010 Murasaki Shikibu, *The Tale of Genji*; Sei Shonagon, *The Pillow Book*	c. 1000 Medical works written; expansion of printing
	1002 Dissolution of caliphate of Cordova		Temple of Shiva built in Tanjore, south India
		c. 1010 Completion of *Book of Kings*, Persian heroic poem, by Ferdowsi	
	c. 1055 Occupation of Baghdad by Seljuk Turks		
	1066 Norman Conquest of England	c. 1020–1160 Andalusian courtly love poets, including Ibn Zaydun (d. 1070), Wallada (d. 1077), Ibn Quzman (d. 1160)	c. 1080 Bayeux tapestry depicts Norman Conquest.
	1085 Fall of Toledo; Spanish Reconquest begins.		
	1095 Pope Urban II preaches the First Crusade.		Cathedral schools; access to Latin classics
	1099 Christians sack Jerusalem.		

one-half of the world knew only itself; its encounter with the other half awaited the European oceanic voyages of exploration of the sixteenth and seventeenth centuries.

DEVELOPMENT OF THE ARTS AND LITERATURE

Medieval architecture, painting, manuscript illumination, music, dance, and other expressions of culture and the arts flowered in many lands from the first to the fourteenth centuries. Developments in stonework and advances in architectural design contributed to the range, magnitude, and aesthetic beauty of the great buildings of the period, from public forums to mosques to cathedrals. It might be said that great medieval cities such as Constantinople, Baghdad, and Chang-an contained the foremost works of art of the period in their architecture alone. Many societies also were able to preserve beautiful paintings, tapestries, pottery, and other works for more than a millennium. In addition, MANUSCRIPT ILLUMINATIONS enabled religious and civil institutions and wealthy families to appreciate the art of the book. Illuminated manuscripts from around the world are still regarded as testaments to medieval civilizations.

In India, China, Japan, Arabia, Persia, and northern Europe, earlier literatures were collected by newly centralized authorities; the traditions of the past were

Date	History and Politics	Literature	Science, Culture, and Technology
1100–1200		c. 1100 *The Song of Roland* composed	
		1100–1250 Courtly love literature in the south of France spreads throughout Europe.	
	1127 Invasion of north China; Sung dynasty retreats to the south.	1126–1198 Ibn Rushd (Averroes), philosopher	1122–1204 Eleanor of Aquitaine, patroness of the arts
		c. 1141–c. 1221 Farid ud-Din Attar, Sufi poet	
		c. 1145–c. 1217 Ibn Jubayr, traveler	
		c. 1160 Courtly romances *Breton lais* of Marie de France	

available once more. Much of this preservation took place during the early medieval centuries, often under the influence of the flourishing courts of these new societies. Some of the indigenous Indian literature was preserved in Sanskrit despite India's variety of cultures, religions, and languages. Chinese high culture developed out of the religious, philosophical, and literary works it inherited from antiquity. Buddhism, Confucianism, and Daoism flavored Chinese poetry and art during the Tang dynasty in the eighth century. Ancient Japanese poetry was collected by monks writing in an improvised version of Chinese characters in Japan in the eighth and ninth centuries. Islamic literature flourished after the Muslim conquests of the seventh century, first in Baghdad and later in Cordova. Islamic rulers sponsored the translation of pre-Islamic national epics such as Arabic odes, or QASIDAH, and the voluminous Persian *Epic of the Kings.* The stories and poems of ancient England, some derived from Germanic oral literature, were carefully preserved by Latin clerics in the tenth century who recorded them in Anglo-Saxon.

PRIMARY LITERARY FORMS, GENERALLY IN POETRY

In early medieval societies concerned with the building of secure capitals and well-defended fortresses, courtly audiences favored epic tales of confrontation

Date	History and Politics	Literature	Science, Culture, and Technology
1100–1200 (cont.)		1160–1233 Ibn al-Athir, historian	
		1165–1240 Ibn Arabi, philosopher	
	1171–1193 Rule of Saladin, who expels Crusaders from Jerusalem in 1187.	1174 Andreas Capellanus, *The Art of Courtly Love*	
	1180–1185 Gempei Wars between Heike and Genji clans; end of Heian dynasty in Japan.		
	1185–1333 Kamakura period—fall of aristocracy, rule by military warrior class in Japan		
	1193 Islamic Turks capture Delhi, rule north India.		1195 Construction of Chartres Cathedral, France

with human and supernatural forces. Later, as wars were waged at a distance and castles became more elegant and commodious, romances emphasized the pomp and circumstance of courtly life. The relationship of epics and romances to the societies of their times suggests a broad connection between literature and society.

Most EPICS evolved out of the oral traditions of tribal societies and were intended to glorify the heroes of the past or mourn the passing of a heroic age. Epics reflect on a remote time in history and reflect the societies from which they emerge. The Babylonian *Epic of Gilgamesh* (1800 B.C.E.) and the Greek epics of Homer, *The Iliad* and *The Odyssey* (eighth century B.C.E.), are the stories of ancient Mesopotamia and Greece, respectively. Medieval epics include the English *Beowulf* (tenth century), the Persian *Book of Kings* (tenth century), the French *Song of Roland* (c. 1100), and the Japanese *Tale of the Heike* (fourteenth century). The tale of Chingis Khan, preserved in *The Secret History of the Mongols* (thirteenth century), is composed of oral epic material. A subcategory of the epic is the LITERARY EPIC, a written work without a predecessor in an oral tradition. Virgil's *Aeneid* (first century C.E.) is the greatest literary epic of classical antiquity. Dante's *Inferno* (fourteenth century), a sophisticated literary work indebted to the *Aeneid* but

Date	History and Politics	Literature	Science, Culture, and Technology
1200–1300	1204 Christians sack Constantinople.	c. 1200 Aristotle translated into Latin (on natural history, metaphysics, ethics, politics)	c. 1200 Founding of universities of Paris and Oxford
	1208 Albigensian Crusade against heretics in south of France	1207–1273 Jalaloddin Rumi, Sufi poet	1209 Francis of Assisi founds the Franciscan order.
	1212 Battle of Las Navas de Talosa outside Toledo; decisive battle of the Reconquest of Spain		
	1215 Chingis Khan, ruler of Mongols, invades China.		
	1258 Sack of Baghdad by Mongol invaders	1273 Thomas Aquinas, *Summa Theologica*	
	1274–1275 Marco Polo visits China.		
	1279 Mongols conquer south China.		
	1291 Fall of Acre signals end of Crusader states in Asia Minor.		
		1298 Marco Polo, *Travels*	

addressed to a Christian audience, displays encyclopedic scope and grandeur as well as a complex relationship with the past.

The ancient ODE often centers on the themes of celebration and remembrance found in epics. The Arabian *Mu'allaqah* of Imru' al-Quays, composed in the sixth century, is such an ode, called a *qasidah* in Arabic. The CHOKA, or long poems, written by the Japanese poet Kakinomoto Hitomaro in the late seventh century, often about public occasions but always imbued with personal sentiment, can also be thought of as odes, though they are part of a radically different tradition. Even some of the Sufi poems composed by the Persian writer Rumi in the thirteenth century, while literary and mystical in intention, can be regarded as odes because they share in a contemplative, reflective tradition.

The ROMANCE is a literary work produced within courtly society, usually appearing later in time than the epic and reflecting a later stage of social development. Rather than simply glorifying communal life or the role of the warrior-hero in the manner of many epics, the romance looks inside castle walls to uncover love intrigues and expound tales of chivalrous and refined behavior. Romances like the Japanese *The Tale of Genji* (eleventh century) and the Norman-French *Lay of Chevrefoil* (twelfth century) give expression to the concerns of an elite courtly society trying to preserve its genteel way of life.

Date	History and Politics	Literature	Science, Culture, and Technology
1300–1400		c. 1300 *Thousand and One Nights* completed.	c. 1300 Giotto paints murals on life of St. Francis in Assisi.
		1321 Dante, *The Divine Comedy*	
	1338–1573 Muromachi period; landowners and the military share governance in Japan.		
	1348 Bubonic plague kills one-third of world's population.	1353 Boccaccio, *Decameron*	
		1364–1433 Zeami Moto-kiyo (1364–1443), creator of the *Nō* drama	
		1371 *The Tale of the Heike*, Japanese literary epic of the Gempei Wars	
		1377 Ibn Battuta, traveler and philosopher, dies.	
		1386 Chaucer, *The Canterbury Tales*	

LYRIC POETRY is common to nearly all world cultures, and although each society develops its own distinct conventions, lyrics around the world share certain features. Often they derive from songs; some are later set to music. Typically, a lyric poem captures emotion in a single scene or moment. Whereas more lengthy reflections are largely restricted to odes, lyric poetry focuses on a defining image or thought in order to express a poet's feelings. Although medieval lyric poetry was often encouraged by the courts and royal households and often addressed the subject of love, not all medieval lyrics were designed with the wealthy in mind or spoke of romantic love. Some medieval lyrics were cosmopolitan and sexually explicit. Others were mystical, even when they seemed to be talking about romantic love, while still others held social conventions up to ridicule. Diverse examples of lyric poetry in the Middle Period include the fierce Tamil poetry of love and war from the south of India in the second and third centuries; pastoral Chinese poetry, including the works of Tao Qian in the fifth century and the poets of the Tang dynasty in the eighth century; Japanese court poetry from the *Kokinshu* anthology of the early tenth century; Arabic and Jewish love poetry from Spain in the tenth and eleventh centuries; Provençal courtly love poetry of the twelfth century and its northern European counterparts of the thirteenth and fourteenth centuries; and Rumi's shorter Persian mystical poems of the thirteenth century.

LATER NARRATIVE FORMS, OFTEN IN PROSE

Several medieval literary forms are early examples of genres that achieved greater renown in later centuries. St. Augustine's *Confessions* (fifth century) is often called the first true AUTOBIOGRAPHY. Other texts in this vein include Ibn Ishaq's BIOGRAPHY of the prophet Muhammad (seventh century), which later helped to inspire a series of Muslim biographies and autobiographies. Other medieval literature falls under the heading of historical writings, which includes accounts of the Crusades written by Muslim, Christian, and Byzantine authors in the twelfth and thirteenth centuries and the astonishing reports concerning the life and death of Joan of Arc in France in the fifteenth century. Diaries and personal reminiscences were considered literature by Muslim writers starting around the tenth century. Japanese women's diaries and reminiscences of their lives at court helped to introduce vernacular Japanese writing to the educated reading public. One brilliant example is Sei Shonagon's *The Pillow Book,* written in the eleventh century.

The TRAVEL NARRATIVES of the time comprised prose accounts of religious pilgrimages as well as business and diplomatic journeys to and from the Far East. These writings, which reveal how much knowledge of the world medieval people had acquired, sometimes present nearly identical journeys through very different eyes. Compare *The Travels of Marco Polo,* recounting a trip from Italy to China, and

The Travels of Ibn Battuta, whose author journeys from Baghdad to India and China, both of which were written in the fourteenth century. Another form of travel literature concerned popular religious pilgrimages to holy shrines. Margery Kempe's account of her extraordinary travels, religious experiences, and controversies with authorities shows how far the form had developed by the end of the Middle Period (early fifteenth century). Marco Polo, Ibn Battuta, and Marjorie Kempe, whose motives for travel varied greatly, were all forerunners of the modern middle class.

What today is called FICTION may have begun with Lady Murasaki's prose romance *The Tale of Genji* (eleventh century). Other works of early fiction are the tales of *The Thousand and One Nights* (thirteenth and fourteenth centuries, but collected earlier), the popular romantic stories in *The Decameron* of Boccaccio (early fourteenth century), and the poetic narratives of the religious pilgrims in *The Canterbury Tales* of Chaucer (late fourteenth century). The Japanese epic *The Tale of the Heike* (fourteenth century), although derived from an oral tradition and reminiscent of epic material, is a semifictionalized account of a defining national experience.

At first, work acknowledged as fiction had its detractors. Chinese and Japanese scholars did not count it a serious literary form, saying it originated in village storytelling and lacked the disciplined use of literary conventions found in traditional literature. Islamic scholars, who accorded other prose writings a higher place, regarded fiction as an unworthy form, chiefly on moral grounds. In Europe and elsewhere in the West, the delayed popularity of fiction in part resulted from the difficulty of reproducing long works before the development of printing in the fifteenth century. With the advent of printed books, longer imaginative works of all kinds found a large reading audience.

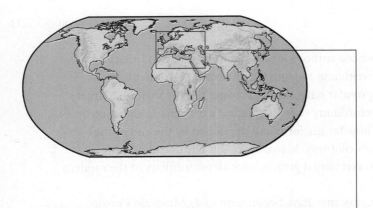

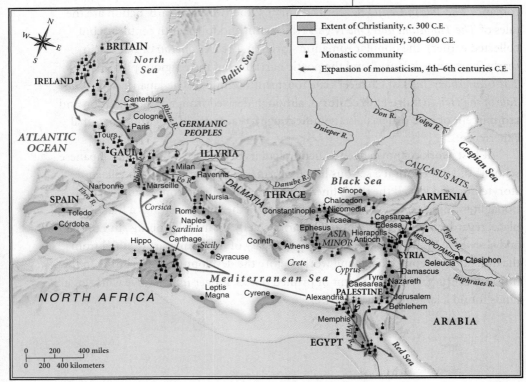

The Spread of Christianity, 300–600

By 300 C.E., Christian congregations existed in many cities and towns of the Roman Empire, though Christians were still a distinct minority. In the early fourth century, the Roman emperor Constantine converted to Christianity, moving the capital to Constantinople as the empire declined. By 600 C.E. Christianity had spread from end to end of the former empire.

THE NEAR EAST
Christianity and Islam

At the end of the Ancient World, the Mediterranean region bore witness to rapid political and religious development. Roman religion was once POLYTHEISTIC; the names of its gods and goddesses derived from the Greek PANTHEON. With the death of Augustus Caesar in 14 C.E., the Roman emperors themselves were declared gods. The next great wave of religious feeling came with the rise of Christianity in the Near East, along with the mystery religions of Dionysus and Orpheus in Greece, Isis in Egypt, and Mithras in Persia. Until the end of the third century, the Christian church competed for attention with these popular rivals. The ecumenical tendency of Christianity—especially its desire to expand its circle of believers—and the ethical core it inherited from Judaism became the keys to its success with both the general population and sponsoring governments.

THE CHRISTIAN ENTERPRISE

Public support for Christianity increased as Roman civil authority waned. In 313, Emperor Constantine granted the Christians his protection. In 330, he built an Eastern imperial capital in Constantinople, on the ruins of the old Greek city of Byzantium at the southern edge of the Black Sea leading to the Mediterranean. The division of the seat of the Roman Empire into Western and Eastern capitals was mirrored in the creation of an Eastern Christian enterprise at Constantinople. The resplendent new capital, with its special emphasis on Greek civilization, became the new center of Christian learning. For centuries, Constantinople was the showpiece of Christian culture, benefiting from the capital's rich trading connections throughout the Far East. Constantinople's glory endured until the twelfth and thirteenth centuries, when it was humiliated and finally occupied by the Crusaders.

Politically, Christianity's alliance with the Western and Eastern capitals of the Roman Empire secured its position for a time. Intellectually, however, the

Samaritan Woman at the Well

The earliest Christians were persecuted by the Romans for their faith. This wall fresco was found in the catacombs beneath the streets of Rome, where Christians had secret meeting places and tombs. Here, Christ, pictured in Roman garb, approaches a Samaritan woman, a story told in the Gospel of St. John. It was not until the fourth century that Christianity was established as the official religion of the Roman Empire, guaranteeing its survival. (Scala / Art Resource, NY)

Christians still needed to meld the Greco-Roman and the Judeo-Christian traditions together. The most advanced Christian writers had been educated in Greek and Roman rhetoric, literature, and philosophy. In the fourth century, three great "fathers" of the early church who were later canonized as saints—St. Ambrose (c. 340–397), St. Jerome (340–420), and St. Augustine (354–430)—further secured the intellectual position of Christianity in the Roman Empire by reconciling their own classical learning with the Christian faith. St. Ambrose, Bishop of Milan, stoutly defended Christian doctrine, opposing even the emperor when it became necessary to protect the sanctity of the church. St. Jerome directed the copying of the Greek and Roman classics and produced the first great translation of the Bible from Hebrew and Greek into Latin—the Latin Vulgate Bible. St. Augustine, the bishop of Hippo, in North Africa, addressed his most important spiritual writings, *The Confessions* (c. 400) and *The City of God* (426), to the needs of his time. Although by the time of Augustine's death Hippo lay under siege and the western Roman Empire was being torn apart, Christianity had prevailed. It had become the dominant religious and cultural force of the regions of the former Roman Empire and was well positioned to deal with Rome's successors.

THE CHRISTIAN CULTURAL LEGACY

The story of Jesus, his life, teachings, and resurrection, as told in the four Gospels of Matthew, Mark, Luke, and John in the New Testament, is the foundation of Christian worship. In addition, certain medieval Christian practices have influenced Western society. Among these, four deserve mention. First is the practice of scriptural interpretation as conducted by the early church fathers. Second is the Christian acceptance of the Greek and Latin classics as literature fit for a Christian audience. Third is the practice of charity and tolerance taught by Jesus and exemplified in his life. Fourth is the emphasis placed on the City of God, a world that awaits the believer after the fall of the City of Man. While none of these traditions took hold without controversy, especially the idea of tolerance, all set important intellectual, artistic, and moral standards that have served the Christian religion to this day.

Following the teachings of St. Jerome and St. Augustine, Christians interpreted Hebrew Scriptures, which they called the Old Testament, as a sign of future events that would take place after the coming of Christianity. Thus, the story of the prophet Moses was compared to the later story of the coming of Christ. The two stories are provided with a HISTORICAL and a SYMBOLIC interpretation. In its historical aspect, Moses' rescue of the nation of Israel by crossing the Red Sea is said to anticipate Christ's redemption of humanity. In its symbolic aspect, the spiritual life of every Christian is supposed to be linked with the history of the world, so personal salvation follows the deliverance of the children of Israel and the redemption brought about by Jesus. The poet Dante uses this symbolism in *The Divine Comedy* (thirteenth century) when he envisions the progression of the individual soul to heaven as a single aspect of the entirety of God's purpose.

The Christian church fathers generally deemed the Greek and Roman classics acceptable literature, though doing so was not always simple. Both St. Jerome and St. Augustine agonized over the sinfulness they detected in their own love of the classics. Nevertheless, the church's tolerance prepared the way for the study of classical learning by later Christian scholars. The fact that Jews, Christians, and Muslims loved literature and wished to preserve worldly knowledge ensured the further development of that knowledge through the medieval period. Among the great contributions of medieval learning were Christian Neoplatonism and studies of ancient works of philosophy and the natural sciences in both Arabic and Latin.

Because Jesus had shown love and respect for common people, especially the poor, medieval Christians felt that they should practice humility and service to others. This intention, while not always put into action, encouraged such practices as evangelism, pilgrimage, education, and charity, and inspired some Christians to work for the betterment of society. Humility and service were often referred to in medieval times, especially in sermons and in the works of such humanistic authors as Geoffrey Chaucer, the poet of *The Canterbury Tales,* in the late fourteenth century.

Christian millennial piety, the belief that the world as people knew it was coming to an end and that immediate salvation would be theirs, played a role in the Christian enterprise throughout the Middle Period. As the year one thousand C.E. approached, many Christians practiced extreme acts of worship, some of it self-destructive, thinking that the end was near. Also throughout the medieval period, the doctrine contained in Jesus' saying "My kingdom is not of this world" flavored Christian practices and attitudes, from the zeal of the first Crusaders to the spiritual practices of those who withdrew from the world and lived a cloistered existence.

While noting these predominant features of Christian belief in the Middle Period, it is also necessary to state that medieval Christians, in obvious contrast to their professed intentions, often acted in a violent and domineering fashion. The Christian Crusades of the twelfth and thirteenth centuries, aimed at taking the Holy Land from the Muslims, brought untold suffering to Muslims, Jews, and Christians alike. While it can be argued that the Crusades were a response to the Muslim holy wars of the seventh and eighth centuries, documents from the period suggest that the Christian attacks were often motivated by greed and politics, resulting in horrific acts of cruelty and theft. Taken as a whole, the Crusades are comparable to other notorious medieval campaigns such as the Germanic pillaging of the Roman Empire in the fifth century and the Mongol invasion of Asia, the Near East, and Europe in the thirteenth century.

THE RISE OF ISLAM

Arabia felt the reverberations of intense social and religious ferment in the seventh century. In the city of Mecca, in what today is Saudi Arabia, the merchants of the Quraysh tribe had always paid minimal attention to religious observance while focusing on personal profit. Muhammad (c. 570–632), an orphan child born of a poor clan in Mecca, grew up to become a camel driver and eventually a respected member of the business community. But greater things lay in store. At about age forty, the future prophet of the religion of Islam began receiving visions from the angel Gabriel—visions that determined his career as a preacher. Calling existing

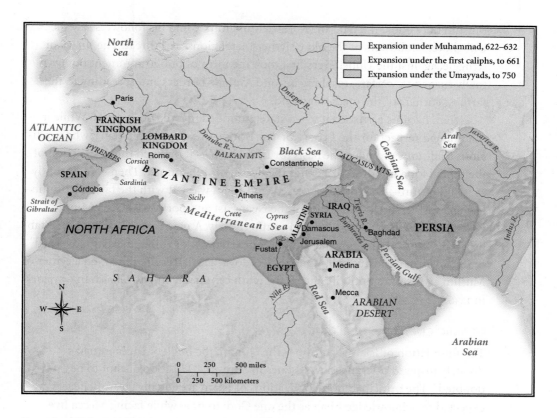

Expansion of Islam to 750
Beginning with Muhammad's campaigns, Islamic armies, in little more than a century, conquered a vast region made up of diverse peoples, cultures, climates, and living conditions. The force uniting these territories was the religion of Islam, which gathered all believers into one community, the umwah.

religious practices into question, Muhammad upset the ways of the Quraysh. He became both a successful preacher and a hunted man. Fleeing Mecca in 622, Muhammad took his followers to the city of Medina, founded the religion of Islam, and began to fight the tribes of Arabia, including the Quraysh of Mecca. When he died in 632, Muhammad's Muslim followers already ruled most of Arabia.

The astounding vitality of Islam as a religious faith rests largely on its universal claims. Borrowing from both the Hebrew Scriptures and the New Testament, it honors the prophets of the past, from Moses to Jesus Christ, but denies the divinity of Jesus, indeed of any man, including Muhammad himself. Muhammad was the Messenger, seen as completing the work of the Jewish and Christian prophets and delivering the Word of God, which his followers transcribed verbatim in the

Muslim holy book, the Qur'an (Koran). Muhammad and his followers saw the Unbelievers, followers of the old polytheistic religions, as a threat. The JIHAD, or struggle, against the Unbelievers first took the form of public argument but eventually turned to warfare, reaching beyond Arabia's borders and spreading to the farthest corners of the medieval world.

Islam became a THEOCRACY—a state grounded in a religious belief. While it maintained respect for the PEOPLE OF THE BOOK—Jews and Christians, whose religious traditions provided the basis for Islam itself—it pursued the destruction of the infidel for a hundred years after the death of Muhammad. Then—as abruptly as it had begun—the conquest ceased, and Islam was left with the task of administering a vast territory, consisting of the Near East and portions of Asia Minor, Egypt and North Africa, Spain, and southern Italy. A new Eastern capital was established in Baghdad in 750, while a different CALIPHATE, or ruling dynasty, governed in the Spanish (Andalusian) capital of Cordova. The latter site remained a center of Muslim civilization until the end of the tenth century, falling to Christian warriors in 1236.

ISLAMIC CULTURAL HERITAGE

The foundation of Islamic culture is the Qur'an, the book of Muhammad's divinely inspired utterances. As it states in Sura 2:1, "This Book is not to be doubted." The principal moral obligations of Islam are equally clear: Believers are expected to acknowledge Allah as the one God; to pray while facing Mecca five times a day; to engage in fasting, especially in the Islamic month of Ramadan; to make a religious pilgrimage to Mecca at least once in their lifetimes; and to assist the needy. The observance of public law was a religious practice in Muslim society; and the Muslim "church" was a community of believers with no priests, only selected prayer leaders. Muhammad was followed by a CALIPH, or "successor," a man known to be a defender of the faith and a guardian of the faithful. The exact formula for Muhammad's succession was unstated at the time of his death, leading to controversy and dissension in later days.

The Qur'an was considered the greatest literary work as well as the holy book of Islam. Its variety, comprehensiveness, and style were praised in commentaries that expanded on its meaning. Arabian and Persian grammars and rhetorical treatises were written with the Qur'an as their principal source of inspiration as early as the eighth century. Besides the Qur'an, poetry was seen as the preeminent classical Arabian literature. Many rules and formulas were prescribed for its composition. Scientific and philosophical writings, including commentaries on the Qur'an, held the next highest place. Humanistic writings, essays on topics of interest, were given the name of ADAB and were also highly valued. Fiction was viewed as a

The Near East: The Dome of the Rock (687–698 C.E.)

The Dome of the Rock was built during the rule of Caliph Abd al-Malik a little more than half a century after the death of Muhammad. It marks the spot where, according to the Qur'an, the Prophet ascended into the heavens in a spiritual dream or journey. The Dome also symbolizes the Islamic conception of the relationship between the Jewish, Christian, and Muslim faiths. It is raised over the rock on which Abraham is believed to have prepared his son Isaac as a sacrifice to Jehovah, the same ground on which the Temple of Solomon was later twice built and twice destroyed. The Dome is also situated near the Church of the Holy Sepulchre, the place where Christ is believed to have been crucified, and several of the Dome's principal architectural features strive to imitate or surpass those of that Christian monument. The architectural style of the Dome of the

The Dome of the Rock. *A contemporary view of Jerusalem with the Dome of the Rock in the distance. (The Art Archive / Dagli Orti)*

Rock came from its Muslim builders, with its beautifully colored inner pillars encircling the Rock; the octagonal outer wall, once done in mosaics but later replaced by sea-blue porcelain; and the Dome itself, a wooden curved cupola about seventy-five feet in diameter covered in gold.

The Jewish heritage of the site begins with the story of Abraham and Isaac and continues with the construction of Solomon's Temple, erected over the Rock itself on a level plateau in about 950 B.C.E. Constantly falling under attack after the death of Solomon, the temple finally was destroyed by the Babylonian warrior Nebuchadnezzar in 587 B.C.E. Languishing in captivity until 539, the remaining peoples of Judah returned to Jerusalem and rebuilt the Temple beginning in 520. The area was conquered again by Alexander the Great in the fourth century B.C.E. and faced further invasion and desecration until the time of the Roman emperors. Rebuilt by King Herod in 20 B.C.E. in an effort to win the admiration of the Jews, the Temple was finally destroyed by the Roman general Titus in 70 C.E. All that was left of the Second Temple of Solomon was a portion of the western edifice now known as the Wailing Wall, a site of Jewish prayer and mourning.

Early in the seventh century C.E., Bedouin tribes from Arabia led an explosive wave of conquest prompted by the teachings of the Prophet Muhammad and the faith of Islam. Five years after Muhammad's death in 632, Muslim soldiers were encamped outside the gates of Jerusalem. Muhammad's own injunction that a new temple be built over the ruins of the old was followed to the letter, resulting in the Dome of the Rock, the greatest monument to the Muslim faith. Today this monument stands as a commemoration both of Muhammad's ascent into heaven and his followers' determination to prevail in the Holy Land.

vehicle of village gossip, not deserving of great notice. This bias against fiction has endured in the Muslim world until modern times.

ISLAMIC INTELLECTUAL HERITAGE

The greatest achievement of the early Islamic authors is *The Life of Muhammad* by Ibn Ishaq (704–767). This lengthy and complicated book about Muhammad, written a little more than a hundred years after the Prophet's death, uses as its source material a collection of oral narratives, letters, legal documents, poetry written for special occasions, and battle accounts. For stories passed down for several generations, Ibn Ishaq lists every transmitter of the tale, even commenting from time to time by his use of words like *alleges* on the reliability of his sources. He does not produce a "master narrative" that gives the appearance of utter certainty, a common literary device in the West. Instead he leaves final verification of the information he provides to the reader. This scrupulous method of presentation makes the unedited material almost unreadable at times, but it also prepares the way for what came after Ibn Ishaq: equally scrupulous biographies of other famous men, biographies of the less famous, and — still in the Middle Period — autobiographies.

www   For more information about the culture and context of the Near East in the Middle Period, see *World Literature Online* at bedfordstmartins.com/worldlit.

∾ THE NEW TESTAMENT
FIRST CENTURY–SECOND CENTURY C.E.

A collection of documents from the early Christian community written in the first two centuries after Jesus' death, the New Testament brings together the Hebraic and Hellenic strands of Western culture. The New Testament, which centers on the life and teachings of a Jewish prophet, was written in Greek. Its message was meant to replace the law and covenant between Moses, the Jewish people, and God. Instead of a religion restricted to God's chosen people, the Jews, the new covenant was put forth as a bond with all humankind, and Christianity proclaimed itself a world religion for all people.

www For quizzes on the New Testament, see *World Literature Online* at bedfordstmartins .com/worldlit.

Christian Evangelism. The twenty-seven books of the New Testament were written in less than a century, beginning about 50 C.E. with Paul's early letters. Shortly before his death in about 29 C.E.,[1] Jesus instructed his followers to "go into all the world and preach the gospel," and the books of the New Testament reflect various aspects of that mission. From its beginnings as a sect in Jerusalem after Jesus' death, Christianity soon spread throughout the Mediterranean. Saint Stephen, the first Christian martyr, who was killed about 34 C.E., prophesied the destruction of the Temple in Jerusalem and prompted a persecution of the Christians in Jerusalem by zealous Jews. Those fleeing this persecution scattered and established churches in other places, especially at Antioch, in Asia Minor, a center of early Christian evangelism. In these new religious centers, Gentile, or non-Jewish, converts soon outnumbered the Jewish members of the sect, and early Christians concentrated on extending their message beyond the Jewish community in Palestine. Paul's letters, the earliest writings of the New Testament, recount the apostle's missionary activities in the fifth decade of the first century as he established and encouraged new churches in the areas surrounding Palestine. The gospels and the other later books of the New Testament met the growing need in these early churches for historical, ethical, and theological documents explaining a movement that was spreading far beyond its place of origin. Written in Greek, the international language of the day, the New Testament exported the Christian message from Palestine to the whole Mediterranean world.

The Gospels. Shorter and less varied than the Hebrew Scriptures, the New Testament is made up of four major kinds of writing: biography, history, letters, and apocalyptic vision. The first four books, the Gospels

---

[1] 29 C.E.: Jesus was thirty-three at the time of his death. The calendar that divided "B.C." (before Christ) and "A.D." (after Christ) was developed by the sixth-century monk Dionysius Exiguus, who was several years off in determining the date of Jesus' birth. Jesus was actually born sometime between 6 and 4 B.C.E.

He [the translator]
will find one English
book and one only,
where, as in the *Iliad*
itself, perfect plain-
ness of speech is
allied with perfect
nobleness; and that
book is the Bible.

– MATTHEW ARNOLD,
Critic, 1861

of Matthew, Mark, Luke, and John, tell the life of Jesus from different perspectives. Writing several decades after the death of Jesus, the gospel writers were not simply biographers; first and foremost they were evangelists
who told the life of Jesus to win converts to Christianity from communities of Greek, Roman, and Jewish readers. Their narratives, which
emphasize the supernatural and mythic elements of Jesus' life, were based
largely on oral stories that circulated in the Christian community and
differ at times in their facts, such as who was responsible for Jesus' death.

The Gospel of Mark, generally believed to be the first of the gospels,
written around 65 or 70 C.E., is the shortest and most matter-of-fact of
the four. More than the other gospels, it seems to be addressed to a
Roman readership. In Mark, Jesus is presented realistically, even journal-
istically, by a writer who may have been present during the last week of
Jesus' ministry and who traveled with Paul on one of his missionary journeys. Although he may have been an eyewitness to some of the events he
describes, Mark probably based most of his gospel on oral stories about
Jesus. His plain and vigorous style matches the simple, unembellished
story that he tells. Because many of the episodes and teachings in Mark's
biography reappear in the Gospels of Matthew and Luke, scholars believe
that these two later accounts — written between 80 and 95 C.E. — were
based on Mark's work. Because they tell essentially the same story and
work from a common outline or synopsis of Jesus' life, these three gospels
are often referred to as the SYNOPTIC GOSPELS. By comparing the three and
noting their differences and similarities, scholars have been able to date
their composition and establish the authorship and intent of each. The
Gospels of Matthew and Luke are longer than that of Mark and the added
material in the two later gospels has distinct similarities, leading scholars
to assume the existence of a second source, a lost "Q Document," that
both later writers used along with Mark's gospel. As Matthew is significantly concerned with placing Jesus in a Jewish context, his gospel is
sometimes called the Jewish gospel. He traces Jesus' genealogy back to
King David, presents him as the Messiah, and often relates his teachings
to those of the Hebrew Scriptures. Luke, a physician who addresses his
work to a Gentile, largely Greek, audience, presents Jesus as a human and
heroic figure.

Written much later, about 130 C.E., the Gospel of John, whose author
is unknown but who is not the John of the Book of Revelation, is less
interested in biography than are its three predecessors. Instead, this
gospel, sometimes called the "spiritual gospel," develops a theological and
symbolic interpretation of Jesus' life and message and is addressed to an
audience of Christians who sought to understand the meaning of Jesus'
life and message.

Paul's Letters and the Early Church.   The Acts of the Apostles, the fifth
book of the New Testament, is thought to have been written by Luke. A
work of church history, Acts describes the evangelistic efforts of the early
apostles and the formation of the early Christian church. These subjects
are important as well in the letters of Paul and of the other early apostles

Head of Christ, third century C.E.
Christ's life and teachings were written down in the New Testament and disseminated by his faithful followers, becoming the foundation for a new world religion. This early stone inlay depicting the head of Christ already shows him with a halo, a beard, and a gentle demeanor. (© Scala/Art Resource, NY)

that make up about half of the New Testament. Although they do not appear first in the New Testament as it is ordered today, Paul's letters were probably the first written, composed in the decade between 50 and 60 C.E. Most of them are addressed to the fledgling churches in Asia Minor, Greece, and Italy that Paul himself helped to establish and visited on his evangelistic journeys around the Mediterranean. Paul began his life as Saul of Tarsus—a city in Cilicia in what is now Turkey—the son of parents who were Pharisees, strict followers of Jewish laws. Saul became an enforcer of those laws and a persecutor of the followers of "the way," the new Christians. But, according to tradition, as he was traveling on the road from Jerusalem to Damascus, he was blinded by a light from heaven and was converted to Christianity. Under his Christian name, Paul became the most important of the apostles. His missionary work moved the center of Christianity from Jerusalem to Antioch, in Asia Minor, and his message combined the ethical dimension of Judaism with elements from Greek and Oriental MYSTERY RELIGIONS.[2] His letters, written before the Gospels and addressed to a Gentile rather than a Jewish audience, take up practical matters having to do with church organization, ethical and moral issues, and points of theology and belief. They develop the doctrine of the early Christian church.

---

[2] **Greek and Oriental mystery religions:** Underground sects that provided an emotional and ritual alternative to the formal practices of the established religions of ancient Greece and Rome. The secret rites of some of these cults derived from the Near Eastern worship of such deities as Cybele, Isis, and Mithras. The mystery cults offered a balm for persecution and suffering by promising a messiah, and immortality.

Those who talk of the Bible as a "monument of English prose" are merely admiring it as a monument over the grave of Christianity.

– T. S. ELIOT, Poet and Critic, 1935

The Apocalypse.   The last book of the twenty-seven in the established canon of the New Testament, the Revelation of St. John the Divine, is an example of apocalyptic writing that presents a cryptic vision of the future, especially of the final days, the Second Coming of Christ, and the Last Judgment. If the Bible is viewed as a single work presenting a spiritual history of humankind from the Creation on, then John's vision of the future rounds out that history and gives ultimate meaning to the whole, from Adam's Fall to Christ's redeeming sacrifice to the judgment at the end of time.

Jesus and Socrates.   Socrates and Jesus have often been compared. Both teachers had devoted students and passionate followers who were subjected to controversial trials because of their association with these iconoclasts. One way to look at Socrates is to see him as a man who challenged the conventional ideas of his time. He rejected many of the traditional aspects of heroism to define a new type of ideal. Rather than defeating external enemies, Socrates sought to know himself and to define for himself standards of right conduct. His "internalization" of the self might be taken as his most significant and heroic achievement, a heroism confirmed by his uncompromising choice of dying for his beliefs. Jesus could be said similarly to have "internalized" the Hebraic tradition. In place of the law and the external rules so important to the Pharisees, Jesus taught inner commitment and a belief in the power of love that could lead to surprising and transforming action—"turning the other cheek" when harmed and caring for the sick and hungry. Jesus also, like Socrates, accepted his own condemnation by the authorities and execution. In the stories of Jesus and Socrates an evolution of the heroic ideal can be seen. Both men revise the traditions of their times, modifying the ideals of the Greek warrior or the Hebrew patriarch in some interestingly similar ways. In both cases, the revisions became more widespread than the traditions they challenged.

"The Great Code."   The New Testament tells the story of Jesus and places it in historical and prophetic contexts. From a Christian point of view, the New Testament fulfills the Old Testament, so that many Christian readings of the Bible find foreshadowings, or "types," of Christ in the ancient Hebrew patriarchs. Adam and Joseph and Moses are completed by Jesus; he becomes the "antitype" who fulfills their historical roles and gives ultimate meaning to their stories. As the "second Adam," Jesus redeems Adam's original sin, for the fallen condition of man in the Hebrew Scriptures is resolved by Jesus' sacrifice. Such "typological" readings see the Bible as much more than a loosely connected collection of songs, histories, myths, and stories by many different writers from many different epochs. They see it as a unified story revealing all of human history, past, present, and future. Whatever one's position, one cannot deny the significance of the Bible in Western culture. It is not only a fund of stories, an anthology of literature, and a handbook of ethics. It is for the West, as Northrop Frye has called it, "the great code," the cosmic diagram of promise and fulfillment through which Westerners plot their history and tell the stories of their lives.

■ CONNECTIONS

Hebrew Scriptures (Book 1), *In the World:* **The Good Life (Book 1).** Many literary classics seek to define the rules by which one can live a good or righteous life. When Jesus states many of his ideals in the Sermon on the Mount, he recognizes that he is challenging some of the laws of the Hebrew Scriptures, such as "an eye for an eye" retribution. Consider the ways in which the Sermon on the Mount challenges or modifies the Ten Commandments. How does it compare with the prescriptions found in *In the World:* The Good Life?

The Epic of Gilgamesh **(Book 1);** Homer, *The Iliad* and *The Odyssey* **(Book 1);** Virgil, *The Aeneid* **(Book 1).** The biographies of heroes usually tell of unusual or supernatural happenings in the hero's birth and childhood, a ceremony in which the hero is invested with his or her mission, and accounts of heroic deeds performed by him or her. Consider several of the heroes in Books 1 and 2 of this anthology—Moses, Achilles, Inanna, Gilgamesh, Aeneas, Socrates, the Buddha, St. Joan, and Muhammad, for example. What qualities, events, and deeds mark each of them as heroic? Do the differences in the extraordinary circumstances in the lives of each indicate variations in their heroic ideals?

Chaucer, "The Wife of Bath's Prologue," p. 904; The Qur'an (Koran), p. 97. St. Paul is sometimes characterized as one of the primary promulgators of patriarchal ideas in Christian culture. Consider his advice on marriage and the roles of men and women in his First Letter to the Corinthians. Is his stance sexist? How does Chaucer's Wife of Bath respond to Paul's writings? How do they compare with Sura 4 of the Qur'an?

■ FURTHER RESEARCH

Modern Translations
The New English Bible. 1970.
The New Revised Standard Version. 1989.

Commentary
Alter, Robert and Frank Kermode. *The Literary Guide to the Bible.* 1987.
Beardslee, W. A. *Literary Criticism of the New Testament.* 1970.
Enslin, Morton Scott. *Christian Beginnings.* 1956.
Frye, Northrop. *The Great Code: The Bible and Literature.* 1981.
———. *Words with Power: Being a Second Study of 'The Bible and Literature.'* 1990.
Gabel, John B., and Charles B. Wheeler. *The Bible as Literature: An Introduction.* 1990.
Kee, Howard Clark, Franklin W. Young, and Karlfried Froehlich. *Understanding the New Testament.* 1973.
Pritchard, John Paul. *A Literary Approach to the New Testament.* 1972.

FROM

❧ Luke 1–3

Translated by Edgar Goodspeed (American Version)

[THE BIRTH, YOUTH, AND BAPTISM OF JESUS]

American Version

Chapter 1 ⁵ In the days when Herod° was king of Judea, there was a priest named Zechariah who belonged to the division of Abijah. His wife was also a descendant of Aaron, and her name was Elizabeth. ⁶ They were both upright in the sight of God, blamelessly observing all the Lord's commands and requirements. ⁷ They had no children, for Elizabeth was barren; and they were both advanced in life.

⁸ Once when he was acting as priest before God, when his division was on duty, it fell to his lot, ⁹ according to the priests' practice, to go into the sanctuary of the Lord and burn the incense, ¹⁰ while all the throng of people was outside, praying at the hour of the incense offering. ¹¹ And an angel of the Lord appeared to him, standing at the right of the altar of incense. ¹² When Zechariah saw him he was startled and overcome with fear. ¹³ And the angel said to him, "Do not be afraid,

---

The Gospels. These passages from the Gospels of Matthew and Luke describe some of the major events in Jesus' life: his birth, boyhood, and baptism in Luke; the Sermon on the Mount in Matthew, which states many of the key ideas of Jesus' ministry; some parables from Matthew and Luke, the illustrative stories by which Jesus often taught; and, finally, Luke's account of Jesus' betrayal, crucifixion, and resurrection. These selections provide only some highlights of the entire gospel story; they leave out much of Jesus' ministry, most of his teachings, and nearly all of the miracles he performed. They also do not illustrate the differences among the various gospel accounts. Nevertheless, they do present an outline of an extraordinary life, and of the signs and tokens that accompanied Jesus' birth and death, marking him as a supernatural figure. Although these markers link his story with that of Moses and the Jewish patriarchs from the Hebrew Scriptures as well as with the mythic warriors of Greece and Rome who were said to have descended from the gods, the content of Jesus' message and his life's story broke with the heroic ideals of the past. Jesus preached a new covenant, a new ethic of love, and his life articulated a wholly new heroism.

A note on the translation. The modern American translation of the New Testament by Edgar Goodspeed (1961) has been chosen for its clarity and readability. The classic English translation, the King James Version done in 1611, includes many texts whose poetic language has so influenced later writers that we have also included some of those familiar passages from King James in blue next to their Goodspeed counterparts. These examples include the nativity, the Sermon on the Mount, and the Lord's Prayer. We think you'll find the variations fascinating, as we do — an exercise showing how important a particular translation can be.

1, 5: **Herod:** Ruler of Palestine, including Judea, or southern Palestine, from 37 to 4 B.C.E., under authority of the Roman emperor Augustus Caesar.

American Version

Zechariah, for your prayer has been heard. Your wife Elizabeth will bear you a son, and you are to name him John. ¹⁴ This will bring gladness and delight to you, and many will rejoice over his birth. ¹⁵ For he will be great in the sight of the Lord. He will drink no wine or strong drink, but he will be filled with the holy Spirit from his very birth, ¹⁶ and he will turn many of Israel's descendants to the Lord their God. ¹⁷ He will go before him with the spirit and the power of Elijah,° to reconcile fathers to their children, and to bring the disobedient back to the wisdom of upright men, to make a people perfectly ready for the Lord." ¹⁸ Zechariah said to the angel, "How am I to know that this is so? [. . .]

¹⁹ The angel answered, "I am Gabriel. I stand in the very presence of God. I have been sent to speak to you and tell you this good news [. . .]

American Version

²⁶ In the sixth month the angel Gabriel was sent by God to a town in Galilee called Nazareth, ²⁷ to a maiden there who was engaged to be married to a man named Joseph, a descendant of David. The maiden's name was Mary. ²⁸ And the angel went into the town and said to her, "Good morning, favored woman! The Lord be with you!" ²⁹ But she was startled at what he said, and wondered what this greeting meant. ³⁰ And the angel said to her, "Do not be afraid, Mary, for you have gained God's approval. ³¹ You are to become a mother and you will give birth to a son, and you are to name him Jesus.° ³² He will be great and will be called the Son of the Most High. The Lord God will give him the throne of his forefather David, ³³ and he will reign over Jacob's house forever; his reign will have no end."

King James Version

26 And in the sixth month the angel Gabriel was sent from God unto a city of Galilee, named Nazareth, 27 To a virgin espoused to a man whose name was Joseph, of the house of David; and the virgin's name *was* Mary. 28 And the angel came in unto her, and said, Hail, *thou that art* highly favoured, the Lord *is* with thee: blessed *art* thou among women. 29 And when she saw *him,* she was troubled at his saying, and cast in her mind what manner of salutation this should be.
30 And the angel said unto her, Fear not, Mary: for thou hast found favour with God. 31 And, behold, thou shalt conceive in thy womb, and bring forth a son, and shalt call his name JESUS. 32 He shall be great, and shall be called the Son of the Highest; and the Lord God shall give unto him the throne of his father David: 33 And he shall reign over the house of Jacob for ever; and of his kingdom there shall be no end. [. . .]

1, 17: **Elijah:** According to the prophesy in Malachi 4, Elijah was to prepare the way for the Messiah.

1, 31: **Jesus:** The name Jesus, the Greek form of the Hebrew name Yeshua, or Joshua, means "he shall serve."

American Version

³⁴ Mary said to the angel, "How can this be, when I have no husband?" ³⁵ The angel answered, "The holy Spirit will come over you, and the power of the Most High will overshadow you. For that reason your child will be called holy, and the Son of God. ³⁶ And your relative, Elizabeth, although she is old, is going to give birth to a son, and this is the sixth month with her who was said to be barren. ³⁷ For nothing is ever impossible for God." ³⁸ And Mary said, "I am the Lord's slave. Let it be as you say." Then the angel left her.

³⁹ In those days Mary set out and hurried to the hill-country, to a town in Judah, ⁴⁰ and she went to Zechariah's house and greeted Elizabeth. ⁴¹ When Elizabeth heard Mary's greeting, the babe stirred within her. ⁴² And Elizabeth was filled with the holy Spirit and she gave a great cry, and said,

"You are the most favored of
women,
And blessed is your child!
43   Who am I,
To have the mother of my Lord
come to me?

44   "For the moment your greeting
reached my ears,
The child stirred with joy within
me!
45   Blessed is she who has believed,
For what the Lord has promised her
will be fulfilled!"

46   And Mary said,
"My heart extols the Lord,
47   My spirit exults in God my Savior.
48   For he has noticed his slave in her
humble station,

For from this time all the ages will
think me favored!

49   "For the Almighty has done
wonders for me,
How holy his name is!
50   He shows his mercy age after age
To those who fear him.

51   "He has done mighty deeds with his
arm,
He has routed the proud-minded,
52   He has dethroned monarchs and
exalted the poor,
53   He has satisfied the hungry with
good things, and sent the rich
away empty-handed.

54   "He has helped his servant Israel
Remembering his mercy,
55   As he promised our forefathers
To have mercy on Abraham and his
descendants forever!"

⁵⁶ So Mary stayed with her about three months, and then returned home.

⁵⁷ Now the time came for Elizabeth's child to be born, and she gave birth to a son. ⁵⁸ Her neighbors and relatives heard of the great mercy the Lord had shown her, and they came and congratulated her. ⁵⁹ On the eighth day they came to circumcise the child, and they were going to name him Zechariah, after his father. ⁶⁰ But his mother said, "No! He is to be named John." ⁶¹ They said to her, "There is no one among your relatives who bears that name." ⁶² But they made signs to the child's father and asked him what he wished to have the child named. ⁶³ He asked for a writing tablet, and wrote, "His name is John." ⁶⁴ And they were all amazed. Then his voice and the use of his tongue were immediately

American Version

restored, and he blessed God aloud.
65 And all their neighbors were overcome with fear, and all over the hill-
country of Judea all these stories
were told, 66 and everyone who
heard them kept them in mind, and
said, "What is this child going to be?"
For the Lord's hand was with him.

67 And his father Zechariah was
filled with the holy Spirit and he
uttered a divine message, saying,

68   "Blessings on the Lord, the God of
        Israel,
      Because he has turned his attention
        to his people, and brought
        about their deliverance,
69   And he has produced a mighty
        Savior for us
      In the house of his servant David.

70   "By the lips of his holy prophets he
        promised of old to do this —
71   To save us from our enemies and
        from the hands of all who hate
        us,
72   Thus showing mercy to our
        forefathers,
      And keeping his sacred agreement,

73   "And the oath that he swore to our
        forefather Abraham,
74   That we should be delivered from
        the hands of our enemies,
75   And should serve him in holiness
        and uprightness, unafraid,
      In his own presence all our lives.

76   "And you, my child, will be called a
        prophet of the Most High,
      For you will go before the Lord to
        make his way ready,
77   Bringing his people the knowledge
        of salvation
      Through the forgiveness of their
        sins.

78   "Because the heart of our God is
        merciful,
      And so the day will dawn upon us
        from on high,
79   To shine on men who sit in dark-
        ness and the shadow of death,
      And guide our feet into the way of
        peace."

80 And the child grew up and
became strong in the Spirit, and he
lived in the desert until the day when
he proclaimed himself to Israel.

American Version

[THE BIRTH]

Chapter 2   1 In those days an
edict was issued by the Emperor
Augustus that a census of the whole
world should be taken. 2 It was the
first census, taken when Quirinius
was governor of Syria. 3 So everyone
went to his own town to register.
4 And Joseph went up from Galilee
from the town of Nazareth to Judea
to the city of David called Bethlehem, because he belonged to the
house and family of David, 5 to

King James Version

Chapter 2   And it came to pass in
those days, that there went out a
decree from Cesar Augustus, that all
the world should be taxed. 2 (*And*
this taxing was first made when Cyre-
nius was governor of Syria.) 3 And
all went to be taxed, every one into
his own city. 4 And Joseph also went
up from Galilee, out of the city of
Nazareth, into Judea, unto the city of
David, which is called Bethlehem,
(because he was of the house and

American Version

register with Mary, who was engaged to him and who was soon to become a mother. 6 While they were there, the time came for her child to be born, 7 and she gave birth to her first-born son; and she wrapped him up, and laid him in a manger, for there was no room for them at the inn.

8 There were some shepherds in that neighborhood keeping watch through the night over their flock in the open fields. 9 And an angel of the Lord stood by them, and the glory of the lord shone around them, and they were terribly frightened. 10 The angel said to them, "Do not be frightened, for I bring you good news of a great joy that is to be felt by all the people, 11 for today, in the town of David, a Savior for you has been born who is your Messiah and Lord. 12 And this will prove it to you: You will find a baby wrapped up and lying in a manger." 13 Suddenly there appeared with the angel a throng of the heavenly army, praising God, saying,

14   "Glory to God in heaven and on
           earth!
       Peace to the men he favors!"

15 When the angels left them and returned to heaven, the shepherds said to one another, "Come! Let us go over to Bethlehem, and see this thing that has happened, that the Lord has told us of!" 16 And they hurried there, and found Mary and Joseph, with the baby lying in the manger. 17 When they saw this, they told what had been said to them about this child. 18 And all who heard it were

King James Version

lineage of David,) 5 To be taxed with Mary his espoused wife, being great with child. 6 And so it was, that, while they were there, the days were accomplished that she should be delivered. 7 And she brought forth her firstborn son, and wrapped him in swaddling clothes, and laid him in a manger; because there was no room for them in the inn.
8 And there were in the same country shepherds abiding in the field, keeping watch over their flock by night. 9 And, lo, the angel of the Lord came upon them, and the glory of the Lord shone round about them; and they were sore afraid. 10 And the angel said unto them, Fear not: for, behold, I bring you good tidings of great joy, which shall be to all people. 11 for unto you is born this day in the city of David a Saviour, which is Christ the Lord. 12 And this *shall be* a sign unto you; Ye shall find the babe wrapped in swaddling clothes, lying in a manger. 13 And suddenly there was with the angel a multitude of the heavenly host praising God, and saying, 14 Glory to God in the highest, and on earth peace, good will toward men.
15 And it came to pass, as the angels were gone away from them into heaven, the shepherds said one to another, Let us now go even unto Bethlehem, and see this thing which is come to pass, which the Lord hath made known unto us. 16 And they came with haste, and found Mary and Joseph, and the babe lying in a manger. 17 And when they had seen *it,* they made known abroad the saying which was told them concerning this child. 18 And all they that heard

American Version	King James Version
amazed at what the shepherds told them, ¹⁹ but Mary treasured up all they had said, and pondered over it. ²⁰ And the shepherds went back glorifying God and praising him for all that they had heard and seen in fulfilment of what they had been told.	*it* wondered at those things which were told them by the shepherds. 19 But Mary kept all these things, and pondered *them* in her heart. 20 And the shepherds returned, glorifying and praising God for all the things that they had heard and seen, as it was told unto them.

American Version

²¹ When he was eight days old and it was time to circumcise him, he was named Jesus, as the angel had named him, before his birth was first expected.

²² When their purification period under the Law of Moses was over, they took him up to Jerusalem to present him to the Lord, ²³ in fulfilment of the requirement of the Law of the Lord, "Every first-born male shall be considered consecrated to the Lord,"° ²⁴ and to offer the sacrifice prescribed in the Law of the Lord, "A pair of turtle-doves or two young pigeons." ²⁵ Now there was a man in Jerusalem named Symeon, an upright, devout man, who was living in expectation of the comforting of Israel, and under the influence of the holy Spirit. ²⁶ It had been revealed to him by the holy Spirit that he should not die without seeing the Lord's Messiah. ²⁷ And under the Spirit's influence he went into the Temple, and when Jesus' parents brought him there to do for him what the Law required, ²⁸ Symeon also took him in his arms and blessed God, and said,

²⁹   "Now, Master, you will let your slave
go free

In peace, as you promised,
³⁰   For my eyes have seen your
salvation
³¹   Which you have set before all the
nations,
³²   A light of revelation for the
heathen,
And a glory to your people
Israel!"

³³ The child's father and mother were astonished at what Symeon said. ³⁴ And he gave them his blessing, and said to Mary, the child's mother, "This child is destined to cause the fall and rise of many in Israel, and to be a portent that will be much debated— ³⁵ you yourself will be pierced to the heart—and so the thoughts of many minds will be revealed." ³⁶ There was also a prophetess there named Hannah, the daughter of Phanuel, who belonged to the tribe of Asher. She was very old, for after her girlhood she had been married for seven years, ³⁷ and she had been a widow until she was now eighty-four. She never left the Temple, but worshipped night and day with fasting and prayer. ³⁸ She came up just at that time and gave thanks to God and spoke about the child to all who were living in

---

2, 23: "Every first-born . . . Lord": See Exodus 13:2.

American Version

expectation of the liberation of Jerusalem. ³⁹ When they had done everything that the Law of the Lord required, they returned to Galilee, to their own town of Nazareth.

⁴⁰ And the child grew up and became strong and thoughtful, with God's blessing resting on him.

⁴¹ His parents used to go to Jerusalem every year at the Passover Festival. ⁴² And when he was twelve years old, they went up as usual to the festival and made their customary stay. ⁴³ When they started back the boy Jesus stayed behind in Jerusalem without his parents' knowledge. ⁴⁴ They supposed that he was somewhere in the party, and traveled until the end of the first day's journey, and then they looked everywhere for him among their relatives and acquaintances. ⁴⁵ As they could not find him, they went back to Jerusalem in search of him. ⁴⁶ And on the third day they found him in the Temple, sitting among the teachers, listening to them and asking them questions, ⁴⁷ and everyone who heard him was astonished at his intelligence and at the answers he made. ⁴⁸ When his parents saw him they were amazed, and his mother said to him. "My child, why did you treat us like this? Here your father and I have been looking for you, and have been very anxious." ⁴⁹ He said to them, "How did you come to look for me? Did you not know that I must be at my Father's house?" ⁵⁰ But they did not understand what he told them. ⁵¹ And he went back with them to Nazareth and obeyed them. And his

mother treasured all these things up in her mind.

⁵² As Jesus grew older he gained in wisdom and won the approval of God and men.

Chapter 3   In the fifteenth year of the reign of the Emperor Tiberius,° when Pontius Pilate was governor of Judea, and Herod governor of Galilee, while his brother Philip was governor of the territory of Iturea and Trachonitis, and Lysanias was the governor of Abilene, ² in the high priesthood of Annas and Caiaphas, a message from God came to Zechariah's son John in the desert. ³ And he went all through the Jordan Valley preaching repentance and baptism in order to obtain the forgiveness of sins, ⁴ as the book of the sermons of the prophet Isaiah says,

> "Hark! Someone is shouting in the
>   desert,
> Get the Lord's way ready!
> Make his paths straight.
> ⁵   Every hollow must be filled up,
> And every mountain and hill
>   leveled.
> What is crooked is to be made
>   straight,
> And the rough roads are to be made
>   smooth,
> ⁶   And all mankind is to see how God
>   can save!"

⁷ So he would say to the crowds that came out there to be baptized by him, "You brood of snakes! Who warned you to fly from the wrath that is coming? ⁸ Then produce fruit that will be consistent with your professed repentance! And do not begin to say to yourselves, 'We have Abra-

---

3, 1: fifteenth year . . . Tiberius: 26 or 27 C.E.

American Version

ham for our forefather,' for I tell you, God can produce descendants for Abraham right out of these stones! ⁹ But the axe is already lying at the roots of the trees. Any tree that fails to produce good fruit is going to be cut down and thrown into the fire." ¹⁰ The crowds would ask him, "Then what ought we to do?" ¹¹ And he answered, "The man who has two shirts must share with the man who has none, and the man who has food must do the same." ¹² Even tax-collectors came to be baptized, and they said to him, "Master, what ought we to do?" ¹³ He said to them, "Do not collect any more than you are authorized to." ¹⁴ And soldiers would ask him, "And what ought we to do?" He said to them, "Do not extort money or make false charges against people, but be satisfied with your pay."

¹⁵ As all this aroused people's expectations, and they were all wondering in their hearts whether John was the Christ, ¹⁶ John said to them all, "I am only baptizing you in water, but someone is coming who is stronger than I am, whose shoes I am not fit to untie. He will baptize you in the holy Spirit and in fire. ¹⁷ He has his winnowing fork in his hand, to clean up his threshing-floor, and store his wheat in his barn, but he will burn up the chaff with inextinguishable fire."

¹⁸ So with many varied exhortations he would preach the good news to the people, ¹⁹ but Herod the governor, whom he condemned because of Herodias, his brother's wife,° and all the wicked things Herod had done, ²⁰ crowned them all by putting John in prison.

²¹ Now when all the people were baptized and when Jesus also after his baptism was praying, heaven opened ²² and the holy Spirit came down upon him in the material shape of a dove, and there came a voice from heaven,

"You are my Son, my Beloved! You are my Chosen!" [. . .]

↶ Matthew 5–7

Translated by Edgar Goodspeed (American Version)

[THE SERMON ON THE MOUNT]

American Version	*King James Version*
Chapter 5 When he saw the crowds of people he went up on the mountain. There he seated himself, and when his disciples had come up	*Chapter 5* And seeing the multitudes, he went up into a mountain: and when he was set, his disciples came unto him:

3, 19: **whom he condemned . . . wife:** John had objected that Herod's marriage to Herodias, his brother Philip's wife, was unlawful.

American Version | *King James Version*

American Version

to him, 2 he opened his lips to teach them. And he said,

3 "Blessed are those who feel their spiritual need, for the Kingdom of Heaven belongs to them!

4 "Blessed are the mourners, for they will be consoled!

5 "Blessed are the humble-minded, for they will possess the land!

6 "Blessed are those who are hungry and thirsty for uprightness, for they will be satisfied!

7 "Blessed are the merciful, for they will be shown mercy!

8 "Blessed are the pure in heart, for they will see God!

9 "Blessed are the peacemakers, for they will be called God's sons!

10 "Blessed are those who have endured persecution for their uprightness, for the Kingdom of Heaven belongs to them!

11 "Blessed are you when people abuse you, and persecute you, and falsely say everything bad of you, on my account. 12 Be glad and exult over it, for you will be richly rewarded in heaven, for that is the way they persecuted the prophets who went before you!

13 "You are the salt of the earth! But if salt loses its strength, how can it be made salt again? It is good for nothing but to be thrown away and trodden underfoot. 14 You are the light of the world! A city that is built upon a hill cannot be hidden.

15 People do not light a lamp and put it under a peck-measure; they put it on its stand and it gives light to everyone in the house. 16 Your light must burn in that way among men so that they will see the good

King James Version

2 And he opened his mouth, and taught them, saying,

3 Blessed *are* the poor in spirit: for theirs is the kingdom of heaven.

4 Blessed *are* they that mourn: for they shall be comforted.

5 Blessed *are* the meek: for they shall inherit the earth.

6 Blessed *are* they which do hunger and thirst after righteousness: for they shall be filled.

7 Blessed *are* the merciful: for they shall obtain mercy.

8 Blessed *are* the pure in heart: for they shall see God.

9 Blessed *are* the peacemakers: for they shall be called the children of God.

10 Blessed *are* they which are persecuted for righteousness' sake: for theirs is the kingdom of heaven.

11 Blessed are ye, when *men* shall revile you, and persecute *you,* and shall say all manner of evil against you falsely, for my sake. 12 Rejoice, and be exceeding glad: for great *is* your reward in heaven: for so persecuted they the prophets which were before you.

13 ¶ Ye are the salt of the earth: but if the salt have lost his savour, wherewith shall it be salted? it is thenceforth good for nothing, but to be cast out, and to be trodden under foot of men. 14 Ye are the light of the world. A city that is set on a hill cannot be hid. 15 Neither do men light a candle, and put it under a bushel, but on a candlestick; and it giveth light unto all that are in the house. 16 Let your light so shine before men, that they may see your good works, and glorify your Father which is in heaven.

American Version

you do, and praise your Father in heaven.

17 "Do not suppose that I have come to do away with the Law or the Prophets. I have not come to do away with them but to enforce them. 18 For I tell you, as long as heaven and earth endure, not one dotting of an *i* or crossing of a *t* will be dropped from the Law until it is all observed. 19 Anyone, therefore, who weakens one of the slightest of these commands, and teaches others to do so, will be ranked lowest in the Kingdom of Heaven; but anyone who observes them and teaches others to do so will be ranked high in the Kingdom of Heaven. 20 For I tell you that unless your uprightness is far superior to that of the scribes and Pharisees,° you will never even enter the Kingdom of Heaven!

21 "You have heard that the men of old were told 'You shall not murder,' and 'Whoever murders will have to answer to the court.' 22 But I tell you that anyone who gets angry with his brother will have to answer to the court, and anyone who speaks contemptuously to his brother will have to answer to the great council, and anyone who says to his brother 'You cursed fool!' will have to answer for it in the fiery pit! 23 So when you are presenting your gift at the altar, if you remember that your brother has any grievance against you, 24 leave your gift right there before the altar and go and make up with your brother; then come back and present your gift. 25 Be quick and come to

King James Version

17 ¶ Think not that I am come to destroy the law, or the prophets: I am not come to destroy, but to fulfil. 18 For verily I say unto you, Till heaven and earth pass, one jot or one tittle shall in no wise pass from the law, till all be fulfilled. 19 Whosoever therefore shall break one of these least commandments, and shall teach men so, he shall be called the least in the kingdom of heaven: but whosoever shall do and teach *them,* the same shall be called great in the kingdom of heaven. 20 For I say unto you, That except your righteousness shall exceed *the righteousness* of the scribes and Pharisees, ye shall in no case enter into the kingdom of heaven.

21 ¶ Ye have heard that it was said by them of old time, Thou shalt not kill; and whosoever shall kill shall be in danger of the judgment: 22 But I say unto you, That whosoever is angry with his brother without a cause shall be in danger of the judgment: and whosoever shall say to his brother, 'Raca,' shall be in danger of the council: but whosoever shall say, 'Thou fool,' shall be in danger of hell fire. 23 Therefore if thou bring thy gift to the altar, and there rememberest that thy brother hath aught against thee; 24 Leave there thy gift before the altar, and go thy way; first be reconciled to thy brother, and then come and offer thy gift. 25 Agree with thine adversary quickly, while thou art in the way with him; lest at any time the adversary deliver thee to the judge, and the judge deliver thee to

---

5, 20: **Pharisees:** A Jewish sect that insisted on strict observance of the Mosaic law.

American Version

terms with your opponent while you are on the way to court with him, or he may hand you over to the judge, and the judge may hand you over to the officer, and you will be thrown into prison. 26 I tell you, you will never get out again until you have paid the last penny!

27 "You have heard that men were told 'You shall not commit adultery.' 28 But I tell you that anyone who looks at a woman with desire has already committed adultery with her in his heart. 29 But if your right eye makes you fall, tear it out and throw it away, for you might better lose one part of your body than have it all thrown into the pit! 30 If your right hand makes you fall, cut it off and throw it away, for you might better lose one part of your body than have it all go down to the pit!

31 "They were told, 'Anyone who divorces his wife must give her a certificate of divorce.' 32 But I tell you that anyone who divorces his wife on any ground, except unfaithfulness, makes her commit adultery, and anyone who marries her after she is divorced commits adultery.

33 "Again, you have heard that the men of old were told, 'You shall not swear falsely, but you must fulfil your oaths to the Lord.' 34 But I tell you not to swear at all, either by heaven, for it is God's throne, 35 or by the earth, for it is his footstool, or by Jerusalem, for it is the city of the great king. 36 You must not swear by your own head, for you cannot make one single hair white or black. 37 But your way of speaking must be 'Yes' or 'No.' Anything that goes beyond that comes from the evil one.

King James Version

the officer, and thou be cast into prison. 26 Verily I say unto thee, Thou shalt by no means come out thence, till thou hast paid the uttermost farthing.

27 ¶ Ye have heard that it was said by them of old time, Thou shalt not commit adultery: 28 But I say unto you, That whosoever looketh on a woman to lust after her hath committed adultery with her already in his heart. 29 And if thy right eye offend thee, pluck it out, and cast *it* from thee: for it is profitable for thee that one of thy members should perish, and not *that* thy whole body should be cast into hell. 30 And if thy right hand offend thee, cut it off, and cast *it* from thee: for it is profitable for thee that one of thy members should perish, and not *that* thy whole body should be cast into hell. 31 It hath been said, Whosoever shall put away his wife, let him give her a writing of divorcement. 32 But I say unto you, That whosoever shall put away his wife, saving for the cause of fornication, causeth her to commit adultery: and whosoever shall marry her that is divorced committeth adultery.

33 ¶ Again, ye have heard that it hath been said by them of old time, Thou shalt not forswear thyself, but shalt perform unto the Lord thine oaths: 34 But I say unto you, Swear not at all; neither by heaven; for it is God's throne: 35 Nor by the earth; for it is his footstool: neither by Jerusalem; for it is the city of the great King. 36 Neither shalt thou swear by thy head, because thou canst not make one hair white or black. 37 But let your communication be, 'Yea, yea'; 'Nay, nay': for whatsoever is more than these cometh of evil.

American Version

38 "You have heard that they were told, 'An eye for an eye and a tooth for a tooth.' 39 But I tell you not to resist injury, but if anyone strikes you on your right cheek, turn the other to him too; 40 and if anyone wants to sue you for your shirt, let him have your coat too. 41 And if anyone forces you to go one mile, go two miles with him. 42 If anyone begs from you, give to him, and when anyone wants to borrow from you, do not turn away.

43 "You have heard that they were told, 'You must love your neighbor and hate your enemy.' 44 But I tell you, love your enemies and pray for your persecutors, 45 so that you may show yourselves true sons of your Father in heaven, for he makes his sun rise on bad and good alike, and makes the rain fall on the upright and the wrongdoers. 46 For if you love only those who love you, what reward can you expect? Do not the very tax-collectors do that? 47 And if you are polite to your brothers and no one else, what is there remarkable in that? Do not the very heathen do that? 48 So you are to be perfect, as your heavenly Father is.

Chapter 6 "But take care not to do your good deeds in public for people to see, for, if you do, you will get no reward from your Father in heaven. 2 So when you are going to give to charity, do not blow a trumpet before yourself, as the hypocrites do, in the synagogues and the streets, to make people praise them. I tell you, that is all the reward they will get! 3 But when you give to charity, your own left hand must not know what your right hand is doing, 4 so that your charity may be secret, and

King James Version

38 ¶ Ye have heard that it hath been said, An eye for an eye, and a tooth for a tooth: 39 But I say unto you, That ye resist not evil: but whosoever shall smite thee on thy right cheek, turn to him the other also. 40 And if any man will sue thee at the law, and take away thy coat, let him have *thy* cloak also. 41 And whosoever shall compel thee to go a mile, go with him twain. 42 Give to him that asketh thee, and from him that would borrow of thee turn not thou away.

43 ¶ Ye have heard that it hath been said, Thou shalt love thy neighbour, and hate thine enemy. 44 But I say unto you, Love your enemies, bless them that curse you, do good to them that hate you, and pray for them which despitefully use you, and persecute you; 45 That ye may be the children of your Father which is in heaven: for he maketh his sun to rise on the evil and on the good, and sendeth rain on the just and on the unjust. 46 For if ye love them which love you, what reward have ye? do not even the publicans the same? 47 And if ye salute your brethren only, what do ye more *than others*? do not even the publicans so? 48 Be ye therefore perfect, even as your Father which is in heaven is perfect.

Chapter 6 Take heed that ye do not [sic] your alms before men, to be seen of them: otherwise ye have no reward of your Father which is in heaven.

2 Therefore when thou doest *thine* alms, do not sound a trumpet before thee, as the hypocrites do in the synagogues and in the streets, that they may have glory of men. Verily I say unto you, They have their reward.

American Version

your Father who sees what is secret will reward you.

⁵ "When you pray, you must not be like the hypocrites, for they like to pray standing in the synagogues and in the corners of the squares, to let people see them. I tell you, that is the only reward they will get! ⁶ But when you pray, go into your own room, and shut the door, and pray to your Father who is unseen, and your Father who sees what is secret will reward you. ⁷ And when you pray, do not repeat empty phrases as the heathen do, for they imagine that their prayers will be heard if they use words enough. ⁸ You must not be like them. For God, who is your Father, knows what you need before you ask him. ⁹ This, therefore, is the way you are to pray:

    'Our Father in heaven,
    Your name be revered!
10   Your kingdom come!
    Your will be done on earth as it is
      done in heaven!
11   Give us today bread for the day,
12   And forgive us our debts, as we have
      forgiven our debtors.
13   And do not subject us to
      temptation,
    But save us from the evil one.'

¹⁴ For if you forgive others when they offend you, your heavenly Father will forgive you too. ¹⁵ But if you do not forgive others when they offend you, your heavenly Father will not forgive you for your offenses.

¹⁶ "When you fast, do not put on a gloomy look, like the hypocrites, for they neglect their personal appearance to let people see that they are fasting. I tell you, that is all the

King James Version

3 But when thou doest alms, let not thy left hand know what thy right hand doeth: 4 That thine alms may be in secret: and thy Father which seeth in secret himself shall reward thee openly.

5 ¶ And when thou prayest, thou shalt not be as the hypocrites *are:* for they love to pray standing in the synagogues and in the corners of the streets, that they may be seen of men. Verily I say unto you, They have their reward. 6 But thou, when thou prayest, enter into thy closet, and when thou hast shut thy door, pray to thy Father which is in secret; and thy Father which seeth in secret shall reward thee openly. 7 But when ye pray, use not vain repetitions, as the heathen *do:* for they think that they shall be heard for their much speaking. 8 Be not yet therefore like unto them: for your Father knoweth what things ye have need of, before ye ask him. 9 After this manner therefore pray ye: Our Father which art in heaven, Hallowed be thy name. 10 Thy kingdom come. Thy will be done in earth, as *it is* in heaven. 11 Give us this day our daily bread. 12 And forgive us our debts, as we forgive our debtors. 13 And lead us not into temptation, but deliver us from evil: For thine is the kingdom, and the power, and the glory, for ever. Amen. 14 For if ye forgive men their trespasses, your heavenly Father will also forgive you: 15 But if ye forgive not men their trespasses, neither will your Father forgive your trespasses. 16 ¶ Moreover when ye fast, be not, as the hypocrites, of a sad countenance: for they disfigure their faces, that they may appear unto men to

American Version

reward they will get. ¹⁷ But when you fast, perfume your hair and wash your face, ¹⁸ so that no one may see that you are fasting, except your Father who is unseen, and your Father who sees what is secret, will reward you.

¹⁹ "Do not store up your riches on earth, where moths and rust destroy them, and where thieves break in and steal them, ²⁰ but store up your riches in heaven, where moths and rust cannot destroy them, and where thieves cannot break in and steal them. ²¹ For wherever your treasure is, your heart will be also. ²² The eye is the lamp of the body. If then your eye is sound, your whole body will be light, ²³ but if your eye is unsound, your whole body will be dark. If, therefore, your very light is darkness, how deep the darkness will be! ²⁴ No slave can belong to two masters, for he will either hate one and love the other, or stand by one and make light of the other. You cannot serve God and money. ²⁵ Therefore, I tell you, do not worry about life, wondering what you will have to eat or drink, or about your body, wondering what you will have to wear. Is not life more important than food, and the body than clothes? ²⁶ Look at the wild birds. They do not sow or reap, or store their food in barns, and yet your heavenly Father feeds them. Are you not of more account than they? ²⁷ But which of you with all his worry can add a single hour to his life? ²⁸ Why should you worry about clothing? See how the wild flowers grow. They do not toil or spin, ²⁹ and yet I tell you, even Solomon in all his splendor was

King James Version

fast. Verily I say unto you, They have their reward. 17 But thou, when thou fastest, anoint thine head, and wash thy face; 18 That thou appear not unto men to fast, but unto thy Father which is in secret: and thy Father which seeth in secret shall reward thee openly.

19 ¶ Lay not up for yourselves treasures upon earth, where moth and rust doth corrupt, and where thieves break through and steal: 20 But lay up for yourselves treasures in heaven, where neither moth nor rust doth corrupt, and where thieves do not break through nor steal: 21 For where your treasure is, there will your heart be also. 22 The light of the body is the eye: if therefore thine eye be single, thy whole body shall be full of light. 23 But if thine eye be evil, thy whole body shall be full of darkness. If therefore the light that is in thee be darkness, how great *is* that darkness!

24 ¶ No man can serve two masters: for either he will hate the one, and love the other; or else he will hold to the one, and despise the other; Ye cannot serve God and mammon. 25 Therefore I say unto you, Take no thought for your life, what ye shall eat, or what ye shall drink; nor yet for your body, what ye shall put on. Is not the life more than meat, and the body than raiment? 26 Behold the fowls of the air: for they sow not, neither do they reap, nor gather into barns; yet your heavenly Father feedeth them. Are ye not much better than they? 27 Which of you by taking thought can add one cubit unto his stature? 28 And why take ye thought for raiment? Consider the

American Version

never dressed like one of them.
30 But if God so beautifully dresses the wild grass, which is alive today and is thrown into the furnace tomorrow, will he not much more surely clothe you, you who have so little faith? 31 So do not worry and say, 'What shall we have to eat?' or 'What shall we have to drink?' or 'What shall we have to wear?' 32 For these are all things the heathen are in pursuit of, and your heavenly Father knows well that you need all this. 33 But you must make his kingdom, and uprightness before him, your greatest care, and you will have all these other things besides. 34 So do not worry about tomorrow, for tomorrow will have worries of its own. Let each day be content with its own ills.

Chapter 7 "Pass no more judgments upon other people, so that you may not have judgment passed upon you. 2 For you will be judged by the standard you judge by, and men will pay you back with the same measure you have used with them. 3 Why do you keep looking at the speck in your brother's eye, and pay no attention to the beam that is in your own? 4 How can you say to your brother, 'Just let me get that speck out of your eye,' when all the time there is a beam in your own? 5 You hypocrite! First get the beam out of your own eye, and then you can see to get the speck out of your brother's eye.

6 "Do not give what is sacred to dogs, and do not throw your pearls before pigs, or they will trample them under their feet and turn and tear you in pieces. 7 Ask, and what you ask will be given you. Search, and

King James Version

lilies of the field, how they grow; they toil not, neither do they spin:
29 And yet I say unto you, That even Solomon in all his glory was not arrayed like one of these. 30 Wherefore, if God so clothe the grass of the field, which to day is, and to morrow is cast into the oven, *shall he* not much more *clothe* you, O ye of little faith? 31 Therefore take no thought, saying, What shall we eat? or, What shall we drink? or, Wherewithal shall we be clothed? 32 (For after all these things do the Gentiles seek:) for your heavenly Father knoweth that ye have need of all these things. 33 But seek ye first the kingdom of God, and his righteousness; and all these things shall be added unto you. 34 Take therefore no thought for the morrow: for the morrow shall take thought for the things of itself. Sufficient unto the day *is* the evil thereof.

Chapter 7 Judge not, that ye be not judged. 2 For with what judgment ye judge, ye shall be judged: and with what measure ye mete, it shall be measured to you again. 3 And why beholdest thou the mote that is in thy brother's eye, but considerest not the beam that is in thine own eye? 4 Or how wilt thou say to thy brother, Let me pull out the mote out of thine eye; and, behold, a beam *is* in thine own eye? 5 Thou hypocrite, first cast out the beam out of thine own eye; and then shalt thou see clearly to cast out the mote out of thy brother's eye.
6 ¶ Give not that which is holy unto the dogs, neither cast ye your pearls before swine, lest they trample them under their feet, and turn again and rend you.
7 ¶ Ask, and it shall be given you;

American Version

you will find what you search for. Knock, and the door will open to you. 8 For it is always the one who asks who receives, and the one who searches who finds, and the one who knocks to whom the door opens. 9 Which of you men when his son asks him for some bread will give him a stone? 10 Or if he asks for a fish, will he give him a snake? 11 So if you, bad as you are, know enough to give your children what is good, how much more surely will your Father in heaven give what is good to those who ask him for it! 12 Therefore, you must always treat other people as you would like to have them treat you, for this sums up the Law and the Prophets.

13 "Go in at the narrow gate. For the road that leads to destruction is broad and spacious, and there are many who go in by it. 14 But the gate is narrow and the road is hard that leads to life, and there are few that find it.

15 "Beware of the false prophets, who come to you disguised as sheep but are ravenous wolves underneath. 16 You can tell them by their fruit. Do people pick grapes off thorns, or figs off thistles? 17 Just so any sound tree bears good fruit, but a poor tree bears bad fruit. 18 No sound tree can bear bad fruit, and no poor tree can bear good fruit. 19 Any tree that does not bear good fruit is cut down and burned. 20 So you can tell them by their fruit. 21 It is not everyone who says to me 'Lord! Lord!' who will get into the Kingdom of Heaven, but only those who do the will of my Father in heaven. 22 Many will say to me on that Day, 'Lord! Lord! Was it

King James Version

seek, and ye shall find; knock, and it shall be opened unto you: 8 For every one that asketh receiveth; and he that seeketh findeth; and to him that knocketh it shall be opened. 9 Or what man is there of you, whom if his son ask bread, will he give him a stone? 10 Or if he ask a fish, will he give him a serpent? 11 If ye then, being evil, know how to give good gifts unto your children, how much more shall your Father which is in heaven give good things to them that ask him? 12 Therefore all things whatsoever ye would that men should do to you, do ye even so to them: for this is the law and the prophets.

13 ¶ Enter ye in at the strait gate: for wide *is* the gate, and broad *is* the way, that leadeth to destruction, and many there be which go in thereat: 14 Because strait *is* the gate, and narrow *is* the way, which leadeth unto life, and few there be that find it.

15 ¶ Beware of false prophets, which come to you in sheep's clothing, but inwardly they are ravening wolves. 16 Ye shall know them by their fruits. Do men gather grapes of thorns, or figs of thistles? 17 Even so every good tree bringeth forth good fruit; but a corrupt tree bringeth forth evil fruit. 18 A good tree cannot bring forth evil fruit, neither *can* a corrupt tree bring forth good fruit. 19 Every tree that bringeth not forth good fruit is hewn down, and cast into the fire. 20 Wherefore by their fruits ye shall know them.

21 ¶ Not every one that saith unto me, Lord, Lord, shall enter into the kingdom of heaven; but he that doeth the will of my Father which is

American Version

not in your name that we prophesied, and by your name that we drove out demons, and by your name that we did many mighty acts?' 23 Then I will say to them plainly, 'I never knew you! Go away from me, you do wrong!'

24 "Everyone, therefore, who listens to this teaching of mine and acts upon it, will be like a sensible man who built his house on rock. 25 And the rain fell, and the rivers rose, and the winds blew, and beat about that house, and it did not go down, for its foundations were on rock. 26 And anyone who listens to this teaching of mine and does not act upon it, will be like a foolish man who built his house on sand. 27 And the rain fell, and the rivers rose, and the winds blew and beat about that house, and it went down, and its downfall was complete."

28 When Jesus had finished this discourse, the crowds were astounded at his teaching, for he taught them like one who had authority and not like their scribes.

King James Version

in heaven. 22 Many will say to me in that day, Lord, Lord, have we not prophesied in thy name? and in thy name have cast out devils? and in thy name done many wonderful works? 23 And then will I profess unto them, I never knew you: depart from me, ye that work iniquity.

24 ¶ Therefore whosoever heareth these sayings of mine, and doeth them, I will liken him unto a wise man, which built his house upon a rock: 25 And the rain descended, and the floods came, and the winds blew, and beat upon that house; and it fell not: for it was founded upon a rock. 26 And every one that heareth these sayings of mine, and doeth them not, shall be likened unto a foolish man, which built his house upon the sand: 27 And the rain descended, and the floods came, and the winds blew, and beat upon that house; and it fell: and great was the fall of it. 28 And it came to pass, when Jesus had ended these sayings, the people were astonished at his doctrine: 29 For he taught them as *one* having authority, and not as the scribes.

FROM

 # Matthew 13, 25

Translated by Edgar Goodspeed

[TEACHINGS OF JESUS: PARABLES]

American Version

[THE PARABLE OF THE SOWER]

Chapter 13   That same day Jesus went out of his house and was sitting on the seashore. 2 And such great crowds gathered about him that he

got into a boat and sat down in it, while all the people stood on the shore. 3 And he told them many things in figures, and said to them, "A sower went out to sow, 4 and as he

American Version

was sowing, some of the seed fell by the path and the birds came and ate it up, ⁵ and some fell on rocky ground where there was not much soil and it sprang up at once, because the soil was not deep, ⁶ but when the sun came up it was scorched and withered up, because it had no root. ⁷ And some of it fell among the thorns, and the thorns grew up and choked it out. ⁸ And some fell on good soil, and yielded some a hundred, some sixty, and some thirtyfold. ⁹ Let him who has ears listen!"

¹⁰ His disciples came up and said to him, "Why do you speak to them in figures?" ¹¹ He answered, "You are permitted to know the secrets of the Kingdom of Heaven, but they are not. ¹² For people who have will have more given to them, and will be plentifully supplied, and from people who have nothing even what they have will be taken away. ¹³ This is why I speak to them in figures, because though they look they do not see, and though they listen they do not hear or understand. ¹⁴ They are a fulfilment of Isaiah's prophecy,°

> " 'You will listen and listen, and
>   never understand,
> And you will look and look, and
>   never see!
¹⁵   For this nation's mind has grown
>   dull,
> And they hear faintly with their ears,
> And they have shut their eyes,
> So as never to see with their eyes,
> And hear with their ears,
> And understand with their minds,
>   and turn back,
> And let me cure them!'

¹⁶ But blessed are your eyes, for they do see, and your ears, for they do hear. ¹⁷ For I tell you, many prophets and upright men have longed to see what you see, and could not see it, and to hear what you hear, and could not hear it. ¹⁸ You must listen closely then to the figure of the sower. ¹⁹ When anyone hears the teaching of the kingdom and does not understand it, the evil one comes and robs him of the seed that has been sown in his mind. That is what was sown along the path. ²⁰ And what was sown upon the rocky soil means the man who hears the message and at once accepts it joyfully, ²¹ but it takes no real root in him, and lasts only a little while, and when trouble or persecution comes because of the message, he gives it up at once. ²² And what was sown among the thorns means the man who listens to the message, and then the worries of the time and the pleasure of being rich choke the message out, and it yields nothing. ²³ And what was sown in good ground means the man who listens to the message and understands it, and yields one a hundred, and another sixty, and another thirtyfold." [. . .]

[THE PARABLE OF THE TALENTS]

Chapter 25 ¹⁴ "For it is just like a man who was going on a journey, and called in his slaves, and put his property in their hands. ¹⁵ He gave one five thousand dollars, and another two thousand, and another one thousand; to each according to

---

13, 14: Isaiah's prophecy: Isaiah 5:9–10.

American Version

his ability. ¹⁶ Then he went away. The man who had received the five thousand dollars immediately went into business with the money, and made five thousand more. ¹⁷ In the same way the man who had received the two thousand made two thousand more. ¹⁸ But the man who had received the one thousand went away and dug a hole in the ground and hid his master's money. ¹⁹ Long afterward, their master came back and settled accounts with them. ²⁰ And the man who had received the five thousand dollars came up bringing him five thousand more, and said, 'Sir, you put five thousand dollars in my hands; here I have made five thousand more.' ²¹ His master said to him, 'Well done, my excellent, faithful slave! you have been faithful about a small amount; I will put a large one into your hands. Come, share your master's enjoyment!' ²² And the man who had received the two thousand came up and said, 'Sir, you put two thousand dollars into my hands; here I have made two thousand more.' ²³ His master said to him, 'Well done, my excellent,

faithful slave! you have been faithful about a small amount; I will put a large one into your hands. Come! share your master's enjoyment.' ²⁴ And the man who had received the one thousand came up and said, 'Sir, I knew you were a hard man, who reaped where you had not sown, and gathered where you had not threshed, ²⁵ and I was frightened, and I went and hid your thousand dollars in the ground. Here is your money!' ²⁶ His master answered, 'You wicked, idle slave! You knew that I reaped where I had not sown and gathered where I had not threshed? ²⁷ Then you ought to have put my money in the bank, and then when I came back I would have gotten my property with interest. ²⁸ So take the thousand dollars away from him, and give it to the man who has the ten thousand, ²⁹ for the man who has will have more given him, and will be plentifully supplied, and from the man who has nothing even what he has will be taken away. ³⁰ And put the good-for-nothing slave out into the darkness outside, to weep and grind his teeth there.'" [...]

FROM

∾ Luke 10, 15

Translated by Edgar Goodspeed (American Version)

[TEACHINGS OF JESUS: PARABLES]

American Version   *King James Version*

[THE GOOD SAMARITAN]

Chapter 10 ²⁵ Then an expert in the Law got up to test him and said, "Master, what must I do to make sure of eternal life?" ²⁶ Jesus said to him,

Chapter 10 ²⁵ ¶ And, behold, a certain lawyer stood up, and tempted him, saying, Master, what shall I do to inherit eternal life? ²⁶ He said

American Version

"What does the Law say? How does it read?" 27 He answered, "'You must love the Lord your God with your whole heart, your whole soul, your whole strength, and your whole mind,' and 'your neighbor as you do yourself.'" 28 Jesus said to him, "You are right. Do that, and you will live." 29 But he, wishing to justify his question, said, "And who is my neighbor?" 30 Jesus replied, "A man was on his way down from Jerusalem to Jericho, when he fell into the hands of robbers, and they stripped him and beat him and went off leaving him half dead. 31 Now a priest happened to be going that way, and when he saw him, he went by on the other side of the road. 32 And a Levite° also came to the place, and when he saw him, he went by on the other side. 33 But a Samaritan° who was traveling that way came upon him, and when he saw him he pitied him, 34 and he went up to him and dressed his wounds with oil and wine and bound them up. And he put him on his own mule and brought him to an inn and took care of him. 35 The next day he took out a dollar and gave it to the innkeeper and said, 'Take care of him, and whatever more you spend I will refund to you on my way back.' 36 Which of these three do you think proved himself a neighbor to the man who fell into the robbers' hands?" 37 He said, "The man who took pity on him." Jesus said to him, "Go and do so yourself!"

King James Version

unto him, What is written in the law? how readest thou? 27 And he answering said, Thou shalt love the Lord thy God with all thy heart, and with all thy soul, and with all thy strength, and with all thy mind; and thy neighbour as thyself. 28 And he said unto him, Thou hast answered right: this do, and thou shalt live. 29 But he, willing to justify himself, said unto Jesus, And who is my neighbour? 30 And Jesus answering said, A certain *man* went down from Jerusalem to Jericho, and fell among thieves, which stripped him of his raiment, and wounded *him*, and departed, leaving *him* half dead. 31 And by chance there came down a certain priest that way; and when he saw him, he passed by on the other side. 32 And likewise a Levite, when he was at the place, came and looked *on him*, and passed by on the other side. 33 But a certain Samaritan, as he journeyed, came where he was; and when he saw him, he had compassion *on him*, 34 And went to *him*, and bound up his wounds, pouring in oil and wine, and set him on his own beast, and brought him to an inn, and took care of him. 35 And on the morrow when he departed, he took out two pence, and gave *them* to the host, and said unto him, Take care of him: and whatsoever thou spendest more, when I come again, I will repay thee. 36 Which now of these three, thinkest thou, was neighbour unto him that fell among the thieves? 37 And he said, He that shewed mercy on him. Then said Jesus unto him, Go, and do thou likewise.

10, 32: **Levite:** A lay associate of the priest.
10, 33: **Samaritan:** A foreigner, not expected to show sympathy to a Jew.

American Version   *King James Version*

[THE PRODIGAL SON]

Chapter 15 ¹¹ And he said, ¹² "A man had two sons. The younger of them said to his father, 'Father, give me my share of the property.' So he divided his property between them. ¹³ Not many days later, the younger son gathered up all he had, and went away to a distant country, and there he squandered his property by fast living. ¹⁴ After he had spent it all, a severe famine arose in that country, and he began to be in want. ¹⁵ And he went and hired himself out to a resident of the country, and he sent him into his fields to tend pigs. ¹⁶ And he was ready to fill himself with the pods the pigs were eating, and no one would give him anything. ¹⁷ When he came to himself he said, 'How many hired men my father has, who have more than enough to eat, and here I am, dying of hunger! ¹⁸ I will get up, and go to my father and say to him, "Father, I have sinned against heaven and in your eyes; ¹⁹ I no longer deserve to be called your son; treat me like one of your hired men!"' ²⁰ And he got up and went to his father. But while he was still a long way off, his father saw him, and pitied him, and ran and fell on his neck, and kissed him. ²¹ His son said to him, 'Father, I have sinned against heaven, and in your eyes; I no longer deserve to be called your son; treat me like one of your hired men!' ²² But his father said to his slave, 'Make haste and get out the best robe, and put it on him, and put a ring on his hand, and shoes on his feet; ²³ and get the calf we are fattening, and kill it, and let us feast and	*Chapter 15* 11 ¶ And he said, A certain man had two sons: 12 And the younger of them said to *his* father, Father, give me the portion of goods that falleth *to me*. And he divided unto them *his* living. 13 And not many days after the younger son gathered all together, and took his journey into a far country, and there wasted his substance with riotous living. 14 And when he had spent all, there arose a mighty famine in that land; and he began to be in want. 15 And he went and joined himself to a citizen of that country; and he sent him into his fields to feed swine. 16 And he would fain have filled his belly with the husks that the swine did eat: and no man gave unto him. 17 And when he came to himself, he said, How many hired servants of my father's have bread enough and to spare, and I perish with hunger! 18 I will arise and go to my father, and will say unto him, Father, I have sinned against heaven and before thee, 19 And am no more worthy to be called thy son: make me as one of thy hired servants. 20 And he arose, and came to his father. But when he was yet a great way off, his father saw him, and had compassion, and ran, and fell on his neck, and kissed him. 21 And the son said unto him, Father, I have sinned against heaven, and in thy sight, and am no more worthy to be called thy son. 22 But the father said to his servants, Bring forth the best robe, and put *it* on him; and put a ring on his hand, and shoes on *his* feet: 23 And bring hither the fatted calf, and kill *it;* and

American Version

celebrate, 24 for my son here was dead, and he has come to life; he was lost, and he is found!' So they began to celebrate. 25 But his elder son was in the field. When he came in and approached the house, he heard music and dancing, 26 and he called one of the servants to him and asked him what it meant. 27 He said to him, 'Your brother has come, and your father has killed the calf he has been fattening, because he has gotten him back alive and well.' 28 But he was angry and would not go into the house. And his father came out and urged him. 29 And he said to his father, 'Here I have served you all these years, and have never disobeyed an order of yours, and you have never given me a kid, so that I could entertain my friends. 30 But when your son here came, who has eaten up your property with women of the street, for him you killed the calf you have been fattening!' 31 But he said to him, 'My child, you have been with me all the time, and everything I have is yours. 32 But we had to celebrate and be glad, because your brother was dead, and has come to life, and was lost and is found!'"

King James Version

let us eat, and be merry: 24 For this my son was dead, and is alive again; he was lost, and is found. And they began to be merry. 25 Now his elder son was in the field: and as he came and drew nigh to the house, he heard music and dancing. 26 And he called one of the servants, and asked what these things meant. 27 And he said unto him, Thy brother is come; and thy father hath killed the fatted calf, because he hath received him safe and sound. 28 And he was angry, and would not go in: therefore came his father out, and entreated him. 29 And he answering said to *his* father, Lo, these many years do I serve thee, neither transgressed I at any time thy commandment; and yet thou never gavest me a kid, that I might make merry with my friends: 30 But as soon as this thy son was come, which hath devoured thy living with harlots, thou hast killed for him the fatted calf. 31 And he said unto him, Son, thou art ever with me, and all that I have is thine. 32 It was meet that we should make merry, and be glad: for this thy brother was dead, and is alive again; and was lost, and is found.

FROM

❧ Luke 22–24

Translated by Edgar Goodspeed

[THE BETRAYAL, TRIAL, CRUCIFIXION, AND RESURRECTION OF JESUS]

American Version

Chapter 22   The festival of Unleavened Bread, which is called the Passover, was approaching.
2 And the high priests and the scribes were casting about for a way to put him to death, for they were afraid of the people.

3 But Satan entered into Judas, who was called Iscariot, a member of the Twelve. 4 And he went off and discussed with the high priests and captains of the Temple how he could betray him to them. 5 And they were delighted and agreed to pay him for it. 6 And he accepted their offer, and watched for an opportunity to betray him to them without a disturbance.

7 When the day of Unleavened Bread came, on which the Passover lamb had to be sacrificed, 8 Jesus sent Peter and John, saying to them, "Go and make preparations for us to eat the Passover." 9 They said to him, "Where do you want us to prepare it?" 10 He said to them, "Just after you enter the city, you will meet a man carrying a pitcher of water. Follow him to the house to which he goes, 11 and say to the man of the house, 'Our Master says to you, "Where is the room where I can eat the Passover supper with my disciples?"' 12 And he will show you a large room upstairs with the necessary furniture. Make your preparations there." 13 So they went and found everything just as he had told them, and they prepared the Passover supper.

14 When the time came, he took his place at the table, with the apostles about him. 15 And he said to them, "I have greatly desired to eat this Passover supper with you before I suffer. 16 For I tell you, I will never eat one again until it reaches its fulfilment in the Kingdom of God."
17 And when he was handed a cup, he thanked God, and then said, "Take this and share it among you, for I tell you, 18 I will not drink the product of the vine again until the Kingdom of God comes." 19 And he took a loaf of bread and thanked God, and broke it in pieces, and gave it to them, saying, "This is my body. 21 Yet look! The hand of the man who is betraying me is beside me on the table!
22 For the Son of Man is going his way, as it has been decreed, but alas for the man by whom the Son of Man is betrayed!" 23 And they began to discuss with one another which of them it was who was going to do this.

24 A dispute also arose among them, as to which one of them ought to be considered the greatest. 25 But he said to them, "The kings of the heathen lord it over them, and their authorities are given the title of Benefactor. 26 But you are not to do so, but whoever is greatest among

American Version

you must be like the youngest, and the leader like a servant. 27 For which is greater, the man at the table, or the servant who waits on him? Is not the man at the table? Yet I am like a servant among you. 28 But it is you who have stood by me in my trials. 29 So just as my Father has conferred a kingdom on me 30 I confer on you the right to eat and drink at my table in my kingdom, and to sit on thrones and judge the twelve tribes of Israel! 31 O Simon, Simon! Satan has obtained permission to sift all of you like wheat, 32 but I have prayed that your own faith may not fail. And afterward you yourself must turn and strengthen your brothers." 33 Peter said to him, "Master, I am ready to go to prison and to death with you!" 34 But he said, "I tell you, Peter, the cock will not crow today before you deny three times that you know me!" [. . .]

39 And he went out of the city and up on the Mount of Olives as he was accustomed to do, with his disciples following him. 40 And when he reached the spot, he said to them, "Pray that you may not be subjected to trial." 41 And he withdrew about a stone's throw from them, and kneeling down he prayed 42 and said, "Father, if you are willing, take this cup away from me. But not my will but yours be done!" 45 When he got up from his prayer, he went to the disciples and found them asleep from sorrow. 46 And he said to them. "Why are you asleep? Get up, and pray that you may not be subjected to trial!"

47 While he was still speaking, a crowd of people came up, with the man called Judas, one of the Twelve, at their head, and he stepped up to Jesus to kiss him. 48 Jesus said to him, "Would you betray the Son of Man with a kiss?" 49 Those who were about him saw what was coming and said, "Master, shall we use our swords?" 50 And one of them did strike at the high priest's slave and cut his right ear off. 51 But Jesus answered, "Let me do this much!" And he touched his ear and healed him. 52 And Jesus said to the high priests, captains of the Temple, and elders who had come to take him, "Have you come out with swords and clubs as though I were a robber? 53 When I was among you day after day in the Temple you never laid a hand on me! But you choose this hour, and the cover of darkness!"

54 Then they arrested him and led him away and took him to the house of the high priest. And Peter followed at a distance. 55 And they kindled a fire in the middle of the courtyard and sat about it, and Peter sat down among them. 56 A maid saw him sitting by the fire and looked at him and said, "This man was with him too." 57 But he denied it, and said, "I do not know him." 58 Shortly after, a man saw him and said, "You are one of them too!" But Peter said, "I am not!" 59 About an hour later, another man insisted, "This man was certainly with him too, for he is a Galilean!" 60 But Peter said, "I do not know what you mean." And immediately, just as he spoke, a cock crowed. 61 And the master turned and looked at Peter, and Peter remembered the words the Master had said to him — "Before the cock crows today, you

American Version

will disown me three times." 62 And he went outside and wept bitterly.

63 The men who had Jesus in custody flogged him and made sport of him, 64 and they blindfolded him, and asked him, "Show that you are a prophet! Who was it that struck you?" 65 And they said many other abusive things to him.

66 As soon as it was day, the elders of the people and the high priests and scribes assembled, and brought him before their council, and said to him, 67 "If you are the Christ, tell us so." But he said to them, "If I tell you, you will not believe me, 68 and if I ask you a question, you will not answer me. 69 But from this time on, the Son of Man will be seated at the right hand of God Almighty!" 70 And they all said, "Are you the Son of God then?" And he said to them, "I am, as you say!" 71 Then they said, "What do we want of testimony now? We have heard it ourselves from his own mouth!"

Chapter 23   Then they arose in a body and took him to Pilate, 2 and they made this charge against him: "Here is a man whom we have found misleading our nation, and forbidding the payment of taxes to the emperor, and claiming to be an anointed king himself." 3 And Pilate asked him, "Are you the king of the Jews?" He answered, "Yes." 4 And Pilate said to the high priests and the crowd, "I cannot find anything criminal about this man." 5 But they persisted and said, "He is stirring up the people all over Judea by his teaching. He began in Galilee and he has come here." 6 When Pilate heard this, he asked if the man was a Galilean

7 and learning that he belonged to Herod's jurisdiction he turned him over to Herod, for Herod was in Jerusalem at that time.

8 When Herod saw Jesus he was delighted, for he had wanted for a long time to see him, because he had heard about him and he hoped to see some wonder done by him. 9 And he questioned him at some length, but he made him no answer. 10 Meanwhile the high priests and the scribes stood by and vehemently accused him. 11 And Herod and his guards made light of him and ridiculed him, and they put a gorgeous robe on him and sent him back to Pilate. 12 And Herod and Pilate became friends that day, for they had been at enmity before.

13 Pilate summoned the high priests and the leading members of the council and the people, 14 and said to them, "You brought this man before me charged with misleading the people, and here I have examined him before you and not found him guilty of any of the things that you accuse him of. 15 Neither has Herod, for he has sent him back to us. You see he has done nothing to call for his death. 16 So I will teach him a lesson and let him go." 18 But they all shouted out,

"Kill him, and release Barabbas for us!" 19 (He was a man who had been put in prison for a riot that had taken place in the city and for murder.) 20 But Pilate wanted to let Jesus go, and he called out to them again. 21 But they kept on shouting, "Crucify him! Crucify him!" 22 And he said to them a third time, "Why, what has he done that is wrong? For I have

American Version

found nothing about him to call for his death. So I will teach him a lesson and let him go." 23 But they persisted with loud outcries in demanding that he be crucified, and their shouting won. 24 And Pilate pronounced sentence that what they asked for should be done. 25 He released the man they asked for, who had been put in prison for riot and murder, and handed Jesus over to their will.

26 As they led Jesus away, they seized a man named Simon, from Cyrene,° who was coming in from the country, and put the cross on his back, for him to carry behind Jesus. 27 He was followed by a great crowd of people and of women who were beating their breasts and lamenting him. 28 But Jesus turned to them and said, "Women of Jerusalem, do not weep for me but weep for yourselves and for your children, 29 for a time is coming when they will say, 'Happy are the childless women, and those who have never borne or nursed children!' 30 Then people will begin to say to the mountains, 'Fall on us!' and to the hills, 'Cover us up!' 31 For if this is what they do when the wood is green, what will happen when it is dry?"

32 Two criminals were also led out to execution with him. 33 When they reached the place called the Skull, they crucified him there, with the criminals one at his right and one at his left. 34 And they divided up his clothes among them by drawing lots for them, while the people stood looking on. 35 Even the leading councilors jeered at him, and said, "He has saved others, let him save himself, if he is really God's Christ, his Chosen One!" 36 The soldiers also made sport of him, coming up and offering him sour wine, 37 saying, "If you are the king of the Jews, save yourself!" 38 For there was a notice above his head, "This is the king of the Jews!"

39 One of the criminals who were hanging there, abused him, saying, "Are you not the Christ? Save yourself and us too!" 40 But the other reproved him and said, "Have you no fear even of God when you are suffering the same penalty? 41 And we are suffering it justly, for we are only getting our deserts, but this man has done nothing wrong." 42 And he said, "Jesus, remember me when you come into your kingdom!" 43 And he said to him, "I tell you, you will be in paradise with me today!" 44 It was now about noon, and darkness came over the whole country, and lasted until three in the afternoon, 45 as the sun was in eclipse. And the curtain before the sanctuary was torn in two. 46 Then Jesus gave a loud cry, and said, "Father, I intrust my spirit to your hands!" With these words he expired. 47 When the captain saw what had happened he praised God, and said, "This man was really innocent!" 48 And all the crowds that had collected for the sight, when they saw what happened, returned to the city beating their breasts. 49 And all his

---

23, 26: from Cyrene: In North Africa.

American Version

acquaintances and the women who had come with him from Galilee, stood at a distance looking on.

50 Now there was a man named Joseph, a member of the council, a good and upright man, 51 who had not voted for the plan or action of the council. He came from the Jewish town of Arimathea and lived in expectation of the Kingdom of God. 52 He went to Pilate and asked for Jesus' body. 53 Then he took it down from the cross and wrapped it in linen and laid it in a tomb hewn in the rock, where no one had yet been laid. 54 It was the Preparation Day, and the Sabbath was just beginning. 55 The women who had followed Jesus from Galilee followed and saw the tomb and how his body was put there. 56 Then they went home, and prepared spices and perfumes.

Chapter 24   On the Sabbath they rested in obedience to the commandment, but on the first day of the week, at early dawn, they went to the tomb, taking spices they had prepared. 2 But they found the stone rolled back from the tomb, 3 and when they went inside they could not find the body. 4 They were in great perplexity over this, when suddenly two men in dazzling clothing stood beside them. 5 The women were frightened and bowed their faces to the ground, but the men said to them, "Why do you look among the dead for him who is alive? 6 Remember what he told you while he was still in Galilee, 7 when he said that the Son of Man must be handed over to wicked men and be crucified and rise again on the third day." 8 Then they remembered his words, 9 and

they went back from the tomb and told all this to the eleven and all the rest. 10 They were Mary of Magdala and Joanna and Mary, James's mother; and the other women also told this to the apostles. 11 But the story seemed to them to be nonsense and they would not believe them. 13 That same day two of them were going to a village called Emmaus, about seven miles from Jerusalem 14 and they were talking together about all these things that had happened. 15 And as they were talking and discussing them, Jesus himself came up and went with them, 16 but they were prevented from recognizing him. 17 And he said to them, "What is all this that you are discussing with each other on your way?" 18 They stopped sadly, and one of them named Cleopas said to him, "Are you the only visitor to Jerusalem who does not know what has happened there lately?" 19 And he said, "What is it?" They said to him, "About Jesus of Nazareth, who in the eyes of God and of all the people was a prophet mighty in deed and word, 20 and how the high priests and our leading men gave him up to be sentenced to death, and had him crucified. 21 But we were hoping that he was to be the deliverer of Israel. Why, besides all this, it is three days since it happened. 22 But some women of our number have astounded us. They went to the tomb early this morning 23 and could not find his body, but came back and said that they had actually seen a vision of angels who said that he was alive. 24 Then some of our party went to the tomb and found things just as the women had said, but they did not see him."

25 Then he said to them, "How foolish you are and how slow to believe all that the prophets have said! 26 Did not the Christ have to suffer thus before entering upon his glory?" 27 And he began with Moses and all the prophets and explained to them the passages all through the Scriptures that referred to himself. 28 When they reached the village to which they were going, he acted as though he were going on, 29 but they urged him not to, and said, "Stay with us, for it is getting toward evening, and the day is nearly over." 30 So he went in to stay with them. And when he took his place with them at table, he took the bread and blessed it and broke it in pieces and handed it to them. 31 Then their eyes were opened and they knew him, and he vanished from them. 32 And they said to each other, "Did not our hearts glow when he was talking to us on the road, and was explaining the Scriptures to us?" 33 And they got up immediately and went back to Jerusalem, and found the eleven and their party all together, 34 and learned from them that the Master had really risen and had been seen by Simon. 35 And they told what had happened on the road, and how they had known him when he broke the bread in pieces.

36 While they were still talking of these things, he himself stood among them. 37 They were startled and panic stricken, and thought they saw a ghost. 38 But he said to them, "Why are you so disturbed, and why do doubts arise in your minds? 39 Look at my hands and feet, for it is I myself! Feel of me and see, for a ghost has not flesh and bones, as you see I have." 41 But they could not yet believe it for sheer joy and they were amazed. And he said to them, "Have you anything here to eat?" 42 And they gave him a piece of broiled fish, 43 and he took it and ate it before their eyes.

44 Then he said to them, "This is what I told you when I was still with you — that everything that is written about me in the Law of Moses and the Prophets and the Psalms must come true." 45 Then he opened their minds to the understanding of the Scriptures, 46 and said to them, "The Scriptures said that Christ should suffer as he has done, and rise from the dead on the third day, 47 and that repentance leading to the forgiveness of sins should be preached to all the heathen in his name. 48 You are to be witnesses to all this, beginning at Jerusalem. 49 And I will send down upon you what my Father has promised. Wait here in the city until you are clothed with power from on high."

50 And he led them out as far as Bethany. Then he lifted up his hands and blessed them. 51 And as he was blessing them, he parted from them. 52 And they went back with great joy to Jerusalem, 53 and were constantly in the Temple, blessing God.

❧ First Corinthians: 1, 7, 11–13, 15

Translated by Edgar Goodspeed

[PAUL: ON THE CHRISTIAN LIFE]

American Version

Chapter 1   Paul, by the will of God called as an apostle of Jesus Christ, and our brother Sosthenes, 2 to the church of God at Corinth, to those who are consecrated by union with Christ Jesus, and called as God's people, like all those anywhere who call on the name of Jesus Christ, their Lord as well as ours; 3 God our Father and the Lord Jesus Christ bless you and give you peace.

4 I am always thanking God about you, for the blessing God has given you through Christ Jesus. 5 For you have grown rich in everything through union with him—in power of expression and in capacity for knowledge. 6 So your experience has confirmed the testimony that I bore to Christ, 7 and there is no gift that you lack even while you are waiting for our Lord Jesus Christ to reappear, 8 and at the Day of our Lord Jesus Christ he will insure your complete vindication. 9 God can be depended on, and it was he who called you to this fellowship with his Son, Jesus Christ our Lord. [. . .]

Chapter 7   As to the matters of which you wrote me, it is an excellent thing for a man to remain unmarried. 2 But there is so much immorality that every man had better have a wife of his own, and every woman a husband of her own. 3 The husband must give his wife what is due her, and the wife must do the same by her husband. 4 A wife cannot do as she likes with her own person; it is her husband's; and in the same way a husband cannot do as he likes with his own person; it is his wife's. 5 You must not refuse each other what is due, unless you agree to do so for a while, to devote yourselves to prayer, and then to come together again, so that Satan may not tempt you through your lack of self-control. 6 But I mean this as a concession, not a command. 7 I should like to have

---

First Corinthians. Paul's First Letter to the Corinthians (57 C.E.) was addressed to the Christian community of Corinth, a bustling port city in Greece. In the letter, Paul addresses numerous issues troubling the new church, especially the divisions and factions among its members, their relations with the secular community around them, and the relation of Christian practices to those of other religions. In the selections here Paul gives counsel on marriage and sexuality, advice that still sparks debate and has literary reverberations in such works as Chaucer's "The Wife of Bath." Paul's celebration of Christian love (Chapter 13) is the most famous passage in all of his letters. His doctrinal discussion of the Resurrection, the key event in his theological reconstruction of Christ's significance, follows. The modern American translation by Edgar Goodspeed has been chosen as a clearer, more accurate and more accessible version of Paul's dense prose than the more familiar King James Version. Included, however, is a parallel text of Chapter 13 from the King James Version.

7, 7: as I am myself: Paul was unmarried.

American Version

everyone be just as I am myself;° but each one has his own special gift from God, one of one kind, and one of another.

⁸ To all who are unmarried and to widows, I would say this: It is an excellent thing if they can remain single as I am. ⁹ But if they cannot control themselves, let them marry. For it is better to marry than to be on fire with passion. ¹⁰ To those already married my instructions are — and they are not mine, but the Lord's — that a wife is not to separate from her husband. ¹¹ If she does separate, she must remain single or else become reconciled to him. And a husband must not divorce his wife. ¹² To other people I would say, though not as Christ's command, if a Christian has a wife who is not a believer, and she is willing to live with him, he must not divorce her, ¹³ and a woman who has a husband who is not a believer, but is willing to live with her, must not divorce her husband. ¹⁴ For the husband who is not a believer is consecrated through union with his wife, and the woman who is not a believer is consecrated through union with her Christian husband, for otherwise your children would be unblessed, but, as it is, they are consecrated. ¹⁵ But if the one who is not a believer wishes to separate, let the separation take place. In such cases the brother or sister is not a slave; God has called you to live in peace. ¹⁶ For how do you wives know whether you will save your husbands? Or how do you husbands know whether you will save your wives?

¹⁷ Only, everyone must continue in the station which the Lord has appointed for him, and in which he was when God's call came to him. This is the rule I make in all the churches. ¹⁸ If a man was circumcised when he was called,° he must not try to alter it. If a man was uncircumcised when he was called, he must not have himself circumcised. ¹⁹ Being circumcised or being uncircumcised does not make any difference; all that matters is keeping God's commands. ²⁰ Everyone ought to remain in the station in which he was called. ²¹ If you were a slave when you were called, never mind. Even if you can gain your freedom, make the most of your present condition instead. ²² For a slave who has been called to union with the Lord is a freedman of the Lord, just as a free man who has been called is a slave of Christ. ²³ You have been bought and paid for; you must not let yourselves become slaves to men. ²⁴ Brothers, everyone must remain in fellowship with God in the station in which he was called.

²⁵ About unmarried women I have no command of the Lord to give you, but I will give you my opinion as that of one on whom through the Lord's mercy you can depend.

²⁶ This, then, is my opinion in view of the present distress — that it is a good thing for a man to remain just as he is. ²⁷ If you are united to a wife, do not seek to be released. If you are not, do not seek a wife. ²⁸ But if you do marry, there is no sin in that. And if a girl marries, it is no

---

7, 18: when he was called: That is, at the time of his call to Christianity.

American Version

sin. But those who marry will have worldly trouble, which I would like to spare you. ²⁹ But this I do say, brothers. The appointed time has grown very short. From this time on those who have wives should live as though they had none, ³⁰ and those who mourn as though they did not mourn, and those who are glad as though they were not glad, and those who buy anything as though they did not own it, ³¹ and those who mix in the world, as though they were not absorbed in it. For the present shape of the world is passing away. ³² I want you to be free from all anxiety. An unmarried man is concerned about the Lord's work, and how he can please the Lord. ³³ A married man is concerned about worldly affairs, and how he can please his wife, and so his interests are divided. ³⁴ An unmarried woman or a girl is concerned about the Lord's work, so as to be consecrated in body and spirit, but the woman who marries is concerned with worldly affairs, and how she can please her husband. ³⁵ It is for your benefit that I say this, not to put a halter on you, but to promote good order, and to secure your undivided devotion to the Lord.

³⁶ But if a man thinks he is not acting properly toward the girl to whom he is engaged, if his passions are too strong, and that is what ought to be done, let him do as he pleases; it is no sin; let them be married. ³⁷ But a man who has definitely made up his mind, under no constraint of passion but with full self-control, and who has decided in his own mind to keep her as she is, will be doing what is right. ³⁸ So the man who marries her does what is right, and the man who refrains from doing so does even better.

³⁹ A wife is bound to her husband as long as he lives. If her husband dies, she is free to marry anyone she pleases so long as he is a Christian. ⁴⁰ But she will be happier, in my judgment, if she remains as she is, and I think I have God's spirit as well as other people. [. . .]

Chapter 11   ² I appreciate your always remembering me, and your standing by the things I passed on to you, just as you received them. ³ But I want you to understand that Christ is the head of every man, while a woman's head is her husband, and Christ's head is God. ⁴ Any man who offers prayer or explains the will of God with anything on his head disgraces his head, ⁵ and any woman who offers prayer or explains the will of God bareheaded disgraces her head, for it is just as though she had her head shaved. ⁶ For if a woman will not wear a veil, let her cut off her hair too. But if it is a disgrace for a woman to have her hair cut off or her head shaved, let her wear a veil. ⁷ For a man ought not to wear anything on his head, for he is the image of God and reflects his glory; while woman is the reflection of man's glory. ⁸ For man was not made from woman, but woman from man, ⁹ and man was not created for woman, but woman was for man. ¹⁰ That is why she ought to wear upon her head something to symbolize her subjection, out of respect to the angels, if to nobody else. ¹¹ But in union with the Lord, woman is not independent of man nor man of woman. ¹² For just

American Version

as woman was made from man, man is born of woman, and both like everything else really come from God. ¹³ Judge for yourselves. Is it proper for a woman to offer prayer to God with nothing on her head? ¹⁴ Does not nature itself teach you that for a man to wear his hair long is degrading, ¹⁵ but a woman's long hair is her pride? For her hair is given her as a covering. ¹⁶ But if anyone is disposed to be contentious about it, I for my part recognize no other practice in worship than this, and neither do the churches of God. [. . .]

Chapter 12 About spiritual gifts, brothers, I do not want you to be misinformed. ² You know that when you were heathen you would stray off, as impulse directed, to idols that could not speak. ³ Therefore, I must tell you that no one who is speaking under the influence of the Spirit of God ever says, "Curse Jesus!" and no one can say, "Jesus is Lord!" without being under the influence of the holy Spirit.

⁴ Endowments vary, but the Spirit is the same, ⁵ and forms of service vary, but it is the same Lord who is served, ⁶ and activities vary, but God who produces them all in us all is the same. ⁷ Each one is given his spiritual illumination for the common good. ⁸ One man receives through the Spirit the power to speak wisely, another, by the same Spirit, receives the power to express knowledge, ⁹ another, from his union with the same Spirit receives faith, another, by one and the same Spirit, the ability to cure the sick, ¹⁰ another, the working of wonders, another, inspiration in preaching, another, the

power of distinguishing the true Spirit from false ones, another, various ecstatic utterances, and another, the ability to explain them. ¹¹ These are all produced by one and the same Spirit, and apportioned to each of us just as the Spirit chooses.

¹² For just as the body is one and yet has many parts, and all the parts of the body, many as they are, form one body, so it is with Christ. ¹³ For we have all — Jews or Greeks, slaves or free men — been baptized in one spirit to form one body, and we have all been saturated with one Spirit. ¹⁴ For the body does not consist of one part but of many. ¹⁵ If the foot says, "As I am not a hand, I am not a part of the body," that does not make it any less a part of the body. ¹⁶ And if the ear says, "As I am not an eye, I am not a part of the body," that does not make it any less a part of the body. ¹⁷ If all the body were eye, how would we hear? If it were all ear, how could we have a sense of smell? ¹⁸ As it is, God has arranged the parts, every one of them in the body as he wished them to be. ¹⁹ If they were all one part, where would the body be? ²⁰ As it is, there are many parts, but one body. ²¹ The eye cannot say to the hand, "I do not need you," or the head to the feet, "I do not need you." ²² On the contrary, the parts of the body that are considered most delicate are indispensable, ²³ and the parts of it that we think common, we dress with especial care, and our unpresentable parts receive especial attention ²⁴ which our presentable parts do not need. God has so adjusted the body and given such especial distinction to its inferior

American Version

parts ²⁵ that there is no clash in the body, but its parts all alike care for one another. ²⁶ If one part suffers, all the parts share its sufferings. If a part has honor done it, all the parts enjoy it too. ²⁷ Now you are Christ's body, and individually parts of it. ²⁸ And God has placed people in the church, first as apostles, second as inspired preachers, third as teachers, then wonder-workers; then come ability to cure the sick, helpfulness, administration, ecstatic speaking. Is everyone an apostle? ²⁹ Is everyone an inspired preacher? Is everyone a teacher? Is everyone a wonder-worker? ³⁰ Is everyone able to cure the sick? Can everyone speak ecstatically? Can everyone explain what it means? ³¹ But you must cultivate the higher endowments.

American Version

   Chapter 13   I will show you a far better way. If I can speak the languages of men and even of angels, but have no love, I am only a noisy gong or a clashing cymbal.° ² If I am inspired to preach and know all the secret truths and possess all knowledge, and if I have such perfect faith that I can move mountains, but have no love, I am nothing. ³ Even if I give away everything I own, and give myself up, but do it in pride, not love, it does me no good. ⁴ Love is patient and kind. Love is not envious or boastful. It does not put on airs. ⁵ It is not rude. It does not insist on its rights. It does not become angry. It is not resentful. ⁶ It is not happy over injustice, it is only happy with truth. ⁷ It will bear anything, believe anything, hope for anything, endure anything. ⁸ Love will never die out. If there is inspired preaching, it will pass away. If there is ecstatic speaking, it will cease. If there is knowledge, it will pass away. ⁹ For our knowledge is imperfect and our

King James Version

Chapter 13   Though I speak with the tongues of men and of angels, and have not charity, I am become *as* sounding brass, or a tinkling cymbal.
2 And though I have *the gift of* prophecy, and understand all mysteries, and all knowledge; and though I have all faith, so that I could remove mountains, and have not charity, I am nothing.
3 And though I bestow all my goods to feed *the poor,* and though I give my body to be burned, and have not charity, it profiteth me nothing.
4 Charity suffereth long, *and* is kind; charity envieth not; charity vaunteth not itself, is not puffed up,
5 Doth not behave itself unseemly, seeketh not her own, is not easily provoked, thinketh no evil;
6 Rejoiceth not in iniquity, but rejoiceth in the truth;
7 Beareth all things, believeth all things, hopeth all things, endureth all things.
8 Charity never faileth: but whether *there be* prophecies, they shall fail;

13, 1: gong . . . cymbal: Gongs and cymbals were musical instruments used in pagan worship.

American Version	King James Version

preaching is imperfect. 10 But when perfection comes, what is imperfect will pass away. 11 When I was a child, I talked like a child, I thought like a child, I reasoned like a child. When I became a man, I put aside my child-ish ways. 12 For now we are looking at a dim reflection in a mirror, but then we shall see face to face. Now my knowledge is imperfect, but then I shall know as fully as God knows me. 13 So faith, hope, and love endure. These are the great three, and the greatest of them is love.

whether *there be* tongues, they shall cease; whether *there be* knowledge, it shall vanish away.
9 For we know in part, and we prophesy in part.
10 But when that which is perfect is come, then that which is in part shall be done away.
11 When I was a child, I spake as a child, I understood as a child, I thought as a child: but when I became a man, I put away childish things.
12 For now we see through a glass, darkly; but then face to face: now I know in part; but then shall I know even as also I am known.
13 And now abideth faith, hope, charity, these three; but the greatest of these *is* charity.

American Version

Chapter 15   Now I want to remind you, brothers, of the form in which I presented to you the good news I brought, which you accepted and have stood by, 2 and through which you are to be saved, if you hold on, unless your faith has been all for nothing. 3 For I passed on to you, as of first importance, the account I had received, that Christ died for our sins, as the Scriptures foretold, 4 that he was buried, that on the third day he was raised from the dead, as the Scriptures foretold, 5 and that he was seen by Cephas, and then by the Twelve. 6 After that he was seen by more than five hundred brothers at one time, most of whom are still alive, although some of them have fallen asleep. 7 Then he was seen by

James, then by all the apostles, 8 and finally he was seen by me also, as though I were born at the wrong time. 9 For I am the least important of the apostles, and am not fit to be called an apostle, because I once per-secuted God's church. 10 But by God's favor I have become what I am, and the favor he showed me has not gone for nothing, but I have worked harder than any of them, although it was not really I but the favor God showed me. 11 But whether it was I or they, this is what we preach, and this is what you believed.
12 Now if what we preach about Christ is that he was raised from the dead, how can some of you say that there is no such thing as a resurrec-tion of the dead? 13 If there is no

American Version

resurrection of the dead, then Christ was not raised, ¹⁴ and if Christ was not raised, there is nothing in our message; there is nothing in our faith either, ¹⁵ and we are found guilty of misrepresenting God, for we have testified that he raised Christ, when he did not do it, if it is true that the dead are never raised. ¹⁶ For if the dead are never raised, Christ was not raised; ¹⁷ and if Christ was not raised, your faith is a delusion; you are still under the control of your sins. ¹⁸ Yes, and those who have fallen asleep in trust in Christ have perished. ¹⁹ If we have centered our hopes on Christ in this life, and that is all, we are the most pitiable people in the world.

²⁰ But the truth is, Christ was raised from the dead, the first to be raised of those who have fallen asleep. ²¹ For since it was through a man that we have death, it is through a man also that we have the raising of the dead. ²² For just as because of their relation to Adam all men die, so because of their relation to Christ they will all be brought to life again. ²³ But each in his own turn; Christ first, and then at Christ's coming those who belong to him. ²⁴ After that will come the end, when he will turn over the kingdom to God his Father, bringing to an end all other government, authority, and power, ²⁵ for he must retain the kingdom until he puts all his enemies under his feet. ²⁶ The last enemy to be overthrown will be death, ²⁷ for everything is to be reduced to subjection and put under Christ's feet. But when it says that everything is subject to him, he is evidently excepted who

reduced it all to subjection to him. ²⁸ And when everything is reduced to subjection to him, then the Son himself will also become subject to him who has reduced everything to subjection to him, so that God may be everything to everyone.

²⁹ Otherwise, what do people mean by having themselves baptized on behalf of their dead? If the dead do not rise at all, why do they have themselves baptized on their behalf? ³⁰ Why do we ourselves run such risks every hour? ³¹ By the very pride I take in you, brothers, through our union with Christ Jesus our Lord, I face death every day. ³² From the human point of view, what good is it to me that I have fought wild animals here in Ephesus? If the dead do not rise at all, "Let us eat and drink, for we will be dead tomorrow!" ³³ Do not be misled. Bad company ruins character. ³⁴ Return to your sober sense as you ought, and stop sinning, for some of you are utterly ignorant about God. To your shame I say so.

³⁵ But someone will say, "How can the dead rise? What kind of a body will they have when they come back?" ³⁶ You foolish man, the very seed you sow never comes to life without dying first; ³⁷ and when you sow it, it has not the form it is going to have, but is a naked kernel, perhaps of wheat or something else; ³⁸ and God gives it just such a form as he pleases, so that each kind of seed has a form of its own. ³⁹ Flesh is not all alike; men have one kind, animals another, birds another, and fish another. ⁴⁰ There are heavenly bodies, and there are earthly bodies, but the beauty of the heavenly bodies is

American Version

of one kind, and the beauty of the earthly bodies is of another. ⁴¹ The sun has one kind of beauty, and the moon another, and the stars another; why, one star differs from another in beauty. ⁴² It is so with the resurrection of the dead. ⁴³ The body is sown in decay, it is raised free from decay. It is sown in humiliation, it is raised in splendor. It is sown in weakness, it is raised in strength. ⁴⁴ It is a physical body that is sown, it is a spiritual body that is raised. If there is a physical body, there is a spiritual body also. ⁴⁵ This is also what the Scripture says: "The first man Adam became a living creature." The last Adam has become a life-giving Spirit. ⁴⁶ It is not the spiritual that comes first, but the physical, and then the spiritual. ⁴⁷ The first man is of the dust of the earth; the second man is from heaven. ⁴⁸ Those who are of the earth are like him who was of the earth, and those who are of heaven are like him who is from heaven, ⁴⁹ and as we have been like the man of the earth, let us also try to be like the man from heaven. ⁵⁰ But I can tell you this, brothers: flesh and blood cannot share in the Kingdom of God, and decay will not share in what is imperishable. ⁵¹ I will tell you a secret. We shall not all fall asleep, but we shall all be changed, ⁵² in a moment, in the twinkling of an eye, at the sound of the last trumpet. For the trumpet will sound, and the dead will be raised free from decay, and we shall be changed. ⁵³ For this perishable nature must put on the imperishable, and this mortal nature must put on immortality. ⁵⁴ And when this mortal nature puts on immortality, then what the Scripture says will come true — "Death has been triumphantly destroyed. ⁵⁵ Where, Death, is your victory? Where, Death, is your sting?"

⁵⁶ Sin is the sting of death, and it is the Law that gives sin its power. ⁵⁷ But thank God! He gives us victory through our Lord Jesus Christ. ⁵⁸ So my dear brothers, be firm and unmoved, and always devote yourselves to the Lord's work, for you know that through the Lord your labor is not thrown away.

ST. AUGUSTINE
354–430

www For links to more information about St. Augustine, a quiz on *The Confessions,* and information about the twenty-first-century relevance of St. Augustine, see *World Literature Online* at bedfordstmartins .com/worldlit.

Of the three great doctors of the Latin church in the first millennium of Christianity, the most celebrated is St. Augustine. St. Ambrose (340–397), bishop of Milan, increased the followers of the Christian faith by his ministry and established the church as a strong voice in the secular world; St. Jerome (340–420), a great scholar, translated the Scriptures from their original Hebrew and Greek, creating the Latin Vulgate Bible, the greatest spiritual resource of the European Middle Ages. However, it was Augustine, Bishop of Hippo (an ancient city in present-day Algeria), who more than any other won the hearts and minds of his contemporaries to Christianity. His *Confessions* (397–98) and *The City of God* (413–26) are considered his greatest writing achievements; he also wrote a number of theological works that helped establish the basis of Christian doctrine. Today St. Augustine is reckoned as the most important early Christian philosopher, rivaled only by St. Thomas Aquinas (1225–1274)[1] in the thirteenth century.

tuh-GAS-tee

Augustine's Life. Born in **Tagaste**, North Africa, in 354, Aurelius Augustinus was the son of a pagan town councilor and a Christian mother. He was probably descended from the dark-skinned Europeanized North African people later known as Berbers.[2] By the time of Augustine's birth, Christianity had established itself as the official religion of the Roman Empire. This did not necessarily mean, however, that a young man of promising abilities would become a Christian. Despite the pleadings of his mother, Monica, Augustine was never baptized in his youth. Educated for a public career like his father, he excelled in his early studies during a licentious period in Carthage (present-day Tunis, in North Africa). For the next nine years, while he taught rhetoric, Augustine followed the doctrine of **MANICHEANISM**,[3] which saw good and evil as the operative forces in the universe. He studied other philosophical systems as well, coming under the influence of **NEOPLATONISM**,[4] which

---

[1] **St. Thomas Aquinas** (1225–1274): Italian scholastic theologian who, as a follower of Aristotle, reformed Catholic philosophy when he created a complete philosophical system in his *Summa Theologica,* completed in 1273.

[2] **Berbers:** Semitic tribal people who occupied North Africa before being scattered by Bedouin raiders in the twelfth century.

[3] **Manicheanism:** Founded by Mani (216–276 C.E.), this dualistic religion migrated from Persia to all parts of the Roman Empire (third to fifth century) and, eventually, eastward to China (seventh century) and Turkey (eighth and ninth centuries). Its emphasis on the existence of two forces, Light (goodness) and Darkness (evil), in constant conflict with each other, marked it as a Christian heresy.

[4] **Neoplatonism:** Beliefs derived from the Greek philosopher Plato (c. 427–347 B.C.E.) that adapted themselves to several religions, especially Christianity. Major elements of Christian Neoplatonism, which flourished from the time of the writings of Plotinus (205–270 C.E.) to the end of the Middle Period, included the separation of the soul and the body, the nature of the heavenly cosmos, and the relationship of divine Ideas to Christian spirituality.

emphasized the soul's striving for perfection in an imperfect world. In 384, Augustine began to accept Christian teachings. Through his reading of the Epistles of St. Paul, he embraced the doctrine of grace, which he found essential to conversion. In 387, at the age of thirty-two, he was baptized a Christian by his chief spiritual advisor, Bishop Ambrose of Milan.

After the death of his mother the following year, Augustine entered monastic society, rising in the Catholic hierarchy to become bishop of Hippo in his native North Africa in 396. He spent the rest of his life ministering to his diocese and writing works of theology and moral philosophy. In his later years, the Roman Empire rapidly disintegrated; Rome was sacked by **Alaric** and the Goths[5] in 410, and Hippo itself lay under siege by the VANDALS at the time of Augustine's death in 430.[6] Augustine's bones were transported twice in subsequent centuries to protect them from desecration: from Hippo, which was again under attack by the Vandals, to the island of Sardinia in 497; and from Sardinia, under Saracen attack, to Italy in 722.

AL-uh-rik

His Principal Writings.   *The Confessions* is the first truly autobiographical work written in the West. Its honesty, passion, and personal relevance have guaranteed it a secure place in the Western literary canon. Augustine's struggle to embrace Christianity is one of the great stories in the history of Europe, and his conversion, the dramatic climax of the book, became the model for all such subsequent accounts. This work also provides unparalleled insight into the life of a favored young man growing up during the last days of the Roman Empire. *The City of God,* written near the end of Augustine's life, celebrates the superiority of the heavenly City of God at a time when Rome was failing. Augustine's other writings take up the issues he had wrestled with as a convert, such as the nature of the Trinity, the idea of evil, the authority of the priesthood, the relationship between free will and determinism, and the doctrine of grace and its role in salvation. A notable feature of all his work is its practical utility in the service of the spirit: Augustine writes to state beliefs, solve problems, and influence other human beings. In doing so he often forges a close personal bond with the reader.

The Pattern of *The Confessions.*   *The Confessions* covers the period from Augustine's childhood to his struggles over his faith in adulthood to his conversion to Christianity. The autobiographical portion of the work ends with the death of his mother, Monica, in 388, when Augustine was thirty-three. The text's three concluding chapters explain and extol

---

[5] **Alaric . . . Goths:** Alaric, leader of the Visigoths, took advantage of Roman military weakness to threaten northern Italy in 406. When the emperor fled to Ravenna, the Visigoths sacked Rome for three days in 410, greatly demoralizing the Romans and those who depended on them. In those dark days St. Jerome wrote, "My tongue sticks to the roof of my mouth, and sobs choke my speech."

[6] **Hippo itself . . . 430:** The Vandals, a Germanic people, swept through Gaul (France) and Spain and across the Straits of Gibraltar into North Africa, seizing Hippo in 430. They established a kingdom in Carthage and terrorized the Mediterranean area as pirates and raiders throughout the fifth century.

Baptism Scene, third century C.E.

After his conversion and baptism at the age of thirty-two, St. Augustine became one of the fathers of the Latin church, helping to establish the very basis of Christian doctrine. (Erich Lessing / Art Resource, NY)

Christian doctrine, with the last being a scriptural interpretation of Genesis. In Catholic terms, the work is a *confession* by nature of its threefold emphasis on admission of sin, declaration of faith, and praise of God. First, Augustine confesses the sins of his childhood, his sins of the flesh beginning in adolescence, his misguided faith as a young man, and the sin of pride that held him back from fully accepting Christianity. Second, through the story of his conversion, Augustine acknowledges his faith in God. And in the closing chapters of the work, Augustine praises God by expounding doctrine on such matters as memory, time and eternity, form and matter, and Creation.

Consciousness of Sin.   The early chapters of *The Confessions* reveal Augustine's extreme consciousness of sin. For instance, he states that as a child he loved classical romances too much: "I wept over the dead **Dido**, 'who sought her end by the sword.' I forsook you [God], and I followed after your lowest creatures" (Book I, ch. 13).[7] He writes that at the age of sixteen "the madness of lust . . . took me completely under its scepter, and I clutched it with both hands" (Book II, ch. 2). About the same time, he and his companions slipped into a walled garden and stole pears from

DIGH-doh

---

[7] **"I wept . . . lowest creatures"**: This refers to Dido the queen of Carthage, whose suicide is depicted in Book IV of Virgil's *Aeneid*. Dido is one of God's "lowest creatures" because she is a pagan and a suicide as well as the creation of a work of fiction.

a neighbor's tree. "Those pears I gathered solely that I might steal," he writes, "for if I put any of that fruit in my mouth, my sin was its seasoning" (Book II, ch. 6). The details of his wrongdoings—some of them palpable, some that might have been the product of a guilty conscience—are everywhere, with Augustine's own interpretations of them never far behind. Not surprisingly, St. Augustine was one of the major exponents of the doctrine of original sin in the early church.[8]

From Doubt to Conversion.   In his twenties, the self-described young sensualist rose in the intellectual world of Carthage, where he conducted his studies. At first, he writes, he found the Holy Scriptures "unworthy of comparison with the nobility of Cicero's writings" (Book III, ch. 5), and a bishop whom his mother sent to speak to him found him unripe for religious instruction.[9] But after traveling to Rome and then to Milan, where he met Bishop Ambrose, he became a CATECHUMEN in the Catholic faith. Step by step, his reading of the PLATONISTS led him to consider the Epistles of Paul in the New Testament. Now, with the combination of his reading and his exposure to Christian doctrine, Augustine moved toward conversion. The most famous passage in *The Confessions* begins in Augustine's backyard in Milan. There, in a small garden attached to his house, he finds himself driven by "the tumult in my breast" (Book VIII, ch. 8). Excoriating himself for his sins, uncertain of where to turn with his faith, he finds himself interrupted by a new sound:

> And lo, I heard from a nearby house, a voice like that of a boy or a girl, I know not which, chanting and repeating over and over, "Take up and read, take up and read." (Book VIII, ch. 12)

Opening his book of the Epistles of Paul, Augustine read the first passage he saw:

> Not in rioting and drunkenness, not in chambering and impurities, not in strife and envying; but put you on the Lord Jesus Christ, and make not provision for the flesh in its concupiscences. (*Romans* 13:13–14. Cited in *The Confessions* Book VIII, ch. 12)

His conversion followed. The holy text and the living Augustine had been joined. Clearly he hoped that his own story would serve others, leading them to the Bible so that it might act upon them as it had upon him.

Keys to Interpretation.   Crucial to Augustine's work is his scriptural interpretation. The core of *The Confessions*—its dual status as the first true autobiography in the Western tradition and the first lengthy description of the journey of the Christian soul toward God—is dependent on

---

Augustine (354–430) is the single most important of the Latin church fathers. His works range widely over an enormous number of subjects. In them he puts his own personal stamp on Christian theology, on church-state relations, on the classical tradition, and on Rome as a historical phenomenon. . . . He is the only Latin church father with a truly philosophical mind, who enjoys thinking as an activity in its own right.

– MARCIA L. COLISH, Scholar, 1997

---

[8] **doctrine . . . church:** Augustine believed that all human beings inherit Original Sin caused by the Fall of Adam and Eve, and that only divine grace can restore them to freely seek their salvation. This grace is a gift of God, not the result of human action.

[9] **unripe . . . instruction:** Young St. Augustine was trained in classical Latin rhetoric, derived from the writings of the Roman author and grammarian Marcus Tullius Cicero (106–43 B.C.E.). He snobbishly preferred Cicero's writing to the Latin of the Bible. The bishop sent to Augustine reasoned that the young man was too prideful for conversion.

Never before had a man faced his own soul in this way. Not Heraclitus . . . not Socrates and Plato, for whom everything depended on the good of the soul. "Man," cried Augustine, "is an immense abyss, whose very hairs thou numberest, O Lord. . . . And yet are the hairs of his head more readily numbered than are his affections and the movements of his heart." And he sums up the whole of his awe in one short sentence: "I became a question to myself."

– KARL JASPERS, Critic, 1962

this mode of understanding, which holds that the Old Testament prefigures the New Testament; that is, what is promised under the Old Law is fulfilled in the New Law of Christ. For example, Exodus, the story of the deliverance of the Jewish people from slavery, is fulfilled eternally in the redemption of mankind by Christ. Similarly, Augustine wants to be understood not only as himself but also as a representative of all mankind seeking fulfillment in salvation.

The reader of St. Augustine will also notice the rhetorical energy of *The Confessions.* Even in translation, the work echoes the cadences and rhythms of Augustine's original, which exploits the rich verbal effects of late classical Latin. Trained in the art of rhetoric, or persuasive communication, Augustine embraced literary style as a means of promoting Christian doctrine. Often the energy of his prose comes from a melodic questioning:

> Who will bring to my mind the sins of my infancy? For in your sight no man is clean of sin, not even the infant who has lived but a day upon earth. Who will bring this to my mind? (Book I, ch. 7)

At other times, Augustine endows his arguments with repetitions of imagery, sounds, and sense, much as a poet would or as might be heard today in an excellent sermon:

> Therefore, I defiled the very source of friendship by the filth of concupiscence, and its clear waters I befouled with the lust of hell. Yet foul and vicious as I was, with overflowing vanity, I took pride in being refined and cultured. (Book III, ch. 1)

The Historical Legacy.   In the centuries following St. Augustine's death, Western Europe as it is known today slowly rose out of the ashes of the ruined Roman Empire. When it did, it could claim a Christian culture based on classical foundations. Along with his contemporaries St. Ambrose and St. Jerome, St. Augustine helped establish that foundation. Augustine's special vision offered a reading of Christian theology that, following the Pauline Epistles, saw individual, historical man traveling on a spiritual pilgrimage toward God and salvation. This theme of *HOMO VIATOR,* or man as a traveler through life, is taken up in one way or another by writer after writer throughout the European Middle Ages and beyond. It is most notable of all in Dante's *The Divine Comedy,*[10] finished in 1321. Some later European literary works also follow the Augustinian model: A famous example is Bunyan's Puritan allegory, *Pilgrim's Progress,*[11] written in 1678.

HOH-moh

vee-AH-tore

---

[10] *The Divine Comedy:* Written while Dante was in exile from his native Florence, this epic poem begins "Midway in the journey of our life," when Dante was thirty-five. The first work in the trilogy, *Inferno,* the poet's vision of hell, is presented in this anthology (p. 689).

[11] *Pilgrim's Progress:* An allegorical tale of a Christian sinner traveling through the world, *Pilgrim's Progress* was written in 1678 by Puritan author and preacher John Bunyan (1628–1688).

■ CONNECTIONS

Dante, *Inferno*, p. 689. While St. Augustine's autobiography is not comparable to the poetic dream-vision of *Inferno,* the theological background of the two works is nearly identical. Dante the character, like Augustine, is a *homo viator,* a spiritual wanderer on earth; Dante the poet believes that the soul's sinful state leads to retribution in Hell. What do you think Augustine would have made of Dante's work?

Miguel de Cervantes, *Don Quixote* (Book 3). In Cervantes' novel the hero's quest is represented as a comic work of fiction. This story of a Spanish knight-errant lovingly details the adventures of its misguided romantic hero. Despite the work's satirical tone, the story itself is told against a backdrop of Christian piety. Do you believe *Don Quixote* would have won Augustine's approval or disapproval?

Jean-Jacques Rousseau, *Confessions* (Book 4). Published posthumously in 1782, this work of French philosopher Rousseau (1712–1778) borrows both its title and its tone of self-interrogation from Augustine's classic. Part of the borrowing is ironic; unlike Augustine, Rousseau believed in the natural goodness of human beings and the corrupting influence of institutional life. In comparing the two works, imagine a meeting between Augustine and Rousseau across the centuries. Would they have any grounds for agreement?

■ FURTHER RESEARCH

Translations
Pine-Coffin, R. S., trans. *St. Augustine: Confessions.* 1961.
Ryan, John K., trans. *The Confessions of St. Augustine.* 1960.

Biography and Criticism
Brown, Peter. *Augustine of Hippo.* 1967.
O'Donnell, James J. *Augustine.* 1985.
Smith, Warren Thomas. *Augustine, His Life and Thought.* 1980.

Background and Interpretation
Auerbach, Erich. *Scenes from the Drama of European Literature.* 1959.
Butler, Dom Cuthbert. *Western Mysticism.* 1934.
Clark, Gillian. *Augustine: The Confessions.* 1993.
Gilson, Etienne. *The Christian Philosophy of St. Augustine.* 1960.
Ladner, Gerhard. *The Idea of Reform.* 1959.

■ PRONUNCIATION

Alaric: AL-uh-rik
Dido: DIGH-doh
homo viator: HOH-moh vee-AH-tore, vee-AY-tur
Tagaste: tuh-GAS-tee

∽ The Confessions

Translated by John K. Ryan

BOOK I
CHILDHOOD

Chapter 1: God and the Soul

You are great, O Lord, and greatly to be praised: great is your power and to your wisdom there is no limit.[1] And man, who is a part of your creation, wishes to praise you, man who bears about within himself his mortality, who bears about within himself testimony to his sin and testimony that you resist the proud.[2] Yet man, this part of your creation, wishes to praise you. You arouse him to take joy in praising you, for you have made us for yourself, and our heart is restless until it rests in you. [. . .][3]

Chapter 6: The Infant Augustine

[. . .] What do I want to say, Lord, except that I do not know whence I came into what I may call a mortal life or a living death. Whence I know not. Your consolation and your mercies[4] have raised me up, as I have heard from the parents of my flesh, for by one and in the other you fashioned me in time. I myself do not remember this. Therefore, the comfort of human milk nourished me, but neither my mother nor my nurses filled their own breasts. Rather, through them you gave me an infant's

---

The Confessions. This selection from *The Confessions* includes St. Augustine's classic account of his childhood, including his discussion of Original Sin and its meaning for the Catholic Church (Book I); an account of his boyhood, including the stealing of pears from a neighbor's tree and another disquisition on the nature of sin (Book II); tales of his later youth, from his misbehavior as a student in Carthage to his unwise preoccupation with the secular classics of the great Roman authors, especially Cicero (Book III); Augustine's gradual accommodation to Christian doctrine in Milan, helped by his mother and guided by his spiritual counselor, Bishop Ambrose (Book VI); and Augustine's conversion to Christianity in a garden in Milan, brought about by reading St. Paul (Book VIII). These excerpts focus on Augustine's personal and spiritual growth, two aspects of his development that he would have said were inseparable from each other.

Throughout the European Middle Ages, *The Confessions* was a popular work. It was frequently copied in monasteries and religious houses, enjoying a broader circulation than Augustine's theological treatises. Because of the availability of the Latin original, the first English translation, by a Protestant, Sir Tobie Matthew, did not appear until 1620. A highly improved version was produced by Edward B. Pusey, a British Catholic reformer, in 1838. The first modern translation was by W. H. D. Rouse for the Loeb Classical Library of Harvard University Press in

---

[1] Cf. Ps. 144:3; Ps. 146:5. [All notes to *The Confessions* are the translator's.]

[2] Cf. Jas. 4:6; I Pet. 5:5; Prov. 3:34.

[3] **our heart . . . you:** "Our heart is restless until it rests in you" sums up Augustine's whole teaching on man's relation to God. It is perhaps the most quoted line in *The Confessions*.

[4] **your . . . mercies:** Cf. Ps. 93:19; 68:17.

food in accordance with your law and out of the riches that you have distributed even down to the lowest level of things. You gave me to want no more than you gave, and you gave to those who nursed me the will to give what you gave to them. By an orderly affection they willingly gave me what they possessed so abundantly from you. It was good for them that my good should come from them; yet it was not from them but through them. For from you, O God, come all good things, and from you, my God, comes all my salvation. This I afterwards observed when you cried out to me by means of those things which you bestow both inwardly and outwardly. For at that time I knew how to seek the breast, to be satisfied with pleasant things, and to cry at my bodily hurts, but nothing more.

Later on, I began to laugh, at first when asleep and then when awake. This has been told to me concerning myself, and I believe it, since we see other infants acting thus, although I do not remember such acts of my own. Then little by little I perceived where I was, and I wished to make my wants known to those who could satisfy them. Yet I could not do so, because the wants were within me, while those outside could by no sensible means penetrate into my soul. So I tossed my limbs about and uttered sounds, thus making such few signs similar to my wishes as I could, and in such fashion as I could, although they were not like the truth. When they would not obey me, either because they did not understand or because it would be harmful, I grew angry at older ones who were not subject to me and at children for not waiting on me, and took it out on them by crying. That infants are of this sort I have since learned from those whom I have been able to observe. That I was such a one they have unwittingly taught me better than my nurses who knew me. [. . .]

Chapter 7: The Psychology of Infancy

Graciously hear me, O God. Woe to the sins of men! Yet a man says this and you have mercy upon him, for you have made him, but the sin that is in him you have not made. Who will bring to my mind the sins of my infancy? For in your sight no man is clean of sin,[5] not even the infant who has lived but a day upon earth. Who will bring

---

1912. This text is still useful for anyone who wishes to study Augustine's Latin alongside a facing page English translation.

Our translation of *The Confessions* is an authorized Catholic version by John K. Ryan (1959). Father Ryan notes that "the first and great commandment for a translator of this work is to determine, as far as he can, what St. Augustine thought, and to state it, as far as he can, in our alien tongue." It is one thing to achieve accuracy, another to capture the grammatical and rhetorical effects of St. Augustine's Latin; Ryan produces a literal translation while using the English cognates of Latin words to capture some of the original sound of *The Confessions*. Footnotes to the Ryan edition show borrowings from Holy Scriptures (for instance, "cf. Ps. 144.3") and occasionally other sources of St. Augustine's thought. Bible passages are generally from the Rheims-Douai Catholic Bible; sometimes the location of the texts vary slightly from other English Bibles (for instance, in the numbering of the Psalms).

---

[5] **no man . . . sin:** Cf. Job 25:4.

this to my mind? Does not each little child now do this, for in him I now perceive what I do not remember about myself? How then did I sin at that age? Was it because I cried out as I tried to mouth the breast? Indeed if I did so now — not of course as one gaping for the breast, but for food fitting to my years — I would be laughed at and most justly blamed. Hence at that time I did reprehensible things, but because I could not understand why anyone should blame me, neither custom nor reason allowed me to be blamed. As we grow up, we root out such things and throw them aside. Yet I have never seen anyone knowingly throw aside the good when he purges away the bad.

But even then were these things good: to try to get by crying even what would be harmful if it were given to me, to be bitterly resentful at freemen, elders, my parents, and many other prudent people who would not indulge my whims, when I struck at them and tried to hurt them as far as I could because they did not obey orders that would be obeyed only to my harm? Thus it is not the infant's will that is harmless, but the weakness of infant limbs. I myself have seen and have had experience with a jealous little one; it was not yet able to speak, but it was pale and bitter in face as it looked at another child nursing at the same breast.

Who is unaware of such things? Mothers and nurses claim to make up for them by some sort of correctives. Yet is it really innocence not to allow another child to share in that richly flowing fountain of milk, although it is in great need of help and derives life from that sole source of food? These things are easily put up with not because they are of little or no account, but because they will disappear with increase in age. This you can prove from the fact that the same things cannot be borne with patience when detected in an older person.

Therefore, O Lord my God, you have given to the infant life and a body, which, as we see, you have thus furnished with senses, equipped with limbs, beautified with a shapely form, and, for its complete good and protection, have endowed with all the powers of a living being. For all such things you command me to praise you and to confess you, and to "sing to your name, O Most High."[6] For you are God, all-powerful and good, even if you made only such things. For no other can do this but you, the One, from whom is every measure, you, the absolute Form,[7] who give form to all things and govern all things by your law.

Therefore, O Lord, this age which I do not remember to have lived, which I have taken on trust from others, which I conclude myself to have passed from observing other infants, although such testimonies are most probable, this age I hesitate to join to this life of mine which I have lived in this world. In so far as it belongs to the dark regions of forgetfulness, it is like that which I lived in my mother's womb. But "if I was conceived in iniquity," and if my mother nourished me within her womb in sins,[8] where, I beseech you, O Lord my God, where or when was your servant inno-

---

[6] **"sing . . . High":** Cf. Ps. 91:2.

[7] **the One . . . Form:** God is referred to as the One and the supreme Form or Beauty in terms of Plotinian philosophy.

[8] Cf. Ps. 50:7.

cent? But, see, I now set aside that period. What matters that now to me of which I recall no trace?

Chapter 8: The Growth of Speech

Did I not advance from infancy and come into boyhood? Or rather, did it not come upon me and succeed to my infancy? Yet infancy did not depart: for where did it go? Still, it was no more, for I was no longer an infant, one who could not speak, but now I was a chattering boy. I remembered this, and afterwards I reflected on how I learned to talk. Grown up men did not teach me by presenting me with words in any orderly form of instruction, as they did my letters a little later. But I myself, with that mind which you, my God, gave me, wished by means of various cries and sounds and movements of my limbs to express my heart's feelings, so that my will would be obeyed. However, I was unable to express all that I wished or to all to whom I wished. I pondered over this in memory: when they named a certain thing and, at that name, made a gesture towards the object, I observed that object and inferred that it was called by the name they uttered when they wished to show it to me. That they meant this was apparent by their bodily gestures, as it were by words natural to all men, which are made by change of countenance, nods, movements of the eyes and other bodily members, and sounds of the voice, which indicate the affections of the mind in seeking, possessing, rejecting, or avoiding things. So little by little I inferred that the words set in their proper places in different sentences, that I heard frequently, were signs of things. When my mouth had become accustomed to these signs, I expressed by means of them my own wishes. Thus to those among whom I was I communicated the signs of what I wished to express. I entered more deeply into the stormy society of human life, although still dependent on my parents' authority and the will of my elders. . . .

Chapter 12: Good out of Evil

In boyhood itself, when there was less to be feared in my regard than from youth, I did not love study and hated to be driven to it. Yet I was driven to it, and good was thus done to me, but I myself did not do good. I would have learned nothing unless forced to it. No one does good against his will, even if what he does is good. Nor did those who drove me on do well: the good was done to me by you, my God. They did not see to what use I would put what they forced me to learn, beyond satisfying the insatiable desires of a rich beggary and a base glory. But you, before whom the hairs of our head are numbered,[9] turned to my advantage the error of all those who kept me at my studies. The error of myself, who did not want to study, you used for my chastisement. For I, so small a boy and yet so great a sinner, was not unworthy of punishment. Thus by means of men who did not do well you did well for me, and out of my sinning you justly imposed punishment on me. You have ordered it, and so it is, that every disordered mind should be its own punishment.

---

[9] **The hairs . . . numbered:** Cf. Matt. 10:30.

Chapter 13: Studies in Greek and Latin

Why I detested the Greek language when I was taught it as a little boy I have not yet fully discovered. I liked Latin very much, not the parts given by our first teachers but what the men called grammarians teach us.[10] The first stages of our education, when we learn reading, writing, and arithmetic, I considered no less a burden and punishment than all the Greek courses. Since I was but "flesh, and a wind that goes and does not return,"[11] where could this come from except from sin and vanity of life? Better indeed, because more certain, were those first studies by which there was formed and is formed in me what I still possess, the ability to read what I find written down and to write what I want to, than the later studies wherein I was required to learn by heart I know not how many of Aeneas's wanderings, although forgetful of my own, and to weep over Dido's death, because she killed herself for love, when all the while amid such things, dying to you, O God my life, I most wretchedly bore myself about with dry eyes.

Who can be more wretched than the wretched one who takes no pity on himself, who weeps over Dido's death, which she brought to pass by love for Aeneas,[12] and who does not weep over his own death, brought to pass by not loving you, O God, light of my heart, bread for the inner mouth of my soul, power wedding together my mind and the bosom of my thoughts? I did not love you, and I committed fornication against you,[13] and amid my fornications from all sides there sounded the words, "Well done! Well done!"[14] Love of this world is fornication against you,[15] but "Well done! Well done!" is said, so that it will be shameful for a man to be otherwise. I did not weep over these facts, but I wept over the dead Dido "who sought her end by the sword."[16] I forsook you, and I followed after your lowest creatures, I who was earth, turning to earth. If I had been forbidden to read those tales, I would have grieved because I could not read what would cause me to grieve. Such folly is deemed a higher and more profitable study than that by which I learned to read and write.

Now let my God cry out in my soul, and let your truth say to me, "It is not so. It is not so." Far better is that earlier teaching. See how I am readier to forget the wanderings of Aeneas and all such tales than to read and write. True it is that curtains hang before the doors of the grammar schools, but they do not symbolize some honored mystery but rather a cloak for error. Let not men whom I no longer fear inveigh against me when I confess to you, my God, what my soul desires, and when I

---

[10] **not the parts . . . teach us:** The "first teachers" taught the three *Rs*; the *grammatici* gave more advanced courses, such as composition, rhetoric, and literature.

[11] **"flesh . . . return":** Ps. 77:39.

[12] **Dido's death . . . Aeneas:** As Dido was the legendary queen of Carthage, her story must have been a favorite in African schools.

[13] Cf. Osee 9:1; 4:12.

[14] Ps. 39:16.

[15] Cf. Jas. 4:4.

[16] **"who . . . sword":** Virgil, *Aeneid,* iv, 457.

acquiesce in a condemnation of my evil ways, so that I may love your ways, which are good.[17] Let not these buyers and sellers of literature inveigh against me if I put this question to them: "Did Aeneas ever come to Carthage, as the poet says?" For if I do, the more unlearned will answer that they do not know; the more learned will even deny that it is true. But if I ask them with what letters the name Aeneas is spelled, all who have learned this much will give the right answer in accordance with that agreement and convention by which men have established these characters among themselves. Again, if I should ask which of these would be forgotten with greater inconvenience to our life, to read and write or those poetic fables, who does not discern the answer of every man who has not completely lost his mind? Therefore, as a boy I sinned when I preferred these inane tales to more useful studies, or rather when I hated the one and loved the other. But then, "One and one are two, and two and two are four" was for me a hateful chant, while the wooden horse full of armed men, the burning of Troy, and Creusa's ghost[18] were most sweet but empty spectacles.

Book II
Augustine's Sixteenth Year

Chapter 1: The Depths of Vice

I wish to bring back to mind my past foulness and the carnal corruptions of my soul. This is not because I love them, but that I may love you, my God. Out of love for your love I do this. In the bitterness of my remembrance, I tread again my most evil ways, so that you may grow sweet to me, O sweetness that never fails, O sweetness happy and enduring, which gathers me together again from that disordered state in which I lay in shattered pieces, wherein, turned away from you, the one, I spent myself upon the many.[19] For in my youth, I burned to get my fill of hellish things. I dared to run wild in different darksome ways of love. My comeliness wasted away.[20] I stank in your eyes, but I was pleasing to myself and I desired to be pleasing to the eyes of men.

Chapter 2: Love and Lust

What was there to bring me delight except to love and be loved? But that due measure between soul and soul, wherein lie the bright boundaries of friendship, was not kept. Clouds arose from the slimy desires of the flesh and from youth's seething spring. They clouded over and darkened my soul, so that I could not distinguish the calm light of chaste love from the fog of lust. Both kinds of affection burned confusedly within me and swept my feeble youth over the crags of desire and plunged me into a whirlpool of shameful deeds. Your wrath was raised above me, but I knew it

---

[17] Cf. Jer. 18:11.

[18] **wooden horse . . . ghost:** Cf. *Aeneid*, ii, 772.

[19] The phrases "the one" and "the many" are from Neoplatonic philosophy.

[20] **My comeliness . . . away:** Cf. Dan. 10:8.

not. I had been deafened by the clanking chains of my mortality, the penalty of my pride of soul. I wandered farther away from you, and you let me go. I was tossed about and spilt out in my fornications; I flowed out and boiled over in them, but you kept silent. Ah, my late-found joy! you kept silent at that time, and farther and farther I went from you, into more and more fruitless seedings of sorrow, with a proud dejection and a weariness without rest.

Who might have tempered my misery, turned to good use the fleeting beauties of those lowest things, and put limits to their delights, so that youth's flood might have spent itself on the shore of married life, if rest in such pleasures could not be gained by the end of begetting children, as your law, O Lord, prescribes? Even so do you fashion the offspring of our mortality, for you have power to stretch forth a gentle hand and soften those thorns that had no place in your paradise.[21] For your omnipotence is not far from us, even when we are far from you. Or I might have listened more heedfully to your voice as it sounded from the clouds: "Nevertheless, such shall have tribulation of the flesh. But I spare you."[22] "It is good for a man not to touch a woman."[23] And again: "He that is without a wife is solicitous for the things that belong to God, how he may please God. But he that is with a wife is solicitous for the things of this world, how he may please his wife."[24] I should have listened more heedfully to these words, and having thus been made a eunuch for the sake of the kingdom of heaven,[25] I would have looked with greater joy to your embraces.

But I, poor wretch, foamed over: I followed after the sweeping tide of passions and I departed from you. I broke all your laws, but I did not escape your scourges. For what mortal man can do that? You were always present to aid me, merciful in your anger, and charging with the greatest bitterness and disgust all my unlawful pleasures, so that I might seek after pleasure that was free from disgust, to the end that, when I could find it, it would be in none but you, Lord, in none but you. For you fashion sorrow into a lesson to us.[26] You smite so that you may heal. You slay us, so that we may not die apart from you.[27]

Where was I in that sixteenth year of my body's age, and how long was I exiled from the joys of your house? Then it was that the madness of lust, licensed by human shamelessness but forbidden by your laws, took me completely under its scepter, and I clutched it with both hands. My parents took no care to save me by marriage from plunging into ruin. Their only care was that I should learn to make the finest orations and become a persuasive speaker.

---

[21] **thorns . . . paradise:** Cf. Gen. 3:18; Matt. 22:30.

[22] **"Nevertheless . . . you":** I Cor. 7:28.

[23] **"It is good . . . woman":** I Cor. 7:1.

[24] **"He that . . . wife":** I Cor. 7:32, 33.

[25] **a eunuch . . . heaven:** Cf. Matt. 19:12.

[26] Cf. Ps.93:20: ". . . who frame labor in commandment."

[27] **you fashion . . . us:** Cf. Deut. 32:39.

Chapter 3: A Year of Idleness

In that year my studies were interrupted, with my return from Madauros,[28] the nearby city in which I had already resided to take up the study of literature and oratory, while the money for the longer journey to Carthage was being raised, more by the determination than by the finances of my father, a moderately well-off burgess[29] of Thagaste. To whom do I tell these things? Not to you, my God, but before you I tell them to my own kind, to mankind, or to whatever small part of it may come upon these books of mine. Why do I tell these things? It is that I myself and whoever else reads them may realize from what great depths we must cry unto you.[30] And what is closer to your ears than a contrite heart and a life of faith?[31]

Who at that time did not praise and extol my father because, beyond the resources of his own estate, he furnished his son with everything needed for this long sojourn to be made for purposes of study? No such provision was made for their sons by many far richer citizens. But meanwhile this same father took no pains as to how I was growing up before you, or as to how chaste I was, as long as I was cultivated in speech, even though I was left a desert, uncultivated for you, O God, who are the one true and good Lord of that field which is my heart.[32]

During the idleness of that sixteenth year, when, because of lack of money at home, I lived with my parents and did not attend school, the briars of unclean desires spread thick over my head, and there was no hand to root them out. Moreover, when my father saw me at the baths, he noted how I was growing into manhood and was clothed with stirring youth. From this, as it were, he already took pride in his grandchildren, and found joy in telling it to my mother. He rejoiced over it in that intoxication, wherein this world, from the unseen wine of its own perverse will, tending down towards lower things, forgets you, its creator, and loves your creature more than yourself.[33] But you had already begun to build your temple within my mother's breast and to lay there the foundations of your holy dwelling place. My father, indeed, was still a catechumen, and that a recent one. But she was moved by a holy fear and trembling, and although I was not yet baptized she feared the crooked ways on which walk those who turn their back on you and not their face towards you.[34]

---

[28] Madauros, or Madaura, the present-day Mdaourouch, was about twenty miles from Thagaste. In Augustine's boyhood it was still largely pagan, and he must have been adversely affected by his surroundings and companions.

[29] **father . . . burgess:** Patricius, Augustine's father, had the rights of a Roman citizen. He had some property, but apparently not too much. As a member of the municipal curia, he incurred expenses that must have been a serious burden to him.

[30] **from what great . . . you:** Cf. Ps. 129:1.

[31] **And what is closer . . . faith?:** Cf. Hab. 2:4; Rom. 1:17; Gal. 3:11; Heb. 10:38.

[32] **that field . . . heart:** Cf. I Cor. 3:9.

[33] **loves your creature . . . yourself:** Cf. Rom. 1:25.

[34] **turn their back . . . you:** Cf. Jer. 2:27.

Ah, woe to me! Do I dare to say that you, my God, remained silent when I departed still farther from you? Did you in truth remain silent to me at that time? Whose words but yours were those that you sang in my ears by means of my mother, your faithful servant? Yet none of them sank deep into my heart, so that I would fulfill them. It was her wish, and privately she reminded me and warned me with great solicitude, that I should keep from fornication, and most of all from adultery with any man's wife. Such words seemed to be only a woman's warnings, which I should be ashamed to bother with. But they were your warnings, and I knew it not. I thought that you kept silent and that only she was speaking, whereas through her you did not remain silent to me. In person you were despised[35] by me, by me, her son, "the son of your handmaid,"[36] and your servant.

But I did not know this, and I ran headlong with such great blindness that I was ashamed to be remiss in vice in the midst of my comrades. For I heard them boast of their disgraceful acts, and glory in them all the more, the more debased they were. There was pleasure in doing this, not only for the pleasure of the act, but also for the praise it brought. What is worthy of censure if not vice? But lest I be put to scorn, I made myself more depraved than I was. Where there was no actual deed, by which I would be on equal footing with the most abandoned, I pretended that I had done what I had not done, lest I be considered more contemptible because I was actually more innocent, and lest I be held a baser thing because more chaste than the others.

See with what companions I ran about the streets of Babylon, and how I wallowed in its mire as though in cinnamon and precious ointments![37] That I might cling even more firmly to its very navel, my invisible enemy crushed me under foot and seduced me, for I was easy to seduce. The mother of my flesh, who had fled from the center of Babylon,[38] but lingered in other parts of the city, just as she had warned me against unchastity, so also had some concern over what her husband had said about me, to restrain within the bounds of married love, if it could not be cut back to the quick, what she knew to be a present disease and a future danger. Yet she took no final care for this, because of fear that my prospects would be hindered by the impediment of a wife. These were not those hopes of the life to come which my mother herself had, but those hopes for learning, which, as I knew, both parents desired too much: he, because he almost never thought of you, and only of vain things for me; she, because she thought that the usual studies would be not only no obstacle but even of some help to me in attaining to you. Thus recalling things as far as I can, I conjecture that such were my parents' attitudes. Meanwhile, the lines of liberty at play were loosened over me beyond any just severity and the result was dissolution and various punishments. In all these things, my God, there was a mist that darkened for me the serene light of your truth, and my "iniquity came forth as it were from fatness."[39]

---

[35] **you were despised:** Cf. I Thess. 4:8; II Sam. 12:9.

[36] **"the son . . . handmaid":** Ps. 115:16.

[37] **cinnamon . . . ointments:** Cf. Cant. 4:14.

[38] **fled from . . . Babylon:** Cf. Jer. 50:8; 51:6. Babylon is here used as a synonym for a city of idolatry and vice.

[39] **"iniquity . . . fatness":** Ps. 72:7.

Chapter 4: The Stolen Fruit

Surely, Lord, your law punishes theft, as does that law written on the hearts of men, which not even iniquity itself blots out. What thief puts up with another thief with a calm mind? Not even a rich thief will pardon one who steals from him because of want. But I willed to commit theft, and I did so, not because I was driven to it by any need, unless it were by poverty of justice, and dislike of it, and by a glut of evil-doing. For I stole a thing of which I had plenty of my own and of much better quality. Nor did I wish to enjoy that thing which I desired to gain by theft, but rather to enjoy the actual theft and the sin of theft.

In a garden nearby to our vineyard there was a pear tree, loaded with fruit that was desirable neither in appearance nor in taste. Late one night to which hour, according to our pestilential custom, we had kept up our street games, a group of very bad youngsters set out to shake down and rob this tree. We took great loads of fruit from it, not for our own eating, but rather to throw it to the pigs; even if we did eat a little of it, we did this to do what pleased us for the reason that it was forbidden.

Behold my heart, O Lord, behold my heart upon which you had mercy in the depths of the pit. Behold, now let my heart tell you what it looked for there, that I should be evil without purpose and that there should be no cause for my evil but evil itself. Foul was the evil, and I loved it. I loved to go down to death. I loved my fault, not that for which I did the fault, but I loved my fault itself. Base in soul was I, and I leaped down from your firm clasp even towards complete destruction, and I sought nothing from the shameful deed but shame itself!

Chapter 5: Why Men Sin

There is a splendor in beautiful bodies, both in gold and silver and in all things. For the sense of touch, what is suitable to it affords great pleasure, and for each of the other senses there is a just adaptation of bodily things. Worldly honor, too, and the power to command and to rule over others have their own appeal, and from them issues greed for revenge. But even to gain all these objects, we must not depart from you, O Lord, or fall away from your law. This life which we live here has its own allurements, which come from its own particular mode of beauty and its agreement with all these lower beauties. The friendship of men, bound together by a loving tie, is sweet because of the unity that it fashions among many souls. With regard to all these things, and others of like nature, sins are committed when, out of an immoderate liking for them, since they are the least goods, we desert the best and highest goods, which are you, O Lord our God, and your truth and your law. These lower goods have their delights, but none such as my God, who has made all things, for in him the just man finds delight, and he is the joy of the upright of heart.[40]

When there is discussion concerning a crime and why it was committed, it is usually held that there appeared possibility that the appetites would obtain some of these goods, which we have termed lower, or there was fear of losing them. These

---

[40] **my God . . . heart:** Cf. Ps. 63:11.

things are beautiful and fitting, but in comparison with the higher goods, which bring happiness, they are mean and base. A man commits murder: why did he do so? He coveted his victim's wife or his property; or he wanted to rob him to get money to live on; or he feared to be deprived of some such thing by the other; or he had been injured, and burned for revenge. Would anyone commit murder without reason and out of delight in murder itself? Who can believe such a thing? Of a certain senseless and utterly cruel man[41] it was said that he was evil and cruel without reason. Nevertheless, a reason has been given, for he himself said, "I don't want to let my hand or will get out of practice through disuse."[42] Why did he want that? Why so? It was to the end that after he had seized the city by the practice of crime, he would attain to honors, power, and wealth, and be free from fear of the law and from trouble due to lack of wealth or from a guilty conscience. Therefore, not even Catiline himself loved his crimes, but something else, for sake of which he committed them.

Chapter 6: The Anatomy of Evil

What was it that I, a wretch, loved in you, my act of theft, my deed of crime done by night, done in the sixteenth year of my age? You were not beautiful, for you were but an act of thievery. In truth, are you anything at all, that I may speak to you? The fruit we stole was beautiful, for it was your creation, O most beautiful of all beings, creator of all things, God the good, God the supreme good and my true good. Beautiful was the fruit, but it was not what my unhappy soul desired. I had an abundance of better pears, but those pears I gathered solely that I might steal. The fruit I gathered I threw away, devouring in it only iniquity, and that I rejoiced to enjoy. For if I put any of that fruit into my mouth, my sin was its seasoning. But now, O Lord my God, I seek out what was in that theft to give me delight, and lo, there is no loveliness in it. I do not say such loveliness as there is in justice and prudence, or in man's mind, and memory, and senses, and vigorous life, nor that with which the stars are beautiful and glorious in their courses; or the land and the sea filled with their living kinds, which by new births replace those that die, nor even that flawed and shadowy beauty found in the vices that deceive us.

For pride imitates loftiness of mind, while you are the one God, highest above all things. What does ambition seek, except honor and glory, while you alone are to be honored above all else and are glorious forever? The cruelty of the mighty desires to be feared: but who is to be feared except the one God, and from his power what can be seized and stolen away, and when, or where, or how, or by whom? The caresses of the wanton call for love; but there is naught more caressing than your charity, nor is anything to be loved more wholesomely than your truth, which is beautiful and bright above all things. Curiosity pretends to be a desire for knowledge, while you know all things in the highest degree. Ignorance itself and folly are cloaked over with the names of simplicity and innocence, because nothing more

---

[41] **a certain . . . man:** Augustine refers to Lucius Sergius Catiline (c. 108–62 B.C.E.) against whom Cicero delivered four powerful orations.

[42] **"I don't . . . disuse":** Cf. Sallust, *De Catilina*, xvi.

simple than you can be found. What is more innocent than you, whereas to evil men their own works are hostile? Sloth seeks rest as it were, but what sure rest is there apart from the Lord? Luxury of life desires to be called plenty and abundance; you are the fullness and the unfailing plenty of incorruptible pleasure. Prodigality casts but the shadow of liberality, while you are the most affluent giver of all good things. Avarice desires to possess many things, and you possess all things. Envy contends for excellence: what is more excellent than you? Anger seeks vengeance: who takes vengeance with more justice than you?[43] Fear shrinks back at sudden and unusual things threatening what it loves, and is on watch for its own safety. But for you what is unusual or what is sudden? Or who can separate you from what you love? Where, except with you, is there firm security? Sadness wastes away over things now lost in which desire once took delight. It did not want this to happen, whereas from you nothing can be taken away.

Thus the soul commits fornication when it is turned away from you and, apart from you, seeks such pure, clean things as it does not find except when it returns to you. In a perverse way, all men imitate you who put themselves far from you, and rise up in rebellion against you. Even by such imitation of you they prove that you are the creator of all nature, and that therefore there is no place where they can depart entirely from you.

What, therefore, did I love in that theft of mine, in what manner did I perversely or viciously imitate my Lord? Did it please me to go against your law, at least by trickery, for I could not do so with might? Did it please me that as a captive I should imitate a deformed liberty, by doing with impunity things illicit bearing a shadowy likeness of your omnipotence? Behold, your servant flees from his Lord and follows after a shadow![44] O rottenness! O monstrous life and deepest death! Could a thing give pleasure which could not be done lawfully, and which was done for no other reason but because it was unlawful?

Chapter 7: *Grace That Keeps and Heals*

"What shall I render to the Lord,"[45] for he recalls these things to my memory, but my soul is not made fearful by them? Lord, I will love you, and give thanks to you, and confess to your name,[46] since you have forgiven me so many evils and so many impious works. To your grace and to your mercy I ascribe it that you have dissolved my sins as if they were ice. To your grace I ascribe also whatsoever evils I have not done. For what evil is there that I, who even loved the crime for its own sake, might not have done? I confess that you have forgiven me all my sins, both those which I have done by my own choice and those which, under your guidance, I have not committed.

Who is the man who will reflect on his weakness, and yet dare to credit his chastity and innocence to his own powers, so that he loves you the less, as if he had

---

[43] **who takes . . . you?**: Cf. Rom. 12:19.

[44] **your servant . . . a shadow**: Cf. Job 7:2, as known to Augustine.

[45] **"What . . . Lord"**: Ps. 115:12.

[46] Cf. Ps. 53:8.

little need for that mercy by which you forgive sins to those who turn to you. There may be someone who has been called by you, and has heeded your voice, and has shunned those deeds which he now hears me recalling and confessing of myself. Let him not laugh to scorn a sick man who has been healed by that same physician who gave him such aid that he did not fall ill, or rather that he had only a lesser ill. Let him therefore love you just as much, nay even more. For he sees that I have been rescued from such depths of sinful disease by him who, as he also sees, has preserved him from the same maladies.

Book III
Later Youth

Chapter 1: A Student at Carthage

I came to Carthage, where a caldron of shameful loves seethed and sounded about me on every side.[47] I was not yet in love, but I was in love with love, and by a more hidden want I hated myself for wanting little. I sought for something to love, for I was in love with love; I hated security, and a path free from snares.[48] For there was a hunger within me from a lack of that inner food, which is yourself, my God. Yet by that hunger I did not hunger, but was without desire for incorruptible food, not because I was already filled with it, but because the more empty I was, the more distaste I had for it. Therefore, my soul did not grow healthy, but it was ulcered over, and it cast outside itself and in its misery was avid to be scratched by the things of sense,[49] things that would not be loved if they lacked all soul. To love and to be loved was sweet to me, and all the more if I enjoyed my loved one's body.

Therefore, I defiled the very source of friendship by the filth of concupiscence, and its clear waters I befouled with the lust of hell. Yet foul and vicious as I was, with overflowing vanity, I took pride in being refined and cultured. I plunged headlong into love, whose captive I desired to be. But my God, my mercy, with how much gall did you sprinkle all that sweetness of mine, and how good you were to do it![50] For I was loved, and I had gained love's bond of joy. But in my joy I was bound about with painful chains of iron, so that I might be scourged by burning rods of jealousy, and suspicion, and fear, and anger, and quarreling.

Chapter 2: A Lover of Shows

The theater enraptured me, for its shows were filled with pictures of my own miseries and with tinder for my fires. Why is it that a man likes to grieve over doleful and tragic events which he would not want to happen to himself? The spectator likes to experience grief at such scenes, and this very sorrow is a pleasure to him. What is this

---

[47] **I came . . . every side:** In the Latin, *sartago*, here translated as caldron, repeats the sound of *Carthago*, as we would say, "London, a dungeon." Carthage was notorious for vice.

[48] **path . . . snares:** Cf. Wisd. 14:11.

[49] **it was ulcered . . . sense:** Cf. Job 2:7, 8.

[50] **with how much gall . . . to do it:** Cf. Plato, *Gorgias*, 509, for this thought.

but a pitiable folly? For the more a man is moved by these things, the less free is he from such passions. However, when he himself experiences it, it is usually called misery; when he experiences it with regard to others, it is called mercy.[51] But what sort of mercy is to be shown to these unreal things upon the stage? The auditor is not aroused to go to the aid of the others; he is only asked to grieve over them. Moreover, he will show greater approval of the author of such representations, the greater the grief he feels. But if men's misfortunes, whether fictitious or of ancient times, are put on in such manner that the spectator does not feel sorrow, then he leaves in disgust and with disapproval. If grief is aroused in him, he remains in the theater, full of attention and enjoying himself.

Tears and sorrow, therefore, are objects of love. Certainly, every man likes to enjoy himself. But while no man wants to be wretched, does he nevertheless want to be merciful? Now since mercy cannot exist apart from grief, is it for this sole reason that grief is loved? This also has friendship as its source and channel. But where does it go? Where does it flow? Why does it run down into a torrent of boiling pitch,[52] into those immense surges of loathsome lusts? For into these it is changed, and by its own choice it is turned from the purity of heaven into something distorted and base. Shall mercy, therefore, be cast aside? By no means. At certain times, therefore, sorrows may be loved. But shun uncleanness, O my soul! With God as my keeper, the God of our fathers, worthy to be praised and exalted above all forever,[53] shun uncleanness!

Today still I feel compassion, but in those days at the theater I felt joy together with the lovers when by shameful means they had joy in one another, although those things were only pretended in the show, and when they lost each other, I became sad like one who feels compassion. Both situations gave me delight. But now I have more pity for one who rejoices in a shameful deed than for one who has suffered, so to speak, damage to a pernicious pleasure or loss of some vile joy. This is surely the truer mercy, and sorrow finds no delight in it. Although any man who sorrows over a sinner is commended for his act of charity, yet one who shows fraternal mercy prefers rather that there be no occasion for his sorrow. If there is a good will that is at the same time bad-willed, which cannot be, then only a truly and sincerely merciful man can wish that there might be some unfortunates, so that he could show mercy to them. Hence, a certain kind of sorrow can be commended, but none can be loved. Such mercy is yours, O Lord God, for you love our souls with a purity of love more deep and wide than that we have for ourselves, and you are unalterably merciful, because you suffer no wound from sorrow. "And for these things who is sufficient."[54]

But in my wretchedness at that time I loved to feel sorrow, and I sought out opportunities for sorrow. In the false misery of another man as it was mimicked on the stage, that actor's playing pleased me most and had the strongest attraction for

---

[51] **mercy:** Mercy, or compassion.

[52] **boiling pitch:** Cf. Isa. 34:9.

[53] Cf. Dan. 3:52.

[54] **"And for these . . . sufficient":** II. Cor. 2:16.

me which struck tears from my eyes. What wonder was it that I, an unhappy sheep straying from your flock and impatient of your protection, should be infected with loathsome sores? Hence came my love for such sorrows, by which I was not pierced deep down — for I did not like to suffer such things, but only to look at them — and by which when they were heard and performed, I was scratched lightly, as it were. As a result as though from scratches made by fingernails, there followed a burning tumor and horrid pus and wasting away. Such was my life, but was it truly life, my God?

Chapter 3: The Wreckers

Your faithful mercy hovered above me but from afar. Upon what great evils did I waste myself, and what a sacrilegious desire for knowledge did I pursue, so that it might bring me, a deserter from you, down into the depths of apostasy and into the deceitful service of demons! To them I made a sacrifice of my evil deeds, by all of which you scourged me. Even during the celebration of your mysteries, within the walls of your church, I dared to desire and to arrange an affair for procuring the fruit of death. Hence you scourged me with heavy punishments, but nothing in proportion to my faults, O you my most mighty mercy, my God, my refuge from those terrible dangers amid which I wandered, too proud of neck, so that I might depart far from you, loving my own ways and not yours, loving a fugitive's freedom!

Moreover, my studies, which were called honorable, were directed to the practice of law, so that I might excel at it and become so much the more distinguished because so much the more crafty. So great is the blindness of men, who even glory in their blindness! I was already the leading student in the school of rhetoric, and in my pride I rejoiced and I was swollen up with vanity. However, I was much more reserved than others, as you know, O Lord. I kept entirely apart from the acts of wreckage which were perpetrated by the wreckers — this cruel and diabolical name is a sort of emblem of their sophistication — among whom I lived with a sort of shameless shame, since I was not one of them. I associated with them and sometimes took pleasure in their friendship. But I always abhorred their deeds, that is, their acts of wreckage, by which they wantonly mocked at the natural shyness of the new students. By their coarse tricks they overturned this modesty, and thus they provided for their own perverted fun. Nothing is more like the acts of demons than their conduct. How could they be better named than as wreckers? For they themselves had been altogether overturned and perverted in the first instance by devils who laugh at them and through trickery secretly seduce them in the very way in which they love to deride and trick others.

Chapter 4: Cicero's Influence

Among such associates of my callow youth I studied the treatises on eloquence, in which I desired to shine, for a damnable and inflated purpose, directed towards empty human joys. In the ordinary course of study I came upon a book by a certain Cicero,[55]

---

[55] **a certain Cicero:** Cicero was, of course, a familiar author to Augustine. Apparently, he says "a certain Cicero" to indicate detachment from a pagan author.

whose tongue almost all men admire but not his heart. This work contains his exhortation to philosophy and is called *Hortensius*. This book changed my affections. It turned my prayers to you, Lord, and caused me to have different purposes and desires. All my vain hopes forthwith became worthless to me, and with incredible ardor of heart I desired undying wisdom. I began to rise up,[56] so that I might return to you. I did not use that book to sharpen my tongue: that I seemed to purchase with the money my mother gave to me, since I was in my nineteenth year and my father had died two years before. I did not use it, then, to sharpen my tongue, nor did it impress me by its way of speaking but rather by what it spoke.

How I burned, O my God, how I burned with desire to fly away from earthly things and upwards to you, and yet I did not know what you would do with me! For with you there is wisdom.[57] Love of wisdom has the name philosophy in Greek, and that book set me on fire for it. There are some who may lead others astray by means of philosophy, coloring and falsifying their errors with that great, and beauteous, and honest name. Almost all such men, both of Cicero's time and of earlier periods, are marked out and refuted in that book. There also he makes clear the salutary warning of your Spirit, given to us through your good and devout servant: "Beware lest any man deceive you through philosophy and vain deceit, according to the tradition of man, according to the elements of the world, and not according to Christ: For in him dwells all the fulness of the Godhead corporeally."[58] At that time, as you, the light of my heart, do know, these apostolic words were not yet known to me. But I was delighted with the exhortation only because by its argument I was stirred up and enkindled and set aflame to love, and pursue, and attain and catch hold of, and strongly embrace not this or that sect, but wisdom itself, whatsoever it might be. In so great a blaze only this checked me, that Christ's name was not in it. For this name, O Lord, according to your mercy,[59] this name of my Savior, your Son, my tender heart had holily drunken in with my mother's milk and kept deep down within itself. Whatever lacked this name, no matter how learned and polished and veracious it was, could not wholly capture me.

Chapter 5: Introduction to Sacred Scripture

I accordingly decided to turn my mind to the Holy Scriptures and to see what they were like. And behold, I see something within them that was neither revealed to the proud nor made plain to children, that was lowly on one's entrance but lofty on further advance, and that was veiled over in mysteries. None such as I was at that time could enter into it, nor could I bend my neck for its passageways. When I first turned to that Scripture, I did not feel towards it as I am speaking now, but it seemed to me unworthy of comparison with the nobility of Cicero's writings. My swelling pride

---

[56] **I began . . . up:** Cf. Luke 15:18–20 for the parable of the prodigal son.

[57] **For with . . . wisdom:** Cf. Job 12:13.

[58] **"Beware . . . corporeally":** Col. 2:8, 9.

[59] Cf. Ps. 24:7.

turned away from its humble style, and my sharp gaze did not penetrate into its inner meaning. But in truth it was of its nature that its meaning would increase together with your little ones, whereas I disdained to be a little child and, puffed up with pride, I considered myself to be a great fellow.

BOOK VI
YEARS OF STRUGGLE

Chapter 1: The Widow's Son

"My hope from my youth,"[60] where were you, and where had you gone?[61] Was it not you who created me, and made me different from the beasts of the field, and made me wiser than the birds of the air?[62] But I walked in darkness, and upon a slippery way,[63] and I sought for you outside myself, but I did not find you, the God of my heart.[64] I went down into the depth of the sea,[65] and I lost confidence, and I despaired of finding the truth.

But now my mother, strong in her love, had come to me, for she had followed me over land and sea, kept safe by you through all her perils. In the midst of storms at sea, she reassured the sailors themselves, by whom inexperienced travelers upon the deep are accustomed to be comforted, and promised them that they would reach port in safety, for you had promised this to her in a vision.[66] She found me in great danger because of my despair at ever finding the truth. Yet when I told her that I was no longer a Manichean, although not a Catholic Christian, she did not leap with joy, as if she had heard something unexpected. The reason was that she had already been assured with regard to that aspect of my wretched state, in which she bewailed me as one dead, but yet destined to be brought back to life by you. In thought she put me before you on a bier, so that you might say to a widow's son, "Young man, I say to you, arise!"[67] Then would he revive, and begin to speak, and you would deliver him to his mother. Therefore, her heart did not pound in turbulent exultation when she heard that what she daily implored you with her tears to do was already done in so great a part. For although I had not yet attained to the truth, I had now been rescued from falsehood. Rather, she was all the more certain that you, who had promised the whole, would grant what still remained. Hence most calmly and with a heart filled with confidence, she replied to me how she believed in Christ that before she departed from this life she would see me a faithful Catholic. This much she said to me. But to you, O fountain of mercies, she multiplied her prayers and tears, so that

---

[60] Ps. 70:5.

[61] Cf. Ps. 10:1.

[62] Cf. Job 35:10, 11.

[63] Cf. Ps. 34:6; Isa. 50:10.

[64] Cf. Ps. 72:26.

[65] Cf. Ps. 67:23.

[66] Cf. Acts 27:21–26.

[67] Luke 7:14.

you would speed your help[68] and enlighten my darkness.[69] More zealously still she would hasten to the church, and she would hang on the words of Ambrose, as on "a fountain of water springing up into life everlasting."[70] For she loved that man as though he were an angel of God,[71] because she had learned that through him I had been brought in the meantime to the wavering, doubtful state in which I then was. She felt sure that through this state I was to pass from sickness to health, with a more acute danger intervening, throug[h] ~~which doctors call the~~ crisis.

Chapt[er]

One time when she had brought and wine, as was her custom in keeper. As soon as she learned accepted it in so devout and obed she became an accuser of her c Addiction to wine did not captu hatred of truth, as it does so mar as the intoxicated object to a wat val foods, which were to be mer out more than a single small cup would take a little for sake of c that seemed fit to be honored which she would set out in all s and tepid, she would share in sma[ll portions] sought devotion and not pleasure.

As soon as she found that by order of that famous preacher and patron of devotion such things were not to be done, not even by those who would do them in a sober fashion, so that no opportunity would be offered for sots to get drunk, and because such tributes to the dead were too much like Gentile superstitions, she most willingly gave them up. Instead of a basket filled with the fruits of the earth, she learned to bring to the martyrs' memorials a breast filled with purer oblations. Thus she would give what she could to the poor, and thus would the communication of the Lord's body be celebrated in those places where, in imitation of his passion, the martyrs were immolated and received their crowns.

Yet it seems to me, O Lord my God, and so stands my heart on this matter in your sight, that perhaps it would not have been easy for my mother to forego that

---

[68] Cf. Ps. 69:2.

[69] Cf. Ps. 17:29.

[70] John 4:14.

[71] Cf. Gal. 4:14.

[72] **she had brought . . . his command:** Following St. Ambrose's example, Augustine later helped to stop the custom in Africa. The objections were twofold, as he indicates: there were associations with pagan customs and they were the occasion of drinking and revelry.

custom, if it had been forbidden by someone whom she did not love as she loved Ambrose. She loved him greatly because of my salvation, while he loved her because of her most devout life, in which, so fervent in spirit[73] among her good works, she frequented the church. Hence when he saw me, he would often break forth in her praise, and congratulate me for having such a mother. But he did not know what sort of son she had, for I doubted all things, and I thought that the way to life[74] could not be found.

Chapter 3: The Example and Words of St. Ambrose

I had not yet groaned in prayer for you to come to my help, but my mind was intent on questioning and restless for argument. Ambrose himself I believed to be a happy man, as the world judges such things, because so many powerful persons showed him honor. His celibacy alone appeared to me to be a hard thing. But what hopes he held, what struggles against temptations arising from his exalted station, what comforts amid adversities, how sweet the joys of that secret mouth within his heart as it fed upon and savored again the bread you gave him—such things I could not guess at, nor had I any experience of them.

He did not know the passions that seethed within me, nor my pit of danger. Yet I was unable to ask of him what I wanted and in the way I wanted, for crowds of busy men, to whose troubles he was a slave, shut me away from both his ear and his mouth. When he was not with them, and this was but a little while, he either refreshed his body with needed food or his mind with reading. When he read, his eyes moved down the pages and his heart sought out their meaning, while his voice and tongue remained silent. Often when we were present—for no one was forbidden entry, and it was not his custom to have whoever came announced to him—we saw him reading to himself, and never otherwise. After sitting for a long time in silence—who would dare to annoy a man so occupied?—we would go away. We thought that in that short time which he obtained for refreshing his mind, free from the din of other men's problems, he did not want to be summoned to some other matter. We thought too that perhaps he was afraid, if the author he was reading had expressed things in an obscure manner, then it would be necessary to explain it for some perplexed but eager listener, or to discuss some more difficult questions, and if his time were used up in such tasks, he would be able to read fewer books than he wished to. However, need to save his voice, which easily grew hoarse, was perhaps the more correct reason why he read to himself. But with whatever intention he did it, that man did it for a good purpose.[75]

Certainly, no opportunity was given me to ask what I desired to ask of so holy an oracle of yours, his breast, unless the matter could be heard quickly. But my surging

---

[73] Cf. Acts 18:25; Rom. 12:11.

[74] Cf. Prov. 6:23; 10:17; 15:10.

[75] The present passage is reported to be one of the few descriptions of silent reading in ancient literature. The detail with which Augustine describes St. Ambrose's custom indicates how unusual silent reading must have been.

passions needed full leisure in him to whom they might be poured out, but this they never found. I heard him, indeed, every Sunday as he was "rightly handling the word of truth"[76] before the people. More and more was I convinced that all the knots of the wily calumnies that those men who had deceived us wove against the sacred books could be loosened. When I found that "man was made by you to your image,"[77] was understood by your spiritual sons, whom you had regenerated by grace in our Catholic Mother, not as though they believed and thought of you as limited by the shape of the human body—although what a spiritual substance would be like I did not surmise even in a weak and obscure manner[78]—I blushed joyfully because I had barked for so many years, not against the Catholic faith but against the fantasies of a carnal imagination. Rash and irreverent had I been in that I talked about and condemned things I should have inquired into and learned about. But you, most high and most near at hand, most secret and most present, in whom there are no members, some greater and others smaller, who are everywhere whole and entire, who are never confined in place, and who surely are not in our corporeal shape, you have yet made man to your own image.[79] And behold, from head to foot he is contained in space!

Chapter 4: Errors Refuted; Truth Not Yet Found

Therefore, since I did not understand how this, your image, should subsist, I should have knocked[80] and proposed the question, "How is this to be believed?" instead of insultingly opposing it, as if it were believed as I thought. So much the more sharply did concern over what I could hold with certainty gnaw at my very vitals, so much the more shame did I feel at being so long deluded and deceived by a promise of certainties and for gabbling in childish error and ardor over so many uncertainties as if they were certain.[81] That they were false afterwards became clear to me. Certain it was that they were uncertain, and that at one time they had been taken for certain by me, when with blind belligerence I would attack your Catholic Church, although I had not yet discovered that it teaches true doctrines, and that it does not teach those with which I had seriously charged it. Thus I was in the course of being refuted and converted. I rejoiced, my God, that the one only Church, the body of your Only-begotten Son,[82] in which the name of Christ had been put upon me as an infant, had no place for such infantile nonsense. Nor in its sound doctrine would it maintain one that would confine you, the creator of all things, in a space, however high and wide, yet bounded on every side by the shape of human members.

---

[76] "rightly . . . truth": II Tim. 2:15.

[77] Cf. Gen. 9:6.

[78] Cf. I Cor. 13:12.

[79] Cf. Gen. 1:26.

[80] knocked: Cf. Matt. 7:7: "Knock, and it shall be opened to you."

[81] uncertainties . . . certain: Augustine's Manichean errors.

[82] Cf. Col. 1:18–24.

I rejoiced also that the ancient scriptures of the law and the prophets were now set before me for reading, not with that eye which once looked on them as absurdities, when I argued as if your saints understood them in that way, whereas in truth they did not thus understand them. I was glad when I often heard Ambrose speaking in his sermons to the people as though he most earnestly commended it as a rule that "the letter kills, but the spirit quickens."[83] For he would draw aside the veil of mystery and spiritually lay open things that interpreted literally seemed to teach unsound doctrine. He would say nothing that caused me difficulty, although he would state things which I did not as yet know to be true. I held back my heart from all assent, fearing to fall headlong, and died all the more from that suspense. I wished to be made just as certain of things that I could not see, as I was certain that seven and three make ten. I was not so mad as to think that even this last could not be known, but I wanted other things to be known with the same certainty, whether bodily things that were not present to my senses, or spiritual things, which I did not know how to conceive except in a corporeal way. By believing I could have been healed, so that my mind's clearer sight would be directed in some way to your truth, which endures forever[84] and is lacking in nothing. But as often happens, just as a man who has had trouble with a poor physician fears to entrust himself even to a good one, so it was with my soul's health. In truth, it could never be healed except by believing, but lest it believe what was false, it refused to be cured and it resisted the hands of you who have compounded the remedies of faith, and have applied them to the diseases of the whole world, and to them you have given great efficacy.

Chapter 5: The Authority of the Scriptures

From that time forward I preferred Catholic teaching. I thought that on its part it was more moderate and not at all deceptive to command men to believe what was not demonstrated, either because it was a matter that could be demonstrated, but perhaps not to everyone, or because it was indemonstratable, than for others to make a mockery of credulity by rash promises of sure knowledge, and then commanding that so many most fabulous and absurd things be accepted on trust because they could not be demonstrated. Then, little by little, O Lord, with a most mild and merciful hand you touched and calmed my heart. I considered how countless were the things that I believed, although I had not seen them nor was I present when they took place. Such were so many events in human history, so many things about places and cities that I had not seen, so many things about my friends, so many things about physicians, so many things about countless other men. Unless we believed these things, nothing at all could be done in this life. Lastly, I thought of how I held with fixed and unassailable faith that I was born of certain parents, and this I could never know unless I believed it by hearing about them. By all this you persuaded me that not those who believe in your books, which you have established with such mighty authority among almost all nations, but those who do not believe

---

[83] II Cor. 3:6.

[84] Cf. Ps. 116:2.

in them are the ones to be blamed, and not to be given a hearing, if they should perhaps say to me: "How do you know that these are the books of the one true and most truthful God, dispensed by his Spirit to the human race?" This truth most above all was to be believed, for no hostile and slanderous questions, so many of which I had read in philosophers who contradict one another, could extort from me the answer that I would at any time believe that you do not exist, whatsoever might be your nature (for this I did not know), or that the governance of human affairs did not belong to you.

Sometimes I believed this more strongly and at other times in a more feeble way. But always I believed both that you are and that you have care for us, although I did not know either what must be thought concerning your substantial being or what way led up to you or back to you. Therefore, since we were too weak to find the truth by pure reason, and for that cause we needed the authority of Holy Writ, I now began to believe that in no wise would you have given such surpassing authority throughout the whole world to that Scripture, unless you wished that both through it you be believed in and through it you be sought. Now that I had heard many things in those writings explained in a probable manner, I referred the absurdity that used there to cause me difficulty to the depths of their mysteries. To me, that authority seemed all the more venerable and worthy of inviolable faith, because they were easy for everyone to read and yet safeguarded the dignity of their hidden truth within a deeper meaning, by words completely clear and by a lowly style of speech making itself accessible to all men, and drawing the attention of those who are not light of heart.[85] Thus it can receive all men into its generous bosom, and by narrow passages lead on to you a small number of them,[86] although these are more numerous than if it did not stand out with such lofty authority and if it had not attracted throngs into the bosom of its holy humility.

I thought over these things, and you were present to me. I uttered sighs, and you gave ear to me. I wavered back and forth, and you guided me. I wandered upon the broad way[87] of the world, but you did not forsake me.

Book VIII
The Grace of Faith

Chapter 5

Thus by the burdens of this world I was sweetly weighed down, just as a man often is in sleep. Thoughts wherein I meditated upon you were like the efforts of those who want to arouse themselves but, still overcome by deep drowsiness, sink back again. Just as no man would want to sleep forever, and it is the sane judgment of all men that it is better to be awake, yet a man often defers to shake off sleep when a heavy

---

[85] Cf. Ecclus. 19:4.

[86] **Thus it can . . . number of them:** Augustine makes a contrast between the many and the few (cf. Matt. 7:13, 14 and 20:16), but it is to the effect that the simplicity of the Scriptures has an appeal to all men, while a smaller number are led on to a deeper study of them.

[87] Cf. Matt. 7:13.

languor pervades all his members, and although the time to get up has come, he yields to it with pleasure even although it now irks him. In like manner, I was sure that it was better for me to give myself up to your love than to give in to my own desires. However, although the one way appealed to me and was gaining mastery, the other still afforded me pleasure and kept me victim. I had no answer to give to you when you said to me, "Rise, you who sleep, and arise from the dead, and Christ will enlighten you."[88] When on all sides you showed me that your words were true, and I was overcome by your truth, I had no answer whatsoever to make, but only those slow and drowsy words, "Right away. Yes, right away." "Let me be for a little while." But, "Right away—right away" was never right now, and "Let me be for a little while" stretched out for a long time.

In vain was I delighted with your law according to the inward man, when another law in my members fought against the law of my mind, and led me captive in the law of sin which was in my members.[89] For the law of sin is force of habit, whereby the mind is dragged along and held fast, even against its will, but still deservedly so, since it was by its will that it had slipped into the habit. Unhappy man that I was! Who would deliver me from the body of this death, unless your grace through Jesus Christ our Lord?[90]

Chapter 8: In the Garden

Then, during that great struggle in my inner house, which I had violently raised up against my own soul in our chamber,[91] in my heart, troubled both in mind and in countenance, I turn upon Alypius and cry out to him: "What is the trouble with us? What is this? What did you hear? The unlearned rise up and take heaven by storm,[92] and we with all our erudition but empty of heart, see how we wallow in flesh and blood! Are we ashamed to follow, because they have gone on ahead of us? Is it no shame to us not even to follow them?" I said some such words, and my anguish of mind tore me from him, while astounded he looked at me and kept silent. I did not speak in my usual way. My brow, cheeks, eyes, color, and tone of voice spoke of my state of mind more than the words that I uttered.

Attached to our lodging there was a little garden; we had the use of it, as of the whole house, for our host, the owner of the house, did not live in it. The tumult within my breast hurried me out into it, where no one would stop the raging combat that I had entered into against myself, until it would come to such an end as you knew of, but as I knew not. I suffered from a madness that was to bring health, and I was in a death agony that was to bring life: for I knew what a thing of evil I was, but I did not know the good that I would be after but a little while. I rushed, then, into the garden, and Alypius followed in my steps. Even when he was present I was not less

---

[88] Eph. 5:14.

[89] Cf. Rom. 7:22, 23.

[90] Cf. Rom. 7:24, 25.

[91] Cf. Isa. 26:20; Matt. 6:6.

[92] Cf. Matt. 11:12.

alone—and how could he desert me when I was reduced to such a state? We sat down as far as we could from the house. Suffering from a most fearful wound, I quaked in spirit, angered by a most turbulent anger, because I did not enter into your will and into a covenant with you,[93] my God. For all my bones cried out[94] to me to enter into that covenant, and by their praises they lifted me up to the skies. Not by ships, or in chariots, or on foot do we enter therein; we need not go even so far as I had gone from the house to the place where we were sitting. For not only to go, but even to go in thither was naught else but the will to go, to will firmly and finally, and not to turn and toss, now here, now there, a struggling, half-maimed will, with one part rising upwards and another falling down.

Finally, in the shifting tides of my indecision, I made many bodily movements, such as men sometimes will to make but cannot, whether because they lack certain members or because those members are bound with chains, weakened by illness, or hindered in one way or another. If I tore my hair, and beat my forehead, if I locked my fingers together and clasped my knees, I did so because I willed it. But I could have willed this and yet not done it, if the motive power of my limbs had not made its response. Therefore I did many things in which to will was not the same as the ability to act. Yet I did not do that which I wanted to do with an incomparably greater desire, and could have done as soon as I willed to act, for immediately, when I made that act of will, I would have willed with efficacy. In such an act the power to act and the will itself are the same, and the very act of willing is actually to do the deed. Yet it was not done: it was easier for the body to obey the soul's most feeble command, so that its members were moved at pleasure, than for the soul to obey itself and to accomplish its own high will wholly within the will.

Chapter 11: The Voice of Continence

Thus I was sick and tormented, and I upbraided myself much more bitterly than ever before. I twisted and turned in my chain, until it might be completely broken, although now I was scarcely held by it, but still held by it I was. Within the hidden depths of my soul, O Lord, you urged me on. By an austere mercy you redoubled the scourges[95] of fear and shame, lest I should give in again, and lest that thin little remaining strand should not be broken through but should grow strong again and bind me yet more firmly.

Within myself I said: "Behold, let it be done now, now let it be done," and by those words I was already moving on to a decision. By then I had almost made it, and yet I did not make it. Still, I did not slip back into my former ways; but close by I stood my ground and regained my breath. Again I tried, and I was but a little away from my goal, just a little away from it, and I all but reached it and laid hold of it. Yet I was not quite there, and I did not reach it, and I did not catch hold of it. I still hesitated to die to death and to live to life, for the ingrown worse had more power over

---

[93] Cf. Ezech. 16:8.

[94] Cf. Ps. 34:10.

[95] **redoubled the scourges:** Cf. *Aeneid*, v, 457.

me than the untried better. The nearer came that moment in time when I was to become something different, the greater terror did it strike into me. Yet it did not strike me back, nor did it turn me away, but it held me in suspense.

My lovers of old, trifles of trifles and vanities of vanities,[96] held me back. They plucked at my fleshy garment, and they whispered softly: "Do you cast us off?" and "From that moment we shall no more be with you forever and ever!" and again, "From that moment no longer will this thing and that be allowed to you, forever and ever!" What did they suggest by what I have called "this thing and that," what, O my God, did they suggest? May your mercy turn away all that from your servant's soul! What filth did they suggest! What deeds of shame! But now by far less than half did I hear them. For now it was not as if they were openly contradicting me, face to face, but as if they were muttering behind my back, and as if they were furtively picking at me as I left them, to make me look back again. Yet they did delay me, for I hesitated to tear myself away, and shake myself free of them, and leap over to that place where I was called to be. For an overpowering habit kept saying to me, "Do you think that you can live without them?"

But now it asked this in a very feeble voice. For from that way in which I had set my face and where I trembled to pass, there appeared to me the chaste dignity of continence, serene and joyous, but in no wanton fashion, virtuously alluring, so that I would come to her and hesitate no longer. To lift me up and embrace me, she stretched forth her holy hands, filled with varied kinds of good examples. Many were the boys and girls, there too a host of youths, men and women of every age, grave widows and aged virgins, and in all these continence herself was in no wise barren but a fruitful mother[97] of children, of joys born of you, O Lord, her spouse.

She smiled upon me with an enheartening mockery, as if to say: "Cannot you do what these youths and these maidens do? Or can these youths and these maidens do this of themselves, and not rather in the Lord their God? The Lord their God gave me to them. Why do you stand on yourself, and thus stand not at all? Cast yourself on him. Have no fear. He will not draw back and let you fall. Cast yourself trustfully on him: he will receive you and he will heal you." I felt great shame, for I still heard the murmurings of those trifles, and still I delayed and hung there in suspense. Again she smiled, as if to say: "Turn deaf ears to those unclean members of yours upon the earth, so that they may be mortified. They tell you of delights, but not as does the law of the Lord your God."[98] This debate within my heart was solely of myself against myself. But Alypius, standing close by my side, silently awaited the outcome of my strange emotion.

Chapter 12: The Voice as of a Child

But when deep reflection had dredged out of the secret recesses of my soul all my misery and heaped it up in full view of my heart, there arose a mighty storm, bring-

---

[96] Cf. Eccles. 1:2.

[97] Cf. Ps. 112:9.

[98] Cf. Ps. 118:85.

ing with it a mighty downpour of tears. That I might pour it all forth with its own proper sounds, I arose from Alypius's side—to be alone seemed more proper to this ordeal of weeping—and went farther apart, so that not even his presence would be a hindrance to me. Such was I at that moment, and he sensed it, for I suppose that I had said something in which the sound of my voice already appeared to be choked with weeping. So I had arisen, while he, in deep wonder, remained there where we were sitting. I flung myself down, how I do not know, under a certain fig tree, and gave free rein to my tears.[99] The floods burst from my eyes, an acceptable sacrifice to you.[100] Not indeed in these very words but to this effect I spoke many things to you: "And you, O Lord, how long?[101] How long, O Lord, will you be angry forever?[102] Remember not our past iniquities."[103] For I felt that I was held by them, and I gasped forth these mournful words, "How long, how long? Tomorrow and tomorrow? Why not now? Why not in this very hour an end to my uncleanness?"

Such words I spoke, and with most bitter contrition I wept within my heart. And lo, I heard from a nearby house, a voice like that of a boy or a girl, I know not which, chanting and repeating over and over, "Take up and read. Take up and read." Instantly, with altered countenance, I began to think most intently whether children made use of any such chant in some kind of game, but I could not recall hearing it anywhere. I checked the flow of my tears and got up, for I interpreted this solely as a command given to me by God to open the book and read the first chapter I should come upon. For I had heard how Anthony had been admonished by a reading from the Gospel at which he chanced to be present, as if the words read were addressed to him: "Go, sell what you have, and give to the poor, and you shall have treasure in heaven, and come, follow me,"[104] and that by such a portent he was immediately converted to you.

So I hurried back to the spot where Alypius was sitting, for I had put there the volume of the apostle when I got up and left him. I snatched it up, opened it, and read in silence the chapter on which my eyes first fell: "Not in rioting and drunkenness, not in chambering and impurities, not in strife and envying; but put you on the Lord Jesus Christ, and make not provision for the flesh in its concupiscences."[105] No further wished I to read, nor was there need to do so. Instantly, in truth, at the end of this sentence, as if before a peaceful light streaming into my heart, all the dark shadows of doubt fled away.

Then, having inserted my finger, or with some other mark, I closed the book, and, with a countenance now calm, I told it all to Alypius. What had taken place in him, which I did not know about, he then made known to me. He asked to see what

---

[99] Cf. *Aeneid,* vii, 499.

[100] Cf. Ps. 50:19.

[101] Ps. 6:4.

[102] Ps. 78:5.

[103] Ps. 78:8.

[104] Matt. 19:21.

[105] Rom. 13:13, 14.

I had read: I showed it to him, and he looked also at what came after what I had read for I did not know what followed. It was this that followed: "Now him that is weak in the faith take unto you,"[106] which he applied to himself and disclosed to me. By this admonition he was strengthened, and by a good resolution and purpose, which were entirely in keeping with his character, wherein both for a long time and for the better he had greatly differed from me, he joined me without any painful hesitation.

Thereupon we went in to my mother; we told her the story, and she rejoiced. We related just how it happened. She was filled with exultation and triumph, and she blessed you, "who are able to do above that which we ask or think."[107] She saw that through me you had given her far more than she had long begged for by her piteous tears and groans. For you had converted me to yourself, so that I would seek neither wife nor ambition in this world, for I would stand on that rule of faith where, so many years before, you had showed me to her. You turned her mourning into a joy[108] far richer than that she had desired, far dearer and purer than that she had sought in grandchildren born of my flesh.[109]

---

[106] Rom. 14:1.

[107] Cf. Eph. 3:20.

[108] Cf. Ps. 29:12.

[109] **she had sought . . . flesh:** Monica had made efforts to arrange a lawful marriage for her son. Cf. *Confessions*, Book VI, ch. 13.

THE QUR'AN
651–652

The Qur'an, or Koran, which means "reading" or "recital," is the sacred text of the nation of believers called Islam, the third major religion to originate in the Middle East after Judaism and Christianity. For believers in Islam, or Muslims, the **Qur'an** is not considered a book of prophecy, but is the Word of God, **Allah**, delivered in the Arabic language between the years 610–632 C.E. to the prophet Muhammad; it completes the earlier prophecies of the great prophets of the Hebrew Scriptures and the New Testament, including Abraham, Moses, David, and Jesus. Muslims believe that the earthly Qur'an is a copy of the divine Qur'an that, inscribed in gold on tablets of marble in heaven, exists for eternity and is in all aspects — religious, moral, historical — the only true guide to the conduct of life. All important tasks begun by believing Muslims are undertaken "in the name of God, the Compassionate, the Merciful." The monotheism of the Qur'an and its ascription to Muhammad as its divine Messenger are contained in the first two lines of the prayer, "There is no god but Allah, and Muhammad is his prophet." Strictly speaking, the Qur'an cannot be translated; versions in other languages may be used for the purposes of teaching and conversion, but the true Word of God is in Arabic alone. Far from limiting the spread of the Qur'an and Islam — whose followers number nearly one billion — this belief has served as a powerful protector of the Arabic language throughout the world.

The political and cultural impact of the religion of Islam and its holy book can hardly be overstated. A language, a religion, and a culture were carried abroad together during the expansion of Muslim territory in the seventh and early eighth centuries. By the time of the death of Muhammad in 632 C.E., Islam, which means "submitting oneself to God," was already well established throughout Arabia. Muhammad's followers initiated a period of *jihad*,[1] or holy war, during which they moved out of the Arabian peninsula, conquering Syria, Persia, Armenia, Egypt, and eventually North Africa, Spain, and a large part of Asia Minor. The Muslim expansion under the **Umayyad** dynasty[2] reached Constantinople in 718 and southern France in 732, one hundred years after Muhammad's death.

koo-RAHN
AH-luh

jih-HAHD

oo-MIGH-yad

---

[1] *jihad:* In its sense of "holy war," *jihad* first referred to the struggle of the people of Medina, Muhammad's followers, against the "unbelievers" of Mecca. When Muslim armies moved out of Arabia across North Africa and Spain and followed the trade routes through Asia Minor in the seventh and eighth centuries, the meaning of *jihad* expanded. By that time, a permanent state of war was believed to exist between Islam and nations of unbelievers beyond the borders of Islam. After the Islamic armies ceased advancing, the concept of *jihad* changed again to mean a spiritual obligation to convert unbelievers, and a relationship of tolerance gradually was established between the Muslim world and its neighbors. Orthodox Muslims today usually define *jihad* as self-discipline or a struggle for the faith, not a call to arms.

[2] **Umayyad dynasty:** Formed from a distant branch of Muhammad's family in 661. Under this dynasty the capital was moved to Damascus, in Syria. The dynasty's limited claim to ancestry, its poor administrative record, and a series of political crises led to its overthrow in 749.

uh-BAS-id

Muslim culture took hold in the conquered territories, coming to full flower under the **Abbasid** dynasty,[3] located in Baghdad, between 750 and 950. Except in times of JIHAD, other religions were tolerated in the Muslim world, and this relative openness made possible great intellectual advances in philosophy, the arts, and science. Even to this day, Islam's inclusiveness has had much to do with its widespread acceptance: Its believers come from many races in all parts of the world.

The Prophet Muhammad.   Muhammad was born about 570 C.E. in the trading town of Mecca near the west coast of Arabia to a poor clan, the Hashim, of the Quraysh tribe. Orphaned as a child, he worked as a young man for his uncle Abu-Talib as a camel driver on caravans. About 595 he married **Khadijah**, a rich widow who tested him by having him lead her trading caravan to Syria before proposing marriage to him. Muhammad's marriage prospered, and together he and his wife had four daughters whom they were able to marry to substantial men in the community. While Muhammad was busy attaining a position of prominence himself and brooding over the fate of Mecca, he had a vision of the angel Gabriel who said to him:

kah-DEE-jah

> Recite in the name of your Lord who created — created man from
> clots of blood.
> Recite! Your Lord is the Most Bountiful One, who by the pen
> taught man what he did not know.

This was the first fragment of the Qur'an. (It is now the opening lines of Sura 96.) After an interval of two to three years, Muhammad's visions began again, sometimes in dreams and sometimes in daytime reveries. Over a period of twenty-two years the entire Qur'an was transmitted to him in this way. As far as is known, Muhammad was illiterate. But he recited the received verses to his followers, who memorized them, and eventually the verses were recorded by scribes — according to legend, on anything they could find, including parchment, leather, palm leaves, even camel bones.

Muhammad began preaching in Mecca about 613, three years after receiving the first of his visions. Like other prophets throughout history, he preached at a time of frustration and social unrest, and he called for a renewal of faith; at the same time, he introduced new religious beliefs and practices. The chief topics of his early preaching included God's goodness and power, the necessity to meet God for judgment, the proper response to God of gratitude and worship, the need to exhibit generosity, and his own vocation as God's prophet. Soon Muhammad encountered opposition from some of the rich merchants in Mecca, having to do with several aspects of his preaching. To these wealthy businessmen, Muhammad's insistence on generosity toward the poor suggested a condemnation of excessive wealth. Moreover, Muhammad's avowal that he was the Prophet

www   For a quiz on the Qur'an, see *World Literature Online* at bedfordstmartins .com/worldlit.

---

[3] **Abbasid dynasty:** This dynasty, established in 750, proclaimed an end to "secular Arab" rule and moved the capital to Baghdad, in Iraq. Deeply influenced by its neighbor Persia, the Abbasid regime enjoyed its "golden age" late in the eighth century.

Arabia in
Muhammad's
Lifetime

*In the last decade of
his life, Muhammad
gained control of vir-
tually all of western
Arabia. After
Muhammad's death
in 632, the Prophet's
followers took Islam
into the north, into
Persian and Byzan-
tine territories.*

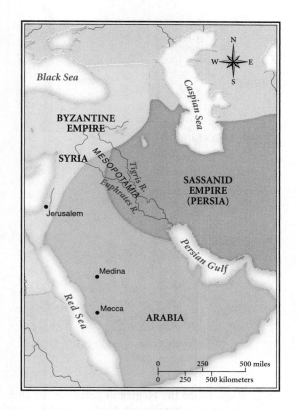

Arabia in Muhammad's Lifetime

of God made the merchants think he was trying to seize political control
of Mecca. Finally, Muhammad recanted the so-called satanic verses that
favored the worship of certain idols, saying they had been received in a
false vision sent by the devil. After considering the issue further, Muhammad opposed the worship of any images whatever, and denounced polytheism. As the Qur'an states, "There is no god but God." It is likely that
the local merchants supported the shrines around Mecca because of their
proximity to the centers of trade and commerce from which they benefited, and for this reason they opposed Muhammad's condemnation of
idol worship.

The Hegira. Under pressure from the Meccan merchants, Muhammad's followers began to migrate, first to Abyssinia around 615 and later
to Medina in 622. The reasons for the twofold migration are still debated,
but it is known that Muhammad's clan, the Hashim, came under political
pressure in Mecca in 616, and both Muhammad's uncle and protector,
Abu-Talib, and Muhammad's wife, Khadijah, died in 619. Facing hostility
at home, Muhammad began to negotiate with emissaries from Medina,
another coastal city in western Arabia, and in September 622 fled Mecca
in the middle of the night, arriving in Medina with his supporters. This

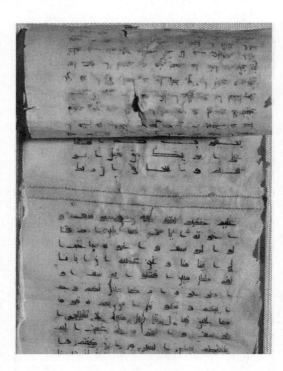

Abbasid Qur'an, ninth century
The Qur'an, Islam's holy book, recounts the Word of God as told to Muhammad, the Prophet and divine Messenger. The holy Qur'an informs the daily life and culture of all its followers. It is the central text of one of the great world religions whose millions of adherents inhabit countries all over the world. (Detail The Art Archive / Turkish and Islamic Art Museum, Istanbul / Dagli Orti)

hih-JIGH-ruh; HIJ-ruh

oom-WAH

HAHJ

KAY-lif AHTH-mun
ZIDE IB-un THAH-bit

emigration, called the **Hegira** in Latin (or hijrah in Arabic), established Muhammad as a dignitary in Medina. He became the city's chief arbiter of disputes, and soon the city became a community of believers, or *UMWAH,* under Muhammad's spiritual leadership.

In the remaining decade of his life, Muhammad subdued opposition in Medina, confronted and defeated his old opponents in Mecca, and became virtual ruler of western Arabia. The continuing conflict between the Byzantine empire and Persia to the north and east enhanced the position of the new Arabian Muslims, since they represented a religiously-based community of impressive numbers and relative stability. In March 632, Muhammad led a holy pilgrimage, or *HAJJ,* to Mecca, a "pilgrimage of farewell" in his case, that has since become common practice for every Muslim, who is expected to make the journey at least once in his or her lifetime. Muhammad died in Medina on June 8, 632.

The Text of the Qur'an.   In 651–652 C.E., under the CALIPH **Othman,** Muhammad's secretary **Zaid Ibn Thabit** collected the prophet's recitations and edited them into 114 suras, or chapters, creating the Qur'an in Arabic. All alternative versions were destroyed, thereby fixing the canonical text that has been passed down virtually unchanged to the present. Each of the 114 suras is titled with a word, such as "Women" or "Jonah," suggesting its contents. The suras vary in length from nearly three hundred verses to a few words; although the shortest suras were often the earliest, all suras now are arranged in descending order, from the longest to the shortest, in the Qur'an. Partly because of this arrangement, the Qur'an as a whole is not connected by a narrative thread, and indeed its longer suras jump from subject to subject. The style of the suras varies considerably as well. Some of the short suras have the power of a brief sermon, including moral exhortations to lead a good life, while the long chapters detail prescriptions for the improvement of the society of the believers, often legalistic in tone.

The fact that the Qur'an is considered holy, a direct message from God, makes it comparable to the Torah—the Books of Genesis, Exodus, Leviticus, Numbers, and Deuteronomy in the Hebrew Scriptures. Muhammad is rarely named in the Qur'an; he is usually called **al-Rasul**, or "Messenger." Although the influence of the Qur'an on later Arabic literature has been tremendous, Muhammad rejected attempts to see himself as a gifted poet or storyteller. In fact, for many centuries Muslims regarded serious literature as limited to works touching on philosophy, ethics, morals, or spiritual concerns; storytelling was generally dismissed as unworthy of concern. Poetry, which was held in high esteem before the Qur'an, continued to flourish after Muhammad's death.

ahl-rah-SOOL

The Book for Believers: The Story of the Cow.   From the start the Qur'an states its purpose clearly. The Word of God is intended for believers, so that they may follow the right path. As **Sura** 2: The Cow says, "This Book is not to be doubted. It is a guide for the righteous." Sura 2 begins by distinguishing believers from unbelievers; in the story Moses brings his followers a command from God to sacrifice a cow. They are at first incredulous. Muhammad compares this incredulity to the reluctance of "People of the Book"—Christians and Jews—to believe in his prophecy, clinging instead to what they already know. The figure of Abraham is used to explain the presence of the *KA'BAH*, the sacred House of the Black Stone, in Mecca, following the injunction: "Make the place where Abraham stood a place of worship."[4] Thus Sura 2 emphasizes the continuity of prophecy that began with Abraham and has its completion in Muhammad. Also in Sura 2, the nature of righteousness is defined:

SOO-rah

KAH-buh

> Righteousness does not consist in whether you face towards the East or the West. The Righteous man is he who believes in God and the Last Day, in the angels and the Book and the prophets; who, though he loves it dearly, gives away his wealth to kinsfolk, to orphans, to the destitute, to the traveler in need and to beggars, and for the redemption of captives; who attends to his prayers and renders the alms levy; who is true to his promises and steadfast in adversity and in times of war. Such are the true believers; such are the God-fearing. (2:176)

---

[4] **the Ka'bah . . . worship:** This is the destination of holy pilgrimage *(hajj)* for Muslims, the site of prayer where they pay reverence to the Black Stone. The Stone is kept in the *Ka'bah*, a cubical house in the center of Mecca.

Men and Women.   To modern-day Western readers, the ancient religious texts of the Middle East, especially the Hebrew Scriptures and the Qur'an, treat women harshly, subordinating them to their husbands and calling for punishment for such offenses as disloyalty and infidelity. One frequently cited passage in Sura 4 of the Qur'an leaves little doubt as to this position.

> Men have authority over women because God has made the one superior to the other, and because they spend their wealth to maintain them. Good women are obedient. They guard their unseen parts because God has guarded them. As for those from whom you fear disobedience, admonish them, forsake them in beds apart, and beat them. Then if they obey you, take no further action against them. Surely God is high, supreme. (4:34)

On the other hand, the Qur'an contains passages demonstrating respect for women within the limits of their assigned roles. The beginning of Sura 4: Women, for example, reminds believers of the common origin of all humanity, and pledges to honor motherhood in particular.

> You people! Have fear of your Lord, who created you from a single soul. From that soul he created its spouse, and through them He bestrewed the earth with countless men and women.
> Fear God, in whose name you plead with one another, and honor the Mothers who bore you. God is ever watching you. (4:1–2)

The Qur'an also prescribes Islamic laws governing inheritance, including provisions for women, children, orphans, the disabled, and even slaves. While these laws still discriminate against women, who could inherit only half the sum that a similarly situated male would inherit, they insist on compassion and respect for surviving families, the poor, and those otherwise unable to support themselves. It should be remembered that the enactment of strict laws against such offenses as the taking of the widow of a deceased male relative by his brother — a common practice of the day — represented a gain for women of the time, grounding the treatment of women in a context of respect for human rights, no matter how limited it might seem according to a modern perspective.

The Story of the Table.   In Sura 5: The Table the angel Gabriel addresses Jews and Christians ("People of the Book"), chastising them for falling away from their covenant with God. Then he addresses the Apostle Muhammad, explaining that the Jewish Torah and the Christian Gospels are precursors to the "Book with the truth" (the Qur'an). He also addresses the People of the Book, in an interesting passage, concerning the question of religious tolerance.

> We have ordained a law and assigned a path for each of you. Had God pleased, He could have made of you one community: but it is His wish to prove you by that which He has bestowed upon you. Vie with each other in good works, for to God shall you all return and He will resolve your differences for you. (5:49)

While conceding nothing to what are regarded as the false beliefs of the Jews and Christians, this passage clarifies why Muslims are encouraged to tolerate these faiths, in the hope that their practitioners will adopt Islam voluntarily.

In particular, this chapter militates against the Christian belief in the divinity of Jesus. At the end of the chapter, the following story is told: The disciples request of Jesus that the Lord send them down a table of food from heaven. In reply, God sends down the table, but also tests Jesus, asking him whether he ever has said to mankind, "Worship me and my mother as gods besides God." Jesus denies this, saying that he has only said "Serve God, my Lord and your Lord." God then declares that the righteous will be saved, and is praised as all-powerful.

Joseph.   Unique in the Qur'an, Sura 12: Joseph is a narrative closely parallel to Hebrew Scriptures (see Genesis 37, 39–50). The Joseph of the Qur'an is a prophet of God, but he is not specifically identified with the Hebrews. Cruelly abandoned by his older brothers, he withstands many hardships in Egyptian exile until they arrive to enjoy his hospitality, unaware of his identity. He sends them home to request of their father that they return with his other brother, whom he favors. When they do, Joseph keeps his favorite brother with him, forcing the older brothers to abandon this brother as well. When the brothers return again in disgrace, he forgives them, cures his grieving father's blindness, and invites his entire family to join him. By enduring hardship without complaint, Joseph has won the reward of the righteous, and he shares his newly gained prosperity with his errant brothers.

In the Qur'an version of the story, Joseph resists seduction by his Egyptian master's wife. After he is tempted, he awaits a sign from God before he refuses her. The wayward wife is treated more tolerantly than she is in Hebrew Scriptures. When she confesses her attempt to seduce Joseph to the women of the city, she uses the excuse that they, too, would have been attracted had he appeared before them. Joseph is unjustly imprisoned as a result of this episode, but his forbearance of this hardship only adds to his stature. When he wins his release from prison, encounters his brothers, and is finally reunited with his grieving father he is quick to praise God for his deliverance.

> "This . . . is the meaning of my old vision: my Lord has fulfilled it. He has been gracious to me. He has released me from prison and brought you out of the desert after Satan had stirred up strife between me and my brothers. My Lord is gracious to whom he will. He alone is all-knowing and wise." (12:100)

The story of Joseph in the Qur'an differs from the original Hebrew version in disassociating Joseph from the Jewish people and taking a more tolerant view of his sexual temptation. It emphasizes that righteousness has a double origin, in the good deeds of the individual and the grace of God.

Visions of Heaven and Hell.   The linked sections, Sura 55: The Merciful and Sura 56: That Which Is Coming describe the joy of creation, man's choice between heaven and hell, and the two states of existence after death. Some of the lyricism and the sensual imagery in the descriptions of the

[T]he Koran is everything to the devout Moslem: It is history, sacred and profane; it is prayer; it is a code of civil and religious law; it is a guide to conduct and meditation. . . . The non-Moslem may be captivated by its beauty, may discern its sharply characterized styles and manifold literary subtleties, but he can never fully understand or appreciate how the Koran has superintended all genuine Moslem thought and fashioned the Moslem soul.

– JAMES KRITZECK, Scholar, 1964

One of the most dramatic of these [first] conversions was that of Umar ibn al-Khattab, who was devoted to the old paganism, passionately opposed to Muhammad's message, and determined to wipe out the new sect. But he was also an expert in Arabian poetry, and the first time he heard the words of the Quran he was overcome by their extraordinary eloquence. As he said, the language broke through all his reservations about its message: "When I heard the Qur'an my heart was softened and I wept, and Islam entered me."

– KAREN ARMSTRONG, Historian, 2000

gardens of the saved recall Psalms or even The Song of Solomon from the Hebrew Scriptures. These short suras are among the most inspired — and the most controversial — in the Qur'an.

The Concluding Suras.   Several of the concluding suras are fine examples of the richness and range of the shorter pieces. Sura 93: Daylight is an admonition to treat the lowly of this world with care and respect. Sura 96: Clots of Blood is believed to be Muhammad's first vision, when he is called upon to recite the messages he receives. Sura 109: The Unbelievers seems to be a charm to keep the godless away. Sura 110: Help foresees a day when "God's help and victory come, and you see men embrace God's faith in multitudes." Characteristically, it advises humility. Sura 112: Oneness is often seen as a summary of the spiritual message of the Qur'an.

The Abiding Qur'an.   After centuries of conflict among Jews, Christians, and Muslims, the Qur'an is one of the least understood books in the West. While it is based on many of the prophecies found in the Hebrew Scriptures and the New Testament, it differs markedly from Judaism and especially Christianity in some major tenets. It recognizes neither original sin nor the divinity of Jesus. Muhammad himself is only human, while the message he receives is divine. God is all-powerful, and human conduct is subjected to close scrutiny. Moral behavior is carefully prescribed, especially with regard to what would be called ethics and property rights today. Prayer rituals and religious pilgrimages are a part of the prescribed way of life. Little consideration is given to the individual, because God's ways are beyond man's comprehension or ability to predict, so man need not arrive at an understanding of God. There is no priesthood in Islam, but a community of believers guided by an imam, a man who sets the time and leads the chanting for prayer.

The idea of *jihad*, which ordinarily means "struggle," vigilance over one's own moral and spiritual behavior, has also the broader meaning of holy warfare. Holy wars against the unbeliever certainly have existed in Islamic history, most notably in its first hundred years. Muslim conduct, however, generally has been restrained by a strict code of ethics that is full of prohibitions against aggressive behavior. Muslims are not supposed to strike the first blow and are forbidden to exact unequal punishment or vengeance. The same orthodoxy that insists on moral absolutism helps to maintain the Islamic code of justice in law and political conduct, which considers the nature of the enemy. Tolerance is a prominent feature of Islamic thought, extending particularly to the "People of the Book," Jews and Christians, whom Muslims usually have regarded as capable of redemption rather than enemies to be mistreated. From a scholarly perspective, one sees in the sufferings of the twentieth and twenty-first centuries how linked Islamic civilization is to Judaism and Christianity and how the fate of all three societies is inextricably connected.

■ CONNECTIONS

Hebrew Scriptures (Book 1); New Testament. Although Islam regards the prophets of the Hebrew Scriptures and the New Testament as having been divinely inspired, only Muhammad is the true Prophet, the deliverer of The Book, the final Word of God. Compare the teachings of the Qur'an with the Biblical texts it cites. Does the Qur'an treat the scriptural texts with accuracy and respect?

St. Augustine, *The Confessions*, p. 70. St. Augustine, who lived approximately two hundred years before Muhammad and spent most of his adult life in North Africa, shared some qualities with the Islamic apostle, including his searching intelligence, his strong monotheism, and his emphasis on living an ethical and moral life. Augustine did not, however, subscribe to the same religious beliefs as Muhammad or lead a political and social movement based on his faith. Compare the characters and piety of these two men. What major differences do you find between them?

Ibn Ishaq, *The Life of Muhammad*, p. 134. This story of the life of Muhammad establishes a context for his prophecies for Western readers. Most of our personal knowledge of Muhammad comes from this encyclopedic work, completed more than a hundred years after his death. The Qur'an itself also deals with certain moments from Muhammad's life. How much more of his life, if any, does one need to know to understand the Qur'an?

■ FURTHER RESEARCH

Translations
Arberry, A. J. *The Koran Interpreted.* 1955.
Dawood, N. J. *The Koran.* Revised ed., 1990.
Rodwell, J. M. *The Koran.* 1909.

Studies and Interpretations
Abu-Hamdiyyah, Mohammad. The Qur'an: *An Introduction.* 2000.
Bell, Richard. *Introduction to the* Koran. 1953.
Cleary, Thomas. *The Essential* Koran: *The Heart of Islam.* 1993.
Pickethall, M. M. *The Meaning of the Glorious Koran.* 1963.

Muhammad and Islam
Gibb, H. A. R. *Mohammedanism: An Historical Survey.* 2d ed. 1953.
Guillaume, Alfred. *Islam.* 1956.
Schacht, Joseph, with C. E. Bosworth, eds. *The Legacy of Islam.* 1974.
Watt, Montgomery. *Muhammad: Prophet and Statesman.* 1961.

■ PRONUNCIATION

Abbasid: uh-BAS-id, AB-uh-sid
Allah: AH-luh, AH-lah
al-Rasul: ahl-rah-SOOL
caliph Othman: KAY-lif AHTH-mun, ooth-MAHN
hajj: HAHJ
hijrah: HIJ-ruh
Hegira: hih-JIGH-ruh, HEJ-uh-ruh
jihad: jih-HAHD
Ka'bah: KAH-buh, KAH-uh-buh
Khadijah: kah-DEE-juh
Qur'an: koo-RAHN, koh-RAHN
sura: SOO-rah
umwah: oom-WAH
Umayyad: oo-MIGH-yad
Zaid Ibn Thabit: ZIDE IB-un THAH-bit

The Koran

Translated by N. J. Dawood

Sura 1: The Exordium

1:1

In the name of God
the compassionate
the merciful

Praise be to God, Lord of the Universe,
The Compassionate, the Merciful,
Sovereign of the Day of Judgement!
You alone we worship, and to You alone
we turn for help.
Guide us to the straight path,

1:7

The path of those whom You have favoured,
Not of those who have incurred Your wrath,
Nor of those who have gone astray.

The Qur'an. The text of the Qur'an was established by Zaid Ibn Thabit under the caliph Othman from 651 to 652 C.E. This editorial enterprise included the consolidation of the work into 114 suras, the destruction of other versions, the titling of each sura with a descriptive name, and the arrangement of the suras generally from the longest to the shortest. This effort produced not only the sacred book of the Muslims but also the definitive work of classical Arabic prose that stands at the forefront of Arabic language studies.

Western selections from the Qur'an have tended to include suras whose themes derive from Hebrew scriptural or New Testament themes. While this may help members of a Western audience identify with what they are reading, the moral and spiritual message of the Qur'an itself may be better sought elsewhere in the work. The sections of the Qur'an presented here include some of the Hebrew and Christian stories, but they also focus on aspects of Islamic belief itself. Because the longer suras often deal with several strands of subject matter, the three presented here have been edited to illustrate specific directions of thought. Here the Qur'an—like Hebrew Scriptures and the New Testament—is not treated as sacred scripture, but as material for academic study.

According to Islamic tradition, translations of the Qur'an have always been considered mere interpretations of the Arabic original. Muslims the world over learn Arabic passages for reciting, even while reading the work in their own vernacular languages. The bias against translation out of Arabic is magnified in the case of a language such as English, since it is hard to find English equivalents for key Arabic expressions or even to spell Arabic words consistently in English. A case in point is the word *Qur'an* itself. Until recently, the conventional spelling of the word in English has been *Koran* (the spelling used by Dawood's translation reprinted here). The newly adopted spelling is consistent with the rules governing other spellings of Arabic words in English.

Another difficulty comes when scholars try to arrange the suras in the Qur'an in the order in which they may have been received by Muhammad. Such efforts not only go against Islamic canonical practice, but they involve a great deal of speculation. The English translation and

FROM

SURA 2: THE COW

In the Name of God, the Compassionate, the Merciful

2:1 *Alif lām mīm.* This Book is not to be doubted. It is a guide for the righteous, who believe in the unseen and are steadfast in prayer; who give in alms[1] from what We gave them; who believe in what has been revealed to you[2] and what was revealed before you, and have absolute faith in the life to come. These are rightly guided by their Lord; these shall surely triumph.

As for the unbelievers, it is the same whether or not you forewarn them; they will not have faith. God has set a seal upon their hearts and ears; their sight is dimmed and grievous punishment awaits them.

There are some who declare: 'We believe in God and the Last Day,' yet they are no true believers. They seek to deceive God and those who believe in Him: but they 2:10 deceive none save themselves, though they may not perceive it. There is a sickness in their hearts which God has aggravated: they shall be sternly punished for the lies they tell.

When they are told: 'You shall not do evil in the land,' they reply: 'Surely we are doing only what is good.' But it is they who are the evil-doers, though they may not perceive it.

And when they are told: 'Believe as others believe,' they reply: 'Are we to believe as fools believe?' It is they who are the fools, if they but knew it!

When they meet the faithful, they declare: 'We, too, are believers.' But when alone with their devils they say to them: 'We follow none but you: we were only mocking.' God will mock them and keep them long in sin, ever straying from the right path.

Such are those that barter guidance for error: they profit nothing, nor are they 2:17 on the right path. They are like one who kindled a fire, but as soon as it lit up all 2:18 around him God put it out and left him in darkness: they do not see. Deaf, dumb, and blind, they will never return to the right path.

Or like those who, beneath a dark storm-cloud charged with thunder and lightning, thrust their fingers into their ears at the sound of every thunder-clap for fear of

---

"chronological" arrangement by J. M. Rodwell (1909) is one example of speculative editing of the Qur'an. On the other hand, the present translation by N. J. Dawood features the traditional sura arrangement. This translation was completed in 1956 with several revisions since then. Recently the translator has substituted the word "God" for "Allah," apparently because Islamic belief holds that Allah is differently named by different cultures, and God is a more universal term in English.

In most of the Qur'an, the angel Gabriel speaks to Muhammad, but sometimes Gabriel recalls God or Christ speaking to the believers or the unbelievers. Therefore the pronouns "we," "you," and "they" sometimes may be ambiguous. The issue of who is being addressed is discussed where necessary in the footnotes.

---

[1] **give in alms:** Or, "give to the cause."   [2] **you:** Muhammad.

death (God thus encompasses the unbelievers). The lightning almost snatches away their sight: whenever it flashes upon them they walk on, but as soon as it darkens they stand still. Indeed, if God pleased, He could take away their hearing and their sight: God has power over all things.

You people! Serve your Lord, who has created you and those who have gone before you, so that you may guard yourselves against evil; who has made the earth a bed for you and the sky a dome, and has sent down water from the sky to bring forth fruits for your sustenance. Do not knowingly set up other gods beside God.

2:23   If you doubt what We have revealed to Our servant, produce one chapter comparable to it. Call upon your idols to assist you, if what you say be true. But if you fail (as you are sure to fail), then guard yourselves against the Fire whose fuel is men and stones, prepared for the unbelievers.

Proclaim good tidings to those who have faith and do good works. They shall dwell in gardens watered by running streams: whenever they are given fruit to eat they will say: 'This is what we used to eat before,' for they shall be given the like. Wedded to chaste spouses, they shall abide therein for ever.

God does not disdain to make comparison with a gnat or with a larger creature. The faithful know that it is the truth from their Lord, but the unbelievers ask: 'What could God mean by this comparison?'

By such comparisons God confounds many and enlightens many. But He con-
2:27   founds none except the evil-doers, who break His covenant after accepting it, and put asunder what He has bidden to be united, and perpetrate corruption in the land. These will surely be the losers. [. . .]

2:67   When Moses said to his people: 'God commands you to sacrifice a cow,' they replied: 'Are you trifling with us?'

'God forbid that I should be so foolish!' he rejoined.

'Call on your Lord,' they said, 'to make known to us what kind of cow she shall be.'

He replied: 'Your Lord says: "Let her be neither an old cow nor a young heifer, but in between." Do, therefore, as you are bidden.'

'Call on your Lord,' they said, 'to make known to us what her colour shall be.'

He replied: 'Your Lord says: "Let the cow be yellow, a rich yellow, pleasing to those that see it."'

2:70   'Call on your Lord,' they said, 'to make known to us the exact type of cow she shall be; for to us cows look all alike. If God wills we shall be rightly guided.'

Moses replied: 'Your Lord says: "Let her be a healthy cow, not worn out with ploughing the earth or watering the field; a cow free from any blemish."'

'Now you have told us all,' they answered. And they slaughtered a cow, after they had nearly declined to do so. [. . .]

2:122   Children of Israel, remember the favour I have bestowed upon you, and that I exalted you above the nations. Guard yourselves against a day on which no soul shall stand for another: when no ransom shall be accepted from it, no intercession avail it, no help be given it.

When his Lord put Abraham to the proof by enjoining on him certain commandments and Abraham fulfilled them, He said: 'I have appointed you a leader of mankind.'

'And what of my descendants?' asked Abraham.

'My covenant,' said He, 'does not apply to the evil-doers.'

We made the House³ a resort and a sanctuary for mankind, saying: 'Make the place where Abraham stood a house of worship.' We enjoined Abraham and Ishmael to cleanse Our House for those who walk round it, who meditate in it, and who kneel and prostrate themselves.

'Lord,' said Abraham, 'make this a secure land and bestow plenty upon its people, those of them that believe in God and the Last Day.'

'As for those that do not,' He answered, 'I shall let them live awhile, and then shall drag them to the scourge of the Fire: an evil fate.'

2:127   Abraham and Ishmael built the House and dedicated it, saying: 'Accept this from us, Lord. You are the One that hears all and knows all. Lord, make us submissive to You; make of our descendants a community that will submit to You. Teach us our rites of worship and turn to us with mercy; You are the Forgiving One, the Merciful. Lord, send forth to them an apostle of their own who shall declare to them Your revelations, and shall instruct them in the Book and in wisdom, and shall purify them of sin. You are the Mighty, the Wise One.'

Who but a foolish man would renounce the faith of Abraham? We chose him
2:131   in this world, and in the world to come he shall abide among the righteous. When his Lord said to him: 'Submit,' he answered: 'I have submitted to the Lord of the Universe.'

2:132   Abraham enjoined the faith on his children, and so did Jacob, saying: 'My children, God has chosen for you the true faith. Do not depart this life except in full submission.'

Were you present when death came to Jacob? He said to his children: 'What will you worship when I am gone?' They replied: 'We will worship your God and the God of your forefathers Abraham and Ishmael and Isaac: the One God. To Him we will submit.'

That community has passed away. Theirs is what they did and yours what you have done. You shall not be questioned about their actions.

They say: 'Accept the Jewish or the Christian faith and you shall be rightly guided.'

Say: 'By no means! We believe in the faith of Abraham, the upright one. He was no idolater.'

2:136   Say: 'We believe in God and that which has been revealed to us; in what was revealed to Abraham, Ishmael, Isaac, Jacob, and the tribes; to Moses and Jesus and the other prophets by their Lord. We make no distinction among any of them, and to Him we submit.'

If they accept your faith, they shall be rightly guided; if they reject it, they shall surely be in schism. Against them God is your all-sufficient defender. He hears all and knows all.

---

³ **the House:** The Ka'bah in Mecca.

We take on God's own dye. And who has a better dye than God's? Him will we worship.

Say: 'Would you dispute with us about God, who is our Lord and your Lord? We shall both be judged by our works. To Him alone we are devoted.

'Do you claim that Abraham, Ishmael, Isaac, Jacob, and the tribes, were all Jews or Christians?' Say: 'Who knows better, you or God? Who is more wicked than the man who hides a testimony he has received from God? God is never heedless of what you do.'

2:141   That community has passed away. Theirs is what they did and yours what you have done. You shall not be questioned about their actions. [. . .]

2:176   Righteousness does not consist in whether you face towards the East or the West. The righteous man is he who believes in God and the Last Day, in the angels and the Book and the prophets; who, though he loves it dearly, gives away his wealth to kinsfolk, to orphans, to the destitute, to the traveller in need and to beggars, and for the redemption of captives; who attends to his prayers and renders the alms levy; who is true to his promises and steadfast in trial and adversity and in times of war. Such are the true believers; such are the God-fearing.

2:178   Believers, retaliation is decreed for you in bloodshed: a free man for a free man, a slave for a slave, and a female for a female. He who is pardoned by his aggrieved brother shall be prosecuted according to usage and shall pay him a liberal fine. This is a merciful dispensation from your Lord. He that transgresses thereafter shall be sternly punished.

Men of understanding! In retaliation you have a safeguard for your lives; perchance you will guard yourselves against evil.

It is decreed that when death approaches, those of you that leave property shall bequeath it equitably to parents and kindred. This is a duty incumbent on the righteous. He that alters a will after hearing it shall be accountable for his crime. God hears all and knows all.

2:182   He that suspects an error or an injustice on the part of a testator and brings about a settlement among the parties incurs no guilt. God is forgiving and merciful.

2:183   Believers, fasting is decreed for you as it was decreed for those before you; perchance you will guard yourselves against evil. Fast a certain number of days, but if any one among you is ill or on a journey, let him fast a similar number of days later; and for those that cannot endure it there is a penance ordained: the feeding of a poor man. He that does good of his own accord shall be well rewarded; but to fast is better for you, if you but knew it.

In the month of Ramaḍān the Koran was revealed, a book of guidance for mankind with proofs of guidance distinguishing right from wrong.[4] Therefore whoever of you is present in that month let him fast. But he who is ill or on a journey shall fast a similar number of days later on.

God desires your well-being, not your discomfort. He desires you to fast the whole month so that you may magnify God and render thanks to Him for giving you His guidance.

---

[4] **with proofs . . . wrong:** Alternatively: "with proofs of guidance and salvation."

2:186   If My servants question you about Me, tell them that I am near. I answer the prayer of the suppliant when he calls to Me; therefore let them answer My call and put their trust in Me, that they may be rightly guided.

It is now lawful for you to lie with your wives on the night of the fast; they are a comfort to you as you are to them. God knew that you were deceiving yourselves. He has relented towards you and pardoned you. Therefore you may now lie with them and seek what God has ordained for you. Eat and drink until you can tell a white thread from a black one in the light of the coming dawn. Then resume the fast till nightfall and do not approach them, but stay at your prayers in the mosques.

These are the bounds set by God: do not approach them. Thus He makes known His revelations to mankind that they may guard themselves against evil.

2:188   Do not devour one another's property by unjust means, nor bribe the judges with it in order that you may wrongfully and knowingly usurp the possessions of other men.

2:189   They question you about the phases of the moon. Say: 'They are seasons fixed for mankind and for the pilgrimage.'

Righteousness does not consist in entering your dwellings from the back.[5] The righteous man is he that fears God. Enter your dwellings by their doors and fear God, so that you may prosper.

Fight for the sake of God those that fight against you, but do not attack them first. God does not love aggressors.

Slay them wherever you find them. Drive them out of the places from which they drove you. Idolatry is more grievous than bloodshed. But do not fight them within the precincts of the Holy Mosque unless they attack you there; if they attack you put them to the sword. Thus shall the unbelievers be rewarded: but if they mend their ways, know that God is forgiving and merciful.

2:193   Fight against them until idolatry is no more and God's religion reigns supreme. But if they desist, fight none except the evil-doers.

A sacred month for a sacred month: sacred things too are subject to retaliation. If anyone attacks you, attack him as he attacked you. Have fear of God, and know that God is with the righteous.

Give generously for the cause of God and do not with your own hands cast yourselves into destruction. Be charitable; God loves the charitable.

2:196   Make the pilgrimage and visit the Sacred House for His sake. If you cannot, send such offerings as you can afford and do not shave your heads until the offerings have reached their destination. But if any of you is ill or suffers from an ailment of the head, he must do penance either by fasting or by almsgiving or by offering a sacrifice.

If in peacetime anyone among you combines the visit with the pilgrimage, he must offer such gifts as he can afford; but if he lacks the means let him fast three days during the pilgrimage and seven when he has returned; that is, ten days in all. That is incumbent on him whose family are not present at the Holy Mosque. Have fear of God: know that God is stern in retribution.

---

[5] **entering . . . back:** A custom of pagan Arabs returning from pilgrimage.

2:197   Make the pilgrimage in the appointed months. He that intends to perform it in those months must abstain from sexual intercourse, obscene language, and acrimonious disputes while on pilgrimage. God is aware of whatever good you do. Provide well for yourselves: the best provision is piety. Fear Me, then, you that are endowed with understanding.

It shall be no offence for you to seek the bounty of your Lord. When you come running from 'Arafāt[6] remember God as you approach the sacred monument. Remember Him that gave you guidance when you were in error. Then go out from the place whence the pilgrims will go out and implore the forgiveness of God. God is forgiving and merciful. And when you have fulfilled your sacred duties, remember God as you remember your forefathers or with deeper reverence.

There are some who say: 'Lord, give us abundance in this world.' These shall
2:201   have no share in the world to come. But there are others who say: 'Lord, give us what is good both in this world and in the world to come, and keep us from the torment of the Fire.' These shall have a share, according to what they did. Swift is God's reckoning.

Give glory to God on the appointed days. He that departs on the second day incurs no sin, nor does he who stays on longer, if he truly fears God. Have fear of God, then, and know that you shall all be gathered before Him.

There are some whose views on this life please you: they even call on God to vouch for that which is in their hearts; whereas in fact they are the deadliest of your
2:205   opponents. No sooner do they leave you than they hasten to do evil in the land, destroying crops and cattle. God does not love evil.
2:206   When they are told: 'Have fear of God,' vanity carries them off to sin. Sufficient for them shall be Hell, an evil resting-place.

But there are others who would give away their lives in order to find favour with God. God is compassionate to His servants.

Believers, submit all of you to God and do not walk in Satan's footsteps; he is your inveterate foe. If you lapse after the veritable signs that have been shown to you, know that God is mighty and wise.

Are they waiting for God to come down to them in the shadow of a cloud, with all the angels? Their fate will have been settled then. To God shall all things return.

Ask the Israelites how many conspicuous signs We gave them. He that tampers with the gift of God after it is bestowed on him shall find that God is stern in retribution.

For the unbelievers the life of this world is decked with all manner of temptations. They scoff at the faithful, but those that fear God shall be above them on the Day of Resurrection. God gives unstintingly to whom He will.
2:213   Mankind were once but one community. Then God sent forth prophets to give them good news and to warn them, and with these He sent down the Book with the Truth, that it might serve as arbiter in the disputes of men. (None disputed it save those to whom it was given, and that was through envy of one another, after veritable

---

[6] **'Arafāt:** A location near Mecca.

signs had been vouchsafed them.) So God guided by His will those who believed in the truth which had been disputed. God guides whom He will to a straight path.

Did you suppose that you would go to Paradise untouched by the suffering which was endured by those before you? Affliction and adversity befell them; and so shaken were they that each apostle, and those who shared his faith, cried out: 'When will God's help come?' God's help is ever near.

2:215   They will ask you about almsgiving. Say: 'Whatever you bestow in charity must go to parents and to kinsfolk, to the orphans and to the destitute and to the traveller in need. God is aware of whatever good you do.'

2:216   Fighting is obligatory for you, much as you dislike it. But you may hate a thing although it is good for you, and love a thing although it is bad for you. God knows, but you know not.

They ask you about the sacred month. Say: 'To fight in this month is a grave offence; but to debar others from the path of God, to deny Him, and to expel His worshippers from the Holy Mosque, is far more grave in His sight. Idolatry is more grievous than bloodshed.'

They will not cease to fight against you until they force you to renounce your faith — if they are able. But whoever of you recants and dies an unbeliever, his works shall come to nothing in this world and in the world to come. Such men shall be the tenants of the Fire, wherein they shall abide for ever.

Those that have embraced the Faith, and those that have fled their land and fought for the cause of God, may hope for God's mercy. God is forgiving and merciful. [. . .]

FROM

SURA 4: WOMEN

In the Name of God, the Compassionate, the Merciful

4:1   YOU PEOPLE! Have fear of your Lord, who created you from a single soul. From that soul He created its spouse, and through them He bestrewed the earth with countless men and women.

Fear God, in whose name you plead with one another, and honour the mothers who bore you. God is ever watching you.

Give orphans the property which belongs to them. Do not exchange their valuables for worthless things or cheat them of their possessions; for this would surely be a grievous sin. If you fear that you cannot treat orphans[7] with fairness, then you may marry other women who seem good to you: two, three, or four of them. But if you fear that you cannot maintain equality among them, marry one only or any slave-girls you may own. This will make it easier for you to avoid injustice.

Give women their dowry as a free gift; but if they choose to make over to you a part of it, you may regard it as lawfully yours.

---

[7] **orphans:** Orphan girls.

4:5   Do not give the feeble-minded the property with which God has entrusted you for their support; but maintain and clothe them with its proceeds, and speak kind words to them.

4:6   Put orphans to the test until they reach a marriageable age. If you find them capable of sound judgement, hand over to them their property, and do not deprive them of it by squandering it before they come of age.

Let not the rich guardian touch the property of his orphan ward; and let him who is poor use no more than a fair portion of it for his own advantage.

When you hand over to them their property, call in some witnesses; sufficient is God's accounting of your actions.

Men shall have a share in what their parents and kinsmen leave; and women shall have a share in what their parents and kinsmen leave: whether it be little or much, they shall be legally entitled to a share.

If relatives, orphans, or needy men are present at the division of an inheritance, give them, too, a share of it, and speak kind words to them.

Let those who are solicitous about the welfare of their young children after their own death take care not to wrong orphans. Let them fear God and speak for justice.

4:10   Those that devour the property of orphans unjustly, swallow fire into their bellies; they shall burn in a mighty conflagration.

God has thus enjoined you concerning your children:

A male shall inherit twice as much as a female. If there be more than two girls, they shall have two-thirds of the inheritance; but if there be one only, she shall inherit the half. Parents shall inherit a sixth each, if the deceased have a child; but if he leave no child and his parents be his heirs, his mother shall have a third. If he have brothers, his mother shall have a sixth after payment of any legacy he may have bequeathed or any debt he may have owed.

You may wonder whether your parents or your children are more beneficial to you. But this is the law of God; surely God is all-knowing and wise.

4:12   You shall inherit the half of your wives' estate if they die childless. If they leave children, a quarter of their estate shall be yours after payment of any legacy they may have bequeathed or any debt they may have owed.

Your wives shall inherit one quarter of your estate if you die childless. If you leave children, they shall inherit one-eighth, after payment of any legacy you may have bequeathed or any debt you may have owed.

If a man or a woman leave neither children nor parents and have a brother or a sister, they shall each inherit one-sixth. If there be more, they shall equally share the third of the estate, after payment of any legacy he may have bequeathed or any debt he may have owed, without prejudice to the rights of the heirs. That is a commandment from God. God is all-knowing, and gracious.

4:13   Such are the bounds set by God. He that obeys God and His apostle shall dwell for ever in gardens watered by running streams. That is the supreme triumph. But he that defies God and His apostle and transgresses His bounds, shall be cast into a Fire wherein he will abide for ever. Shameful punishment awaits him.

If any of your women commit a lewd act, call in four witnesses from among yourselves against them; if they testify to their guilt confine them to their houses till death overtakes them or till God finds another way for them.

4:16   If two men among you commit a lewd act, punish them both. If they repent and mend their ways, let them be. God is forgiving and merciful.

God forgives those who commit evil in ignorance and then quickly turn to Him in penitence. God will pardon them. God is all-knowing and wise. But He will not forgive those who do evil and, when death comes to them, say: 'Now we repent!' Nor those who die unbelievers: for them We have prepared a woeful scourge.

4:19   Believers, it is unlawful for you to inherit the women of your deceased kinsmen against their will, or to bar them from re-marrying, in order that you may force them to give up a part of what you have given them, unless they be guilty of a proven lewd act. Treat them with kindness; for even if you dislike them, it may well be that you dislike a thing which God has meant for your own abundant good.

4:20   If you wish to replace one wife with another, do not take from her the dowry you have given her even if it be a talent of gold. That would be improper and grossly unjust; for how can you take it back when you have lain with each other and entered into a firm contract?

You shall not marry the women whom your fathers married: all previous such marriages excepted. That was an evil practice, indecent and abominable.

Forbidden to you are your mothers, your daughters, your sisters, your paternal and maternal aunts, the daughters of your brothers and sisters, your foster-mothers, your foster-sisters, the mothers of your wives, your step-daughters who are in your charge, born of the wives with whom you have lain (it is no offence for you to marry your step-daughters if you have not consummated your marriage with their mothers), and the wives of your own begotten sons. You are also forbidden to take in marriage two sisters at one and the same time: all previous such marriages excepted.

4:24 Surely God is forgiving and merciful. Also married women, except those whom you own as slaves. Such is the decree of God. All women other than these are lawful for you, provided you court them with your wealth in modest conduct, not in fornication. Give them their dowry for the enjoyment you have had of them as a duty; but it shall be no offence for you to make any other agreement among yourselves after you have fulfilled your duty. Surely God is all-knowing and wise.

4:25   If any one of you cannot afford to marry a free believing woman, let him marry a slave-girl who is a believer (God best knows your faith: you are born one of another). Marry them with the permission of their masters and give them their dowry in all justice, provided they are honourable and chaste and have not entertained other men. If after marriage they commit adultery, they shall suffer half the penalty inflicted upon free adulteresses. Such is the law for those of you who fear to commit sin: but if you abstain, it will be better for you. God is forgiving and merciful.

4:26   God desires to make this known to you and to guide you along the paths of those who have gone before you, and to turn to you with mercy. God is all-knowing and wise.

God wishes to forgive you, but those who follow their own appetites wish to see you stray grievously into error. God wishes to lighten your burdens, for man was created weak.

Believers, do not consume your wealth among yourselves in vanity, but rather trade with it by mutual consent.

Do not kill yourselves. God is merciful to you, but he that does that through wickedness and injustice shall be burned in fire. That is easy enough for God.

If you avoid the enormities you are forbidden, We shall pardon your misdeeds and usher you in with all honour. Do not covet the favours by which God has exalted some among you above others. Men shall be rewarded according to their deeds, and women shall be rewarded according to their deeds. Rather implore God to bestow on you His gifts. Surely God has knowledge of all things.

To every parent and kinsman We have appointed heirs who will inherit from them. As for those with whom you have entered into agreements, let them, too, have their share. Surely God bears witness to all things.

4:34   Men have authority over women because God has made the one superior to the other, and because they spend their wealth to maintain them. Good women are obedient. They guard their unseen parts because God has guarded them. As for those from whom you fear disobedience, admonish them, forsake them in beds apart, and beat them. Then if they obey you, take no further action against them. Surely God is high, supreme.

If you fear a breach between a man and his wife, appoint an arbiter from his people and another from hers. If they wish to be reconciled, God will bring them together again. Surely God is all-knowing and wise. [. . .]

FROM

Sura 5: The Table

In the Name of God, the Compassionate, the Merciful

5:15   [. . .] People of the Book! Our apostle has come to reveal to you much of what you have hidden of the Scriptures, and to forgive you much. A light has come to you from God and a glorious Book, with which God will guide to the paths of peace those that seek to please Him; He will lead them by His will from darkness to the light; He will guide them to a straight path.

Unbelievers are those who declare: 'God is the Messiah, the son of Mary.' Say: 'Who could prevent God, if He so willed, from destroying the Messiah, the son of Mary, his mother, and all the people of the earth? God has sovereignty over the heavens and the earth and all that lies between them. He creates what He will; and God has power over all things.'

5:18   The Jews and the Christians say: 'We are the children of God and His loved ones.' Say: 'Why then does He punish you for your sins? Surely you are mortals of His own creation. He forgives whom He will and punishes whom He pleases. God has sovereignty over the heavens and the earth and all that lies between them. All shall return to Him.'

5:19   People of the Book! Our apostle has come to you with revelations after an interval which saw no apostles, lest you say: 'No one has come to give us good news or to warn us.' Now someone has come to give you good news and to warn you. God has power over all things. [. . .]

5:35   Believers, have fear of God and seek the right path to Him. Fight valiantly for His cause, so that you may triumph.

As for the unbelievers, if they offered all that the earth contains and as much besides to redeem themselves from the torment of the Day of Resurrection, it shall not be accepted from them. Woeful punishment awaits them.

They will strive to get out of the Fire, but get out of it they shall not. Lasting punishment awaits them. [. . .]

5:40   Did you not know that God has sovereignty over the heavens and the earth? He punishes whom He will and forgives whom He pleases. God has power over all things.

5:41   Apostle, do not grieve for those who plunge headlong into unbelief; those who say with their tongues: 'We believe,' but have no faith in their hearts, and those Jews who listen to lies and listen to others who have not come to you. They tamper with words out of their context and say: 'If this be given you, accept it; if not, then beware!'

You cannot help a man if God intends to try him. Those whose hearts God does not intend to purify shall be held up to shame in this world, and in the world to come grievous punishment awaits them.

They listen to falsehoods and practise what is unlawful. If they come to you, give them your judgement or avoid them. If you avoid them, they can in no way harm you; but if you do act as their judge, judge them with fairness. God loves those that deal justly.

But how will they come to you for judgement when they already have the Torah which enshrines God's own judgement? Soon after, they will turn their backs: they are no true believers.

5:44   We have revealed the Torah, in which there is guidance and light. By it the prophets who submitted to God judged the Jews, and so did the rabbis and the divines, according to God's Book which had been committed to their keeping and to which they themselves were witnesses.

Have no fear of man; fear Me, and do not sell My revelations for a paltry sum. Unbelievers are those who do not judge according to God's revelations.

We decreed for them a life for a life, an eye for an eye, a nose for a nose, an ear for an ear, a tooth for a tooth, and a wound for a wound. But if a man charitably forbears from retaliation, his remission shall atone for him. Transgressors are those that do not judge according to God's revelations.

After them We sent forth Jesus son of Mary, confirming the Torah already revealed, and gave him the Gospel, in which there is guidance and light, corroborating what was revealed before it in the Torah: a guide and an admonition to the

5:47   righteous. Therefore let those who follow the Gospel judge according to what God has revealed therein. Evil-doers are those that do not judge according to God's revelations.

5:48   And to you We have revealed the Book with the truth. It confirms the Scriptures which came before it and stands as a guardian over them. Therefore give judgement among men according to God's revelations, and do not yield to their whims or swerve from the truth made known to you.

We have ordained a law and assigned a path for each of you. Had God pleased, He could have made of you one community: but it is His wish to prove you by that which He has bestowed upon you. Vie with each other in good works, for to God shall you all return and He will resolve your differences for you. [...]

5:65   If the People of the Book accept the true faith and keep from evil, We will pardon them their sins and admit them to the gardens of delight. If they observe the Torah and the Gospel and what has been revealed to them from their Lord, they shall enjoy abundance from above and from beneath.

There are some among them who are righteous men; but there are many among them who do nothing but evil.

Apostle, proclaim what has been revealed to you from your Lord; if you do not, you will surely fail to convey His message. God will protect you from all men. God does not guide the unbelievers.

Say: 'People of the Book, you will attain nothing until you observe the Torah and the Gospel and that which has been revealed to you from your Lord.' [...]

5:75   The Messiah, the son of Mary, was no more than an apostle: other apostles passed away before him. His mother was a saintly woman. They both ate earthly food.

See how We make plain to them Our revelations. See how they ignore the truth.

Say: 'Will you serve instead of God that which can neither harm nor help you? God is He who hears all and knows all.'

Say: 'People of the Book! Do not transgress the bounds of truth in your religion. Do not yield to the desires of those who have erred before; who have led many astray and have themselves strayed from the even path.' [...]

One day God will gather all the apostles and ask them: 'How were you received?' 5:110 They will reply: 'We have no knowledge. You alone know what is hidden.' God will say: 'Jesus son of Mary, remember the favour I bestowed on you and on your mother: how I strengthened you with the Holy Spirit, so that you preached to men in your cradle and in the prime of manhood; how I instructed you in the Book and in wisdom, in the Torah and in the Gospel; how by My leave you fashioned from clay the likeness of a bird and breathed into it so that, by My leave, it became a living bird; how, by My leave, you healed the blind man and the leper, and by My leave restored the dead to life; how I protected you from the Israelites when you had come to them with clear signs: when those of them who disbelieved declared: "This is but plain sorcery"; how, when I enjoined the disciples to believe in Me and in My apostle, they replied: "We believe; bear witness that we submit."'

'Jesus son of Mary,' said the disciples, 'can your Lord send down to us from heaven a table spread with food?'

He replied: 'Have fear of God, if you are true believers.'

5:113   'We wish to eat of it,' they said, 'so that we may reassure our hearts and know that what you said to us is true, and that we may be witnesses of it.'

5:114   'Lord,' said Jesus son of Mary, 'send down to us from heaven a table spread with food, that it may mark a feast for the first of us and the last of us: a sign from You. Give us our sustenance; You are the best provider.'

God replied: 'I am sending one to you. But whoever of you disbelieves hereafter shall be punished as no man will ever be punished.'

Then God will say: 'Jesus son of Mary, did you ever say to mankind: "Worship me and my mother as gods besides God?"'

'Glory be to You,' he will answer, 'I could never have claimed what I have no right to. If I had ever said so, You would have surely known it. You know what is in my mind, but I know not what is in Yours. You alone know what is hidden. I told them only what You bade me. I said: "Serve God, my Lord and your Lord." I 5:117 watched over them while living in their midst, and ever since You took me to Yourself, You have been watching them. You are the witness of all things. If You punish them, they surely are Your servants; and if You forgive them, surely You are mighty and wise.'

God will say: 'This is the day when their truthfulness will benefit the truthful. They shall for ever dwell in gardens watered by running streams. God is pleased with them, and they are pleased with Him. That is the supreme triumph.'

5:120   God has sovereignty over the heavens and the earth and all that they contain. He has power over all things.

Sura 12: Joseph

In the Name of God, the Compassionate, the Merciful

12:1 *Alif lām rā'*. These are the verses of the Glorious Book. We have revealed the Koran in the Arabic tongue so that you may grow in understanding.

12:3   In revealing this Koran We will recount to you the best of narratives, though before it you were heedless.

Joseph said to his father: 'Father, I dreamt of eleven stars and the sun and the moon; I saw them prostrate themselves before me.'

'My son,' he replied, 'say nothing of this dream to your brothers, lest they plot evil against you: Satan is the sworn enemy of man. Even thus shall you be chosen by your Lord. He will teach you to interpret visions, and will perfect His favour to you and to the house of Jacob, as He perfected it to your forefathers Abraham and Isaac before you. Your Lord is all-knowing and wise.'

Surely in Joseph and his brothers there are signs for doubting men.

They said to each other: 'Surely Joseph and his brother are dearer to our father than ourselves, though we are many. Truly, our father is much mistaken. Let us slay Joseph, or cast him away in some far-off land, so that we may have no rivals in our father's love, and after that be honourable men.'

12:10   One of the brothers said: 'Do not slay Joseph; but, if you must, rather cast him into a dark pit. Some caravan will take him up.'

They said to their father: 'Why do you not trust us with Joseph? Surely we wish him well. Send him with us tomorrow, that he may play and enjoy himself. We will take good care of him.'

He replied: 'It would much grieve me to let him go with you; for I fear lest the wolf should eat him when you are off your guard.'

They said: 'If the wolf could eat him despite our number, then we should surely be lost!'

And when they took him with them, they resolved to cast him into a dark pit.

We revealed to him Our will, saying: 'You shall tell them of all this when they will not know you.'

12:17   At nightfall they returned weeping to their father. They said: 'We went off to compete together, and left Joseph with our packs. The wolf devoured him. But you 12:18 will not believe us, though we speak the truth.' And they showed him their brother's shirt, stained with false blood.

'No!' he cried. 'Your souls have tempted you to evil. Sweet patience! God alone can help me bear the loss you speak of.'

And a caravan passed by, who sent their water-bearer to the pit. And when he had let down his pail, he cried: 'Rejoice! A boy!'

They concealed him as part of their merchandise. But God knew what they did. They sold him for a trifling price, for a few pieces of silver. They cared nothing for him.

The Egyptian who bought him said to his wife: 'Be kind to him. He may prove useful to us, or we may adopt him as our son.'

Thus We established Joseph in the land, and taught him to interpret dreams. God has power over all things, though most men may not know it. And when he reached maturity We bestowed on him wisdom and knowledge. Thus do We reward the righteous.

12:23   His master's wife attempted to seduce him. She bolted the doors and said: 'Come!'

'God forbid!' he replied. 'My lord has treated me with kindness. Wrongdoers shall never prosper.'

She made for him, and he himself would have succumbed to her had he not seen a sign from his Lord. Thus did We shield him from wantonness, for he was one of Our faithful servants.

They both rushed to the door. She tore his shirt from behind. And at the door they met her husband.

She cried: 'Shall not the man who wished to violate your wife be thrown into prison or sternly punished?'

Joseph said: 'It was she who attempted to seduce me.'

'If his shirt is torn from the front,' said one of her people, 'she is speaking the truth and he is lying. If it is torn from behind, then he is speaking the truth, and she is lying.'

12:28   And when her husband saw that Joseph's shirt was rent from behind, he said to 12:29 her: 'This is but one of your tricks. Your cunning is great indeed! Joseph, say no more about this. Woman, ask pardon for your sin. You have assuredly done wrong.'

In the city, women were saying: 'The Prince's wife has sought to seduce her servant. She has conceived a passion for him. We can see that she has clearly gone astray.'

When she heard of their intrigues, she invited them to a banquet prepared at her house. To each she gave a knife, and ordered Joseph to present himself before them. When they saw him, they were amazed at him and cut their hands, exclaiming: 'God preserve us! This is no mortal, but a gracious angel.'

'This is he,' she said, 'on whose account you blamed me. I attempted to seduce him, but he was unyielding. If he declines to do my bidding, he shall be thrown into prison and shall be held in scorn.'

'Lord,' said Joseph, 'sooner would I go to prison than give in to their advances. Shield me from their cunning, or I shall yield to them and lapse into folly.'

12:34   His Lord answered his prayer and warded off their wiles from him. He hears all and knows all.

Yet, for all the evidence they had seen, they thought it right to jail him for a time.

Two young men entered the prison with him. One said: 'I dreamt that I was pressing grapes.' And the other: 'I dreamt I was carrying a loaf upon my head, and the birds came and ate of it. Tell us the meaning of these dreams, for we can see you are a man of virtue.'

Joseph replied: 'Whatever food you are provided with, I can divine for you its meaning, even before it reaches you. This knowledge my Lord has given me, for I have left the faith of those that disbelieve in God and deny the life to come. I follow the faith of my forefathers, Abraham, Isaac and Jacob. We will serve no idols besides God. Such is the grace which God has bestowed on us and on all mankind. Yet most men do not give thanks.

'Fellow prisoners! Are sundry gods better than God, the One who conquers all? 12:40   Those you serve besides Him are nothing but names which you and your fathers have devised and for which God has revealed no sanction. Judgement rests only with God. He has commanded you to worship none but Him. That is the true faith: yet most men do not know it.

12:41   'Fellow prisoners, one of you will serve his lord with wine. The other will be crucified, and the birds will peck at his head. That is the answer to your question.'

And Joseph said to the prisoner who he knew would survive: 'Remember me in the presence of your lord.'

But Satan made him forget to mention Joseph to his lord, so that he stayed in prison for several years.

The king said: 'I saw seven fatted cows which seven lean ones devoured; also seven green ears of corn and seven others dry. Tell me the meaning of this vision, my nobles, if you can interpret visions.'

They replied: 'They are but a medley of dreams; nor are we skilled in the interpretation of dreams.'

Thereupon the man who had been freed remembered after all that time. He said: 'I shall tell you what it means. Give me leave to go.'

12:46   'Joseph,' he said, 'man of truth, tell us of the seven fatted cows which seven lean ones devoured; also of the seven green ears of corn and the other seven which were dry: so that I may go back to my masters and inform them.'

He replied: 'You shall sow for seven consecutive years. Leave in the ear the corn you reap, except a little which you may eat. There shall follow seven hungry years which will consume all but a little of what you stored. Then will come a year of abundant rain, in which the people will press the grape.'

The king said: 'Bring this man before me.'

But when the envoy came to him, Joseph said: 'Go back to your master and ask him about the women who cut their hands. My master knows their cunning.'

12:51   The king questioned the women, saying: 'What made you attempt to seduce Joseph?'

'God forbid!' they replied. 'We know no evil of him.'

'Now the truth must come to light,' said the Prince's wife. 'It was I who attempted to seduce him. He has told the truth.'

12:52 'From this,' said Joseph, 'my lord will know that I did not betray him in his absence, and that God does not guide the mischief of the treacherous. Not that I claim to be free from sin: man's soul is prone to evil, except his to whom my Lord has shown mercy. My Lord is forgiving and merciful.'

The king said: 'Bring him before me. I will choose him for my own.'

And when he had spoken with him, the king said: 'You shall henceforth dwell with us, honoured and trusted.'

Joseph said: 'Give me charge of the granaries of the land. I shall husband them wisely.'

Thus did We establish Joseph in the land, and he dwelt there as he pleased. We bestow Our mercy on whom We will, and shall never deny the righteous their reward. Surely better is the recompense of the life to come for those who believe in God and keep from evil.

12:58 Joseph's brothers arrived and presented themselves before him. He recognized them, but they knew him not. And when he had given them their provisions, he said: 'Bring me your other brother from your father. Do you not see that I give just measure and am the best of hosts? If you refuse to bring him, you shall have no measure, nor shall you come near me again.'

They replied: 'We will endeavour to fetch him from his father. This we will surely do.'

He said to his servants: 'Put their silver[8] into their packs, so that they may discover it when they return to their people. Perchance they will come back.'

When they returned to their father, they said: 'Father, corn is henceforth denied us. Send our brother with us and we shall have our measure. We will take good care of him.'

12:64 He replied: 'Am I to trust you with him as I once trusted you with his brother? But God is the best of guardians: and of all those that show mercy He is the most merciful.'

12:65 When they opened their packs, they discovered that their money had been returned to them. 'Father,' they said, 'what more can we desire? Here is our money paid back to us. We will buy provisions for our people, and take good care of our brother. We should receive an extra camel-load; a camel-load should be easy enough.'

He replied: 'I will not send him with you until you promise in God's name to bring him back to me, unless the worst befall you.'

And when they had given him their pledge, he said: 'God is the witness of what we say. My sons, do not enter from one gate; enter from different gates. In no way can I shield you from the might of God; judgement is His alone. In Him I have put my trust. In Him let the faithful put their trust.'

And when they entered as their father bade them, he could in no way shield them from the might of God. It was but a wish in Jacob's soul which he had thus

---

[8] **silver:** Literally, merchandise.

fulfilled. He was possessed of knowledge which We had given him. But most men have no knowledge.

12:69   When they went in to Joseph, he embraced his brother, and said: 'I am your brother. Do not grieve at what they did.'

And when he had given them their provisions, he hid a drinking-cup in his brother's pack.

Then a crier called out after them: 'Travellers, you are surely thieves!'

They turned back, and asked: 'What have you lost?'

'We miss the king's drinking-cup,' they replied. 'He that brings it shall have a camel-load of corn. I pledge my word for it.'

'In God's name,' they cried, 'you know we did not come to do evil in the land. We are no thieves.'

The Egyptians said: 'What punishment shall be his who stole it, if you prove to be lying?'

They replied: 'He in whose pack the cup is found shall render himself your bondsman. Thus do we punish the wrongdoers.'

12:76   Joseph searched their bags before his brother's, and then took out the cup from his brother's bag.

Thus We directed Joseph. By the king's law he had no right to seize his brother: but God willed otherwise. We exalt whom We will to a lofty station: and above those that have knowledge there is One who is all-knowing.

12:77   They said: 'If he has stolen — know then that a brother of his stole before him.'

But Joseph kept his secret and revealed nothing to them. He said: 'Your deed was worse. God best knows the things you speak of.'

They said: 'Noble prince, this boy has an aged father. Take one of us, instead of him. We can see you are a generous man.'

He replied: 'God forbid that we should take any but the man with whom our property was found: for then we should surely be unjust.'

When they despaired of him, they went aside to confer in private. The eldest said: 'Do you not know that your father took from you a pledge in God's name, and that long ago you did your worst with Joseph? I will not stir from the land until my

12:81   father gives me leave or God makes known to me His judgement: He is the best of judges. Return to your father and say to him: "Father, your son has stolen. We testify only to what we know. How could we guard against the unforeseen? Inquire at the city where we lodged, and from the caravan with which we travelled. We surely speak the truth."'

'No!' cried their father. 'Your souls have tempted you to evil. But I will have sweet patience. God may bring them all to me. He alone is all-knowing and wise.' And he turned away from them, crying: 'Alas for Joseph!' His eyes went white with grief, and he was oppressed with silent sorrow.

His sons exclaimed: 'In God's name, will you not cease to think of Joseph until you ruin your health and die?'

He replied: 'I complain to God of my sorrow and sadness. God has made known

12:87   to me things that you know not. Go, my sons, and seek news of Joseph and his brother. Do not despair of God's spirit; none but unbelievers despair of God's spirit.'

12:88   And when they went in to him, they said: 'Noble prince, we and our people are scourged with famine. We have brought but little money. Give us our full measure, and be charitable to us: God rewards the charitable.'

'Do you know,' he replied, 'what you did to Joseph and his brother? You are surely unaware.'

They cried: 'Can you indeed be Joseph?'

'I am Joseph,' he answered, 'and this is my brother. God has been gracious to us. Those that keep from evil and endure with fortitude, God will not deny them their reward.'

'By the Lord,' they said, 'God has exalted you above us all. We have indeed done wrong.'

He replied: 'None shall reproach you this day. May God forgive you: of all those that show mercy He is the most merciful. Take this shirt of mine and throw it over my father's face: he will recover his sight. Then return to me with all your people.'

12:94   When the caravan departed their father said: 'I feel the breath of Joseph, though you will not believe me.'

'In God's name,' said those who heard him, 'it is but your old illusion.'

And when the bearer of good news arrived, he threw Joseph's shirt over the old man's face, and he regained his sight. He said: 'Did I not tell you, God has made known to me what you know not?'

His sons said: 'Father, implore forgiveness for our sins. We have indeed done wrong.'

He replied: I shall implore my Lord to forgive you. He is forgiving and merciful.'

And when they went in to Joseph, he embraced his parents and said: 'Welcome to Egypt, safe, if God wills!'

12:100   He helped his parents to a couch, and they all fell on their knees and prostrated themselves before him.

'This,' said Joseph to his father, 'is the meaning of my old vision: my Lord has fulfilled it. He has been gracious to me. He has released me from prison, and brought you out of the desert after Satan had stirred up strife between me and my brothers. My Lord is gracious to whom He will. He alone is all-knowing and wise.

12:101   'Lord, You have given me authority and taught me to interpret dreams. Creator of the heavens and the earth, my Guardian in this world and in the world to come! Allow me to die in submission, and admit me among the righteous.'

That which We have now revealed to you[9] is a tale of the unknown. You were not present when Joseph's brothers conceived their plans and schemed against him. Yet strive as you may, most men will not believe.

You shall demand of them no recompense for this. It is but an admonition to all mankind.

Many are the marvels of the heavens and the earth; yet they pass them by and pay no heed to them. The greater part of them believe in God only if they can worship other gods besides Him.

---

[9] **you:** Muhammad.

Are they confident that God's scourge will not fall upon them, or that the Hour of Doom will not overtake them unawares, without warning?

12:108   Say: 'This is my path. With sure knowledge I call on you to have faith in God, I and all my followers. Glory be to God! I am no idolater.'

Nor were the apostles whom We sent before you other than mortals inspired by Our will and chosen from among their people.

Have they not travelled the land and seen what was the end of those who disbelieved before them? Surely better is the life to come for those that keep from evil. Can you not understand?

And when at length Our apostles despaired and thought they were denied, Our help came down to them, delivering whom We pleased. The evil-doers could not be

12:111   saved from Our scourge. Their annals point a moral to men of understanding.

This[10] is no invented tale, but a confirmation of previous scriptures, an explanation of all things, a guide and a blessing to true believers.

SURA 55: THE MERCIFUL[11]

In the Name of God, the Compassionate, the Merciful

IT IS the Merciful who has taught the Koran.

55:1   He created man and taught him articulate speech. The sun and the moon pursue their ordered course. The plants and the trees bow down in adoration.

He raised the heaven on high and set the balance of all things, that you might not transgress that balance. Give just weight and full measure.

He laid the earth for His creatures, with all its fruits and blossom-bearing palm, chaff-covered grain and scented herbs. Which of your Lord's blessings would you[12] deny?

He created man from potter's clay, and the jinn from smokeless fire. Which of your Lord's blessings would you deny?

The Lord of the two easts[13] is He, and the Lord of the two wests. Which of your Lord's blessings would you deny?

55:19   He has let loose the two oceans:[14] they meet one another. Yet between them
55:20   stands a barrier which they cannot overrun. Which of your Lord's blessings would you deny?

Pearls and corals come from both. Which of your Lord's blessings would you deny?

His are the ships that sail like mountains upon the ocean. Which of your Lord's blessings would you deny?

---

[10] **This:** The Qur'an.

[11] **The Merciful:** Compare this chapter with *Psalms* 137.

[12] **you:** This is a plural form of *you*, addressed to humanity and the *jinn*, sometimes mischievous spirits who cohabit with man. See the next verse.

[13] **the two easts:** The points at which the sun rises in summer and in winter.

[14] **the two oceans:** Salt water and fresh water.

All that lives on earth is doomed to die. But the face of your Lord will abide for ever, in all its majesty and glory. Which of your Lord's blessings would you deny?

All who dwell in heaven and earth entreat Him. Each day some mighty task engages Him. Which of your Lord's blessings would you deny?

Mankind and jinn, We shall surely find the time to judge you! Which of your Lord's blessings would you deny?

Mankind and jinn, if you have power to penetrate the confines of heaven and earth, then penetrate them! But this you shall not do except with Our own authority. Which of your Lord's blessings would you deny?

55:35   Flames of fire shall be lashed at you, and molten brass. There shall be none to help you. Which of your Lord's blessings would you deny?

When the sky splits asunder, and reddens like a rose or stainèd leather (which of your Lord's blessings would you deny?), on that day neither man nor jinnee will be asked about his sins. Which of your Lord's blessings would you deny?

The wrongdoers will be known by their looks; they shall be seized by their forelocks and their feet. Which of your Lord's blessings would you deny?

That is the Hell which the sinners deny. They shall wander between fire and water fiercely seething. Which of your Lord's blessings would you deny?

But for those that fear the majesty of their Lord there are two gardens (which of your Lord's blessings would you deny?) planted with shady trees. Which of your Lord's blessings would you deny?

55:51   Each is watered by a flowing spring. Which of your Lord's blessings would you deny?

55:52   Each bears every kind of fruit in pairs. Which of your Lord's blessings would you deny?

They shall recline on couches lined with thick brocade, and within reach will hang the fruits of both gardens. Which of your Lord's blessings would you deny?

Therein are bashful virgins whom neither man nor jinnee will have touched before. Which of your Lord's blessings would you deny?

Virgins as fair as corals and rubies. Which of your Lord's blessings would you deny?

Shall the reward of goodness be anything but good? Which of your Lord's blessings would you deny?

And beside these there shall be two other gardens (which of your Lord's blessings would you deny?) of darkest green. Which of your Lord's blessings would you deny?

55:66   A gushing fountain shall flow in each. Which of your Lord's blessings would you deny?

Each planted with fruit-trees, the palm and the pomegranate. Which of your Lord's blessings would you deny?

In each there shall be virgins chaste and fair. Which of your Lord's blessings would you deny?

Dark-eyed virgins, sheltered in their tents (which of your Lord's blessings would you deny?), whom neither man nor jinnee will have touched before. Which of your Lord's blessings would you deny?

They shall recline on green cushions and fine carpets. Which of your Lord's blessings would you deny?

55:78   Blessed be the name of your Lord, the Lord of majesty and glory!

SURA 56: THAT WHICH IS COMING

In the Name of God, the Compassionate, the Merciful

WHEN THAT which is coming comes—and no soul shall then deny its coming—

56:1 some shall be abased and others exalted.

When the earth shakes and quivers, and the mountains crumble away and scat-

56:6 ter abroad into fine dust, you shall be divided into three multitudes: those on the right (blessed shall be those on the right); those on the left (damned shall be those on the left); and those to the fore (foremost shall be those). Such are they that shall be brought near to their Lord in the gardens of delight: a whole multitude from the men of old, but only a few from the latter generations.

They shall recline on jewelled couches face to face, and there shall wait on them immortal youths with bowls and ewers and a cup of purest wine (that will neither pain their heads nor take away their reason); with fruits of their own choice and flesh of fowls that they relish. And theirs shall be the dark-eyed houris, chaste as virgin pearls: a guerdon for their deeds.

There they shall hear no idle talk, no sinful speech, but only the greeting, 'Peace! Peace!'

56:27   Those on the right hand—happy shall be those on the right hand! They shall recline on couches raised on high in the shade of thornless sidrs and clusters of talh;[15] amidst gushing waters and abundant fruits, unforbidden, never-ending.

We created the houris and made them virgins, loving companions for those on the right hand: a multitude from the men of old, and a multitude from the latter generations.

As for those on the left hand (wretched shall be those on the left hand!) they shall dwell amidst scorching winds and seething water: in the shade of pitch-black smoke, neither cool nor refreshing. For they have lived in comfort and persisted in the heinous sin,[16] saying: 'When we are once dead and turned to dust and bones, shall we be raised to life? And our forefathers, too?'

Say: 'Those of old, and those of the present age, shall be brought together on an appointed day. As for you sinners who deny the truth, you shall eat the fruit of the Zaqqūm tree and fill your bellies with it. You shall drink scalding water: yet you shall

56:55 drink it as the thirsty camel drinks.'

56:56   Such shall be their fare on the Day of Reckoning.

---

[15] **talh:** Acacia trees.   [16] **the heinous sin:** Idolatry.

We created you: will you not believe then in Our power?

Behold the semen you discharge: did you create it, or We?

It was We that ordained death among you. Nothing can hinder Us from replacing you by others like yourselves or transforming you into beings you know nothing of.

You surely know of the First Creation. Why, then, do you not reflect? Consider the seeds you grow. Is it you that give them growth, or We? If We pleased, We could turn your harvest into chaff, so that, filled with wonder, you would exclaim: 'We are laden with debts! Surely we have been robbed!'

Consider the water which you drink. Was it you that poured it from the cloud, or We? If We pleased, We could turn it bitter. Why, then, do you not give thanks?

Observe the fire which you light. Is it you that create its wood, or We? A reminder for man We made it, and for the traveller a comfort.

56:74   Praise, then, the name of your Lord, the Supreme One.

I swear by the shelter of the stars (a mighty oath, if you but knew it) that this is a glorious Koran, safeguarded in a book which none may touch except the purified; a revelation from the Lord of the Universe.

Would you scorn a scripture such as this, and earn your daily bread denying it?

When under your very eyes a man's soul is about to leave him (We are nearer to him than you, although you cannot see Us), why do you not restore it, if you will not be judged hereafter? Answer this, if what you say be true!

Thus, if he is favoured, his lot will be repose and plenty, and a garden of delight. If he is one of those on the right hand, he will be greeted with, 'Peace be with you!' by those on the right hand.

But if he is an erring disbeliever, his welcome will be scalding water, and he will burn in Hell.

56:96   This is surely the indubitable truth. Praise, then, the name of your Lord, the Supreme One.

SURA 93: DAYLIGHT

In the Name of God, the Compassionate, the Merciful

93:1   BY THE light of day, and by the dark of night, your Lord has not forsaken you,[17] nor does He abhor you.

The life to come holds a richer prize for you than this present life. You shall be gratified with what your Lord will give you.

93:6   Did He not find you an orphan and give you shelter?

Did He not find you in error and guide you?

Did He not find you poor and enrich you?

93:11   Therefore do not wrong the orphan, nor chide away the beggar. But proclaim the goodness of your Lord.

---

[17]**you:** Muhammad.

SURA 96: CLOTS OF BLOOD

In the Name of God, the Compassionate, the Merciful

96:1 RECITE IN the name of your Lord who created—created man from clots of blood.

Recite! Your Lord is the Most Bountiful One, who by the pen taught man what he did not know.

Indeed, man transgresses in thinking himself his own master: for to your Lord all things return.

Observe the man who rebukes Our servant when he prays. Think: does he follow the right guidance or enjoin true piety?

96:13 Think: if he denies the Truth and pays no heed, does he not realize that God observes all?

No. Let him desist, or We will drag him by the forelock, his lying, sinful forelock. Then let him call his helpmates. We will call the guards of Hell.

96:19 No, never obey him! Prostrate yourself and come nearer.

SURA 109: THE UNBELIEVERS

In the Name of God, the Compassionate, the Merciful

109:1 SAY: 'UNBELIEVERS, I do not worship what you worship, nor do you worship what I worship. I shall never worship what you worship, nor will you ever worship what I
109:6 worship. You have your own religion, and I have mine.'

SURA 110: HELP

In the Name of God, the Compassionate, the Merciful

110:1 WHEN GOD's help and victory come, and you see men embrace God's faith in multi-
110:3 tudes, give glory to your Lord and seek His pardon. He is ever disposed to mercy.

SURA 112: ONENESS

In the Name of God, the Compassionate, the Merciful

112:1 SAY: 'GOD is One, the Eternal God. He begot none, nor was He begotten. None is
112:4 equal to Him.'

༂ MUHAMMAD IBN ISHAQ
704–767

see-RAHT
ahn-nah-BEE
IB-un is-HAHK

The Life of Muhammad (**Sirat an-Nabi**), the most complete biography of Muhammad, was compiled by **Muhammad Ibn Ishaq**, the grandson of a freed slave, in the eighth century, about one hundred years after the Prophet's death. This collection of stories and oral legends, poetry, and accounts of Muhammad's raids provides the life story of Muhammad only alluded to in the Qur'an (Koran), where he is the Messenger rather than the subject of the story. While *The Life of Muhammad* is comparable in some respects to the Gospels of the New Testament, it differs in that it is understood by Muslims to be a secular work, not to be equated with the Qur'an. Its importance, however, should not be underestimated. The life story of Muhammad — the supreme political leader and founder of the nation of Islam as well as its Messenger of God — demanded a unique kind of representation for the Muslims of the eighth century, intent as they were on continuing the Prophet's work by spreading their faith throughout the world.

Literary Form and Content.   To these Muslims the literary status of the biography of Muhammad was highly important. Although other first-hand accounts of the life of the Prophet had been assembled (**Wahb ibn Munabbih**, an ambitious historian, had collected stories of Muhammad before Ibn Ishaq began to write), *The Life* was viewed as *the* work of its kind, helping to establish an entire literary genre, the SIRA,[1] or exemplary life story. *The Life* consists of a number of literary forms, the most important of which is the *HADITH*, the report of a saying of Muhammad on a particular subject. Imbedded in the text are also examples of a form of poetry called *MARATHI* (originally meaning "dirge"), verse written on an important occasion. The text also contains a written legal agreement concerning the scope of Muhammad's authority over the people of Medina. Finally, in order to relate the events of Muhammad's embattled later life, *The Life* relies on *MAGHAZI*, legendary accounts of "the raids of the Prophet." A number of literary devices were brought together to tell Muhammad's story.[2]

WAH-hub IB-un
moo-NAH-bee

SEE-rah

hah-DEETH

muh-RAH-thee

muh-GAH-zee

The Life begins with the tale of Muhammad's miraculous birth, reminiscent of the story of the birth of Jesus in the Gospels. Accounts of the

---

[1] *sira:* This term, first applied to the biography of Muhammad, was later applied to other narratives of exemplary lives, such as Ibn Shaddad's biography of the great warrior Saladin (d. 1193). Later writers like al-Mu'ayyad al-Shirazi (d. 1077) wrote autobiographies that were also called *sira* as the meaning of the term expanded.

[2] **Muhammad's story:** Ibn Ishaq also relied on the rhetorical traditions of Hebrew Scriptures and the Greek New Testament. While the use of the edifying story, the celebratory ode, or the battle narrative does not begin with *The Life of Muhammad,* by bringing together such different forms in a single literary work Ibn Ishaq and his followers founded a brilliant Islamic method of writing.

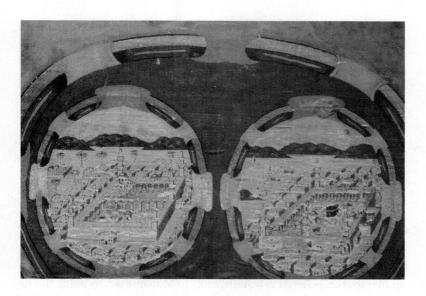

Mecca, ninth century

This detail from an illuminated Qur'an shows Mecca and the tomb of Muhammad. All Muslims are strongly encouraged to perform a hajj, *a pilgrimage to the holy site of Mecca, at least once in their life. (The Art Archive / Turkish and Islamic Art Museum, Istanbul / Dagli Orti)*

infancy of Muhammad were taken from legends, for the most part; only his status as a poor orphan is actually mentioned in the Qur'an. The stories of his later childhood and maturity, including his marriage to the wealthy merchant **Khadijah**, all suggest his future vocation as a prophet. Particularly noteworthy is the work's concentration on Muhammad's personal qualities, including his deep seriousness at all times and his forceful nature, as well as on his efforts to decide matters of great importance to his people. His traits would later be imitated by the faithful. The events of Muhammad's subsequent life, including the revelations of the angel Gabriel in the desert, Muhammad's vocation as a preacher in Mecca, his founding of a community of believers, their flight to Medina and eventual triumphant return to Mecca, and the wars against the polytheists and unbelievers throughout Arabia, are treated in the rest of the narrative. Many details of Muhammad's adult life, such as his struggles against the merchant lords of Mecca and his meetings with the citizens of Medina, were passed down orally through personal accounts and family histories. The battle stories, or *maghazi*, from his later years were already being collected by a new class of historians in his lifetime, creating a new genre.

This short outline only begins to suggest the drama of Muhammad's life, his inner turmoil before his resolution to become the Prophet of

kah-DEE-juh

www For links to more information about Ibn Ishaq and a quiz on *The Life of Muhammad,* see *World Literature Online* at bedfordstmartins .com/worldlit.

God, followed by the fulfillment of his promise in the destiny of Islam. In *The Life,* despite his fierce devotion to Islam, Muhammad never loses his humanity, experiencing doubt in the midst of revelation and exercising compassionate judgment in his victories over the chiefs of Mecca. Although his life is held by others to be exemplary, he often protests that he should not be the subject of religious veneration, for he is only human, a prophet chosen by God, while God is without bounds. As **Abu Bakr** says to the mourners after his death, "O men, if anyone worships Muhammad, Muhammad is dead; if anyone worships God, God is alive, immortal."

The Reading of the Text.   In *The Life of Muhammad,* Ibn Ishaq takes considerable care to indicate the source of each story about Muhammad. His frequent use of the *isnad,* or attribution, sometimes frustrates one's desire to "get on with the story." But historical necessities dictated this practice. The need to cite sources came from the presence of many false stories about Muhammad, circulated by friends and enemies alike. Often Ibn Ishaq includes more than one version of a story, and sometimes he quotes sources believed to be unfriendly to Muhammad; by doing this he wishes to provide his contemporaries with a narrative they can submit to common sense, judging it according to the credibility of the individuals who knew Muhammad and reported things about him.

While *The Life* deliberately leaves final judgment to the reader, its melange of forms creates a variety of effects: wonder, entertainment, instruction, and moral edification. Ibn Ishaq modestly directs the reader through the maze of detail. Hoary old legends are often prefaced with the cautionary "It is alleged," and some stories end with the intentionally equivocal "God knows best."

The Beginnings of Islamic Scholarship.   During and after the composition of *The Life of Muhammad,* many works were written to explain Islam and its traditions. These included commentaries on the Qur'an as well as scholarly treatments of history, jurisprudence, political philosophy, natural philosophy, and theology. Thus was laid the foundation for Islamic culture in the centuries to come. The decisive role of later Islamic translators in preserving the classics of Greek and Latin, especially the works of Plato and Aristotle, further illustrates a love of documentation suggested early on in Ibn Ishaq's treatment of the story of Muhammad.

■ **CONNECTIONS**

The New Testament, p. 23. The Gospels of Matthew, Luke, Mark, and John are counted as Holy Scripture, while Ibn Ishaq's *The Life of Muhammad* is viewed as a secular work. Differences and similarities of treatment are key to an understanding of the two religions of Christianity and Islam. What might the historical reasons have been for revealing the words of Jesus through his disciples? Why might Muhammad's life story have been separated for the most part from the Qur'an (Koran)?

St. Augustine, *The Confessions,* p. 70. *The Confessions* is the autobiography of a man of God, while *The Life of Muhammad* is a collection of stories about the Prophet of

ah-BOO BAH-kur

is-NAHD

God who has brought God's Word to fulfillment. Augustine and Muhammad, who lived in a similar time and place, both struggled to embrace a belief in God. How would you compare the two individuals and the stories of their lives?

The Koran, p. 106. *The Life of Muhammad* is closely related to the text of the Qur'an, sometimes even furnishing a background for passages written there. *The Life* may help to put certain suras or chapters of the relatively unstructured Qur'an into better perspective. Find examples and try to allow your reading of *The Life* to support your reading of the Qur'an. What passages in particular does it help you to understand more clearly?

■ **FURTHER RESEARCH**

Text
Ibn Ishaq, Muhammad. *The Life of Muhammad.* Trans. A. Guillaume. 1955.

Discussion and Commentary
Allen, Roger. *An Introduction to Arabic Literature.* 2000.
Lichtenstadter, Ilse. *Introduction to Classical Arabic Literature.* 1974.
Reynolds, Dwight F. *Interpreting the Self: Autobiography in the Arabic Literary Tradition.* 2001.
Watt, W. Montgomery. *Muhammad: Prophet and Statesman.* 1961.

■ **PRONUNCIATION**

Abu Bakr (Abū Bakr): ah-BOO BAH-kur
Abu Talib (Abū Ṭālib): ah-BOO TAH-lib
al-Mab'ath: ahl-mah-BAHTH
Hadith: hah-DEETH
Ibn Hisham: IB-un hih-SHAHM
Ibn Ishaq: IB-un is-HAHK
isnad: is-NAHD
Khadija (Khadīja): kah-DEE-juh
maghazi: muh-GAH-zee
marathi: muh-RAH-thee
Mubtada: moob-TAH-dah
Ramadan (Ramaḍān): RAH-muh-dahn
sira: SEE-rah
Sirat-an-Nabi: see-RAHT ahn-nah-BEE
Wahb ibn Munabbih: WAH-hub IB-un moo-NAH-bee

FROM

∾ The Life of Muhammad

Translated by Alfred Guillaume

[MUHAMMAD'S CHILDHOOD AND EARLY MANHOOD]

What Was Said to Āmina When She Had Conceived the Apostle

It is alleged in popular stories (and only God knows the truth) that Āmina d. Wahb, the mother of God's apostle, used to say when she was pregnant with God's apostle that a voice said to her, 'You are pregnant with the lord of this people and when he is born say, "I put him in the care of the One from the evil of every envier; then call him Muhammad."' As she was pregnant with him she saw a light come forth from her by which she could see the castles of Buṣrā in Syria. Shortly afterwards 'Abdullah the apostle's father died while his mother was still pregnant.

The Birth of the Apostle and His Suckling

The apostle was born on Monday, 12th Rabī'u'l-awwal, in the year of the elephant. [. . .]

Ḥalīma the apostle's foster-mother used to say that she went forth from her country with her husband and little son whom she was nursing, among the women of her tribe, in search of other babies to nurse. This was a year of famine when they were destitute. She was riding a dusky she-donkey of hers and an old she-camel which did not yield a drop of milk. They could not sleep the whole night because of

---

The Life of Muhammad.   By the time Muhammad Ibn Ishaq compiled this biography, three generations after the death of the Prophet, others already had begun to undertake the same effort. But Ibn Ishaq's thoroughness in tracking down stories and his combination of different literary genres helped to make his work superior to that of the other biographers. According to the English translator Alfred Guillaume, "No book known to the Arabs or to us can compare in comprehensiveness, arrangement, or systematic treatment." Even so, this version of *The Life of Muhammad* was further edited by Ibn Hisham (d. c. 835–840). Scholars believe it contains most of Ibn Ishaq's original text, however, in part because stories unfavorable to Muhammad survived the editing process.

Ibn Hisham's edition of *The Life* is divided into three sections: the first consisting mostly of ancient legends, the second concerning Muhammad's life and mission, and the third his migration to Medina, his raids, and his death. The first section, the *Mubtada,* is initially a retelling of Hebrew Scriptures, beginning with creation and continuing through the descent of man, from Adam to the time before the birth of Jesus. Stories of South Arabian kings that Ibn Ishaq culled from other legends as well as the birth and early life of Muhammad follow. The second part, called *al-Mab'ath,* begins with Muhammad's calling while at Mecca to become a prophet and ends with his flight to Medina. The stories from Mecca are somewhat imprecise, while those from Medina are better documented. The third section, more than two-thirds of the length of the book, consists of *maghazi,*

the weeping of her hungry child. She had no milk to give him, nor could their she-camel provide a morning draught, but we were hoping for rain and relief. 'I rode upon my donkey which had kept back the other riders through its weakness and emaciation so that it was a nuisance to them. When we reached Mecca, we looked out for foster children, and the apostle of God was offered to every one of us, and each woman refused him when she was told he was an orphan, because we hoped to get payment from the child's father. We said, "An orphan! and what will his mother and grandfather do?" and so we spurned him because of that. Every woman who came with me got a suckling except me, and when we decided to depart I said to my husband: "By God, I do not like the idea of returning with my friends without a suckling; I will go and take that orphan." He replied, "Do as you please; perhaps God will bless us on his account." So I went and took him for the sole reason that I could not find anyone else. I took him back to my baggage, and as soon as I put him in my bosom, my breasts overflowed with milk which he drank until he was satisfied, as also did his foster-brother. Then both of them slept, whereas before this we could not sleep with him. My husband got up and went to the old she-camel and lo, her udders were full; he milked it and he and I drank of her milk until we were completely satisfied, and we passed a happy night. In the morning my husband said: "Do you know, Ḥalīma, you have taken a blessed creature?" I said, "By God, I hope so." . . .

We ceased not to recognize this bounty as coming from God for a period of two years, when I weaned him. He was growing up as none of the other children grew and by the time he was two he was a well-made child. We brought him to his mother, though we were most anxious to keep him with us because of the blessing which he brought us. I said to her: "I should like you to leave my little boy with me until he

---

or battle stories, and ends with the death of Muhammad. The *maghazi,* often a retelling of previously existing accounts, are quite specific.

The stories of these selections from Ibn Ishaq's narrative touch on the most important times in Muhammad's life. They include his birth; his adoption; his miraculous "cleansing" by two strangers dressed in white; the care of the young Muhammad; his marriage to the wealthy merchant Khadija; his becoming an evangelist at forty; his first vision of Gabriel in the month of Ramadan; the call of God; Muhammad's reception of the Koran; Khadija's acceptance of Islam; Muhammad's learning of the correct method of prayer; his preaching in Mecca; his confrontation with the merchants over worshipping false idols; the first effort of the Quraysh tribe to expel Muhammad from Mecca, foiled by his uncle and protector, Abu Talib; the flight of Muhammad and his followers to Medina; his raids and battles to convert the "unbelievers"; the triumphant return to Mecca; Muhammad's request to die and join Paradise at once rather than conquer the world and live a long life; the death of Muhammad; and the dispute between 'Umar and Abu Bakr and its meaning for Islam's future.

A note on the translation. In this anthology's excerpts from the translation by Alfred Guillaume, the subtitles given to sections of the work have been retained, some of the attributions introducing the stories have been cut, and the stories have been edited for length. Most of the notes, including references to the Qur'an, are taken from the Guillaume edition; a few passages requiring further explanation have been footnoted by the editors. The diacritical marks were supplied by the translator.

becomes a big boy, for I am afraid on his account of the pest[1] in Mecca." We persisted until she sent him back with us.

Some months after our return he and his brother were with our lambs behind the tents when his brother came running and said to us, "Two men clothed in white have seized that Qurayshī brother of mine and thrown him down and opened up his belly, and are stirring it up." We ran towards him and found him standing up with a livid face. We took hold of him and asked him what was the matter. He said, "Two men in white raiment came and threw me down and opened up my belly and searched therein for I know not what." So we took him back to our tent. [. . .]

Thaur b. Yazīd [. . .] told me that some of the apostle's companions asked him to tell them about himself. He said: 'I am what Abraham my father prayed for and the good news of Jesus. When my mother was carrying me she saw a light proceeding from her which showed her the castles of Syria. I was suckled among the B. Sa'd b. Bakr, and while I was with a brother of mine behind our tents shepherding the lambs, two men in white raiment came to me with a gold basin full of snow. Then they seized me and opened up my belly, extracted my heart and split it; then they extracted a black drop from it and threw it away; then they washed my heart and my belly with that snow until they had thoroughly cleaned them. Then one said to the other, weigh him against ten of his people; they did so and I outweighed them. Then they weighed me against a hundred and then a thousand, and I outweighed them. He said, "Leave him alone, for by God, if you weighed him against all his people he would outweigh them."' [. . .]

Āmina Dies and the Apostle Lives
with His Grandfather

The apostle lived with his mother Āmina d. Wahb and his grandfather 'Abdu'l-Muttalib in God's care and keeping like a fine plant, God wishing to honour him. When he was six years old his mother Āmina died. [. . .] Thus the apostle was left to his grandfather for whom they made a bed in the shade of the Ka'ba. His sons used to sit round the bed until he came out to it, but none of them sat upon it out of respect for him. The apostle, still a little boy, used to come and sit on it and his uncles would drive him away. When 'Abdu'l-Muttalib saw this he said: 'Let my son alone, for by Allah he has a great future.' Then he would make him sit beside him on his bed and would stroke his back with his hand. It used to please him to see what he did.

Abū Ṭālib Becomes Guardian of the Apostle

After the death of 'Abdu'l-Muttalib the apostle lived with his uncle Abū Ṭālib, for (so they allege) the former had confided him to his care because he and 'Abdullah, the apostle's father, were brothers by the same mother, Fāṭima d. 'Amr b. 'Ā'idh b. 'Abd b. 'Imrān b. Makhzūm. It was Abū Ṭālib who used to look after the apostle after the death of his grandfather and he became one of his family. . . .

---

[1] **pest:** Plague.

The Story of Bahira

[. . .] The apostle of God grew up, God protecting him and keeping him from the vileness of heathenism because he wished to honour him with apostleship, until he grew up to be the finest of his people in manliness, the best in character, most noble in lineage, the best neighbour, the most kind, truthful, reliable, the furthest removed from filthiness and corrupt morals, through loftiness and nobility, so that he was known among his people as 'The trustworthy' because of the good qualities which God had implanted in him. The apostle, so I was told, used to tell how God protected him in his childhood during the period of heathenism, saying, 'I found myself among the boys of Quraysh carrying stones such as boys play with; we had all uncovered ourselves, each taking his shirt and putting it round his neck as he carried the stones. I was going to and fro in the same way, when an unseen figure slapped me most painfully saying, "Put your shirt on"; so I took it and fastened it on me and then began to carry the stones upon my neck wearing my shirt alone among my fellows.'

The Apostle of God Marries Khadīja

Khadīja was a merchant woman of dignity and wealth. She used to hire men to carry merchandise outside the country on a profit-sharing basis, for Quraysh were a people given to commerce. Now when she heard about the prophet's truthfulness, trustworthiness, and honourable character, she sent for him and proposed that he should take her goods to Syria and trade with them, while she would pay him more than she paid others. He was to take a lad of hers called Maysara. The apostle of God accepted the proposal, and the two set forth until they came to Syria.

The apostle stopped in the shade of a tree near a monk's cell, when the monk came up to Maysara and asked who the man was who was resting beneath the tree. He told him that he was of Quraysh, the people who held the sanctuary; and the monk exclaimed: 'None but a prophet ever sat beneath this tree.'

Then the prophet sold the goods he had brought and bought what he wanted to buy and began the return journey to Mecca. The story goes that at the height of noon when the heat was intense as he rode his beast, Maysara saw two angels shading the apostle from the sun's rays. When he brought Khadīja her property she sold it and it amounted to double or thereabouts. Maysara for his part told her about the two angels who shaded him and of the monk's words. Now Khadīja was a determined, noble, and intelligent woman possessing the properties with which God willed to honour her. So when Maysara told her these things she sent to the apostle of God and—so the story goes—said: 'O son of my uncle I like you because of our relationship and your high reputation among your people, your trustworthiness and good character and truthfulness.' Then she proposed marriage. Now Khadīja at that time was the best born woman in Quraysh, of the greatest dignity and, too, the richest. All her people were eager to get possession of her wealth if it were possible. [. . .]

The apostle of God told his uncles of Khadīja's proposal, and his uncle Ḥamza b. 'Abdu'l-Muṭṭalib went with him to Khuwaylid b. Asad and asked for her hand and he married her.

She was the mother of all the apostle's children except Ibrāhīm, namely al-Qāsim (whereby he was known as Abu'l-Qāsim); al-Ṭahir, al-Ṭayyib,[2] Zaynab, Ruqayya, Umm Kulthūm, and Fāṭima.

Al-Qāsim, al-Ṭayyib, and al-Ṭahir died in paganism. All his daughters lived into Islam, embraced it, and migrated with him to Medina. [. . .]

The Prophet's Mission

When Muhammad the apostle of God reached the age of forty God sent him in compassion to mankind, 'as an evangelist to all men'.[3] . . .

Al-Zuhrī related [. . .] that when Allah desired to honour Muhammad and have mercy on His servants by means of him, the first sign of prophethood vouchsafed to the apostle was true visions, resembling the brightness of daybreak, which were shown to him in his sleep. And Allah, she said, made him love solitude so that he liked nothing better than to be alone.

'Abdu'l-Malik [. . .] the Thaqafite who had a retentive memory related to me from a certain scholar that the apostle at the time when Allah willed to bestow His grace upon him and endow him with prophethood would go forth for his affair and journey far afield until he reached the glens of Mecca and the beds of its valleys where no house was in sight; and not a stone or tree that he passed by but would say, 'Peace unto thee, O apostle of Allah.' And the apostle would turn to his right and left and look behind him and he would see naught but trees and stones. Thus he stayed seeing and hearing so long as it pleased Allah that he should stay. Then Gabriel came to him with the gift of God's grace whilst he was on Ḥirā' in the month of Ramaḍān. [. . .]

When it was the night on which God honoured him with his mission and showed mercy on His servants thereby, Gabriel brought him the command of God. 'He came to me,' said the apostle of God, 'while I was asleep, with a coverlet of brocade whereon was some writing, and said, "Read!" I said, "What shall I read?" He pressed me with it so tightly that I thought it was death; then he let me go and said, "Read!" I said, "What shall I read?" He pressed me with it again so that I thought it was death; then he let me go and said "Read!" I said, "What shall I read?" He pressed me with it the third time so that I thought it was death and said "Read!" I said, "What then shall I read?"—and this I said only to deliver myself from him, lest he should do the same to me again. He said:

"Read in the name of thy Lord who created,
Who created man of blood coagulated.
Read! Thy Lord is the most beneficent,
Who taught by the pen,
Taught that which they knew not unto men."[4]

---

[2] **al-Ṭahir, al-Ṭayyib:** Two epithets (The Pure, The Good) applied to one son, 'Abdullah. Of Khadija's six children by Muhammad, the two sons died and the four daughters lived.

[3] **'as an evangelist to all men':** Sura 34.27.

[4] **'Read in . . . not unto men':** Sura 96.1–5.

So I read it, and he departed from me. And I awoke from my sleep, and it was as though these words were written on my heart. Now none of God's creatures was more hateful to me than an (ecstatic) poet or a man possessed: I could not even look at them. I thought, Woe is me poet or possessed—Never shall Quraysh say this of me! I will go to the top of the mountain and throw myself down that I may kill myself and gain rest. So I went forth to do so and then when I was midway on the mountain, I heard a voice from heaven saying, "O Muhammad! thou art the apostle of God and I am Gabriel." I raised my head towards heaven to see who was speaking, and lo, Gabriel in the form of a man with feet astride the horizon, saying, "O Muhammad! thou art the apostle of God and I am Gabriel." I stood gazing at him, moving neither forward nor backward; then I began to turn my face away from him, but towards whatever region of the sky I looked, I saw him as before. And I continued standing there, neither advancing nor turning back, until Khadīja sent her messengers in search of me and they gained the high ground above Mecca and returned to her while I was standing in the same place; then he parted from me and I from him, returning to my family. And I came to Khadīja and sat by her thigh and drew close to her. She said, "O Abū'l-Qāsim,[5] where hast thou been? By God, I sent my messengers in search of thee, and they reached the high ground above Mecca and returned to me." I said to her, "Woe is me poet or possessed." She said, "I take refuge in God from that O Abū'l-Qāsim. God would not treat you thus since he knows your truthfulness, your great trustworthiness, your fine character, and your kindness. This cannot be, my dear. Perhaps you did see something." "Yes, I did," I said. Then I told her of what I had seen; and she said, "Rejoice, O son of my uncle, and be of good heart. Verily, by Him in whose hand is Khadīja's soul, I have hope that thou wilt be the prophet of this people."' [. . .]

[Muhammad's Call and Preaching in Mecca]

The Beginning of the Sending Down of the Qurān

The apostle began to receive revelations in the month of Ramaḍān. In the words of God, 'The month of Ramaḍān in which the Qurān was brought down as a guidance to men, and proofs of guidance and a decisive criterion.'[6] [. . .]

Then revelation came fully to the apostle while he was believing in Him and in the truth of His message. He received it willingly, and took upon himself what it entailed whether of man's goodwill or anger. Prophecy is a troublesome burden— only strong, resolute messengers can bear it by God's help and grace, because of the opposition which they meet from men in conveying God's message. The apostle carried out God's orders in spite of the opposition and ill treatment which he met with.

Khadīja, Daughter of Khuwaylid, Accepts Islam

Khadīja believed in him and accepted as true what he brought from God, and helped him in his work. She was the first to believe in God and His apostle, and in the truth

---

[5] **Abū'l-Qāsim**: Muhammad's name of honor.

[6] **'The month . . . criterion'**: Sura 2.18.

of his message. By her God lightened the burden of His prophet. He never met with contradiction and charges of falsehood, which saddened him, but God comforted him by her when he went home. She strengthened him, lightened his burden, proclaimed his truth, and belittled men's opposition. May God Almighty have mercy upon her! [. . .]

Then revelations stopped for a time so that the apostle of God was distressed and grieved. Then Gabriel brought him the Sūra of the Morning, in which his Lord, who had so honoured him, swore that He had not forsaken him, and did not hate him. God said, 'By the morning and the night when it is still, thy Lord hath not forsaken nor hated thee,'[7] meaning that He has not left you and forsaken you, nor hated you after having loved you. 'And verily, the latter end is better for you than the beginning,' i.e. What I have for you when you return to Me is better than the honour which I have given you in the world. 'And your Lord will give you and will satisfy you,' i.e. of victory in this world and reward in the next. 'Did he not find you an orphan and give you refuge, going astray and guided you, found you poor and made you rich?' God thus told him of how He had begun to honour him in his earthly life, and of His kindness to him as an orphan poor and wandering astray, and of His delivering him from all that by His compassion.

'Do not oppress the orphan and do not repel the beggar.' That is, do not be a tyrant or proud or harsh or mean towards the weakest of God's creatures.

'Speak of the kindness of thy Lord,' i.e. tell about the kindness of God in giving you prophecy, mention it and call men to it.

So the apostle began to mention secretly God's kindness to him and to his servants in the matter of prophecy to everyone among his people whom he could trust.

The Prescription of Prayer

The apostle was ordered to pray and so he prayed. Ṣāliḥ b. Kaisān from 'Urwa b. al-Zubayr from 'Ā'isha told me that she said, 'When prayer was first laid on the apostle it was with two prostrations for every prayer: then God raised it to four prostrations at home while on a journey the former ordinance of two prostrations held.'

A learned person told me that when prayer was laid on the apostle Gabriel came to him while he was on the heights of Mecca and dug a hole for him with his heel in the side of the valley from which a fountain gushed forth, and Gabriel performed the ritual ablution as the apostle watched him. This was in order to show him how to purify himself before prayer. Then the apostle performed the ritual ablution as he had seen Gabriel do it. Then Gabriel said a prayer with him while the apostle prayed with his prayer. Then Gabriel left him. The apostle came to Khadīja and performed the ritual for her as Gabriel had done for him, and she copied him. Then he prayed with her as Gabriel had prayed with him, and she prayed his prayer. [. . .]

---

[7] **'By the morning . . . hated thee':** Sura 93.

'Alī B. Abū Ṭālib the First Male to Accept Islam

'Alī was the first male to believe in the apostle of God, to pray with him and to believe in his divine message, when he was a boy of ten. God favoured him in that he was brought up in the care of the apostle before Islam began. [. . .]

The Apostle's Public Preaching and the Response

People began to accept Islam, both men and women, in large numbers until the fame of it was spread throughout Mecca, and it began to be talked about. Then God commanded His apostle to declare the truth of what he had received and to make known His commands to men and to call them to Him. Three years elapsed from the time that the apostle concealed his state until God commanded him to publish his religion, according to information which has reached me. Then God said, 'Proclaim what you have been ordered and turn aside from the polytheists.'[8] And again, 'Warn thy family, thy nearest relations, and lower thy wing[9] to the followers who follow thee.' And 'Say, I am the one who warns plainly'.[10] [. . .]

When the apostle's companions prayed they went to the glens so that their people could not see them praying, and while Sa'd b. Abū Waqqāṣ was with a number of the prophet's companions in one of the glens of Mecca, a band of polytheists came upon them while they were praying and rudely interrupted them. They blamed them for what they were doing until they came to blows, and it was on that occasion that Sa'd smote a polytheist with the jawbone of a camel and wounded him. This was the first blood to be shed in Islam.

When the apostle openly displayed Islam as God ordered him his people did not withdraw or turn against him, so far as I have heard, until he spoke disparagingly of their gods. When he did that they took great offence and resolved unanimously to treat him as an enemy, except those whom God had protected by Islam from such evil, but they were a despised minority. Abū Ṭālib his uncle treated the apostle kindly and protected him, the latter continuing to obey God's commands, nothing turning him back. When Quraysh saw that he would not yield to them and withdrew from them and insulted their gods and that his uncle treated him kindly and stood up in his defence and would not give him up to them, some of their leading men went to Abū Ṭālib. [. . .] They said, 'O Abū Ṭālib, your nephew has cursed our gods, insulted our religion, mocked our way of life[11] and accused our forefathers of error; either you must stop him or you must let us get at him, for you yourself are in the same position as we are in opposition to him and we will rid you of him.' He gave them a conciliatory reply and a soft answer and they went away.

The apostle continued on his way, publishing God's religion and calling men thereto. In consequence his relations with Quraysh deteriorated and men withdrew

---

[8] 'Proclaim . . . polytheists': Sura 15.94.   [9] **lower thy wing:** Deal gently with. Sura 26.214.   [10] **'Say, I am . . . plainly':** Sura 15.8, 9.   [11] **our way of life:** *Ahlam*, the civilization of the pre-Islamic Arabs.

from him in enmity. They were always talking about him and inciting one another against him. Then they went to Abū Ṭālib a second time and said, 'You have a high and lofty position among us, and we have asked you to put a stop to your nephew's activities but you have not done so. By God, we cannot endure that our fathers should be reviled, our customs mocked and our gods insulted. Until you rid us of him we will fight the pair of you until one side perishes,' or words to that effect. Thus saying, they went off. Abū Ṭālib was deeply distressed at the breach with his people and their enmity but he could not desert the apostle and give him up to them.

Ya'qūb [. . .] told me that he was told that after hearing these words from the Quraysh Abū Ṭālib sent for his nephew and told him what his people had said. 'Spare me and yourself,' he said. 'Do not put on me a burden greater than I can bear.' The apostle thought that his uncle had the idea of abandoning and betraying him, and that he was going to lose his help and support. He answered, 'O my uncle, by God, if they put the sun in my right hand and the moon in my left on condition that I abandoned this course, until God has made it victorious, or I perish therein, I would not abandon it.' Then the apostle broke into tears, and got up. As he turned away his uncle called him and said, 'Come back, my nephew,' and when he came back, he said, 'Go and say what you please, for by God I will never give you up on any account.'

When the Quraysh perceived that Abū Ṭālib had refused to give up the apostle, and that he was resolved to part company with them, they went to him with 'Umāra b. al-Walīd b. al-Mughīra and said, according to my information, 'O Abū Ṭālib, this is 'Umāra, the strongest and most handsome young man among Quraysh, so take him and you will have the benefit of his intelligence and support; adopt him as a son and give up to us this nephew of yours, who has opposed your religion and the religion of your fathers, severed the unity of your people, and mocked our way of life, so that we may kill him. This will be man for man.' He answered, 'By God, this is an evil thing that you would put upon me, would you give me your son that I should feed him for you, and should I give you my son that you should kill him? By God, this shall never be.' Al-Muṭ'im b. 'Adīy said, 'Your people have treated you fairly and have taken pains to avoid what you dislike. I do not think that you are willing to accept anything from them.' Abū Ṭālib replied, 'They have not treated me fairly, by God, but you have agreed to betray me and help the people against me, so do what you like,' or words to that effect. So the situation worsened, the quarrel became heated and people were sharply divided, and openly showed their animosity to their opponents. . . .

Then the Quraysh incited people against the companions of the apostle who had become Muslims. Every tribe fell upon the Muslims among them, beating them and seducing them from their religion. God protected His apostle from them through his uncle, who, when he saw what Quraysh were doing, called upon B. Hāshim and B. al-Muṭṭalib to stand with him in protecting the apostle. This they agreed to do, with the exception of Abū Lahab, the accursed enemy of God. [. . .]

How the Apostle Was Treated by His Own People

[. . .] Yaḥyā b. 'Urwa b. al-Zubayr on the authority of his father from 'Abdullah b. 'Amr b. al-'Āṣ told me that the latter was asked what was the worst way in which Quraysh showed their enmity to the apostle. He replied: 'I was with them one day when the notables had gathered in the Ḥijr and the apostle was mentioned. They said that they had never known anything like the trouble they had endured from this fellow; he had declared their mode of life foolish, insulted their forefathers, reviled their religion, divided the community, and cursed their gods. What they had borne was past all bearing, or words to that effect.'

While they were thus discussing him the apostle came towards them and kissed the black stone, then he passed them as he walked round the temple. As he passed they said some injurious things about him. This I could see from his expression. He went on and as he passed them the second time they attacked him similarly. This I could see from his expression. Then he passed the third time, and they did the same. He stopped and said, 'Will you listen to me O Quraysh? By him who holds my life in His hand I bring you slaughter.' This word so struck the people that not one of them but stood silent and still; even one who had hitherto been most violent spoke to him in the kindest way possible, saying, 'Depart, O Abū'l-Qāsim, for by God you are not violent.' So the apostle went away, and on the morrow they assembled in the Ḥijr, I being there too, and they asked one another if they remembered what had taken place between them and the apostle so that when he openly said something unpleasant they let him alone. While they were talking thus the apostle appeared, and they leaped upon him as one man and encircled him, saying, 'Are you the one who said so-and-so against our gods and our religion?' The apostle said, 'Yes, I am the one who said that.' And I saw one of them seize his robe. Then Abū Bakr interposed himself weeping and saying, 'Would you kill a man for saying Allah is my Lord?' Then they left him. That is the worst that I ever saw Quraysh do to him.

One of the family of Umm Kulthūm, Abū Bakr's daughter, told me that she said, 'Abū Bakr returned that day with the hair of his head torn. He was a very hairy man and they had dragged him along by his beard.'

The First Migration to Abyssinia

When the apostle saw the affliction of his companions and that though he escaped it because of his standing with Allah and his uncle Abū Ṭālib, he could not protect them, he said to them: 'If you were to go to Abyssinia it would be better for you, for the king will not tolerate injustice and it is a friendly country, until such time as Allah shall relieve you from your distress.' Thereupon his companions went to Abyssinia, being afraid of apostasy and fleeing to God with their religion. This was the first hijra in Islam. [. . .]

The Night Journey and the Ascent to Heaven

Ziyād b. 'Abdullah al-Bakkā'ī [. . .] told me the following: Then the apostle was carried by night from the mosque at Mecca to the Masjid al-Aqṣā, which is the temple of Aelia, when Islam had spread in Mecca among the Quraysh and all the tribes.

The following account reached me from 'Abdullah b. Mas'ūd and Abū Sa'īd al-Khudrī, and 'Ā'isha the prophet's wife, and Mu'āwiya b. Abū Sufyān, and al-Hasan b. Abū'l-Ḥasan al-Baṣrī, and Ibn Shihāb al-Zuhrī and Qatāda and other traditionists, and Umm Hāni' d. of Abū Ṭālib. It is pieced together in the story that follows, each one contributing something of what he was told about what happened when he was taken on the night journey. The matter of the place[12] of the journey and what is said about it is a searching test and a matter of God's power and authority wherein is a lesson for the intelligent; and guidance and mercy and strengthening to those who believe. It was certainly an act of God by which He took him by night in what way He pleased[13] to show him His signs which He willed him to see so that he witnessed His mighty sovereignty and power by which He does what He wills to do.

According to what I have heard 'Abdullah b. Mas'ūd used to say: Burāq, the animal whose every stride carried it as far as its eye could reach on which the prophets before him used to ride was brought to the apostle and he was mounted on it. His companion (Gabriel) went with him to see the wonders between heaven and earth, until he came to Jerusalem's temple. There he found Abraham the friend of God, Moses, and Jesus assembled with a company of the prophets, and he prayed with them. Then he was brought three vessels containing milk, wine, and water respectively. The apostle said: 'I heard a voice saying when these were offered to me: If he takes the water he will be drowned and his people also; if he takes the wine he will go astray and his people also; and if he takes the milk he will be rightly guided and his people also. So I took the vessel containing milk and drank it. Gabriel said to me, You have been rightly guided and so will your people be, Muhammad.'

I was told that al-Ḥasan said that the apostle said: 'While I was sleeping in the Ḥijr Gabriel came and stirred me with his foot. I sat up but saw nothing and lay down again. He came a second time and stirred me with his foot. I sat up but saw nothing and lay down again. He came to me the third time and stirred me with his foot. I sat up and he took hold of my arm and I stood beside him and he brought me out to the door of the mosque and there was a white animal, half mule, half donkey, with wings on its sides with which it propelled its feet, putting down each forefoot at the limit of its sight and he mounted me on it. Then he went out with me keeping close to me. [. . .]

In his story al-Ḥasan said: 'The apostle and Gabriel went their way until they arrived at the temple at Jerusalem. There he found Abraham, Moses, and Jesus among a company of the prophets. The apostle acted as their imam in prayer. Then he was brought two vessels, one containing wine and the other milk. The apostle took the milk and drank it, leaving the wine. Gabriel said: "You have been rightly guided to the way of nature[14] and so will your people be, Muhammad. Wine is forbidden you." Then the apostle returned to Mecca and in the morning he told Quraysh what had happened. Most of them said, "By God, this is a plain absurdity! A caravan takes a month to go to Syria and a month to return and can Muhammad do the return journey in one night?" Many Muslims gave up their faith; some went to Abū Bakr and said, "What do you think of your friend now, Abū Bakr? He alleges

---

[12] **the place:** or (masra) "time."

[13] **in what way He pleased:** This leaves open the question of whether it was an actual physical journey or a nocturnal vision.

[14] **the way of nature:** Or, "the true primeval religion."

that he went to Jerusalem last night and prayed there and came back to Mecca." He replied that they were lying about the apostle; but they said that he was in the mosque at that very moment telling the people about it. Abū Bakr said, "If he says so then it is true. And what is so surprising in that? He tells me that communications from God from heaven to earth come to him in an hour of a day or night and I believe him, and that is more extraordinary than that at which you boggle!" He then went to the apostle and asked him if these reports were true, and when he said they were, he asked him to describe Jerusalem to him.' [. . .]

One of Abū Bakr's family told me that 'Ā'isha the prophet's wife used to say: 'The apostle's body remained where it was but God removed his spirit by night.' [. . .]

I have heard that the apostle used to say, 'My eyes sleep while my heart is awake.' Only God knows how revelation came and he saw what he saw. But whether he was asleep or awake, it was all true and actually happened. [. . .]

The Ascent to Heaven

One whom I have no reason to doubt told me on the authority of Abū Sa'īd al-Khudrī: I heard the apostle say, 'After the completion of my business in Jerusalem a ladder was brought to me finer than any I have ever seen. It was that to which the dying man looks when death approaches. My companion mounted it with me until we came to one of the gates of heaven called the Gate of the Watchers. An angel called Ismā'īl was in charge of it, and under his command were twelve thousand angels each of them having twelve thousand angels under his command.' As he told this story the apostle used to say, 'and none knows the armies of God but He.'[15] When Gabriel brought me in, Ismā'īl asked who I was, and when he was told that I was Muhammad he asked if I had been given a mission,[16] and on being assured of this he wished me well.

A traditionist who had got it from one who had heard it from the apostle told me that the latter said: 'All the angels who met me when I entered the lowest heaven smiled in welcome and wished me well except one who said the same things but did not smile or show that joyful expression which the others had. And when I asked Gabriel the reason he told me that if he had ever smiled on anyone before or would smile on anyone hereafter he would have smiled on me; but he does not smile because he is Mālik, the Keeper of Hell. I said to Gabriel, he holding the position with regard to God which he has described to you "obeyed there, trustworthy,"[17] "Will you not order him to show me hell?" And he said, "Certainly! O Mālik, show Muhammad Hell." Thereupon he removed its covering and the flames blazed high into the air until I thought that they would consume everything. So I asked Gabriel

---

[15] 'and none knows . . . but He': Sura 74.34.

[16] given a mission: Or perhaps simply "sent for."

[17] 'obeyed there, trustworthy': Sura 81.21.

to order him to send them back to their place which he did. I can only compare the effect of their withdrawal to the falling of a shadow, until when the flames retreated whence they had come, Mālik placed their cover on them.'

In his tradition Abū Saʿīd al-Khudrī said that the apostle said: 'When I entered the lowest heaven I saw a man sitting there with the spirits of men passing before him. To one he would speak well and rejoice in him saying: "A good spirit from a good body" and of another he would say "Faugh!" and frown, saying: "An evil spirit from an evil body." In answer to my question Gabriel told me that this was our father Adam reviewing the spirits of his offspring; the spirit of a believer excited his pleasure, and the spirit of an infidel excited his disgust so that he said the words just quoted.

'Then I saw men with lips like camels; in their hands were pieces of fire like stones which they used to thrust into their mouths and they would come out of their posteriors. I was told that these were those who sinfully devoured the wealth of orphans.

'Then I saw men in the way of the family of Pharaoh,[18] with such bellies as I have never seen; there were passing over them as it were camels maddened by thirst when they were cast into hell, treading them down, they being unable to move out of the way. These were the usurers.

'Then I saw men with good fat meat before them side by side with lean stinking meat, eating of the latter and leaving the former. These are those who forsake the women which God has permitted and go after those he has forbidden.

'Then I saw women hanging by their breasts. These were those who had fathered bastards on their husbands.'

Jaʿfar b. ʿAmr told me from al-Qāsim b. Muhammad that the apostle said: 'Great is God's anger against a woman who brings a bastard into her family. He deprives the true sons of their portion and learns the secrets of the harim.'

To continue the tradition of Saʿīd al-Khudrī: 'Then I was taken up to the second heaven and there were the two maternal cousins Jesus, Son of Mary, and John, son of Zakariah. Then to the third heaven and there was a man whose face was as the moon at the full. This was my brother Joseph, son of Jacob. Then to the fourth heaven and there was a man called Idrīs. "And we have exalted him to a lofty place."[19] Then to the fifth heaven and there was a man with white hair and a long beard, never have I seen a more handsome man than he. This was the beloved among his people Aaron son of ʿImrān. Then to the sixth heaven, and there was a dark man with a hooked nose like the Shanūʾa. This was my brother Moses, son of ʿImrān. Then to the seventh heaven and there was a man sitting on a throne at the gate of the immortal mansion.[20] Every day seventy thousand angels went in not to come back until the resurrection day. Never have I seen a man more like myself. This was my father Abraham. Then he took me into Paradise and there I saw a damsel with dark red lips and I asked her to

---

[18] 'in the way of . . . Pharaoh': Cf. Sura 40.49, "Cast the family of Pharaoh into the worst of all punishments."

[19] 'And we have . . . place': Sura 19.58.

[20] the immortal mansion: In view of what follows this would seem to mean Paradise itself.

whom she belonged, for she pleased me much when I saw her, and she told me "Zayd b. Ḥāritha." The apostle gave Zayd the good news about her.'

From a tradition of 'Abdullah b. Mas'ūd from the prophet there has reached me the following: When Gabriel took him up to each of the heavens and asked permission to enter he had to say whom he had brought and whether he had received a mission and they would say 'God grant him life, brother and friend!' until they reached the seventh heaven and his Lord. There the duty of fifty prayers a day was laid upon him.

The apostle said: 'On my return I passed by Moses and what a fine friend of yours he was! He asked me how many prayers had been laid upon me and when I told him fifty he said, "Prayer is a weighty matter and your people are weak, so go back to your Lord and ask him to reduce the number for you and your community." I did so and He took off ten. Again I passed by Moses and he said the same again; and so it went on until only five prayers for the whole day and night were left. Moses again gave me the same advice. I replied that I had been back to my Lord and asked him to reduce the number until I was ashamed, and I would not do it again. He of you who performs them in faith and trust will have the reward of fifty prayers.' [. . .]

The Apostle Receives the Order to Fight

The apostle had not been given permission to fight or allowed to shed blood before the second 'Aqaba. He had simply been ordered to call men to God and to endure insult and forgive the ignorant. The Quraysh had persecuted his followers, seducing some from their religion, and exiling others from their country. They had to choose whether to give up their religion, be maltreated at home, or to flee the country, some to Abyssinia, others to Medina.

When Quraysh became insolent towards God and rejected His gracious purpose, accused His prophet of lying, and ill treated and exiled those who served Him and proclaimed His unity, believed in His prophet, and held fast to His religion, He gave permission to His apostle to fight and to protect himself against those who wronged them and treated them badly.

The first verse which was sent down on this subject from what I have heard from 'Urwa b. al-Zubayr and other learned persons was: 'Permission is given to those who fight because they have been wronged. God is well able to help them,—those who have been driven out of their houses without right only because they said God is our Lord. Had not God used some men to keep back others, cloisters and churches and oratories and mosques wherein the name of God is constantly mentioned would have been destroyed. Assuredly God will help those who help Him. God is Almighty. Those who if we make them strong in the land will establish prayer, pay the poor-tax, enjoin kindness, and forbid iniquity. To God belongs the end of matters.[21] The meaning is: 'I have allowed them to fight only because they have been unjustly treated while their sole offence against men has been that they worship God. When

---

[21] 'To God . . . matters': Sura 22.40–42.

they are in the ascendant they will establish prayer, pay the poor-tax, enjoin kind-ness, and forbid iniquity, i.e. the prophet and his companions all of them.' Then God sent down to him: 'Fight them so that there be no more seduction,'[22] i.e. until no believer is seduced from his religion. 'And the religion is God's,' i.e.[,] Until God alone is worshipped.

When God had given permission to fight and this clan of the Anṣār had pledged their support to him in Islam and to help him and his followers, and the Muslims who had taken refuge with them, the apostle commanded his companions, the emi-grants of his people and those Muslims who were with him in Mecca, to emigrate to Medina and to link up with their brethren the Anṣār. 'God will make for you brethren and houses in which you may be safe.' So they went out in companies, and the apostle stayed in Mecca waiting for his Lord's permission to leave Mecca and migrate to Medina. [. . .]

[CAMPAIGNS FROM MEDINA, OCCUPATION OF MECCA, CONQUEST OF ARABIA, DEATH OF THE PROPHET]

The Hijra of the Prophet

After his companions had left, the apostle stayed in Mecca waiting for permission to migrate. Except for Abū Bakr and 'Alī, none of his supporters were left but those under restraint and those who had been forced to apostatize. The former kept asking the apostle for permission to emigrate and he would answer, 'Don't be in a hurry; it may be that God will give you a companion.' Abū Bakr hoped that it would be Muhammad himself.

When the Quraysh saw that the apostle had a party and companions not of their tribe and outside their territory, and that his companions had migrated to join them, and knew that they had settled in a new home and had gained protectors, they feared that the apostle might join them, since they knew that he had decided to fight them. So they assembled in their council chamber, the house of Quṣayy b. Kilāb where all their important business was conducted, to take counsel what they should do in regard to the apostle, for they were now in fear of him. [. . .]

Thereupon Abū Jahl said that he had a plan which had not been suggested hith-erto, namely that each clan should provide a young, powerful, well-born, aristocratic warrior; that each of these should be provided with a sharp sword; then that each of them should strike a blow at him and kill him. Thus they would be relieved of him, and responsibility for his blood would lie upon all the clans. The B. 'Abdu Manāf could not fight them all and would have to accept the blood-money which they would all contribute to. The shaykh exclaimed: 'The man is right. In my opinion it is the only thing to do.' Having come to a decision the people dispersed.

Then Gabriel came to the apostle and said: 'Do not sleep tonight on the bed on which you usually sleep.' Before much of the night had passed they assembled at his

---

[22] 'Fight them . . . seduction': Sura 2.198.

door waiting for him to go to sleep so that they might fall upon him. When the apostle saw what they were doing he told 'Alī to lie on his bed and to wrap himself in his green Ḥaḍramī mantle; for no harm would befall him. He himself used to sleep in this mantle.

Yazīd b. Ziyād on the authority of Muhammad b. Ka'b. al-Quraẓī told me that when they were all outside his door Abū Jahl said to them: 'Muhammad alleges that if you follow him you will be kings of the Arabs and the Persians. Then after death you will be raised to gardens like those of the Jordan. But if you do not follow him you will be slaughtered, and when you are raised from the dead you will be burned in the fire of hell.' The apostle came out to them with a handful of dust saying: 'I do say that. You are one of them.' God took away their sight so that they could not see him and he began to sprinkle the dust on their heads as he recited these verses: 'Ya Sīn, by the wise Quran. Thou art of those that art sent on a straight path, a revelation of the Mighty the Merciful' as far as the words 'And we covered them and they could not see.'[23] When he had finished reciting not one of them but had dust upon his head. Then he went wherever he wanted to go and someone not of their company came up and asked them what they were waiting for there. When they said that they were waiting for Muhammad he said: 'But good heavens Muhammad came out to you and put dust on the head of every single man of you and then went off on his own affairs. Can't you see what has happened to you?' They put up their hands and felt the dust on their heads. Then they began to search and saw 'Alī on the bed wrapped in the apostle's mantle and said, 'By God it is Muhammad sleeping in his mantle.' Thus they remained until the morning when 'Alī rose from the bed and then they realized that the man had told them the truth. [. . .]

It was then that God gave permission to his prophet to migrate. Now Abū Bakr was a man of means, and at the time that he asked the apostle's permission to migrate and he replied 'Do not hurry; perhaps God will give you a companion,' hoping that the apostle meant himself he bought two camels and kept them tied up in his house supplying them with fodder in preparation for departure. [. . .]

When the apostle decided to go he came to Abū Bakr and the two of them left by a window in the back of the latter's house and made for a cave on Thaur, a mountain below Mecca. Having entered, Abū Bakr ordered his son 'Abdullah to listen to what people were saying and to come to them by night with the day's news. He also ordered 'Āmir b. Fuhayra, his freedman, to feed his flock by day and to bring them to them in the evening in the cave. Asmā' his daughter used to come at night with food to sustain them.

The two of them stayed in the cave for three days. When Quraysh missed the apostle they offered a hundred she-camels to anyone who would bring him back. During the day 'Abdullah was listening to their plans and conversation and would come at night with the news. 'Āmir used to pasture his flock with the shepherds of Mecca and when night fell would bring them to the cave where they milked them and slaughtered some. When 'Abdullah left them in the morning to go to Mecca,

[23] 'And we . . . see': Sura 36, 1–8.

'Āmir would take the sheep over the same route to cover his tracks. When the three days had passed and men's interest waned, the man they had hired came with their camels and one of his own. [. . .]

When Abū Bakr brought the two camels to the apostle he offered the better one to him and invited him to ride her. But the apostle refused to ride an animal which was not his own and when Abū Bakr wanted to give him it he demanded to know what he had paid for it and bought it from him. They rode off, and Abū Bakr carried 'Āmir his freedman behind him to act as a servant on the journey.

I was told that Asmā' said, 'When the apostle and Abū Bakr had gone, a number of Quraysh including Abū Jahl came to us and stood at the door. When I went out to them they asked where my father was and when I said that I did not know Abū Jahl, who was a rough dissolute man, slapped my face so violently that my earring flew off. Then they took themselves off and we remained for three days without news until a man of the Jinn came from the lower part of Mecca singing some verses in the Arab way. And lo people were following him and listening to his voice but they could not see him, until he emerged from the upper part of Mecca saying the while:

God the Lord of men give the best of his rewards
To the two companions who rested in the two tents of Umm Ma'bad.
They came with good intent and went off at nightfall.
May Muhammad's companion prosper!
May the place of the Banū Ka'b's woman bring them luck,
For she was a look-out for the believers.'

Asmā' continued: 'When we heard his words we knew that the apostle was making for Medina. [. . .]

The Expedition of 'Ubayda b. al-Ḥārith

During that stay in Medina the apostle sent 'Ubayda b. al-Ḥārith b. al-Muṭṭalib with sixty or eighty riders from the emigrants, there not being a single one of the Anṣār among them. He went as far as water in the Hijaz below Thanīyatu'l-Murra, where he encountered a large number of Quraysh. No fighting took place except that Sa'd b. Abū Waqqāṣ shot an arrow on that day. It was the first arrow to be shot in Islam. [. . .]

The Expedition of 'Abdullah b. Jaḥsh and the Coming
Down of 'They Will Ask You about the Sacred Month'

The apostle sent 'Abdullah b. Jaḥsh b. Ri'āb al-Asadī in Rajab on his return from the first Badr. He sent with him eight emigrants, without any of the Anṣār. He wrote for him a letter, and ordered him not to look at it until he had journeyed for two days, and to do what he was ordered to do, but not to put pressure on any of his companions. . . .

When 'Abdullah had travelled for two days he opened the letter and looked into it, and this is what it said: 'When you have read this letter of mine proceed until you reach Nakhla between Mecca and Al-Ṭā'if. Lie in wait there for Quraysh and find out for us what they are doing.' Having read the letter he said, 'To hear is to obey.' Then he said to his companions, 'The apostle has commanded me to go to Nakhla to lie in wait there for Quraysh so as to bring him news of them. He has forbidden me to put pressure on any of you, so if anyone wishes for martyrdom let him go forward, and he who does not, let him go back; as for me I am going on as the prophet has ordered.' So he went on, as did all his companions, not one of them falling back. He journeyed along the Ḥijāz until at a mine called Baḥrān above al-Furuʿ, Saʿd and ʿUtba lost the camel which they were riding by turns, so they stayed behind to look for it, while ʿAbdullah and the rest of them went on to Nakhla. A caravan of Quraysh carrying dry raisins and leather and other merchandise of Quraysh passed by them, ʿAmr b. al-Ḥaḍramī (349), ʿUthmān b. Abdullah b. al-Mughīra and his brother Nau-fal the Makhzūmites, and al-Ḥakam b. Kaysān, freedman of Hishām b. al-Mughīra being among them. When the caravan saw them they were afraid of them because they had camped near them. ʿUkkāsha, who had shaved his head, looked down on them, and when they saw him they felt safe and said, 'They are pilgrims, you have nothing to fear from them.' The raiders took council among themselves, for this was the last day of Rajab, and they said, 'If you leave them alone tonight they will get into the sacred area and will be safe from you; and if you kill them, you will kill them in the sacred month,' so they were hesitant and feared to attack them. Then they encouraged each other, and decided to kill as many as they could of them and take what they had. Wāqid shot ʿAmr b. al-Ḥaḍramī with an arrow and killed him, and ʿUthmān and al-Ḥakam surrendered. Naufal escaped and eluded them. ʿAbdullah and his companions took the caravan and the two prisoners and came to Medina with them. One of ʿAbdullah's family mentioned that he said to his companions, 'A fifth of what we have taken belongs to the apostle.' (This was before God had appointed a fifth of the booty to him.) So he set apart for the apostle a fifth of the caravan, and divided the rest among his companions.

When they came to the apostle, he said, 'I did not order you to fight in the sacred month,' and he held the caravan and the two prisoners in suspense and refused to take anything from them. When the apostle said that, the men were in despair and thought that they were doomed. Their Muslim brethren reproached them for what they had done, and the Quraysh said 'Muhammad and his companions have vio-lated the sacred month, shed blood therein, taken booty, and captured men.' The Muslims in Mecca who opposed them said that they had done it in Shaʿbān. The Jews turned this raid into an omen against the apostle. ʿAmr b. al-Ḥaḍramī whom Wāqid had killed they said meant *ʿamaratiʾl-ḥarb* (war has come to life), al-Ḥaḍramī meant *ḥaḍaratiʾl-ḥarb* (war is present), and Wāqid meant *waqadatiʾl-ḥarb* (war is kindled); but God turned this against them, not for them, and when there was much talk about it, God sent down to his apostle: 'They will ask you about the sacred month, and war in it. Say, war therein is a serious matter, but keeping people from the way of God and disbelieving in Him and in the sacred mosque and driving out His people therefrom is more serious with God.'[24] i.e. If you have killed in the sacred month, they have kept you back from the way of God with their unbelief in Him, and from the sacred mosque, and have driven you from it when you were its people.

---

[24] **'They will ask . . . God':** Sura 2.214.

This is a more serious matter with God than the killing of those of them whom you have slain. 'And seduction is worse than killing.' i.e. They used to seduce the Muslim in his religion until they made him return to unbelief after believing, and that is worse with God than killing. 'And they will not cease to fight you until they turn you back from your religion if they can.' . . .

And when the Quran came down about that and God relieved the Muslims of their anxiety in the matter, the apostle took the caravan and the prisoners. [. . .]

The Causes That Led
to the Occupation of Mecca

[. . .] The apostle entered Mecca on the day of the conquest and it contained 360 idols which Iblīs had strengthened with lead. The apostle was standing by them with a stick in his hand, saying, 'The truth has come and falsehood has passed away; verily falsehood is sure to pass away' (Sūra 17. 82). Then he pointed at them with his stick and they collapsed on their backs one after the other.

When the apostle prayed the noon prayer on the day of the conquest he ordered that all the idols which were round the Ka'ba should be collected and burned with fire and broken up. Faḍāla b. al-Mulawwiḥ al-Laythī said commemorating the day of the conquest:

> Had you seen Muhammad and his troops
> The day the idols were smashed when he entered,
> You would have seen God's light become manifest
> And darkness covering the face of idolatry.

[. . .] Quraysh had put pictures in the Ka'ba including two of Jesus son of Mary and Mary (on both of whom be peace!). I. Shihāb said: Asmā' d. Shaqr said that a woman of Ghassān joined in the pilgrimage of the Arabs and when she saw the picture of Mary in the Ka'ba she said, 'My father and my mother be your ransom! You are surely an Arab woman!' The apostle ordered that the pictures should be erased except those of Jesus and Mary.

A traditionist told me that the apostle stood at the door of the Ka'ba and said: 'There is no God but Allah alone; He has no associate. He has made good His promise and helped His servant. He has put to flight the confederates alone. Every claim of privilege[25] or blood or property are abolished by me except the custody of the temple and the watering of the pilgrims. The unintentionally slain[26] in a quasi-intentional way by club or whip, for him the bloodwit is most severe: a hundred camels, forty of them to be pregnant. O Quraysh, God has taken from you the haughtiness of paganism and its veneration of ancestors. Man springs from Adam and Adam sprang from dust.' Then he read to them this verse: 'O men, We created you from male and female

---

[25] **claim of privilege:** Especially inherited authority.

[26] **unintentionally slain:** That is, a victim of manslaughter.

and made you into peoples and tribes that you may know one another: of a truth the most noble of you in God's sight is the most pious'[27] to the end of the passage. Then he added, 'O Quraysh, what do you think that I am about to do with you?' They replied, 'Good. You are a noble brother, son of a noble brother.' He said, 'Go your way for you are the freed ones.' [. . .]

The Year of the Deputations, A.H. 9

When the apostle had gained possession of Mecca, and had finished with Tabūk, and Thaqīf had surrendered and paid homage, deputations from the Arabs came to him from all directions.

In deciding their attitude to Islam the Arabs were only waiting to see what happened to this clan of Quraysh and the apostle. For Quraysh were the leaders and guides of men, the people of the sacred temple, and the pure stock of Ishmael son of Abraham; and the leading Arabs did not contest this. It was Quraysh who had declared war on the apostle and opposed him; and when Mecca was occupied and Quraysh became subject to him and he subdued it to Islam, and the Arabs knew that they could not fight the apostle or display enmity towards him they entered into God's religion 'in batches' as God said, coming to him from all directions. God said to His prophet: 'When God's help came and the victory, and you saw men entering into God's religion in batches, then glorify God with praise and ask His pardon for He is most forgiving,'[28] i.e. praise God for His having made your religion victorious, and ask His pardon, for He is most forgiving.

The Farewell Pilgrimage

In the beginning of Dhū'l-Qa'da the apostle prepared to make the pilgrimage[29] and ordered the men to get ready.

'Abdu'l-Raḥmān b. al-Qāsim from his father al-Qāsim b. Muhammad from 'Ā'isha the prophet's wife told me that the apostle went on pilgrimage on the 25th Dhū'l-Qa'da.

Neither he nor the men spoke of anything but the pilgrimage, until when he was in Sarif and had brought the victims with him as also some dignitaries had done, he ordered the people to remove their pilgrim garments except those who brought victims.[30] That day my menses were upon me and he came in to me as I was weeping and asked me what ailed me, guessing correctly what was the matter. I told him he was right and said I wished to God that I had not come out with him on the journey this year. He said 'Don't say that, for you can do all that the pilgrims do except go

---

[27] **O men . . . most pious:** Sura 49.13.

[28] **When God's help . . . most forgiving:** Sura 110.

[29] **to make the pilgrimage:** The pilgrimage, or *hajj*, to Mecca remains an obligation of all Muslims. It must be completed at least once in a lifetime. [Editors' note]

[30] **victims:** Animals intended for ritual sacrifice. [Editors' note]

round the temple.' The apostle entered Mecca and everyone who had no sacrificial victim, and his wives, took off the pilgrim garment. When the day of sacrifice came I was sent a lot of beef and it was put in my house. When I asked what it was they said that the apostle had sacrificed cows on behalf of his wives. When the night that the pebbles were thrown duly came the apostle sent me along with my brother 'Abdu'l-Raḥmān and let me perform the 'umra from al-Tan'īm in place of the 'umra which I had missed. [. . .]

Then the apostle continued his pilgrimage and showed the men the rites and taught them the customs of their *ḥajj*. He made a speech in which he made things clear. He praised and glorified God, then he said: 'O men, listen to my words. I do not know whether I shall ever meet you in this place again after this year. Your blood and your property are sacrosanct until you meet your Lord, as this day and this month are holy. You will surely meet your Lord and He will ask you of your works. I have told you. He who has a pledge let him return it to him who entrusted him with it; all usury is abolished, but you have your capital. Wrong not and you shall not be wronged. God has decreed that there is to be no usury and the usury of 'Abbās b. 'Abdu'l-Muṭṭalib is abolished, all of it. All blood shed in the pagan period is to be left unavenged. The first claim on blood I abolish is that of b. Rabī'a b. al-Ḥārith b. 'Abdu'l-Muṭṭalib (who was fostered among the B. Layth and whom Hudhayl killed). It is the first blood shed in the pagan period which I deal with. Satan despairs of ever being worshipped in your land, but if he can be obeyed in anything short of worship he will be pleased in matters you may be disposed to think of little account, so beware of him in your religion. [. . .]

You have rights over your wives and they have rights over you. You have the right that they should not defile your bed and that they should not behave with open unseemliness. If they do, God allows you to put them in separate rooms and to beat them but not with severity. If they refrain from these things they have the right to their food and clothing with kindness. Lay injunctions on women kindly, for they are prisoners with you having no control of their persons. You have taken them only as a trust from God, and you have the enjoyment of their persons by the words of God, so understand my words, O men, for I have told you. I have left with you something which if you will hold fast to it you will never fall into error—a plain indication, the book of God and the practice of His prophet, so give good heed to what I say.

Know that every Muslim is a Muslim's brother, and that the Muslims are brethren. It is only lawful to take from a brother what he gives you willingly, so wrong not yourselves. O God, have I not told you?

I was told that the men said 'O God, yes,' and the apostle said 'O God, bear witness.' [. . .]

[. . .] The apostle completed the *ḥajj* and showed men the rites, and taught them what God had prescribed as to their *ḥajj*, the station, the throwing of stones, the circumambulation of the temple, and what He had permitted and forbidden. It was the pilgrimage of completion and the pilgrimage of farewell because the apostle did not go on pilgrimage after that.

The Beginning of the Apostle's Illness

While matters were thus the apostle began to suffer from the illness by which God took him to what honour and compassion He intended for him shortly before the end of Ṣafar or in the beginning of Rabīʿuʾl-awwal. It began, so I have been told, when he went to Baqīʿuʾl-Gharqad in the middle of the night and prayed for the dead. Then he returned to his family and in the morning his sufferings began.

'Abdullah b. 'Umar from 'Ubayd b. Jubayr, a freedman of al-Ḥakam b. Abūʾl-ʿĀṣ. [. . .] a freedman of the apostle, said: In the middle of the night the apostle sent for me and told me that he was ordered to pray for the dead in this cemetery and that I was to go with him. I went; and when he stood among them he said, 'Peace upon you, O people of the graves! Happy are you that you are so much better off than men here. Dissensions have come like waves of darkness one after the other, the last being worse than the first.' Then he turned to me and said, 'I have been given the choice between the keys of the treasuries of this world and long life here followed by Paradise, and meeting my Lord and Paradise (at once).' I urged him to choose the former, but he said that he had chosen the latter. Then he prayed for the dead there and went away. Then it was that the illness through which God took him began.

[. . .] Āʾisha, the prophet's wife, said: The apostle returned from the cemetery to find me suffering from a severe headache and I was saying, 'O my head!' He said, 'Nay, ʿĀʾisha, O *my* head!' Then he said, 'Would it distress you if you were to die before me so that I might wrap you in your shroud and pray over you and bury you?' I said, 'Methinks I see you if you had done that returning to my house and spending a bridal night therein with one of your wives.' The apostle smiled and then his pain overcame him as he was going the round of his wives, until he was overpowered in the house of Maymūna. He called his wives and asked their permission to be nursed in my house, and they agreed.

The Apostle's Illness in the House of 'Āʾisha

'The apostle went out walking between two men of his family, one of whom was al-Faḍl b. al-ʿAbbās. His head was bound in a cloth and his feet were dragging as he came to my house. [. . .]

Then the apostle's illness worsened and he suffered much pain. He said, 'Pour seven skins of water from different wells over me so that I may go out to the men and instruct them.' We made him sit down in a tub belonging to Ḥafṣa d. 'Umar and we poured water over him until he cried, 'Enough, enough!'

Al-Zuhrī said that Ayyūb b. Bashīr told him that the apostle went out with his head bound up and sat in the pulpit. The first thing he uttered was a prayer over the men of Uḥud asking God's forgiveness for them and praying for them a long time; then he said, 'God has given one of his servants the choice between this world and that which is with God and he has chosen the latter.' Abū Bakr perceived that he meant himself and he wept, saying, 'Nay, we and our children will be your ransom.' He replied, 'Gently, Abū Bakr,' adding, 'See to these doors that open on to the mosque and shut them except one from Abū Bakr's house, for I know no one who is a better friend to me than he.' [. . .]

Al-Zuhrī said, Ḥamza b. 'Abdullah b. 'Umar told me that 'Ā'isha said: 'When the prophet became seriously ill he ordered the people to tell Abū Bakr to superintend the prayers.[31] 'Ā'isha told him that Abū Bakr was a delicate man with a weak voice who wept much when he read the Quran. He repeated his order nevertheless, and I repeated my objection. He said, "You are like Joseph's companions; tell him to preside at prayers." My only reason for saying what I did was that I wanted Abū Bakr to be spared this task, because I knew that people would never like a man who occupied the apostle's place, and would blame him for every misfortune that occurred, and I wanted Abū Bakr to be spared this.' [. . .]

Al-Zuhrī said that Anas b. Mālik told him that on the Monday on which God took His apostle he went out to the people as they were praying the morning prayer. The curtain was lifted and the door opened and out came the apostle and stood at 'Ā'isha's door. The Muslims were almost seduced from their prayers for joy at seeing him, and he motioned to them that they should continue their prayers. The apostle smiled with joy when he marked their mien in prayer, and I never saw him with a nobler expression than he had that day. Then he went back and the people went away thinking that the apostle had recovered from his illness. Abū Bakr returned to his wife in al-Sunḥ. . . .

Abū Bakr b. 'Abdullah b. Abū Mulayka told me that when the Monday came the apostle went out to morning prayer with his head wrapped up while Abū Bakr was leading the prayers. When the apostle went out the people's attention wavered, and Abū Bakr knew that the people would not behave thus unless the apostle had come, so he withdrew from his place; but the apostle pushed him in the back, saying, 'Lead the men in prayer,' and the apostle sat at his side praying in a sitting posture on the right of Abū Bakr. When he had ended prayer he turned to the men and spoke to them with a loud voice which could be heard outside the mosque: 'O men, the fire is kindled, and rebellions come like the darkness of the night. By God, you can lay nothing to my charge. I allow only what the Quran allows and forbid only what the Quran forbids.' . . .

Ya'qūb b. 'Utba from al-Zuhrī from 'Urwa from 'Ā'isha said: The apostle came back to me from the mosque that day and lay in my bosom. A man of Abū Bakr's family came in to me with a toothpick in his hand and the apostle looked at it in such a way that I knew he wanted it, and when I asked him if he wanted me to give it him he said Yes; so I took it and chewed it for him to soften it and gave it to him. He rubbed his teeth with it more energetically than I had ever seen him rub before; then he laid it down. I found him heavy in my bosom and as I looked into his face, lo his eyes were fixed and he was saying, 'Nay, the most Exalted Companion is of paradise.' I said, 'You were given the choice and you have chosen, by Him Who sent you with the truth!' And so the apostle was taken. . . .

---

[31] **to superintend the prayers:** As this office was a sign of leadership, A'isha assumed that Muhammad wished Abū Bakr to succeed him. [Editors' note]

Al-Zuhrī said, and Saʿīd b. al-Musayyib from Abū Hurayra told me: When the apostle was dead ʿUmar got up and said: 'Some of the disaffected will allege that the apostle is dead, but by God he is not dead: he has gone to his Lord as Moses b. ʿImrān went and was hidden from his people for forty days, returning to them after it was said that he had died. By God, the apostle will return as Moses returned and will cut off the hands and feet of men who allege that the apostle is dead.' When Abū Bakr heard what was happening he came to the door of the mosque as ʿUmar was speaking to the people. He paid no attention but went in to ʿĀʾisha's house to the apostle, who was lying covered by a mantle of Yamanī cloth. He went and uncovered his face and kissed him, saying, 'You are dearer than my father and mother. You have tasted the death which God had decreed: a second death will never overtake you.' Then he replaced the mantle on the apostle's face and went out. ʿUmar was still speaking and he said, 'Gently, ʿUmar, be quiet.' But ʿUmar refused and went on talking, and when Abū Bakr saw that he would not be silent he went forward to the people who, when they heard his words, came to him and left ʿUmar. Giving thanks and praise to God he said: 'O men, if anyone worships Muhammad, Muhammad is dead: if anyone worships God, God is alive, immortal.' Then he recited this verse: 'Muhammad is nothing but an apostle. Apostles have passed away before him. Can it be that if he were to die or be killed you would turn back on your heels? He who turns back does no harm to God and God will reward the grateful.'[32] By God, it was as though the people did not know that this verse had come down until Abū Bakr recited it that day. The people took it from him and it was (constantly) in their mouths. ʿUmar said, 'By God, when I heard Abū Bakr recite these words I was dumbfounded so that my legs would not bear me and I fell to the ground; knowing that the apostle was indeed dead.'

---

[32] 'Muhammad is . . . the grateful': Sura 3.138.

Kings, Conquerors, and Fighting Saints

As the story of the life of the prophet Muhammad suggests, Islamic culture grew from a love of the Book—both the Qur'an and the literature created in its service beginning in the eighth century. In Arabic literature, biographies soon followed the model narrative of the life of Muhammad, which had been assembled from many individual stories. Of course, this is not a unique situation. All of ancient literature is full of accounts of the lives of the great, from the legendary Babylonian king Gilgamesh to Moses, David, Solomon, and other patriarchs of the Hebrew Scriptures; from Jesus, whose life is recorded in the Christian Gospels, to Buddha, whose story is told in the writings of **Ashvaghosha**; from the historical Caesars in ancient Rome to the Christian saints; from the emperors of China and Japan to the members of the ruling dynasties of India.

ush-vuh-GOH-shuh

MEDIEVAL HEROES: THE STORIES

Although a single model for the stories of rulers and other great men and women in the Middle Period does not exist, it is often possible to locate specific models of these narratives in classical literature. Many cultures praise their heroes by recalling stories from the past, often imitating the form of previous biographies, as can be seen in some of the life stories of famous kings, conquerors, and warrior saints of the Middle Period: **Charlemagne** (742–814), king of the Franks and Holy Roman Emperor; Alexius I (1048–1118), fated member of a famous dynasty of Byzantine emperors; **Saladin** (1137–1193), sultan of Egypt and Syria and commander of the Muslim armies in the Third Crusade; **Chingis Khan** (c. 1160–1227), Mongol

SHAR-luh-mane

SAL-uh-din

CHING-giz-KAHN

ولاه ارسل الى تمنع المعالى قابوس رسولا وطلباته ان يلم اليهم اخا ولا فاجابهما اسمع معهم من جاء نص مهم مدمع ب
سرلي ذلك ايضا واناى وسط الكيلاتين الذين يلعبون بروسهم ومذوقت الحيبة ولا يعلون برقا بصم على السيوف ومذوقت الحمابة وحاصل
قابوس ذيهب عنه الناموس ويكون فضله فى معرض الخطر من شعلة السنه اكى الاسن كل من لعة استنهم   فلما وصل ذلك الجواب ال
بنته وتميم عوه على المكاوحة والمقا تله وكتب الى مؤبد الدوله يامر بتهيبة اسباب المناهضة وترتها الحبادة قابوس و خرجوا من الرت وتوجهوا الى خ
عسكر كبير من الترك والعرب والديلم وخرجوا بلاد قابوس الى وقتت على طريقه عمر وتمت واد خطوها فى تصرف ذرف ذول بهم حتى نزلوا باسنا ا باد واد باد بم
جرحان لحد يظهامن عض هؤلاء بها فانها كانت دار ملكه   فلما وصل مؤبد الدوله سوى الصفوف وانطت السبوف   دما الكامل مطر الكامر من السحاب ف

Mongol Warriors, fourteenth century

Under the fierce and phenomenally successful warrior leader Chingis Khan, the Mongols conquered a vast territory stretching from China in the east to the Balkans in the west. This Muslim illuminated manuscript shows a heavily armed group of Mongol warriors, an ominous sight for any army. (The Art Archive / Edinburgh University Library)

warrior who was called "the world conqueror" by one of his foes; and Joan of Arc (1412–1431), referred to as *la Pucelle,* or the Maid, in her brief lifetime and canonized half a millennium after her death as Saint Joan.

With one exception, the stories of these individuals were preserved in written histories. Charlemagne's biographer, Einhard, served under the great king in his own court and wrote about Charlemagne shortly after his death. Einhard's biography borrows quite consciously from Suetonius' Latin life of Augustus Caesar (first century c.e.). The tribulations of Alexius I as Byzantine emperor were soon molded into an epic by his gifted and fiercely determined daughter, Anna Comnena, as an apologia for his life's work. Although written in Greek, the literary model for this biography was *The Aeneid,* the literary epic of the Roman poet Virgil (first century c.e.). Saladin's deeds were recorded in Muslim accounts of the Crusades written contemporaneously with the campaigns, and his life was treated in biographies soon after his own death. The model for these later narratives was *The Life of Muhammad* (p. 134), a work completed by Ibn Ishaq in the eighth century c.e. Chroniclers of the times recorded the life, trial, and condemnation of Joan of Arc. Ironically, perhaps, the complete account of her life resembles that of a medieval saint's tale, including her martyrdom, even though some of its authors were Joan's enemies.

The Mongol version of the story of Chingis Khan has no literary model for several reasons. It began as a collection of oral legends; made into a loosely alliterative narrative several decades after his death, it was intended to be recited only to his descendants and royal successors. Eventually, it saw the light of day as the major portion of a Chinese work called *The Secret History of the Mongols.* It is perhaps fitting that this tale is the hardest to come by in written form. Chingis Khan ruthlessly attacked European and Muslim societies, which were committed to the writing of history, often visiting fiery destruction on their great libraries.

CHARLEMAGNE, "TYPE" OF THE CHRISTIAN KING

On Christmas Day, 800, Charles the Great (Charlemagne) was crowned Holy Roman Emperor in St. Peter's Cathedral in Rome. Apparently Pope Leo III surprised him with the coronation; as his biographer Einhard says, "He made it clear that he would not have entered the cathedral that day . . . if he had known in advance what the Pope was planning to do." Charlemagne was being rewarded for having expanded Frankish territory in Europe as well as for embracing the cause of the Christian Church enthusiastically while defending the pope against his enemies. The Papacy had owed some form of tribute to Charlemagne and his family for some time. Charlemagne's grandfather Charles Martel had defeated the Muslims at Tours in southern France in 732, ending their drive through Europe

Charlemagne with His Son, Pepin, tenth century
Charlemagne is remembered not only as a great Christian warrior and king but also as a promoter of culture and an able administrator. He is pictured in a manuscript here with his son, Pepin, giving instructions to a court clerk. (The Art Archive/Biblioteca del Duomo, Modena/Dagli Orti)

and forcing them back to Andalusia (Spain). While the territory recaptured by Charlemagne rapidly diminished again after his death, the Franks remained strong enough in their various branches to lead the First Crusade nearly two centuries later, in 1095, and Charlemagne's image as the ideal Christian king endured.

Charlemagne was a giant for his time—he stood six foot three inches—and his feats of valor on the battlefield were substantial. Equally impressive to later historians was his promotion of a revival of culture, the Carolingian Renaissance, in the Frankish kingdom. He persuaded the monk Alcuin (c. 732–804), a scholar from Britain, to introduce the study of literature, philosophy, and the arts to his court. Charlemagne's reforms in education helped to create a tradition of scholars who influenced European education for three hundred years, until the rise of the universities in the twelfth century.

ALEXIUS I, BYZANTINE EMPEROR

mas-uh-DOH-nee-un

With the end of the **Macedonian** dynasty in 1056 C.E., the Byzantine empire fell into decline. The Seljuk Turks, Muslim converts who warred even with their own brethren, routed the Byzantine army at the Battle of Manzikert in Asia Minor in 1071. Existing tensions among the Muslim, Byzantine, and Christian civilizations were exacerbated by the **Seljuks**, and conflicts among these groups disrupted life throughout the region. By the end of the eleventh century, traders and religious pilgrims traveling in the desert to the Holy Land were subject to molestation by armies and bandit chieftains.

SEL-jooks

When Alexius Comnenus was crowned Emperor Alexius I in **Constantinople** in 1081, he sought to keep potential enemies at bay—the Normans from Sicily, the Seljuk Turks from Asia Minor, and other groups from the Balkans. However, he miscalculated when he sought the assistance of Pope Urban II, his nominal Christian ally in Rome, in 1095. Instead of sending a limited number of mercenaries to protect pilgrimages to the Holy Land as Alexius had requested, Urban preached the beginning of the First Crusade, designed to promote the influence of the Catholic Church, send large numbers of restless Frankish knights far from their European homes, punish the Muslims, and raid the Middle East for treasure. Within a year, Frankish Crusaders and their dependents began appearing on the eastern shores of the Mediterranean. Committed to defending Constantinople from attack, Alexius decided that the Christian supporters he had requested were more dangerous to the city than his original enemies. Edging away from the alliance, he appeared to aid the Christian cause as the Crusaders then turned their attention to the conquest of Jerusalem, but in truth he was horrified by the brutal and chaotic Frankish armies.

kahn-stan-tih-NOH-pul

Alexius I was fortunate in two respects. He saved Constantinople from invasion for at least a century. And, thanks to the creative gifts of his daughter, Anna Comnena, his reign was recorded in one of the best medieval biographies extant. Haughty, learned, and a gifted student of classical literature, Anna set out to vindicate her father's courage and intelligence and in the process created a moving portrait of the most powerful ruler in Asia Minor during his greatest crisis.

SALADIN, THE MIRROR OF HIS AGE

It is often said of Saladin that he was as respected by his enemies as he was by his followers. A brilliant strategist on the battlefield, he was also prodigiously generous, remarkably learned, and an effective statesman. He won some of his victories through negotiation. His crowning achievement was his nearly bloodless conquest of Jerusalem in 1187, a stark contrast to the Christian massacre of Muslim and Jewish inhabitants of the city in 1099. Even so, he displayed some of the violence that comes with absolute power. After a decisive victory over Christian forces on his way to Jerusalem in the battle of Hittin in 1187, he pardoned King Guy of Jerusalem and freed other Christians, but he also murdered his enemy **Reynald of Chatillon** and ordered the beheading of two hundred Christian knights from the religious orders, an atrocity in which it is said he took great pleasure.

ray-NOH, shah-tee-YAWNG

A privileged young man of Turkish descent, Saladin in 1156 was named deputy governor of Damascus, reputedly the most populous city in the world. He studied under **al-Ghazali** (1058–1110), the famous Sufi philosopher, but carefully followed the precepts of the Syrian ruler **Nur al-Din** in both civil and military matters. Between 1164 and 1169, Saladin fought in three Syrian campaigns in Egypt, becoming the leader of the Syrian army at the age of thirty. In 1171, acting under Nur al-Din's orders, Saladin established the Abbasid caliphate in Egypt. Thus he became master of Egypt and, upon the death of Nur al-Din in 1174, the most powerful figure in Islam, second in all the Middle East only to the Byzantine emperor. He spent the next decade consolidating his authority in Egypt and Syria.

ahl-gah-ZAH-lee

noor-ahl-DEEN

Responding to the massacre of a caravan of merchants on their way to Damascus by Reynald of Chatillon in 1186, Saladin took up the war against the Christians. Two great armies assembled in Hittin, in the Jordan River valley, in 1187. Thousands of mounted knights and more than ten thousand infantry on each side faced off in full armor in the burning heat of the Jordanian summer. To test the mettle of the Christian army, Saladin attacked the town of Tiberias, situated between the Jordanian hills and Lake Galilee. The Christians coming to rescue the city, overcome by the heat, were slaughtered by Saladin's forces. It was at this time that Saladin spared King Guy of Jerusalem, killed Reynald of Chatillon, and sent two hundred Christian knights to their deaths. After the siege of Jerusalem, which took two weeks, Saladin spared the occupants of the city, arranged for the evacuation of Christians, and discouraged looting by his troops. He restored the sacred shrines of Islam, including the Dome of the Rock, but did not desecrate the Holy Sepulchre or other Christian shrines. In subsequent military action, Saladin captured many of the cities along the peninsula leading to Jerusalem but failed to conquer Tyre, a major port city. This proved to be a costly error: Christian warriors of the Third Crusade (1189–1193) hung onto a tenuous beachhead in the Middle East as a result.

CHINGIS KHAN, WORLD CONQUEROR

Even before the death of Saladin in 1193, word of the rise of Mongol tribes in Manchuria, Mongolia, and eastern Turkestan had reached Islam. At a council in 1206 a successful young tribal leader called **Temujin** (c. 1162–1227) was given the name of Chingis Khan, meaning "Illustrious Leader of the Mongols." By the time of his death twenty years later, his armies had conquered most of north China, devastated the eastern Persian empire, and circled the Caspian Sea. Ten years after his death, the Mongols invaded Eastern Europe, and after several more decades they controlled most of the Eurasian continent. No conquest approaching this scale had ever occurred. Equally astonishing, however, was the disintegration of the same empire, beginning after the death of Chingis Khan's grandson Kublai Khan in 1294 and reaching completion in 1368.

jooz-jah-NEE,
jooz-JAH-NEE

The Muslim historian **Juzjani** describes Chingis Khan as "a man of tall stature, of vigorous build, robust in body, the hair on his face scanty and turned white, with cat's eyes, possessed of great energy, discernment, genius, and understanding, awe-inspiring, a butcher, just, resolute, an overthrower of enemies, intrepid, sanguinary, and cruel." As a soldier Chingis Khan was a great innovator, outfitting his mounted troops with light armor, small and sturdy horses, and a short stirrup that enabled them to fire arrows accurately at a gallop. Their bows were very heavy, with a 160–pound pull, and their armor-piercing arrows were accurate at several hundred yards. As an administrator, he introduced writing in Turkish script, organized a strong civil service in the defeated territories, and revitalized the economies of captured regions for the benefit of the Mongols. He encouraged religious tolerance and protected trade over the Silk

Road. He also promulgated a legal code that combined liberal reforms with severe penalties for lawbreakers.

What stirs historians about Chingis Khan, however, is his extreme cruelty. The deaths he caused must have numbered in the millions. His indiscriminate murder of entire populations, sparing only accomplished artisans and civil servants whom he could press into service in his army of occupation, was unheard of before his time. Apparently, he wanted to instill terror to solidify his rule, but his rampant genocide still defies explanation. To Muslim historians especially, he was the epitome of evil, the "world conqueror."

JOAN OF ARC, MYSTIC AND WARRIOR

The fabled life of Joan of Arc was as brief as it was astounding. Born in the French province of Lorraine to landed peasants in 1412, Joan heard the voice of God in the wind and in the village chapel bells in her early adolescence and journeyed to the castle at **Vaucouleurs** to offer her services to Charles, **dauphin** of France (the eldest son of

voh-koo-LUR

doh-FAN

Joan of Arc, 1429
The life and legend of Joan of Arc have resonated for ages. This drawing, from a French parliamentary council register detailing the events surrounding the victory at Orleans, is thought to be the only extant portrait of her. The lethal sword Joan is holding contrasts with her feminine clothing. (The Art Archive/Dagli Orti)

the French king), in 1428. She proposed, outrageously, that she would lead the dauphin's army and deliver France from the English invaders who controlled most of his country. Even more amazingly, Charles consented to her doing so, and she led his troops into battle. The army accepted her leadership, although aware that this spectacle might lead to charges of heresy from the church, and fought with extraordinary success under her command; Joan refused to allow the soldiers to loot or pillage any towns they captured. She won a great victory at **Orleans**, breaking an English siege of the city, and again defeated the English in open battle at Patay in June 1429. Under her protection the dauphin was crowned King Charles VII of France at **Reims** in July of the same year. But in the spring of 1430, after Joan failed to take several suburbs of Paris, she was defeated and captured by French Burgundian allies of the English. Sold to her enemies, she was tried as a heretic and burned at the stake on May 30, 1431.

Joan's emergence into history was recorded in a great number of journals and official records. Her uncanny three years of service to Charles VII, her insistence on her communication with God and His angels, her beauty and purity, her prowess in battle, her mannish clothing, her refusal to compromise, and her ultimate choice of martyrdom mark her as a unique national hero. Her life and death also represent for many the end of the European Middle Ages, the last breath of chivalry and idealism in a world given over to small intrigues and low purposes. No wonder that even in modern times many in France claim her as their own.

On July 20, 1456, twenty-five years after her execution, Joan of Arc was rehabilitated by the Catholic Church in **Rouen**, France, something her mother lived to see. On May 9, 1920, more than five hundred years after her birth, Joan of Arc was canonized as a saint. Her saint's day is celebrated on July 10, a national holiday in France.

■ CONNECTIONS

Ibn Ishaq, *The Life of Muhammad,* **p. 134.** It has been argued that the growth of European culture in the ninth century was a consequence of the Muslim invasion of Europe less than a century before. As one historian famously put it, "Without Muhammad, Charlemagne would have been inconceivable." What effect did Muhammad have on Charlemagne, the Frankish leader whose grandfather Charles

ohr-lay-AWNG

REEMZ, RANGS

roo-AWNG

Martel stopped the Muslim invasion of Europe at Tours in 732; on Saladin, the Muslim leader who was often viewed as a spiritual descendant of Muhammad; and on later history in general?

The Song of Roland, p. 546. *The Song of Roland* and the literature of the Crusades depict Charlemagne as a heroic figure whose story inspired the participation of the Franks in the First Crusade two centuries after his death. How does the figure of Charlemagne presented by biographer Einhard compare with the character Charlemagne in the Crusade epic *The Song of Roland*?

The Epic of Gilgamesh (Book 1); Shahnama. In the thirteenth century, Chingis Khan, known as the "world conqueror," was seen in an epic dimension hitherto reserved for the warriors of ancient legend. How was Chingis Khan like or unlike the epic hero Gilgamesh and the tragic hero Rostam in the Persian epic *Shahnama*?

■ **FURTHER RESEARCH**

Translations and Studies

Charlemagne

Einhard. *The Life of Charlemagne.* Trans. Eileen Frichow and Edwin Zeydel. 1972.

Thorpe, Lewis, trans. *Einhard and Notker the Stammerer: Two Lives of Charlemagne.* 1969.

Emperor Alexius

Angold, Michael. *The Byzantine Empire, 1025–1204: A Political History.* 1997.

Comnena, Anna. *The Alexiad.* Trans. E. R. A. Sewter. 1969.

Dalven, Rae. *Anna Comnena.* 1972.

Runciman, Steven. *The First Crusade.* Abridged ed. 1980.

Saladin

Gabrieli, Francesco. *Arab Historians of the Crusades.* Trans. E. J. Costello. 1969.

Newby, P. H. *Saladin in His Time.* 1983.

Reynolds, Dwight F. *Interpreting the Self: Autobiography in the Arabic Literary Tradition.* 2001.

Chingis Khan

Boyle, John A., trans. *Juvaini: The History of the World-Conqueror.* 1958.

Cleaves, Francis W., trans. *The Secret History of the Mongols.* 1982.

Kahn, Paul. *The Secret History of the Mongols.* 1998.

Morgan, David. *The Mongols.* 1986.

Saunders, J. J. *The History of the Mongol Conquests.* 1971.

Joan of Arc

Pernoud, Régine. *Joan of Arc: By Herself and Her Witnesses.* 1969.

Wheeler, Bonnie, and Charles T. Wood. *Fresh Verdicts on Joan of Arc.* 1996.

■ **PRONUNCIATION**

Alexiad: uh-LEK-see-ad
al-Ghazali: ahl-gah-ZAH-lee
Ashvaghosha: ush-vuh-GOH-shuh
Charlemagne: SHAR-luh-mane
Chingis Khan: CHING-giz KAHN
Constantinople: kahn-stan-tih-NOH-pul
dauphin: doh-FAN
Juzjani: jooz-jah-NEE, jooz-JAH-nee

Macedonian: mas-uh-DOH-nee-un
Nur al-Din: noor-ahl-DEEN
Orleans: ohr-lay-AWNG
Reims: REEMZ, RANGS
Reynald of Chatillon: ray-NOH, shah-tee-YAWNG
Rouen: roo-AWNG
Saladin: SAL-uh-din
Seljuks: SEL-jooks
Tatar: TAH-tar
Temujin: TEM-oo-jin
Vaucouleurs: voh-koo-LUR

∾ EINHARD
c. 770–840

Most of what is known about Einhard, the first biographer of Charlemagne, comes from an introduction to his famous work written by an eminent man of letters, Walafrid Strabo, the abbot of Reichenau. Einhard was born in an eastern Frankish domain, educated at the monastery of Fulda, and sent to the court of Charlemagne at Aix-la-Chappelle shortly after 791. Talented and of good family, he adjusted well to life at the brilliant court. Strabo depicts the tiny Einhard and the strapping King Charles as close confidantes; their relationship helps validate the information in the biography, much of which Einhard learned firsthand. From other documents it is known that after the death of Charlemagne Einhard became a favorite of Louis the Pious, was named abbot of several monasteries, and received significant grants of land. He wrote four works, of which *A Life of Charlemagne,* composed between 829 and 836, is the best known.

Einhard's *Life of Charlemagne* painstakingly depicts its subject. Working from contemporary sources Einhard compiled an account of the military campaigns undertaken before his arrival at Charlemagne's court, and concerning Charlemagne's life and death he wrote from memory. Throughout his work he follows the literary model of Suetonius' *Lives of the Caesars.* In Einhard's time, imitation was not regarded as plagiarism but rather as a form of compliment. The picture of Charlemagne that Einhard wished to present was in many respects a conventional portrait with an ancient pedigree.

In succeeding generations Charlemagne became the subject of statuary, epic poetry, legends, ballads, and chronicle histories. His feats of war, which extended the Frankish frontier and created an approach to northern Spain, helped inspire the Frankish Crusaders in 1095. In *The Song of Roland,* composed around 1100, Charlemagne is portrayed as the ideal

Equestrian Statuette of Charlemagne, ninth century

This small statue of an emperor holding an orb (representing the world) is thought to be either Charlemagne or his grandson, Charles the Bald, who was said to resemble him. The plump face, droopy mustache, and simple attire all correspond with Einhard's description of Charlemagne. (Louvre)

Christian king. Nearly two hundred years later he became the subject of an expanded biography by a scribe named Primat, *The Chronicles of St. Denis,* which presents an even more flattering and romantic picture of the ruler. By this time he was presented as a "mirror for princes," a model for future generations.

FROM

❧ A Life of Charlemagne

Translated by Lewis Thorpe

BOOK III

The Emperor's Private Life

What has gone before is a fair picture of Charlemagne and all that he did to protect and enlarge his kingdom, and indeed to embellish it. I shall now speak of his intellectual qualities, his extraordinary strength of character, whether in prosperity or adversity, and all the other details of his personal and domestic life. [. . .]

The Emperor was strong and well built. He was tall in stature, but not excessively so, for his height was just seven times the length of his own feet. The top of his head was round, and his eyes were piercing and unusually large. His nose was slightly longer than normal, he had a fine head of white hair and his expression was gay and good-humoured. As a result, whether he was seated or standing, he always appeared masterful and dignified. His neck was short and rather thick, and his stomach a trifle too heavy, but the proportions of the rest of his body prevented one from noticing these blemishes. His step was firm and he was manly in all his movements. He spoke distinctly, but his voice was thin for a man of his physique. His health was good, except that he suffered from frequent attacks of fever during the last four years of his life, and towards the end he was lame in one foot. Even then he continued to do exactly as he wished, instead of following the advice of his doctors, whom he came positively to dislike after they advised him to stop eating the roast meat to which he was accustomed and to live on stewed dishes.

He spent much of his time on horseback and out hunting, which came naturally to him, for it would be difficult to find another race on earth who could equal the Franks in this activity. He took delight in steam-baths at the thermal springs and loved to exercise himself in the water whenever he could. He was an extremely strong swimmer and in this sport no one could surpass him. It was for this reason that he built his palace at Aachen[1] and remained continuously in residence there during the last years of his life and indeed until the moment of his death. He would invite not only his sons to bathe with him, but his nobles and friends as well, and occasionally even a crowd of his attendants and bodyguards, so that sometimes a hundred men or more would be in the water together.

He wore the national dress of the Franks.[2] Next to his skin he had a linen shirt and linen drawers; and then long hose and a tunic edged with silk. He wore shoes on his feet and bands of cloth wound round his legs. In winter he protected his chest and shoulders with a jerkin made of otter skins or ermine. He wrapped himself in a blue cloak and always had a sword strapped to his side, with a hilt and belt of gold or silver. Sometimes he would use a jewelled sword, but this was only on great feast days or when ambassadors came from foreign peoples. He hated the clothes of other countries, no matter how becoming they might be, and he would never consent to wear them. The only exception to this was one day in Rome when Pope Hadrian entreated him to put on a long tunic and a Greek mantle, and to wear shoes made in the Roman fashion; and then a second time, when Leo, Hadrian's successor, persuaded him to do the same thing. On feast days he walked in procession in a suit of cloth of gold, with jewelled shoes, his cloak fastened with a golden brooch and with a crown of gold and precious stones on his head. On ordinary days his dress differed hardly at all from that of the common people.

He was moderate in his eating and drinking, and especially so in drinking; for he hated to see drunkenness in any man, and even more so in himself and his friends. All the same, he could not go long without food, and he often used to complain that fasting made him feel ill. He rarely gave banquets and these only on high

---

[1] Aachen: Charlemagne's capital, known in French as Aix-la-Chappelle, is located in present-day northern Germany.

[2] the national dress of the Franks: Charlemagne wore the clothing a knight might wear under armor or a coat of mail. Only the linen was expensive, having come from the Orient. Otter and ermine were everyday furs.

feast days, but then he would invite a great number of guests. His main meal of the day was served in four courses, in addition to the roast meat which his hunters used to bring in on spits and which he enjoyed more than any other food. During his meal he would listen to a public reading or some other entertainment. Stories would be recited for him, or the doings of the ancients told again. He took great pleasure in the books of Saint Augustine and especially in those which are called *The City of God.*

He was so sparing in his use of wine and every other beverage that he rarely drank more than three times in the course of his dinner. In summer, after his midday meal, he would eat some fruit and take another drink; then he would remove his shoes and undress completely, just as he did at night, and rest for two or three hours. During the night he slept so lightly that he would wake four or five times and rise from his bed. When he was dressing and putting on his shoes he would invite his friends to come in. Moreover, if the Count of the Palace told him that there was some dispute which could not be settled without the Emperor's personal decision, he would order the disputants to be brought in there and then, hear the case as if he were sitting in tribunal and pronounce a judgement. If there was any official business to be transacted on that day, or any order to be given to one of his ministers, he would settle it at the same time.

He spoke easily and fluently, and could express with great clarity whatever he had to say. He was not content with his own mother tongue, but took the trouble to learn foreign languages. He learnt Latin so well that he spoke it as fluently as his own tongue; but he understood Greek better than he could speak it. He was eloquent to the point of sometimes seeming almost garrulous.

He paid the greatest attention to the liberal arts; and he had great respect for men who taught them, bestowing high honours upon them. When he was learning the rules of grammar he received tuition from Peter the Deacon of Pisa, who by then was an old man, but for all other subjects he was taught by Alcuin, surnamed Albinus, another Deacon, a man of the Saxon race who came from Britain and was the most learned man anywhere to be found. Under him the Emperor spent much time and effort in studying rhetoric, dialectic and especially astrology.[3] He applied himself to mathematics and traced the course of the stars with great attention and care. He also tried to learn to write. With this object in view he used to keep writing-tablets and notebooks under the pillows on his bed, so that he could try his hand at forming letters during his leisure moments; but, although he tried very hard, he had begun too late in life and he made little progress.

Charlemagne practised the Christian religion with great devotion and piety, for he had been brought up in this faith since earliest childhood. This explains why he built a cathedral of such great beauty at Aachen, decorating it with gold and silver, with lamps, and with lattices and doors of solid bronze. He was unable to find marble columns for his construction anywhere else, and so he had them brought from Rome and Ravenna.

---

[3] **Alcuin . . . astrology:** Charlemagne asked Alcuin (735–804) to join his court in 782. Alcuin was the architect of the Carolingian revival of learning.

As long as his health lasted he went to church morning and evening with great regularity, and also for early-morning Mass, and the late-night hours. He took the greatest pains to ensure that all church ceremonies were performed with the utmost dignity, and he was always warning the sacristans to see that nothing sordid or dirty was brought into the building or left there. He donated so many sacred vessels made of gold and silver, and so many priestly vestments, that when service time came even those who opened and closed the doors, surely the humblest of all church dignitaries, had no need to perform their duties in their everyday clothes.

He made careful reforms in the way in which the psalms were chanted and the lessons read. He was himself quite an expert at both of these exercises, but he never read the lesson in public and he would sing only with the rest of the congregation and then in a low voice.

He was most active in relieving the poor and in that form of really disinterested charity which the Greeks call *eleemosyna*. He gave alms not only in his own country and in the kingdom over which he reigned, but also across the sea in Syria, Egypt, Africa, Jerusalem, Alexandria and Carthage. Wherever he heard that Christians were living in want, he took pity on their poverty and sent them money regularly. It was, indeed, precisely for this reason that he sought the friendship of kings beyond the sea, for he hoped that some relief and alleviation might result for the Christians living under their domination.

Charlemagne cared more for the church of the holy Apostle Peter in Rome than for any other sacred and venerable place. He poured into its treasury a vast fortune in gold and silver coinage and in precious stones. He sent so many gifts to the Pope that it was impossible to keep count of them. Throughout the whole period of his reign nothing was ever nearer to his heart than that, by his own efforts and exertion, the city of Rome should regain its former proud position. His ambition was not merely that the church of Saint Peter should remain safe and protected thanks to him, but that by means of his wealth it should be more richly adorned and endowed than any other church. However much he thought of Rome, it still remains true that throughout his whole reign of forty-seven years he went there only four times to fulfil his vows and to offer up his prayers.

These were not the sole reasons for Charlemagne's last visit to Rome. The truth is that the inhabitants of Rome had violently attacked Pope Leo, putting out his eyes and cutting off his tongue, and had forced him to flee to the King for help.[4] Charlemagne really came to Rome to restore the Church, which was in a very bad state indeed, but in the end he spent the whole winter there. It was on this occasion that he received the title of Emperor and Augustus. At first he was far from wanting this. He made it clear that he would not have entered the cathedral that day at all, although it was the greatest of all the festivals of the Church, if he had known in advance what the Pope was planning to do. Once he had accepted the title, he endured with great patience the jealousy of the so-called Roman Emperors, who were most indignant at what had happened. He overcame their hostility only by the

---

[4] **The truth . . . help:** In fact, Pope Leo was not mutilated; he was assaulted in 799 but escaped his pursuers.

sheer strength of his personality, which was much more powerful than theirs. He was for ever sending messengers to them, and in his dispatches he called them his brothers.

Now that he was Emperor, he discovered that there were many defects in the legal system of his own people, for the Franks have two separate codes of law which differ from each other in many points. He gave much thought to how he could best fill the gaps, reconcile the discrepancies, correct the errors and rewrite the laws which were ill-expressed. None of this was ever finished; he added a few sections, but even these remained incomplete. What he did do was to have collected together and committed to writing the laws of all the nations under his jurisdiction which still remained unrecorded.

At the same time he directed that the age-old narrative poems, barbarous enough, it is true, in which were celebrated the warlike deeds of the kings of ancient times, should be written out and so preserved. He also began a grammar of his native tongue. [. . .]

∾ ANNA COMNENA
1083–1153

Anna Comnena was the oldest child of Alexius Comnenus, Emperor Alexius I of Byzantium. After the death of her father in 1118, Comnena tried to block the succession to the throne of her brother John; as a result, she was sent into lifelong exile. In 1137, following the death of her talented husband, Nicephorous Bryennius, she began to reshape his fragmentary history of the reign of her father, calling her Greek work *The Alexiad*, after Virgil's *Aeneid*. The completed work is marked by Comnena's extreme partiality toward her father's memory, her disappointment in the later political direction of the Byzantine empire, and a noteworthy sourness of tone; it also reflects a high degree of literary training and the superior writing skills of this isolated widow. Comnena took at least eleven years, until 1148, to finish *The Alexiad*.

uh-LEK-see-ad

Between 1056 and the beginning of Alexius I's reign in 1081, Byzantium had undergone a precipitous decline. Deeply threatened from the moment he ascended the throne, Alexius used all his cunning to build alliances among his friends and to keep his enemies off balance. After fighting successive wars with the Normans, the Scythians, and the Turks, the emperor faced a new set of problems in 1096. Word reached him of a massive invasion of Christians from the west, aggressors whom Comnena later refers to as Celts, Normans, and Latins (they were primarily Norman Franks). Anna's description of this event relies completely on the notion that an itinerant preacher, Peter the Hermit, stirred up the First Crusade by preaching in the churches of Europe; she never cites the communication between Pope Urban II and her father that apparently led to the coming of the Crusaders. Even so, Comnena's narrative is both dramatic and instructive. It shows Alexius I initially overwhelmed by the onslaught of Franks, then cleverly winning concessions from them as they grew in size and potential menace. His treatment of Peter the Hermit, whom he regarded as a holy innocent, was remarkably kind; his response to Hugh of Vermandois, the blustering brother of the king of France, was humorously tactful. The narrative is energized throughout by Anna Comnena's salty style and her unabashed prejudices concerning the characters in her story.

Following its original publication *The Alexiad* was last mentioned in 1223; a copy of the manuscript was later discovered and published in Germany in 1610. The work was mocked and derided by Edward Gibbon, the magisterial author of *The History of the Decline and Fall of the Roman Empire,* in 1788. In the twentieth century, however, Western scholars improved their valuation of *The Alexiad,* noting both its literary value and its importance as a Byzantine view of medieval history.

FROM

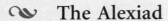 # The Alexiad

Translated by E. R. A. Sewter

BOOK TEN

[. . .] A certain Kelt, called Peter, with the surname Koukoupetros,[1] left to worship at the Holy Sepulchre and after suffering much ill-treatment at the hands of the Turks and Saracens who were plundering the whole of Asia, he returned home with difficulty. Unable to admit defeat, he wanted to make a second attempt by the same route, but realizing the folly of trying to do this alone (worse things might happen to him) he worked out a clever scheme. He decided to preach in all the Latin countries. A divine voice, he said, commanded him to proclaim to all the counts in France that all should depart from their homes, set out to worship at the Holy Shrine and with all their soul and might strive to liberate Jerusalem from the Agarenes. Surprisingly, he was successful. It was as if he had inspired every heart with some divine oracle. Kelts assembled from all parts, one after another, with arms and horses and all the other equipment for war. Full of enthusiasm and ardour they thronged every highway, and with these warriors came a host of civilians, outnumbering the sand of the sea shore or the stars of heaven, carrying palms and bearing crosses on their shoulders. There were women and children, too, who had left their own countries. Like

---

[1] **A certain Kelt, called Peter . . . :** Peter Koukoupetros, later called Peter the Hermit. Alternatively viewed as a holy man and a charlatan, he gathered perhaps twenty thousand followers on his way to the Holy Land with little encouragement from Pope Urban.

tributaries joining a river from all directions they streamed towards us in full force, mostly through Dacia. The arrival of this mighty host was preceded by locusts,[2] which abstained from the wheat but made frightful inroads on the vines. The prophets of those days interpreted this as a sign that the Keltic army would refrain from interfering in the affairs of Christians but bring dreadful affliction on the barbarian Ishmaelites, who were the slaves of drunkenness and wine and Dionysos. The Ishmaelites are indeed dominated by Dionysos and Eros; they indulge readily in every kind of sexual licence, and if they are circumcised in the flesh they are certainly not so in their passions. In fact, the Ishmaelites are nothing more than slaves — trebly slaves — of the vices of Aphrodite.[3] Hence they reverence and worship Astarte and Ashtaroth, and in their land the figure of the moon and the golden image of Chobar[4] are considered of major importance. Corn, because it is not heady and at the same time is most nourishing, has been accepted as the symbol of Christianity. In the light of this the diviners interpreted the references to vines and wheat. So much for the prophecies. The incidents of the barbarians' advance followed in the order I have given and there was something strange about it, which intelligent people at least would notice. The multitudes did not arrive at the same moment, nor even by the same route — how could they cross the Adriatic *en masse* after setting out from different countries in such great numbers? — but they made the voyage in separate groups, some first, some in a second party and others after them in order, until all had arrived, and then they began their march across Epirus. Each army, as I have said, was preceded by a plague of locusts, so that everyone, having observed the phenomenon several times, came to recognize locusts as the forerunners of Frankish battalions. They had already begun to cross the Straits of Lombardy in small groups when the emperor summoned certain leaders of the Roman forces and sent them to the area round Dyrrachium and Avlona, with instructions to receive the voyagers kindly and export from all countries abundant supplies for them along their route; then to watch them carefully and follow, so that if they saw them making raids or running off to plunder the neighbouring districts, they could check them by light skirmishes. These officers were accompanied by interpreters who understood the Latin language; their duty was to quell any incipient trouble between natives and pilgrims. I would like here to give a clearer and more detailed account of the matter.

The report of Peter's preaching spread everywhere, and the first to sell his land and set out on the road to Jerusalem was Godfrey.[5] He was a very rich man, extremely proud of his noble birth, his own courage and the glory of his family. (Every

---

[2] **The arrival of this mighty host was preceded by locusts:** Anna Comnena reports the folk belief that the locusts were a judgment against the Muslim Turks.

[3] **The Ishmaelites . . . Aphrodite:** Comnena repeats the often-heard accusation that the Muslims were dissolute drunkards.

[4] **Aphrodite . . . the golden image of Chobar:** Aphrodite, Astarte, Ashtaroth are three Greek mythological names for the same goddess of love. Chobar is the name given by the Saracens to the goddess of love.

[5] **The report . . . Godfrey:** Godfrey of Bouillon, Duke of Lorraine. Often praised as a model of chivalry, Godfrey argued with Alexius before accepting his terms for safe conduct to the Holy Land.

Kelt desired to surpass his fellows.) The upheaval that ensued as men *and* women took to the road was unprecedented within living memory. The simpler folk were in very truth led on by a desire to worship at Our Lord's tomb and visit the holy places, but the more villainous characters (in particular Bohemond and his like) had an ulterior purpose, for they hoped on their journey to seize the capital itself, looking upon its capture as a natural consequence of the expedition. Bohemond disturbed the morale of many nobler men because he still cherished his old grudge against the emperor. Peter, after his preaching campaign, was the first to cross the Lombardy Straits, with 80,000 infantry and 100,000 horsemen. He reached the capital via Hungary.[6] The Kelts, as one might guess, are in any case an exceptionally hotheaded race and passionate, but let them once find an inducement and they become irresistible.

The emperor knew what Peter had suffered before from the Turks and advised him to wait for the other counts to arrive, but he refused, confident in the number of his followers. He crossed the Sea of Marmora and pitched camp near a small place called Helenopolis. Later some Normans, 10,000 in all, joined him but detached themselves from the rest of the army and ravaged the outskirts of Nicaea, acting with horrible cruelty to the whole population; they cut in pieces some of the babies, impaled others on wooden spits and roasted them over a fire; old people were subjected to every kind of torture. The inhabitants of the city, when they learnt what was happening, threw open their gates and charged out against them. A fierce battle ensued, in which the Normans fought with such spirit that the Nicaeans had to retire inside their citadel. The enemy therefore returned to Helenopolis with all the booty. There an argument started between them and the rest (who had not gone on the raid) — the usual quarrel in such cases — for the latter were green with envy. That led to brawling, whereupon the daredevil Normans broke away for a second time and took Xerigordos by assault.

The sultan's reaction was to send Elkhanes with a strong force to deal with them. He arrived at Xerigordos and captured it; of the Normans some were put to the sword and others taken prisoner. At the same time Elkhanes made plans to deal with the remainder, still with Koukoupetros. He laid ambushes in suitable places, hoping that the enemy on their way to Nicaea would fall into the trap unawares and be killed. Knowing the Keltic love of money he also enlisted the services of two determined men who were to go to Peter's camp and there announce that the Normans, having seized Nicaea, were sharing out all the spoils of the city. This story had an amazing effect on Peter's men; they were thrown into confusion at the words 'share' and 'money'; without a moment's hesitation they set out on the Nicaea road in complete disorder, practically heedless of military discipline and the proper arrangement which should mark men going off to war. As I have said before, the Latin race at all times is unusually greedy for wealth, but when it plans to invade a country, neither reason nor force can restrain it. They set out helter-skelter, regardless of their individual companies. Near the Drakon they fell into the Turkish ambuscade and

---

[6] **He reached . . . Hungary:** Peter's crusaders arrived at Constantinople on August 1, 1096. They continued, attacking the city of Nicaea in September.

were miserably slaughtered. So great a multitude of Kelts and Normans died by the Ishmaelite sword that when they gathered the remains of the fallen, lying on every side, they heaped up, I will not say a mighty ridge or hill or peak, but a mountain of considerable height and depth and width, so huge was the mass of bones. Some men of the same race as the slaughtered barbarians later, when they were building a wall like those of a city, used the bones of the dead as pebbles to fill up the cracks. In a way the city became their tomb. To this very day it stands with its encircling wall built of mixed stones and bones.

When the killing was over, only Peter with a handful of men returned to Helenopolis. The Turks, wishing to capture him, again laid an ambush, but the emperor, who had heard of this and indeed of the terrible massacre, thought it would be an awful thing if Peter also became a prisoner. Constantine Euphorbenus Catacalon (already mentioned often in this history) was accordingly sent with powerful contingents in warships across the straits to help him. At his approach the Turks took to their heels. Without delay Catacalon picked up Peter and his companions (there were only a few) and brought them in safety to Alexius, who reminded Peter of his foolishness in the beginning and added that these great misfortunes had come upon him through not listening to his advice. With the usual Latin arrogance Peter disclaimed responsibility and blamed his men for them, because (said he) they had been disobedient and followed their own whims. He called them brigands and robbers, considered unworthy therefore by the Saviour to worship at His Holy Sepulchre. Some Latins, after the pattern of Bohemond and his cronies, because they had long coveted the Roman Empire and wished to acquire it for themselves, found in the preaching of Peter an excuse and caused this great upheaval by deceiving more innocent people. They sold their lands on the pretence that they were leaving to fight the Turks and liberate the Holy Sepulchre.

A certain Hugh,[7] brother of the King of France, with all the pride of a Nauatos in his noble birth and wealth and power, as he was about to leave his native country (ostensibly for a pilgrimage to the Holy Sepulchre) sent an absurd message to the emperor proposing that he (Hugh) should be given a magnificent reception: 'Know, Emperor, that I am the King of Kings, the greatest of all beneath the heavens. It is my will that you should meet me on my arrival and receive me with the pomp and ceremony due to my noble birth.' When this letter reached Alexius, John the son of Isaac the sebastocrator happened to be Duke of Dyrrachium, and Nicolas Mavrocatacalon, commander of the fleet, had anchored his ships at intervals round the harbour there. From this base he made frequent voyages of reconnaissance to prevent pirate ships sailing by unnoticed. To these two men the emperor now sent urgent instructions: the Duke was to keep watch by land and sea for Hugh's arrival and inform Alexius at once when he came; he was also to receive him with great pomp; the admiral was exhorted to keep a constant vigil—there must be no relaxation or negligence whatever.

---

[7] **A certain Hugh:** Hugh of Vermandois, brother of King Philip of France. Despite his pomposity, he carried little authority in France.

Hugh reached the coast of Lombardy safely and forthwith despatched envoys to the Duke of Dyrrachium. There were twenty-four of them in all, armed with breast-plates and greaves of gold and accompanied by Count William the Carpenter and Elias (who had deserted from the emperor at Thessalonica). They addressed the duke as follows: 'Be it known to you, Duke, that our Lord Hugh is almost here. He brings with him from Rome the golden standard of St. Peter.[8] Understand, more-over, that he is supreme commander of the Frankish army. See to it then that he is accorded a reception worthy of his rank and yourself prepare to meet him.' While the envoys were delivering this message, Hugh came down via Rome to Lombardy, as I have said, and set sail for Illyricum from Bari, but on the crossing he was caught by a tremendous storm. Most of his ships, with their rowers and marines, were lost. Only one ship, his own, was thrown up on the coast somewhere between Dyrra-chium and a place called Pales, and that was half-wrecked. Two coastguards on the lookout for his arrival found him, saved by a miracle. They called to him, 'The duke is anxiously waiting for your coming. He is very eager to see you.' At once he asked for a horse and one of them dismounted and gave him his own gladly. When the duke saw him, saved in this way, and when he had greeted him, he asked about the voyage and heard of the storm which had wrecked his ships. He encouraged Hugh with fine promises and entertained him at a magnificent banquet. After the feasting Hugh was allowed to rest, but he was not granted complete freedom. John the duke had immediately informed the emperor of the Frank's adventures and was now awaiting further instructions. Soon after receiving the news Alexius sent Bouto-umites to Epidamnos (which we have on numerous occasions called Dyrrachium) to escort Hugh, not by the direct route but on a detour through Philippopolis to the capital. He was afraid of the armed Keltic hordes coming on behind him. Hugh was welcomed with honour by the emperor, who soon persuaded him by generous largess and every proof of friendship to become his liege-man and take the custom-ary oath of the Latins.[9]

---

[8] "He brings . . . St. Peter.": That is, he took up the cross of the crusades.

[9] Hugh was welcomed . . . Latins: Alexius demanded, despite his show of cordiality, that visiting knights with armed supporters declare loyalty to the Byzantine state. This was intended to curb thievery or violence against the empire. Hugh was persuaded to do this, to the disgust of some other knights.

✍ BAHA AD-DIN
1145–1234

One of Saladin's principal biographers, Baha ad-Din Ibn Shaddad entered the sultan's service in 1188 as his military judge and remained in his household until the leader's death in 1193. His biography of Saladin, largely based on personal observation, is noted for its sincerity and conviction. Although Baha ad-Din's style may seem somewhat artificial to the modern reader, with frequent allusions to articles of the Islamic faith and to his own conversations with the sultan (in which he appears to play a major role), it is nevertheless much less contrived than that of some of his contemporaries. One of the pleasures of his narrative is the simple virtue he often discovers in Saladin, a necessarily complex historical figure. Along with the biography of Saladin by Imad al-Din (1125–1201),

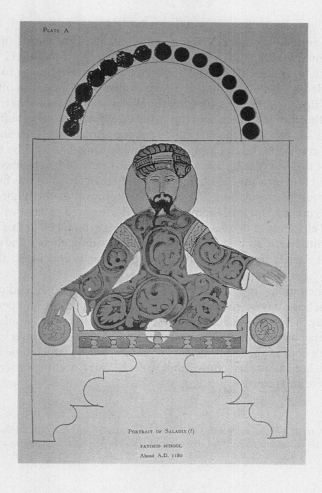

PLATE A

PORTRAIT OF SALADIN (?)

FATIMID SCHOOL.
About A.D. 1180

Portrait of Saladin, 1180
A miniature portrait of the great Muslim leader and general from a Persian literary text shows him at rest in a highly stylized pose. (British Library)

which gives the most complete account of the fall of Jerusalem, *A Life of Saladin* helped shape Islamic biography and effectively establish the image of Saladin as the great prince of the Muslim warriors.

The highly regarded opening of Baha ad-Din's work touches on Saladin's virtues as a leader. It is interesting to compare this passage, with its distinctively Muslim style, with Einhard's description of Charlemagne's noble qualities in *A Life of Charlemagne*.

FROM

∽ A Life of Saladin

Translated by Francesco Gabrieli
Translated into English by E. J. Costello

Saladin's Character

One of the authentic canonical traditions[1] contains these words of the Prophet: 'Islām rests on five pillars: the asseveration that there is no god but God; prayer; the paying of the legal tithe; the fast of ramadān; and the Pilgrimage to God's Sacred House (at Mecca).' Now Saladin was a man of firm faith, one who often had God's name on his lips. He drew his faith from the evidence duly studied in the company of the most authoritative scholars and the greatest lawyers, acquiring sufficient competence to take his part in a theological discussion should one arise in his presence, although of course he did not adopt the technical language used by the specialists. The result of this was that his faith was free of any taint of heterodoxy, and speculation never led him into any theological error or heresy. His faith was firm, within the bounds of healthy speculation, and it had the approval of the highest authorities. The imām Qutb ad-Din an-Nisaburi compiled for him a catechism containing all the essential elements of dogma, and he was so deeply attached to this that he taught it to all his little sons so that it should be impressed on their minds from earliest childhood. I myself have heard him instructing them and heard them repeat it before him.

As for the canonic prayers, he performed them assiduously, and used to pray in public; in fact one day he remarked that it was years since he had performed them any other way. When he was ill he would send for one imām and would force himself to rise and pray with him. [. . .] He never omitted the canonic prayer except when he was at death's door in the last three days of his life, during which time he was unconscious. If the hour of prayer came round while he was travelling he would dismount from his horse and pray.

---

[1] **One of the . . . traditions:** Meaning a Hadith, a saying from a collection of wisdom attributed to the prophet Muhammad or his immediate circle. It is a conventional way of beginning or augmenting a narrative.

As for the legal alms-giving, he died without leaving a large enough estate to be subject to it, for his extra-canonic gifts had consumed all his wealth. Of all that he had been master of, he left in his treasury when he died forty-seven Nasirite drachmas and a single piece of Tyrian gold. Nor did he leave houses, estates, gardens, villages, fields or any other material possession.

As for ramadān, there were ramadāns that he should have made up, because of illness at various times. The qadi al-Fadil[2] kept an exact record of these days, which Saladin began to make up when he was at Jerusalem in the year of his death, persevering in the fast for more than the prescribed month. He had still two ramadāns to make up for, that illness and involvement in the Holy War had kept him from observing; fasting did not suit his temperament, and God inspired him to fast in that year to make good his omissions. [. . .] The doctor was not in favour of it, but Saladin would not listen to him. 'Anything might happen,' he said, as if he had been inspired to pay his debt of conscience, and fasted long enough to discharge whatever he had owed to God.

As for the Pilgrimage, he had always wanted and intended to go, in particular in the year of his death. He made a decision to go then, and ordered the preparations to be made. We got together provisions for the journey and were ready to set out when lack of time and shortage of the money necessary to equip himself as became a man of his standing prevented his departure. He put it off until the next year, but God decreed otherwise, as often happens in the experience of men both great and small.

He loved to hear the noble Qur'ān recited; he examined the imām whose job it was and required him to be learned in Qur'anic studies and to have a perfect knowledge and understanding of the text. At night, when he was in his room, he would ask anyone who was awake to recite two, three or four suras of the Qur'ān while he listened. In public audiences he would ask whoever had been appointed to the office to recite twenty or so verses. Once he passed a child reciting the Qur'ān to its father, and the recitation pleased him so much that he called the child to him and assigned to him a part of his personal daily food and bequeathed to the child and his father part of an estate. He was humble and sensitive of heart, quick to weep, and used often to be moved to tears by hearing the Qur'ān recited. [. . .]

He venerated deeply the laws of the Faith, believed in the resurrection of the body, the reward of Paradise for the virtuous and of Hell for the sinners, and accepted all the teachings of Holy Scripture with an open heart. He hated philosophers, heretics, materialists and all the opponents of the Law. For this reason he commanded his son al-Malik az-Zahir, Prince of Aleppo, to punish a young man called as-Suhrawardi[3] who called himself an enemy of the Law and a heretic. His son had the man arrested for what he had heard of him and informed the Sultan, who commanded that he be put to death. So he was killed, and left hanging on the cross for several days. [. . .]

---

[2] **qadi al-Fadil:** Saladin's closest counselor.

[3] **to punish . . . as-Suhrawardi:** While Saladin was liberal in many respects, he did not shrink from extreme measures when he felt they were necessary.

His Justice

Abu Bakr the Truthful[4]—God look kindly on him—said that the Prophet—God bless and preserve him—said: 'The just prince is God's shadow on earth, and his mercy. [. . .] The just prince's day's work shall be held equal in value to that of sixty pious men, each devoted to worshipping God and working for the benefit of his own soul.' Saladin was just, benign, merciful, quick to help the weak against the strong. Every Monday and Thursday he would give an audience and administer justice in public session, in the presence of the lawyers, qadis and scholars. He listened to the litigants, for all had access to him, great and small, old, hale and sick. Whether on journeys or at home he was ready to perform this office, always ready to receive the supplications addressed to him and to remove the abuses brought to his notice. [. . .] I myself saw a man from Damascus, one Ibn Zuháir, come with a complaint against Saladin's nephew Taqi ad-Din. He sent requesting the latter to appear before a tribunal, and although Taqi ad-Din was one of the people he loved and respected most he did not allow personal feeling to affect his judgment. [. . .]

Examples of His Generosity

The Prophet said: 'When the generous man stumbles God takes his hand,' and many other *hadīth* speak of generosity. Saladin's was too widespread to be recorded here and too well known to need mention: [. . .] He used to give away whole provinces; when he conquered Amida, Qara Arslān's son asked him for it and he gave it to him. I myself saw a whole series of deputations appear before him in Jerusalem when he had decided to leave for Damascus and there was no gold left in the treasury to give these people. I was so insistent on his giving them something that he sold a village belonging to the public revenue and distributed to them what he was given for it without keeping a single *drachma.* He was as generous when he was poor as when he was rich, and his treasurers kept certain reserves concealed from him for fear that some financial emergency might arise. For they knew that the moment he heard of their existence he would spend them.

I heard Saladin say in the course of conversation, 'There might be a man here who looks on money as one looks on the dust in the road,' by which he seemed to be referring to himself. He would give even more than the postulant asked, but I have never heard him say 'We gave so-and-so so much.' He spread largesse with a generous hand, smiling as cheerfully on the recipient as if he had hardly given him anything. His gifts bestowed honour even more than money. The people knew what he was like and solicited his generosity at every moment, but I never heard him say 'I have already given over and over again; how much more must I give?' [. . .] As for enumerating his gifts or giving details, no one could hope to get them straight. Let me just say that I heard his chief administrator say, when we were discussing Saladin's bounty: 'We counted the horses he gave away on the plain of Acre and the

---

[4] **Abu Bakr the Truthful:** Another Hadith used as a conventional opening. Abu Bakr was the direct successor to Muhammad.

number reached 10,000,' and anyone with experience of his generosity would find even that a small number. O Lord, You inspired his generosity, You who are the most generous, therefore be generous to him in your mercy and grace, O most merciful of the merciful!

His Courage and Steadfastness

The Prophet is reported to have said: 'God loves courage, even in the killing of a serpent.' Saladin was indeed one of the most courageous of men; brave, gallant, firm, intrepid in any circumstance. I remember when he was encamped facing a great Frankish army which was continuously growing with the addition of re-inforcements and auxiliaries, and all the time his strength of will and tenacity of purpose increased. One evening more than seventy enemy ships arrived—I counted them myself—between the *'asr*[5] prayer and sunset, and their only effect seemed to be to incense him the more. When winter came he had disbanded his army and faced the enemy with only a small detachment of troops. I asked Baliān ibn Barzān how many there were—he was one of the great Frankish kings of Palestine, and had an audience of the Sultan on the day when peace was signed—and he replied through the interpreter: 'The Prince of Sidon (another of their kings and commanders) and I came from Tyre to join our army. When we came within sight of them we laid a wager on the size of the army. He guessed 500,000, I guessed 600,000.' 'And how many of them are dead?' 'Killed in battle, 100,000; died of sickness or drowned, God alone knows.' And of all that multitude only a small minority returned home. [. . .]

I never saw him find the enemy too numerous or too powerful. He would ponder and deliberate, exposing each aspect of the situation and taking the necessary steps to deal with it, without becoming angry, for he was never irate. On the day of the great battle on the plain of Acre the centre of the Muslim ranks was broken, drums and flags fell to the ground, but he stood firm with a handful of men until he was able to withdraw all his men to the hill and then lead them down into battle again, shaming them into turning and fighting, so that although there were almost 7,000 infantry and cavalry killed that day God gave the Muslims victory over their enemies. He stood firm before overwhelming hordes of enemy soldiers until it became clear to him that the Muslims were exhausted, and then he agreed to a truce at the enemy's request. The Franks were also exhausted and had suffered even heavier losses than we, but they could expect reinforcements, as we could not, so that peace was in our interest, as emerged clearly from the developments that followed. When he was ill, which happened often, or throughout the most appalling crises he stayed firmly in camp; the camp-fires of each side could be seen clearly by the other; we heard the sound of their bells[6] and they heard our call to prayer, until everything resolved itself in the pleasantest and most acceptable manner. [. . .]

---

[5] **the 'asr:** The first afternoon prayer.

[6] **their bells:** Or, more accurately, *nawaqis,* or clappers, calling the Christians to prayer.

His Endurance and Determination
to Win Merit in God's Eyes

Almighty God said: '. . . and then they fought for God's cause, and endured, and your Lord is forgiving and merciful.'[7] I saw him on the plain of Acre smitten with such a painful malady; boils covering him from waist to knees, so that he could not sit down, but lay on his side in his tent. He could not be served his food, since he could not sit, so he ordered that it should be divided among those present. In spite of all this he remained in his tent in the camp, close by the enemy, and when he had disposed his troops in left and right wings and a central block, in battle order, he (mounted his horse and) remained on horseback from the dawn to the midday prayer, and from early afternoon to sunset, inspecting his battalions notwithstanding the painful throbbing of his abscesses. When I marvelled at him he said: 'When I am on my horse all pain ceases until I dismount'—a gift of Providence! [. . .]

I was there [. . .] when he was brought the news of the death of Taqi ad-Din (his nephew). We were with a small detachment of men attacking the Franks below Ramla, and the enemy were at Yazūr, a short gallop away. [. . .] Then he took out the letter, read it, and wept pitifully enough to move to tears even those who did not know the reason for his weeping. Finally, in a voice thick with tears, he said: 'Taqi ad-Din is dead.' He began to weep again, as did everyone else. After a time I took a hold on myself and said: 'God forgive us for the state we are in: consider where you are and on what you are engaged, then leave off weeping and turn to other things.' The Sultan replied: 'Yes, God forgive us.' He repeated this several times, adding, 'Let no one know of this!' He called for rose-water and bathed his eyes, then sent for food and summoned the others to approach again. No one knew what had happened until the enemy withdrew to Jaffa and we to Natrūn, where our supplies were.

He was deeply attached to his infant sons and showed great affection for them. Nevertheless he endured separation and resigned himself to their being far away from him, putting up with the discomforts of a life of squalor when he could have behaved quite differently, in order to gain merit in God's eyes and dedicate himself to the Holy War against God's enemies. My God, he left all this in the hope that You would approve of him; approve of him therefore and have mercy on him!

Examples of His Humanity and Forgiveness

God has said: '. . . and those among men who pardon others, and God loves those who act rightly.'[8] He was indulgent to those who failed and slow to wrath. I was on duty at his side at Marj 'Uyūn before the Franks attacked Acre—may God make its reconquest easy!—It was his custom to ride on for as long as possible and then to dismount and have food served, which he would eat in company with his men before retiring to sleep in his private tent. When he awoke he would pray, and then withdraw, with me in attendance on him, to read a section of *hadīth* or Law: among other works that he read with me was an anthology of Suláim ar-Razi, including the four

---

[7] ". . . and then . . . merciful": Another *hadith*. Qur'an 16:111.
[8] ". . . and those . . . rightly": Another *hadith*. Qur'an 3:128.

sections of the Law. One day he dismounted as usual and food was served. He was about to rise when he was told that it was almost the hour of prayer, so he sat down again and said: 'Let us pray, and then let us go to bed.' He sat and talked wearily. Everyone except his personal servants had withdrawn, when suddenly there appeared an ancient mamlūk whom he held in high esteem, who presented him with a plea from someone fighting in the Holy War. 'I am tired now,' said the Sultan, 'present it again a little later,' but the man would not comply with this request. He held the plea up to the Sultan's august face, opening it so that he could read it. Saladin read the name written at the top, recognized it and said: 'A worthy man.' 'Well then,' said the other, 'Your Majesty will inscribe your *placet*.' 'But there is no inkwell here,' said the Sultan, for he was sitting at the opening of the tent, blocking the entrance, while the inkstand was at the back of the tent, which was a big one. But his interlocutor observed: 'There is the inkstand, at the back of the tent!' which was nothing if not an invitation to Saladin to bring that very inkwell out. The Sultan turned, saw the inkstand and said: 'By Allāh, you are right!' He leaned on his left elbow, stretched out his right hand, took the inkstand, signed the plea. . . . Then I said: 'God said to His prophet: "You are truly a magnanimous man,"[9] and it seems to me that Your Majesty shares this quality with him,' to which Saladin replied: 'It did not cost anything: we heard what he wanted, and we wanted to recompense him.' If a similar thing had happened to a private individual he would have lost his temper; and who would have been capable of replying to one of his subordinates in this way? This is the perfection of kindness and generosity, 'and God will not let such goodness go unrewarded.'[10]

His Unfailing Goodness

[. . .] Saladin was a pleasant companion, affectionate and shrewd, well versed in genealogy and the battles of the Arabs, their history and the genealogy of their horses, and the wonders and curiosities of the country; so much so that anyone who had the pleasure of his company would learn things that he could have heard from no one else. He put his companions at their ease and drew them out; he would ask one about one's health, how one looked after oneself, how one was eating and drinking and all about oneself. Conversation in his circle was unusually honest, though no one was spoken of except in praise; he liked to hear only good of people and had a very restrained tongue; in fact I have never heard him speak ill of someone with enjoyment. It was the same when he wrote; he never wrote a line of insult to a Muslim. He observed all his obligations faithfully. Every time an orphan was brought before him he invoked God's mercy on his dead parents, consoled the child and provided the father's bread. If there were a trustworthy old man in the orphan's family he would entrust the child to him, and if not he secured to the child an adequate portion of his father's salary and entrusted him to someone who would see to his upbringing. The sight of an old man moved him to pity, and he would give him alms. He kept these noble qualities all his life, until God raised him to the seat of His mercy and the home of His grace.

---

[9] **"You are truly a magnanimous man"**: Qur'ān 58:4.

[10] **'and God . . . unrewarded'**: Qur'an 9:121.

(ANONYMOUS)
THIRTEENTH CENTURY

The story of the life of Chingis Khan was transcribed from oral legends several decades after his death, probably during a great assembly of the ruling dynasty of the Mongols on the banks of the Keluren River. It was composed in the spoken Mongolian of the court, then transcribed into a Turkish script that was modified to fit the sounds of the Mongolian language. After a brief beginning that deals in legend, the narrative covers the period from the rule of Chingis Khan to the end of the reign of his son Ogodei Khan. Although access to the work was carefully guarded, some of it was narrated to the Persian scholar Rashid al-Din early in the fourteenth century. In the late fourteenth century, after the defeat of the Mongol empire, the work was translated into Chinese and entitled *The Secret History of the Mongols (Yuan Ch'ao Pi Shih)*.

Chingis Khan Fighting Chinese in Mountains, 1397
In a thundering fury, Chingis Khan and his Mongol warriors attack Chinese forces in a steep mountainous terrain. At its height, the Mongol empire stretched from China to eastern Europe. (The Art Archive / British Library)

Nothing resembling a complete version of the work, even in Chinese, was available in the West until the twentieth century. It was finally translated into English, in as complete a version as possible, by Frances W. Cleaves in the 1950s; the Cleaves translation was rendered into narrative verse by Paul Kahn in 1984. As Kahn notes in his translation, the original Mongolian text, an oral, alliterative narrative, fell somewhere between prose and poetry. The present title of the work, *The Origin of Chingis Khan,* was originally the first line of the Mongolian version.

The narrative of *The Origin of Chingis Khan* is plain-spoken and bold. His rise to power and his many conquests are captured in a rough, straightforward style. He is seen as a man fair in his judgment but holding the life and death of his enemies in his hands. Many passages in the narrative show Chingis Khan deciding how to proceed—whether against an enemy in the field, an old friend turned foe, or his own sons. In the first selection Chingis Khan is locked in battle with his Tatar enemies in 1202 during the Mongolian Wars. He must decide how to deal with not only the captured Tatars but also three of his warriors, Altan, Khuchar, and Daritai, who disobey orders, and his younger half brother Belgutei who unintentionally betrays the murderous plan of the Mongols to the enemy. In the second selection Jamugha, once Chingis Khan's best friend and now his sworn enemy, is captured. Chingis Khan generously offers Jamugha the opportunity to share his kingdom, but the old man chooses death instead, a decision the Mongol leader reluctantly honors. In the final selection, Chingis Khan determines who will succeed him among his four sons Jochi, Chagadai, Ogodei, and Tolui—for the moment, they too are captives of his awesome power of determination. Perhaps surprisingly, the words of his wife are important; women in the life of Chingis Khan exert a powerful influence over him.

This work is not for the fainthearted: Chingis Khan is arguably the most terrible warrior in history. But the narrative itself has an eerie appeal, moving from one situation to another with a highly intelligent leader undertaking a series of barbaric conquests.

FROM

ꙮ The Origin of Chingis Khan

Translated by Paul Kahn

[1. The War with the Tatars]

At the end of that winter
in the autumn of the Year of the Dog,
Chingis Khan assembled his army at Seventy Felt Cloaks
to go to war with the four Tatar clans.[1]

---

[1] **to go to war ... Tatar clans:** The Tatars were the neighbors and traditional enemies of the Mongols.

Before the battle began
Chingis Khan spoke with his soldiers and set down these rules:
"If we overcome their soldiers
no one will stop to gather their spoils.
When they're beaten and the fighting is over
10   then there'll be time for that.
We'll divide their possessions equally among us.
If we're forced to retreat by their charge
every man will ride back to the place where we started our attack.
Any man who doesn't return to his place for a counterattack will be killed."
Chingis Khan met the Tatar at Seventy Felt Cloaks
and made them retreat.
He surrounded them
and drove them back into their camp at Ulkhui Shilugeljid.
But as they destroyed the army of the four Tatar clans
20   Altan, Khuchar and Daritai ignored the orders Chingis had set down
and they stopped with their men to gather the spoils.
When Chingis Khan heard this, he said:
"They've broken their word,"
and he sent Jebe and Khubilai to punish them.
They took away from them everything they had gathered
and left them with nothing at all.
Having destroyed the Tatar army and taken their spoils,
a council was called to decide what to do with the captives.
Chingis Khan presided over the great council
30   in a tent set away from the rest of the camp.
They said to each other:
"Since the old days
the Tatar have fought our fathers and grandfathers.
Now to get our revenge for all the defeats,
to get satisfaction for the deaths of our grandfathers and fathers,
we'll kill every Tatar man taller than the linch-pin on the wheel of a cart.
We'll kill them until they're destroyed as a tribe.
The rest we'll make into slaves and disperse them among us."
That being what they decided to do,
40   they filed out of the tent.
As they came out the door of the council tent
the Tatar chief, Yeke Cheren, asked Belgutei:[2]
"What have you decided?"
Belgutei told him:
"We've decided to kill every man taller than the linch-pin on the wheel of a cart."
Hearing that, Yeke Cheren warned all the Tatar survivors
and they threw up a fort to fight us off.

---

[2] **Belgutei:** Chingis Khan's younger half brother.

We had to storm this fort
and many of our soldiers were killed.
50 Then after we'd finally forced the Tatar to surrender their fort
and were measuring them against the height of a linch-pin and executing them,
they saw there was no way to escape death.
They said to each other:
"Every man place a knife in his sleeve.
When the Mongol comes to kill you,
take that man as your pillow."[3]
And we lost many more of our soldiers.
When all of the Tatar men taller than the height of a linch-pin were dead,
Chingis Khan made this decree:
60 "Because Belgutei revealed the decision we'd reached in the great council
many of our soldiers have died.
From now on Belgutei won't be allowed to take part in such councils.
He'll be in charge outside the council tent until it is over.
Let him judge the fights in the camp
and the men accused of lying and theft.
After the council is over and we've all drunk the holy wine
only then will Belgutei and Daritai be allowed to enter the tent." [. . .]

[2. The Capture of Jamugha]

When Chingis Khan defeated the Naiman army
Jamugha[4] had been with the Naiman
and in the battle all of his people were taken away.
He had escaped with only five followers
and become a bandit in the Tangnu Mountains.
One day he and his companions were lucky enough to kill a great mountain sheep,
and as they sat around the fire roasting the mutton
Jamugha said to his companions:
"What nobleman's sons are so lucky today
10 to have such a feast of roast mutton to eat?"
But even as he said this
his five followers seized him,
and binding Jamugha they brought him to Chingis Khan.
Because he'd been captured this way, Jamugha said:
"Tell my anda,[5] the Khan,
'Black crows have captured a beautiful duck.
Peasants and slaves have laid hands on their lord.
My anda the Khan will see this and know what to do.

---

[3] take that man as your pillow: Expression meaning "kill him."
[4] Jamugha: Leader of the Jadaran clan and the closest peer to Chingis Khan. After a falling-out due to mutual suspicion, Jamugha has fought against Chingis Khan for the Kereyid, Naiman, and other groups.
[5] my anda: Blood brother or declared ally. This is a ceremonial, not a casual, tie.

Brown vultures have captured a mandarin duck.
20   Slaves and servants have conspired against their lord.
Surely my holy anda will know how to respond to this.'"
When he heard Jamugha's words Chingis Khan made a decree:
"How can we allow men who lay hands on their own lord to live?
Who could trust people like this?
Such people should be killed
along with all their descendants!"
He brought before Jamugha the men who had seized him,
these men who had betrayed their own lord,
and in their lord's presence their heads were cut off.
30   Then Chingis Khan said:
"Tell Jamugha this.
'Now we two are together.
Let's be allies.
Once we moved together like the two shafts of a cart,
but you thought about separating from me and you left.
Now that we're together again in one place
let's each be the one to remind the other of what he forgot;
let's each be the one to awaken the other's judgment whenever it sleeps.
Though you left me you were always my anda.
40   On the day when we met on the battlefield
the thought of trying to kill me brought pain to your heart.
Even though you went your own way
the day when we met as enemies in war
the thought that I would die brought you pain.
If you ask me, "When did this happen?"
I'll tell you it was when I met the Kereyid at the sands of Khalakhaljid.
You sent me a messenger
to inform me about what you'd said to our father, Ong Khan.
That was the service you did for me there.
50   Then again when we fought with the Naiman
you sent me a messenger telling me how you'd terrified the Naiman.
They were killed by your mouth;
your words made them die.
You told me their own fear would kill them.
That was the service you did for me there.'"
Jamugha answered him:
"Long ago when we were children in the Khorkhonagh Valley
I declared myself to be your anda.
Together we ate the food which is never digested
60   and spoke words to each other which are never forgotten,
and at night we shared one blanket to cover us both.
Then it was as if people came between us with knives,
slashing our legs and stabbing our sides,

and we were separated from each other.
I thought to myself,
'We've made solemn promises to each other'
and my face was so blackened by the winds of shame
that I couldn't bring myself to show my face,
this shameful windburned face,
70   before the warm face of my anda, the Khan.
I thought to myself,
'We've spoken words to each other that are never forgotten'
and my face was so red from the heat of my shame
that I went far away from you,
unable to show this burned, peeling face
before the clear face of my anda, whose memory is long.
And now my anda the Khan wants to favor me,
and says to me, 'Let's be allies.'
When I should have been his ally I deserted him.
80   Now, my anda, you've pacified every nation;
you've united every tribe in the world.
The Great Khan's throne has given itself to you.
Now that the world is ready for you
what good would I be as your ally?
I'd only invade your dreams in the dark night
and trouble your thoughts in the day.
I'd be like a louse on your collar,
like a thorn under your shirt.
I was brought up by my father's grandmothers.
90   I went wrong when I strove to be a better man than my anda.
In this life, of the two of us,
it's my name that's reached from sunrise to sunset;
it's Jamugha who's reached the end of his days.
My anda has a wise mother.
Having been born a great hero,
he has skillful young brothers.
Having many fine men by his side,
he's always been greater than I am.
As for me,
100 since I lost both my parents when I was young,
I have no younger brothers.
My wife is a babbling fool.
I can't trust the men at my side.
Because of all this
my anda, whose destiny is Heaven's will,
has surpassed me in everything.
My anda, if you want to favor me,
then let me die quickly and you'll be at peace with your heart.

When you have me killed, my anda,
110 see that it's done without shedding my blood.
Once I am dead and my bones have been buried high on a cliff
I will protect your seed and the seed of your seed.
I will become a prayer to protect you.
My very nature is different than yours.
I've been crushed by my anda's generosity and greatness.
Remember these words that I've spoken
and repeat them to each other morning and night.
Now let me die quickly."
Hearing this Chingis Khan spoke:
120 "Though my anda deserted me
and said many things against me,
I've never heard that he ever wanted me dead.
He's a man we all might learn from
but he's not willing to stay with us.
If I simply ordered him to be killed
there isn't a diviner in the world who could justify it.
If I harmed this man's life without good reason
it would bring a curse on us.
Jamugha is a noble and important man.
130 You can speak to him and give him this reason.
Tell him,
'One time in the past
because Jochi Darmala and Taichar stole a herd of horses from one another,
Anda Jamugha, you broke your oath
and attacked me at Seventy Marshes.
I was forced to run from you there,
retreating to the refuge of Jerene Narrows.
That time you put fear in my heart.
Now I say "Let's be allies" but you refuse me.
140 When I try to spare your life you won't allow it.'
So speak to Jamugha and tell him,
'Allow this man to kill you
according to your own wishes,
without shedding your blood.'"
And Chingis Khan made a decree, saying:
"Execute Jamugha without shedding his blood
and bury his bones with all due honor."
He had Jamugha killed and his bones properly buried. [. . .]

[3. Determining the Succession]
Once Chingis Khan heard that his hundred ambassadors led by Ukhuna
had been arrested and killed by the Moslems, he said:
"How did the Moslems break my golden reins?

I'll go to war with them to get satisfaction for this crime;
to win revenge for their killing of Ukhuna and my hundred ambassadors."
His Tatar wife, Yesui Khatun, spoke:
"The Khan will cross the high mountain passes,
cross over wide rivers,
waging a long war far from home.
10   Before he leaves has he thought about setting his people in order?
There is no eternity for all things born in this world.
When your body falls like an old tree
who will rule your people,
these fields of tangled grasses?
When your body crumbles like an old pillar
who will rule your people,
these great flocks of birds?
Which of your four heroic sons will you name?
What I've said everyone knows is true,
20   your sons, your commanders, all the common people,
even someone as low as myself.
You should decide now who it will be."
Chingis Khan replied:
"Even though she's only a woman,
what Yesui says is quite right.
My commanders, my sons, Bogorchu, Mukhali, and the others,
none of you have had the nerve to say this to me.
I've been forgetting it as if I won't follow my ancestors someday.
I've been sleeping like I won't someday be taken by death.
30   Jochi, you are my eldest son.
What do you say?"
But before Jochi could speak, Chagadai spoke up:
"When you tell Jochi to speak
do you offer him the succession?
How could we allow ourselves to be ruled
by this bastard son of a Merkid?"
Jochi rose up and grabbed Chagadai by the collar, saying:
"I've never been set apart from my brothers by my father the Khan.
What gives you the right to say that I'm different?
40   What makes you any better than I am?
Maybe your heart is harder than mine,
that's the only difference I can see.
If you can shoot an arrow farther than I can,
I'll cut off my thumb and throw it away.
If you can beat me at wrestling,
I'll lay still on the ground where I fall.
Let the word of our father the Khan decide."
The two brothers grasped each other by the collar.
Bogorchu pulling Jochi back by his arm

50 and Mukhali holding back Chagadai,
    when Koko Chos, always standing at Chagadai's side, spoke:
    "Chagadai, how can you say such things!
    Of all his sons, your father had highest hopes for you.
    In the time before you were born
    the stars in the heavens were spinning around.
    Everyone was fighting each other.
    Unable to sleep in their own beds,
    they constantly stole from each other.
    The crust of the earth was pitching back and forth.
60 All the nations were at war with each other.
    Unable to lie beneath their own blankets,
    they attacked each other every day.
    When your mother was stolen by the Merkid
    she didn't want it to happen.
    It happened when one nation came armed to fight with another.
    She didn't run away from her home.
    It happened when one nation attacked the other.
    She wasn't in love with another man.
    She was stolen by men who had come to kill other men.
70 The way you speak will harden the butter
    and sour the milk of your own mother's love for you.
    Weren't you born from the same warm womb as Jochi?
    Didn't you and Jochi spring from a single hot womb?
    If you insult the mother who gave you your life from her heart,
    if you cause her love for you to freeze up,
    even if you apologize to her later the damage is done.
    If you speak against the mother who brought you to life from her own belly
    even if you take back what you've said the damage is done.
    Your father the Khan has built this whole nation.
80 He tied his head to his saddle
    poured his own blood into great leather buckets,
    never closed his eyes nor put his ear to a pillow.
    His own sleeve was his pillow and the skirt of his jacket his bed.
    He quenched his thirst with his own spittle
    and ate the flesh between his own teeth for his supper,
    fighting on till the sweat of his forehead soaked through to the soles of his feet
    and the sweat of his feet reached up to his forehead.
    Your mother fought there beside him,
    working together,
90 she placed her headdress on top of her head
    and tucked in the ends of her skirt.
    She fastened her headdress firm on her head
    and pulled in the waist of her skirt.
    She raised up her children,

giving each of you half the food that passed by her mouth.
Out of her great compassion she even blocked her own mouth
and gave all her food to you,
leaving her own stomach empty.
She pulled you up by the shoulders and said to herself,
100 'How can I make these children as tall as great men?'
She stretched you up by the neck, saying,
'How can I make him a man?'
She cleaned out your diapers
and lifted your feet to teach you to walk.
She brought you up to the shoulders of men,
to the flanks of the horses.
Don't you think she wants to see you all find happiness?
Our holy Khatun raised you up
with a heart as bright as the Sun,
110 a heart as wide as the Sea."
Then Chingis Khan spoke:
"How can you say this about Jochi?
Jochi is my eldest son, isn't he?
Don't ever say that again."
Hearing this, Chagadai smiled and said:
"I won't say anything about whether Jochi is stronger than I am,
nor answer this boast that his ability is greater than mine.
I'll only say that the meat you kill with words
can't be carried home for your dinner.
120 You can't clothe yourself in the skin of an animal
you only say you've killed.
Jochi and I are your two eldest sons.
Together we'll give all our strength to our father the Khan.
We'll cut down the one of us who strays from his promise.
We'll cut the feet from the one of us who falls behind.
Brother Ogodei is honest.
Let's agree on Ogodei.
If Ogodei stays at the side of our father,
if our father instructs him in how to wear the hat of the Great Khan,
130 that will be fine."
Hearing this Chingis Khan spoke:
"Jochi, what do you say?
Speak up!"
and Jochi said:
"Chagadai speaks for me.
The two of us will give all our strength to him.
Let's agree on Ogodei."
So Chingis Khan made a decree:
"Why say you'll stay together?

140   Mother Earth is broad and her rivers and waters are numerous.
Make up your camps far apart
and each of you rule your own kingdom.
I'll see to it that you are separated.
Don't forget what you've pledged today, Jochi and Chagadai.
Don't do anything that will give men cause to insult you.
Don't give men cause to laugh at your promises.
In the past Altan and Khuchar gave their word like this
and they didn't keep it.
You know what happened to them.
150   I'll give you each a band of people,
people who had once been the possession of Altan and Khuchar.
Seeing these people you won't forget your promises.
Now Ogodei, what do you say?
Tell me!"
Ogodei answered:
"If my father the Khan commands me to speak
what can I say to him?
Can I answer him no and decline?
I will say that I'll do the best my ability will allow.
160   Long after this day
if my descendants are so empty of bravery
that wrapped up in sweet grass an ox won't even eat them,
wrapped up in rich fat a dog won't even smell them,
they'll be as likely to miss the broadside of an elk with their bow
as strike the head of a rat.
That's all I have to say for myself."
Chingis Khan made a decree:
"Then Ogodei agrees.
Now Tolui, what do you say?
170   Speak up!"
And Tolui said:
"I'll stay beside my elder brother.
I'll remind him of anything he forgets
and waken his judgment whenever it sleeps.
I'll stay by his side and help him press on.
I'll lend him all my strength in long wars and quick fights."
Chingis Khan approved of all this and made a decree:
"Each of my brothers Khasar, Alchidai, Odchigin, and Belgutei
have appointed one of their sons to govern after them.
180   Likewise I've appointed one of my sons to rule.
If all of you respect this decree then all will go well.
And if the descendants of Ogodei are so empty of bravery
that wrapped in sweet grass an ox won't even eat them,
wrapped in rich fat a dog won't even smell them,
then some other one of my descendants will be found to succeed him." [. . .]

Joan of Arc and Witnesses
c. 1429–1456

Joan of Arc found many unexpected partisans to help in her struggle against her enemies during her lifetime; her posthumous fortunes were equally dramatic. Her rehabilitation by the Catholic Church in 1456 came only twenty-five years after her execution. During a successful military campaign of King Charles VII of France against the Burgundians and the English, Joan's trial records were recovered at Rouen in 1449. In 1450, Charles, whose kingship Joan had supported, commanded the examination of Joan's condemnation:

> Whereas formerly Joan the Maid was taken and apprehended by our ancient enemies and adversaries the English, and brought to this town of Rouen, against whom they caused to be brought proceedings . . . to such point that, by means of that trial and great hatred which our enemies had against her, they brought about her death iniquitously and against right reason, very cruelly; therefore we would know the truth of the said trial proceedings and the manner accordingly to which it was carried on and proceeded with. . . . The information [gathered] by you in this matter, bring it close and sealed before us and the people of our council.

The trial records included the sworn testimony of witnesses and the interrogation of Joan herself; also preserved were eyewitness accounts of her execution. In addition to looking at these records, the king's councilor called seven of the original witnesses to testify again under the less intimidating conditions of French authority. These proceedings were handed over to the king and then to the ecclesiastical court, which, no longer dominated by English politics, reversed its earlier decision and

The Liberation of Orleans, fifteenth century
This manuscript illustration shows Joan of Arc triumphantly telling King Charles VII of her victory at Orleans. She is holding aloft a white banner on which is painted an image of God holding an orb; He is flanked by two angels. (The Art Archive / Centre Jeanne d'Arc, Orleans / Dagli Orti)

exonerated Joan of all blame. The town records of Rouen indicate that after Joan's vindication a municipal celebration was held on July 27, 1456, for which the town provided "ten pints and chopines of wine . . . twelve chickens, two rabbits, twelve pigeons, etc." Joan's mother, Isabelle Romee, may have attended; two years later she died peacefully in a small town nearby.

Some of the events of Joan's life remain a mystery. Joan herself stated many times that her life was driven by God's commandment and that her successes were guided by divine providence. Others have suggested quite another range of explanation for her behavior, from mental disease to witchcraft, but these views fall far short of either historical proof or true elucidation. Professional historians at least agree on the facts of her life; as her great twentieth-century French interpreter Régine Pernoud has pointed out: "The text of the two trials, and the public and private papers which confirm the conclusions from those texts, make Joan one of the best-documented people in history, one of those about whom we are really well-informed."

The following texts are translations from the original documents provided by Régine Pernoud in her monumental work *Joan of Arc: By Herself and Her Witnesses,* translated into English by Edward Hyams (1966). Pernoud's sources are cited before each selection.

FROM

∾ Joan of Arc by Herself and Her Witnesses

Translated by Régine Pernoud
Translated into English by Edward Hyams

From Joan's Testimony at Her Trial
of Condemnation, 1431

JOAN: When I was thirteen years old, I had a voice from God to help me govern my conduct. And the first time I was very fearful. And came this voice, about the hour of noon, in the summer-time, in my father's garden; I had not fasted on the eve preceding that day. I heard the voice on the right-hand side, towards the church; and rarely do I hear it without a brightness. This brightness comes from the same side as the voice is heard. It is usually a great light. When I came to France, often I heard this voice. . . . The voice was sent to me by God and, after I had thrice heard this voice, I knew that it was the voice of an angel. This voice has always guarded me well and I have always understood it clearly.

Question: What sort of help say you that this voice has brought you for the salvation of your soul?

JOAN: It has taught me to conduct myself well, to go habitually to church. It told me that I, Joan, should come into France. . . . This voice told me, twice or thrice a week, that I, Joan, must go away and that I must come to France and that my father must know nothing of my leaving. The voice told me that I should go to France and I could not bear to stay where I was. The voice told me that I should raise the siege laid to the city of Orleans. The voice told me also that I should make my way to Robert de Baudricourt in the fortress of Vaucouleurs, the Captain of that place, that he would give me people to go with me. And me, I answered it that I was a poor girl who knew not how to ride nor lead in war.

Question: Have you some other sign that these voices are good spirits?

JOAN: Saint Michael assured me of it before the voices came.

Question: How did you know it was Saint Michael?

JOAN: I knew it by his speech and by the language of the Angels, and I believe firmly that they were Angels. [. . .]

Question: Of these versions which you say you had, did you mention them to your parish priest or to any other churchman?

JOAN: No, but to Robert de Baudricourt only, and to my King. My voices did not oblige me to hold this secret, but I feared greatly to reveal it for fear of the Burgundians, lest they prevent my journey; and above all I greatly feared my father, that he might prevent me from making my journey.

Question: Did you think you were doing well in going away without the permission of your father and your mother, since we must honour our father and our mother?

JOAN: In all other things I did obey my father and my mother, save in this leaving them, but afterwards I wrote to them about it and they gave me their forgiveness.

Question: When you left your father and your mother, did you think you were committing a sin?

JOAN: Since God commanded it, it had to be. Since God commanded it, had I had a hundred fathers, and a hundred mothers, had I been a King's daughter, I should have departed.

Question: Did you ask your voices whether you could tell your father and your mother of your setting forth?

JOAN: As for my father and my mother, my voices would have been satisfied that I tell them, had it not been for the pain it would have caused them if I had announced my departure. As for me, I would not have told them anything in the world. The voices left it to me to tell my father and my mother, or to keep silent. . . . And them within so little of going out of their senses the time I left to go to the town of Vaucouleurs. [. . .]

Testimony of Jean de Metz, at the Trial of Rehabilitation, 1456

[. . .] When Joan the Maid came to the place and town of Vaucouleurs, in the diocese of Toul, I saw her, dressed in poor clothes, women's clothes, red; she lodged at the house of one Henri Le Royer of Vaucouleurs. I spoke to her, saying, 'My dear girl, what are you doing here? Must it not be that the King be cast out of the kingdom and we become English?' And the Maid answered me, 'I am come here to a King's Chamber' (i.e., to a royalist place) 'to talk with Robert de Baudricourt that he may be willing to lead me or send me to the King, but he pays no attention to me nor to my words. And yet, before we are in mid-Lent, I must be at the King's side, though I wear my feet to the knees. For indeed there is nobody in all the world, neither king nor duke, nor daughter of the King of Scotland, nor any other who can recover the kingdom for France. And there will be no help (for the kingdom) if not from me. Although I would rather have remained spinning at my mother's side, for it is not my condition, yet must I go and must I do this thing, for my Lord wills that I do so.' I asked her who was her Lord. And she told me that it was God. Whereupon I, Jean, who bear witness here, promised the Maid, putting my hand in hers in a gesture of good faith, that, God helping, I would lead her to the King. And I asked her when she wished to set out. She said to me, 'Rather today than tomorrow and tomorrow than later.' Then I asked her if she wanted to go in her own clothes. She replied that she would rather have men's clothes. Then I gave her clothes and hose of my servants that she might don them. And that done, the inhabitants of Vaucouleurs had men's clothes made for her and shoes and all things necessary to her and they delivered to her a horse which cost about sixteen francs. When she was dressed and had a horse, with a safe conduct from the lord Charles, Duke of Lorraine, the Maid went to speak with that lord and I went with her to the city of Toul. And when she returned to Vaucouleurs, [. . .] myself and Bertrand de Poulengy and two of his servants and Colet de Vienne, King's Messenger, and one Richard, an archer, we conducted the Maid to the King who was at Chinon, at my expense and Bertrand's. [. . .]

Leaving the town of Vaucouleurs, for fear of the English and the Burgundians who were everywhere across our road to the King, we sometimes moved at night. And we kept on the road for a period of eleven days, riding towards the town of Chinon; and making my way beside her, I asked her if she would do what she said, and the Maid always told us to have no fear and that she had a mandate to do this thing, for her brothers in Paradise told her what she had to do; that for four or five years already her brothers in Paradise and her Lord, to wit God, had been telling her that she must go to the war to recover the Kingdom of France. On our way, Bertrand and I, we lay down with her, and the Maid lay beside me, keeping on her doublet and hose; and I, I feared (respected) her so that I would never have dared make advances to her, and I say upon oath that neither did I have for her desire nor carnal motion. . . . On her way she would have liked to hear mass, for she often said to us, 'If we could hear mass, we should do well.' But, to my knowledge, we only heard mass twice upon our way. I had great confidence in the Maid's sayings, and I was fired by her sayings and with love for her, divine as I believe. I believe that she was sent by God; never did she swear, she liked to hear mass and she crossed herself with the sign of the Cross. And thus we took her to the King, to the place of Chinon, as secretly as we could.

Testimony of Simon Charles, President
of the Chamber of Accounts,
at the Trial of Rehabilitation, 1456

The year when Joan went to seek the King, I had been sent by him with an embassy to Venice and I returned about the month of March. At the time I heard Jean de Metz, who had escorted Joan, say that she was with the King. I know that, when Joan arrived in Chinon, there was deliberation in counsel to decide whether the King should hear her or not. To start with they sent to ask her why she was come and what she was asking for. She was unwilling to say anything without having spoken to the King, yet was she constrained by the King to say the reasons for her mission. She said that she had two (reasons) for which she had a mandate from the King of Heaven; one, to raise the siege of Orleans, the other to lead the King to Rheims for his sacring. Which being heard, some of the King's counsellors said that the King should on no account have faith in Joan (believe her), and the others that since she said that she was sent by God, and that she had something to say to the King, the King should at least hear her.

However, it was the King's will that she be first examined by clerks and churchmen, which was done. And at last, albeit with difficulties, it was decided that the King would listen to her. [. . .] After having heard her, the King appeared radiant. Thereafter, still not wishing to do anything without having the advice of churchmen, he sent Joan to Poitiers that she be examined by the clerks of the University of Poitiers. When he knew that she had been examined and it was reported to him that they had found nothing but what was good in her, the King had arms (armour) made for her and entrusted her to his men of war, and she was given command in the matter of the war. [. . .]

From Joan's Testimony
at Her Trial of Condemnation, 1431

JOAN: When I was at Tours or at Chinon I sent to seek a sword which was in the church of Sainte-Catherine of Fierbois, behind the altar, and it was found at once all covered with rust.

Question: How did you know that this sword was there?

JOAN: This sword was in the earth, all rusty, and there were upon it five crosses and I knew it by my voices and I had never seen the man who went to seek this sword. I wrote to the prelates of the place that if they please I should have the sword and they sent it to me. It was not very deep under ground behind the altar, as it seems to me, but I do not know exactly whether it was before or behind the altar. I think that I wrote at the time that it was behind the altar. After this sword had been found, the prelates of the place had it rubbed, and at once the rust fell from it without difficulty. There was an arms merchant of Tours who went to seek it, and the prelates of that place gave me a sheath, and those of Tours also, with them, had two sheaths made for me: one of red velvet and the other of cloth-of-gold, and I myself had another made of right strong leather. But when I was captured, it was not that sword which I had. I always wore that sword until I had withdrawn from Saint-Denis after the assault against Paris.

Question: Had you, when you went to Orleans, a standard, and of what colour?

JOAN: I had a standard whose field was sewn with fleurs-de-lys and there was the world figured and two angels at the sides and its colour was white, (and) of *boucassin* canvas. And there, it seems to me, were written the names of Jesus and of Mary, and they were embroidered in silk. . . .

Question: Which did you like the better, your standard or your sword?

JOAN: I liked better, even forty times, my standard than my sword.

Question: Who caused you to have this painting on the standard done?

JOAN: I have told you often enough that I did nothing but by God's commandment. I
   bore this standard when we went forward against the enemy to avoid killing
   anyone. I have never killed anyone. [. . .]

From the Journal of the Siege [of Orleans], 1429

The Friday following twenty-ninth of the same month, came into Orleans certain
news that the King was sending by the Sologne way victuals, powder, canon and
other equipments of war under the guidance of the Maid, who came from Our Lord
to re-victual and comfort the town and raise the siege—by which were those of
Orleans much comforted. And because it was said that the English would take pains
to prevent the victuals, it was ordered that all take up arms throughout the city.
Which was done.

   This day also arrived fifty foot soldiers equipped with *guisarmes* and other war
gear. They came from the country of Gatinais where they had been in garrison.

   This same day there was a great skirmish because the French wished to give
place and time for the victuals to enter, which were brought to them. [. . .] While this
skirmish was making, entered into the town the victuals and the artillery which the
Maid had brought as far as Checy. To meet her went out to that village the Bastard of
Orleans and other knights, esquires and men of war from Orleans and elsewhere,
right joyful at her coming, who all made her great reverence and handsome cheer
and so did she to them; and they concluded all together that she should not enter
into Orleans before nightfall, to avoid the tumult of the people. . . . At eight o'clock,
despite all the English who never attempted to prevent it, she entered, armed at all
points, riding upon a white horse; and she caused her standard to be borne before
her, which was likewise white, on which were two angels, holding each a fleur-de-lys
in their hands; and on the pennon was painted an annunciation (this is the image of
Our Lady having before her an angel giving her a lily). [. . .]

Testimony of Jean Pasquerel, from the Trial of Rehabilitation, 1456

I rose early and celebrated mass. And Joan went out against the fortress of the bridge
where was the Englishman Classidas. And the assault lasted there from the morning
until sunset. In this assault, after the morning meal, Joan, as she had predicted, was
struck by an arrow above the breast, and when she felt herself wounded she was afraid
and wept, and was consoled as she said. And some soldiers, seeing her so wounded,
wanted to apply a charm to her wound, but she would not have it, saying: 'I would
rather die than do a thing which I know to be a sin or against the will of God.' And
that she knew well that she must die one day, but knew not when or how or at what
time of the day. But if to her wound could be applied a remedy without sin, she was
very willing to be cured. And they put on to her wound olive oil and lard. And after
that had been applied, Joan made her confession to me, weeping and lamenting.

Testimony of the Bastard of Orleans, from the Trial of Rehabilitation, 1456

The assault lasted from the morning until eight o'clock of vespers, so that there was hardly hope of victory that day. So that I was going to break off and wanted the army to withdraw towards the city. Then the Maid came to me and required me to wait yet a while. She herself, at that time, mounted her horse and retired alone into a vineyard, some distance from the crowd of men. And in this vineyard she remained at prayer during one half of a quarter of an hour. Then she came back from that place, at once seized her standard in hand and placed herself on the parapet of the trench, and the moment she was there the English trembled and were terrified. And the king's soldiers regained courage and began to go up, charging against the boulevard without meeting the least resistance. [. . .]

From the Journal of the Siege [of Orleans], 1429

No sooner had the attack recommenced than the English lost all power to resist longer and thought to make their way from the boulevard into the Tourelles, but few among them could escape, for the four or five hundred soldiers they numbered were all killed or drowned, excepting some few whom were taken prisoners, and these not great lords. And thinking to save themselves the bridge broke under them, which was great disorder to the English forces and great pity for the valiant French, who for their ransom might have had much money *(grand finance)*.

Testimony of Jean Pasquerel, from the Trial of Rehabilitation, 1456

Joan returned to the charge, crying and saying: 'Classidas, Classidas, yield thee, yield thee to the King of Heaven; thou hast called me 'whore,' me; I take great pity on thy soul and thy people's!' Then Classidas, armed (as he was) from head to foot, fell into the river of Loire and was drowned. And Joan, moved by pity, began to weep much for the soul of Classidas and the others who were there drowned in great numbers. And that day all the English who were beyond the bridge were taken or killed.

Testimony of the Bastard of Orleans, 1456

The place where the King made a halt with his army was before the city of Troyes. Once there, he held council with the lords of his blood and the other captains of war to consider whether they should set themselves before the city and lay siege to it or take it, or if it would be better to march past it, going directly to Rheims and leaving this city of Troyes. The King's council was divided between diverse opinions and they wondered what was best to be done. Then the Maid came and entered into the council and spoke these words or nearly: 'Noble Dauphin, order that your people go and besiege the town of Troyes and stay no longer in council, for, in God's name, within three days I will take you into the city of Troyes by love or by force or by courage, and false Burgundy will stand amazed (*sera toute stupéfaite*).' Then the Maid crossed at once with the King's army and left the encampment beside the moats, and made admirable dispositions such as could not have done (better) two or three of the most famous and experienced soldiers. And she worked so well that night that on the morrow the bishop and the citizens of the city made their obedience to the King, shaking and trembling. And subsequently it was learned that from the moment when she advised the King not to go away from the city, the inhabitants lost heart and did nothing but seek refuge and flee into the churches. This city being reduced to royal obedience, the King went away to Rheims where he found total obedience and he was there consecrated and crowned. [. . .]

Testimony of Georges Chastellain, Northern Departmental Archives, 1430

The French, with their Maid, were beginning to retreat very slowly, as finding no advantage over their enemies but rather perils and damage. Wherefore the Burgundians [. . .] did great damage among the French. Of which the Maid, passing the nature of women, took all the brunt, and took great pains to save her company, remaining behind as captain and bravest of her troop. And there Fortune allowed that her glory at last come to an end and that she bear arms no longer; an archer, a rough man and a sour, full of spite because a woman of whom so much had been heard should have overthrown so many valiant men, dragged her to one side by her cloth-of-gold cloak and pulled her from her horse, throwing her flat on the ground; never could she find recourse or succour in her men, try though they might to remount her, but a man of arms called the Bastard of Wandomme, who arrived at the moment of her fall, pressed her so hard that she gave him her faith (word, parole), for he declared himself to be a nobleman. He, more joyful than if he had had a King in his hands, took her hastily to Margny, and there held her in his keeping until that day's work was done. [. . .]

Testimony of Jean Massieu, Usher, at the Trial of Rehabilitation, 1456

When she was abandoned by the Church I was still with her and with great devoutness she asked to have the cross. Hearing that, an Englishman who was present made a little cross of wood from the end of a stick, which he gave her and devoutly she received and kissed it, making pious lamentations to God our Redeemer who had suffered on the Cross, for our redemption, of which Cross she had sign and representation. And she put this cross into her bosom, between her flesh and her clothes, and furthermore asked humbly that I enable her to have the cross from the church so that she could have it continually before her eyes until death. And I so contrived that the parish clerk of Saint-Sauveur brought it to her. Which being brought, she embraced it long and closely and retained it until she was bound to the stake. Brother Isambart had gone with the parish clerk to fetch the cross. The pious woman asked, requested and begged me, as I was near her at her end, that I would go to the near-by church and fetch the cross to hold it raised right before her eyes until the threshold of death, that the cross which God hung upon be continually before her eyes in her lifetime. Being in the flames she ceased not until the end to proclaim and confess aloud the holy name of Jesus, imploring and invoking without cease the help of the saints in paradise. And what is more, in giving up the ghost and bowing her head, uttered the name of Jesus as a sign that she was fervent in the faith of God.

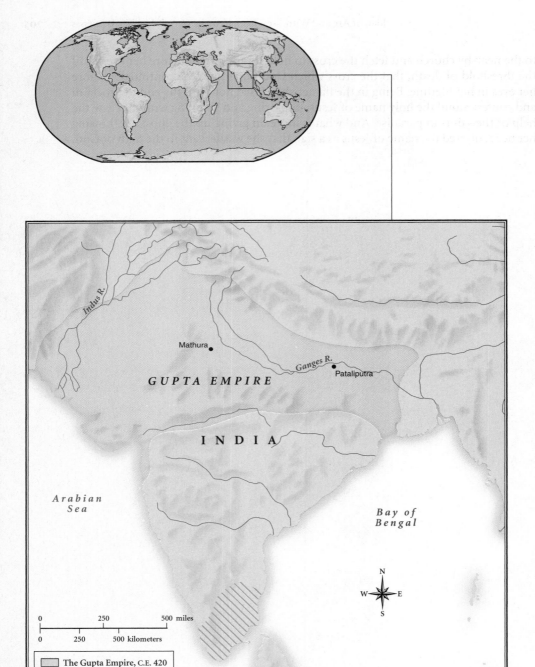

The Gupta Empire, c. 400

The Aryan Gupta dynasty was the first to unify India after the collapse of the Mauryan empire about five hundred years earlier. By 400, Aryan peoples had solidified their dominance over the Dravidian-speaking people of the south of India. While Sanskrit was the official language of the Gupta empire, the Dravidians produced a literary culture in the Tamil language.

INDIA
North and South

⮌ The culture of classical India continued to dominate Indian society during the Middle Period while India's political and ethnographic boundaries were being redefined. The **VEDAS**, works of sacred knowledge collected and written down in Sanskrit by the **ARYANS**, invaders from central Asia in the second millennium B.C.E., articulated the core beliefs of Indian society by 500 B.C.E. The Hindu religion was modified by its contact with two great rivals, **BUDDHISM** and **JAINISM**, beginning in the sixth century B.C.E. The Sanskrit epic *Ramayana,* written in the middle of the first millennium B.C.E., describes the steady movement of the Aryans into southern India and their encounter with the southern **DRAVIDIAN**-speaking cultures. The Aryans justified their expansion by claiming their racial and cultural superiority, calling it "righteous conquest according to the Sacred Law."

THE MAURYA EMPIRE AND ITS AFTERMATH

When the Macedonian ruler Alexander the Great ventured near the Indian border-lands in 330 B.C.E., his soldiers were turned back by a local warlord, Chandragupta, who proceeded to establish the Maurya empire in northern India in 323. A later Mauryan ruler, Ashoka the Great (r. 273–232), renounced warfare and dispatched Buddhist missionaries as far as Syria, Egypt, and Macedonia to promote the cause of understanding. The Maurya empire fell into decline after Ashoka's death and ended with the murder of its last king in 184 B.C.E.

In the five hundred years between the end of the **MAURYA EMPIRE** and the beginning of the **GUPTA DYNASTY**, several societies exchanged control of the northern region. The Indo-Greeks, introduced into northern India at the time of Alexander the Great, ruled along the northwestern border between 255 and 145 B.C.E. Later, the consolidation of the Chinese empire and the drying up of pasture land in northern China drove nomadic tribes from China toward the border of northern India. These tribes in turn pushed other peoples southward into India. The Northern Shakas (100 B.C.E.–73 C.E.) and the Kushanas (70–150 C.E.) were both displaced peoples from the central Asian steppes. The Kushana king Kanishka (r. 115–40 C.E.) gained control of much of northern India, became a patron of the Buddhist faith, and conducted successful land trade all the way to Rome. Elsewhere in India, the Satavahana kingdom (35 B.C.E.–210 C.E.) reached across the Indian peninsula, maintaining a sea trade with Southeast Asia. Meanwhile the northern Aryan culture, adopted in many kingdoms and principalities, continued to influence all peoples with whom it came into contact. The Dravidian-speaking kingdoms to the south were gradually absorbed by the Aryans, with the exception of three feuding kingdoms, the Chola along the west coast, the Chera in the region of Malabar, and the Pandya at the southern tip of the Indian peninsula. In these kingdoms, the Tamil language, a branch of the Dravidian languages, was spoken.

IN THE SOUTH: TAMIL SOCIETY

The origins of the Dravidians are still debated. Separate theories suggest that they were either an ancient people from a stone age society or considerably later Mediterranean migrants. Their language is completely distinct from all the Indo-European languages, including Sanskrit. By 150 C.E. the Tamil kingdoms at the southern tip of India assumed the leading role among the Dravidians.

The Tamil, though great warriors, were not barbarians. They took writing seriously, working in carefully prescribed poetic forms. At three conferences held in the city of Madurai between 100 and 250 C.E. the Tamil poets compiled a formal description of their work, the TOLKAPPIYAM, which defined the types of poetry they wrote and its appropriate subject matter, including the regions of the land, the flowers and vegetation appropriate to those regions, and so on. At these same meetings, the Tamil compiled eight anthologies of poetry—three puram, collections of poetry usually written in a man's voice on the topics of worldly experience and war, and five AKAM, works containing poems usually written in a woman's voice that refer to inner experience and emphasize love. The poems of love and war written by the Tamil between the first and third centuries remain part of India's cultural heritage.

THE RISE AND FALL OF THE GUPTAS

The Gupta dynasty began in the former territory of the Maurya empire in northeastern India in the early fourth century. Chandragupta I (r. 320–335 C.E.), taking his name from the first Mauryan ruler, established the Gupta kingdom. His son Samudragupta (r. 335–376 C.E.) led an expedition south, enhancing his claim as ruler of India. Samudragupta's son, Chandragupta II (r. 376–415 C.E.), was the greatest of the Gupta kings, extending the kingdom across the entire north and establishing a strong central authority. He established an effective administrative bureaucracy and initiated important public works projects. Trade routes passing through the two capital cities, Ujjayini to the west and the seaport city of Tamralipti to the east, provided access to Rome and the Mediterranean in one direction and China and Southeast Asia in the other. Caravans and pilgrimages increased between India and China, enabling Buddhism to spread rapidly from India to the rest of Asia. The increasingly wealthy Gupta capitals became rich depositories of culture and the arts.

The Guptas ruled with unaccustomed liberality. They allowed local kings to keep their titles as long as they declared obedience to the empire. This feudal form of military organization did not hold up against the invasion of the Huns from northern China during the fifth century. In 480 C.E. the Huns overran northern India, in 500 C.E. western India as well. Under their pressure the Gupta dynasty collapsed in 550 C.E. For six hundred years following the end of the Guptas, India remained decentralized. Small kingdoms often reflected no more than the local economy and tribal history of their regions.

GUPTA LITERARY CULTURE

Sanskrit was the basis of Gupta literary culture. The language provided the means for academic studies, not only in grammar and linguistics but also in philosophy, law, religion, the humanities, and scientific and mathematical writing. The major literary works at the time of the Guptas were courtly epics, adaptations of heroic epics written in poetic stanzas; dramas, written in mixed prose and poetry; short lyric poems governed by formal rules of rhetoric and grammar; and longer poems, primarily devoted to instruction and satire.

The most important Gupta author was Kalidasa (fl. early fifth century C.E.), a poet and playwright and the elder statesman of Indian literature. In his masterwork, the drama *Shakuntala,* Kalidasa draws from a tale in the ancient epic *Mahabharata,* working in the elaborate tradition of Sanskrit drama with its emphasis on emotional development achieved through a series of interlocking scenes. While the subject of *Shakuntala,* the recognition of the king's child as his own and the testing of the constancy in love between the king and his young bride, is relatively uncomplicated, the separation of King Dusyanta and Shakuntala during the play provides emotional intensity, and the scenes of estrangement, danger, and hardship add suspense to the drama. Nature figures deeply in the outcome, on both a realistic and symbolic level. The play is not "romantic" in the western sense, but focuses on the

Palace Scene, fourth to sixth century
Sometimes called the golden age of Hindu history, the Gupta dynasty was noted for its culture and cosmopolitanism. In this palace scene depicted on an exterior fresco in Madhya Pradesh, various castes and ethnic groups are shown. (SEF/Art Resource, NY)

conflict within each character between his or her emotional attachments and sense of obligation to social norms. The commonplace comparison of Kalidasa to Shakespeare is based on the relationship each master playwright establishes with his audience, creating several levels of recognition and understanding at the same time, and the ability each has to draw on a wide range of emotions and treat matters of immediate concern to his society.

India: The Gupta Dynasty and the Reign of Chandragupta II (376–415 C.E.)

The Gupta dynasty (320–550), is regarded as the golden age of classical Indian civilization. Under King Chandragupta II (376–415), known as Vikramaditya ("The Sun of Power"), the Gupta empire reached its zenith, unifying most of central and northern India for the first time since the end of the Mauryan period in the second century B.C.E. Politically, the Gupta period was marked by religious tolerance, peace, and stability. Representatives of all three major Indian religions — Hinduism, Jainism, and Buddhism — were welcomed at the court. With the Guptas' major enemies subdued, the states of northern India were brought into confederation, promoting travel, trade, and scholarship. For this reason the Gupta period was also a time of cultural renaissance, when literature, the visual arts, sculpture, architecture, and the sciences flourished.

In addition to the works of Kalidasa, the magnificent court poet believed to have lived during the reign of Chandragupta II, the Gupta period saw the publication of Vishnu Sharma's *Pachatantra,* a collection of fables similar to those of Aesop, and the *Kamasutra* of Vatsayana, the classic work on the art of lovemaking. The lavishly painted Ajinta caves, a series of Buddhist temples carved out of rock, date from the second half of the fifth century. Another cave, the Hindu rock temple at Elephanta, honors the lord Shiva with a massive three-headed statue. Also in the fifth century, mathematicians developed the numerical system later known as Arabic numerals and the decimal system based on the number ten. And the astronomer Aryabatta calculated Pi as 3.1416 and the length of the solar year as 365.358 days.

Vikrama and Urvasi, fifth to sixth century C.E. *A Gupta dynasty relief sculpture of the legendary first century Indian King Vikrama and the Hindu goddess Urvasi. (Borromeo / Art Resource, NY)*

The achievements of the Gupta civilization were perhaps best described by the Chinese Buddhist monk Faxian, who kept a journal of his travels to India during the reign of Chandragupta II. "Indian cities are prosperous," he wrote, "and stretch far and wide. There are many guest houses for tourists. There are hospitals providing free medical services for the poor. The viharas and temples are majestic. People are free to choose their occupations. There are no restrictions on the movement of the people. Government officers and soldiers are paid their salaries regularly. People are not addicted to drinks. They shun violence. The administration provided by the Gupta rulers is fair and just."

www For more information about the culture and context of India in the Middle Period, see *World Literature Online* at bedfordstmartins.com/worldlit.

THE TAMIL ANTHOLOGIES
C. 100–250

SAN-skrit
SUNG-gum

EH-ree-un

druh-VID-ee-un

TOLE-kah-pee-yum

Although Tamil court poetry is one of the outstanding achievements of Indian literature, its physical and intellectual separation from the dominant **Sanskrit** culture of northern India has kept it from receiving the attention it deserves. Eight Tamil *sangams* or poetry anthologies, containing more than 2,300 poems ascribed to over 400 authors, comprise the literary expression of southern India during its busiest period of economic expansion and maritime trade from the first to third centuries C.E. The poems also mark the end of an era for the Tamil people, a feudal society anticipating the invasion of the much larger **Aryan** population to the north. The predicament the society faced of material abundance bearing within it the seeds of its destruction may partly explain the peculiar dichotomy of the poems, some of which praise fertility and romantic adventure in a woman's voice and others that celebrate the warrior's code of ethics and mourn the fall of kings from a man's perspective.

The Uniqueness of the Tamil. The Aryans of the north, bent on justifying their invasion of the south, described the southern **Dravidian**-speaking tribes as barbarians. It is true that the three principal Tamil kingdoms, Chola, Chera, and Pandya, had persisted for many years in an almost constant state of warfare among themselves as the Aryans gathered around them. The social contrast between the warriors of the Tamil lyrics and their refined counterparts of the Sanskrit epics is reminiscent of that between the early Germanic tribesmen and their Roman opponents of approximately the same period. Yet in the case of the Tamil, the so-called barbarians had developed an extremely sophisticated poetry relying on the conventions of an educated society of poets, both men and women. The same cannot be said for the Germanic invaders of late imperial Rome.

The Tamil branch of the Dravidian language, a non-Indo-European language completely unrelated to Sanskrit, remained unadulterated through several centuries of contact before beginning to acquire some Sanskrit vocabulary and imitate Sanskrit grammatical inflections. For this and other reasons, most scholars today agree that until the third century C.E., Tamil culture was essentially distinct from Aryan culture. No matter how great a sense of foreboding the Tamil people may have had about the Aryans, the two societies had not yet collided at the time of the writing of the Tamil anthologies; the war the poems speak of takes place exclusively between competing Tamil kings.

The Character of Tamil Poetry. According to legend, Tamil poets held three great "academies" or literary assemblies in and around the city of Madurai between 100 and 250 C.E. The first anthologies to represent the Tamil tradition are believed to have been written at the third assembly. At the same time a formal grammar, called ***Tolkappiyam*** (Ancient Compo-

**Nymphs,
second century**
*This fresco, painted
after the height of the
Tamil period, is from
Sri Lanka (formerly
Ceylon), a stronghold
of Dravidian, Tamil
culture. (The Art
Archive / Dagli Orti)*

sition), was created to classify the rhetorical features of Tamil poetry. The first prominent feature of the poetry lay in its metrical pattern and rhyme scheme. The meter consisted of a four-foot line in which two metrical units make up a foot. The rhyme scheme developed over time: The first syllables of each line in a two-line couplet were often rhymed, while first syllables of each line in a longer stanza were often ALLITERATED (begun with the same consonant to produce a similar sound). The effect was a highly sonorous, chanting rhythm that suited the energy of the poetry.

The imagery of Tamil poetry was carefully fitted to the natural landscape of south India. The mountains and valleys, deserts and plains made up a beautiful and diverse natural setting hospitable to fruits and flowers, fit for agriculture and grazing, and productive beyond the immediate needs of the inhabitants. The south also had its seacoast, which provided access to the Persian Gulf, the Red Sea, and the Mediterranean Sea. The poetry of the Tamil made direct use of these surroundings. They were associated with five specific regions: the hills, the dry land, the jungle and woodlands, the cultivated plains, and the coast. Their subject matter matched the features of the land, so that the parting of lovers or the laying waste of enemies took place in the dry lands while the hillsides provided the setting for the trysting of lovers or the raiding of cattle. Similarly, natural events such as monsoon rains and flowers like the jasmine and *kurinci* (a wild mountain bloom) represented emotions ranging from unrequited longing to satisfied passion. The familiar animals of

www For a quiz on *The Tamil Anthologies,* see *World Literature Online* at bedfordstmartins .com/worldlit.

The love poems take one small event, one image that seems trivial, and with that material describe an intense human experience in a sudden and wonderful way, creating in a few words a richness of suggestion and feeling that resonates in the reader's mind long afterward. The war poems contrast the demands of society with human needs, pointing out a dilemma that is the source of most tragedy. As the poems take up these issues — how a person may experience, how he may exist with the unfeeling conventions and demands of society — they offer no simple answers. What they do is to consider them with a complexity and profundity that seems inexhaustible, a continuous source of insight and pleasure.

— GEORGE L. HART III, scholar, translator, 1979

South India, including the tiger, the elephant, and the cobra, also figured both realistically and symbolically in the poems of the Tamil.

The Subject of the Poetry.   The poetry that flourished for a few centuries was vigorous, ambitious, and outspoken, like the well-trained poets who composed it. It was divided into two main types, *akam* ("inner" poems, chiefly concerning passion and the personal emotions) and *puram* ("outer" poems, mostly having to do with warfare and the state of society). Dramatic types such as the heroine and her female companions, the male lover, and the romantic soldier dominated the *akam* poetry, often speaking forcefully in their own voices. The more formal *puram* poems were less expressions of the individual ego than they were representative songs of the entire community, a people often under siege and therefore united in self-defense. Sometimes the two modes of writing were combined, as in the poems in which mothers pray that their dead sons have performed valiantly on the battlefield so that their memories would be praised.

Five of the eight Tamil anthologies consisted of *akam* while the other three contained *puram*. The love encounters in the *akam* poems usually are bounded by the house, the village, the city walls, or the protected hillside on which the lovers lie. Some *akam* poems were written from the woman's point of view; some *akam* poets actually were women. In contrast, the *puram* poems generally reflected a man's world, especially with regard to his freedom of movement and his stereotypic detachment from emotion. The tone of *puram* poetry was often elevated, as when kings were the objects of description. Women could write *puram* poetry as well, as in neither form of verse is "a man's point of view" or "a woman's point of view" revealed through the gender of the poet himself or herself. Despite the different roles assumed by men and women in the poetry, the poets themselves were regarded as equals, whether male or female, and they treated their subject matter virtually identically.

The Poems of Love.   Four of the *akam* poems included here are short lyrics from the *Kuruntokai* anthology, the most extensive collection of love poetry. They conventionally begin with the titles "What She Said" or "What He Said." These poems reflect the Tamil view of love in which the man dominates and the woman, though passionate, must await his initiative. Different scenarios are played out in these poems: a woman complains that she has been "taken" by a man, whom she calls a thief; a woman reacts to nature's harshness by longing to lie on her lover's breast; a man desires his lover but fears she is not ready to receive him; and a woman has sent her lover away only to miss him. All focus on the drama of the moment and are tied in with natural locations and images.

The Poems of War.   Connected as it is with conduct on a grand scale, *puram* poetry often reveals a deeper understanding of character and event than *akam*. "A King's Double Nature" from the *Patirruppattu* anthology is both a courtier's advice to other bards and his own expression of praise for his patron. This king is fierce, certainly, but he is also beneficent. After describing the region's bountiful countryside and the high sea cliffs manned by the king's warriors, the poet again regards the king, this time as "tender among tender women." One might say that the king's "feminine side" is made as important as his status as a warrior. In another poem, contained in yet another anthology, the *Purananuru,* a beleaguered king is viewed as a complex personality. "A King's Last Words" begins with his bitter reflection that even a stillborn child is stabbed with a sword so that he can receive a warrior's funeral; how then can this king stand for his humiliation at the hands of his captors? It is cause, surely, for suicide. The harshness of the warrior ethic is again shown in the poem "Mothers," in which a mother depicts her son as a fierce animal who once slept in her womb but now joins others on the battlefield. "A Chariot Wheel," written by the well-known woman poet Auvaiyar, praises tribal warriors as the deliberately crafted products of not only their mothers, but also the whole society.

Other *puram* poetry constitutes an even higher level of literary achievement. In "His Hill," a lament on the death of the noted King Pari, the poet Kapilar describes the double nature of the king, as in the first of the *puram* selections. This king, he says, will not be defeated by a gigantic army with many war elephants and charioteers, but he can be conquered by a procession of musicians and female dancers. "A Woman and Her Dying Warrior" dramatizes a sorrowful scene in which a woman assists her mortally wounded husband up a hill to some shade. "A Leaf in Love and War" contrasts a leaf used to adorn women's intimate apparel with the leaf worn into battle as an emblem by a soldier, now soaked with his life's blood. The almost unbearable poem "Mothers" tells the story of a mother who finds the mutilated body of her son on a battlefield, rejoicing more than she did on the day she gave him birth that he has died a hero's death.

The range of these poems is as startling as their depth is compelling. Not only are the love poems capable of treating many moods, situations, and attitudes with dramatic insight and the poems of war able to convey with penetrating awareness the agonies and desperate hopes of a warrior society, but many of the poems are able to combine the themes of love and war as well. Two of the most affecting of these are "A Woman and Her Dying Warrior" and "A Leaf in Love and War," in which image and reflection, a woman's part and warrior's voice come together with a combined force of tragedy and pathos we would expect only from a work of drama. In a nation intimate with the violence of war, human affirmation takes on the role of a heroic encounter with fate.

The End of Tamil Culture.   Six of the eight anthologies were almost certainly written in the third century, as the great era of the Tamil poets was coming to a close. For the next several hundred years, as the northern Aryan culture exerted greater influence, Tamil poetry took on a religious, didactic tone. By the sixth century, epics glorifying earlier Tamil culture began to appear. Though one such work, *Silappadigaram* ("The Jeweled Anklet"), presenting a domestic tragedy against the backdrop of a king's court, contains poetry reminiscent of the Tamil lyric, it lacks coherence

SIH-lah-puh-dee-gah-rum

ruh-MAH-yuh-num
KAHM-bahn

and basically reflects the decline of Tamil culture. The last Tamil poem to achieve recognition was a version of the Sanskrit ***Ramayanam*** completed in the ninth century by the poet **Kamban**. The great work of Tamil literary culture remains the collection of poems of love and war written from the first to the third century.

■ CONNECTIONS

In the Tradition: **Courtly Love Lyrics, p. 628.** While many of the poems in both the *akam* and *puram* traditions are comparable to the poetry of chivalry of other courtly societies, the particular combination of interests reflected in the Tamil poems is most closely mirrored by the courtly love lyrics of Spain and the South of France. What would account for these similarities?

Beowulf, **p. 482.** Some of the depictions of warrior culture in the lyric poetry of early Tamil society are reminiscent of Anglo-Saxon verse, including *Beowulf.* This is especially true in the portrayal of the wisdom of kings and the tragic determination of warrior heroes in both. Why might the Tamil and Anglo-Saxon expressions of war resemble each other?

■ FURTHER RESEARCH

Translations
Hart, George L. III. *Poets of the Tamil Anthologies: Ancient Poems of Love and War.* 1985.
Ramanujan, A. K. *Love Poems from a Classical Tamil Anthology.* 1967.
———. *Poems of Love and War: From the Eight Anthologies and Ten Long Poems of Classical Tamil.* 1985.

Cultural History
Basham, A. L. *The Wonder that Was India.* 1959.

Literary Criticism
Hart, George L. III. *The Poems of Ancient Tamil: Their Milieu and Their Sanskrit Counterparts.* 1975.
Kailasapathy, K. *Tamil Heroic Poetry.* 1969.
Zvelebil, Kamil. *The Smile of Murugan: On Tamil Literature of South India.* 1973.

■ PRONUNCIATION

akam: ah-KAHM
Aryan: EH-ree-un
Dravidian: druh-VID-ee-un
Kamban: KAHM-bahn
kurinci: KOO-rin-chee
puram: POO-rum
Ramayanam: ruh-MAH-yuh-num
sangam: SUNG-gum
Sanskrit: SAN-skrit
Silappadigaram: SIH-luh-puh-dee-gah-rum
Tolkappiyam: TOLE-kah-pee-yum

FROM

❧ The Tamil Anthologies

Translated by A. K. Ramanujan

FROM

KURUNTOKAI

25: WHAT SHE SAID

Only the thief was there, no one else.
And if he should lie, what can I do?

> There was only
> a thin-legged heron standing
> on legs yellow as millet stems
> and looking
>   for lampreys
> in the running water
>
> when he took me.

Kapilar

The Tamil Anthologies. The poetry of the Tamil people was first codified in the *Tolkappiyam*, which serves even today as an introduction to both the poetic forms themselves and the elaborate system of classification by which mood and subject matter are related to location in the poems. It is still unclear whether the *Tolkappiyam* was created to direct the writing of the lyrics or written after the fact to describe the practices of Tamil poets. It is probably safe to say that this elaborate rhetorical work, rich in ingenuity, was both prescriptive *and* descriptive. At the very least, it negates the idea that Tamil poetry consists of spontaneous creations composed without regard to formal rhetorical principles. Still, readers do not need to know the formal rules of their composition to enjoy these poems. Often it is enough to "follow the image" — to trace the figures of speech used in a poem and trust them to lead to its meaning.

Translations of the Tamil lyrics into English were first brilliantly rendered by A. K. Ramanujan in *The Interior Landscape* (1967) and *Poems of Love and War* (1985). One of Ramanujan's students, George L. Hart III, translated more poems in *Poets of the Tamil Anthologies* (1979). Ramanujan's translations are used here for their superior poetic quality, but Hart's practice of arranging the poems in the sequence in which they appear in the original anthologies is followed.

68: What She Said

The bare root of the bean is pink
like the leg of a jungle hen,
and herds of deer attack its overripe pods.

For the harshness
of this season of morning dew
there is no cure

but the breast of my man.

Allūr Nanmullai

131: What He Said

Her arms have the beauty
of a gently moving bamboo.
Her large eyes are full of peace.
She is far away,
her place is not easy to reach.

My heart is frantic
with haste,

a plowman with a single plow
on land all wet
10   and ready for seed.

Ōrērulavanār

325: What She Said

When he said,
                "I'll go! I'll go!"
I thought he was playing
at going, as usual,
and said,
                "Go then,
leave me alone!"

Where is he now,
protective as a father,
O where?

The place between my breasts
10   is filled with tears,

a pool where
black-legged white heron
feed on fish.

Naṉṉākaiyār

FROM

PATIRRUPPATTU

60: A KING'S DOUBLE NATURE:

a guide to singers

His armies love massacre,
he loves war,
yet gifts
flow from him ceaselessly.

Come, dear singers,
let's go and see him in Naravu[1]

where, on trees
no ax can fell,
fruits ripen, unharmed
by swarms of bees,
egg-shaped, ready
for the weary traveler
in fields of steady, unfailing harvests;

where warriors with bows
that never tire of arrows
shiver
but stand austere
in the sea winds
mixed with the lit cloud
and the spray of seafoam.

There he is,
in the town of Naravu,
tender among tender women.

Kākkaipāṭiṇiyār Nacceḷḷaiyār

10

20

---

[1] **Naravu:** A town in the kingdom of Chera, on the southern coast of India. A description of orchards and a fortified seacoast follows.

FROM

PUṟANĀṈŪṞU

74: A King's Last Words,

in jail, before he takes his life

> If a child of my clan should die,
> if it is born dead,
> a mere gob of flesh
> not yet human,
>
> they will put it to the sword,
> to give the thing
> a warrior's death.
>
> Will such kings
> bring a son into this world
> to be kept now
> like a dog at the end of a chain,
>
> who must beg,
> because of a fire in the belly,
> for a drop of water,
>
> and lap up a beggar's drink
> brought by jailers,
> friends who are not friends?

Cēramāṉ Kaṇaikkāl Irumpoṟai

86: Mothers

> You stand against the pillar
> of my hut and ask:
>   Where is your son?
>
> I don't really know.
> This womb was once
> a lair
> for that tiger.
>
> You can see him now
> only on battlefields.

Kāvaṟpeṇṭu

87: A Chariot Wheel

Enemies,
take care
when you enter
the field of battle
and face
our warrior

who is like a chariot wheel
made thoughtfully over a month
by a carpenter
10   who tosses off eight chariots
in a day.

Auvaiyār

109: His Hill

Pāri's Paṟampu hill[2]
is quite a place.

Even if all three of you kings
should surround it
with your great drums of war,
remember
it has four things
not grown under the plows
of plowmen:

10   one, wild rice
grows in the tiny-leaved bamboos;
two, ripening jackfruit,
crammed with segments
of sweet flesh;
three, down below
grow sweet potatoes
under fat creepers;
four,
beehives break

---

[2] **Pāri's Paṟampu hill:** Pari, the patron of the poet Kapilar, was a chieftain who controlled the hill named after him and about three hundred small villages. He was besieged by the three kings of Chera, Chola, and Pandya, captured by deception, and put to death.

20   as their colors ripen
      to a purple,
      and the rich tall hill
      drips with honey.

      The hill is wide as the sky,
      the pools flash like stars.
      Even if you have
      elephants
      tied to every tree there,
      and chariots
30   standing in every field,
      you will never take the hill.
      He will not give in
      to the sword.

          But I know a way
          to take it:

                  pick carefully
          your lute-strings, string little lutes,
          and with your dancing women
                  with dense fragrant hair
          behind you,

40   go singing and dancing
          to Pāri,

          and he'll give you
          both hill and country.

                                        Kapilar

255: A WOMAN AND HER DYING WARRIOR

      I cannot cry out,
      I'm afraid of tigers.
      I cannot hold you,
      your chest is too wide
      for my lifting.

      Death
      has no codes
      and has dealt you wrong,
      may he
10   shiver as I do!

Hold my wrist
of bangles,
let's get to the shade
of that hill.
Just try and walk a little.

Vaṇparaṇar

271: A LEAF IN LOVE AND WAR

The chaste trees, dark-clustered,
blend with the land
that knows no dryness;
the colors on the leaves
mob the eyes.

> We've seen those leaves
> on jeweled women,
> on their mounds
> of love.

10   Now the chaste wreath lies slashed
on the ground, so changed, so mixed
with blood, the vulture snatches it
with its beak,
thinking it raw meat.

> We see this too
> just because a young man
> in love with war
> wore it for glory.

Veṟipāṭiya Kāmakkaṇṇiyār

278: MOTHERS

The old woman's shoulders
were dry, unfleshed,
with outstanding veins;
her low belly
was like a lotus pad.

When people said
her son had taken fright,
had turned his back on battle
and died,

10   she raged
and shouted,

    "If he really broke down
    in the thick of battle,
    I'll slash these breasts
    that gave him suck,"

and went there,
sword in hand.

Turning over body after fallen body,
she rummaged through the blood-red field
20   till she found her son,
quartered, in pieces,

and she rejoiced
more than on the day
she gave him birth.

Kākkaipāṭiṇiyār Naccellaiyār

✆ KALIDASA

FL. EARLY FIFTH CENTURY

uh-bij-NYAH-nuh
shuh-KOON-tuh-luh

shuh-KOON-tuh-luh

www For links to
more information
about Kalidasa
and a quiz on
Shakuntala, see *World
Literature Online* at
bedfordstmartins
.com/worldlit.

When *Shakuntala* (***Abhijñanasakuntala***) was first translated into English by William Jones in 1789, the play caused a sensation in Europe, especially in Germany where Goethe said the play made a "transcendental impression" on him, and in a poetic tribute counseled readers: "If you want to designate both the heaven and earth by a common name / I refer you to the ***Sákuntalā . . .***" Goethe's excitement came from his having discovered a work that in every way fulfilled what he would later define as "world literature," a work that speaks across centuries and transcends the particularities of its cultural origins. Kalidasa's masterwork is also the finest example of Sanskrit drama from classical India, a literature similar in its mythic subject matter and its origins in ancient ritual to Greek drama.

An Obscure Life.   Little is known about Kalidasa beyond the fact that he is named as the author in the prologues of three surviving plays. Even the time when he lived is a matter of speculation, with scholars suggesting dates that range over several centuries. Hints in the plays and circumstantial historical evidence have led most commentators to locate him during the reign of the third Gupta ruler, **Chandragupta** II (376–415), at the height of India's classical golden age.

According to a popular legend, Kalidasa was orphaned as an infant, raised in illiteracy by an oxcart driver, married by fraud to a princess who cast him out when she discovered his ignorance, and ultimately given the power of poetry by the goddess Kali. From this mythic biography the playwright and poet earned the name Kalidasa, meaning "the slave of Kali." His plays, however, would indicate that he was a highly educated and well-traveled man, not an ignorant peasant. His descriptions of court life suggest that he was probably a court poet and perhaps an emissary for the king. His references to Ujjayini, one of the great cities of Gupta India, indicate that he probably lived there as a member of the intelligentsia. And his descriptions of nature reveal him to have been a close observer of the natural world especially drawn to the mountains of north India. He holds a position of utmost prominence in Indian literature, similar to that of Homer, Dante, or Shakespeare in the West.

Seven works have been attributed to Kalidasa: two volumes of poetry, two epics, and three plays. The earliest was probably the poem *The Gathering of the Seasons (Raghuramsam),* which describes nature at different times of the year and compares the beauty of nature to the beauty of a woman; nature and the woman ultimately become one. The long lyric poem *The Cloud Messenger (Meghadutam)* tells of a love message transmitted from central India to the Himalayas by a cloud. The two epics *Raghu's Dynasty (Raghuvamsam)* and *The Birth of Kumara (Kumarasambhavam)* treat mythological subjects. Kalidasa is most remembered for his plays, *Malavika and Agnimitra (Malavikagnimitram), Urvasi Won*

chun-druh-GOOP-tuh

Lovers, 475–510 C.E.

Shakuntala, *Kalidasa's epic play, is essentially a love story, the romantic tale of the courtship, secret marriage, separation, and reunion of King Dushyanta and the semidivine Shakuntala. (Lovers. Wallpainting. Scala / Art Resources, NY)*

This fusion of esthetic and spiritual, of sensual and religious values is perhaps unknown, in equal measure, in any other country. Kalidasa is the best exponent of this singularly Indian approach to life. His imagination dwells on love which seems at first to be of the earth, but which leads imperceptibly into heavenly vistas. What appears as gross sensuality is soon transformed into domestic felicity, which culminates in divine ecstasy.

– K. KRISHNAMOORTHY, critic, 1972

Kalidasa understood in the fifth century what Europe did not learn until the nineteenth, and even now comprehends only imperfectly: that the world was not made for man, that man reaches his full stature only as he realises the dignity and worth of life that is not human.

– ARTHUR W. RYDER, critic, 1912

nah-tyuh-SHAHS-truh

by Valor (*Vikramorvasiyam*), and his masterwork, *Shakuntala and the Ring of Recollection*. All three plays develop essentially the same story, that of a king separated from his beloved but ultimately reunited with her, a masterplot of Sanskrit drama.

Sanskrit Drama.   Sanskrit was the literary language of classical India. Codified and formalized in the fourth century B.C.E., it became, like classical Arabic or church Latin, a formal written language distinct from the spoken language in everyday use. While such languages may be appropriate for epic poems and religious ritual, they do not work well in drama, especially with characters whose speech is meant to sound like that of real people. Kalidasa and other early Sanskrit dramatists solved this problem by using two languages. Kings, gods, and other important male characters spoke in Sanskrit verse. Women and men of lower castes, including the **BRAHMIN** buffoon, spoke in vernacular languages, and often in prose.

Like Greek drama in the West, Sanskrit drama probably has its roots in religious ritual. The prayers that begin and end the action are one indication of this heritage, as is the underlying theme in all the plays that compares the human order under a king to the divine order ruled by Indra, the ruling deity in the Hindu **PANTHEON** of gods. Also like Greek drama, Sanskrit drama also has its book of theory, the *The Treatise on Drama* (**Natyashastra**), comparable to *The Poetics* of Aristotle. The date and authorship of *The Treatise* are still in dispute. Like *Poetics*, *Treatise* analyzes the elements of drama, discussing literary components like character and plot as well as such theatrical concerns as costume, gesture, movement, and the physical layout of theaters. Theatrical elements, especially gesture and dance, play a more important role in Indian drama than similar elements (called "spectacle" by Aristotle) do in the drama of the West.

Aristotle's focus on tragedy in *The Poetics* elevated that genre to preeminence in the West. *The Treatise* concentrates on the *NATAKA*,[1] or heroic romance, the genre to which *Shakuntala* and Kalidasa's other plays belong. To achieve its goal of "pleasurable instruction," the *nataka* tells a well-known story, often from one of the heroic epics. Its central character is a mythic figure, a warrior-king with divine elements in his ancestry. Unlike the Greek tragic heroes, whose flaws bring suffering and usually death, the Sanskrit hero-kings are idealized types and the dramatic action is heroic and comic rather than tragic. In Sanskrit drama, plot, character, and language combine with music, dance, gesture, and other theatricalities to create an emotional mood, or *RASA*,[2] shared by author, actors, and members of the audience. Of the eight possible *rasas* identified in *The*

---

[1] *nataka:* Of the ten genres recognized in Indian dramatic theory, the *nataka,* or heroic romance, is the most important. It presents a familiar story, usually from one of the epics, about a mythic hero, most times a king. In the *nataka* the emotional effect, or *rasa,* must be either erotic, heroic, or a combination of the two.

[2] *rasa:* Indian dramatic theory identifies eight *rasas* (aesthetic emotions) that can focus a drama: the erotic, the heroic, the disquieting, the furious, the comic, the marvellous, the horrible, and the pathetic. Only two are appropriate to the *nataka* form, the erotic and the heroic.

Treatise, only two are present in the *nataka,* the erotic and the heroic. Instead of a CATHARSIS of pity and fear, the Indian heroic romance seeks to induce a mood of harmony and peace, as the love story embodying the erotic *rasa* and the kingship story embodying the heroic *rasa* are resolved together and harmoniously in the end. The effect of the play, then, is to affirm the connection between the divine and the human realms as the central characters fulfill the roles they have been born to play in the cosmic order.

Shakuntala.   Kalidasa faithfully follows these dramatic conventions in *Shakuntala.* The hero and heroine are both semidivine figures. King **Dushyanta** is descended from the great King **Puru** and can trace his ancestry back to the lunar dynasty of Indian legend. Early in the play he establishes that Shakuntala is not the daughter of a Brahmin sage from a caste beneath his own warrior caste but is also of semidivine ancestry, the daughter of a royal sage and a celestial nymph. Dushyanta has all the attributes of a perfect ruler: He is generous, intelligent, a great hunter, a fine painter, a protector of his people, and the warrior called by Indra to battle the gods' enemies. Shakuntala embodies the virtues her culture admires in women, modesty and submissiveness, but also displays a significant measure of self-respect and energy, actively seeking celestial refuge, for instance, for herself and her child after the king's rejection. The other conventional role in the drama is that of the Buffoon, the king's companion **Madhavya**, who is much like one of Shakespeare's fools, speaking plain truth to the king. The action of *Shakuntala* follows the story of Dushyanta and Shakuntala, their courtship and secret marriage, and their separation as the king returns to court to take up his royal duties. Their reunion, which affirms the marriage and establishes the harmony of the ruler pair, also reveals the heir to Dushyanta, his son, Bharata, destined to become the great ruler of India and the subject of the epic poem *Mahabharata.*

The *Mahabharata* was in fact the source for Kalidasa's play, a familiar story that he elaborated and refined. The original story had only three characters, the king, Shakuntala, and Kanva. Kalidasa gave richness and depth to these central figures by adding minor characters such as Shakuntala's two attendants, the members of the King's entourage, and, later in the play, the fisherman and the policemen. He also added Durvasas's curse and the ring, devices that give probability to the action and absolve the king from responsibility for his forgetfulness. Instead of appearing as a ruthless Don Juan, the king, when he resists the physical attractions of Shakuntala because he believes she is another man's wife, shows himself a restrained man and a devoted ruler.

Kalidasa's distinctive contribution to the story is most evident in the poetry of the play and in his evocation of character and setting. Although Shakuntala and Dushyanta are idealized stock characters, they are given depth and complexity by their companions. **Anasuya**'s seriousness and **Priyamvada**'s playful teasing reveal contrasting sides of Shakuntala's character, while Madhavya and the king's other attendants similarly add dimension to the sovereign's character. The settings are especially significant,

doosh-YAHN-tuh;
POO-roo

MAH-duv-yuh

uh-nuh-SOO-yuh
pree-yum-VAH-duh

even though Sanskrit plays were, like Shakespeare's, performed on a bare stage. The poetry of the opening acts evokes the natural green world where Shakuntala is identified with the deer and the jasmine flowers and the king with the bee that disrupts Shakuntala's repose. This setting is more than just scenic; it is a sacred grove, an earthly paradise where hunting ceases and animals and humans live together in a peaceable kingdom. Shakuntala, whose name alludes to the shakunta birds who nurtured and protected her as an infant before she was adopted by the sage Kanva, is a child of nature. In this sacred and sensual setting, the passions of the king and the maiden are aroused, culminating in the inevitable natural marriage at the end of Act III.

When the king is recalled to the city, his conflict between duty (*DHARMA*) and sensual desire (*KAMA*), the main theme of the *nataka* genre, is brought into focus. Dushyanta prolongs his stay in the sacred grove by claiming he has a duty to protect the place and by sending Madhavya in his place to respond to the summons. When he does return to his duties, the demands of kingship absorb all of his attention and erase memories of the forest and of his marriage, an amnesia made dramatically believable by **Durvasas**' spell. The royal city, with its palace intrigues and official duties, is Dushyanta's milieu. It is also home to a barren marriage. When Shakuntala arrives she is out of place, for she signifies nature. So unnatural is the city that the mango flowers in the palace's pleasure garden "bloom without spreading pollen," symbolic of the barrenness of the king's urban marriage. In this setting the king is unable to recognize Shakuntala, and he drives her away. Remorseful after the ring restores his memory, he cancels the festival of spring.

Resolution is achieved in a *DEUS EX MACHINA*[3] ending. After Dushyanta serves as a warrior for the god Indra, he is reunited with Shakuntala in a celestial garden recalling the sacred grove of the play's opening scenes. This transcendental reunion resolves the conflict between duty and desire and amends the earlier barrenness of Dushyanta's reign as he recognizes his and Shankutala's son, Bharata, who is destined to become India's founding monarch.

door-VAH-sus

■ **CONNECTIONS**

Euripides, *Medea* (Book 1). Both *Shakuntala* and Euripides' *Medea* are plays that develop the story of "the woman scorned." Consider the differences in the characterizations of the hero and the heroine in the two plays. What is the *rasa* of *Medea*? Of *Shakuntala*? Do their *deus ex machina* endings serve different purposes?

Sophocles, *Oedipus Rex* (Book 1); Machiavelli, *The Prince* (Book 3). Many works of world literature treat the theme of kingship: the qualities of a good ruler, the dangers of holding power, the relations between ruler and ruled. Sophocles' *Oedipus Rex*

---

[3] *deus ex machina:* Latin for "god from the machine," this phrase originally was applied to Greek plays, especially those by Euripides, in which resolution of the conflict was achieved by the interventions of a god who was lowered onto the stage mechanically. In its broader use, the phrase is applied to any plot whose resolution comes by means of an improbable or fortuitous device from outside the action.

can be read as a study of a king whose power makes him deny his human weaknesses, leading to the play's tragic conclusion. In *Shakuntala,* the king consolidates his power and brings divine blessings on his rule. Are the qualities of a good ruler the same in the two plays? How might any divergences between the Greek and Indian worldviews explain the differences between these two plays? Which of the two rulers would better qualify for Machiavelli's approval as a prince?

Goethe, *Faust* (Book 5). One of Kalidasa's great admirers in the West, the German poet and dramatist Goethe devoted many years to his masterwork, *Faust,* a long dramatic poem with many resemblances to *Shakuntala.* Its cosmic setting; its mythic hero from a familiar story; its mixture of poetry and prose, and elevated language and street slang; its philosophical and spiritual themes; and its comic "theological" ending all bear comparison to Kalidasa's work. In what ways are *Shakuntala* and *Faust* different?

■ FURTHER RESEARCH

Lal, P. *Great Sanskrit Plays.* 1964.
Ragan, Chandra, ed. and trans. *Kalidasa: The Loom of Time.* 1989.
Stoler Miller, Barbara, ed. and trans. *Theater of Memory: The Plays of Kalidasa.* 1984.
Wells, Henry W. *The Classical Drama of India.* 1963.

■ PRONUNCIATION

Abhijñanasakuntala: uh-bij-NYAH-nuh shuh-KOON-tuh-luh, uh-bid-YAH-nuh
Anasūyā: uh-nuh-SOO-yuh
Aparājitā: uh-puh-RAH-jih-tuh
Ayodhyā: uh-YOH-dyuh
Bharatavarsa: bah-ruh-tuh-VAR-shuh
Chandragupta: chun-druh-GOOP-tuh, chahn-druh-
Caturikā: chuh-TOO-rih-kah
Dhanamitra: duh-nuh-MIT-ruh
Durvāsas: door-VAH-sus
Duṣyanta: doosh-YAHN-tuh
Haṁsapadikā: hawng-suh-PAH-dih-kuh
Hastināpura: hus-tih-NAH-poo-ruh
Jayanta: JIGH-yun-tuh
Karabhaka: kuh-ruh-BAH-kuh
Māḍhavya: MAH-duv-yuh
Madhukarikā: muh-doo-KAH-rih-kuh
Mārīca: muh-REE-chuh
Marīci: muh-REE-chee
Mitrāvasu: mih-TRAH-vuh-soo
moksha: MOKE-shuh
Natyashastra: nah-tyuh-SHAHS-truh
Parabhṛtikā: puh-ruh-BUR-tih-kuh
Priyaṃvadā: pree-yum-VAH-duh
Puru: POO-roo
Raivataka: righ-VAH-tuh-kuh
Śakuntalā: shuh-KOON-tuh-luh
śamī: SHUH-mee, SHAH-mee
Sānumatī: sah-NOO-muh-tee
Śāradvata: shuh-RUD-vuh-tuh
Śārṅgarava: sharng-guh-RUH-vuh

If you would enjoy the flowers of early years / and the fruits of age advanced, / If you want to have something that charms, / something that is enchanting, / If you want to designate both the heaven / and the earth by a common name, / I refer you to the Sákuntala and thus express these all.

—JOHANN WOLFGANG VON GOETHE, Poet, eighteenth century

Sarvadamana: sar-vuh-DAH-muh-nuh
śirīṣa: shih-REE-shuh
Somarāta: soh-muh-RAH-tuh
Somatīrtha: soh-muh-TEER-tuh
sṛṅgāra: shurng-GAH-ruh
Sūcaka: SOO-chuh-kuh
svabhāvokti: svuh-buh-VOKE-tee, swuh-
svarga: SVAR-guh
svayaṃvara: svuh-YUM-vuh-ruh, swuh-
Taralikā: tuh-RAH-lih-kuh
Triśaṅku: tree-SHAHNG-koo
Triṣṭubh: TRISH-toob
Vasumatī: vuh-soo-MUH-tee, -MAH-tee
Vātāyana: vah-TAH-yuh-nuh
Vetravatī: vay-truh-VUH-tee, -VAH-tee
vidūṣaka: vih-DOO-shuh-kuh
Viṣṇu: VISH-noo
Viśvāmitra: vish-vuh-MIT-ruh
Yakṣī: YUK-shee, YAHK-

✑ Śakuntalā and the Ring of Recollection

Translated by Barbara Stoler Miller

CHARACTERS

Players in the prologue:
DIRECTOR, *Director of the players and manager of the theater.*
ACTRESS, *The lead actress.*

Principal roles:
KING, *Duṣyanta, the hero; ruler of Hastināpura; a royal sage of the lunar dynasty of Puru.*
ŚAKUNTALĀ, *The heroine; daughter of the royal sage Viśvāmitra and the celestial nymph Menakā; adoptive daughter of the ascetic Kaṇva.*
BUFFOON, *Māḍhavya, the king's comical brahman companion.*

Shakuntala. Ever since William Jones first introduced this work to the West with his English translation in 1789, it has intrigued Western readers and translators. Kalidasa's poetry, especially his evocation and celebration of nature, spoke to the European Romantics, who also viewed nature as infused with spirit, but there is nothing otherworldly about his poetry. Through his close observation of plants and animals he was able to produce natural imagery with an almost scientific accuracy, and his characters speak in a language that's appropriate to their position in the real world. In *Shakuntala,* the king and the gods speak an elevated poetry; the policemen speak the argot of the precinct house. As a poet, Kalidasa might be described as a Romantic Realist.

Mixing a love story with serious theological issues usually produces a tragedy in the West, plays like *Romeo and Juliet* and *Antony and Cleopatra.* For Kalidasa the mixture is the stuff of cosmic comedy. His audience knew that the ring would be found and the proper order of the universe affirmed by the end of the play. Not only would the separated lovers be reunited but also their marriage would produce a son who would become India's heroic founding monarch as well. The

Members of Kaṇva's hermitage:

ANASŪYĀ *and* PRIYAṂVADĀ, *Two young female ascetics; friends of Śakuntalā.*

KAṆVA, *Foster father of Śakuntalā and master of the hermitage; a sage belonging to the lineage of the divine creator Marīci, and thus related to Mārīca.*

GAUTAMĪ, *The senior female ascetic.*

ŚĀRṄGARAVA *and* ŚĀRADVATA, *Kaṇva's disciples.*

Various inhabitants of the hermitage: a monk with his two pupils, two boy ascetics (named Gautama and Nārada), a young disciple of Kaṇva, a trio of female ascetics.

Members of the king's forest retinue:

CHARIOTEER, *Driver of the king's chariot.*

GUARD, *Raivataka, guardian of the entrance to the king's quarters.*

GENERAL, *Commander of the king's army.*

KARABHAKA, *Royal messenger.*

Various attendants, including Greco-Bactrian bow-bearers.

Members of the king's palace retinue:

CHAMBERLAIN, *Vātāyana, chief officer of the king's household.*

PRIEST, *Somarāta, the king's religious preceptor and household priest.*

DOORKEEPER, *Vetravatī, the female attendant who ushers in visitors and presents messages.*

PARABHṚTIKĀ *and* MADHUKARIKĀ, *Two maids assigned to the king's garden.*

CATURIKĀ, *A maidservant.*

City dwellers:

MAGISTRATE, *The king's low-caste brother-in-law; chief of the city's policemen.*

POLICEMEN, *Sūcaka and Jānuka.*

FISHERMAN, *An outcaste.*

Celestials:

MĀRĪCA, *A divine sage; master of the celestial hermitage in which Śakuntalā gives birth to her son; father of Indra, king of the gods, whose armies Duṣyanta leads.*

ADITI, *Wife of Mārīca.*

MĀTALI, *Indra's charioteer.*

SĀNUMATĪ, *A nymph; friend of Śakuntalā's mother Menakā.*

Various members of Mārīca's hermitage: two female ascetics, Mārīca's disciple Gālava.

BOY, *Sarvadamana, son of Śakuntalā and Duṣyanta; later known as Bharata.*

Offstage voices:

VOICES OFFSTAGE, *From the backstage area or dressing room; behind the curtain, out of view of the audience. The voice belongs to various players before they enter the stage, such as the monk, Śakuntalā's friends, the buffoon, Mātali; also to figures who never enter the stage, such as the angry sage Durvāsas, the two bards who chant royal panegyrics* (vaitālikau).

VOICE IN THE AIR, *A voice chanting in the air from somewhere offstage: the bodiless voice of Speech quoted in Sanskrit by Priyaṃvadā; the voice of a cuckoo who represents the trees of the forest blessing Śakuntalā in Sanskrit; the voice of Haṃsapadikā singing a Prakrit love song.*

---

separation of Shakuntala and Dushyanta, far from threatening a catharsis of pity and fear, anticipates a celebration of love and cosmic order.

Translators of Kalidasa's work are sometimes awed by its antiquity and its serious themes, casting it into almost scriptural language. Barbara Stoler Miller, whose translation is presented here, nicely captures the many different voices in Kalidasa's play. Her rendering of this work written more than fifteen hundred years ago makes it seem almost contemporary. We have retained her use of diacritical marks such as the Ś in Śakuntala that indicates an English *sh* sound. The pronunciation guide includes a rendering that indicates an unmarked sounding of the words.

The setting of the play shifts from the forest hermitage (Acts I–IV) to the palace (Acts V–VI) to the celestial hermitage (Act VII). The season is early summer when the play begins and spring during the sixth act; the passage of time is otherwise indicated by the birth and boyhood of Śakuntalā's son.

ACT I

The water that was first created,
the sacrifice-bearing fire, the priest,
the time-setting sun and moon,
audible space that fills the universe,
what men call nature, the source of all seeds,
the air that living creatures breathe—
through his eight embodied forms,
may Lord Śiva come to bless you![1]

Prologue

DIRECTOR: [*Looking backstage.*] If you are in costume now, madam, please come on
10   stage!
ACTRESS: I'm here, sir.
DIRECTOR: Our audience is learned. We shall play Kālidāsa's new drama called
        Śakuntalā and the Ring of Recollection. Let the players take their parts to heart!
ACTRESS: With you directing, sir, nothing will be lost.
DIRECTOR: Madam, the truth is:

> I find no performance perfect
> until the critics are pleased;
> the better trained we are
> the more we doubt ourselves.

20 ACTRESS: So true . . . now tell me what to do first!
DIRECTOR: What captures an audience better than a song?
        Sing about the new summer season and its pleasures:

> To plunge in fresh waters
> swept by scented forest winds
> and dream in soft shadows
> of the day's ripened charms.

ACTRESS: [*Singing.*]

> Sensuous women
> in summer love

---

[1] **The water . . . to bless you:** This benedictory verse, or *nandi,* is one of the traditional rituals recited before the performance of a Sanskrit play. It is addressed to Śiva, or Shiva, the patron god of creation and the drama who is manifest in the eight forms listed in the verse: water, fire, the priest, Sun, Moon, space, earth, and air.

weave
30 flower earrings
from fragile petals
of mimosa
while wild bees
kiss them gently.

DIRECTOR: Well sung, madam! Your melody enchants the audience. The silent theater is like a painting. What drama should we play to please it?

ACTRESS: But didn't you just direct us to perform a new play called *Śakuntalā and the
Ring of Recollection*?

DIRECTOR: Madam, I'm conscious again! For a moment I forgot.

40 The mood of your song's melody
carried me off by force,
just as the swift dark antelope
enchanted King Duṣyanta.

[*They both exit; the prologue ends. Then the* KING *enters with his* CHARIOTEER, *in a chariot, a
bow and arrow in his hand, hunting an antelope.*]

CHARIOTEER: [*Watching the* KING *and the antelope.*]

I see this black buck move
as you draw your bow
and I see the wild bowman Śiva,
hunting the dark antelope.[2]

KING: Driver, this antelope has drawn us far into the forest. There he is again:

The graceful turn of his neck
50 as he glances back at our speeding car,
the haunches folded into his chest
in fear of my speeding arrow,
the open mouth dropping
half-chewed grass on our path —
watch how he leaps, bounding on air,
barely touching the earth.

[*He shows surprise.*]

Why is it so hard to keep him in sight?

CHARIOTEER: Sir, the ground was rough. I tightened the reins to slow the chariot and
the buck raced ahead. Now that the path is smooth, he won't be hard to catch.

60 KING: Slacken the reins!

CHARIOTEER: As you command, sir. [*He mimes the speeding chariot.*] Look!

---

[2] **I see . . . the dark antelope:** Here, the Charioteer compares the king as a hunter with the god Śiva, who pursued the creator-god Prajapati who had taken the form of an antelope.

> Their legs extend as I slacken the reins,
> plumes and manes set in the wind, ears angle back;
> our horses outrun their own clouds of dust,
> straining to match the antelope's speed.

KING: These horses would outrace the steeds of the sun.[3]

> What is small suddenly looms large,
> split forms seem to reunite,
> bent shapes straighten before my eyes —
> 70   from the chariot's speed
> nothing ever stays distant or near.

CHARIOTEER: The antelope is an easy target now. [*He mimes the fixing of an arrow.*]

VOICE OFFSTAGE: Stop! Stop, king! This antelope belongs to our hermitage! Don't kill him!

CHARIOTEER: [*Listening and watching.*] Sir, two ascetics are protecting the black buck from your arrow's deadly aim.

KING: [*Showing confusion.*] Rein in the horses!

CHARIOTEER: It is done!

[*He mimes the chariot's halt. Then a* MONK *enters with* TWO PUPILS, *his hand raised.*]

MONK: King, this antelope belongs to our hermitage.

80   Withdraw your well-aimed arrow! Your weapon should rescue victims, not destroy the innocent!

KING: I withdraw it. [*He does as he says.*]

MONK: An act worthy of the Puru dynasty's shining light!

> Your birth honors
> the dynasty of the moon!
> May you beget a son
> to turn the wheel of your empire!

THE TWO PUPILS: [*Raising their arms.*] May you beget a son to turn the wheel of your empire!

90   KING: [*Bowing.*] I welcome your blessing.

MONK: King, we were going to gather firewood. From here you can see the hermitage of our master Kaṇva on the bank of the Mālinī river. If your work permits, enter and accept our hospitality.

> When you see the peaceful rites of devoted ascetics,
> you will know how well your scarred arm protects us.

KING: Is the master of the community there now?

MONK: He went to Somatīrtha, the holy shrine of the moon, and put his daughter Śakuntalā in charge of receiving guests.
Some evil threatens her, it seems.

---

[3] **steeds of the sun:** Horses that pull the chariot of the sun-god.

100   KING: Then I shall see her. She will know my devotion and commend me to the great
       sage.

    MONK: We shall leave you now.

[He exits with his pupils.]

    KING: Driver, urge the horses on! The sight of this holy hermitage will purify us.

    CHARIOTEER: As you command, sir. *[He mimes the chariot's speed.]*

    KING: *[Looking around.]* Without being told one can see that this is a grove where
       ascetics live.

    CHARIOTEER: How?

    KING: Don't you see —

> Wild rice grains under trees
110   where parrots nest in hollow trunks,
> stones stained by the dark oil
> of crushed ingudī nuts,
> trusting deer who hear human voices
> yet don't break their gait,
> and paths from ponds streaked
> by water from wet bark cloth.

    CHARIOTEER: It is perfect.

    KING: *[Having gone a little inside.]* We should not disturb the grove! Stop the chariot
      and let me get down!

120   CHARIOTEER: I'm holding the reins. You can dismount now, sir.

    KING; *[Dismounting.]* One should not enter an ascetics' grove in hunting gear. Take
      these! *[He gives up his ornaments and his bow.]* Driver, rub down the horses
      while I pay my respects to the residents of the hermitage!

    CHARIOTEER: Yes, sir!

[He exits.]

    KING: This gateway marks the sacred ground. I will enter. *[He enters, indicating he
    feels an omen.]*

> The hermitage is a tranquil place,
> yet my arm is quivering . . .
> do I feel a false omen of love
> or does fate have doors everywhere?

130   VOICE OFFSTAGE: This way, friends!

    KING: *[Straining to listen.]* I think I hear voices to the right of the grove. I'll find out.

[Walking around and looking.]

    Young female ascetics with watering pots cradled on their hips are coming to
    water the saplings. *[He mimes it in precise detail.]* This view of them is sweet.

> These forest women have beauty
> rarely seen inside royal palaces —
> the wild forest vines far surpass
> creepers in my pleasure garden.

I'll hide in the shadows and wait.

[ŚAKUNTALĀ *and her two friends enter, acting as described.*]

ŚAKUNTALĀ: This way, friends!

140 ANASŪYĀ: I think Father Kaṇva cares more about the trees in the hermitage than he cares about you. You're as delicate as a jasmine, yet he orders you to water the trees.

ŚAKUNTALĀ: Anasūyā, it's more than Father Kaṇva's order. I feel a sister's love for them. [*She mimes the watering of trees.*]

KING: [*To himself.*] Is this Kaṇva's daughter? The sage does show poor judgment in imposing the rules of the hermitage on her.

> The sage who hopes to subdue
> her sensuous body by penances
> is trying to cut firewood
150 > with a blade of blue-lotus leaf.

Let it be! I can watch her closely from here in the trees. [*He does so.*]

ŚAKUNTALĀ: Anasūyā, I can't breathe! Our friend Priyaṁvadā tied my bark dress too tightly! Loosen it a bit!

ANASŪYĀ: As you say. [*She loosens it.*]

PRIYAṀVADĀ: [*Laughing.*] Blame your youth for swelling your breasts. Why blame me?

KING: This bark dress fits her body badly, but it ornaments her beauty . . .

> A tangle of duckweed adorns a lotus,
> a dark spot heightens the moon's glow,
160 > the bark dress increases her charm—
> beauty finds its ornaments anywhere.

ŚAKUNTALĀ: [*Looking in front of her.*] The new branches on this mimosa tree are like fingers moving in the wind, calling to me. I must go to it! [*Saying this, she walks around.*]

PRIYAṀVADĀ: Wait, Śakuntalā! Stay there a minute! When you stand by this mimosa tree, it seems to be guarding a creeper.

ŚAKUNTALĀ: That's why your name means "Sweet-talk."

KING: "Sweet-talk" yes, but Priyaṁvadā speaks the truth about Śakuntalā:

> Her lips are fresh red buds,
> her arms are tendrils,
170 > impatient youth is poised
> to blossom in her limbs.

ANASŪYĀ: Śakuntalā, this is the jasmine creeper who chose the mango tree in marriage, the one you named "Forestlight." Have you forgotten her?

ŚAKUNTALĀ: I would be forgetting myself? [*She approaches the creeper and examines it.*] The creeper and the tree are twined together in perfect harmony. Forestlight has just flowered and the new mango shoots are made for her pleasure.

PRIYAṀVADĀ: [*Smiling.*] Anasūyā, don't you know why Śakuntalā looks so lovingly at Forestlight?

ANASŪYĀ: I can't guess.

180 PRIYAṀVADĀ: The marriage of Forestlight to her tree makes her long to have a husband too.

ŚAKUNTALĀ: You're just speaking your own secret wish. [*Saying this, she pours water from the jar.*]

KING: Could her social class be different from her father's?[4] There's no doubt!

> She was born to be a warrior's bride,
> for my noble heart desires her—
> when good men face doubt,
> inner feelings are truth's only measure.

Still, I must learn everything about her.

ŚAKUNTALĀ: [*Flustered.*] The splashing water has alarmed a bee. He is flying from the
190   jasmine to my face. [*She dances to show the bee's attack.*]

KING: [*Looking longingly.*]

> Bee, you touch the quivering
> corners of her frightened eyes,
> you hover softly near
> to whisper secrets in her ear;
> a hand brushes you away,
> but you drink her lips' treasure—
> while the truth we seek defeats us,
> you are truly blessed.

ŚAKUNTALĀ: This dreadful bee won't stop. I must escape. [*She steps to one side, glanc-*
200   *ing about.*] Oh! He's pursuing me. . . . Save me! Please save me! This mad bee is chasing me!

BOTH FRIENDS: [*Laughing.*] How can we save you? Call King Duṣyanta. The grove is under his protection.

KING: Here's my chance. Have no fear . . . [*With this half-spoken, he stops and speaks to himself.*] Then she will know that I am the king. . . . Still, I shall speak.

ŚAKUNTALĀ: [*Stopping after a few steps.*] Why is he still following me?

KING: [*Approaching quickly.*]

> While a Puru king rules the earth
> to punish evildoers,
> who dares to molest
210   these innocent young ascetics?

[*Seeing the* KING, *all act flustered.*]

---

[4] **her social class . . . father's:** The Hindu caste system forbade marrying outside one's class. Kaṇva's daughter, a Brahmin, would not have been eligible to marry a king of the warrior caste.

ANASŪYĀ: Sir, there's no real danger. Our friend was frightened when a bee attacked her. [*She points to* ŚAKUNTALĀ.]

KING: [*Approaching* ŚAKUNTALĀ.] Does your ascetic practice go well? [ŚAKUNTALĀ *stands speechless.*]

ANASŪYĀ: It does now that we have a special guest. Śakuntalā, go to our hut and bring the ripe fruits. We'll use this water to bathe his feet.[5]

KING: Your kind speech is hospitality enough.

PRIYAṀVADĀ: Please sit in the cool shadows of this shade tree and rest, sir.

KING: You must also be tired from your work.

ANASŪYĀ: Śakuntalā, we should respect our guest. Let's sit down. [*All sit.*]

220   ŚAKUNTALĀ: [*To herself.*] When I see him, why do I feel an emotion that the forest seems to forbid?

KING: [*Looking at each of the girls.*] Youth and beauty complement your friendship.

PRIYAṀVADĀ: [*In a stage whisper.*] Anasūyā, who is he? He's so polite, fine looking, and pleasing to hear. He has the marks of royalty.

ANASŪYĀ: I'm curious too, friend. I'll just ask him. [*Aloud.*] Sir, your kind speech inspires trust. What family of royal sages do you adorn? What country mourns your absence? Why does a man of refinement subject himself to the discomfort of visiting an ascetics' grove?

ŚAKUNTALĀ: [*To herself.*] Heart, don't faint! Anasūyā speaks your thoughts.

230   KING: [*To himself.*] Should I reveal myself now or conceal who I am? I'll say it this way: [*Aloud.*] Lady, I have been appointed by the Puru king as the officer in charge of religious matters. I have come to this sacred forest to assure that your holy rites proceed unhindered.

ANASŪYĀ: Our religious life has a guardian now.

[ŚAKUNTALĀ *mimes the embarrassment of erotic emotion.*]

BOTH FRIENDS: [*Observing the behavior of* ŚAKUNTALĀ *and the* KING; *in a stage whisper.*] Śakuntalā, if only your father were here now!

ŚAKUNTALĀ: [*Angrily.*] What if he were?

BOTH FRIENDS: He would honor this distinguished guest with what he values most in life.

ŚAKUNTALĀ: Quiet! Such words hint at your hearts' conspiracy. I won't listen.

240   KING: Ladies, I want to ask about your friend.

BOTH FRIENDS: Your request honors us, sir.

KING: Sage Kaṇva has always been celibate, but you call your friend his daughter. How can this be?

ANASŪYĀ: Please listen, sir. There was a powerful royal sage[6] of the Kauśika clan . . .

KING: I am listening.

ANASŪYĀ: He begot our friend, but Kaṇva is her father because he cared for her when she was abandoned.

---

[5] **to bathe his feet:** A traditional act of hospitality.

[6] **royal sage:** Viśvāmitra, born into the warrior caste, attained the spiritual powers of a Brahmin sage.

KING: "Abandoned"? The word makes me curious. I want to hear her story from the beginning.

250   ANASŪYĀ: Please listen, sir. Once when this great sage was practicing terrible austerities on the bank of the Gautamī river, he became so powerful that the jealous gods sent a nymph named Menakā to break his self-control.

KING: The gods dread men who meditate.

ANASŪYĀ: When springtime came to the forest with all its charm, the sage saw her intoxicating beauty . . .

KING: I understand what happened then. She is the nymph's daughter.

ANASŪYĀ: Yes.

KING: It had to be!

> No mortal woman could give birth to such beauty—
260   lightning does not flash out of the earth.

[ŚAKUNTALĀ *stands with her face bowed. The* KING *continues speaking to himself.*]

My desire is not hopeless. Yet, when I hear her friends teasing her about a bridegroom, a new fear divides my heart.

PRIYAMVADĀ: [*Smiling, looking at* ŚAKUNTALĀ, *then turning to the* KING.] Sir, you seem to want to say more.

[ŚAKUNTALĀ *makes a threatening gesture with her finger.*]

KING: You judge correctly. In my eagerness to learn more about your pious lives, I have another question.

PRIYAMVADĀ: Don't hesitate! Ascetics can be questioned frankly.

KING: I want to know this about your friend:

> Will she keep the vow of hermit life
270   only until she marries . . .
> or will she always exchange
> loving looks with deer in the forest?

PRIYAMVADĀ: Sir, even in her religious life, she is subject to her father, but he does intend to give her to a suitable husband.

KING: [*To himself.*] His wish is not hard to fulfill.

> Heart, indulge your desire—
> now that doubt is dispelled,
> the fire you feared to touch
> is a jewel in your hands.

280   ŚAKUNTALĀ: [*Showing anger.*] Anasūyā, I'm leaving!

ANASŪYĀ: Why?

ŚAKUNTALĀ: I'm going to tell Mother Gautamī that Priyamvadā is talking nonsense.

ANASŪYĀ: Friend, it's wrong to neglect a distinguished guest and leave as you like.

[ŚAKUNTALĀ *starts to go without answering.*]

KING: [*Wanting to seize her, but holding back, he speaks to himself.*] A lover dare not act on his impulsive thoughts!

I wanted to follow the sage's daughter,
but decorum abruptly pulled me back;
I set out and returned again
without moving my feet from this spot.

290 PRIYAṀVADĀ: [*Stopping* ŚAKUNTALĀ.] It's wrong of you to go!

ŚAKUNTALĀ: [*Bending her brow into a frown.*] Give me a reason why!

PRIYAṀVADĀ: You promised to water two trees for me. Come here and pay your debt
before you go! [*She stops her by force.*]

KING: But she seems exhausted from watering the trees:

Her shoulders droop, her palms
are red from the watering pot—
even now, breathless sighs
make her breasts shake;
beads of sweat on her face
300   wilt the flower at her ear;
her hand holds back
disheveled locks of hair.

Here, I'll pay her debt!

[*He offers his ring. Both friends recite the syllables of the name on the seal and stare at each
other.*]

Don't mistake me for what I am not! This is a gift from the king to identify me as
his royal official.

PRIYAṀVADĀ: Then the ring should never leave your finger. Your word has already
paid her debt. [*She laughs a little.*] Śakuntalā, you are freed by this kind man . . .
or perhaps by the king. Go now!

ŚAKUNTALĀ: [*To herself.*] If I am able to . . . [*Aloud.*] Who are you to keep me or
310   release me?

KING: [*Watching* ŚAKUNTALĀ.] Can she feel toward me what I feel toward her? Or is
my desire fulfilled?

She won't respond directly to my words,
but she listens when I speak;
she won't turn to look at me,
but her eyes can't rest anywhere else.

VOICE OFFSTAGE: Ascetics, be prepared to protect the creatures of our forest grove!
King Duṣyanta is hunting nearby!

Dust raised by his horses' hooves
320   falls like a cloud of locusts swarming
at sunset over branches of trees
where wet bark garments hang.

In terror of the chariots, an elephant
charged into the hermitage
and scattered the herd of black antelope,

like a demon foe of our penances—
his tusks garlanded with branches
from a tree crushed by his weight,
his feet tangled in vines

330   that tether him like chains.

[*Hearing this, all the girls are agitated.*]
KING: [*To himself.*] Oh! My palace men are searching for me and wrecking the grove. I'll have to go back.
BOTH FRIENDS: Sir, we're all upset by this news. Please let us go to our hut.
KING: [*Showing confusion.*] Go, please. We will try to protect the hermitage.

[*They all stand to go.*]
BOTH FRIENDS: Sir, we're ashamed that our bad hospitality is our only excuse to invite you back.
KING: Not at all. I am honored to have seen you.

[ŚAKUNTALĀ *exits with her two friends, looking back at the* KING, *lingering artfully.*]
I have little desire to return to the city. I'll join my men and have them camp near the grove. I can't control my feelings for Śakuntalā.

340   My body turns to go,
my heart pulls me back,
like a silk banner
buffeted by the wind.

[*All exit.*]

ACT II

[*The* BUFFOON *enters, despondent.*]
BUFFOON: [*Sighing.*] My bad luck! I'm tired of playing sidekick to a king who's hooked on hunting. "There's a deer!" "There's a boar!" "There's a tiger!" Even in the summer midday heat we chase from jungle to jungle on paths where trees give barely any shade. We drink stinking water from mountain streams foul with rusty leaves. At odd hours we eat nasty meals of spit-roasted meat. Even at night I can't sleep. My joints ache from galloping on that horse. Then at the crack of dawn, I'm woken rudely by a noise piercing the forest. Those sons of bitches hunt their birds then. The torture doesn't end—now I have sores on top of my bruises. Yesterday, we lagged behind. The king chased a buck into the hermitage.
10   As luck would have it, an ascetic's daughter called Śakuntalā caught his eye. Now he isn't even thinking of going back to the city. This very dawn I found him wide-eyed, mooning about her. What a fate! I must see him after his bath. [*He walks around, looking.*] Here comes my friend now, wearing garlands of wild flowers. Greek women carry his bow in their hands.[7] Good! I'll stand here pretending my arms and legs are broken. Maybe then I'll get some rest.

---

[7] **Greek women . . . hands:** Probably women from Asia Minor who were employed by the Gupta rulers as bodyguards and bow-bearers.

[*He stands leaning on his staff. The* KING *enters with his retinue, as described.*]

KING: [*To himself.*]

> My beloved will not be easy to win,
> but signs of emotion revealed her heart—
> even when love seems hopeless,
> mutual longing keeps passion alive.

20   [*He smiles.*] A suitor who measures his beloved's state of mind by his own desire is a fool.

> She threw tender glances
> though her eyes were cast down,
> her heavy hips swayed
> in slow seductive movements,
> she answered in anger
> when her friend said, "Don't go!"
> and I felt it was all for my sake . . .
> but a lover sees in his own way.

30   BUFFOON: [*Still in the same position.*] Dear friend, since my hands can't move to greet you, I have to salute you with my voice.

KING: How did you cripple your limbs?

BUFFOON: Why do you ask why I cry after throwing dust in my eyes yourself?

KING: I don't understand.

BUFFOON: Dear friend, when a straight reed is twisted into a crooked reed, is it by its own power, or is it the river current?

KING: The river current is the cause.

BUFFOON: And so it is with me.

KING: How so?

40   BUFFOON: You neglect the business of being a king and live like a woodsman in this awful camp. Chasing after wild beasts every day jolts my joints and muscles till I can't control my own limbs anymore. I beg you to let me rest for just one day!

KING: [*To himself.*] He says what I also feel. When I remember Kaṇva's daughter, the thought of hunting disgusts me.

> I can't draw my bowstring
> to shoot arrows at deer
> who live with my love
> and teach her tender glances.

BUFFOON: Sir, you have something on your mind. I'm crying in a wilderness.

50   KING: [*Smiling.*] Yes, it is wrong to ignore my friend's plea.

BUFFOON: Live long! [*He starts to go.*]

KING: Dear friend, stay! Hear what I have to say!

BUFFOON: At your command, sir!

KING: When you have rested, I need your help in some work that you will enjoy.

BUFFOON: Is it eating sweets? I'm game!

KING: I shall tell you. Who stands guard?

GUARD: [*Entering.*] At your command, sir!

KING: Raivataka! Summon the general!

[*The* GUARD *exits and reenters with the* GENERAL.]

GUARD: The king is looking this way, waiting to give you his orders. Approach him,
60   sir!

GENERAL: [*Looking at the* KING.] Hunting is said to be a vice, but our king prospers.

> Drawing the bow only hardens his chest,
> he suffers the sun's scorching rays unburned,
> hard muscles mask his body's lean state—
> like a wild elephant, his energy sustains him.

[*He approaches the* KING.] Victory, my lord! We've already tracked some wild
beasts. Why the delay?

KING: Mādhavya's[8] censure of hunting has dampened my spirit.

GENERAL: [*In a stage whisper, to the* BUFFOON.] Friend, you stick to your opposition!
70   I'll try to restore our king's good sense. [*Aloud.*] This fool is talking nonsense.
Here is the king as proof:

> A hunter's belly is taut and lean,
> his slender body craves exertion;
> he penetrates the spirit of creatures
> overcome by fear and rage;
> his bowmanship is proved
> by arrows striking a moving target—
> hunting is falsely called a vice.
> What sport can rival it?

80 BUFFOON: [*Angrily.*] The king has come to his senses. If you keep chasing from forest
to forest, you'll fall into the jaws of an old bear hungry for a human nose . . .

KING: My noble general, we are near a hermitage; your words cannot please me now.

> Let horned buffaloes plunge into muddy pools!
> Let herds of deer huddle in the shade to eat grass!
> Let fearless wild boars crush fragrant swamp grass!
> Let my bowstring lie slack and my bow at rest!

GENERAL: Whatever gives the king pleasure.

KING: Withdraw the men who are in the forest now and forbid my soldiers to disturb
the grove!

90
> Ascetics devoted to peace
> possess a fiery hidden power,

---

[8] Mādhavya: The Buffoon.

like smooth crystal sunstones
that reflect the sun's scorching rays.

GENERAL: Whatever you command, sir!

BUFFOON: Your arguments for keeping up the hunt fall on deaf ears!

[*The* GENERAL *exits.*]

KING: [*Looking at his* RETINUE.] You women, take away my hunting gear! Raivataka, don't neglect your duty!

RETINUE: As the king commands!

[*They exit.*]

BUFFOON: Sir, now that the flies are cleared out, sit on a stone bench under this shady
100   canopy. Then I'll find a comfortable seat too.

KING: Go ahead!

BUFFOON: You first, sir!

[*Both walk about, then sit down.*]

KING: Mādhavya, you haven't really used your eyes because you haven't seen true beauty.

BUFFOON: But you're right in front of me, sir!

KING: Everyone is partial to what he knows well, but I'm speaking about Śakuntalā, the jewel of the hermitage.

BUFFOON: [*To himself.*] I won't give him a chance! [*Aloud.*] Dear friend, it seems that you're pursuing an ascetic's daughter.

110   KING: Friend, the heart of a Puru king wouldn't crave a forbidden fruit . . .

The sage's child is a nymph's daughter,
rescued by him after she was abandoned,
like a fragile jasmine blossom
broken and caught on a sunflower pod.

BUFFOON: [*Laughing.*] You're like the man who loses his taste for dates and prefers sour tamarind! How can you abandon the gorgeous gems of your palace?

KING: You speak this way because you haven't seen her.

BUFFOON: She must be delectable if you're so enticed!

KING: Friend, what is the use of all this talk?

120   The divine creator imagined perfection
and shaped her ideal form in his mind —
when I recall the beauty his power wrought,
she shines like a gemstone among my jewels.

BUFFOON: So she's the reason you reject the other beauties!

KING: She stays in my mind:

A flower no one has smelled,
a bud no fingers have plucked,
an uncut jewel, honey untasted,
unbroken fruit of holy deeds —

130   I don't know who is destined
to enjoy her flawless beauty.

BUFFOON: Then you should rescue her quickly! Don't let her fall into the arms of some ascetic who greases his head with iṅgudī oil!

KING: She is someone else's ward and her guardian is away.

BUFFOON: What kind of passion did her eyes betray?

KING: Ascetics are timid by nature:

Her eyes were cast down in my presence,
but she found an excuse to smile—
modesty barely contained the love
140   she could neither reveal nor conceal.

BUFFOON: Did you expect her to climb into your lap when she'd barely seen you?

KING: When we parted her feelings for me showed despite her modesty.

"A blade of kuśa grass
pricked my foot,"
the girl said for no reason
after walking a few steps away;
then she pretended to free
her bark dress from branches
where it was not caught
150   and shyly glanced at me.

BUFFOON: Stock up on food for a long trip! I can see you've turned that ascetics' grove into a pleasure garden.

KING: Friend, some of the ascetics recognize me. What excuse can we find to return to the hermitage?

BUFFOON: What excuse? Aren't you the king? Collect a sixth of their wild rice as tax!

KING: Fool! These ascetics pay tribute that pleases me more than mounds of jewels.

Tribute that kings collect
from members of society decays,
but the share of austerity
160   that ascetics give lasts forever.

VOICE OFFSTAGE: Good, we have succeeded!

KING: [*Listening.*] These are the steady, calm voices of ascetics.

GUARD: [*Entering.*] Victory, sir! Two boy ascetics are waiting near the gate.

KING: Let them enter without delay!

GUARD: I'll show them in. [*He exits; reenters with the boys.*] Here you are!

FIRST BOY: His majestic body inspires trust. It is natural when a king is virtually a sage.

His palace is a hermitage
with its infinite pleasures,
the discipline of protecting men
170   imposes austerities every day—

pairs of celestial bards praise
his perfect self-control,
adding the royal word "king"
to "sage," his sacred title.

SECOND BOY: Gautama, is this Duṣyanta, the friend of Indra?[9]
FIRST BOY: Of course!
SECOND BOY:

It is no surprise that this arm of iron
rules the whole earth bounded by dark seas—
when demons harass the gods, victory's hope
180   rests on his bow and Indra's thunderbolt.

BOTH BOYS: [*Coming near.*] Victory to you, king!
KING: [*Rising from his seat.*] I salute you both!
BOTH BOYS: To your success, sir! [*They offer fruits.*]
KING: [*Accepting their offering.*] I am ready to listen.
BOTH BOYS: The ascetics know that you are camped nearby and send a petition to you.
KING: What do they request?
BOTH BOYS: Demons are taking advantage of Sage Kaṇva's absence to harass us. You
    must come with your charioteer to protect the hermitage for a few days!
KING: I am honored to oblige.
190   BUFFOON: [*In a stage whisper.*] Your wish is fulfilled!
KING: [*Smiling.*] Raivataka, call my charioteer! Tell him to bring the chariot and
    my bow!
GUARD: As the king commands!   [*He exits.*]
BOTH BOYS: [*Showing delight.*]

Following your ancestral duties
suits your noble form—
the Puru kings are ordained
to dispel their subjects' fear.

KING: [*Bowing.*] You two return! I shall follow.
BOTH BOYS: Be victorious!   [*They exit.*]
200   KING: Mādhavya, are you curious to see Śakuntalā?
BUFFOON: At first there was a flood, but now with this news of demons, not a drop
    is left.
KING: Don't be afraid! Won't you be with me?
BUFFOON: Then I'll be safe from any demon . . .
GUARD: [*Entering.*] The chariot is ready to take you to victory . . . but Karabhaka has
    just come from the city with a message from the queen.
KING: Did my mother send him?

---

[9] **Indra:** Lord of heaven, ruler of the gods, the god of thunder and rain, and the sustainer of the universe; comparable to Zeus in the Greek pantheon.

GUARD: She did.

KING: Have him enter then.

210   GUARD: Yes. [*He exits; reenters with* KARABHAKA.] Here is the king. Approach!

KARABHAKA: Victory, sir! Victory! The queen has ordered a ceremony four days from now to mark the end of her fast. Your Majesty will surely give us the honor of his presence.

KING: The ascetics' business keeps me here and my mother's command calls me there. I must find a way to avoid neglecting either!

BUFFOON: Hang yourself between them the way Triśańku hung between heaven and earth.[10]

KING: I'm really confused . . .

My mind is split in two
220   by these conflicting duties,
like a river current split
by boulders in its course.

[*Thinking.*] Friend, my mother has treated you like a son. You must go back and report that I've set my heart on fulfilling my duty to the ascetics. You fulfill my filial duty to the queen.

BUFFOON: You don't really think I'm afraid of demons?

KING: [*Smiling.*] My brave brahman, how could you be?

BUFFOON: Then I can travel like the king's younger brother.

KING: We really should not disturb the grove! Take my whole entourage with you!

230   BUFFOON: Now I've turned into the crown prince!

KING: [*To himself.*] This fellow is absent-minded. At any time he may tell the palace women about my passion. I'll tell him this: [*Taking the* BUFFOON *by the hand, he speaks aloud.*] Dear friend, I'm going to the hermitage out of reverence for the sages. I really feel no desire for the young ascetic Śakuntalā.

What do I share with a rustic girl
reared among fawns, unskilled in love?
Don't mistake what I muttered
in jest for the real truth, friend!

[*All exit.*]

ACT III

[*A disciple of* KAṆVA *enters, carrying kuśa grass for a sacrificial rite.*]

DISCIPLE: King Duṣyanta is certainly powerful. Since he entered the hermitage, our rites have not been hindered.

Why talk of fixing arrows?
The mere twang of his bowstring

---

[10] **the way Triśańku . . . heaven and earth:** A mythic king who ends up suspended between heaven and earth as a result of a struggle between Viśvāmitra and the gods.

clears away menacing demons
as if his bow roared with death.

I'll gather some more grass for the priests to spread on the sacrificial altar. [*Walking around and looking, he calls aloud.*] Priyaṁvadā, for whom are you bringing the ointment of fragrant lotus root fibers and leaves? [*Listening.*] What are you saying? Śakuntalā is suffering from heat exhaustion? They're for rubbing on her body? Priyaṁvadā, take care of her! She is the breath of Father Kaṇva's life. I'll give Gautamī this water from the sacrifice to use for soothing her.

[*He exits; the interlude ends. Then the* KING *enters, suffering from love, deep in thought, sighing.*]

KING:

> I know the power ascetics have
> and the rules that bind her,
> but I cannot abandon my heart
> now that she has taken it.

[*Showing the pain of love.*] Love, why do you and the moon both contrive to deceive lovers by first gaining our trust?

> Arrows of flowers and cool moon rays
> are both deadly for men like me—
> the moon shoots fire through icy rays
> and you hurl thunderbolts of flowers.

[*Walking around.*] Now that the rites are concluded and the priests have dismissed me, where can I rest from the weariness of this work? [*Sighing.*] There is no refuge but the sight of my love. I must find her. [*Looking up at the sun.*] Śakuntalā usually spends the heat of the day with her friends in a bower of vines on the Mālinī riverbank. I shall go there. [*Walking around, miming the touch of breeze.*] This place is enchanted by the wind.

> A breeze fragrant with lotus pollen
> and moist from the Mālinī waves
> can be held in soothing embrace
> by my love-scorched arms.

[*Walking around and looking.*]

> I see fresh footprints
> on white sand in the clearing,
> deeply pressed at the heel
> by the sway of full hips.

I'll just look through the branches. [*Walking around, looking, he becomes joyous.*] My eyes have found bliss! The girl I desire is lying on a stone couch strewn with flowers, attended by her two friends. I'll eavesdrop as they confide in one another. [*He stands watching.* ŚAKUNTALĀ *appears as described, with her two friends.*]

40 BOTH FRIENDS: [*Fanning her affectionately.*] Śakuntalā, does the breeze from this lotus leaf please you?
ŚAKUNTALĀ: Are you fanning me?

[*The friends trade looks, miming dismay.*]
KING: [*Deliberating.*] Śakuntalā seems to be in great physical pain. Is it the heat or is it what is in my own heart? [*Miming ardent desire.*] My doubts are unfounded!

> Her breasts are smeared with lotus balm,
> her lotus-fiber bracelet hangs limp,
> her beautiful body glows in pain—
> love burns young women like summer heat
> but its guilt makes them more charming.

50 PRIYAMVADĀ: [*In a stage whisper.*] Anasūyā, Śakuntalā has been pining since she first saw the king. Could he be the cause of her sickness?
ANASŪYĀ: She must be suffering from lovesickness. I'll ask her ... [*Aloud.*] Friend, I have something to ask you. Your pain seems so deep ...
ŚAKUNTALĀ: [*Raising herself halfway.*] What do you want to say?
ANASŪYĀ: Śakuntalā, though we don't know what it is to be in love, your condition reminds us of lovers we have heard about in stories. Can you tell us the cause of your pain? Unless we understand your illness, we can't begin to find a cure.
KING: Anasūyā expresses my own thoughts.
ŚAKUNTALĀ: Even though I want to, suddenly I can't make myself tell you.
60 PRIYAMVADĀ: Śakuntalā, my friend Anasūyā means well. Don't you see how sick you are? Your limbs are wasting away. Only the shadow of your beauty remains ...
KING: What Priyamvadā says is true:

> Her cheeks are deeply sunken,
> her breasts' full shape is gone,
> her waist is thin, her shoulders bent,
> and the color has left her skin—
> tormented by love,
> she is sad but beautiful to see,
> like a jasmine creeper
70 > when hot wind shrivels its leaves.

ŚAKUNTALĀ: Friends, who else can I tell? May I burden you?
BOTH FRIENDS: We insist! Sharing sorrow with loving friends makes it bearable.
KING:

> Friends who share her joy and sorrow
> discover the love concealed in her heart—
> though she looked back longingly at me,
> now I am afraid to hear her response.

ŚAKUNTALĀ: Friend, since my eyes first saw the guardian of the hermits' retreat, I've felt such strong desire for him!

KING: I have heard what I want to hear.

80
> My tormentor, the god of love,
> has soothed my fever himself,
> like the heat of late summer
> allayed by early rain clouds.

ŚAKUNTALĀ: If you two think it's right, then help me to win the king's pity. Otherwise, you'll soon pour sesame oil and water[11] on my corpse . . .

KING: Her words destroy my doubt.

PRIYAṂVADĀ: [*In a stage whisper.*] She's so dangerously in love that there's no time to lose. Since her heart is set on the ornament of the Puru dynasty, we should rejoice that she desires him.

90 ANASŪYĀ: What you say is true.

PRIYAṂVADĀ: [*Aloud.*] Friend, by good fortune your desire is in harmony with nature. A great river can only descend to the ocean. A jasmine creeper can only twine around a mango tree.

KING: Why is this surprising when the twin stars of spring serve the crescent moon?

ANASŪYĀ: What means do we have to fulfill our friend's desire secretly and quickly?

PRIYAṂVADĀ: "Secretly" demands some effort. "Quickly" is easy.

ANASŪYĀ: How so?

PRIYAṂVADĀ: The king was charmed by her loving look; he seems thin these days from sleepless nights.

100 KING: It's true . . .

> This golden armlet
> slips to my wrist
> without touching the scars
> my bowstring has made;
> its gemstones are faded
> by tears of secret pain
> that every night wets my arm
> where I bury my face.

PRIYAṂVADĀ: [*Thinking.*] Compose a love letter and I'll hide it in a flower. I'll deliver
110   it to his hand on the pretext of bringing an offering to the deity.

ANASŪYĀ: This subtle plan pleases me. What does Śakuntalā say?

ŚAKUNTALĀ: I'll try my friend's plan.

PRIYAṂVADĀ: Then compose a poem to declare your love!

ŚAKUNTALĀ: I'm thinking, but my heart trembles with fear that he'll reject me.

KING: [*Delighted.*]

> The man you fear will reject you
> waits longing to love you, timid girl—

---

[11] **sesame oil and water:** Used in traditional Hindu funeral rites.

a suitor may lose or be lucky,
but the goddess always wins.

120 BOTH FRIENDS: Why do you belittle your own virtues? Who would cover his body
with a piece of cloth to keep off cool autumn moonlight?

ŚAKUNTALĀ: [*Smiling.*] I'm trying to follow your advice. [*She sits thinking.*]

KING: As I gaze at her, my eyes forget to blink.

> She arches an eyebrow,
> struggling to compose the verse —
> the down rises on her cheek,
> showing the passion she feels.

ŚAKUNTALĀ: I've thought of a verse, but I have nothing to write it on.

PRIYAMVADĀ: Engrave the letters with your nail on this lotus leaf! It's as delicate as a
parrot's breast.

130 ŚAKUNTALĀ: [*Miming what* PRIYAMVADĀ *described.*] Listen and tell me this makes
sense!

BOTH FRIENDS: We're both paying attention.

ŚAKUNTALĀ: [*Singing.*]

> I don't know
> your heart,
> but day and night
> for wanting you,
> love violently
> tortures
> my limbs,
140 > cruel man.

KING: [*Suddenly revealing himself.*]

> Love torments you, slender girl,
> but he completely consumes me —
> daylight spares the lotus pond
> while it destroys the moon.

BOTH FRIENDS: [*Looking, rising with delight.*] Welcome to the swift success of love's
desire!

[ŚAKUNTALĀ *tries to rise.*]

KING: Don't exert yourself!

> Limbs lying among crushed petals
> like fragile lotus stalks
150 > are too weakened by pain
> to perform ceremonious acts.

ANASŪYĀ: Then let the king sit on this stone bench!

[*The* KING *sits;* ŚAKUNTALĀ *rises in embarrassment.*]

PRIYAṀVADĀ: The passion of two young lovers is clear. My affection for our friend makes me speak out again now.

KING: Noble lady, don't hesitate! It is painful to keep silent when one must speak.

PRIYAṀVADĀ: We're told that it is the king's duty to ease the pain of his suffering subjects.

KING: My duty, exactly!

PRIYAṀVADĀ: Since she first saw you, our dear friend has been reduced to this sad
160   condition. You must protect her and save her life.

KING: Noble lady, our affection is shared and I am honored by all you say.

ŚAKUNTALĀ: [*Looking at* PRIYAṀVADĀ.] Why are you keeping the king here? He must be anxious to return to his palace.

KING:

> If you think that my lost heart
> could love anyone but you,
> a fatal blow strikes a man
> already wounded by love's arrows!

ANASŪYĀ: We've heard that kings have many loves. Will our dear friend become a sorrow to her family after you've spent time with her?

170 KING: Noble lady, enough of this!

> Despite my many wives,
> on two the royal line rests—
> sea-bound earth
> and your friend.

BOTH FRIENDS: You reassure us.

PRIYAṀVADĀ: [*Casting a glance.*] Anasūyā, this fawn is looking for its mother. Let's take it to her!

[*They both begin to leave.*]

ŚAKUNTALĀ: Come back! Don't leave me unprotected!

BOTH FRIENDS: The protector of the earth is at your side.

180 ŚAKUNTALĀ: Why have they gone?

KING: Don't be alarmed! I am your servant.

> Shall I set moist winds in motion
> with lotus-leaf fans to cool your pain,
> or rest your soft red lotus feet
> on my lap to stroke them, my love

ŚAKUNTALĀ: I cannot sin against those I respect!

[*Standing as if she wants to leave.*]

KING: Beautiful Śakuntalā, the day is still hot.

> Why should your frail limbs
> leave this couch of flowers

190   shielded by lotus leaves
           to wander in the heat?

[*Saying this, he forces her to turn around.*]

ŚAKUNTALĀ: Puru king, control yourself! Though I'm burning with love, how can I
     give myself to you?

KING: Don't fear your elders! The father of your family knows the law. When he finds
     out, he will not blame you.

           The daughters of royal sages often marry
           in secret[12] and then their fathers bless them.

ŚAKUNTALĀ: Release me! I must ask my friends' advice!

KING: Yes, I shall release you.

200   ŚAKUNTALĀ: When?

KING:

           Only let my thirsting mouth
           gently drink from your lips,
           the way a bee sips nectar
           from a fragile virgin blossom.

[*Saying this, he tries to raise her face.* ŚAKUNTALĀ *evades him with a dance.*]

VOICE OFFSTAGE: Red goose,[13] bid farewell to your gander! Night has arrived!

ŚAKUNTALĀ: [*Flustered.*] Puru king, Mother Gautamī is surely coming to ask about
     my health. Hide behind this tree!

KING: Yes.

[*He conceals himself and waits. Then* GAUTAMĪ *enters with a vessel in her hand, accompanied
by* ŚAKUNTALĀ'*s two friends.*]

BOTH FRIENDS: This way, Mother Gautamī!

210   GAUTAMĪ: [*Approaching* ŚAKUNTALĀ.] Child, does the fever in your limbs burn less?

ŚAKUNTALĀ: Madam, I do feel better.

GAUTAMĪ: Kuśa grass and water will soothe your body. [*She sprinkles* ŚAKUNTALĀ'*s
     head.*] Child, the day is ended. Come, let's go back to our hut! [*She starts to go.*]

ŚAKUNTALĀ: [*To herself.*] My heart, even when your desire was within reach, you
     were bound by fear. Now you'll suffer the torment of separation and regret.
     [*Stopping after a few steps, she speaks aloud.*] Bower of creepers, refuge from my
     torment, I say goodbye until our joy can be renewed . . . [*Sorrowfully,* ŚAKUN-
     TALĀ *exits with the other women.*]

KING: [*Coming out of hiding.*] Fulfillment of desire is fraught with obstacles.

           Why didn't I kiss her face
220   as it bent near my shoulder,

---

[12] **marry in secret:** The king invokes the *gandharva* form of marriage, a secret union by mutual consent that is
permitted for the warrior caste under Hindu law. By the beginning of Act IV, this secret marriage is assumed to
have taken place.

[13] **Red goose:** Also known as the sheldrake, this bird and her mate were said to be inseparable by day but
doomed to be parted every night.

her fingers shielding lips
that stammered lovely warning?

Should I go now? Or shall I stay here in this bower of creepers that my love
enjoyed and then left?

I see the flowers her body pressed
on this bench of stone,
the letter her nails inscribed
on the faded lotus leaf,
the lotus-fiber bracelet
230   that slipped from her wrist—
my eyes are prisoners
in this empty house of reeds.

VOICE IN THE AIR: King!

When the evening rituals begin,
shadows of flesh-eating demons swarm
like amber clouds of twilight,
raising terror at the altar of fire.

KING: I am coming.

[*He exits.*]

ACT IV

[*The two friends enter, miming the gathering of flowers.*]
ANASŪYĀ: Priyaṁvadā, I'm delighted that Śakuntalā chose a suitable husband for
herself, but I still feel anxious.
PRIYAṀVADĀ: Why?
ANASŪYĀ: When the king finished the sacrifice, the sages thanked him and he left.
Now that he has returned to his palace women in the city, will he remember us
here?
PRIYAṀVADĀ: Have faith! He's so handsome, he can't be evil. But I don't know what
Father Kaṇva will think when he hears about what happened.
ANASŪYĀ: I predict that he'll give his approval.
10 PRIYAṀVADĀ: Why?
ANASŪYĀ: He's always planned to give his daughter to a worthy husband. If fate
accomplished it so quickly, Father Kaṇva won't object.
PRIYAṀVADĀ: [*Looking at the basket of flowers.*] We've gathered enough flowers for
the offering ceremony.
ANASŪYĀ: Shouldn't we worship the goddess who guards Śakuntalā?
PRIYAṀVADĀ: I have just begun. [*She begins the rite.*]
VOICE OFFSTAGE: I am here!
ANASŪYĀ: [*Listening.*] Friend, a guest is announcing himself.
PRIYAṀVADĀ: Śakuntalā is in her hut nearby, but her heart is far away.
20 ANASŪYĀ: You're right! Enough of these flowers!

[*They begin to leave.*]

VOICE OFFSTAGE: So . . . you slight a guest . . .

> Since you blindly ignore
> a great sage like me,
> the lover you worship
> with mindless devotion
> will not remember you,
> even when awakened —
> like a drunkard who forgets
> a story he just composed!

30 PRIYAṂVADĀ: Oh! What a terrible turn of events! Śakuntalā's distraction has offended someone she should have greeted. [*Looking ahead.*] Not just an ordinary person, but the angry sage Durvāsas himself cursed her and went away in a frenzy of quivering, mad gestures. What else but fire has such power to burn?

ANASŪYĀ: Go! Bow at his feet and make him return while I prepare the water for washing his feet!

PRIYAṂVADĀ: As you say.   [*She exits.*]

ANASŪYĀ: [*After a few steps, she mimes stumbling.*] Oh! The basket of flowers fell from my hand when I stumbled in my haste to go. [*She mimes the gathering of flowers.*]

PRIYAṂVADĀ: [*Entering.*] He's so terribly cruel! No one could pacify him! But I was

40 able to soften him a little.

ANASŪYĀ: Even that is a great feat with him! Tell me more!

PRIYAṂVADĀ: When he refused to return, I begged him to forgive a daughter's first offense, since she didn't understand the power of his austerity.

ANASŪYĀ: Then? Then?

PRIYAṂVADĀ: He refused to change his word, but he promised that when the king sees the ring of recollection, the curse will end. Then he vanished.

ANASŪYĀ: Now we can breathe again. When he left, the king himself gave her the ring engraved with his name. Śakuntalā will have her own means of ending the curse.

PRIYAṂVADĀ: Come friend! We should finish the holy rite we're performing for her.

[*The two walk around, looking.*]

50 Anasūyā, look! With her face resting on her hand, our dear friend looks like a picture. She is thinking about her husband's leaving, with no thought for herself, much less for a guest.

ANASŪYĀ: Priyaṁvadā, we two must keep all this a secret between us. Our friend is fragile by nature; she needs our protection.

PRIYAṂVADĀ: Who would sprinkle a jasmine with scalding water?

[*They both exit; the interlude ends. Then a* DISCIPLE *of* KAṆVA *enters, just awakened from sleep.*]

DISCIPLE: Father Kaṇva has just returned from his pilgrimage and wants to know the exact time. I'll go into a clearing to see what remains of the night. [*Walking around and looking.*] It is dawn.

The moon sets over the western mountain
as the sun rises in dawn's red trail—
rising and setting, these two bright powers
portend the rise and fall of men.

When the moon disappears, night lotuses
are but dull souvenirs of its beauty—
when her lover disappears, the sorrow
is too painful for a frail girl to bear.

ANASŪYĀ: [*Throwing aside the curtain and entering.*] Even a person withdrawn from worldly life knows that the king has treated Śakuntalā badly.

DISCIPLE: I'll inform Father Kaṇva that it's time for the fire oblation. [*He exits.*]

ANASŪYĀ: Even when I'm awake, I'm useless. My hands and feet don't do their work. Love must be pleased to have made our innocent friend put her trust in a liar . . . but perhaps it was the curse of Durvāsas that changed him . . . otherwise, how could the king have made such promises and not sent even a message by now? Maybe we should send the ring to remind him. Which of these ascetics who practice austerities can we ask? Father Kaṇva has just returned from his pilgrimage. Since we feel that our friend was also at fault, we haven't told him that Śakuntalā is married to Duṣyanta and is pregnant. The problem is serious. What should we do?

PRIYAṂVADĀ: [*Entering, with delight.*] Friend, hurry! We're to celebrate the festival of Śakuntalā's departure for her husband's house.

ANASŪYĀ: What's happened, friend?

PRIYAṂVADĀ: Listen! I went to ask Śakuntalā how she had slept. Father Kaṇva embraced her and though her face was bowed in shame, he blessed her: "Though his eyes were filled with smoke, the priest's oblation luckily fell on the fire. My child, I shall not mourn for you . . . like knowledge given to a good student I shall send you to your husband today with an escort of sages."

ANASŪYĀ: Who told Father Kaṇva what happened?

PRIYAṂVADĀ: A bodiless voice was chanting when he entered the fire sanctuary. [*Quoting in Sanskrit.*]

Priest, know that your daughter
carries Duṣyanta's potent seed
for the good of the earth—
like fire in mimosa wood.

ANASŪYĀ: I'm joyful, friend. But I know that Śakuntalā must leave us today and sorrow shadows my happiness.

PRIYAṂVADĀ: Friend, we must chase away sorrow and make this hermit girl happy!

ANASŪYĀ: Friend, I've made a garland of mimosa flowers. It's in the coconut-shell box hanging on a branch of the mango tree. Get it for me! Meanwhile I'll prepare the special ointments of deer musk, sacred earth, and blades of dūrvā grass.

PRIYAṂVADĀ: Here it is!

[ANASŪYĀ *exits;* PRIYAṂVADĀ *gracefully mimes taking down the box.*]

100   VOICE OFFSTAGE: Gautamī! Śārṅgarava and some others have been appointed to escort Śakuntalā.

PRIYAMVADĀ: [*Listening.*] Hurry! Hurry! The sages are being called to go to Hastināpura.

ANASŪYĀ: [*Reentering with pots of ointments in her hands.*] Come, friend! Let's go!

PRIYAMVADĀ: [*Looking around.*] Śakuntalā stands at sunrise with freshly washed hair while the female ascetics bless her with handfuls of wild rice and auspicious words of farewell. Let's go to her together.

[*The two approach as* ŚAKUNTALĀ *enters with* GAUTAMĪ *and other female ascetics, and strikes a posture as described. One after another, the female ascetics address her.*]

FIRST FEMALE ASCETIC: Child, win the title "Chief Queen" as a sign of your husband's high esteem!

110   SECOND FEMALE ASCETIC: Child, be a mother to heroes!

THIRD FEMALE ASCETIC: Child, be honored by your husband!

BOTH FRIENDS: This happy moment is no time for tears, friend.

[*Wiping away her tears, they calm her with dance gestures.*]

PRIYAMVADĀ: Your beauty deserves jewels, not these humble things we've gathered in the hermitage.

[*Two boy ascetics enter with offerings in their hands.*]

BOTH BOYS: Here is an ornament for you!

[*Everyone looks amazed.*]

GAUTAMĪ: Nārada, my child, where did this come from?

FIRST BOY: From Father Kaṇva's power.

GAUTAMĪ: Was it his mind's magic?

SECOND BOY: Not at all! Listen! You ordered us to bring flowers from the forest trees
120   for Śakuntalā.

> One tree produced this white silk cloth,
> another poured resinous lac to redden her feet—
> the tree nymphs produced jewels in hands
> that stretched from branches like young shoots.

PRIYAMVADĀ: [*Watching* ŚAKUNTALĀ.] This is a sign that royal fortune will come to you in your husband's house.

[ŚAKUNTALĀ *mimes modesty.*]

FIRST BOY: Gautama, come quickly! Father Kaṇva is back from bathing. We'll tell him how the trees honor her.

SECOND BOY: As you say.

[*The two exit.*]

130   BOTH FRIENDS: We've never worn them ourselves, but we'll put these jewels on your limbs the way they look in pictures.

ŚAKUNTALĀ: I trust your skill.

[*Both friends mime ornamenting her. Then* KAṆVA *enters, fresh from his bath.*]

KAṆVA:

> My heart is touched with sadness
> since Śakuntalā must go today,
> my throat is choked with sobs,
> my eyes are dulled by worry—
> if a disciplined ascetic
> suffers so deeply from love,
> how do fathers bear the pain
> of each daughter's parting?

140

[*He walks around.*]

BOTH FRIENDS: Śakuntalā, your jewels are in place; now put on the pair of silken cloths.

[*Standing,* ŚAKUNTALĀ *wraps them.*]

GAUTAMĪ: Child, your father has come. His eyes filled with tears of joy embrace you.
    Greet him reverently!

ŚAKUNTALĀ: [*Modestly.*] Father, I welcome you.

KAṆVA: Child,

> May your husband honor you
> the way Yayāti honored Śarmiṣṭhā.
> As she bore her son Puru,[14]
> may you bear an imperial prince.

150 GAUTAMĪ: Sir, this is a blessing, not just a prayer.

KAṆVA: Child, walk around the sacrificial fires!

[*All walk around;* KAṆVA *intoning a prayer in Vedic meter.*]

> Perfectly placed around the main altar,
> fed with fuel, strewn with holy grass,
> destroying sin by incense from oblations,
> may these sacred fires purify you!

You must leave now! [*Looking around.*] Where are Śārṅgarava and the others?

DISCIPLE: [*Entering.*] Here we are, sir!

KAṆVA: You show your sister the way!

ŚĀRṄGARAVA: Come this way!

[*They walk around.*]

160 KAṆVA: Listen, you trees that grow in our grove!

> Until you were well watered
> she could not bear to drink;
> she loved you too much

---

[14]Yayāti . . . Śarmiṣṭhā . . . Puru: Yayāti and Śarmiṣṭhā are the parents of Puru, the king whose service to others characterized the rulers of the Paurava dynasty. Duṣyanta is descended from Puru and is one of the Paurava rulers.

to pluck your flowers for her hair;
the first time your buds bloomed,
she blossomed with joy—
may you all bless Śakuntalā
as she leaves for her husband's house.

[*Miming that he hears a cuckoo's cry.*]

170

The trees of her forest family
have blessed Śakuntalā—
the cuckoo's melodious song
announces their response.

VOICE IN THE AIR:

May lakes colored by lotuses mark her path!
May trees shade her from the sun's burning rays!
May the dust be as soft as lotus pollen!
May fragrant breezes cool her way!

[*All listen astonished.*]

GAUTAMĪ: Child, the divinities of our grove love you like your family and bless you.
We bow to you all!

ŚAKUNTALĀ: [*Bowing and walking around; speaking in a stage whisper.*] Priyaṁvadā,

180   though I long to see my husband, my feet move with sorrow as I start to leave
the hermitage.

PRIYAṀVADĀ: You are not the only one who grieves. The whole hermitage feels this
way as your departure from our grove draws near.

Grazing deer
drop grass,
peacocks
stop dancing,
vines loose
pale leaves

190   falling
like tears.

ŚAKUNTALĀ: [*Remembering.*] Father, before I leave, I must see my sister, the vine
Forestlight.

KAṆVA: I know that you feel a sister's love for her. She's right here.

ŚAKUNTALĀ: Forestlight, though you love your mango tree, turn to embrace me with
your tendril arms! After today, I'll be so far away . . .

KAṆVA:

Your merits won you the husband
I always hoped you would have
and your jasmine has her mango tree—

200   my worries for you both are over.

Start your journey here!

ŚAKUNTALĀ: [*Facing her two friends.*] I entrust her care to you.

BOTH FRIENDS: But who will care for us? [*They wipe away their tears.*]

KAṆVA: Anasūyā, enough crying! You should be giving Śakuntalā courage!

[*All walk around.*]

ŚAKUNTALĀ: Father, when the pregnant doe who grazes near my hut gives birth, please send someone to give me the good news.

KAṆVA: I shall not forget.

ŚAKUNTALĀ: [*Miming the interrupting of her gait.*] Who is clinging to my skirt?

[*She turns around.*]

KAṆVA: Child,

210   The buck whose mouth you healed with oil
       when it was pierced by a blade of kuśa grass
       and whom you fed with grains of rice—
       your adopted son will not leave the path.

ŚAKUNTALĀ: Child, don't follow when I'm abandoning those I love! I raised you when you were orphaned soon after your birth, but now I'm deserting you too. Father will look after you. Go back! [*Weeping, she starts to go.*]

KAṆVA: Be strong!

       Hold back the tears that blind
       your long-lashed eyes—
220   you will stumble if you cannot see
       the uneven ground on the path.

ŚĀRṄGARAVA: Sir, the scriptures prescribe that loved ones be escorted only to the water's edge. We are at the shore of the lake. Give us your message and return!

ŚAKUNTALĀ: We shall rest in the shade of this fig tree.

[*All walk around and stop;* KAṆVA *speaks to himself.*]

KAṆVA: What would be the right message to send to King Duṣyanta? [*He ponders.*]

ŚAKUNTALĀ: [*In a stage whisper.*] Look! The wild goose cries in anguish when her mate is hidden by lotus leaves. What I'm suffering is much worse.

ANASŪYĀ: Friend, don't speak this way!

       This goose spends
230   every long night
       in sorrow
       without her mate,
       but hope lets her
       survive
       the deep pain
       of loneliness.

KAṆVA: Śārṅgarava, speak my words to the king after you present Śakuntalā!

ŚĀRṄGARAVA: As you command, sir!

KAṆVA:

240
    Considering our discipline,
    the nobility of your birth
    and that she fell in love with you
    before her kinsmen could act,
    acknowledge her with equal rank
    among your wives—
    what more is destined for her,
    the bride's family will not ask.

ŚĀRṄGARAVA: I grasp your message.

KAṆVA: Child, now I must instruct you. We forest hermits know something about worldly matters.

250 ŚĀRṄGARAVA: Nothing is beyond the scope of wise men.

KAṆVA: When you enter your husband's family:

    Obey your elders, be a friend to the other wives!
    If your husband seems harsh, don't be impatient!
    Be fair to your servants, humble in your happiness!
    Women who act this way become noble wives;
    sullen girls only bring their families disgrace.

But what does Gautamī think?

GAUTAMĪ: This is good advice for wives, child. Take it all to heart!

KAṆVA: Child, embrace me and your friends!

260 ŚAKUNTALĀ: Father, why must Priyaṁvadā and my other friends turn back here?

KAṆVA: They will also be given in marriage. It is not proper for them to go there now. Gautamī will go with you.

ŚAKUNTALĀ: [*Embracing her father.*] How can I go on living in a strange place, torn from my father's side, like a vine torn from the side of a sandalwood tree growing on a mountain slope?

KAṆVA: Child, why are you so frightened?

    When you are your husband's honored wife,
    absorbed in royal duties and in your son,
    born like the sun to the eastern dawn,
270
    the sorrow of separation will fade.

[ŚAKUNTALĀ *falls at her father's feet.*]

Let my hopes for you be fulfilled!

ŚAKUNTALĀ: [*Approaching her two friends.*] You two must embrace me together!

BOTH FRIENDS: [*Embracing her.*] Friend, if the king seems slow to recognize you, show him the ring engraved with his name!

ŚAKUNTALĀ: Your suspicions make me tremble!

BOTH FRIENDS: Don't be afraid! It's our love that fears evil.

ŚĀRṄGARAVA: The sun is high in the afternoon sky. Hurry, please!

ŚAKUNTALĀ: [*Facing the sanctuary.*] Father, will I ever see the grove again?

KAṆVA:

> When you have lived for many years
> 280 as a queen equal to the earth
> and raised Duṣyanta's son
> to be a matchless warrior,
> your husband will entrust him
> with the burdens of the kingdom
> and will return with you
> to the calm of this hermitage.

GAUTAMĪ: Child, the time for our departure has passed. Let your father turn back! It would be better, sir, if you turn back yourself. She'll keep talking this way forever.

KAṆVA: Child, my ascetic practice has been interrupted.

290 ŚAKUNTALĀ: My father's body is already tortured by ascetic practices. He must not grieve too much for me!

KAṆVA: [Sighing.]

> When I see the grains of rice
> sprout from offerings you made
> at the door of your hut,
> how shall I calm my sorrow!

[ŚAKUNTALĀ exits with her escort.]

BOTH FRIENDS: [Watching ŚAKUNTALĀ.] Śakuntalā is hidden by forest trees now.

KAṆVA: Anasūyā, your companion is following her duty. Restrain yourself and return with me!

BOTH FRIENDS: Father, the ascetics' grove seems empty without Śakuntalā. How can
300 we enter?

KAṆVA: The strength of your love makes it seem so. [Walking around in meditation.] Good! Now that Śakuntalā is on her way to her husband's family, I feel calm.

> A daughter belongs to another man—
> by sending her to her husband today,
> I feel the satisfaction
> one has on repaying a loan.

[All exit.]

ACT V

[The KING and the BUFFOON enter; both sit down.]

BUFFOON: Pay attention to the music room, friend, and you'll hear the notes of a song strung into a delicious melody . . . the lady Haṃsapadikā is practicing her singing.

KING: Be quiet so I can hear her!

VOICE IN THE AIR: [Singing.]

> Craving sweet
> new nectar,

> you kissed
> a mango bud once—
> how could you
> forget her, bee,
> to bury your joy
> in a lotus

KING: The melody of the song is passionate.

BUFFOON: But did you get the meaning of the words?

KING: I once made love to her. Now she reproaches me for loving Queen Vasumatī. Friend Mādhavya, tell Haṃsapadikā that her words rebuke me soundly.

BUFFOON: As you command! [*He rises.*] But if that woman grabs my hair tuft, it will be like a heavenly nymph grabbing some ascetic . . . there go my hopes of liberation![15]

KING: Go! Use your courtly charm to console her.

BUFFOON: What a fate!

[*He exits.*]

KING: [*To himself.*] Why did hearing the song's words fill me with such strong desire? I'm not parted from anyone I love . . .

> Seeing rare beauty,
> hearing lovely sounds,
> even a happy man
> becomes strangely uneasy . . .
> perhaps he remembers,
> without knowing why,
> loves of another life
> buried deep in his being.

[*He stands bewildered. Then the* KING'S CHAMBERLAIN *enters.*]

CHAMBERLAIN: At my age, look at me!

> Since I took this ceremonial bamboo staff
> as my badge of office in the king's chambers
> many years have passed; now I use it
> as a crutch to support my faltering steps.

A king cannot neglect his duty. He has just risen from his seat of justice and though I am loath to keep him longer, Sage Kaṇva's pupils have just arrived. Authority to rule the world leaves no time for rest.

> The sun's steeds were yoked before time began,
> the fragrant wind blows night and day,

---

[15] **if that woman . . . liberation:** The Buffoon is comparing his chances of being released from the grip of the courtesan to the ascetic's hopes for liberation from *karma*.

the cosmic serpent always bears earth's weight,[16]
and a king who levies taxes has his duty.

Therefore, I must perform my office. [*Walking around and looking.*]

Weary from ruling them like children,
he seeks solitude far from his subjects,
like an elephant bull who seeks cool shade
after gathering his herd at midday.

50 [*Approaching.*] Victory to you, king! Some ascetics who dwell in the forest at the foothills of the Himālayas have come. They have women with them and bring a message from Sage Kaṇva. Listen, king, and judge!

KING: [*Respectfully.*] Are they Sage Kaṇva's messengers?

CHAMBERLAIN: They are.

KING: Inform the teacher Somarāta that he should welcome the ascetics with the prescribed rites and then bring them to me himself. I'll wait in a place suitable for greeting them.

CHAMBERLAIN: As the king commands.   [*He exits.*]

KING: [*Rising.*] Vetravatī, lead the way to the fire sanctuary.

DOORKEEPER: Come this way, king!

60 KING: [*Walking around, showing fatigue.*] Every other creature is happy when the object of his desire is won, but for kings success contains a core of suffering.

High office only leads to greater greed;
just perfecting its rewards is wearisome—
a kingdom is more trouble than it's worth,
like a royal umbrella one holds alone.

TWO BARDS OFFSTAGE: Victory to you, king!

FIRST BARD:

You sacrifice your pleasures every day
to labor for your subjects—
as a tree endures burning heat
70 to give shade from the summer sun.

SECOND BARD:

You punish villains with your rod of justice,
you reconcile disputes, you grant protection—
most relatives are loyal only in hope of gain,
but you treat all your subjects like kinsmen.

KING: My weary mind is revived. [*He walks around.*]

DOORKEEPER: The terrace of the fire sanctuary is freshly washed and the cow is waiting to give milk for the oblation. Let the king ascend!

---

[16] **cosmic serpent . . . earth's weight:** In Hindu mythology the earth rests on the cosmic serpent Sesa.

KING: Vetravatī, why has Father Kaṇva sent these sages to me?

> Does something hinder their ascetic life?
> Or threaten creatures in the sacred forest?
> Or do my sins stunt the flowering vines?
> My mind is filled with conflicting doubts.

DOORKEEPER: I would guess that these sages rejoice in your virtuous conduct and come to honor you.

[*The ascetics enter;* ŚAKUNTALĀ *is in front with* GAUTAMĪ; *the* CHAMBERLAIN *and the* KING'S PRIEST *are in front of her.*]

CHAMBERLAIN: Come this way, sirs!

ŚĀRṄGARAVA: Śaradvata, my friend:

> I know that this renowned king is righteous
> and none of the social classes follows evil ways,
> but my mind is so accustomed to seclusion
> that the palace feels like a house in flames.

ŚĀRADVATA: I've felt the same way ever since we entered the city.

> As if I were freshly bathed, seeing a filthy man,
> pure while he's defiled, awake while he's asleep,
> as if I were a free man watching a prisoner,
> I watch this city mired in pleasures.

ŚAKUNTALĀ: [*Indicating she feels an omen.*] Why is my right eye twitching?

GAUTAMĪ: Child, your husband's family gods turn bad fortune into blessings! [*They walk around.*]

PRIEST: [*Indicating the* KING.] Ascetics, the guardian of sacred order has left the seat of justice and awaits you now. Behold him!

ŚĀRṄGARAVA: Great priest, he seems praiseworthy, but we expect no less.

> Boughs bend, heavy with ripened fruit,
> clouds descend with fresh rain,
> noble men are gracious with wealth —
> this is the nature of bountiful things.

DOORKEEPER: King, their faces look calm. I'm sure that the sages have confidence in what they're doing.

KING: [*Seeing* ŚAKUNTALĀ.]

> Who is she? Carefully veiled
> to barely reveal her body's beauty,
> surrounded by the ascetics
> like a bud among withered leaves.

DOORKEEPER: King, I feel curious and puzzled too. Surely her form deserves closer inspection.

KING: Let her be! One should not stare at another man's wife!

ŚAKUNTALĀ: [*Placing her hand on her chest, she speaks to herself.*] My heart, why are you quivering? Be quiet while I learn my noble husband's feelings.

PRIEST: [*Going forward.*] These ascetics have been honored with due ceremony. They have a message from their teacher. The king should hear them!

KING: I am paying attention.

SAGES: [*Raising their hands in a gesture of greeting.*] May you be victorious, king!

120 KING: I salute you all!

SAGES: May your desires be fulfilled!

KING: Do the sages perform austerities unhampered?

SAGES:

> Who would dare obstruct the rites
> of holy men whom you protect —
> how can darkness descend
> when the sun's rays shine?

KING: My title "king" is more meaningful now. Is the world blessed by Father Kaṇva's health?

SAGES: Saints control their own health. He asks about your welfare and sends this

130 message . . .

KING: What does he command?

ŚĀRṄGARAVA: At the time you secretly met and married my daughter, affection made me pardon you both.

> We remember you to be a prince of honor;
> Śakuntalā is virtue incarnate —
> the creator cannot be condemned
> for mating the perfect bride and groom.

And now that she is pregnant, receive her and perform your sacred duty together.

GAUTAMĪ: Sir, I have something to say, though I wasn't appointed to speak:

140
> She ignored her elders
> and you failed to ask her kinsmen —
> since you acted on your own,
> what can I say to you now?

ŚAKUNTALĀ: What does my noble husband say?

KING: What has been proposed?

ŚAKUNTALĀ: [*To herself.*] The proposal is as clear as fire.

ŚĀRṄGARAVA: What's this? Your Majesty certainly knows the ways of the world!

> People suspect a married woman who stays
> with her kinsmen, even if she is chaste —
150
> a young wife should live with her husband,
> no matter how he despises her.

KING: Did I ever marry you?

ŚAKUNTALĀ: [*Visibly dejected, speaking to herself.*] Now your fears are real, my heart!

ŚĀRṄGARAVA:

> Does one turn away from duty in contempt
> because his own actions repulse him?

KING: Why ask this insulting question?

ŚĀRṄGARAVA:

> Such transformations take shape
> when men are drunk with power.

KING: This censure is clearly directed at me.

160 GAUTAMĪ: Child, this is no time to be modest. I'll remove your veil. Then your husband will recognize you.

[*She does so.*]

KING: [*Staring at* ŚAKUNTALĀ.]

> Must I judge whether I ever married
> the flawless beauty they offer me now?
> I cannot love her or leave her, like a bee
> near a jasmine filled with frost at dawn.

[*He shows hesitation.*]

DOORKEEPER: Our king has a strong sense of justice. Who else would hesitate when beauty like this is handed to him?

ŚĀRṄGARAVA: King, why do you remain silent?

KING: Ascetics, even though I'm searching my mind, I don't remember marrying this
170 lady. How can I accept a woman who is visibly pregnant when I doubt that I am the cause?

ŚAKUNTALĀ: [*In a stage whisper.*] My lord casts doubt on our marriage. Why were my hopes so high?

ŚĀRṄGARAVA: It can't be!

> Are you going to insult the sage
> who pardons the girl you seduced
> and bids you keep his stolen wealth,
> treating a thief like you with honor?

ŚĀRADVATA: Śārṅgarava, stop now! Śakuntalā, we have delivered our message and the
180 king has responded. He must be shown some proof.

ŚAKUNTALĀ: [*In a stage whisper.*] When passion can turn to this, what's the use of reminding him? But, it's up to me to prove my honor now. [*Aloud.*] My noble husband . . . [*She breaks off when this is half-spoken.*] Since our marriage is in doubt, this is no way to address him. Puru king, you do wrong to reject a simple-hearted person with such words after you deceived her in the hermitage.

KING: [*Covering his ears.*] Stop this shameful talk!

> Are you trying to stain my name
> and drag me to ruin—
> like a river eroding her own banks,
> soiling water and uprooting trees?

190

ŚAKUNTALĀ: Very well! If it's really true that fear of taking another man's wife turns you away, then this ring will revive your memory and remove your doubt.

KING: An excellent idea!

ŚAKUNTALĀ: [*Touching the place where the ring had been.*] I'm lost! The ring is gone from my finger. [*She looks despairingly at* GAUTAMĪ.]

GAUTAMĪ: The ring must have fallen off while you were bathing in the holy waters at the shrine of the goddess near Indra's grove.

KING: [*Smiling.*] And so they say the female sex is cunning.

ŚAKUNTALĀ: Fate has shown its power. Yet, I will tell you something else.

200   KING: I am still obliged to listen.

ŚAKUNTALĀ: One day, in a jasmine bower, you held a lotus-leaf cup full of water in your hand.

KING: We hear you.

ŚAKUNTALĀ: At that moment the buck I treated as my son approached. You coaxed it with the water, saying that it should drink first. But he didn't trust you and wouldn't drink from your hand. When I took the water, his trust returned. Then you jested, "Every creature trusts what its senses know. You both belong to the forest."

KING: Thus do women further their own ends by attracting eager men with the
210   honey of false words.

GAUTAMĪ: Great king, you are wrong to speak this way. This child raised in an ascetics' grove doesn't know deceit.

KING: Old woman,

> When naive female beasts show cunning,
> what can we expect of women who reason?
> Don't cuckoos let other birds nurture
> their eggs and teach the chicks to fly?

ŚAKUNTALĀ: [*Angrily.*] Evil man! You see everything distorted by your own ignoble heart. Who would want to imitate you now, hiding behind your show of justice,
220   like a well overgrown with weeds?

KING: [*To himself.*] Her anger does not seem feigned; it makes me doubt myself.

> When the absence of love's memory
> made me deny a secret affair with her,
> this fire-eyed beauty bent her angry brows
> and seemed to break the bow of love.

[*Aloud.*] Lady, Duṣyanta's conduct is renowned, so what you say is groundless.

ŚAKUNTALĀ: All right! I may be a self-willed wanton woman! But it was faith in the Puru dynasty that brought me into the power of a man with honey in his words and poison in his heart. [*She covers her face at the end of the speech and weeps.*]

230 ŚĀRṄGARAVA: A willful act unchecked always causes pain.

> One should be cautious
> in forming a secret union—
> unless a lover's heart is clear,
> affection turns to poison.

KING: But sir, why do you demean me with such warnings? Do you trust the lady?

ŚĀRṄGARAVA: [*Scornfully.*] You have learned everything backwards.

> If you suspect the word of one
> whose nature knows no guile,
> then you can only trust
240 people who practice deception.

KING: I presume you speak the truth. Let us assume so. But what could I gain by deceiving this woman?

ŚĀRṄGARAVA: Ruin.

KING: Ruin? A Puru king has no reason to want his own ruin!

ŚĀRADVATA: Śārṅgarava, this talk is pointless. We have delivered our master's message and should return.

> Since you married her, abandon her or take her—
> absolute is the power a husband has over his wife.

GAUTAMĪ: You go ahead.

[*They start to go.*]

250 ŚAKUNTALĀ: What? Am I deceived by this cruel man and then abandoned by you? [*She tries to follow them.*]

GAUTAMĪ: [*Stopping.*] Śārṅgarava my son, Śakuntalā is following us, crying pitifully. What will my child do now that her husband has refused her?

ŚĀRṄGARAVA: [*Turning back angrily.*] Bold woman, do you still insist on having your way?

[ŚAKUNTALĀ *trembles in fear.*]

> If you are what the king says you are,
> you don't belong in Father Kaṇva's family—
> if you know that your marriage vow is pure,
> you can bear slavery in your husband's house.

Stay! We must go on!

260 KING: Ascetic, why do you disappoint the lady too?

> The moon only makes lotuses open,
> the sun's light awakens lilies—

a king's discipline forbids him
to touch another man's wife.

ŚĀRṄGARAVA: If you forget a past affair because of some present attachment, why do
you fear injustice now?

KING: [*To the* PRIEST.] Sir I ask you to weigh the alternatives:

> Since it's unclear whether I'm deluded
> or she is speaking falsely—
> should I risk abandoning a wife
> or being tainted by another man's?

270

PRIEST: [*Deliberating.*] I recommend this . . .

KING: Instruct me! I'll do as you say.

PRIEST: Then let the lady stay in our house until her child is born. If you ask why: the
wise men predict that your first son will be born with the marks of a king who
turns the wheel of empire. If the child of the sage's daughter bears the marks,
congratulate her and welcome her into your palace chambers. Otherwise, send
her back to her father.

KING: Whatever the elders desire.

280 PRIEST: Child, follow me!

ŚAKUNTALĀ: Mother earth, open to receive me!

[*Weeping,* ŚAKUNTALĀ *exits with the* PRIEST *and the hermits. The* KING, *his memory lost
through the curse, thinks about her.*]

VOICE OFFSTAGE: Amazing! Amazing!

KING: [*Listening.*] What could this be?

PRIEST: [*Reentering, amazed.*] King, something marvelous has occurred!

KING: What?

PRIEST: When Kaṇva's pupils had departed,

> The girl threw up her arms and wept,
> lamenting her misfortune . . . then . . .

KING: Then what?

PRIEST:

290

> Near the nymph's shrine a ray of light
> in the shape of a woman carried her away.

[*All mime amazement.*]

KING: We've already settled the matter. Why discuss it further?

PRIEST: [*Observing the* KING.] May you be victorious!

[*He exits.*]

KING: Vetravatī, I am bewildered. Lead the way to my chamber!

DOORKEEPER: Come this way, my lord! [*She walks forward.*]

KING:

> I cannot remember marrying
> the sage's abandoned daughter,

but the pain my heart feels
makes me suspect that I did.

[*All exit.*]

ACT VI

[*The* KING's *wife's brother, who is city* MAGISTRATE, *enters with two policemen leading a* MAN *whose hands are tied behind his back.*]

BOTH POLICEMEN: [*Beating the* MAN.] Speak, thief? Where'd you steal this handsome ring with the king's name engraved in the jewel?

MAN: [*Showing fear.*] Peace, sirs! I wouldn't do a thing like that.

FIRST POLICEMAN: Don't tell us the king thought you were some famous priest and gave it to you as a gift!

MAN: Listen, I'm a humble fisherman who lives near Indra's grove.

SECOND POLICEMAN: Thief, did we ask you about your caste?

MAGISTRATE: Sūcaka, let him tell it all in order! Don't interrupt him!

BOTH POLICEMEN: Whatever you command, chief!

10 MAN: I feed my family by catching fish with nets and hooks.

MAGISTRATE: [*Mocking.*] What a pure profession![17]

MAN:

> The work I do
> may be vile
> but I won't deny
> my birthright —
> a priest
> doing his holy rites
> pities the animals
> he kills.

20 MAGISTRATE: Go on!

MAN: One day as I was cutting up a red carp, I saw the shining stone of this ring in its belly. When I tried to sell it, you grabbed me. Kill me or let me go! That's how I got it!

MAGISTRATE: Jānuka, I'm sure this ugly butcher's a fisherman by his stinking smell. We must investigate how he got the ring. We'll go straight to the palace.

BOTH POLICEMEN: Okay. Go in front, you pickpocket!

[*All walk around.*]

MAGISTRATE: Sūcaka, guard this villain at the palace gate! I'll report to the king how we found the ring, get his orders, and come back.

BOTH POLICEMEN: Chief, good luck with the king!

[*The* MAGISTRATE *exits.*]

---

[17] **a pure profession:** A sarcastic comment about fishing, a profession that requires the killing of animals.

30 FIRST POLICEMAN: Jānuka, my hands are itching to tie on his execution garland.[18] [*He points to the* MAN.]

MAN: You shouldn't think about killing a man for no reason.

SECOND POLICEMAN: [*Looking.*] I see our chief coming with a letter in his hand. It's probably an order from the king. You'll be thrown to the vultures or you'll see the face of death's dog[19] again . . .

MAGISTRATE: [*Entering.*] Sūcaka, release this fisherman! I'll tell you how he got the ring.

FIRST POLICEMAN: Whatever you say, chief!

SECOND POLICEMAN: The villain entered the house of death and came out again. [*He unties the prisoner.*]

MAN: [*Bowing to the* MAGISTRATE.] Master, how will I make my living now?

40 MAGISTRATE: The king sends you a sum equal to the ring. [*He gives the money to the* MAN.]

MAN: [*Bowing as he grabs it.*] The king honors me.

FIRST POLICEMAN: This fellow's certainly honored. He was lowered from the execution stake and raised up on a royal elephant's back.

SECOND POLICEMAN: Chief, the reward tells me this ring was special to the king.

MAGISTRATE: I don't think the king valued the stone, but when he caught sight of the ring, he suddenly seemed to remember someone he loved, and he became deeply disturbed.

FIRST POLICEMAN: You served him well, chief!

SECOND POLICEMAN: I think you better served this king of fish. [*Looking at the fisherman with jealousy.*]

50 MAN: My lords, half of this is yours for your good will.

FIRST POLICEMAN: It's only fair!

MAGISTRATE: Fisherman, now that you are my greatest and dearest friend, we should pledge our love over kadamba-blossom wine. Let's go to the wine shop!

[*They all exit together; the interlude ends. Then a nymph named* SĀNUMATĪ *enters by the skyway.*]

SĀNUMATĪ: Now that I've performed my assigned duties at the nymph's shrine, I'll slip away to spy on King Duṣyanta while the worshipers are bathing. My friendship with Menakā makes me feel a bond with Śakuntalā. Besides, Menakā asked me to help her daughter. [*Looking around.*] Why don't I see preparations for the spring festival in the king's palace? I can learn everything by using my mental powers, but I must respect my friend's request. So be it! I'll make myself invis-

60 ible and spy on these two girls who are guarding the pleasure garden.

[SĀNUMATĪ *mimes descending and stands waiting. Then a* MAID *servant named Parabhṛtikā, "Little Cuckoo," enters, looking at a mango bud. A* SECOND MAID, *named Madhukarikā, "Little Bee," is following her.*]

---

[18] **execution garland:** Condemned prisoners were dressed in sacrificial robes and garlands at the time of execution.

[19] **death's dog:** In Hindu mythology, the path of death is guarded by two four-eyed dogs.

FIRST MAID:

> Your pale green stem
> tinged with pink
> is a true sign
> that spring has come—
> I see you,
> mango-blossom bud,
> and I pray
> for a season of joy.

SECOND MAID: What are you muttering to yourself?

70 FIRST MAID: A cuckoo goes mad when she sees a mango bud.

SECOND MAID: [*Joyfully rushing over.*] Has the sweet month of spring come?

FIRST MAID: Now's the time to sing your songs of love.

SECOND MAID: Hold me while I pluck a mango bud and worship the god of love.

FIRST MAID: Only if you'll give me half the fruit of your worship.

SECOND MAID: That goes without saying . . . our bodies may be separate, but our lives are one . . . [*Leaning on her friend, she stands and plucks a mango bud.*] The mango flower is still closed, but this broken stem is fragrant. [*She makes the dove gesture with her hands.*]

> Mango blossom bud,
> I offer you to Love
80 > as he lifts
> his bow of passion.
> Be the first
> of his flower arrows
> aimed at lonely girls
> with lovers far away!

[*She throws the mango bud.*]

MAGISTRATE: [*Angrily throwing aside the curtain and entering.*] Not now, stupid girl! When the king has banned the festival of spring, how dare you pluck a mango bud!

BOTH MAIDS: [*Frightened.*] Please forgive us, sir. We don't know what you mean.

90 CHAMBERLAIN: Did you not hear that even the spring trees and the nesting birds obey the king's order?

> The mango flowers bloom without spreading pollen,
> the red amaranth buds, but will not bloom,
> cries of cuckoo cocks freeze though frost is past,
> and out of fear, Love holds his arrow half-drawn.

BOTH MAIDS: There is no doubt about the king's great power!

FIRST MAID: Sir, several days ago we were sent to wait on the queen by Mitrāvasu, the king's brother-in-law. We were assigned to guard the pleasure garden. Since we're newcomers, we've heard no news.

100   CHAMBERLAIN: Let it be! But don't do it again!

BOTH MAIDS: Sir, we're curious. May we ask why the spring festival was banned?

SĀNUMATĪ: Mortals are fond of festivals. The reason must be serious.

CHAMBERLAIN: It is public knowledge. Why should I not tell them? Has the scandal of Śakuntalā's rejection not reached your ears?

BOTH MAIDS: We only heard from the king's brother-in-law that the ring was found.

CHAMBERLAIN: [*To himself.*] There is little more to tell. [*Aloud.*] When he saw the ring, the king remembered that he had married Śakuntalā in secret and had rejected her in his delusion. Since then the king has been tortured by remorse.

> Despising what he once enjoyed,
110 > he shuns his ministers every day
> and spends long sleepless nights
> tossing at the edge of his bed —
> when courtesy demands that
> he converse with palace women,
> he stumbles over their names,
> and then retreats in shame.

SĀNUMATĪ: This news delights me.

CHAMBERLAIN: The festival is banned because of the king's melancholy.

BOTH MAIDS: It's only right.

120   VOICE OFFSTAGE: This way, sir!

CHAMBERLAIN: [*Listening.*] The king is coming. Go about your business!

BOTH MAIDS: As you say.

[*Both maids exit. Then the* KING *enters, costumed to show his grief, accompanied by the* BUFFOON *and the* DOORKEEPER.]

CHAMBERLAIN: [*Observing the* KING.] Extraordinary beauty is appealing under all conditions. Even in his lovesick state, the king is wonderful to see.

> Rejecting his regal jewels,
> he wears one golden bangle
> above his left wrist;
> his lips are pale with sighs,
> his eyes wan from brooding at night —
130 > like a gemstone ground in polishing,
> the fiery beauty of his body
> makes his wasted form seem strong.

SĀNUMATĪ: [*Seeing the* KING.] I see why Śakuntalā pines for him though he rejected and disgraced her.

KING: [*Walking around slowly, deep in thought.*]

> This cursed heart slept
> when my love came to wake it,
> and now it stays awake
> to suffer the pain of remorse.

SĀNUMATĪ: The girl shares his fate.

140 BUFFOON: [*In a stage whisper.*] He's having another attack of his Śakuntalā disease. I doubt if there's any cure for that.

CHAMBERLAIN: [*Approaching.*] Victory to the king! I have inspected the grounds of the pleasure garden. Let the king visit his favorite spots and divert himself.

KING: Vetravatī, deliver a message to my noble minister Piśuna: "After being awake all night, we cannot sit on the seat of justice today. Set in writing what your judgment tells you the citizens require and send it to us!"

DOORKEEPER: Whatever you command!   [*She exits.*]

KING: Vātāyana, attend to the rest of your business!

CHAMBERLAIN: As the king commands!   [*He exits.*]

150 BUFFOON: You've cleared out the flies. Now you can rest in some pretty spot. The garden is pleasant now in this break between morning cold and noonday heat.

KING: Dear friend, the saying "Misfortunes rush through any crack" is absolutely right:

> Barely freed by the dark force
> that made me forget Kaṇva's daughter,
> my mind is threatened by an arrow
> of mango buds fixed on Love's bow.

BUFFOON: Wait, I'll destroy the love god's arrow with my wooden stick. [*Raising his staff, he tries to strike a mango bud.*]

KING: [*Smiling.*] Let it be! I see the majesty of brahman bravery. Friend, where may I
160 sit to divert my eyes with vines that remind me of my love?

BUFFOON: Didn't you tell your maid Caturikā, "I'll pass the time in the jasmine bower. Bring me the drawing board on which I painted a picture of Śakuntalā with my own hand!"

KING: Such a place may soothe my heart. Show me the way!

BUFFOON: Come this way!

[*Both walk around; the nymph* SĀNUMATĪ *follows.*]
The marble seat and flower offerings in this jasmine bower are certainly trying to make us feel welcome. Come in and sit down!

[*Both enter the bower and sit.*]

SĀNUMATĪ: I'll hide behind these creepers to see the picture he's drawn of my friend. Then I'll report how great her husband's passion is.

[*She does as she says and stands waiting.*]

170 KING: Friend, now I remember everything. I told you about my first meeting with Śakuntalā. You weren't with me when I rejected her, but why didn't you say anything about her before? Did you suffer a loss of memory too?

BUFFOON: I didn't forget. You did tell me all about it once, but then you said, "It's all a joke without any truth." My wit is like a lump of clay, so I took you at your word . . . or it could be that fate is powerful . . .

SĀNUMATĪ: It is!

KING: Friend, help me!

BUFFOON: What's this? It doesn't become you! Noblemen never take grief to heart. Even in storms, mountains don't tremble.

180   KING: Dear friend, I'm defenseless when I remember the pain of my love's bewilderment when I rejected her.

> When I cast her away, she followed her kinsmen,
> but Kaṇva's disciple harshly shouted, "Stay!"
> The tearful look my cruelty provoked
> burns me like an arrow tipped with poison.

SĀNUMATĪ: The way he rehearses his actions makes me delight in his pain.

BUFFOON: Sir, I guess that the lady was carried off by some celestial creature or other.

KING: Who else would dare to touch a woman who worshiped her husband? I was told that Menakā is her mother. My heart suspects that her mother's compan-

190   ions carried her off.

SĀNUMATĪ: His delusion puzzled me, but not his reawakening.

BUFFOON: If that's the case, you'll meet her again in good time.

KING: How?

BUFFOON: No mother or father can bear to see a daughter parted from her husband.

KING:

> Was it dream or illusion or mental confusion,
> or the last meager fruit of my former good deeds?
> It is gone now, and my heart's desires are
> like riverbanks crumbling of their own weight.

BUFFOON: Stop this! Isn't the ring evidence that an unexpected meeting is destined

200   to take place?

KING: [*Looking at the ring.*] I only pity it for falling from such a place.

> Ring, your punishment is proof
> that your face is as flawed as mine—
> you were placed in her lovely fingers,
> glowing with crimson nails, and you fell.

SĀNUMATĪ: The real pity would have been if it had fallen into some other hand.

BUFFOON: What prompted you to put the signet ring on her hand?

SĀNUMATĪ: I'm curious too.

KING: I did it when I left for the city. My love broke into tears and asked, "How long

210   will it be before my noble husband sends news to me?"

BUFFOON: Then? What then?

KING: Then I placed the ring on her finger with this promise:

> One by one, day after day,
> count each syllable of my name!
> At the end, a messenger will come
> to bring you to my palace.

But in my cruel delusion, I never kept my word.

SĀNUMATĪ: Fate broke their charming agreement!

BUFFOON: How did it get into the belly of the carp the fisherman was cutting up?

220 KING: While she was worshiping at the shrine of Indra's wife, it fell from her hand into the Gaṅgā.[20]

BUFFOON: It's obvious now!

SĀNUMATĪ: And the king, doubtful of his marriage to Śakuntalā, a female ascetic, was afraid to commit an act of injustice. But why should such passionate love need a ring to be remembered?

KING: I must reproach the ring for what it's done.

BUFFOON: [*To himself.*] He's gone the way of all madmen . . .

KING:

> Why did you leave her delicate finger
> and sink into the deep river?

230 of course . . .

> A mindless ring can't recognize virtue,
> but why did I reject my love?

BUFFOON: [*To himself again.*] Why am I consumed by a craving for food?

KING: Oh ring! Have pity on a man whose hate is tormented because he abandoned his love without cause! Let him see her again!

[*Throwing the curtain aside, the maid* CATURIKĀ *enters, with the drawing board in her hand.*]

CATURIKĀ: Here's the picture you painted of the lady. [*She shows the drawing board.*]

BUFFOON: Dear friend, how well you've painted your feelings in this sweet scene. My eyes almost stumble over the hollows and hills.

SĀNUMATĪ: What skill the king has! I feel as if my friend were before me.

KING:

240
> The picture's imperfections are not hers,
> but this drawing does hint at her beauty.

SĀNUMATĪ: Such words reveal that suffering has increased his modesty as much as his love.

BUFFOON: Sir, I see three ladies now and they're all lovely to look at. Which is your Śakuntalā?

SĀNUMATĪ: Only a dim-witted fool like this wouldn't know such beauty!

KING: You guess which one!

BUFFOON: I guess Śakuntalā is the one you've drawn with flowers falling from her loosened locks of hair, with drops of sweat on her face, with her arms hanging limp and tired as she stands at the side of a mango tree whose tender shoots are gleaming with the fresh water she poured. The other two are her friends.

---

[20] **the Gaṅgā:** The river Ganges.

KING: You are clever! Look at these signs of my passion!

> Smudges from my sweating fingers
> stain the edges of the picture
> and a tear fallen from my cheek
> has raised a wrinkle in the paint.

Caturikā, the scenery is only half-drawn. Go and bring my paints!

CATURIKĀ: Noble Māḍhavya, hold the drawing board until I come back!

KING: I'll hold it myself.   [*He takes it, the maid exits.*]

260

> I rejected my love when she came to me,
> and how I worship her in a painted image—
> having passed by a river full of water,
> I'm longing now for an empty mirage.

BUFFOON: [*To himself.*] He's too far gone for a river now! He's looking for a mirage!
[*Aloud.*] Sir, what else do you plan to draw here?

SĀNUMATĪ: He'll want to draw every place my friend loved.

KING:

> I'll draw the river Mālinī
> flowing through Himālaya's foothills
> where pairs of wild geese nest in the sand

270

> and deer recline on both riverbanks,
> where a doe is rubbing her left eye
> on the horn of a black buck antelope
> under a tree whose branches
> have bark dresses hanging to dry.

BUFFOON: [*To himself.*] Next he'll fill the drawing board with mobs of ascetics wearing long grassy beards.

KING: Dear friend, I've forgotten to draw an ornament that Śakuntalā wore.

BUFFOON: What is it?

SĀNUMATĪ: It will suit her forest life and her tender beauty.

KING:

280

> I haven't drawn the mimosa flower on her ear,
> its filaments resting on her cheek,
> or the necklace of tender lotus stalks,
> lying on her breasts like autumn moonbeams.

BUFFOON: But why does the lady cover her face with her red lotus-bud fingertips and stand trembling in fear? [*Looking closely.*] That son-of-a-bee who steals nectar from flowers is attacking her face.

KING: Drive the impudent rogue away!

BUFFOON: You have the power to punish criminals. You drive him off!

KING: All right! Bee, favored guest of the flowering vines, why do you frustrate yourself by flying here?

290

A female bee waits on a flower,
thirsting for your love —
she refuses to drink
the sweet nectar without you.

SĀNUMATĪ: How gallantly he's driving him away!

BUFFOON: When you try to drive it away, this creature becomes vicious.

KING: Why don't you stop when I command you?

Bee, if you touch the lips of my love
that lure you like a young tree's virgin buds,
300   lips I gently kissed in festivals of love,
I'll hold you captive in a lotus flower cage.

BUFFOON: Why isn't he afraid of your harsh punishment? [*Laughing, he speaks to himself.*] He's gone crazy and I'll be the same if I go on talking like this. [*Aloud.*] But sir, it's just a picture!

KING: A picture? How can that be?

SĀNUMATĪ: When I couldn't tell whether it was painted, how could he realize he was looking at a picture?

KING: Dear friend, are you envious of me?

My heart's affection made me feel
310   the joy of seeing her —
but you reminded me again
that my love is only a picture.

[*He wipes away a tear.*]

SĀNUMATĪ: The effects of her absence make him quarrelsome.

KING: Dear friend, why do I suffer this endless pain?

Sleepless nights prevent our meeting in dreams;
her image in a picture is ruined by my tears.

SĀNUMATĪ: You have clearly atoned for the suffering your rejection caused Śakuntalā.

CATURIKĀ: [*Entering.*] Victory my lord! I found the paint box and started back right away . . . but I met Queen Vasumatī with her maid Taralikā on the path and she
320   grabbed the box from my hand, saying, "I'll bring it to the noble lord myself!"

BUFFOON: You were lucky to get away!

CATURIKĀ: The queen's shawl got caught on a tree. While Taralikā was freeing it, I made my escape.

KING: Dear friend, the queen's pride can quickly turn to anger. Save this picture!

BUFFOON: You should say, "Save yourself!" [*Taking the picture, he stands up.*] If you escape the woman's deadly poison, then send word to me in the Palace of the Clouds.   [*He exits hastily.*]

SĀNUMATĪ: Even though another woman has taken his heart and he feels indifferent to the queen, he treats her with respect.

330 DOORKEEPER: [*Entering with a letter in her hand.*] Victory, king!

KING: Vetravatī, did you meet the queen on the way?

DOORKEEPER: I did, but when she saw the letter in my hand, she turned back.

KING: She knows that this is official and would not interrupt my work.

DOORKEEPER: King, the minister requests that you examine the contents of this letter. He said that the enormous job of reckoning the revenue in this one citizen's case had taken all his time.

KING: Show me the letter! [*The girl hands it to him and he reads barely aloud.*] What is this? "A wealthy merchant sea captain named Dhanamitra has been lost in a shipwreck and the laws say that since the brave man was childless, his accumu-

340   lated wealth all goes to the king." It's terrible to be childless! A man of such wealth probably had several wives. We must find out if any one of his wives is pregnant!

DOORKEEPER: King, it's said that one of his wives, the daughter of a merchant of Ayodhyā, has performed the rite to ensure the birth of a son.[21]

KING: The child in her womb surely deserves his parental wealth. Go! Report this to my minister!

DOORKEEPER: As the king commands! [*She starts to go.*]

KING: Come here a moment!

DOORKEEPER: I am here.

350   KING: Is it his offspring or not?

> When his subjects lose a kinsman,
> Duṣyanta will preserve the estates—
> unless there is some crime.
> Let this be proclaimed.

DOORKEEPER: It shall be proclaimed loudly. [*She exits; reenters.*] The king's order will be as welcome as rain in the right season.

KING: [*Sighing long and deeply.*] Families without offspring whose lines of succession are cut off lose their wealth to strangers when the last male heir dies. When I die, this will happen to the wealth of the Puru dynasty.

360   DOORKEEPER: Heaven forbid such a fate!

KING: I curse myself for despising the treasure I was offered.

SĀNUMATĪ: He surely has my friend in mind when he blames himself.

KING:

> I abandoned my lawful wife, the holy ground
> where I myself planted my family's glory,
> like earth sown with seed at the right time,
> ready to bear rich fruit in season.

SĀNUMATĪ: But your family's line will not be broken.

CATURIKĀ: [*In a stage whisper.*] The king is upset by the story of the merchant. Go and bring noble Mādhavya from the Palace of the Clouds to console him!

370   DOORKEEPER: A good idea!

[*She exits.*]

---

[21] **the rite . . . a son:** A rite (*pumsavana*) performed in the third month of pregnancy.

KING: Duṣyanta's ancestors are imperiled.

> Our fathers drink the yearly libation
> mixed with my childless tears,
> knowing that there is no other son
> to offer the sacred funeral waters.

[*He falls into a faint.*]

CATURIKĀ: [*Looking at the bewildered* KING.] Calm yourself, my lord!

SĀNUMATĪ: Though a light shines, his separation from Śakuntalā keeps him in a state of dark depression. I could make him happy now, but I've heard Indra's consort consoling Śakuntalā with the news that the gods are hungry for their share of the ancestral oblations and will soon conspire to have her husband welcome his lawful wife. I'll have to wait for the auspicious time, but meanwhile I'll cheer my friend by reporting his condition.

> [*She exits, flying into the air.*]

VOICE OFFSTAGE: Help! Brahman-murder!

KING: [*Regaining consciousness, listening.*] Is it Māḍhavya's cry of pain? Who's there?

DOORKEEPER: King, your friend is in danger. Help him!

KING: Who dares to threaten him?

DOORKEEPER: Some invisible spirit seized him and dragged him to the roof of the Palace of the Clouds.

KING: [*Getting up.*] Not this! Even my house is haunted by spirits.

> When I don't even recognize
> the blunders I commit every day,
> how can I keep track
> of where my subjects stray?

VOICE OFFSTAGE: Dear friend! Help! Help!

KING: [*Breaking into a run.*] Friend, don't be afraid! I'm coming!

VOICE OFFSTAGE: [*Repeating the call for help.*] Why shouldn't I be afraid? Someone is trying to split my neck in three, like a stalk of sugar cane.

KING: [*Casting a glance.*] Quickly, my bow!

BOW-BEARER: [*Entering with a bow in hand.*] Here are your bow and quiver.

[*The* KING *takes his bow and arrows.*]

VOICE OFFSTAGE:

> I'll kill you as a tiger kills struggling prey!
> I'll drink fresh blood from your tender neck!
> Take refuge now in the bow Duṣyanta lifts
> to calm the fears of the oppressed!

KING: [*Angrily.*] How dare you abuse my name? Stop, carrion-eater! Or you will not live! [*He strings his bow.*] Vetravatī, lead the way to the stairs!

DOORKEEPER: This way, king.

[*All move forward in haste.*]

KING: [*Searching around.*] There is no one here!

VOICE OFFSTAGE: Help! Help! I see you. Don't you see me? I'm like a mouse caught by a cat! My life is hopeless!

410 KING: Don't count on your powers of invisibility! My magical arrows will find you. I aim this arrow:

> It will strike its doomed target
> and spare the brahman it must save —
> a wild goose can extract the milk
> and leave the water untouched.

[*He aims the arrow. Then Indra's charioteer* MĀTALI *enters, having released the* BUFFOON.]

MĀTALI: King!

> Indra sets demons as your targets;
> draw your bow against them!
> Send friends gracious glances
420 rather than deadly arrows!

KING: [*Withdrawing his arrow.*] Mātali, welcome to great Indra's charioteer!

BUFFOON: [*Entering.*] He tried to slaughter me like a sacrificial beast and this king is greeting him with honors!

MĀTALI: [*Smiling.*] Your Majesty, hear why Indra has sent me to you!

KING: I am all attention.

MĀTALI: There is an army of demons descended from one-hundred-headed Kāla-nemi, known to be invincible . . .

KING: I have already heard it from Nārada, the gods' messenger.

MĀTALI:

> He is invulnerable to your friend Indra,
430 so you are appointed to lead the charge —
> the moon dispels the darkness of night
> since the sun cannot drive it out.

Take your weapon, mount Indra's chariot, and prepare for victory!

KING: Indra favors me with this honor. But why did you attack Mādhavya?

MĀTALI: I'll tell you! From the signs of anguish Your Majesty showed, I knew that you were despondent. I attacked him to arouse your anger.

> A fire blazes when fuel is added;
> a cobra provoked raises its hood —
> men can regain lost courage
440 if their emotions are aroused.

KING: [*In a stage whisper.*] Dear friend, I cannot disobey a command from the lord of heaven. Inform my minister Piśuna of this and tell him this for me:

> Concentrate your mind on guarding my subjects!
> My bow is strung to accomplish other work.

BUFFOON: Whatever you command!

[*He exits.*]

MĀTALI: Mount the chariot, Your Majesty!

[*The* KING *mimes mounting the chariot; all exit.*]

ACT VII

[*The* KING *enters with* MĀTALI *by the skyway, mounted on a chariot.*]

KING: Mātali, though I carried out his command, I feel unworthy of the honors Indra gave me.

MĀTALI: [*Smiling.*] Your Majesty, neither of you seems satisfied.

> You belittle the aid you gave Indra
> in face of the honors he conferred,
> and he, amazed by your heroic acts,
> deems his hospitality too slight.

KING: No, not so! When I was taking leave, he honored me beyond my heart's desire and shared his throne with me in the presence of the gods:

10
> Indra gave me a garland of coral flowers
> tinged with sandalpowder from his chest,
> while he smiled at his son Jayanta,
> who stood there barely hiding his envy.

MĀTALI: Don't you deserve whatever you want from Indra?

> Indra's heaven of pleasures has twice
> been saved by rooting out thorny demons—
> your smooth-jointed arrows have now done
> what Viṣṇu once did with his lion claws.[22]

KING: Here too Indra's might deserves the praise.

20
> When servants succeed in great tasks,
> they act in hope of their master's praise—
> would dawn scatter the darkness
> if he were not the sun's own charioteer?

MĀTALI: This attitude suits you well! [*He moves a little distance.*] Look over there, Your Majesty! See how your own glorious fame has reached the vault of heaven!

> Celestial artists are drawing your exploits
> on leaves of the wish-granting creeper[23]

---

[22] what Viṣṇu . . . lion claws: Half man, half horse, the god Viṣṇu once killed a demon.

[23] the wish-granting creeper: The *kalpalata* vine that grows in Indra's heaven.

with colors of the nymphs' cosmetic paints,
and bards are moved to sing of you in ballads.

30   KING: Mātali, in my desire to do battle with the demons, I did not notice the path we
took to heaven as we climbed through the sky yesterday. Which course of the
winds are we traveling?

MĀTALI:

They call this path of the wind Parivaha—
freed from darkness by Viṣṇu's second stride,
it bears the Gaṅgā's three celestial streams
and turns stars in orbit, dividing their rays.

KING: Mātali, this is why my soul, my senses, and my heart feel calm. [*He looks at the
chariot wheels.*] We've descended to the level of the clouds.

MĀTALI: How do you know?

KING:

40   Crested cuckoos fly between the spokes,
lightning flashes glint off the horses' coats,
and a fine mist wets your chariot's wheels—
all signs that we go over rain-filled clouds.

MĀTALI: In a moment you'll be back in your own domain, Your Majesty.

KING: [*Looking down.*] Our speeding chariot makes the mortal world appear fantastic. Look!

Mountain peaks emerge as the earth descends,
branches spread up from a sea of leaves,
fine lines become great rivers to behold—

50   the world seems to hurtle toward me.

MĀTALI: You observe well! [*He looks with great reverence.*] The beauty of earth is
sublime.

KING: Mātali, what mountain do I see stretching into the eastern and western seas,
rippled with streams of liquid gold, like a gateway of twilight clouds?

MĀTALI: Your Majesty, it is called the "Golden Peak," the mountain of the demigods,
a place where austerities are practiced to perfection.

Mārīca, the descendant of Brahmā,
a father of both demons and gods,
lives the life of an ascetic here

60   in the company of Aditi, his wife.

KING: One must not ignore good fortune! I shall perform the rite of circumambulat-
ing the sage.

MĀTALI: An excellent idea!

[*The two mime descending.*]

KING: [*Smiling.*]

> The chariot wheels make no sound,
> they raise no clouds of dust,
> they touch the ground unhindered—
> nothing marks the chariot's descent.

MĀTALI: It is because of the extraordinary power that you and Indra both possess.
KING: Mātali, where is Mārīca's hermitage?
MĀTALI: [*Pointing with his hand.*]

70
> Where the sage stands staring at the sun,
> as immobile as the trunk of a tree,
> his body half-buried in an ant hill,
> with a snake skin on his chest,
> his throat pricked by a necklace
> of withered thorny vines,
> wearing a coil of long matted hair
> filled with nests of śakunta birds.

KING: I do homage to the sage for his severe austerity.
MĀTALI: [*Pulling hard on the chariot reins.*] Great king, let us enter Mārīca's her-
80   mitage, where Aditi nurtures the celestial coral trees.
KING: This tranquil place surpasses heaven. I feel as if I'm bathing in a lake of nectar.
MĀTALI: [*Stopping the chariot.*] Dismount, Your Majesty!
KING: [*Dismounting.*] Mātali, what about you?
MĀTALI: I have stopped the chariot. I'll dismount too. [*He does so.*] This way, Your
     Majesty! [*He walks around.*] You can see the grounds of the ascetics' grove ahead.
KING: I am amazed!

> In this forest of wish-fulfilling trees
> ascetics live on only the air they breathe
> and perform their ritual ablutions
90
> in water colored by golden lotus pollen.
> They sit in trance on jeweled marble slabs
> and stay chaste among celestial nymphs,
> practicing austerities in the place
> that others seek to win by penances.

MĀTALI: Great men always aspire to rare heights! [*He walks around, calling aloud.*] O
     venerable Śakalya, what is the sage Mārīca doing now? What do you say? In
     response to Aditi's question about the duties of a devoted wife, he is talking in a
     gathering of great sages' wives.
KING: [*Listening.*] We must wait our turn.
100 MĀTALI: [*Looking at the KING.*] Your Majesty, rest at the foot of this aśoka tree. Mean-
     while, I'll look for a chance to announce you to Indra's father.
KING: As you advise . . . [*He stops.*]

MĀTALI: Your Majesty, I'll attend to this.   [*He exits.*]

KING: [*Indicating he feels an omen.*]

> I have no hope for my desire.
> Why does my arm throb in vain?
> Once good fortune is lost,
> it becomes constant pain.

VOICE OFFSTAGE: Don't be so wild! Why is his nature so stubborn?

KING: [*Listening.*] Unruly conduct is out of place here. Whom are they reprimand-
110   ing? [*Looking toward the sound, surprised.*] Who is this child, guarded by two
female ascetics? A boy who acts more like a man.

> He has dragged this lion cub
> from its mother's half-full teat
> to play with it, and with his hand
> he violently tugs its mane.

[*The* BOY *enters as described, with two female ascetics.*]

BOY: Open your mouth, lion! I want to count your teeth!

FIRST ASCETIC: Nasty boy, why do you torture creatures we love like our children?
You're getting too headstrong! The sages gave you the right name when they
called you "Sarvadamana, Tamer-of-everything."

120   KING: Why is my heart drawn to this child, as if he were my own flesh? I don't have a
son. That is why I feel tender toward him . . .

SECOND ASCETIC: The lioness will maul you if you don't let go of her cub!

BOY: [*Smiling.*] Oh, I'm scared to death! [*Pouting.*]

KING:

> This child appears to be
> the seed of hidden glory,
> like a spark of fire
> awaiting fuel to burn.

FIRST ASCETIC: Child, let go of the lion cub and I'll give you another toy!

BOY: Where is it? Give it to me! [*He reaches out his hand.*]

130   KING: Why does he bear the mark of a king who turns the wheel of empire?

> A hand with fine webs connecting the fingers
> opens as he reaches for the object greedily,
> like a single lotus with faint inner petals
> spread open in the red glow of early dawn.

SECOND ASCETIC: Suvratā, you can't stop him with words! The sage Mārkaṇḍeya's
son left a brightly painted clay bird in my hut. Get it for him!

FIRST ASCETIC: I will!   [*She exits.*]

BOY: But until it comes I'll play with this cub.

KING: I am attracted to this pampered boy . . .

140
> Lucky are fathers whose laps give refuge
> to the muddy limbs of adoring little sons
> when childish smiles show budding teeth
> and jumbled sounds make charming words.

SECOND ASCETIC: Well, he ignores me. [*She looks back.*] Is one of the sage's sons here? [*Looking at the* KING.] Sir, please come here! Make him loosen his grip and let go of the lion cub! He's tormenting it in his cruel child's play.

KING: [*Approaching the* BOY, *smiling.*] Stop! You're a great sage's son!

> When self-control is your duty by birth,
> why do you violate the sanctuary laws
150
> and ruin the animals' peaceful life,
> like a young black snake in a sandal tree?

SECOND ASCETIC: Sir, he's not a sage's son.

KING: His actions and his looks confirm it. I based my false assumption on his presence in this place. [*He does what she asked; responding to the* BOY's *touch, he speaks to himself.*]

> Even my limbs feel delighted
> from the touch of a stranger's son —
> the father at whose side he grew
> must feel pure joy in his heart.

SECOND ASCETIC: [*Examining them both.*] It's amazing! Amazing!

160 KING: What is it, madam?

SECOND ASCETIC: This boy looks surprisingly like you. He doesn't even know you, and he's acting naturally.

KING: [*Fondling the child.*] If he's not the son of an ascetic, what lineage does he belong to?

SECOND ASCETIC: The family of Puru.

KING: [*To himself.*] What? His ancestry is the same as mine . . . so this lady thinks he resembles me. The family vow of Puru's descendants is to spend their last days in the forest.

> As world protectors they first choose
170
> palaces filled with sensuous pleasures,
> but later, their homes are under trees
> and one wife shares the ascetic vows.

[*Aloud.*] But mortals cannot enter this realm on their own.

SECOND ASCETIC: You're right, sir. His mother is a nymph's child. She gave birth to him here in the hermitage of Mārīca.

KING: [*In a stage whisper.*] Here is a second ground for hope! [*Aloud.*] What famed royal sage claims her as his wife?

SECOND ASCETIC: Who would even think of speaking the name of a man who rejected his lawful wife?

180 KING: [*To himself.*] Perhaps this story points to me. What if I ask the name of the boy's mother? No, it is wrong to ask about another man's wife.

FIRST ASCETIC: [*Returning with a clay bird in her hand.*] Look, Sarvadamana, a śakunta! Look! Isn't it lovely?

BOY: Where's my mother?

BOTH ASCETICS: He's tricked by the similarity of names.[24] He wants his mother.

SECOND ASCETIC: Child, she told you to look at the lovely clay śakunta bird.

KING: [*To himself.*] What? Is his mother's name Śakuntalā? But names can be the same. Even a name is a mirage . . . a false hope to herald despair.

BOY: I like this bird! [*He picks up the toy.*]

190 FIRST ASCETIC: [*Looking frantically.*] Oh, I don't see the amulet-box on his wrist!

KING: Don't be alarmed! It broke off while he was tussling with the lion cub. [*He goes to pick it up.*]

BOTH ASCETICS: Don't touch it! Oh, he's already picked it up! [*With their hands on their chests, they stare at each other in amazement.*]

KING: Why did you warn me against it?

FIRST ASCETIC: It contains the magical herb called Aparājitā,[25] honored sir. Mārīca gave it to him at his birth ceremony. He said that if it fell to the ground no one but his parents or himself could pick it up.

KING: And if someone else does pick it up?

FIRST ASCETIC: Then it turns into a snake and strikes.

KING: Have you two seen it so transformed?

200 BOTH ASCETICS: Many times.

KING: [*To himself, joyfully.*] Why not rejoice in the fulfillment of my heart's desire? [*He embraces the child.*]

SECOND ASCETIC: Suvratā, come, let's tell Śakuntalā that her penances are over. [*Both ascetics exit.*]

BOY: Let me go! I want my mother!

KING: Son, you will greet your mother with me.

BOY: My father is Duṣyanta, not you!

KING: This contradiction confirms the truth.

[ŚAKUNTALĀ *enters, wearing the single braid of a woman in mourning.*]

ŚAKUNTALĀ: Even though Sarvadamana's amulet kept its natural form instead of changing into a snake, I can't hope that my destiny will be fulfilled. But maybe what my friend Sānumatī reports is right.

210 KING: [*Looking at* ŚAKUNTALĀ.] It is Śakuntalā!

> Wearing dusty gray garments,
> her face gaunt from penances,

---

[24] **the similarity of names:** The boy confuses the word *śakunta* (bird) with *Śakuntalā* (woman of birds).

[25] **Aparājitā:** An herb whose name means invincible.

her bare braid[26] hanging down —
she bears with perfect virtue
the trial of long separation
my cruelty forced on her.

ŚAKUNTALĀ: [*Seeing the* KING *pale with suffering.*] He doesn't resemble my noble husband. Whose touch defiles my son when the amulet is protecting him?

BOY: [*Going to his mother.*] Mother, who is this stranger who calls me "son"?

220 KING: My dear, I see that you recognize me now. Even my cruelty to you is transformed by your grace.

ŚAKUNTALĀ: [*To herself.*] Heart, be consoled! My cruel fate has finally taken pity on me. It is my noble husband!

KING:

Memory chanced to break my dark delusion
and you stand before me in beauty,
like the moon's wife Rohiṇī
as she rejoins her lord after an eclipse.

ŚAKUNTALĀ: Victory to my noble husband! Vic . . . [*She stops when the word is half-spoken, her throat choked with tears.*]

KING: Beautiful Śakuntalā,

230 Even choked by your tears,
the word "victory" is my triumph
on your bare pouting lips,
pale-red flowers of your face.

BOY: Mother, who is he?

ŚAKUNTALĀ: Child, ask the powers of fate!

KING: [*Falling at* ŚAKUNTALĀ's *feet.*]

May the pain of my rejection
vanish from your heart;
delusion clouded my weak mind
and darkness obscured good fortune —
240 a blind man tears off a garland,
fearing the bite of a snake.

ŚAKUNTALĀ: Noble husband, rise! Some crime I had committed in a former life surely came to fruit and made my kind husband indifferent to me.

[*The* KING *rises.*]

But how did my noble husband come to remember this woman who was doomed to pain?

---

[26] **bare braid:** A sign that a woman is separated from her lover.

KING: I shall tell you after I have removed the last barb of sorrow.

> In my delusion I once ignored
> a teardrop burning your lip—
> let me dry the tear on your lash
250 > to end the pain of remorse!

[*He does so.*]

ŚAKUNTALĀ: [*Seeing the signet ring.*] My noble husband, this is the ring!

KING: I regained my memory when the ring was recovered.

ŚAKUNTALĀ: When it was lost, I tried in vain to convince my noble husband who I was.

KING: Let the vine take back this flower as a sign of her union with spring.

ŚAKUNTALĀ: I don't trust it. Let my noble husband wear it!

[MĀTALI *enters.*]

MĀTALI: Good fortune! This meeting with your lawful wife and the sight of your son's face are reasons to rejoice.

KING: The sweet fruit of my desire! Mātali, didn't Indra know about all this?

260 MĀTALI: What is unknown to the gods? Come Your Majesty! The sage Mārīca grants you an audience.

KING: Śakuntalā, hold our son's hand! We shall go to see Mārīca together.

ŚAKUNTALĀ: I feel shy about appearing before my elders in my husband's company.

KING: But it is customary at a joyous time like this. Come! Come!

[*They all walk around. Then* MĀRĪCA *enters with* ADITI; *they sit.*]

MĀRĪCA: [*Looking at the* KING.]

> Aditi, this is king Duṣyanta,
> who leads Indra's armies in battle;
> his bow lets your son's thunderbolt
> lie ready with its tip unblunted.

ADITI: He bears himself with dignity.

270 MĀTALI: Your Majesty, the parents of the gods look at you with affection reserved for a son. Approach them!

KING: Mātali, the sages so describe this pair.

> Source of the sun's twelve potent forms,
> parents of Indra, who rules the triple world,
> birthplace of Viṣṇu's primordial form,
> sired by Brahmā's sons, Marīci and Dakṣa.

MĀTALI: Correct!

KING: [*Bowing.*] Indra's servant, Duṣyanta, bows to you both.

MĀRĪCA: My son, live long and protect the earth!

280 ADITI: My son, be an invincible warrior!

ŚAKUNTALĀ: I worship at your feet with my son.
MĀRĪCA:

> Child, with a husband like Indra
> and a son like his son Jayanta,
> you need no other blessing.
> Be like Indra's wife Paulomī!

ADITI: Child, may your husband honor you and may your child live long to give both families joy! Be seated!

[*All sit near* MĀRĪCA.]
MĀRĪCA: [*Pointing to each one.*]

> By the turn of fortune,
> virtuous Śakuntalā, her noble son,
> and the king are reunited —
> faith and wealth with order.

KING: Sir, first came the success of my hopes, then the sight of you. Your kindness is unparalleled.

> First flowers appear, then fruits,
> first clouds rise, then rain falls,
> but here the chain of events is reversed —
> first came success, then your blessing.

MĀTALI: This is the way the creator gods give blessings.
KING: Sir, I married your charge by secret marriage rites. When her relatives brought her to me after some time, my memory failed and I sinned against the sage Kaṇva, your kinsman. When I saw the ring, I remembered that I had married his daughter. This is all so strange!

> Like one who doubts the existence
> of an elephant who walks in front of him
> but feels convinced by seeing footprints,
> my mind has taken strange turns.

MĀRĪCA: My son, you need not take the blame. Even your delusion has another cause. Listen!
KING: I am attentive.
MĀRĪCA: When Menakā took her bewildered daughter from the steps of the nymph's shrine and brought her to my wife, I knew through meditation that you had rejected this girl as your lawful wife because of Durvāsas' curse, and that the curse would end when you saw the ring.
KING: [*Sighing.*] So I am freed of blame.
ŚAKUNTALĀ: [*To herself.*] And I am happy to learn that I wasn't rejected by my husband without cause. But I don't remember being cursed. Maybe the empty heart

of love's separation made me deaf to the curse . . . my friends did warn me to show the ring to my husband . . .

MĀRĪCA: My child, I have told you the truth. Don't be angry with your husband!

320
> You were rejected when the curse
> that clouded memory made him cruel,
> but now darkness is lifted
> and your power is restored—
> a shadow has no shape
> in a badly tarnished mirror,
> but when the surface is clean
> it can easily be seen.

KING: Sir, here is the glory of my family! [*He takes the child by the hand.*]

MĀRĪCA: Know that he is destined to turn the wheel of your empire!

330
> His chariot will smoothly cross
> the ocean's rough waves
> and as a mighty warrior
> he will conquer the seven continents.
> Here he is called Sarvadamana,
> Tamer-of-everything;
> later when his burden is the world,
> men will call him Bharata, Sustainer.[27]

KING: Since you performed his birth ceremonies, we can hope for all this.

ADITI: Sir, let Kaṇva be told that his daughter's hopes have been fulfilled. Menakā,
340 who loves her daughter, is here in attendance.

ŚAKUNTALĀ: [*To herself.*] The lady expresses my own desire.

MĀRĪCA: He knows everything already through the power of his austerity.

KING: This is why the sage was not angry at me.

MĀRĪCA: Still, I want to hear his response to this joyful reunion. Who is there?

DISCIPLE: [*Entering.*] Sir, it is I.

MĀRĪCA: Gālava, fly through the sky and report the joyous reunion to Kaṇva in my own words: "The curse is ended. Śakuntalā and her son are embraced by Duṣyanta now that his memory is restored."

DISCIPLE: As you command, sir!   [*He exits.*]

350 MĀRĪCA: My son, mount your friend Indra's chariot with your wife and son and return to your royal capital!

KING: As you command, sir!

---

[27] **Bharata, Sustainer:** According to Indian mythical geography, the earth consists of seven islands surrounded by seven seas. The legendary Bharata, celebrated for his dharmic rule, was called the Sustainer. He created an empire of such great extent that all of India came to be called Bharata, or Bharatavarṣa. (Translator's note.)

MĀRĪCA: My son, what other joy can I give you?
KING: There is no greater joy, but if you will:

> May the king serve nature's good!
> May priests honor the goddess of speech!
> And may Śiva's dazzling power
> destroy my cycle of rebirths![28]

[*All exit.*]

---

[28] **May the king . . . rebirths:** The traditional ending of all Sanskrit plays; in this verse the king calls for the blessings of the gods on himself and the universal order.

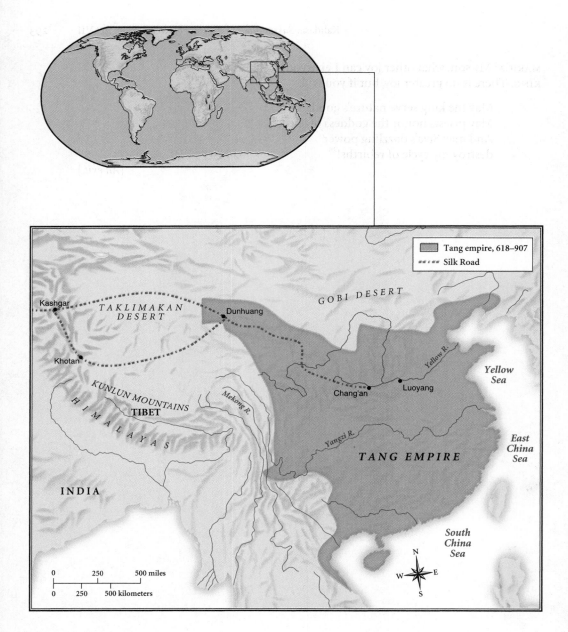

The Tang Empire, c. 750

Under the Tang dynasty, a unified China enjoyed increased prosperity and growth. Travel routes such as the Silk Road helped spread Tang influence from the heartland of China west to Tibet through central Asia, to the Middle East.

CHINA
From the Collapse of the Han Dynasty to the Mongol Invasions

In 220 C.E., barbarians invaded China, bringing an end to the Han dynasty. Soon after, beginning in 317, invading nomads developed a stable society in north China. In south China in the same period, a new culture grew up around the Yangtze River valley. The Sui dynasty (581–617), the Tang dynasty (618–907), and the northern and southern Sung dynasties (960–1279) eventually united the separate regions of China. Then in 1215, Mongols invaded the north and reached the south in 1279, ending a thousand-year period of flourishing Chinese culture. The developments that occurred during the Sui and Tang dynasties have been compared to those of the European **MIDDLE AGES**, while the advances of the Sung dynasties have been compared to the European **RENAISSANCE**. These are accurate comparisons insofar as each period comprised four general stages: the disorientation brought about by a barbarian invasion, a period of recovery on the part of social institutions, a period of high culture, and a process of consolidation and preservation.

THE EARLY PERIOD: DYNASTIES OF THE NORTH AND SOUTH

From the beginning of the fourth century to the end of the sixth, the situation of China can be discussed in terms of the north and the south. In north China, nomadic tribes slowly became settled agricultural people. Their fear of new invasions from the northern steppes motivated them to produce a strong military force and a centralized government. In the south, earlier Chinese migrants had settled into the basin of the Yangtze River and the area around Canton. As they did, they colonized the indigenous peoples from the river valley, mountains, and seacoast, taking many as slaves. Unifying this diverse region was extremely difficult; instead, wealthy families established local courts that ruled by controlling the native labor force and local trade. By the fifth and sixth centuries, this aristocratic system of rule was well established.

The rise of the Sui dynasty in 581 put an end to the rule of separate nomadic dynasties in the north. Eight years later, the Sui dynasty unified China, a situation that would last until the tenth century, or through the Tang dynasty. Unification brought the southern Yangtze culture into the national mainstream, opened up the seacoasts for northern trade, and brought about a massive public-works program. After floods, riots, and an unpopular war led to a rebellion against the Sui dynasty, the Tang dynasty was formed in 618.

THE TANG DYNASTY (618–907)

The Tang dynasty began well. Aristocratic families of north China headed the government, commanded the imperial guards and palace troops of the army, and helped create a well-organized bureaucracy composed of scholars and clerks. The new rulers instituted governmental reforms and rebuilt the military, which opposed Turkish armies to the north and west and safeguarded the northern border. They intensified the breeding of horses, animals that were indispensable for military activity and private enjoyment and whose importance is confirmed in many artworks of the period. The Tang rulers also completed an effective system of canals, originally intended to speed communications but later instrumental in transporting rice from the south.

The ancient city of Chang'an (Ch'ang-an), restored by the Sui dynasty in 583, became the western capital of the Tang dynasty in the early seventh century. Conceived as a vast cosmopolitan center, it was a meeting place for traders, merchants, soldiers, artists, entertainers, religious pilgrims, courtiers, and government bureaucrats. Along with Baghdad, Chang'an was one of the great cities of the world in the eighth and ninth centuries. Built in the shape of a rectangle whose outer walls ran six miles from east to west and five miles from north to south, the city was crisscrossed by fourteen avenues north to south and eleven east to west. The imperial city, located at the north end, was protected by double walls; adjacent to it was the palace, famed for its works of art and cultural performances. The population of the walled city of Chang'an in the eighth century was approximately one million, with as many people living outside its walls.

The first weakening of Tang rule occurred during a military rebellion of 755 in which a northern general, An Lushan, marched south from Peking in defiance of the ruler Tang Xuanzong (r. 712–756) to occupy Chang'an. His entrance into the city was unopposed. Although the rebel armies were defeated in 757, the shock of the rebellion dealt a blow to Tang authority and eventually led to the weakening of the aristocracy, the creation of military regions, the formation of mercenary armies, the ceding of public lands to the wealthy, the closure of borders, and a sharp decline in foreign trade. The Tang dynasty dissolved under the weight of

Two Horsemen, seventh century C.E.

With the unification of the northern and southern dynasties in the sixth century, Chinese culture flourished. From its great capital, Chang'an, the Tang dynasty (618–907) furthered the consolidation begun in the previous century and oversaw a literary flowering in poetry. During the Tang dynasty, horse breeding for both military and private purposes was strongly encouraged. (Wallpainting. Dun Huang. Giraudon/Art Resource, NY)

expenses required to support its numerous military regions and its mercenary army, which fell into disorder in the ninth century. Tang rulers deserted Chang'an in 885 and yielded to a new emperor in 907.

FROM THE SUNG DYNASTY TO THE MONGOL INVASIONS

During a transition period of fifty years, China was divided into the Five Dynasties, each under separate military control. For the next three hundred years the Sung dynasty held power, first as the northern Sung (960–1126) and then as the southern Sung (1127–1279). This progressive dynasty was finally destroyed by the Mongol invasions, beginning in the north in 1215 and proceeding south in 1279. The Sung had recognized the Mongol threat by the twelfth century but were powerless to stop it.

The Mongols conquered Manchuria and north China in 1215, Russia in 1243, and Baghdad and the Abbasid empire in 1258. At first, under the rule of Chingis Khan (r. 1206–1227), the Mongols devastated the lands they conquered, destroying crops and livestock and putting civilian populations to the sword. Liberalizing their policies somewhat after the death of Chingis Khan, the Mongols continued to adopt reforms through the era of Kubilai Khan (r. 1274–1294), mainly for their own benefit. Having entered China during a period of economic expansion, they modified their political and economic behavior in order to increase their prosperity. Their heavy taxation, however, eventually provoked peasant revolts, and their policy of distributing paper money barely disguised their practice of spiriting silver and gold out of China for their own use. Although occupation remained burdensome, Mongol rulers did not force China into isolation from the rest of the world. In the thirteenth century, travelers from abroad still journeyed in and out of China. Contact with Muslim society, conducted through Mongol intermediaries, remained a source of enrichment for the Chinese.

CULTURE IN THE EARLY PERIOD

The cultural development in China in the early period (fourth to sixth centuries) was distinctly uneven. The dynasties of north China showed little interest in the arts, focusing instead on stability and self-defense. But the local courts of south China, especially among the new Yangtze family dynasties, took a radical turn. Instead of following CONFUCIANISM, the philosophy of the Chinese classical period, southern artists, writers, and performers focused on the values of spontaneity and artistic sensibility as well as the separation of the artist from the concerns of everyday society. Landscape painting and the writing of literary criticism and lyric poetry occupied artists during the fourth century. About this time Buddhism also began to contribute significantly to Chinese cultural life. The new religion was accepted in the north as a partial antidote to the grim militaristic society that existed there. In the south, BUDDHISM and DAOISM were equally embraced for their reverence for nature. Early period landscape painting and classical poetry reflect these values.

A great innovator in Chinese poetry, Tao Qian (Tao Ch'ien), was born in southeastern China in 365. He witnessed the influx of northern aristocratic families to the Yangtze valley and lived to see the breakup of the eastern Jin (Chin) dynasty in 420. A Daoist, he withdrew from civilization to live on his family farm near Poyang Lake, thus helping to create the popular image of the poet as recluse. Resigning from a minor government post at the age of forty, he retired to the countryside in 406, living the rest of his days, he writes, "unconcerned with success or failure." Both the substance of his poetry and his way of life became objects of emulation for the later Tang poets. Tao Qian died in 427.

Court Ladies,
tenth century
*Ladies of the court
receive instructions in
adornment in what is
thought to be a Tang
dynasty painted
scroll. (British
Museum)*

THE CULTURE OF THE TANG DYNASTY

During the Tang dynasty, the Buddhism that had taken root in China became a highly
visible Chinese export. Scholarly Buddhist monks and pious Chinese laymen served as
important cultural models whenever religious pilgrims traveled to India or the West.
The Buddhist monk Xuanzang (596–664) who helped to establish this pattern, toured
India, the Near East, and the Middle East, taking extensive notes on his journeys, and
translated Chinese literature into Sanskrit and Indian literature into Chinese.

The first half of the eighth century marked the greatest period of Tang culture.
The capital at Chang'an was a brilliant center of civilization. Although Confucianism still dominated the civil service, the well-established Buddhist monasteries
recruited many followers, and the Chinese artistic leaning toward self-expression
continued to develop in painting and poetry. The Tang poets, following the writings of Tao Qian (365–427), demonstrated an attitude of independence, developed
an ethical justification for living apart from society, and cultivated an interest in
nature poetry in particular.

THE POETS OF THE TANG DYNASTY

Three of the four great poets of the Tang dynasty—Wang Wei (c. 699–761), Li Bai
(Li Po; 701–762), and Du Fu (Tu Fu; 712–770)—lived during the reign of Tang
Xuanzong (r. 712–756), who possessed among other qualities a sincere affection
for the arts. Though these Tang poets were not afraid of controversy and sometimes reflected the ills of society, their major claim to greatness lay in personal

TIME AND PLACE

China: The Silk Road, Highway to the World

The Silk Road was an ancient network of trade routes spanning nearly eight thousand miles from Chang'an, China, to port cities along the eastern Mediterranean. Coastal cities such as Acre, Constantinople, and Antioch and trading centers such as Damascus prospered as a result of its existence. The Silk Road passed through such central Asian cities as Kashgar, Samarkand, and Bukhara west of the Takla Makan Desert, and through present-day Afghanistan to what are now Jaipur, India; Tehran, Iran; and Ankara, Turkey.

This ancient trading route first developed before the first millennium B.C.E., when horses and camels were domesticated along the deserts and steppes of central Asia. Well before the Han dynasty (206 B.C.E.–220 C.E.) took over the easternmost portion of the route, Chinese silk was transported to the Mediterranean and beyond across a network of routes in central Asia. By means of force and diplomacy, the Han dynasty extended its control over the Silk Road from Chang'an to

beyond the Takla Makan Desert, creating a regional commercial network. Trade flourished, with China sending silk, herbs, jade, and luxury goods to the West in exchange for horses, glassware, gold, silver, woolens, and even ivory. Goods from China reached as far as Greece, Rome, and parts of Europe, changing hands several times en route to terminal points along the Mediterranean. There was no actual contact between the Chinese traders themselves and their Mediterranean, Roman, or European buyers until much later.

During the late Han period, Buddhist monks began traveling this road on treks from India, making converts, establishing monasteries, and conveying manuscripts of holy texts along the way and giving rise to the massive Buddhist stone carvings and cave temples found in mountains from China to what is today Afghanistan. Famous Buddhist travelers, including Faxian and Xuanzang, followed the Silk Road to India to recover Buddhist scriptures and to learn more about the

expression, with its style, clarity, originality, and depth of feeling. The later Tang poet Bo Juyi (Po Chu-i; 772–846) expressed a more critical view of his society in a time of waning prosperity. All the poets were influenced in one way or another by the Chinese religions — native Confucianism and Daoism, and imported Buddhism — though in general the detachment, irony, and spirit of contemplation found in their poems places them closest to the Buddhist tradition. Wang Wei was a devoted Buddhist, preferring his home in the mountains to the city life of Chang'an. Li Bai, with his unpredictable nature and love of spontaneity, is considered a Daoist. Du Fu, the most orderly of the Tang poets, seems closer to Confucianism. Bo Juyi is what might be thought of as a social poet; in the next generation, the trenchant quality of his work endeared the Japanese to his writings.

www For more information about the culture and context of China in the Middle Period, see *World Literature Online* at bedfordstmartins.com/worldlit.

TIME AND PLACE

China: The Silk Road, Highway to the World *continued*

Buddhist religion. Thus not only goods but ideas traveled the Silk Road, the information highway of its time.

With the demise of the Han dynasty in the third century, China's control over the eastern segment of the routes collapsed. But with the rise of the Tang dynasty in 618, Chinese trade once again dominated the Silk Road, extending deep into central Asia and supplying an increasing demand for silk, tea, and hand-

Tang Troops, 870–907.   A Tang dynasty cave painting found along the Silk Road. [Bridgeman]

crafted items. Chang'an became one of the richest cities in the world, a cosmopolitan center where new fashions and practices from the Arabic world mixed with traditional Chinese customs and attire. In 751, however, a Muslim army defeated the Chinese at the battle of Talas River, and forces from Tibet cut off China's access to the Silk Road in the north. It was at Talas River that Arabs captured Chinese soldiers skilled in making paper, a technology that was later transmitted to the Arab world and Europe. With the collapse of the Tang dynasty in 907 and the advent of sea trade across the Indian Ocean, Silk Road trade with China was reduced to a trickle.

Later travelers of the Middle Period from the West, such as Friar William of Rubruck, Giovanni da Pian de Carpine, and Marco Polo, still used many parts of the Silk Road. But by the beginning of the Ming dynasty in 1368, China's trade was conducted primarily along new maritime routes through the straits of Molucca and into the Indian Ocean.

MISSION TO JAPAN AND THE END OF AN ERA

Beginning in the seventh century, Chinese delegations brought cultural knowledge of all sorts to an eager Japanese society: Chinese political, social, and legal organization; the Chinese language system; literature and literary criticism; technology and science; and religion, including Buddhism all had a major impact on Japanese life in the seventh and eighth centuries. By the time of the Japanese Nara dynasty (710–784), cultural curiosity toward China had become systematic cultural borrowing. Merchants and traders came and went; shipping routes were established.

At the same time, nationalist and xenophobic currents in both countries began to circulate. In the ninth century, China began to close off its borders; in 845 it issued a decree prohibiting foreign religions, including Buddhism. The shock of this edict, even though the ruling was eventually reversed, sent a message to Japan, Korea, and neighboring states that the openness of Chinese culture was coming to an end.

❧ TAO QIAN
365–427

tow-CHYEN

TOW yoo-en-MING

From his own time to the present, **Tao Qian** (Tao Ch'ien) has been known as the premier poet of the Six Dynasties Period (222–589), a time of political turmoil and instability in China. Known for his sincerity, integrity, and love of nature, Tao Qian, also known by his courtesy title, **Tao Yuanming** (T'ao Yüan-ming), is much like the nineteenth-century American writer Henry David Thoreau (1817–1862). Both men led reclusive lives of voluntary simplicity in the country, both cultivated a keen sense of place in their lives and in their work, and both blended philosophy, autobiography, and close observation of their everyday lives and their immediate environment in their writings. Moreover, both writers are seen as the founders of new literary traditions in their respective countries: Tao Qian, of Chinese nature poetry, and Thoreau, of American nature writing.

A Quiet Life in Turbulent Times. Tao Qian was born in 365 in a small town near what is today the city of Jiujang, Jiangxi province, in southeastern China. He grew up among thick forests, deep gorges, spectacular waterfalls, and the nearby Poyang Lake, towered over by Mount Lushan, a major center then and today for Buddhism and Daoism. Just before Tao Qian was born, the regions south of the Yangtze River had become a refuge for native Chinese people from the north. After the collapse of the Later Han dynasty (25–220), political and economic chaos had broken out in northern China, leaving its boundaries vulnerable to invasions by nomadic tribes (related to the Tatars or Huns) from the Gobi Desert region known as the Xiongnu. At the end of the third century, thousands of aristocratic families and officials fled the north and settled in the relatively more stable Yangtze valley. At Nanking, south of Jiujang, the eastern Jin (Chin) dynasty (317–420) managed to fend off the invaders, but just seven years before Tao Qian's death, infighting among powerful families and rebel uprisings in the region led to the collapse of the Jin and the founding of the Liu Song (Liu Sung) dynasty (420–589 C.E.).

The chaos and disorder of the times had led many of Tao Qian's contemporaries to seek individual spiritual solace in the doctrines of **BUDDHISM**[1] and **DAOISM**[2] rather than in the state-oriented **CONFUCIANISM**[3] that

www For links to more information about Tao Qian and a quiz on his poetry, see *World Literature Online* at bedfordstmartins .com/worldlit.

---

[1] **Buddhism:** A religion that formed in India in the sixth century B.C.E. based on the teachings of Siddhartha Gautama (the Buddha). While Buddhism has branched into several strands, its central teaching is that desire causes suffering, so that to find peace one must learn to live without desire. In order to attain happiness *(nirvana),* one must follow an "eight-fold path" that includes the practice of right action and right mindfulness.

[2] **Daoism:** A religious philosophy (also spelled "Taoism") stemming from the work of Zhuangzi (Chuang Tzu; c. 369–c. 286 B.C.E.) and Laozi (Lao Tzu; seventh to fifth century B.C.E.); Daoism teaches that inner peace, spiritual freedom, and salvation come from the effacement of desire and an assimilation of human activity into the dao (Tao), or the Way, the underlying principle of unity that governs the universe. Its emphasis on quietism

Daoist Deities Vase, 256–316 C.E.
During the economic and political disruptions of the Six Dynasties Period, Tao Qian, like many others, found respite and comfort in the doctrines of Daoism and its emphasis on the cultivation of the way. (The Art Archive / Genius of China Exhibition)

had predominated under the Han dynasty. Following the breakdown of the Han dynasty, many became more interested in schools of thought and religions emphasizing the cultivation of the self as opposed to the subordination of the self to the state. CONFUCIANISM, a religious philosophy based on the teachings of the Chinese philosopher Confucius (551–479 B.C.E.), promoted the virtues of self-discipline, filial piety, social hierarchy, political order, and respect for tradition. Under the Han, Confucianism had solidified as a state religion, and its emphasis on discipline, hierarchy, and order permeated the bureaucratic and military institutions of China. It was also during the Han that Buddhism first appeared in China, and that Daoism, originally a highly individualistic philosophy, took the form of a religious institution. Stressing sometimes esoteric doctrines about the nature of being, the importance of personal enlightenment, and the renunciation of worldly pursuits, Buddhism and

and individual salvation conflicted with the tenets of Confucianism, which emphasized right action and social virtue.

[3] **Confucianism:** A religious philosophy developed by the Chinese philosopher Confucius (551–479 B.C.E.) that exerted an enormous influence over subsequent Chinese moral, political, social, and religious thought and practice. Its basic tenets promote virtue, filial piety, political order, social hierarchy, and respect for tradition.

At a time when Chinese poetry on the whole was marked by ornate diction and elaborate rhetorical devices, T'ao Yüan-ming [Tao Qian] chose to write in a relatively plain and simple style — in translation he may even sound rather flat on first reading.

– BURTON WATSON, Critic, 1984

Daoism offered disciplined means to turn away from troubles, and Buddhism, with its promise of salvation, showed the way to deliverance from worldly concerns and cares altogether. A Daoist, Tao Qian was just one of many Chinese intellectuals who cultivated withdrawal from the bustle of the world, and his poetry and prose exalted the image of the eccentric poet-hermit, abandoning the chaos of the world for the freedom and serenity of the Great Way, the dao. The hermit-poet in exile would become a favorite stance for many Chinese poets, from the Tang dynasty (618–907) to the present.

The Reluctant Bureaucrat.   Despite his desire to lead a life apart, Tao Qian somewhat reluctantly served in minor government posts in his district, always letting it be known that he preferred a solitary life to even the least demanding of official positions. After serving as a military advisor in Koam Weo (Chien-Wei), he was appointed the governor of Beng-ze (Peng-tse), his last public office. In 406 Tao Qian retired from office for good and returned home to his farm. His poem "The Return" (translated as "Back Home Again Chant" by David Hinton on p. 309), one of the most famous poems in China, commemorates and celebrates his return to the simple but sparing life of the small farmer. He spent his later years with his family, drinking wine with friends, and composing poetry. In "The Gentleman of the Five Willows," a brief autobiographical piece, Tao Qian draws a somewhat idealized sketch of himself as a poet of little means for his class and with little care for the business of the world in his old age. Of himself he writes, "He was utterly unconcerned with success or failure and so lived out his days." The circumstances surrounding his death in 427, the date recorded in the historical annals, are not known.

Tao Qian's Poetry and Prose.   Tao Qian's poetry and prose mark a turning point in Chinese poetry. While some of the poems in the ancient *Book of Songs* (*Shi Jing*),[4] as well as poems by Yuchan (Yü Ch'an; 286–339) and Sunchuo (Sun Ch'o; 320–377) already show an interest in the beauties of landscape and dynamic forces of the natural world, Tao Qian and his contemporary Xie Lingyun (Hsieh Ling-yün; 385–433) are known as the founders of Chinese nature poetry. Such poetry does not treat nature as beautiful scenery, though it is partly that; rather it seeks to engage the essential, active principles that drive the natural world in all its diversity, a poetry in which the poet identifies with the life world of which he recognizes himself as a part. As David Hinton explains in his introduction to Tao Qian's poems, Tao Qian cultivated the art of the moment, what the Chinese call *tzu-jan* (*ziran*), that which comes about spontaneously or naturally. To dwell in the moment and to open oneself to the spontaneous is to attain a sense of unity with the dao, the principle of unity that governs all of creation — to attain, in short, unity with nature. One way

---

[4] **Book of Songs:** (*Shi Jing; Shih ching*) Also known as the *Poetry Classic, Book of Poems,* and *Book of Odes,* this is the oldest Chinese anthology of poems, dating from the ninth to the sixth centuries B.C.E. Written primarily in four-character verse, these poems treat a variety of subjects and form the foundation for later Chinese verse.

of cultivating this unity was to withdraw from the world and lead the life of a scholar-recluse or hermit, seeking enlightenment while wandering through the country. Although Tao Qian acknowledged the possibility of such an ascetic retirement, in his writing and in his preferred way of living he affirmed the values of the simple but active life of the small farmer. His poetry celebrates the country life of a self-sufficient farmer who tends his fields by day and reads books and writes poetry by night. It recounts the necessity of enduring a poor harvest, bad weather, and the threat of near starvation and appreciates the rare moments of serenity and quiet joy found in better days or in the detached clarity brought on by drinking wine. As seen in his writings, Tao Qian performs all his activities — from hoeing weeds and filling the rice jar to wandering the mountains and playing the *koto* — with an active mindfulness that brings him close to the unifying force that rolls through mountains and rivers and the bodies and minds of all beings. It is in this context that Tao Qian's numerous poems on drinking wine must be understood; he saw wine as a means of breaking down the acquired habits of knowing and being that prevented people from participating fully in the spontaneity of the present moment.

Tao Qian was a master of prose as well as poetry. He wrote prose poems known as rhapsodies (*fu*), such as "Back Home Again Chant," that usually begin with a prose preface and thereafter mix verse and prose in lines of varying length. He also wrote four-character poems in the style of the *Book of Songs* (*Shi Jing*). Primarily, however, Tao Qian wrote in the five-syllable verse form that would come to be known as GUSHI (*ku-shih*), a form that he helped to perfect. The *gushi* or "old-style" verse consists of even-numbered, alternately rhymed lines of five characters each. As might be expected, Tao Qian's works are remarkable for their simplicity of language and precision of image. The fifth-century poet Zhong Rong (469–518) described Tao Qian's literary style as "spare and limpid, with scarcely a superfluous word." Tang dynasty poets such as Li Bai (Li Po; 701–762) and Bo Juyi (Po Chui; 772–846) were drawn to Tao Qian's poetry not only for its evocation of feeling, sincerity, and themes of retirement from society but also for its conveyance of subtle complexity in a deceptively simple, economical style. Tao Qian's grasp of the identity between human beings and nature as well as his ideals of simplicity and detachment continue to influence our thinking about our place in nature.

> Tao Yuanming [Tao Qian] was great precisely because he was *not* all serenity.
>
> – Lu Xun, Writer, d. 1936

■ **CONNECTIONS**

Matsuo Bashō, "The Narrow Road through the Backcountry" (Book 4). Tao Qian's poetry, which contains many allusions to earlier poems in the *Book of Songs,* has been widely acclaimed for its profound engagement with nature. Similarly, Bashō's *The Narrow Road,* which is also highly allusive, suggests an awakened appreciation of the moment and of the environment. Consider the works of these two poets as examples of nature writing. What is the view of nature one gets from each writer? How does their work convey a sense of immediacy and transparency?

William Wordsworth, "Lines Composed a Few Miles above Tintern Abbey; Ode: Intimations of Immortality" (Book 5). While conveying a strong sense of rustic simplicity and love of nature, Tao Qian's poetry also takes a philosophical perspective on society. Likewise, Wordsworth, often considered one of the Romantic era's preeminent nature poets, presents not so much a description of nature in his work as a philosophy of nature and society. What values and ideas do Tao Qian and Wordsworth have in common? Are any of their shared values inflected with cultural or philosophical differences?

Li Bai (Li Po), "Drinking Alone Beneath the Moon," p. 335; John Keats, "Ode to a Nightingale" (Book 5). Many of Tao Qian's poems, like those of Keats, are elegiac in tone, expressions of ways of coping with the troubles of the world. Moreover, like Li Bai but in contrast to Keats, Tao Qian presents a favorable image of drinking wine as a means of enhancing poetic inspiration and achieving a mental clarity that transcends the world of sorrows. Consider the elegiac character of these poets. Why might Keats, in contrast to his Chinese predecessors, have rejected wine as an agency of transcendence?

■ **FURTHER RESEARCH**

Acker, William. *T'ao the Hermit.* 1952.
Chang, H. C. *Chinese Literature 2: Nature Poetry.* 1977.
Davis, Albert Richard. *T'ao Yüang-ming: His Works and Their Meaning.* 1984.
Hightower, James Robert. *The Poetry of T'ao Ch'ien.* 1970.
Hinton, David. *The Selected Poems of T'ao Chien.* 1993.
Kwong, Charles Yim-Tze. *Tao Qian and the Chinese Poetic Tradition: The Quest for Cultural Identity.* 1995.

■ **PRONUNCIATION**

Tao Qian (T'ao Ch'ien): tow-CHYEN, tow-CHEN
Tao Yuanming: TOW yoo-en-MING

❧ The Gentleman of the Five Willow Trees[1]

Translated by James Robert Hightower

I don't know where this gentleman was born and I am not sure of his name, but beside his house were five willow trees, from which he took his nickname. He was of a placid disposition and rarely spoke. He had no envy of fame or fortune. He was fond of reading, without puzzling greatly over difficult passages. When he came across something to his liking he would be so delighted he would forget his meals. By nature he liked wine, but being poor could not always come by it. Knowing the cir-

---

[1]**The Gentleman . . . Trees:** In this idealized sketch of a life written when he was a young man, Tao Qian projects an idealized image of himself into the future.

The Poems of Tao Qian. Although Tao Qian was recognized in his own time as a principled recluse of great integrity, his works did not achieve wide acclaim until the Tang dynasty, when his philosophical views based on Buddhist and Daoist teachings influenced poets such as Li Bai (Li Po; 701–762) and Bo Juyi (Po Chui; 772–846). He left behind nearly 130 poems written in various styles,

cumstances, his friends and relatives would invite him over when they had wine. He could not drink without emptying his cup, and always ended up drunk, after which he would retire, unconcerned about what might come. He lived alone in a bare little hut which gave no adequate shelter against rain and sun. His short coat was torn and patched, his cooking pots were frequently empty, but he was unperturbed. He used to write poems for his own amusement, and in them can be seen something of what he thought. He had no concern for worldly success, and so he ended his days.

❧ Substance, Shadow, and Spirit[1]

Translated by James Robert Hightower

Noble or base, wise or stupid, none but cling tenaciously to life. This is a great delusion. I have put in the strongest terms the complaints of Substance and Shadow and then, to resolve the matter, have made Spirit the spokesman for naturalness. Those who share my tastes will all get what I am driving at.

I Substance to Shadow

Earth and heaven endure forever,
Streams and mountains never change.
Plants observe a constant rhythm,
Withered by frost, by dew restored.
But man, most sentient being of all,
In this is not their equal.
He is present here in the world today,
Then leaves abruptly, to return no more.
No one marks there's one man less—
Not even friends and family think of him;
The things that he once used are all that's left

---

[1]**Substance . . . Spirit:** While not strictly allegorical, the conversation among these three figures reflects the differences between Confucianism (Shadow, with its emphasis on doing good in the world and achieving fame) and two kinds of Daoism—one that emphasizes ritual, diet, and breathing practices (Substance) and one that stresses surrender to the natural forces of life and death (Spirit).

---

from four-character and five-character verse *(shi)* to mixed prose and poetry forms known as rhapsodies, or *fu*. His work is available in many English translations, the variety of which is represented here by selections from the "standard" translations of James Robert Hightower as well as from the more recent and highly regarded translations by David Hinton. These interpretations convey the clarity and simplicity of Tao Qian's original language and style while rendering his verse into a meter attuned to the ear of English speakers.

To catch their eye and move them to grief.
I have no way to transcend change,
That it must be, I no longer doubt.
I hope you will take my advice:
When wine is offered, don't refuse.

II Shadow to Substance

No use discussing immortality
When just to keep alive is hard enough.
Of course I want to roam in paradise,
But it's a long way there and the road is lost.
In all the time since I met up with you
We never differed in our grief and joy.
In shade we may have parted for a time,
But sunshine always brings us close again.
Still this union cannot last forever —
Together we will vanish into darkness.
The body goes; that fame should also end
Is a thought that makes me burn inside.
Do good, and your love will outlive you;
Surely this is worth your every effort.
While it is true, wine may dissolve care
That is not so good a way as this.

III Spirit's Solution

The Great Potter[2] cannot intervene —
All creation thrives of itself.
That Man ranks with Earth and Heaven
Is it not because of me?
Though we belong to different orders,
Being alive, I am joined to you.
Bound together for good or ill
I cannot refuse to tell you what I know:
The Three August Ones[3] were great saints
But where are they living today?

---

[2] **The Great Potter:** Literally, "The Great Potter's Wheel," upon which all created beings are shaped; the Great Potter is the agent of creation and change.

[3] **The Three August Ones:** Fu Xi, "The Mythical Emperor"; Shen Nang, "The Divine Farmer"; and Huang Di, "The Yellow Emperor." These legendary figures were associated with medical lore and long life.

Though P'eng-tsu[4] lasted a long time
He still had to go before he was ready.
Die old or die young, the death is the same,
Wise or stupid, there is no difference.
Drunk every day you may forget,
But won't it shorten your life span?
Doing good is always a joyous thing
But no one has to praise you for it.
Too much thinking harms my life;
20   Just surrender to the cycle of things,
Give yourself to the waves of the Great Change
Neither happy nor yet afraid.
And when it is time to go, then simply go
Without any unnecessary fuss.

---

[4] **P'eng-tsu:** (Peng Tsu) A man who supposedly lived 800 years and became a symbol of longevity.

∾ Back Home Again Chant[1]

Translated by David Hinton

We were destitute. I worked hard farming, but we never had enough: the house was full of kids, and the rice-jar always empty. And though people have made their living like this for countless generations, I never quite caught on, so everyone kept pushing me to find government work. Finally I decided they were right, but had no idea where to begin. Before long I had to do some traveling, and some important people I met seemed impressed by me. Then, when my uncle took an interest in our bitter poverty, I found myself appointed to office in a small town. At that time, since the land was still full of trouble, I was leery about serving far away. But P'eng-tse was only thirty miles from here, and the receipts from government fields were enough to keep me in wine, so I took the job. The first few days went well enough; then all I wanted was to be home with my family again. Why the sudden change of heart? My nature comes of itself. It isn't something you can force into line. Hunger and cold may cut deep, but turning on myself that way felt like a sickness. Serving the public good, I was nothing more than a mouth and belly serving themselves. Seeing this, and thinking of the ideals I'd always held, I was sad and utterly ashamed of my fine public spirit. And yet, I still thought I should hold out until next year's harvest before packing up and slipping away in the night. But soon my younger sister, Chang's wife, died in Wu-chang,[2] and forgetting everything in the rush to get there, I

---

[1] **Back . . . Chant:** This poem is often translated as "The Return."

[2] **Wu-chang:** In what is today Hopei.

escaped, leaving my duties behind. After holding office more than eighty days, from mid-autumn into winter, I turned what happened into my heart's content.

My piece is called *Back Home Again,* and this preface was written in the 11th month, *Yi* year of the snake.[3]

Back home—
with fields and gardens all weeds back home,
how can I stay here, my heart a slave to the body?
Why live this dismal life, this lonely grief?
You can't argue with what's been done, I know,
but the future's there to be made. Not too far
gone down this road of delusion, I can see
where I'm right today, yesterday I was wrong.

Far from home, the boat rocking on gentle
10   swells, my robe snaps in billowing winds.
Asking travelers how the road ahead is,
I wonder how morning light can be so dim,
but seeing our house, suddenly
happy, I break into a run.
Servants greet me gleefully,
and my kids there at the gate.
Our three paths are grown over,
but pines and chrysanthemums
survived. And taking everyone
20   inside, I find wine waiting.
Pouring a cup from the winejar, I smile, happy
to see these courtyard trees. At the window
my presumptions drift away south. How easily
content I am in this cramped little place.
Here, garden strolls bring joy day after day:
our gate always closed, propped on my old-folk's
walking-stick, I go a little ways, then rest,
and turning my head, look far away. Clouds
leaving mountain peaks drift without a thought,
30   and tired of flight, birds think of return.
At sunset, light fading slowly away, I linger
fondly over a lone pine, nowhere I'd rather be.

Back home again—
O let me keep to myself, my wandering ended.
Let the world and I give each other up.
If I left again, what would I go looking for?

---

[3] *Yi* year of the snake: 405 C.E.

It's loving family voices that make me happy,
koto and books that keep worried grief away.
And farmers here tell me spring has arrived. Soon,
40   there'll be work out in the western fields.
Sometimes in a covered cart,
sometimes rowing a lone boat—
I'll search out sheltered streams and quiet pools,
follow mountain paths up through the hills.
Trees revel in the joy of their lavish blossoms,
and murmuring springs flow again. In these
ten thousand things, each following its season
away perfectly, I touch that repose in which
life ends, done and gone.
50   This form I am in the world can't last much longer.
Why not let things carry my heart away with them?
What good is it, agonizing over the way things are going?
Getting rich isn't what I want. And who
expects to end in some celestial village?
My dream is to walk out all alone into a lovely
morning—maybe stop to pull weeds in the garden,
maybe climb East Ridge and chant, settling into
my breath, or sit writing poems beside a clear
stream. I'll ride change back to my final home,
60   rejoicing in heaven's way. How can it ever fail me?

Home Again among Gardens and Fields

Translated by David Hinton

I

Nothing like the others, even as a child,
rooted in a love for hills and mountains,

I fell into their net of dust, that one
departure a blunder lasting thirteen years.

But a tethered bird longs for its forest,
a pond fish its deep waters. So now, my

land out on the south edge cleared, I
nurture simplicity among gardens and fields,

home again. I've got nearly two acres here,
10   and four or five rooms in my thatch hut.

Elms and willows shade the eaves out back,
and in front, peach and plum spread wide.

Distant—village people lost in distant
haze, kitchen smoke hangs above wide-open

country. Here, dogs bark deep in back roads,
and roosters crow from mulberry treetops.

No confusion within the gate, no dust,
my empty home harbors idleness to spare.

Back again: after so long in that trap,
20   I've returned to all that comes of itself.

FROM

∾ A Reply to Secretary Kuo[1]

Translated by James Robert Hightower

I

The trees before the house grow thick, thick
In midsummer they store refreshing shade.
The gentle southern breeze arrives on time,
It soothes my heart as it blows and whirls my gown.
I have renounced the world to have my leisure
And occupy myself with lute and books.
The garden produce is more than plentiful—
Of last year's grain some is left today.
What one can do oneself has its limits;
10   More than enough is not what I desire.
I crush the grain to brew a first-rate wine
And when it is ripe I pour myself a cup.
My little son, who is playing by my side,
Has begun to talk, but cannot yet pronounce.
Here is truly something to rejoice in
It helps me to forget the badge of rank.
The white clouds I watch are ever so far away—
How deep my yearning is for ages past.

---

[1] **Secretary Kuo:** Secretary Guo, an unidentified magistrate.

∾ In the Sixth Month of 408, Fire

Translated by James Robert Hightower

I built my thatched hut in a narrow lane,
Glad to renounce the carriages of the great.
In midsummer, while the wind blew long and sharp,
Of a sudden grove and house caught fire and burned.
In all the place not a roof was left to us
And we took shelter in the boat[1] by the gate.

Space is vast this early autumn evening,
The moon, nearly full, rides high above.
The vegetables begin to grow again
But the frightened birds still have not returned.
Tonight I stand a long time lost in thought;
A glance encompasses the Nine Heavens.[2]
Since youth I've held my solitary course
Until all at once forty years have passed.
My outward form follows the way of change
But my heart remains untrammelled still.
Firm and true, it keeps its constant nature,
No jadestone is as strong, adamantine.
I think back to the time when East-Gate[3] ruled
When there was grain left out in the fields
And people, free of care, drummed full bellies,
Rising mornings and coming home to sleep.
Since I was not born in such a time,
Let me just go on watering my garden.

---

[1] **the boat:** Presumably a houseboat.

[2] **Nine Heavens:** That is, the sky, which was said to have nine divisions, or layers.

[3] **East-Gate:** According to myth, a ruler of ancient China during a golden age of such abundance that none went hungry and there was no need to store food.

∾ Reading *The Classic of Mountains and Seas*[1]

Translated by David Hinton

It's early summer. Everything's lush.
Our house set deep among broad trees,

birds delight in taking refuge here.
I too love this little place. And now

the plowing and planting are finished,
I can return to my books again and read.

Our meager lane nowhere near well-worn
roads, most old friends turn back. Here,

I ladle out spring wine with pleasure,
and pick vegetables out in the garden.

And coming in from the east, thin rain
arrives on a lovely breeze. My eyes

wander *Tales of Emperor Mu,*[2] float along
on *Mountains and Seas* pictures. . . .

Look around. All time and space within
sight—if not here, where will joy come?

10

---

[1] *The Classic of Mountains and Seas:* An ancient book of sometimes fanciful geography that contained, at least in the edition to which Tao Qian refers here, illustrations.

[2] *Tales of Emperor Mu:* A narrative describing the marvelous adventures of King Mu of the Zhou (Chou) dynasty as he traveled outside of China.

Elegy for Myself

Translated by David Hinton

It's the late-autumn pitch-tone, *Wu-yi,*[1] *Ting*[2] year of the hare. The heavens are cold now, and the nights long. Geese pass, traveling south in desolate, windswept skies. Leaves turn yellow and fall. I, Master T'ao, will soon leave this inn awaiting travelers, and return forever to my native home. Everyone grieves. Mourning together, they've gathered here tonight for these farewell rites. They're making offerings to me: elegant foods and libations of crystalline wine. I look into their already blurred faces, listen to their voices blending away into silence.

Hu-ooo! Ai-tsai hu-ooo!

> Boundless—this vast heap earth,
> this bottomless heaven, how perfectly
>
> boundless. And among ten thousand
> things born of them, to find myself
>
> a person somehow, though a person
> fated from the beginning to poverty
>
> alone, to those empty cups and bowls,
> thin clothes against winter cold.
>
> Even hauling water brought such joy,
> and I sang under a load of firewood:
>
> this life in brushwood-gate seclusion
> kept my days and nights utterly full.
>
> Spring and autumn following each other
> away, there was always garden work—
>
> some weeding here or hoeing there.
> What I tended I harvested in plenty,
>
> and to the pleasure of books, *koto*
> strings added harmony and balance.

10

---

[1] *Wu-yi:* (Wu-i) One of the twelve pitch tones of ancient music, each corresponding to one of the twelve months (in this case, October).

[2] *Ting:* In the solar cycle, the year of the rabbit; here 427 C.E.

I'd sun in winter to keep warm,
20   and summers, bathe in cool streams.

Never working more than hard enough,
I kept my heart at ease always,

and whatever came, I rejoiced in all
heaven made of my hundred-year life.

Nothing more than this hundred-year
life — and still, people resent it.

Afraid they'll never make it big,
hoarding seasons, they clutch at

days, aching to be treasured alive
30   and long remembered in death. Alone,

alone and nothing like them, I've
always gone my own way. All their

esteem couldn't bring me honor, so
how can mud turn me black? Resolute

here in my little tumbledown house,
I swilled wine and scribbled poems.

Seeing what fate brings, our destiny
clear, who can live without concern?

But today, facing this final change,
40   I can't find anything to resent:

I lived a life long and, cherishing
solitude always, abundant. Now

old age draws to a close, what more
could I want? Hot and cold pass

away and away. And absence returns,
something utterly unlike presence.

My wife's family came this morning,
and friends hurried over tonight.

50   They'll take me out into the country,
      bury me where the spirit can rest

      easy. O dark journey. O desolate
      grave, gate opening into the dark

      unknown. An opulent coffin Huan's[3]
      disgrace, Yang's[4] naked burial a joke,

      it's empty — there's nothing in death
      but the empty sorrows of distance.

      Build no gravemound, plant no trees —
      just let the days and months pass

60   away. I avoided it my whole life,
      so why invite songs of praise now?

      Life is deep trouble. And death,
      why should death be anything less?

Hu-ooo! Ai-tsai hu-ooo!

---

[3] **Huan:** The figure Huan Tui is said to have ordered an elaborate stone coffin that took more than three years to complete.

[4] **Yang:** Yang Wang-sun (first century B.C.E.) commanded that he be buried naked.

Poets of the Tang Dynasty

The Tang dynasty (618–907) is known as the golden age of Chinese classical poetry. It was a time of great fruition in Chinese culture brought about in part by the opening of China to outside cultural influences in dance, music, and architecture from central Asia, the steppe region, India, Persia, and Tibet as well as the Islamic world. The capital city of Chang'an (Ch'ang-an), with a population of nearly two million people, was one of the greatest cities in the world and boasted a rich cosmopolitanism. Located on the Wei River in Jingji (Shenshi) Province, Chang'an was a locus of trade from central Asia and a city bustling with merchants, travelers, and intellectuals representing various countries. People from Turkey, Korea, Tibet, India and Persia were able to mix with the Chinese, and ZOROASTRIANS,[1] Christians, Jews, and BUDDHISTS came into contact with CONFUCIANISTS[2] and DAOISTS.[3] Moreover, the Tang, particularly in the seventh century, was an era when Chinese rulers such as Xuanzong (Hsuan Tsung; 712–756) not only patronized poetry but were often distinguished poets themselves. As in the later Japanese

---

[1] Zoroastrians: Adherents of a religion founded in ancient Persia by Zoroaster (c. 628–c. 551 B.C.E.); its basic teaching is that there are spirits of good at war with spirits of evil.

[2] Confucianists: Followers of a religious philosophy founded by the Chinese philosopher Confucius (551–479 B.C.E.) that exerted an enormous influence over subsequent Chinese moral, political, social, and religious thought and practice. Its basic tenets promote virtue, filial piety, political order, social hierarchy, and respect for tradition.

[3] Daoists: Subscribers to a religious philosophy stemming from the work of Laozi (Lao Tzu; seventh to fifth century B.C.E.) and Zhuangzi (Chuang Tzu; c. 369–c. 286 B.C.E.); Daoism (Taoism) teaches that inner peace and spiritual freedom and salvation come from the effacement of desire and an assimilation of human activity into the dao (Tao), or the Way, the underlying principle of unity that governs the universe.

court society depicted in Lady Murasaki's[4] *Tale of Genji,* composing poetry was not only a mark of education and accomplishment in China but also an essential means of communication. In contrast to Japan, however, in Tang-dynasty China writing poetry was a pastime and means of entertainment for all educated people. Merchants and officials wrote poems in transacting their business; friends and lovers used poems to make their feelings known to each other; and Buddhist and Daoist monks wrote poems as part of their spiritual practices. At parties and social gatherings, poetry and song were as much a part of the celebration as was wine, and in Chang'an, popular courtesans were known for their songs as well as their charms. In short, poetry permeated the culture of the Tang, giving rise to thousands of poems, ranging from the conventional to the occasional masterpiece.

The literary brilliance of the Tang era shines through in two eighteenth-century Chinese anthologies: *The Complete Tang Poems* (*Chuan Tang Shih*), a compendium of almost forty-nine thousand poems by more than two thousand two hundred poets, and the *Three Hundred Poems of the T'ang* (*Tang-shi san-bai-shou*), a still popular anthology of slightly more than three hundred poems edited by Sun Zhu in 1763. While many of the works in these voluminous anthologies display moments of brilliance and insight, most do not rise above formula and cliché. Among the hundreds of conventional and imitative poets, **Wang Wei** (c. 699–761), **Li Bai** (Li Po; 701–762), **Du Fu** (Tu Fu; 712–770), and **Bo Juyi** (Po Chü-i; 772–846) are standouts for their depth of feeling, stylistic innovation, clarity of expression, and originality. The work of these four poets has attained the status of world literature and spawned a legion of admirers, imitators, and translators that continues to grow in China and throughout the world even today.

THE TANG DYNASTY AND ITS POETS

The Tang dynasty began after the murder of Yangdi (Yang Ti), the last of the Sui[5] emperors, in 618, when the general Li Yuan took over

> The difference between T'ang poetry and the *Book of Poetry* is the difference between a carefully arranged flower twig in a vase, where every angle and curve is carefully studied, and the luxuriant growth of a wild garden.
>
> – LIN YU-TANG, critic, 1942

wahng-WAY; lee-BIGH

doo-FOO; boh-joo-EE

---

[4] Lady Murasaki (973–1030 C.E.): An early master of Japanese prose fiction and the author of Japan's first and perhaps still greatest novel, *The Tale of Genji* (*Genji Monogatari*).

[5] the Sui: The Sui dynasty, founded by General Yang Jian (r. 581–604), lasted only from 581 to 618 C.E. but was important in uniting the northern and southern regions of China under a central authority and implementing

The Emperor Xuanzong Watching His Favorite Concubine, Yang Guifei, Mount a Horse (left side of scroll), 712–756

The Tang emperor Xuanzong, pictured on the right side of this scroll, was not only a poet but also an important patron of the arts. Wang Wei, Li Bai, and Du Fu all produced some of China's greatest poetry during his reign and under his patronage. The beautiful and treacherous Yang Guifei can be seen in this painting mounting a horse. She would eventually be involved in a rebellion against the emperor and executed. (See page 321 for the right half of this scroll.) (The Art Archive / Freer Gallery of Art)

power and declared a new dynasty. Nine years later, the younger of his two sons, Li Shimin (Li Shih-min), took over the throne from his father and became the emperor Tang Taizong (T'ang T'ai-tsung; r. 626–49). Taizong turned out to be a highly effective leader, securing and expanding China's borders, revising its system of laws, and bringing peace and prosperity to the land. Taizong and his successors, including his son Gaozong (Kao Tsung; r. 635–684) presided over a flourishing in the arts, particularly in sculpture and poetry. They strengthened the *CHIN-SHI* system[6] of civil service examinations in order to bring diverse talent from the population into the

---

a system of common weights and measures as well as common laws, and inaugurating the Chinese system of civil service examinations.

[6] ***chin-shi* system:** First begun in the Sui dynasty (581–618 C.E.) under Yang Jian and formalized during the Tang era, the *chin-shi* system of civil service examinations brought bright and talented men from all over China into the government bureaucracy.

The Emperor Xuanzong Watching His Favorite Concubine, Yang Guifei, Mount a Horse
(right side of scroll), 712–756
(See page 320 for the left half of this scroll.) (The Art Archive/Freer Gallery of Art)

bureaucracy, and they founded a major center of learning, the
Imperial Academy, in the increasingly cosmopolitan capital city.
Though she had effectively ruled since 684, after the death of her
husband in 690 Gaozong's wife Wu Zetian (Wu Tse-t'ien; r. 684–705)
in an unprecedented move proclaimed herself emperor. Under
Empress Wu writing poetry became a required part of the new *chin-
shi,* the gateway to all government positions. Spurred by the competitive atmosphere of these examinations, many students, scholars,
and officials matched wits and talent in poetry contests.

THE AN LUSHAN REBELLION

After Wu's reign, Tang Xuanzong (r. 712–756), a poet and patron of
the arts, presided for many years over a prosperous Chinese culture
and society. It was under his reign that Wang Wei, Li Bai, and Du Fu
wrote what many consider China's greatest poetry. But Xuanzong
was eventually brought down, in part because of his relationship
with the beautiful but scheming concubine Yang Guifei (Yang Kuei-
fei; 719–756). Under the influence of Yang Guifei, Xuanzong gradually abandoned the Confucian austerity for which his court was

Female Musician, 619–906
Poetry and music permeated every aspect of Tang-dynasty society. In the booming capital city of Chang'an (Ch'ang-an), courtesans were as well versed in the musical arts as they were in other forms of artistic expression. (Werner Forman / Art Resource, NY)

known and respected, turning increasingly to lavish spending on luxuries and on the military. He replaced loyal court officials with protégés of Yang Guifei, among whom was the Turkish-born general An Lushan, whom Yang Guifei adopted as a son. The favoritism lavished on An Lushan led to a rivalry that erupted in the An Lushan Rebellion of 755, when An Lushan seized the eastern capital of Luoyang and declared himself emperor. Soon Xuanzong was forced to flee from Chang'an, which was occupied by the rebel forces. An Lushan was killed by his own men, and the rebellion was eventually put down. For her role in the intrigue, Yang Guifei was executed, and her story—that of a beautiful concubine who brings down an empire—became a favorite narrative of Chinese and Japanese writers, including Du Fu and Bo Juyi. After the rebellion, the central authority of the Tang emperor at Chang'an was weakened. Increased power and rivalry among landed families as well as peasant revolts and constant incursions along the borders further eroded the empire until it finally fell in 907. China was then left in a state of political chaos until 960, when General Zhao Guangyin founded the Song empire. In their poetry, Du Fu and Bo Juyi in particular record the decline of the Tang, an ending they observed with some bitterness and regret.

THE RISE OF BUDDHISM

In the early years of the Tang, Buddhism, which had been growing in China since the second century C.E., became increasingly influential, and Buddhist monasteries became important centers of learning and culture. New sects with distinctively Chinese orientations were founded, including the Tiantai (T'ien-t'ai; Tendai in Japan), the Chan (Zen in Japan), and the popular Pure Land Buddhism.[7] Although a challenge to native Confucianism, a thisworldly religious philosophy stressing duty to family and state, Buddhist sects often found common ground with Daoism (Taoism). Many Tang poets, some of whom were monks, were drawn to Buddhism's otherworldliness, its sense of the insubstantiality of worldly things, and its emphasis on enlightenment and salvation by means of disciplined practice and grace. A body of poetry known as the Cold Mountain Poems, supposedly written by the monk Han Shan (c. 600–800), captures the stern serenity of Chan Buddhism, while the writings of Wang Wei evoke the contemplative serenity and the sense of impermanence and emptiness of things taught in Tiantai. None of the poets whose work is presented here, however, can be tied strictly to a particular sect or religious philosophy, though certain tendencies can be seen in their work. Wang Wei and Bo Juyi, for example, are most heavily influenced by Buddhism; Du Fu, by Confucianism; and Li Bai, by Daoism.

---

[7] **Tiantai . . . Pure Land Buddhism:** Tiantai (T'ien T'ai; Tendai in Japan), Chan (Zen in Japan), and Pure Land are three types of Buddhist thought and practice developed in China. Tiantai Buddhism, founded by the Chinese monk Zhiyi (Chih-i; 538–597), takes as its central doctrine the Lotus Sutra. Involving a rigorous study of doctrine with a strict regimen of meditative practice, Tiantai appealed primarily to educated people of leisure or to those willing to become monks. Chan Buddhism, also known as the Meditation School, emphasized the stripping away of conceptual thinking by means of riddles and meditative practices designed to empty the mind and achieve a clear intuition of the nature of things. Harmonizing well with Daoism (Taoism), Chan was popular among poets, artists, and intellectuals. Pure Land, a more utopian belief, emphasized salvation through faith — rebirth into the Western Paradise through the grace of Buddha Amitabha. The simple utterance of Amitabha's name was thought to bring deliverance from suffering.

TANG POETRY AND POETICS

In Chinese, the word for poetry in general, *shi*, means the natural expression or outward manifestation of intense feeling. In the words of "The Canon of Shun" in the *Book of History*,[8] "Poetry expresses in words the intent of the heart." In this context, expression of feeling transcends the private emotions of the writer, for when expressed in its purest form the "intent of the heart" corresponds to the dao, or the underlying principle of nature that encompasses all being. For the poets of early China, the signs or patterns *(wen)* of calligraphic writing were reproductions of natural patterns such as the veins in leaves, the markings of birds, or the shapes of stones, themselves a revelation of the deeper, universal design of the dao.[9] To write poetry, then, was to come to recognize the dao in oneself as it corresponded to the dao in nature and in the cosmos. The Han dynasty poet Lu Ji (261–303 C.E.) characterizes this process when he writes that the poet "traps heaven and earth / In the cage of form."

Tang-era poets drew from and made innovations to a variety of past poetic forms. The earliest forms of Chinese lyric poetry, *shi,* are found in the *Classic of Poetry (Shi jing),* a collection of court poems, folk songs, and ritual hymns dating to the eleventh century B.C.E. and compiled sometime in the seventh century B.C.E. These poems, of varying length, generally were written in four-character (four-syllable) lines whose every other line rhymed. During the Han dynasty (206 B.C.E.–220 C.E.), poets developed from this basic four-character line the five- to seven-syllable verse form known as *GUSHI* ("old style verse"), which in turn became the basis for later developments, including the *LUSHI* ("regulated verse"), a form originating in the Tang era. As perfected by the Tang poets, the *lushi* is a highly structured form of poetry consisting of eight lines of five or seven syllables and emphasizing aesthetic balance and order.

---

[8] *Book of History:* (*Xu Kin, Shu King,* or *Shang-shu*) An ancient collection of documents on history and politics written in prose and dating back to the early years of the Zhou dynasty (c. 1027–256 B.C.E.), if not before. One of the earliest works of history and a foundation for Confucian ideas, it describes among other things history as a process of change and delineates the important "Mandate of Heaven," which said that emperors ruled by divine right but if or when an emperor violated his office that mandate would rightfully pass to another.

[9] **the dao:** Translated as "the Way," *dao (Tao)* refers to the basic principle of order that underlies the cosmos in Daoist thought; it is said to be the origin of all things as well as the path to peace and salvation. For Laozi (Lao Tzu), the dao is unknowable and cannot be spoken; hence, it can only be intuited.

The *lushi* form, however, was not the only, and not always the preferred, form for the poets featured in the selections that follow. Wang Wei, Li Bai, Du Fu, and Bo Juyi wrote in a variety of poetic genres, including the *gushi;* the YUEFU, or folk ballads, which during the Han evolved into literary ballads written in quatrains of five-character lines; and the FU, or "rhapsody," another Han-dynasty development that mixes introductions with lines of verse of various metrical lengths. Li Bai, with his penchant for strong drink and his wild nature, preferred the freedom of the *yuefu* to the strict regimen of the *lushi,* a form more suited to the Confucian Du Fu. The famous distinction in style between Li Bai and Du Fu is in many ways comparable to that between European Romanticism and Neo-classicism: the inspired genius versus the master craftsman. Li Bai, however, wrote *lushi* and *gushi* as well as *yuefu.* The *yuefu* form, derived from folk ballads, was adapted by the Tang poets—most of whom experienced at some point in their lives a form of political ostracism or exile—to write poems criticizing society and its politics. This "new ballad," or "new *yuefu,*" was perfected in particular by the second generation poet Bo Juyi, who used the form to criticize the social abuses he witnessed after the An Lushan Rebellion. Both Li Bai and Bo Juyi also experimented with the *ci (tz'u),* a lyrical form with varied line lengths modeled on songs introduced from central Asia. Until Li Bai and Bo Juyi, *ci* had been thought of as a low form of poetry.

THE PROBLEM OF TRANSLATION

The twentieth-century American poet Robert Frost once said, "Poetry is what gets lost in translation," and most poets and editors wholeheartedly agree. Poetry works on the senses as well as on the intellect, and rhythm, rhyme, balance, and colloquialism inevitably are muted, if not lost altogether, even in the best translations. While some translators try especially hard to preserve the integrity of the structure, form, rhythm, and music of a poem, others attempt to do justice to its subtle innuendoes or to capture its literal meaning. Selecting translations always vexes editors, but the difficulty of selection becomes particularly acute when it comes to poems translated into English from non-European languages such as Sanskrit, Chinese, or Japanese, whose sound structures, grammatical features,

> Savor his poetry, and there is a painting in each poem; look carefully at his paintings, and each one contains a poem.
> – SU DONGPO on Wang Wei, writer, 2000

and systems of writing depart drastically from Western languages. Unlike English, the Chinese poetic language is paratactic. That is, in Chinese the relationships between words are not fixed by articles, linking words, and indicators of tense, agency, and number to the extent that they are in English. On the subject of translating Chinese, Yip Wai-lim gives the example of *sung-feng,* a common poetic phrase that literally means "pine-wind." Should the English translator render the phrase as "wind in the pine," "the wind in the pines," "the wind blowing through the pine trees," or "pine wind"? Translators of even the shortest Chinese poem face endless decisions like this one as well as others that are more complex.

■ CONNECTIONS

Laozi (Lao Tzu), Dao De Jing (Tao Te Ching) (Book 1); Zhuangzi (Chuang Tzu), Writings (Book 1). The influence of Daoism (Taoism) on Tang-dynasty poetry was quite strong, and many of the poems in this section allude to the writings of Laozi and Zhuangzi. Examine the tenets of Daoism as they are insinuated in those writings. How do Tang dynasty poets express those beliefs?

The Man'Yoshu, p. 1018; *The Kokinshu,* p. 1051. The poems of the *Man'yoshu* and *Kokinshu* treat a variety of themes similar to those found in Tang dynasty poetry: the impermanence and mutability of life, poverty and asceticism, social injustice, the parting of friends and lovers, the passing of the seasons, and love of nature. Though many of the poems in these collections allude to Chinese models, they are often celebrated for their distinctive Japanese character. Closely examine some pairs of comparable poems from the Tang dynasty poets and from their near contemporaries in Japan. What distinguishes the Chinese from the Japanese poems? (Li Bai's "Ch'ang-kan Village Song," for example, might be compared with Hitomaro's longer poems, called *choka,* in the *Man'Yoshu.*)

Anna Akhmatova, Poems (Book 6). Some of the Tang dynasty poets, particularly Du Fu and Bo Juyi, capture a sense of social injustice and societal decline in their work. Du Fu's handling of the collective suffering of the Chinese people in a poetry that is at once compassionate and sparse, imagistic and formally balanced, anticipates the way Anna Akhmatova collapses private and collective grief in her brilliant poem *Requiem.* How is Du Fu's or Bo Juyi's evocation of sorrow and grief like or unlike Akhmatova's?

■ FURTHER RESEARCH

Background/History

Chen, Kenneth. *The Chinese Transformation of Buddhism.* 1973.
Cheng, François. *Chinese Poetic Writing.* 1982.
Hightower, James, and Florence Chia-Ying Yeh. *Studies in Chinese Poetry.* 1998.
Liu, James. *The Art of Chinese Poetry.* 1962.
Liu, Wu-chi. *An Introduction to Chinese Literature.* 1966.
Mair, Victor H. *The Columbia History of Chinese Literature.* 2002.
Owen, Stephen. *The Great Age of Chinese Poetry: The High Tang.* 1981.
———. *Traditional Chinese Poetry and Poetics: An Omen of the World.* 1985.
Yip, Wai-lim. *Chinese Poetry: Major Modes and Genres.* 1976.

Criticism and Translations

Wang Wei

Robinson, G. W. *Wang Wei: Poems*. 1973.
Wagner, Marsha. *Wang Wei*. 1981.
Yu, Pauline. *The Poetry of Wang Wei*. 1980.

Li Bai (Li Po)

Cooper, Arthur. *Li Po and Tu Fu*. 1973.
Hinton, David. *The Selected Poems of Li Po*. 1996.
Waley, Arthur. *Poetry and Career of Li Po*. 1950.

Du Fu (Tu Fu)

Davis, A. R. *Tu Fu*. 1971.
Hawkes, David. *A Little Primer of Tu Fu*. 1967.
Hinton, David. *The Selected Poems of Tu Fu*. 1988, 1989.

Bo Juyi (Po Chü-i)

Hinton, David. *The Selected Poems of Po Chü-i*. 1999.
Waley, Arthur. *The Life and Times of Po Chü-i*. 1949.
Watson, Burton. *Po Chü-i: Selected Poems*. 2000.

■ PRONUNCIATION

Bo Juyi (Po Chü-i): boh-joo-EE
Du Fu (Tu Fu): doo-FOO
Li Bai (Li Po): lee-BIGH (lee POH)
Wang Wei: wahng-WAY

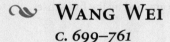

WANG WEI
c. 699–761

Wang Wei was born into an aristocratic family living in what is now the Province of Shanxi (Shansi). A gifted youth of great accomplishment in poetry, painting, and music, Wang Wei, when he was about sixteen, moved to the capital city of Chang'an (Ch'ang-an) where he was well received in the court. In 723 he passed the *chin-shi* civil service examination and began a career as a mid level official, serving as Assistant Secretary of Music in Chang'an before being transferred to the provinces after a minor infraction caused him to lose favor. After taking on the role of the poet in exile, a persona that Du Fu (Tu Fu) and Li Bai (Li Po) would also adopt, Wang Wei returned to city life briefly before purchasing an estate on the Wang River in the mountains south of Chang'an. Here Wang Wei began to cultivate in his poetry and painting the deep appreciation for and sensitivity to landscape and nature for which he is celebrated. Though he would return to the active life of Chang'an in 734 after the death of his wife, his estate on the Wang River served as a retreat for the poet for the rest of his life.

During his government service, Wang Wei was sent on diplomatic missions to various regions of China. When the An Lushan Rebellion took place in 755, Wang Wei was taken by the rebels, imprisoned, and eventually forced to work for them. When the rebellion was quashed by imperial forces, Wang Wei was at first accused of collaboration with the rebels. But the intervention of his brother and two poems displaying his loyalty to Emperor Xuanzong that he had written while with the rebels saved Wang Wei from execution. Restored to favor in the court, Wang Wei was appointed Right Assistant Director of the Council of State in 759, two years before he died.

Wang Wei was a devoted Buddhist with little desire for worldly success. As can be seen in his poetry, as he grew older he preferred the quiet serenity of his home in the mountains to the noise of the bustling capital, the clear light of the moon to the flickering lanterns of the palace. The Buddhist character of his poetry has been aptly described by Pauline Yu who observes that it lies not in doctrinal statements but in attitude: "His contemplative, dispassionate observations of the sensory world affirm its beauty at the same time as they call its ultimate reality into question, by emphasizing its vagueness, relativity, and 'emptiness.'" A poet with a highly visual sensibility, Wang Wei is famous for his depiction of landscape, which he blends with a consciousness of the illusory nature of worldly things. Moving between the concrete and the abstract, between the perceiving subject and the object, Wang Wei disturbs the fixed landscape with an awareness of mutability and the relativity of sensuous experience. The empty mountains, endless spaces, and mists without resting places of his poetry suggest the transience of human experience in contrast to the constant movement and cycles of seasonal change in nature. Thus, Wang Wei's mountains and rivers are often elusive, intimating a purer world just beyond what can be grasped by the five senses.

Group of Musicians, 618–906 C.E.

Music was an integral part of Tang-dynasty culture. Wang Wei was an accomplished musician as well as an outstanding poet. (Earthenware. Israel Museum)

ॐ **To Subprefect Chang**[1]

Translated by Irving Y. Lo

In late years, I love only the stillness,
The world's affairs no longer trouble my heart.
Looking at myself: no far-reaching plans;
All I know: to return to familiar woods—
The pine winds blow and loosen my sash;
The mountain moon shines upon me playing the lute.
You ask for reasons for failure or success—
Fisherman's song enters the riverbanks deep.

---

[1] Subprefect Chang: A midlevel government official (vice-magistrate) and a friend of Wang Wei.

FROM

ॐ **The Wang River Collection**[1]

HUATZU HILL

Translated by G. W. Robinson

Flying birds away into endless spaces
Ranged hills all autumn colours again.
I go up Huatzu Hill and come down—
Will my sadness never come to its end?

DEER PARK

Translated by Sam Hamill

No sign of men on the empty mountain,
only faint echoes from below.

Refracted light enters the forest,
shining through green moss above.

---

[1] The Wang River Collection: These poems all celebrate various scenic sites at Wang Wei's estate at Lantian in the Wang River valley southeast of Chang'an. The twenty poems of the collection, along with answering poems by Wang Wei's friend Pei Di, were written when Pei Di visited Wang Wei's retreat sometime after 746. Wang Wei's poems written at Huazi (Huatzu) Hill, Deer Park, Lake Yi, and Bamboo Lodge are presented here.

At Lake Yi

Translated by Sam Hamill

Flutes echo from the far shore
as we pause at sunset to bid farewell.

Green mountains, inverted on the lake,
plunge through pure white clouds.

Bamboo Mile Lodge

Translated by Burton Watson

Alone I sit in dark bamboo,
strumming the lute, whistling away;
deep woods that no one knows,
where a bright moon comes to shine on me.

Hermitage at Chung-nan Mountain

Translated by Sam Hamill

Growing older, I grow into the Tao:[1]
now I make my home in southern mountains,

and go there on a whim to wander alone.
But even in all this splendor, things remain empty.[2]

I climb to the headwaters
where clouds rise up from emptiness.

If I chance to meet another hermit in the woods,
we talk and laugh and never even think of home.

---

[1] Tao: "The Way," or dao, here referring to the path toward enlightenment accessed through Buddhist practices and teachings. Chinese Buddhists, Confucianists, and Daoists use the term *Dao* to mean the path of enlightenment, though that path involves different practices for each religion.

[2] But . . . things remain empty: This line suggests the transcendence of material distinctions and differences through an intuition of the underlying unity of all things.

❧ Crossing the Yellow River

Translated by Sam Hamill

A little boat on the great river
whose waves reach the end of the sky—

suddenly a great city, ten thousand
houses dividing sky from wave.

Between the towns there are
hemp and mulberry trees in the wilds.

Look back on the old country:
wide waters; clouds; and rising mist.

❧ Seeing Someone Off

Translated by Irving Y. Lo

Dismounting, I offer you wine
And ask, "Where are you bound?"
You say, "I've found no fame or favors;
"I must return to rest in the South Mountain."
You leave, and I ask no more—
White clouds drift on and on.

❧ LI BAI
701–762

Li Bai (Li Po) ranks with Du Fu (Tu Fu) as one of the greatest poets of the celebrated golden Tang era in China. Known in Japan as the great master Rihaku, Li Bai exerted a profound influence on Chinese and Japanese literature, and through the translations of Ezra Pound and Arthur Waley, on American poets of the Beat generation. Because of his deep feeling for nature, his brash disregard for convention, and his love of the common people, Li Bai has often been compared to European Romantic poets such as Goethe and Wordsworth. As in the work of those poets, a melancholy strain of loss and regret tempers even Li Bai's most celebratory poems, and scenes of conviviality and union with nature are often revisited as memories only.

Li Bai, 1510–1551

The celebrated poet Li Bai (Li Po) is shown here in a garden with friends and admirers in a sixteenth-century Chinese painting. (The Art Archive / Private Collection, Paris / Dagli Orti)

The Itinerant Poet.   Li Bai was born, probably in Chinese Turkestan west of Kansu, in 701, just before the end of the reign of Empress Wu. His family apparently had a remote ancestor, Li Gao, in common with the imperial family, although near the end of the Sui dynasty (c. 610) one of his relatives was banished for some unknown crime or for political reasons. Li Bai seems to have spent his childhood in Sichuan, where he studied the Confucian classics and practiced swordsmanship, poetry, and other gentlemanly arts. In his mid-twenties he left home to travel throughout northern and central China, taking advantage of the improved roads and bridges and greater assurance of safety made possible by the Tang dynasty. Li Bai's penchant for traveling continued throughout his life; his numerous poems thanking friends for their hospitality and the number of places mentioned in his poetry testify to his love of being on the road. After taking up residence in Yun Meng, Li Bai is said to have married the granddaughter of a former prime minister (this story may be apocryphal), and eventually moved to Shansi. Sometimes called the Old Wine Genius, Li Bai lost the first of his four wives because he spent too much time with a group of fellow poets who came to be called the Six Idlers of the Bamboo Valley.

In his extensive travels, Li Bai had occasion to meet and befriend many important people, among them the Daoist priests Wu Yun and Hou Jizhang (Ho Chi-chang)—from whom Li Bai received the name "Banished Immortal"—as well as the emperor himself, Xuanzong, who granted Li Bai patronage and appointed him to the prestigious Han Lin Academy. In the service of Xuanzong, Li Bai was commissioned to write various commemorative poems, tributes, and even edicts, all in verse. In the short time he was in the service of the court (742–44), Li Bai amplified his reputation for drunkenness, giving rise to numerous stories (some apocryphal) about his life. Du Fu (Tu Fu), who wrote a number of poems praising and jesting with his friendly rival, names Li Bai among "Eight Immortals of the Wine Cup," in which he quips, "Does his Majesty know that his humble servant is a drunken angel."

After leaving Chang'an, Li Bai used Shandong as a base for continuing travels. When in 755 the revolt of An Lushan forced the emperor to flee the capital, Li Bai, who was in the service of one of the emperor's sons, was arrested and sentenced to death. His life was spared by the minister of war, and Li Bai was banished to southwestern China. Eventually an amnesty enabled him to return to the region of the lower Yangtze, where he died in 762. Legend has it that Li Bai drowned in a drunken stupor, falling off a boat as he tried to embrace the moon reflected in the water, but it may well be that he died of pneumonia or another natural cause.

Although he studied Daoism (Taoism), Li Bai celebrated — often with a pensive, melancholy sense of regret and longing — wine, romance, love, and friendship in his work. With its author's high-spirited rebellion against poetic and social conventions and his emphasis on worldly indulgence, Li Bai's poetry stood in direct opposition to the rigid hierarchy of the Confucian tradition in China. The boastful, reckless, and iconoclastic quality of his poetry has made Li Bai one of China's best-known poets and earned for him from time to time the disfavor of state-commissioned *literati* — Confucianist and Communist — interested in enforcing conformity.

Some of Li Bai's most celebrated poems are presented here, including examples of the drinking songs and occasional poems he wrote about leaving friends and lovers.

❧ Going to Visit Tai-T'ien Mountain's Master[1] of the Way without Finding Him

Translated by David Hinton

A dog barks among the sounds of water.
Dew stains peach blossoms. In forests,

I sight a few deer, then at the creek,
hear nothing of midday temple bells.

Wild bamboo parts blue haze. A stream
hangs in flight beneath emerald peaks.

No one knows where you've gone. Still,
for rest, I've found two or three pines.

---

[1] **Tai-t'ien (Daitian) Mountain's Master:** Sacred to Daoists, this mountain is where the legendary Liu Chen (Liu Ch'en) was said to have met with divine maidens.

Ch'ang-Kan Village Song[1]

Translated by David Hinton

These bangs not yet reaching my eyes,
I played at our gate, picking flowers,

and you came on your horse of bamboo,
circling the well, tossing green plums.

We lived together here in Ch'ang-kan,
two little people without suspicions.

At fourteen, when I became your wife,
so timid and betrayed I never smiled,

I faced wall and shadow, eyes downcast.
A thousand pleas: I ignored them all.

At fifteen, my scowl began to soften.
I wanted us mingled as dust and ash,

and you always stood fast here for me,
no tower vigils awaiting your return.

At sixteen, you sailed far off to distant
Yen-yü Rock in Ch'ü-t'ang Gorge,[2] fierce

June waters impossible, and howling
gibbons called out into the heavens.

At our gate, where you lingered long,
moss buried your tracks one by one,

deep green moss I can't sweep away.
And autumn's come early. Leaves fall.

It's September now. Butterflies appear
in the west garden. They fly in pairs,

---

[1] "Ch'ang-Kan Village Song": This poem is well known as Ezra Pound's translation "The River Merchant's Wife." Ch'ang-kan (Changkan; today, Nanjing) was a port town on the Yangtze, China's longest river.

[2] Yen-yü . . . Ch'ü-t'ang Gorge: The Ch'ü-t'ang was a hazardous gorge along the Yangtze River near the remote city of Kuei-chou (Guizhou); the dangerous Yen-yü Rock lies in the midst of the river in the gorge.

and it hurts. I sit heart-stricken
at the bloom of youth in my old face.

Before you start back from out beyond
all those gorges, send a letter home.

I'm not saying I'd go far to meet you,
30 no further than Ch'ang-feng[3] Sands.

---

[3] **Ch'ang-feng:** A remote northern town on the Yangtze.

Drinking Alone beneath the Moon

Translated by David Hinton

1

Among the blossoms, a single jar of wine.
No one else here, I ladle it out myself.

Raising my cup, I toast the bright moon,
and facing my shadow makes friends three,

though moon has never understood wine,
and shadow only trails along behind me.

Kindred a moment with moon and shadow,
I've found a joy that must infuse spring:

I sing, and moon rocks back and forth;
10 I dance, and shadow tumbles into pieces.

Sober, we're together and happy. Drunk,
we scatter away into our own directions:

intimates forever, we'll wander carefree
and meet again in Star River[1] distances.

---

[1] **Star River:** The Milky Way. It was thought that the great rivers of China formed a cyclic pattern: flowing east into the sea, then mounting to the sky to become the Star River, then returning to earth in the west at the rivers' source.

2

Surely, if heaven didn't love wine,
there would be no Wine Star in heaven,

and if earth didn't love wine, surely
there would be no Wine Spring on earth.

Heaven and earth have always loved wine,
so how could loving wine shame heaven?

I hear clear wine called enlightenment,
and they say murky wine is like wisdom:

once you drink enlightenment and wisdom,
why go searching for gods and immortals?

Three cups and I've plumbed the great Way,[2]
a jarful and I've merged with occurrence

appearing of itself. Wine's view is lived:
you can't preach doctrine to the sober.

3

It's April in Ch'ang-an, these thousand
blossoms making a brocade of daylight.

Who can bear spring's lonely sorrows, who
face it without wine? It's the only way.

Success or failure, life long or short:
our fate's given by Changemaker at birth.

But a single cup evens out life and death,
our ten thousand concerns unfathomed,

and once I'm drunk, all heaven and earth
vanish, leaving me suddenly alone in bed,

forgetting that person I am even exists.
Of all our joys, this must be the deepest.

---

[2] **the great Way:** The dao (Tao), or the basic principle of order that underlies the cosmos in Daoist thought; it is said to be the origin of all things as well as the path to peace and enlightenment.

❧ Searching for Master Yung

Translated by Jerome P. Seaton

So many cliffs, jade blue to scour the sky,
I've rambled, years uncounted,
Brushed aside the clouds, and sought the Ancient Way,[1]
Or leaned against a tree and listened to streams flow.
Sunwarmed blossoms: the blue ox sleeps.
Tall pines: the white cranes resting.
Words came, with the river sunset.
Alone, I came down, through the cold mist.

---

[1] **the Ancient Way:** The dao (Tao), the basic principle of order that underlies the cosmos in Daoist thought; it is said to be the origin of all things as well as the path to peace and enlightenment.

❧ Seeing Off a Friend

Translated by Jerome P. Seaton

Green mountains border Northern Rampart.
Clear water curls by Eastern Wall.
Here, we'll make our parting.
There, lonely brambles stretch ten thousand *li*.
Floating clouds: the traveler's thoughts.
Falling sun: the old friend's feelings.
Touch hands, and now you go,
Muffled sighs, and the post horse, neighing.

❧ Teasing Tu Fu

Translated by David Hinton

Here on the summit of Fan-k'o Mountain, it's Tu Fu
under a midday sun sporting his huge farmer's hat.

How is it you've gotten so thin since we parted?
Must be all those poems you've been suffering over.

Drinking in the Mountains with a Recluse

Translated by David Hinton

Drinking together among mountain blossoms, we
down a cup, another, and yet another. Soon drunk,

I fall asleep, and you wander off. Tomorrow morning,
if you think of it, grab your *ch'in*[1] and come again.

---

[1] *ch'in:* An ancient Chinese stringed instrument similar to a zither; ancestor to the Japanese *koto*.

Sent to My Two Little Children in the East of Lu[1]

Translated by Burton Watson

Wu land mulberry leaves grow green,
already Wu silkworms have slept three times.
I left my family in the east of Lu;
who sows our fields there on the dark side of Mt. Kuei?[2]
Spring chores too long untended,
river journeys that leave me dazed —
south winds blow my homing heart;
it soars and comes to rest before the wine tower.
East of the tower a peach tree grows,
branches and leaves brushed with blue mist,
10   a tree I planted myself,
parted from it these three years.
The peach now is tall as the tower
and still my journey knows no return.
P'ing-yang, my darling girl,
picks blossoms, leaning by the peach,
picks blossoms and does not see me;
her tears flow like a welling fountain.
The little boy, named Po-ch'in,

---

[1] Lu: Lu is the ancient name for Shandong (Shantung) Province, where Li Bai left his family while traveling in the south, which he refers to here as Wu, the name of an ancient kingdom in southeast China.

[2] Mt. Kuei: Mt. Gui, a mountain in Shandong.

20 is shoulder high to his elder sister;
side by side they walk beneath the peach—
who will pat them with loving hands?
I lose myself in thoughts of them;
day by day care burns out my heart.
On this piece of cut silk I'll write my far-away thoughts
and send them floating down the river Wen-yang.[3]

---

[3] Wen-yang: A river in Shandong.

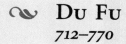

✍ Du Fu
712–770

Though relatively neglected in his own day, subsequent generations of Chinese readers came to consider the Confucian poet Du Fu (Tu Fu) China's greatest poet. A versatile and innovative master of all the forms of poetry practiced in the High Tang era, Du Fu also displayed in his poetry what at the time was an unprecedented concern for the personal and social consequences of historical change. Du Fu's poetry engages both the historical and personal events in his life to such a high degree that he is often called a poet-historian. Unlike the poetry of Wang Wei, whose meditative descriptions of nature give one a feeling of timelessness, Du Fu's work records with sadness and compassion the harsh realities of everyday life, the suffering of the poor, and, in his later poetry, the decline of the Tang dynasty after the An Lushan Rebellion of 755. He also criticizes those who fail to live up to the Confucian standards of duty and piety, particularly targeting the corrupt officials of Emperor Xuanzong's court. Du Fu's own life was marked by disappointment and failure, and in his poetry the boundary between public and private experience often blurs.

 Du Fu was born in 712 to a family of midlevel scholar-officials. His mother was the great-granddaughter of the former emperor Taizong, and his grandfather was Du Shenyan, an important court poet in the previous generation. Though he showed promise as a youth, Du Fu twice failed the *chin-shi* examinations (in 735 and 747), and despite his family's connections was unable to obtain special appointment to a government position. He spent much of his life traveling throughout China, cultivating his art as a poet, working on his painting and musical skills, and relying on the generosity of distant family members and other patrons for support and patronage. In 744 or 745 the as-yet unacknowledged Du Fu met the already-famous Li Bai (Li Po), inaugurating one of literary

Du Fu, eighteenth
century
*A late portrait
of an older and
contemplative Du Fu
(Tu Fu). (The Art
Archive / British
Library)*

history's most celebrated friendships. The disciplined and humble Confucian Du Fu may seem an unlikely friend for the irreverent and reckless Daoist Li Bai, who teased Du Fu for laboring too hard and suffering too much over his poetry. Despite their different sensibilities, or perhaps because of them, the two poets developed a strong friendship and each devoted several poems to the other.

Du Fu was offered a government post in 755, the year of the An Lushan Rebellion. Though he was not in Chang'an when it was seized, he was cut off from the court party fleeing to the west and like Wang Wei was soon captured and held by the rebels. Escaping his captors, Du Fu joined Xuanzong's court in exile at Sichuan and returned with them to Chang'an when it was recaptured in 757. Though the post he had so long tried to secure now seemed within his grasp, he managed to offend the court and was exiled to Huazhou where he held a minor post. Unhappy with his job, Du Fu left it behind and took to traveling again. He spent two years in Chengdu, the capital of Sichuan province, where he held the title of assistant deputy in the Ministry of Works and served as a military advisor. Despite the instability in his life, Du Fu was particularly productive in his later years when he was again dependent on the good grace of patrons. In fact, the poems of his later years are imbued with an intensity and a sense of peace and dignity, signifying that Du Fu was able to rise above his misfortune. These poems also show Du Fu continuing to experiment with new poetic forms. When his patron at Chengdu died, Du Fu undertook several voyages down the Yangtze River toward the lakes region in central China. Weakened by illness, Du Fu died in 770, most likely while on the Yangtze.

Du Fu's Confucian sensibilities are evident in his poetry, noted for its technical perfection. He was drawn to the technical challenges posed by the *lushi,* or regulated verse, of which form he is still considered the undisputed master. In the formal perfection of his style, he manages to present his personal suffering in an objective light, tying it to the larger events taking place in China and blurring the distinction between his personal plight and the collective misfortune of the Chinese people in a time of great difficulty. The following translations by a variety of respected translators demonstrate the versatility of Du Fu's style and the variety in the English versions of his work.

❧ To Li Po° on a Winter Day

Li Bai

Translated by Sam Hamill

Alone in my secluded hut,
I think of you all day, Li Po.

Whenever I read of friendship,
I remember your friendly poems.

Harsh winds tatter your old clothes
as you search for the wine of endless life.

Unable to go with you, I remember only
that old hermitage we'd hoped to make a home.

P'eng-Ya Song

Translated by David Hinton

I remember long ago slipping away
in precarious depths of night. The moon
bright on Po-shui Mountain, I eluded
rebel armies and fled with my family

far north by foot on P'eng-ya Road.[1]
By then, most people we met had lost all
shame. Scattered bird cries haunted
valleys. No one returned the way we came.

My silly, starved girl bit me and screamed.
Afraid tigers and wolves might hear,
I cradled her close, holding her mouth,
but she squirmed loose, crying louder still.

Looking after us gallantly, my little boy
searched out sour-plum feasts. Of ten days,
half were all thunder and rain — mud
and more mud to drag ourselves through.

We didn't plan for rain. Clothes ever
colder, the road slippery, an insufferable
day's travel often took us but a few short
miles by nightfall. Wild fruit replaced

what little food we had carried with us.
Low branches became our home. We left dew-
splashed rocks each morning, and passed
nights at the smoke-scored edge of heaven.

We had stopped at T'ung-chia Marsh,
planning to cross Lu-tu Pass, when you
took us in, Sun Tsai, old friend, your
kindness towering like billowing clouds.

---

[1] **I remember . . . P'eng-ya Road:** This poem records the arduous 140-mile journey along the P'eng-ya Road from Fengxian, where Du Fu (Tu Fu) had moved his family, to Fuzhou, where he hoped to secure their safety from the An Lushan Rebellion. (See also "Moonlit Night.")

30 Dusk already become night, you hung lanterns
out and swung door after door wide open.
You soothed our feet with warm water
and cut paper charms to summon our souls,

then called your wife and children in, their
eyes filling with tears for us. My chicks
soon drifted away in sleep, but you brought
them back, offering choice dishes of food.

You and I, you promised, will be forever
bound together like two dear brothers.
And before long, you emptied our rooms,
40 leaving us to joy and peace and rest.

In these times overrun with such calamity,
how many hearts are so open and generous?
A year of months since we parted, and still
those Mongols spin their grand catastrophes.

How long before I've grown feathers and wings
and settled beside you at the end of flight?

Moonlit Night

Translated by David Hinton

Tonight at Fu-chou,[1] this moon she watches
Alone in our room. And my little, far-off
Children, too young to understand what keeps me
Away, or even remember Ch'ang-an. By now,

Her hair will be mist-scented, her jade-white
Arms chilled in its clear light. When
Will it find us together again, drapes drawn
Open, light traced where it dries our tears?

---

[1] **Fu-chou:** (Fuzhou) The city more than two hundred miles north of Chang'an (Ch'ang-an) where Du Fu (Tu Fu) escaped with his family (see "P'eng-ya Song") at the time of the An Lushan Rebellion. Leaving his wife and children behind in Fuzhou, Du Fu was captured and taken to Chang'an where somehow he managed to elude imprisonment and execution.

Dreaming of Li Po

Translated by David Hinton

Death at least gives separation repose.
Without death, its grief can only sharpen.
You wander out in malarial southlands,
and I hear nothing of you, exiled

old friend. Knowing I think of you
always now, you visit my dreams, my heart
frightened it is no living spirit
I dream. Endless miles—you come

10   so far from the Yangtze's sunlit maples
night shrouds the passes when you return.
And snared as you are in their net,
with what bird's wings could you fly?

Filling my room to the roof-beams, the moon
sinks. You nearly linger in its light,
but the waters deepen in long swells,
unfed dragons—take good care old friend.

Restless Night

Translated by Burton Watson

The cool of bamboo invades my room;
moonlight from the fields fills the corners of the court;
dew gathers till it falls in drops;
a scattering of stars, now there, now gone.
A firefly threading the darkness makes its own light;
birds at rest on the water call to each other;
all these lie within the shadow of the sword—
Powerless I grieve as the clear night passes.

∿ Flying from Trouble

Translated by Florence Ayscough

At fifty a white-headed old man,
South, North, I fly from troubles of the State.

Coarse cloth wound round dried bones.
Walk back, forth; alas am still not warm.

∿ Spring Night, Delighted by Rain

Translated by David Hinton

Lovely rains, knowing their season,
Always appear in spring. Entering night
Secretly on the wind, they silently
Bless things with such delicate abundance.

Clouds fill country lanes with darkness,
The one light a riverboat lamp. Then
Dawn's view opens: all bathed reds, our
Blossom-laden City of Brocade Officers.[1]

---

[1] **City of Brocade Officers:** The city of Chengdu, the southern capital where Emperor Xuanzong set up office while in exile during the An Lushan Rebellion, was well known for its brocades, the production of which was overseen by government-appointed officers.

Thoughts, Traveling at Night

Translated by David Hinton

In delicate beach-grass, a slight breeze.
The boat's mast teetering up into solitary
Night, plains open away beneath foundering stars.
A moon emerges and, the river vast, flows.

How will poems bring honor? My career
Lost to age and sickness, buffeted, adrift
On the wind—is there anything like it? All
Heaven and earth, and one lone sand-gull.

Bo Juyi
772–846

Like Du Fu, Bo Juyi (Po Chü-i; 772–846) wrote many poems criticizing government inefficiency and corruption and sympathizing with the suffering of the people. Whereas Du Fu (Tu Fu) was a master of *lushi,* or regulated verse, Bo Juyi is known for his innovations in the *yuefu,* the ballad form he adapted to write poems of social criticism. Also in contrast to Du Fu whose poetic talent went largely unnoticed in his lifetime, Bo Juyi enjoyed tremendous popularity while alive. He once said that when he walked the nearly four thousand leagues from Chang'an (Ch'ang-an) to Jiangxi he found his poems everywhere, posted at village schools, monasteries, and inns, but that he regretted that his best work was neglected in favor of what he thought of as literary trifles. His popularity, which extended to Japan, was in large part due to the simplicity of his style. According to legend, after composing his poems Bo Juyi would read them to a peasant woman and revise any lines that she could not understand. Whether the story is true or not, as the Sinologist and translator Burton Watson points out, it has survived because it so well captures the spirit of the poet's work. Bo Juyi's popularity may also be attributed to the topical and romantic themes of some of his poems, such as those found in his most famous work, *The Song of Unending Sorrow,* about the tragic love between Emperor Xuanzong and his villainous concubine Yang Guifei. Many of his poems also focus on gardening, eating, keeping pets, drinking wine, and making money—everyday matters that broadened the parameters of what was considered appropriate subject matter for poetry.

The son of a poor scholar-official at Xinzheng in Henan (Honan) Province, Bo Juyi was born in 772. His early years, like those of many young men born in similar circumstances, were spent studying for the *chin-shi* civil service examinations, which he passed in 800. Three years later, having passed an advanced examination, he began a career as a government official in Chang'an, eventually gaining an appointment to Han-Lin Academy in 807. Bo Juyi was married in 808 and began his important friendship with Yuan Zhen (779–831), the author of *The Story of Ying-ying.* Here, too, he got himself into trouble by writing poems critical of the government; he was stripped of his rank and sent into exile as a marshal to Jiujiang (Xunyang) in 815. At the time of his banishment, he had been back in the capital only a year after observing three years of mourning near the river Wei following the death of his mother in 811. In exile, Bo Juyi began to study Chan Buddhism with monks at local temples on Mount Lu, where he eventually built a retreat celebrated in his poetry. After three years in Jiujiang, Bo Juyi was transferred to Zhongzhou in Sichuan Province, and in 819 he returned to Chang'an where he served as an assistant secretary in an office issuing official edicts. Before retiring from government service, Bo Juyi served as the governor of Hangzhou (822–24), the governor of Suzhou (825–26), the senior librarian of the Imperial Library at Chang'an (827), and the governor of Henan Province at Luoyang (829–31), the eastern capital. During this time Bo Juyi kept up his study of Buddhism and continued writing poetry. In 832 he finally settled in at the Xiangshan Monastery on the river Yi south of Luoyang, where he lived until his death in 846.

Despite his later practice of Chan Buddhism, Bo Juyi early on held a Confucian notion that poetry should serve as an agent of moral improvement. While Bo Juyi's poems of social criticism, the "new *yuefu*" or "new ballads," received a great deal of attention in his own time (and have continued to), he also wrote lyric poems, *lushi* and *kushi,* of great intensity, clarity, and simplicity. Recent critics have seen in his lyric poetry an expression of his Chan Buddhism, whose practitioners seek to dissolve the ego so that the mind is emptied of all attachments and the true reality of things may appear in its profound simplicity and transparency. Bo Juyi's poems are always intensely personal, even as they embrace the objective world and the tumultuous society in which he lived. The selections that follow, rendered into English by Arthur Waley and the prizewinning translator David Hinton, transport the power of both types of Bo Juyi's poetry to the modern reader.

Watching the Reapers

Translated by Arthur Waley

Tillers of the earth have few idle months:
In the fifth month[1] their toil is double-fold.
A south wind visits the fields at night;
Suddenly the ridges are covered with yellow corn.
Wives and daughters shoulder baskets of rice,
Youths and boys carry flasks of wine,
In a long train, to feed the workers in the field —
The strong reapers toiling on the southern hill,
Whose feet are burned by the hot earth they tread,

10 Whose backs are scorched by the flames of the shining sky
Tired they toil, caring nothing for the heat,
Grudging the shortness of the long summer day.
A poor woman with a young child at her side
Follows behind, to glean the unwanted grain.
In her right hand she holds the fallen ears,
On her left arm a broken basket hangs.
Listening to what they said as they worked together
I heard something that made me very sad:
They lost in grain-tax[2] the whole of their own crop;

20 What they glean here is all they will have to eat.

And I to-day — in virtue of what desert
Have I never once tended field or tree?
My government-pay is three hundred "stones";
At the year's end I have still grain in hand.
Thinking of this, secretly I grew ashamed
And all day the thought lingered in my head.

---

[1] the fifth month: The middle of summer

[2] grain-tax: Excessive taxation to finance the extravagances of Xuanzong's court and military adventures placed a heavy burden on the peasants and eventually led to peasant revolts.

Passing T'ien-mên Street in Ch'ang-an and Seeing a Distant View of Chung-nan Mountains

Translated by Arthur Waley

The snow has gone from Chung-nan;[1] spring is almost come.
Love in the distance its blue colours, against the brown of the streets.
A thousand coaches, ten thousand horsemen pass down the Nine Roads;
Turns his head and looks at the mountains—not one man!

---

[1] **Chung-nan:** Chongnan, a mountain to the south of Ch'ang-an.

An Old Charcoal Seller

Translated by David Hinton

An old charcoal seller
cuts firewood and sears it to charcoal below South Mountain,

his face smeared with dust and ash the color of woodsmoke,
his hair gone grizzled and grey, his ten fingers utter black,

and yet daring such hopes for the profits he'll take home
once the charcoal's all sold: warm robes to wear, food to eat.

His clothes are worn so miserably thin, and yet he worries
charcoal's selling too cheap, so he hopes for colder weather,

then one night an inch of snow falls in the city's foothills
and at dawn he takes his cart crackling through ruts of ice.

A tired ox and hungry man: the sun is already high when
they pause to rest in marketplace mud outside the south gate

and two riders no one knows appear in a dashing flourish:
one an envoy dressed in yellow, the other a servant in white.

The envoy carries an imperial warrant, and after reading it out,
he chases the ox away, turns the cart and takes it off north.

A cart like that easily carries a thousand pounds of charcoal,
but a palace envoy hurries it away without a second thought:

half a length of crimson lace and a few yards of fine damask
20   draped over the old ox's neck: isn't that a fair enough price?

✺ Buying Flowers

Translated by David Hinton

Late spring in this emperor's city,[1]
horses and carts clattering past:

it's peony season on the avenues
and the people stream out to buy.

They won't be this cheap for long.
At these prices, anyone can buy.

Showing five delicate whites amid
hundreds of huge luminous reds,

they rig canopies to shelter them
10   and bamboo screens to shield them,

sprinkle them, stand them in mud,
keeping their color rich and fresh.

Families come back day after day:
people just can't shake their spell.

Happening by the flower markets,
an old man from a farm somewhere

gazes down and sighs to himself,
a sigh no one here could fathom:

a single clutch of bottomless color
20   sells for taxes on ten village farms.

---

[1] this emperor's city: Chang'an (Ch'ang-an), the capital city.

Winter Night

Translated by David Hinton

Those I love scattered away, poor
and far too sick for friendly visits,

I'm shut up inside, no one in sight.
Lying in this village study alone,

the wick cold and lampflame dark,
wide open drapes torn and tattered,

I listen as the snow begins to fall
again, that hiss outside the window.

Older now, sleeping less and less,
I get up in the night and sit intent,

mind utterly forgotten. How else
can I get past such isolate silence?

Body visiting this world steadfast,
mind abandoned to change limitless:

it's been like this four years now,
one thousand three hundred nights.

 # On the Boat, Reading
Yüan Chen's[1] Poems

Translated by David Hinton

I sit up with a scroll of your poems, reading before a lamp.
When I'm done, the lamp's flickering low and dawn's far off.

My eyes ache. I put out the lamp and sit in the dark. Waves
blown by headwinds: the sound of them slapping at the boat.

---

[1] Yüan-Chen: Yuan Zhen (d. 831), a close friend and poet in honor of whom Bo Juyi wrote many poems.

Idle Song

Translated by David Hinton

After such painstaking study of empty-gate dharma,[1]
everything life plants in the mind has dissolved away:

there's nothing left now but that old poetry demon.
A little wind or moon, and I'm chanting an idle song.

---

[1] **empty-gate dharma:** The way of Chan Buddhism, which involves meditation aimed at emptying the mind of both subjectivity, or identity, and objective reality.

Madly Singing in the Mountains

Translated by Arthur Waley

There is no one among men that has not a special failing;
And my failing consists in writing verses.
I have broken away from the thousand ties of life;
But this infirmity still remains behind.
Each time that I look at a fine landscape,
Each time that I meet a loved friend,
I raise my voice and recite a stanza of poetry
And marvel as though a God had crossed my path.
Ever since the day I was banished to Hsün-yang[1]
Half my time I have lived among the hills.
And often, when I have finished a new poem,
Alone I climb the road to the Eastern Rock.
I lean my body on the banks of white Stone;
I pull down with my hands a green cassia branch.
My mad singing startles the valleys and hills;
The apes and birds all come to peep.
Fearing to become a laughing-stock to the world,
I choose a place that is unfrequented by men.

---

[1] **Hsün-yang:** Xunyang, a city on the Yangtze in the district of Jiujiang (Jiangzhou) where Bo Juyi was exiled in 815.

Autumn Pool

Translated by David Hinton

My body's idle, doing perfectly nothing,
and mind, thinking perfectly nothing,

now more than ever. In this old garden
tonight, I've returned to my autumn pool,

shoreline dark now birds have settled in,
bridge incandescent under a rising moon.

Chestnut scents swell, adrift on a breeze,
and the cinnamon's a confusion of lit dew.

So much solitude in this far end of quiet,
an isolate mystery no one finally knows:

just a few words haunting a far-off mind,
asking why it took so long coming here.

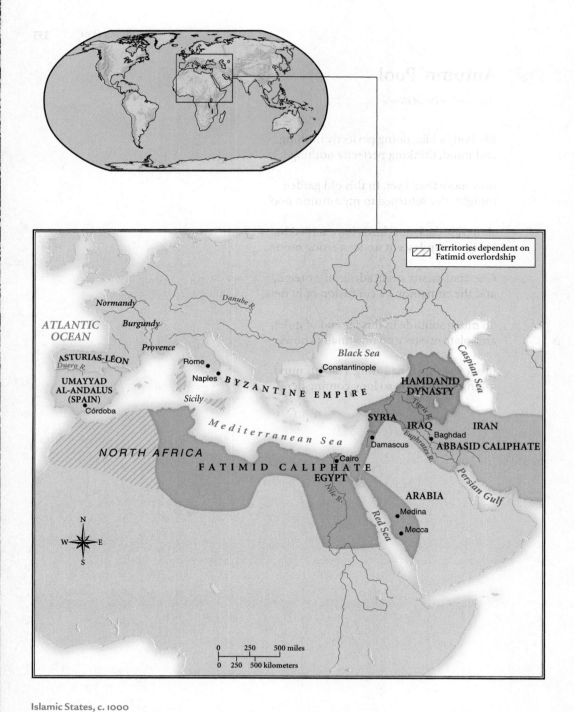

Islamic States, c. 1000

In 750, one caliph ruled the territory from Spain to India, but by 1000, the once-united Islamic world had fragmented, resulting in several caliphates and ruling dynasties.

ARABIA AND PERSIA
The World of Islam

Islamic culture began with the Qur'an (Koran) and the biography of Muhammad, texts treated in this anthology in "The Near East: Christianity and Islam." Those who established Islam during the seventh and early eighth centuries influenced the medieval period with, in particular, three new ways of approaching the world: First was the early Muslim belief that a special relationship existed among Jews, Christians, and themselves, all of whom were **PEOPLE OF THE BOOK**, capable of finding God through their study of the prophets; second was the reverence Muslims displayed for scholarship during the seventh century, while the biography of Muhammad was being assembled; third was the remarkable generosity Islamic scholars displayed in sharing their knowledge with other peoples in both Baghdad and Cordova. The learning they made available crucially influenced later European thought and benefited the medieval world as a whole.

The major periods of Islamic rule following the death of Muhammad—those of the "rightly guided" CALIPHS in Medina (630–661), the Umayyad dynasty in Damascus (661–750), and the Abbasid dynasty in Baghdad (750–1258)—contained serious political problems and weaknesses. The debate over the succession after Muhammad's death left a bitter legacy that divided Muslims for centuries. The failure of the first caliphs, or "successors," to establish unity forced a reconsideration of how political power should be dispensed. Even the successful Umayyad dynasty finally could not overcome internal family divisions as well as the heightened expectations of the conquered territories, with the result that they came to a sudden end in 750. And the even greater achievements of the Abbasid dynasty were undercut by the weakening of Abbasid rule in Baghdad in the tenth century, leading to the loss of conquered territories to other Muslim dynasties and caliphates. Despite these setbacks, Islamic culture continued to develop and to transform the Middle Period.

Chess Players, 1282
After its founding in the seventh century, Islamic religion and culture spread throughout
Europe, Africa, and the Near East, encompassing and embracing many geographies,
cultures, and peoples. This miniature showing two chess players is from an Andalusian
illuminated manuscript. (El Escorial / Giraudon / The Art Resource)

THE EBB AND FLOW OF DYNASTIES

The first four caliphs after the death of Muhammad in 632 were called *rashidun,* or
"rightly guided," based on the fact that all four rulers had been either friends or in
one case a relative of the Prophet. Men from different families did not constitute a
dynasty, and for the time being the seat of Islam remained in Medina. But later,
with the conquest of more and more territory, the once-intimate nature of the
relationships around Muhammad as well as the unquestioned importance of
Arabia as the center of the Islamic world lost immediacy and strength.

The first caliph, the Prophet's close associate Abu Bakr, argued that the Islamic
state should remain a single community. True to his word, he unified all of Arabia
during his short reign (632–634). Next, under Caliph Umar ibn al-Khattab
(634–644), the Arabs exploded into Iraq, Syria, and Egypt, winning a decisive battle
against the Persians in 637. Under Uthman ibn Affan (644–656), the Muslims

extended their territory across North Africa into Libya as well as further north and east through Asia Minor. In 656, Uthman was assassinated in an attack that was shocking and repugnant to most Muslims. He was succeeded in 656 by Muhammad Ali, Muhammad's closest surviving relative and an original contender for succession after Muhammad's death. Muhammad Ali ruled under constant threat. Even his favorite wife Aisha accused him of failing to pursue the assassins of Uthman and helped to lead the campaign against him. After five contentious years, Muhammad Ali was murdered. Mu'awiyah, the prince of Syria, succeeded him, and the capital was moved from Medina to Damascus. In effect, Islam had outgrown the place of its origins.

THE UMAYYAD DYNASTY

The Umayyad dynasty was formed with Mu'awiyah at its head in 661. In the next hundred years, the Umayyads transformed the conquered territories into a single unified Muslim state. Damascus became a glorious capital adorned in jeweled and perfumed splendor. The Umayyads completed building the Dome of the Rock in Jerusalem in 691, Islam's claim on the Holy City. Arabic replaced Persian as the language of the court in Damascus, bolstering the claim of continuity of Arab culture despite the relocation of the capital to Syria. And in 711, the Muslims expanded their territory once again with the conquest of what today is Spain. The Muslim incursion into Europe was halted at Tours, in southern France, in 732, when the Frankish leader, Charles Martel, defeated the Muslim army. Abandoning any further advances in Europe, the Muslims returned to Spain, then called Andalusia.

Two major enemies undermined the Umayyad dynasty in the middle of the eighth century: the SHI'ITE followers of the ill-starred Muhammad Ali, whom they viewed as a martyr after his political murder in 661, and a large group of non-Arab Muslims, including Persians who had been passed over for advancement by the Umayyads. An uneasy alliance of these two groups drove out the Umayyads in 750, and the Abbasid dynasty was installed. In a sense, the Umayyads had been depleted by their successes. Through painful and sometimes brutal internal struggle they had constructed an empire out of an Arabian religious enclave; now they were forced to make way for a more forward-looking dynasty. In the next two centuries, Islamic culture would reach its apotheosis.

THE ABBASID DYNASTY

The new rulers of the Abbasid dynasty, who in 750 had managed to build an alliance between two groups with little in common, chose between their supporters once in office. Rejecting the narrowly sectarian Shi'ites, the Abbasids favored the Persians, noted for their sophistication and bureaucratic skills. The Abbasid caliph

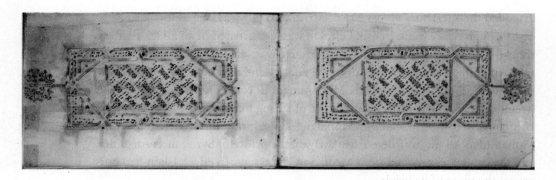

Abbasid Qur'an, ninth century
Islamic culture flowered under the Abassid dynasty. This figure shows a book from
central Islamic lands; there are no illustrations other than the decorative letters. (The
Metropolitan Museum of Art. Gift of Philip Hafer, 1937. All rights reserved.)

Al-Mansur even built a new capital city in Baghdad, at the western edge of the old
Persian empire. The splendor of the Abbasid court, decorated in Persian fashion,
was matched by the brilliance of Baghdad itself, the center of a commercial
network that spread beyond the distant borders of Islam to the ends of the known
earth: to China, Scandinavia, and Africa.

The greatest prosperity of the Abbasids came during the rule of Harun
al-Rashid (r. 786–809). Harun, a contemporary of Charlemagne, once dazzled the
Frankish leader with the gift of an elephant. Harun's reputation for flamboyance is
probably responsible for his depiction as the tyrannical caliph in *The Thousand
and One Nights,* the renowned Arabic story collection completed in the thirteenth
and fourteenth centuries. In actuality, Harun was celebrated for his endowment of
scholarship and the arts; in Baghdad and across the Islamic world, he created the
greatest meeting ground for philosophers, mathematicians, scientists, legal scholars, poets, and artists in the Middle Period. He also established an efficient
bureaucracy modeled after that of the Persian empire, drained the swamps, and
enhanced public works. Harun was not, however, a particularly enlightened ruler
by modern political standards. His society depended heavily on the slave trade with
sub-Saharan Africa, and he reduced women to a lower status than provided for in
the Qur'an.

The Abbasid dynasty eventually declined, partly from lack of a commercial
infrastructure. Over vast stretches of land where transportation was often limited
to camel caravans or sailing ships, communications were nearly impossible. Tax
collection was extraordinarily difficult. Local chieftains who had built up sizeable
armies for their own protection eventually broke off from Baghdad. Finally, the
Abbasids themselves capitulated: Persians took over the rule of Baghdad in all but

name after 950, and the city was occupied in 1055 by the Seljuk Turks, who used it to stage a bloody invasion of Byzantium. Although Islam recovered from most of the devastation of the Crusades during the later twelfth century, Baghdad never regained its former glory. It was conquered again by the Mongols in 1258, the date usually cited as the end of the Abbasid dynasty. In truth, the Abbasids had ruled effectively from 750 to about 950.

THE ANDALUSIAN EXPERIENCE

Andalusia was occupied by Muslims in 711; its Umayyad rulers survived a purge attempt by the Abbasids in 750. In 756 Abdul Raman al-Amawi became the Umayyad caliph of Andalusia, and his dynasty lasted for more than two hundred years. By the tenth century Cordova was the leading city of Andalusia, with a population of a half million. Its jewel-encrusted palace and the administrative capital of az-Zahra were built in the time of an-Nasir li-Din Allah (r. 912–961), at the height of Cordova's prestige. The University of Cordova and its library were for a time the largest in Europe; the university was home to thousands of students and the library to some four hundred thousand manuscripts. Although religious tolerance existed among Jews, Christians, and Muslims in this period in Cordova, Muslim culture prevailed. Alvaro, the Christian bishop of Cordova in the middle of the ninth century, lamented that none of his flock seemed to understand Christian doctrine while many wrote poetry in Arabic better than the Arabs did.

Conditions gradually worsened for the Muslims in Andalusia as Christians from the north continued to recover territory, although the progress of the Reconquest, as the Christian Spaniards called it, was very slow. Though the caliphate of Cordova was dissolved in 1002, and the city was sacked by Berbers in 1013, it recovered and remained Muslim for more than two hundred years. Toledo fell to the Christians in 1085, and the province of Aragon joined Catalonia on the Christian side in 1140. In 1212 the pope declared a Crusade against the Muslims in Spain, and a decisive battle was fought at Las Navas de Talosa outside of Toledo the same year. Cordova finally fell in 1236. In 1492, the year Columbus sailed for America, the Muslims were formally expelled along with remaining Jews from Spain; those not actually forced to leave were expected to convert to Christianity. Many remaining Christianized Muslims, called "Moriscos," were either slaughtered or expelled under the later reign of King Phillip III between 1609 and 1611.

RECLAIMING THE ANCIENT LITERATURES OF THE ARABS AND PERSIANS

After the rise of the Abbasid Dynasty in 750, a conscious effort of cultural restoration arose throughout Islam. Scholars reclaimed the ancient odes of Arabia and the epic *Shahnama* from the *Book of Kings* of ancient Iran (Persia). The Arabian odes, greatly loved in the century before Islamic rule, were edited during the early Muslim period, even though Muhammad himself had referred to one of their authors, the notorious poet and outlaw chieftain Imru' al-Qays (d. 540), as "the leader of the poets into hellfire." Imru' al-Qays's *Mu'allaqah* helped establish the pattern for other Arabic qasidah, or odes. Its themes of life in the desert, the seductive powers of women, and the joys of the hunt as well as its melancholy reflections on the past came to permeate the work of the poet's contemporaries and that of succeeding generations of poets. The Persian *Book of Kings* was composed with the active participation of Persian loyalists for several centuries after the Abbasid occupation of Baghdad. Finished in the early eleventh century by the Persian compiler Abu al-Qasem Ferdowsi after decades of work accumulating stories, poems, and oral legends, it won the patronage of the Abbasids, still the cultural arbiters of the day.

FORMS OF EXPRESSION OF ISLAMIC CULTURE

Although Baghdad lost its political autonomy in the middle of the tenth century and the northern cities of Andalusia fell under attack from Spanish Christians late in the eleventh century, Islamic culture persisted in both locations. In Cordova and other centers of Andalusian culture, humanistic writing known as *ADAB* — polite literature on a variety of subjects highlighting the sensibilities and interests of the writer — flourished. Love songs were performed in the brilliant courts, musicology was studied across cultures, and Jewish and vernacular Spanish elements flavored the Arabic poetry of the period. Prominent among the eleventh-century writers from Cordova is Ibn Hazm (994–1064), a philosopher, essayist, and poet. Others representing the richness and diversity of Andalusian poetry include Ibn Faraj (d. 976), Ibn Zaydun (1004–1070), Wallada (d. 1077), Ibn al-Labbana (d. 1113), and Ibn Quzman (ca. 1080–1160). At least one Jewish writer, the poet and philosopher Judah ha-Levi (c. 1070–1141), was deemed equal in stature to the era's Arab writers. Unlike the prim and scholarly Ibn Hazm, many of the Arab poets led stormy and scandalous lives at court. Their writings still retain their shock value today.

THE INTELLECTUAL ACCOMPLISHMENT OF BAGHDAD AND CORDOVA

The Arab love of learning created the conditions for important breakthroughs. All the fields of study covered in the Qur'an — astronomy, mathematics, philosophy, medicine, law, art, and literature — received support in the new capitals of Baghdad and Cordova, resplendent centers of culture an4d education. The Islamic philosophers Ibn Sina *(Avicenna)* (980–1037) and Ibn Rushd *(Averroes)* (1126–1198) and the Jewish philosopher Moses Maimonides (1135–1204) all sought to reconcile religion and philosophy, largely by reinvestigating the writings of the ancient Greek philosophers Plato and Aristotle. In fact, it was this interest on the part of philosophers and scientists that was largely responsible for the translation of ancient Greek writings into Arabic, from which they were later translated into Latin. European philosopher St. Thomas Aquinas (1225–1274), known for reconciling Greek and Christian philosophies, depended in part on the translations and commentaries of twelfth-century Arabic philosophers.

CRUSADERS AND TRAVELERS

Crusade and travel literature also figured heavily in the writings of the Arabs of this period. Muslim historians of the Crusades, such as Imad al-Din (1125–1201), Baha ad-Din (1145–1234) and Ibn al-Athir (1160–1233), wrote both general histories and biographies of such figures as Saladin, the Turkish sultan and leader of the Third Crusade (1137–93). At about the same time, the Syrian gentleman Usamah Ibn Munqidh (1095–1190) wrote his reminiscences, including a sophisticated and amusing account of his life with the Franks during the period of Christian occupation. This period's travel literature, reflecting the contradictions and dangers of the times, is equally compelling. Ibn Jubayr (c. 1145–c. 1217) undertook an arduous pilgrimage to Mecca in 1183, visiting Cairo, Medina, Baghdad, and Nineveh along the way; on the return journey he made an unscheduled stop in Sicily, when he was shipwrecked. The world traveler Ibn Battuta (1304–1377) surpasses even the elegance of Ibn Jubayr with his particularly moving descriptions of Jerusalem, Mecca, and Constantinople.

SUFISM OF THE TWELFTH AND THIRTEENTH CENTURIES

Sufism, the mystical branch of Islamic belief, came to prominence in the ninth century. Its roots lie in the Qur'an, especially in Muhammad's visions of the angel Gabriel and his ascension through the heavens in a mystical dream. According to Sufi belief, the soul may enjoy direct union with God through mystical practices. In the early stages of Sufism, Islamic authorities sometimes viewed its practitioners as heretics. These suspicions were enhanced by the tendency of Shi'ites — political outcasts at the time — to find sanctuary in Sufi circles. Sufi spiritual leader Husayn ibn Mansur al-Hallaj (b. 857) was executed in Baghdad in 922 for both his political intrigues and his spiritual beliefs. Specifically, he was condemned for announcing "I am the Truth" and thus declaring his unity with the godhead. Later, the philosopher Muhyi al-Din ibn Arabi (1165–1240) wrote extensively on Sufi doctrine. In his masterwork, *The Meccan Revelations,* he proclaimed "unity of being," the idea that all that exists is God, who has created human beings the better to know himself. Ibn Arabi's second major doctrine, the Perfect Human Being, counsels the imitation of God in order to approximate the image of the divine.

Sufism produced great literature, perhaps owing to its struggle to express the ineffable in the written word and thus locate divinity in the material world. The poet Farid ud-Din Attar (c. 1145–c. 1221) wrote the mystical yet entertaining *The Conference of the Birds,* a long poem of religious instruction. A native of Persia, Attar faced many challenges in his lifetime, including accusations of heresy and the threat of Mongol invasion. In *The Conference of the Birds,* the point of the story rests on a pun. A hoopoe (similar to a hornbill) calls the birds together to go on a pilgrimage to seek their god, the Simorgh. When they reach their destination, thirty birds are left. In Persian "thirty birds" is *si morgh,* also the name of their god. At the end of their journey they find their god is no longer distinguishable from them; they have become one with the divine.

The poetry of Jalaloddin Rumi (1207–1283) expresses Sufism in terms of spiritual practice. Rumi's poetry combines advice to the Sufi initiate with insight into the nature of Sufi experience. In "A Basket of Fresh Bread," Rumi acknowledges the importance of having a spiritual teacher, but he also places responsibility for attaining closeness with God on the individual. He summarizes his irritation with a spiritual initiate in the lines: "There is a basket of fresh bread on your head, / and yet you go door to door asking for crusts." Rumi's poetry is full of surprising images conducive to mystical insight, what he called "rough metaphors of what happens to the lover." Often his sayings are paradoxical. In "The Gift of Water," the jugs of water from the Tigris River become "perfect" when they break and the pieces of glass and the water are dispersed.

LITERATURE AS ENTERTAINMENT: *THE THOUSAND AND ONE NIGHTS*

The stories contained in *The Thousand and One Nights,* or *The Arabian Nights,* are drawn from many periods and parts of the world. The first known written collection of the tales, *A Thousand Legends,* is dated at 850; their supposed setting is the court of Harun al-Rashid (766–809), the caliph of Baghdad at the height of the Abbasid dynasty. Notwithstanding this acknowledgment of the golden age of Islamic culture, *The Thousand and One Nights* is indifferent to the canonical tastes of Arabic and Persian literature. Full of mixed literary forms, nonstandard language, irreverent parodies of the court, and risqué subject matter, *The Thousand and One Nights* is still regarded in some Islamic quarters as inappropriate reading.

Taken together, the stories in *The Thousand and One Nights* picture the court of Harun al-Rashid in all its splendor, an abundance that is also decadence. The relationship of the beautiful and clever Shahrazad to the despotic but gullible sultan Shahrayar is, after all, that of a slave to her master. The circular nature of the storytelling, with the end of one tale leading to the beginning of the next, affirms the triumph of Shahrazad's endless work of creation. Caught in the spell of her own art, she literally talks circles around the caliph. Finally, he is instructed, indeed overwhelmed, by the goodness as well as the resourcefulness of the young woman.

TIME AND PLACE

Arabia and Persia:
Baghdad in the Reign of Harun al-Rashid (786–809)

In 750, more than a hundred years after the death of the prophet Muhammad, the Abbasid dynasty rose to power in the Muslim world. The ruling Arabs of the young dynasty had formed an uneasy alliance with Shi'ite Muslims on one hand and non-Arabic peoples on the other to bring down the Umayyads, the first Muslim dynasty. The center of the Muslim world shifted from Damascus, Syria, with its ancient Roman associations, to the new city of Baghdad, built near the ruins of the old Persian capital of Ctesiphon. Baghdad soon surpassed even Damascus as a center of culture and intellectual ferment. Scholars from much of the known world — including Persia, India, and Egypt — came together to enrich one another's understanding. The urban lifestyle of Baghdad, at once rich and eclectic, would influence the development of other cities throughout the Islamic world, including Cairo in Egypt and Toledo in Andalusia (Spain).

Baghdad's architecture reflected its great wealth, its role as the capital of the Islamic world, and its ambition. The central palace in Baghdad, seldom seen by outsiders to the royal court, took on a mysterious, romantic aura in the minds of the citizens. Stupendous mosques, with precious metals and rich mosaics, were built to house the faithful. Minaret towers, tall, graceful, and flowing, were positioned inside the mosque compounds to call Muslims to prayer five times a day.

Baghdad, which began to decline in the tenth century, still played its role as the capital for several hundred years while the world of Islam gradually took on a regional character. Islamic trade routes linked the major cities of central and southwest Asia, North Africa, and the African coast on the Indian Ocean until the thirteenth century. Baghdad finally fell to the invasion of the Mongols in 1258. Its architectural heritage, however, has lasted into modern times; recently, aerial bombing has taken its toll.

Al-Kazimayn Mosque, eighth to thirteenth century.
A contemporary view of the Abbasid-era Al-Kazimayn Mosque in Baghdad, Iraq. (The Art Archive / Dagli Orti)

www   For more information about the culture and context of Arabia and Persia in the Middle Period, see *World Literature Online* at bedfordstmartins.com/worldlit.

❧ IMRU' AL-QAYS
D. 540

moo-ah-lah-KAH;
im-ROO ahl-KISE

KAH-buh

The *Mu'allaqah* of **Imru' al-Qays** derives its name from the work's inclusion in a group of seven poems called the *mu'allaqat,* or "suspended odes." In the sixth century this group of poems was named the masterwork of Arabic poetry. In recognition of their worth, the poems were embroidered on rare Egyptian cloth in gold letters and suspended inside the shrine of the **Kaaba** in Mecca, the holiest site in Islam. At least this is the story told by later scholars of the Islamic period, who regarded these odes as the foundation of Arabic poetry. The ode by Imru' al-Qays, regarded as the finest of them all, has influenced writing in Arabic ever since. Its grand theme of life in the desert, its obsession with the seductive power of women, its epic comparison of lovemaking with the joys of the hunt, its tone of melancholy, and its reflection on the events of the past all mark it as one of the great odes of world literature, comparable to the eighth-century odes of Kakinomoto Hitomaro in the Japanese anthology *Man'yoshu;* the thirteenth-century mystical odes of the Persian poet **Rumi**; and the longer poems and odes of the nineteenth-century English Romantic poets William Wordsworth and John Keats.

mahn-YOH-shoo
roo-MEE

The Poet and His Age. Imru' al-Qays was the notoriously prodigal son of the Bedouin chief **Hujr**,[1] ruler of **Kindah** and sworn enemy of the **Banu Asad** tribe that declined to pay him tribute. The story of Imru' al-Qays and his wanderings is told repeatedly in the AKHBAR, or historical accounts of the time. While still a young man, he was expelled from his father's lands due to his reckless behavior, including his seduction of his cousin **'Unayzah**. He was later denied his rightful inheritance following his father's murder and the overthrow of the family dynasty. Now an outlaw popularly known as "the vagabond king," he sought revenge against his father's murderers but was never satisfied with his efforts.[2] He joined the court of the Byzantine emperor Justinian in 530 and eventually was commissioned to lead an army against their common Persian enemy. During his sojourn of ten years at the court, however, he had undertaken a scandalous love affair with the emperor's daughter. Fearing Justinian's wrath after the affair's disclosure, Imru' al-Qays departed for Arabia with his commission. According to legend he died as the result of donning a poisoned robe that was Justinian's parting gift in 540, his mission unfulfilled.

HOO-jur; KIN-dah
bah-NOO ah-SAHD
AHK-bar

oo-NIGH-zuh

www For links to more information about Imru' al-Qays and a quiz on the *Mu'allaqah,* see *World Literature Online* at bedfordstmartins .com/worldlit.

---

[1] **Hujr:** Hujr Ibn al-Harith, the father of Imru' al-Qays, took over stewardship of the Banu Asad tribe when he became king of Kindah, an area in south central Arabia in the fifth and sixth centuries. When the Banu Asad refused to pay Hujr tribute, he attacked them. He was killed by members of the tribe, either on the battlefield or after being taken prisoner.

[2] **never satisfied with his efforts:** Imru' al-Qays is alleged to have sworn over his father's body, "Wine and women are forbidden to me until I have killed a hundred of the Banu Asad!" His followers began to desert him as he continued to avenge himself against the Banu Asad and related tribes.

The Poet's Vocation and His Theme. Imru' al-Qays managed to compile a large body of poetry despite his erratic and violent life. Later poets would follow in his path, portraying the wild life of the desert wanderer while relying on princely patronage—though they were more cautious with their lives and honor than Imru' al-Qays had been. Poems set in the desert were already common in the oral poetry of Bedouin nomads. In certain ways the romance conjured by this setting is comparable to that of the "Wild West" in the United States or the **gaucho** tales of the Argentine **pampas**. The works document the poet's affinity with his horse or camel and his path of solitude and danger through an arid wasteland, broken up by occasional fighting or encounters with women. Added to this are the poet's reflections on the joys and sorrows of the past, broadly hinting of tragic themes. In the case of Imru' al-Qays's poetry, the poet is also a king's son[3] looking for those who killed his father and robbed him of his rightful possessions.

GOW-choh
PAHM-pus

The Form of the _Qasidah._ The early QASIDAH, or ode, was a loosely constructed, orally recited poem of several dozen to sixty or so rhymed couplets expressing reflection and sentiment; by the sixth century, more definite rules of composition had come into favor. The odes usually told of life in the desert and some matters of romance in a tone of either lamentation or self-glorification. Because of the length of these odes, several topics were often covered in a single work. The poems' structure consisted of an opening NASIB, or nostalgic prelude, involving memories of a place or loved one; a RAHIL, or "disengagement," telling of a solitary journey on horseback or camelback, or metaphorically, of the separation of the poet from the source of his sorrowful memory; and, finally, the core of the poem, a FAKHR, celebrating the significance of the poet's life or a community's renewal, an affirmation in which nature might participate by offering dramatic storms or which a tribal society might help to achieve through victories in battle.

kuh-SEE-duh

nah-SEEB
ruh-HEEL

FAH-keer

Divisions of the _Mu'allaqah._ In the opening _nasib_ of the _Mu'allaqah,_ the poet, stopped at the ruins of an encampment, remembers his separation from his loved one there many years before. As he recalls what happened, his two friends warn him against excessive grief, but he tells them his cure lies in his tears, for this was the place where his beloved **Fatimah** parted from him with her tribe (verses 4–6).

    In the _rahil,_ at the encouragement of his companions, the poet recalls his past love exploits, including the time he sacrificed his camel to feed some adoring maidens ("the virgins") as well as the time he entered the **howdah** or canopied carrier of his cousin 'Unayzah to enjoy her favors. He also remembers a woman who nursed her child to keep it satisfied during their lovemaking (17). Then his thoughts return to the lady Fatimah, whom he accuses of cruelty. To be with her, he had to invade her

FAT-ih-muh

HOW-duh

---

[3] **a king's son:** Translator Suzanne Pinckney Stetkevych argues that the _Mu'allaqah_ is the threefold story of a prodigal son, his royal father's murder, and the son's quest for revenge.

In the words of the Prophet Muham-mad, Imru' al-Qays was "the leader of the poets into hell-fire."

— SUZANNE PINCKNEY STETKEVYCH, translator, 1993

hostile family encampment and carry her across the desert. He praises her beauty for many lines, finally confiding that his heart refuses solace for its love for her (42). The poet then attempts to separate himself from the joys and sorrows of his life. He laments his life in the wilds, describing his journeys far from home "where the wolf howled." Indeed, like the wolf he cannot hold onto possessions (verses 7–52).

In the concluding section, the *fakhr,* the mood changes. The poet remembers going out in the mornings on his stallion, an animal full of life and power that he admires. He describes a hunt in which his horse caught up with the lead animals of a herd of oryx and the feast that followed. Interrupted in this recital by a flash of lightning, he remembers a past storm and its initially catastrophic, then regenerative flooding of the countryside. Truly, he thinks, death and destruction lead to revival (verses 53–82).

Interpretations.   While the broad outlines of the *Mu'allaqah* are apparent, its verbal complexity and difficult allusions have led scholars to interpret it in several ways. It is clear enough that Imru' al-Qays draws on his own life story for this portrait of a reckless young man who is a seducer of women. The story of the poet's attempted seduction of the virgins and of the fulfillment of his desires with a nursing mother were undoubtedly (and successfully) designed to shock his audience. There is even a certain wickedness in the description of the oryx cows as "virgins" later in the poem. Beyond that, the speaker stubbornly refuses to give up his romantic obsession. Even the celebrated description of the rejuvenation of nature at the end of the work is not a formula for a personal change of heart. The poet remains suspended sorrowfully between the past and present; his relationship to his tribesmen is one of old affection rather than new purpose. While the symbolic action of the poem may move his audience dramatically, the situation of the speaker with respect to his life does not change.

Although the [*Mu'allaqah*] is one of the best known and most admired in the Arabic language, not everyone praised it. According to the literary theorist al-Baquillani, writing in the tenth century, this poem was full of ludicrous implausi-bilities and detest-able features "which frighten the ear, terrify the heart, and put a strain on the tongue."

— ROBERT IRWIN, scholar, 1999

■ CONNECTIONS

The Epic of Gilgamesh (Book 1). In Imru' al-Qays's *Mu'allaqah,* the descriptions of the horse, the hunt scene, and the beauty of the women whom the speaker has loved are reminiscent of the Sumerian *Epic of Gilgamesh.* In what way can a *qasidah,* or ode, recited in the first person and reflecting back on the speaker's life, recall a heroic epic of a godly king from an earlier time? Does *Mu'allaqah* contain features of thought or language reminiscent of epic poetry?

Song of Solomon (Book 1). The sensual descriptions of love in *Mu'allaqah* resemble those in the Hebrew Song of Solomon. The supposed purpose of the Song of Solomon is to symbolize the soul's search for the love of God. In Imru' al-Qays's *qasidah,* is the speaker on a quest? If so, beyond maidens and warfare, what is he seeking? Does he find it? How can you tell?

William Wordsworth, "Lines Composed a Few Miles above Tintern Abbey" and *Ode: Intimations of Immortality* (Book 5); John Keats, "Ode to a Nightingale" and "Ode on a Grecian Urn" (Book 5). Wordsworth's reflective poem recalling a visit to a ruined abbey is similar in tone to the *Mu'allaqah.* Wordsworth and Keats are famous for their odes that share some of the passionate uses of memory found in Imru' al-Qays's work. In what ways are the Arabian and the English poetry different from one another?

■ FURTHER RESEARCH

Translations and Commentaries

Arberry, A. J. *The Seven Odes: The First Chapter in Arabic Literature*. 1957.

Stetkevych, Suzanne Pinckney. *The Mute Immortals Speak: Pre-Islamic Poetry and the Poetics of Ritual*. 1993.

Literary Anthologies and Criticism

Hamori, Andras. *On the Art of Medieval Arabic Literature*. 1974.

Irwin, Robert. *Night and Horses and the Desert: An Anthology of Classical Arabic Literature*. 2000.

Sells, Michael. *Desert Tracings: Six Classic Arabian Odes*. 1989.

Stetkevych, Jaroslav. *Muhammad and the Golden Bow*. 1996.

Turner, Victor. *The Ritual Process: Structure and Anti-Structure*. 1977.

Zwettler, Michael. *The Oral Tradition of Classical Arabic Poetry*. 1972.

■ PRONUNCIATION

akhbar: AHK-bar

Banu Asad: bah-NOO ah-SAHD

Banu 'Udhra: bah-NOO OOTH-ruh

colocynth: KOH-luh-sinth

fakhr: FAH-keer, FAH-kur

Fatimah: FAT-ih-muh

gaucho: GOW-choh

howdah: HOW-duh

Hujr Ibn al-Harith: HOO-jur IB-un ahl-HAH-rith

Imru' al Qays: im-ROO ahl-KISE

Kaaba: KAH-buh, KAH-uh-buh

Kindah: KIN-dah

Man'yoshu: mahn-YOH-shoo

Mu'allaqah, mu'allaqat: moo-ah-lah-KAH, -KAHT

nasib: nah-SEEB

pampas: PAHM-pus

qasidah: kuh-SEE-duh

rahil: ruh-HEEL

Rumi: roo-MEE

'Unayzah: oo-NIGH-zuh

The Mu'allaqah of Imru' al-Qays

Translated by Suzanne Pinckney Stetkevych

1. Halt, two friends, and we will weep
          for the memory of one beloved
    And an abode at Siqṭ al-Liwā
          between al-Dakhūl, then Hawmal,
2. Then Tūḍiḥ, then al-Miqrāt,[1] whose trace
          was not effaced
    By the two winds weaving over it
          from south and north.
3. You see the droppings
          of white antelope
    Scattered on its outer grounds and lowlands
          like peppercorns,
4. As if I, on the morning
          that they loaded up their beasts,[2]
    Before the tribe's acacia trees,
          were splitting colocynth.[3]
5. My companions, halting there
          their mounts for me,

The Mu'allaqah of Imru' al-Qays. The Arabic *qasidahs* of the sixth century reflect a millennium of oral tradition during which the poetry adopted conventions of theme, structure, and rhyme. As with most Arabic literature, the appeal of the *Mu'allaqah* depends on its being spoken or performed in the original language, which contains many allusive references concerning places, events, and customs known to Imru' al-Qays. Despite the loss of these elements in English translation, we sense the writer's passion preserved in the ancient form of his *Mu'allaqah*.

Imru' al-Qays's *Mu'allaqah* is praised by Arabic scholars for its highly artistic rendering of the *qasidah* form. The *nasib* (verses 1–6) introduces the poet and his companions, who have stopped at the ruins of an old encampment where he recalls the story of how he lost his beloved. The *rahil,* or journey portion (verses 7–52) tells of the many amorous episodes and lonely wanderings that have brought the poet joy and sorrow in his life but have not offered him any peace. In the beginning of the *fakhr,* the final section, the poet remembers the heroic activities in which he has engaged on his mighty horse, culminating in a great hunt (verses 53–70). At this point the poet is interrupted by a

---

[1] **al-Dakhūl . . . al-Miqrāt:** Not all place names have been identified. The names al-Dakhūl and Hawmal may involve puns associated with sexual potency, while Tūḍiḥ and al-Miqrāt refer to clarity and a pool where water gathers, respectively.

[2] **on the morning . . . beasts:** The poet remembers the day that his beloved Fāṭimah and her tribesmen, the Banu 'Udhra, departed from this spot.

[3] **colocynth:** A bitter, hard fruit sometimes compared in taste to an orange.

Say, Do not perish out of grief,
 control yourself!

6. Surely my cure is tears
  poured forth;
 Then, at a worn-out trace is there
  a place for weeping?

7. [Console yourself] As was your wont before her
  with Umm al-Ḥuwayrith
 And her neighbor at Mount Ma'sal,
  Umm al-Rabāb![4]

8. When they arose there wafted from them
  musk as redolent
 As the east breeze when it bears
  the scent of clove.

9. Then my eyes, out of ardent love, sent down
  a flood of tears upon my neck
 Till my sword belt was soaked
  in tears.

10. Did you not have many a fine day
  from them?
 And best of all the day
  at Dārat Juljul?[5]

11. And the day when, for the virgins,
  I hocked my mount,[6]

---

flash of lightning and recalls a storm that once destroyed an encampment and flooded a valley but finally restored life to the desert (lines 71–82). In this way the poet moves from loss to rejuvenation, from bittersweet memories to the rebirth of nature, fulfilled in brilliant imagery. Full of dramatic scenes and wild deeds, this ode confidently reflects the life of its author and sets a high standard for poets to follow him.

 A handful of English poets have attempted to translate this famous pre-Islamic ode. The formal demands of the *qasidah* require hemstitch couplets (two long lines, each divided in half) rhymed at the end of each line with the same rhyme continued throughout the poem. While it is easy to rhyme in this fashion in Arabic, it is difficult in English. Translators therefore generally attempt to reproduce the running rhythm of the long-line couplets without the rhymes. The two best translations of Imru' al-Qays's *Mu'allaqah* are those of A. J. Arberry (1957) and Suzanne Pinckney Stetkevych (1993). We have chosen the latter version partly because it faithfully repeats the hemstitch or broken-line character of each of the couplets. Footnotes to the text follow the notes of Stetkevych where possible.

---

[4] **Umm al-Ḥuwayrith . . . Umm al-Rabāb:** Two women the poet has loved in the past. *Umm* means "mother."

[5] **the day / at Dārat Juljul?:** The poet's companions remind him of a notorious picnic at which he slaughtered his prize camel and gave out tidbits of the meat to impress a group of maidens.

[6] **hocked my mount:** Cut the hind legs of his camel to incapacitate him before slaughtering him.

> —What an amazing sight!—they made off
>   with her saddle and its gear!

12. Then through the day the virgins
        tossed her meat,
     And her fat like twisted fringes
        of white Damascus silk.

13. And the day I entered the howdah,
        'Unayzah's howdah,[7]
     Then she said, Woe to you! You'll make me
        go on foot.

14. She kept saying, when the high-sided saddle
        listed with our weight,
     You have hocked my camel, O Imru' al-Qays,
        So get down!

15. Keep going, I said to her,
        slacken his reins,
     But don't drive me away from your
        twice-to-be-tasted fruit!

16. Then many a woman like you, pregnant and nursing,
        have I visited by night,
     And distracted from her amuleted
        one-year-old.

17. When he cried from behind her, she turned
        her upper half toward him,
     But the half that was beneath me
        did not budge.

18. And one day on a sand dune's back
        she rebuffed me,[8]
     And swore an oath never
        to be broken.

19. O Fātimah, don't try me
        with your teasing,
     [Or] if you have resolved to cut me off,
        then do it gently.

20. Are you deluded about me because
        your love is my slayer
     And whatever you command my heart
        it does?

21. If something of my character
        has hurt you,

---

[7] **'Unayzah's howdah:** 'Unayzah is the poet's cousin; his affair with her produced a scandal. A *howdah* is the covered platform on top of a camel.

[8] **one day . . . she rebuffed me:** Here the poet's attention returns to Fātimah, the object of his grieving.

Then pull my clothes away from yours,
> they will slip off.

22. Your eyes do not shed tears
> but to pierce
with your two shafts the pieces of
> my slaughtered heart.

23. Many an "egg" of the curtained quarters,[9]
> whose tent none dares to seek,
I took my pleasure with her,
> unhurried.

24. I stole past guards
> to get to her, past clansmen
Eager, could they conceal it,
> to slay me.

25. When the Pleiades spread out[10]
> across the sky
Like a girdle's spread-out pleats,
> alternating gold and gems,

26. I came when she, before the tent curtain,
> had shed her clothes for sleep,
And was clad in nothing but
> an untied shift.

27. She said, God's oath! There's no way
> to dissuade you,
And I don't see the veil lift
> from your error.

28. I led her forth from her tent,
> walking as she trailed
Over our tracks the train
> of her gown of figured silk.

29. Then, when we had crossed
> the clan's enclosure
And made our way to a sandy hollow
> surrounded by long-winding dunes,

30. I drew her temples toward me, and she
> leaned over me
With hollow waist, but plump the place
> that anklets ring.

31. Slender-waisted, white,
> not flabby,

---

[9] an "egg" . . . quarters: Recalls the ostrich egg; refers to the maiden's pale complexion.
[10] when the Pleiades spread out: See verses 46–48.

Her collarbone shone like
    a polished mirror.

32. Now hiding, now baring a cheek
    long and wide,
She guards herself with the glance
    of a wild doe at Wajrah with fawn,

33. And a neck like the neck
    of the white antelope,
Not overly long when she raises it,
    or lacking ornament.

34. A head of hair, jet-black,
    adorns her back,
Luxuriant as a bunch of dates
    on a cluster-laden palm.

35. Some of its locks are
    secured on top,
While others stray between the plaited
    and the loose.

36. A waist delicate, like
    a twisted bowstring, trim,
A lower leg like the papyrus reed,
    well-watered, tender.

37. In the forenoon crumbs of musk
    still deck her bed,
And she, late morning sleeper, still is clad
    in sleeping gown, ungirded.

38. She grasps with fingers, soft, uncalloused,
    as if they were
The worms of Zaby[11] or the supple tooth sticks
    of the *ishil* tree.[12]

39. When night falls she lights up the dark
    as if she were
A lamp in the night cell
    of an anchorite.[13]

40. At one like her the staid man
    gazes with ardor
When she stands in her full stature between
    woman's gown and maiden's shift,

41. Like the first inviolate bloom,
    white mixed with yellow,

---

[11] worms of Zaby: Sand worms.

[12] tooth sticks / of the *ishil* tree: Toothpicks were regarded as a mark of refinement. The *ishil* tree is related to the tamarisk.

[13] A lamp . . . of an anchorite: See "the sudden flare of a monk's lamp," verse 72.

Nurtured on water limpid and unmuddied
    by alighting traveler.

42. [Grown] men find consolation from
    the follies of their youth,
But my heart refuses solace for
    its love for you.

43. How many an enemy,
    quarreling over you,
Not neglectful of advice or of rebuke,
    did I repel?

44. Many a night like the billowing sea
    let down its veils over me
With all kinds of cares
    to test me.

45. Then I said to it when
    it stretched out its spine,
Followed with its hindquarters,
    and heaved its ponderous breast,

46. Alas, long night, will you not dispel,
    revealing dawn,
Though the dawn of day will be
    no better for me.

47. Then, oh what a night you are!
    as if its stars
Were all bound by tight-twisted ropes
    to Mount Yadhbul,[14]

48. As if the Pleiades were
    in midcourse suspended
By flaxen cords
    from obdurate rock.

49. And many a waterskin of the clans
    have I borne its leathern strap
Upon my shoulder, submissive
    and much traveled.

50. And many a riverbed, a bare waste like
    the belly of an ass, I crossed,
Where the wolf howled like an outcast profligate
    with many mouths to feed.

51. So when he howled I said to him,
    Our lot is meager sustenance
If you have not gained wealth,
    [for I have none].

---

[14] **Mount Yadhbul:** The "firmly rooted mountain," one of the foundations of the earth.

52. Each of us when he acquires a thing,
        it soon escapes him,
    Whoever tills your tilth and mine,
        it will leave lean.

53. I would ride forth early,[15]
        the birds still in their nests,
    On a steed sleek and swift,
        a shackle for wild game, huge.

54. Now wheeling, now charging, advancing, retreating,
        all at once,
    Like a mighty boulder the torrent has washed
        down from the heights.

55. A dark bay from whose back
        the saddle pad slips,
    Like raindrops
        from hard rock,

56. Despite leanness, spirited
        as if his bursting gallop,
    When he seethes with heat
        were a cauldron's boil,

57. Pouring forth his gallop
        when, despite fatigue, the coursers
    On the hard and trampled plain
        stir up the dust.

58. The slender youth he makes slip
        from his back,
    The robes of the rugged, bulky rider
        he sends flying out behind,

59. Streaming like a boy's button-on-a-string,
        when he has tightly twisted it
    By his hands' successive circling
        the connecting string.

60. He has the flanks of a gazelle fawn,
        the ostrich's two legs,
    The wolf's lope,
        the fox cub's canter.

61. Huge-ribbed, when you look from behind,
        a full tail blocks the gap between his legs,
    Reaching almost to the ground,
        not crooked.

62. As if when he heads off there were mounted
        on his rump a stone

---

[15] **I would ride forth early:** Here the poet recites the stories of his horse rather than the more traditional subject of camels.

A bride pounds perfumes with or on which
    colocynth is crushed,

63. As if the blood of the herd's front-runners
    upon his throat
    Were henna juice upon an old man's
    combed and hoary head.

64. Then there appeared before us an oryx herd
    as if its cows were virgins[16]
    Circling round a sacred stone
    in long-trained gowns.

65. They turned about like alternated onyx beads
    upon the neck
    Of a child nobly uncled in the clan
    from dam and sire.

66. Then he let us catch
    the herd's lead runners
    And outstripped those that lagged
    in an unbroken cluster.

67. One after the other, he hit
    a bull and cow,
    And yet was not awash
    with sweat.

68. Then the meat cooks kept on cooking
    both meat laid upon the rocks
    To roast well-done, and meat
    quick boiled in cauldrons.

69. And our glance, in the evening,
    almost failed before him,
    To whatever spot the eye was raised,
    dazzled, it dropped.

70. All night he remained, his saddle and bridle
    upon him,
    All night he stood beneath my eye, not
    loosed to graze.

71. O friend, do you see the lightning?
    There is its flash—
    Like two hands shining in a high-crowned
    cumulus!

72. Its flash illumining the sky, or like
    the sudden flare of a monk's lamp,
    When, tilting it, he soaks with oil
    the tightly twisted wick.

---

[16] **oryx herd . . . virgins:** The white Arabian antelope with elegant cylindrical horns. The cows were especially prized for their tender meat.

73. Between Dārij and al-ʿUdhayb I sat with my companions
    to watch the storm,
    How distant was the object
    of my gaze!

74. Over Mount Qaṭan, as I read the signs,
    the right flank of its downpour falls,
    Over Mount al-Sitār,[17] then Mount Yadhbul,
    falls the left.

75. Then in the forenoon it was pouring
    its water down around Kutayfah,
    Overturning the lofty *kanahbal* trees
    upon their beards.

76. It passed its fringes over
    Mount Qanān,
    And drove the white-footed mountain goats
    down every path.

77. In Taymāʾ[18] it did not leave
    a single palm trunk standing,
    Or a single castle but
    those built of stone.

78. As if Mount Thabīr in the foremost
    of its rains
    Were a tribal chieftain wrapped
    in a striped cloak,

79. As if the peaks of Mount Mujaymir's crest
    at morning
    Ringed with the torrent's dross
    were the whorl of a spindle,

80. It deposited its load on
    the low-lying desert
    Like a Yemeni alighting with
    his [fabric]-laden bags,

81. As if, early in the morning,
    the songbirds of the valley
    Had drunk a morning draught
    of fine spiced wine,

82. As if the wild beasts drowned at evening
    in its remotest stretches
    Were wild onions'
    plucked-out bulbs.

---

[17] Mount al-Sitār: *Al-Sitār* means "veil."

[18] Taymāʾ: A location west of the Sinai Peninsula surrounded by low mountains.

⌘ ABU AL-QASEM FERDOWSI
932–1025

The Persian *Book of Kings (Shahnama)* by **Abu al-Qasem Ferdowsi** (Firdausi) is one of the great national epics of world literature. Certainly its scope is unsurpassed. It begins with the creation of the universe, continues through the dynasties of mythological Iranian kings, takes up the legendary account of the Iranian wars against the Turks,[1] proceeds to the deeds of Alexander the Great,[2] and concludes with a heavily fictionalized account of the Parthian and **Sasanian** dynasties (247 B.C.E.–651 C.E.) up to the fall of the Iranians to the Muslims in 651. Three hundred years would pass after this defeat before the *Shahnama* was composed in its final written form, a long heroic poem under Ferdowsi's authorship. Including myth, legend, folk tradition, and written history, and involving epic battle scenes as well as interludes of courtly romance, the *Shahnama* can be compared to other great national epics, including the Babylonian *Epic of Gilgamesh*,[3] the Greek *Iliad*,[4] the English *Beowulf*,[5] and the French *Song of Roland*.[6] Of all the episodes in the 45,000-line *Shahnama*, the most famous is the tragic killing of the young knight Sohrab by his father, the legendary warrior-hero Rostam.

shah-nah-MAH;
ah-BOO ahl-KAH-sim
feer-DOW-see

sas-AY-nee-un

GIL-guh-mesh; IL-ee-ud

The Writing of the Poem. The writing of the *Shahnama*, begun under Muslim court encouragement in the second half of the tenth century by **Daqiqi** of **Tus**,[7] was temporarily halted when Daqiqi was murdered by a servant around 970 with scarcely a thousand lines completed. The work

dah-KEE-kee; TOOS

---

[1] **Iranian wars against the Turks:** The Turks were the traditional enemies of Iran. Although the *Shahnama* situates the Turkish wars in antiquity, the period that would have framed the Iranian attitude about the Turks was the sixth and seventh centuries C.E., before the end of the Sasanian dynasty in 651.

[2] **Alexander the Great:** Macedonian ruler born in 356 B.C.E. who ruled from 336 to 323 B.C.E. His conquest of the Persian (Iranian) empire has been called the greatest military campaign in the history of the ancient world. The largely legendary source for the deeds of Alexander is the Greek *Alexander Romance* (second century C.E.); in *Shahnama*, Ferdowsi "domesticates" Alexander by making him into an Iranian prince.

[3] **Epic of Gilgamesh:** A Sumerian epic of a king of Uruk who may have lived about 2700 B.C.E.; the text is preserved on tablets dating from the seventh century B.C.E. Gilgamesh, like Rostam, is a figure of mythic proportions.

[4] **Iliad:** Epic poem of the Trojan War from the Greek perspective, attributed to Homer, a blind poet from the eighth century B.C.E.

[5] **Beowulf:** Anglo-Saxon epic poem composed between the eighth and tenth centuries C.E. about a hero's struggle against two monsters besieging a friendly king's court and his own battle fifty years later with a marauding dragon.

[6] **Song of Roland:** Epic poem of the death of Roland, leader of the rear guard of Charlemagne's army, at Rencesvals in northern Spain in 778 C.E. The poem was composed around 1100, at the beginning of the European Crusades to the Holy Land, and is generally regarded as the national epic of the Franks.

[7] **Daqiqi of Tus:** A young man who had become a court poet of the Samanid dynasty (ended in 999). The portion of the *Shahnama* that he completed related to ancient religious doctrine.

Scene from the *Shahnama*, 1330–1340 C.E.
This scene from the Shahnama, *or Book of Kings (gouache on paper), shows the final episode in the saga of the great hero Rostam and his faithful horse, Rakhsh. (British Museum/All rights reserved.)*

mah-MOOD;
GUZ-nuh

then was taken up by Abu al-Qasem Ferdowsi,[8] a member of the Iranian *dehqan,* or landed gentry, also from the city of Tus. Working tirelessly for decades, Ferdowsi expanded the poem to about fifty thousand lines. Patronage proved hard to obtain as the work drew near its conclusion, probably due to changing political currents. The nationalistic values of *dehqan* society, the pre-Muslim religious material in the poem, and the use of archaic Iranian language and verse forms may have proved irritating to its formerly favorable patron, **Mahmud** of **Ghazna**. As a result, Ferdowsi was poorly rewarded and was even in political danger for a time. Nevertheless, the work was circulated soon after its completion and was paid the greatest of compliments by fellow poets: imitation and downright theft. Competitor epics were produced using its same archaic language, poetic forms, and plot elements as the *Shahnama.*

The epic material put into written verse by Ferdowsi included leg-

---

[8] **Abu al-Qasem Ferdowsi:** Ferdowsi was a well-educated, wealthy man who belonged to a group of devotees of Iranian history and culture. His patron, Mahmud of Ghazna, was a liberal Muslim ruler who favored the preservation of ancient stories.

endary tales of heroes that undoubtedly had been sung once as lays at court.[9] The actions of the heroes — fighting, feasting, and hunting — had been meant as entertainment for a courtly audience. Such heroes were supposed to be faithful to their king and brave in war but not reflective in the sense of having self-doubts that would make them vulnerable to failure. Similarly, the "tragedy" of **Sohrab** and **Rostam** does not come about through weakness in the hero but rather is determined by fate. This story constitutes but a small part of the *Shahnama;* its great popularity appears to come from its archetypal power[10] as a world story (it appears in other versions in the ancient literature of Germany, Ireland, and Russia) and its subsequent status in Iran as a folk legend shared by an entire culture.

SOH-rahb;
ROH-stahm

The Subject of Kingship.   The *Shahnama,* literally a "book of kings," is the story of the kings of Iran. The modern reader seeking an understanding of Ferdowsi and his task might do well to compare his epic with the history plays of the English dramatist William Shakespeare.[11] Linguistically, the Persian language Ferdowsi wrote in is to modern Persian what Shakespeare's English is to present-day English. Shakespeare's kings are given dramatic individuality through portrayals of their thoughts and behavior. Though Ferdowsi covers a greater span of history than does Shakespeare, starting as he does at the beginning of time, and though he does not depict each king's character so carefully or regularly as the English dramatist, he does differentiate between good deeds and bad, and by implication between good kings and bad. And some key figures of the *Shahnama,* especially the mythical-legendary Rostam, are drawn in great detail.

The larger-than-life Rostam, who assumes extraordinary prominence in the work, lives for many generations, reaffirming his role as savior of Iran in battle after battle. His virtues include his pride and ungovernable strength. Along with his awesome power comes a dangerous failure to reflect. In this way he is like other ancient heroes, including the Babylonian Gilgamesh and **Achilles**[12] of Homer's *Iliad.*

uh-KIL-eez

The Story of Rostam.   The story of Rostam comes from the **Sistan** Cycle, a collection of stories not originally associated with the tales of the

see-STAHN

---

[9] **The epic material . . . lays at court:** All the stories Ferdowsi collected had some basis in oral or written literature, and lays — tales set to musical accompaniment — were one of the popular means of their transmission.

[10] **its archetypal power:** An archetype may be defined as an image or a story that appears in many cultures and symbolizes a universal category of thought. The modern originator of this meaning of the term was the Swiss psychologist C. G. Jung (1875–1961).

[11] **William Shakespeare:** English playwright (1564–1616) and author of thirty-seven plays, of which ten make up a cycle of the histories of British kings. For centuries British schoolchildren derived much of their knowledge of the history of England directly or indirectly from Shakespeare's history plays.

[12] **Gilgamesh . . . Achilles:** With roots in ancient mythology and legend, these heroes made their mark through physical strength rather than wisdom. Gilgamesh was feared as a threat to the city he had built, and Achilles, motivated by wrath, not reason, nearly lost the Trojan War for the Greeks by his refusal to fight when he was most needed.

ZAHL

roo-dah-BAH

too-RAHN
kigh-yah-NYAHN
KIGH kah-OOS

tah-mee-NAH

ah-frah-see-YAHB

Iranian dynasty but later assimilated into the national epic. Rostam is the son of **Zal**, who himself was abandoned by his father, Sam, after being born with white hair, thought to be an augury of doom. Eventually, Zal and Sam are reconciled, and Zal falls in love with **Rudabé**, daughter of the king of Kabul.[13] When Rostam, their son, is born, he is already gigantic, requiring ten wet-nurses to feed him. While still a boy, he kills the king's white elephant after it has gone on a rampage. As Rostam grows up, relations between Iran and its neighbor **Turan** (Turkey) steadily worsen. The newly formed **Keyanian** dynasty fights the Turkish invaders. Rostam comes to the aid of the second Keyanian king, **Kay Kavus**, fighting his way through mountainous countryside in a series of battles against ferocious creatures to reach the embattled king. Along the way he marries and spends one night with the beautiful **Tahmina**, daughter of a local ruler, and she becomes pregnant with their future son, Sohrab.

At first Sohrab is raised unaware of his origins, and Tahmina hides the news of his birth from his father, fearing that Rostam will take Sohrab to live with him. When Sohrab is told who his father is, he decides to conquer the realm of Kay Kavus and deliver it to his father to rule. To accomplish this he forms an alliance with the Turkish shah **Afrasiyab**, while Kavus forms an alliance with Rostam. As a result, an army led by Sohrab meets an army led by Rostam in the field. To spare their armies, the two leaders agree to single combat. Neither son nor father knows the identity of his opponent, until in the third day of battle Rostam, temporarily pinning Sohrab to the ground but lacking the strength to hold him there, stabs him with his knife. The dying son asks his attacker's name, and the full tragedy is revealed.

The Nature of Historical Epic.   The epic poem *Shahnama* presents its own version of history. Emerging from creation, the Iranians name their first king and establish their first dynasty. The beginning of this work is mythological: hero-kings fight mythical beasts and supernatural beings to establish the realm, and the people can hope to prosper only after these forces have been subdued. In the second period, with supernatural beings still lurking in the darkness, the nature of the struggle changes. Folk heroes such as Rostam supplant the authority of hero-kings and survive for hundreds of years, leading the people to victories over tyrants and foreign enemies. Here the Iranian epic begins to assume a folkloric character, and Turan emerges as the great national enemy. Finally, after the story of Alexander the Great, a real king about whom many legends have been created and recorded, legend converges with fact. The tales of the Sasanian dynasty, leading up to the fall of Iran to Muslim invaders in the seventh century, establish the historic boundaries of the Iranian nation, enabling Ferdowsi to write his great work. Mythology, legendary hero tales, and historical narrative mark the stages of development of the *Shahnama* and, by extension, the consciousness of the Iranian people.

www   For links to more information about Abu al-Qasem Ferdowsi and a quiz on *The Tragedy of Sohrab and Rostam,* see *World Literature Online* at bedfordstmartins .com/worldlit.

---

[13] **daughter of the king of Kabul:** The women of Kabul, the present-day capital of Afghanistan, were celebrated for their beauty.

Begun at the behest of a liberal Muslim ruler, the *Shahnama* was permitted only because the time of the original Iranian kingdom had passed. Throughout the next millennium, Iran operated under Muslim authority. The enmity with Turkey remained, as did the quest for Iranian national glory, but the world that Iran was now a part of was too multifarious and complex for a single work of literature to define. Still, Ferdowsi's great epic helped carve out an Iranian identity for the ages.

■ **CONNECTIONS**

The Epic of Gilgamesh (Book 1). The hero of this ancient Babylonian story, famed for his strength, suffers a great loss with the sickness and death of his friend, Enkidu, and demonstrates nobility of character in his mourning. Compare Gilgamesh's grief with that of Rostam for his son. Will Rostam be much changed by his tragedy?

Homer, *The Iliad* (Book 1). *The Iliad* centers on "the wrath of Achilles," who deserts his fellow warriors only to return in time to ensure victory over Hector, the Trojan champion. Compare the behavior of Sohrab and Rostam, who conduct their final struggle, more or less unaware of the plight of their respective armies, with that of Achilles. Is pride responsible for their misfortune?

Beowulf, p. 489. In the first part of this epic poem, the young warrior Beowulf fights on behalf of the Swedish court against the monster Grendel and his mother. That strength is contrasted with Beowulf's weakness in the second part of the work, when he fights to protect his own kingdom from a dragon fifty years later. Compare the young and feckless Beowulf with Sohrab, and the elder Beowulf with Rostam. How do youth and age affect the conduct of an epic hero?

■ **FURTHER RESEARCH**

Translation and Commentary
Clinton, Jerome W. *The Tragedy of Sohrab and Rostam: From the Persian National Epic, the Shahname of Abol-Qasem Ferdowsi.* Rev. ed. 1996.

Literary History and Criticism
Davidson, Olga M. *Poet and Hero in the Persian Book of Kings.* 1994.
Davis, Dick. *Epic and Sedition: The Case of the Shahname.* 1992.
Hanaway, W. L. "The Iranian Epics." In *Heroic Epic and Saga,* edited by F. Oinas. 1978.
Levy, Reuben. *An Introduction to Persian Literature.* 1969.
Noldeke, T. *The Iranian National Epic.* 1979.
Rypka, J. *History of Iranian Literature.* 1968.

■ **PRONUNCIATION**

Abu al-Qasem Ferdowsi: ah-BOO ahl-KAH-sim feer-DOW-see
Achilles: uh-KIL-eez
Afrasiyab: ah-frah-see-YAHB
Daqiqi of Tus: dah-KEE-kee, TOOS
Gilgamesh: GIL-guh-mesh
Iliad: IL-ee-ud
Kay Kavús: KIGH kah-OOS
Keyanian: kigh-yah-NYAHN
Mahmud, Ghazna: mah-MOOD, GUZ-nuh
Rostám: ROH-stahm, ROO-stahm, roo-STAHM
Rudabé: roo-dah-BAH

The *Shahnama* is indeed an epic of the people such as no other nation has ever produced, with its materials going back to the beginning of time. . . . Firdausi therefore did not invent the legends he set down, but transmitted in verse form a general picture of the past glories of Iran, which from its appearance on the stage of history played an important part in civilizing the world.

– REUBEN LEVY, 1969, scholar

Sasanian: sas-AY-nee-un
Shahnama: shah-nah-MAH, shaw-hnaw-MAW
Sistan: see-STAHN
Sohráb: SOH-rahb, -hrahb
Tahmina: tah-mee-NAH, tah-hmee-NAH
Turán: too-RAHN
Zal: ZAHL
Zoroastrian: zoh-roh-AS-tree-un

FROM

ꙮ The Tragedy of Sohráb and Rostám

Translated by Jerome W. Clinton

THE FIRST BATTLE

[Sohráb] rode onto the battlefield, armed with
His lance and wondering at his mother's words.[1]
Upon the field of war they chose a narrow
Space to meet and fought with shortened lance.
When neither points nor bindings held,
They reined their horses in and turned aside,
And then with Indian swords renewed their fight,
Sparks pouring from their iron blades like rain.
With blows they shattered both their polished swords.

The Tragedy of Sohráb and Rostám. The story of Sohrab and Rostam found in Ferdowsi's *Shah-nama,* or *Book of Kings,* begins when Rostam, the ruler of Zabolestan and a warrior in the service of Iran, is attacked by Turkish warriors while hunting in the Turkish borderlands and loses his horse, Rakhsh. He reaches the city of Semengan, where he is treated royally while city officials look for his horse. That evening he meets Tahmina, daughter of the local shah, who offers to sleep with him and give him a son. Rostam "sealed firm his bond with her that night" (whether they actually married is disputable, due to textual corruption). Rostam departs in the morning, and nine months later Sohrab is born, rosy-faced and healthy. Sohrab soon grows to enormous size, and when he is twelve his mother reveals to him that he is Rostam's son. She swears him to secrecy, however, fearing that otherwise Rostam will claim him and take him away from her forever.

The youthful Sohrab, already sensing his power, hatches a plot. He will convene an army of Turkish soldiers and attack Kay Kavus, the shah of Iran—not in opposition to the Iranians, but in order to hand his father, Rostam, the Iranian throne. He will then return to Turan and attack the Turkish shah, Afrasiyab, whom he now serves, so that he and his father may rule adjoining countries. But the cunning shah Afrasiyab, who hears of the plot, preempts the youthful Sohrab's designs by welcoming his plan to invade Iran and offering his best officers to direct the battle. At

---

[1] **his mother's words:** Sohráb's mother, Tahmina, had told him Rostám was his father.

10 Such blows as these will fall on Judgment Day.
And then each hero seized his heavy mace.
The battle had now wearied both their arms.
Although their mounts were neighing and both heroes
Groaned with pain, they bent them with their might.
The armor flew from their two steeds; the links
That held their coats of mail burst wide apart.
Both mounts stood still; nor could their masters move.
Not one could lift a hand or arm to fight.
Their bodies ran with sweat, dirt filled their mouths,
20 And heat and thirst had split their tongues. Once more
They faced each other on that plain — the son
Exhausted and the father weak with pain.
Oh, world! How strange your workings are! From you
Comes both what's broken and what's whole as well.
Of these two men, neither was stirred by love.
Wisdom was far off, the face of love not seen.
From fishes in the sea to wild horses on
The plain, all beasts can recognize their young.
But man who's blinded by his wretched pride
30 Cannot distinguish son from foe.
      Rostám said to himself, "I've never seen
A warlike crocodile that fought like this.

---

the same time Afrasiyab arranges for the utmost secrecy concerning the identity of Sohrab, so that Rostam will not know his son when he meets him in battle.

    After Sohrab's first victory in the field, Kay Kavus enlists the support of his great champion, Rostam. Rostam discounts the idea that the leader of the Turkish forces could be Sohrab, as he knows the boy is only twelve years old. Unfortunately, Sohrab, a mythological hero, has already completely matured and thus appears much older than his age. When the two armies converge and Sohrab establishes his dread reputation among the enemy warriors of Kay Kavus, Rostam dresses for battle and meets Sohrab alone on the field. When Sohrab asks his opponent whether he is Rostam, Rostam lies, downplaying his legendary strength by pretending he is not a member of the nobility. "I have no throne, no palace, and no crown," he tells Sohrab. Sohrab, who had hoped he had finally met his father, prepares instead to face his mysterious enemy, and the battle that will last three days is joined. It is here that the text picks up the action of the story.

    The *Shahnama* gradually impressed itself on the consciousness of Europe. It was known in England by the eighteenth century and first translated into English in 1814. Other translations followed throughout Europe, though they were limited by the need to drastically shorten the epic poem, the corruption of available manuscripts, and the tendency of translators to depart from the original text whenever it suited them. British poet Matthew Arnold wrote a famous version of the fight between father and son entitled "The Story of Sohrab and Rustum" (1853), but no serviceable English version of the complete poem exists to the present day. This excerpt rendered by Jerome W. Clinton is taken from what is generally regarded as the best available English translation.

    A note on the translation: All notes are adapted from the translator's.

My battle with the Div Sepíd[2] seems nothing now.
Today my heart despaired of my own strength
While these two armies watched us here;
A youth who's seen but little of the world,
And who is neither noble nor well known,
Has made me weary of my destiny."
When both their steeds had rested and they had
40 Recovered from the pain and shame of war,
These mighty warriors, one ancient and
The other still a youth, both strung their bows.
But since each wore a breast plate and a tiger-
Skin cuirass, their arrows could not penetrate.
Although each now despaired before his foe,
They closed and seized each other round the waist.
Rostám, who in the heat of battle, could wrench
Huge stones from the flinty earth with his bare hands,
Now grasped Sohráb around the waist,
50 And sought with all his strength to wrest him from
His horse's back. The youth budged not at all.
The hero's mighty grip left him unmoved.
These lion-slayers both grew weary then.
They paused to rest and ease their wounds awhile.
And then once more Sohráb drew out his mace,
And pressed his thighs into his horse's flanks.
He struck Rostám upon the shoulder once,
A fearful blow that made him wince with pain.
Sohráb just laughed at him, "Oh, *pahlaván!*[3]
60 It seems you cannot bear a warrior's blow.
This steed of yours in battle is an ass.
Or is it that his master's hands grow weak?
Although you're tall as any cypress tree,
An old man who would play the youth's a fool."
     But each was wearied by the other now.
The earth seemed strait to them, the end unsure.
They turned their steeds aside and left the field,
Abandoning their hearts and souls to grief.
Great Tahamtán[4] attacked the Turkish host
70 Just like a leopard when he spies his prey.
When that fierce wolf appeared within their ranks,
The army of Turán all turned and fled.
Sohráb had turned his horse toward Irán,

---

[2] **Div Sepíd:** The white demon, a fearsome monster Rostám had to fight in order to join forces with Kay Kavús.
[3] *pahlaván:* One formally designated as a hero.
[4] **Great Tahamtán:** Another name for Rostám, meaning "huge body."

And fell upon their camp in swift assault.
He launched himself into their very midst,
Slaughtering many heroes with his mace.
Rostám grew anxious when he learned of this.
He thought that he would surely harm Kavús—
This wondrous Turk who had so suddenly
80   Appeared with chest and arms adorned for war.
He galloped swiftly to his army's camp,
So greatly was Rostám distressed by this.
Within the army's heart he saw Sohráb.
He'd turned the river there wine red with blood.
His spear was drenched in gore, his breast and arms
As well. He seemed a hunter drunk with sport.
Rostám grew sick at heart as he looked on,
And roared in anger like a fearsome lion.
"You cruel bloodthirsty Turk! Which of the men
90   Assembled here has challenged you to fight?
Why did you raise your hand in war to them?
Why slaughter them, a wolf among the flock?"
Sohráb replied, "The army of Turán
Was blameless in this fight as well. You first
Attacked, though none was keen to challenge you."
"The day's grown dark," Rostám replied, "but when
Once more the world-illuming sun's bright blade
Appears, there'll be a gibbet and a throne
Set side by side upon this plain of war.
100   The whole bright world now lies beneath the sword.
Although your blade's familiar with the smell
Of milk, may you live long and never die.
Let us return at dawn with our keen swords.
Go now; await the World Creator's wish."

THE INTERVAL

They left and then the sky turned black. The circling
Sphere looked down and wondered at Sohráb.
It seemed that he'd been formed for war and strife.
He rested not a moment from attack.
The steed he rode was made of steel, his soul
110   A wonder, and his body hardened brass.
Sohráb came to his camp when night had fallen,
His body scoured with wounds. He asked Humán,[5]

---

[5] **Humán:** The Turkish general sent by Afrasiyab to aid Sohráb in battle and to prevent him from learning his father's identity.

"Today the rising sun filled all the world
With weapons and the sounds of war. Tell me,
What damage did he wreak upon our host,
That horseman with a hero's neck and lion's charge?"
Humán replied, "The shah's command to me
Was that the army should not stir from here.
We were quite unprepared. We had not looked
120 To fight at all today. When suddenly
A fierce and warlike man approached our camp,
And turned to face this broad-ranged company,
It seemed he'd just returned from drinking or
From battling singlehanded with some foe."
Sohráb replied, "And yet he did not slay
A single man from all this numerous host,
While I slew many heroes from Irán,
And made that campground muddy with their blood.
But now it's time to spread the board and feast.
130 Come, let's ease our hearts with ruby wine."
       While on the other side, Rostám reviewed
His troops and spoke a while with Giv.[6] "How did
The battle-tried Sohráb fare here today?
Did he attack the camp? How did he fight?"
Heroic Giv replied to Tahamtán,
"I've never seen a hero quite like him.
He galloped to the army's very heart.
And there within that host made straight for Tus,
For he was armed and mounted, lance in hand.
140 And while Gorgín dismounted, he sat firm.
He came and when he saw him with his lance,
He galloped toward him like a raging lion.
He bent his heavy mace upon his chest.
Its force unloosed his helmet from his head.
Tus saw that he must fail, and turned and fled.
Then many other warriors challenged him,
But none among those heroes had his strength.
Only Piltán's the equal of this youth.
And yet we still held fast our ancient rule,
150 And held the army in a single rank.
No horseman went to fight with him alone
While he paraded on the field of war."
Rostám was grieved at this report. He turned
His face toward the camp of Shah Kavús.

---

[6] **Giv**: An Iranian hero whom the poet sets opposite Humán as Rostám's advisor.

When Kay Kavús saw him entering his tent,
He sat the *pahlaván* close by his throne.
Rostám described Sohráb to him, and spoke
At length of his great stature and his strength.
"None in this world has ever seen a child
160 Half grown who is so brave, so lionlike.
His head brushes against the stars above,
The earth below bends at his body's weight.
His arms and thighs are like a camel's limbs,
And yet to me they seemed more massive still.
We fought at length with heavy mace and sword,
With bow and arrow, and with lasso too.
No feint or weapon did we leave untried.
And finally I said, 'Before this time
I've lifted many heroes from their seats,'
170 And seized him round the waist and grasped his belt.
I thought to pluck him from his horse's back
And hurl him like the others to the ground.
The hurricane that shakes a granite peak
Would not disturb that worthy in his seat.
Tomorrow when he rides into the field,
My only hope's to fight him hand to hand.
And though I'll strive, I don't know who will win.
Nor do I know what choice Yazdán[7] will make.
Strength, victory, and fame all come from Him
180 Who has created both the sun and moon."
Kavús replied, "Then may the Pure Lord split
In two the hearts of all who wish you ill!
Tonight before the Maker of the World
I'll press my brow and cheeks against the earth.
For strength and greatness come from Him alone.
By his command the moon sends down its light.
Once more may He renew your hopes, and raise
Your name aloft in triumph to the sun."
Rostám replied, "By the glory of the shah,
190 May the hopes of those who wish him well be heard."
       Brave Tahamtán returned to camp, his soul
Distressed, his mind prepared for war.
His brother, Zavaré, approached him with
An anxious heart. "How did you fare today?"
Rostám first called for food, and ate his fill,
Then purged his heart of all his grief and fear.

---

[7]**Yazdán:** One of the names of God.

He spoke to Zavaré, advising him,
"Be vigilant of heart, do nothing rash.
Tomorrow, just at dawn, when I must meet
200   That warlike Turk in battle once again,
You bring the army and my standard to
The field, my throne and golden boots as well.
Be standing at the door of my pavilion
When the shining sun begins to rise.
If in this fight I gain the victory,
I will not linger on the battlefield.
But should the matter turn out otherwise,
Don't weep for me, and do not seek revenge.
Neither enter the field to fight alone,
210   Nor yet prepare yourself for general war.
Return together to Zabolestán,[8]
Once you are there, seek out my father, Zal.
Then you must try to ease my mother's heart.
This is the fate Yazdán decreed for me.
Tell her she should not mourn for me too long,
For she will do herself no good by that.
No one has lived for all eternity.
I've no complaint against the circling sphere.
In battle have I strangled many demons,
220   And lions, crocodiles, and leopards too.
I've leveled forts and towers to the ground,
And there's no man who's ever vanquished me.
The man who mounts a horse and gallops off
To fight, is he not knocking on death's door?
And if you live a thousand years, or more,
At last, the end of all will be the same.
When she's content, then tell Dastán,[9] 'Don't turn
Your back upon the monarch of the world.
Should he make war, do not be slack in your
230   Support, obey his word in everything.
We all are mortal, young and old alike.
There's none who lives for all eternity.'"
For half that night their words were of Sohráb.
The other half they spent in restful sleep.
    In the Turkish camp, Sohráb with all his friends
Had passed the night with wine and minstrelsy.
Musing, to Humán he said, "This lion who

---

[8] Zabolestán: The home country of Rostám.

[9] Dastán: Rostám's father, also known as Zal.

Engages me so fiercely on the field,
Is not one whit less tall than I, and when
240 Engaged in single combat has no fear.
His shoulders, chest, and neck are so like mine,
It seems some craftsman marked them with a rule.
I see in him the signs my mother told
Me of. That makes me hesitate a little.
I think that he must be Rostám, for in
This world few *pahlaváns* can equal him.
I must not in confusion rush to meet
My father here in combat face to face."
Humán replied, "I've met Rostám in war,
250 And seen him battle many times. I've heard
How that brave hero used his heavy mace
When he was fighting in Mazandarán.
This horse of his is very like Rostám's,
But he has not the hoof or rump of Rakhsh."

THE SECOND DAY

The shining sun spread wide its radiance,
The raven tucked its head beneath its wings,
Tahmatán put on his tiger-skin cuirass,
And sat astride his huge, fierce elephant.
To his seat he bound his rope in sixty coils,
260 And in his hand he grasped an Indian sword.
He galloped to the field, the place where they
Would fight, and there put on his iron helm.
All bitterness is born of precedence.
Alas when it is yoked to greedy pride!
     Sohráb stood up and armed himself. His head
Was filled with war, his heart with revelry.
Shouting his cry he rode into the field,
Within his hand, he held his bullhide mace.
He greeted him, a smile upon his lips,
270 As though they'd spent the night in company.
"How did you sleep? How do you feel today?
And how have you prepared yourself to fight?
Let's put aside this mace and sword of war.
Cast strife and wrong down to the ground.
Let us dismount and sit together now,
And smooth our brows with wine. And let us make
A pact before the World Preserving Lord,
That we'll repent of all our warlike plans.
Until another comes who's keen to fight,

280 Make peace with me and let us celebrate.
     My heart is ever moved by love for you,
     And wets my face with tears of modesty.
     I'm sure you're from a noble line; come then,
     Recite for me the line of your descent.
     Aren't you the son of brave Dastán, the son
     Of Sam?[10] Aren't you the *pahlaván* Rostám?"
     "Oh, shrewd ambitious youth," Rostám replied,
     "Before this hour we never spoke like this.
     Last night our words were of the coming fray.
290 Your tricks won't work with me; don't try again.
     Though you are but a youth, I am no child,
     And I'm prepared to fight you hand to hand.
     So let's begin our strife. Its end will be
     As the Keeper of the World commands it should.
     I've traveled long through hills and valleys too.
     And I'm no man for guile, deceits, and lies."
     Sohráb replied, "Such words do not befit
     A warrior who's so advanced in years.
     I wished that you might die upon your bed,
300 And that your soul would leave in its own time;
     That those you leave behind could keep your bones,
     Immure your flesh, but let your spirit fly.[11]
     But if your life is in my grasp, then as
     Yazdán commands, let us lock hands and fight."
          They both dismounted from their horses and
     In helmet and mail they approached each other
     with care. They tied their horses to a stone,
     Then advanced on foot, their hearts as cold as earth.
     Each seized the other and they grappled until
310 Their bodies ran with sweat and blood. Sohráb
     Was like a maddened elephant; he struck
     Rostám a blow and felled him to the earth.
     Then like a lion in the hunt whose claws
     Have thrown a mighty stallion to the ground,
     Sohráb sat firmly on the chest of huge
     Rostám, fist, face, and mouth all smeared with dirt,
     And from his belt he drew his polished knife,
     As he bent down to sever head from trunk.
     Rostám cried out, "Oh, lion-slaying chief,

---

[10] **Sam:** Rostám's grandfather.

[11] **Immure . . . spirit fly:** Refers to the Zoroastrian religious practice of leaving the dead exposed until their skeletons have been picked clean by vultures. The bones are then collected and placed in an ossuary.

320 And master of the sword and mace and rope!
    The custom of our nation is not thus.
    Our faith commands us to another way.
    Whoever in a wrestling match first throws
    His noble adversary to the ground,
    And pins him to the earth, may not cut off
    His head, not even if he seeks revenge.
    But if he fells him twice, he's earned that right,
    And all will call him Lion if he does."
    By that deceit he shrewdly sought to free
330 Himself from this fierce dragon's mortal grip.
        The brave youth bowed his head and yielded
    To the old man's words, and said no more,
    But loosed his grip and rushed off to the plain,
    A lion who has seen a deer race by.
    He hunted eagerly and gave no thought
    To him with whom he'd fought so recently.
    When it grew late, Humán came swiftly to
    The field, and asked him how the battle'd gone.
    Sohráb informed Humán of all he'd done,
340 And what Rostám had said to him. The brave
    Humán just heaved a sigh and said, "Dear youth,
    I see that you've grown weary of your life.
    I fear for this stout neck and arms and chest,
    This hero's waist and royal legs and feet.
    You caught a tiger firm within your trap,
    Then spoiled your work by letting him escape.
    You'll see what consequence this foolish act
    Of yours will have when next you meet to fight."
    He spoke, despairing of his life. He paused
350 A while in grief, still wondering at his deed.
        Sohráb returned toward his army's camp,
    Perplexed at heart and angry with himself.
    A shah once wisely spoke a proverb on
    This point, "Despise no foe, however mean."
    Rostám, when he'd escaped from his foe's hand,
    Sprang up like a blade of hardened steel, and rushed
    Off to a flowing stream that was nearby,
    For he was like a man who'd been reborn.
    He drank his fill, and when he'd washed his face
360 And limbs, he bowed before his Lord in prayer.
    He asked for strength and victory; he did
    Not know what sun and moon might hold in store,
    Or if the heavens as they wheeled above
    Would wish to snatch the crown from off his head.

Then pale of face and with an anxious heart,
He left the stream to meet his foe once more.
While like a maddened elephant, Sohráb
With bow and lasso galloped on the plain.
He wheeled and shouted as he chased his prey;
370 His yellow steed leaped high and tore the earth.
Rostám could not but stand in awe of him;
He sought to take his measure for the fight.
And when the lion-slayer saw him there,
The arrogance of youth boiled up in him.
"Hail him who fled the lion's claws,
And kept himself apart from his fierce blows."

THE DEATH OF SOHRÁB

Again they firmly hitched their steeds, as ill-
Intentioned fate revolved above their heads.
Once more they grappled hand to hand. Each seized
380 The other's belt and sought to throw him down.
Whenever evil fortune shows its wrath,
It makes a block of granite soft as wax.
Sohráb had mighty arms, and yet it seemed
The skies above had bound them fast. He paused
In fear; Rostám stretched out his hands and seized
That warlike leopard by his chest and arms.
He bent his strong and youthful back, and with
A lion's speed, he threw him to the ground.
Sohráb had not the strength; his time had come.
390 Rostám was sure he'd not stay down for long.
He swiftly drew a dagger from his belt
And tore the breast of that stout-hearted youth.
He writhed upon the ground; groaned once aloud,
Then thought no more of good and ill. He told
Rostám, "This was the fate allotted me.
The heavens gave my key into your hand.
It's not your fault. It was this hunchback Fate,
Who raised me up then quickly cast me down.
While boys my age still spent their time in games,
400 My neck and shoulders stretched up to the clouds.
My mother told me who my father was.
My love for him has ended in my death.
Whenever you should thirst for someone's blood,
And stain your silver dagger with his gore,
Then Fate may thirst for yours as well, and make
Each hair upon your trunk a sharpened blade.

Now should you, fishlike, plunge into the sea,
Or cloak yourself in darkness like the night,
Or like a star take refuge in the sky,
410 And sever from the earth your shining light,
Still when he learns that earth's my pillow now,
My father will avenge my death on you.
A hero from among this noble band
Will take this seal and show it to Rostám.
'Sohráb's been slain, and humbled to the earth,'
He'll say, 'This happened while he searched for you.'"
     When he heard this, Rostám was near to fainting.
The world around grew dark before his eyes.
And when Rostám regained his wits once more,
420 He asked Sohráb with sighs of grief and pain,
"What sign have you from him—Rostám? Oh, may
His name be lost to proud and noble men!"
"If you're Rostám," he said, "you slew me while
Some evil humor had confused your mind.
I tried in every way to draw you forth,
But not an atom of your love was stirred.
When first they beat the war drums at my door,
My mother came to me with bloody cheeks.[12]
Her soul was racked by grief to see me go.
430 She bound a seal upon my arm, and said
'This is your father's gift, preserve it well.
A day will come when it will be of use.'
Alas, its day has come when mine has passed.
The son's abased before his father's eyes.
My mother with great wisdom thought to send
With me a worthy *pahlaván* as guide.
The noble warrior's name was Zhende Razm,[13]
A man both wise in action and in speech.
He was to point my father out to me,
440 And ask for him in every gathering,
But Zhende Razm, that worthy man, was slain.
And at his death my star declined as well.
Now loose the binding of my coat of mail,
And look upon my naked, shining flesh."
When Rostám undid his armor's ties, and saw

---

[12] **with bloody cheeks:** In Persian poetry, intense grief is indicated by bloody tears.

[13] **Zhende Razm:** The Turkish warrior sent with Sohráb to counsel him and ensure that he recognizes his father. Rostám kills Zhende Razm, however, during a spying expedition to the Turkish camp, before his battle with his son.

That seal, he tore his clothes and wept.
"Oh, brave and noble youth, and praised among
All men, whom I have slain with my own hand!"
He wept a bloody stream and tore his hair;
450 His brow was dark with dust, tears filled his eyes.
Sohráb admonished him, "But this is worse.
You must not fill your eyes with tears. It does
No good to slay yourself with grief. Not now.
What's happened here is what was meant to be."
     When the radiant sun had left the sky,
And Tahamtán had not returned to camp,
Some twenty cavaliers rode off to see
How matters stood upon the field of war.
They saw two horses standing on the plain,
460 Both caked with dirt. Rostám was somewhere else.
Because they did not see his massive form
Upon the battlefield and mounted on
His steed, the heroes thought that he'd been slain.
The nobles all grew fearful and perplexed.
They sent a message swiftly to the shah,
"The throne of majesty has lost Rostám."
From end to end the army cried aloud,
And suddenly confusion filled the air.
Kavús commanded that the horns and drums
470 Be sounded, and his marshal, Tus, approached.
Then Kavús spoke, "Be quick, and gallop your horse
From here to view the battlefield,
And see how matters stand with bold Sohráb.
Must we lament the passing of Irán?
If by his hand the brave Rostám's been slain,
Who from Irán will dare approach this foe?
We must plan to strike a wide and general blow;
We dare not tarry long upon this field."
     And while a tumult rose within their camp,
480 Sohráb was speaking with brave Tahamtán,
"The situation of the Turks has changed
In every way now that my days are done.
Be kind to them, and do not let the shah
Pursue this war or urge his army on.
It was for me the Turkish troops rose up,
And mounted this campaign against Irán.
I it was who promised victory, and I
Who strove in every way to give them hope.
They should not suffer now as they retreat.

490 Be generous with them, and let them go."
        Rostám swiftly mounted Rakhsh, but as he did,
    His eyes bled tears, his lips were chilled with sighs.
    He wept as he approached the army's camp,
    His heart was filled with pain at what he'd done.
    When they first spied his face, the army of Irán
    Fell prostrate to the earth in gratitude,
    And loudly praised the Maker of the World,
    That he'd returned alive and well from war.
    But when they saw him with chest and clothes
500 All torn, his body heavy and his face
    Begrimed by dust, they asked him with one voice,
    "What does this mean? Why are you sad at heart?"
    He told them of his strange and baffling deed,
    Of how he'd slain the one he held most dear.
    They all began to weep and mourn with him,
    And filled the earth and sky with loud lament.
    At last he told the nobles gathered there,
    "It seems my heart is gone, my body too.
    Do not pursue this battle with the Turks.
510 The evil I have done is quite enough."
    And when he left that place, the *pahlaván*
    Returned with weary heart to where he lay.
    The noble lords accompanied their chief,
    Men like Gudárz and Tus and Gostahám.
    The army all together loosed their tongues,
    And gave advice and counsel to Rostám,
    "Yazdán alone can remedy this wound;
    He yet may ease this burden's weight for you."
    He grasped a dagger in his hand, and made
520 To cut his worthless head from his own trunk.
    The nobles hung upon his arm and hand,
    And tears of blood poured from their eyes.
    Gudárz said to Rostám, "What gain is there
    If by your death you set the world aflame?[14]
    Were you to give yourself a hundred wounds,
    How would that ease the pain of brave Sohráb?
    If some time yet remains for him on earth,
    He'll live, and you'll remain with him, at peace.
    But if this youth is destined to depart,

---

[14] **you set the world aflame:** If Rostám died, Kay Kavús would be defenseless against the further onslaught of Afrasiyab.

530   Look on the world, who's there that does not die?
       The head that wears a helmet and the head
       That wears a crown, to death we all are prey."

ROSTÁM ASKS KAY KAVÚS FOR THE NUSHDARÚ

       Rostám called wise Gudárz and said to him,
       "Depart from here upon your swiftest steed,
       And take a message to Kavús the shah.
       Tell him what has befallen me. With my
       Own dagger I have torn the breast of my
       Brave son—oh, may Rostám not live for long!
       If you've some recollection of my deeds,
540   Then share with me a portion of my grief,
       And from your store send me the *nushdarú*,[15]
       That medicine which heals whatever wound.
       It would be well if you sent it to me
       With no delay, and in a cup of wine.
       By your good grace, my son may yet be cured,
       And like his father stand before your throne."
       The *sepahbód*[16] Gudárz rode like the wind,
       And gave Kavús the message from Rostám.
             Kavús replied, "If such an elephant
550   Should stay alive and join our royal court,
       He'll make his father yet more powerful.
       Rostám will slay me then, I have no doubt.
       When I may suffer evil at his hands,
       What gift but evil should I make him now?
       You heard him, how he said, 'Who is Kavús?
       If he's the shah, then who is Tus?' And with
       That chest and neck, that mighty arm and fist,
       In this wide world, who's there to equal him?
       Will he stand humbly by my royal seat,
560   Or march beneath my banner's eagle wings?"
             Gudárz heard his reply, then turned and rode
       Back to Rostám as swift as wind-borne smoke.
       "The evil nature of the shah is like
       The tree of war, perpetually in fruit.
       You must depart at once and go to him.
       Perhaps you can enlighten his dark soul."

---

[15] *nushdarú:* A panacea or magical cure that only the shah can dispense.

[16] *sepahbód:* Shah or general.

ROSTÁM MOURNS SOHRÁB

Rostám commanded that a servant bring
A robe and spread it by the river's bank.
He gently laid Sohráb upon the robe,
570 Then mounted Rakhsh and rode toward the shah.
But as he rode, his face toward the court,
They overtook him swiftly with the news,
"Sohráb has passed from this wide world; he'll need
A coffin from you now, and not a crown.
'Father!' he cried, then sighed an icy wind,
Then wept aloud and closed his eyes at last."
    Rostám dismounted from his steed at once.
Dark dust replaced the helmet on his head.
He wept and cried aloud, "Oh, noble youth,
580 And proud, courageous seed of *pahlaváns!*
The sun and moon won't see your like again,
No more will shield or mail, nor throne or crown.
Who else has been afflicted as I've been?
That I should slay a youth in my old age
Who is descended from world-conquering Sam,
Whose mother's seed's from famous men as well.
It would be right to sever these two hands.
No seat be mine henceforth save darkest earth.
What father's ever done a deed like this?
590 I deserve abuse and icy scorn, no more.
Who else in all this world has slain his son,
His wise, courageous, youthful son?
How Zal the golden will rebuke me now,
He and the virtuous Rudabé as well.
What can I offer them as my excuse?
What plea of mine will satisfy their hearts?
What will the heroes and the warriors say
When word of this is carried to their ears?
And when his mother learns, what shall I say?
600 How can I send a messenger to her?
What shall I say? Why did I slay him when
He'd done no crime? Why blacken all his days?
How will her father, that worthy *pahlaván,*
Report this to his pure and youthful child?
He'll call this seed of Sam a godless wretch,
And heap his curses on my name and line.
Alas, who could have known this precious child
Would quickly grow to cypress height, or that
He'd raise this host and think of arms and war,

610 Or that he'd turn my shining day to night."
        Rostám commanded that the body of
His son be covered with a royal robe.
He'd longed to sit upon the throne and rule;
His portion was a coffin's narrow walls.
The coffin of Sohráb was carried from
The field. Rostám returned to his own tent.
They set aflame Sohráb's pavilion while
His army cast dark dust upon their heads.
They threw his tents of many colored silk,
620 His precious throne and leopard saddle cloth
Into the flames, and tumult filled the air.
        Rostám lamented, "Oh, youthful conqueror!
Alas, that stature and that noble face!
Alas, that wisdom and that manliness!
Alas, what sorrow and heart-rending loss—
Mother far off, slain by his father's hand."
His eyes wept bloody tears, he tore the earth,
And rent the kingly garments on his back.
        Then all the *pahlaváns* and Shah Kavús
630 Sat with him in the dust beside the road.
They spoke to him with counsel and advice—
In grief Rostám was like one driven mad—
"This is the way of fortune's wheel. It holds
A lasso in this hand, a crown in that.
As one sits happily upon his throne,
A loop of rope will snatch him from his place.
Why is it we should hold the world so dear?
We and our fellows must soon travel on.
The longer we have thought about our wealth,
640 The sooner we must face that earthy door.
If heaven's wheel knows anything of this,
Or if its mind is empty of our fate,
The turning of the wheel it cannot know,
Nor can it understand the reason why.
One must lament that he should leave this world,
Yet what this means at last, I do not know."
        Then Kay Kavús spoke to Rostám at length,
"From Mount Alborz down to the frailest reed,
The turning heavens carry all away.
650 You must not fix your heart upon this world.
One sets off quickly on the road, and one
Will take more time, but all pass on to death.
Content your heart with his departure and
Give careful heed to what I tell you now.

If you should bring the heavens down to earth,
Or set the world aflame from end to end,
You won't recall from death the one who's gone.
His soul's grown ancient in that other dwelling.
Once from afar I saw his arms and neck,
660 His lofty stature and his massive chest.
The times impelled him and his martial host
To come here now and perish by your hand.
What can you do? What remedy is there
For death? For how long can you mourn and weep?"
    Rostám replied, "Though he himself is gone,
Humán still sits upon this ample plain,
His Turkish and his Chinese chiefs as well.
Retain no hint of enmity toward them,
But strengthened by Yazdán and your command,
670 Let Zavaré guide all their army home."
    "Oh, famous *pahlaván*," said Shah Kavús,
"This war has caused you suffering and loss.
Though they have done me many grievous wrongs,
And though Turán has set Irán aflame,
Because my heart can feel your heavy pain,
I'll think no more of them and let them go."

ROSTÁM CONVEYS HIS SON TO ZABOLESTÁN

Kavús, whose radiance outshone the sun,
Commanded that his brother stay as guide.
Then Zavaré approached the royal throng,
680 The clothes upon his body torn to shreds.
He sent a message to Humán which said,
The sword of vengeance stays within its sheath.
You are commander of this army now,
Observe their conduct well, and do not sleep.
The shah departed from the field and led
His army to Irán; Rostám remained
To wait until brave Zavaré returned,
And brought him news of how that army'd fared.
When Zavaré returned at break of day,
690 Rostám commanded that the troops form ranks
At once, then led them toward Zabolestán.
    When news of their arrival reached Dastán,
All in Sistán[17] went forth to meet Rostám;

---

[17] Sistán: The province north of Zabolestan, also ruled by Rostám and his family.

They came to him prostrate with pain and grief.
When first he looked upon that wooden bier,
Dastán dismounted from his golden saddle.
Rostám came forward then, on foot. His clothes
Were torn to shreds, his heart was pierced by grief.
The heroes one and all let fall their arms,
700 And bowed down to the earth before his bier.
Zal spoke, "This was a strange event indeed.
Sohráb could lift the heavy mace; of this
The greatest in the land would speak with awe.
No mother in the world will bear his like."
And Zal spoke on; his eyes were filled with tears
His tongue with words of praise for bold Sohráb.

When Tahamtán had reached his palace gate,
He cried aloud and set the coffin down.
He wrenched the nails out, threw the lid aside,
710 And drew the shroud off as his father watched,
Showing his son's body to those noble men.
It was as if the heavens burned with grief.
Those famous heroes tore their clothes and wept;
Like dust their cries ascended to the clouds.
From end to end the palace seemed a tomb,
In which a lion had been laid to rest.
It seemed as though great Sam was lying there.
The battle'd wearied him, and now he slept.
He covered him again with gold brocade,
720 And firmly closed the coffin's narrow lid.
"If now I build Sohráb a golden tomb
And strew it round with fragrant, sable musk,
When I am gone, it won't remain for long.
If that's not so, yet so it seems to me."
With horses' hooves they built a warrior's tomb,
And all the world went blind with weeping there.

Thus spoke Bahrám the wise and eloquent,
"Don't bind yourself too closely to the dead,
For you yourself will not remain here long.
730 Prepare yourself to leave, and don't be slow.
One day your sire gave you a turn at life.
The turn is at its end, that's only right.
That's how it is, the secret why's unknown.
The door is locked; nor will the key be found.
You won't discover it, don't even try!
And if you do, you'll spend your life in vain."

It is a tale that's filled with tears and grief.
The tender heart will rage against Rostám.

∾ FARID UD-DIN ATTAR

C. 1145–C. 1221

fah-REED

oo-DEEN ah-TAR

jah-lah-loo-DEEN

roo-MEE

sah-nah-EE

One of three great Persian Sufi poets of the twelfth and thirteenth centuries, **Farid ud-Din Attar** is less well known today than his younger contemporary **Jalaloddin Rumi** (1207–1283), but his most famous poem, *The Conference of the Birds,* remains a perennial best-seller in the Islamic world. All three of the great medieval Persian poets—**Sana'i** (d. 1150), author of *The Garden of the Truth (Hadiqatu'l Haqiqat),* Attar, and Rumi— wrote in the mathnavi[1] form, a long didactic verse form employing a structure similar to the HEROIC COUPLET[2] in the West. All also treated subjects inspired by their engagement with Sufism, the mystical tradition of Islam. As a child Rumi met Attar and received the gift of a volume of his work; later on Rumi counted Attar as one of his mentors: "Attar was the spirit and Sana'i its two eyes"; he wrote, "I followed on Sana'i and Attar."

Attar's most important work, *The Conference of the Birds (Manteq at-Tair),* like Dante's *Divine Comedy* and Chaucer's *Canterbury Tales* is an account of a spiritual pilgrimage. All the stories in Attar's collection, unlike those in *The Canterbury Tales,* are intended to illustrate the spiritual allegory of the journey. The Western work *The Conference of the Birds* most resembles is the later allegory by English Evangelical John Bunyan (1628–1688), *The Pilgrim's Progress* (1678), which describes the journey of Christian from the City of Destruction to the Celestial City, a work whose popularity with English readers was exceeded only by the Bible. *The Conference of the Birds* has enjoyed a similar popularity with readers in the Islamic world.

An Obscure Life. Even the dates of Attar's birth and death are uncertain. He was born in the city of Neishapour in what is now northeastern Iran—also the home of the famous Persian poet Omar Khayyam (died c. 1123), author of *The Rubaiyat*—sometime around 1145. His name Attar, from the Persian word for perfume, identifies him as a perfumer, pharmacist, and medical practitioner, a profession he inherited from his father. Educated in medicine, Arabic, and theosophy at an Islamic school in Mashhad, he first started his work life in his father's pharmacy before taking off several years to travel throughout the Middle East—to Egypt, Syria, Arabia, Turkestan, and India as well as important cities in Persia. Such travels were common at the time, particularly for Muslims on a

www For links to more information about Farid ud-Din Attar and a quiz on *The Conference of the Birds,* see *World Literature Online* at bedfordstmartins .com/worldlit.

---

[1] **mathnavi:** Persian poetic form used for romantic, epic, didactic, and other poems whose subjects demanded lengthy treatment. The *mathnavi* uses a verse structure similar to that of the heroic couplet in the West in which each line is made up of two rhyming halves.

[2] **heroic couplet:** A two-line, rhymed, iambic-pentameter stanza that completes its thought within its two-line form. Alexander Pope (1688–1744) is the most accomplished practitioner of the form in English; in this couplet from *An Essay on Criticism,* he writes: "True wit is nature to advantage dressed,/What oft was thought, but ne'er so well expressed."

Attar was the spirit and Sana'i its two eyes; / I followed on Sana'i and Attar.

– RUMI, poet

Phoenix Tile, 1270–80 C.E.

In Attar's spiritual allegory The Conference of the Birds, *a group of birds led by a hoopoe (similar to a hornbill) take a journey toward enlightenment. (British Museum/ All rights reserved.)*

spiritual quest and for poets who, like the troubadours of the West, went off in search of poetic inspiration. After several years of travel, Attar returned to Neishapour and to his profession as a druggist and doctor.

One legend has it that Attar wrote 114 literary works, a number equal to the number of suras in the Qur'an (Koran), but the true number was probably far fewer. Today he is remembered largely for two works, *Memorials of the Saints (Tadhkirat al-Auliya)*, a collection of anecdotes about the lives of Islamic saints, and *The Conference of the Birds*. How Attar became a believer in **SUFISM** and the details of his spiritual life are unknown, although one plausible story claims that he was accused of heresy, a real danger for a believer in Sufism, which challenged the role of the established religious authorities. Even his death remains a mystery. One account reports that he died at the hands of the Mongols who invaded northern Persia in 1229 and were said to have massacred all 1.7 million **Neishapour** inhabitants. Attar probably died earlier than the time of

nee-shah-POOR

the invasion, and his career marks the end of a great age of poetry in Persia. His younger follower, Rumi, would survive to write Persian poetry only by escaping to Turkey and eventually to Asia Minor.

Sufism.   Like mystics in all regions, Sufis sought a direct, unmediated experience of the divine, and they practiced meditation and other spiritual disciplines as ways of achieving purification and approaching God. Some Sufi sects, which practice a form of dance as a spiritual discipline, are sometimes referred to as "whirling dervishes." *Sufi*, from the Arabic word for a wearer of wool, originally identified the mystical practitioners by the coarse cloth that was used in their clothing, similar to the hair shirts worn by some Western mystics who disciplined the body to free the spirit. Sufi doctrine asserts that God alone exists, extending the Islamic notion that there is no absolute reality except for God. This belief does not lead to PANTHEISM, which asserts that everything is divine, but rather to MONISM, to the one truth that God alone is. This doctrine, along with their rejection of institutional mediators between humans and God, often brought Sufis dangerously close to heresy in the eyes of established Islamic clergy. **Mansur al-Hallaj**, for example, a tenth-century Sufi, after experiencing the unity of all things, was executed in Baghdad in 922 for asserting "I am the truth," or "I am God." Attar considered al-Hallaj, who appeared to him in a dream, one of his important teachers.

The goal of Sufi practice is the extinction of the ego and the total identification of the believer with the divine, a state the Sufis describe as love. The process of arriving at this unified consciousness, the Way *(tariqah)*, has several stages: repentance, avoiding doubt, abstinence, poverty, perseverance, trust in God, and contentment. These spiritual states, which may overlap and will not necessarily occur in any particular order, make up the stages of the spiritual journey undertaken by the believer. They are also the spiritual beliefs and ideas on which Attar's poetry is based.

The Conference of the Birds.   Attar's famous poem translates the doctrines and disciplines of Sufism into popular ALLEGORY,[3] a narrative in which the characters, settings, and episodes are meant to stand for another order of persons, places, and events. In the poem's allegorical FRAME NARRATIVE,[4] a hoopoe — a bird similar to the hornbill found in Europe,

> Attar, along with Chaucer and Dante, was a great genius of community and how that involves the path toward enlightenment.
>
> – COLEMAN BARKS, critic

mahn-SOOR
ahl-hah-LEJ

---

[3] **allegory:** A narrative in which the characters, settings, and episodes are meant to stand for other persons, places, and events. Traditionally, most allegories correlate to spiritual concepts, as in Dante's *Divine Comedy* (1321) and John Bunyan's *The Pilgrim's Progress* (1678). Some later allegories, such as George Orwell's *Animal Farm* (1946), an allegory of the Bolshevik Revolution in Russia, connect their stories to political, historical, or sociological subjects.

[4] **frame narrative:** A story that frames another story or stories, such as the story of the pilgrimage to Canterbury that frames the many tales in Chaucer's *Canterbury Tales*. Although this device has been used by authors from classical times to the present, it was especially popular with writers in the thirteenth, fourteenth, and fifteenth centuries, such as Dante, Boccaccio, and Marguerite de Navarre. The most elaborate use of the frame narrative is probably that in *The Thousand and One Nights*, in which there are frame narratives within frame narratives.

Like Chaucer's *Canterbury Tales*, [*The Conference of the Birds*] is a group of stories bound together by the convention of a pilgrimage, and as in Chaucer's work the convention allows the author to present a panorama of contemporary society; both poems can accommodate widely differing tones and subjects, from the scatological to the exalted and pathetic (and, occasionally, it must be admitted, the bathetic); both authors delight in quick character sketches and brief vignettes of quotidian life.

– AFKHAM DARBANDI
AND DICK DAVIS,
1984, critics

Africa, and Asia — calls a conference of birds to organize an expedition of all birds to seek their god, the Simorgh. At first the birds are enthusiastic, but when they consider the difficulty of the journey they manufacture excuses for why they are unable to go. The nightingale, for example, says he must remain behind to sing for the lovers who listen for his song, and the duck claims that he will be unable to stay clean while traveling. The hoopoe, who represents a spiritual teacher or Sufi master, answers each bird's excuses with a brief theological challenge and a story, parable, or fable to illustrate his point. After challenging all the birds' excuses, the hoopoe responds to their questions about the journey, its difficulties, with similar tales and fables. Finally, before setting out, the hoopoe describes each of the seven valleys of the Way that the birds will pass through on their journey: the quest, love, insight and mystery, detachment, bewilderment, poverty and nothingness, and unity. He illustrates each of these spiritual challenges with stories. The actual journey takes up only a few pages of the poem. Only thirty birds arrive at the final destination. When they meet their god, the Simorgh, whose name means thirty *(si)* birds *(morgh)*, they allegorically fulfill the purpose of their quest. They discover that their god is not separate from them. The Simorgh is themselves; the birds have become one with the divine.

To answer his fellow birds' objections and questions, the hoopoe draws on episodes from the Qur'an, historical anecdotes, folktales, animal fables, and legends. Typically, his stories are brief, and many were probably familiar to the poem's readers. Each makes a particular point, which is often explained by the hoopoe as he introduces a story or links one story with the next. Since there are no words to describe the mystical experience or the spiritual stages leading to it, the poet must speak in metaphors. Just as the birds' journey stands for the process of spiritual discipline and growth in the poem, so carnal love represents unity with the divine, sleep suggests spiritual contemplation, and intoxication stands for religious ecstasy. A number of the hoopoe's stories seem to transgress the strictures of Islam which, for example, forbids drinking and illicit sexuality. In "The Story of the Princess Who Loved a Slave," the hoopoe addresses spiritual bewilderment through a forbidden relationship across class lines, the couple's sexual fulfillment symbolizing spiritual ecstasy and understanding. Such stories may have been meant to challenge readers to abandon conventional dogmas and give fresh consideration to their spiritual condition. Partly because they portrayed transgressive behaviors such as drinking and sexual license in positive ways, the Sufis were seen by some as heretics.

The hoopoe's commentary frames all his stories, however, so their theological purpose is not forgotten. While reading the poem, the reader may also experience the unity of the divine and the human, for finally there is no distinction between worldly and spiritual love.

■ CONNECTIONS

The Thousand and One Nights, p. 441. *The Conference of the Birds,* like *Thousand and One Nights,* is a collection of Islamic stories enclosed within a frame narrative. A frame narrative can serve to give the individual stories it contains larger significance, directing the reader to interpret them as illustrations of larger thematic issues. Attar's frame narrative is much more explicit about the significance of the tales it encompasses and the connections among them than the frame in *Thousand and One Nights*. Is Attar's scheme simplistically didactic? How does Shahrazad indicate the thematic significance of the tales she tells?

Boccaccio, *The Decameron,* "The Tale of Tancred and Ghismonda," p. 850. Like Boccaccio's tale of Tancred and Ghismonda, Attar's "Story of the Princess Who Loved a Slave" is about a ruler's daughter who loves outside accepted class lines. Consider the differences between the two stories, especially the ways in which they are resolved. How might these differences indicate the intentions of the two authors? What reasons might there be for the tragic way in which Boccaccio's story ends and the comic resolution of Attar's?

William Shakespeare, Sonnet 130: "My mistress' eyes are nothing like the sun" (Book 3). In Sonnet 130, Shakespeare makes fun of the clichéd poetic hyperbole often used to celebrate a lover's beauty. In "The Story of the Princess Who Loved a Slave" Attar employs such clichéd comparisons to describe the princess and her lover. How do the differences between the two works make such expressions appropriate or inappropriate?

■ FURTHER RESEARCH

Translations
Darbandi, Afkham, and Dick Davis. *The Conference of the Birds.* 1984.
Nott, C. S. *The Conference of the Birds.* 1971.

Commentary and Background
Levy, Reuben. *An Introduction to Persian Literature.* 1969.
Morris, James Winston. "Reading *The Conference of the Birds.*" In *Approaches to the Asian Classics,* edited by William Theodore de Bary and Irene Bloom. 1990.

■ PRONUNCIATION

Azra'el: AZ-ray-el
Bismillah: bis-MIL-uh
Farid ud-Din Attar: fah-REED oo-DEEN ah-TAR, AT-ur
Jalaloddin Rumi: jah-lah-loo-DEEN roo-MEE
Ka'abah: KAH-buh, KAH-uh-buh
Mansur al-Hallaj: mahn-SOOR ahl-hah-LEJ
Neishapour: nee-shah-POOR
Sana'i: sah-nah-EE

FROM

∿ The Conference of the Birds

Translated by Afkham Darbandi and Dick Davis

THE BIRDS ASSEMBLE AND THE HOOPOE TELLS THEM OF THE SIMORGH

The world's birds gathered for their conference
And said: 'Our constitution makes no sense.
All nations in the world require a king;
How is it we alone have no such thing?
Only a kingdom can be justly run;
We need a king and must inquire for one.'

They argued how to set about their quest.
The hoopoe fluttered forward; on his breast
There shone the symbol of the Spirit's Way
10   And on his head Truth's crown, a feathered spray.
Discerning, righteous and intelligent,
He spoke: 'My purposes are heaven-sent;
I keep God's secrets, mundane and divine,
In proof of which behold the holy sign
Bismillah[1] etched for ever on my beak.
No one can share the grief with which I seek
Our longed-for Lord, and quickened by my haste
My wits find water in the trackless waste.

The Conference of the Birds.   The following selections from this Farid ud-Din Attar poem written in the late twelfth or early thirteenth century are taken from the first English translation of the complete poem, that by Afkham Darbandi and Dick Davis published in 1984. This translation in rhymed couplets captures the character of Attar's *mathnavi* verse form, which rhymes the two halves of each line.

   The poem itself traces the pilgrimage of a group of birds from its shaky beginning to its fulfillment, when the birds meet their god, the Simorgh. These excerpts from the work begin as the hoopoe, who represents the Islamic Sufi teacher, proposes the pilgrimage; include the hoopoe's response to the bird who asserts that he is unable to abandon his material pleasures and go on the journey as well as the hoopoe's stories describing the spiritual test of the Valley of Bewilderment; and conclude, where the work itself ends, as the remaining group of thirty birds meet the Simorgh, their god. These selections are characteristic of the poem as a whole, ranging from brief anecdotes such as "The Restless Fool and the Dervish" to more sustained stories such as "The Story of the Princess Who Loved a Slave."

   A note on the translation. The notes are the editors' unless otherwise indicated.

---

[1] *Bismillah:* "In the name of God": the opening words of the Qur'an (Koran). [Translator's note.]

    I come as Solomon's close friend and claim
20 The matchless wisdom of that mighty name
    (He never asked for those who quit his court,
    But when I left him once alone he sought
    With anxious vigilance for my return—
    Measure my worth by this great king's concern!).
    I bore his letters—back again I flew—
    Whatever secrets he divined I knew;
    A prophet loved me; God has trusted me;
    What other bird has won such dignity?
    For years I travelled over many lands,
30 Past oceans, mountains, valleys, desert sands,
    And when the Deluge rose I flew around
    The world itself and never glimpsed dry ground;
    With Solomon I set out to explore
    The limits of the earth from shore to shore.
    I know our king—but how can I alone
    Endure the journey to His distant throne?
    Join me, and when at last we end our quest
    Our king will greet you as His honoured guest.
    How long will you persist in blasphemy?
40 Escape your self-hood's vicious tyranny—
    Whoever can evade the Self transcends
    This world and as a lover he ascends.
    Set free your soul; impatient of delay,
    Step out along our sovereign's royal Way:
    We have a king; beyond Kaf's[2] mountain peak
    The Simorgh lives, the sovereign whom you seek,
    And He is always near to us, though we
    Live far from His transcendent majesty.
    A hundred thousand veils of dark and light
50 Withdraw His presence from our mortal sight,
    And in both worlds no being shares the throne
    That marks the Simorgh's power and His alone—
    He reigns in undisturbed omnipotence,
    Bathed in the light of His magnificence—
    No mind, no intellect can penetrate
    The mystery of His unending state:
    How many countless hundred thousands pray
    For patience and true knowledge of the Way
    That leads to Him whom reason cannot claim,
60 Nor mortal purity describe or name;

---

[2] **Kaf:** A city in northwestern Saudi Arabia.

There soul and mind bewildered miss the mark
And, faced by Him, like dazzled eyes, are dark —
No sage could understand His perfect grace,
Nor seer discern the beauty of His face.
His creatures strive to find a path to Him,
Deluded by each new, deceitful whim,
But fancy cannot work as she would wish;
You cannot weigh the moon like so much fish!
How many search for Him whose heads are sent
70   Like polo-balls in some great tournament
From side to giddy side — how many cries,
How many countless groans assail the skies!
Do not imagine that the Way is short;
Vast seas and deserts lie before His court.
Consider carefully before you start;
The journey asks of you a lion's heart.
The road is long, the sea is deep — one flies
First buffeted by joy and then by sighs;
If you desire this quest, give up your soul
80   And make our sovereign's court your only goal.
First wash your hands of life if you would say:
"I am a pilgrim of our sovereign's Way";
Renounce your soul for love; He you pursue
Will sacrifice His inmost soul for you. [. . .]

An Ostentatious Bird

Another bird declared: 'My happiness
Comes from the splendid things which I possess:
My palace walls inlaid with gold excite
Astonishment in all who see the sight.
They are a world of joy to me — how could
90   I wrench my heart from this surpassing good?
There I am king; all bow to my commands —
Shall I court ruin in the desert sands?
Shall I give up this realm, and live without
My certain glory in a world of doubt?
What rational mind would give up paradise
For wanderings filled with pain and sacrifice?'

The Hoopoe Answers Him

The hoopoe said: 'Ungrateful wretch! Are you
A dog that you should need a kennel too?
This world's a kennel's filthy murk at best;
100   Your palace is a kennel with the rest.

If it seems paradise, at your last breath
You'll know it is your dungeon after death.
There'd be no harm in palaces like yours,
Did not the thought of death beat at our doors.

A King Who Built a Splendid Palace

A king who loved his own magnificence
Once built a palace and spared no expense.
When this celestial building had been raised,
The gorgeous carpets and its splendour dazed
The crowd that pressed around—a servant flung
110   Trays heaped with money to the scrabbling throng.
The king now summoned all his wisest friends
And said: "What do I lack? Who recommends
Improvements to my court?" "We must agree,"
They said, "no man could now or ever see,
In all the earth, a palace built like this."
An old ascetic spoke. "One thing's amiss,"
He said; "there's one particular you lack.
This noble structure has a nasty crack
(Though if it weren't for that it would suffice
120   To be the heavenly court of paradise)."
The king replied: "What crack? Where is it? Where?
If you've come here for trouble, then take care!"
The man said: "Lord, it is the truth I tell—
And through that crack will enter Azra'el.[3]
It may be you can block it, but if not,
Then throne and palace are not worth a jot!
Your palace now seems like some heavenly prize,
But death will make it ugly to your eyes;
Nothing remains for ever and you know—
130   Although you live here now—that this is so.
Don't pride yourself on things that cannot last;
Don't gallop your high-stepping horse so fast.
If one like me is left to indicate
Your faults to you, I pity your sad fate."

A Merchant Gives a Party

To gratify his busy self-esteem,
A merchant built a mansion like a dream,
And when the preparations were all done,

---

[3] Azra'el: The angel of death. [Translators' note.]

He regally invited everyone
To an enormous entertainment there,
140   At which they'd feast and dutifully stare.
But running self-importantly around,
He met a begging fool, who stood his ground
And mocked the merchant's diligence. "My lord,"
He said, "I'm desolate (O, rest assured!)
That I can't come and drink your health, but I'm
So busy that I really haven't time—
You will forgive me?" and he gave a grin.
"Of course," the merchant answered, taken in.

THE SPIDER

You've seen an active spider work—he seems
150   To spend his life in self-communing dreams;
In fact the web he spins is evidence
That he's endowed with some far-sighted sense.
He drapes a corner with his cunning snare
And waits until a fly's entangled there,
Then dashes out and sucks the meagre blood
Of his bewildered, buzzing, dying food.
He'll dry the carcass then, and live off it
For days, consuming bit by tasty bit—
Until the owner of the house one day
160   Will reach up casually to knock away
The cunning spider's home—and with her broom
She clears both fly and spider from the room.

Such is the world, and one who feeds there is
A fly trapped by that spider's subtleties;
If all the world is yours, it will pass by
As swiftly as the blinking of an eye;
And though you boast of kings and patronage,
You are a child, an actor on a stage.
Don't seek for wealth unless you are a fool;
170   A herd of cows is all that you can rule!
Whoever lives for banners, drums and glory
Is dead; the dervish understands this story
And calls it windy noise—winds vainly flap
The banners, hollowly the brave drums tap.
Don't gallop on the horse of vanity;
Don't pride yourself on your nobility.
They skin the leopard for his splendid pelt;
They'll flay you too before your nose has smelt
A whiff of danger. When your life's made plain,

180 Which will be better, death or chastening pain?
You cannot hold your head up then—obey!
How long must you persist in childish play?
Either give up your wealth or lay aside
The rash pretensions of your crazy pride.
Your palace and your gardens! They're your gaol,
The dungeon where your ruined soul will wail.
Forsake this dusty pride, know what it's worth;
Give up your restless pacing of the earth.
To see the Way, look with the eyes of thought;
190 Set out on it and glimpse the heavenly court—
And when you reach that souls' asylum, then
Its glory will blot out the world of men.

THE RESTLESS FOOL AND THE DERVISH

A fool dashed onward at a reckless pace
Till in the desert he came face to face
With one who wore the ragged dervish cloak,
And asked: "What is your work?" The dervish spoke:
"Poor shallow wretch, can you not see I faint
With this strict pressure of the world's constraint?"
"Constraint? That can't be right," the man replied;
200 "The empty desert stretches far and wide."
The dervish said: "If there is no strict Way,
How has it led you to me here today?"

A myriad promises beguile your mind,
But flames of greed are all that you can find.
What are such flames? Tread down the world's desire,
And like a lion shun this raging fire.
Accomplish this, and you will find your heart;
There waits your palace, pure in every part.
Fire blocks the path, the goal is long delayed—
210 Your heart's a captive and your soul's afraid,
But in the midst of such an enterprise
You will escape this universe of lies.
When worldly pleasures cloy, prepare to die—
The world gives neither name nor truth, pass by!
The more you see of it the less you see,
How often must I warn you to break free?

SEEING THE WORLD

A mourner following a coffin cried:
"You hardly saw the world, and yet you've died."

A fool remarked: "Such noise! You'd think that he
220   Had seen the world himself repeatedly!"

If you would take the world with you, you must
Descend with all the world unseen to dust;
You rush to savour life, and so life goes
While you ignore the balm for all its woes;
Until the Self is sacrificed your soul
Is lost in filth, divided from its goal.

A perfumed wood was burning, and its scent
Made someone sigh with somnolent content.
One said to him: "Your sigh means ecstasy;
230   Think of the wood, whose sigh means misery".'
[. . .]

THE VALLEY OF BEWILDERMENT

Next comes the Valley of Bewilderment,
A place of pain and gnawing discontent—
Each second you will sigh, and every breath
Will be a sword to make you long for death;
Blinded by grief, you will not recognize
The days and nights that pass before your eyes.
Blood drips from every hair and writes "Alas"
Beside the highway where the pilgrims pass;
In ice you fry, in fire you freeze—the Way
240   Is lost, with indecisive steps you stray—
The Unity you knew has gone; your soul
Is scattered and knows nothing of the Whole.
If someone asks: "What is your present state;
Is drunkenness or sober sense your fate,
And do you flourish now or fade away?"
The pilgrim will confess: "I cannot say;
I have no certain knowledge any more;
I doubt my doubt, doubt itself is unsure;
I love, but who is it for whom I sigh?
250   Not Moslem, yet not heathen; who am I?
My heart is empty, yet with love is full;
My own love is to me incredible."

THE STORY OF THE PRINCESS WHO LOVED A SLAVE

A great king had a daughter whose fair face
Was like the full moon in its radiant grace,

She seemed a Joseph,[4] and her dimpled chin
The well that lovely youth was hidden in —
Her face was like a paradise; her hair
Reduced a hundred hearts to love's despair;
Her eyebrows were two bows bent back to shoot
260   The arrows of love's passionate dispute;
The pointed lashes of her humid eyes
Were thorns strewn in the pathway of the wise;
The beauty of this sun deceived the train
Of stars attendant on the moon's pale reign;
The rubies of her mouth were like a spell
To fascinate the angel Gabriel —
Beside her smile, her sweet, reviving breath,
The waters of eternal life seemed death;
Whoever saw her chin was lost and fell
270   Lamenting into love's unfathomed well;
And those she glanced at sank without a sound —
What rope could reach the depths in which they drowned?
It happened that a handsome slave was brought
To join the retinue that served at court,
A slave, but what a slave! Compared with him
The sun and moon looked overcast and dim.
He was uniquely beautiful — and when
He left the palace, women, children, men
Would crowd into the streets and market-place,
280   A hundred thousand wild to see his face.
One day the princess, by some fateful chance,
Caught sight of this surpassing elegance,
And as she glimpsed his face she felt her heart,
Her intellect, her self-control depart —
Now reason fled and love usurped its reign;
Her sweet soul trembled in love's bitter pain.
For days she meditated, struggled, strove,
But bowed at last before the force of love
And gave herself to longing, to the fire
290   Of passionate, insatiable desire.

Attendant on the daughter of the king
Were ten musicians, slave girls who could sing
Like nightingales — whose captivating charms

---

[4] **Joseph:** The story of Joseph, the favorite son of Jacob, recounted in the twelfth sura of the Qur'an and in the Hebrew Scriptures, is frequently alluded to in *The Conference of the Birds*. Since Joseph was said to be of unsurpassed beauty, he is frequently compared to heroes and heroines as the standard for beauty.

Would rival David's[5] when he sang the psalms.
The princess set aside her noble name
And whispered to these girls her secret shame
(When love has first appeared who can expect
The frenzied lover to be circumspect?),
Then said: "If I am honest with this slave
300   And tell my love, who knows how he'll behave?
My honour's lost if he should once discover
His princess wishes that she were his lover!
But if I can't make my affection plain
I'll die, I'll waste away in secret pain;
I've read a hundred books on chastity
And still I burn—what good are they to me?
No, I must have him; this seductive youth
Must sleep with me and never know the truth—
If I can secretly achieve my goal
310   Love's bliss will satisfy my thirsting soul."
Her girls said: "Don't despair; tonight we'll bring
Your lover here and he won't know a thing."
One of them went to him—she simpered, smiled,
And O! how easily he was beguiled;
He took the drugged wine she'd prepared—he drank,
Then swooned—unconscious in her arms he sank,
And in that instant all her work was done;
He slept until the setting of the sun.
Night came and all was quiet as the grave;
320   Now, stealthily, the maidens brought this slave,
Wrapped in a blanket, to their mistress' bed
And laid him down with jewels about his head.
Midnight: he opened his dazed, lovely eyes
And stared about him with a mute surprise—
The bed was massy gold; the chamber seemed
An earthly paradise that he had dreamed;
Two candles made of ambergris burnt there
And with their fainting fragrance filled the air;
The slave girls made such music that his soul
330   Seemed beckoned onward to some distant goal;
Wine passed from hand to hand; the candles' light
Flared like a sun to drive away the night.
But all the joys of this celestial place
Could not compare with her bewitching face,

---

[5] David (c. 1012–c. 972 B.C.E.): King of the ancient Hebrews whose story is told in both the Hebrew Scriptures and the Qur'an. Traditionally regarded as the author of many of the Psalms.

At which he stared as if struck senseless, dumb,
Lost both to this world and the world to come—
His heart acknowledged love's supremacy;
His soul submitted to love's ecstasy;
His eyes were fixed on hers, while to his ears
340 The girls' song seemed the music of the spheres;
He smelt the burning candles' ambergris;
His mouth burnt with the wine, then with her kiss;
He could not look away, he could not speak,
But tears of eloquence coursed down his cheek—
And she too wept, so that each kiss was graced
With salty sweetness mingled in one taste,
Or he would push aside her stubborn hair
And on her lovely eyes in wonder stare.
Thus, in each other's arms, they passed the night
350 Until, worn out by sensual delight,
By passion, by the vigil they had kept,
As dawn's cool breeze awoke, the young man slept.

Then, as he slept, they carried him once more
And laid him gently on his own hard floor.
He woke, he slowly knew himself again—
Astonishment, regret, grief's aching pain
Swept over him (though what could grief achieve?
The scene had fled and it was vain to grieve).
He bared his body, ripped his tattered shirt,
360 Tore out his hair, besmeared his head with dirt—
And when his friends asked what assailed his heart,
He cried: "How can I say? Where could I start?
No dreamer, no, no seer could ever see
What I saw in that drunken ecstasy;
No one in all the world has ever known
The bliss vouchsafed to me, to me alone—
I cannot tell you what I saw; I saw
A stranger sight than any seen before."
They said: "Try to remember what you've done,
370 And of a hundred joys describe just one."
He answered: "Was it me who saw that face?
Or did some other stand there in my place?
I neither saw nor heard a thing, and yet
I saw and heard what no man could forget."
A fool suggested: "It's some dream you had;
Some sleepy fantasy has sent you mad."
He asked: "Was it a dream, or was it true?
Was I drunk or sober? I wish I knew—

The world has never known a state like this,
380 This paradox beyond analysis,
Which haunts my soul with what I cannot find,
Which makes me speechless speak and seeing blind.
I saw perfection's image, beauty's queen,
A vision that no man has ever seen
(What is the sun before that face? — God knows
It is a mote, a speck that comes and goes!).
But did I see her? What more can I say?
Between this 'yes' and 'no' I've lost my way!"

THE GRIEVING MOTHER AND THE SUFI

Beside her daughter's grave a mother grieved.
390 A sufi said: "This woman has perceived
The nature of her loss; her heart knows why
She comes to mourn, for whom she has to cry —
She grieves, but knowledge makes her fortunate:
Consider now the sufi's wretched state!
What daily, nightly vigils I must keep
And never know for whom it is I weep;
I mourn in lonely darkness, unaware
Whose absence is the cause of my despair.
Since she knows what has caused her agony,
400 She is a thousand times more blest than me —
I have no notion of what makes me weep,
What prompts the painful vigils I must keep.
My heart is lost, and here I cannot find
That rope by which men live, the rational mind —
The key to thought is lost; to reach this far
Means to despair of who and what you are.
And yet it is to see within the soul —
And at a stroke — the meaning of the Whole."

THE MAN WHO HAD LOST HIS KEY

A sufi heard a cry: "I've lost my key;
410 If it's been found, please give it back to me —
My door's locked fast; I wish to God I knew
How I could get back in. What can I do?"
The sufi said: "And why should you complain?
You know where this door is; if you remain
Outside it — even if it is shut fast —
Someone no doubt will open it at last.
You make this fuss for nothing; how much more

Should I complain, who've lost both key and door!"
But if this sufi presses on, he'll find
420 The closed or open door which haunts his mind.
Men cannot understand the sufis' state,
That deep Bewilderment which is their fate.
To those who ask: "What can I do?" reply:
"Bid all that you have done till now goodbye!"
Once in the Valley of Bewilderment
The pilgrim suffers endless discontent,
Crying: "How long must I endure delay,
Uncertainty? When shall I see the Way?
When shall I know? O, when?" But knowledge here
430 Is turned again to indecisive fear;
Complaints become a grateful eulogy
And blasphemy is faith, faith blasphemy.

The Old Age of Sheikh Nasrabad

Sheikh Nasrabad made Mecca's pilgrimage[6]
Twice twenty times, yet this could not assuage
His yearning heart. This white-haired sheikh became
A pilgrim of the pagans' sacred flame,
A naked beggar in whose heart their fire
Was mirrored by the blaze of his desire.
A passer-by said: "Shame on you, O sheikh,
440 Shame on these wretched orisons you make;
Have you performed the Moslems' pilgrimage
To be an infidel in your old age?
This is mere childishness; such blasphemy
Can only bring the sufis infamy.
What sheikh has followed this perverted way?
What is this pagan fire to which you pray?"
The sheikh said: "I have suffered from this flame,
Which burnt my clothes, my house, my noble name,
The harvest of my life, all that I knew,
450 My learning, wisdom, reputation too —
And what is left to me? — Bewilderment,
The knowledge of my burning discontent;
All thoughts of reputation soon depart
When such fierce conflagrations fire the heart.
In my despair I turn with equal hate

---

[6] **Mecca's pilgrimage:** All Muslims were and are instructed to make a pilgrimage to Mecca at least once during their lifetime.

Both from the Ka'abah[7] and this temple's gate—
If this Bewilderment should come to you
Then you will grieve, as I am forced to do."

A NOVICE SEES HIS DEAD MASTER

A novice in whose heart the faith shone bright
460 Met with his teacher in a dream one night
And said: "I tremble in bewildered fear;
How is it, master, that I see you here?
My heart became a candle when you went,
A flame that flickers with astonishment;
I seek Truth's secrets like a searching slave—
Explain to me your state beyond the grave!"
His teacher said: "I cannot understand—
Amazed, I gnaw the knuckles of my hand.
You say that you're bewildered—in this pit
470 Bewilderment seems endless, infinite!
A hundred mountains would be less to me
Than one brief speck of such uncertainty!"
[. . .]

THE BIRDS DISCOVER THE SIMORGH

The thirty birds read through the fateful page
And there discovered, stage by detailed stage,
Their lives, their actions, set out one by one—
All that their souls had ever been or done:
And this was bad enough, but as they read
They understood that it was they who'd led
The lovely Joseph into slavery—
480 Who had deprived him of his liberty
Deep in a well, then ignorantly sold
Their captive to a passing chief for gold.[8]
(Can you not see that at each breath you sell
The Joseph you imprisoned in that well,
That he will be the king to whom you must
Naked and hungry bow down in the dust?)

---

[7] Ka'abah: The sanctuary in Mecca said to have been originally constructed by Adam and reconstructed by the prophet Abraham and his son Ishmael, who were given a black stone, now in the building, to do so, and purified of idol worship by the Prophet Muhammad.

[8] led the lovely Joseph . . . for gold: Joseph's brothers, jealous of their father's favoritism, cast Joseph into a well and sold him into slavery. (See Sura 12, p. 119.)

The chastened spirits of these birds became
Like crumbled powder, and they shrank with shame.
Then, as by shame their spirits were refined
490 Of all the world's weight, they began to find
A new life flow towards them from that bright
Celestial and ever-living Light—
Their souls rose free of all they'd been before;
The past and all its actions were no more.
Their life came from that close, insistent sun
And in its vivid rays they shone as one.
There in the Simorgh's[9] radiant face they saw
Themselves, the Simorgh of the world—with awe
They gazed, and dared at last to comprehend
500 They were the Simorgh and the journey's end.
They see the Simorgh—at themselves they stare,
And see a second Simorgh standing there;
They look at both and see the two are one,
That this is that, that this, the goal is won.
They ask (but inwardly; they make no sound)
The meaning of these mysteries that confound
Their puzzled ignorance—how is it true
That 'we' is not distinguished here from 'you'?
And silently their shining Lord replies:
510 'I am a mirror set before your eyes,
And all who come before my splendour see
Themselves, their own unique reality;
You came as thirty birds and therefore saw
These selfsame thirty birds, not less nor more;
If you had come as forty, fifty—here
An answering forty, fifty, would appear;
Though you have struggled, wandered, travelled far,
It is yourselves you see and what you are.'
(Who sees the Lord? It is himself each sees;
520 What ant's sight could discern the Pleiades?
What anvil could be lifted by an ant?
Or could a fly subdue an elephant?)
'How much you thought you knew and saw; but you
Now know that all you trusted was untrue.
Though you traversed the Valleys' depths and fought
With all the dangers that the journey brought,
The journey was in Me, the deeds were Mine—

---

[9] **the Simorgh:** The meaning of this crucial moment depends on a pun: *si* means "thirty," *morgh* means "bird(s)." . . . It was probably this pun which suggested the idea of the poem to Attar. [Translators' note.]

You slept secure in Being's inmost shrine.
And since you came as thirty birds, you see
530 These thirty birds when you discover Me,
The Simorgh, Truth's last flawless jewel, the light
In which you will be lost to mortal sight,
Dispersed to nothingness until once more
You find in Me the selves you were before.'
Then, as they listened to the Simorgh's words,
A trembling dissolution filled the birds—
The substance of their being was undone,
And they were lost like shade before the sun;
Neither the pilgrims nor their guide remained.
540 The Simorgh ceased to speak, and silence reigned.

❧ JALALODDIN RUMI
1207–1283

www For links to
more information
about Rumi and a
quiz on *The Essential
Rumi,* see *World
Literature Online* at
bedfordstmartins
.com/worldlit.

For more than seven hundred years the poetry of Rumi has been a source of inspiration to followers of Islam. And because he deals with the whole range of the spiritual journey, from the sacredness of ordinary experience to the more esoteric and sophisticated teachings of MYSTICISM,[1] Rumi has had a wide following among non-Muslims as well, including Jews, Christians, Hindus, and Buddhists. British scholars produced literal but sometimes unreadable translations of Rumi's poems at the beginning of the twentieth century, but only recently has Rumi become available in English translations that begin to do justice to his poetic style and imagery. In the hands of modern translators, Rumi speaks to people of a wide variety of national and religious backgrounds. The enthusiastic modern revival of Rumi's poetry in the West coincides with a rebirth of interest in Islamic culture, non-Western spiritual traditions like Daoism and Buddhism, and the Eastern practices of yoga, tai chi chuan, and meditation.

The thirteenth century was a turbulent time across the Middle East. Early in the century Mongol armies conquered established communities from China to eastern Europe and the shores of the Mediterranean. From the eleventh to late in the thirteenth century, Europe was taken up with the Crusades, the struggle between Christians and Muslims for control of Palestine, or the Holy Land. It was a stressful time when prophets rose

---

[1] mysticism: The term *mysticism* refers to a direct, ecstatic, personal experience of the divine, but by definition, the mystical experience transcends language and learning.

Rumi Frontispiece,
1453
This sumptuously
decorated fifteenth-
century copy of
Rumi's poems testifies
to the work's
popularity through
the centuries. (The
Art Archive / Bodleian
Library, Oxford / The
Bodleian Library)

up preaching reform and renewal, and there was a revived interest in the mystical practices of established religions. Scholars of mysticism suggest that the various mystical groups around the world tend to resemble one another more closely than they resemble the established religions from which they arise. Around 1200, ZEN BUDDHISM[2] enjoyed a revival in Japan. About that same time, while a Muslim dynasty took power in much of India, the mystical religion of Hinduism, the BHAKTI,[3] moved across northern India. And the mystical branches of Judaism and Christianity were fed by the teachings of Moses Maimonides (1135–1204) and Meister Eckhart[4] (c. 1260–1327), respectively.

Rise of Sufism.   The thirteenth-century golden age of Islam was supported by the spread of Sufism, the mystical orders within Islam that seek

---

[2] **Zen Buddhism:** Zen teaches the path of *zazen,* sitting meditation, as the quickest route to enlightenment. (See Glossary, p. 1212.)

[3] **Bhakti:** Bhakti teaches the path of ecstatic surrender to God, usually in personal form, as a means to union with God. (See Glossary, p. 1189.)

[4] **Eckhart:** Besides Eckhart, Francis of Assisi (c. 1181–1226) and Hildegard von Bingen (1098–1152), among others, promoted Christian mysticism.

a personal experience of God, whom the Sufis refer to as "the Beloved."[5]
Imam Ali (598–661), the Prophet Muhammad's son-in-law, is thought to
be the first Sufi, but Sufism first became popular in the eighth and ninth

bah-yuh-ZEED
bes-tah-MEE

centuries through figures like **Bayazid Bestami** (d. 877).[6] Early Sufism
resembled Christian mysticism in its use of rosaries, mantras, and vows
of poverty and silence; Sufis were never encouraged, however, to retreat
from life into monasteries and celibacy. They were fully engaged in life
in the world; they married and had families. A subgroup known as
the dervishes practiced asceticism and wandered from village to village
preaching and dancing. The roots of Sufism lie in the Qur'an and
Muhammad's mystical visions of the angel Gabriel, but the Qur'an
teaches that believers can expect to encounter God in the world: "To God
belongs the East and the West, in whatever direction you turn to look,
there is the Face of God."

Moving from Afghanistan to Turkey.   Jalaloddin Rumi was born on
September 30, 1207, in Balkh, Afghanistan, which at the time was part of
the Persian empire. Situated near the Silk Road, along which traveled not
only goods but ideas, Balkh was a center of both Islamic and Buddhist

jah-lahl-oo-DEEN

learning. To Persians, Rumi is known as **Jalaloddin** Balkhi, "Glory of the
faith from Balkh." (The name Rumi, used only in the West, means "the
one from Roman Anatolia.") Rumi's father, Bahauddin Walad, was a theologian, teacher, and Sufi mystic. Because Mongol armies under the leadership of Chingis Khan (c. 1162–1227) began to invade the eastern reaches
of the Persian empire in 1219, Rumi's father moved the family westward
to the city of Konya in the Seljuk empire, in what today is Turkey. The
Seljuk king invited Bahauddin Walad to administer a new *madrasa,* or
college, in Konya.

Under the instruction of Burhanuddin Meliaqqiq, a student of
Rumi's father, Rumi mastered the disciplines of Arabic grammar, the

sah-NEE-yuh

Qur'an, and Islamic law as well as the writers **Sana'i** and Attar.[7] The story
is told that when Rumi was twelve years old and traveling with his father,

fah-REED
oo-DEEN ah-TAR

he met the famous poet **Farid ud-Din Attar**. Recognizing something special in the young Rumi, Attar gave him a book about the soul's journey
through the material world, the *Asranama.* After his father died, Rumi
took over his college while still in his late twenties and became the spiri-

SHEEK, SHAKE

tual master, the Shaykh, or **Sheikh**, of the Sufi community in Konya.
Despite the fact that he was an accomplished teacher of Islamic lore and

---

[5] **Sufis . . . Beloved:** The mystical orders of Islam — of which there are several — are called Sufis. The name *sufi*
comes from *suf,* meaning "wool" (the Sufis wore woolen cloaks), and *safa,* meaning "purity." A *darvesh,* or
dervish, meaning "poor" or "beggar" in Persian, is a member of a Sufi order dedicated to a life of poverty. The
name for God, "the Beloved" links human and divine love.

[6] **Bestami:** Bayazid Bestami was a famous Muslim mystic who advocated an ecstatic path to God, or "spiritual
drunkenness."

[7] **Sana'i and Attar:** The Sufi movement was supported by writers like Hakim Sana'i (died c. 1150), who wrote
The Orchard of Truth (Hadiqat al-haqiqa), and Farid ud-Din Attar (c. 1145–c. 1221), the famous author of *The
Conference of the Birds* (see p. 406).

known by the titles *Maulana,* "Our Master," and *Hazrat,* "Saint," Rumi had not yet, according to tradition, had a direct mystical experience of the divine.

Shams of Tabriz.   Rumi's life changed significantly in the fall of 1244 when at the age of thirty-seven he met the wandering mystic, **Shams-e Tabriz,**[8] meaning "the Glorious Sun of Tabriz," who was older than Rumi, maybe as old as sixty, and thought to be a "wild dervish." In one version of this encounter Shams asks Rumi who was greater, Muhammad or Bestami. Hearing the question, Rumi faints. When he recovers, Rumi answers that Muhammad was greater because his whole life was a spiritual quest while Bestami had been satisfied with one swallow of the divine.

SHAHMS eh-tah-BREEZ

Shams and Rumi spent countless hours together, chanting, praying, and dancing. Some say the attraction between them was that of master and student. If Rumi's earlier association with the Muslim faith was primarily intellectual, then his association with Shams led to a personal experience of God. It is said that the deep love Rumi and Shams had for each other opened up the divine ocean of love, the loving nature of God. Two things seem clear: First, Shams was the occasion for a profound transformation in Rumi, either as the medium for Rumi's ecstatic experience of God or through his example; second, their relationship caused dissension in the Sufi community.

After about a year and a half, Shams disappeared. When Rumi heard that Shams was in the Syrian city of Damascus, he sent his son Sultan Walad to persuade him to return. The two were reunited, and again they enjoyed extended conversations and dancing. Shams even married a girl from Rumi's household. On December 5, 1248, however, Shams again disappeared, this time for good. One theory is that he was murdered by jealous young men in the community, led by Allaedin, another of Rumi's sons, and thrown down a well. Rumi searched for Shams once more and, to fill the void, devoted himself to Sufi practices and teaching. And he began to recite poetry. One story has it that Shams told Rumi while they were still together to throw all his scholarly works into a well; when they rose again from the water the pages were blank, ready for Rumi's poetry. After a time, Rumi realized that he had absorbed Shams into his psyche and felt that Shams spoke through him. In fact, Rumi called his large poetry collection of quatrains and odes *The Works of Shams of Tabriz (Divani Shamsi Tabriz).*

All manifestations of the mystical spirit are fundamentally the same, and we shall not be astonished to encounter in remote lands and different ages of the world "one set of principles variously combined."
– R. A. NICHOLSON, 1975, historian

According to tradition, Rumi created his poems while whirling around a column in the tradition of the dervishes; his recitations were written down by his followers. He founded the Mawlawiyya (Mevlevi) Sufi order, known in the West as the "whirling dervishes" apparently in honor of Rumi's practice. Rumi's tomb in Konya, which is the seat of the Mawlawiyya Sufis, attracts pilgrims from around the world.

---

[8] **Shams-e Tabriz:** Shams, also known as Shamsruddin and Shams Din, was like the wandering, unaffiliated mendicants of both the Christian and Hindu traditions during the Middle Ages. His full name is Shamsruddin Muhammad-ebne Ali-ebne Molkdad.

roo-bigh-YAHT

Major Works. In *The Works of Shams of Tabriz,* which contains about two thousand quatrains and thirty-four hundred odes, Rumi uses poetic forms that were common to Persian poetry. In Persian, the QUATRAIN, or RUBA'I (plural, *ruba'iyat*), is an intricate form consisting of four lines of equal length, with each line divided into halves and the first, second, and fourth lines rhyming. The ODE, or GHAZAL, is equally complex; of its ten lines, the first four rhyme like the quatrain's, and then every other half line rhymes. Rumi's second major work, *Spiritual Couplets (Mathnawi),* is six books of poetry that were dictated to Husam Chelebi, Rumi's scribe, comprising a wide variety of didactic material, from folklore and animal fables to humorous parables and ecstatic lyrics. *Spiritual Couplets* has been called by some scholars "the Qur'an in Persian."

The selections presented in the following pages represent the wide variety of Rumi's poetry. "A Basket of Fresh Bread" provides an introduction to Rumi's essential message: God's presence can be experienced in ordinary people, places, and events. Since God is everywhere all the time, God is right here, right now. Several of the poems that follow deal with why the presence of God is nevertheless difficult to experience, and why one usually requires guidance from a spiritual master. "I Come Before Dawn," "Checkmate," and "Only Breath" deal with how people get trapped by their desires, their application of religious labels, their shortsightedness, and their unwillingness to simply open their hearts. Divine love, they suggest, transcends all sectarianism, all the divisions inherent in the labels of Judaism, Islam, and Christianity. The message in "When you are with everyone but me" and "The Food Sack" is that mind and knowledge, common sense and logic, can inhibit mystical visions. "The Gift of Water" engages the symbolism of water, a metaphor common to the discourse of most religions, be it the primordial waters, the waters of life, the waters of the psyche or soul, or the baptism of immortality.

The underlying message of these poems is that there is a unity behind all reality, akin to the Qur'an's *La'illaha il'Allahu,* "There's no reality but God; there is only God," a statement to which all mystics of whatever religious persuasion could agree.

Translations. Contemporary interest in Rumi and his poetry has led to a number of modern translations, and as with any translation, the results can vary a great deal. The original Persian of the quatrain numbered 1159 in Furuzanfar's standard edition, *Kulliyat-e Shams* (1957–66), reproduced below, illustrates the conventional rhyme scheme of the quatrain form:

> Eyjaan-o jahaan, jaan-o jahaan, gom kardam
> Eymaah, zameen-o aasemaan, gom kardam
> Mei bar kaf-e man manah, benah bar dahanam
> Kaz masti-e to, raah-e dahaan gom kardam

Shahram T. Shiva provides this literal translation:

> O life and \ the world \ life and \ the world \ lost \ I have
> O moon \ earth and \ the sky \ lost \ I have

> Nowhere have the impulses of Eastern and Western spirituality been more vividly expressed than in the works of the Sufi saint, Jalaluddin Rumi. His poetry is a boundless fusion of all time and cultures, all mysteries and truths; his every word came from a place of love and inspiration, a place where the soul and its Creator are one.
>
> – JONATHAN STAR, 1992, translator and poet

wine \ on \ palm of \ mine \ don't place \ place [it] \ in \ my
    mouth
because of \ drunkenness of \ you \ way to \ mouth \ lost \ I have

    (*Rending the Veil*, p. 155)

Shiva is also responsible for this poetic interpretation of the quatrain:

O life and the world, I have lost both life and the world.
O bright Moon, I have lost the earth and the sky.
Don't place more wine in my hand, pour it in my mouth.
I am so drunk on you that I have lost the way to my mouth.

This same quatrain has been rendered by Jonathan Star:

I am so drunk
I have lost the way in
    and the way out.
I have lost the earth, the moon, and the sky!
Don't put another cup of wine in my hand,
    pour it in my mouth—
For I have lost the way to my mouth!

    (*A Garden Beyond Paradise*, p. 40)

And by Coleman Barks:

Gone, inner and outer,
no moon, no ground or sky.
Don't hand me another glass of wine.
Pour it in my mouth.
I've lost the way to my mouth.

    (*The Essential Rumi*, pp. 5–6)

    In this quatrain, Rumi is describing the disorienting state of being filled or enraptured by God's love, whereby the distinctions between inner and outer, up and down are dissolved. The poem appears to be addressed to *Saaqi*, the manifestation of God as a wine-bearer, who provides divine ecstasy through the wine of love. Each of the above translations has its virtues. Shiva's renderings are closest to the original, connecting drunkenness to "you," or God, in the last line. Emphasizing the nature of ecstasy, Star leads off with drunkenness, something that is mentioned only later in the original. Barks's version is quite lean, only implying intoxication.

    Coleman Barks's translations appear in the following pages. Barks had this to say about his and his collaborator John Moyne's intentions: "John Moyne and I try to be faithful to the images, the tone as we hear it, and the spiritual information coming through. We have not tried to reproduce any of the dense musicality of the Persian originals. It has seemed appropriate to place Rumi in the strong tradition of American free verse, which has the inner searching, the delicacy, and the simple groundedness that also characterizes Rumi's poetry."

> It is the Persian of Rumi that is all-encompassing. It is the Persian of Rumi that heals spiritual wounds. It is the Persian of Rumi that initiates the seeker into the world of the unknown.
>
> – SHAHRAM T. SHIVA,
> 1995, translator

■ CONNECTIONS

Farid ud-Din Attar, *The Conference of the Birds,* **p. 406; Dante,** *The Inferno,* **p. 689.** The mystical experience in literature is commonly portrayed as a journey that leads to enlightenment or an ecstatic vision. Attar tells of the pilgrimage of a group of birds and Dante writes of one man's descent into the underworld and his subsequent ascent to heaven to portray the necessary conditioning of the soul for a beatific vision. What metaphors does Rumi employ to suggest the necessary preparations for an ecstatic encounter with the divine?

Hebrew Scriptures, Song of Songs (Book 1). When God is manifest in the natural world, the distance between the sensual and the spiritual can be narrow to nonexistent. The Song of Songs indicates the passion and intimacy of God's love through images of plants and animals. How do Rumi's images of bread and water convey the proximity of the divine?

Geoffrey Chaucer, "The Wife of Bath's Tale," p. 924. In Western literature, such as "The Wife of Bath's Tale," the attractions of the physical world are portrayed as barriers to spiritual experience, while in Eastern literature it is the mind and the personal ego that seem to get in the way of the mystical. According to Rumi, what are the distractions that prevent humans from experiencing God's love?

■ FURTHER RESEARCH

Translations
Arberry, A. J., trans. *Mystical Poems of Rumi.* 1979.
————. *The Rubaiyat of Jalal al-din Rumi.* 1949.
Nicholson, Reynold, trans. *The Mathnawi of Jalaluddin Rumi.* 1925–1940.
Shiva, Shahram T. *Rending the Veil: Literal and Poetic Translations of Rumi.* 1995.
Star, Jonathan, and Shahram T. Shiva. *A Garden Beyond Paradise: The Mystical Poetry of Rumi.* 1992.

Background and Commentary
Arberry, A. J. *Sufism: An Account of the Mystics of Islam.* 1968.
Chittick, William. *The Sufi Path of Love.* 1983.
Friedlander, Ira. *The Whirling Dervishes.* 1991.
Hakim, Khalifa Abdul. *The Metaphysics of Rumi.* 1977.
Iqbal, Afzal. *The Life and Work of Jalaloddin Rumi.* 1983.
Schimmel, Annemarie. *Mystical Dimensions of Islam.* 1975.
————. *The Triumphal Sun: A Study of the Works of Jalaloddin Rumi.* 1978.

■ PRONUNCIATION

Farid ud-Din Attar: fah-REED oo-DEEN ah-TAR, AT-ur
Bayazid Bestami: bah-yuh-ZEED bes-tah-MEE
Hakim Sana'i: hah-KEEM sah-NEE-yuh
Jalaloddin: jah-lahl-oo-DEEN
Mahmud Shabestari: mah-MOOD shah-bes-tah-REE, mah-HMOOD
Rabi'a of Basra: rah-BEE-yah, BAHS-ruh
ruba'iyat: roo-bigh-YAHT
Shams-e Tabriz: SHAHMS eh-tah-BREEZ
Sheikh: SHEEK, SHAKE

FROM

ɷ The Essential Rumi

Translated by Coleman Barks

A Basket of Fresh Bread

The Prophet Muhammad said,
                    "There is no better companion
on this way than what you do. Your actions will be
your best friend, or if you're cruel and selfish,
your actions will be a poisonous snake
that lives in your grave."
               But tell me,
can you do the good work without a teacher?
Can you even know what it is without the presence
of a Master? Notice how the lowest livelihood
requires some instruction.
                   First comes knowledge,
then the doing of the job. And much later,
perhaps after you're dead, something grows
from what you've done.
               Look for help and guidance
in whatever craft you're learning. Look for a generous
teacher, one who has absorbed the tradition he's in.

Look for pearls in oyster shells.
Learn technical skill from a craftsman.

Whenever you meet genuine spiritual teachers,
be gentle and polite and fair with them.

10

The Essential Rumi. Rumi's individual poems were not originally titled in Persian. Translator Coleman Barks provided titles for most of the selections here. "A Basket of Fresh Bread" comes from the *Mathnawi* and deals with the need for spiritual guidance and for looking inside rather than outside the self for the divine. The divine experience is immediate and manifest, rather than distant and transcendent. "I Come Before Dawn" and "Checkmate" also come from the *Mathnawi*, and deal with resistance to God's love as well as the fact that the soul must be tested and trained. "When you are with everyone but me" is a quatrain from *The Works of Shams* that uses paradox for instruction, and "The Food Sack," from the *Mathnawi*, describes a moment of epiphany wherein a common object, an empty food sack, becomes an emblem of spiritual quest. In "The Gift of Water," also from the *Mathnawi*, a lovely parable introduces a spiritual lesson about divine reality. "Only Breath" is a reworking of a translation quoted in Pir Ilayat Khan's *The Message in Our Time* (New York: Harper & Row, 1978, p. 426); the mystical experience of the Beloved transcends all religious labels, all the limitations of time and space.

20   Ask them questions, and be eager
        for answers. Never condescend.

        If a master tanner wears an old, threadbare smock,
        that doesn't diminish his mastery.

        If a fine blacksmith works at the bellows
        in a patched apron, it doesn't affect
        how he bends the iron.
                            Strip away your pride,
        and put on humble clothes.
                            If you want to learn theory,
        talk with theoreticians. That way is oral.

        When you learn a craft, practice it.
        That learning comes through the *hands*.

30   If you want dervishhood, spiritual poverty,
        and emptiness, you must be friends with a sheikh.[1]

        Talking about it, reading books, and doing practices
        don't help. Soul receives from soul that knowing.

        The mystery of spiritual emptiness
        may be living in a pilgrim's heart, and yet
        the knowing of it may not yet be his.

        Wait for the illuminating openness,
        as though your chest were filling with light,
        as when God said,
                            Did We not expand you?
                                            (Qur'an 94:1)

40   Don't look for it outside yourself.
        You are the source of milk. Don't milk others!

        There is a milk fountain inside you.
        Don't walk around with an empty bucket.

        You have a channel into the ocean, and yet
        you ask for water from a little pool.

        Beg for that love expansion. Meditate only
        on THAT. The Qur'an says,

---

[1] **sheikh:** Also Sheik or Shaykh, the title for an Islamic teacher, master, or official.

And He is with you
(57:4).
There is a basket of fresh bread on your head,
and yet you go door to door asking for crusts.

50 Knock on your inner door. No other.
Sloshing knee-deep in fresh riverwater, yet
you keep wanting a drink from other people's waterbags.

Water is everywhere around you, but you see only
barriers that keep you from water.
The horse is beneath the rider's thighs, and still
he asks, "Where's my horse?"
                    Right there, under you!
"Yes, this is a horse, but where's the horse?"
                    Can't you see!
"Yes, I can see, but whoever saw such a horse?"

Mad with thirst, he can't drink from the stream
60 running so close by his face. He's like a pearl
on the deep bottom, wondering, inside his shell,
Where's the ocean?
                    His mental questionings
form the barrier. His physical eyesight
bandages his knowing. Self-consciousness
plugs his ears.
                    Stay bewildered in God,
and only that.
                    Those of you who are scattered,
simplify your worrying lives. There is *one*
righteousness: Water the fruit trees,
and don't water the thorns. Be generous
70 to what nurtures the spirit and God's luminous
reason-light. Don't honor what causes
dysentery and knotted-up tumors.

Don't feed both sides of yourself equally.
The spirit and the body carry different loads
and require different attentions.
                    Too often
we put saddlebags on Jesus[2] and let the donkey

---

[2] **Jesus:** In several poems Rumi shows his admiration for Jesus as a spiritual master, although in "One Who Wraps Himself," which is about the need for actively participating in society, Rumi states, "Do not practice solitude like Jesus. Be *in* / the assembly, and take charge of it."

run loose in the pasture.
                              Don't make the body do
what the spirit does best, and don't put a big load
on the spirit that the body could carry easily.

I COME BEFORE DAWN

Muhammad says,
                "I come before dawn
to chain you and drag you off."
It's amazing, and funny, that you have to be pulled away
from being tortured, pulled out
into this Spring garden,
                              but that's the way it is.

Almost everyone must be bound and dragged here.
Only a few come on their own.

Children have to be made to go to school at first.
Then some of them begin to like it.
                              They run to school.
They expand with the learning.
10   Later, they receive money
because of something they've learned at school,
and they get really excited. They stay up all night,
as watchful and alive as thieves!

Remember the rewards you get for being obedient!

There are two types on the path. Those who come
against their will, the blindly religious people, and those
who obey out of love. The former have ulterior motives.
They want the midwife near, because she gives them milk.
The others love the beauty of the nurse.

20 The former memorize the prooftexts of conformity,
and repeat them. The latter disappear
into whatever draws them to God.

Both are drawn from the source.
Any movings from the mover.
Any love from the beloved.

CHECKMATE

Borrow the beloved's eyes.
Look through them and you'll see the beloved's face
everywhere. No tiredness, no jaded boredom.
"I shall be your eye and your hand and your loving."
Let that happen, and things
you have hated will become helpers.

A certain preacher always prays long and with enthusiasm
for thieves and muggers that attack people
on the street. "Let your mercy, O Lord,
cover their insolence."
He doesn't pray for the good,
but only for the blatantly cruel.
Why is this? his congregation asks.

"Because they have done me such generous favors.
Every time I turn back toward the things they want.
I run into them, they beat me, and leave me nearly dead
in the road, and I understand, again, that what they want
is not what I want. They keep me on the spiritual path.
That's why I honor them and pray for them."

Those that make you return, for whatever reason,
to God's solitude, be grateful to them.
Worry about the others, who give you
delicious comforts that keep you from prayer.
Friends are enemies sometimes,
and enemies friends.

There is an animal called an *ushghur,* a porcupine.
If you hit it with a stick, it extends its quills
and gets bigger. The soul is a porcupine,
made strong by stick-beating.

So a prophet's soul is especially afflicted,
because it has to become so powerful.

A hide is soaked in tanning liquor and becomes leather.
If the tanner did not rub in the acid,
the hide would get foul-smelling and rotten.

The soul is a newly skinned hide, bloody and gross.
Work on it with manual discipline,
and the bitter tanning acid of grief,
and you'll become lovely, and *very* strong.

40   If you can't do this work yourself, don't worry.
You don't even have to make a decision,
one way or another. The Friend, who knows
a lot more than you do, will bring difficulties,
and grief, and sickness,

                as medicine, as happiness,

as the essence of the moment when you're beaten,
when you hear *Checkmate,* and can finally say,
with Hallaj's voice,[3]

          I trust you to kill me.

WHEN YOU ARE WITH EVERYONE BUT ME

When you are with everyone but me,
    you're with no one.
When you are with no one but me,
    you're with everyone.

Instead of being so bound up *with* everyone,
    be everyone.
When you become that many, you're nothing.
    Empty.

THE FOOD SACK

One day a sufi sees an empty food sack hanging on a nail.
He begins to turn and tear his shirt, saying,
Food for what needs no food!
A cure for hunger!

His burning grows and others join him,
shouting and moaning in the love-fire.

An idle passerby comments, "It's only an empty sack."

The sufi says, *Leave. You want what we do not want.*
You are not a lover.

---

[3] **Hallaj's voice:** Mansur Al-Hallaj is the Sufi mystic martyred in Baghdad in 922 for saying *"Ana'l-Haqq,"* or "I am the truth," "I am God." [Translator's note.]

10 A lover's food is the love of bread,
    not the bread. No one who really loves,
    loves existence.

    Lovers have nothing to do with existence.
    They collect the interest without the capital.

    No wings, yet they fly all over the world. No hands,
    but they carry the polo ball from the field.

    That dervish got a sniff of reality.
    Now he weaves baskets of pure vision.

    Lovers pitch tents on a field of nowhere.
20 They are all one color like that field.

    A nursing baby does not know the taste of roasted meat.
    To a spirit the foodless scent is food.

    To an Egyptian, the Nile looks bloody.
    To an Israelite, clear.
    What is a highway to one is disaster to the other.

THE GIFT OF WATER

Someone who doesn't know the Tigris River exists
brings the caliph who lives near the river
a jar of fresh water. The caliph accepts, thanks him,
and gives in return a jar filled with gold coins.

"Since this man has come through the desert,
he should return by water." Taken out by another door,
the man steps into a waiting boat
and sees the wide freshwater of the Tigris.
He bows his head, "What wonderful kindness
10 that he took my gift."

Every object and being in the universe is
a jar overfilled with wisdom and beauty,
a drop of the Tigris that cannot be contained
by any skin. Every jarful spills and makes the earth
more shining, as though covered in satin.
If the man had seen even a tributary

of the great river, he wouldn't have brought
the innocence of his gift.

Those that stay and live by the Tigris
20   grow so ecstatic that they throw rocks at the jugs,
and the jugs become perfect!
                              They shatter.
The pieces dance, and water . . . .
                              Do you see?
Neither jar, nor water, nor stone,
                                   nothing.

You knock at the door of reality,
shake your thought-wings, loosen
your shoulders,
                              and open.

ONLY BREATH

Not Christian or Jew or Muslim, not Hindu,
Buddhist, sufi, or zen. Not any religion

or cultural system. I am not from the East
or the West, not out of the ocean or up

from the ground, not natural or ethereal, not
composed of elements at all. I do not exist,

am not an entity in this world or the next,
did not descend from Adam and Eve or any

origin story. My place is placeless, a trace
10   of the traceless. Neither body or soul.

I belong to the beloved, have seen the two
worlds as one and that one call to and know,

first, last, outer, inner, only that
breath breathing human being.

THE THOUSAND AND ONE NIGHTS
THIRTEENTH CENTURY–FOURTEENTH CENTURY

The collection of tales known as *The Thousand and One Nights* or *The Arabian Nights* is undoubtedly the best-known work of Middle Eastern literature in the West, where the stories of Ali Baba, Aladdin, and Sindbad are as familiar as Cinderella and Little Red Riding Hood and have been made into movies by Hollywood studios on an almost annual basis. From the time of their first translation into French at the beginning of the eighteenth century, the tales have been perennial favorites, prompting many translations, imitations, sequels, and revisions. Even before the eighteenth century, the folk process that had transmitted these stories from one generation to the next in the East had allowed for some of them to reach the West, so that analogous stories appear in the works of such writers as Boccaccio, Chaucer, and Shakespeare.[1] Once they were in general circulation, Scottish novelist Robert Louis Stevenson (1850–1894) claimed that the Arabian stories were even more popular than Shakespeare. In "A Gossip on Romance" (1882), he asserts: "There is one book, for example, more generally loved than Shakespeare, that captivates in childhood, and still delights in age—I mean the *Arabian Nights*—where you shall look in vain for moral or for intellectual interest.... Adventure, on the most naked terms, furnishes forth the entertainment and is found enough."

www For a quiz on *The Thousand and One Nights*, see *World Literature Online* at bedfordstmartins.com/worldlit.

History of the Tales. The stories collected in *The Thousand and One Nights* are deeply rooted in an oral tradition. Romantic accounts tell of traders traveling the Silk Road between Asia and the West who gathered at caravanseries, or inns, in the evenings to exchange the stories eventually collected in *Arabian Nights*. While some of the tales may date back to pre-Islamic times, the first written collection, *A Thousand Legends* (*Hazar Afsanah*) is dated at about 850 C.E. The earliest extant manuscript is a single page dating from 879 that contains the opening dedication, the mention of two characters, Dinarzad and **Shahrazad**, and a few lines in which the former asks the latter to tell a story.

shih-heh-ruh-ZAHD

The earliest substantial manuscript of *The Arabian Nights*, from Syria, is dated between the second half of the thirteenth century and the first half of the fourteenth century. This manuscript, now in the Louvre, in Paris, was the basis of the first European translation, by Antoine Galland (1646–1715) into French, published in 1704. Galland purchased the manuscript in Istanbul while serving there as an assistant to the French ambassador. That manuscript did not contain 1,001 stories or even 1,001 nights. Clearly, the title was not originally intended literally but rather

---

[1] **Boccaccio . . . Shakespeare:** Analogous versions of "The Story of the Sleeper Awakened" from *The Arabian Nights* are found in *The Decameron* (1353) by Italian Giovanni Boccaccio and in English playwright William Shakespeare's *The Taming of the Shrew* (1594). English poet Geoffrey Chaucer's "The Squire's Tale," from *The Canterbury Tales* (c. 1387), is similar to the Arabian story "The Ebony Horse."

Illustration from *The Thousand and One Nights,* **1760–70**
With the translation in 1704 of The Thousand and One Nights *into French, the West became captivated by a collection of tales already famous in other parts of the world. This illustration of the work is from an eighteenth-century Indian manuscript produced during the reign of the Mughals, Muslim rulers of India. (The Art Archive / Bodleian Library, Oxford / The Bodleian Library)*

was meant to indicate "numerous" stories. Galland's version, comprising 281 nights, added stories from sources other than the Syrian manuscript. Its popularity encouraged Galland and others to seek out or invent the "lost" stories to bring the inventory up to 1,001. This process of discovering or inventing the complete canon of the tales was pursued by both Western translators and Middle Eastern editors. During the European Enlightenment of the eighteenth century the awakened interest in "the Orient," the term used by Europeans to describe the Asian lands to their east, gave added impetus to this pursuit. Egyptian editors were particularly successful in both recovering missing material and creating new tales. By the end of the nineteenth century, editions that included a full 1,001 nights had been published. Richard Burton's monumental sixteen-volume translation published in 1885–1888 collected all the tales and rendered them unabridged, accompanied by elaborate footnotes on Middle Eastern culture, especially sexual customs. Burton sought to shock as well as educate his Victorian audience. Since other editors and translators had removed or censored the erotic tales and passages, Burton's edition, in spite of its idiosyncrasies and excesses of style, became the standard English edition of the work, for adults at least, until the 1980s.

In 1984 Muhsin Mahdi, a professor of Arabic at Harvard, working from both Syrian and Egyptian manuscripts, constructed an "archetype" edition of the work, an edition including only those tales on which the earliest Syrian manuscript was based. Mahdi's edition, published in 1984 in Arabic as *Alf Laylah Wa Laylah,* did not contain the popular tales of Sindbad, Ali Baba and the Forty Thieves, or Aladdin, all of which Mahdi judged to be later additions. The English translation of Mahdi's work by Husain Haddawy (1990) is now considered the most accessible version in English. The excerpts presented in these pages come from that edition, though the "Conclusion" that rounds out the frame narrative, a section that was not part of the medieval Syrian manuscript or the Mahdi edition, has been added from an earlier translation.

Although the Mahdi edition is most times thought of as the authoritative scholarly text, some scholars have questioned its assumptions. To judge one edition or time period to be more "authentic" than others for a work that emerged from an oral tradition and that continued to accrue new materials over its published life, some argue, distorts the folk process that created the work and that continues to change it. The stories of Sindbad, Ali Baba, and Aladdin, although possibly later additions, seem to many central to the tradition that is *The Arabian Nights;* after first publishing his translation of the Mahdi edition, Husain Haddawy came out with an expanded translation in 1996 that includes these famous tales. Rather than the work of a single author or even a single period, the original *Thousand and One Nights* was an ongoing project, like the building of a cathedral, that spanned generations, even centuries. Argentine author Jorge Luis Borges (1899–1986) used just such a metaphor to describe the work's creation: "To erect the palace of *The 1001 Nights,*" he wrote, "took generations of men, and those men are our benefactors, as we have inherited this inexhaustible book, this book capable of so much metamorphosis." Even today writers are revising the story of Shahrazad and the sultan and devising new "Arabian Nights" tales. Among the many

Read Sindbad the
Sailor's voyages and
you will be sick of
Aeneas's.

  – HORACE WALPOLE,
    in a letter to Mary
    Berry, 1789, novelist

recent additions to the tradition are sequels to the Shahrazad story by American novelist John Barth (*Chimera,* 1972), Egyptian novelist Naguib Mahfouz (*Arabian Nights and Days,* 1982), and Indian feminist Githa Haribaran (*When Dreams Travel,* 1999).

History and Society.   The stories in *Arabian Nights* come from many different times. Some of the oldest tales are pre-Islamic, and many can be traced to India. Other stories were added over the centuries, by both Eastern and Western interpolators, so that the editions that exist today include tales from pre-Islamic times up to the nineteenth century. The archetypal text assembled by Muhsin Mahdi represents a medieval version of the work based on the earliest surviving manuscript from fourteenth-century Syria. Since this version was the ultimate source for nearly all Western translations, the Islamic context of the tales and the magical city of Baghdad that figures in many of them have become defining characteristics of the collection. Daniel Beaumont describes *The Arabian Nights* as stories that "wear the garb of the late medieval [. . .] Arab-Islamic world, the eras of the Mamluks and the Ottomans, that is. Thus, stories about the Abbasid caliph Harun al-Rashid, who ruled about six centuries before Ottoman Turks established their power, may reflect popular notions about how an Ottoman sultan lived in the fifteenth century [. . .] more than they reflect [. . .] the way Harun lived six hundred years earlier."

hah-ROON
ahl-rah-SHEED

The Baghdad of Caliph **Harun al-Rashid** (766–809), the setting of many of the tales, is imagined as the center of a magical kingdom with Harun as its enlightened ruler. The largest city west of China, with a population of at least a half million, Baghdad in the eighth century was reportedly an architectural wonder. At its center was the Round City of Mansur, the *Madinat al-Salaam,* or City of Peace, constructed by Harun's grandfather al-Mansur, the second caliph, in 762. The city, according to ninth-century observer al-Jahiz, appeared as if it had been "poured into a mould and cast." The caliph's domed palace was situated at the center of the perfectly circular city, which was 3,000 yards in diameter and contained three additional concentric circular walls between the palace and the city's edge. Four gates in the outer circle were aligned with roads that radiated to the four corners of the kingdom. The beauty of the palaces, the gardens, and the city as a whole, and the luxurious way of life pursued by the caliph, are celebrated in many stories in *Thousand and One Nights* as a golden age of Islamic culture. By the end of Harun's reign at the beginning of the ninth century, when tensions in the far-flung empire sparked wars between Harun's sons, the Round City was destroyed. Founded in the thirteenth century, the Ottoman empire in Turkey was pushing into Asia Minor and eastern Europe in the fourteenth century. The glory of Harun's earlier Muslim empire projected a model and ideal for the young and ambitious Ottomans.

The *Nights* in Arabic Literature.   Although *The Arabian Nights* is probably the best-known work of Arabic literature in the West, the work that characterizes Islamic culture for many Westerners, it is not representative of Arabic literature. Unlike other works of classical Arabic literature, the

Nights is written primarily in prose rather than poetry; it uses a mixture of literary styles, especially a colloquial, nonliterary language; and its frequently risqué subject matter departs from the usual philosophical and historical subjects of Arabic writings. Most Islamic scholars discount the importance of *Nights* and consider its popularity in the West unfortunate, for it has reinforced Western stereotypes of Arabs as devious tricksters, superstitious know-nothings, and misogynistic despots indulging in exotic luxury and decadent sensuality. Nevertheless, this popular collection of stories is almost the only literature about the common people in medieval Islamic culture, as most classical Arabic literature treats the lives of the rich and powerful and avoids fiction in favor of historical accounts. *The Arabian Nights* is almost alone in Arabic literature in celebrating the imagined worlds possible only in fiction. Like the stories in the *Nights,* the folk and fairy tales of the West also employ stereotypes, indulge in bawdy jokes, and delight in the impossible. The stories in Boccaccio's *Decameron* (1353); Charles Perrault's *Tales from Times Past with Morals* (1697), a collection including "Little Red Riding Hood" and "Cinderella"; and the folktales gathered by Romantic collectors like the Brothers Grimm (1812–15) are comparable works in the Western tradition.

In stories that celebrate the fanciful—miraculous incidents and worlds conceivable only in the imagination—chance plays a large role; this may be a perspective peculiar to common people, whose lives were often determined by others. In the Middle Ages, before science provided at least the illusion of control, the threat of plague that prompts the stories in Boccaccio's *Decameron* and the vagaries of arbitrary despots that occasion the action in many of the Arabian tales, for example, were perceived as uncontrollable realities. Indeed the stories offer solace to those adversely affected by unpredictable forces. Escaping the plague or surviving despotism at times may have been determined by chance, and fanciful stories, with their coincidences and miracles, suggest that chance can sometimes work in one's favor.

Although the individual stories in *The Thousand and One Nights* are noted for their power to entertain rather than to instruct or moralize, the collection as a whole does have a plot and a serious point to make. The frame narrative of Shahrazad and the despotic sultan Shahrazar is the story of an encounter between despotic male power, which asserts control through destruction, and the life-affirming female principle, devoted to creativity and survival. Shahrazar, who discovered his wife's infidelity and deception, vows to sleep with a new virgin every night and have her put to death in the morning so as never to be betrayed again. Shahrazad's storytelling challenges his despotism and suggests that art can save lives, not only Shahrazad's and her sister's but also those of the sultan, his brother, and their subjects, for the rulers are ultimately changed by listening to Shahrazad's tales. The very form of the narrative, with stories generating stories within stories, affirms a principle of creative generation, creative vitality triumphing over destructive negativity. By the end of the thousand and one nights of storytelling, the sultan has been transformed. Rather than fearing betrayal and disappointment, he delights in Shahrazad's storytelling and trusts in her fidelity. Furthermore, he passes these life-affirming attitudes onto his brother. Finally, he

I used to wish the *Arabian Tales* were true: my imagination ran on unknown influences, magic powers and talismans.

– CARDINAL JOHN HENRY NEWMAN. *Apologia pro Vita Sua,* 1864, Author

is ready to learn that he has unknowingly fathered two children during the three-year-period that has passed. By the end of *The Arabian Nights*, creation — both of life and art — has displaced fear and violence.

■ CONNECTIONS

Giovanni Boccaccio, *The Decameron*, p. 850; Geoffrey Chaucer, *The Canterbury Tales*, p. 885; Marguerite de Navarre, *The Heptameron* (Book 3). Three great works of fiction from the late Middle Ages and the early Renaissance in the West — Chaucer's *Canterbury Tales*, Boccaccio's *Decameron*, and de Navarre's *Heptameron* — are collections of stories told within a larger narrative. Consider the ways in which the stories in each of these works relate to their frame narrative. In each case, is the frame narrative more important than the individual tales it comprises? How significant is the teller of each of the tales?

Homer, *The Odyssey* (Book 1); Virgil, *The Aeneid* (Book 1). The journey narratives in Homer's *Odyssey* and Virgil's *Aeneid* frame the individual episodes in the story of these two heroes, such as Odysseus's series of adventures and escapes. Aeneas's recounting his trials to Dido and others in Carthage lends a seductive power to his storytelling, similar to the appeal of Shahrazad's. Consider the journey that frames each of the heroic narratives. How do the stories within that journey relate to the journey itself? How does Shahrazad's frame story differ from a travel narrative? Could those differences be attributed to the gender of the storytellers?

Rabindranath Tagore, "The Hungry Stones" (Book 5); Alifa Rifaat, "My World of the Unknown" (Book 6). Many storytellers have employed the narrative techniques of *The Arabian Nights*. Two examples in *The Bedford Anthology of World Literature* are Tagore, who employs a frame narrative in "The Hungry Stones" to tell a story of a haunted palace, and Rifaat, whose story of an ethereal serpent in "My World of the Unknown" recalls the supernatural atmosphere of *Nights*.

■ FURTHER RESEARCH

Translations

Burton, Richard. *A Plain and Literal Translation of the Arabian Nights Entertainments, Now Entitled the Book of the Thousand Nights and a Night.* 1885–88. Several contemporary versions and selections from this translation are available.
Haddawy, Husain. *The Arabian Nights.* 1990.

Criticism and Commentary

Beaumont, Daniel E. *Slave of Desire: Sex, Love and Death in The 1001 Nights.* 2002.
Gerhardt, Mia. *The Art of Story-telling: A Literary Study of the Thousand and One Nights.* 1963.
Hovannisian, Richard, and Georges Sabagh, eds. *The Thousand and One Nights in Arabic Literature and Society.* 1997.
Irwin, Robert. *The Arabian Nights: A Companion.* 1994.
Mahdi, Muhsin. *The Thousand and One Nights.* 1995.
Pinault, David. *Story-telling Techniques in the Arabian Nights.* 1992.
Sallis, Eva. *Sheherazade through the Looking Glass: The Metamorphosis of the Thousand and One Nights.* 1999.

■ PRONUNCIATION

Dinarzad, Dunyazād: dee-nar-ZAHD
Harun al-Rashid: hah-ROON ahl-rah-SHEED
Shahrayar, Shahryār: shah-rah-YAHR
Shahrazad, Shahrazād: shah-rah-ZAHD (= Scheherazade, which is shih-heh-ruh-ZAHD)

FROM

❧ The Arabian Nights

Translated by Husain Haddawy

FOREWORD

In the Name of God the Compassionate, The Merciful.
In Him I Trust

Praise be to God, the Beneficent King, the Creator of the world and man, who raised the heavens without pillars and spread out the earth as a place of rest and erected the mountains as props and made the water flow from the hard rock and destroyed the race of Thamud, 'Ad, and Pharaoh of the vast domain.[1] I praise Him the Supreme Lord for His guidance, and I thank Him for His infinite grace.

To proceed, I should like to inform the honorable gentlemen and noble readers that the purpose of writing this agreeable and entertaining book is the instruction of those who peruse it, for it abounds with highly edifying histories and excellent lessons for the people of distinction, and it provides them with the opportunity to learn the art of discourse, as well as what happened to kings from the beginnings of time. This book, which I have called *The Thousand and One Nights,* abounds also with splendid biographies that teach the reader to detect deception and to protect himself from it, as well as delight and divert him whenever he is burdened with the cares of life and the ills of this world. It is the Supreme God who is the True Guide.

The Arabian Nights. Selections from this work have been taken from two translations. The opening of the frame story and the tales of the first eight nights are from the best contemporary English translation, by Husain Haddawy of the "archetype" text developed by Muhsin Mahdi, and the conclusion of the frame narrative, which appears in later versions of the story only, is from the early twentieth century translation by Powys Mathers.

In the frame narrative, the cruel sultan Shahrayar avenges his wife's infidelity by sleeping with a new virgin each evening and having her killed in the morning, and the imaginative Shahrazad, one of the virgins, saves her life and transforms the sultan through storytelling. Her first eight tales indicate the variety of stories in the *Nights* and are examples of tales that lead into or enclose other tales and comment obliquely on the issues in the frame narrative. The vizier begins the tale-telling with the stories he tells to his daughter, Shahrazad, as he attempts to discourage her from going to the sultan. When the animal fable, "The Ox and the Donkey," fails to convince her, he goes on to the related story of "The Merchant and His Wife," which also fails to deter her. Shahrazad turns out to be a more successful storyteller than her father, for she succeeds in keeping the sultan from cutting off her head and ultimately converts him into a good king, a loving husband, and a father.

A note on the translation: Notes are editors' unless otherwise specified. The spelling of names (i.e., Shahrayar, Shahrazar) vary from text to text.

---

[1]**Thamud . . . vast domain:** No specific Egyptian pharaoh is referred to here. Thamud and 'Ad were two neighboring tribes on the Arabian peninsula who were destroyed by natural disasters. They are referred to in pre-Islamic poetry and the Qur'an, and their destruction is cited as an example of God's wrath against blasphemy. [Translator's note.]

PROLOGUE: [THE STORY OF KING SHAHRAYAR
AND SHAHRAZAD, HIS VIZIER'S DAUGHTER]

It is related—but God knows and sees best what lies hidden in the old accounts of bygone peoples and times—that long ago, during the time of the Sasanid dynasty,[2] in the peninsulas of India and Indochina, there lived two kings who were brothers. The older brother was named Shahrayar, the younger Shahzaman. The older, Shahrayar, was a towering knight and a daring champion, invincible, energetic, and implacable. His power reached the remotest corners of the land and its people, so that the country was loyal to him, and his subjects obeyed him. Shahrayar himself lived and ruled in India and Indochina, while to his brother he gave the land of Samarkand to rule as king.

Ten years went by, when one day Shahrayar felt a longing for his brother the king, summoned his vizier[3] (who had two daughters, one called Shahrazad, the other Dinarzad) and bade him go to his brother. Having made preparations, the vizier journeyed day and night until he reached Samarkand.[4] When Shahzaman heard of the vizier's arrival, he went out with his retainers to meet him. He dismounted, embraced him, and asked him for news from his older brother, Shahrayar. The vizier replied that he was well, and that he had sent him to request his brother to visit him. Shahzaman complied with his brother's request and proceeded to make preparations for the journey. In the meantime, he had the vizier camp on the outskirts of the city, and took care of his needs. He sent him what he required of food and fodder, slaughtered many sheep in his honor, and provided him with money and supplies, as well as many horses and camels.

For ten full days he prepared himself for the journey; then he appointed a chamberlain in his place, and left the city to spend the night in his tent, near the vizier. At midnight he returned to his palace in the city, to bid his wife good-bye. But when he entered the palace, he found his wife lying in the arms of one of the kitchen boys. When he saw them, the world turned dark before his eyes and, shaking his head, he said to himself, "I am still here, and this is what she has done when I was barely outside the city. How will it be and what will happen behind my back when I go to visit my brother in India? No. Women are not to be trusted." He got exceedingly angry, adding, "By God, I am king and sovereign in Samarkand, yet my wife has betrayed me and has inflicted this on me." As his anger boiled, he drew his sword and struck both his wife and the cook. Then he dragged them by the heels and threw them from the top of the palace to the trench below. He then left the city and, going to the vizier, ordered that they depart that very hour. The drum was struck, and they set out on their journey, while Shahzaman's heart was on fire because of what his wife had done to him and how she had betrayed him with some cook, some kitchen boy. They

---

[2] **Sasanid dynasty:** A dynasty of Persian kings who ruled from c. 226 to 641 C.E. [Translator's note.]

[3] **vizier:** The highest state official or administrator under a caliph or a king; literally, "one who bears burdens." [Translator's note.]

[4] **Samarkand:** A city in what today is Uzbekistan.

journeyed hurriedly, day and night, through deserts and wilds, until they reached the land of King Shahrayar, who had gone out to receive them.

When Shahrayar met them, he embraced his brother, showed him favors, and treated him generously. He offered him quarters in a palace adjoining his own, for King Shahrayar had built two beautiful towering palaces in his garden, one for the guests, the other for the women and members of his household. He gave the guest house to his brother, Shahzaman, after the attendants had gone to scrub it, dry it, furnish it, and open its windows, which overlooked the garden. Thereafter, Shahzaman would spend the whole day at his brother's, return at night to sleep at the palace, then go back to his brother the next morning. But whenever he found himself alone and thought of his ordeal with his wife, he would sigh deeply, then stifle his grief, and say, "Alas, that this great misfortune should have happened to one in my position!" Then he would fret with anxiety, his spirit would sag, and he would say, "None has seen what I have seen." In his depression, he ate less and less, grew pale, and his health deteriorated. He neglected everything, wasted away, and looked ill.

When King Shahrayar looked at his brother and saw how day after day he lost weight and grew thin, pale, ashen, and sickly, he thought that this was because of his expatriation and homesickness for his country and his family, and he said to himself, "My brother is not happy here. I should prepare a goodly gift for him and send him home." For a month he gathered gifts for his brother; then he invited him to see him and said, "Brother, I would like you to know that I intend to go hunting and pursue the roaming deer, for ten days. Then I shall return to prepare you for your journey home. Would you like to go hunting with me?" Shahzaman replied, "Brother, I feel distracted and depressed. Leave me here and go with God's blessing and help." When Shahrayar heard his brother, he thought that his dejection was because of his homesickness for his country. Not wishing to coerce him, he left him behind, and set out with his retainers and men. When they entered the wilderness, he deployed his men in a circle to begin trapping and hunting.

After his brother's departure, Shahzaman stayed in the palace and, from the window overlooking the garden, watched the birds and trees as he thought of his wife and what she had done to him, and sighed in sorrow. While he agonized over his misfortune, gazing at the heavens and turning a distracted eye on the garden, the private gate of his brother's palace opened, and there emerged, strutting like a dark-eyed deer, the lady, his brother's wife, with twenty slave-girls, ten white and ten black. While Shahzaman looked at them, without being seen, they continued to walk until they stopped below his window, without looking in his direction, thinking that he had gone to the hunt with his brother. Then they sat down, took off their clothes, and suddenly there were ten slave-girls and ten black slaves dressed in the same clothes as the girls. Then the ten black slaves mounted the ten girls, while the lady called, "Mas'ud, Mas'ud!" and a black slave jumped from the tree to the ground, rushed to her, and, raising her legs, went between her thighs and made love to her. Mas'ud topped the lady, while the ten slaves topped the ten girls, and they carried on till noon. When they were done with their business, they got up and washed themselves. Then the ten slaves put on the same clothes again, mingled with the girls, and once more there appeared to be twenty slave-girls. Mas'ud himself jumped over the garden wall and disappeared, while the slave-girls and the lady sauntered to the private gate, went in and, locking the gate behind them, went their way.

All of this happened under King Shahzaman's eyes. When he saw this spectacle of the wife and the women of his brother the great king—how ten slaves put on women's clothes and slept with his brother's paramours and concubines and what Mas'ud did with his brother's wife, in his very palace—and pondered over this calamity and great misfortune, his care and sorrow left him and he said to himself, "This is our common lot. Even though my brother is king and master of the whole world, he cannot protect what is his, his wife and his concubines, and suffers misfortune in his very home. What happened to me is little by comparison. I used to think that I was the only one who has suffered, but from what I have seen, everyone suffers. By God, my misfortune is lighter than that of my brother." He kept marveling and blaming life, whose trials none can escape, and he began to find consolation in his own affliction and forget his grief. When supper came, he ate and drank with relish and zest and, feeling better, kept eating and drinking, enjoying himself and feeling happy. He thought to himself, "I am no longer alone in my misery; I am well."

For ten days, he continued to enjoy his food and drink, and when his brother, King Shahrayar, came back from the hunt, he met him happily, treated him attentively, and greeted him cheerfully. His brother, King Shahrayar, who had missed him, said, "By God, brother, I missed you on this trip and wished you were with me." Shahzaman thanked him and sat down to carouse with him, and when night fell, and food was brought before them, the two ate and drank, and again Shahzaman ate and drank with zest. As time went by, he continued to eat and drink with appetite, and became lighthearted and carefree. His face regained color and became ruddy, and his body gained weight, as his blood circulated and he regained his energy; he was himself again, or even better. King Shahrayar noticed his brother's condition, how he used to be and how he had improved, but kept it to himself until he took him aside one day and said, "My brother Shahzaman, I would like you to do something for me, to satisfy a wish, to answer a question truthfully." Shahzaman asked, "What is it, brother?" He replied, "When you first came to stay with me, I noticed that you kept losing weight, day after day, until your looks changed, your health deteriorated, and your energy sagged. As you continued like this, I thought that what ailed you was your homesickness for your family and your country, but even though I kept noticing that you were wasting away and looking ill, I refrained from questioning you and hid my feelings from you. Then I went hunting, and when I came back, I found that you had recovered and had regained your health. Now I want you to tell me everything and to explain the cause of your deterioration and the cause of your subsequent recovery, without hiding anything from me." When Shahzaman heard what King Shahrayar said, he bowed his head, then said, "As for the cause of my recovery, that I cannot tell you, and I wish that you would excuse me from telling you." The king was greatly astonished at his brother's reply and, burning with curiosity, said, "You must tell me. For now, at least, explain the first cause."

Then Shahzaman related to his brother what happened to him with his own wife, on the night of his departure, from beginning to end, and concluded, "Thus all the while I was with you, great King, whenever I thought of the event and the misfortune that had befallen me, I felt troubled, careworn, and unhappy, and my health deteriorated. This then is the cause." Then he grew silent. When King Shahrayar heard his brother's explanation, he shook his head, greatly amazed at the deceit of women, and prayed to God to protect him from their wickedness, saying, "Brother, you were fortunate in killing your wife and her lover, who gave you good reason to feel troubled, careworn, and ill. In my opinion, what happened to you has never happened to anyone else. By God, had I been in your place, I would have killed at least a hundred or even a thousand women. I would have been furious; I would have gone mad. Now praise be to God who has delivered you from sorrow and distress. But tell me what has caused you to forget your sorrow and regain your health?" Shahzaman replied, "King, I wish that for God's sake you would excuse me from telling you." Shahrayar said, "You must." Shahzaman replied, "I fear that you will feel even more troubled and careworn than I." Shahrayar asked, "How could that be, brother? I insist on hearing your explanation."

Shahzaman then told him about what he had seen from the palace window and the calamity in his very home — how ten slaves, dressed like women, were sleeping with his women and concubines, day and night. He told him everything from beginning to end (but there is no point in repeating that). Then he concluded, "When I saw your own misfortune, I felt better — and said to myself, 'My brother is king of the world, yet such a misfortune has happened to him, and in his very home.' As a result I forgot my care and sorrow, relaxed, and began to eat and drink. This is the cause of my cheer and good spirits."

When King Shahrayar heard what his brother said and found out what had happened to him, he was furious and his blood boiled. He said, "Brother, I can't believe what you say unless I see it with my own eyes." When Shahzaman saw that his brother was in a rage, he said to him, "If you do not believe me, unless you see your misfortune with your own eyes, announce that you plan to go hunting. Then you and I shall set out with your troops, and when we get outside the city, we shall leave our tents and camp with the men behind, enter the city secretly, and go together to your palace. Then the next morning you can see with your own eyes."

King Shahrayar realized that his brother had a good plan and ordered his army to prepare for the trip. He spent the night with his brother, and when God's morning broke, the two rode out of the city with their army, preceded by the camp attendants, who had gone to drive the poles and pitch the tents where the king and his army were to camp. At nightfall King Shahrayar summoned his chief chamberlain and bade him take his place. He entrusted him with the army and ordered that for three days no one was to enter the city. Then he and his brother disguised themselves and entered the city in the dark. They went directly to the palace where Shahzaman resided and slept there till the morning. When they awoke, they sat at the palace window, watching the garden and chatting, until the light broke, the day dawned, and the sun rose. As they watched, the private gate opened, and there emerged as usual the wife of King Shahrayar, walking among twenty slave-girls. They made their way under the tree until they stood below the palace window where the two kings sat. Then they took off their women's clothes, and suddenly there were ten slaves, who mounted the ten girls and made love to them. As for the lady, she called, "Mas'ud, Mas'ud," and a black slave jumped from the tree to the ground, came to her, and said, "What do you want, you slut? Here is Sa'ad al-Din Mas'ud." She laughed and fell on her back, while the slave mounted her and like the others did his business with her. Then the black slaves got up, washed themselves, and, putting on the same clothes, mingled with the girls. Then they walked away, entered the palace, and locked the gate behind them. As for Mas'ud, he jumped over the fence to the road and went on his way.

When King Shahrayar saw the spectacle of his wife and the slave-girls, he went out of his mind, and when he and his brother came down from upstairs, he said, "No one is safe in this world. Such doings are going on in my kingdom, and in my very palace. Perish the world and perish life! This is a great calamity, indeed." Then he turned to his brother and asked, "Would you like to follow me in what I shall do?" Shahzaman answered, "Yes. I will." Shahrayar said, "Let us leave our royal state and roam the world for the love of the Supreme Lord. If we should find one whose misfortune is greater than ours, we shall return. Otherwise, we shall continue to journey through the land, without need for the trappings of royalty." Shahzaman replied, "This is an excellent idea. I shall follow you."

Then they left by the private gate, took a side road, and departed, journeying till nightfall. They slept over their sorrows, and in the morning resumed their day journey until they came to a meadow by the seashore. While they sat in the meadow amid the thick plants and trees, discussing their misfortunes and the recent events, they suddenly heard a shout and a great cry coming from the middle of the sea. They trembled with fear, thinking that the sky had fallen on the earth. Then the sea parted, and there emerged a black pillar that, as it swayed forward, got taller and taller, until it touched the clouds. Shahrayar and Shahzaman were petrified; then they ran in terror and, climbing a very tall tree, sat hiding in its foliage. When they looked again, they saw that the black pillar was cleaving the sea, wading in the water toward the green meadow, until it touched the shore. When they looked again, they saw that it was a black demon, carrying on his head a large glass chest with four steel locks. He came out, walked into the meadow, and where should he stop but under the very tree where the two kings were hiding. The demon sat down and placed the glass chest on the ground. He took out four keys and, opening the locks of the chest, pulled out a full-grown woman. She had a beautiful figure, and a face like the full moon, and a lovely smile. He took her out, laid her under the tree, and looked at her, saying, "Mistress of all noble women, you whom I carried away on your wedding night, I would like to sleep a little." Then he placed his head on the young woman's lap, stretched his legs to the sea, sank into sleep, and began to snore.

Meanwhile, the woman looked up at the tree and, turning her head by chance, saw King Shahrayar and King Shahzaman. She lifted the demon's head from her lap and placed it on the ground. Then she came and stood under the tree and motioned to them with her hand, as if to say, "Come down slowly to me." When they realized that she had seen them, they were frightened, and they begged her and implored her, in the name of the Creator of the heavens, to excuse them from climbing down. She replied, "You must come down to me." They motioned to her, saying, "This sleeping demon is the enemy of mankind. For God's sake, leave us alone." She replied, "You must come down, and if you don't, I shall wake the demon and have him kill you." She kept gesturing and pressing, until they climbed down very slowly and stood before her. Then she lay on her back, raised her legs, and said, "Make love to me and satisfy my need, or else I shall wake the demon, and he will kill you." They replied, "For God's sake, mistress, don't do this to us, for at this moment we feel nothing but dismay and fear of this demon. Please, excuse us." She replied, "You must," and insisted, swearing, "By God who created the heavens, if you don't do it, I shall wake my husband the demon and ask him to kill you and throw you into the sea." As she persisted, they could no longer resist and they made love to her, first the older brother, then the younger. When they were done and withdrew from her, she said to them, "Give me your rings," and, pulling out from the folds of her dress a small purse, opened it, and shook out ninety-eight rings of different fashions and color. Then she asked them, "Do you know what these rings are?" They answered, "No." She said, "All the owners of these rings slept with me, for whenever one of them made love to me, I took a ring from him. Since you two have slept with me, give me your rings, so that I may add them to the rest, and make a full hundred. A hundred men have known me under the very horns of this filthy, monstrous cuckold, who has imprisoned me in this chest, locked it with four locks, and kept me in the middle of this raging, roaring sea. He has guarded me and tried to keep me pure and chaste, not realizing that nothing can prevent or alter what is predestined and that when a woman desires something, no one can stop her." When Shahrayar and Shahzaman heard what the young woman said, they were greatly amazed, danced with joy, and said, 'O God, O God! There is no power and no strength, save in God the Almighty, the Magnificent. 'Great is women's cunning.'" Then each of them took off his ring and handed it to her. She took them and put them with the rest in the purse. Then sitting again by the demon, she lifted his head, placed it back on her lap, and motioned to them, "Go on your way, or else I shall wake him."

They turned their backs and took to the road. Then Shahrayar turned to his brother and said, "My brother Shahzaman, look at this sorry plight. By God, it is worse than ours. This is no less than a demon who has carried a young woman away on her wedding night, imprisoned her in a glass chest, locked her up with four locks, and kept her in the middle of the sea, thinking that he could guard her from what God had foreordained, and you saw how she has managed to sleep with ninety-eight men, and added the two of us to make a hundred. Brother, let us go back to our kingdoms and our cities, never to marry a woman again. As for myself, I shall show you what I will do."

Then the two brothers headed home and journeyed till nightfall. On the morning of the third day, they reached their camp and men, entered their tent, and sat on their thrones. The chamberlains, deputies, princes, and viziers came to attend King Shahrayar, while he gave orders and bestowed robes of honor, as well as other gifts. Then at his command everyone returned to the city, and he went to his own palace and ordered his chief vizier, the father of the two girls Shahrazad and Dinarzad, who will be mentioned below, and said to him, "Take that wife of mine and put her to death." Then Shahrayar went to her himself, bound her, and handed her over to the vizier, who took her out and put her to death. Then King Shahrayar grabbed his sword, brandished it, and, entering the palace chambers, killed every one of his slave-girls and replaced them with others. He then swore to marry for one night only and kill the woman the next morning, in order to save himself from the wickedness and cunning of women, saying, "There is not a single chaste woman anywhere on the entire face of the earth." Shortly thereafter he provided his brother Shahzaman with supplies for his journey and sent him back to his own country with gifts, rarities, and money. The brother bade him good-bye and set out for home.

Shahrayar sat on his throne and ordered his vizier, the father of the two girls, to find him a wife from among the princes' daughters. The vizier found him one, and he slept with her and was done with her, and the next morning he ordered the vizier to put her to death. That very night he took one of his army officers' daughters, slept with her, and the next morning ordered the vizier to put her to death. The vizier, who could not disobey him, put her to death. The third night he took one of the merchants' daughters, slept with her till the morning, then ordered his vizier to put her to death, and the vizier did so. It became King Shahrayar's custom to take every night the daughter of a merchant or a commoner, spend the night with her, then have her put to death the next morning. He continued to do this until all the girls perished, their mothers mourned, and there arose a clamor among the fathers and mothers, who called the plague upon his head, complained to the Creator of the heavens, and called for help on Him who hears and answers prayers.

Now, as mentioned earlier, the vizier, who put the girls to death, had an older daughter called Shahrazad and a younger one called Dinarzad. The older daughter, Shahrazad, had read the books of literature, philosophy, and medicine. She knew poetry by heart, had studied historical reports, and was acquainted with the sayings of men and the maxims of sages and kings. She was intelligent, knowledgeable, wise, and refined. She had read and learned. One day she said to her father, "Father, I will tell you what is in my mind." He asked, "What is it?" She answered, "I would like you to marry me to King Shahrayar, so that I may either succeed in saving the people or perish and die like the rest." When the vizier heard what his daughter Shahrazad said, he got angry and said to her, "Foolish one, don't you know that King Shahrayar has sworn to spend but one night with a girl and have her put to death the next morning? If I give you to him, he will sleep with you for one night and will ask me to put you to death the next morning, and I shall have to do it, since I cannot disobey him." She said, "Father, you must give me to him, even if he kills me." He asked, "What has possessed you that you wish to imperil yourself?" She replied, "Father, you must give me to him. This is absolute and final." Her father the vizier became furious and said to her, "Daughter, 'He who misbehaves, ends up in trouble,' and 'He who considers not the end, the world is not his friend.' As the popular saying goes, 'I would be sitting pretty, but for my curiosity.' I am afraid that what happened to the donkey and the ox with the merchant will happen to you." She asked, "Father, what happened to the donkey, the ox, and the merchant?" He said:

[The Tale of the Ox and the Donkey]

There was a prosperous and wealthy merchant who lived in the countryside and labored on a farm. He owned many camels and herds of cattle and employed many men, and he had a wife and many grown-up as well as little children. This merchant was taught the language of the beasts, on condition that if he revealed his secret to anyone, he would die; therefore, even though he knew the language of every kind of animal, he did not let anyone know, for fear of death. One day, as he sat, with his wife beside him and his children playing before him, he glanced at an ox and a donkey he kept at the farmhouse, tied to adjacent troughs, and heard the ox say to the donkey, "Watchful one, I hope that you are enjoying the comfort and the service you are getting. Your ground is swept and watered, and they serve you, feed you sifted barley, and offer you clear, cool water to drink. I, on the contrary, am taken out to plow in the middle of the night. They clamp on my neck something they call yoke and plow, push me all day under the whip to plow the field, and drive me beyond my endurance until my sides are lacerated, and my neck is flayed. They work me from nighttime to nighttime, take me back in the dark, offer me beans soiled with mud and hay mixed with chaff, and let me spend the night lying in urine and dung. Meanwhile you rest on well-swept, watered, and smoothed ground, with a clean trough full of hay. You stand in comfort, save for the rare occasion when our master the merchant rides you to do a brief errand and returns. You are comfortable, while I am weary; you sleep, while I keep awake."

When the ox finished, the donkey turned to him and said, "Greenhorn, they were right in calling you ox, for you ox harbor no deceit, malice, or meanness. Being sincere, you exert and exhaust yourself to comfort others. Have you not heard the saying 'Out of bad luck, they hastened on the road'? You go into the field from early morning to endure your torture at the plow to the point of exhaustion. When the plowman takes you back and ties you to the trough, you go on butting and beating with your horns, kicking with your hoofs, and bellowing for the beans, until they toss them to you; then you begin to eat. Next time, when they bring them to you, don't eat or even touch them, but smell them, then draw back and lie down on the hay and straw. If you do this, life will be better and kinder to you, and you will find relief."

As the ox listened, he was sure that the donkey had given him good advice. He thanked him, commended him to God, and invoked His blessing on him, and said, "May you stay safe from harm, watchful one." All of this conversation took place, daughter, while the merchant listened and understood. On the following day, the plowman came to the merchant's house and, taking the ox, placed the yoke upon his neck and worked him at the plow, but the ox lagged behind. The plowman hit him, but following the donkey's advice, the ox, dissembling, fell on his belly, and the plowman hit him again. Thus the ox kept getting up and falling until nightfall, when the plowman took him home and tied him to the trough. But this time the ox did not bellow or kick the ground with his hoofs. Instead, he withdrew, away from the trough. Astonished, the plowman brought him his beans and fodder, but the ox only smelled the fodder and pulled back and lay down at a distance with the hay and straw, complaining till the morning. When the plowman arrived, he found the trough as he had left it, full of beans and fodder, and saw the ox lying on his back, hardly breathing, his belly puffed, and his legs raised in the air. The plowman felt sorry for him and said to himself, "By God, he did seem weak and unable to work." Then he went to the merchant and said, "Master, last night, the ox refused to eat or touch his fodder."

The merchant, who knew what was going on, said to the plowman, "Go to the wily donkey, put him to the plow, and work him hard until he finishes the ox's task." The plowman left, took the donkey, and placed the yoke upon his neck. Then he took him out to the field and drove him with blows until he finished the ox's work, all the while driving him with blows and beating him until his sides were lacerated and his neck was flayed. At nightfall he took him home, barely able to drag his legs under his tired body and his drooping ears. Meanwhile the ox spent his day resting. He ate all his food, drank his water, and lay quietly, chewing his cud in comfort. All day long he kept praising the donkey's advice and invoking God's blessing on him. When the donkey came back at night, the ox stood up to greet him, saying, "Good evening, watchful one! You have done me a favor beyond description, for I have been sitting in comfort. God bless you for my sake." Seething with anger, the donkey did not reply, but said to himself, "All this happened to me because of my miscalculation. 'I would be sitting pretty, but for my curiosity.' If I don't find a way to return this ox to his former situation, I will perish." Then he went to his trough and lay down, while the ox continued to chew his cud and invoke God's blessing on him.

"You, my daughter, will likewise perish because of your miscalculation. Desist, sit quietly, and don't expose yourself to peril. I advise you out of compassion for you." She replied, "Father, I must go to the king, and you must give me to him." He said, "Don't do it." She insisted, "I must." He replied, "If you don't desist, I will do to you what the merchant did to his wife." She asked, "Father, what did the merchant do to his wife?" He said:

[The Tale of the Merchant and His Wife]

After what had happened to the donkey and the ox, the merchant and his wife went out in the moonlight to the stable, and he heard the donkey ask the ox in his own language, "Listen, ox, what are you going to do tomorrow morning, and what will you do when the plowman brings you your fodder?" The ox replied, "What shall I do but follow your advice and stick to it? If he brings me my fodder, I will pretend to be ill, lie down, and puff my belly." The donkey shook his head, and said, "Don't do it. Do you know what I heard our master the merchant say to the plowman?" The ox asked, "What?" The donkey replied, "He said that if the ox failed to get up and eat his fodder, he would call the butcher to slaughter him and skin him and would distribute the meat for alms and use the skin for a mat. I am afraid for you, but good advice is a matter of faith; therefore, if he brings you your fodder, eat it and look alert lest they cut your throat and skin you." The ox farted and bellowed.

The merchant got up and laughed loudly at the conversation between the donkey and the ox, and his wife asked him, "What are you laughing at? Are you making fun of me?" He said, "No." She said, "Tell me what made you laugh." He replied, "I cannot tell you. I am afraid to disclose the secret conversation of the animals." She asked, "And what prevents you from telling me?" He answered, "The fear of death." His wife said, "By God, you are lying. This is nothing but an excuse. I swear by God, the Lord of heaven, that if you don't tell me and explain the cause of your laughter, I will leave you. You must tell me." Then she went back to the house crying, and she continued to cry till the morning. The merchant said, "Damn it! Tell me why you are crying. Ask for God's forgiveness, and stop questioning and leave me in peace." She said, "I insist and will not desist." Amazed at her, he replied, "You insist! If I tell you what the donkey said to the ox, which made me laugh, I shall die." She said, "Yes, I insist, even if you have to die." He replied, "Then call your family," and she called their two daughters, her parents and relatives, and some neighbors. The merchant told them that he was about to die, and everyone, young and old, his children, the farmhands, and the servants began to cry until the house became a place of mourning. Then he summoned legal witnesses, wrote a will, leaving his wife and children their due portions, freed his slave-girls, and bid his family good-bye, while everybody, even the witnesses, wept. Then the wife's parents approached her and said, "Desist, for if your husband had not known for certain that he would die if he revealed his secret, he wouldn't have gone through all this." She replied, "I will not change my mind," and everybody cried and prepared to mourn his death.

Well, my daughter Shahrazad, it happened that the farmer kept fifty hens and a rooster at home, and while he felt sad to depart this world and leave his children and relatives behind, pondering and about to reveal and utter his secret, he overheard a dog of his say something in dog language to the rooster, who, beating and clapping his wings, had jumped on a hen and, finishing with her, jumped down and jumped on another. The merchant heard and understood what the dog said in his own language to the rooster, "Shameless, no-good rooster. Aren't you ashamed to do such a thing on a day like this?" The rooster asked, "What is special about this day?" The dog replied, "Don't you know that our master and friend is in mourning today? His wife is demanding that he disclose his secret, and when he discloses it, he will surely die. He is in this predicament, about to interpret to her the language of the animals, and all of us are mourning for him, while you clap your wings and get off one hen and jump on another. Aren't you ashamed?" The merchant heard the rooster reply, "You fool, you lunatic! Our master and friend claims to be wise, but he is foolish, for he has only one wife, yet he does not know how to manage her." The dog asked, "What should he do with her?"

The rooster replied, "He should take an oak branch, push her into a room, lock the door, and fall on her with the stick, beating her mercilessly until he breaks her arms and legs and she cries out, 'I no longer want you to tell me or explain anything.' He should go on beating her until he cures her for life, and she will never oppose him in anything. If he does this, he will live, and live in peace, and there will be no more grief, but he does not know how to manage." Well, my daughter Shahrazad, when the merchant heard the conversation between the dog and the rooster, he jumped up and, taking an oak branch, pushed his wife into a room, got in with her, and locked the door. Then he began to beat her mercilessly on her chest and shoulders and kept beating her until she cried for mercy, screaming, "No, no, I don't want to know anything. Leave me alone, leave me alone. I don't want to know anything," until he got tired of hitting her and opened the door. The wife emerged penitent, the husband learned good management, and everybody was happy, and the mourning turned into a celebration.

"If you don't relent, I shall do to you what the merchant did to his wife." She said, "Such tales don't deter me from my request. If you wish, I can tell you many such tales. In the end, if you don't take me to King Shahrayar, I shall go to him by myself behind your back and tell him that you have refused to give me to one like him and that you have begrudged your master one like me." The vizier asked, "Must you really do this?" She replied, "Yes, I must."

Tired and exhausted, the vizier went to King Shahrayar and, kissing the ground before him, told him about his daughter, adding that he would give her to him that very night. The king was astonished and said to him, "Vizier, how is it that you have found it possible to give me your daughter, knowing that I will, by God, the Creator of heaven, ask you to put her to death the next morning and that if you refuse, I will have you put to death too?" He replied, "My King and Lord, I have told her every-thing and explained all this to her, but she refuses and insists on being with you tonight." The king was delighted and said, "Go to her, prepare her, and bring her to me early in the evening."

The vizier went down, repeated the king's message to his daughter, and said, "May God not deprive me of you." She was very happy and, after preparing herself and packing what she needed, went to her younger sister, Dinarzad, and said, "Sister, listen well to what I am telling you. When I go to the king, I will send for you, and when you come and see that the king has finished with me, say, 'Sister, if you are not sleepy, tell us a story.' Then I will begin to tell a story, and it will cause the king to stop his practice, save myself, and deliver the people." Dinarzad replied, "Very well."

At nightfall the vizier took Shahrazad and went with her to the great King Shahrayar. But when Shahrayar took her to bed and began to fondle her, she wept, and when he asked her, "Why are you crying?" she replied, "I have a sister, and I wish to bid her good-bye before daybreak." Then the king sent for the sister, who came and went to sleep under the bed. When the night wore on, she woke up and waited until the king had satisfied himself with her sister Shahrazad and they were by now all fully awake. Then Dinarzad cleared her throat and said, "Sister, if you are not sleepy, tell us one of your lovely little tales to while away the night, before I bid you good-bye at daybreak, for I don't know what will happen to you tomorrow." Shahrazad turned to King Shahrayar and said, "May I have your permission to tell a story?" He replied, "Yes," and Shahrazad was very happy and said, "Listen":

The First Night
[THE STORY OF THE MERCHANT AND THE DEMON]

It is said, O wise and happy King, that once there was a prosperous merchant who had abundant wealth and investments and commitments in every country. He had many women and children and kept many servants and slaves. One day, having resolved to visit another country, he took provisions, filling his saddlebag with loaves of bread and with dates, mounted his horse, and set out on his journey. For many days and nights, he journeyed under God's care until he reached his destina-tion. When he finished his business, he turned back to his home and family. He jour-neyed for three days, and on the fourth day, chancing to come to an orchard, went in to avoid the heat and shade himself from the sun of the open country. He came to a spring under a walnut tree and, tying his horse, sat by the spring, pulled out from the saddlebag some loaves of bread and a handful of dates, and began to eat, throwing the date pits right and left until he had had enough. Then he got up, performed his ablutions, and performed his prayers.

But hardly had he finished when he saw an old demon, with sword in hand, standing with his feet on the ground and his head in the clouds. The demon approached until he stood before him and screamed, saying, "Get up, so that I may kill you with this sword, just as you have killed my son." When the merchant saw and heard the demon, he was terrified and awestricken. He asked, "Master, for what crime do you wish to kill me?" The demon replied, "I wish to kill you because you have killed my son." The merchant asked, "Who has killed your son?" The demon replied, "You have killed my son." The merchant said, "By God, I did not kill your son. When and how could that have been?" The demon said, "Didn't you sit down, take out some dates from your saddlebag, and eat, throwing the pits right and left?" The merchant replied, "Yes, I did." The demon said, "You killed my son, for as you were throwing the stones right and left, my son happened to be walking by and was struck and killed by one of them, and I must now kill you." The merchant said, "O my lord, please don't kill me." The demon replied, "I must kill you as you killed him—blood for blood." The merchant said, "To God we belong and to God we return. There is no power or strength, save in God the Almighty, the Magnificent. If I killed him, I did it by mistake. Please forgive me." The demon replied, "By God, I must kill you, as you killed my son." Then he seized him and, throwing him to the ground, raised the sword to strike him. The merchant began to weep and mourn his family and his wife and children. Again, the demon raised his sword to strike, while the merchant cried until he was drenched with tears, saying, "There is no power or strength, save in God the Almighty, the Magnificent." Then he began to recite the following verses:

> Life has two days: one peace, one wariness,
> And has two sides: worry and happiness.
> Ask him who taunts us with adversity,
> "Does fate, save those worthy of note, oppress?
> Don't you see that the blowing, raging storms
> Only the tallest of the trees beset,
> And of earth's many green and barren lots,
> Only the ones with fruits with stones are hit,
> And of the countless stars in heaven's vault
> None is eclipsed except the moon and sun?
> You thought well of the days, when they were good,
> Oblivious to the ills destined for one.
> You were deluded by the peaceful nights,
> Yet in the peace of night does sorrow stun."

When the merchant finished and stopped weeping, the demon said, "By God, I must kill you, as you killed my son, even if you weep blood." The merchant asked, "Must you?" The demon replied, "I must," and raised his sword to strike.

But morning overtook Shahrazad, and she lapsed into silence, leaving King Shahrayar burning with curiosity to hear the rest of the story. Then Dinarzad said to her sister Shahrazad, "What a strange and lovely story!" Shahrazad replied, "What is this compared with what I shall tell you tomorrow night if the king spares me and lets me live? It will be even better and more entertaining." The king thought to himself, "I will spare her until I hear the rest of the story; then I will have her put to death the next day." When morning broke, the day dawned, and the sun rose; the king left to attend to the affairs of the kingdom, and the vizier, Shahrazad's father, was amazed and delighted. King Shahrayar governed all day and returned home at night to his quarters and got into bed with Shahrazad. Then Dinarzad said to her sister Shahrazad, "Please, sister, if you are not sleepy, tell us one of your lovely little tales to while away the night." The king added, "Let it be the conclusion of the story of the demon and the merchant, for I would like to hear it." Shahrazad replied, "With the greatest pleasure, dear, happy King":

The Second Night

It is related, O wise and happy King, that when the demon raised his sword, the merchant asked the demon again, "Must you kill me?" and the demon replied, "Yes." Then the merchant said, "Please give me time to say good-bye to my family and my wife and children, divide my property among them, and appoint guardians. Then I shall come back, so that you may kill me." The demon replied, "I am afraid that if I release you and grant you time, you will go and do what you wish, but will not come back." The merchant said, "I swear to keep my pledge to come back, as the God of Heaven and earth is my witness." The demon asked, "How much time do you need?" The merchant replied, "One year, so that I may see enough of my children, bid my wife good-bye, discharge my obligations to people, and come back on New Year's Day." The demon asked, "Do you swear to God that if I let you go, you will come back on New Year's Day?" The merchant replied, "Yes, I swear to God."

After the merchant swore, the demon released him, and he mounted his horse sadly and went on his way. He journeyed until he reached his home and came to his wife and children. When he saw them, he wept bitterly, and when his family saw his sorrow and grief, they began to reproach him for his behavior, and his wife said, "Husband, what is the matter with you? Why do you mourn, when we are happy, celebrating your return?" He replied, "Why not mourn when I have only one year to live?" Then he told her of his encounter with the demon and informed her that he had sworn to return on New Year's Day, so that the demon might kill him.

When they heard what he said, everyone began to cry. His wife struck her face in lamentation and cut her hair, his daughters wailed, and his little children cried. It was a day of mourning, as all the children gathered around their father to weep and exchange good-byes. The next day he wrote his will, dividing his property, discharged his obligations to people, left bequests and gifts, distributed alms, and engaged reciters to read portions of the Quran in his house. Then he summoned legal witnesses and in their presence freed his slaves and slave-girls, divided among his elder children their shares of the property, appointed guardians for his little ones, and gave his wife her share, according to her marriage contract. He spent the rest of the time with his family, and when the year came to an end, save for the time needed for the journey, he performed his ablutions, performed his prayers, and, carrying his burial shroud, began to bid his family good-bye. His sons hung around his neck, his daughters wept, and his wife wailed. Their mourning scared him, and he began to weep, as he embraced and kissed his children good-bye. He said to them, "Children, this is God's will and decree, for man was created to die." Then he turned away and, mounting his horse, journeyed day and night until he reached the orchard on New Year's Day.

He sat at the place where he had eaten the dates, waiting for the demon, with a heavy heart and tearful eyes. As he waited, an old man, leading a deer on a leash, approached and greeted him, and he returned the greeting. The old man inquired, "Friend, why do you sit here in this place of demons and devils? For in this haunted orchard none come to good." The merchant replied by telling him what had happened to him and the demon, from beginning to end. The old man was amazed at the merchant's fidelity and said, "Yours is a magnificent pledge," adding, "By God, I shall not leave until I see what will happen to you with the demon." Then he sat down beside him and chatted with him. As they talked . . .

But morning overtook Shahrazad, and she lapsed into silence. As the day dawned, and it was light, her sister Dinarzad said, "What a strange and wonderful story!" Shahrazad replied, "Tomorrow night I shall tell something even stranger and more wonderful than this."

The Third Night

When it was night and Shahrazad was in bed with the king, Dinarzad said to her sister Shahrazad, "Please, if you are not sleepy, tell us one of your lovely little tales to while away the night." The king added, "Let it be the conclusion of the merchant's story." Shahrazad replied, "As you wish":

I heard, O happy King, that as the merchant and the man with the deer sat talking, another old man approached, with two black hounds, and when he reached them, he greeted them, and they returned his greeting. Then he asked them about themselves, and the man with the deer told him the story of the merchant and the demon, how the merchant had sworn to return on New Year's Day, and how the demon was waiting to kill him. He added that when he himself heard the story, he swore never to leave until he saw what would happen between the merchant and the demon. When the man with the two dogs heard the story, he was amazed, and he too swore never to leave them until he saw what would happen between them. Then he questioned the merchant, and the merchant repeated to him what had happened to him with the demon.

While they were engaged in conversation, a third old man approached and greeted them, and they returned his greeting. He asked, "Why do I see the two of you sitting here, with this merchant between you, looking abject, sad, and dejected?" They told him the merchant's story and explained that they were sitting and waiting to see what would happen to him with the demon. When he heard the story, he sat down with them, saying, "By God, I too like you will not leave, until I see what happens to this man with the demon." As they sat, conversing with one another, they suddenly saw the dust rising from the open country, and when it cleared, they saw the demon approaching, with a drawn steel sword in his hand. He stood before them without greeting them, yanked the merchant with his left hand, and, holding him fast before him, said, "Get ready to die." The merchant and the three old men began to weep and wail.

But dawn broke and morning overtook Shahrazad, and she lapsed into silence. Then Dinarzad said, "Sister, what a lovely story!" Shahrazad replied, "What is this compared with what I shall tell you tomorrow night? It will be even better; it will be more wonderful, delightful, entertaining, and delectable if the king spares me and lets me live." The king was all curiosity to hear the rest of the story and said to himself, "By God, I will not have her put to death until I hear the rest of the story and find out what happened to the merchant with the demon. Then I will have her put to death the next morning, as I did with the others." Then he went out to attend to the affairs of his kingdom, and when he saw Shahrazad's father, he treated him kindly and showed him favors, and the vizier was amazed. When night came, the king went home, and when he was in bed with Shahrazad, Dinarzad said, "Sister, if you are not sleepy, tell us one of your lovely little tales to while away the night." Shahrazad replied, "With the greatest pleasure":

The Fourth Night

It is related, O happy King, that the first old man with the deer approached the demon and, kissing his hands and feet, said, "Fiend and King of the demon kings, if I tell you what happened to me and that deer, and you find it strange and amazing, indeed stranger and more amazing than what happened to you and the merchant, will you grant me a third of your claim on him for his crime and guilt?" The demon replied, "I will." The old man said:

[THE FIRST OLD MAN'S TALE]

Demon, this deer is my cousin, my flesh and blood. I married her when I was very young, and she a girl of twelve, who reached womanhood only afterward. For thirty years we lived together, but I was not blessed with children, for she bore neither boy nor girl. Yet I continued to be kind to her, to care for her, and to treat her generously. Then I took a mistress, and she bore me a son, who grew up to look like a slice of the moon. Meanwhile, my wife grew jealous of my mistress and my son. One day, when he was ten, I had to go on a journey. I entrusted my wife, this one here, with my mistress and son, bade her take good care of them, and was gone for a whole year. In my absence my wife, this cousin of mine, learned soothsaying and magic and cast a spell on my son and turned him into a young bull. Then she summoned my shepherd, gave my son to him, and said, "Tend this bull with the rest of the cattle." The shepherd took him and tended him for a while. Then she cast a spell on the mother, turning her into a cow, and gave her also to the shepherd.

When I came back, after all this was done, and inquired about my mistress and my son, she answered, "Your mistress died, and your son ran away two months ago, and I have had no news from him ever since." When I heard her, I grieved for my mistress, and with an anguished heart I mourned for my son for nearly a year. When the Great Feast of the Immolation[5] drew near, I summoned the shepherd and ordered him to bring me a fat cow for the sacrifice. The cow he brought me was in reality my enchanted mistress. When I bound her and pressed against her to cut her throat, she wept and cried, as if saying, "My son, my son," and her tears coursed down her cheeks. Astonished and seized with pity, I turned away and asked the shepherd to bring me a different cow. But my wife shouted, "Go on. Butcher her, for he has none better or fatter. Let us enjoy her meat at feast time." I approached the cow to cut her throat, and again she cried, as if saying, "My son, my son." Then I turned away from her and said to the shepherd, "Butcher her for me." The shepherd butchered her, and when he skinned her, he found neither meat nor fat but only skin and bone. I regretted having her butchered and said to the shepherd, "Take her all for yourself, or give her as alms to whomever you wish, and find me a fat young bull from among the flock." The shepherd took her away and disappeared, and I never knew what he did with her.

Then he brought me my son, my heartblood, in the guise of a fat young bull. When my son saw me, he shook his head loose from the rope, ran toward me, and, throwing himself at my feet, kept rubbing his head against me. I was astonished and touched with sympathy, pity, and mercy, for the blood hearkened to the blood and the divine bond, and my heart throbbed within me when I saw the tears coursing over the cheeks of my son the young bull, as he dug the earth with his hoofs. I turned away and said to the shepherd, "Let him go with the rest of the flock, and be kind to him, for I have decided to spare him. Bring me another one instead of him." My wife, this very deer, shouted, "You shall sacrifice none but this bull." I got angry and replied, "I listened to you and butchered the cow uselessly. I will not listen to you and kill this bull, for I have decided to spare him." But she pressed me, saying, "You must butcher this bull," and I bound him and took the knife . . .

But dawn broke, and morning overtook Shahrazad, and she lapsed into silence, leaving the king all curiosity for the rest of the story. Then her sister Dinarzad said, "What an entertaining story!" Shahrazad replied, "Tomorrow night I shall tell you something even stranger, more wonderful, and more entertaining if the king spares me and lets me live."

---

[5] **Great Feast of the Immolation:** A four-day Muslim feast that celebrates the pilgrimage to Mecca; marked by the slaughtering of sheep and cattle as sacrificial offerings to God. [Translator's note.]

The Fifth Night

The following night, Dinarzad said to her sister Shahrazad, "Please, sister, if you are not sleepy, tell us one of your little tales." Shahrazad replied, "With the greatest pleasure":

I heard, dear King, that the old man with the deer said to the demon and to his companions:

I took the knife and as I turned to slaughter my son, he wept, bellowed, rolled at my feet, and motioned toward me with his tongue. I suspected something, began to waver with trepidation and pity, and finally released him, saying to my wife, "I have decided to spare him, and I commit him to your care." Then I tried to appease and please my wife, this very deer, by slaughtering another bull, promising her to slaughter this one next season. We slept that night, and when God's dawn broke, the shepherd came to me without letting my wife know, and said, "Give me credit for bringing you good news." I replied, "Tell me, and the credit is yours." He said, "Master, I have a daughter who is fond of soothsaying and magic and who is adept at the art of oaths and spells. Yesterday I took home with me the bull you had spared, to let him graze with the cattle, and when my daughter saw him, she laughed and cried at the same time. When I asked her why she laughed and cried, she answered that she laughed because the bull was in reality the son of our master the cattle owner, put under a spell by his stepmother, and that she cried because his father had slaughtered the son's mother. I could hardly wait till daybreak to bring you the good news about your son."

Demon, when I heard that, I uttered a cry and fainted, and when I came to myself, I accompanied the shepherd to his home, went to my son, and threw myself at him, kissing him and crying. He turned his head toward me, his tears coursing over his cheeks, and dangled his tongue, as if to say, "Look at my plight." Then I turned to the shepherd's daughter and asked, "Can you release him from the spell? If you do, I will give you all my cattle and all my possessions." She smiled and replied, "Master, I have no desire for your wealth, cattle, or possessions. I will deliver him, but on two conditions: first, that you let me marry him; second, that you let me cast a spell on her who had cast a spell on him, in order to control her and guard against her evil power." I replied, "Do whatever you wish and more. My possessions are for you and my son. As for my wife, who has done this to my son and made me slaughter his mother, her life is forfeit to you." She said, "No, but I will let her taste what she has inflicted on others." Then the shepherd's daughter filled a bowl with water, uttered an incantation and an oath, and said to my son, "Bull, if you have been created in this image by the All-Conquering, Almighty Lord, stay as you are, but if you have been treacherously put under a spell, change back to your human form, by the will of God, Creator of the wide world." Then she sprinkled him with the water, and he shook himself and changed from a bull back to his human form.

As I rushed to him, I fainted, and when I came to myself, he told me what my wife, this very deer, had done to him and to his mother. I said to him, "Son, God has sent us someone who will pay her back for what you and your mother and I have suffered at her hands." Then, O demon, I gave my son in marriage to the shepherd's daughter, who turned my wife into this very deer, saying to me, "To me this is a pretty form, for she will be with us day and night, and it is better to turn her into a pretty deer than to suffer her sinister looks." Thus she stayed with us, while the days and nights followed one another, and the months and years went by. Then one day the shepherd's daughter died, and my son went to the country of this very man with whom you have had your encounter. Some time later I took my wife, this very deer, with me, set out to find out what had happened to my son, and chanced to stop here. This is my story, my strange and amazing story.

The demon assented, saying, "I grant you one-third of this man's life."

Then, O King Shahrayar, the second old man with the two black dogs approached the demon and said, "I too shall tell you what happened to me and to these two dogs, and if I tell it to you and you find it stranger and more amazing than this man's story will you grant me one-third of this man's life?" The demon replied, "I will." Then the old man began to tell his story, saying . . .

But dawn broke and morning overtook Shahrazad, and she lapsed into silence. Then Dinarzad said, "This is an amazing story," and Shahrazad replied, "What is this compared with what I shall tell you tomorrow night if the king spares me and lets me live!" The king said to himself, "By God, I will not have her put to death until I find out what happened to the man with the two black dogs. Then I will have her put to death, God the Almighty willing."

The Sixth Night

When the following night arrived and Shahrazad was in bed with King Shahrayar, her sister Dinarzad said, "Sister, if you are not sleepy, tell us a little tale. Finish the one you started." Shahrazad replied, "With the greatest pleasure":

I heard, O happy King, that the second old man with the two dogs said:

[THE SECOND OLD MAN'S TALE]

Demon, as for my story, these are the details. These two dogs are my brothers. When our father died, he left behind three sons, and left us three thousand dinars,[6] with which each of us opened a shop and became a shopkeeper. Soon my older brother, one of these very dogs, went and sold the contents of his shop for a thousand dinars, bought trading goods, and, having prepared himself for his trading trip, left us. A full year went by, when one day, as I sat in my shop, a beggar stopped by to beg. When I refused him, he tearfully asked, "Don't you recognize me?" and when I looked at him closely, I recognized my brother. I embraced him and took him into

---

[6] **dinars:** Gold coins, the basic Muslim monetary unit. [Translator's note.]

the shop, and when I asked him about his plight, he replied, "The money is gone, and the situation is bad." Then I took him to the public bath, clothed him in one of my robes, and took home with me. Then I examined my books and checked my balance, and found out that I had made a thousand dinars and that my net worth was two thousand dinars. I divided the amount between my brother and myself, and said to him, "Think as if you have never been away." He gladly took the money and opened another shop.

Soon afterward my second brother, this other dog, went and sold his merchandise and collected his money, intending to go on a trading trip. We tried to dissuade him, but he did not listen. Instead, he bought merchandise and trading goods, joined a group of travelers, and was gone for a full year. Then he came back, just like his older brother. I said to him, "Brother, didn't I advise you not to go?" He replied tearfully, "Brother, it was foreordained. Now I am poor and penniless, without even a shirt on my back." Demon, I took him to the public bath, clothed him in one of my new robes, and took him back to the shop. After we had something to eat, I said to him, "Brother, I shall do my business accounts, calculate my net worth for the year, and after subtracting the capital, whatever the profit happens to be, I shall divide it equally between you and myself." When I examined my books and subtracted the capital, I found out that my profit was two thousand dinars, and I thanked God and felt very happy. Then I divided the money, giving him a thousand dinars and keeping a thousand for myself. With that money he opened another shop, and the three of us stayed together for a while. Then my two brothers asked me to go on a trading journey with them, but I refused, saying, "What did you gain from your ventures that I can gain?"

They dropped the matter, and for six years we worked in our stores, buying and selling. Yet every year they asked me to go on a trading journey with them, but I refused, until I finally gave in. I said, "Brothers, I am ready to go with you. How much money do you have?" I found out that they had eaten and drunk and squandered everything they had, but I said nothing to them and did not reproach them. Then I took inventory, gathered all I had together, and sold everything. I was pleased to discover that the sale netted six thousand dinars. Then I divided the money into two parts, and said to my brothers, "The sum of three thousand dinars is for you and myself to use on our trading journey. The other three thousand I shall bury in the ground, in case what happened to you happens to me, so that when we return, we will find three thousand dinars to reopen our shops." They replied, "This is an excellent idea." Then, demon, I divided my money and buried three thousand dinars. Of the remaining three I gave each of my brothers a thousand and kept a thousand for myself. After I closed my shop, we bought merchandise and trading goods, rented a large seafaring boat, and after loading it with our goods and provisions, sailed day and night, for a month.

But morning overtook Shahrazad, and she lapsed into silence. Then her sister Dinarzad said, "Sister, what a lovely story!" Shahrazad replied, "Tomorrow night I shall tell you something even lovelier, stranger, and more wonderful if I live, the Almighty God willing."

The Seventh Night

The following night Dinarzad said to her sister Shahrazad, "For God's sake sister, if you are not sleepy, tell us a little tale." The king added, "Let it be the completion of the story of the merchant and the demon." Shahrazad replied, "With the greatest pleasure":

I heard, O happy King, that the second old man said to the demon:

For a month my brothers, these very dogs, and I sailed the salty sea, until we came to a port city. We entered the city and sold our goods, earning ten dinars for every dinar. Then we bought other goods, and when we got to the seashore to embark, I met a girl who was dressed in tatters. She kissed my hands and said, "O my lord, be charitable and do me a favor, and I believe that I shall be able to reward you for it." I replied, "I am willing to do you a favor regardless of any reward." She said, "O my lord, marry me, clothe me, and take me home with you on this boat, as your wife, for I wish to give myself to you. I, in turn, will reward you for your kindness and charity, the Almighty God willing. Don't be misled by my poverty and present condition." When I heard her words, I felt pity for her, and guided by what God the Most High had intended for me, I consented. I clothed her with an expensive dress and married her. Then I took her to the boat, spread the bed for her, and consummated our marriage. We sailed many days and nights, and I, feeling love for her, stayed with her day and night, neglecting my brothers. In the meantime they, these very dogs, grew jealous of me, envied me for my increasing merchandise and wealth and coveted all our possessions. At last they decided to betray me and, tempted by the Devil, plotted to kill me. One night they waited until I was asleep beside my wife; then they carried the two of us and threw us into the sea.

When we awoke, my wife turned into a she-demon and carried me out of the sea to an island. When it was morning, she said, "Husband, I have rewarded you by saving you from drowning, for I am one of the demons who believe in God. When I saw you by the seashore, I felt love for you and came to you in the guise in which you saw me, and when I expressed my love for you, you accepted me. Now I must kill your brothers." When I heard what she said, I was amazed and I thanked her and said, "As for destroying my brothers, this I do not wish, for I will not behave like them." Then I related to her what had happened to me and them, from beginning to end. When she heard my story, she got very angry at them, and said, "I shall fly to them now, drown their boat, and let them all perish." I entreated her, saying, "For God's sake, don't. The proverb advises 'Be kind to those who hurt you.' No matter what, they are my brothers after all." In this manner, I entreated her and pacified her. Afterward, she took me and flew away with me until she brought me home and put me down on the roof of my house. I climbed down, threw the doors open, and dug up the money I had buried. Then I went out and, greeting the people in the market, reopened my shop. When I came home in the evening, I found these two dogs tied up, and when they saw me, they came to me, wept, and rubbed themselves against me. I started, when I suddenly heard my wife say, "O my lord, these are your brothers." I asked, "Who has done this to them?" She replied, "I sent to my sister and asked her to do it. They will stay in this condition for ten years, after which they may be delivered." Then she told me where to find her and departed. The ten years have passed, and I was with my brothers on my way to her to have the spell lifted, when I met this man, together with this old man with the deer. When I asked him about himself, he told me about his encounter with you, and I resolved not to leave until I found out what would happen between you and him. This is my story. Isn't it amazing?

The demon replied, "By God, it is strange and amazing. I grant you one-third of my claim on him for his crime."

Then the third old man said, "Demon, don't disappoint me. If I told you a story that is stranger and more amazing than the first two would you grant me one-third of your claim on him for his crime?" The demon replied, "I will." Then the old man said, "Demon, listen":

But morning overtook Shahrazad, and she lapsed into silence. Then her sister said, "What an amazing story!" Shahrazad replied, "The rest is even more amazing." The king said to himself, "I will not have her put to death until I hear what happened to the old man and the demon; then I will have her put to death, as is my custom with the others."

The Eighth Night

The following night Dinarzad said to her sister Shahrazad, "For God's sake, sister, if you are not sleepy, tell us one of your lovely little tales to while away the night." Shahrazad replied, "With the greatest pleasure":

I heard, O happy King, that the third old man told the demon a story that was even stranger and more amazing than the first two. The demon was very much amazed and, swaying with delight, said, "I grant you one-third of my claim on him for his crime." Then the demon released the merchant and departed. The merchant turned to the three old men and thanked them, and they congratulated him on his deliverance and bade him good-bye. Then they separated, and each of them went on his way. The merchant himself went back home to his family, his wife, and his children, and he lived with them until the day he died. But this story is not as strange or as amazing as the story of the fisherman. . . .

FROM

∾ The Book of the Thousand Nights and One Night

Translated by Powys Mathers

CONCLUSION

'Such, O auspicious King,' said Shahrazād, 'is the tender tale of Prince Jasmine and Princess Almond. I have told it as I heard it. But Allāh knows all!'

Then she fell silent, and King Shahryār cried: 'O Shahrazād, that was a noble and admirable story! O wise and subtle one, you have taught me many lessons, letting me see that every man is at the call of Fate; you have made me consider the words of kings and peoples passed away; you have told me some things which were strange, and many that were worthy of reflection. I have listened to you for a thousand nights and one night, and now my soul is changed and joyful, it beats with an appetite for life. I give thanks to Him Who has perfumed your mouth with so much eloquence and has set wisdom to be a seal upon your brow!'

Little Dunyazād rose quite up from her carpet, and ran to throw her arms about her sister, crying: 'O Shahrazād, how soft and delicate are your words, how moving and delightful! With what a savour they have filled our hearts! Oh, how beautiful are your words, my sister!'

Shahrazād leaned over the child and, as she embraced her, whispered some words which caused her to glide from the room, as camphor melts before the sun.

Shahrazād stayed alone with Shahryār, but, as he was preparing to take this marvellous bride between his joyful arms, the curtains opened and Dunyazād reappeared, followed by a nurse with twin children hanging at her breasts. A third child hurried after them on all fours.

Shahrazād embraced the three little ones and then ranged them before Shahryār; her eyes filled with tears, as she said: 'O King of time, behold these three whom Allāh has granted to us in three years.'

While Shahryār kissed the children and was moved with joy through all his body to touch them, Shahrazād said again: 'Your eldest son is more than two years old, and these twins will soon be one. Allāh protect them from the evil-eye! You remember, O King of time, that I was absent through sickness for twenty days between the six hundred and seventy-ninth night of my telling and the seven hundredth. It was during that absence that I gave birth to the twins. They pained and wearied me a great deal more than their elder brother in the previous year. With him I was so little disturbed that I had no need to interrupt the tale of Sympathy the Learned, even for one night.'

She fell silent, and King Shahryār, looking from her to his sons and from his sons to her, could say no word.

Then little Dunyazād turned from kissing the infants a twentieth time, and said to Shahryār: 'Will you cut off my sister's head, O King? Will you destroy the mother of your sons, and leave three little kings to miss her love?'

'Be quiet and have no fear, young girl,' answered King Shahryār, between two fits of sobbing. It was not for a long time that he could master his emotion, and say: 'O Shahrazād, I swear by the Lord of Pity that you were already in my heart before the coming of these children. He had given you gifts with which to win me; I loved you in my soul because I had found you pure, holy, chaste, tender, straightforward, unassailable, ingenious, subtle, eloquent, discreet, smiling, and wise. May Allāh bless you, my dear, your father and mother, your root and race! O Shahrazād, this thousand and first night is whiter for us than the day!' When he had said these things, he rose and embraced the woman's head.

Shahrazād took her King's hand and carried it to her lips, her heart, and her brow, saying: 'O lord of time, I beg you to call your old wazīr, that he may rejoice at my salvation and partake in the benediction of this night.'

So the King sent for his wazīr, and the old man entered carrying Shahrazād's winding-sheet over his arm, for he was sure that her hour had come at last. Shahryār rose in his honour and kissed him between the eyes, saying: 'O father of Shahrazād, O begetter of benediction, Allāh has raised up your daughter to be the salvation of my people. Repentance has come to me through her!' Joy penetrated the old man's heart so suddenly that he fell into a swoon. When rose-water had brought him to himself, Shahrazād and Dunyazād kissed his hand, and he blessed them. The rest of that night passed for them all in a daze of happiness.

Shahryār sent for his brother Shahzamān, King of Samarkand al-Ajam, and went out to meet his coming with a glorious retinue. The city was gay with flags, and in the streets and markets the people burnt incense, sublimated camphor, aloes, Indian musk, nard and ambergris. They put fresh henna upon their fingers and saffron upon their faces. Drums, flutes, clarinets, fifes, cymbals and dulcimers filled every ear with a rejoicing sound.

While great feasts were being given at the royal expense, King Shahryār took his brother aside and spoke of the life which he had led with Shahrazād for the last three years. He recounted for Shahzamān's benefit some of the maxims, phrases, tales, proverbs, jests, anecdotes, characteristics, marvels, poems, and recitations which he had heard during that time. He praised the wazīr's daughter for her eloquence, wisdom, purity, piety, sweetness, honesty and discretion. 'She is my wife,' he said, 'the mother of my children.'

When King Shahzamān had a little recovered from his astonishment, he said: 'Since you have been so fortunate, I too will marry. I will marry Shahrazād's sister, the little one, I do not know her name. We shall be two brothers married to two sure and honest sisters; we will forget our old misfortune. That calamity touched me first, and then through me it reached to you. If I had not discovered mine, you would never have known of yours. Alas, my brother, I have been mournful and loveless during these years. Each night I have followed your example by taking a virgin to my bed, and every morning I have avenged our ills upon her life. Now I will follow you in a better deed, and marry your wazīr's second daughter.'

Shahryār went joyfully to Shahrazād and told her that his brother had, of his own accord, elected Dunyazād for his bride. 'We consent, O King of time,' she said, 'on condition that your brother stays henceforth with us. I could not bear to be separated from my little sister, even for one hour. I brought her up and educated her;

she could not part from me. If Shahzamān will give this undertaking, Dunyazād shall be his slave. If not, we will keep her.'

When Shahzamān heard Shahrazād's answer, he said: 'As Allāh lives, my brother, I had intended no less than to remain with you always. I feel now that I can never abide to be parted from you again. As for the throne of Samarkand, Allāh will send to fill it.' 'I have longed for this,' answered King Shahryār. 'Join with me in thanks to Allāh, my brother, that He has brought our hearts together again after so many months!'

The kādi[1] and witnesses were summoned, and a marriage contract was written out for King Shahzamān and Dunyazād. Rejoicing and illuminations with coloured fire followed upon the news of this; and all the city ate and drank at the King's expense for forty days and forty nights. The two brothers and two sisters entered the hammām[2] and bathed there in rose-water, flower-water, scented willow-water, and perfumed water of musk, while eagle wood and aloes were burned about them.

Shahrazād combed and tressed her little sister's hair, and sprinkled it with pearls. Then she dressed her in a robe of antique Persian stuff, stitched with red gold and enhanced by drunken animals and swooning birds embroidered in the very colours of life. She put a fairy collar about her neck, and Dunyazād became below her fingers fairer than Alexander's wife.

When the two Kings had left the hammām and seated themselves upon their thrones, the bridal company, the wives of the amīrs[3] and notables, stood in two motionless lines to right and left. Time came, and the sisters entered between these living walls, each sustaining the other, and having the appearance of two moons in one night sky.

Then the noblest ladies there took Dunyazād by the hand and, after removing her robes, dressed her in a garment of blue satin, a sea tint to make reason fail upon her throne. A poet said of her:

> Her veil is torn from the bright blue
> Which all the stars are hasting to,
> Her lips control a hive of bees,
> And roses are about her knees,
> The white flakes of the jasmine twine
> Round her twin sweetness carnaline,
> Her waist is a slight reed which stands
> Swayed on a hill of moving sands.

Shahzamān came down to be the first to look upon her. When he had admired her in this dress, he sat upon his throne again, and this was a signal for the second change. So Shahrazād and the women clad their bride in a robe of apricot silk. As she passed before her husband's throne, she justified the words of the poet:

> You are more fair than a summer moon
>   On a winter night, you are more fair.
>   I said when I saw your falling hair:

---

[1] **kādī**: A local judge. [2] **hammām**: A public bath. [3] **amīrs**: Military officers of the caliphs.

'Night's black fain wing is hiding day.'
'A cloud, but lo! the moon is there,'
You, rose child, found to say.

When Shahzamān had come down and admired her in this dress, Shahrazād put a tunic of grenade[4] velvet upon her sister. A poet said:

Red and slight as a running deer,
    Small as a child with his father's bow,
    Yet you so shine that when you go
The sun will fly and night appear.

After this Dunyazād was habited in citron yellow silk with lines of pictures. A poet has said:

You are the fortunate moon which shone
    On the road I used to take
    Many a glad night for the sake
Of a once desirous one;
    Yet if now a lover nears,
    Unrecking silver fire,
Your breasts' two crimson granite spears
    Are proof against desire.

Shahrazād led her slowly before the Kings and all the company of guests. Shahzamān looked upon his bride and then, by returning to his place, gave signal for the final change. Shahrazād kissed the child long upon the mouth, and then dressed her in a robe of green, sewn with red gold and pearls. With careful fingers she pulled out the lines of this, and then set a light diadem of emeralds on her sister's brow. It was upon her arm that this small branch of ban, this camphor girl, walked through the hall. A poet has been inspired to sing:

Green leaves as fairly shade the red pomegranate flowers
    As you your light chemise.
I ask its name which suits your golden check,
You ponder and then speak:
    'It has no name, for it is my chemise.'
Yet I will call it murderer of ours,
    A murderous chemise . . . .

Shahrazād slipped her hand to her sister's waist, and they walked before the Kings and between the guests toward the inner chambers. Then the Queen undressed little Dunyazād and laid her upon the bed with such recommendations as were suitable. They kissed and wept in each other's arms for a little, as it was the first night for which they had been separated.

That was a white and joyful night for the two brothers and the two sisters, it was a fair continuation of the thousand and one which had gone before, a love tale better than them all, the dawn of a new era for the subjects of King Shahryār.

---

[4]**grenade**: Pomegranate.

When the brothers had come from the hammām in the morning and joined their wives, the wazīr sought permission to enter. They rose in his honour and the two women kissed his hand; but, when he asked for the day's orders, the four said with one voice: 'O father, we wish that you should give commands in the future and not receive them. That is why we make you King of Samarkand al-Ajam.' 'I yield my throne to you,' said Shahzamān; and Shahryār cried: 'I will only give you leave to do so, my brother, if you will consent to share my royalty and reign with me day and day about.' 'I hear and I obey,' said Shahzamān.

The wazīr kissed his daughters in farewell, embraced the three little sons, and departed for Samarkand al-Ajam at the head of a magnificent escort. Allāh had written him security in his journey, and the inhabitants of his new kingdom hailed his coming with delight. He reigned over them in all justice and became a King among great Kings. So much for him.

After these things, King Shahryār called together the most renowned annalists and proficient scribes from all the quarters of Islam, and ordered them to write out the tales of Shahrazād from beginning to end, without the omission of a single detail. So they sat down and wrote thirty volumes in gold letters, and called this sequence of marvels and astonishments: THE BOOK OF THE THOUSAND NIGHTS AND ONE NIGHT. Many faithful copies were made, and King Shahryār sent them to the four corners of his empire, to be an instruction to the people and their children's children. But he shut the original manuscript in the gold cupboard of his reign and made his wazīr of treasure responsible for its safe keeping.

King Shahryār and Queen Shahrazād, King Shahzamān and Queen Dunyazād, and Shahrazād's three small sons, lived year after year in all delight, knowing days each more admirable than the last and nights whiter than days, until they were visited by the Separator of friends, the Destroyer, the Builder of tombs, the Inexorable, the Inevitable.

Such are the excellent tales called THE THOUSAND NIGHTS AND ONE NIGHT, together with all that is in them of wonder and instruction, prodigy and marvel, astonishment and beauty.

But Allah knows all! He alone can distinguish between the true and the false. He knows all!

Now everlasting glory and praise be unto Him
Who rests Intangible amid Eternity;
Who, changing all things, yet Himself changes not;
Who is the Master of the Seen and of the Unseen;
Who alone Lives!
And prayer and peace with benediction
be upon the King's Chosen,
our Lord Muhammad,
Prince of Messengers,
Jewel of the World,
our hope for an auspicious
END!

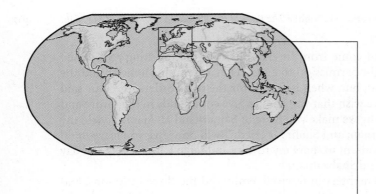

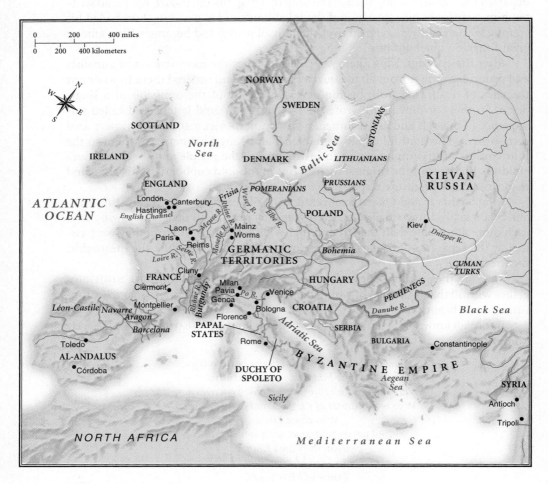

Europe and the Mediterranean, c. 1050

By 1050, several political entities had divided Europe. The German king presided over territories that reached from Rome to the North Sea; to the east, Kievan Russia was being forged from a mix of Scandinavian and Slavic populations; to the south was the Byzantine empire; and in al-Andalus and North Africa was the Muslim world. The next centuries, however, would show how weak these large states actually were.

EUROPE
From Epic to Romance and Beyond

The concept of the European Middle Ages was first formulated during the Italian RENAISSANCE, when scholars wished to identify the period between the classical age of Greece and Rome and their own era. This medieval age can be broken down into four parts: the first period consists of Roman influence, the creation of Germanic tribal identity, and the rise of kingdoms (100–800 C.E.); the second period extends from the development of the system of feudalism to the beginning of the Crusades (800–1100); the third period includes the Crusades and the consolidation of major European institutions (1100–1300); and the fourth period marks the transition from the medieval to the modern world (1300–1500). The key development of the European Middle Ages was the political, economic, and social formation of Europe and its growing interaction with the Near East, the Middle East, the Far East, North Africa, and Asia.

Broadly speaking, the literary production of the Middle Period follows these historical divisions and the events that define them. The earliest literature reflects the Latin culture of the Catholic Church and the restoration of the heroic literature of the continent, such as the Anglo-Saxon *Beowulf*. The literature of the next period reflects the courts of the feudal period, up to the time of the *Song of Roland*. The literature of the third period reflects the growth of the courts and their enthusiasm for romances and the love poetry of the south of France. The literature of the fourth period reflects a broader and more cosmopolitan outlook, nourished in the cities and towns; there is greater access to the Greek and Latin classics and the education provided in schools and universities. At this time, sophisticated writers like Dante, Boccaccio, and Chaucer incorporated the stories of diverse lands and cultures into their work, taking them from religious and secular sources alike. And for the first time women writers appeared as significant voices in European writing.

The Coronation of Charlemagne, fourteenth century

Pope Leo's coronation of the Frankish king Charlemagne as emperor in 800 C.E. marked the restoration of the Roman Empire, the formal joining of Church and State, the consecration of Europe as an idea, and the start of a cultural revival through which learning and the arts would receive recognition. This event is depicted here in the fourteenth-century illuminated French manuscript, The Chronicles of France. (The Art Archive/Bibliothèque Municipale, Castres/Dagli Orti)

FROM ROME TO THE GERMANIC STATES

Because Roman military rule never included adequate economic planning for the development of conquered regions, Rome's economy stagnated as its territory expanded. Cities declined from lack of trade. Finally, the Roman army itself weakened, especially in the Germanic regions, so that increasingly the Roman legions in the north were actually composed of Franks and other Germans. Slowly the Germanic tribes gathered strength and overcame the Romans. Though life was uniformly hard and cruel in the northern warrior societies, a new system of ethics, justice, and social organization was slowly taking shape, a combination of ancient tribal customs and Roman practices. By the beginning of the sixth century, those newly in possession of the land — the Ostrogoths in what was later Italy, the Visigoths in what was later southern France and Spain, the Franks and other Germanic tribes in what was later northern France and Germany, and the Anglo-Saxons in what had been Roman and Celtic Britain — had established a certain stability. Meanwhile, the Catholic Church was adapting to the expansion of the Germanic tribal states. After Pope Leo I (r. 440–61) consolidated papal authority in Rome, the Frankish king Clovis (r. 481–511) extended protection to the church, much as the Roman emperors had in the fourth century.

At the end of the sixth century, Pope Gregory the Great (r. 590–604) sent Benedictine monks and other members of the clergy to convert tribal chieftains from central Europe west to the British Isles. The rudimentary Latin culture of the missionaries consisted of the Bible, a brief liturgical handbook, the Benedictine Rule for establishing monasteries, and Gregory's treatise on pastoral care. The missionaries often made their case for conversion within the framework of the native culture of Germanic society. The British historian The Venerable Bede (d. 735) reports that after speaking to a priest, a pagan counselor tried to persuade his king to convert to Christianity by using traditional Anglo-Saxon eloquence. He spoke as follows:

> [A] sparrow flies swiftly in one door of the hall, and out through another. While he is inside, he is safe from the winter storms; but after a few moments of comfort, he vanishes from sight into the wintry world from which he came. Even so, man appears on earth for a little while; but of what went before this life or of what follows, we know nothing. Therefore, if this new teaching has brought any more certain knowledge, it seems only right that we should follow it.

The conversion missions were quite successful. The literature of the period contains many sermons, poems, and passages from the Bible translated into the Germanic languages with the same penchant for dramatic effect.

The Auzon Casket, eighth century C.E.
This early casket, named after the French town in which it was found in the nineteenth century, is remarkable for its depictions of scenes from Roman, Jewish, Christian, and Germanic traditions. It is thought to have been built in Northumbria (England) sometime during the first half of the eighth century. On the left of the visible panel is a scene from Germanic legend and on the right is the Adoration of the Magi. (British Museum)

THE EARLY FRANKISH KINGDOM

Politically speaking, the European continent just emerging from Roman authority was still largely unconscious of itself. Ironically, the development of European consciousness awaited pressure from outside the region. When the Prophet Muhammad, driven out of his native city of Mecca, took up arms and swept through Arabia until his death in 632, he set in motion a "holy war" that would propel the Islamic faithful through Syria, Persia, and Egypt, into North Africa, and across the Mediterranean to the Iberian Peninsula (now Spain and Portugal). For a hundred years Europe could not halt Islam's advance to the north, until finally the Franks defeated Islamic warriors at Tours in 732.

The Carolingians, named after Charles Martel, ruler of the Franks from 714 to 741, were an impoverished people dependent on a crude agricultural system. Although based far to the north, it was they who managed to overcome the Muslims at Tours. But the honor of uniting the Franks under the Papacy was reserved for Martel's grandson, Charlemagne (768–814). Under Charlemagne's authority, Frankish holdings were extended into what is now Italy, Bavaria, Austria, and northern

Germany. (A minor battle against the Basques in the Pyrenees in 778 that caused the death of one of Charlemagne's lords was depicted in the great epic of feudal society, *The Song of Roland,* a work written down at the end of the eleventh century.)

THE FORMATION OF EUROPE

Charlemagne was crowned emperor by Pope Leo III on Christmas Day in 800 C.E., in his northern capital at Aix-la-Chapelle (Aachen). Whether or not one believes that he was taken by surprise by the pope's appearance at his coronation, as reported by his biographer, the event served the interests of both Rome and the Carolingians. It marked the restoration of the Roman Empire, the formal joining of church and state, the consecration of Europe as an idea, and the start of a cultural revival through which learning and the arts would receive recognition. This moment of glory, however, was relatively brief. After the death of Charlemagne, the grandiose conception of an empire that would stretch from the North Sea to the Mediterranean faltered as a result of the economic underdevelopment of the entire area, the persistence of local cultures with their own languages and customs, and the fragmentation brought about by Viking raids from the north. Since the dissolution of the original Roman Empire, trading opportunities were limited, roads poorly developed, and towns few and primitive. Efforts to raise taxes from local barons were hampered by inefficiency and the poverty of the estates. In addition, invaders from the north attacked outposts near the sea and isolated, unguarded monasteries, taking over territory in Normandy and the British Isles. England itself fell to the Norman Conquest in 1066 in which Norman French troops seized the throne and significantly changed the direction of British language, culture, and society.

Overall, the Carolingian cultural revival was important both for what it did and did not accomplish. Charlemagne, barely literate himself, imported scholars from the scattered centers of learning across Europe to begin a program of cultural restoration. The Bible was purged of centuries of scribal errors, schools were established under the royal court, monasteries were scrutinized and abuses corrected, and the Benedictine Rule was expanded to provide a better guide to monastic life. Few original works of literary or philosophical merit, however, were produced. Although Charlemagne prohibited the writing of love poems in the vernacular by nuns, Latin hymns and secular lyrics were composed in monasteries, preparing for a broader literature in the vernacular languages later on.

FEUDALISM BEFORE THE CRUSADES

In the later ninth and early tenth centuries, as the Carolingian dynasty faltered, a feudal system began to develop in Europe that would enable baronial estates to protect themselves against foreign raids and to cope with the time's harsh economic circumstances. Each feudal enclave consisted of the lord of an estate and a landed class of knights, who pledged, along with their lesser vassals and serfs, to defend the lord against his enemies. Ties of obedience were created and feudal society grew out of this vertical system of loyalties. A worldview based on these ties was necessarily a limited one, and the typical literature of the day emphasized rigidly determined knightly virtues, conceived of as service to the lord and faith in God, to be maintained even in the worst of situations. But European feudal society as a whole, especially in the Frankish kingdoms, was never completely stable. With the beginning of the First Crusade in 1095, feudal society, which had depended on the division of Europe into small entities, gave way to the expansion of Christendom and the reorganization of Europe on a broader political and military basis.

THE FIRST CRUSADE

The new warfare between Christians and Muslims began in the eleventh century, when Muslim control of Andalusia, or Spain, began to weaken. As the century ended, Christian forces slowly began recapturing Spanish cities and driving the Muslims out; but the Reconquest, as it was called, took another four hundred years to complete. Meanwhile, deep in Asia Minor, Muslim Turks were interfering with Christian pilgrims traveling to Jerusalem, and Emperor Alexius I of Constantinople, powerless to stop them, asked for Western aid. Following a fiery sermon by Pope Urban II, the First Crusade was launched by the Franks and their allies in 1095 to occupy the Holy Land. Once begun, the First Crusade took on a character of its own. The capture of Jerusalem from the Muslims in 1099 precipitated one of the worst massacres in human history. Christian eyewitnesses reported that for days the streets of the city ran with Muslim and Jewish blood.

The impact of the First Crusade was as much economic as it was religious or political. By gaining control of a vast area in Asia Minor, the Crusaders secured the Mediterranean as a trade route to the Far East; thus one consequence of the Crusade was the liberation of Europe from economic stagnation. And with the new prosperity, the fixed order of the feudal system came to an end. A new society was forming, one with a different economic base, worldview, and cultural values.

ECONOMIC AND SOCIAL TRANSFORMATION

Free from the threat of outside invasion and benefiting from the economic rewards of the First and Second Crusades, European society of the early twelfth century underwent dramatic changes. Trade and commerce developed, first in the coastal towns and cities and then across the continent. From landlocked areas, farmers and serfs began to flock to town centers, which clamored for independence from surrounding baronial estates. Everywhere towns and cities began to demand independence from the countryside. In schools administrated by the larger churches and the new cathedrals, education changed from the strict regimen of the Benedictines, who taught grammar, rhetoric, and logic according to narrowly defined monastic usage, to classically influenced models. There was even a change in books deemed worthy of study. The Latin poet Ovid was now read in full: *The Metamorphoses* was no longer edited to exclude its bawdy stories, and *The Art of Love,* always viewed with a certain distaste by the church, was freely consulted.

The fighting of the Crusades, which persisted through the twelfth and thirteenth centuries, took place far from European soil; at the same time, this mobilization of Europe over many years tended to create a broader consciousness in its population. The motive for warfare changed from a feudal obligation to defend the local lord to a choice to serve God and country in foreign lands; the latter choice was often viewed by younger knights as an opportunity to display their courage and noble breeding. The military class of knights was transformed from a hardscrabble army to an honorable assembly charged with a holy cause. On European soil, jousting tournaments took the place of battles, and the lower aristocracy occupied itself with maintaining its estates and providing hospitality and entertainment. Castles and manors, no longer the narrow, fortified spaces they were in the tenth century, became rich, commodious quarters suitable for lavish display. As a result of these changes, tastes changed and a new audience emerged at court. The new literature looked to the idealized knighthood that the courts themselves were beginning to create.

CHIVALRY AND THE DEVELOPMENT OF ROMANCE

Ideals of chivalry, some imported from the Near and Middle East after the First Crusade, came to dominate the knightly code of ethics. Proper behavior was considered an important attribute of true knighthood, and the great romances of the twelfth century by the French writer Chrétien de Troyes and the German Wolfram von Eschenbach stress the necessity to display "courtesy" or good breeding. Women at court were seen as educators of men in good behavior, while the theories of courtly love from the south of France insisted — rather fancifully — that the only true love was the secret and possibly adulterous love of a knight for his aristocratic lady. Such a knight was twice subjugated by his love — the lady was above him in social class and favored over him by gender. The audience for this material was a mixed courtly society of knights and ladies, along with their retainers and some of their wealthy followers from the towns.

The legendary figure of Eleanor, duchess of Aquitaine (1122–1204), hovered over Anglo-Norman and French court life in this period, helping to give birth to the courtly romance. Eleanor was the granddaughter of the first troubadour poet in the southern French province of Aquitaine. The child bride of Louis VII, king of France, in 1137, she joined her first husband on the Second Crusade in 1147. In 1152, tiring of the confining life of the French monarchy in Paris, she divorced Louis to marry Henry Plantagenet, duke of Normandy, later Henry II of England (1154–1189). Eleanor reigned as queen of England until 1170, when she returned to Poitiers in the south of France. There she revived the troubadour song tradition her grandfather had initiated in the courts of southern France. She also brought with her stories of King Arthur, immortalized in Geoffrey of Monmouth's legendary *History of the Kings of Britain* (1140). King Arthur, the stories go, lived in a supernatural realm populated by the fairies, magicians, and fantasy knights of Celtic legend. In an atmosphere laden with the miraculous, these knights were easily separated from their feudal ties to experience new adventures.

THE NEW SPIRITUALITY AND THE DECLINE OF THE PAPACY

In the twelfth and early thirteenth centuries, the Catholic Church developed spiritually and artistically. Saint Bernard of Clairvaux (1090–1153), a Cistercian monk who preached the call to the Second Crusade, led a reform movement inside the church that emphasized the mystical association of the believer with God. Following in the spirit of St. Bernard's entreaties, two new religious orders arose at the beginning of the thirteenth century. The Dominicans focused on their preaching mission while the Franciscans were known for the simplicity and piety attributed to their founder, St. Francis of Assisi (1182–1226). St. Francis's spiritual sufferings and his concern for the condition of the poor gained him a huge popular following. After his death, he became the first major subject of the Italian painter Giotto di Bondone (1267–1337), whose *Histories of St. Francis* decorate the lower panels of the nave in the Basilica of Assisi.

Later in the century, the new European monarchies, built around strong nation-states like England and France, began to clamor for control of the church. The inauguration of Pope Clement V in 1305 marked the beginning of the decline of papal authority. Under attack from various heads of state, Clement moved the papacy from Rome to Avignon, in the south of France, where it remained until 1376. The new popular spirituality encouraged by the religious orders and the decline of the papacy coexisted in the Roman Catholic experience of the thirteenth century: while the piety of common people helped to create a spiritual revival, the corruption of church officials led to the humiliation of the church by the princes of Europe. Both the spiritual and the worldly aspects of religious life were of major concern to the Italian poet Dante Alighieri (1265–1321), a Florentine exile who wrote *The Divine Comedy* early in the fourteenth century. Dante's visionary verse trilogy describes a spiritual dream in which the poet visits Hell, Purgatory, and Heaven. Dante locates many great lords, popes, and prominent citizens of Florence in Hell, providing the poet the opportunity for satire as well as fiery condemnation.

END OF AN ERA

Italian cities were the first to fully reflect the economic improvement brought about by increased trade with the Near East in the thirteenth century. Prosperity spread to the north in the later fourteenth century. Both the new prosperity and the decline of the papacy strengthened the developing governments in the new nations of England, France, and Spain. In the fifteenth century, these states would develop strong monarchies that would dominate European political life for centuries to come. The overall increase in secular authority also helped create a new climate in which the state, the city, and the individual became the dominant moral and cultural forces, while the ideals of the church and of the feudal and courtly societies lost influence.

In the chaos of the fourteenth century, increasingly secularized writers enjoyed a new status. Authors such as Giovanni Boccaccio (1313–1375) and Geoffrey Chaucer (c. 1340–1400), trained in the schools of the cities and towns, expressed faith in trade and progress—Chaucer's father was a wine merchant and the poet himself was clerk of the works for the English royal household. They were individuals, no longer writing merely because they were attached to wealthy patrons who expected it of them, but writing in greater part out of personal motivation. They were still Christians, but Christianity no longer dictated all the terms of worldly behavior. Above all, they possessed a perspective on the passing of a millennium—a thousand years during which, by and large, the City of God had taken precedence over the City of Man.

THE CREATION OF EUROPEAN CULTURE

One way to look at the formation of Europe is to see it as the story Europe tells about itself: Europe was based on the ideals of Greek and Roman civilization. It adopted Christianity as the Roman Empire declined and produced from within its own ranks a new civilization, starting with Charlemagne. In areas conquered by the Europeans, the "barbarians" were suppressed and their literature rescued and collected by the conquerors. In the case of Islam, the Christian Crusades in the Middle East at the beginning of the twelfth century resulted in the capture of Jerusalem and much of the Holy Land, although eventually Muslims reconquered this territory. In Spain, the Christians ultimately prevailed, driving the Muslims into Africa and the Near East. Since 1492, the year of the Muslim expulsion from Spain and, coincidentally, the year of Columbus's first voyage to America, Europe has maintained its cultural identity and geographic stability despite shifts of power and influence.

It is a story subject to debate. The "barbarian" inheritance of social organization, law, and culture received from the Germanic tribes of the first to fifth centuries is arguably as important to modern-day Europeans as the classical heritage of Greece and Rome. Charlemagne, king of the Franks, was a descendant of the same "barbarians" whom the Romans had tried so savagely to repress; in any case, his dynasty crumbled soon after his death. The influence of Islam on Europe can be said to be much greater than Europe ever admitted; in Spain, medieval Europe benefited from Islamic art and architecture, music, philosophy, law, medicine, science, translation of the Greek and Roman classics, and trade. Finally, Europe never has maintained a stable cultural identity: From the "discovery" of America to its importation of "guest workers" today, it has taken part in a continuous cultural exchange, often weighted in its favor, with other nations of the world.

FROM EPIC TO ROMANCE

Every society has its myths and texts, cultural themes that are important to its growth and survival. Germanic tribal societies had their own heroic stories of larger-than-life human figures, among them EPICS such as *Beowulf*. Typically, in stories that celebrate the life of the tribe, the hero saves his people from monsters or leads them into battle, the outcome of which is governed by Fate. There is often an elegiac tone to these works, since no man lives forever and the greatest societies weaken and die.

The beginning of the twelfth century, the period of the Christian Crusades, marked a transition period in European literature. Although *The Song of Roland* retains some of the values of the heroic epic, its hero, now completely human, fights and dies with the name of God on his lips, and his opponent is the pagan infidel, not a monster. This was the literature of the "Church militant," suitable for recitation to the armies of Europe as they rode off under the papal banner to the First Crusade. It combined the feudal principle of service to one's lord with the new idea of the Christian warrior, for now knights were fighting for the glory of God and the destruction of the heathen, and they were promised eternal salvation as a reward for their service.

The next stage of literary development marked a new departure. The courtly literature of the twelfth century was ROMANCE. While its hero was still a knight, the world around him had softened considerably; indeed, he existed in a world made up partly of fantasy and partly the rules of social decorum, or chivalry. The religious version of courtly romance literature took the form of stories of holy pilgrimage, wherein the characters were models of appropriate behavior. Sometimes the courtly romance and the literature of pilgrimages merged, as in the twelfth-century romance *Perceval, the Knight of the Grail* by Chrétien de Troyes, whose young knight goes in quest of the Holy Grail, the cup used according to legend by Christ at the Last Supper.

THE THEME OF LOVE

In the late medieval period, treatises on love, theories of love, and accounts of both sublimated and sexual love abounded, even in religious settings. There is considerable evidence that the European interest in love themes derived at least in part from the Arabic literature of Andalusia (Spain) in the tenth and eleventh centuries. As is true of Andalusian love poetry, some of the great European expressions of romantic love of this time took the form of poetry, especially the Provencal lyrics of the twelfth century. This literature emerged at about the same time that monastic Christianity's monopoly on education was being disturbed, and previously questionable works such as Ovid's *Art of Love* found their way into the schools and universities.

Medieval conventions regarding love were connected with social class. As the court priest Andreas Capellanus writes in the twelfth-century *Art of Courtly Love,* love is understood differently according to whether it takes place between members of the nobility, the peasantry, or the clergy (though the latter is immoral, Capellanus hints of his interest in the subject). For the nobility, love is complicated, with distinctions of rank and custom to be observed. Love among the peasantry is bawdy and direct; Capellanus views it as animal passion with no human qualities at all. This double standard is still at work in the writings of Boccaccio and Chaucer in the fourteenth century, in the courtly affairs of knights and ladies and the earthy love stories of the town and the countryside.

THE THEME OF TRAVEL AND THE RISE OF THE INDIVIDUAL

Whether undertaken for adventure, pilgrimage, or trade, travel was an important theme of medieval European literature during the time of the Crusades. The Europeans were not the first great travelers; others had already come from Asia to discover the Middle East or taken to the Silk Road from the Middle East to China with their goods. Pilgrimage literature was a venerable tradition in both Islam and Europe by the eleventh century, and expeditions from Europe to India and China began in earnest in the twelfth and thirteenth centuries. Travelers often wrote memorable accounts of their journeys, such as that of Venetian trader Marco Polo (1254–1324). But the most loved work of medieval European travel literature was a literary fabrication, an assemblage of earlier accounts. Neverthe-less, *Mandeville's Travels,* written in the fourteenth century, enjoyed enormous popularity for centuries.

Other transformations in literature near the end of the Middle Ages reflected what could be called the individualization of experience. For instance, while Chaucer frames his *Canterbury Tales* in a pilgrimage narrative, his interest in human personality is more modern than medieval. Boccaccio, Chaucer's Italian predecessor, treated personality in a similarly modern fashion. And fifteenth-century English writer Margery Kempe's account of her pilgrimage to the Holy Land is so blunt and realistic that it transforms the literary genre it belongs to. After Kempe it is hard to find pilgrimage literature in the old sense at all—so much had the personality of the narrator come to dominate the purpose of the journey.

THE DIVINE COMEDY: THE GREAT SYNTHESIS

Dante's *Divine Comedy* is a combination of all the literary categories discussed thus far: the epic, the romance, courtly love literature, and the travel narrative. Influ-enced by certain books of the Bible and the Qur'an (Koran), it imitates visionary prophecy. But it is also much more: an incisive exposure of the contemporary world lost to the madness of sin, and the tragedy of human existence seen from the point of death. Ultimately, it contains the hope of redemption. It is titled a "comedy" simply because, in Aristotelian terms, the story turns out well: Dante the pilgrim is granted a vision of Paradise in the end.

Dante saw the humiliation of the papacy and the depravity of people every-where at the end of the Middle Ages and asked what had become of Christian Europe under its popes and kings, its creeds and dynasties. Any possibility of belief in the just actions of the papal armies and the holy wars had ended with the exhaustion of the Crusades; Dante had witnessed the Christian defeat in his life-time. For the individual soul there remained the hope of salvation in the doctrine of the grace of God. But what had man, acting in the name of God, made of man? It was the secular Dante, the inquisitor of history, who sent shivers up the spines of worldly men by asking questions they could hardly answer.

www For more information about the culture and context of Europe in the Middle Period, see *World Literature Online* at bedfordstmartins.com/worldlit.

Europe: Chartres Cathedral of Notre Dame (Twelfth and Thirteenth Centuries)

The Gothic cathedrals of Europe were created during a time of tremendous social and cultural ferment. In the twelfth century these great edifices, with their spacious interiors, towering vaulted roofs, brilliant high windows, massive columns supported by buttresses, and tall single or double spires were first erected in France, then in Germany and England. Perhaps the most beautiful and the longest standing without major alteration is the Chartres Cathedral in the province of Orleans in northern France. The original church was destroyed by fire in 1134. Construction of the cathedral, with its two magnificent towers, royal portal, and rose window, was halted by a second fire in 1194. From then on, the job of building this massive sanctuary continued unabated through the thirteenth century, with the nave, transept, and choir having all been completed by 1220.

The character of a medieval European cathedral was determined by its use of the symbolic imagery of the Christian faith and by the particular imagination and competence of its master builder—in how he exploited the possibilities of stone and glass; in his choice of the weight and height of the structure's ceilings, walls, and towers; in his design of the buttresses that supported the outer walls. Christian imagery was depicted in stained-glass windows, in sculptures adorning the inner walls as well as the outer edifice, and in the cruciform design, or the cross shape, of the cathedral itself. The enormity of Chartres can be partially comprehended in the height of its spires (350 and 375 feet) and in the area and height of its windows. By 1260, 22,000 square feet of glass had been installed in 186 windows of approximately half the height of the cathedral's walls. The beautiful glass windows, including many originals; the massive grouped sculptures along the outer

ledges of the cathedral; the majestic height of the nave, or central section, as seen from within the church; and the structure's grand yet graceful flying buttresses remain today. Entire books have been written and films created to interpret the design and meaning of this great cathedral.

Chartres Cathedral is a shining example of the new culture of cathedrals and universities that emerged in Europe in the twelfth century, out of which also came Scholasticism, a synthesis of religion and philosophy most memorably stated in *Summa Theologica* by St. Thomas Aquinas in the thirteenth century. The bringing together of the work of the ancient Greek philosophers and the faith of the Christian fathers, the concept of intelligence guided by God's grace, dominated the period. Chartres cathedral, a symphony of glass and stone, is a consummate artistic expression of this synthesis.

Chartres Cathedral. The great Gothic cathedral of Notre Dame de Chartres in Chartres, France. (The Art Archive / Dagli Orti)

❧ BEOWULF

EIGHTH CENTURY—TENTH CENTURY

While *Beowulf* is renowned as one of the world's great poems, it also holds many mysteries. Despite the efforts of generations of scholars, no one is certain exactly when or where it was written or who it was written by. The major events in the work—**Beowulf**'s fights with two monsters, Grendel and Grendel's mother, and his final battle with a dragon—were drawn from ancient Scandinavian legends. The poem's allusions to the kings and peoples of northern Europe date primarily from the fifth and sixth centuries; the story most likely was brought to England by Germanic invaders a little later. The poem, first composed orally, was written down in Anglo-Saxon somewhere between the eighth and tenth centuries, accounting for its "Christian coloring," which was probably added once the poem reached England. Thematically, *Beowulf* belongs to an ancient epic tradition found in a number of early societies. Like the Sumerian hero Gilgamesh and the Greek hero Achilles from Homer's *Iliad,* Beowulf is stronger and wiser than other men, though a mortal. *Beowulf* emphasizes the hero's role as the protector of his people, while also showing that no man is secure before fate, or knows what awaits him after death. It contrasts the strength of the young warrior with his vulnerability fifty years later; in fact, the hero's death anticipates the end of his warrior society. For this reason, the ending of *Beowulf* is considered an elegy, both for its hero and for the culture he represents.

Ancient and Christian.   *Beowulf* reflects three distinct cultural systems: the ancient culture of Scandinavia, with its folktales of monsters and demons and its fatalistic view of human impotence before the gods; the Scandinavian and Germanic tribal societies of early medieval Europe, with their cautionary tales of the rise and fall of kingdoms and their reliance on custom and the will of the community as arbiters of human conduct; and the culture of the Anglo-Saxon author, stressing the Christian ideals of humility and righteousness. These earlier northern European traditions and Christianity coexist uneasily at times in the text. In the last lines of the poem, Beowulf is eulogized for his kindness and gentleness, suggesting Christian virtues, but also for his eagerness for fame, an attribute of pagan heroes. Attempts to interpret the poem as a religious allegory in which paganism is overcome by Christianity ultimately are unconvincing; instead, the story laments the passing of one culture through the eyes of another.

The epic of *Beowulf* has recognizable Scandinavian and Germanic ancestors. The Old Norse prose epic ***Volsungasaga***, drawn from Germanic and Scandinavian legends of the fifth through the eighth centuries, was probably composed during the age of the Vikings (800–1070), though it survives only in a manuscript from the thirteenth century. The ***Nibelungenlied***, a south German courtly epic composed at the beginning of the thirteenth century, invokes the same cycle of heroic stories. Both

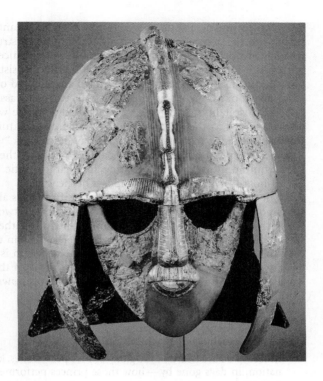

Anglo-Saxon Helmet, seventh century
This magnificent helmet is one of only four Anglo-Saxon helmets in existence. The eyebrows are thin strands of silver wire and garnet, and each ends in a gilt boar's head. Between the eyebrows, two gilded dragons' heads lie nose to nose, with the upper one's body running in a low crest over the crown of the helmet. The helmet was recovered from the site of the ship burial at Sutton Hoo in 1939. (British Museum)

these works contain the theme of the "final battle," a myth about the destruction of the gods at the end of the heroic era. Other works nearly contemporary with *Beowulf* consist of battle descriptions composed in alliterative poetry, including the Old German *Hildebrandslied* and the Anglo-Saxon *Battle of Finnsburh*, a story repeated in *Beowulf* itself.

The Christian beliefs represented in *Beowulf* arrived in England after the migration of the Germanic tribes in the fifth and sixth centuries. The church historian The Venerable Bede (673–735) writes in his *Ecclesiastical History of the English People* (731) about the poet Caedmon, who composed Anglo-Saxon Christian poetry in the latter half of the seventh century. Sermons and other Christian writings in Anglo Saxon also attest to the restatement of Christian doctrine from Latin sources in the vernacular English language.

Oral Formulaic Poetry and the Language of *Beowulf*.   The proof of the Scandinavian (Germanic) origins of *Beowulf* lies in its language and verse form. The manuscript of the poem comes from a period when scribes attached to royal courts and monasteries were encouraged to record the poetry and prose of the vernacular language. *Beowulf* is composed in the traditional poetic meter termed oral-formulaic poetry (referring to its manner of composition) or alliterative poetry (referring to its formal features).

www   For quizzes on *Beowulf*, see *World Literature Online* at bedfordstmartins .com/worldlit.

The general structure
of the poem . . . is
essentially a balance,
an opposition of
ends and beginnings.
In its simplest terms
it is a contrasted
description of two
moments in a great
life, rising and
setting; an elabora-
tion of the ancient
and intensely moving
contrast between
youth and age, first
achievement and
final death. . . .
   —J. R. R. TOLKIEN,
   scholar and editor,
   1936

Oral-formulaic poetry is verse that is either chanted or spoken, perhaps to the accompaniment of a harp or other instrument, using a number of stock phrases or formulas in order to enhance the poet's opportunities for expression. The formulas usually consist of descriptive phrases: for instance, a ruler may be called a "shepherd of his people," a "ring-giver," or a "shield" in time of war. His wife, who assists the king by offering hospitality to visitors, may be called a "peace weaver" or "cup bearer" as well as the queen. Even the elements of nature are assigned stock epithets: for instance, the ocean may be called a "whale-road." In Anglo-Saxon poetry there are many parallel names for the things that are most commonly described, resulting in a large poetic vocabulary, or "word-hoard," available to the composer of the work.

The standard form of Anglo-Saxon versification is alliterative four-stress poetry. Each verse line is made up of four feet, two to each half a line with a pause halfway through the line. Alliteration, the repetition of a single sound at the beginning of words, often occurs in two or three of the four stressed words in a line, at least one of which is found in each half line, and is usually governed by the first letter of the first stressed word in the second half line. In the opening lines of *Beowulf*, the alliterative sounds have been italicized:

Hwaet! We *G*ar-Dena in *g*ear-dagum
*Th*eod-cyninga, *th*rym gefrunon,
Hu tha *ae*thelingas *e*llen fremedon!

Indeed, we have heard of the glory of the Spear-Danes, kings of the nation, in days gone by—how those princes performed deeds of courage.[1]

Although irregularity in the verse form is frequent, the four-stress line and alliteration clearly dominate the sound of the poem as a whole. English verse translations, while they use a modern vocabulary, usually mimic some of the poetic features of the original. Prose translations, such as the one used in this anthology, are generally more accurate renderings of the original meaning but lose much of the aural quality, the music, of the original.

Effects of the Poetry.   *Beowulf* is a narrative poem whose action moves ahead step by step. This simple style is called PARATAXIS, from the Greek meaning "putting one after the other." The narrative becomes more complex when the writer embellishes the main story with other tales. These secondary narratives range from anecdotes or historical references taking up a few lines to self-contained stories with an implied relationship to the main story, called DIGRESSIONS.

A special case of embellishment comes when the poet steps out of the time frame of the narrative to refer to more recent history—history known to himself and his audience—that reflects on the main story. Often this commentary is ironic; it undercuts the mood of the poem. An

---

[1] The spelling and punctuation in the first three lines of *Beowulf* in Anglo-Saxon have been adapted for modern English; the prose translation is by Michael Swanton.

example is when King Hrothgar of the Geats erects a great hall in which he shows his beneficence to his followers by distributing gifts. In the middle of the description of the hall, the poet mentions a future fire, known to the audience, resulting from a feud within the ruling family that later destroys the hall:

> The hall rose up high, lofty and wide-gabled; awaited the furious surge of hostile flames. The day was not yet near when violent hatred between son-in-law and father-in-law should be born of deadly malice.

Irony also appears in Anglo-Saxon literature in the form of understatement. For example, after Beowulf is killed by the dragon near the end of the poem, his loyal young retainer, **Wiglaf**, chastises his companions who have run away from the dragon-fight. With mock politeness he remarks: "Too few defenders thronged about the prince when the evil time came upon him." He adds bluntly that these companions will have neither a share of the dragon's treasure nor the benefits of their lord's protection that they once enjoyed. Finally, furious, he declares: "To any warrior death is better than a life of disgrace!"

WIG-lahf

The Flow of the Epic.   As *Beowulf*'s narrative begins, the young lord Beowulf of the Geats travels across the sea to **Heorot** Hall, ruled by King **Hrothgar** in the land of the Danes. Heorot is in crisis: It has sustained bloody raids by **Grendel**, a monster who has been devouring its thanes (knights). Beowulf and his men are warmly greeted by the lords of Heorot, with the exception of **Unferth**, a Danish champion who insults him by belittling his physical prowess and courage. After getting the better of Unferth in a verbal duel, Beowulf retires for the night with his men in the great hall. When all is dark and the men are asleep, Grendel steals upon them and feasts on one of Beowulf's men. Beowulf grapples with the monster, tearing off his arm at the shoulder. Mortally wounded, Grendel flees. In the morning, Beowulf follows his bloody trail to a swampy pool where he has died. Heorot Hall celebrates Beowulf's feat with a great feast, and his deed is memorialized in song. But that night a second monster invades the hall and kills **Aeschere**, the chief advisor of King Hrothgar. At daybreak Beowulf tracks this monster to the same pool. In an underwater chamber, Beowulf discovers and kills Grendel's mother, who had attacked the hall to avenge the death of her son; thus he purges the evil from Heorot at last. After another celebration at Hrothgar's court, Beowulf returns to the kingdom of the Geats where he shares the gifts he has received with his own king, **Hygelac**. He is given a great hall and land of his own, and one section of the poem ends.

HEH-oh-rote
HROHTH-gar
GREN-dul

UN-furth

ASH-hay-ruh

HIH-yuh-lak

Epic and Elegy.   A different world is depicted in the final part of the poem. Beginning with an account of the Geats over the fifty years of Beowulf's reign, it turns to the story of a dragon and his hoard of ancient treasure, abandoned by a royal house centuries before. The dragon, disturbed by the theft of a cup from his treasure-hoard by a fugitive from the court of Beowulf, burns down Beowulf's stronghold. Beowulf pursues

Here at the end of this poem there is only the structure men make, a frail shell around their solidarity, fated to have only a brief space of time before the final burning. It is a boundary situation. . . . The Geats' riding [around the burial mound] and their speaking of the words of praise draw the audience into the poet's circle of human solidarity. We too can see and honor, always against the terrible darkness, Beowulf's qualities: strength, mercy, gentleness, and above all an unquenchable passion for glory.

– EDWARD B. IRVING JR., 1989, critic

koh-mih-TAH-toos

the dragon, taking with him eleven retainers and the man who stole the cup, or flagon. In the dragon-fight, Beowulf's sword, Naegling, and his other defenses fail him. Seeing this, his retainers flee except for the youthful Wiglaf, who tells Beowulf to take heart and joins the battle. Finally, the dragon bites Beowulf on the neck. Wiglaf strikes the dragon a mortal blow and Beowulf disembowels it. Feeling the dragon's poison begin to take effect, Beowulf commands Wiglaf to show him the treasure. He then orders its burial in a barrow overlooking the sea, gives Wiglaf his collar, ring, and helmet, and names him the last of his royal line. The Geats prepare Beowulf for cremation and the treasure for burial. Wiglaf delivers the eulogy. It is fitting, the poet concludes, to mourn such a great king.

The dragon-fight shows the Geats in dissolution. The recovery of the dragon's treasure is meaningless, since it is soon buried again. There can be no celebration in the great hall—it has been destroyed by the dragon—and Beowulf's followers have deserted him in his hour of need. Wiglaf inherits the throne but will have no successor. The circle of society formed by the giving of gifts and the telling of stories of the heroes of the past will soon be broken. A famous speech sometimes called "the song of the last survivor" mourns the passing of heroic society:

> Hold now, you earth, the possession of warriors, now that the heroes cannot! Indeed, it was from you that the great men formerly won it. Death in war, fierce mortal havoc, has carried off every man of my people who forsook this life, saw the last joys in the hall. I have none who bears the sword or polishes the plated flagon, precious drinking-cup; the company of tried warriors has passed elsewhere.

Although it is not clear that the single existing manuscript of *Beowulf* contains the complete epic, it appears that the Anglo-Saxon author joined the stories of the youthful and the aging Beowulf by framing both with a story of the death and burial of heroes. The beginning of the story, celebrating the life and death of the Danish hero Scyld Scefing, foreshadows the hero's cremation and the burial of the treasure at the end of *Beowulf*. This together with the "song of the last survivor" confirms the elegiac status of the poem and helps to establish the epic as a great work of world literature.

Past, Present, Future.   The Anglo-Saxon audience of *Beowulf* knew firsthand of the loss of a way of life depicted in the epic. The great heroes of the past had gone from the earth, and their treasures were scattered, destroyed, or expended. There remained only echoes of the old society, such as the ideal of the **comitatus,** men who banded together in the interest of protection and stability. In part at least, *Beowulf* was an attempt to preserve the memories of the past and inspire those living to rise to noble actions. Although its monsters and dragon were only symbols, they reminded the audience that their enemies were real, threatening them whenever their vigilance decreased.

Interpretations of *Beowulf* have varied greatly over the last two hundred years. In the nineteenth century, the poem was viewed as an antiquity, a way of directly reading the age of heroes; the Christian element was largely ignored as an irrelevant addition. For a time in the twentieth century, especially during World War II in England, the poem was regarded as a fable of the heroism necessary to preserve civilization. Recent critics tend to view the poem as a reflection of the values and interests of late Anglo-Saxon culture, written down sometime after the demise of the Germanic society it dramatizes. But the poem also raises questions about epic poets and their audience, including whatever drives one to construct a heroic past out of legends and stories. What did *Beowulf* mean in its own time? Who preserved it, and why? These and related questions invite further speculation.

If, as some scholars now suggest, the poem was completed as late as the end of the tenth century, it existed in writing for less than a hundred years before the Battle of Hastings in 1066, in which the Norman French conquered the Anglo-Saxons and established a new society in England. Those who recalled the legends of their ancestors in *Beowulf* rapidly faded from the scene, overwhelmed by the Norman Conquest and the reshaping of English language and culture. So *Beowulf,* a work celebrating antiquity, became irrelevant to the newly created Anglo-Norman society and for centuries vanished from memory.

■ CONNECTIONS

The Epic of Gilgamesh (Book 1). The earliest known epic, this work deals with a larger-than-life hero whose society is tragically dependent on him. How do the strengths of Gilgamesh and Beowulf also suggest their weaknesses, and how might mortality be their greatest weakness? What are the similarities and differences between these heroes?

The New Testament, p. 28. The Christ of the Gospels of Matthew and Luke is another kind of epic hero. Christ brings spiritual power into the world while Beowulf embodies physical strength; both he and Beowulf can be said to have been sacrificed. Attempts have been made to see Beowulf as a Christian hero. What might be the possibilities and limitations of this position?

The Song of Roland, **p. 546.** Roland is a hero who dies in defense of his people. In what sense do Beowulf and Roland share the idea of struggling to save humanity?

■ FURTHER RESEARCH

Editions and Translations

Chickering, Howell D. *Beowulf: A Dual-Language Edition. Translated with Introduction and Commentary.* 1977.
Liuzza, R. M. *Beowulf: A New Verse Translation.* 2000.
Mitchell, Bruce, and Fred C. Robinson. *Beowulf: An Edition.* 1998.

Translations and Selected Criticism

Donoghue, Daniel, ed. *Beowulf: Verse Translation, Authoritative Text, Contexts, Criticism.* Trans. Seamus Heaney. 2002.
Howe, Nicholas, ed. *Beowulf: Prose Translation, Backgrounds and Contexts, Criticism.* Trans. E. Talbot Donaldson. 2002.

Anthologies of Literary Criticism

Baker, Peter S., ed. *Beowulf: Basic Readings.* 1995.

Bjork, Robert E., and John D. Niles, eds. *A Beowulf Handbook*. 1997.
Fry, Donald K., ed. *The Beowulf Poet*. 1968.
Nicholson, Lewis B., ed. *An Anthology of Beowulf Criticism*. 1963.

Works of Literary Criticism
Bonjour, A. *The Digressions in Beowulf*. 1950.
Hill, John. *The Cultural World in Beowulf*. 1995.
Irving, Edward B. *Rereading Beowulf*. 1989.
Niles, John D. *Beowulf: The Poem and Its Tradition*. 1983.
Stanley, E. G. *In the Foreground: Beowulf*. 1994.

■ PRONUNCIATION

Anglo-Saxon pronunciation is basically consistent. All consonants and vowels are pronounced, and long vowels sound as they did before the time of Shakespeare: *ah, ei, ee, oh, oo*. The short *a* sounds roughly equivalent to the short *o* in *hop*. A short final *e* is pronounced unaccented, as *uh*. Diphthongs are pronounced as a single syllable, with the first vowel predominating: *Healfdene*, for example, sounds like HAY-ulf-day-nuh. While most consonants are pronounced as in modern English, there are some exceptions: *sc* is pronounced like modern *sh* (scip, ship); *cg* like modern *dg* (ecg, edge); *h* after a vowel like German *ch* (ich, ach); *c* before *i* or *e* like *ch* in child (cild, child); *c* after *i, e* like soft *ch* (micel, much); *g* before *i* or *e* like *y* in yet (giefu, gift); *g* after *i, e* like *y* in yet (hefig, heavy); and the special symbols þ (thorn) and ð (eth) which interchangeably produce the "th" sound.

In Anglo-Saxon versification, the first syllable of a word is generally stressed, as in BAY-oh-woolf (Beowulf). Pronunciation guides for the most important Anglo-Saxon names in the text are given below.

Aeschere: ASH-hay-ruh, ASH-heh-ruh
Beowulf: BAY-oh-woolf
Freawaru: FRAY-ah-wah-roo
Grendel: GREN-dul
Heorot: HEH-oh-rote
Hrothgar: HROHTH-gar
Hygd: HEED, HEE-yid
Hygelac: HIH-yuh-lak
Naegling: NAY-ling
Unferth: UN-furth, OON-fehrth
Wealhtheow: WAY-ahl-thay-oh, WEH-ahlh-theh-oh
Wiglaf: WEE-lahf, WIG-lahf

ꙮ Beowulf

Translated by Michael Swanton

Indeed, we have heard of the glory of the Spear-Danes, kings of the nation in days gone by—how those princes performed deeds of courage. (1–3)

Often Scyld Scefing[1] dragged away the mead benches from bands of foes, from many tribes—struck terror into the Heruli.[2] From the time when first he was found destitute (he received consolation for that) he flourished beneath the skies, prospered in honours until every one of those who dwelt around about him across the whale's road had to obey him, pay him tribute. That was a great king! (4–11)

Later a son was born to him, a young man in the court, whom God sent to be a comfort to the people. He had perceived the cruel distress they once suffered when for a long time they lacked a king. Therefore the Lord of Life, the Ruler of Glory, granted him honour in the world; Beowulf[3] was renowned, the fame of Scyld's son spread widely throughout the Danish lands. So it is that a young man while still in his father's protection ought to do good deeds, making liberal rich gifts, so that when he comes of age good companions will stand by him, lend aid to the people

---

Beowulf. According to the numbering of its manuscript, *Beowulf* is divided into forty-three sections not counting the opening, which tells of Scyld Scefing's miraculous arrival, life, death, and funeral. Brief subheadings have been assigned here to each section of the poem.

Some of the poem's digressions, or secondary narratives, require explanation. Often they express the memory of an incident that comes to mind in light of a present situation in the epic. Usually, these digressions rely on the audience's familiarity with Scandinavian (Germanic) history and culture. A few digressions refer to things that happened *after* the action described in the poem, adding further significance to the narrated events. Brief notes on the digressions are included as necessary. The common themes of *Beowulf*—such as the behavior expected of a king, the fight against the creatures of darkness, and the transience of the things of this world—do not require explanation.

A note on the translation: Verse translations of *Beowulf* often keep the rhythm and sound of the original text while giving up literal accuracy. Prose translations—such as the one reprinted here by Michael Swanton—are more literal but lose the formal quality of the Anglo-Saxon poetry. Students may want to compare the prose version presented here with a line-by-line poetic translation, or with the original with an interlinear translation. For this purpose, the corresponding line numbers of the original poem are located in parentheses at the end of each prose paragraph.

The footnotes to the text generally are taken from Swanton's notes, either completely or in part, often greatly abbreviated, since they were originally written for a scholarly edition. Notes written entirely by this anthology's editors are so marked.

---

[1] **Scyld Scefing:** Legendary founder of the Danish royal house whose story introduces the poem. [Editors' note.]

[2] **the Heruli:** Germanic mercenaries who fought for the Romans; they were subdued by the Danes in the fourth century C.E.

[3] **Beowulf:** This Beowulf, son of Scyld Scefing, is not the young hero of the poem, a Geat who comes to support the Danes in their need. [Editors' note.]

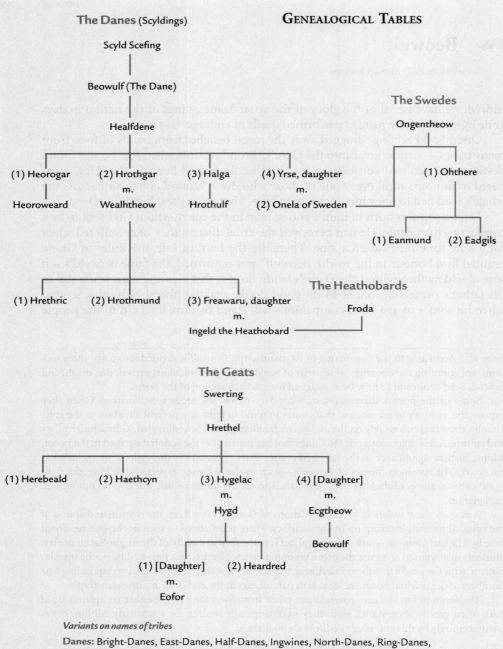

The Danes (Scyldings)

Scyld Scefing

Beowulf (The Dane)

Healfdene

(1) Heorogar   (2) Hrothgar   (3) Halga   (4) Yrse, daughter
               m.

Heoroweard   Wealhtheow   Hrothulf   (2) Onela of Sweden

(1) Hrethric   (2) Hrothmund   (3) Freawaru, daughter
               m.
     Ingeld the Heathobard

The Swedes

Ongentheow

(1) Ohthere

(1) Eanmund   (2) Eadgils

The Heathobards

Froda

The Geats

Swerting

Hrethel

(1) Herebeald   (2) Haethcyn   (3) Hygelac   (4) [Daughter]
              m.   m.

Hygd   Ecgtheow

Beowulf

(1) [Daughter]   (2) Heardred
     m.
    Eofor

Variants on names of tribes

Danes: Bright-Danes, East-Danes, Half-Danes, Ingwines, North-Danes, Ring-Danes, South-Danes, Spear-Danes, West-Danes. Also, Scyldings: Battle-Scyldings, Honor-Scyldings, Victory-Scyldings.

Geats: Sea-Geats, War-Geats, Weders (Weather-Geats).

Swedes: Scylfings.

Merovingians: includes the Franks and the Hetware.

when war comes. Among all nations it is by praiseworthy deeds that a man shall prosper. (12–25)

Then at his destined hour Scyld, still very active, passed away to go into the keeping of the Lord. Those who were his dear companions carried him down to the surge of the sea as he himself had instructed when, friend of the Scyldings, he governed with words. The beloved leader of the land had been long in possession. (26–31)

There at the landing-place stood the curved prow, ice-covered, ready to put out, a prince's vessel.[4] Then they laid down the beloved ruler, the distributor of rings, in the bosom of the ship, the famous man by the mast. Many treasures, jewels from distant lands, were brought there. I have not heard of a craft more splendidly furnished with weapons of war and battle garments, with swords and coats of mail. On his breast lay many treasures which were to go with him far out into the power of the flood. In no way did they provide him with lesser gifts, treasures of the nation, than did those who at the beginning when he was still a child sent him off alone over the waves. Furthermore they set up a golden banner high over his head; they let the sea carry him, gave him up to the ocean. Their spirits were sad, their hearts sorrowful. Men cannot say for certain, neither councillors in the hall nor warriors beneath the skies, who received that cargo. (32–52)

1. [THE BUILDING OF HEOROT]

Then in that stronghold the beloved king of the people, Beowulf of the Scyldings, was for a long time famous among the nations (his father had passed elsewhere, the chief from his land) until to him in turn was born lofty Healfdene. He ruled the noble Scyldings for as long as he lived, old and savage in war. To him, the leader of armies, there were born into the world in succession four children: Heorogar and Hrothgar and Halga the Good; I have heard that Yrse was Onela's[5] queen, the beloved bed-fellow of the War-Scylfing. (53–63)

Then success in war, glory in battle, was granted to Hrothgar, so that his friends and kinsmen gladly obeyed him until the youthful band of companions grew into a mighty troop of young warriors. It came into his mind that he would instruct men to build a greater mead-hall than the children of men had ever heard of, and therein he would distribute to young and old everything which God had given him — except for public land and the lives of men. I have heard how then orders for the work were

---

[4] **a prince's vessel:** An archaeological expedition at Sutton Hoo, England, in 1939 discovered an Anglo-Saxon royal burial ship of the late sixth or early seventh century similarly laden with weapons and armor. [Editors' note.]

[5] **Onela:** The Swedish king Onela would later cause harm to the Geats. [Editors' note.]

◀ **Genealogies of the northern European tribes in *Beowulf*.**

Since the Anglo-Saxon poetic vocabulary relies on the frequent use of synonyms, the name of a people such as the Danes or the Geats may have many variants. In the same way, a hero or other prominent character may be referred to as the son or daughter of either parent, or through some other affiliation of kinship. This genealogy shows the more important family connections.

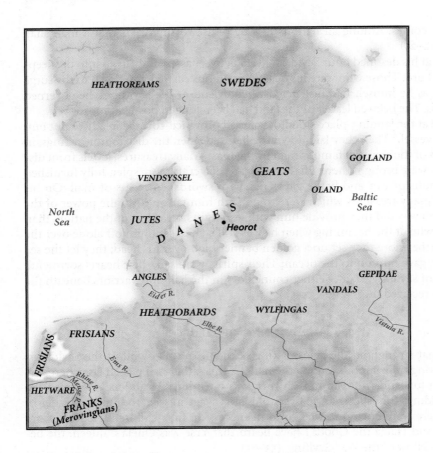

Peoples and Places in *Beowulf*

The history and legends depicted in Beowulf took place in a northern Europe peopled by warring tribes, particularly the Danes, Swedes, and Geats. Heorot is the presumed location of Hrothgar's hall, around which most of the action is centered in the first part of the story.

given to many peoples throughout this world to adorn the nation's palace. So in time — rapidly as men reckon it — it came about that it was fully completed, the greatest of hall buildings. He who ruled widely with his words gave it the name Heorot.[6] He did not neglect his vow; he distributed rings, treasure at the banquet. The hall rose up high, lofty and wide-gabled: awaited the furious surge of hostile flames.[7] The day was not yet near when violent hatred between son-in-law and father-in-law should be born of deadly malice. (64–85)

---

[6] Heorot: Literally, "hart," a male deer.

[7] awaited . . . flames: Hrothgar's palace would be destroyed during a later feud among his kinsmen.

Then the powerful demon, he who abode in darkness, found it hard to endure this time of torment, when every day he heard loud rejoicing in the hall. There was the sound of the harp, the clear song of the minstrel. He who could recount the creation of men in far off times, spoke; he told how the Almighty made the earth, a bright-faced plain which the waters encircle, set up in triumph the radiance of sun and moon as light for those dwelling on land, and adorned the corners of the earth with branches and leaves, how also he created life for every kind of thing that moves about alive. Thus these noble men lived blessedly in joy, until a certain fiend from hell began to wreak evil. That grim demon was called Grendel, a notorious prowler of the borderlands, who held the wastelands, swamp and fastness. Unhappy creature, he lived for a time in the home of the monster race after God had condemned them as kin of Cain. The Eternal Lord avenged the murder whereby he killed Abel;[8] he got no joy from that feud, but Providence drove him far away from mankind for that crime. Thence were born all evil broods: ogres and elves and goblins — likewise the giants who for a long time strove against God; he paid them their reward for that. (86–114)

2. [Grendel's Attacks on Heorot]

Then, after night had come, Grendel went to seek out the lofty house to see how, after their beer-drinking, the Ring-Danes had settled into it. Inside he found a band of noblemen, asleep after the banquet; they had no thought of sorrow, of the misery destined for men. Straightaway the creature of damnation was ready, grim and greedy, savage and cruel, and seized thirty thanes from their rest. From there he turned, exulting in plunder, to go back home, to seek out his dwelling with that glut of slaughter. (115–125)

Then in the half-light before dawn Grendel's war-strength was revealed to men; then after the feast arose weeping, a great cry in the morning. The famous prince, a leader of proven merit, sat joyless; when they examined the tracks of that loathsome, accursed demon, the mighty one suffered, grieved for his thanes. That struggle was too fierce, loathsome and long-lasting. Nor was there longer interval, but the next night he again wrought more murderous havoc, vengeful acts and wickedness, and felt no remorse; he was too intent on it. Then it was easy to find the man who was seeking a couch for himself elsewhere, a bed among the outbuildings farther away, once this 'hall-thane's' hatred was made clear by manifest proof. Whoever escaped the fiend held himself afterwards farther off and more securely. Thus one held sway over all and strove against right until the best of houses stood deserted. (126–146a)

This went on for a long time: for a period of twelve years the Scyldings' friend suffered affliction, every kind of woe and deep sorrows. Wherefore sadly in songs it became generally known among the children of men that Grendel had long waged war on Hrothgar, maintained fierce malice, feud and enmity, constant conflict over

---

[8] **he killed Abel:** In medieval times, it was commonly held that all monsters were descended from Cain, who kills his brother, Abel, in the Book of Genesis and is banished from Eden.

many seasons. He wanted no friendship with any man of the Danish force, would not withdraw his deadly hostility, or pay compensation; nor need any of the councillors there expect a handsome reparation at the killer's hands. But the monster, dark shadow of death, went on persecuting both tried warriors and youths, lay in wait and ensnared them; in perpetual darkness he ruled the misty wastelands. Men do not know where those who share hell's secrets will direct their paths. (146b–164)

Thus the enemy of mankind, this dreadful solitary, would often commit many crimes, bitter humiliations. On dark nights he dwelt in the treasure-decked hall, Heorot. Because of Providence he could not approach the precious throne, the source of gifts; nor did he feel his love. (165–169)

That was a great misery and heartbreak for the Scyldings' friend. Many a powerful man often sat in council, sought a plan, what action would be best for a stout-hearted man to take against the terror of sudden onslaughts. At times they took vows of idol-worship at heathen shrines,[9] prayed aloud that the slayer of souls would render aid against the nation's calamities. Such was their custom, the hope of heathens; they turned their minds towards hell; they were ignorant of Providence, the Judge of deeds, they knew not the Lord God, nor indeed did they know how to worship the Protector of Heaven, the Ruler of Glory. It will go ill for him who as a result of terrible malice must thrust his soul into the fire's embrace—to expect no comfort, nothing to change. Well will it be for him who after the day of his death may seek out the Lord and ask for peace in the embrace of the Father. (170–188)

3. [BEOWULF'S JOURNEY TO DENMARK]

Thus the son of Healfdene constantly brooded on the sorrow of his time, nor could the wise hero set aside his grief; that strife which had befallen the people, cruel and malicious distress, worst of night-horrors, was too harsh, loathsome and long-lasting. (189–193)

At home, a great man among the Geats,[10] a thane of Hygelac, heard of Grendel's deeds. In strength he was the mightiest among mankind in that day and age, noble and powerful. He ordered a good seagoing vessel to be made ready for him; he said that he wished to seek out over the swan's road the war-king, the famous prince, since he had need of men. Wise men in no way reproached him for that venture, though he was dear to them; they encouraged the man renowned for his spirit, examined the omens. From the people of the Geats the great man had picked champions, the bravest he could find; he went down to the water-borne timbers as one of fifteen. A skilled seaman pointed out the line of the coast. (194–209)

The time came; the boat lay on the waves, afloat beneath the cliff. Eager heroes stepped aboard at the prow; the tide turned, sea against the sand; soldiers carried

---

[9] **vows . . . heathen shrines:** The poet here has the Danes reverting to paganism in their moment of dread; actually, they were not converted to Christianity until the eleventh century.

[10] **a great man . . . Geats:** Beowulf of the Geats, the hero of the poem, is first described here. His actual name is not given until he arrives at Heorot Hall in line 343. [Editors' note.]

bright trappings, splendid battle-gear, into the bosom of the vessel; men shoved out the well-braced timbers, warriors on a willing journey. (210–216)

Then driven by the wind, the ship travelled over the sea-waves, floating foamy-necked, just like a bird, until in due course on the following day its curved prow had come to where the voyagers could sight land, shining sea-cliffs, steep promontories and broad headlands. The sea then was crossed, the voyage at an end. The men of the Weders[11] quickly set foot on level ground, moored the sea-borne timbers; their mail-shirts, the garments of war, rang out. They thanked God that the sea voyage had been easy for them. (217–228)

Then from the rampart the Scyldings' watchman, whose duty it was to guard the sea-cliffs, saw bright shields carried over the bulkhead, war-equipment ready for use. Curiosity pricked his mind as to who these men were. So Hrothgar's thane went down to the shore, riding on horseback; he forcefully brandished the mighty shaft in his hands, questioned them in formal words: (229–236)

'What manner of armed men are you who have come thus protected by mail, bringing a tall ship over the seaways, over the water to this place? For a long time I have been guardian of this frontier, kept watch on the sea, so that no enemies might harry the land of the Danes with a shipborne force. Never have shield-bearers made so open an approach; and yet you had no ready knowledge of the soldiers' password approved by kinsmen. I have never seen a mightier warrior on earth than is a certain one among you, a hero in armour. That is no mere serving-man decked out with weapons, unless his appearance and unique form belie him. Now I must know your origin before you go any further from here as spies, deeper into the land of the Danes. Now you foreigners, sea-voyagers, pay attention to my frank opinion: you would do best to announce quickly where you are coming from.' (237–257)

4. [BEOWULF'S PURPOSE]

The chief of them, the leader of the company, answered him, unlocked his store of words: 'We are men of the Geatish people and the companions of Hygelac's hearth. My father was well known among the nations, a noble war-leader called Ecgtheow. He lived on for many years before in old age he passed away from his court; every councillor throughout all parts of the earth remembers him well. We have come in good faith to seek out your leader, Healfdene's son, defender of his people; advise us well. We have important business with the famous lord of the Danes; there should be no secret from what I understand of it. (258–272a)

You will know, if what we have heard tell is in fact so, that among the Scyldings some kind of ravager, mysterious persecutor, displays in the terror he creates on dark nights, unheard of malice, humiliation and carnage. I can give Hrothgar advice about this from a generous heart, how he, wise and good, might overcome the enemy, and his surging anxieties grow cooler—if change is ever to come to him, relief from the

---

[11] **the Weders:** Another name for the Geats. For other alternative names for tribal societies, see the list provided.

affliction of miseries. Otherwise he will ever after suffer great hardship, times of distress, for as long as the best of houses remains there in its lofty position.' (272b–285)

The watchman, fearless officer, spoke from where he sat on his horse: 'A sharp shield-fighter who thinks clearly must know the difference between the two things: words and deeds. I gather, then, that here is a troop loyal towards the lord of the Scyldings. Proceed, bearing weapons and armour; I will guide you. Moreover, I will instruct my young thanes to guard your ship honourably against all enemies, the newly-tarred vessel on the sand, until the timbers with curved prow carry back the beloved man over the sea's currents to the Weders' coastline. May it be granted to one of such noble deeds that he survive the onslaught of battle unharmed.' (286–300)

Then they proceeded to journey onwards. The boat lay quietly, rode on its moorings, a broad-bosomed ship fast at anchor. Above their cheek-guards, adorned with gold, shone the boar image; bright and fire-hardened, it stood guard over men's lives.[12] Warlike hearts were excited; the men hastened, moved onwards together until they could see the timbered hall, splendid and decked with gold. Of all buildings beneath the skies, this in which the great ruler dwelt was the most famous to those who inhabit the earth; its radiance shone over many lands. The battle-brave man then pointed out to them the splendid bright dwelling of proud men, so that they might proceed directly to it. The notable warrior turned his horse and thereupon spoke these words: 'It is time for me to leave. May the Almighty Father keep you in grace, safe in your exploit! I will return to the sea to keep watch against hostile bands.' (301–319)

5. [BEOWULF'S ARRIVAL AT HEOROT]

The road was paved with stone, a path guiding the group of men. The war-mail shone, hard with hand-forged links; the bright iron rings sang on their armour. When they first arrived, striding up to the hall in their grim gear, the sea-weary men laid broad shields, wonderfully strong discs, against the wall of the building; then they sank to the bench—coats of mail, the battle-dress of men, rang out. The javelins that were the seamen's arms, stood all together, a forest of ash-wood shafts, steel-grey above. The iron-clad troop was well-equipped with weapons. (320–331a)

Then a proud hero there questioned the champions about their lineage: 'From whence do you bring these gold-plated shields, grey mail-shirts and visored helmets, this pile of battle-shafts? I am Hrothgar's messenger and officer. I have never seen foreigners—so many men—more brave in bearing. I imagine that it was through daring and greatness of heart that you sought out Hrothgar, and in no way as a result of banishment! The proud prince of the Weders, renowned for courage, answered him; stern beneath his helmet, he spoke these words in reply: 'We are the companions of Hygelac's table; Beowulf is my name. I wish to tell my errand to Healfdene's son, the famous commander your chief, if, good as he is, he will grant that we might

---

[12] **the boar image . . . lives:** Such a helmet, worn by a seventh-century Mercian warrior, was discovered at an archaeological dig at Derbyshire, England. Also see illustration, p. 483.

approach him.' Wulfgar spoke—he was a prince of the Vandals,[13] his bold spirit, valour and wisdom known to many: 'Respecting this, I will ask the friend of the Danes, the Scyldings' lord, distributor of rings, famous prince, about your venture, as you have requested, and rapidly make known to you the answer the noble man thinks fit to give me.' (331b–355)

Then he turned away swiftly to where Hrothgar, old and quite grey, sat with his band of warriors; the man renowned for courage went forward till he stood squarely in front of the lord of the Danes—he knew the custom of the company. Wulfgar spoke to his friend and leader: 'Men of the Geats have journeyed here, come from afar over the ocean's expanse. These champions call their chief Beowulf. They have asked that they might exchange words with you, my prince. Do not refuse them your response, gracious Hrothgar: from their fighting-gear they seem worthy of the respect of warriors; at any rate the chief who has led these warlike men is valiant.' (356–370)

6. [BEOWULF'S OFFER TO HROTHGAR]

Hrothgar spoke, protector of the Scyldings: 'I knew him when he was a boy. His late father was called Ecgtheow; it was to him that Hrethel of the Geats gave in marriage his only daughter; now his son has come here, a strong man, to visit a faithful friend. Moreover, seafarers who have carried rich gifts there to the Geats as a token of our regard, have said that he has in the grip of his hand the strength of thirty men, one renowned in battle. Holy God in his mercy has sent him to us, the West Danes, to meet the terror of Grendel, or so I hope. I shall offer the great man treasures for his impetuous courage. Make haste, bid them enter to see the noble company of kinsmen assembled together. Say also to them in your speech that they are welcome to the Danish people!' (371–389a)

Then Wulfgar went to the door of the hall and from inside announced these words: 'My victorious leader, the chief of the East Danes, has bidden me tell you that he knows of your lineage, and you are welcome to him here, brave-hearted men from across the surging sea. You may now go to see Hrothgar in your war-dress and beneath battle-visors; leave here your war-shields and spears, deadly shafts, to await the outcome of your talk.' (389b–398)

The mighty one then arose with many a warrior about him, a splendid band of thanes; some waited there to guard their war-trappings as the bold man instructed them. Together they hastened as the warrior directed under Heorot's roof. The battle-brave man, bold beneath his helmet, advanced till he stood by the hearth. Beowulf spoke—the mail-coat on him shone, an armour net woven with a smith's ingenuity: (399–406)

'Hail to you, Hrothgar! I am kinsman and young thane of Hygelac. In my youth I have undertaken many glorious deeds. The affair of Grendel became well known to

---

[13] **prince of the Vandals:** Hrothgar's court apparently attracted noblemen from distant regions. By the fifth century C.E. the main force of the Vandals had migrated far to the south, across Spain to North Africa.

me on my native soil; seafarers say that this hall, the best of buildings, stands empty and useless to all warriors once the evening light is hidden beneath heaven's firmament. Thereupon my people, the noblest, wise men, advised me that I should seek you out, prince Hrothgar, because they knew the power of my strength. They themselves had looked on when, stained with the blood of foes, I came back from the struggle in which I destroyed a race of ogres, bound five of them, and killed watermonsters in the waves by night; I suffered dire straits, avenged the Weders' wrong, utterly crushed those fierce creatures — they asked for trouble. And now I alone shall settle matters with that monster, with the demon Grendel. (407–426a)

Now therefore, chief of the Bright-Danes, bulwark of the Scyldings, I wish to make one request of you: that you do not refuse me, defence of fighting men, noble friend of nations, now that I have come so far, that I alone may cleanse Heorot with my company of warriors, this band of brave men. Also, I have heard that in his recklessness the monster disdains weapons. Therefore, so that my leader Hygelac may be glad at heart on my account, I scorn to carry sword or broad shield, yellow disc, into battle; but I shall grapple with the enemy with my bare hands and fight to the death, foe against foe. He whom death then takes must trust to the judgement of the Lord. (426b–441)

I imagine that, if he is able to prevail, he will fearlessly devour the people of the Geats in the war-hall, as he has often done to a force of triumphant men. You will have no need to cover my head if death takes me, for he will have me dripping with gore; he will carry away the bloody corpse, intent on eating it. The lone prowler will devour it remorselessly, staining his wasteland retreat; you will no longer need to trouble yourself about caring for my body. If war should take me, send to Hygelac this best of battle-clothing, most excellent of garments, that protects my breast; it is a legacy from Hrethel, the work of Weland.[14] Fate will always go as it must!' (442–455)

7. [HROTHGAR'S TALE OF GRENDEL]

Hrothgar spoke, protector of the Scyldings: 'Beowulf my friend, you have sought us out to fight in our defence and out of good will. A blow by your father brought about the greatest of feuds, when with his own hand he killed Heatholaf among the Wylfings. After that the kindred of the Weders could not keep him for fear of war. Thence he sought out the people of the South Danes, the Honoured-Scyldings, over the rolling waves. At that time I was first ruling the nation of the Danes, and in my youth held a broad kingdom, a rich stronghold of heroes. By then my elder brother Heorogar, Healfdene's son, was dead and lifeless — he was better than I! Thereupon I settled the feud by payment; I sent ancient treasures over the crest of the waves to the Wylfings — he swore oaths to me. (456–472)

It grieves my heart to tell any man what humiliation, sudden violence, Grendel has inflicted on me in Heorot with his notions of hatred. My hall-troop, fighting-

---

[14] **Weland:** The legendary Germanic blacksmith of the gods.

band, has shrunk; fate has swept them away in Grendel's terror. God could easily sever the mad ravager from his deeds! (473–479)

So often champions, drunk with beer, have vowed over the ale-cups that they would await Grendel's attack in the beer-hall with terrible blades. Then in the morning when day dawned, this mead-hall, noble court, was stained with gore, all the bench-boards drenched with blood, the hall full of gore fallen from swords. I had all the fewer faithful men, dear companions, for death had taken them off. Now, sit down to the banquet and in happiness reveal victorious deeds to the triumphant men, as your mood may prompt you.' (480–490)

Then a bench in the beer-hall was cleared for the men of the Geats all together; the stout-hearted men went to sit there, proud in their strength. The thane who carried in his hands a decorated ale-cup did his duty, poured out the sweet drink. From time to time a minstrel sang, a clear voice in Heorot. There was rejoicing among heroes, no small company of Danes and Weders. (491–498)

8. [UNFERTH CHALLENGES BEOWULF]

Unferth[15] spoke, Ecglaf's son who sat at the feet of the Scyldings' lord, let loose hostile thoughts; the bold seafarer Beowulf's venture caused him great vexation, for he did not wish that any other man in the world should ever achieve more glorious deeds beneath the heavens than himself: 'Are you the Beowulf who contended against Breca, competed in swimming on the open sea, where in your pride you two explored the flood, and risked your lives in deep water for the sake of a foolish boast? Nor could any man, neither friend nor foe, dissuade the both of you from that disastrous venture when you swam out to sea. There you both embraced the tides with your arms, measured the seaways, struck out with your hands, glided across the ocean; the sea surged with waves, with winter's swell. For seven days you two toiled in the power of the water. He beat you at swimming, had the greater strength; then in the morning the water carried him to the coast of the Heatho-Ræmas. From there, beloved of his people, he sought out his dear country, the land of the Brondings, the fair peaceful stronghold where he ruled over a nation, fortress and treasures. The son of Beanstan in fact accomplished all he had boasted against you. So although you have been successful everywhere in the onslaught of battle, in grim warfare, I imagine the outcome will be the worse for you if you dare wait all night long near at hand for Grendel.' (499–528)

Beowulf spoke, the son of Ecgtheow: 'Well, Unferth my friend, drunk with beer you have talked a great deal about Breca, told of his adventure. I claim for a fact that I had greater strength in the sea, hardship on the waves, than any other man. As boys we two came to an agreement and boasted—we were both then still in our youth— that we would risk our lives out on the ocean; and we did just that. As we swam in

---

[15] Unferth: Unferth holds influence in Hrothgar's court; he is twice referred to as a spokesman or orator. His taunting of Beowulf is a form of testing found in other epic tales.

the sea we each took a naked sword, strong in our hands; we meant to defend our-selves against whales. He was quite unable to float far away from me across the waves of the flood, to move more quickly in the water; nor would I leave him. So we stayed together on the sea for the space of five days until the flood, the surging sea, drove us apart; the coldest of weather, darkening night and the battle-fierce north wind turned against us. (529–548a)

The waves were savage; the anger of the sea-fish was aroused. My body-armour, hard with hand-forged links, afforded help against the enemies there; the woven war-garment, decked with gold, lay on my breast. A fierce, hostile ravager dragged me to the bottom, held fast in the grasp of the grim creature. Nevertheless it was given to me that I should reach the monster with the point of my war-sword; the onslaught of battle carried off the mighty sea-beast by my hand. (548b–558)

9. [BEOWULF ANSWERS. THE FEAST]

Frequently these loathsome assailants pressed hard upon me thus; I served them with my dear sword, as was fitting. The wicked evildoers had no joy whatever in that glut, feeding off me sitting round a banquet at the bottom of the sea. But in the morning, wounded by blades, they lay along the sand of the shore, put to sleep by swords, so that never again would they hinder the passage of ocean voyagers across the high seas. (559–568)

Light came from the east, the bright beacon of God; the ocean grew calm so that I could see promontories, windswept ramparts of the sea. Fate will often spare a man not yet destined for death, when his courage is good. In any case it befell me that I struck down nine sea-monsters with the sword. I have not heard tell of a harder fight by night beneath the vault of heaven, nor of a man under greater stress in the tides; yet I escaped from the grasp of foes alive, exhausted from the exploit. Then the sea, the flood with its currents, the surging waters, carried me away to the land of the Lapps. (569–581a)

I have never heard ought of such skilful conflicts, such terror of swords, told about you. I do not boast too much in saying that in the game of war never yet has Breca—nor either of you—performed so valuable a deed with shining swords—although *you* became the slayer of your brothers, your closest kin; for that you shall suffer damnation in hell, clever as you are! (581b–589)

I tell you for a fact, son of Ecglaf, that the dreadful monster Grendel would never have committed so many terrible deeds against your chief, humiliation in Heorot, if your heart and mind were as warlike as you yourself claim. But he has found out that he need not fear a feud, a dreadful storm of blades, from your people, not be so frightened of the Victorious-Scyldings. He takes his toll, shows mercy to none of the people of the Danes; but he takes his pleasure, puts to sleep and despatches, expect-ing no opposition from the Spear-Danes. But very soon now I shall show him the Geats' strength and courage in battle. Then when the morning light of another day, the sun clothed in radiance, shines from the south over the children of men, he who will may again go brave to the mead-drinking!' (590–606)

Then, grey-haired and renowned in battle, the distributor of treasure was joyful;

the prince of the Bright-Danes, the shepherd of his nation, counted on help, having heard in Beowulf a steadfast resolve. (607–610)

There was laughter among the heroes; a jubilant sound rose up, talk was cheerful. Wealhtheow,[16] Hrothgar's queen, stepped forth, mindful of etiquette; decked with gold, she greeted the men in the hall, and then the noble woman gave the goblet first to the guardian of the East Danes' homeland; bade him who was loved by the people be happy at the beer-drinking. He, the king renowned for victories, gladly partook of the banquet and hall-goblet. Then the lady of the Helmings went about everywhere among both tried warriors and youths, passed round the precious cup, until the moment arrived when she, a noble-hearted queen, circlet-adorned, carried the mead-goblet to Beowulf. She greeted the prince of the Geats and, perfect in speech, thanked God that her wish was fulfilled, that she might count on some warrior for help against wickedness. (611–628a)

A fighter, savage in slaughter, he took the goblet from Wealhtheow and then, eager for battle, made a speech; Beowulf spoke, son of Ecgtheow: 'When I put to sea, occupied an ocean-going boat with my band of men, I resolved that I should once for all carry out the wish of your people, or else fall in slaughter, fast in the grip of the enemy. I shall achieve this deed of heroic courage, or else meet my final hour in this mead-hall.' These words, the Geat's vaunting speech, pleased the woman well; decked with gold, the noble queen of the nation went to sit by her lord. (628b–641)

Then again as of old, brave words were spoken within the hall, the nation joyful, the sound of a victorious people, until presently the son of Healfdene determined to seek his evening's rest. He knew that the monster had planned an attack on the lofty hall from the time they should be unable to see the light of the sun and, night growing dark over everything, the shadowy shapes of dusk should stride forth, black under the clouds. The whole company rose. Then one man saluted the other, Hrothgar Beowulf, and wished him good luck, mastery of the wine-hall, and spoke these words: 'Never before, since I could lift hand and shield, have I entrusted the Danes' glorious hall to any man, except now to you. Now take and guard the best of houses; think of fame, show great courage, keep watch against the enemy! You shall lack nothing you desire if you escape this courageous deed alive.' (642–661)

10. [THE WATCH]

Then Hrothgar, the Scyldings' refuge, with his band of heroes went out of the hall; the war-leader wished to seek out Wealhtheow the queen for his bed-fellow. The King of Glory, so men heard tell, had appointed a hall-guard against Grendel; he discharged a special duty on behalf of the chief of the Danes: mounted guard against ogres. Indeed, the prince of the Geats readily trusted in his brave strength, the favour of Providence, as he put off his iron mail, the helmet from his head, gave his decorated sword, the choicest of iron, to an attendant, and bade him take charge of the war-gear. (662–674)

---

[16] **Wealhtheow:** The name Wealhtheow may be British or Celtic in origin.

Then before the great man got on to his bed, Beowulf of the Geats spoke vaunting words: 'I do not reckon myself inferior in warlike vigour, for deeds of battle, than Grendel does himself; therefore I will not put him to sleep, take away his life, with a sword, although I easily could. He knows nothing of such noble matters—that he might strike against me, hew at the shield—renowned though he may be for hostile deeds. But in the night we both shall dispense with the sword, if he dare seek a fight without weapons. And then may the wise God, the holy Lord, assign the glory to whichever side seems to him appropriate.' (675–687)

The battle-brave man then laid himself down, a pillow received the hero's cheek, and around him many a bold seaman sank to his couch in the hall. Not one of them thought that he would ever return from there to seek out his beloved country, nation and noble stronghold where he was raised; for they had heard that deadly slaughter had already carried off all too many of the Danish people in that wine-hall. But to these, the people of the Weders, the Lord granted comfort and support, success in battle to be woven into their destiny, inasmuch as through the might of one man, his sole powers, they all overcame their foe. The truth was made known that Almighty God has ruled mankind down the ages. (688–702a)

The creature that prowls in shadows came stalking through the black night. The marksmen who had to guard that gabled building were asleep—all but one. It was known to men that, if Providence did not wish it, the spectral ravager could not drag them away beneath the shadows. But he, lying awake in anger for the enemy, awaited the outcome of the conflict, his heart swollen with rage. (702b–709)

11. [GRENDEL'S ATTACK]

Then out of the wasteland came Grendel, advancing beneath the misty slopes; he carried the wrath of God. The wicked ravager intended to ensnare someone of the human race in that lofty hall. He strode beneath the clouds until he could most clearly make out the wine-hall, the treasure-house of men, gleaming with gold plate. That was not the first time he had sought out the home of Hrothgar. Never in all the days of his life, before nor since, did he have worse luck in meeting thanes in a hall. (710–719)

The creature, bereft of joys, came on, making his way to the hall. The door, fastened with fire-forged bars, gave way immediately once he touched it with his hands; intent on evil, swollen with rage he thrust open the mouth of the building. After that the fiend advanced, angry at heart, swiftly stepped on to the patterned floor. From his eyes, very like fire, there gleamed an ugly light. Within the hall he saw many warriors, a band of kinsmen sleeping, a troop of young warriors all together. Then his heart laughed; the dreadful monster intended that, before day came, he should have severed life from the body of each one of them, now the chance of a glut of feasting had come his way. (720–734a)

It was not his destiny that, when that night was over, he should taste more of mankind. Very powerful, Hygelac's kinsman watched for how the wicked ravager would set about his sudden onslaughts. The monster did not think to delay it, but for a start he quickly seized a sleeping warrior, tore him apart without resistance, bit into the bones' links, drank the blood from the veins, swallowed great chunks; he had soon devoured all of the lifeless man — feet and fists. He stepped forward closer, then clutched with his hand at the stout-hearted warrior on his couch; the fiend groped towards him with open palm. He promptly realised this malicious intention and sat right up so as to drive back the arm. The patron of crimes soon discovered that nowhere in the world, in no corner of the earth, had he encountered a mightier hand-grip in any other man. In his mind he grew fearful in spirit; for all that, he could not escape any sooner. His spirit longed to be gone, wanted to flee into the darkness, seek out the company of devils. His plight there was unlike anything he had ever encountered in all the days of his life. (734b–757)

Then Hygelac's great kinsman recalled his speech of that evening, stood erect and laid firm hold on him. Fingers cracked; the ogre was striving to escape; the warrior took a step forward. The notorious creature intended to slip into the open whenever he could, and thence flee away into the swamp retreat; he knew his fingers' power to be in the grip of a wrathful man. That was a sorry journey that the pernicious ravager had taken to Heorot. (758–766)

The noble hall resounded — became for all the Danes, those who dwelt in the city, for each valiant man, for warriors, a bitter cup. Both fierce occupants of the house were enraged. The building re-echoed; it was a miracle that the wine-hall withstood those bold in battle — that it did not fall to the ground, the fair earthly dwelling; but inside and out it was too firmly made fast with iron bands, skilfully forged. There, as I have heard, where the fierce ones struggled, many a mead-bench set with gold collapsed from its base. The councillors of the Scyldings had never imagined that any man could ever shatter it in any way, tear it apart by cunning, splendid and adorned with antlers — unless the embrace of fire should swallow it up in flame. (767–782a)

A strange sound rose up, repeatedly. Dire terror came upon the North Danes, upon every one of those who from the rampart heard that shriek, heard the enemy of God chant his terrible lay, a song of defeat, the thrall of hell howl with pain. He who was the strongest of men in might in that day and age held him fast. (782b–790)

12. [Beowulf Wins the Fight]

The warriors' defence did not wish that murderous visitant to leave alive on any account: he did not reckon his life of use to any people. (791–794a)

Then many a warrior of Beowulf's drew out an ancient heirloom, wished to defend the life of the noble leader, famous prince, if they could. One thing they did not know, stern-minded men of battle, when they joined in the struggle and thought to hack at him on every side, to seek his life — no war-sword, not the choicest of iron in the world, would touch the evil ravager, for with a spell he had rendered victorious weapons, all blades, useless. His departure from life at that time was to be wretched, and the alien visitant would have to travel far away into the power of fiends. Then he who, wicked in heart, had committed crimes against mankind for so long — he was in feud with God — found that his flesh would not serve him, but Hygelac's bold kinsman had him by the hand. As long as he was alive, each was hateful to the other. The dreadful monster suffered bodily pain; a huge wound appeared plain on his shoulder; sinews sprang apart, the bones' links broke. Triumph in battle was allotted to Beowulf. Grendel, mortally wounded, had to flee from there beneath the swampy slopes, to seek out a joyless dwelling; he knew all too well that the end of his life had come, the full number of his days. (794b–823a)

As a consequence of that deadly onslaught, the desire of all the Danes was achieved. He who had recently come from afar, wise and stout-hearted, had thus cleansed Hrothgar's hall, saved it from persecution. He rejoiced in that night's work, in deeds of famous courage. The prince of the Geatish men had fulfilled his boast to the East Danes, and so remedied all the distress, the evil sorrow which they earlier endured and had to suffer through dire necessity—no little trouble. It was manifest proof when the battle-brave man set the hand, arm and shoulder, up under the curved roof—there was the whole of Grendel's grasp complete. (823b–836)

13. [Celebration at Heorot]

Then in the morning, as I have heard, there was many a warrior around that gift-hall; leaders of the nation travelled from far and near, through distant regions, to examine that marvel, the tracks of the foe. His separation from life was in no way thought sorrowful by any of the men who examined the footprints of the inglorious creature—how, weary at heart, overcome in violence, doomed and put to flight, he left traces of his life-blood from there all the way to the water-monsters' lake. There the water was welling with blood, the dreadful swirl of waves all mingled with hot gore, welled with sword-blood. Doomed to death he hid himself when, bereft of joys, he laid down his life, the heathen soul, in the swamp refuge; there hell received him. (837–852)

From there old companions, and many a young man also, returned again from their joyful journey, riding from the lake, high-spirited on horseback, warriors on glossy steeds. Then Beowulf's fame was proclaimed; many repeatedly declared that nowhere in the wide world, south or north between the seas, was there any shield-bearer nobler than he under the expanse of heaven, nor more worthy of power. Yet in no way did they reproach their friend and leader, the gracious Hrothgar, for he was a great king. (853–863)

At times, where the paths seemed fair, were known to be good, those renowned in battle allowed their steeds to gallop, to run races. At times one of the king's thanes, a man filled with high-sounding words, with a memory for stories, who remembered a multitude of all kinds of old legends, improvised a new poem linked in true metre; again the man began by his art to relate Beowulf's exploit and skilfully to tell an apt tale, varying his words.[17] (864–874a)

---

[17] **the man began . . . words:** These lines describe Anglo-Saxon versification, including the major poetic techniques of alliteration and elegant choice in language. The minstrel weaves ancient stories and allusions to them into his poetry.

He spoke of all he had heard tell about Sigemund,[18] about courageous deeds—many strange things—of the struggle of the son of Wæls, his remote journeys, feuds and crimes, about which the children of men knew little except for Fitela, to whom he would speak of such matters, as uncle to nephew, since they were always friends in need in every conflict; they had laid low with their swords very many of the race of ogres. No little glory accrued to Sigemund after the day of his death, since, bold in battle, he had slain a serpent, guardian of a treasure-hoard. He, a prince's son, had ventured alone on that daring deed beneath the grey rock; Fitela was not with him; nevertheless it befell him that his sword pierced the wondrous serpent so that it stuck in the wall, noble iron; the dragon died a violent death. By his courage the terrifying man had brought it about that he might enjoy the hoard of rings at his own pleasure; the offspring of Wæls loaded a seagoing boat, carried bright treasure into the bosom of the ship; heat consumed the serpent. (874b–897)

Of all exiles, he, the defence of fighting men, was the most widely renowned among the nations for deeds of courage—so much had he prospered of old—after the battle-prowess, the strength and courage of Heremod[19] ceased; among the Jutes he was betrayed into the power of enemies, and quickly despatched. Surging misery had crippled him too long; he became a cause for deadly anxiety to his people, to all the nobles. For in earlier times many a prudent man often grieved over the stout-hearted one's career—the same who had counted on him for a remedy against disasters, counted on the fact that the prince's son should prosper, succeed to his father's rank, guard the people, treasure-hoard and stronghold, the realm of heroes, homeland of the Scyldings. The kinsman of Hygelac became the dearer to his friends, to all mankind: crime took possession of the other! (898–915)

Racing at times, they measured the yellow road with their steeds. By then the morning light was advanced and hastening on. Many a strong-minded man went to the great hall to look at the strange wonder. The king himself, guardian of ring-hoards, famed for his virtues, also stepped forth majestically from his marriage-bower with a large troop; and his queen with him measured the path to the mead-hall with a company of maidens. (916–924)

14. [HROTHGAR'S GRATITUDE AND BEOWULF'S REPLY]

Hrothgar spoke—he went to the hall, stood on the steps,[20] gazed at the steep roof shining with gold, and at Grendel's hand: 'For this sight thanks may at once be given

---

[18] **Sigemund:** The story of Sigemund is told in the Old Norse *Volsungasaga* and later in the Middle High German *Nibelungenlied*. In both, the slayer of the dragon is Siegfried, the son of Sigemund. *Beowulf*'s version may be closer to the original source.

[19] **Heremod:** Heremod was an ancient Danish king who showed great promise in his youth but later proved a bad ruler. Miserly and bloodthirsty, he was expelled from his kingdom and eventually slain while living among his former enemies.

[20] **Hrothgar . . . on the steps:** Hrothgar, returning to Heorot Hall from Wealhtheow's private dwelling, stares at the hand and forearm of Grendel, which are nailed to the building.

to the Almighty! I have endured many afflictions, violence at the hands of Grendel: God, the Guardian of Glory, can always work marvel upon marvel. It was only recently that I despaired of ever living to see any remedy for my woes, since the best of houses stood bloodstained with sword-gore, a far-reaching woe to every one of the councillors who despaired of ever defending the peoples' fortress from its enemies, from demons and evil spirits. Now through the might of the Lord, a man has accomplished the deed that previously all of us with our skill could not contrive. Indeed, whichever maiden gave birth to such a son among mankind may well say— if she is still alive—that eternal Providence was kind to her in her child-bearing. (925–945a)

Now Beowulf, best of men, I will cherish you in my heart as a son; keep true henceforth to this new friendship. You shall lack nothing in the world you desire if it lies in my power. I have often enough conferred rewards for lesser deeds, honouring with riches a slighter warrior, weaker in combat. You yourself have ensured with deeds that your glory will live for ever. May the Almighty reward you with good things, as he has just done!' (945b–956)

Beowulf spoke, the son of Ecgtheow: 'We undertook the fight, that deed of courage, with great good will, daringly risked the strength of an unknown creature. I dearly wish that you could have seen him, the foe himself in his trappings, exhausted to the point of death! I thought to bind him quickly on his deathbed with a firm grasp so that, unless his body should slip away, he would have to lie struggling for life in the grip of my hand. I could not prevent him going, since Providence did not wish it, nor did I hold him, mortal enemy, closely enough for that; the fiend was too exceedingly strong in his movement. Nevertheless, to save his life he relinquished his fist—the arm and shoulder—to remain behind, although the wretched creature bought no comfort at all by that; weighed down with sins, the loathsome despoiler will not live any the longer, for pain has clutched him close in a forceful grip, in deadly fetters. There, stained with crime, the creature must await the great Judgement, whatever resplendent Providence should wish to impose on him.' (957–979)

Ecglaf's son[21] was then the more silent a man in boasting talk about deeds of war, when, thanks to the hero's might, princes examined the hand, the fingers of the fiend, up towards the high roof. From in front, each fixed nail was just like steel, every talon on the hand of the heathen warrior a hideous spike. Everyone agreed that there was no old and ancient iron of stern men would touch him, would sever the monster's bloody battle-fist. (980–990)

15. [The Feast and Giving of Gifts]

Then it was quickly commanded that Heorot should be decorated within by hands; there were many, both men and women, who made ready that wine-hall, a building for guests. Along the walls tapestries shone adorned with gold, many a wonderful thing to look at for all men who gaze at such things. That bright house, all made firm

---

[21] **Ecglaf's son:** Unferth. [Editors' note.]

within by iron bands, was much damaged, its hinges sprung apart; only the roof escaped entirely sound when the monster, guilty of criminal deeds, turned in flight, despairing of life. That is not easy to flee from—let him try it who will—but compelled by necessity one must seek out the place prepared for those who dwell on the earth, those who bear souls, the children of men, where, after the banquet, one's flesh shall sleep fast in its bed of death. (991–1008a)

Then was occasion and time for the son of Healfdene to go into the hall; the king himself would share in the banquet. I have never heard that a nation behaved more nobly around their treasure-giver in so large a company. Then men of high renown sat at the benches, rejoiced in the feast; those kinsmen, stout-hearted Hrothgar and Hrothulf, courteously partook of many a goblet of mead in that lofty hall. Heorot was filled with friends; in no way, as yet, did the race of Scyldings practise treacherous arts.[22] (1008b–1019)

Then, as a reward for victory, Healfdene's brand[23] presented Beowulf with a golden banner, decorated war-standard, a helmet and coat of mail; many saw a famous costly sword carried before the hero. Beowulf partook of a goblet in the hall; he had no need to be ashamed in front of the marksmen for that rich gift. I have not heard of many men more heartily giving to others on the ale-bench four such treasures decked with gold. Across the crown of the helmet a crest bound with wires gave protection to the head from without, so that no storm-hardened legacy of files might badly injure him when the bold shield-warrior had to advance against fierce foes. Then the defence of warriors commanded eight steeds with gold-plated bridles to be led into the hall through the precincts. On one of them lay a skilfully decorated saddle, enriched with jewels: that had been the high-king's war-seat when Healfdene's son wished to take part in the play of swords; the valour of the far-famed man never failed at the front, when the slaughtered were falling. And then the refuge of Ing's Friends conferred possession of the both, horses and weapons, on Beowulf; he bade him make good use of them. So manfully did the famous prince, guardian of the treasure-hoard of heroes, reward the onslaught of battle with steeds and jewels, that no one who wishes to speak the truth in fairness will ever disparage them. (1020–1049)

16. [The Finnsburh Tale: Part I]

In addition the leader of warriors bestowed a treasure, an heirloom, on each of those on the mead-benches who had undertaken the ocean voyage with Beowulf; and he caused gold to be paid in recompense for the one whom earlier Grendel in his wickedness had killed—as he would more of them if wise God and the man's courage had not averted that fate. Providence governed all mankind, just as it still does now; wherefore discernment, forethought of mind, is best in everything. He

---

[22] **in no way . . . treacherous arts:** This refers to later dissension among the Danes, culminating in the usurpation of the royal throne by Hrothgar's nephew Hrothulf.

[23] **Healfdene's brand:** Hrothgar, the "brand," or sword, of the Danes.

who is going to enjoy the world for long in these troublesome times must live through much of good and of evil. (1050–1062)

There in the presence of Healfdene's war-leader, song and music joined together, the joyful wood was plucked, a story often rehearsed when, to entertain the hall, Hrothgar's minstrel would recite down the mead-benches: (1063–1067)

Together with Finn's offspring, Hnæf of the Scyldings, hero of the Half-Danes, had to fall in a Frisian slaughter,[24] when the disaster befell them. Indeed, Hildeburh had no cause to praise the loyalty of the Jutes; guiltless, she was deprived of her loved ones, a son and a brother, in that shield-play; wounded by the javelin, they fell to their fate; she was a sad woman! Not without cause did the daughter of Hoc lament the decree of Providence when, after morning came, she could see beneath the heavens the violent slaughter of kinsmen, where earlier she possessed the greatest of earthly pleasure. (1068–1079a)

The conflict carried off all Finn's thanes, save for only a few, so that he could in no way in that meeting-place fight to a finish the battle with Hengest the prince's thane, nor by warfare dislodge the survivors of the disaster. So they offered them terms: that they should entirely clear for them another building, a hall and throne, so that they might share equal power with the children of the Jutes; and the son of Folcwalda should every time honour the Danes with rich gifts, treat Hengest's troop well with rings, precious treasures of plated gold, to the same extent as he would have wished to encourage the Frisian kin in the beer-hall. (1079b–1094)

Then on both sides they put their trust in a firm peace-treaty. Finn declared to Hengest, with oaths of indisputable sincerity, that in accordance with the judgement of his councillors he would treat the survivors of the disaster with honour, provided that no man there should break the treaty by word or deeds, nor ever complain by means of a malicious contrivance, that, having lost their prince, they were following their ring-giver's slayer, since this was forced on them by necessity; if, however, any of the Frisians by rash speech should continually call the deadly hatred to mind, then it would have to be settled with the edge of the sword. (1095–1106)

The funeral pyre was prepared, and fine gold brought from the hoard: the finest of the warriors of the War-Scyldings was ready on the fire. Upon the pyre was easily to be seen: blood-stained mail-shirt, the swine-image all golden, a boar as hard as iron, many a prince destroyed by wounds; notable men had fallen in the slaughter. Then Hildeburh commanded her own son to be committed to the flames on Hnæf's pyre, the body to be burned, and to be placed on the fire shoulder to shoulder with

---

[24] **fall in a Frisian slaughter:** This story is unknown outside of *Beowulf* and a fragment of another Anglo-Saxon poem, *Battle at Finnsburh*. It tells of a warrior's conflict between his duty to avenge the slaying of his leader and his obligation to uphold a sworn oath. In the story, Finn, the king of Frisia, has married a Danish princess, Hildeburh, in an effort to make peace between the Frisians and Danes. But when Hildeburh's brother Hnaef and his Danish followers visit her at Finnsburh, they are attacked by a dissident band of Frisians. After the fight, both Hnaef and Finn's son by Hildeburh lie dead. The warrior Hengest assumes leadership of the surviving Danes and a truce is declared, extending protection to the Danish guests of the Frisians under the condition that no one speak of the fight again. But after two Frisians, Guthlaf and Oslaf, lament the tragedy, violating the oath of silence, Hengest and his Danish companions avenge the death of Hnaef, killing Finn, seizing his treasure, and carrying Hildeburh back to her own people.

his uncle. The woman mourned, chanted a dirge. The warrior ascended; the greatest of funeral-fires curled up towards the clouds, roared in front of the burial-mound; heads melted away, gaping wounds, terrible bites in the body, burst open as the blood gushed out. Fire, the most ravenous of spirits, swallowed up all those of both nations whom war had carried off; their glory was gone. (1107–1124)

17. [The Finnsburh Tale: Part II]

Bereft of friends, the fighting men then went to seek out their dwellings, to see the Frisian land, their homes and great stronghold. But Hengest remained with Finn through the slaughter-stained winter—quite disastrously. He remembered his homeland, though he could not drive curved prow onto the water. The sea surged with storms, fought against the wind; winter locked the waves in fetters of ice until another year came to the courts of men, just as it still does now—those periods of gloriously bright weather that always observe their due season. (1125–1136a)

Then winter was gone, the bosom of the earth beautiful. The exile, the guest, longed to be quit of these courts; he thought more particularly of avenging his wrongs than of the sea-voyage—whether he could contrive some occasion for violence, for he brooded inwardly about the children of the Jutes. So he did not hinder the way of the world when Hunlaf's son placed Battle-flame, the best of swords, in his lap; its edges were well known to the Jutes. (1136b–1145)

So also a cruel death by the sword befell in turn the bold-hearted Finn in his own home, after Guthlaf and Oslaf bewailed the grim attack, sorrow following their sea-journey, blamed him for their share of woes; the restless heart could not be restrained in the breast. Then the hall was reddened with the life-blood of foes, Finn killed too, the king among his bodyguard, and the queen taken. The Scylding marksmen carried away to their ships all the household property of the king of that country, whatever jewels, skilfully-wrought gems, they could find in the home of Finn. With a sea-voyage they carried the noble woman away to the Danes, led her to her people. (1146–1159a)

The song, the minstrel's lay, was sung. Once again mirth arose, the sound from the benches rang out clearly, cup-bearers served wine in wondrous vessels. Then Wealhtheow came forth, wearing a golden circlet, and went to where those two fine men, uncle and nephew, sat; as yet there was friendship between them, each trusting the other. There also the spokesman Unferth sat at the feet of the lord of the Scyldings; both of them trusted his spirit, believed that he had great courage, although he had not been honourable towards his kinsmen in the play of swords. (1159b–1168a)

Then the lady of the Scyldings spoke: 'Take this goblet, my noble prince, distributor of treasure. Be glad, gold-friend of warriors, and speak to the Geats with kindly words, as a man ought to do. Be gracious towards the Geats, mindful of the gifts you now possess from far and near. They told me that you wish to take the warrior to be a son to you. Heorot, the fair ring-hall, is cleansed. Rejoice, while you may, in many rewards, and when you must go forth to face the decree of destiny, bequeath people and kingdom to your kinsmen. I know my gracious Hrothulf—that he will treat these youths honourably if you, friend of the Scyldings, should leave the world before him; I think that he will repay our offspring well, if he remembers all the favours we both bestowed on him for his pleasure and his honour while he was still a child.' (1168b–1187)

Then she turned to the bench where her boys, Hrethric and Hrothmund, and the sons of the warriors were, young men together; there sat the great man, Beowulf of the Geats, beside the two brothers. (1188–1191)

18. [THE CELEBRATION CONTINUES]

A goblet was carried to him and a toast offered in words, and twisted gold was presented with good will: two bracelets, dress and rings, and the greatest necklace of those I have heard spoken of on earth. I have learned of no better treasure-hoard of heroes beneath the heavens since Hama carried off to his fair stronghold the collar of the Brosings,[25] jewel and rich setting; he fled from Eormanric's treacherous hatred, chose eternal gain. Hygelac of the Geats, grandson of Swerting, had that circlet with him on his last venture when beneath the banner he defended treasure, guarded the spoils of slaughter. Fate carried him off when, out of pride, he went looking for trouble, a feud with the Frisians.[26] The powerful prince wore that ornament, the precious stones, across the bowl of the waves; he fell dead beneath his shield. The body of the king then fell into the hands of the Franks, his breast armour and the collar together; lesser fighting-men plundered the slain after the battle-shearing, men of the Geats remained on the field of corpses. (1192–1214a)

The hall resounded with noise. Wealhtheow spoke; before the company she said: 'Beloved Beowulf, enjoy this collar with good fortune, young man, and make good use of this garment, national treasures, and prosper well. Prove yourself with your might, and show kindness to these boys with counsel; I shall remember to reward you for that. You have brought it about that down the ages men far and near will respect you as widely as the sea, the home of the winds, encircles the cliffs. May you be fortunate, prince, for as long as you live! I wish you well of your rich treasures. Be kind in your deeds to my son, you who are possessed of joy! Here every warrior is true to the other, gentle of heart, faithful to the leader of men; the thanes are united, the nation quite prepared, the noble men, having drunk, will do as I ask.' (1214b–1231)

Then she went to her seat. There was the finest of banquets; men drank wine. They did not know the fate, the grim destiny ordered of old, as it came to pass for many a warrior after evening had come and Hrothgar had gone to his chamber, the

---

[25] **since Hama . . . the Brosings:** Hama (Heimir) is accused of having stolen jewels from Eormenric (d. 375), king of the Ostrogoths, following a family dispute.

[26] **feud with the Frisians:** This is one of a series of allusions to the Geatish king Hygelac's final adventure, which indirectly leads to Beowulf's assumption of the throne. Apparently flushed with his victory over the Swedes at the battle of Ravenswood (lines 2922–98), Hygelac rashly turns his attention to the Franks. After a successful raid, he is caught among the rear guard of his returning army by the Frankish leader Theudebert, in a battle in which Beowulf plays a heroic part (lines 2499–508). Hygelac dies along with most of his followers in the battle, the Franks recover their plundered treasure, and Beowulf escapes (lines 2359–68).

powerful man to his couch. Countless warriors guarded the building, as earlier they often did; they cleared the bench-board; it was spread over with bedding and pillows. One among the beer-drinkers, ripe and doomed to die, stooped to his couch in the hall. They set at their heads their war-discs, shields of bright wood. There on the bench above each prince was easily to be seen a towering battle-helmet, ringed mail, a magnificent strong shaft. It was their custom always to be ready for war both at home and on an expedition, in case at any time such need befell their leader; they were a fine nation. (1232–1250)

19. [The Attack of Grendel's Mother]

Then they sank into sleep. One among them paid sorely for his night's rest, as had so often befallen them since Grendel occupied the gold-hall, perpetrated misdeeds until his end came, death in consequence of sins. It came to be seen, widely known among men, that there was still an avenger who survived the loathsome creature for a long while after the conflict. (1251–1258a)

Grendel's mother, a woman, she-monster, brooded on her misery, she who had to dwell in dreadful waters, cold currents, after Cain killed his only brother, his father's son, by the sword; stained he then went out, marked by murder, to flee the joys of mankind, and occupied the wilderness. Thence sprang many a fated demon; one of these was Grendel, the hateful savage outcast who at Heorot had found one man watchful, awaiting the conflict. There the monster came to grips with him; however, he remembered the power of his strength, the ample gift that God had given him, and counted on the Almighty for help, comfort and support; by that he overcame the fiend, laid low the hellish demon. Then humiliated he went off, the foe of mankind, bereft of joy, to seek out the mansion of death. And his mother, still ravenous and gloomy at heart, purposed to go on a sorry journey to avenge the death of her son. (1258b–1278)

She came then to Heorot where the Ring-Danes slept all around the hall. Immediately then there came a reverse for the warriors, once Grendel's mother made her way in. The terror was the less dreadful by just so much as the power of women, the war-terror of a female, is that of an armed man when the patterned blade of a hammer-forged sword, stained with blood, mighty of edge, shears through the boar-crest above opposing helmets. (1279–1287)

Then in the hall the hard-edged sword was drawn, from above the seats many a broad disc lifted firmly by the hand; none thought of helmet, of broad mail when the horror came upon him. She was in a hurry, wanted to be gone from there, to save her life now she was discovered. Swiftly she had taken firm grasp of one of the princes as she went towards the swamp. He whom she destroyed on his couch was to Hrothgar the most beloved of heroes between the seas, having the rank of companion, a powerful shield-fighter, a man of great renown. Beowulf was not there, for earlier, after the treasure-giving, a separate lodging had been assigned to the famous Geat. There was uproar in Heorot; she had taken, covered in gore, the hand she knew; grief was renewed, come again to the dwellings. That was not a good bargain, where those on both sides had to pay with the lives of friends! Then the wise king, grizzled warrior, was troubled at heart when he knew his chief thane to be lifeless, the dearest man to be dead. (1288–1309)

Swiftly Beowulf, the man blessed with victory, was fetched to the chamber. At daybreak he went together with his warriors, the princely champion himself with his companions, to where the wise man waited to see whether, after tidings of woe, the Almighty would ever bring about some change on his behalf. The man who was distinguished in war strode across the floor with his bodyguard—the hall timbers resounded—so that he might address the wise lord of the Friends of Ing with words; he asked if the night had been pleasant, according to his desires. (1310–1320)

20. [HROTHGAR'S DESCRIPTION OF THE HAUNTED LAKE]

Hrothgar spoke, protector of the Scyldings: 'Do not ask for good tidings! Sorrow is come again to the people of the Danes. Æschere is dead—the eldest brother of Yrmenlaf, my confidant and my councillor, closest comrade when we defended our heads in the fray, when troops clashed, struck against boar-crests. Whatever a warrior should be, a prince of proven merit, that Æschere was! Now a restless murderous demon has slain him in Heorot with her hands. I do not know which way the dreadful creature took her journey back, exulting over the carcass, made infamous by the glut. She has taken vengeance for the quarrel—that last night you killed Grendel in a savage manner with fierce grips because for too long he had diminished and destroyed my people. He fell in the fight, his life forfeit; and now another mighty, wicked ravager has come, wishing to avenge her kinsman, and has gone far in pursuing vengeance for the quarrel—so it may seem to many a thane whose heart weeps for his treasure-giver, a bitter affliction in the breast. Now the hand lies low that was willing to fulfill your every desire. (1321–1344)

I have heard that those who dwell in the land, my people, hall-councillors, say this—that they have seen two such huge prowlers in the border regions, alien visitants holding the wastelands. One of these, so far as they could best tell, took the likeness of a woman; the other wretched creature trod the paths of exile in the form of a man, save that he was bigger than any other human; from days of old those who dwell on the earth have called him 'Grendel'; they know of no father, whether any such dark demon was begotten before them. They occupy a secret land, wolf-haunted slopes, windswept crags, dangerous swamp tracks where the mountain stream passes downwards under the darkness of the crags, water under the earth. It is not far from here, measured in miles, that the lake stands; over it hang frost-covered groves, trees held fast by their roots overshadow the water. There each night may be seen a fearful wonder—fire on the flood. No one alive among the children of men is wise enough to know the bottom. Although the strong-antlered stag, roaming the heath, may seek out the forest when driven from afar, hard pressed by hounds, he will sooner yield up life and spirit on the bank than hide his head there. That is not a pleasant place! From it a surging wave rises up black to the clouds when the wind stirs up hostile storms, till the air grows dim, the skies weep. (1345–1376a)

Now once again help depends on you alone. You do not yet know the region, the dangerous place where you might find the deeply sinful creature; seek it out if you dare! I will recompense you for the quarrel with money as I did before, with ancient treasures, twisted gold, if you make your way back again.' (1376b–1382)

21. [THE JOURNEY TO THE LAKE]

Beowulf spoke, the son of Ecgtheow: 'Do not be sorrowful, wise man! It is better for anyone that he should avenge his friend, rather than mourn greatly. Each of us must await the end of life in this world; let him who can, achieve glory before death; afterwards, when lifeless, that will be best for a noble man. Rise up, guardian of the kingdom; let us go swiftly to examine the trail of Grendel's relative. I promise you this: she will not escape under cover, neither in the bosom of the earth, nor in the mountain forest, nor at the bottom of the ocean, go where she will. For today, have patience in every affliction, as I expect you to.' (1383–1396)

The old man then leapt up, thanked God, the mighty Lord, for what the hero had said. Then a horse was bridled for Hrothgar, a steed with braided mane. The wise ruler moved off in state; the troop of shield-bearers marched forth. The tracks could be widely seen along the forest paths, the trail over the ground where she went straight on over the murky wasteland, carrying a lifeless young thane, the best of those who watched over their home with Hrothgar. Then the son of princes advanced over steep rocky slopes by a narrow path, a constricted route where only one could pass at a time, an unfamiliar way, precipitous crags, many a lair of water-monsters. He went in front with a few knowledgeable men to examine the ground, until suddenly he found mountain trees leaning out over a grey rock, a cheerless wood; below lay the water, gory and turbid. There was anguish at heart for all the Danes, for the Scyldings' friends, for many a thane to suffer, distress for each of the warriors, when on the cliff above the water they came upon Æschere's head. (1397–1421)

The flood welled with blood, with hot gore — the people gazed at it. From time to time a horn sang out its eager battle-call. The troop all sat down; they saw then upon the water many of the serpent race, strange sea-dragons exploring the deep, also water-monsters lying on the slopes of the crags, such as those that in the morning-time often attend a miserable journey on the sail-way, serpents and wild beasts. They fell away, fierce and swollen with rage; they understood the clear sound, the war-horn ringing. With an arrow from his bow the prince of the Geats parted one of them from life, from its battle with the waves, when a hard warshaft stuck in its vitals; it was slower in swimming on the water when death carried it off. Swiftly the water's strange offspring was hard-pressed in the waves with savagely-barbed boar-spears, violently assailed and dragged on to the crag; men examined the terrifying visitant. (1422–1441a)

Beowulf dressed himself in warrior's clothing, had no fear at all for his life. The hand-woven war-mail, broad and cunningly adorned, would have to explore the deep — it was able to protect his frame so that no warlike grip, no malicious grasp of any hostile creature, might injure his breast, his life. And a shining helmet guarded the head that would have to disturb the lake bottom, seek out the turbid depths—it was decorated with rich ornament, encircled with a chain-mail guard, just as the weapon-smith had wrought it in days of old, wonderfully formed it, set about with boar-images so that thereafter no sword or battle-blade might bite into it. (1441b–1454)

Not least among the mighty aids was that which Hrothgar's spokesman lent him in his need—a hafted blade called Hrunting;[27] it was foremost among ancient treasures; the edge was iron, marked with poisoned stripes, hardened in the gore of battle. In combat it had never failed any of those who grasped it in their hands when daring to set out on perilous journeys to the meeting-place of foes. That was not the first time it would have to accomplish a deed of courage. When he lent the weapon to the better fighter, surely the son of Ecglaf, skilled in strength, did not remember what he had said previously when drunk with wine. He himself did not dare risk his life, perform noble deeds of valour beneath the turmoil of waves; there he forfeited glory, his reputation for courage. It was not so with the other man, once he had dressed himself for war. (1455–1472)

22. [BEOWULF ATTACKS GRENDEL'S MOTHER]

Beowulf spoke, the son of Ecgtheow: 'Now, famous son of Healfdene, wise ruler, gold-friend of men, now that I am ready to set out on this venture, consider what we two talked about earlier—that if I should relinquish life in your cause, you would always take the role of my father when I passed away. If battle should take me, be the guardian of my young thanes, my close companions. Also, beloved Hrothgar, send to Hygelac the precious things you bestowed on me. Then, when he gazes on that treasure, the leader of the Geats, Hrethel's son, may understand from the gold that I found a generous distributor of rings, enjoyed him while I could. And let Unferth, a man widely known, have this old heirloom, my beautiful wave-patterned sword, hard of edge; I shall achieve fame for myself with Hrunting, or else death will take me.' (1473–1491)

With these words the prince of the Weder-Geats turned away boldly, would wait for no reply at all; the water's surge received the warrior. It was part of a day before he could catch sight of the level bottom. (1492–1496)

Straight away she who for a hundred seasons had kept watch on the flood's expanse, grim and greedy, fiercely ravenous, discovered that some man from up above was exploring the dwelling-place of monsters. Then she clutched at him, seized the warrior in a dreadful grip; yet for all that, she failed to injure the healthy body; ring-mail shielded him externally so that she could not thrust her hateful fingers through the war-dress, the interlocked shirt on his limbs. Then, when she came to the bottom, the water-wolf carried the commander of rings into her lair, so that—no matter how resolute he might be—he was unable to wield his weapons; and a host of weird creatures harried him in the deep; many a sea-beast tore at his battle-shirt; monsters pursued him. Then the hero realised that he was in some sort

---

[27] **Hrunting:** Unferth gives the famous sword to Beowulf; it will fail him in the fight. [Editors' note.]

of enemy hall, where no water could harm him at all, nor could the flood's sudden grip touch him because of the vaulted hall. He saw fire-light, a pale gleam shining brightly. (1497–1517)

Then the great man perceived the accursed creature of the depths, the powerful lake-wife. He made a mighty onslaught with his war-sword, his hand not withholding the blow, so that the ring-adorned thing sang a greedy war-song on her head. Then the newcomer discovered that the battle-brand would not bite, harm her life, but the edge failed the prince in his need. It had endured many hand-to-hand encounters before, often sheared through helmet, war-coat of a doomed man; it was the first occasion for this precious treasure that its glory failed. (1518–1528)

Again Hygelac's kinsman was resolute, in no way slack in courage, remembering famous deeds. Then the angry champion threw down the patterned blade, inlaid with ornament, so that it lay on the ground, rigid and steel-edged; he put his trust in strength, his mighty hand-grip. So ought a man to do when he means to gain long-lasting praise in battle; he cares nothing for his life. (1529–1536)

Then the prince of the War-Geats seized Grendel's mother by the shoulder—he felt no remorse for the quarrel. Now swollen with rage, battle-hardened, he dragged his mortal enemy so that she fell to the floor. Swiftly she paid him back again with fierce grips, and clutched at him. Weary at heart, the strongest of fighters, of foot-soldiers, then stumbled so that he took a fall. (1537–1544)

Then she sat upon the visitor to the hall and drew her knife, broad and bright-edged; she wished to avenge her son, her sole offspring. On his shoulder lay a woven breast-net; that protected his life, prevented entry by point and by edge. Ecgtheow's son, the champion of the Geats, would have fared badly beneath the wide ground then, had the war-mail, hard war-net, not afforded help, and holy God brought about victory in battle. Once he stood up again, the wise Lord, Ruler of the Heavens, easily decided it with justice. (1545–1556)

23. [BEOWULF'S VICTORY: RETURN TO HEOROT]

Then he saw among the armour a victory-blessed blade, an ancient sword made by ogres, firm in its edges, the pride of fighters; it was the choicest of weapons, save that it was larger than any other man might carry out to battle-play—fine and splendid, the work of giants. He seized the belted hilt, the Scyldings' daring champion, savage and deadly grim, drew the patterned blade; despairing of life, he struck angrily so that it bit her hard on the neck, broke the bone-rings; the sword passed straight through the doomed body. She fell dead on the floor; the sword was bloody; the man rejoiced in his work. (1557–1569)

Light shone, brightness gleamed within, just as the candle of the sky shines clearly from heaven. He looked about the building, then turned by the wall; angry and resolute, Hygelac's thane raised his weapon firmly by the hilt. The edge was not useless to the warrior, for he wished swiftly to repay Grendel for those many onslaughts he had made on the West Danes—much more frequent than that one occasion when he slew the companions of Hrothgar's hearth in their sleep, devoured fifteen men of the Danish nation while they slept, and as many others carried away, loathsome plunder. He had paid him his reward for that, the fierce champion, to the effect that he now saw Grendel lying on his couch, sated with war, lifeless, so much had he been injured earlier in the battle at Heorot. The corpse split open when, after death, it suffered a blow, a hard sword-stroke, and thus he cut off his head. (1570–1590)

Straight away the wise men who were gazing at the water with Hrothgar saw that the surging waves were all troubled, the sea stained with blood. The aged men, grey-haired, spoke together of the great man, saying that they did not expect to see the prince return, exulting in victory, to seek out the famous king; to many it seemed certain that the sea-wolf had destroyed him. The ninth hour of the day had come. The bold Scyldings forsook the crag; the gold-friend of men went back to his home. The visitors sat on, sick at heart, and stared at the lake; they wished—and did not expect—that they might see their friend and leader himself. (1591–1604a)

Then, because of the battle-gore, that sword, the fighting blade, began to dwindle into icicles of war. It was a marvel of marvels how it all melted away, just like the ice when the Father, he who has power over times and seasons, loosens the fetters of frost, unbinds the water's bonds; that is true Providence. The prince of the Weder-Geats took no more precious possessions from that dwelling, although he saw many there, but only the head together with the hilt, shining with treasure; the sword itself had already melted, the patterned blade burned away: the blood was too hot for it, the alien demon that had died there too poisonous. He who in the conflict had survived the battle-fall of foes, straight away took to swimming, plunged upwards through the water. The currents, vast tracts, were all cleansed when the alien demon gave up the days of her life and this transitory state. (1604b–1622)

Then the protector of seafarers, swimming with a brave heart, came to land; he rejoiced in the sea-plunder, the great burden he had with him. A splendid band of thanes went to meet him, thanked God, rejoiced in their prince—that they were allowed to see him safe. Then helmet and mail-coat were quickly loosened from the strong man. The lake grew still, the waters beneath the clouds, stained with the gore of slaughter. (1623–1631)

They journeyed forth from there with joyful hearts, retracing their footsteps, measured the path, the familiar road. Men brave as kings carried the head from the cliff by the water—difficult for any two of the great-hearted men. Four had laboriously to convey Grendel's head on the corpse-stake to the gold-hall, until presently they came striding to the hall, fourteen brave Geats, bold in war; among them the leader of men, proud in their midst, trod the fields by the mead-hall. Then the chief of thanes, a man bold in his deeds, enriched by glory, a hero brave in battle, came striding in to greet Hrothgar. The head of Grendel was carried in by the hair on to the hall floor where people were drinking—an object of horror to the warriors and the lady with them, a marvellous spectacle; men looked at it. (1632–1650)

24. [BEOWULF'S REPORT; HROTHGAR'S ADVICE]

Beowulf spoke, the son of Ecgtheow: 'Well, son of Healfdene, prince of Scyldings, we have gladly brought you this sea-plunder which you look on here, as a token of success. I hardly came through it alive, the underwater conflict, engaged in the business not without difficulty. The battle would have ended at once had God not shielded me. I could accomplish nothing with Hrunting in the fight, fine though that weapon may be. But the Ruler of men granted me that I should see hanging, beautiful on the wall, an enormous ancient sword—he has often guided the friendless thus—so that I might wield that weapon. Then in the conflict, when my opportunity came, I struck down the guardians of that house. Then that war-sword, the patterned blade, burned away as the blood gushed out, the hottest of battle-gore. I have brought back that hilt from the foes, avenged the evil deeds, the slaughter of Danes, as was fitting. I promise you, then, that you may sleep in Heorot free from care, with your band of men and every thane of your people, tried warriors and youths—that you need not fear deadly injury to your soldiers from that quarter, as you did before, prince of Scyldings!' (1651–1676)

Then the golden hilt, the ancient work of giants, was given into the hand of the old hero, the grizzled war-leader. After the fall of the devils it passed, the work of marvellous smiths, into the possession of the lord of the Danes; and when the angry-hearted creature, the enemy of God, forsook this world—and his mother too—it passed into the power of the best of earthly kings between the seas, of those who distributed wealth in the Danish realm. (1677–1686)

Hrothgar spoke, examining the hilt, ancient heirloom.[28] On it there was engraved the origin of the ancient strife, when the flood, the gushing ocean, slew the race of giants—they suffered fearfully. That was a nation estranged from the eternal Lord; therefore the Ruler gave them their final reward through the surge of water. On the plates of shining gold was thus correctly marked in runic lettering, set down and told, for whom that sword, the choicest of irons, with twisted hilt and serpentine patterns, had first been wrought. (1687–1698a)

Then the wise man, the son of Healfdene, spoke (everyone was silent): 'Well, one who furthers truth and justice among the people, an old guardian of the homeland who remembers all that has passed, may say that this warrior was born the better man. Your glory, Beowulf my friend, will be exalted among every nation, throughout distant regions. You carry all this power of yours with patience and prudence of mind. I shall fulfil my friendship towards you, just as we spoke together a short time ago. You shall become a comfort to your people, a help to heroes, given to endure for a very long time. (1698b–1709a)

Heremod, the offspring of Ecgwela, was not thus to the Honoured-Scyldings; he did not grow to be a delight to them, but to bring slaughter and deadly injury to the Danish people. His heart swollen with rage, he destroyed the companions of his table, close comrades, until alone, he, the famous prince, turned away from the joys of men. Although mighty God had raised him up in strength, had advanced him above all men in the pleasures of power, nevertheless within his breast the secrets of

---

[28] **the hilt, ancient heirloom:** The hilt of the sword originally belonging to the monsters depicts the story of the flood, written in runic letters of the old Germanic alphabet and surrounded by a serpentine pattern of lines. Hrothgar interprets the runes, which have magical and symbolic qualities. [Editors' note.]

his heart grew blood-thirsty; in no way did he give rings to the Danes for the sake of glory. Joyless he survived to suffer the pain of that strife, a lasting injury to the people. Teach yourself from this, understand nobility! Wise with the passing winters, I have recited this story for your benefit. (1709b–1724a)

It is a marvel to tell how mighty God in his ample spirit distributes to mankind wisdom, homeland and heroism. He has power over all things. Sometimes he allows the thoughts of the heart of a man of famous race to follow his desire, grants him the joy of land in his own country, a safe stronghold of men to rule over, makes regions of the world subject to him thus, an ample kingdom, so that in his unwisdom he himself cannot conceive an end to it. He lives in abundance; neither sickness nor old age afflict him at all, no evil sorrow darkens his spirit, no enmity anywhere reveals violent hatred, but the whole world turns at his will. He knows nothing worse — (1724b–1739)

25. [Hrothgar's Advice Continues]

— until within him great arrogance grows and flourishes; then the watchman, the guardian of the soul slumbers; bound in cares, that sleep will be too deep, the slayer very near who wickedly shoots with an arrow from his bow. Then he who knows not how to protect himself will be stricken beneath his helmet in the breast with a bitter shaft, with the crooked mysterious promptings of the evil demon. That which he has held so long seems too little for him; angry-minded, he covets, never giving away plated rings in display. And because of the great honours which God, the Ruler of Glory, had earlier bestowed on him, he forgets and neglects what is ordained for the future. In the end it happens as a matter of course that the transitory flesh declines, falls doomed; another man takes over who, not obsessed by fear, will distribute the treasures, the warrior's former wealth, without reluctance. (1740–1756)

Guard yourself against that pernicious wickedness, beloved Beowulf, best of men, and choose for yourself the better part — eternal gains; do not be obsessed by arrogance, famous champion! Now for a time there is glory in your strength; yet soon it shall be that sickness or sword-edge will part you from your power — or the fire's embrace, or the flood's surge, or blade's attack, or spear's flight, or dreadful old age; or else the brightness of the eyes will fade and grow dim; presently it will come about that death shall overpower you, noble man. (1757–1768)

Thus for a hundred seasons I ruled the Ring-Danes beneath the skies, and secured them from war by spear and sword-edge against many nations throughout the world, so that I did not reckon on any opponent beneath the expanse of heaven. Well, there came a set-back to me in my own country, misery following merriment, when Grendel, the old enemy, became my invader. Because of that persecution I have constantly borne great anxiety of mind. Thanks be to Providence, the eternal Lord, that after ancient tribulation I have lived long enough to gaze with my eyes on that blood-stained head! Distinguished in battle, go now to your seat, join in the joy of the banquet. When morning comes, a great many treasures shall be shared between us.' (1769–1784)

The Geat was glad at heart, went at once to take his seat as the wise man bade. Then once again, as before, a feast was agreeably spread for those men renowned for courage who sat in the hall. The cover of night grew dark, black over the noble men. The band of companions all rose; the grey-haired man, the old Scylding, wished to seek out his bed. The Geat, renowned shield-fighter, was particularly well pleased to rest. Straight away a hall-thane who out of courtesy attended to all the needs of a thane—such as a seafaring warrior had to have in those days—led him forth, weary from his exploit, having come from afar. (1785–1798)

Then the great-hearted man took his rest. The building towered up, gabled and decked with gold; within it the guest slept, until the black raven, cheerful at heart, announced the joy of the sky.[29] Then came brightness advancing, radiance following shadows. The soldiers made haste, the princes were eager to journey back to their people. Bold in spirit, the visitor wished to seek out his ship, far from there. (1799–1806)

Then the brave man commanded Hrunting to be carried to the son of Ecglaf, commanded him to take his sword, the precious iron; he gave him thanks for the loan of it, said that he reckoned it a good friend in war, strong in battle, by none of his words disparaged the edge of the blade: that was a gallant man. And then the fighting-men, eager for the journey, were ready in their armour. The prince, precious to the Danes, went to the dais where the other was, the hero brave in battle addressed Hrothgar. (1807–1816)

26. [The Geats Depart]

Beowulf spoke, the son of Ecgtheow: 'Now we seafarers, come from afar, wish to say that we are anxious to seek out Hygelac. We have been properly, delightfully entertained here; you have treated us well. If while on earth I might in any way earn more of the love of your heart than I have yet done, by warlike deeds, I shall be ready at once, leader of men. If over the expanse of the flood I learn that those dwelling round about threaten you with terrible things, as those hating you have sometimes done, I will bring a thousand thanes, heroes to your aid. As for Hygelac, leader of the Geats, guardian of the nation, I know that, young though he may be, he would be willing to assist me by words and deeds, so that I might show my esteem for you and carry a forest of spears to help you, the support of strength where you have need of men. If then Hrethric, the prince's son, decides to come to the courts of the Geats, he will be able to find many friends there; distant countries are well sought by one who is himself strong.' (1817–1839)

Hrothgar spoke to him in reply: 'The wise Lord sent that speech into your mind; I have never heard a man of so young an age talk more sagaciously. You are mighty in strength and prudent in spirit, sensible in speech. I think it likely, if it comes about

---

[29] **the black raven . . . sky:** A bird intimately linked with Woden, the Norse god of war, the raven is usually associated with war and carnage. But in both Old Norse and Latin literature the raven is considered a prophetic bird that can signal either good or evil.

that the spear, sword-grim war, sickness or iron, take Hrethel's offspring, your chief, the guardian of the nation, and you are still living, that the Sea-Geats would have no better man to choose as king and guardian of the treasure-hoard of heroes, if you wish to hold your kinsman's kingdom. The longer I know them, the better your mind and spirit please me, beloved Beowulf. You have brought it about that there shall be mutual friendship between the nations, the people of the Geats and the Spear-Danes, and conflict, the acts of malice in which they previously engaged, shall rest; for as long as I rule the broad kingdom there shall be treasures in common — many a man greet another with great gifts across the gannet's bath; the curved vessel shall bring presents and tokens of love across the sea. I know the people to be stead-fast both towards foe and towards friend, blameless in every respect in the ancient manner.' (1840–1865)

Then moreover the defence of warriors, Healfdene's kinsman, gave him in the hall twelve treasures, bade him seek out his own dear people in safety with these presents, come back again quickly. Then the prince of the Scyldings, a king great in nobility, kissed the best of thanes, and clasped him by the neck; tears fell from the grey-haired man. Being old and very wise, two things might be expected, the second more strongly — that they would not see one another again, brave in the council. That man was so loved by him that he could not restrain the breast's surging; but a hidden yearning for the beloved man burned in the blood, fixed in the heart-strings. (1866–1880a)

Beowulf departed, trod the grassy earth, a warrior proud in the gold, exulting in treasure. The sea-traveller, which rode at anchor, awaited its master. Then on the journey Hrothgar's gift was often praised. That was a peerless king, faultless in every respect, until old age, which has often ruined many, took from him the joys of strength. (1880b–1887)

27. [THE ARRIVAL AT HYGELAC'S COURT: THE TALE OF THRYTH]

Then the band of great-hearted young men came to the flood; they wore ring-mail, an interlocked shirt on their limbs. The guard at the coast noticed the return of the warriors, as he had done before. He did not greet the guests with defiance from the top of the cliff, but rode to meet them, declared that the soldiers in shining armour going down to the ship would be welcome to the people of the Weders. Then on the sand the broad seagoing vessel, the curved prow, was loaded with battle-dress, steeds and treasures; the mast towered up over wealth from Hrothgar's hoard. He gave the boat-guard a gold-inlaid sword, so that thereafter he was the more honoured on the mead-bench on account of that treasure, the heirloom. (1888–1903a)

The vessel forsook the land of the Danes, moved out to stir the deep water. Then at the mast the sail was made fast by a rope, a fine sea-dress; the water-borne timbers creaked. The wind over the billows did not hinder the wave-floater from its journey. The sea-traveller advanced, floated foamy-necked over the waves, the clamped prow over the ocean currents, until they could descry the Geatish cliffs, familiar head-lands. Driven by the breeze, the craft pressed forward, grounded on land. (1903b–1913)

Swiftly the landing-guard, he who, eager for the beloved men, had for a long time before gazed far out across the currents, was ready by the water. He moored the broad-bosomed ship in the sand, fast by its anchor-ropes, lest the force of the waves should drive the superb timbers away. Then he commanded that the princes' wealth, the ornaments and plated gold, be carried up; they would not have to go far from there to seek the distributor of treasure, Hygelac son of Hrethel, where he himself dwelt with his companions, near to the sea-wall. (1914–1924)

The building was splendid, the king most renowned, high in the hall — Hæreth's daughter Hygd very young, wise, accomplished, though she had lived few winters within the enclosed stronghold; yet she was not mean, not too niggardly in gifts of treasured wealth to the people of the Geats. Thryth,[30] imperious queen of the nation, showed haughtiness, a terrible sin. There was no brave man among the dear companions, save for her overlord, who by day dared venture to gaze at her with his eyes; but he might reckon deadly fetters, twisted by hand, assured for him; that after seizure, the sword would be prescribed, the patterned blade should settle it, make known a violent death. Such a thing is no queenly custom for a lady to practise, peerless though she may be — that a 'peace-weaver' should take the life of a beloved man on account of a fancied insult. (1925–1943)

However, Hemming's kinsman put a stop to that. Those drinking ale told another tale — that she brought about fewer acts of malice, injuries to the people, as soon as she was given, adorned with gold, to the young champion, the dear prince, when at her father's bidding she sought out Offa's hall in a journey across the yellowish flood. There she subsequently occupied the throne well, famous for virtue, while living made good use of the life destined for her, maintained a profound love for the chief of heroes — the best, as I have heard, of all mankind, of the entire race between the seas. Indeed Offa, a spear-bold man, was widely honoured for gifts and battles; he held his homeland with wisdom. Thence sprang Eomer, to be a help to heroes — a kinsman of Hemming, grandson of Garmund, skilful in conflicts. (1944–1962)

28. [Hygelac's Welcome: The Tale of Freawaru]

Then the bold man himself went along the sand with his bodyguard, treading the beach, the wide shores. The world's candle shone, the sun hastening from the south. They made their way, going eagerly, to where they heard that the defence of warriors, the slayer of Ongentheow,[31] the great young war-king, was dealing out rings in the

---

[30] **Thryth:** After speaking of Hygd, the young and virtuous bride of Hygelac, the poet considers the story of Thryth, who is said to have changed her malevolent character after her marriage to Offa, king of the Angles, sometime later in the fourth century. The story of King Offa's good effect on Thryth may have been intended as an indirect compliment to Offa's descendant, Offa II, king of Mercia (757–796). Based on their interpretation of these lines, some scholars claim that the final version of *Beowulf* was composed at the end of the eighth century, under the protection of the Mercian court.

[31] **slayer of Ongentheow:** This distinction is given to Hygelac, though his follower Eofor actually killed the Swedish king.

stronghold. Beowulf's journey was quickly made known to Hygelac — that there in the precincts the defence of fighting-men, his shield-companion, came walking alive to the court, safe from the game of war. The floor within was swiftly cleared for those who were coming on foot, as the powerful man commanded. (1963–1976)

Then he who had come safely through combat sat down facing him, kinsman facing kinsman, after he had greeted the faithful leader of men with ceremonial speech, sincere words. Hæreth's daughter moved through the spacious building with mead-cups, cared for the people, carried flagons of drink to the hands of the Hæth-nas. (1977–1983a)

Hygelac began courteously to question his comrade in that lofty hall; curiosity pricked him as to what the adventures of the Sea-Geats had been: 'How did you fare on the journey, beloved Beowulf, when you suddenly resolved to seek out combat far off across the salt water, battle at Heorot? And did you in any way remedy the widely-known woes of the famous prince, Hrothgar? I have brooded over this with anxiety of mind, surging grief, mistrusting the venture of my beloved man. I long begged you that you should in no way approach that murderous demon, letting the South Danes settle the war against Grendel themselves. I give thanks to God that I was allowed to see you safe.' (1983b–1998)

Beowulf, the son of Ecgtheow, spoke: 'My leader Hygelac, the famous encounter is openly known to many men — what period of conflict came about between Grendel and me in the place where he brought an abundance of sorrows to the Victorious-Scyldings, constant misery. I avenged everything, so that none of Grendel's kin on earth — not he who, encompassed by deceit, lives longest of all that loathsome race — will have cause to boast of that pre-dawn clash. (1999–2009a)

There I first came to the ring-hall to greet Hrothgar. Straight away, when he knew my purpose, the famous kinsman of Healfdene assigned me a seat facing his own sons. The company was joyful; in my whole life I have not seen beneath the vault of heaven a greater rejoicing in mead among those sitting in the hall. At times the famous queen, peace-pledge of the nations, passed through the entire building, encouraged the young warriors; often she presented a twisted circlet to a man before she went to her seat; at times Hrothgar's daughter carried an ale-cup before the tried men, to each of the warriors in turn. I heard those sitting in the hall call her Freawaru, as she presented the studded treasure to heroes. (2009b–2024a)

Young, adorned with gold, she is promised to the gracious son of Froda.[32] That has been agreed upon by the Scyldings' friend, the guardian of the kingdom, and he considers it good advice that, by means of this woman, he should settle their share of slaughterous feuds, of conflicts. It seldom happens after the fall of a prince that the deadly spear rests for even a little while — worthy though the bride may be! (2024b–2031)

---

[32] **son of Froda:** Froda and his son Ingeld were Heathobards, a people in a longstanding feud with the Danes. Apparently, after Froda is killed, Hrothgar attempts to secure peace by marrying his daughter Freawaru to Ingeld. Beowulf guesses correctly that this attempt will fail. Eventually, Hrothgar and his kinsmen kill Ingeld when he attacks them while visiting Heorot.

It may displease the prince of the Heathobards and every thane of those peoples when he goes in the hall with the girl, that the noble sons of the Danes are splendidly entertained; upon them will glisten the heirlooms of ancestors, hard and ring-adorned, the treasure of Heathobards for as long as they could wield those weapons— (2032–2038)

29. [THE TALE OF FREAWARU; BEOWULF'S ACCOUNT CONTINUES]

—until in the play of shields they brought their dear companions and their own lives to destruction. (2039–2040)

Then he who sees the ring, an old spear-fighter who remembers all the death of men by darts—grim will be his spirit—will speak over the beer, sad in mind, begin to test the mettle of a young champion, to awaken the violence of war through the thought of his heart, and will speak these words: 'Can you, my friend, recognise the sword, the precious iron which your father beneath his war-visor carried into the fray on his last expedition, where the Danes, the bold Scyldings, slew him, had mastery of the battlefield when, after the fall of heroes, Withergyld lay dead? Now some son or other of those slayers walks in the hall, exulting in the trappings, boasts of the killing and wears the treasure which by rights you should possess!' (2041–2056)

On every occasion thus he will provoke and prompt the mind with bitter words, until the moment comes that the girl's thane will sleep stained with blood from the bite of a sword, his life forfeit, because of his father's deeds; the other will escape with his life, knowing the land well. So then the sworn oaths of warriors will be broken on both sides; after that deadly hatred will well up in Ingeld, and because of surging anxiety, his love for his wife will grow cooler. Therefore I do not reckon the faith of the Heathobards, their great alliance with the Danes, to be without deceit, a firm friendship. (2057–2069a)

I shall speak once again about Grendel, so that you may clearly know, distributor of treasure, how the hand-to-hand combat of heroes turned out. After the gem of heaven had glided over the earth, the angry demon came, a dreadful hostility in the dusk, to visit us where, unharmed, we kept watch over the hall. There the battle was fatal to Hondscioh, a deadly injury to the doomed man; he was the first to lie dead, girded champion. Grendel destroyed the famous young thane with his mouth, swallowing the entire body of the beloved man. Nevertheless the bloody-toothed slayer, intent on destruction, did not wish to go out of the gold-hall empty-handed; but, renowned for strength, he made trial of me, clutching with an eager hand. A pouch hung there, wide and wonderful, made fast with cunning clasps; it had been entirely fashioned with ingenuity, the skill of the devil, and dragon-skins. He wished, the bold source of wicked deeds, to put me inside it, guiltless, as one of many; he could not do so, once I stood upright in anger. (2069b–2092)

It is too long to tell how I paid that scourge of the people back again for every evil deed. By my actions there, my prince, I brought honour to your people. He escaped away, enjoyed the delight of life for a little while; however, his right hand remained behind, a spoor in Heorot, and he went from there humiliated, mournful at heart sank to the bottom of the lake. (2093–2100)

30. [Beowulf's Account Continues]

The Scyldings' friend rewarded me for that deadly onslaught with much plated gold, many treasures, when morning came and we had sat down to the banquet. There was story and song. The old Scylding, who had heard many things, told of times far off; sometimes the battle-brave man plucked the joyful wood, the pleasing harp, sometimes he recited a story, true and sorrowful, sometimes the great-hearted king told aright a strange tale; sometimes, again, the old war-fighter, bowed with age, would lament his youth, his strength in battle; the heart welled within when, wise with winters, he remembered so much. (2101–2114)

So all day long we took our pleasure there, until another night came to men. Then in turn Grendel's mother was swiftly ready for the avenging of wrongs, took a sorry journey. Death, the war-hatred of the Weders, had carried off the son. The hideous woman avenged her child, boldly destroyed a warrior; there it was that life departed from Æschere, sage old councillor. Not when morning came, could the people of the Danes burn him, sated with war, in the blaze, neither lay the beloved man on the pyre; she had carried the body off in a fiend's embrace beneath a mountain stream. To Hrothgar that was the most grievous of sorrows of those which had long befallen the chieftain of the people. (2115–2130)

Then, troubled in mind, the prince implored me that, for your sake, I should display heroism in the tumult of waters, should risk life, should achieve a glorious deed; he promised me reward. Then, as is widely known, I found in the surge a terrible grim guardian of the deep. There for a time we locked, hand-to-hand; the water welled with blood, and in that war-hall I cut off the head of Grendel's mother with a great blade. I hardly got away from there alive — I was not yet doomed to die; but the defence of warriors, Healfdene's kinsman, again bestowed on me many treasures. (2131–2143)

31. [An Exchange of Gifts: Interlude]

The king of that nation lived thus in the traditional manner; I lost no reward whatever, the recompense of strength, but Healfdene's son gave me treasures of my own choosing; these I wish to bring to you, warrior king, to present with good will. All favour is still dependent on you; I have few close kinsmen except for you, Hygelac!' (2144–2151)

Then he commanded them to carry in the boar-standard, symbol of chieftaincy, towering battle-helmet, the grey mail-coat, the splendid war-sword, and related their story: 'The wise ruler, Hrothgar, presented me with this battle-garb; he commanded me in one speech that I should first tell you about his gracious gift. He said that King Heorogar, the prince of the Scyldings, had it for a long while; nevertheless he would not give it, the breast-armour, to his son, bold Heoroweard, faithful to him though he was. Make good use of it all!' (2152–2162)

I heard that four swift steeds, all alike, yellow as apples, followed those adornments. He made over to him the gracious gift of steeds and treasures. So ought a kinsman to act, never weave a web of malice for the other with secret craft, devise the death of a close comrade. Hygelac's nephew, stern in combats, was very faithful to him, and each was mindful of the other's profit. I heard that he presented to Hygd the neck-ring, the wonderful adorned treasure, that Wealhtheow, a prince's daughter, had given him, together with three horses, graceful and bright with saddles; after receiving the ring her breast was thenceforward honoured. (2163–2176)

Thus Ecgtheow's son, a man well known for battles, for great deeds, displayed his bravery, acted with honour; never did he slay the companions of his hearth when drunk; his heart was not savage but, brave in battle, with the greatest strength among mankind, he held the ample gift which God had bestowed on him. He had long been despised, since the children of the Geats did not reckon him a fine man, nor would the leader of the Weders do him great honour on the mead-bench; they firmly believed him to be slothful, a feeble prince.[33] There came to the man blessed with glory a change from all troubles. (2177–2189)

Then the defence of warriors, a king renowned in battle, commanded them to fetch in Hrethel's heirloom, decked with gold; there was not then among the Geats a better treasure in the shape of a sword. He laid that in Beowulf's lap, and bestowed on him seven thousand hides,[34] a hall and princely throne. Both of them alike owned inherited land in that country, a dwelling, ancestral rights—to the other in particular, whose rank was higher, a wide kingdom. (2190–2199)

In clashes of battle in later days—after Hygelac lay dead, and battle-blades beneath the shield's shelter had been the death of Heardred when the War-Scylfings, bold battle-fighters, sought him out among his victorious nation, assailed the nephew of Hereric with enmity—it came to pass that then the broad kingdom came into Beowulf's hand.[35] (2200–2208a)

For fifty winters he held it well—he was then a wise king, an old guardian of the homeland—until there began to hold sway in the dark nights a certain creature, a dragon, which in a lofty dwelling kept watch over a hoard, a high stone barrow; beneath lay a passage unknown to men. Into this some man or other had gone, who got near to the heathen hoard, whose hand seized a flagon, large, adorned with treasure. Nor did it afterwards conceal the fact, though it had been tricked by a thief's cunning while sleeping; the men of the people dwelling there found that out when it was swollen with rage. (2208b–2220)

---

[33] **a feeble prince:** This allusion to Beowulf's sluggish youth seems at odds with the hero's own account, but sloth is a common motif concerning young heroes of folklore, including two Old Norse sagas related to *Beowulf*.

[34] **seven thousand hides:** The unit of land known as a "hide" originally meant the land necessary to support one family. Beowulf's estate must have been very extensive; according to one Anglo-Saxon historian, seven thousand hides was the size of South Mercia.

[35] **it came to pass . . . hand:** In this transition, intended to cover fifty years, the events leading to Beowulf's rule are necessarily brief. See lines 2354–96.

32. [The Plundering of the Dragon's Hoard]

He who grievously despoiled it did not break into the serpent's hoard on purpose by his own choice at all; but in sore distress, the slave of one or another hero's son fled from hostile blows, in need of a dwelling, and made his way inside there, a man troubled by sin. As soon as he looked inside, a terrible horror arose in the stranger; however, the poor wretch [escaped the dreadful serpent]. When the sudden attack came upon him [he took with him] a precious cup. There were many such ancient treasures in that earthen house, just as in days gone by some man or other had carefully hidden precious jewels there, the immense legacy of a noble race.[36] Death had carried off them all in former times, and the one man remaining of the tried warriors of the people, he who lived there longest, a guardian mourning his friends, expected the same fate as theirs — that only for a little while would he be allowed to enjoy the long-accumulated treasures. (2221–2241a)

A barrow stood all ready on open ground near the sea-waves, new by the headland, secure in its powers of confinement. Into this the keeper of the rings carried a large amount of what was worth hoarding, noble treasures, plated gold, spoke few words: (2241b–2246)

'Hold now, you earth, the possession of warriors, now that the heroes cannot! Indeed, it was from you that the great men formerly won it. Death in war, fierce mortal havoc, has carried off every man of my people who forsook this life, saw the last of joys in the hall. I have none who bears the sword or polishes the plated flagon, precious drinking-cup; the company of tried warriors has passed elsewhere. The hard helmet, decorated with gold, must be reft of its plates; the polishers who should burnish the war-visor are asleep; so also the war-coat, which endured the bite of iron over the splintering of shields, falls to pieces along with the warrior; nor can the mail's rings travel far with the war-leader, side-by-side with heroes. There is no delight in the harp, mirth in the singing wood, nor does a fine hawk swoop through the hall, nor the swift steed stamp in the courtyard. Baleful death has despatched many of the human race!' (2247–2266)

Thus, sad in mind, the lone survivor lamented his grief, unhappy, moved through day and night until the surge of death touched his heart. (2267–2270a)

The ancient pre-dawn scourge who, burning, seeks out barrows — the smooth-skinned, malicious dragon who flies by night encircled in fire — found the delightful hoard standing open. Those who dwell on earth greatly fear it. It is its nature to seek out a hoard in the earth where, wise with winters, it guards heathen gold; it is none the better for that. (2270b–2277)

Thus for three hundred winters the scourge of the nation held a particularly immense treasure-house in the earth, until a certain man enraged its heart; he

---

[36] **immense legacy of a noble race:** The tale of this treasure is revealed in brief passages throughout the poem. Long ago it was consigned to the earth by noble princes, with a curse laid on it. Discovered by a warrior race, it was used until all but one of its members succumbed to the curse. The sole survivor reburied the treasure in an ancient funeral mound. There the hoard was found by the dragon, who watched over it for three hundred years until the theft of the cup roused his anger.

carried to his leader the plated flagon, asked his lord for peace-conditions. So the hoard was ransacked, the hoard of rings diminished, the wretched man granted his request. The prince examined the ancient work of men for the first time. (2278–2286)

Then the serpent awoke, a new grievance arose; it moved rapidly along the rock, ruthless in heart, discovered the enemy's footprint—with stealthy craft he had stepped too far forward near to the dragon's head. Thus a man not fated to die, whom the favour of the Ruler protects, can survive miseries and banishment with ease. The guardian of the hoard eagerly searched along the ground, wanted to find the man who had treated it cruelly while it slept; hot and savage at heart, it frequently circled all round the mound on the outside; there was no man in that wilderness; however, it rejoiced in anticipation of conflict, an act of war; sometimes it turned back into the barrow, searched for the precious cup; it soon discovered that some man had tampered with the gold, the princely treasure. (2287–2302a)

With difficulty, the guardian of the hoard waited until evening came. Then the keeper of the barrow was swollen with rage, the loathsome creature wanted to pay them back for the precious drinking-cup with fire. Then to the serpent's gratification, the day had passed; it would not stay longer within the walls, but set out with flame, ready with fire. The beginning was terrible to the people in the land, just as presently it would end with bitterness for their treasure-giver. (2302b–2311)

33. [THE DRAGON ATTACKS THE GEATISH STRONGHOLD]

Then the visitant began to spew forth coals of fire, to burn the bright houses; the light of burning arose, bringing terror upon men. The loathsome creature flying in the air wished to leave nothing there alive. From far and near the serpent's warfare, cruelly hostile malice, was widely evident, how the warlike scourge persecuted and humiliated the people of the Geats. It darted back to the hoard, its secret, splendid hall, before daytime. It had encircled those who dwelt in the land with flame, fire and burning; it put its trust in the barrow, warfare and the rampart; the expectation deceived it. (2312–2323)

Then the truth of the horror was quickly made known to Beowulf—that his own home, the finest of buildings, the Geats' throne, source of gifts, had melted away in the burning surges. That was a distress to the spirit of the great man, the greatest of sorrows to the mind. The wise man supposed that he had bitterly offended the Ruler, eternal Lord, by breaking some ancient law; his breast within surged with dark thoughts, which was unusual for him. (2324–2332)

The fiery dragon had utterly crushed with coals of fire the fortress of the people from the seaboard to the interior. The war-king, the prince of the Weders, planned revenge on it for this. The defence of fighting-men, the leader of warriors, commanded to be made for him a wonderful war-shield all of iron; he knew very well that forest wood could not help him—limewood against flame. The seafarer, a prince of proven merit, had to meet the end of his days, his life in the world—and the dragon as well, long though it had held the hoarded wealth. (2333–2344)

Then the ruler of rings disdained to seek out the wide-flying creature with a troop, an extensive force; he had no fear for himself in the combat, nor did he make much of the serpent's war-power, strength and courage, because, risking danger, he had previously survived many violent situations, clashes of battle, since he, a man blessed with victory, had cleansed Hrothgar's hall and crushed to death in battle Grendel's kin, of loathsome race. (2345–2354a)

Not the least of hand-to-hand encounters was that where they slew Hygelac, when the king of the Geats, lord and friend of the people, died by blood-drinking blades in the onslaught of war in Frisia, the offspring of Hrethel beaten down by the sword. Beowulf came away from there by his own strength, engaged in a feat of swimming;[37] he held in his arm the battle-gear of thirty warriors when he turned to the water. The Hetware[38] had no cause at all for exultation in the conflict of troops when they carried limewood shields against him; few came back from that battle-fighter to seek out their homes. (2354b–2366)

Then the son of Ecgtheow, a wretched solitary, swam over the expanse of tides back to his people. There Hygd offered him hoard and kingdom, rings and a princely throne; now that Hygelac was dead, she did not trust that her son knew how to hold the throne of his homeland against foreign nations. Nevertheless the destitute people could not in any way persuade the prince to become lord over Heardred or agree to accede to royal power. However, he upheld him among the people with friendly counsels, good-will with honour, until he became older and ruled the Weder-Geats. (2367–2379a)

Exiled men, the sons of Ohthere, sought him out from over the sea;[39] they had rebelled against the protector of the Scylfings, a famous prince, the best of the sea-kings, of those who distributed treasure in the Swedish kingdom. That was to mark his end; because of his hospitality, Hygelac's son received a mortal wound by strokes from a sword. And when Heardred lay dead, Ongentheow's son went back to seek his home again—allowed Beowulf to hold the princely throne, rule the Geats. That was a great king! (2379b–2390)

34. [BEOWULF PREPARES TO FIGHT AND SPEAKS TO THE GEATS]

In later days he was mindful of requiting the prince's fall—became a friend to the destitute Eadgils; across the wide sea he advanced the cause of Ohthere's son among the people with fighters and weapons. Later he took vengeance with cold expeditions that brought sorrow—deprived the king of life. (2391–2396)

---

[37] **Beowulf . . . swimming:** The story of Beowulf's heroism after the defeat of Hygelac continues in this tale of his strength as a swimmer, already established with his boast to Unferth (lines 506 ff.).

[38] **The Hetware:** Frankish allies of the Frisians who fought against Hygelac. [Editors' note.]

[39] **Exiled men . . . sea:** After the murder of Heardred, son of Hygelac, by the Swedish king Onela, Beowulf assumed the Geatish throne. He befriended Eadgils, son of the former Swedish king Ohthere, in his fight to recover the throne from his uncle Onela. [Editors' note.]

Thus he, the son of Ecgtheow, had come safely through every conflict, danger-ous onslaught, deeds of courage, until that particular day when he had to fight against the serpent. Then the leader of the Geats, swelling with rage, went as one of twelve to view the dragon. He had learned by then for what reason this feud had arisen, dire malice to men; the famous precious vessel had come into his lap through the hand of the informant. The thirteenth man in that band was he who had been responsible for the beginning of that strife, the slave who, mournful in mind, humil-iated, had to lead the way from there to the place. Against his will he went to where he knew the singular earthen hall to be, a mound covered in soil near to the surging water, the tumult of the waves, which within was full of decorated objects and fili-gree. The hideous guardian, ready, bold in war, held the golden treasures, old beneath the earth; it was no easy merchandise for any man to win. (2397–2416)

Then the king, bold in conflict, sat on the headland, as the gold-friend of the Geats wished the companions of his hearth good fortune. His spirit was mournful, restless and ready for death—the fate very close which should meet the old man, seek out the soul's hoard, divide asunder life from body; the life of the prince was not wrapped in flesh for long then. Beowulf spoke, the son of Ecgtheow: 'In youth I came safely through many an onslaught in war, period of conflict; I remember it all. I was seven winters old when the commander of treasure, the lord and friend of the people, took me on from my father.[40] King Hrethel kept and maintained me, gave me treasure and banquet, remembering our relationship; I was no more hated by him as a warrior in the strongholds during his lifetime, than any of his sons: Here-beald and Hæthcyn, or my Hygelac. A bed of violent death was spread for the eldest, inappropriately by the actions of a kinsman when Hæthcyn, his lord and friend, struck him with an arrow from a horn bow, missed the mark and shot his kinsman, one brother the other, with a bloody dart.[41] That was a conflict without compensa-tion, a wicked crime wearying to ponder in the heart; but nevertheless, the prince had to relinquish life unavenged. (2417–2443)

Just so, it is a sad thing for an old man to endure if his son should swing young on the gallows. Then he may recite a story, a sorrowful song, as his son hangs, a profit to the raven, and he, old and wise with years, cannot afford him any help. Regularly each morning he is reminded of his offspring's journey elsewhere; he does not care to wait for another heir within the stronghold when the first has completed his trial of deeds in the compulsion of death. Moved with sorrow, he sees in his son's cham-ber a deserted wine-hall, a windswept resting-place bereft of joy. The horsemen sleep, heroes in darkness; there is no sound of harp, mirth in the courts, as once there was— (2444–2459)

---

[40] **took me on from my father:** It was a frequent practice among the Germanic peoples for youths to be sent away from their overprotective parents to be trained in the customs of heroic society. In Beowulf's case, he was sent to the royal household of an uncle, King Hrethel.

[41] **shot his kinsman . . . dart:** When Hrethel's son Haethcyn accidentally killed his brother Herebeald, there was no way for the father to avenge his son's death, either by payment or punishment. Similarly, neither com-pensation nor retribution can be exacted for anyone killed by the legal process, as in a hanging.

35. [The Speech Ends. The Battle Begins]

— then he goes to his couch, chants a dirge for the lost one. The land and dwelling-place seemed all too roomy for him; so the Weders' protector felt sorrow welling in the heart for Herebeald; he could in no way settle the feud with the life-slayer; nor yet could he persecute the battle-warrior with acts of hatred, although he was not loved by him. Then with the sorrow which had befallen him he forsook the joys of men, chose God's light; when he passed from life he left his offspring, as a prosperous man does, land and the national stronghold. (2460–2471)

After Hrethel died there was hostility and strife between Swedes and Geats, a mutual grievance across the broad water, severe warlike conflict; and the offspring of Ongentheow were brave, bold in war, wanted to keep no peace over the sea, but often committed dreadful malicious slaughter around Mares' Hill. As is well known, my dear kinsman avenged that feud and crime, although one of them bought it with his life, a hard bargain; the war was fatal to Hæthcyn, leader of the Geats. I heard that then in the morning one kinsman took vengeance for the other with the edge of the sword on the slayer, when Ongentheow sought out Eofor;[42] the war-helmet split apart, the aged Scylfing fell, made pale by the sword; the hand remembered enough feuds, did not withhold the mortal blow. (2472–2489)

As it was granted me, I repaid with my bright sword in the battle the treasures he bestowed on me; he gave me estate, dwelling, delight in homeland. There was no need, not any cause, for him to seek out to hire for a price a worse fighting-man among the Gifthas[43] or among the Spear-Danes or in the Swedish kingdom. I would always go before him in the troop, alone in the van; and while life lasts I shall do battle for as long as this sword endures that has stood by me early and late, ever since I slew the Franks' champion Dæghrefn with my hand in the presence of tried warriors. In no way could he bring to the Frisian king the ornament adorning the breast, but the standard-bearer fell in the contest, a prince with courage; nor was a sword-edge his slayer, but a warlike grip broke his heart's surge, his bone frame. Now the edge of the blade, hand and hard sword, must fight for the hoard.' (2490–2509)

Beowulf spoke, uttered vaunting words for the last time: 'I engaged in many a war in my youth; an old guardian of the people, I will seek out the feud, achieve a deed of glory, if the wicked ravager will come out of the earthen hall to meet me!' (2510–2515)

Then he addressed each of the men, bold helmet-bearers, dear companions, for the last time: 'I would not carry a sword, a weapon, against the serpent if I knew how else, in accordance with my boast, I could grapple with the monster as once I did with Grendel; but here I expect hot battle-fire and poisonous breath; therefore I have shield and mail-coat upon me. I will not retreat one footstep from the guardian of

---

[42] **when Ongentheow . . . Eofor:** At the battle of Ravenswood, Hygelac was avenged for the death of his brother Haethcyn by his follower Eofor's killing of the Swedish king Ongentheow.

[43] **Gifthas:** An East Germanic people, some of whom remained in the north to form part of Danish society.

the barrow, but at the rampart it shall be for us both as fate, the Providence ruling every man, shall decree. I am resolute in spirit, so I will abstain from boasts against the war-flier. You wait on the barrow, men in armour, protected by mail-coats, to see which of us two can better endure wounds in the deadly onslaught. It is not your exploit, nor is it any man's measure but mine alone that he should pit strength against the monster, display heroism. I shall win the gold with courage, or else war, fierce deadly evil, will take your lord!' (2516–2537)

Then the renowned champion rose, leaning on his shield, bold beneath his helmet, carried his mail-shirt beneath the rocky cliff, trusted in a single man's might—such is not the way of a coward! Then he who, great in manly virtues, had survived so many a war, crash of battle when troops clashed, saw arches of rock standing in the rampart through which a stream gushed out of the barrow; the surge of that brook was hot with deadly fire; because of the dragon's flame he could not survive for any length of time in the hollow near the hoard without being burned. Then, swollen with rage as he was, the prince of the Weder-Geats let a cry break forth from his breast: the stout-hearted stormed; clear in battle, the voice came roaring in beneath the grey rock. Hatred was aroused as the guardian of the hoard recognised human speech; there was no more time to sue for peace. First the monster's breath came out from the rock, a hot battle-vapour; the earth resounded. The man beneath the barrow, the leader of the Geats, swung his round shield against the terrible visitant. Then the heart of the coiled creature was incited to seek combat. The great war-king had already drawn his sword, an ancient heirloom very sharp of its edges. Each of them, intent on havoc, felt horror at the other. Resolute, the prince of friends stood by his tall shield while the serpent quickly coiled itself together; in his armour he waited. (2538–2568)

Then burning, coiled, it went gliding out, hastened to its fate. The shield protected the famous prince well in life and limb for less time than he anticipated; there on that occasion for the first time he had to manage without fate assigning him triumph in battle. The leader of the Geats swung his hand, struck the patterned horror with the fine heirloom so that the burnished edge gave way on the bone, bit less strongly than the nation's king had need, hard-pressed by troubles. (2569–2580a)

Then as a result of the battle-blow the heart of the barrow's guardian was savage, threw out a deadly fire; the flames of battle sprang wide. The gold-friend of the Geats boasted of no glorious victories; the naked war-sword failed in combat as it should not have done, iron of proven merit. It was no pleasant exploit, for the famous kinsman of Ecgtheow would forsake the face of the earth; against his will he must inhabit a dwelling in some other place, just as every man must relinquish the days loaned him. It was not long before they came together again, those terrible foes. The guardian of the hoard took heart once again—its breast surged with breath; encircled by fire, he who formerly ruled a nation suffered severe straits. (2580b–2595)

In no way did his close companions, sons of princes, take up a stand in a band around him with honour in battle, but they turned to the wood, saved their lives. In one of them a spirit welled with sorrows; nothing can ever set aside friendship in him who means well. (2596–2601)

36. [WIGLAF JOINS THE FIGHT.
BEOWULF IS WOUNDED]

He was called Wiglaf, son of Weohstan, a much-loved shield-fighter, a prince of the Scylfings, kinsman of Ælfhere. He saw his leader of men suffer the heat beneath his war-visor. Then he remembered the property which formerly he granted him, the wealthy dwelling-place of the Wægmundings, each rightful share of common land, such as his father possessed. He could not then restrain himself; hand grasped shield, the yellow limewood, drew an ancient sword that was known among men as an heirloom of Ohthere's son Eanmund. In combat Weohstan had become his slayer when a friendless exile, and carried off to his kinsmen a brightly-burnished helmet, ringed mail, an ancient sword made by ogres. Onela granted him all that—his relative's war-gear, ready battle-trappings; he did not talk of a feud, although he had laid low his brother's child. He kept the adornments, sword and coat of mail, for many a season until his son was able to display heroism like his father before him; then among the Geats he gave him countless war-gear of all kinds when, aged, he passed away from life on his journey hence. This was the first time for the young champion that he had to stand the onslaught of war with his noble leader. His heart's spirit did not melt, nor did the heirloom of his kinsman fail in the fray. The serpent found that out after they had come together. (2602–2630)

Wiglaf spoke, said many a fitting word to his companions—his spirit was mournful: 'I remember the occasion on which we drank mead, when in the beer-hall we promised our lord, who gave us these rings, that we would repay him for the war-equipment, the helmets and hard sword, if any such need as this were to befall him. For that reason he chose us of his own accord from the army for this adventure, thought us worthy of glories—and gave me these treasures—because he reckoned us good spear-fighters, bold helmet-bearers, though for our sake the lord, the people's guardian, thought to perform this deed of courage alone, since he of all men had achieved the greatest glories, audacious deeds. (2631–2646a)

Now the day has come when our leader of men has need of the strength of good warriors. Let us go forward, assist the battle-leader while the heat, the grim terrible fire, lasts. For myself, God knows that I would much prefer that coals of fire should embrace my flesh with my gold-giver. I do not think it proper that we should carry our shields back home unless we can first fell the foe, defend the life of the Weders' prince. I certainly know that his past deeds were not such that he alone among the tried warriors of the Geats should suffer distress, go down in combat; both of us shall together share sword and helmet, coat of mail and battle-clothing.' (2646b–2660)

Then he advanced through the deadly smoke, carried his war-helmet to the aid of his lord, spoke in few words: 'Beloved Beowulf, carry through all well, for long ago in the days of your youth you declared that you would never allow your reputation to decline for as long as you lived. Now, resolute prince, renowned for deeds, you must defend your life with all your might; I will aid you!' (2661–2668)

After these words, the serpent, angry, a dreadful malicious spirit, came on a second time, glowing with surges of fire, to seek out his enemies, the hated men. The fire advanced in waves, burned the shield right up to the boss; coat of mail could afford the young spear-fighter no help; but the young man courageously went behind his kinsman's shield when his own was destroyed by coals of fire. Then the war-king was again mindful of glorious deeds, struck with the war-sword in great strength so that, driven by violence, it stuck in the head. Nægling shattered; Beowulf's sword, old and patterned grey, failed in combat. It was not granted him that edges of iron might help him in the battle; the hand was too strong which, as I heard, over-taxed every blade with its stroke, when he carried into combat a weapon hardened with wounds; it was none the better for him. (2669–2687)

Then a third time, when it had opportunity, the scourge of the nation, the dangerous fire-dragon, was mindful of feuds, rushed upon the brave man, hot and battle-grim, clenched his entire neck between sharp tusks; he became ensanguined with life-blood; gore welled up in waves. (2688–2693)

37. [THE DRAGON'S DEATH]

Then, as I have heard, at the need of the nation's king the warrior by his side displayed courage, skill and daring, as was natural to him. He did not bother about the head, so the hand of the brave man, warrior in armour, was burned as he helped his kinsman by striking the spiteful creature somewhat lower down, so that the sword, shining and plated, sank in, so that thereupon the fire began to abate. Then the king himself, again in control of his senses, drew the deadly knife, keen and battle-sharp, that he wore on his mail; the protector of the Weders cut the serpent open in the middle. They felled the foe—courage had driven out its life—and they had cut it down together, kindred noblemen. That is what a man should be, a thane in time of need! (2694–2709a)

For the prince that was the moment of victory, brought about by his own deeds—work in the world. Then the wound which the earth-dragon had inflicted on him earlier began to burn and swell; straight away he found that the poison within welled up with deadly evil in his breast. Then thinking deeply, the prince went till he sat on a bank by the rampart; he looked at the giant's work—how the enduring earthen hall held within it stone arches fast on pillars. Then with his hands that most excellent thane bathed his friend and leader, the famous prince, bloodstained, sated with battle, and unfastened his helmet. (2709b–2723)

Beowulf spoke—talked despite his hurt, pitiful mortal wound; he knew well enough that he had come to the end of his span of days, joy in the earth; then all the number of his days was passed away, death exceedingly near: 'I would have wanted to present the war-garb to my son, if it had been granted that any heir belonging to my body should succeed me. I held this nation for fifty winters; there was no nation's king among those dwelling around who dared approach me with allies in war, threaten with terror. At home I awaited what was destined, held well what was mine, sought no treacherous quarrels, nor did I unjustly swear many oaths. Sick with mortal wounds, I can rejoice in all this; indeed, when life passes from my body, the Ruler of men has no cause to blame me for the wicked murder of kinsmen. (2724–2743a)

Now you go quickly, beloved Wiglaf, to examine the hoard beneath the grey rock, now that the serpent lies low, sleeping from a grievous wound, bereft of treasure. Make haste now, so that I may appreciate the ancient wealth, gold possessions, may eagerly examine the brilliant precious jewels, so that because of the treasure's richness I may the more easily leave my life and country which I have held for so long.' (2743b–2751)

38. [Beowulf's Death-Speech]

Then, I heard, after this speech Weohstan's son quickly obeyed his wounded leader, injured in combat, carried his ring-mail, the woven battle-shirt, beneath the roof of the barrow. Then as he went along the bank, the brave young thane, exulting in victory, saw many a precious jewel, gold glittering lying on the ground, wonderful things on the wall throughout the lair of the serpent, the ancient pre-dawn flier, pitchers standing, the vessels of men of old, stripped of their ornaments, lacking a polisher. There was many an old and rusty helmet, many a bracelet skilfully twisted. Treasure, gold in the earth, can easily overwhelm any of the human race, hide it who will! (2752–2766)

Also he saw hanging high above the hoard a banner, all gold, the finest of wonderful hand-wrought things, woven with the fingers' skill; from it there shone a light so that he could discern the level ground, survey the works of art. There was not any sign of the serpent there, for the blade's edge had carried him off. Then, I heard, one man plundered the hoard in the mound, the ancient work of giants, loaded his bosom with bowls and dishes at his own choice; he also took the banner, the brightest of signs. The aged lord's sword—its edge was iron—had earlier injured that which for a long time had been guardian of the treasures, carried hot flaming terror for the sake of the hoard, fiercely welling up in the middle of the night, until it died a violent death. (2767–2782)

The messenger made haste, eager to return, urged on by the ornaments; anxiety pricked him, a man bold in spirit, as to whether he would find the Weders' prince, deprived of strength, still alive in the place where earlier he had left him. Then with those treasures he found the famous prince his leader, dripping with blood, at the end of his life. Again he began to splash him with water, until the beginning of speech broke from his breast's hoard. (2783–2792a)

Then the hero spoke, an aged man in distress—examined the gold: 'I give words of thanks to the Lord of all, the King of Glory, eternal Ruler, for these adornments which I gaze on here, that I was able to acquire such things for my people before the moment of death. Now that I have paid for the hoard of treasures with the life allotted me, you must attend to the people's needs henceforth; I can remain here no longer! Bid those famous for war to build a fine mound after the pyre on the headland by the sea; it shall tower high on Whale's Cape as a remembrance to my people, so that seafarers when they drive their tall ships from afar across the mists of the flood will thereafter call it Beowulf's Barrow.' (2792b–2808)

The valiant prince took the golden collar from his neck, presented to the thane, the young spear-fighter, gold-adorned helmet, ring and coat of mail, bade him make good use of them. 'You are the last left of our race, the Wægmundings; fate has swept away all my kinsmen, courageous warriors, as destiny decreed; I must follow them.' (2809–2816)

That was the aged man's final word from the thoughts of his heart before he was to choose the pyre, hot, fierce surges; the soul passed from his breast to seek the glory of the righteous. (2817–2820)

39. [WIGLAF'S CHALLENGE]

Then it went hard with the young man when he saw the most beloved on the ground at the end of his life in a pitiful condition. The slayer, the terrible earth-dragon, likewise lay dead, bereft of life, overwhelmed in destruction. The coiled serpent could no longer rule the ring-hoard, but edges of iron, hard, notched by battle, the hammers' legacy, had carried it off, so that the wide-flier, stilled by wounds, had sunk to the earth near the treasure-house. In no way did it whirl, playing in the air in the middle of the night, display its form, proud of precious possessions; but it fell to the ground as a result of the war-leader's handiwork. Yet, so far as I have heard, there was no man possessed of strength in the land, daring in every action though he were, whom it benefited to rush against the breath of the poisonous scourge, or to disturb the ring-hall with his hands, if he found the guardian awake who dwelt in the barrow. The mass of noble treasures was paid for by Beowulf with death; they had each come to the end of this transitory life. (2821–2845a)

It was not long then before those slow to do battle forsook the wood, ten frail faith-breakers together, who earlier did not dare bring darts into play at their leader's great need; but, ashamed, they carried their shields, battle-dress, to where the aged man lay dead; they gazed at Wiglaf. Exhausted he sat, the foot-soldier, by the shoulders of his lord, sought to rouse him with water; he did not succeed at all. Dearly though he would wish, he could not keep earthly life in the chieftain, nor turn aside anything ordained by the Ruler. The judgement of God would rule the actions of every man, as he still does. (2845b–2859)

Then it was easy to get from the young man a grim answer to him who earlier lost his courage. Wiglaf the son of Weohstan spoke, sick, sad in spirit—looked at the unloved ones: 'Well, he who wants to speak the truth can say that the leader of men who gave you those treasures, the war-equipment with which you stand there—when he, as a prince to his thanes, often presented helmet and mail-coat to those sitting on ale-benches in the hall, of the most splendid kind he could find anywhere, far or near—that, when conflict befell him, he had woefully completely thrown away the war-gear. The people's king had no reason at all to boast about comrades in arms; however, God, the Ruler of victories, granted him that when there was need for courage he avenged himself alone with the edge of the sword. I could do little to protect his life in the battle, but nevertheless I undertook beyond my measure to help my kinsman. When I struck the deadly foe with the sword it was ever the weaker, the fire surged less strongly from its head. Too few defenders thronged about the prince when the evil time came upon him. Now the receiving of treasure and giving of swords, all delight in native land, beloved home, must cease for your race;

once princes afar off should hear of your flight, inglorious action, every man of the tribe will have to wander, stripped of rights in the land. To any warrior death is better than a life of disgrace!' (2860–2891)

40. [THE MESSENGER'S SPEECH]

Then he commanded that the deed of battle be announced to the enclosure high on the cliff-edge, where the warriors, troop of shield-bearers, sat mournful at heart all morning long, expecting one of two things: the last day or the return of the beloved man. He who rode to the headland kept back little of the new tidings, but spoke truthfully in the hearing of them all: (2892–2899)

'Now he who grants the desires of the people of the Weders, the leader of the Geats, is fast on his death-bed, lies on a couch of slaughter, as a result of the serpent's actions. At his side lies the deadly enemy stricken with knife-wounds; with his sword he could not inflict injury of any kind on the monster. Wiglaf son of Weohstan sits by Beowulf, one warrior by the lifeless other, in weariness of heart keeps watch by the heads of friend and of foe. (2900–2910a)

Now the people can expect a period of conflict,[44] once the fall of the king becomes openly known abroad among Franks and Frisians. The bitter grievance against the Hugas was brought about when Hygelac came journeying with a sea-borne army into the land of the Frisians, where the Hetware subdued him in battle, with greater forces brought it about that the mailed fighter had to bow in death; the chieftain fell in the troop, in no way gave adornments to tried warriors. The favour of the Merovingian has been denied us ever since. (2910b–2921)

Nor do I expect the least friendship or loyalty from the Swedish nation; for it was widely known that Ongentheow took the life of Hæthcyn Hrethling near Ravenswood when the men of the Geats in their arrogance first went looking for the War-Scylfings. Straight away Ohthere's wise father, old and terrible, struck a return blow, cut down the sea-king; he rescued the aged woman, his wife of former years, the mother of Onela and Ohthere, stripped of gold; and then he pursued his mortal enemies until with difficulty they escaped into Ravenswood without their lord. (2922–2935)

Then with a great army he besieged those whom the swords had left, exhausted with wounds; frequently throughout the night he promised miseries to the wretched band, said that in the morning he would cut them to pieces with the blade's edge — some on gallows-trees as sport for the birds. Together with daybreak comfort returned to their grieving minds when they heard Hygelac's battle-cry, horn and trumpet, as the great man came following their track with the tried warriors of the people. (2936–2945)

---

[44] **Now the people . . . conflict:** In his speech, the messenger describes the enmity of the Franks (or Merovingians) and the Frisians on one hand, and the bitter hostility of the Swedes after the battle of Ravenswood on the other, repeating the history of Geatish battles in greater detail. It is part of his ceremonial task to give warning about the future. [Editors' note.]

41. [THE MESSENGER CONCLUDES.
THE GEATS VISIT THE SCENE OF BATTLE]

The bloody trail of Swedes and Geats, the deadly onslaught of men, was widely visible—how those peoples had awakened the feud between them. Then old, mourning much, the great man went with his kinsmen to seek his stronghold; the warrior Ongentheow turned aside to higher ground. He had heard of Hygelac's warfare, the proud man's skill in battle; he did not trust in resistance, that he could fight off the seamen, defend hoard, women and children from the war-voyagers; thence the old man drew back behind an earthen rampart. (2946–2957a)

Then pursuit was given to the people of the Swedes, Hygelac's banners over-ran the place of refuge once the Hrethlings pressed forward to the enclosure. There the white-haired Ongentheow was brought to bay by the edges of swords, so that the nation's king had to consent to the sole decree of Eofor. Wulf Wonreding had struck him angrily with his weapon so that as a result of the blow, blood spurted forth from the veins beneath his hair. However, he was not afraid, the aged Scylfing, but once he turned towards him, the nation's king swiftly repaid the deadly blow with a worse exchange. Wonred's brave son could not give the old fellow a return blow, for he had first sheared through the helmet on his head, so that he had to sink down, stained with blood—fell to the ground. He was not yet doomed, for he recovered, though the wound hurt him. As his brother lay there, the stern thane of Hygelac let his broad blade, an ancient sword made by ogres, break the gigantic helmet behind the shield-wall; then the king sank down, the people's guardian was mortally stricken. (2957b–2981)

When it was open to them that they might control the place of slaughter, there were many who bandaged his kinsman, speedily lifted him up. Meanwhile, one warrior plundered the other, took from Ongentheow iron coat of mail, hard hilted sword, and his helmet as well; he carried the grizzled man's equipment to Hygelac. He accepted the trappings and courteously promised him rewards among the people, and fulfilled it thus; when he came home the leader of the Geats, Hrethel's offspring, repaid Eofor and Wulf for that battle-onslaught with copious treasures; he bestowed on each of them a hundred thousands'-worth of land and linked rings— no man on earth need reproach him for those rewards—after they had achieved fame by fighting; and then he gave Eofor his only daughter, an ornament to the home, as a pledge of good faith. (2982–2998)

That is the feud and the enmity, deadly hatred of men, for which I expect the people of the Swedes will come looking for us, once they hear that our lord has lost his life—he who earlier held hoard and kingdom against those who hated us, after the fall of heroes furthered the good of the people, the bold Scyldings, and displayed still more heroism. (2999–3007a)

Now it is best to make haste that we may look there upon the nation's king and bring him, who gave us rings, on his way to the pyre. Not just a single share shall melt away with the brave man, for there is a hoard of treasures, countless gold, grimly purchased; and now in the end he has bought these rings with his own life. These the fire shall devour, flame enfold—no warrior to wear a jewel in remembrance, no bright girl to have the adornment of rings about her neck; but mournful at heart, stripped of gold, they will have to tread an alien land, not once but often, now that the leader of armies has laid aside laughter, merriment and joyful mirth. Wherefore many a spear, chill in the morning, shall be grasped with the fists, lifted in the hand — in no way shall the sound of the harp awaken the fighting-men, but the dark raven, eager for the doomed, shall speak of much, tell the eagle how he fared at the meal when with the wolf he plundered the slain.' (3007b–3027)

Thus the bold man was the teller of grievous news; he did not much lie in respect of facts or words. The whole company rose up; unhappy, they went below Eagles' Crag to gaze on the wondrous sight with welling tears. Then they found the lifeless man on the sand, keeping to his bed of rest, he who had given them rings in former times; the final day had come to pass for the great man then, when the war-king, the prince of the Weders, perished by a wondrous death. (3028–3037)

First they saw there a very remarkable creature, the loathsome serpent lying on the open ground there opposite; the fiery dragon, terrible patterned horror, was scorched with live coals. It measured fifty feet long as it lay; at one time it had delight in the air by night, came down again to seek out its den; then it was fixed by death, had made its last use of earthen caverns. (3038–3046)

Beside it stood bowls and pitchers, dishes and precious swords lying rusty, eaten through, as if they had rested a thousand winters there in the bosom of the earth. Moreover, that exceedingly great heritage, the gold from men of years gone by, was bound by an incantation, so that no man could touch the ring-hall unless God himself, the true King of victories — he is the protection of men — should grant to him whom he wished, whatever man seemed fit to him, power to open the hoard. (3047–3057)

42. [The Funeral Preparations]

It was evident then that the venture had not benefited the creature that wrongfully kept hidden within, in misery beneath the rampart. Earlier the guardian had slain a man like few others; the feud was then cruelly avenged. It is a mystery where a warrior renowned for courage may meet the end of his destined life, when a man may no longer dwell in the mead-hall with his kinsmen. So it was with Beowulf when he sought out the barrow's guardian, a treacherous contest; he himself did not know by what means his departure from the world should be brought about. The famous princes who put it there had laid a curse, that until doomsday the man who should pillage the place would be guilty of sin, confined in pagan shrines, fast in hell-bonds, punished with evils. He had never before examined more eagerly the owner's legacy, abundant gold. (3058–3075)

Wiglaf spoke, the son of Weohstan: 'Often many a warrior has to endure distress owing to the will of one man, as has befallen us. By no counsel could we persuade the beloved prince, guardian of the kingdom, not to approach the keeper of the gold, but let it lie where it had long been, to live in its dwelling until the world's end; he kept to his great destiny. (3076–3084a)

The hoard, grimly acquired, has been examined. The fate that impelled the nation's king towards it was too great! I have been in there and gazed around at all the precious trappings of the building, once the way was open to me—the journey within beneath the earthen rampart not allowed in any friendly fashion. In haste, I seized in my hands a huge great load of hoarded treasures, and carried it out here to my king. He was still alive then, alert and conscious. The aged man spoke many things in his distress, and commanded me to address you, asked that in remembrance of your friend's deeds you should construct at the site of the pyre a high barrow, huge and glorious, because as long as he could still rejoice in a prosperous stronghold he was the worthiest fighter among men throughout the wide world. (3084b–3100)

Let us now make haste to seek out and see for a second time the heap of precious jewels, the wonder beneath the rampart. I will direct you so that you may examine close up rings and thick gold in plenty. Let the bier be ready, rapidly prepared, when we come out, and then let us carry our lord, the beloved man to where he must long abide in the keeping of the Ruler.' (3101–3109)

The son of Weohstan, a hero brave in battle, then bade them command many a hero, those who possessed buildings, that they carry wood for the pyre from afar to where he who possessed the nation, the great man, lay: 'Now live coals must devour the commander of fighters—the flame grow dark—him who often endured the iron shower when, driven from strings, the storm of arrows passed over the shield-wall, when shaft, eager with feathered flights, did its duty, urged on the barb.' (3110–3119)

Well, Weohstan's prudent son called forth together seven men from the king's bodyguard of thanes, the noblest, and as one of eight battle-warriors went in beneath the evil roof; the one who walked in front carried a flaming torch in his hand. There was no lottery then to decide who should pillage that hoard, once the men saw that any part of it remained unguarded in the hall, lay wasting; little did anyone grieve that they should hastily carry the precious jewels outside. Also they pushed the dragon, the serpent, over the cliff, let the wave take it, the flood embrace the guardian of the ornaments. Then twisted gold was loaded on a wagon, a countless number of things, and the prince, the grizzled battle-warrior, carried to Whale's Cape. (3120–3136)

43. [BEOWULF'S FUNERAL]

Then the people of the Geats prepared a pyre for him on the earth, unstinted, hung about with helmets, battle-shields and bright coats of mail, as his wish was. In the midst the lamenting heroes then laid down the famous prince, the beloved lord. Then on the mount the fighting-men began to kindle the greatest of funeral-fires; woodsmoke climbed up, black over the blaze, roaring flame mingled with weeping—the swirling wind fell still—until it had broken the bone frame, hot at the heart. With cheerless spirits they bewailed their souls' sorrow, the death of their leader. Likewise, a Geatish woman, sorrowful, her hair bound up, sang a mournful lay, chanted clamorously again and again that she sorely feared days of lamentation for herself, a multitude of slaughters, the terror of an army, humiliation and captivity. Heaven swallowed up the smoke. (3137–3155)

Then the people of the Weders constructed on the promontory a mound which was high and broad, to be seen far and near by those voyaging across the waves, and in ten days had built up a monument to the man renowned in battle; they surrounded the remains of the fire with a rampart, the finest that the most skilful men could devise. In the barrow they placed rings and brooches, all such trappings as men disposed to strife had earlier taken from the hoard; they let the earth keep the warriors' treasure, gold in the dust, where it still remains now, as useless to men as it was before. (3156–3168)

Then those brave in battle, the children of princes, twelve in all, rode round the mound, would lament their grief, bewail their king, recite a lay and speak about the man. They praised his heroism and acclaimed the nobility of his courageous deeds. It is fitting that a man should thus honour his friend and leader with words, love him in spirit, when he must needs be led forth from the flesh. Thus the people of the Geats, the companions of his hearth, mourned the fall of their lord; they said that among the world's kings he was the gentlest of men and the most courteous, the most kindly to his people and the most eager for renown. (3169–3182)

❧ THE SONG OF ROLAND
LATE ELEVENTH CENTURY

shawn-SAWNG-
duh-ziest

When it was performed before a French audience at the end of the eleventh century, *The Song of Roland (Le Chanson de Roland)* must have constituted entertainment of the highest order. This heroic epic, a ***chanson de geste*** or "tale of deeds," depicted the tragic defeat of Roland, a courageous leader of Charlemagne's army, in Spain three centuries earlier at the hands of the Saracens. To the contemporary audience it signified the leadership of the Franks in the First Crusade, begun in 1096.[1] It established the image of the legendary Roland as the perfect Christian knight within the social and moral framework of the new era. Thus, Frankish patriotism was served, even after the Crusades themselves came under scrutiny and the victories of the early Crusaders were reversed. Eventually, however, the spirit of *The Song of Roland* came to an end. The European courtly literature that replaced it expressed a totally different view of culture and society.

www For quizzes on *The Song of Roland,* see *World Literature Online* at bedfordstmartins .com/worldlit.

---

[1] **First Crusade, begun in 1096:** Pope Urban preached the First Crusade in 1095. Translator Frederick Goldin points out that *The Song of Roland* contributed to the new spirit of the Crusades: Chroniclers reported that Crusaders riding off to battle sang verses from the epic.

The Carolingian Empire under Charlemagne, 768–814
The conquests of Charlemagne temporarily united almost all of Western Europe.
Although this empire was divided into three parts by the Treaty of Verdun in 843, it was
substantially reunited as the Holy Roman Empire in the twelfth century.

The Story of Roland. Only scraps of information remain about the historical Roland. In Einhard's *Life of Charlemagne*,[2] written about 830, an account of the Frankish king's unsuccessful wars in Spain relates that the Basques of the northern Pyrenees ambushed the rear guard of Charlemagne's army, "forced them down into the valley beneath, joined battle with them and killed them to the last man." In this battle some members of the Frankish nobility died, including "Roland, Lord of the Breton Marches." The date of the battle was August 15, 778.

---

[2] *Life of Charlemagne:* Einhard served Charlemagne at his court in Aix-la-Chapelle from 791 until the king's death in 814. His is the only contemporary biography of the Frankish king.

toor-PANG

gah-nuh-LAWNG

We shall never know
what it was that
turned the obscure
disaster which befell
the rear guard of
Charlemagne's army
on 15 August 778,
when Roland count
of Brittany was
killed, into one of the
most memorable
incidents in Christian
epic. No doubt, like
many other military
disasters, it was
relieved by some
signal act of heroism
of which "history"
has left no record.
But the story lived.

– R. W. SOUTHERN,
scholar, 1953

The story of Roland resurfaces more than three centuries later as his battle against the Saracens in the poetic epic *The Song of Roland*. In this carefully conceived story, Roland is accompanied by his friends, Oliver, Archbishop Turpin, and others while he is hounded and betrayed by his enemy, his uncle Ganelon. Of these men, **Turpin** was a historical figure, but reportedly nowhere near the battle in question; the others are known only through the poem itself, though they probably were part of an older cycle of stories already familiar to French audiences. What was certainly new, however, was the poem's treatment of Muslims: It names the Saracens as the foe when in fact they were allies who had enlisted Charlemagne's support in suppressing a common enemy.[3]

The plot of *The Song of Roland* is simple. Because of the connivance of **Ganelon** with the enemy, the rear guard of Charlemagne's army under the leadership of the young count Roland is separated from the main force and attacked by the Saracens. Roland, too proud to call for help, refuses to sound the battle horn, or olifant, until the situation is hopeless and his forces are about to be massacred. Finally, Charlemagne, hearing the belated note of the horn, counterattacks, but too late to save his army. He drives the foe from the field, buries Roland and his company of knights, then captures, arraigns, and executes the traitors within his own ranks. The poet, apparently uninterested in creating suspense, repeatedly reminds the listener of the plot of the story as the action unfolds.

A Christian Epic.   *The Song of Roland*, a patriotic poem and a paean to the spirit of the Crusades, elevates with its stately, repetitious stanzas the figure of Roland to the status of exemplary Christian knight, emphasizing his courage, his steadfastness, his faith in God, and his role as a defender of both the crown and the Catholic Church. Roland is also firmly placed in a larger context: He is the Christian warrior just as Charlemagne is the Christian king.[4] It is for this reason that the epic does not end with the death of Roland; the rest of the poem, which details the rout of the Saracens and the capture, torture, and execution of Ganelon and his men, confirms the restoration of the authority of both Charlemagne and militant Christianity. At the epic's end, the aged Charlemagne plucks his beard and cries out, "How weary is my life!" — but then rises out of bed to rescue another Christian king held under siege by the Saracens.

In the moral and ethical framework of the knightly epic, every character stands for a specific virtue and may also have specific faults. Roland is strong but often rash; his uninstructed courage does not contain an

---

[3] **suppressing a common enemy:** Charlemagne had formed an alliance with the Saracens against a rebel leader, al-Arabi, in order to increase Frankish influence in southern Europe. Al-Arabi's resistance was more effective than had been anticipated, and Charlemagne was leaving Spain without a clear-cut victory when the rear guard of his troops was attacked by Basques on the Spanish frontier.

[4] **He is the . . . Christian king:** The reciprocal ties joining Roland and Charlemagne were part of the hierarchal structure of loyalties common throughout feudal society in the European Middle Ages. All his vassal knights, including Roland, are bound to Charlemagne, while he is bound to protect them.

Scenes from *The Song of Roland,* twelfth century
A relief frieze at St. Pierre Cathedral, in Angouleme, France, depicts scenes from the great feudal epic, The Song of Roland. *(Giraudon / Art Resource, NY)*

equal measure of wisdom.[5] Oliver, his friend, lacking Roland's strength, is wise: He angrily upbraids Roland for not calling for help sooner than he does. Ganelon, meanwhile, is the archvillain led by jealousy, false pride, and a desire for revenge to betray not only Roland but the entire Frankish kingdom.

Art or Propaganda?   *The Song of Roland* is organized in LAISSES, or stanzas, composed of a varied number of ten-syllable lines whose concluding line is repeated as a refrain at the end of subsequent stanzas. The action moves briskly, even with this device of incremental repetition, with the poem's language concentrated in a manner unique among major works of Western literature. There is a pictorial quality to the descriptions of its leading characters, as if they had just stepped down from stained-glass windows or emerged from a medieval illuminated manuscript. The description of Charlemagne, though dignified, economical, and conventional, includes certain stylistic idiosyncrasies as well, such as his habit of stroking or pulling his beard. And there is particular artistry in the economical rendering of emotional states, such as the description of Ganelon's anger at Roland in council or the encounter between Roland and Oliver over the sounding of the battle horn. The gestures of the characters are often larger than life, most tellingly in the case of Roland, who

LES

---

[5] **his uninstructed courage . . . wisdom:** The poet is playing off conventional stereotypes, or "topics," that frequently appear in medieval literature. Roland exemplifies the virtue of *fortitudo* (strength), while his friend Oliver is known for his *sapientia* (wisdom, or in this case, common sense).

literally blows his brains out while sounding the olifant. The work's realism is pointed, with its descriptions of the killing, maiming, and gore on the battlefield perhaps unparalleled in epic poetry. This realism extends to its portrayal of emotion, as in the dignified scene of the burial of Roland and his peers by the grieving king. Perhaps the most famous rhetorical feature of the poem is its method of opposing two qualities within a single line, as when the poet states, "Pagans are wrong and Christians are right" (stanza 79) or "Roland is good, and Oliver is wise" (stanza 87).

The extreme partisanship of the poem disturbs many readers, especially in light of the more sophisticated treatments of the Christian invaders by Muslim writers during the Crusades. The medieval Catholic institution of *ecclesia militans,* the church militant, told its warrior knights that dying in battle against the infidel (in this case, the Muslims) ensured their salvation. It is hard to find another instance before modern times in which political fervor and religious fanaticism produced a more brutal, less forgiving type of warrior than the Christian Crusader of this period. Thus, the composition of *The Song of Roland* is a powerful work in which subjective political emotion completely overwhelms objective "distance."

ih-KLEE-zhee-uh
MIH-lih-tanz

The Love of War.   The only love expressed in *The Song of Roland* seems to be that of the warrior for warfare and for his fellow warriors. The love that Roland and his company express for one another completely overshadows the forgettable presence in the work of Roland's fiancé, who dies almost unnoticed by collapsing in Charlemagne's arms at the news of Roland's death. Even the Muslim warriors receive their due: Though crueler than the Christian knights and owing their allegiance to the devil, they are comparable as warriors, and the poem's sympathetic descriptions of battle tend to valorize their actions. This love of war in *The Song of Roland* is nowhere else so evident in Western literature except *The Iliad,* a work with which *Roland* invites comparison.

■ CONNECTIONS

Homer, *The Iliad* (Book 1). Homer's *Iliad* is admired for the realism of its battle scenes; it has also been intensely criticized for its glorification of war. Like *The Iliad, The Song of Roland* contains particularly graphic and gruesome battlefield scenes. The love of war is apparent in both epics. How do you think their audiences received these works? What might have influenced their response?

***Beowulf,* p. 489.** In the second episode of this epic poem, the dragon fight, Beowulf holds the fate of his entire society in his hands as he enters what he correctly believes will be his last battle. Compare and contrast the attitudes of Beowulf and Roland as they go into battle, each anticipating death. Both men may be said to be "eager for fame," though in a different sense. How do they differ and how does this difference weigh on their spirits?

***In the World:* Muslim and Christian at War, p. 578.** The glorification of the Franks in *The Song of Roland* can be contrasted with the description of the Frankish Crusaders in *The Anonymous History of the First Crusade,* a report from the Muslim writer Ibn al-Athir, and with later remarks about the Franks in *The Book of Reflections* by

Usamah Ibn Munqidh. How did the Franks behave in the Crusades? Did they behave differently from their enemies? Why or why not?

■ SUGGESTED READINGS

Translations with Commentary
Brault, Gerard J. *The Song of Roland: An Analytical Edition.* 2 vols. 1978.
Goldin, Frederick, trans. *The Song of Roland.* 1978.
Owen, D. D. R. *The Song of Roland: The Oxford Text.* 1972.

History and Criticism
Cook, Robert Francis. *The Sense of the Song of Roland.* 1987.
Jones, George Fenwick. *The Ethos of the Song of Roland.* 1963.
Le Gentil, Pierre. *The Song of Roland.* Trans. Frances F. Beer. 1969.
Lejeune, Rita and Jacques Stiennon. *The Legend of Roland in the Middle Ages.* Trans. Christine Trollope. 1971.
Owen, D. D. R. *The Legend of Roland: A Pageant of the Middle Ages.* 1973.
Vance, Eugene. *Reading the Song of Roland.* 1970.

Roland and Medieval Culture
Auerbach, Erich. *Mimesis.* 1953. 83–107.
Southern, R. W. *The Making of the Middle Ages.* 1953. 241–246.

Related Literature
Thorpe, Lewis, trans. *Einhard and Notker the Stammerer: Two Lives of Charlemagne.* 1969.

■ PRONUNCIATION

Aix (la Chapelle): EKS (lah-shah-PEL)
Apollin: ah-poh-LANG
Aude: ODE
Blancandrin: blawng-kawng-DRANG
chanson de geste: shawn-SAWNG duh-ZHEST
Chanson de Roland: shawn-SAWNG duh-roh-LAWNG
Durendal: doo-rawn-DAHL
ecclesia militans: ih-KLEE-zhee-uh MIH-lih-tanz, eh-KLAY-zee-uh MIH-lih-tahnz
Ganelon: gah-nuh-LAWNG
laisse: LES
Mahum: mah-OOM
Marsilion: mar-see-lee-AWNG
Munjoie: moon-ZHWAH
Naimon: neh-MAWNG
Rencesvals: rawngs-VAL
Turpin: toor-PANG

[It appears to me that] . . . the first elevated style of the European Middle Ages arose at the moment when the single event [was] filled with life. [. . .] Confronting the reality of life, this style is neither able nor willing to deal with its breadths or depths. [. . .] It simplifies the events of the past by stylizing and idealizing them. The feeling it seeks to arouse in its auditor is admiration and amazement for a distant world [. . .], whose instincts and ideals [. . .] evolve in such uncompromising purity and freedom, in comparison with the friction and resistance of real life, as his practical existence could not possibly attain.

– ERICH AUERBACH, scholar, on *The Song of Roland,* 1953

❧ The Song of Roland

Translated and annotated by Frederick Goldin

1

Charles the King, our emperor, the Great,
has been in Spain for seven full years,
has conquered the high land down to the sea.
There is no castle that stands against him now,
no wall, no citadel left to break down—
except Saragossa, high on a mountain.
King Marsilion holds it, who does not love God,
who serves Mahumet and prays to Apollin.
He cannot save himself: his ruin will find him there. AOI.[1]

2

10 King Marsilion was in Saragossa.
He has gone forth into a grove, beneath its shade,
and he lies down on a block of blue marble,
twenty thousand men, and more, all around him.
He calls aloud to his dukes and his counts:

The Song of Roland. The earliest known manuscript of the poem is the so-called Oxford version, written in the Anglo-Norman dialect of French between 1125 and 1150 and derived from an earlier text probably composed between 1095 and 1100. A legendary poetic tradition concerning Roland and the battle of Rencesvals must have existed for several centuries before the written composition of the poem. The finished work describes a period in history that the contemporary audience already associated with antiquity. As translator Frederick Goldin points out, "By the time of the Oxford version it was the remote and therefore the glorious and exemplary past, a golden age."

The original form appears to have been oral-formulaic poetry, broadly similar to other epics in the European tradition. The themes, episodes, and motifs of the poem are expressed in repeated poetic formulae. Significant concluding lines sometimes are repeated in as many as five succeeding stanzas, producing a sense of increasing dramatic intensity.

Undoubtedly *The Song of Roland* was popular among the Franks who fought in the Crusades; they must have memorized long passages in order to recite them to companions along the way. Thus it appears to have enjoyed a prolonged oral history *after* the time of its written composition. Even today, the poem recited in its original language has a nearly hypnotic effect on its audience.

The present version is edited to produce a narrative of the fatal battle of Roland with the Saracens; it ends with Roland's death and burial, leaving out the story of Charlemagne's revenge against the foe and the trial and execution of Ganelon and the other traitors within the Christian ranks. The footnotes are derived from the edition of Frederick Goldin.

---

[1] AOI: These three mysterious letters appear at certain moments throughout the text, 180 times in all. No one has ever adequately explained them, but every reader feels their effect.

"Listen, my lords, to the troubles we have.
The Emperor Charles of the sweet land of France
has come into this country to destroy us.
I have no army able to give him battle,
I do not have the force to break his force.
20   Now act like my wise men: give me counsel,
save me, save me from death, save me from shame!"
No pagan there has one word to say to him
except Blancandrin, of the castle of Valfunde.

3

One of the wisest pagans was Blancandrin,
brave and loyal, a great mounted warrior,
a useful man, the man to aid his lord;
said to the King: "Do not give way to panic.
Do this: send Charles, that wild, terrible man,
tokens of loyal service and great friendship:
30   you will give him bears and lions and dogs,
seven hundred camels, a thousand molted hawks,
four hundred mules weighed down with gold and silver,
and fifty carts, to cart it all away:
he'll have good wages for his men who fight for pay.
Say he's made war long enough in this land:
let him go home, to France, to Aix,[2] at last—
come Michaelmas[3] you will follow him there,
say you will take their faith, become a Christian,
and be his man with honor, with all you have.
40   If he wants hostages, why, you'll send them,
ten, or twenty, to give him security.
Let us send him the sons our wives have borne.
I'll send my son with all the others named to die.
It is better that they should lose their heads
than that we, Lord, should lose our dignity
and our honors—and be turned into beggars!" AOI.

4

Said Blancandrin: "By this right hand of mine
and by this beard that flutters on my chest,
you will soon see the French army disband,

---

[2] **Aix:** Aachen (Aix-la-Chapelle), capital of Charlemagne's empire.
[3] **Michaelmas:** Either September 29 or October 16.

50 the Franks will go to their own land, to France.
When each of them is in his dearest home,
King Charles will be in Aix, in his chapel.
At Michaelmas he will hold a great feast—
that day will come, and then our time runs out,
he'll hear no news, he'll get no word from us.
This King is wild, the heart in him is cruel:
he'll take the heads of the hostages we gave.
It is better, Lord, that they lose their heads
than that we lose our bright, our beautiful Spain—
60 and nothing more for us but misery and pain!"
The pagans say: "It may be as he says."

5

King Marsilion brought his counsel to end,
then he summoned Clarin of Balaguét,
Estramarin and Eudropin, his peer,
and Priamun, Guarlan, that bearded one,
and Machiner and his uncle Maheu,
and Joüner, Malbien from over-sea,
and Blancandrin, to tell what was proposed.
From the worst of criminals he called these ten.
70 "Barons, my lords, you're to go to Charlemagne;
he's at the siege of Cordres, the citadel.
Olive branches are to be in your hands—
that signifies peace and humility.
If you've the skill to get me an agreement,
I will give you a mass of gold and silver
and lands and fiefs, as much as you could want."
Say the pagans: "We'll benefit from this!" AOI.

8

The Emperor is secure and jubilant:
he has taken Cordres, broken the walls,
knocked down the towers with his catapults.
80 And what tremendous spoils his knights have won—
gold and silver, precious arms, equipment.
In the city not one pagan remained
who is not killed or turned into a Christian.
The Emperor is in an ample grove,
Roland and Oliver are with him there,
Samson the Duke and Ansëis the fierce,

Geoffrey d'Anjou, the King's own standard-bearer;
and Gerin and Gerer, these two together always,
90 and the others, the simple knights, in force:
fifteen thousand from the sweet land of France.
The warriors sit on bright brocaded silk;
they are playing at tables to pass the time,
the old and wisest men sitting at chess,
the young light-footed men fencing with swords.
Beneath a pine, beside a wild sweet-briar,
there was a throne, every inch of pure gold.
There sits the King, who rules over sweet France.
His beard is white, his head flowering white.
100 That lordly body! the proud fierce look of him! —
if someone should come here asking for him,
there'd be no need to point out the King of France.
The messengers dismounted, and on their feet
they greeted him in all love and good faith.

9

Blancandrin spoke, he was the first to speak,
said to the King: "Greetings, and God save you,
that glorious God whom we all must adore.
Here is the word of the great king Marsilion:
he has looked into this law of salvation,
110 wants to give you a great part of his wealth,
bears and lions and hunting dogs on chains,
seven hundred camels, a thousand molted hawks,
four hundred mules packed tight with gold and silver,
and fifty carts, to cart it all away;
and there will be so many fine gold bezants,
you'll have good wages for the men in your pay.
You have stayed long — long enough! — in this land,
it is time to go home, to France, to Aix.
My master swears he will follow you there."
120 The Emperor holds out his hands toward God,
bows down his head, begins to meditate. AOI.

10

The Emperor held his head bowed down;
never was he too hasty with his words:
his custom is to speak in his good time.
When his head rises, how fierce the look of him;
he said to them: "You have spoken quite well.

King Marsilion is my great enemy.
Now all these words that you have spoken here—
how far can I trust them? How can I be sure?"
130 The Saracen: "He wants to give you hostages.
How many will you want? ten? fifteen? twenty?
I'll put my son with the others named to die.
You will get some, I think, still better born.
When you are at home in your high royal palace,
at the great feast of Saint Michael-in-Peril,[4]
the lord who nurtures me will follow you,
and in those baths—the baths God made for you—
my lord will come and want to be made Christian."
King Charles replies: "He may yet save his soul." AOI.

12

140 The Emperor goes forth beneath a pine,
calls for his barons to complete his council:
Ogier the Duke, and Archbishop Turpin,
Richard the Old, and his nephew Henri;
from Gascony, the brave Count Acelin,
Thibaut of Reims, and his cousin Milun;
and Gerer and Gerin, they were both there,
and there was Count Roland, he came with them,
and Oliver, the valiant and well-born;
a thousand Franks of France, and more, were there.
150 Ganelon came, who committed the treason.
Now here begins the council that went wrong. AOI.

14

The Emperor has told them what was proposed.
Roland the Count will never assent to that,
gets to his feet, comes forth to speak against it;
says to the King: "Trust Marsilion—and suffer!
We came to Spain seven long years ago,
I won Noples for you, I won Commibles,
I took Valterne and all the land of Pine,
and Balaguer and Tudela and Seville.

---

[4] **Saint Michael-in-Peril:** The epithet "in the peril of the sea" was applied to the famous sanctuary of Saint Michael on the Normandy coast because it could be reached only on foot at low tide, and pilgrims were endangered by the incoming tide; eventually the phrase was applied to the saint himself.

160 And then this king, Marsilion, played the traitor:
he sent you men, fifteen of his pagans —
and sure enough, each held an olive branch;
and they recited just these same words to you.
You took counsel with all your men of France;
they counseled you to a bit of madness:
you sent two Counts across to the Pagans,
one was Basan, the other was Basile.
On the hills below Haltille, he took their heads.
They were your men. Fight the war you came to fight!
170 Lead the army you summoned on to Saragossa!
Lay siege to it all the rest of your life!
Avenge the men that this criminal murdered!" AOI.

15

The Emperor held his head bowed down with this,
and stroked his beard, and smoothed his mustache down,
and speaks no word, good or bad, to his nephew.
The French keep still, all except Ganelon:
he gets to his feet and comes before King Charles,
how fierce he is as he begins his speech;
said to the King: "Believe a fool — me or
180 another — and suffer! Protect your interest!
When Marsilion the King sends you his word
that he will join his hands[5] and be your man,
and hold all Spain as a gift from your hands
and then receive the faith that we uphold —
whoever urges that we refuse this peace,
that man does not care, Lord, what death we die.
That wild man's counsel must not win the day here —
let us leave fools, let us hold with wise men!" AOI.

20

"My noble knights," said the Emperor Charles,
190 "choose me one man:[6] a baron from my march,
to bring my message to King Marsilion."

---

[5] **he will join his hands:** Part of the gesture of homage; the lord enclosed the joined hands of his vassal with his own hands.

[6] **one man:** Charlemagne wants them to choose a baron from an outlying region and not one of the Twelve Peers, the circle of his dearest men.

And Roland said: "Ganelon, my stepfather."
The French respond: "Why, that's the very man!
pass this man by and you won't send a wiser."
And hearing this Count Ganelon began to choke,
pulls from his neck the great furs of marten
and stands there now, in his silken tunic,
eyes full of lights, the look on him of fury,
he has the body, the great chest of a lord;
200 stood there so fair, all his peers gazed on him;
said to Roland: "Madman, what makes you rave?
Every man knows I am your stepfather,
yet you named me to go to Marsilion.
Now if God grants that I come back from there,
you will have trouble: I'll start a feud with you,
it will go on till the end of your life."
Roland replies: "What wild words—all that blustering!
Every man knows that threats don't worry me.
But we need a wise man to bring the message:
210 if the King wills, I'll gladly go in your place."

21

Ganelon answers: "You will not go for me. AOI.
You're not my man, and I am not your lord.
Charles commands me to perform this service:
I'll go to Marsilion in Saragossa.
And I tell you, I'll play a few wild tricks
before I cool the anger in me now."
When he heard that, Roland began to laugh. AOI.

26

Said Ganelon: "Lord, give me leave to go,
since go I must, there's no reason to linger."
220 And the King said: "In Jesus' name and mine,"
absolved him and blessed him with his right hand.
Then he gave him the letter and the staff.

28

Ganelon rides to a tall olive tree,
there he has joined the pagan messengers.
And here is Blancandrin, who slows down for him:
with what great art they speak to one another.
Said Blancandrin: "An amazing man, Charles!

conquered Apulia, conquered all of Calabria,
crossed the salt sea on his way into England,
230   won its tribute, got Peter's pence[7] for Rome:
what does he want from us here in our march?"
Ganelon answers: "That is the heart in him.
There'll never be a man the like of him." AOI.

29

Said Blancandrin: "The Franks are a great people.
Now what great harm all those dukes and counts do
to their own lord when they give him such counsel:
they torment him, they'll destroy him, and others."
Ganelon answers: "Well, now, I know no such man
except Roland, who'll suffer for it yet.
240   One day the Emperor was sitting in the shade:
his nephew came, still wearing his hauberk,
he had gone plundering near Carcassonne;
and in his hand he held a bright red apple:
'Dear Lord, here, take,' said Roland to his uncle;
'I offer you the crowns of all earth's kings.'
Yes, Lord, that pride of his will destroy him,
for every day he goes riding at death.
And *should* someone kill him we would have peace." AOI.

30

Said Blancandrin: "A wild man, this Roland!
250   wants to make every nation beg for his mercy
and claims a right to every land on earth!
But what men support him, if that is his aim?"
Ganelon answers: "Why, Lord, the men of France.
They love him so, they will never fail him.
He gives them gifts, masses of gold and silver,
mules, battle horses, brocaded silks, supplies.
And it is all as the Emperor desires:
he'll win the lands from here to the Orient." AOI.

31

Ganelon and Blancandrin rode on until
260   each pledged his faith to the other and swore

---

[7] **Peter's pence:** A tribute of one penny per house "for the use of Saint Peter," that is, for the pope in Rome.

they'd find a way to have Count Roland killed.
They rode along the paths and ways until,
in Saragossa, they dismount beneath a yew.
There was a throne in the shade of a pine,
covered with silk from Alexandria.
There sat the king who held the land of Spain,
and around him twenty thousand Saracens.
There is no man who speaks or breathes a word,
poised for the news that all would like to hear.
270   Now here they are: Ganelon and Blancandrin.

32

Blancandrin came before Marsilion,
his hand around the fist of Ganelon,
said to the King: "May Mahumet save you,
and Apollin, whose sacred laws we keep!
We delivered your message to Charlemagne:
when we finished, he raised up both his hands
and praised his god. He made no other answer.
Here he sends you one of his noble barons,
a man of France, and very powerful.
280   You'll learn from him whether or not you'll have peace."
"Let him speak, we shall hear him," Marsilion answers. AOI.

33

But Ganelon had it all well thought out.
With what great art he commences his speech,
a man who knows his way about these things;
said to the King "May the Lord God save you,
that glorious God, whom we must all adore.
Here is the word of Charlemagne the King:
you are to take the holy Christian faith;
he will give you one half of Spain in fief.
290   If you refuse, if you reject this peace,
you will be taken by force, put into chains,
and then led forth to the King's seat at Aix;
you will be tried; you will be put to death:
you will die there, in shame, vilely, degraded."
King Marsilion, hearing this, was much shaken.
In his hand was a spear, with golden feathers.
He would have struck, had they not held him back. AOI.

38

King Marsilion went forth into the orchard,
he takes with him the greatest of his men;
300 Blancandrin came, that gray-haired counselor,
and Jurfaleu, Marsilion's son and heir,
the Algalife, uncle and faithful friend.
Said Blancandrin: "Lord, call the Frenchman back.
He swore to me to keep faith with our cause."
And the King said: "Go, bring him back here, then."
He took Ganelon's right hand by the fingers,
leads him into the orchard before the King.
And there they plotted that criminal treason. AOI.

43

"Dear Lord Ganelon," said Marsilion the King,
310 "I have my army, you won't find one more handsome:
I can muster four hundred thousand knights!
With this host, now, can I fight Charles and the French?"
Ganelon answers: "No, no, don't try that now,
you'd take a loss: thousands of your pagans!
Forget such foolishness, listen to wisdom:
send the Emperor so many gifts
there'll be no Frenchman there who does not marvel.
For twenty hostages — those you'll be sending —
he will go home: home again to sweet France!
320 And he will leave his rear-guard behind him.
There will be Roland, I do believe, his nephew,
and Oliver, brave man, born to the court.
These Counts are dead, if anyone trusts me.
Then Charles will see that great pride of his go down,
he'll have no heart to make war on you again." AOI.

44

"Dear Lord Ganelon," said Marsilion the King,
"What must I do to kill Roland the Count?"
Ganelon answers: "Now I can tell you that.
The King will be at Cize, in the great passes,
330 he will have placed his rear-guard at his back:
there'll be his nephew, Count Roland, that great man,
and Oliver, in whom he puts such faith,
and twenty thousand Franks in their company.
Now send one hundred thousand of your pagans

against the French — let them give the first battle.
The French army will be hit hard and shaken.
I must tell you: your men will be martyred.
Give them a second battle, then, like the first.
One will get him, Roland will not escape.
340 Then you'll have done a deed, a noble deed,
and no more war for the rest of your life!" AOI.

45

"If someone can bring about the death of Roland,
then Charles would lose the right arm of his body,
that marvelous army would disappear —
never again could Charles gather such forces.
Then peace at last for the Land of Fathers!"
When Marsilion heard that, he kissed his neck.
Then he begins to open up his treasures. AOI.

46

Marsilion said, "Why talk. . . .
350 No plan has any worth which one. . . .[8]
Now swear to me that you will betray Roland."
Ganelon answers: "Let it be as you wish."
On the relics in his great sword Murgleis
he swore treason and became a criminal. AOI.
. . .

52

Marsilion took Ganelon by the shoulder
and said to him: "You're a brave man, a wise man.
Now by that faith you think will save your soul,
take care you do not turn your heart from us.
I will give you a great mass of my wealth,
360 ten mules weighed down with fine Arabian gold;
and come each year, I'll do the same again.
Now you take these, the keys to this vast city:
present King Charles with all of its great treasure;
then get me Roland picked for the rear-guard.
Let me find him in some defile or pass,
I will fight him, a battle to the death."

---

[8] **Lines 347, 348:** Parts of these lines are unintelligible in the manuscript.

Ganelon answers: "It's high time that I go."
Now he is mounted, and he is on his way. AOI.

54

The Emperor rose early in the morning,
370 the King of France, and has heard mass and matins.
On the green grass he stood before his tent.
Roland was there, and Oliver, brave man,
Naimon the Duke, and many other knights.
Ganelon came, the traitor, the foresworn.
With what great cunning he commences his speech;
said to the King: "May the Lord God save you!
Here I bring you the keys to Saragossa.
And I bring you great treasure from that city,
and twenty hostages, have them well guarded.
380 And good King Marsilion sends you this word:
Do not blame him concerning the Algalife:
I saw it all myself, with my own eyes:
four hundred thousand men, and all in arms,
their hauberks on, some with their helms laced on,
swords on their belts, the hilts enameled gold,
who went with him to the edge of the sea.
They are in flight: it is the Christian faith—
they do not want it, they will not keep its law.
They had not sailed four full leagues out to sea
390 when a high wind, a tempest swept them up.
They were all drowned; you will never see them;
if he were still alive, I'd have brought him.
As for the pagan King, Lord, believe this:
before you see one month from this day pass,
he'll follow you to the Kingdom of France
and take the faith—he will take your faith, Lord,
and join his hands and become your vassal.
He will hold Spain as a fief from your hand."
Then the King said: "May God be thanked for this.
400 You have done well, you will be well rewarded."
Throughout the host they sound a thousand trumpets.
The French break camp, strap their gear on their pack-horses.
They take the road to the sweet land of France. AOI.

55

King Charlemagne laid waste the land of Spain,
stormed its castles, ravaged its citadels.

The King declares his war is at an end.
The Emperor rides toward the land of sweet France.
Roland the Count affixed the gonfanon,
raised it toward heaven on the height of a hill;
410   the men of France make camp across that country.
Pagans are riding up through these great valleys,
their hauberks on, their tunics of double mail,
their helms laced on, their swords fixed on their belts,
shields on their necks, lances trimmed with their banners.
In a forest high in the hills they gathered:
four hundred thousand men waiting for dawn.
God, the pity of it! the French do not know! AOI.

56

The day goes by; now the darkness of night.
Charlemagne sleeps, the mighty Emperor.
420   He dreamt he was at Cize, in the great passes,
and in his fists held his great ashen lance.
Count Ganelon tore it away from him
and brandished it, shook it with such fury
the splinters of the shaft fly up toward heaven.
Charlemagne sleeps, his dream does not wake him.

57

And after that he dreamed another vision:
he was in France, in his chapel at Aix,
a cruel wild boar was biting his right arm;
saw coming at him—from the Ardennes—a leopard,
430   it attacked him, fell wildly on his body.
And a swift hound running down from the hall
came galloping, bounding over to Charles,
tore the right ear off that first beast, the boar,
turns, in fury, to fight against the leopard.
And the French say: It is a mighty battle,
but cannot tell which one of them will win.
Charlemagne sleeps, his dream does not wake him. AOI.

58

The day goes by, and the bright dawn arises.
Throughout that host. . . .[9]

---

[9]**Throughout . . . host . . . :** Second hemistich of line 438 is unintelligible in the manuscript.

440 The Emperor rides forth with such fierce pride.
   "Barons, my lords," said the Emperor Charles,
   "look at those passes, at those narrow defiles—
   pick me a man to command the rear-guard."
   Ganelon answers: "Roland, here, my stepson.
   You have no baron as great and brave as Roland."
   When he hears that, the King stares at him in fury;
   and said to him: "You are the living devil,
   a mad dog—the murderous rage in you!
   And who will precede me, in the vanguard?"
450 Ganelon answers, "Why, Ogier of Denmark,
   you have no baron who could lead it so well."

63

   The Emperor calls forth Roland the Count:
   "My lord, my dear nephew, of course you know
   I will give you half my men, they are yours.
   Let them serve you, it is your salvation."
   "None of that!" said the Count. "May God strike me
   if I discredit the history of my line.
   I'll keep twenty thousand Franks—they are good men.
   Go your way through the passes, you will be safe.
460 You must not fear any man while I live."

64

   Roland the Count mounted his battle horse. AOI.
   Oliver came to him, his companion.
   And Gerin came, and the brave Count Gerer,
   and Aton came, and there came Berenger,
   and Astor came, and Ansëis, fierce and proud,
   and the old man Gerard of Roussillon,
   and Gaifier, that great and mighty duke.
   Said the Archbishop: "I'm going, by my head!"
   "And I with you," said Gautier the Count,
470 "I am Count Roland's man and must not fail him."
   And together they choose twenty thousand men. AOI.

67

   And the Twelve Peers are left behind in Spain,
   and twenty thousand Franks are left with them.
   They have no fear, they have no dread of death.

The Emperor is going home to France.
Beneath his cloak, his face shows all he feels.
Naimon the Duke is riding beside him;
and he said to the King: "What is this grief?"
And Charles replies: "Whoever asks me, wrongs me.
480 I feel such pain, I cannot keep from wailing.
France will be destroyed by Ganelon.
Last night I saw a vision brought by angels:
the one who named my nephew for the rear-guard
shattered the lance between my fists to pieces.
I have left him in a march among strangers.
If I lose him, God! I won't find his like." AOI.

68

King Charles the Great cannot keep from weeping.
A hundred thousand Franks feel pity for him;
and for Roland, an amazing fear.
490 Ganelon the criminal has betrayed him;
got gifts for it from the pagan king,
gold and silver, cloths of silk, gold brocade,
mules and horses and camels and lions.
Marsilion sends for the barons of Spain,
counts and viscounts and dukes and almaçurs,
and the emirs, and the sons of great lords:
four hundred thousand assembled in three days.
In Saragossa he has them beat the drums,
they raise Mahumet upon the highest tower:
500 no pagan now who does not worship him
and adore him. Then they ride, racing each other,
search through the land, the valleys, the mountains;
and then they saw the banners of the French.
The rear-guard of the Twelve Companions
will not fail now, they'll give the pagans battle.

79

They arm themselves in Saracen hauberks,
all but a few are lined with triple mail;
they lace on their good helms of Saragossa,
gird on their swords, the steel forged in Vienne;
510 they have rich shields, spears of Valencia,
and gonfanons of white and blue and red.

They leave the mules and riding horses now,
mount their war horses and ride in close array.
The day was fair, the sun was shining bright,
all their armor was aflame with the light;
a thousand trumpets blow: that was to make it finer.
That made a great noise, and the men of France heard.
Said Oliver: "Companion, I believe
we may yet have a battle with the pagans."
520 Roland replies: "Now may God grant us that.
We know our duty: to stand here for our King.
A man must bear some hardships for his lord,
stand everything, the great heat, the great cold,
lose the hide and hair on him for his good lord.
Now let each man make sure to strike hard here:
let them not sing a bad song about us!
Pagans are wrong and Christians are right!
They'll make no bad example of me this day!" AOI.

80

Oliver climbs to the top of a hill,
530 looks to his right, across a grassy vale,
sees the pagan army on its way there;
and called down to Roland, his companion:
"That way, toward Spain: the uproar I see coming!
All their hauberks, all blazing, helmets like flames!
It will be a bitter thing for our French.
Ganelon knew, that criminal, that traitor,
when he marked us out before the Emperor."
"Be still, Oliver," Roland the Count replies.
"He is my stepfather — my stepfather.
540 I won't have you speak one word against him."

83

Said Oliver: "The pagan force is great;
from what I see, our French here are too few.
Roland, my companion, sound your horn then,
Charles will hear it, the army will come back."
Roland replies: "I'd be a fool to do it.
I would lose my good name all through sweet France.
I will strike now, I'll strike with Durendal,
the blade will be bloody to the gold from striking!

These pagan traitors came to these passes doomed!
550 I promise you, they are marked men, they'll die." AOI.

86

Said Oliver: "I see no blame in it—
I watched the Saracens coming from Spain,
the valleys and mountains covered with them,
every hillside and every plain all covered,
hosts and hosts everywhere of those strange men—
and here we have a little company."
Roland replies: "That whets my appetite.
May it not please God and his angels and saints
to let France lose its glory because of me—
560 let me not end in shame, let me die first.
The Emperor loves us when we fight well."

87

Roland is good, and Oliver is wise,
both these vassals men of amazing courage:
once they are armed and mounted on their horses,
they will not run, though they die for it, from battle.
Good men, these Counts, and their words full of spirit.
Traitor pagans are riding up in fury.
Said Oliver: "Roland, look—the first ones,
on top of us—and Charles is far away.
570 You did not think it right to sound your olifant:
if the King were here, we'd come out without losses.
Now look up there, toward the passes of Aspre—
you can see the rear-guard: it will suffer.
No man in that detail will be in another."
Roland replies: "Don't speak such foolishness—
shame on the heart gone coward in the chest.
We'll hold our ground, we'll stand firm—we're the ones!
We'll fight with spears, we'll fight them hand to hand!" AOI.

89

And now there comes the Archbishop Turpin.
580 He spurs his horse, goes up into a mountain,
summons the French; and he preached them a sermon:
"Barons, my lords, Charles left us in this place.
We know our duty: to die like good men for our King.

Fight to defend the holy Christian faith.
Now you will have a battle, you know it now,
you see the Saracens with your own eyes.
Confess your sins, pray to the Lord for mercy.
I will absolve you all, to save your souls.
If you die here, you will stand up holy martyrs,
590   you will have seats in highest Paradise."
The French dismount, cast themselves on the ground;
the Archbishop blesses them in God's name.
He commands them to do one penance: strike.

91

Roland went forth into the Spanish passes
on Veillantif, his good swift-running horse.
He bears his arms—how they become this man!—
grips his lance now, hefting it, working it,
now swings the iron point up toward the sky,
the gonfanon all white laced on above—
600   the golden streamers beat down upon his hands:
a noble's body, the face aglow and smiling.
Close behind him his good companion follows;
the men of France hail him: their protector!
He looks wildly toward the Saracens,
and humbly and gently to the men of France;
and spoke a word to them, in all courtesy:
"Barons, my lords, easy now, keep at a walk.
These pagans are searching for martyrdom.
We'll get good spoils before this day is over,
610   no king of France ever got such treasure!"
And with these words, the hosts are at each other. AOI.

92

Said Oliver: "I will waste no more words.
You did not think it right to sound your olifant,
there'll be no Charles coming to your aid now.
He knows nothing, brave man, he's done no wrong;
those men down there—they have no blame in this.
Well, then, ride now, and ride with all your might!
Lords, you brave men, stand your ground, hold the field!
Make up your minds, I beg you in God's name,
620   to strike some blows, take them and give them back!
Here we must not forget Charlemagne's war cry."
And with that word the men of France cried out.

A man who heard that shout: Munjoie! Munjoie!
would always remember what manhood is.
Then they ride, God! look at their pride and spirit!
and they spur hard, to ride with all their speed,
come on to strike — what else would these men do?
The Saracens kept coming, never fearing them.
Franks and pagans, here they are, at each other.

93

630   Marsilion's nephew is named Aëlroth.
He rides in front, at the head of the army,
comes on shouting insults against our French:
"French criminals, today you fight our men.
One man should have saved you: he betrayed you.
A fool, your King, to leave you in these passes.
This is the day sweet France will lose its name,
and Charlemagne the right arm of his body."
When he hears that — God! — Roland is outraged!
He spurs his horse, gives Veillantif its head.
640   The Count comes on to strike with all his might,
smashes his shield, breaks his hauberk apart,
and drives: rips through his chest, shatters the bones,
knocks the whole backbone out of his back,
casts out the soul of Aëlroth with his lance;
which he thrusts deep, makes the whole body shake,
throws him down dead, lance straight out,[10] from his horse;
he has broken his neck; broken it in two.
There is something, he says, he must tell him:
"Clown! Nobody! Now you know Charles is no fool,
650   he never was the man to love treason.
It took his valor to leave us in these passes!
France will not lose its name, sweet France! today.
Brave men of France, strike hard! The first blow is ours!
We're in the right, and these swine in the wrong!" AOI.

104

The battle is fearful and wonderful
and everywhere. Roland never spares himself,

---

[10] **lance straight out (*pleine sa hanste*, "with his full lance")**: The lance is held, not thrown, and used to knock the enemy from his horse. To throw one's weapons is savage and ignoble.

strikes with his lance as long as the wood lasts:
the fifteenth blow he struck, it broke, was lost.
Then he draws Durendal, his good sword, bare,
660   and spurs his horse, comes on to strike Chernuble,
smashes his helmet, carbuncles shed their light,
cuts through the coif, through the hair on his head,
cut through his eyes, through his face, through that look,
the bright, shining hauberk with its fine rings,
down through the trunk to the fork of his legs,
through the saddle, adorned with beaten gold,
into the horse; and the sword came to rest:
cut through the spine, never felt for the joint;
knocks him down, dead, on the rich grass of the meadow;
670   then said to him: "You were doomed when you started,
Clown! Nobody! Let Mahum help you now.
No pagan swine will win this field today."

110

The battle is fearful and full of grief.
Oliver and Roland strike like good men,
the Archbishop, more than a thousand blows,
and the Twelve Peers do not hang back, they strike!
the French fight side by side, all as one man.
The pagans die by hundreds, by thousands:
whoever does not flee finds no refuge from death,
680   like it or not, there he ends all his days.
And there the men of France lose their greatest arms;
they will not see their fathers, their kin again,
or Charlemagne, who looks for them in the passes.
Tremendous torment now comes forth in France,
a mighty whirlwind, tempests of wind and thunder,
rains and hailstones, great and immeasurable,
bolts of lightning hurtling and hurtling down:
it is, in truth, a trembling of the earth.
From Saint Michael-in-Peril to the Saints,
690   from Besançon to the port of Wissant,[11]
there is no house whose veil of walls does not crumble.
A great darkness at noon falls on the land,
there is no light but when the heavens crack.

---

[11] **Saint Michael-in-Peril . . . port of Wissant:** It is clear that these four points mark out the France of the tenth century, the realm of the last Carolingians.

No man sees this who is not terrified,
and many say: "The Last Day! Judgment Day!
The end! The end of the world is upon us!"
They do not know, they do not speak the truth:
it is the worldwide grief for the death of Roland.

112

      King Marsilion comes along a valley
700 with all his men, the great host he assembled:
twenty divisions, formed and numbered by the King,
helmets ablaze with gems beset in gold,
and those bright shields, those hauberks sewn with brass.
Seven thousand clarions sound the pursuit,
and the great noise resounds across that country.
Said Roland then: "Oliver, Companion, Brother,
that traitor Ganelon has sworn our deaths:
it is treason, it cannot stay hidden,
the Emperor will take his terrible revenge.
710 We have this battle now, it will be bitter,
no man has ever seen the like of it.
I will fight here with Durendal, this sword,
and you, my companion, with Halteclere —
we've fought with them before, in many lands!
how many battles have we won with these two!
Let no one sing a bad song of our swords." AOI.

128

      Count Roland sees the great loss of his men,
calls on his companion, on Oliver:
"Lord, Companion, in God's name, what would you do?
720 All these good men you see stretched on the ground.
We can mourn for sweet France, fair land of France!
a desert now, stripped of such great vassals.
Oh King, and friend, if only you were here!
Oliver, Brother, how shall we manage it?
What shall we do to get word to the King?"
Said Oliver: "I don't see any way.
I would rather die now than hear us shamed." AOI.

129

      And Roland said: "I'll sound the olifant,
Charles will hear it, drawing through the passes,

730 I promise you, the Franks will return at once."
Said Oliver: "That would be a great disgrace,
a dishonor and reproach to all your kin,
the shame of it would last them all their lives.
When I urged it, you would not hear of it;
you will not do it now with my consent.
It is not acting bravely to sound it now—
look at your arms, they are covered with blood."[12]
The Count replies: "I've fought here like a lord." AOI.

130

And Roland says: "We are in a rough battle.
740 I'll sound the olifant, Charles will hear it."
Said Oliver: "No good vassal would do it.
When I urged it, friend, you did not think it right.
If Charles were here, we'd come out with no losses.
Those men down there—no blame can fall on them."
Oliver said: "Now by this beard of mine,
If I can see my noble sister, Aude,
once more, you will never lie in her arms!" AOI.

131

And Roland said: "Why are you angry at me?"
Oliver answers: "Companion, it is your doing.
750 I will tell you what makes a vassal good:
it is judgment, it is never madness;
restraint is worth more than the raw nerve of a fool.
Frenchmen are dead because of your wildness.
And what service will Charles ever have from us?
If you had trusted me, my lord would be here,
we would have fought this battle through to the end,
Marsilion would be dead, or our prisoner.
Roland, your prowess—had we never seen it!
And now, dear friend, we've seen the last of it.
760 No more aid from us now for Charlemagne,
a man without equal till Judgment Day,
you will die here, and your death will shame France.
We kept faith, you and I, we were companions;

---

[12] **It is not . . . blood:** Some have found these lines difficult. Oliver means: We have fought this far—look at the enemy's blood on your arms: It is too late, it would be a disgrace to summon help when there is no longer any chance of being saved. Roland thinks that is the one time when it is not a disgrace.

and everything we were will end today.
We part before evening, and it will be hard." AOI.

132

Turpin the Archbishop hears their bitter words,
digs hard into his horse with golden spurs
and rides to them; begins to set them right:
"You, Lord Roland, and you, Lord Oliver,
770 I beg you in God's name do not quarrel.
To sound the horn could not help us now, true,
but still it is far better that you do it:
let the King come, he can avenge us then —
these men of Spain must not go home exulting!
Our French will come, they'll get down on their feet,
and find us here — we'll be dead, cut to pieces.
They will lift us into coffins on the backs of mules,
and weep for us, in rage and pain and grief,
and bury us in the courts of churches;
780 and we will not be eaten by wolves or pigs or dogs."
Roland replies, "Lord, you have spoken well." AOI.

133

Roland has put the olifant to his mouth,
he sets it well, sounds it with all his strength.
The hills are high, and that voice ranges far,
they heard it echo thirty great leagues away.
King Charles heard it, and all his faithful men.
And the King says: "Our men are in a battle."
And Ganelon disputed him and said:
"Had someone else said that, I'd call him liar!" AOI.

134

790 And now the mighty effort of Roland the Count:
he sounds his olifant; his pain is great,
and from his mouth the bright blood comes leaping out,
and the temple bursts in his forehead.
That horn, in Roland's hands, has a mighty voice:
King Charles hears it drawing through the passes.
Naimon heard it, the Franks listen to it.
And the King said: "I hear Count Roland's horn;
he'd never sound it unless he had a battle."

Says Ganelon: "Now no more talk of battles!
800   You are old now, your hair is white as snow,
the things you say make you sound like a child.
You know Roland and that wild pride of his—
what a wonder God has suffered it so long!
Remember? he took Noples without your command:
the Saracens rode out, to break the siege;
they fought with him, the great vassal Roland.
Afterwards he used the streams to wash the blood
from the meadows: so that nothing would show.
He blasts his horn all day to catch a rabbit,
810   he's strutting now before his peers and bragging—
who under heaven would dare meet him on the field?
So now: ride on! Why do you keep on stopping?
The Land of Fathers lies far ahead of us." AOI.

135

The blood leaping from Count Roland's mouth,
the temple broken with effort in his forehead,
he sounds his horn in great travail and pain.
King Charles heard it, and his French listen hard.
And the King said: "That horn has a long breath!"
Naimon answers: "It is a baron's breath.
820   There is a battle there, I know there is.
He betrayed him! and now asks you to fail him!
Put on your armor! Lord, shout your battle cry,
and save the noble barons of your house!
You hear Roland's call. He is in trouble."

136

The Emperor commanded the horns to sound,
the French dismount, and they put on their armor:
their hauberks, their helmets, their gold-dressed swords,
their handsome shields; and take up their great lances,
the gonfalons of white and red and blue.
830   The barons of that host mount their war horses
and spur them hard the whole length of the pass;
and every man of them says to the other:
"If only we find Roland before he's killed,
we'll stand with him, and then we'll do some fighting!"
What does it matter what they say? They are too late.

140

Roland looks up on the mountains and slopes,
sees the French dead, so many good men fallen,
and weeps for them, as a great warrior weeps:
"Barons, my lords, may God give you his grace,

840 may he grant Paradise to all your souls,
make them lie down among the holy flowers.
I never saw better vassals than you.
All the years you've served me, and all the times,
the mighty lands you conquered for Charles our King!
The Emperor raised you for this terrible hour!
Land of France, how sweet you are, native land,
laid waste this day, ravaged, made a desert.
Barons of France, I see you die for me,
and I, your lord—I cannot protect you.

850 May *God* come to your aid, that God who never failed.
Oliver, brother, now I will not fail *you*.
I will die here—of grief, if no man kills me.
Lord, Companion, let us return and fight."

142

When a man knows there'll be no prisoners,
what will that man not do to defend himself!
And so the Franks fight with the fury of lions.
Now Marsilion, the image of a baron,
mounted on that war horse he calls Gaignun,
digs in his spurs, comes on to strike Bevon,

860 who was the lord of Beaune and of Dijon;
smashes his shield, rips apart his hauberk,
knocks him down, dead, no need to wound him more.
And then he killed Yvorie and Yvon,
and more: he killed Gerard of Rousillon.
Roland the Count is not far away now,
said to the pagan: "The Lord God's curse on you!
You kill my companions, how you wrong me!
You'll feel the pain of it before we part,
you will learn my sword's name by heart today";

870 comes on to strike—the image of a baron.
He has cut off Marsilion's right fist;
now takes the head of Jurfaleu the blond—
the head of Jurfaleu! Marsilion's son.
The pagans cry: "Help, Mahumet! Help us!
Vengeance, our gods, on Charles! the man who set

these criminals on us in our own land,
they will not quit the field, they'll stand and die!"
And one said to the other: "Let *us* run then."
And with that word, some hundred thousand flee.
880   Now try to call them back: they won't return. AOI.

145

The Saracens, when they saw these few French,
looked at each other, took courage, and presumed,
telling themselves: "The Emperor is wrong!"
The Algalife rides a great sorrel horse,
digs into it with his spurs of fine gold,
strikes Oliver, from behind, in the back,
shattered the white hauberk upon his flesh,
drove his spear through the middle of his chest;
and speaks to him: "Now you feel you've been struck!
890   Your great Charles doomed you when he left you in this pass.
That man wronged us, he must not boast of it.
I've avenged all our dead in you alone!"

147

Oliver feels he is wounded to death,
will never have his fill of vengeance, strikes,
as a baron strikes, where they are thickest,
cuts through their lances, cuts through those buckled shields,
through feet, through fists, through saddles, and through flanks.
Had you seen him, cutting the pagans limb
from limb, casting one corpse down on another,
900   you would remember a brave man keeping faith.
Never would he forget Charles' battle-cry,
Munjoie! he shouts, that mighty voice ringing;
calls to Roland, to his friend and his peer:
"Lord, Companion, come stand beside me now.
We must part from each other in pain today." AOI.

148

Roland looks hard into Oliver's face,
it is ashen, all its color is gone,
the bright red blood streams down upon his body,
Oliver's blood spattering on the earth.
910   "God!" said the Count, "I don't know what to do,
Lord, Companion, your fight is finished now.

There'll never be a man the like of you.
Sweet land of France, today you will be stripped
of good vassals, laid low, a fallen land!
The Emperor will suffer the great loss";
faints with that word, mounted upon his horse. AOI.

149

Here is Roland, lords, fainted on his horse,
and Oliver the Count, wounded to death:
he has lost so much blood, his eyes are darkened—
920   he cannot see, near or far, well enough
to recognize a friend or enemy:
struck when he came upon his companion,
strikes on his helm, adorned with gems in gold,
cuts down straight through, from the point to the nasal,[13]
but never harmed him, he never touched his head.
Under this blow, Count Roland looked at him;
and gently, softly now, he asks of him:
"Lord, Companion, do you mean to do this?
It is Roland, who always loved you greatly.
930   You never declared that we were enemies."
Said Oliver: "Now I hear it is you—
I don't see you, may the Lord God see you.
Was it you that I struck? Forgive me then."
Roland replies: "I am not harmed, not harmed,
I forgive you, Friend, here and before God."
And with that word, each bowed to the other.
And this is the love, lords, in which they parted.

150

Oliver feels: death pressing hard on him;
his two eyes turn, roll up into his head,
940   all hearing is lost now, all sight is gone;
gets down on foot, stretches out on the ground,
cries out now and again: *mea culpa!*
his two hands joined, raised aloft toward heaven,
he prays to God: grant him His Paradise;
and blesses Charles, and the sweet land of France,
his companion, Roland, above all men.
The heart fails him, his helmet falls away,

---

[13] **nasal:** The nosepiece protruding down from the cone-shaped helmet.

the great body settles upon the earth.
The Count is dead, he stands with us no longer.
950 Roland, brave man, weeps for him, mourns for him,
you will not hear a man of greater sorrow.

156

Roland the Count fights well and with great skill,
but he is hot, his body soaked with sweat;
has a great wound in his head, and much pain,
his temple broken because he blew the horn.
But he must know whether King Charles will come;
draws out the olifant, sounds it, so feebly.
The Emperor drew to a halt, listened.
"Seigneurs," he said, "it goes badly for us—
960 My nephew Roland falls from our ranks today.
I hear it in the horn's voice: he hasn't long.
Let every man who wants to be with Roland
ride fast! Sound trumpets! Every trumpet in this host!"
Sixty thousand, on these words, sound, so high
the mountains sound, and the valleys resound.
The pagans hear: it is no joke to them;
cry to each other: "We're getting Charles on us!"

160

Say the pagans: "We were all born unlucky!
The evil day that dawned for us today!
970 We have lost our lords and peers, and now comes Charles—
that Charlemagne!—with his great host. Those trumpets!
that shrill sound on us—the trumpets of the French!
And the loud roar of that Munjoie! This Roland
is a wild man, he is too great a fighter—
What man of flesh and blood can ever hope
to bring him down? Let us cast at him, and leave him there."

168

Now Roland feels that death is very near.
His brain comes spilling out through his two ears;
prays to God for his peers: let them be called;
980 and for himself, to the angel Gabriel;
took the oliphant: there must be no reproach!
took Durendal his sword in his other hand,
and farther than a crossbow's farthest shot

he walks toward Spain, into a fallow land,
and climbs a hill: there beneath two fine trees
stand four great blocks of stone, all are of marble;
and he fell back, to earth, on the green grass,
has fainted there, for death is very near.

169

High are the hills, and high, high are the trees;
990 there stand four blocks of stone, gleaming of marble.
Count Roland falls fainting on the green grass,
and is watched, all this time, by a Saracen:
who has feigned death and lies now with the others,
has smeared blood on his face and on his body;
and quickly now gets to his feet and runs—
a handsome man, strong, brave, and so crazed with pride
that he does something mad and dies for it:
laid hands on Roland, and on the arms of Roland,
and cried: "Conquered! Charles's nephew conquered!
1000 I'll carry this sword home to Arabia!"
As he draws it, the Count begins to come round.

170

Now Roland feels: *someone taking his sword!*
opened his eyes, and had one word for him:
"I don't know you, you aren't one of ours";
grasps that olifant that he will never lose,
strikes on the helm beset with gems in gold,
shatters the steel, and the head, and the bones,
sent his two eyes flying out of his head,
dumped him over stretched out at his feet dead;
1010 and said: "You nobody! how could you dare
lay hands on me—rightly or wrongly: how?
Who'll hear of this and not call you a fool?
Ah! the bell-mouth of the olifant is smashed,
the crystal and the gold fallen away."

171

Now Roland the Count feels: his sight is gone;
gets on his feet, draws on his final strength,
the color on his face lost now for good.
Before him stands a rock; and on that dark rock
in rage and bitterness he strikes ten blows:

1020 the steel blade grates, it will not break, it stands unmarked.
"Ah!" said the Count, "Blessed Mary, your help!
Ah Durendal, good sword, your unlucky day,
for I am lost and cannot keep you in my care.
The battles I have won, fighting with you,
the mighty lands that holding you I conquered,
that Charles rules now, our King, whose beard is white!
Now you fall to another: it must not be
a man who'd run before another man!
For a long while a good vassal held you:
1030 there'll never be the like in France's holy land."

172

Roland strikes down on that rock of Cerritania:
the steel blade grates, will not break, stands unmarked.
Now when he sees he can never break that sword,
Roland speaks the lament, in his own presence:
"Ah Durendal, how beautiful and bright!
so full of light, all on fire in the sun!
King Charles was in the vales of Moriane
when God sent his angel and commanded him,
from heaven, to give you to a captain count.
1040 That great and noble King girded it on me.
And with this sword I won Anjou and Brittany,
I won Poitou, I won Le Maine for Charles,
and Normandy, that land where men are free,
I won Provence and Aquitaine with this,
and Lombardy, and every field of Romagna,
I won Bavaria, and all of Flanders,
all of Poland, and Bulgaria, for Charles,
Constantinople, which pledged him loyalty,
and Saxony, where he does as he wills;
1050 and with this sword I won Scotland and Ireland,
and England, his chamber, his own domain—
the lands, the nations I conquered with this sword,
for Charles, who rules them now, whose beard is white!
Now, for this sword, I am pained with grief and rage:
Let it not fall to pagans! Let me die first!
Our Father God, save France from that dishonor."

174

Now Roland feels: death coming over him,
death descending from his temples to his heart.

He came running underneath a pine tree
1060 and there stretched out, face down, on the green grass,
lays beneath him his sword and the olifant.
He turned his head toward the Saracen hosts,
and this is why: with all his heart he wants
King Charles the Great and all his men to say,
he died, that noble Count, a conqueror;
makes confession, beats his breast often, so feebly,
offers his glove, for all his sins, to God. AOI.

176

Count Roland lay stretched out beneath a pine;
he turned his face toward the land of Spain,
1070 began to remember many things now:
how many lands, brave man, he had conquered;
and he remembered: sweet France, the men of his line,
remembered Charles, his lord, who fostered him:
cannot keep, remembering, from weeping, sighing;
but would not be unmindful of himself:
he confesses his sins, prays God for mercy:
"Loyal Father, you who never failed us,
who resurrected Saint Lazarus from the dead,
and saved your servant Daniel from the lions:
1080 now save the soul of me from every peril
for the sins I committed while I still lived."
Then he held out his right glove to his Lord:
Saint Gabriel took the glove from his hand.
He held his head bowed down upon his arm,
he is gone, his two hands joined, to his end.
Then God sent him his angel Cherubin
and Saint Michael, angel of the sea's Peril;
and with these two there came Saint Gabriel:
they bear Count Roland's soul to Paradise.

204

1090 King Charles has reached the field of Rencesvals;
and comes upon the dead, and weeps for them;
said to the French: "Seigneurs, keep at a walk,
for I must ride ahead by myself now:
it is for my nephew, I would find him.
I was at Aix one day, at a high feast,
there were my valiant knights, all of them boasting
of great assaults, the battles they would fight.

There was one thing that I heard Roland say:
he said he would not die in a strange land
1100　before he'd passed beyond his men and peers,
he'd turn his face toward the enemies' land
and so, brave man, would die a conqueror."
Farther ahead than one could hurl a stick,
beyond them all, he has gone up a hill.

205

The Emperor, as he looks for his nephew,
found in the meadow grass many fair flowers
so bright and red with the blood of our barons;
and he is moved, he cannot keep from weeping.
He came beneath two trees and knew it was
1110　Roland who struck those blows on the three rocks;
and sees his nephew stretched out on the green grass.
Who would wonder at his rage and sorrow? —
gets down on foot; he has come running hard,
and takes in his two hands Roland the Count,
and falls fainting, choked with grief, on his body.

213

The Emperor commands: prepare Roland,
and Oliver, and Archbishop Turpin;
has their bodies opened in his presence,
the hearts received in cloths of silk brocade,
1120　and laid in a coffin of white marble.
Then they took the remains of these good men,
and they wrapped the three lords in deerskin shrouds,
their bodies washed in spiced and fragrant wine.
The King commands, Thibaut and Gebuïn,
Milun the Count, and Othon the Marquis:
"Escort these dead in three carts on their journey";
spread over them rich cloths of Eastern silk. AOI.

Muslim and Christian at War

The Song of Roland, composed at the end of the eleventh century, coincided with the beginning of the First Crusade in 1096. At that time, Christian knights from across Europe joined together ostensibly to come to the aid of Constantinople, but actually to recover Jerusalem from the Muslims and occupy the Holy Land. This "holy war"[1] — formulated according to Christian doctrine in the tenth and eleventh centuries — was partly a belated response to the Muslim conquest of the Middle East nearly four hundred years before. But since Christians and Muslims had found ways to live peaceably together in the interim, especially in Muslim Spain, the Christian Crusades satisfied new political ambitions more than they reflected longstanding political and religious differences. The Crusades helped the Papacy assert itself against not only Muslims but also quarreling factions inside European religious and secular society; they helped European kings consolidate their authority and set the goals for European expansion until the voyages to the New World in the sixteenth century; they provided the unattached knights of Europe with opportunities for acquiring wealth through plunder, taking pressure off their lords to distribute land among them; and they strengthened the hand of the Roman Catholic Church against the Byzantine emperor. But by re-opening the "holy war" with the Muslims, the First Crusade also left Muslims with a bitter determination to repel further Western expansion. The documents of the

---

[1] **"holy war"**: The Christian idea of "holy war," apparent in *The Song of Roland* and other sources, had its origins in St. Augustine's idea of a "just war" and was developed to support the Reconquest in Spain, efforts by Christian warriors to take Spain back from the Muslims who had conquered it in the early eighth century.

Battle between Christians and Muslims, thirteenth century

The beginning of the First Crusade in 1096 inaugurated a new period of conflict between two great world religions for more than two centuries and had lasting repercussions for both sides. The Crusades marked Western Christendom's attempted expansion outside of Europe. Wherever the Christian and Muslim armies collided, it brought about a period of intense cultural interaction. (The Art Archive / Biblioteca Nazionale Marciana, Venice / Dagli Orti)

Crusades show the Christian and Muslim viewpoints from the time of first contact around 1100 to a time some two hundred years later.

MUSLIMS, CHRISTIANS, AND THE BYZANTINE EMPIRE

In the last ten years of his life, from 622 to 632, Muhammad assumed political as well as civil and religious authority over much of Arabia. Muhammad fought his enemies in Mecca and elsewhere in Arabia first by a series of raids and later by territorial conquest. In these battles he followed the words of the Qur'an.

> Fight for the sake of God those that fight against you, but do not attack them first. God does not love aggressors.
>
> Slay them wherever you find them. Drive them out of the places from which they drove you. Idolatry is more grievous than bloodshed. . . .
>
> Fight against them until idolatry is no more and God's religion remains supreme. But if they desist, fight none except the evil-doers.

(SURA 2: *THE COW*. 191–193)

jee-HAHD

His Muslim followers undertook a massive *JIHAD,* or holy war, following his death, breaking out of the Arabian peninsula in every direction. To the north and east they conquered Syria, Armenia, and Persia; they penetrated Asia Minor, where they unsuccessfully besieged Constantinople, the seat of the Byzantine empire, in 718. To the west they conquered Egypt, crossed North Africa, and reached the Straits of Gibraltar, leading to the Iberian Peninsula. Their first contact with the Christian armies of Europe came in 711 after they crossed the Straits of Gibraltar into what is now Spain. Continuing across the Pyrenees mountains into southern France, they were finally stopped by the Merovingian Franks under Charles Martel[2]—

pwah-TYAY

the grandfather of Charlemagne—near **Poitiers** in 732, and retreated to safety back across the Pyrenees. These events marked the far limit of Muslim expansion in the eighth century, resulting in a reconfiguration of the map of what is now identified as Europe, the Middle East, and Asia Minor. The Frankish kingdom, soon to become the seat of Western Christendom, held what is now most of France and Germany; Islam occupied Spain, North Africa, Arabia, most of the Middle East and the trade routes to India; the Byzantine empire, which had lost North Africa, Egypt, Syria, and Palestine to the Muslim invasion, continued to occupy Asia Minor and part of what is now eastern Europe. Italy was contested between the Lombards, Norman Franks, and Byzantine soldiers.

The warlike Muslims of the eighth century soon consolidated their power, attained great wealth, and became the most advanced

---

[2] **Merovingian Franks . . . Charles Martel:** The Merovingian dynasty of Frankish kings lasted from 481 to 751. Charles Martel, mayor of the Merovingian territory of Austrasia from 714 to 741, was the first ruler in the Carolingian family line, which succeeded the Merovingians to power in 751. Charlemagne, the grandson of Charles Martel, ruled as king of the Franks from 768 to 814.

society in the world, with their influence reaching as far as Russia, Scandinavia, and the Far East. The authority of Islam, previously the domain of the **Umayyad** dynasty (661–750), was firmly established in the new capital of Baghdad with the victory of the **Abbasid** dynasty (750–1258), which survived a number of **internecine** wars among Muslims until its gradual dissolution after the eleventh century. For their part, the Christians won major victories in the First Crusade (1096–99), conquering Nicaea, Antioch, and finally Jerusalem, but soon after the Crusade they began losing conquered territory again. They failed to regain this territory in the Second Crusade (1147–48), and lost Jerusalem itself to the Muslim leader **Saladin**[3] in 1187. In the Third Crusade (1189–1193), the Christians failed to regain Jerusalem, and while the Fourth Crusade (1201–1204) resulted in the conquest of Constantinople, temporarily dismembering the Byzantine empire, it failed again to overcome the Muslims. Islam soon recovered its strength in Syria and Egypt and began to force the Christians out of the Middle East early in the thirteenth century. Repeated Christian attempts to recapture Jerusalem also failed; the Crusaders lost their last bridgehead in the region with the fall of **Acre**, a Syrian port, in 1291.

oo-MAH-ydd
uh-BAS-id
in-tur-NES-een

SAH-lah-din

AY-kur

DOCUMENTS OF THE FIRST CRUSADE

The First Crusade was preached by Pope Urban II (1088–99) addressing assembled church officials and members of the French aristocracy in Clermont, France, on November 27, 1095. The Council of Clermont had been assembled to address problems within the Catholic Church, including the breakdown of order throughout its realms. Turning at last from church reform, Pope Urban addressed "another affair that concerns you and God. Hastening to the way, you must help your brothers living in the Orient, who need your aid for which they have already cried out many times."

p. 588

The immediate reason for this undertaking was a plea for assistance from the Byzantine emperor **Alexius Comnenus** (r. 1081–1118), whose armies had been diminished by the Seljuk Turks, a Muslim people, in Asia Minor. Pope Urban called for vengeance on the Turks

uh-LEK-see-us
kahm-NEE-nus

---

[3] **Saladin:** Saladin (1137–1193) held power in Egypt from 1171 until his death, first subjugating Syria and then retaking Jerusalem in 1187. He was highly praised by his supporters and enemies alike for his military skill, enlightened governance, and honesty. (p. 180)

The massacre at Jerusalem profoundly impressed all the world. No one can say how many victims it involved; but it emptied Jerusalem of its Moslem and Jewish inhabitants. Many even of the Christians were horrified by what had been done; and amongst the Moslems, who had been ready hitherto to accept the Franks as another factor in the tangled politics of the time, there was henceforward a clear determination that the Franks must be driven out. It was this bloodthirsty proof of Christian fanaticism that re-created the fanaticism of Islam.

– STEVEN RUNCIMAN, *The First Crusade,* 1980

p. 592

Council of Clermont, 1337

This miniature from a French illuminated manuscript shows the arrival of Pope Urban II in Clermont, France, where he preached before the assembled knights, lords, and church leaders, calling on them to take up arms against the Muslim occupiers of the Holy Land. (Giraudon / Art Resource, NY)

for atrocities committed against Christian pilgrims traveling to Jerusalem, and he prayed for the expulsion of Muslims from Jerusalem. He concluded his call with this promise: "Undertake this journey for the remission of your sins, with the assurance of the imperishable glory of the kingdom of Heaven." Thus the Christian sponsorship of the Crusades combined a call for possession of the Holy Land with a promise of salvation for fallen soldiers.

The Crusaders, largely made up of Franks from northern and southern France, Normandy, and Norman Sicily, made their way by the end of 1096 to Constantinople, where Emperor Alexius had begun to have misgivings about calling on Frankish assistance, fearing that his allies might become his occupiers. As the desire of the Crusaders to conquer the line of Muslim cities on the way to Jerusalem became evident, Alexius withdrew his own armies, but the Frankish army swept south anyway, destroying Antioch in Syria before marching on to Jerusalem. Accounts of the sack of Jerusalem depict the massacre of Muslims within the city walls as well as the incineration of the Jews who had sought refuge in their ancient synagogue. An excerpt from the anonymous *History of the First Crusade,*

Muslim Troops Leaving a Fortress, twelfth century
*The Crusades from a Muslim perspective, from an Egyptian manuscript fragment. (The
Art Archive / British Museum)*

written by an unidentified Frankish Crusader, mixes respect for the
military prowess of the enemy with approval of the massacre of the
inhabitants of Jerusalem. It describes Christian atrocities, including
the robbing of the graves of the Turkish dead at Antioch and the
sacking of the cities of Marra and Jerusalem. Nothing, not even cannibalism, escapes the notice of the chronicler. Accounts such as this
one[4] explain why political relations between Muslims and the West
were soured for centuries.

The same incursions were also recorded by Muslim historians,
working from the accounts of direct participants. The most complete account of the attacks at Antioch, Marra, and Jerusalem from
the Muslim perspective come from **Ibn al-Athir**, p. 596 (1160–1233),   IB-un ahl-ah-THEER
who lived in the time of Saladin. Typical of Muslim historians, Ibn
al-Athir limits his editorial comment while making an extremely
moving presentation, concentrating largely on mistakes made by the

---

[4] **accounts such as this one:** Several accounts of the Christian siege of Jerusalem describe the massacre of Muslims and Jews. The chronicle of the Christian cleric Fulcher of Chartres is typical: "Within this Temple [of Sol-
omon] about ten thousand [Muslims] were beheaded. If you had been there, your feet would have been stained
up to the ankles with the blood of the slain. What more shall I tell? Not one of them was allowed to live. They
did not spare the women and children."

Muslims themselves that contributed to their overwhelming military defeat.

LATER REFLECTIONS ON THE CRUSADE EXPERIENCE

oo-SAH-muh IB-un
moon-KEED

Mindful of this bitter history, the Syrian military officer **Usamah ibn Munqidh**, p. 602 (1095–1190) comments on the morals and behavior of the Franks he encountered during his long life in his autobiography *The Book of Reflections*, written when he was about ninety. Urbane and loquacious, a collector of books as well as a soldier and diplomat, Usamah records for his Muslim audience a series of vignettes of the Franks—doctors, military men, other professionals, and such commoners as he had met—describing the horror he felt as a cultivated Muslim in the presence of the crude and unsophisticated Europeans.

SEN-uh-shul
troo-VEHR
TROO-buh-dohrz

Of course, not all the Franks were uncouth barbarians. The aristocratic knight Conon de Béthune, p. 609 (d. 1224), a participant in the Third and Fourth Crusades (1189–1193 and 1201–1204) who was later named **seneschal** and then regent of Constantinople, was one of the first of the northern French poets, or *trouvères*, to write in the style of the **troubadours**[5] of the south of France. His finely articulated poem to his lady reflects both the idealism of the noble-born Crusaders and their sense of superiority:

> Those who are healthy, young, and rich
> cannot stay home without shame.

In his poem "Alas, Love, what hard leave," Conon de Béthune displays a complete lack of curiosity about the Muslim enemy. His call is to war and glory; he does not describe a life of reflection such as that valued by Usamah Ibn Munqidh.

THE WESTERN INHERITANCE

As long as the Crusades lasted through intervals of peace and war, and as long as Spain remained predominantly Muslim, contact between the two great cultures continued on a regular basis. In periods of peace, cultural ties between the two groups resulted in the

---

[5] *trouvères . . . troubadours:* French troubadour poetry—lyric poems and songs composed by courtiers in the south of France—arose at the court of Guillaume IX, duke of Aquitaine, at the end of the eleventh century. Its influence extended to northern France, where the first *trouvères*, including young nobleman Conon de Béthune, were composing lyrics by the end of the twelfth century.

recovery and translation of much of the literature from Greek and Roman civilization. The culture of Arabic Spain influenced that of southern France, while Europe became aware for the first time of the possibilities of trade and communication via the great trading routes of the East. The eleventh through thirteenth centuries saw the development of European intellectual, social, and cultural life on an unprecedented scale, deriving in large part from Europe's exposure to Arabic and Muslim culture in the preceding centuries. The High Middle Ages of Europe in the twelfth century rested on the foundation of Muslim civilization, found both in the Holy Land during the Crusades and in Spain between the tenth and eleventh centuries.

■ CONNECTIONS

The Song of Roland, **p. 540.** The attitude of the Christian author of *The Song of Roland* toward Muslims parallels the attitude of the Frankish knights of the First Crusade about their enemy. How did the Christians regard the Muslims? How did their opinion of the enemy contribute to their behavior on the battlefield?

The Qur'an, p. 97. The sacred book of Islam, the Qur'an allows *jihad* or holy war in order to defend the faith against unbelievers. The acceptable limits of *jihad* are spelled out in Sura 2: The Cow, 191–193, cited in the text. Were the Muslims operating within the limits of *jihad* during their later territorial conquests in the seventh and eighth centuries? Were they acting within the limits of *jihad* when they came under Christian assault during the First Crusade? How do you account for the difference?

In the Tradition: **Courtly Love Lyrics, p. 628.** "Alas, Love, what hard leave," by Conon de Béthune, can be compared to the love poems of several Provençal poets, including Marcabru, Bernart de Ventadorn, and Raimbaut d'Orange. Themes such as leave-taking to go off to war are treated variously from one society to another. Can you detect a unique tone in the poem of Conon de Béthune that would enable you to discuss his character?

■ FURTHER RESEARCH

Historical Writings on the Crusades

Holt, P. M. *The Age of the Crusades. The Near East from the Eleventh Century to 1517.* 1986.
Maalouf, Amin. *The Crusades through Arab Eyes.* 1984.
Mayer, H. E. *The Crusades.* Trans. J. Gillingham. 1988.
Runciman, Stephen. *A History of the Crusades.* 3 vols. 1951–54.

Source Materials

Gabrieli, F., ed. *Arab Historians of the Crusades.* Trans. E. J. Costello. 1969.
Goldin, Frederick, ed. *Lyrics of the Troubadours and Trouvères.* 1973.
Hallam, E., ed. *Chronicles of the Crusades.* 1989.
Hitti, P. J., ed. *An Arab-Syrian Gentleman and Warrior in the Period of the Crusades.* 1929.
Peters, Edward, ed. *The First Crusade: The Chronicle of Fulcher of Chartres and Other Source Materials.* 1971.

■ PRONUNCIATION

Abbasid: uh-BAS-id, AB-uh-sid
Abul-Muzaffar al-Abiwardi: ah-BOOL moo-ZAH-far ahl-ah-bee-war-DEE

Acre: AH-kur, AY-kur
Alexius Comnenus: uh-LEK-see-us kahm-NEE-nus
Cilicia: sih-LISH-uh
Conon de Béthune: koh-NOHNG duh-bay-TOON, KOH-nahn
farsakh: far-SAHK
Hashim: hah-SHEEM
Ibn al-Athir: IB-un ahl-ah-THEER
internecine: in-tur-NES-een
jihad: jee-HAHD
Marra (Ma'arrat an-Nu'mān): MAH-rah (mah-AH-ree ah-noo-MAHN)
Masjid al-Aqsa: nahs-JEED ahl-AHK-sah
Poitiers: pwah-TYAY
Qawām ad-Daula Kerbuqā: kah-WAHM ah-DOW-lah kehr-BOO-kah
Qusyān: koos-YAHN
Ramadan: RAH-muh-dahn
Ruzbih: rooz-BEEH
Saladin: SAH-lah-din, SAL-uh-din
seneschal: SEN-uh-shul
troubadours: TROO-buh-dohrz
trouvères: troo-VEHR
Umayyad: oo-MAH-yad
Usamah Ibn Munquidh: oo-SAH-muh IB-un moon-KEED, oh-SAH-muh
Yaghi Siyan: YAH-gee see-YAHN

✖ Robert the Monk
FL. 1095

Numerous chronicles recorded Pope Urban's call for the First Crusade at the Council of Clermont in 1095, including Robert the Monk's account in his *History of the Crusade to Jerusalem.* Urban's speech, praised as a masterpiece of its kind, benefited from the strategic arrangement of its parts: an invocation to the Franks; a report of attacks on Christian settlements in the Holy Land; a call to arms; a response to anticipated objections based on safety and personal comfort; a call for unity among the Crusaders themselves; a reminder of the plight of Jerusalem; a response to the rallying cry of the assembled listeners; an injunction that the old and sick should be exempted from service; and an admonition to return from this "pilgrimage" in humility and a spirit of sacrifice.

Pope Urban had political as well as religious reasons for launching this Crusade. His call to arms came after the Council of Clermont had deliberated for days on the reform of the Catholic Church and its role in establishing order and peace throughout Europe. The formation of a volunteer army of knights to support the claims of the Catholic Church abroad would set a strong precedent for the future. It also has been suggested that Pope Urban might have wished to establish a Christian foothold in the Middle East and Asia Minor, with the eventual goal of the

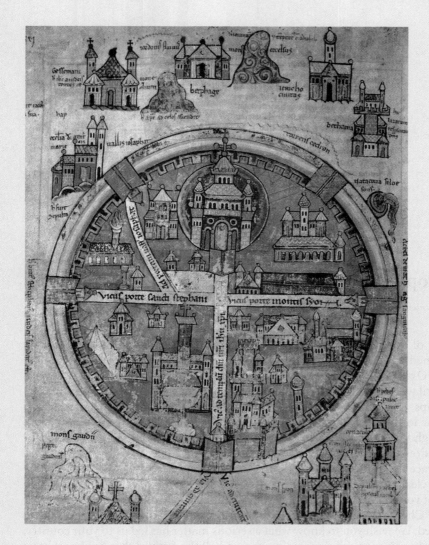

**Map of Jerusalem,
1099**
*This schematic map is
from the* Chronicles
of the Crusades, *by
Robert the Monk,
French abbot of
St. Remy who was
present at the
conquest of Jerusalem
in 1099. (Dagli Orti /
Corbis)*

conquest of Constantinople, the seat of the Byzantine empire and Eastern Christianity, as well as Jerusalem.

Results of the Call.   In his speech, Pope Urban called the Crusaders *pilgrims*; in fact, the Crusades were called "journeys" or "pilgrimages" for nearly the first hundred years, and the knights were given special privileges only over time, as the crusading ideal developed. But the humiliating defeat of groups of Crusaders who actually comported themselves like pilgrims—bringing whole families and households along to risk drownings in sea crossings and separation when attacked, to be hampered by their slowest members, and to be vulnerable because they were insufficiently armed or schooled in warfare—soon forced professional military standards on the "pilgrims." In future campaigns, most Frankish knights left their families and many of their retainers at home.

At first, sending a knight and a small number of supporters on crusade created considerable economic hardship, especially for those left behind on sizeable estates that needed management and care. The burden must have seemed lighter, however, as the Crusades continued, both because of the spirit of sacrifice among the participants and because of increased economic activity among the Crusaders themselves. As the means for establishing long-term credit were created, money circulated more easily, and trade developed between European ports and Eastern cities. Despite the Crusaders' steady loss of previously conquered territory in the East during the later twelfth and thirteenth centuries, the economy of Europe benefited as a whole from the Crusades.

∾   Pope Urban II's Call to the First Crusade

Translated by Frederic Austin Ogg

In the year of our Lord's Incarnation one thousand and ninety-five, a great council was convened within the bounds of Gaul, in Auvergne, in the city which is called Clermont. Over this Pope Urban II presided, with the Roman bishops and cardinals. This council was a famous one on account of the concourse of both French and German bishops, and of princes as well. Having arranged the matters relating to the Church, the lord Pope went forth into a certain spacious plain, for no building was large enough to hold all the people. The Pope then, with sweet and persuasive eloquence, addressed those present in words something like the following, saying:

"Oh, race of Franks, race beyond the mountains,[1] race beloved and chosen by God (as is clear from many of your works), set apart from all other nations by the situation of your country, as well as by your Catholic faith and the honor you render to the holy Church: to you our discourse is addressed, and for you our exhortations are intended. We wish you to know what a serious matter has led us to your country, for it is the imminent peril threatening you and all the faithful that has brought us hither.

"From the confines of Jerusalem and from the city of Constantinople a grievous report has gone forth and has been brought repeatedly to our ears; namely, that a race from the kingdom of the Persians, an accursed race, a race wholly alienated from God, 'a generation that set not their heart aright, and whose spirit was not steadfast with God,'[2] has violently invaded the lands of those Christians and has depopulated them by pillage and fire. They have led away a part of the captives into

---

[1] **beyond the mountains:** The Alps.

[2] **'a generation . . . with God':** Psalms 78:8.

their own country, and a part they have killed by cruel tortures. They have either destroyed the churches of God or appropriated them for the rites of their own religion. They destroy the altars, after having defiled them with their uncleanness. . . . The kingdom of the Greeks[3] is now dismembered by them and has been deprived of territory so vast in extent that it could not be traversed in two months' time.

"On whom, therefore, rests the labor of avenging these wrongs and of recovering this territory, if not upon you—you, upon whom, above all other nations, God has conferred remarkable glory in arms, great courage, bodily activity, and strength to humble the heads of those who resist you? Let the deeds of your ancestors encourage you and incite your minds to manly achievements—the glory and greatness of King Charlemagne and of his son Louis,[4] and of your other monarchs, who have destroyed the kingdoms of the Turks and have extended the sway of the holy Church over lands previously pagan. Let the holy sepulcher of our Lord and Saviour, which is possessed by the unclean nations especially arouse you, and the holy places which are now treated with ignominy and irreverently polluted with the filth of the unclean. Oh most valiant soldiers and descendants of invincible ancestors, do not degenerate, but recall the valor of your ancestors.

"But if you are hindered by love of children, parents, or wife, remember what the Lord says in the Gospel, 'He that loveth father or mother more than me is not worthy of me.'[5] 'Every one that hath forsaken houses, or brethren, or sisters, or father, or mother, or wife, or children, or lands, for my name's sake, shall receive an hundred-fold, and shall inherit everlasting life.'[6] Let none of your possessions restrain you, nor anxiety for your family affairs. For this land which you inhabit, shut in on all sides by the seas and surrounded by the mountain peaks, is too narrow for your large population; nor does it abound in wealth; and it furnishes scarcely food enough for its cultivators. Hence it is that you murder and devour one another, that you wage war, and that very many among you perish in civil strife.

"Let hatred, therefore, depart from among you; let your quarrels end; let wars cease; and let all dissensions and controversies slumber. Enter upon the road of the Holy Sepulcher; wrest that land from the wicked race, and subject it to yourselves. That land which, as the Scripture says, 'floweth with milk and honey'[7] was given by God into the power of the children of Israel. Jerusalem center of the earth; the land is fruitful above all others, like another paradise of delights. This spot the Redeemer of mankind has made illustrious by His advent, has beautified by His sojourn, has consecrated by His passion, has redeemed by His death, has glorified by His burial.

"This royal city, however, situated at the center of the earth, is now held captive by the enemies of Christ and is subjected, by those who do not know God, to the

---

[3] **The kingdom of the Greeks:** The Byzantine empire.

[4] **Charlemagne and of his son Louis:** Charlemagne was king of the Franks from 771 to 814; Louis the Pious succeeded him as king of the Franks from 814 to 840.

[5] **'He that loveth . . . not worthy of me':** Matthew 10:37.

[6] **'Every one that hath . . . everlasting life':** Matthew 19:29.

[7] **'floweth . . . honey':** Numbers 13:27.

worship of the heathen. She seeks, therefore, and desires to be liberated, and ceases not to implore you to come to her aid. From you especially she asks succor, because, as we have already said, God has conferred upon you, above all other nations, great glory in arms. Accordingly, undertake this journey eagerly for the remission of your sins, with the assurance of the reward of imperishable glory in the kingdom of heaven."

When Pope Urban had skillfully said these and very many similar things, he so centered in one purpose the desires of all who were present that all cried out, "It is the will of God! It is the will of God!" When the venerable Roman pontiff heard that, with eyes uplifted to heaven, he gave thanks to God and, commanding silence with his hand, said:

"Most beloved brethren, today is manifest in you what the Lord says in the Gospel, 'Where two or three are gathered together in my name, there am I in the midst of them.'[8] For unless God had been present in your spirits, all of you would not have uttered the same cry; since, although the cry issued from numerous mouths, yet the origin of the cry was one. Therefore I say to you that God, who implanted this in your breasts, has drawn it forth from you. Let that, then, be your war cry in battle, because it is given to you by God. When an armed attack is made upon the enemy, let this one cry be raised by all the soldiers of God: 'It is the will of God! It is the will of God!'

"And we neither command nor advise that the old or feeble, or those incapable of bearing arms, undertake this journey. Nor ought women to set out at all without their husbands, or brothers, or legal guardians. For such are more of a hindrance than aid, more of a burden than an advantage. Let the rich aid the needy; and according to their wealth let them take with them experienced soldiers. The priests and other clerks,[9] whether secular or regular, are not to go without the consent of their bishop; for this journey would profit them nothing if they went without permission. Also, it is not fitting that laymen should enter upon the pilgrimage without the blessing of their priests.

"Whoever, therefore, shall decide upon this holy pilgrimage, and shall make his vow to God to that effect, and shall offer himself to Him for sacrifice, as a living victim, holy and acceptable to God, shall wear the sign of the cross of the Lord on his forehead or on his breast. When he shall return from his journey, having fulfilled his vow, let him place the cross on his back between his shoulders. Thus shall ye, indeed, by this twofold action, fulfill the precept of the Lord, as He commands in the Gospel, 'He that taketh not his cross, and followeth after me, is not worthy of me.'"[10]

---

[8] 'Where two . . . in the midst of them': Matthew 18:20.

[9] other clerks: Members of the clergy.

[10] 'He that taketh . . . worthy of me': Luke 14:27.

HISTORY OF THE FIRST CRUSADE
EARLY TWELFTH CENTURY

The anonymous French *History of the First Crusade* was one of the earliest such chronicles; later annals would follow the two-hundred-year progress of the Christian fighters in the Holy Land. The narrator of the *History* speaks directly from within the action, giving a firsthand account of an attack by the Seljuk Turks as he begins. The reaction of the Crusaders to this massed attack reveals one of the motives for their undertaking:

> There was among us a quiet exchange of words, praising God and taking Counsel and saying: "Be unanimous in every way in the faith of Christ and the victory of the holy cross, for today, if it pleases God, you will all become rich. . . ."

As the narrative resumes, the Christians have their enemies on the run. When the writer praises the Turkish warriors, he does so in terms similar to those in *The Song of Roland:* They are great fighters, but as unbelievers they do not enjoy the favor of God.

As the story turns to the sieges of Antioch, Marra, and Jerusalem, the writer describes at length the deeds of the Franks, which include violating mosques, plundering corpses, engaging in cannibalism, and breaking sacred oaths, resulting in the murder or enslavement of the civilian population. Apparently, the author assumed his readers' sympathy with the Christian cause. The effect of these writings on a modern audience is radically different. Despite obvious exaggerations in the number of Christian and enemy soldiers as well as in the number of citizens slain, the histories of the First Crusade have left an indelible impression of a barbaric assault conducted in the name of religious belief.

Crusader, twelfth century
Detail of a Crusader on the move from a Syrian fresco illustrating a battle between the Knights Templar (a religious military order founded during the Crusades) and the Muslims. (The Art Archive / Templar Chapel, Cressac / Dagli Orti)

FROM

∾ History of the First Crusade

Translated by James B. Ross

THE FIRST CONTACT OF CRUSADERS AND TURKS

Impressions of the People and the Country in Anatolia

The first day of our departure from the city [Constantinople], we reached a bridge and we stayed there two days. The third day our men rose before dawn and, since it was still night, they did not see well enough to hold to the same route, and they divided into two corps which were separated by two days' march. In the first group were Bohemond, Robert of Normandy, the prudent Tancred and many others; in the second were the count of St. Giles, Duke Godfrey, the bishop of Puy, Hugh the Great, the count of Flanders and many others.

The third day [July 1, 1097], the [Seljuk] Turks violently burst upon Bohemond and his companions. At once the Turks began to shriek, scream, and cry out in high voices, repeating some diabolical sound in their own language. The wise Bohemond, seeing the innumerable Turks at a distance, shrieking and crying out in demoniac voices, at once ordered all the knights to dismount and the tents to be pitched quickly. Before the tents were pitched, he said to all the soldiers: "Lords, and valiant soldiers of Christ, here we are confronted on all sides by a difficult battle. Let all the knights advance bravely and let the foot soldiers quickly and carefully pitch the tents."

When all this was done, the Turks had already surrounded us on all sides, fighting, throwing javelins and shooting arrows marvellously far and wide. And we, although we did not know how to resist them nor to endure the weight of so great an enemy, nevertheless we met that encounter with united spirit. And our women on that day were a great help to us, in bearing drinking water to our fighters and perhaps also in always comforting those fighting and defending. The wise Bohemond sent word forthwith to the others, that is, to the count of St. Giles, to Duke Godfrey, Hugh the Great, the bishop of Puy and all the other knights of Christ, to hasten and come quickly to the battle, saying, "If today they wish to fight, let them come bravely." . . .

Our men wondered greatly whence could have sprung such a great multitude of Turks, Arabs, Saracens, and others too numerous to count, for almost all the mountains and hills and valleys and all the plains, both within and without, were covered entirely by that excommunicated race. There was among us a quiet exchange of words, praising God and taking counsel and saying: "Be unanimous in every way in the faith of Christ and the victory of the holy cross, for today, if it pleases God, you will all become rich." . . .

On the approach of our knights, the Turks, Arabs, Saracens, Angulans [unidentifiable], and all the barbarous peoples fled quickly through the passes of the mountains and the plains. The number of the Turks, Persians, Paulicians, Saracens,

Angulans, and other pagans was three hundred and sixty thousand, without counting the Arabs, whose number no one knows except God alone. They fled extremely
quickly to their tents but were not allowed to remain there long. Again they resumed
their flight and we pursued them, killing them during one whole day; and we took
much booty, gold, silver, horses, asses, camels, sheep, cows, and many other things
which we do not know. If the Lord had not been with us in this battle, if He had not
quickly sent us the other division, none of ours would have escaped, because from
the third hour up to the ninth hour the battle continued. But God all-powerful,
pious and merciful, who did not permit His knights to perish nor to fall into the
hands of the enemy, sent aid to us rapidly. But two of our knights died there honourably . . . and other knights and foot soldiers whose names I do not know, found
death there.

Who will ever be wise or learned enough to describe the prudence, the military
skill, and the fortitude of the Turks? They thought to terrorize the race of the Franks
by the threats of their arrows, as they have terrorized the Arabs, Saracens and Arme-
nians, Syrians and Greeks. But, if it pleases God, they will never prevail over such a
great people as ours. In truth they say they are of the race of the Franks and that no
man, except the Franks and themselves, ought rightly to be called a knight. Let me
speak the truth which no one will dare to contest; certainly, if they had always been
firm in the faith of Christ and holy Christianity, if they had been willing to confess
one Lord in three persons, and the Son of God born of a virgin, who suffered, rose
from the dead, ascended into heaven in the sight of His disciples and sent the consolation of the Holy Spirit, and if they had believed in right mind and faith that He
reigns in heaven and on earth, no one could have been found more powerful or
courageous or gifted in war; and nevertheless, by the grace of God, they were conquered by our men. This battle took place on the first of July. . . .

And we kept going on [July–August, 1097], pursuing the most iniquitous Turks
who fled each day before us. . . . And we pursued them through deserts and a land
without water or inhabitants from which we scarcely escaped and got out alive.
Hunger and thirst pressed us on all sides, and there was almost nothing for us to eat,
except the thorns which we pulled and rubbed between our hands; on such food we
lived miserably. In that place there died most of our horses, so that many of our
knights became foot soldiers; and from lack of horses, cattle took the place of war
steeds and in this extreme necessity goats, sheep, and dogs were used by us for
carrying.

Then we began to enter an excellent region, full of nourishment for the body,
of delights and all kinds of good things, and soon we approached Iconium. The inhabitants of this country [probably Armenians] persuaded and warned us to carry
with us skins full of water, because for the journey one day thence there is a great
dearth of water. We did so until we came to a certain river and there we camped for
two days. . . .

We . . . penetrated into a diabolic mountain [in the Antitaurus], so high and so
narrow that no one dared to go before another on the path which lay open on the
mountain; there the horses plunged down and one packhorse dragged over another.

On all sides the knights were in despair; they beat their breasts in sorrow and sadness, wondering what to do with themselves and their arms. They sold their shields and their best coats of mail with helmets for only three or five pennies or for anything at all; those who failed to sell them, threw them away for nothing and proceeded. . . .

Finally [October, 1097] our knights reached the valley in which is situated the royal city of Antioch, which is the capital of all Syria and which the Lord Jesus Christ gave to St. Peter, prince of the apostles, in order that he might recall it to the cult of the holy faith, he who lives and reigns with God the Father in the unity of the Holy Spirit, God through all the ages. Amen. . . .

At the Siege of Antioch

The next day [March 7, 1098], at dawn, some Turks went forth from the city and collected all the fetid corpses of the Turkish dead which they could find on the bank of the river and buried them at the mosque beyond the bridge, before the gate of the city. With the bodies they buried cloaks, bezants [gold coins], pieces of gold, bows, arrows, and many other objects which we cannot name. Our men, hearing that the Turks had buried their dead, all prepared themselves and hastened to the diabolic edifice. They ordered the tombs to be dug up and broken, and dragged from the burial places. They threw all the corpses into a certain ditch and carried the severed heads to our tents so that the number of them should be known exactly. . . . At this sight the Turks mourned exceedingly and were sad unto death for on that day they did nothing in their sorrow except weep and utter cries. . . .

The Taking of Marra

The Saracens, seeing that our men had sapped the wall, were struck with terror and fled within the city. All this took place on Saturday at the hour of vespers, at sunset, December 11th [1098]. Bohemond sent word by an interpreter to the Saracen chiefs that they with their wives and children and other belongings should take refuge in a palace which is above the gate and he himself would protect them from sentence of death.

Then all our men entered the city and whatever of value they found in the houses or hiding places each one took for his own. When day came, wherever they found anyone of the enemy, either man or woman, they killed him. No corner of the city was empty of Saracen corpses, and no one could go through the streets of the city without stepping on these corpses. At length Bohemond seized those whom he had ordered to go to the palace and took from them everything they had, gold, silver, and other ornaments; some he had killed, others he ordered to be led to Antioch to be sold.

Now the stay of the Franks in this city was one month and four days, during which the bishop of Orange died. There were some of our men who did not find there what they needed, both because of the long stay and the pressure of hunger, for outside the city they could find nothing to take. They sawed open the bodies of the dead because in their bellies they found bezants hidden; others cut the flesh in strips and cooked them for eating. . . .

The Sack of Jerusalem

Entering the city [July 15, 1099], our pilgrims pursued and killed Saracens up to the Temple of Solomon, in which they had assembled and where they gave battle to us furiously for the whole day so that their blood flowed throughout the whole temple. Finally, having overcome the pagans, our knights seized a great number of men and women, and they killed whom they wished and whom they wished they let live. . . . Soon the Crusaders ran throughout the city, seizing gold, silver, horses, mules, and houses full of all kinds of goods.

Then rejoicing and weeping from extreme joy our men went to worship at the sepulchre of our Saviour Jesus and thus fulfilled their pledge to Him. . . .

Then, our knights decided in council that each one should give alms with prayers so that God should elect whom He wished to reign over the others and rule the city. They also ordered that all the Saracen dead should be thrown out of the city because of the extreme stench, for the city was almost full of their cadavers. The live Saracens dragged the dead out before the gates and made piles of them, like houses. No one has ever heard of or seen such a slaughter of pagan peoples since pyres were made of them like boundary marks, and no one except God knows their number.

✎ IBN AL-ATHIR
1160–1233

Ibn al-Athir was a Mesopotamian historian, one of three literary brothers, who wrote the compendium of historical knowledge titled *The Collection of Histories,* covering the period from legendary times to 1231. His work treated the period after 1000 C.E., with authority and originality. Though he lived a century after the First Crusade, he studied the defeats at Antioch, Marra, and Jerusalem carefully, seeking the internal causes of the Muslim catastrophe while never sparing the barbarity of the Frankish invaders. His chief faults as a historian were an occasional tendency to treat his sources lightly and a lack of strict observance of chronology in his writing. His depictions of the Muslim leaders **Yaghi Siyan** of Antioch and Kerbuka of Mosul and his characterization of the traitorous guard **Ruzbih** in Antioch are among his memorable portraits. His description of the sack of Jerusalem squares closely with Christian accounts.

YAH-gee see-YAHN

rooz-BEEH

FROM

ᘓ The Collection of Histories

Translated by Francesco Gabrieli, translated from the Italian by E. J. Costello

THE FRANKS SEIZE ANTIOCH

In 1097 the Franks attacked Syria. This is how it all began: Baldwin, their King, a kinsman of Roger the Frank who had conquered Sicily, assembled a great army and sent word to Roger saying: 'I have assembled a great army and now I am on my way to you, to use your bases for my conquest of the African coast. Thus you and I shall become neighbours.'

Roger called together his companions and consulted them about these proposals. 'This will be a fine thing both for them and for us!' they declared, 'for by this means these lands will be converted to the Faith!' At this Roger raised one leg and farted loudly, and swore that it was of more use than their advice. 'Why?' 'Because if this army comes here it will need quantities of provisions and fleets of ships to transport it to Africa, as well as reinforcements from my own troops. Then, if the Franks succeed in conquering this territory they will take it over and will need provisioning from Sicily. This will cost me my annual profit from the harvest. If they fail they will return here and be an embarrassment to me here in my own domain. As well as all this Tamīm will say that I have broken faith with him and violated our treaty, and friendly relations and communications between us will be disrupted. As far as we are concerned, Africa is always there. When we are strong enough we will take it.'

He summoned Baldwin's messenger and said to him: 'If you have decided to make war on the Muslims your best course will be to free Jerusalem from their rule and thereby win great honour. I am bound by certain promises and treaties of allegiance with the rulers of Africa.' So the Franks made ready and set out to attack Syria. [. . .]

When the Franks decided to attack Syria they marched east to Constantinople, so that they could cross the straits and advance into Muslim territory by the easier, land route. When they reached Constantinople, the Emperor of the East refused them permission to pass through his domains. He said: 'Unless you first promise me Antioch, I shall not allow you to cross into the Muslim empire.' His real intention was to incite them to attack the Muslims, for he was convinced that the Turks, whose invincible control over Asia Minor he had observed, would exterminate every one of them. They accepted his conditions and in 1097 they crossed the Bosphorus at Constantinople. [. . .] They broke through in July 1097, crossed Cilicia,[1] and finally reached Antioch, which they besieged.

When Yaghi Siyān, the ruler of Antioch, heard of their approach, he was not sure how the Christian people of the city would react, so he made the Muslims go outside

---

[1] Cilicia: Lesser Armenia.

the city on their own to dig trenches, and the next day sent the Christians out alone to continue the task. When they were ready to return home at the end of the day he refused to allow them. 'Antioch is yours,' he said, 'but you will have to leave it to me until I see what happens between us and the Franks.' 'Who will protect our children and our wives?' they said. 'I shall look after them for you.' So they resigned themselves to their fate, and lived in the Frankish camp for nine months, while the city was under siege.

Yaghi Siyān showed unparalleled courage and wisdom, strength and judgment. If all the Franks who died had survived they would have overrun all the lands of Islām. He protected the families of the Christians in Antioch and would not allow a hair of their heads to be touched.

After the siege had been going on for a long time the Franks made a deal with one of the men who were responsible for the towers. He was a cuirass-maker called Ruzbih whom they bribed with a fortune in money and lands. He worked in the tower that stood over the river-bed, where the river flowed out of the city into the valley. The Franks sealed their pact with the cuirass-maker, God damn him! and made their way to the water-gate. They opened it and entered the city. Another gang of them climbed the tower with ropes. At dawn, when more than 500 of them were in the city and the defenders were worn out after the night watch, they sounded their trumpets. Yaghi Siyān woke up and asked what the noise meant. He was told that trumpets had sounded from the citadel and that it must have been taken. In fact the sound came not from the citadel but from the tower. Panic seized Yaghi Siyān and he opened the city gates and fled in terror, with an escort of thirty pages. His army commander arrived, but when he discovered on enquiry that Yaghi Siyān had fled, he made his escape by another gate. This was of great help to the Franks, for if he had stood firm for an hour, they would have been wiped out. They entered the city by the gates and sacked it, slaughtering all the Muslims they found there. This happened in April/May 1098. As for Yaghi Siyān, when the sun rose he recovered his self control and realized that his flight had taken him several *farsakh*[2] from the city. He asked his companions where he was, and on hearing that he was four *farsakh* from Antioch he repented of having rushed to safety instead of staying to fight to the death. He began to groan and weep for his desertion of his household and children. Overcome by the violence of his grief he fell fainting from his horse. His companions tried to lift him back into the saddle, but they could not get him to sit up, and so left him for dead while they escaped. He was at his last gasp when an Armenian shepherd came past, killed him, cut off his head and took it to the Franks at Antioch.

The Franks had written to the rulers of Aleppo and Damascus to say that they had no interest in any cities but those that had once belonged to Byzantium. This was a piece of deceit calculated to dissuade these rulers from going to the help of Antioch.

---

[2] *farsakh:* One *farsakh* is about four miles.

THE MUSLIM ATTACK ON THE FRANKS, AND ITS RESULTS

When Qawām ad-Daula Kerbuqā[3] heard that the Franks had taken Antioch he mustered his army and advanced into Syria, where he camped at Marj Dabiq. All the Turkish and Arab forces in Syria rallied to him except for the army from Aleppo. [...] When the Franks heard of this they were alarmed and afraid, for their troops were weak and short of food. The Muslims advanced and came face to face with the Franks in front of Antioch. Kerbuqā, thinking that the present crisis would force the Muslims to remain loyal to him, alienated them by his pride and ill-treatment of them. They plotted in secret anger to betray him and desert him in the heat of battle.

After taking Antioch the Franks camped there for twelve days without food. The wealthy ate their horses and the poor ate carrion and leaves from the trees. Their leaders, faced with this situation, wrote to Kerbuqā to ask for safe-conduct through his territory but he refused, saying 'You will have to fight your way out.' Among the Frankish leaders were Baldwin, Saint-Gilles, Godfrey of Bouillon, the future Count of Edessa, and their leader Bohemond of Antioch. There was also a holy man who had great influence over them, a man of low cunning, who proclaimed that the Messiah had a lance buried in the Qusyān, a great building in Antioch:[4] 'And if you find it you will be victorious and if you fail you will surely die.' Before saying this he had buried a lance in a certain spot and concealed all trace of it. He exhorted them to fast and repent for three days, and on the fourth day he led them all to the spot with their soldiers and workmen, who dug everywhere and found the lance as he had told them.[5] Whereupon he cried 'Rejoice! For victory is secure.' So on the fifth day they left the city in groups of five or six. The Muslims said to Kerbuqā: 'You should go up to the city and kill them one by one as they come out; it is easy to pick them off now that they have split up.' He replied: 'No, wait until they have all come out and then we will kill them.' He would not allow them to attack the enemy and when some Muslims killed a group of Franks, he went himself to forbid such behaviour and prevent its recurrence. When all the Franks had come out and not one was left in Antioch, they began to attack strongly, and the Muslims turned and fled. This was Kerbuqā's fault, first because he had treated the Muslims with such contempt and scorn, and second because he had prevented their killing the Franks. The Muslims were completely routed without striking a single blow or firing a single arrow. The last to flee were Suqmān ibn Artūq and Janāh ad-Daula, who had been sent to set an ambush. Kerbuqā escaped with them. When the Franks saw this they were afraid that a trap was being set for them, for there had not even been any fighting to flee from, so they dared not follow them. The only Muslims to stand firm were a detachment of warriors from the Holy Land, who fought to acquire merit in God's eyes and to seek

---

[3] **Qawām ad-Daula Kerbuqā:** The Turkish *amir,* or leader, of Mosul.

[4] **the Qusyān . . . in Antioch:** The Church of St. Peter in Antioch.

[5] **found the lance as he had told them:** This refers to the finding of the Sacred Lance at the instigation of Peter Bartholomew. The Christian versions of this story treat this as a sacred event.

martyrdom. The Franks killed them by the thousand and stripped their camp of food and possessions, equipment, horses and arms, with which they re-equipped themselves.

THE FRANKS TAKE MAʿARRAT AN-NUʿMĀN

After dealing this blow to the Muslims the Franks marched on Maʿarrat an-Nuʿmān[6] and besieged it. The inhabitants valiantly defended their city. When the Franks realized the fierce determination and devotion of the defenders they built a wooden tower as high as the city wall and fought from the top of it, but failed to do the Muslims any serious harm. One night a few Muslims were seized with panic and in their demoralized state thought that if they barricaded themselves into one of the town's largest buildings they would be in a better position to defend themselves, so they climbed down from the wall and abandoned the position they were defending. Others saw them and followed their example, leaving another stretch of wall undefended, and gradually, as one group followed another, the whole wall was left unprotected and the Franks scaled it with ladders. Their appearance in the city terrified the Muslims, who shut themselves up in their houses. For three days the slaughter never stopped; the Franks killed more than 100,000 men and took innumerable prisoners. After taking the town the Franks spent six weeks shut up there, then sent an expedition to ʿArqa, which they besieged for four months. Although they breached the wall in many places they failed to storm it. Munqidh, the ruler of Shaizar, made a treaty with them about ʿArqa and they left it to pass on to Hims. Here too the ruler Janāh ad-Daula made a treaty with them, and they advanced to Acre by way of an-Nawaqir. However they did not succeed in taking Acre.

THE FRANKS CONQUER JERUSALEM

[. . .] After their vain attempt to take Acre by siege, the Franks moved on to Jerusalem and besieged it for more than six weeks. They built two towers, one of which, near Sion, the Muslims burnt down, killing everyone inside it. It had scarcely ceased to burn before a messenger arrived to ask for help and to bring the news that the other side of the city had fallen. In fact Jerusalem was taken from the north on the morning of 15 July 1099. The population was put to the sword by the Franks, who pillaged the area for a week. A band of Muslims barricaded themselves into the Oratory of David[7] and fought on for several days. They were granted their lives in return for surrendering. The Franks honoured their word, and the group left by night for Ascalon. In the Masjid al-Aqsa[8] the Franks slaughtered more than 70,000 people, among them a large number of Imams and Muslim scholars, devout and ascetic men who had left their homelands to live lives of pious seclusion in the Holy Place. The

---

[6] **Maʿarrat an-Nuʿmān:** The city called Marra in the anonymous *History of the First Crusade.*

[7] **Oratory of David:** Called the Tower of David in European sources.

[8] **Masjid al-Aqsa:** The "farthest mosque," site of the worst atrocities.

Franks stripped the Dome of the Rock[9] of more than forty silver candelabra, each of them weighing 3,600 drams, and a great silver lamp weighing forty-four Syrian pounds, as well as a hundred and fifty smaller silver candelabra and more than twenty gold ones, and a great deal more booty. Refugees from Syria reached Baghdād in Ramadan,[10] among them the qadi Abu Sa'd al-Hárawi. They told the Caliph's ministers a story that wrung their hearts and brought tears to their eyes. On Friday they went to the Cathedral Mosque and begged for help, weeping so that their hearers wept with them as they described the sufferings of the Muslims in that Holy City: the men killed, the women and children taken prisoner, the homes pillaged. Because of the terrible hardships they had suffered, they were allowed to break the fast.

It was the discord between the Muslim princes, as we shall describe, that enabled the Franks to overrun the country. Abu l-Muzaffar al-Abiwardi[11] composed several poems on this subject, in one of which he says:

> We have mingled blood with flowing tears, and there is no room left in us
>   for pity(?)
> To shed tears is a man's worst weapon when the swords stir up the embers of war.
> Sons of Islām, behind you are battles in which heads rolled at your feet.
> Dare you slumber in the blessed shade of safety, where life is as soft as an orchard
>   flower?
> How can the eye sleep between the lids at a time of disasters that would waken
>   any sleeper?
> While your Syrian brothers can only sleep on the backs of their chargers, or in
>   vultures' bellies!
> Must the foreigners feed on our ignominy, while you trail behind you the train of
>   a pleasant life, like men whose world is at peace?
> When blood has been spilt, when sweet girls must for shame hide their lovely faces
>   in their hands!
> When the white swords' points are red with blood, and the iron of the brown
>   lances is stained with gore!
> At the sound of sword hammering on lance young children's hair turns white.
> This is war, and the man who shuns the whirlpool to save his life shall grind his
>   teeth in penitence.
> This is war, and the infidel's sword is naked in his hand, ready to be sheathed again
>   in men's necks and skulls.
> This is war, and he who lies in the tomb at Medina seems to raise his voice and
>   cry: 'O sons of Hashim!'[12]
> I see my people slow to raise the lance against the enemy: I see the Faith resting on
>   feeble pillars.

---

[9] **Dome of the Rock:** The rock from which Muhammad was supposed to have ascended to heaven and over which was built the mosque of 'Umar, the chief Muslim monument in Jerusalem.

[10] **Ramadan:** The Muslim holy month of peace.

[11] **Abul-Muzaffar al-Abiwardi:** An Iraqi poet of the eleventh and twelfth centuries.

[12] **'O sons of Hashim!':** Here, Muhammad is imagined rising from his tomb to rebuke his unworthy descendants.

For fear of death the Muslims are evading the fire of battle, refusing to believe that
death will surely strike them.'
Must the Arab champions then suffer with resignation, while the gallant Persians
shut their eyes to their dishonour?

∾ USAMAH IBN MUNQIDH
1095–1190

The valuable autobiography of Usamah ibn Munqidh, *The Book of Reflections,* was written as its author approached the age of ninety. Usamah had
been born in 1095, the year before the Crusades began. The nephew of a
Syrian prince, he was raised and educated as a gentleman and a soldier,
and became a friend of Saladin, the great leader of Egypt. In later life he
often acted as an emissary to the Franks. His reminiscences, written in the
style of serious reflection, concentrate more on hunting and other pursuits of a gentleman than on his impressions of the enemy, but he furnishes enough of the latter to make his works valuable commentaries on
the cultures of both the Syrians and the Franks.

Richard I and Saladin, 1340
*This fourteenth-century illuminated manuscript shows the Crusader King Richard I in
deadly combat with his archenemy, Saladin, one of the most powerful and respected
Muslim warrior-kings. Though they met many times on the field of battle, both men held
a grudging respect for the other's leadership. (The Art Archive / British Museum)*

The stories Usamah tells, often in succession, paint a damning picture of Frankish behavior. While sometimes Usamah expresses his opinion in no uncertain terms, at other times he lets an objective tone censure his Frankish subject, as in this comment:

> Among the Franks are those who have become acclimatized and have associated long with the Moslems. These are much better than the recent comers from the Frankish lands. But they constitute the exception and cannot be treated as a rule.

Usamah's cultured manner, his neat satirical thrusts at the Franks, and his ability to captivate the reader with story after story mark him as an excellent writer of any age.

FROM

ꙮ The Book of Reflections

Translated by Philip K. Hitti

Mysterious are the works of the Creator, the author of all things! When one comes to recount cases regarding the Franks, he cannot but glorify Allah (exalted is he!) and sanctify him, for he sees them as animals possessing the virtues of courage and fighting, but nothing else, just as animals have only the virtues of strength and carrying loads. I shall now give some instances of their doings and their curious mentality.

In the army of King Fulk, son of Fulk, was a Frankish reverend knight who had just arrived from their land in order to make the holy pilgrimage and then return home. He was of my intimate fellowship and kept such constant company with me that he began to call me "my brother." Between us were mutual bonds of amity and friendship. When he resolved to return by sea to his homeland, he said to me:

"My brother, I am leaving for my country and I want thee to send with me thy son (my son, who was then fourteen years old, was at that time in my company) to our country, where he can see the knights and learn wisdom and chivalry. When he returns, he will be like a wise man."

Thus there fell upon my ears words which would never come out of the head of a sensible man; for even if my son were to be taken captive, his captivity could not bring him a worse misfortune than carrying him into the lands of the Franks. However, I said to the man:

"By thy life, this has been exactly my idea. But the only thing that prevented me from carrying it out was the fact that his grandmother, my mother, is so fond of him that she did not this time let him come out with me until she exacted an oath from me to the effect that I would return him to her."

Thereupon he asked, "Is thy mother still alive?" "Yes," I replied. "Well," said he, "disobey her not."

A case illustrating their curious medicine is the following:

The lord of al-Munayṭirah wrote to my uncle asking him to dispatch a physician to treat certain sick persons among his people. My uncle sent him a Christian physician named Thābit. Thābit was absent but ten days when he returned. So we said to him, "How quickly hast thou healed thy patients!" He said:

They brought before me a knight in whose leg an abscess had grown, and a woman afflicted with imbecility. To the knight I applied a small poultice until the abscess opened and became well; and the woman I put on diet and made her humor wet. Then a Frankish physician came to them and said, "This man knows nothing about treating them." He then said to the knight, "Which wouldst thou prefer, living with one leg or dying with two?" The latter replied, "Living with one leg." The physician said, "Bring me a strong knight and a sharp ax." A knight came with the ax. And I was standing by. Then the physician laid the leg of the patient on a block of wood and bade the knight strike his leg with the ax and chop it off at one blow. Accordingly he struck it—while I was looking on—one blow, but the leg was not severed. He dealt another blow, upon which the marrow of the leg flowed out and the patient died on the spot. He then examined the woman and said, "This is a woman in whose head there is a devil which has possessed her. Shave off her hair." Accordingly they shaved it off and the woman began once more to eat their ordinary diet—garlic and mustard. Her imbecility took a turn for the worse. The physician then said, "The devil has penetrated through her head." He therefore took a razor, made a deep cruciform incision on it, peeled off the skin at the middle of the incision until the bone of the skull was exposed, and rubbed it with salt. The woman also expired instantly. Thereupon I asked them whether my services were needed any longer, and when they replied in the negative I returned home, having learned of their medicine what I knew not before.

I have, however, witnessed a case of their medicine which was quite different from that.

The king of the Franks had for treasurer a knight named Bernard [*barnād*], who (may Allah's curse be upon him!) was one of the most accursed and wicked among the Franks. A horse kicked him in the leg, which was subsequently infected and which opened in fourteen different places. Every time one of these cuts would close in one place, another would open in another place. All this happened while I was praying for his perdition. Then came to him a Frankish physician and removed from the leg all the ointments which were on it and began to wash it with very strong vinegar. By this treatment all the cuts were healed and the man became well again. He was up again like a devil.

Another case illustrating their curious medicine is the following:

In Shayzar we had an artisan named abu-al-Fath, who had a boy whose neck was afflicted with scrofula. Every time a part of it would close, another part would open. This man happened to go to Antioch on business of his, accompanied by his son. A Frank noticed the boy and asked his father about him. Abu-al-Fath replied, "This is my son." The Frank said to him, "Wilt thou swear by thy religion that if I prescribe to thee a medicine which will cure thy boy, thou wilt charge nobody fees for prescribing it thyself? In that case, I shall prescribe to thee a medicine which will cure the boy." The man took the oath and the Frank said:

"Take uncrushed leaves of glasswort, burn them, then soak the ashes in olive oil and sharp vinegar. Treat the scrofula with them until the spot on which it is growing is eaten up. Then take burnt lead, soak it in ghee butter [*samn*] and treat him with it. That will cure him."

The father treated the boy accordingly, and the boy was cured. The sores closed, and the boy returned to his normal condition of health.

I have myself treated with this medicine many who were afflicted with such disease, and the treatment was successful in removing the cause of the complaint.

Everyone who is a fresh emigrant from the Frankish lands is ruder in character than those who have become acclimatized and have held long association with the Moslems. Here is an illustration of their rude character.

Whenever I visited Jerusalem I always entered the Aqṣa Mosque, beside which stood a small mosque which the Franks had converted into a church. When I used to enter the Aqṣa Mosque, which was occupied by the Templars [*al-dāwiyyah*], who were my friends, the Templars would evacuate the little adjoining mosque so that I might pray in it. One day I entered this mosque, repeated the first formula, "Allah is great," and stood up in the act of praying, upon which one of the Franks rushed on me, got hold of me and turned my face eastward, saying, "This is the way thou shouldst pray!" A group of Templars hastened to him, seized him and repelled him from me. I resumed my prayer. The same man, while the others were otherwise busy, rushed once more on me and turned my face eastward, saying, "This is the way thou shouldst pray!" The Templars again came in to him and expelled him. They apologized to me, saying, "This is a stranger who has only recently arrived from the land of the Franks and he has never before seen anyone praying except eastward." Thereupon I said to myself, "I have had enough prayer." So I went out, and have ever been surprised at the conduct of this devil of a man, at the change in the color of his face, his trembling, and his sentiment at the sight of one praying towards the *qiblah*.

I saw one of the Franks come to al-Amīr Muʿīn-al-Dīn (may Allah's mercy rest upon his soul!) when he was in the Dome of the Rock, and say to him, "Dost thou want to see God as a child?" Muʿīn-al-Dīn said, "Yes." The Frank walked ahead of us until he showed us the picture of Mary with Christ (may peace be upon him!) as an infant in her lap. He then said, "This is God as a child." But Allah is exalted far above what the infidels say about him!

The Franks are void of all zeal and jealousy. One of them may be walking along with his wife. He meets another man who takes the wife by the hand and steps aside to converse with her while the husband is standing on one side waiting for his wife to conclude the conversation. If she lingers too long for him, he leaves her alone with the conversant and goes away.

Here is an illustration which I myself witnessed:

When I used to visit Nāblus, I always took lodging with a man named Muʿizz, whose home was a lodging house for the Moslems. The house had windows which opened to the road, and there stood opposite to it on the other side of the road a house belonging to a Frank who sold wine for the merchants. He would take some wine in a bottle and go around announcing it by shouting, "So and so, the merchant, has just opened a cask full of this wine. He who wants to buy some of it will find it in such and such a place." The Frank's pay for the announcement made would be the wine in that bottle. One day this Frank went home and found a man with his wife in the same bed. He asked him, "What could have made thee enter into my wife's room?" The man replied, "I was tired, so I went in to rest." "But how," asked he, "didst thou get into my bed?" The other replied, "I found a bed that was spread, so I slept in it." "But," said he, "my wife was sleeping together with thee!" The other replied, "Well, the bed is hers. How could I therefore have prevented her from using her own bed?" "By the truth of my religion," said the husband, "if thou shouldst do it again, thou and I would have a quarrel." Such was for the Frank the entire expression of his disapproval and the limit of his jealousy.

Another illustration:

We had with us a bath-keeper named Sālim, originally an inhabitant of al-Maʿarrah, who had charge of the bath of my father (may Allah's mercy rest upon his soul!). This man related the following story:

"I once opened a bath in al-Maʿarrah in order to earn my living. To this bath there came a Frankish knight. The Franks disapprove of girding a cover around one's waist while in the bath. So this Frank stretched out his arm and pulled off my cover from my waist and threw it away. He looked and saw that I had recently shaved off my pubes. So he shouted, 'Sālim!' As I drew near him he stretched his hand over my pubes and said, 'Sālim, good! By the truth of my religion, do the same for me.' Saying this, he lay on his back and I found that in that place the hair was like his beard. So I shaved it off. Then he passed his hand over the place and, finding it smooth, he said, 'Sālim, by the truth of my religion, do the same to madame [*al-dāma*]' (*al-dāma* in their language means the lady), referring to his wife. He then said to a servant of his, 'Tell madame to come here.' Accordingly the servant went and brought her and made her enter the bath. She also lay on her back. The knight repeated, 'Do what thou hast done to me.' So I shaved all that hair while her husband was sitting looking at me. At last he thanked me and handed me the pay for my service."

Consider now this great contradiction! They have neither jealousy nor zeal, but they have great courage, although courage is nothing but the product of zeal and of ambition to be above ill repute.

Here is a story analogous to the one related above:

I entered the public bath in Ṣūr [Tyre] and took my place in a secluded part. One of my servants thereupon said to me, "There is with us in the bath a woman." When I went out, I sat on one of the stone benches and behold! the woman who was in the bath had come out all dressed and was standing with her father just opposite me. But I could not be sure that she was a woman. So I said to one of my companions, "By Allah, see if this is a woman," by which I meant that he should ask about her. But he went, as I was looking at him, lifted the end of her robe and looked carefully at her. Thereupon her father turned toward me and said, "This is my daughter. Her mother is dead and she has nobody to wash her hair. So I took her in with me to the bath and washed her head." I replied, "Thou hast well done! This is something for which thou shalt be rewarded [by Allah]!"

A curious case relating to their medicine is the following, which was related to me by William of Bures [*kilyām dabūr*], the lord of Ṭabarayyah [Tiberias], who was one of the principal chiefs among the Franks. It happened that William had accompanied al-Amīr Muʿīn-al-Dīn (may Allah's mercy rest upon his soul!) from ʿAkka to Ṭabarayyah when I was in his company too. On the way William related to us the following story in these words:

"We had in our country a highly esteemed knight who was taken ill and was on the point of death. We thereupon came to one of our great priests and said to him, 'Come with us and examine so and so, the knight.' 'I will,' he replied, and walked along with us, while we were assured in ourselves that if he would only lay his hand on him the patient would recover. When the priest saw the patient, he said, 'Bring me some wax.' We fetched him a little wax, which he softened and shaped like the knuckles of fingers, and he stuck one in each nostril. The knight died on the spot. We said to him, 'He is dead.' 'Yes,' he replied, 'he was suffering great pain, so I closed up his nose that he might die and get relief.'

Let this go and let us resume the discussion regarding Harim.

We shall now leave the discussion of their treatment of the orifices of the body to something else.

I found myself in Ṭabarayyah at the time the Franks were celebrating one of their feasts. The cavaliers went out to exercise with lances. With them went out two decrepit, aged women whom they stationed at one end of the race course. At the other end of the field they left a pig which they had scalded and laid on a rock. They then made the two aged women run a race while each one of them was accompanied by a detachment of horsemen urging her on. At every step they took, the women would fall down and rise again, while the spectators would laugh. Finally one of them got ahead of the other and won that pig for a prize.

I attended one day a duel in Nāblus between two Franks. The reason for this was that certain Moslem thieves took by surprise one of the villages of Nāblus. One of the peasants of that village was charged with having acted as guide for the thieves when they fell upon the village. So he fled away. The king sent and arrested his children. The peasant thereupon came back to the king and said, "Let justice be done in my case. I challenge to a duel the man who claimed that I guided the thieves to the village." The king then said to the tenant who held the village in fief, "Bring forth someone to fight the duel with him." The tenant went to his village, where a blacksmith lived, took hold of him and ordered him to fight the duel. The tenant became thus sure of the safety of his own peasants, none of whom would be killed and his estate ruined.

I saw this blacksmith. He was a physically strong young man, but his heart failed him. He would walk a few steps and then sit down and ask for a drink. The one who had made the challenge was an old man, but he was strong in spirit and he would rub the nail of his thumb against that of the forefinger in defiance, as if he was not worrying over the duel. Then came the viscount [*al-biskund*], i.e., the seignior of the town, and gave each one of the two contestants a cudgel and a shield and arranged the people in a circle around them.

The two met. The old man would press the blacksmith backward until he would get him as far as the circle, then he would come back to the middle of the arena. They went on exchanging blows until they looked like pillars smeared with blood. The contest was prolonged and the viscount began to urge them to hurry, saying, "Hurry on." The fact that the smith was given to the use of the hammer proved now of great advantage to him. The old man was worn out and the smith gave him a blow which made him fall. His cudgel fell under his back. The smith knelt down over him and tried to stick his fingers into the eyes of his adversary, but could not do it because of the great quantity of blood flowing out. Then he rose up and hit his head with the cudgel until he killed him. They then fastened a rope around the neck of the dead person, dragged him away and hanged him. The lord who brought the smith now came, gave the smith his own mantle, made him mount the horse behind him, and rode off with him. This case illustrates the kind of jurisprudence and legal decisions the Franks have—may Allah's curse be upon them!

I once went in the company of al-Amīr Muʿīn-al-Dīn (may Allah's mercy rest upon his soul!) to Jerusalem. We stopped at Nāblus. There a blind man, a Moslem, who was still young and was well dressed, presented himself before al-Amīr carrying fruits for him and asked permission to be admitted into his service in Damascus. The Amīr consented. I inquired about this man and was informed that his mother had been married to a Frank whom she had killed. Her son used to practice ruses against the Frankish pilgrims and co-operate with his mother in assassinating them. They finally brought charges against him and tried his case according to the Frankish way of procedure.

They installed a huge cask and filled it with water. Across it they set a board of wood. They then bound the arms of the man charged with the act, tied a rope around his shoulders, and dropped him into the cask, their idea being that in case he was innocent, he would sink in the water and they would then lift him up with the rope so that he might not die in the water; and in case he was guilty, he would not sink in the water. This man did his best to sink when they dropped him into the water, but he could not do it. So he had to submit to their sentence against him— may Allah's curse be upon them! They pierced his eyeballs with red-hot awls.

Later this same man arrived in Damascus. Al-Amīr Muʿīn-al-Dīn (may Allah's mercy rest upon his soul!) assigned him a stipend large enough to meet all his needs and said to a slave of his, "Conduct him to Burhān-al-Dīn al-Balkhi (may Allah's mercy rest upon his soul!) and ask him on my behalf to order somebody to teach this man the Koran and something of Moslem jurisprudence." Hearing that, the blind man remarked, "May triumph and victory be thine! But this was never my thought." "What didst thou think I was going to do for thee?" asked Muʿīn-al-Dīn. The blind man replied, "I thought thou wouldst give me a horse, a mule and a suit of armor and make me a knight." Mu'īn-al-Dīn then said, "I never thought that a blind man could become a knight."

Among the Franks are those who have become acclimatized and have associated long with the Moslems. These are much better than the recent comers from the Frankish lands. But they constitute the exception and cannot be treated as a rule.

Here is an illustration. I dispatched one of my men to Antioch on business. There was in Antioch at that time al-Ra'īs Theodoros Sophianos [*tādrus ibn-al-ṣaffi*], to whom I was bound by mutual ties of amity. His influence in Antioch was supreme. One day he said to my man, "I am invited by a friend of mine who is a Frank. Thou shouldst come with me so that thou mayest see their fashions." My man related the story in the following words:

"I went along with him and we came to the home of a knight who belonged to the old category of knights who came with the early expeditions of the Franks. He had been by that time stricken off the register and exempted from service, and possessed in Antioch an estate on the income of which he lived. The knight presented an excellent table, with food extraordinarily clean and delicious. Seeing me abstaining from food, he said, 'Eat, be of good cheer! I never eat Frankish dishes, but I have Egyptian women cooks and never eat except their cooking. Besides, pork never enters my home.' I ate, but guardedly, and after that we departed.

"As I was passing in the market place, a Frankish woman all of a sudden hung to my clothes and began to mutter words in their language, and I could not understand what she was saying. This made me immediately the center of a big crowd of Franks. I was convinced that death was at hand. But all of a sudden that same knight approached. On seeing me, he came and said to that woman, 'What is the matter between thee and this Moslem?' She replied, 'This is he who has killed my brother Hurso ['*urs*].' This Hurso was a knight in Afāmiyah who was killed by someone of the army of Hamāh. The Christian knight shouted at her, saying, 'This is a bourgeois [*burjāsi*] (i.e., a merchant) who neither fights nor attends a fight.' He also yelled at the people who had assembled, and they all dispersed. Then he took me by the hand and went away. Thus the effect of that meal was my deliverance from certain death."

❧ Conon de Béthune

D. 1224

Conon de Béthune was one of the early *trouvères*, or courtly singers, of northern France. Born into an aristocratic family from the Province of Artois, he participated in the Third Crusade (1189–93) and the fourth Crusade (beginning in 1200), and then served as a diplomat. He was later named regent of Constantinople and spent the rest of his life there. His poems, of which ten have survived, show great variety. A celebrated figure both as a public servant and a poet, by birth and achievement he would have been the social equal of Usamah Ibn Munqidh, though they lived apart and Conon was much younger.

The poem "Alas, Love, what hard leave" follows the polite lyric conventions of the time. First the poet expresses sorrow at parting from his beloved, explaining that he is going to Syria, "the place for the great chivalric deed," to recover Jerusalem and redeem the Franks from shame. He recalls the promise of salvation that the church has extended to the Crusader, and mentions that the old and infirm as well as the clergy will stay behind with the women; for a moment he expresses concern about the chastity of the women who remain behind. But he affirms that any knights who are "healthy, young, and rich" must serve the holy cause. At the close he seeks the blessing owed by God to the Christian warrior while remembering to praise his lady at the same time. The lyric is both artful and conventional: In its excuse to his lady it is a little perfunctory, while in its treatment of the Crusades it iterates several points of Pope Urban's call to arms nearly a century before.

❧ Alas, Love, what hard leave

Translated by Frederick Goldin

Alas, Love, what hard leave
I must take from the best lady
a man ever loved and served.
May God in his goodness lead me back to her
as surely as I part from her in grief.
Alas, what have I said? I do not part from her at all.
If my body goes to serve our Lord,
my heart remains all in her power.

For Him I go sighing into Syria,
for I must not fail my Creator.
Whoever fails Him in this need for help—
do not doubt he shall fail in a greater need.

10

Let the great ones and the little ones know
that *there* is the place for the great chivalric deed,
where one wins Paradise and honor
and praise and the love of his beloved.

God! we have long been brave in idleness,
now we shall see who is brave in deed;
we shall go to avenge the burning shame
20   which ought to make us all angry and ashamed;
for in our time the Holy Place is lost
where God suffered death in agony for us;
if now we let our enemies remain,
our life will be forever more a life of shame.

Whoever does not want a life of misery here,
let him go die joyfully for God,
for the taste of such a death is sweet and good,
for which one wins the precious kingdom.
No, not a single one of them will die into death,
30   but all will be born into glorious life.
Whoever comes back will be full of happiness;
honor to the end of his days will be his wife.

All clergy and aged men
who shall remain behind for charity
will take part, all, in this pilgrimage,
and the ladies who will live in chastity
and keep faith with those who go.
And if through evil counsel they do foolishness,
they will do it with cowards, with scum,
40   for all good men will be gone on this voyage.

God is besieged in his holy heritage;
now we shall see how they come to his aid
whom he let loose from the dark prison
when he died on the Cross the Turks possess.
Be sure of this: those who will not go bring dishonor on their name,
unless they are poor, or old, or sick.
Those who are healthy, young, and rich
cannot stay home without shame.

Alas! I go away weeping from my eyes,
50   I go where God wants to amend my heart,
and I say I shall think of the best in this world
more than the voyage on which I part.

ANDREAS CAPELLANUS
FL. 1170–1186

In the glittering court of **Poitiers** in the south of France in the latter half of the twelfth century, a monk named Andreas Capellanus (Andre the Chaplain) was commissioned to write a treatise by Countess Marie of Champagne, the daughter of Eleanor of **Aquitaine** and one of the wealthiest patrons in France. *The Art of Courtly Love* (literally, *De arte honeste amandi,* or *The Art of Honest Loving*) brought together references to love derived in part from Ovid's Latin classics *The Art of Love* (*Ars amatoria*), *The Cure for Love* (*Remedia amoris*), and *Love* (*Amores*).[1] It also borrowed in both form and content from Arabic scholars of the previous century in Spain, particularly **Ibn Hazm**, author of a treatise on love, *The Dove's Necklace,*[2] written about 1022. Capellanus's treatise portrays dialogues between lovers of similar and different social classes and summarizes "trials" of love, probably conducted for entertainment at the court of Marie of Champagne. The work concludes with a lengthy retraction, "The Rejection of Love," in which Capellanus claims that he has written the book as a warning against carnal love and advises purity and the practice of Christian love instead.

While there is little that is strictly original about *The Art of Courtly Love* except the view it gives of court life in the south of France in the latter half of the twelfth century, scholars have found in it an indication of how the idea of romantic love developed in Europe during the Middle Ages, including the apparent contradiction between love's worldly and spiritual claims. There is a great deal of other literature concerning courtly love from the same period. In the courts of the southernmost regions of France (Gascony, Toulouse, and Provence), properly named **Occitania**, poets and composers—called TROUBADOURS in the Provençal language— had been composing songs that reflected new ideas about love for more than a century before the appearance of Capellanus's work. To the north, where Eleanor of Aquitaine's daughter Marie moved after her marriage to Count Henry of Champagne in 1164, gifted poets including **Chrétien de Troyes**[3] and Marie de France enlarged the discussion of love with their romances and *lais.* Though he was neither the first nor the last commentator on courtly love, Andreas Capellanus was an influential contributor

pwah-TYAY

AH-kwih-tayn
day AR-tay oh-NES-tee
ah-MAHN-dee

ARZ ah-mah-TOH-ree-
uh; reh-MAY-dee-uh
uh-MOH-ris;
ah-MOH-rays;
IB-un HAH-zam

ohk-sih-TAW-nee-uh
TROO-buh-dohrz

kray-TYEN duh-
TRWAH

---

[1] **Ovid** (43 B.C.E.–17 C.E.): Latin poet whose most famous works are *Metamorphoses,* a collection of classic myths and legends, and *The Art of Love,* which exercised an influence throughout the European Middle Ages. His *Cure for Love* recants, sometimes humorously, his earlier advocacy of love.

[2] *The Dove's Necklace:* See the selection from this work by Ibn Hazm (994–1064) in *In the Tradition: The Courtly Love Lyrics of Muslim Spain and the South of France,* on p. 639.

[3] **Chrétien de Troyes** (d. 1183): French poet who wrote major Arthurian romances, including *Perceval, Lancelot,* and *Yvain.* He dedicated *Lancelot* to Marie of Champagne. Marie de France (fl. 1170–1180) was a French poet who wrote short romances, called *Breton lais,* based on Celtic legends in England.

Eleanor of Aquitaine, twelfth to thirteenth century

The patronage of the charismatic Queen Eleanor of Aquitaine (married by turns to the kings of France and England) brought about a poetic flowering the likes of which medieval Europe had never seen. This fresco may be the only extant likeness of Queen Eleanor, shown here with her daughter-in-law, Isabelle of Angoulême. (The Art Archive / Dagli Orti)

to the subject. Reflections of the behavior he helped to codify may be seen in later European writing such as Dante's *Divine Comedy,* the Renaissance love poetry of Petrarch and Shakespeare, the Spanish novel *Don Quixote* by Cervantes and the Romantic poetry and prose of the nineteenth century—even modern popular lyrics and stories.

Capellanus and the Courts of Love.   Capellanus's connection to court and his commission to write *The Art of Courtly Love* is known for certain because he writes about them. From his writings it can be inferred that he was a member of minor orders,[4] that he was a good writer though not a scholar,[5] and that he was caught between the demands of a worldly court

www   For links to more information on Andreas Capellanus and a quiz on *The Art of Courtly Love,* see *World Literature Online* at bedfordstmartins .com/worldlit.

---

[4] **minor orders:** Unaffiliated with one of the large preaching orders; Capellanus was a chapel priest.

[5] **not a scholar:** Although Capellanus probably read Ovid, much of what he cites was available to him through *florilegia*—collections of sayings and bits of wisdom designed for students to memorize. He possessed a good knowledge of the Bible and a rudimentary acquaintance with the sayings of the fathers of the church.

and his own sense of propriety as a priest.[6] Most important, Capellanus was influenced, through his association with the court of Poitiers, by the love lyrics of the Provençal poets who had preceded him and the ethical biases in their work. The court of Poitiers, the ancestral seat of Eleanor of Aquitaine, was the birthplace of poetry in the **Provençal** language; it was there that Eleanor's grandfather, William, duke of Aquitaine (1077–1127), composed the first troubadour poetry that has been preserved. Through the aid of William and his successors, more troubadours were trained to compose lyrics on love and other topics for the enjoyment of the court. The creation of this tradition undoubtedly was enriched by the proximity of Spain,[7] whose Arab and Jewish writings contributed subject matter and poetic forms to the works produced in the Provencal language.

proh-vawn-SAHL

Capellanus, reflecting the biases and stereotypes of the courtly society of which he was a member, describes dialogues concerning love that confirm a strict division among the social classes. In one such exchange, a woman of the court dismisses a potential suitor who happens to be a commoner: "Although good character may ennoble a commoner, still it cannot change his rank to the extent of making him a lord . . . and so it is proper that you should be refused advancement to the love of a countess." She goes on to comment that his physical appearance is unacceptable: "For although soldiers should have long, slender calves and a moderate-sized foot . . . I see that your calves are fat and roundly turned, ending abruptly, and your feet are huge and immensely spread out so that they are as broad as they are long." In a more notorious passage, Capellanus appears to justify rape when the female in question is of low class, saying that since the attraction of a knight to a peasant girl is merely a species of lust, he should satisfy it immediately without any preliminaries and be on his way.

Courtly Love Defined.   The term "courtly love" (*amour courtois* in modern French) was coined by a French scholar to describe the mixture of sexual longing and mystical devotion shown by Sir Lancelot for Queen Guinevere in Chrétien de Troyes's Arthurian romance *Lancelot,* written between 1164 and 1172 under the patronage of Marie of Champagne. The term is also associated with the illicit nature of Lancelot's love, his violation of duty in approaching his king's wife, and the danger this created for Guinevere's reputation. In addition, *courtly love* implies the power of a lady over a knight and his obligation to prove his love through tests of courage and obedience to her wishes. Finally, the term suggests adherence to a refined code of behavior. Capellanus's work, written a few years

ah-MOOR
koor-TWAH

---

[6] **propriety as a priest:** How true a priest Capellanus was is open to question. He flaunts the powers of the priesthood, even remarking at one point that a trained cleric such as himself may make the best lover because of his "experienced knowledge of all things." He boasts of being attractive to nuns but says he has not fallen into temptation for fear of how he would be judged by God and man.

[7] **proximity of Spain:** The exact relationship of Spanish Arabic culture to the Provençal poets has been a matter of controversy for centuries. See *In the Tradition: The Courtly Love Lyrics of Muslim Spain and the South of France,* on p. 628.

before Chrétien's *Lancelot,* takes a similar stance with respect to obedience to love, the elevated status of the woman, the need for secrecy, and the moral problem of illicit behavior.

European scholarship on courtly love has emphasized its contradiction with the Christian beliefs of the time, so that one might speak of the "heresy" of courtly love. Specifically, courtly love has been associated with Catharism, the heretical religious movement in the south of France that was finally crushed by the Albigensian Crusade in 1209. Other scholars have countered that courtly love never really existed, that it was actually a game of the court and was consistent with Christian belief. Recently, a French historian has viewed courtly love as a way to civilize restless young knights, *jovenes,* deprived of an inheritance and roaming the countryside seeking their fortunes. Since the depiction of courtly love certainly varies from text to text, perhaps all these interpretations may be considered to be partly correct.

Studying the words used to describe courtly love in their original contexts may help put the concept as a whole in better perspective. The original title of Andreas Capellanus's treatise, *The Art of Honest Loving,* stressed the situational ethics of love. The Provençal troubadours most frequently using the term FIN'AMOR for courtly love emphasized on the other hand love's refinement or purity. In troubadour songs, however, love is also referred to as *joi,* implying both the modern French *joie* (joy) and *jeu* (game), suggestive of a lighter, livelier approach to the subject. The lady herself is generally addressed as *midons,* or "my lord," in the masculine form. This grammatical transgression of gender may indicate that the adoring lover owes devotion to his lady just as a feudal vassal owes it to his lord. Finally, the treatment of love takes on an altogether cynical aspect in the final chapter of Capellanus's work, "The Rejection of Love," which resembles Ovid's *Cure for Love* while incorporating some of the most scurrilous Christian attacks on women. Here the lady is unceremoniously taken off her pedestal and depicted as a sinful and dangerous character apt to corrupt the man who adores her. In the retraction Capellanus dutifully reports that the love of Christ the Bridegroom is to be preferred.

Contradictions of the Work.   The first part of *The Art of Courtly Love,* "Introduction to the Treatise on Love," defines love as "a certain inborn suffering derived from the sight of and excessive meditation upon the beauty of the opposite sex, which causes each one to wish above all things the embraces of the other and by common desire to carry out all of love's precepts in the other's embrace." Capellanus dedicates his work to his young friend Walter, a "new recruit of Love" who has "recently been wounded by an arrow of his." Full of classical allusions, *The Art of Courtly Love* reads like a new rendering of Ovid's treatises on love. But unlike Ovid, Capellanus does not write an unabashedly candid textbook on seduction. Instead he advises the subordination of love's passion to a civilized code of behavior in a relationship between social equals.

The second part, "How Love May Be Retained," describes how to keep love alive between equals. Capellanus advises first that it should be kept secret, as its revelation to others may destroy it. Moreover, the diffi-

[margin notes:]
joh-VEN-es

fin-ah-MORE

ZHWAH
ZHEU
mee-DOHNZ

culty of its attainment may increase love, while ease of access causes it to diminish. Here Capellanus appears to be defining the nature of illicit passion rather than the civilized behavior he advocated in his introduction. In the third part, "The Rejection of Love," Capellanus advises his friend Walter to give up the pursuit of carnal love altogether and practice the love of God, which leads to salvation. The point of writing the book, he now says, is "not because we consider it advisable for you or any other man to fall in love, but for fear lest you might think us stupid. . . . For God is more pleased with a man who is able to sin and does not, than with a man who has no opportunity to sin." There is no attempt to reconcile this apparent contradiction with the rest of the work, and here Capellanus is like other authors of the later Middle Ages who include retractions[8] of their writings at the end of their works, perhaps with a wink at the reader or at least in order to clear themselves of blame in the eyes of pious readers and officials of the church.

Meaning of the Work. Since modern scholars have disagreed over the interpretation of Andreas Capellanus's work, several points about *The Art of Courtly Love* should be kept in mind. First, Capellanus sometimes cites Ovid and other sources without any attempt to reconcile them with the rest of his text; for that matter, Ovid himself expressed contradictory opinions in his treatises. Moreover, since Capellanus's treatise also subscribes to the tradition of courtly love in the south of France, it contains the prevailing and sometimes contradictory opinions found in the songs and even the practices of the troubadours themselves. Finally, the caution Capellanus expresses near the end of his work may be genuine. If he really is writing a treatise on love to a young man "for fear lest you might think us stupid," then he is in a somewhat compromised position, expounding on a worldly subject with which he, as a priest, is supposed to have limited experience.

There still appears to be a double standard in Capellanus's address to the court of Poitiers on the one hand and his "Rejection of Love" on the other. But Capellanus's work may not be as contradictory as it seems if one accepts the coexistence of a secular worldview alongside that of Christianity. The practice of love, even at court, is part of the ***mundus saeculorum,*** the world of human affairs, which is inherently flawed and unstable. The true design of love as ***caritas,*** or Christian charity, is set forth in Heaven. Obviously an audience could be interested in the former kind of love even while subscribing morally to belief in the latter.[9]

MOON-doos
sigh-koo-LOH-rum
KAH-rih-tahs

---

[8] **like other authors . . . retractions:** Ovid's retraction to *The Art of Love* might have been on Capellanus's mind. Later, Geoffrey Chaucer had this to say at the end of *The Canterbury Tales:* "And if there be anything that displeaseth, I pray that it be charged to my ignorance and not to my will, that surely would have said it better if I had had correct understanding. For our Book sayeth, 'All that is written is written according to our doctrine,' and that is my intent."

[9] **the former . . . latter:** While lust (*luxuria*) was acknowledged as one of the seven deadly sins, in practice it was not taken as seriously as sins of the will, such as pride (*superbia*). Also, what was permissible as entertainment at court might not have been acceptable in a holy place.

The twelfth century has been described as an "age of Ovid" because of the predominant influence of writings by the Classical Latin poet Ovid particularly on the literature of love. Ovidian motifs — love as a fever, a sweet pain or a welcome wound, the beloved as a medicine or an enemy to be overcome — are scattered throughout the lyric poetry of the troubadours. An even more important element of the Ovidian inheritance is [. . .] self-awareness about love as an art of literary composition as much as of emotion. [. . .] A work in this tradition, although not a romance, is Andreas Capellanus's *De Arte honeste amandi (Art of Courtly Love)*. This clever and ironic text humorously applies medieval techniques of intellectual codification and argument to the Ovidian erotic tradition.

— SARAH KAY, scholar, 2000

In the end this little book is an interesting foray into the vagaries of the medieval mind, with results that we find expressed nowhere else in quite the same way. Within this treatise are conversations about the duties and obligations of love between men and women of the courts, debates and even "trials" on the subject of love, and rare glimpses of the actual behavior of highly educated men and women of the time. When read alongside the courtly lyrics of the troubadours, Capellanus's work takes on new life and form, less reality than an imitation of reality — the way the court wished to see itself. Andreas Capellanus the priest was a minor artist who showed his patrons their reflections in a way that they apparently found pleasing.

■ CONNECTIONS

Ibn Hazm, *The Dove's Necklace,* **p. 639.** This eleventh-century Spanish Arabic text explores love's dimensions in somewhat the same fashion as *The Art of Courtly Love.* Notice Ibn Hazm's sophisticated treatment of love (Ibn Hazm was a philosopher as well as a poet) and compare it with the apparent humility of Andreas Capellanus. How might each writer have regarded the other's work?

In the Tradition: **The Courtly Love Lyrics, p. 628.** The Provençal lyrics, designed originally for performance in court, were products of the same society in which Capellanus labored. Since many were composed before Capellanus wrote *The Art of Courtly Love,* it has been conjectured that their idea of *fin'amor* (refinement) is repeated in his writings. What are some of the other similarities between these courtly love songs and *The Art of Courtly Love?* Are they dissimilar in any way?

The Thousand and One Nights, **p. 435.** For a different view of love from the same period, one may go outside European medieval culture and the scholarly Middle Eastern tradition to such works as the anonymous *Thousand and One Nights,* a collection of popular stories culled from many nations. How is the courtly tradition of romance known to Capellanus different from a romance written in the popular tradition?

■ FURTHER RESEARCH

Edition
Capellanus, Andreas. *The Art of Courtly Love.* Parry, John Jay, ed. 1941. Reprint, 1960.

History
Duby, Georges. *The Chivalrous Society.* 1980.
Ferrante, Joan. *The Glory of Her Sex: Women's Roles in the Composition of Medieval Texts.* 1997.
Herr, Friedrich. *The Medieval World.* 1962.
Kelly, Amy. *Eleanor of Aquitaine and the Four Kings.* 1963.

Courtly Love
Boase, R. *The Origin and Meaning of Courtly Love.* 1977.
Kay, Sarah. "Courts, Clerks, and Courtly Love." In Roberta L. Krueger, ed. *Medieval Romance.* 2000.
Newman, F. X., ed. *The Meaning of Courtly Love.* 1968.
Valency, Maurice. *In Praise of Love.* 1958.

Andreas Capellanus
Jackson, W. T. H. "The *De Amore* of Andreas Capellanus and the Practice of Love at Court," in *The Challenge of the Medieval Text.* 1985.

■ PRONUNCIATION

Amores: ah-MOH-rays
amour courtois: ah-MOOR koor-TWAH
Aquitaine: AH-kwih-tayn, ah-kee-TEHN
Ars amatoria: ARZ ah-mah-TOH-ree-uh
caritas: KAH-rih-tahs
Chrétien de Troyes: kray-TYEN duh-TRWAH
De arte honesti amandi: day AR-tay oh-NES-tee ah-MAHN-dee
fin'amor: fin-ah-MORE
florilegia: floh-rih-LEE-jee-uh
Ibn Hazm: IB-un HAH-zum, HAZ-um
jeu: ZHEU
joi, joie: ZHWAH
jovènes: joh-VEN-es
luxuria: look-SOO-ree-uh, loog-ZHOO-
midons: mee-DOHNZ
mundus saeculorum: MOON-doos sigh-koo-LOH-rum
Occitania: ohk-sih-TAW-nee-uh
Poitiers: pwah-TYAY
Provençal: proh-vawn-SAHL
Remedia amoris: reh-MAY-dee-uh uh-MOH-ris
superbia: soo-PEHR-bee-uh, soo-PUR-bee-uh
troubadour: TROO-buh-dohr

☙ The Art of Courtly Love

Translated by John J. Parry

FROM

BOOK I
INTRODUCTION TO THE TREATISE ON LOVE

We must first consider what love is, whence it gets its name, what the effect of love is, between what persons love may exist, how it may be acquired, retained, increased, decreased, and ended, what are the signs that one's love is returned, and what one of the lovers ought to do if the other is unfaithful.

The Art of Courtly Love. The interest that inspired Andreas Capellanus's treatise on love is partly traceable to the enthusiasm in twelfth-century Europe for Ovid's *Art of Love*, which was available in both Latin and the European vernacular languages. Ovid's work, which is considerably bawdier than Capellanus's, had a big following not only among author-practitioners of courtly love but also among authors interested in portraying sensuality, such as the later medieval writers Giovanni Boccaccio (1313–1375) and Geoffrey Chaucer (c. 1340–1400).

Capellanus's book was written at Poitiers under the direction of Marie of Champagne. Marie, who spent most of her married life to the north, in Troyes, visited her mother, Eleanor, in Poitiers

Chapter 1
What Love Is

Love is a certain inborn suffering derived from the sight of and excessive meditation upon the beauty of the opposite sex, which causes each one to wish above all things the embraces of the other and by common desire to carry out all of love's precepts in the other's embrace.

That love is suffering is easy to see, for before the love becomes equally balanced on both sides there is no torment greater, since the lover is always in fear that his love may not gain its desire and that he is wasting his efforts. He fears, too, that rumors of it may get abroad, and he fears everything that might harm it in any way, for before things are perfected a slight disturbance often spoils them. If he is a poor man, he also fears that the woman may scorn his poverty; if he is ugly, he fears that she may despise his lack of beauty or may give her love to a more handsome man; if he is rich, he fears that his parsimony in the past may stand in his way. To tell the truth, no one can number the fears of one single lover. This kind of love, then, is a suffering which is felt by only one of the persons and may be called "single love." But even after both are in love the fears that arise are just as great, for each of the lovers fears that what he has acquired with so much effort may be lost through the effort of someone else, which is certainly much worse for a man than if, having no hope, he sees that his efforts are accomplishing nothing, for it is worse to lose the things you are seeking than to be deprived of a gain you merely hope for. The lover fears, too, that he may offend his loved one in some way; indeed he fears so many things that it would be difficult to tell them.

That this suffering is inborn I shall show you clearly, because if you will look at the truth and distinguish carefully you will see that it does not arise out of any action; only from the reflection of the mind upon what it sees does this suffering come. For when a man sees some woman fit for love and shaped according to his taste, he begins at once to lust after her in his heart; then the more he thinks about her the more he burns with love, until he comes to a fuller meditation. Presently he begins to think about the fashioning of the woman and to differentiate her limbs, to think about what she does, and to pry into the secrets of her body, and he desires to put each part of it to the fullest use. Then after he has come to this complete meditation, love cannot hold the reins, but he proceeds at once to action; straightway he

---

between 1170 and 1174, when Eleanor virtually governed as duchess of Aquitaine; Marie visited again and conducted business with Andreas Capellanus between 1182 and 1186. Some of the detail in *The Art of Courtly Love* concerning court life at Poitiers seems related to the earlier period, but at least one topical reference applies to the years 1184 to 1186, so Capellanus probably began the work in the 1170s and finished it in the 1180s. The only date given in the book is May 1, 1174, the date of a letter from Marie wherein she expresses her opinion concerning a problem of love.

No early manuscript version of *The Art of Courtly Love* survives; the Latin original became popular throughout Europe in the thirteenth century. A French translation appeared in 1287, and Italian and Spanish versions followed in the fourteenth century.

strives to get a helper to find an intermediary. He begins to plan how he may find favor with her, and he begins to seek a place and a time opportune for talking; he looks upon a brief hour as a very long year, because he cannot do anything fast enough to suit his eager mind. It is well known that many things happen to him in this manner. This inborn suffering comes, therefore, from seeing and meditating. Not every kind of meditation can be the cause of love, an excessive one is required; for a restrained thought does not, as a rule, return to the mind, and so love cannot arise from it.

Chapter 2
Between What Persons Love May Exist

Now, in love you should note first of all that love cannot exist except between persons of opposite sexes. Between two men or two women love can find no place, for we see that two persons of the same sex are not at all fitted for giving each other the exchanges of love or for practicing the acts natural to it. Whatever nature forbids, love is ashamed to accept. [. . .]

Chapter 4
What the Effect of Love Is

Now it is the effect of love that a true lover cannot be degraded with any avarice. Love causes a rough and uncouth man to be distinguished for his handsomeness; it can endow a man even of the humblest birth with nobility of character; it blesses the proud with humility; and the man in love becomes accustomed to performing many services gracefully for everyone. O what a wonderful thing is love, which makes a man shine with so many virtues and teaches everyone, no matter who he is, so many good traits of character! There is another thing about love that we should not praise in few words: it adorns a man, so to speak, with the virtue of chastity, because he who shines with the light of one love can hardly think of embracing another woman, even a beautiful one. For when he thinks deeply of his beloved the sight of any other woman seems to his mind rough and rude. [. . .]

Chapter 5
What Persons Are Fit for Love

We must now see what persons are fit to bear the arms of love. You should know that everyone of sound mind who is capable of doing the work of Venus may be wounded by one of love's arrows unless prevented by age, or blindness, or excess of passion. [. . .]

An excess of passion is a bar to love, because there are men who are slaves to such passionate desire that they cannot be held in the bonds of love — men who, after they have thought long about some woman or even enjoyed her, when they see another woman straightway desire her embraces, and they forget about the services they have received from their first love and they feel no gratitude for them. Men of this kind lust after every woman they see; their love is like that of a shameless dog. They should rather, I believe, be compared to asses, for they are moved only by that low nature which shows that men are on the level of the other animals rather than by that true nature which sets us apart from all the other animals by the difference of reason. [. . .]

Chapter 6
In What Manner Love May Be Acquired, and in How Many Ways

It remains next to be seen in what ways love may be acquired. [. . .]

A beautiful figure wins love with very little effort, especially when the lover who is sought is simple, for a simple lover thinks that there is nothing to look for in one's beloved besides a beautiful figure and face and a body well cared for.

[But] a wise woman will seek as a lover a man of praiseworthy character—not one who anoints himself all over like a woman or makes a rite of the care of the body, for it does not go with a masculine figure to adorn oneself in womanly fashion or to be devoted to the care of the body. [. . .]

Likewise, if you see a woman too heavily rouged you will not be taken in by her beauty unless you have already discovered that she is good company besides, since a woman who puts all her reliance on her rouge usually doesn't have any particular gifts of character. As I said about men, so with women—I believe you should not seek for beauty so much as for excellence of character. [. . .] For since all of us human beings are derived originally from the same stock and all naturally claim the same ancestor, it was not beauty or care of the body or even abundance of possessions, but excellence of character alone which first made a distinction of nobility among men and led to the difference of class. [. . .]

Character alone, then, is worthy of the crown of love. Many times fluency of speech will incline to love the hearts of those who do not love, for an elaborate line of talk on the part of the lover usually sets love's arrows a-flying and creates a presumption in favor of the excellent character of the speaker. How this may be I shall try to show you as briefly as I can.

To this end I shall first explain to you that one woman belongs to the middle class, a second to the simple nobility, and a third to the higher nobility. So it is with men: one is of the middle class, another of the nobility, a third of the higher nobility, and a fourth of the very highest nobility. What I mean by a woman of the middle class is clear enough to you; a noblewoman is one descended from an untitled nobleman [vavasor] or a lord, or is the wife of one of these, while a woman of the higher nobility is descended from great lords. The same rules apply to men, except that a man married to a woman of higher or lower rank than himself does not change his rank. A married woman changes her status to match that of her husband, but a man can never change his nobility by marriage. In addition, among men we find one rank more than among women, since there is a man more noble than any of these, that is, the clerk.

. . .

Chapter 11
The Love of Peasants

[. . .] If you should, by some chance, fall in love with a peasant woman, be careful to puff her up with lots of praise, and then, when you find a convenient place, do not hesitate to take what you seek and to embrace her by force. For you can hardly soften their outward inflexibility so far that they will grant you their embraces quietly or permit you to have the solaces you desire unless first you use a little compulsion as a convenient cure for their shyness. We do not say these things, however, because we want to persuade you to love such women, but only so that, if through lack of caution you should be driven to love them, you may know, in brief compass, what to do.

FROM

BOOK II
HOW LOVE MAY BE RETAINED

Chapter 1
How Love, When It Has Been Acquired, May Be Kept

Now since we have already said enough about acquiring love, it is not unfitting that we should next see and describe how this love may be retained after it has once been acquired. The man who wants to keep his love affair for a long time untroubled should above all things be careful not to let it be known to any outsider, but should keep it hidden from everybody; because when a number of people begin to get wind of such an affair, it ceases to develop naturally and even loses what progress it has already made. Furthermore a lover ought to appear to his beloved wise in every respect and restrained in his conduct, and he should do nothing disagreeable that might annoy her. And if inadvertently he should do something improper that offends her, let him straightway confess with downcast face that he has done wrong, and let him give the excuse that he lost his temper or make some other suitable explanation that will fit the case. And every man ought to be sparing of praise of his beloved when he is among other men; he should not spend a great deal of time in places where she is. When he is with other men, if he meets her in a group of women, he should not try to communicate with her by signs, but should treat her almost like a stranger lest some person spying on their love might have opportunity to spread malicious gossip. Lovers should not even nod to each other unless they are sure that nobody is watching them. Every man should also wear things that his beloved likes and pay a reasonable amount of attention to his appearance—not too much because excessive care for one's looks is distasteful to everybody and leads people to despise the good looks that one has. If the lover is lavish in giving, that helps him retain a love he has acquired, for all lovers ought to despise all worldly riches and should give alms to those who have need of them. Also, if the lover is one who is fitted to be a warrior, he should see to it that his courage is apparent to everybody, for it detracts very much from the good character of a man if he is timid in a fight. A lover should always offer his services and obedience freely to every lady, and he ought to root out all his pride and be very humble. Then, too, he must keep in mind the general rule that lovers must not neglect anything that good manners demand or good breeding suggests, but they should be very careful to do everything of this sort. Love may also be retained by indulging in the sweet and delightful solaces of the flesh, but only in such manner and in such number that they may never seem wearisome to the loved one. Let the lover strive to practice gracefully and manfully any act or mannerism which he has noticed is pleasing to his beloved. A clerk should not, of course, affect the manners or the dress of the laity, for no one is likely to please his beloved, if she is a wise woman, by wearing strange clothing or by practicing manners that do not suit his status. Furthermore a lover should make every attempt to be constantly in the company of good men and to avoid completely the society of the wicked. For association with the vulgar makes a lover who joins them a thing of contempt to his beloved. [. . .]

Chapter 2
How Love, Once Consummated, May Be Increased

We shall attempt to show you in a few words how love may be increased after it has been consummated. Now in the first place it is said to increase if the lovers see each other rarely and with difficulty; for the greater the difficulty of exchanging solaces, the more do the desire for them and the feeling of love increase. Love increases, too, if one of the lovers shows that he is angry at the other; for the lover falls at once into a great fear that this feeling which has arisen in his beloved may last forever. Love increases, likewise, if one of the lovers feels real jealousy, which is called, in fact, the nurse of love. Even if he does not suffer from real jealousy, but from a shameful suspicion, still by virtue of this his love always increases and grows more powerful. Love increases, too, if it happens to last after it has been made public; ordinarily it does not last, but begins to fail just as soon as it is revealed. Again, if one of the lovers dreams about the other, that gives rise to love, or if love already exists it increases it. So, too, if you know that someone is trying to win your beloved away from you, that will no doubt increase your love and you will begin to feel more affection for her. I will go further and say that even though you know perfectly well that some other man is enjoying the embraces of your beloved, this will make you begin to value her solaces all the more, unless your greatness of soul and nobility of mind keep you from such wickedness. When you have gone to some other place or are about to go away—that increases your love, and so do the scoldings and beatings that lovers suffer from their parents, for not only does a scolding lecture cause love to increase after it is perfected, but it even gives a perfect reason for beginning a love affair that has not yet started. Frequent dwelling with delight on the thought of the beloved is of value in increasing love; so is the sight of her eyes when you are by yourselves and fearful, and her eager acceptance of a demand for the acts of love. Love is greatly intensified by a carriage and a way of walking that please the beloved, by a readiness to say pretty things, by a pleasant manner of speaking, and by hearing men sing the praises of the loved one. [. . .]

Chapter 3
In What Ways Love May Be Decreased

Now let us see in what ways love may be decreased. Too many opportunities for exchanging solaces, too many opportunities of seeing the loved one, too much chance to talk to each other all decrease love, and so does an uncultured appearance or manner of walking on the part of the lover or the sudden loss of his property. [. . .] Love decreases, too, if the woman finds that her lover is foolish and indiscreet, or if he seems to go beyond reasonable bounds in his demands for love, or if she sees that he has no regard for her modesty and will not forgive her bashfulness. [. . .] Love decreases, too, if the woman considers that her lover is cowardly in battle, or sees that he is unrestrained in his speech or spoiled by the vice of arrogance. [. . .]

Other things which weaken love are blasphemy against God or His saints, mockery of the ceremonies of the Church, and a deliberate withholding of charity from the poor. We find that love decreases very sharply if one is unfaithful to his friend, or if he brazenly says one thing while he deceitfully conceals a different idea in his heart. Love decreases, too, if the lover piles up more wealth than is proper, or if he is too ready to go to law over trifles. [. . .]

Chapter 4
How Love May Come to an End

Now having treated briefly of the lessening of love we shall try next to add for you an explanation of how it may come to an end. First of all we see that love comes to an end if one of the lovers breaks faith or tries to break faith with the other, or if he is found to go astray from the Catholic religion. It comes to an end also after it has been openly revealed and made known to men. So, too, if one of the lovers has plenty of money and does not come to the aid of the other who is in great need and lacks a great many things, then love usually becomes very cheap and comes to an ignominious end. An old love also ends when a new one begins, because no one can love two people at the same time. Furthermore, inequality of love and a fraudulent and deceitful duplicity of heart always drive out love, for a deceitful lover, no matter how worthy he is otherwise, ought to be rejected by any woman. [. . .] Again, if by some chance one of the lovers becomes incapable of carrying out love's duties, love can no longer last between them and deserts them completely. Likewise if one of the lovers becomes insane or develops a sudden timidity, love flees and becomes hateful.

You may, however, ask whether a love once ended can ever come to life again. If this failure of love comes from ignorance of some particular thing, there is no doubt but that it may be revived; however, where it grows out of some misdeed of the lover or of some defect in his nature, we cannot remember any case where it has revived, although we do not say that it cannot, except perhaps in cases where this failure is due to some defect in the lover's nature. And if love should at some time happen to come to life again, we do not think that the lovers would have perfect confidence in each other.

Chapter 5
Indications That One's Love Is Returned

Now that we have thus disposed of these questions and have, in a short space, finished them up, let us add to them a discussion of how to find out whether one's love is returned. [. . .] There are many ways in which a lover can find out the faith of his beloved and test her feelings. If you see that your loved one is missing all sorts of opportunities to meet you or is putting false obstacles in your path, you cannot hope long to enjoy her love. So, too, if you find her, for no reason at all, growing half-hearted about giving you the usual solaces, you may see that her faith is wavering. If you find that she keeps out of your sight more than she was accustomed to do, her feelings are not very stable; and if she tries to hide from your faithful messenger, there is no doubt that she has turned you adrift in the mighty waves and that her love for you is only feigned. [. . .] If at the very moment of delight when she is offering you her sweet solaces the act is more wearisome to her than usual, you need not doubt that she has no love for you. So, too, if she finds more fault with you than usual or demands things that she has not been in the habit of demanding, you may know that your love will not last much longer. Again, if when she is with you or someone else she frequently talks about what you did and what the other man did, without making any distinction between you, or if on some clever pretext she asks what sort of man he is or what sort of character he has, you may know that she is thinking about the love of the other man. Moreover, if you find that she is paying more attention to the care of her person than she had been doing, either her love for you is growing or she is interested in the love of someone else. [. . .]

Chapter 6
If One of the Lovers Is Unfaithful to the Other

If one of the lovers should be unfaithful to the other, and the offender is the man, and he has an eye to a new love affair, he renders himself wholly unworthy of his former love, and she ought to deprive him completely of her embraces. [. . .]

But what if he should be unfaithful to his beloved, — not with the idea of finding a new love, but because he has been driven to it by an irresistible passion for another woman? What, for instance, if chance should present to him an unknown woman in a convenient place or what if at a time when Venus is urging him on to that which I am talking about he should meet with a little strumpet or somebody's servant girl? Should he, just because he played with her in the grass, lose the love of his beloved? We can say without fear of contradiction that just for this a lover is not considered unworthy of the love of his beloved unless he indulges in so many excesses with a number of women that we may conclude that he is overpassionate. But if whenever he becomes acquainted with a woman he pesters her to gain his end, or if he attains his object as a result of his efforts, then rightly he does deserve to be deprived of his former love, because there is strong presumption that he has acted in this way with an eye toward a new one, especially where he has strayed with a woman of the nobility or otherwise of an honorable estate.

[. . .] I know that once when I sought advice I got the answer that a true lover can never desire a new love unless he knows that for some definite and sufficient reason the old love is dead; we know from our own experience that this rule is very true. We have fallen in love with a woman of the most admirable character, although we have never had, or hope to have, any fruit of this love. For we are compelled to pine away for love of a woman of such lofty station that we dare not say one word about it, nor dare we throw ourself upon her mercy, and so at length we are forced to find our body shipwrecked. But although rashly and without foresight we have fallen into such great waves in this tempest, still we cannot think about a new love or look for any other way to free ourself.

But since you are making a special study of the subject of love, you may well ask whether a man can have a pure love for one woman and a mixed or common love with another. We will show you, by an unanswerable argument, that no one can feel affection for two women in this fashion. For although pure love and mixed love may seem to be very different things, if you will look at the matter properly you will see that pure love, so far as its substance goes, is the same as mixed love and comes from the same feeling of the heart. The substance of the love is the same in each case, and only the manner and form of loving are different, as this illustration will make clear to you. Sometimes we see a man with a desire to drink his wine unmixed, and at another time his appetite prompts him to drink only water or wine and water mixed; although his appetite manifests itself differently, the substance of it is the same and unchanged. So likewise when two people have long been united by pure love and afterwards desire to practice mixed love, the substance of the love remains the same in them, although the manner and form and the way of practicing it are different. [. . .]

Chapter 7
Various Decisions in Love Cases

Now then, let us come to various decisions in cases of love:

V.   A certain knight loved his lady beyond all measure and enjoyed her full embrace, but she did not love him with equal ardor. He sought to leave her, but she, desiring to retain him in his former status, opposed his wish. In this affair the Countess of Champagne gave this response: "It is considered very unseemly for a woman to seek to be loved and yet to refuse to love. It is silly for anybody disrespectfully to ask of others what she herself wholly refuses to give to others." [. . .]

IX.   A certain man asked [. . .] [Lady Ermengarde of Narbonne] to make clear where there was the greater affection—between lovers or between married people. The lady gave him a logical answer. She said: "We consider that marital affection and the true love of lovers are wholly different and arise from entirely different sources, and so the ambiguous nature of the word prevents the comparison of the things and we have to place them in different classes. Comparisons of more or less are not valid when things are grouped together under an ambiguous heading and the comparison is made in regard to that ambiguous term. It is no true comparison to say that a name is simpler than a body or that the outline of a speech is better arranged than the delivery."

X.   The same man asked the same lady this question. A certain woman had been married, but was now separated from her husband by a divorce, and her former husband sought eagerly for her love. In this case the lady replied: "If any two people have been married and afterwards separate in any way, we consider love between them wholly wicked." [. . .]

XVI.   A certain knight was in love with a woman who had given her love to another man, but he got from her this much hope of her love—that if it should ever happen that she lost the love of her beloved, then without a doubt her love would go to this man. A little while after this the woman married her lover. The other knight then demanded that she give him the fruit of the hope she had granted him, but this she absolutely refused to do, saying that she had not lost the love of her lover. In this affair the Queen gave her decision as follows: "We dare not oppose the opinion of the Countess of Champagne, who ruled that love can exert no power between husband and wife. Therefore we recommend that the lady should grant the love she has promised." [. . .]

XX. The Queen was also asked which was preferable: the love of a young man or of one advanced in years. She answered this question with wonderful subtlety by saying, "We distinguish between a good and a better love by the man's knowledge and his character and his praiseworthy manners, not by his age. But as regards that natural instinct of passion, young men are usually more eager to gratify it with older women than with young ones of their own age; those who are older prefer to receive the embraces and kisses of young women rather than of the older ones. But on the other hand a woman whether young or somewhat older likes the embraces and solaces of young men better than those of older ones. The explanation of this fact seems to be a physiological one." [. . .]

Chapter 8
The Rules of Love

Let us come now to the rules of love, and I shall try to present to you very briefly those rules which the King of Love is said to have proclaimed with his own mouth and to have given in writing to all lovers. [. . .]

These are the rules.

I.   Marriage is no real excuse for not loving.

II.   He who is not jealous cannot love.

III.   No one can be bound by a double love.

IV.   It is well known that love is always increasing or decreasing.

V.   That which a lover takes against his will of his beloved has no relish.

VI.   Boys do not love until they arrive at the age of maturity.

VII.   When one lover dies, a widowhood of two years is required of the survivor.

VIII.   No one should be deprived of love without the very best of reasons.

IX.   No one can love unless he is impelled by the persuasion of love.

X.	Love is always a stranger in the home of avarice.
XI.	It is not proper to love any woman whom one should be ashamed to seek to marry.
XII.	A true lover does not desire to embrace in love anyone except his beloved.
XIII.	When made public love rarely endures.
XIV.	The easy attainment of love makes it of little value; difficulty of attainment makes it prized.
XV.	Every lover regularly turns pale in the presence of his beloved.
XVI.	When a lover suddenly catches sight of his beloved his heart palpitates.
XVII.	A new love puts to flight an old one.
XVIII.	Good character alone makes any man worthy of love.
XIX.	If love diminishes, it quickly fails and rarely revives.
XX.	A man in love is always apprehensive.
XXI.	Real jealousy always increases the feeling of love.
XXII.	Jealousy, and therefore love, are increased when one suspects his beloved.
XXIII.	He whom the thought of love vexes, eats and sleeps very little.
XXIV.	Every act of a lover ends in the thought of his beloved.
XXV.	A true lover considers nothing good except what he thinks will please his beloved.
XXVI.	Love can deny nothing to love.
XXVII.	A lover can never have enough of the solaces of his beloved.
XXVIII.	A slight presumption causes a lover to suspect his beloved.
XXIX.	A man who is vexed by too much passion usually does not love.
XXX.	A true lover is constantly and without intermission possessed by the thought of his beloved.
XXXI.	Nothing forbids one woman being loved by two men or one man by two women.

The Courtly Love Lyrics of Muslim Spain and the South of France

The creation of the most renowned love lyrics of the European Middle Ages depended on three principal factors: the rich Arabic culture in the Andalusian (Spanish) courts in the eleventh century; the development of the neighboring courts in the south of France in the twelfth and early thirteenth centuries; and the spread of the idea of refined love, of which one example is *The Art of Courtly Love*, written in Latin by Andreas Capellanus between 1174 and 1186. One important feature of this literary movement was the veneration of women; along with it came the sublimation of sexual longing expressed in the poetry. At the same time, themes of knights in combat, so popular at the beginning of the Crusades, gave way to a more idealized form of chivalry, emphasizing the practice of good manners and fidelity to the rules of love at court.

ANDALUSIAN ORIGINS

Following their expansion through Asia Minor, North Africa, and Spain in the eighth century, the conquering Muslims soon developed a more open, tolerant society, declaring that the Christians and Jews living under their authority were **PEOPLE OF THE BOOK** (Hebrew Scriptures and the New Testament) and protecting them within the Islamic state. This protection proved important in Andalusia, under

Lovers, 1344 ▶

While the earliest courtly love poetry had its roots in Muslim Spain, its European counterpart lasted well into the fourteenth century, as this late manuscript illumination of a gentleman paying court to a lady attests. (The Art Archive / Science Academy, Lisbon / Dagli Orti)

whose CALIPHATE (the leading religious and political office) Muslims, Christians, and Jews freely enjoyed mutual commerce and communication. In this way, the population shared a common culture deferential to Islam, and developed a mixed language composed of Spanish, Hebrew, and Arabic elements called *MOZARABIC.*[1]

moh-ZEH-ruh-bik

Andalusia inherited the rich Islamic culture of the Middle East, famous for its architecture, philosophy, literature, music, and courtly society. Borrowing from the ancient Arabic poetic tradition that included the lengthy and complex *QASIDAHS* or odes, Andalusian writers had a sophisticated base on which to create their work. The new poetry, with its apparent spontaneity dictated in part by traditional rules of composition, reflected the cultivation of the courtly society. While the language usually employed for this poetry was Arabic, Jewish writers also adapted Hebrew poetry to fit the new style. Gradually Andalusian poetry adopted vernacular forms of expression from the Mozarabic language, broadening its popular appeal.

kuh-SEE-duhs

Geography played an important role in the contact between Andalusian culture and the south of France. The southern French provinces of **Toulouse**, Aquitaine, and **Provence** were more closely related by travel and trade to northern Spain in the eleventh century than they were to Paris; the major trade route led south through Toledo to **Cordova**, the cultural center of Andalusia. After the interruption occasioned by the Christian conquest of the city of **Toledo** in 1085, Andalusia continued to support peaceful relations among Muslims, Jews, and Christians. The sophisticated Arabic courts greeted poets and performers from southern France who visited Spain as late as the twelfth century.[2]

too-LOOZ;
proh-VAWNS

KORE-duh-vuh
toh-LAY-doh

ARABIC, JEWISH, AND MOZARABIC POETRY

The cosmopolitan culture of Andalusia reached its height in Cordova in the tenth and eleventh centuries. During this time the

---

[1] **Mozarabic:** The word originally meant "one who adopts the manners of the Arabs" and applied to Arabianized Christians. It was later applied to language, meaning the Romance dialect of Andalusia as it was influenced by Hebrew and Arabic. The term accounts for the vernacular language found in the poems included here.

[2] **The sophisticated . . . century:** The Christian Reconquest of Spain, begun under Pope Alexander II (1061–1073), proceeded slowly. Toledo, which fell to the Christians in 1085, became the major point of cultural contact between Christians and Muslims throughout the next century. It remained so until Pope Innocent III declared a Crusade against the Spanish Muslims in 1211.

GHAZAL or love poem developed from the opening lines of the classical *qasidah;* originally distinguished by nostalgia, the *ghazal* became increasingly direct and sensual. Love was either celebrated as a source of exuberant joy or regarded as an unhealthy obsession. Eventually two more poetic forms grew out of the *ghazal.* One, the MUWASHSHAH, contained five or six identically rhymed strophes followed by a short concluding stanza called a KHARJA, expressing direct emotion, usually in Mozarabic. The second form, the ZAJAL, consisted of elaborately rhymed strophes or stanzas in Mozarabic, without the *kharja* ending. The development of these types of love poetry made Andalusian poetry more immediate in tone.

Several trends were at work in Andalusian poetry at this time. **Ibn Hazm**, a young poet and scholar from Cordova, wrote *The Dove's Necklace,* a treatise on love including many of his own poems, in 1022. His poetry and other Arabic and Jewish poetry of his day expressed the ideal of refinement in love, deriving largely from the influence of the Greek philosopher Plato.[3] Some of the poets cited by Ibn Hazm in his treatise, such as Ibn Faraj, carried this idea even further by proclaiming their chastity. Other Arabic love poetry of Ibn Hazm's time was less refined. In the eleventh century the Muslim court of Cordova saw an exchange of poetry between the famous courtier **Ibn Zaydun** and his lover Wallada, the daughter of the last of the caliphs in her family line. Zaydun's meditative *ghazal,* "Written from Al-Zahrā," expresses the melancholy typical of earlier Arabic odes, while Wallada's passionate lyric "To Ibn Zaidun" gives way to obsessive, tormented longing, told directly in the present tense. These pieces may have encouraged later poetic exchanges between male and female writers in the south of France.

In the early twelfth century a number of Jewish poets, including **Judah ha-Levi** (Yehuda Ha Levi), wrote poems in Hebrew employing the Arabic style. His love poems also recall the lush imagery of The Song of Solomon from Hebrew Scriptures. The poem "The Apple" combines Arabic and Hebrew sentiment, describing the captivity of the male lover in terms of courtly love and the physical attributes of his beloved in the language of the Scriptures.

GAZ-ul

moo-WAH-shah
KAR-juh
zah-JAHL

IB-un HAH-zum,
HAZ-um
p. 637

p. 646

IB-un zigh-DOON
p. 647 / p. 648

p. 651
JOO-duh hah-LAY-vee

---

[3] **Plato** (428–347 B.C.E.): At the heart of Ibn Hazm's teachings on love is Plato's *Symposium,* which stresses the sublimation of the passions and the use of the intellect in matters of love.

Further development in Andalusian love poetry came when the conventional Arabic or Hebrew love poems called *muwashshahs* incorporated tag endings called *kharjas,* usually written in Mozarabic. The provocative sayings in the *kharjas* breathed life into the sentiments of the *muwashshahs,* as seen in an elaborate example, "He who has charged the eyes," probably written by **Ibn al-Labbana**, p. 653 in the late eleventh or early twelfth century. Meanwhile, the love poem called the *zajal,* written entirely in the vernacular to express immediacy of feeling, often poked fun at the more spiritual types of courtly love poetry. In one striking *zajal,* "I am madly in love," **Ibn Quzman**, p. 654 celebrates the joys of the tavern rather than the refinement of court.

IB-un ahl-lah-BAH-nuh

IB-un kuz-MAHN

DEVELOPMENTS IN THE SOUTH OF FRANCE

In part because of a booming agricultural economy and an increase in trade generated by the Crusades, rich courts developed in the south of France, especially in Provence, Languedoc, and Aquitaine, in the latter half of the eleventh century. The region was distinguished by its unique language, Provençal, and its cultural refinement. Especially famous was the love poetry composed by professional artists at court called troubadours, who sometimes accompanied themselves on a musical instrument but more often were accompanied by a musician called a *joglar.*

There was a strong historical reason for the patronage of poetry by these courts. Changes in property laws allowed women to inherit estates, and several women, notably Eleanor of Aquitaine and her daughter, Marie of Champagne, established reputations not only as new members of the landed nobility but also as patrons of the arts. They particularly encouraged the composition of songs of love. They also may have been responsible for introducing ideas of jurisprudence into the love poems designed for courtly entertainment. Knights and other court followers were taught to plead a case for their love, and Eleanor and her daughter even passed down "verdicts" on the love pleadings in the court of Poitiers, one of the leading cities in southern France.

The Provençal poetry is often associated with the treatise *The Art of Courtly Love,* written by the twelfth century priest Andreas Capellanus at the court in Poitiers. In it, Capellanus examines the

Troubadour, thirteenth century
*A troubadour plays musical court to two princesses and their attendants. (The Art
Archive / Real Biblioteca de lo Escorial / Dagli Orti)*

phenomenon of *fin'amor,* or refined love, as it was practiced in the
lavish courts of his day. This doctrine of love, which later scholars
would term courtly love, lay behind much of the poetry being
written in the region in the twelfth century. The kind of love discussed by Capellanus includes the sublimation of sexual desire; the
worship of the aristocratic lady of one's choosing; and obedience to
the rules of secrecy and discretion.[4] Some of this work was probably
seen as entertainment, designed to flatter and delight the lord and
lady of the household. But the doctrine of *fin'amor* also may have
been intended to educate all men and women of rank in courtly
society in the etiquette properly attached to love.

---

[4]The kind of love . . . discretion.: See the section on Andreas Capellanus, p. 611.

PROVENÇAL POETRY

gee-YOME

The first Provençal troubadour, **Guillaume IX**, duke of Aquitaine, p. 655, preceded Andreas Capellanus by several generations. He composed love poems in two different styles, bawdy and refined. Eventually his zesty tales of sexual exploits, replete with double meanings and vulgar humor, gave way to more sophisticated poems of *fin'amor*. Guillaume's later patronage encouraged other poets to follow in his footsteps, and also may have influenced their choice of themes.

mar-kuh-BROO

A cautious approach to love can be found in **Marcabru**'s p. 660, "By the fountain in the orchard." Here, a knight attempting to catch a lady's attention defers to her despondency over the absence of her lover, who is off on Crusade. Seeing her innocence reflected in her failure to understand his flirtation, the knight wisely retreats. Later in the twelfth century, Bernart de Ventadorn, p. 661, helped signal the further triumph of refinement over vulgarity in the Provençal tradition. In "My heart is so full of joy," an ironic celebration of the possession of a lady's "image" instead of the lady herself, he purges the subject of love of any crudity and shapes his disappointment into a gently humorous work of art.

One consequence of the poetry of *fin'amor* was the elevation of women to a position of near-adoration. In medieval society this represented a considerable advance for the women at court, surrounded as they were by a hitherto unruly and unmannerly knighthood. And yet, the women still were spoken for, rather than speaking for themselves. Gradually, however, women of high birth developed a poetic idiom of their own. As had happened in the Arabic courts of Spain, some European women became poets and performers. In the following pages, a humorous courtly poem by **Raimbaut d'Orange**, p. 664,

rem-BOH
d'oh-RAWNZH

kah-steh-YOH-sah

troh-bigh-RITS

is followed by two poems by the countess of Dia, p. 666, rumored to have been Raimbaut's lover, and a later work by a woman, **Castelloza**, p. 668, that emphasizes the practical and somber concerns of a woman poet, or TROBAIRITZ such as herself.

THE FATE OF THE LYRIC TRADITION

In both Andalusia and the south of France, the courtly poets suffered a cruel fate in the thirteenth century. In Andalusia, the Spanish Reconquest was virtually assured by the Christian victory over

Muslim forces at Las Navas de Tolosa, between Toledo and Cordova, in 1212. Cordova fell in 1236, and the activity of the remaining Andalusian courts was significantly curtailed. Meanwhile, in 1209 Pope Innocent III preached the Albigensian Crusade, directed against the rulers of the south of France who had tolerated the presence of **Catharist** heretics in their region. The **Cathars** believed in divinity as pure spirit, challenging the Christian belief in the body of Jesus Christ. After the first wave of Crusaders was defeated, King Louis VIII of France provided the pope with an army, and the campaign developed an added objective, the annexation of the south of France. Soon the southern courts and their cultures were all but destroyed and the Provençal language was officially replaced by French. Whatever was left of the old culture was quashed in the middle of the thirteenth century by the heresy hunters of the Catholic Inquisition, who followed the Crusaders into the region.

KATH-ur-ist; KATH-urz

Meanwhile, the love songs of the troubadours and the doctrine of *fin'amor* had spread across Europe, influencing the poets of Spain and Portugal, northern France, Germany, and Italy (including the youthful **Dante Alighieri**). Versions of the same lyrics traveled even farther, to England, Scandinavia, and Russia. Even under the watchful eyes of the Catholic Church the songs of love were revived, only now the "lady" addressed by the Christian poets was the Virgin Mary. And while love poems exist in many forms around the world, the courtly lyrics of Andalusia and Provence set the standard for this poetry in western Europe for an entire millennium.

DAHN-tay
ah-lih-GYAH-ree

■ **CONNECTIONS**

The Tamil Anthology, **p. 212.** The love poems in the second and third century *Tamil Anthology* from India capture the personal voice of the lovers: lyrically in the case of the woman ("What She Said," *Kuruntokai* 25, 68, 325); more circumstantially in the case of the man ("What He Said," *Kuruntokai* 131). How do the personal voices of the women and men in the Arabic and Provençal poetry compare with their counterparts from India?

The Man'yoshu, **p. 1018.** The ancient love poetry of this eighth century Japanese anthology, especially the odes or *chokas* of Kakinomoto Hitomaro, invites comparison with Andalusian love poetry, for example the meditative *ghazal* "Written from Al-Zahrā" by Ibn Zaydun. How do the Japanese *chokas* compare with the Andalusian *ghazal*? How do they differ?

The Kokinshu, **p. 1044.** This tenth-century Japanese poetry anthology contained thousands of five-line poems called *tanka,* which crystallize emotion in a quickly developing image. How do Andalusian poems such as Ibn Hazm's "My Beloved Comes" or Ibn Faraj's "Chastity" resemble the Japanese *tanka*? How do they differ?

■ FURTHER RESEARCH

Anthologies and Collections

Franzen, Cola. *Poems of Arab Andalusia.* 1989.

Goldin, Frederick. *Lyrics of the Troubadours and Trouvères.* 1963.

Monroe, James, ed. *Hispano-Arabic Poetry: A Student Anthology.* 1974.

O'Donoghue, Bernard. *The Courtly Love Tradition.* 1982.

Press, Alan R. *Anthology of Troubadour Lyric Poetry.* 1971.

Wilhelm, James J., ed. *Lyrics of the Middle Ages: An Anthology.* 1990.

History

O'Shea, Stephen. *The Perfect Heresy: The Revolutionary Life and Death of the Medieval Cathars.* 2000.

Sumption, Jonathan. *The Albigensian Crusade.* 1978.

Literary History and Criticism

Bogin, Meg. *The Women Troubadours.* 1980.

Briffault, Robert. *The Troubadours.* 1965.

Dronke, Peter. *Medieval Latin and the Rise of European Love-Lyric.* 2 vols. 1968.

———. *The Medieval Lyric.* 3d ed. 1996.

———. "The Provençal Trobairitz: Castelloza." In *Medieval Women Writers,* edited by Katharina Wilson. 1984.

Glier, Ingeborg. "Troubadours and Minnesang." In Boris Ford, ed. *Medieval Literature, Part Two: The European Inheritance.* 1984.

■ PRONUNCIATION

Andalusian: an-duh-LOO-zhuhn

Aquitaine: AH-kwih-tayn, ah-kee-TAHN

canso: kahn-SOH

Castelloza: kah-steh-YOH-sah

Cathars, Catharist: KATH-urz, KATH-ur-ist

coblas unissonans: KOH-blahs oo-nih-soh-NAHNS

Cordova: KORE-duh-vuh

courtoisie: koor-twah-zee

Dante Alighieri: DAHN-tay ah-lih-GYAY-ree

fin'amor: fin-ah-MORE

ghazal: GAZ-ul

Guillaume: gee-YOME

Ibn al-Labbana: IB-un ahl-lah-BAH-nuh

Ibn Hazm: IB-un HAH-zum, HAZ-um

Ibn Quzman: IB-un kooz-MAHN

Ibn Zaydun: IB-un zigh-DOON

joglar: joh-GLAR

Judah ha-Levi: JOO-duh hah-LAY-vee

kharja: KAR-juh

lais: LAY

Marcabru: mar-kuh-BROO

Mozarabic: moh-ZEH-ruh-bik

muwashshah: moo-WAH-shah

Provençal: proh-vawn-SAHL

Provence: proh-VAWNS, proh-VAWNGS

qasidah: kuh-SEE-duh

Raimbaut d'Orange: rem-BOH doh-RAWNZH

sirvente: seer-VEN-tay

Thibaut de Champagne: TEE-boh duh-shawm-PAH-nyuh

Toledo: toh-LAY-doh
Toulouse: too-LOOZ
trobairitz: troh-bigh-RITS
troubadour: troo-bah-DOHR
vers: VEHRS
zajal: zah-JAHL

∾ Ibn Hazm
994–1064

Ibn Hazm, an Islamic philosopher known for his encyclopedic treatment of the religions of the West and Asia Minor, endured many hardships as a young man. The sack of his native Cordova by Berber tribesmen in 1012, the death of his father later the same year, and the death of his first love in 1013 led to his decision to dedicate himself to serious studies as a moral and spiritual response to an unstable world. He accepted a request less than a decade later to write a treatise on love, stating that those who have grieved excessively should perform an apparently light task in order to strengthen the soul for hard work ahead. He completed the treatise in 1022, before reaching thirty.

The Dove's Necklace.   The treatise entitled *Tawq al-hamamah,* or *The Dove's Necklace,* consisted of thirty chapters "about love and lovers." A remarkable example of Arabic *adab,* or sophisticated writing—what Europeans call *belles lettres*—this frank treatment of love made up partly of the author's own reflections, including his poetry, was attacked by Muslim authorities for "encouraging evil"—language from the Qur'an. Nevertheless, it enjoyed immense popular success in Andalusia and was translated many times over during the European Middle Ages.

   The chief source of Ibn Hazm's philosophy of love is in the writings of Plato, especially *The Symposium.* The importance of love for Ibn Hazm lies in spiritual attainment, though he recognizes physical attraction. Like Plato and most Arabic writers of his own day, Ibn Hazm takes into account homosexual as well as heterosexual love. He distances himself from Christian teaching on one hand and Ovid's *The Art of Love,* with its emphasis on sexual conquest, on the other. At the same time, he does include a "moral" ending to his work—a chapter on continence—somewhat similar to the retractions found in other writers on love, including Ovid and Andreas Capellanus.

   The Dove's Necklace devotes ten chapters to the origins of love; twelve to the circumstances in which love is found; six to the catastrophes to which love is subject; and two to the evils of passion and the superiority of continence (which means sexual restraint rather than complete abstinence). Ibn Hazm concludes his work by listing the calamities he has

Reconciliation, thirteenth century
Very few illustrated manuscripts survive from the Andalusian (Muslim) period in Spanish history. This illustration is from a romance that tells the story of a young merchant who falls in love with a handmaiden (personal servant). In this scene the merchant supplicates the handmaiden's mistress, pleading for her help in winning the heart of his beloved. (From the "Hadith Bayad wa Riyad" manuscript, folio 26v. © Biblioteca Apostolica Vaticana)

endured in his brief lifetime and stating his hope that his good behavior in the world will justify his having written on the subject of love. The excerpt presented here includes material taken primarily from the work's first section, on the origins of love, which addresses the signs of love, falling in love through a description of the beloved, love at first sight, love after a long familiarity, and love because of a single personal quality. The final excerpt comes from a later chapter on the unity of love. These selections exclude Ibn Hazm's poetic interludes and concentrate on the prose writing.

Ibn Hazm also achieved a reputation as a poet. In his poetry, too, he stresses the spiritual aspect of love, an emphasis common among the Muslim upper classes of his time. Thus he borrows from an existing tradition when he writes about love's secrecy, its hidden signs, and its power and authority. In the poem "My Beloved Comes," his seemingly original comparison of the rainbow to the peacock's tail is an example of metaphor long practiced in the refined poetic tradition.

FROM

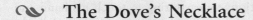 The Dove's Necklace

Translated by A. J. Arberry

Love has certain signs which the intelligent man quickly detects and the shrewd man readily recognizes. Of these the first is the brooding gaze: the eye is the wide gateway of the soul, the scrutinizer of its secrets, conveying its most private thoughts and giving expression to its deepest-hid feelings. You will see the lover gazing at the beloved unblinkingly; his eyes follow the loved one's every movement, withdrawing as he withdraws, inclining as he inclines, just as the chameleon's stare shifts with the shifting of the sun.

The lover will direct his conversation to the beloved even when he purports, however earnestly, to address another: the affection is apparent to anyone with eyes to see. When the loved one speaks, the lover listens with rapt attention to his every word; he marvels at everything the beloved says, however extraordinary and absurd his observations may be; he believes him implicitly even when he is clearly lying, agrees with him though he is obviously in the wrong, testifies on his behalf for all that he may be unjust, follows after him however he may proceed and whatever line of argument he may adopt. The lover hurries to the spot where the beloved is at the moment, endeavours to sit as near to him as possible, sidles up close to him, lays aside all occupations that might oblige him to leave his company, makes light of any matter, however weighty, that would demand his parting from him, is very slow to move when he takes his leave of him.

Other signs of love are that sudden confusion and excitement betrayed by the lover when he unexpectedly sees the one he loves coming upon him unawares, that agitation which overmasters him on beholding someone who resembles his beloved or on hearing his name suddenly pronounced. A man in love will give prodigally, to the limit of his capacity, in a way that formerly he would have refused; as if he were the one receiving the donation, he the one whose happiness is the object in view; all this in order that he may show off his good points, and make himself desirable. How often has the miser opened his purse-strings, the scowler relaxed his frown, the coward leapt heroically into the fray, the clod suddenly become sharp-witted, the boor turned into the perfect gentleman, the stinker transformed into the elegant dandy, the sloucher smartened up, the decrepit recaptured his lost youth, the godly gone wild, the self-respecting kicked over the traces—and all because of love!

All these signs are to be observed even before the fire of love is properly kindled, ere its conflagration truly bursts forth, its blaze waxes fierce, its flames leap up. But when the fire really takes a hold and is firmly established, then you will see the secret whispering, the unconcealed turning away from all present but the beloved.

Other outward signs and tokens of love are the following, which are apparent to all having eyes in their heads: abundant and exceeding cheerfulness at finding oneself with the beloved in a narrow space, and a corresponding depression on being together in a wide expanse; to engage in a playful tug of war for anything the one or the other lays hold of; much clandestine winking; leaning sideways and supporting oneself against the object of one's affection; endeavouring to touch his hand and whatever part of his body one can reach, while engaged in conversation; and drinking the remainder of what the beloved has left in his cup, seeking out the very spot against which his lips were pressed.

There are also contrary signs that occur according to casual provocations and accidental incitements and a variety of motivating causes and stimulating thoughts. Opposites are of course likes, in reality; when things reach the limit of contrariety, and stand at the furthest bounds of divergency, they come to resemble one another. This is decreed by God's omnipotent power, in a manner that baffles entirely the human imagination. Thus, when ice is pressed a long time in the hand, it finally produces the same effect as fire. We find that extreme joy and extreme sorrow kill equally; excessive and violent laughter sends the tears coursing from the eyes. It is a very common phenomenon in the world about us. Similarly with lovers: when they love each other with an equal ardour and their mutual affection is intensely strong, they will turn against one another without any valid reason, each purposely contradicting the other in whatever he may say; they quarrel violently over the smallest things, each picking up every word that the other lets fall and wilfully misinterpreting it. All these devices are aimed at testing and proving what each is seeking in the other.

Now the difference between this sham, and real aversion and contrariness born of deep-seated hatred and inveterate contention, is that lovers are very quickly reconciled after their disputes. You will see a pair of lovers seeming to have reached the extreme limit of contrariety, to the point that you would reckon not to be mended even in the instance of a person of most tranquil spirit and wholly exempt from rancour, save after a long interval, and wholly irreparable in the case of a quarrelsome man; yet in next to no time you will observe them to have become the best of friends once more; silenced are those mutual reproaches, vanished that disharmony; forthwith they are laughing again and playfully sporting together. The same scene may be enacted several times at a single session. When you see a pair of lovers behaving in such a fashion, let no doubt enter your mind, no uncertainty invade your thoughts; you may be sure without hesitation, and convinced as by an unshakable certainty, that there lies between them a deep and hidden secret—the secret of true love. Take this then for a sure test, a universally valid experiment: it is the product only of an equal partnership in love and a true concord of hearts. I myself have observed it frequently.

Another sign is when you find the lover almost entreating to hear the loved one's name pronounced, taking an extreme delight in speaking about him, so that the subject is a positive obsession with him; nothing so much rejoices him, and he is not in the least restrained by the fear that someone listening may realize what he is about, and someone present will understand his true motives. Love for a thing renders you blind and deaf. If the lover could so contrive that in the place where he happens to be there should be no talk of anything but his beloved, he would never leave that spot for any other in the whole world.

It can happen that a man sincerely affected by love will start to eat his meal with an excellent appetite; yet the instant the recollection of his loved one is excited, the food sticks in his throat and chokes his gullet. It is the same if he is drinking or talking—he begins to converse with you gaily enough, then all at once he is invaded by a chance thought of his dear one. You will notice the change in his manner of speaking, the instantaneous failure of his conversational powers; the sure signs are his long silences, the way he stares at the ground, his extreme taciturnity. One moment he is all smiles, lightly gesticulating; the next he has become completely boxed up, sluggish, distrait, rigid, too weary to utter a single word, irritated by the most innocent question.

Love's signs also include a fondness for solitude and a pleasure in being alone, as well as a wasting of the body not accompanied by any fever or ache preventing free activity and liberty of movement. The walk is also an unerring indication and never-deceiving sign of an inward lassitude of spirit. Sleeplessness too is a common affliction of lovers; the poets have described this condition frequently, relating how they watch the stars, and giving an account of the night's interminable length.

Another sign of love is that you will see the lover loving his beloved's kith and kin and the intimate ones of his household, to such an extent that they are nearer and dearer to him than his own folk, himself, and all his familiar friends.

Weeping is a well-known sign of love, except that men differ very greatly from one another in this particular. Some are ready weepers; their tear-ducts are always overflowing, and their eyes respond immediately to their emotions, the tears rolling down at a moment's notice. Others are dry-eyed and barren of tears; to this category I myself belong. This is the result of my habit of eating frankincense to abate the palpitation from which I have suffered since childhood. I will be afflicted by some shocking blow, and at once feel my heart to be splitting and breaking into fragments; I have a choking sensation in my heart more bitter than colocynth, that prevents me from getting my words out properly, and sometimes well nigh suffocates me. My eyes therefore respond to my feelings but rarely, and then my tears are exceedingly sparse.

You will see the lover, when unsure of the constancy of his loved one's feelings for him, perpetually on his guard in a way that he never troubled to be before; he polishes his language, he refines his gestures and his glances, particularly if he has the misfortune and mischance to be in love with one given to making unjust accusations, or of a quarrelsome disposition.

Another sign of love is the way the lover pays attention to the beloved; remembering everything that falls from his lips; searching out all the news about him, so that nothing small or great that happens to him may escape his knowledge; in short, following closely his every movement. Upon my life, sometimes you will see a complete dolt under these circumstances become most keen, a careless fellow turn exceedingly quick-witted.

One of the strangest origins of passion is when a man falls in love through merely hearing the description of the other party, without ever having set eyes on the beloved. In such a case he will progress through all the accustomed stages of love; there will be the sending to and fro of messengers, the exchange of letters, the anxiety, the deep emotion, the sleeplessness; and all this without actual sight of the object of affection. Stories, descriptions of beautiful qualities, and the reporting of news about the fair one have a manifest effect on the soul; to hear a girl's voice singing behind a wall may well move the heart to love, and preoccupy the mind.

All this has occurred to more than one man. In my opinion, however, such a love is a tumbledown building without any foundations. If a man's thoughts are absorbed by passionate regard for one whom he has never seen, the inevitable result is that whenever he is alone with his own reflections, he will represent to himself a purely imaginary picture of the person whose identity he keeps constantly before his mind; no other being than this takes shape in his fantasy; he is completely carried away by his imagination, and visualizes and dreams of her only. Then if some day he actually sees the object of his fanciful passion, either his love is confirmed or it is wholly nullified. Both these alternatives have actually happened and been known.

This kind of romance usually takes place between veiled ladies of guarded palaces and aristocratic households, and their male kinsfolk; the love of women is more stable in these cases than that of men, because women are weak creatures and their natures swiftly respond to this sort of attraction, which easily masters them completely.

Often it happens that love fastens itself to the heart as the result of a single glance. This variety of love is divided into two classes. The first class is the contrary of what we have just been describing, in that a man will fall head over heels in love with a mere form, without knowing who that person may be, what her name is, or where she lives. This sort of thing happens frequently enough.

The second class is the contrary of what we shall be describing in the chapter next following, if God wills. This is for a man to form an attachment at first sight with a young lady whose name, place of abode and origin are known to him. The difference here is the speed or tardiness with which the affair passes off. When a man falls in love at first sight, and forms a sudden attachment as the result of a fleeting glance, that proves him to be little steadfast, and proclaims that he will as suddenly forget his romantic adventure; it testifies to his fickleness and inconstancy. So it is with all things; the quicker they grow, the quicker they decay; while on the other hand slow produced is slow consumed.

Some men there are whose love becomes true only after long converse, much contemplation, and extended familiarity. Such a one is likely to persist and to be steadfast in his affection, untouched by the passage of time; what enters with difficulty goes not out easily. That is my own way in these matters, and it is confirmed by Holy Tradition. For God, as we are informed by our teachers, when He commanded the Spirit to enter Adam's body, that was like an earthen vessel—and the Spirit was afraid, and sorely distressed—said to it, "Enter in unwillingly, and come forth again unwillingly!"

I have myself seen a man of this description who, whenever he sensed within himself the beginnings of a passionate attachment, or conceived a penchant for some form whose beauty he admired, at once employed the device of shunning that person and giving up all association with him, lest his feelings become more intense and the affair get beyond his control, and he find himself completely stampeded. This proves how closely love cleaves to such people's hearts, and once it lays hold of them never looses its grip.

I indeed marvel profoundly at all those who pretend to fall in love at first sight; I cannot easily prevail upon myself to believe their claims, and prefer to consider such love as merely a kind of lust. As for thinking that that sort of attachment can really possess the inmost heart and penetrate the veil of the soul's recess, that I cannot under any circumstances credit. Love has never truly gripped my bowels, save after a long lapse of time and constant companionship with the person concerned, sharing with him all that while my every occupation, be it earnest or frivolous. So I am alike in consolation and in passion; I have never in my life forgotten any romance, and my nostalgia for every former attachment is such that I well nigh choke when I drink and suffocate when I eat. The man who is not so constituted quickly finds complete relief and is at rest again; I have never wearied of anything once I have known it, and neither have I hastened to feel at home with it on first acquaintance. Similarly, I have never longed for a change for change's sake, in any of the things that I have possessed; I am speaking here not only of friends and comrades, but also of all the other things a man uses—clothes, riding-beast, food, and so on.

Life holds no joy for me, and I do nothing but hang my head and feel utterly cast down, ever since I first tasted the bitterness of being separated from those I love. It is an anguish that constantly revisits me, an agony of grief that ceases not for a moment to assail me. My remembrance of past happiness has abated for me every joy that I may look for in the future. I am a dead man, though counted among the living, slain by sorrow and buried by sadness, entombed while yet a dweller on the face of this mortal earth. God be praised, whatever be the circumstances that befall us; there is indeed no other God but He!

As for what transpires at first blush as a result of certain accidental circumstances—physical admiration, and visual enchantment which does not go beyond mere external forms—and this is the very secret and meaning of carnal desire; when carnal desire moreover becomes so overflowing that it surpasses these bounds, and when such an overflow coincides with a spiritual union in which the natural instincts share equally with the soul, the resulting phenomenon is called passionate love. Herein lies the root of the error which misleads a man into asserting that he loves two persons, or is passionately enamoured of two entirely different individuals. All this is to be explained as springing out of carnal desire, as we have just described; it is called love only metaphorically, and not in the true meaning of the term. As for the true lover, his yearning of the soul is so excessive as to divert him from all his religious and mundane occupations; how then should he have room to busy himself with a second love affair?

Know now—may God exalt you!—that love exercises an effective authority, a decisive sovereignty over the soul; its commands cannot be opposed; its ordinances may not be flouted; its rule is not to be transgressed; it demands unwavering obedience, and against its dominion there is no appeal. Love untwists the firmest plaits and looses the tightest strands; it dissolves that which is most solid, undoes that which is most firm; it penetrates the deepest recesses of the heart, and makes lawful things most strictly forbidden.

I have known many men whose discrimination was beyond suspicion, men not to be feared deficient in knowledge, or wanting in taste, or lacking in discernment, who nevertheless described their loved ones as possessing certain qualities not by any means admired by the general run of mankind or approved according to the accepted canons of beauty. Yet those qualities had become an obsession with them, the sole object of their passion, and the very last word (as they thought) in elegance. Thereafter their loved ones vanished, either into oblivion, or by separation, or jilting, or through some other accident to which love is always liable; but those men never lost their admiration for the curious qualities which provoked their approval of them, neither did they ever afterwards cease to prefer these above other attributes that are in reality superior to them.

Let me add a personal touch. In my youth I loved a slave-girl who happened to be a blonde; from that time I have never admired brunettes, not though their dark tresses set off a face as resplendent as the sun, or the very image of beauty itself. I find this taste to have become a part of my whole make-up and constitution since those early days; my soul will not suffer me to acquire any other, or to love any type but that. This very same thing happened to my father also (God be pleased with him!), and he remained faithful to his first preference until the term of his earthly life was done.

Were it not that this world below is a transitory abode of trial and trouble, and paradise a home where virtue receives its reward, secure from all annoyances, I would have said that union with the beloved is that pure happiness which is without alloy, and gladness unsullied by sorrow the perfect realization of hopes and the complete fulfillment of one's dreams.

I have tested all manner of pleasures, and known every variety of joy; and I have found that neither intimacy with princes, nor wealth acquired, nor finding after lacking, nor returning after long absence, nor security after fear, and repose in a safe refuge—none of these things so powerfully affects the soul as union with the beloved, especially if it come after long denial and continual banishment. For then the flame of passion waxes exceeding hot, and the furnace of yearning blazes up, and the fire of eager hope rages ever more fiercely.

The fresh springing of herbs after the rains, the glitter of flowers when the night clouds have rolled away in the hushed hour between dawn and sunrise, the plashing of waters as they run through the stalks of golden blossoms, the exquisite beauty of white castles encompassed by verdant meadows—not lovelier is any of these than union with the well-beloved, whose character is virtuous, and laudable her disposition, whose attributes are evenly matched in perfect beauty. Truly that is a miracle of wonder surpassing the tongues of the eloquent, and far beyond the range of the most cunning speech to describe: the mind reels before it, and the intellect stands abashed.

❧ My Beloved Comes

Translated by Cola Franzen

You came to me just before
the Christians rang their bells.
The half-moon was rising
looking like an old man's eyebrow
or a delicate instep.

And although it was still night,
when you came, a rainbow
gleamed on the horizon,
showing as many colors
as a peacock's tail.

10

Ibn Faraj
D. 976

Ibn Faraj was a practitioner of the sublimated style of love poetry known as 'Udhrite, after a poet of the seventh century. The effect of this poetry is contradictory in that while it praises the absence of sexual gratification it stimulates the reader with sexual imagery. This is not the same phenomenon as the language of chastity that sometimes appears in Ibn Hazm's work. It is more like a heresy of love; by denying sexuality so insistently it exaggerates its importance and calls attention to the lover. In "Chastity," Ibn Faraj uses the unusual metaphor of a muzzled camel to describe the frustration of a man who does not consummate his desire. The themes of 'Udhrite poetry gradually were absorbed into the common stock of Andalusian love poetry; they also resurface later in mystical religious poetry in which abstinence is similarly counted a virtue.

Chastity

Translated by Cola Franzen

Although she was ready to give
herself to me, I abstained
and did not accept
the temptation Satan offered.

She came unveiled in the night.
Illuminated by her face,
night put aside its shadowy
veils as well.

Each one of her glances
could cause hearts to turn over.

But I clung to the divine precept
that condemns lust and reined in
the capricious horses of my passion
so that my instinct
would not rebel against chastity.

And so I passed the night with her
like a thirsty little camel
whose muzzle keeps it from nursing.

20
　She was a field of fruit and flowers
　offering one like me no other enjoyment
　than sight and scent.

　Know then that I am not
　one of those beasts gone wild
　who take gardens for pastures.

∾ IBN ZAYDUN
1004–1070

Ibn Zaydun, the Andalusian master of the themes of passion and longing, was already a famous court poet before he fell in love with Wallada, the daughter of the last Umayyad caliph of Cordova. The story of their ill-fated love affair later became a staple of literary legends in the Arab world. It seems that Wallada emerged better off from this relationship than Ibn Zaydun. While his greatest poetry recalls their love affair with deepest melancholy, she insults him in some of her later work in picturesque language:

> For all his virtue Ibn Zaydun loves rods inside trousers.
> If he spotted a penis up a palm-tree, he'd turn into a whole flock
>   of birds.

At times, however, the writing of the two is so similar in passionate intensity that scholars have argued over who actually wrote the verses in question.

Ibn Zaydun was born in 1004 to an aristocratic family claiming descent from the Quraysh, the tribe of Muhammad in Arabia. After the fall of the Umayyads in Cordova in 1031, Ibn Zaydun became closely connected with the new Jahwarid dynasty, and was almost immediately appointed ambassador to the neighboring Andalusian kingdoms. He lost favor with the Jahwarid king, Abu l'Hazm, a decade later and was imprisoned briefly before escaping and finally being reinstated to his ambassadorial duties. In later life he served as ambassador for the Abbasid government in Seville, eventually helping them to conquer his native Cordova. He died in Seville in 1070.

Ibn Zaydun is most famous for three poems: The "Poem in N," a fiery fifty-two verse *qasidah* that expresses his longing for Wallada; a *ghazal* called "Written from al-Zahrā," set in a beautiful garden outside Cordova; and a prison letter he entitled "The Serious Epistle," begging his sovereign Abu l'Hazm for his release. In "Written from al-Zahrā," included here, Ibn Zaydun recalls the past when he and Wallada met in the place he now returns to. This traditional love poem describes the poet's journey to a place of sanctuary and his recovery of feeling through the restoration of his memories.

Written from Al-Zahrā'

Translated by Cola Franzen

From al-Zahrā'[1]
I remember you with passion.
The horizon is clear,
the earth's face serene.

The breeze grows faint
with the coming of dawn.
It seems to pity me
and lingers, full of tenderness.

The meandering waterway
10   with its silvery waters
shows a sparkling smile.
It resembles a necklace
unclasped and thrown aside.

A day like those delicious ones
now gone by
when seizing the dream of destiny
we were thieves of pleasure.

Today, alone,
I distract myself with flowers
20   that attract my eyes like magnets.
The wind roughhouses with them
bending them over.

The blossoms are eyes.
They see my sleeplessness
and weep for me;
their iridescent tears overflow
staining the calyx.[2]

In the bright sun
red buds light up the rose bushes
30   making the morning
brighter still.

---

[1] **al-Zahrā':** A legendary palace outside of Cordova whose gardens were noted for their opulence and splendor.

[2] **calyx:** The external part of a flower, of a cuplike shape.

Fragrant breaths come from the pome
of the waterlilies,
sleepyheads with eyes
half-opened by dawn.

Everything stirs up the memory
of my passion for you
still intact in my chest
although my chest might seem
40   too narrow to contain it.

If, as I so desire,
we two could again be made one,
that day would be the noblest
of all days.

Would God grant calm to my heart
if it could cease to remember you
and refrain from flying
to your side
on wings trembling with desire?

50   If this passing breeze
would consent to carry me along,
it would put down at your feet
a man worn out by grief.

Oh, my most precious jewel,
the most sublime,
the one preferred by my soul,
as if lovers dealt in jewels!

In times gone by
we demanded of each other
60   payments of pure love
and were happy as colts
running free in a pasture.

But now I am the only one
who can boast of being loyal.
You left me
and I stay here,
still sad, still loving you.

WALLADA

D. 1077

> Wallada was the daughter of the last Umayyad caliph of Cordova and a lover of the famous court poet Ibn Zaydun. Both are believed to have written poems of longing and blame about the other. Wallada's reputation as a passionate, unconventional lover is supported by many stories, such as the one about the lines of verse embroidered on the hem of her robe: "I allow my lovers to caress my cheek, and bestow my kiss on whoever craves it." There were other women poets in the Andalusian courts, ranging in rank from slaves to independent women, most of whom appear to have been professional performers. Wallada is one of several aristocratic female poets whose writing has been preserved. Her favorite form was the *ghazal,* or love poem. Some *ghazals* such as this one are noted for their tone of unrestrained passion and violent, obsessive longing.

To Ibn Zaidun

Translated by James T. Monroe and Deirdre Lashgari

1

Can't we find some way
to meet again
and speak our love?

In winter with you near
no need for coals—
our passion blazed.

Now—cut off, alone
day darkens deep
the fate I feared

Nights pass. You're still away
Longing chains me
and Patience brings no release

Where morning finds you
may God stream down upon your land
refreshing, fertile rain

2

Wait till the darkness is deep;
    be then my guest.
Night knows how to keep
    love's secret best.

20   The sun if it loved as I do
        would hide its light,
full moon not come into view
    stars not journey by night.

❧ JUDAH HA-LEVI
1075–1141

Judah ha-Levi was born in Tudela in northern Andalusia, near the frontier with Christian Spain, in 1075. While still a youth, he journeyed to Granada where he was befriended by the poet Moses Ibn Ezra. After Granada was attacked in 1090, he moved to Castille, leaving there when the Jews fell under persecution in 1109. He wrote brilliant secular poetry until about 1125, when he began to reconsider his vocation. Already considered the greatest Andalusian Jewish poet and cultural authority, he became disenchanted, both with his writing of secular literature and his participation in the Andalusian Jewish community. Finally he decided to travel to Jerusalem, a decision that became the source of some of his most important writing though it also posed personal difficulties for him. Cut off from his own community in Andalusia, he reestablished himself for a time in Egypt. Although he may have died there in 1141 without having completed his pilgrimage to the Holy Land, a legend relates that he was killed by a Muslim as he approached the gates of Jerusalem.

    Like many other Jewish poets, Judah ha-Levi wrote poems in Hebrew though he borrowed many of the conventions of Arabic poetry. Advances in Islamic scholarship actually increased interest in Scriptural studies and the use of Hebrew among the Jews. Ha-Levi's early love songs sometimes incorporated images from The Song of Solomon while using Arabic figures of speech and subject matter. "The Apple," a short lyric poem, is an inspired fusion of Arabic and Hebrew culture.

❧ The Apple

Translated by David Goldstein

You have captured me with your charm, my lady;
You have enslaved me brutally in your prison.
From the very day that we had to part
I have found no likeness to your beauty.
I console myself with a rosy apple,
Whose scent is like the myrrh of your nose and your lips,
Its shape like your breast, and its colour
Like the hue which is seen on your cheeks.

❧ IBN AL-LABBANA
D. 1113

The practitioners of the Andalusian *muwashshah* form of love poetry in the eleventh and twelfth centuries wrote the beginning verses in five or six rhymed stanzas, generally in Arabic or Hebrew, and finished with a short, two- to four-line tag or *kharja* in Mozarabic, the vernacular language consisting of elements of Arabic, Spanish, and Hebrew. Many successful *kharjas* are supposedly spoken by a servant girl and are sexually suggestive; this form has a very dynamic, sensual character.

A *muwashshah* attributed to Ibn al-Labbana (d. 1113) is included in *The House of Embroidery,* an anthology collected by Ibn Sana al-Mulk (d. 1211). The extravagant love language of the first four stanzas is addressed to a man, Ahmad, who is described as dark, slender, sweet smelling, dangerous, and powerful. The intrusion of the girl in the *kharja* at the end of the fifth stanza is unexplained. The translator of the work suggests that "it has no relation to the preceding part of the *muwashshah,* where the poet portrays himself wasting away from unrequited love." Since this *kharja* is used for several other poems as well, it may have been inserted here simply to provide a striking ending.

He who has charged the eyes

Translated by Linda Fish Compton

He who has charged the eyes with cutting swords of Indian metal
And has made sweet basil grow on the side of his cheek
Has inflicted tears and sleeplessness upon the one who is madly in love.
Is there any way to keep silent
  For the lover burdened with tears which reveal, as they flow forth, the secret
   he hides
  Concerning one who wears no jewels, yet is adorned, who is outwardly naive
   and overpowers me with large black eyes?
Oh, I'd give my father as ransom for a black-eyed one who is like the full moon.
He reveals a gem whose kiss is delightful.
His flowerlike cheek blushes at just a thought,
10 So how can I be absolved?
  A speckled serpent crept over the brazilwood, so don't kiss it!
  By magic he appointed an army of Ethiopians, together with Nabateans, to
   kill heroes.

The time has come to emanate light, like the lord of the mountain,
Like a full moon in darkness, with a body as slim as a reed,
Like a branch of beryl in a rounded hillock of camphor.
By the soul of an abandoned one
  I ransom him, even though it makes me an orphan.
   In a sealed place are the teeth of his mouth, and they have been set in order
  Like pearls on strings, with perfumed spaces between, providing my wine and
   my cool water.

Just as you have been endowed with beauty, oh, Ahmad,
20 So is command devoted to you, oh, delicate one.
Your slave is in love with you and subjugated.
Are you going to reprimand me?
  Or will you have mercy and prevent the wasting away of the one in love if he
   becomes ill with grief?
  Woe unto me! I am imprisoned in a sea of fears whose shore is far away. I can
   only cling to the waves.

Sometimes a young girl appears like the full moon rising.
What a breast on a branch of laurel!
Her leaves are a garment more red than the rose.
She spent the night while singing,
  "My darling, make up your mind. Arise! Hurry and kiss my mouth. Come
   embrace
30 My breast and raise my anklets to my earrings. My husband is busy."

IBN QUZMAN

C. 1080–1160

The eleventh century saw a new kind of love poem, the *zajal*, composed wholly in Mozarabic. The master of the *zajal*, Ibn Quzman, was supposedly a distinguished citizen of Cordova, but he delighted in picturing himself as a rake and a drunkard. At least one contemporary, the poet al-Ahwani, agreed, stating that "the major preoccupations of Ibn Quzman's life are money, wine, and love." Other contemporaries also indicated that many of Ibn Quzman's lurid stories about himself were taken from real life.

In the poem "I am madly in love," the speaker carouses with his lover and seduces him after he is drunk. In the same poem he attacks several earlier writers known for their poetry of complaint over unrequited longings. With his confessions of depravity, no doubt Ibn Quzman wanted to shock the complacency of his audience. But his character's boastfulness may have a deeper purpose: It ridicules the restraint recommended by more genteel poets, and it mocks the ideal of courtly love.

Ibn Quzman's style, breezy and unaffected, impressed his generation. He said of his use of the *zajal*, "I cleaned it of the knots that made it ugly . . . I made it easy, but difficul-ly easy; common and rare at the same time, arduous to achieve yet obvious."

I am madly in love

Translated by James T. Monroe

I am madly in love despite the angry behavior of one who finds fault [with me]!
I am the lover of my time:
I fear no one in matters of love!
Love has made me thin, it has turned me pale:
Look, and see how my color has changed!
Yet I can still say "Ah!" O dark-skinned one!
As for my clothes, there is no flesh inside them.
You would not see me
Were it not that I still moan!
10 By God, I am a man enmeshed in love's snares
And my condition proves that I speak the truth.
Moreover, I excel in composing this *zajal*;
Poetry passes through my mind whenever [its sword] is drawn;
As for the sword of my tongue,
No coat of mail can stop it!

654

Spare me the method of Jamīl and ʿUrwa,[1]
Since people have a model in al-Ḥasan.[2]
And say to one who does not follow the method of al-ʿUrwa:
"O you who honor a certain person even more than Ḥātim,
20   What is the method used by a certain debauched fellow
Who is ostracized throughout the land?"
Throw off your restraint in loving the youthful,
And as for the beloved, if you see that his sash is hard to undo,
Give him to drink, and do it again, as often as needed.
Then, if he drinks from the large cup and endures,
Pour him out a second:
He will collapse though he be a lion!
When my beloved drank his cup for you,
And drunkenness made him droop among his seated companions,
30   I redoubled my efforts whenever he raised his head;
My beloved drank; he drank until he keeled over.
There is no safety from me
For one who gets drunk and then falls asleep!

---

[1] **Jamīl and ʿUrwa:** Jamil al-ʿUdhri and ʿUrwat ibm Hizam were two early poets reputed to have developed a love lyric that sang of a languishing, hopeless sentiment, later called ʿUdhrite love.

[2] **al-Ḥasan:** Another poet, also named Abu Nuwas.

✺ GUILLAUME IX, DUKE OF AQUITAINE
1071–1127

Guillaume IX, duke of Aquitaine, was known for his deeds as well as his songs. The lord of an immense domain and leader of the disastrous Crusade of 1101, he was a notorious womanizer and a constant source of irritation for the church. He is important to the courtly love tradition for two reasons: He is often spoken of as the first troubadour poet, and—perhaps because of his rank—his poems, twelve in all, were carefully preserved. As he grew older, his songs changed from bawdy backroom ballads to attacks on the clergy, to showpieces of courtly and religious devotion.

The artistic relationship of Guillaume to the poets of preceding and succeeding generations is somewhat obscure. His relatively sophisticated subject matter, rhyme schemes, and style could not have developed in a vacuum. The earlier poetry that he knew was possibly constructed from the ruins of the Latin tradition and whatever poetry existed in the Romance languages and through contact with the culture of the courts of

Andalusia. As for how Guillaume influenced the generation that followed him, apparently, he began by supporting other troubadours wherever he held court. At Poitiers there appears to have been a poetic line of succession: Guillaume IX was followed by the troubadours Cercamon (fl. 1137–1153) and Marcabru (fl. 1129–1150). (See p. 659.) More significant than this, perhaps, is the fact that Guillaume practiced both "high" and "low" poetry, both of which would have a future with his successors.

VEHR

The song "My companions, I am going to make a **vers** that is refined" is the raucous account of a man with two female lovers, whom he compares to "good and noble horses." His problem is that they will not abide by the arrangement. The women live in two castles within his domain; although one woman is married to another man, the poet boasts that he has first rights to her. The poem is characterized by its chauvinistic point of view and its conspicuous bad taste. For instance, the poet deliberately names the two women, exposing their identities and destroying whatever may be left of their reputations.

A world apart from this poem is the one that begins "Now when we see the meadows once again," one of the early defining texts of the doctrine of courtly love, addressed to a mixed audience of lords and ladies. Here Guillaume practices and preaches the art of refinement. He rebukes himself for having wanted love so much that he has frequently lost it, and he acknowledges that he will never gain love without first obeying its laws. This time he is careful to conceal the identity of his beloved.

Songbook, 1280–1315
A student avows his love for a noble lady in this illustration from a later medieval French songbook. (The Art Archive / Musée Atger, Montpellier / Dagli Orti)

My companions, I am going to make a *vers* that is refined

Translated by Frederick Goldin

My companions,[1] I am going to make a *vers* that is refined,
and it will have more foolishness than sense,
and it will all be mixed with love and joy and youth.

Whoever does not understand it, take him for a peasant,
whoever does not learn it deep in his heart.
It is hard for a man to part from love that he finds to his desire.

I have two good and noble horses for my saddle,
they are good, adroit in combat, full of spirit,
but I cannot keep them both, one can't stand the other.

10 If I could tame them as I wish,
I would not want to put my equipment anywhere else,
for I'd be better mounted then than any man alive.

One of them was the fastest of the mountain horses,
but for a long time now it has been so fierce and shy,
so touchy, so wild, it fights off the currycomb.

The other was nurtured down there around Confolens,
and you never saw a prettier one, I know.
I won't get rid of that one, not for gold or silver.

I gave it to its master as a grazing colt;
20 but I reserved the right
that for every year he had it, I got it for more than a hundred.

You knights, counsel me in this predicament,
no choice ever caused me more embarrassment:
I can't decide which one to keep, Na Agnes or Na Arsen.[2]

Of Gimel I have the castle and the fief,
and with Niol I show myself proud to everyone,
for both are sworn to me and bound by oath.

---

[1] **My companions:** By addressing the poem to his male friends, Guillaume helps to establish its unmannerly type, despite his disclaimer that it is "refined."

[2] **Na Agnes . . . Arsen:** *Na* is the shortened form of *domina,* an address to a lady.

❧ Now when we see the meadows once again

Translated by Frederick Goldin

Now when we see the meadows once again
in flower and the orchards turning green,
streams and fountains running clear,
the breezes and the winds,
it is right that each man celebrate the joy
that makes him rejoice.

Now I must not say anything but good of Love.
Why do I get not one bit of it?
Maybe I wasn't meant for more.
10   And yet how freely
it gives great joy to any man who upholds
its rules.

This is the way it has always been with me:
I never had the joy of what I loved,
and I never will, as I never did.
For I am aware,
I do many things and my heart says,
"It is all nothing."

And so I know less than anyone what pleasure is,
20   because I want what I cannot have.
And yet, one wise saying tells me
the certain truth:
"When the heart is good, its power is good,
if a man knows patience."

Surely no one can ever be Love's
perfect man unless he gives it homage in humility
and is obliging to strangers
and acquaintances,
and to all the people of that realm
30   obedient.

A man who wants to be a lover
must meet many people with obedience,
and must know how to do
the things that fit in court,

and must keep, in court, from speaking
like a vulgar man.

Concerning this *vers* I tell you a man is all the more noble
as he understands it, and he gets more praise;
and all the strophes are built exactly
on the same meter,
and the melody, which I myself am happy about,
is fine and good.

Let my *vers,* since I myself do not,
appear before her,
Mon Esteve, and let it be the witness
for my praise.

MARCABRU
FL. 1129–1150

Marcabru, who although he was low born enjoyed the patronage of the court of Poitiers, could not have differed more from Guillaume IX in his approach. His poems attack other troubadours and advocates of courtly love as hypocritical and depraved, caught up in the vices of the world, while he defends what he calls true love, the love of friendship. Although Marcabru depicts himself as a flawed person who cannot live up to his own ideals, one suspects him of trying to have his argument both ways: Only he, it seems, is honest enough to confess his faults. And is not "the love of friendship" courtly love restored to its original principles of devotion and mutual trust?

The poem "By the fountain in the orchard" maintains a high moral tone despite the narrator's confession of inappropriate desires. In the poem, Marcabru depicts a knight pursuing a lady who is grieving for her lover off fighting in the Crusades. The knight is finally chastened and educated by the lady's fidelity to her absent lover. The portrayal of true love as a virtue is all the more forceful for remaining unstated.

By the fountain in the orchard

Translated by Frederick Goldin

By the fountain in the orchard,
where the grass is green down to the sandy banks,
in the shade of a planted tree,
in a pleasant setting of white flowers
and the ancient song of the new season,
I found her alone, without a companion,
this girl who does not want my company.

She was a young girl, and beautiful,
the daughter of a castle lord.
And just as I reckoned the birds
must be filling her with joy, and the green things,
in this sweet new time,
and she would gladly hear my little speech,
suddenly her whole manner changed.

Her eyes welled up beside the fountain,
and she sighed from the depths of her heart,
"Jesus," she said, "King of the world,
because of You my grief increases,
I am undone by your humiliation,[1]
for the best men of this whole world
are going off to serve you, that is your pleasure.

"With you departs my so
handsome, gentle, valiant, noble friend;
here, with me, nothing of him remains but the great distress,
the frequent desiring, and the tears.
Ai! damn King Louis,
he gave the orders and the sermons,
and grief invaded my heart."

When I heard how she was losing heart,
I came up to her beside the clear stream.
"Beautiful one," I said, "with too much weeping
your face grows pale, the color fades;
you have no reason to despair, now,

---

[1] **your humiliation:** God was humiliated, the lady says, by the failure of the Second Crusade, led by King Louis
VII of France in 1147.

for He who makes the woods burst into leaf
has the power to give you joy in great abundance."

"Lord," she said, "I do believe
that God may pity me
in the next world, time without end,
like many other sinners,
40   but here He wrests from me the one thing
that made my joy increase. Nothing matters now,
for he has gone so far away."

❧ BERNART DE VENTADORN
FL. 1150–1180

One of the most prolific of troubadours, Bernart de Ventadorn also seems
to have struggled constantly against the conventionality of the poetry. One
editor has called him a perpetual aspirant, always seeking his lady's recognition and hoping to be singled out from the rest of her admirers. He also
seeks the audience's recognition as an accomplished performer.

    "My heart is so full of joy" shares with some of the works of Guil-
laume IX a certain outrageousness, as when the poet says he could go
about naked because love protects him from the wind, or asserts that he
would not exchange his love for all the wealth in Pisa. His assertion that
by keeping distant from his beloved he has really won the battle (by possessing the power of her image) is a clever rendering of a familiar theme.
These original maneuvers help make up for the conventional exhortations with which the poem ends.

❧ My heart is so full of joy

Translated by Frederick Goldin

My heart is so full of joy
it changes every nature.
The winter that comes to me
is white red yellow flowers;
my good luck grows
with the wind and the rain,

and so my song mounts up, rises,
and my worth increases.
I have such love in my heart,
such joy, such sweetness,
the ice I see is a flower,
the snow, green things that grow.

I could walk around undressed,
naked in my shirt,
for perfect love protects me
from the cold north wind.
But a man is a fool when he does things out of measure
and doesn't hold himself with courtesy.
Therefore I have kept a watch upon myself
ever since I begged her,
my most beautiful, for love,
and I await such honor
that in place of her riches
I don't want Pisa.

Let her make me keep my distance from her love—
there's still one thing I'm sure of:
I have conquered nothing less
than her beautiful image.
Cut off from her like this I have
such bliss,
that the day I see her again,
not having seen her will not weigh on me.
My heart stays close to Love,
my spirit runs to it there,
but my body is here, in another place,
far from her, in France.

I get good hope from her;
but that does me little good,
because she holds me like this, poised
like a ship on the wave.
I don't know where to take cover
from the sad thoughts that pull me down.
The whole night long I toss and turn
on the edge of the bed.
I bear more pain from love
than Tristan the lover,

10

20

30

40

who suffered many sorrows
for Isolt the blonde.

Ah, God! couldn't I be a swallow
50   and fly through the air
and come in the depths of the night
into her dwelling there.
O gentle lady, o joyful,
your lover dies.
I fear the heart will melt within me
if this lasts a little longer.
Lady, for your love
I join my hands and worship.
Beautiful body of the colors of youth,
60   what suffering you make me bear.

For in this world no enterprise
so draws my thought,
that when I hear any talk of her
my heart does not turn to it
and my face light up,
so that no matter what you hear me saying,
you will always think
I want to laugh.
I love her so with such good love,
70   that many time[s] I weep for it,
because for me the sighs

have a sweeter taste.
Go, messenger, run,
and tell her, the one most beautiful,
of the pain and the sorrow
I bear for her, and the willing death.

RAIMBAUT, COUNT D'ORANGE

FL. 1162–1173

Raimbaut, Count d'Orange, inherited some of the rich estates of Montpellier and Vaucluse. Known for his virtuosity and his habit of calling attention to it in his work, he never achieved his full promise, dying young in an epidemic. The poem beginning "Listen, Lords," is a direct address to an audience of his peers, wittily arguing that he doesn't know what kind of song he is singing because he doesn't know what effect his pursuit is having on his lady. It ends, characteristically, on a note of self-praise.

Listen, Lords . . . but I don't know what

Translated by Frederick Goldin

Listen, Lords . . . but I don't know what
to call this thing I'm about to declaim.
Vers? Estribot? Sirventes? It's none
of these. I can't think up a name,
and don't know how I'd compose such a thing
if I could not finish it and claim
that no one ever saw the like of it made by any man or
  woman in our century or in the other which has passed.[1]

Call me a madman if you like,
it would not make me leave my vow,
10 Lords, to tell you what I feel.
Let no one blame me. I would not set
a penny on this whole Creation,
compared to what I see right now,
and I'll tell you why: because if I started this thing for
  you and did not bring it off, you'd take me for
  a fool: because I prefer six cents in my fist to
  a thousand suns in the sky.

Let my friend never fear he may have done
a thing that weighs on me, I pray:

---

[1] **I don't know what . . . has passed:** By stating his confusion over what kind of poem he is writing, and by the breakdown of metrical form at the end of the first stanza, the poet is parodying certain inept songs, probably those of Guillaume IX.

if he will not help me in my need at once,
let him offer me help after long delay.
But she that conquered me alone
20 deceives me as though it were child's play.
    I say all this because of one lady who makes me pine
        away with beautiful words and a long expectation,
        I don't know why—Lords, can she be good to me?

It's been a good four months—that's more
than a thousand years to me, yes,
since she promised me and swore
to give me what I long for most.
Lady, my heart is your prisoner,
therefore sweeten my bitterness.
Help me, God, *in nomine Patris et Filii et Spiritus sancti!*
    Madam, how will it all turn out?

You make me frolic in my wrath,
30 you make me sing with joyful rage;
and I have left three such as have
no peer, save you, in our age.
Joglar they call me, I go singing
mad with love, in courtly ways.
    Lady, you can do as you please about it, as Na Ayma
        did with the shoulder bone, she stuck it where
        she liked.[2]

Now I conclude my Whatdoyoucallit,
for that is how I've had it baptized;
since I've never heard of a similar thing,
I use the name that I devised;
40 whoever likes it, let him sing,
once he has it memorized,
    and if anyone asks him who made it, he can say: one who
        can do anything, and do it well, when he wants to.

---

[2] **Na Ayma . . . she liked:** Na Ayma must be a lady known to the court. The reference is obscene.

COUNTESS OF DIA
FL. 1160

The first and probably the best of the *trobairitz,* or women poets, the Countess of Dia combined in unique fashion the common song and the courtly lyric. She shares with her female counterparts a demand for personal respect, physical and emotional satisfaction, and above all plain speaking in matters of love. She treats the conventions of courtly love with skepticism: She scrutinizes the behavior of a lover to see whether it matches the standards he has supposedly adopted. Above all, she affirms her own need for satisfaction in her relationships.

The poem beginning "I've lately been in great distress" is direct, with nothing held back, including the fact that the speaker would prefer having her lover to her husband. The countess laments her earlier failure to satisfy her lover's demands but still holds out for control of the relationship. The poem beginning "Of things I'd rather keep in silence I must sing," in which the poet gives a messenger instructions on what to say to a lover who has spurned her, stays within the conventions of courtly love; the poet reminds her lover of their past relationship and demands that he respond to her with more courtesy in the future, warning him also against the excessive pride that may be his undoing.

I've lately been in great distress

Translated by Magda Bogin

I've lately been in great distress
over a knight who once was mine,
and I want it known for all eternity
how I loved him to excess.
Now I see I've been betrayed
because I wouldn't sleep with him;
night and day my mind won't rest
to think of the mistake I made.

How I wish just once I could caress
that chevalier with my bare arms,
for he would be in ecstasy
if I'd just let him lean his head against my breast.
I'm sure I'm happier with him
than Blancaflor with Floris.
My heart and love I offer him,
my mind, my eyes, my life.

Handsome friend, charming and kind,
when shall I have you in my power?
If only I could lie beside you for an hour
and embrace you lovingly—
know this, that I'd give almost anything
to have you in my husband's place,
but only under the condition
that you swear to do my bidding.

Of things I'd rather keep in silence I must sing

Translated by Magda Bogin

Of things I'd rather keep in silence I must sing:
so bitter do I feel toward him
whom I love more than anything.
With him my mercy and fine manners are in vain,
my beauty, virtue and intelligence.
For I've been tricked and cheated
as if I were completely loathesome.

There's one thing, though, that brings me recompense:
I've never wronged you under any circumstance,
and I love you more than Seguin loved Valensa.
At least in love I have my victory,
since I surpass the worthiest of men.
With me you always act so cold,
but with everyone else you're so charming.

I have good reason to lament
when I feel your heart turn adamant
toward me, friend: it's not right another love
take you away from me, no matter what she says.
Remember how it was with us in the beginning
of our love! May God not bring to pass
that I should be the one to bring it to an end.

The great renown that in your heart resides
and your great worth disquiet me,
for there's no woman near or far
who wouldn't fall for you if love were on her mind.
But you, my friend, should have the acumen

to tell which one stands out above the rest.
And don't forget the stanzas we exchanged.

My worth and noble birth should have some weight,
my beauty and especially my noble thoughts;
so I send you, there on your estate,
this song as messenger and delegate.
I want to know, my handsome noble friend,
why I deserve so savage and so cruel a fate.
I can't tell whether it's pride or malice you intend.

But above all, messenger, make him comprehend
that too much pride has undone many men.

CASTELLOZA

FL. 1212

kahn-SOH
KOH-blahs
oo-nih-soh-NAHNS

Castelloza wrote a half century later than the countess of Dia, though she may have known the countess's work. Castelloza came from Auvergne and was married to Turc de Mairona, an influential figure. Her songs are uniform in mood and intensity: They show a brooding spirit, often predicting failure in love. While one should not assume these works are completely autobiographical (her attention to form suggests that she was a professional poet), her speakers are so forceful and passionate that it seems the author herself may have possessed similar qualities.

Her love songs, or *cansos*, consist of five or six stanzas whose rhyme scheme repeats that of the first stanza: These are called *coblas unissonans*. The asymmetrical pattern of each stanza—the first line is shorter than the others—creates an impression of raggedness in the verse. As Castelloza dissects her emotions about her lover in "My friend, if I found you welcoming," she renders him more and more to blame in the mind of the audience, something she must have done deliberately. The provocative last line has survived without scribal changes in only one manuscript: It suggests that the speaker's martyrdom on earth will contribute positively to her status in heaven, while it also appears to tempt her lover's jealousy and possessiveness.

My friend, if I found you welcoming

Translated by Peter Dronke

My friend, if I found you welcoming,
modest and gracious and compassionate,
I'd love you well—whilst now I call to mind
that I find you bad to me, contemptible and proud.

And yet I make songs so as to let others hear
of your good character—for I cannot bear
not to have you praised by all the world,
even when you most hurt me and make me angriest.

I shall never think of you as deserving,
10   or love you with all my heart, loyally,
before I see if it might serve my turn
were I to show you a heart hostile and rancorous. . . .
No, I shan't do it: I don't want to let you say
that I ever had the heart to fail you—
as then you would have some justification
if in any of my acts indeed I failed you.

I know well this way is right for me,
even if everyone says it is unseemly
for a lady to implore a knight on her own account
20   and to preach at him always, at such length.
But those who say this have no means to judge—
for I want to prove, rather than surrender by dying,
that in imploring I am sweetly refreshed,
when I implore the one who makes me think harsh thoughts.

Whoever reproaches me for loving you
is quite mad, since it accords with me so gently—
one who speaks thus does not know how it is with me:
he's never seen you with the eyes with which I saw you
when you told me not to sorrow any more—
30   for, any moment, it could come about
that once again I'd have the joy of that.
Even from saying this my heart takes joy.

I set all other love at naught,
and you must know that no joy ever sustains me
except for yours, that lightens me and revives
where most anguish and most harm beset me.
And I believe through my plaints and lais I will always
have joy in you, my friend—I can't become a convert—
nor do I have joy, or expect any solace,
40   save insofar as I'll gain it while I sleep.

I don't know how to confront you after this,
for by fair means and by foul I have probed
your impassive heart—mine does not weary of the probing.
And I send no messenger—it is I myself who tell you,
and I *shall* die, if you will not lighten me
with any joy; and if you let me die,
you'll commit sin, and be in torment for it,
and at the Judgment I'll be the more desired!

Marie de France
FL. 1170–1180

breh-TAWNG

LAY

Marie de France wrote in Norman French in the second half of the twelfth century. She translated a book of Latin fables and a Latin saint's life, which she said in a preface she had done so that the works might "be understood and available to the layman." She was best loved, however, for twelve original short verse romances known as **Breton** lais.[1] Her contemporary, Denis Piramus, rather quaintly referred to her as "Lady Marie, who wrote in rhyme and composed the verses of **lais** which are not at all true. And so is she much praised because of it and the rhyme loved everywhere; for all love it greatly and hold it dear—counts, barons, and knights." She lived at the same time as Chrétien des Troyes,[2] the peerless French poet of the courtly romance, and apparently drew from the same springs of inspiration. In recent times she has been called by her translators Robert Hanning and Joan Ferrante "perhaps the greatest woman author of the Middle Ages, and certainly the creator of the finest medieval short fiction before Boccaccio and Chaucer."

NOH-bluh RAYS

The Anglo-Norman Poet. Since several of Marie de France's works came from English sources and the surviving manuscripts were found in England, it is believed that she was a member of the Anglo-Norman, or Angevin, aristocracy who lived part of her life in England. The **noble reis** (noble king) to whom she dedicated her *lais* was probably King Henry II of England, who reigned from 1154 to 1189. Some identify Marie as Mary, the Abbess of Shaftesbury from 1181 to 1215, an illegitimate sister of King Henry. This is an interesting possibility; the town of Shaftesbury was the seat of King Alfred the Great, the author of the fables Marie translated, as well as a key locale of the revival of the tales of King Arthur[3] that took place under Henry II.

Whoever she was, Marie de France displayed a remarkable literary background for a woman of her era. Much of what is known about her interests can be found in the prefaces to her works. She was familiar with

---

[1] *Breton lais:* A term characteristically applied to Marie de France's brief verse romances.

[2] **Chrétien de Troyes:** Poet of the northern French courts (fl. 1160–1180) who wrote some of the most famous romances of the European Middle Ages: *Erec and Enide, Cliges, Lancelot or the Knight of the Cart, Yvain,* and *Perceval or the Story of the Grail.* Although there is no conclusive evidence, Marie de France and Chrétien de Troyes probably knew at least some of each other's work; both were influenced by the court of Marie de Champagne.

[3] **revival of the tales of King Arthur:** It behooved Anglo-Norman king Henry II to revive the legends of Celtic Britain, in which ancient local kings fought the Anglo-Saxon enemy. The twelfth-century historians of the Anglo-Norman court, including William of Malmesbury (fl. 1125), Geoffrey of Monmouth (c. 1100–c. 1155), and the poet Wace (c. 1100–1175), developed and amplified the legend of Arthur, an obscure Welsh king of the sixth century. The contemporary Arthurian literature that resulted included the works of Chrétien de Troyes and other writers of romance and legend.

such classics as Aesop's *Fables* and Ovid's *Metamorphoses*[4] and was also acquainted with the Anglo-Norman and Latin literature of her day, including *History of the Kings of Britain* by Geoffrey of Monmouth, the rhymed chronicle **Brut**, and various Anglo-Norman romances.[5] At the same time, the originality of her own work has often been noted. For instance, her *Breton lais* do not resemble the most popular Anglo-Norman romances of her day, the anonymous *Floris and Blanchefleur* (1150) or *Tristan* (1160–1165) by Thomas of Britain. Living in the midst of a literary revival to which she herself was a major contributor, Marie de France developed a unique form of storytelling that treated the courtly love themes of her day with great poetic economy and clarity of language. Her treatment of traditional stories was highly sophisticated, taking for granted her audience's familiarity with the Arthurian romances. Her *Breton lais* were far briefer than other romances, composed in rhymed octa-syllabic couplets that required great compression of meaning.

BROOT

The *Breton Lai*.   The word *lai* originally meant a melody, with or without lyrics, celebrating a tale of adventure; it was redefined by Marie de France to mean a brief narrative poem recited at court. Marie claimed her *lais* were based on Breton or Celtic legends, though she may not have had firsthand knowledge of the language in which those legends appeared. Generally speaking, the poems take love as their topic and the behavior of lovers as their principal subject. While in her verses true love is often rewarded, and insincere or unscrupulous behavior in love is punished, Marie believed that love was always a good in itself, even though it never existed without sacrifice and pain. Women in her poems often arrive at a point of revelation or change, though not all the women are heroes or successful in the end. The poems are marked by "signatures," often the titles of the works, that utilize romantic symbols such as the nightingale, the swan, or in the case of the "The Lay of Chevrefoil," the honeysuckle; frequently these signatures symbolize the meaning at the poem's core.

Despite this seeming consistency of treatment, Marie did not take a single position on the subject of love. She showed respect for her sources, understanding each artist to be bound by the conventions of his or her "matter." Yet she often added a sense of mystery in her writing as well. In "The Lay of Chevrefoil," derived from the Tristan legend, she presents love in its simplest yet most elusive aspect as that which exists and therefore cannot be questioned, a power that makes us both greater and less than ourselves. In the sweep of passion, danger or even death may result

www   For links to more information about Marie de France and a quiz on "The Lay of Chevrefoil" ("The Honeysuckle"), see *World Literature Online* at bedfordstmartins .com/worldlit.

---

[4] *Fables . . . Metamorphoses:* Two of the favorite works of the European Middle Ages. The Greek writer Aesop (sixth century B.C.E.) told moral stories using animals as characters; the Roman author Ovid (43 B.C.E.–17 C.E.) collected legends of men and gods in the *Metamorphoses*.

[5] *History . . . Anglo-Norman romances:* Geoffrey of Monmouth's *History of the Kings of Britain* (1135) enlarged upon the story of King Arthur; Wace's *Brut* (1155) retold the story of Britain in Anglo-Norman verse; romances of the period elaborated on the cycles of Arthurian legend and the legend of Tristan and Iseult.

Mirror of Love,
1320–30
Romantic, courtly
scenes are beautifully
carved onto the back
of this French ivory
mirror. (Giraudon /
Art Resource)

from an unguarded moment; but sometimes luck is on the side of the lovers after all. This open-ended definition of love provides the story-teller with a grand array of possibilities, as Marie undoubtedly knew well.

The Tristan Legend.   Of all the medieval stories of love, the story of Tristan and Iseult[6] is the purest and most tragic. Preserved in a number of fragmentary sources, it derives from a rich body of Celtic legend. In the simplest version, Tristan is a knight in the court of his uncle, King Mark of Cornwall, sent by the king to plead his cause to Iseult, a young girl in Ireland. On their journey back to King Mark's court, Tristan and Iseult are tricked into drinking a magic potion that fills them with undeniable yearning for each other. After many tests of will, they consummate their love. They are then captured and brought before the king for judgment. The king banishes them from his realm, but later seeks them in the forest and finds them sleeping with Tristan's sword between them. He forgives Iseult and takes the couple back. Later, however, Tristan is again forced into exile and is wounded. Iseult looks for him but too late: He has died waiting for her. After Iseult dies beside him, King Mark, repentant, buries them side by side in a chapel; over their graves a vine and a rose inter-twine. Though it was briefly requited, their love remains forever unful-filled; unbidden and unsanctified, criminalized by the king's law, it exists only in a world of possibility.

---

[6] **story of Tristan and Iseult:** The French author Joseph Bedier (1864–1938) distilled the many versions of this story into a simplified core story, which was translated into English as *The Romance of Tristan and Iseult* in 1945. The Bedier edition is a useful introduction to the subject.

"The Lay of Chevrefoil."   In "The Lay of **Chevrefoil**," Marie de France conveys the theme of unfulfilled love with the greatest possible economy. She alludes to the familiar legend of Tristan and Iseult, including the king's anger, the envy of the court, and the necessity that the lovers meet in secret. In the *lai,* the love of Tristan and Iseult is expressed in the image of the honeysuckle and the hazel tree, two plants that require each other in order to survive. In material rife with the makings of melodrama, Marie uses this one reference to suggest the true nature of the lovers' attraction. Their encounter is made possible not so much by craft or guile as by the lovers' perfect, intuitive understanding of each other's thoughts. **Iseult** is not even named in "The Lay of Chevrefoil": Calling her only "the queen," Marie emphasizes both the impossibility and the fragile truth of Iseult and Tristan's love.

Marie's *lai* centers on a happy moment the lovers share in a forest in Cornwall despite the odds against them. About the outcome of their meeting the poet is discreet, saying the pair "took great joy in each other," hastening to add, "He spoke to her as much as he desired, / she told him whatever she liked." Iseult promises Tristan that she will plead for his right to return to King Mark's court, then leaves him. Tristan returns to Wales, where he writes down this *lai* in order, he says, to "remember the words" describing his adventure.

The *Lai* and Courtly Love.   Superficially at least, the story of Tristan and Iseult falls in line with the controversial notion in **Andreas Capellanus's** *The Art of Courtly Love* that the highest form of love is both secretive and adulterous. Since those circumstances are already part of the "matter" of this famous story, they must be respected by Marie. Iseult's attempt to negotiate Tristan's return to Cornwall also adheres to the legend, but without any particular reference to the doctrine of courtly love. The refinement of the couple's love, however, squares nicely with the theories of love being circulated around the courts of Marie of Champagne in the south of France at the time. Since Marie de France wrote many *lais,* some more and some less in conformity with the rules of courtly love, it is up to the reader to decide whether there is a reference to those rules in "The Lay of Chevrefoil" or not.

■ **CONNECTIONS**

Andreas Capellanus, *The Art of Courtly Love,* p. 617. The love ethic of "The Lay of Chevrefoil" can be compared with that of *The Art of Courtly Love.* Is it possible that Marie de France was directly influenced by the work of Capellanus, her contemporary? If so, in what ways does that influence manifest itself?

Lady Murasaki, *The Tale of Genji,* p. 1094. Medieval romances were often closely connected to courts in which knighthood had become a ceremonial occupation as well as a military duty, and where accordingly the "rules" of courtly behavior received great attention. This was as true for Japanese courtly society in the tenth and eleventh centuries as it was for the courts of Europe a bit later. How is Marie de France's miniature version of a European romance like or unlike *The Tale of Genji,* a major work of Japanese courtly literature? How do the rules of courtly behavior influence each work?

shev-ruh-FOIL

ee-SOOLT

ahn-DRAY-us
kah-peh-LAH-noos

■ FURTHER RESEARCH

Edition

Ewart, Alfred, ed. *Marie de France: Lais*. 1944. (Anglo-Norman text.)

Translations

Burgess, Glyn S., and Keith Busby. *The Lais of Marie de France*. 2d ed. 1999.
Hanning, Robert, and Joan Ferrante. *The Lais of Marie de France*. 1978.

Critical Studies

Burgess, Glyn S. *The Lais of Marie de France: Text and Context*. 1987.
Clifford, Paula. *Marie de France: Lais*. 1982.
Mickel, Emanuel J., Jr. *Marie de France*. 1974.

Related Literature

Bedier, Joseph, ed. *The Romance of Tristan and Iseult*. Trans. Hilaire Belloc with Paul
    Rosenfeld. 1945.

■ PRONUNCIATION

Andreas Capellanus: ahn-DRAY-us kah-peh-LAH-noos
Breton: breh-TAWNG, BRET-un
Brut: BROOT
Chevrefoil: shev-ruh-FOIL
Iseult: ee-SOOLT
lai: LAY
noble reis: NOH-bluh RAYS

∽ The Lay of Chevrefoil (The Honeysuckle)

Translated by Robert Hanning and Joan Ferrante

I should like very much
to tell you the truth
about the *lai* men call *Chevrefoil*—
why it was composed and where it came from.
Many have told and recited it to me
and I have found it in writing,
about Tristan and the queen
and their love that was so true,

"The Lay of Chevrefoil." Although Marie de France attained celebrity in her own time, her work was later scattered and laid aside. In 1581 a French scholar, Claude Fauchet, discovered a manuscript of her translation of an English collection of fables written in Latin. He noted the author's own comment: "At the end of this text, which I have written in romance [the vernacular], I shall name myself for the sake of posterity: Marie is my name and I am from France." The thirteenth-century English manuscript later used as a source of Marie's *Breton lais* was cataloged by English scholar Thomas Tyrwhitt while he was editing *The Canterbury Tales* of Geoffrey Chaucer in 1775.

that brought them much suffering
10   and caused them to die the same day.
King Mark was annoyed,
angry at his nephew Tristan;
he exiled Tristan from his land
because of the queen whom he loved.
Tristan returned to his own country,
South Wales, where he was born,
he stayed a whole year;
he couldn't come back.
Afterward he began to expose himself
20   to death and destruction.
Don't be surprised at this:
for one who loves very faithfully
is sad and troubled
when he cannot satisfy his desires.
Tristan was sad and worried,
so he set out from his land.
He traveled straight to Cornwall,
where the queen lived,
and entered the forest all alone—
30   he didn't want anyone to see him;
he came out only in the evening
when it was time to find shelter.
He took lodging that night,
with peasants, poor people.
He asked them for news
of the king—what he was doing.
They told him they had heard
that the barons had been summoned by ban.
They were to come to Tintagel
40   where the king wanted to hold his court;

Marie's works were finally compiled early in the nineteenth century in France. The *Lais* first were translated into English in 1911 by Eugene Mason.

    Anyone with a reading knowledge of French, with the help of footnotes, probably could read Marie's work in the Anglo-Norman original text as edited by Alfred Ewert in 1944. The short, eight-syllable (octasyllabic) lines with rhymed couplets move along briskly:

Asez me plest e bien le voil	It pleases me greatly and I am eager to tell you
Del lai que hum nume Chevrefoil	the truth about the *lai* men call Chevrefoil,
Que la verite vus en cunt	why it was composed and where it came from.
[E] pur quei il fu fet e dunt.	

The Hanning and Ferrante translation presented here abandons the French metrical pattern while keeping the work in free verse. One disputed line is cited in the footnotes.

at Pentecost they would all be there,
there'd be much joy and pleasure,
and the queen would be there too.
Tristan heard and was very happy;
she would not be able to go there
without his seeing her pass.
The day the king set out,
Tristan also came to the woods
by the road he knew
50   their assembly must take.
He cut a hazel tree in half,
then he squared it.
When he had prepared the wood,
he wrote his name on it with his knife.
If the queen noticed it—
and she should be on the watch for it,
for it had happened before
and she had noticed it then—
she'd know when she saw it,
60   that the piece of wood had come from her love.
This was the message of the writing
that he had sent to her:[1]
he had been there a long time,
had waited and remained
to find out and to discover
how he could see her,
for he could not live without her.
With the two of them it was just
as it is with the honeysuckle
70   that attaches itself to the hazel tree:
when it has wound and attached
and worked itself around the trunk,
the two can survive together;
but if someone tries to separate them,
the hazel dies quickly
and the honeysuckle with it.
"Sweet love, so it is with us:
You cannot live without me, nor I without you."
The queen rode along;
80   she looked at the hillside
and saw the piece of wood; she knew what it was,

---

[1]**This was the message . . . sent to her:** It is unclear whether the message is written on the wood (perhaps Tristan's name or something in code) or not. A later editor, Glyn S. Burgess, translates the original, "This was all he wrote, because he had sent her word that he had been there a long time. . . ."

she recognized all the letters.
The knights who were accompanying her,
who were riding with her,
she ordered to stop:
she wanted to dismount and rest.
They obeyed her command.
She went far away from her people
and called her girl
90 Brenguein, who was loyal to her.
She went a short distance from the road;
and in the woods she found him
whom she loved more than any living thing.
They took great joy in each other.
He spoke to her as much as he desired,
she told him whatever she liked.
Then she assured him
that he would be reconciled with the king—
for it weighed on him
100 that he had sent Tristan away;
he'd done it because of the accusation.
Then she departed, she left her love,
but when it came to the separation,
they began to weep.
Tristan went to Wales,
to wait until his uncle sent for him.
For the joy that he'd felt
from his love when he saw her,
by means of the stick he inscribed
110 as the queen had instructed,
and in order to remember the words,
Tristan, who played the harp well,
composed a new *lai* about it.
I shall name it briefly:
in English they call it *Goat's Leaf*
the French call it *Chevrefoil*.
I have given you the truth
about the *lai* that I have told here.

↝ Dante Alighieri

1265–1321

DAHN-tay

ah-lih-GYEH-ree

Certain writers come to represent the age in which they wrote, from whence their influence carries into the modern world: Homer and Confucius from ancient times, Shakespeare from the Elizabethan Age in England, Voltaire from the Enlightenment in Europe, and **Dante Alighieri** in the European Middle Period. In fact, Dante included himself among the six greatest writers of all time in Canto IV of *Inferno,* the first part of his literary masterpiece, *The Divine Comedy,* which like a GOTHIC cathedral embodies the elaborate construct of Christianity in the Middle Period.

At the outset it appears as if *The Divine Comedy* is solely a religious text reflecting the worldview of medieval Christianity: Dante's pilgrim travels the spiritual universe, from the underworld of Hell to the outer reaches of Heaven, a realm systematized into a single worldview and system of values by the medieval Roman Catholic Church. With Satan at the center of the earth and God on the outer circumference of the universe, the relative good or evil of an individual could be measured by his or her proximity to one or the other in the afterlife. Dante's pilgrimage has also been read as an allegorical journey of the soul or a psychological descent into the darkness within and subsequent ascension through knowledge, repentance, and a beatific vision. What gives depth as well as breadth to Dante's epic is the knowledge and history layered into the work, reflecting the diversity of learning in the thirteenth and fourteenth centuries: philosophy, theology, poetry—including works by Muslim poets and scholars[1]—, and Florentine, European, and papal politics. The term *architecture* is often applied to the "towering edifice" that Dante, one of the most learned men of the European Middle Ages, constructed out of words in his *Divine Comedy,* a truly timeless work of art, as interesting and profound today as it was in the fourteenth century.

Transforming Beatrice. Very little is known about Dante's early life in Florence or about his parents, although his father probably accrued some wealth as a money changer; his mother died when he was young. Nothing is known about Dante's formal education, but his scholarly and literary writings suggest that he studied the standard classical and medieval works of literature, rhetoric, and theology. Because of his evident talents he was entertained in the leading families of Florence. He married Gemma Donati in about 1285 with whom he had at least three children, one of whom, Pietro, became an important commentator on the *Comedy.*

Undoubtedly the most important event of Dante's early life was his

BEE-uh-tris

encounter with **Beatrice** Portinari. Nothing is known for certain about

---

[1] **Muslim . . . scholars:** Dante had access to the learning and poetry of Islamic Spain; his descriptions of the infernal regions, the heavens, the circles of the mystic rose, and the choirs of angels are similar to the writings of Islamic poet Ibnu'l-Arabi of Murcia (1165–1240) in *Meccan Revelations.*

Beatrice, and some have questioned her very existence. Tradition, however, has it that Dante first saw her when they were both nine years old, that he fell in love with her at first sight, and, although he saw her only a few times and they married others, that she had a tremendous impact on his life. Beatrice was married to Simone di'Bardi and died in 1290, at twenty-five. It was perhaps her death at such an early age that allowed Dante to idealize her, to transform her into a spiritual symbol of inspiration for the sake of his writings and his own growth as a person. Influenced by the courtly love lyrics of the troubadours of twelfth-century France, especially those concerning love for a married woman,[2] Dante began his apprenticeship as a writer by composing prose and poetry celebrating Beatrice. By 1294 he had written thirty-one poems with prose commentary focusing on his devotion to her, published in a collection titled *The New Life* (*La Vita Nuova*). In this work Beatrice, whose name means "she who blesses," is already a religious, transcendent figure, capable of transformative power. Later she plays an even more important role in *The Divine Comedy,* becoming not only a divine intercessor for the protagonist but also ultimately a member of the inner circle of Christian divinities, the Holy Trinity itself.

www For links to more information about Dante, a quiz on the *Inferno,* and information about the twenty-first-century relevance of Dante, see *World Literature Online* at bedfordstmartins .com/worldlit.

Political Affairs. As a young man Dante became actively involved in the political affairs of Florence, which, with some eighty thousand inhabitants, was a city second only to Paris in size in Europe. When looking at Dante's time, local politics should be seen as part of the larger struggle between the church and secular powers, between the princes of the Roman Catholic Church and the princes of the Holy Roman Empire. Internal wars and divisiveness were tearing apart Florence and Italy in the thirteenth century, and, as a city official, diplomat, and essayist, Dante was passionately involved with the fate of both. In Florence, the **Guelph**, who supported the Papacy, and the **Ghibelline**, who supported the Holy Roman Empire, were engaged in a civil war. On the side of the Guelphs, Dante probably participated in two decisive battles in 1289, Campaldinoa and the taking of Caprona, in which the Ghibellines were finally vanquished. The Guelphs then split over the issue of papal influence in Florence. Dante was a member of the White Guelphs, who sought to preserve an independent republic in Florence. The aristocratic Blacks sought power for themselves through collaboration with Pope Boniface VIII. Dante became one of six guild representatives who governed the city and, when the pope encroached on Florentine politics with threats of excommunication and confiscation of possessions, Dante and two others were sent on a mission to Rome in 1301 to query the pope about whether he intended to become actively involved and support the Blacks. Dante hoped that a secular leader of sufficient stature, such as

GWELF; GIB-uh-leen

---

[2] **love . . . married woman:** The troubadours were aristocratic poets in southern France who often addressed their poems to married ladies of the court from whom they sought patronage and favor. From the courtly love tradition came the idea that illicit love — that is, love outside the married state — was the most intense and inspirational.

the head of the Holy Roman Empire, might unify Italy and thereby bring peace to Florence.

Dante never returned to Florence. In a *coup d'état,* the Blacks gained power and took measures to eliminate the leaders of the Whites. When Dante chose not to return to Florence to face charges, he was sentenced to two years of exile and a large fine. This penalty was subsequently extended to permanent exile with the threat of being burned alive should he return to the city.

Life in Exile.   As an exiled intellectual, Dante temporarily linked up with other exiled Whites and some Ghibellines; after becoming disillusioned with their plans for reentering Florence, he wandered from town to town in Italy, finding temporary lodgings with a variety of patrons. In very poignant lines in the *Paradiso* (Canto XVII), Dante later described the painful experience of exile (Translation by John Ciardi):

> All that you held most dear you will put by
> > and leave behind you; and this is the arrow
> > the longbow of your exile first lets fly.

> You will come to learn how bitter as salt and stone
> > is the bread of others, how hard the way that goes
> > up and downstairs that never are your own.

He had already written several treatises connected to his studies. *The Banquet (Il Convivio)* was an extension of the autobiographical, philosophical *The New Life,* plus an explanation of Dante's literary views. *The Illustrious Vernacular (De vulgari eloquentia),* written in Latin during the same period, defends the use of Italian in serious literature and explores the role of the Italian writer in contemporary society. Later, the *Comedy* itself was written in vernacular Italian, leading to a broader audience and the promotion of cultural identity. Both *The Banquet* and *The Illustrious Vernacular* remained unfinished. A pamphlet written sometime between 1308 and 1317, *Monarchia,* placed hope for healing Italy's afflictions and divisiveness in a clear separation of the powers of the church and state and the investiture of two powerful leaders, a secular emperor and a sacred pope. Crowned in 1308, the new emperor Henry VII began to unite Italy, giving possible substance to Dante's vision; Florence, however, rebuffed him, and then the emperor died suddenly in 1313.

All the learning and the living that underlay Dante's early writings also became part of the complex fabric of the *Comedy,* to which Dante devoted himself for the rest of his life, from 1312 until his death in 1321. Published before the completion of the whole work, the first two parts of Dante's *Comedy,* the *Inferno* and the *Purgatorio,* were immediately recognized as great works of literature. With the work Dante hoped to gain an honorable return to his beloved Florence, but that did not happen. After finishing the last cantos of *Paradiso,* Dante died in Ravenna of malaria at the age of fifty-six in 1321 and was buried there; Florence is still trying to procure his bones. Dante's great work was first called *The Divine Comedy (Divina Commedia)* by a Venetian publisher in 1555.

The Divine Comedy.   *The Divine Comedy* is not an EPIC in the conventional sense, but if by *epic* one means a lengthy and elevated poem that deals with serious issues in a vast or cosmic setting, then Dante's extended narrative certainly qualifies. But his heroes are not Homer's or Virgil's warriors of the battlefield. They are warriors of the spirit, redefining the arena of adventure for the Middle Ages and beyond.

Dante called his monumental work the *Commedia,* a COMEDY because it had a happy ending. The story is essentially that of a pilgrimage by a person named Dante through the three spiritual realms of the Catholic world—Hell, Purgatory, and Heaven—during the Easter season. Because of the importance of the Trinity in Christian theology, the number three plays a key role in Dante's elaborate literary design. Each of the major divisions of the work points to a person of the Trinity and contains thirty-three cantos: the *Inferno,* identified with God the Father and judgment, includes one additional canto as a general introduction; the acts of the Son involving salvation are connected to *Purgatorio;* and the sustaining grace of the Holy Spirit is linked to *Paradiso.* Both *Purgatorio* and *Paradiso* contain thirty-three cantos, bringing the total number of cantos of all three works to one hundred, a perfect number. (The Trinity squared equals nine plus one deity equals ten, which when squared, totals one hundred.) The Trinity is also reflected in the work's complex pattern of three-line stanzas and interlocking rhymes, called TERZA RIMA, in which the first and third lines rhyme and the second line sets up the rhyme for the next stanza. In addition, ideally each line contains eleven syllables, making the total number of syllables in each tercet thirty-three.

The overall geography of Dante's world in the *Comedy* follows generally the cosmic system devised by Ptolemy, the Alexandrian astronomer of the second century. The heavens with their planets revolve around the earth. The geographical center of the earth's surface is Jerusalem; at the eastern edge is the Ganges River and at the western edge of the Mediterranean is the Straits of Gibraltar. Directly opposite from Jerusalem is the mountain of Purgatory. In the center of the earth, at a point farthest from the warmth of God's love in the Heavens, is Hell, where Satan is frozen in ice. All the rivers of Hell, symbolizing the tears of human suffering, flow toward Hell in order to torment its residents.

The *Inferno* begins on the evening of Maundy Thursday, or Holy Thursday, with Dante lost in a wood. At dawn on Good Friday, he meets the poet Virgil, who serves as his guide through Hell, a funnel-shaped region extending from the earth's surface to the center of the earth, a depression formed when Lucifer plunged from Heaven into the earth. Nine separate descending circles are divided into three major divisions; those associated with the mildest of sins are located at the top and those with the worst at the bottom. *Inferno* ends on Easter morning, as Dante and Virgil arrive in Purgatory, a mountain on an island in the sea at the opposite end of the earth from Lucifer's fall.

From the beginning of *Purgatorio,* there is a joyful, hopeful tone totally different from the despair of the *Inferno.* Dante the pilgrim, having learned about avoiding sin in Hell, now learns of the virtues of being

[. . .] A turn to a religious view of man and his fate . . . meant freeing [Dante] as a poet to represent the human with a subtle, many-sided realism that had no parallel in his time, and has not been surpassed since. . . . He can, for the first, fill his poem with many spirits and many voices besides his own, and with all the sights and sounds and smells of God's world.

– FRANCIS FERGUSSON, Critic, 1966

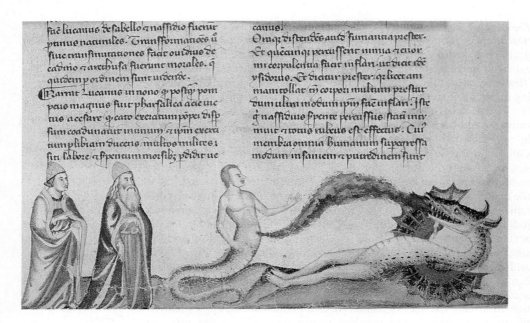

fac lucanus de sabello z nassidio fuerut
ptuius naturalee. Transformationes u
siue transmutationes facit ou diue de
cadnio z arethusa fuerunt morales. q
quidem p ordinem sunt uidende.
Narrat Lucanus in nono q posty pom
peus magnus fuit pharsalica acte uic
tus a cesare q cato exercitum pompei dis p
sum coadunauit innumy z ipm exerci
tum plibiam ducens multos milites s
siti labore a spentum morsib3 perdit ue

canus!
Omq3 distendce auto fumantia prester.
Et quecunq3 percussent nimia zenor
mi corpulentia fuat inflan uc dicit toc
ysidorus. Et dicatur prester qz licec ani
mam collat tn corpou multum prestat
dum ulim modum ipm fac in flan. Iste
q nassidius spente percussus stati inter
muit z totus ruleus est effectus. Cui
membra omnia humanum supgressa
modum infaniem z putredinem sunt

Dante and Virgil, fourteenth century

This illustration from the Inferno *shows Dante and Virgil encountering a dragon and a sea monster. (Giraudon / Art Resource, NY)*

purged of the seven deadly sins on the seven terraces in the middle of Purgatory. In Canto XXVII the poets cross through a wall of fire, a symbol of transformation, into Earthly Paradise. Virgil, having reached a place where he "can discern nothing further," gives a farewell speech. His job as guide comes to an end because Purgatory is as far as reason can carry the individual pilgrim, and Virgil is a virtuous pagan lacking belief in God, with only his reason to guide him. Dante then learns about the Earthly Paradise and experiences the freedom of action associated with being purged of sin. Finally, the epitome of beauty and virtue is introduced, the veiled Beatrice, who becomes Dante's next guide. She scolds Dante for lapsing into material desires, which is perhaps a confession by the poet of his own waywardness. After Dante has been bathed in the river Lethe, washing away all memory of sin, he is allowed to look at Beatrice without her veil and is blinded by the vision. His virtues are strengthened by drinking from the waters of the Eunoe; he is now ready to experience the celestial Paradise. Beatrice leads Dante through the three regions of this realm: the seven planets of ancient astronomy, the circles of fixed stars, and the Empyrean, or highest Heaven, which the pair witness at sunset on the Thursday following Easter.

As the third and final volume of *The Divine Comedy, Paradiso* is a celebration of the starry heavens of an earth-centered cosmos as understood by medieval astronomy. As Dante and Beatrice ascend from planet to planet, various redeemed souls provide scientific explanations for the heavenly bodies. Appropriate Christian doctrines are also discussed. The seven planets plus the circle of fixed stars and the *primum mobile*[3] equal (again) the number nine; the Empyrean, or Heaven, is tenth, a symbol of unity and the totality of the universe. The last three cantos of *Paradiso* picture the saints of the Catholic Church arranged in a mystic white rose with God at its center. Canto XXXII identifies the thrones of the most blessed; Beatrice returns to her eternal throne and St. Bernard of Clairvaux becomes Dante's final guide to a climactic, beatific vision. Bernard's prayers on behalf of Dante lead to a final vision of the Holy Trinity and the oneness of the universe. This culminating vision of God represents a difficult task for the poet: to describe that which by definition transcends words — the ineffable. Dante's answer is to focus on the effect of the vision on its human witness rather than on the vision itself. The result of Dante's artistry is the experience of merging with the divine, the final and ultimate goal of the medieval pilgrim.

Inferno. Because sin is always more interesting than goodness, and because Dante's depictions of sin's punishments are so insightful and imaginative, the *Inferno* has been the most popular volume of the trilogy for modern readers. Canto I begins with the statement that the pilgrim Dante, at thirty-five years of age, has lost his way and found himself in a "dark wood" — a different kind of beginning from those in Homer's epics or Virgil's *Aeneid,* in which a grand theme is explicitly announced. A very visual poet, Dante begins with what seems to be an ordinary situation in accordance with the manner of his narrator, who is a simplified, at times more naive, version of himself. Dante's style, however, becomes more elevated as his pilgrim advances — literally, climbs — to Purgatory and then Paradise. On the literal level, the poem follows the dramatic adventures of this Dante as he journeys through three realms, encountering various sinners and saints from both the ancient world and contemporary Italy, learning from their lives, and progressing from confusion to spiritual illumination.

The first lines of the *Inferno,* however, begin to hint at another layer of meaning, symbolic or allegorical. The pilgrim is at an age when questions traditionally arise about one's spiritual condition; the "dark wood" mirrors the inner confusion and fear people may experience when they reach midlife. When Dante sees the sunrise and decides to climb the Mount of Joy, where he confronts three symbolic animals, it is clear that Dante the poet is deliberately entering into metaphor.

The three animals that rebuff Dante have been variously interpreted. If we are to view them as schematic representations of the journey he will face in Hell, they might be seen as symbols of its three principal regions: Incontinence (lack of restraint), Violence, and Fraud. More traditionally, the leopard may represent lust, the lion pride, and the she-wolf avarice. The latter image is especially convincing, since Dante says his spirit is Defeated by this encounter much in the way that a gambler is defeated by becoming aware of his loss of fortune.

> . . . Dante Alighieri, sometimes described as Shakespeare's one great equal . . . wrote explicitly and extensively about politics, philosophy, science, and especially literature, including a commentary on his own work . . . Dante wrote the story of his own life, presenting not the enigma of silence, but the greater mystery that grows from knowledge of a life.
> – ROBERT PINSKY, Poet, 2001

---

[3] ***primum mobile:*** In the Ptolemaic universe, this is the outermost sphere with the earth as its center, causing all the heavenly bodies to revolve with it.

Enter Virgil, who explains that he has been sent to guide Dante through a descent into Hell and an ascent to Purgatory, where he will be replaced by Beatrice. Virgil stands for reason and conscience as well as the best ideals of the Roman Empire. As a great poet, Virgil was a hero to Dante. Virgil sought to unify the Roman Empire with his own great epic the *Aeneid,* as Dante's poem would do for all of Italy, not just Florence. In addition, Virgil had written the *Fourth Eclogue,* which seemed to many Christians to have predicted the advent of a child messiah and, in Book IV of the *Aeneid,* he had described a descent into Hades, making him an appropriate guide for Dante. As Virgil tells him, Dante is to go on this journey to gain knowledge. Virgil engages in an ongoing dialogue with Dante, answering his questions and probing his understanding.

KAHN-truh PAH-soh

In Canto III, the two poets pass through the Gate of Hell and view for the first time a ***contra passo,*** or symbolic retribution. In Dante's Hell, more picturesque and altogether different from most other literary depictions of Hell, where general horrors engulf an entire group of sinners, individual punishments are fashioned for different sins. Dante's view of accountability was consistent with medieval theology, which held that individuals had free will and therefore chose sin. Thus they could be awarded punishments as individuals, regardless of their family or social situations. For example, because wishy-washy opportunists and the cowardly took no moral stand in life for either good or evil, they are adrift in Hell. Corrupt public officials who accepted bribes are boiled in pitch because, like bribes that cling to the sinner, pitch is sticky. And fortune-tellers and diviners who predicted the future during their time on earth now can look only backwards, as their heads have been turned around.

The first circle of Hell, found in Canto IV, is for virtuous pagans. Modern readers might sympathize with the likes of Homer, Horace, Ovid, and Lucan, but the medieval Christian view was clear on this point: Jesus alone was the gateway to Heaven. Thus the noble and virtuous pagans were held here at the threshold of Hell. Souls guilty of carnal sin are found in Canto V. Those who are led by their desires are blown about by the winds of desire. Dante's method of depicting sinners is to present appropriate examples who would be known to his readers than to develop more complete portraits of just a few of them. He does not analyze the sin abstractly, but rather he vividly shows how people following their desires and yielding to temptation can drift into damnation, as is the case with the most famous couple in *The Divine Comedy,* **Paolo** and **Francesca.** Despite their condemnation, their story is told with great sensitivity and sympathy.

POW-loh
frahn-CHES-kah

CHAH-koh

The first of several political prophecies about Florence is uttered in Canto VI by the glutton **Ciacco** the Hog, who is buried in swill. In subsequent cantos, Dante forthrightly locates his political enemies in various circles of Hell. In Cantos X and XI, the circle reserved for heretics serves as a mezzanine between the upper Hell, for sins of incontinence, and the lower Hell, for violence and fraud. After witnessing the instigators of war boiling in blood, Dante enters the memorable Wood of the Suicides in

Canto XIII, where the Violent Against Themselves are punished and their souls are denied human form. Even though the church considered suicide a sin, **Pier delle Vigne**'s narrative elicits sympathy. In Canto XV, Brunetto Latini, Dante's teacher and mentor, is also treated with delicacy and respect, despite the fact that his sin of homosexuality is acknowledged and punished with a burning rain. This canto is a reminder to the reader that Hell is filled with humans who might not have appeared evil but who nevertheless committed sins. In certain cases, however, Dante seems to be torn between the justice of a particular punishment and sympathy for the vagaries of human nature; after all, most human beings are a mixture of noble sentiments and carnal weaknesses.

At the end of Canto XVII, Virgil and Dante descend into the third and lowest area of Hell—for premeditated fraud—on the back of Geryon, a marvelous monster with the face of a man and a serpent's body. The eighth circle of Hell called the Malebolge (evil ditches) is divided into ten trenches, or **Bolgia**, peopled with different kinds of sinners associated with fraud. The Simoniacs are set upside down in holes and their feet are on fire. Dante locates Ulysses (Odysseus), whom Homer describes in the *Odyssey* as quick-witted and clever, in Bolgia Eight (Canto XXVI), the place for evil counselors. Italians traced their ancestry back to the Trojans, and Odysseus was the architect of the ruse of the wooden horse, which led to the destruction of Troy in the Trojan War. Hidden in a great flame, a proud Ulysses recounts his exploration of the Western ocean. His death by shipwreck on Purgatory Mountain is a symbolic statement that courage and intelligence alone cannot save man.

The climax of the *Inferno* occurs in the last three cantos, when the poets reach the ninth circle of Hell. Here the sinners are so far from the warmth of God's love that they are frozen in a lake of ice, symbolic of the condition of their hearts. One of the lasting images of this section is Ugolino gnawing on the skull of **Ruggieri** in Canto XXXIII, in which **Ugolino** tells their story of betrayal and infamy. The great pathos associated with the starvation of children makes this episode one of the most memorable in the entire poem. In the final canto and at the utter bottom of Hell is the master of evil himself, Satan, with great flapping wings and a treacherous threesome in his mouths: Judas Iscariot, Brutus, and Cassius. For modern readers, Brutus and Cassius may not meet the same standard of evil as the betrayer of Jesus, and the portrait of Satan may not inspire fear.

Dante was a dramatist, a genius who created an imaginary world through which the attentive reader might journey. The encyclopedic, intimidating mountain of saints and sinners, virtues and deadly sins, bits of geography, elaborate political maneuvers from Florence and the Holy Roman Empire—all of which might have a literal, as well as other layers of meaning—fit somehow into Dante's own, esoteric vision of God's plan for the world. The almost immediate fame of the *Comedy* is testified to by several line-by-line commentaries by contemporaries of Dante, as if his work did indeed hold the key to salvation. Today there are hundreds of such line-by-line commentaries.

pee-EHR
deh-lah-VEEN-yay

BOLE-jee-uh

roo-JEH-ree
oo-goh-LEE-no

Dante is an exiled, aggressive, self-righteous, salvation-bent intellectual, humbled only to rise assured and ardent, zealously prophetic, politically messianic, indignant, nervous, muscular, theatrical, energetic — he is at once our brother and our engenderer.

– ALLEN MANDELBAUM,
Translator, 1980

Translation Note.   Italian offers so many possibilities for rhyme. In English, however, *terza rima* is nearly impossible to duplicate. The opening tercets (three-line stanzas) from Canto I of the original Italian *Inferno* provide a sample of Dante's language and form; following the Italian is a prose translation in English by John D. Sinclair:

Nel mezzo del cammin di nostra vita
mi ritrovai per una selva oscura
che la diritta via era smarrita.

Ah quanto a dir qual era è cosa dura
esta selva selvaggia e aspra e forte
che nel pensier rinova la paura!

Tant' è amara che poco è piu morte;
ma per trattar del ben ch'io vi trovai,
dirò dell'altre cose ch'i' v'ho scorte.

In the middle of the journey of our life, I came to myself within a dark wood where the straight way was lost. Ah, how hard a thing it is to tell of that wood, savage and harsh and dense, the thought of which renews my fear! So bitter is it that death is hardly more. But to give account of the good which I found there I will tell of the other things I noted there.

The Robert and Jean Hollander translation presented in full in the following pages stays very close to the language and phrasing of the Italian text in the manner of Sinclair's rendering but in tercets rather than prose, in very readable, contemporary English.

■ **CONNECTIONS**

Chaucer, *The Canterbury Tales*, p. 885. During the Middle Period, the sacred journey was central to Christians, whose ideal destination was Jerusalem, and to Muslims, for whom Mecca was the goal. For both religions the earthly pilgrimage was symbolic of the soul's journey from earth to heaven. In his *Canterbury Tales,* Chaucer tells the stories of pilgrims who must substitute a journey to Canterbury in England for their spiritual nurturance. How does Dante blend symbolic and literal journeys in the *Inferno* to give his pilgrimage depth and relevance?

***Beowulf,* p. 481; Homer *Odyssey* (Book I).** Middle Period writers differ radically in their descriptions of the underworld, depending on whether they were pagan or Christian. Dante, like Christian theologians, transforms the underworld into Hell. Although Dante's Hell, vividly personal, is a dark realm, it is nevertheless lively and passionate. How does Dante's Christian version of hell differ from the pagan or classical versions?

Virgil, *The Aeneid* (Book 1). Roman and Italian writers from Virgil to Dante attempted to create a coherent history for Italy that stretched from myth and legend to the present political-historical reality. Virgil linked the founding of Rome to Aeneas and the Trojan War, which the Greeks won. How does Dante attempt to make a connection between his world and ancient Rome and Greece through his use of Virgil and other classical writers?

■ FURTHER RESEARCH

Translations
Durling, Robert M., trans. *Inferno*. 1996.
Hollander, Robert, and Jean Hollander, trans. *Inferno*. 2000.
Mandelbaum, Allen, trans. *Inferno*. 1980.
Singleton, Charles S., trans. *The Divine Comedy*. 1970.

Bibliography, Biography, and Background
Golino, Carlo. *Dante Alighieri*. 1979.
Lansing, Richard, ed. *The Dante Encyclopedia*. 2000.
Lewis, R. W. B. *Dante*. 2001.
Morgan, Alison. *Dante and the Medieval Other World*. 1990.
Sterns, Monroe. *Dante: Poet of Love*. 1965.
Vossler, K. *Medieval Culture: An Introduction to Dante and His Times*. 1929.

Commentary and Criticism
Auerbach, Erich. *Dante: Poet of the Secular World*. 1961.
Fergusson, Francis. *Dante*. 1966.
Fowlie, Wallace. *A Reading of Dante's "Inferno."* 1981.
Freccero, John, ed. *Dante: A Collection of Critical Essays*. 1965.
Masciandaro, Franco. *Dante as Dramatist*. 1991.
Santayanna, George. *Three Philosophical Poets*. 1927.
Sayers, Dorothy. *Further Papers on Dante*. 1957.
———. *Introductory Papers on Dante*. 1954.

■ PRONUNCIATION

Accorso: ah-KORE-soh
Acheron: AK-uh-rahn
Acre: AH-kruh, AY-kur
Aldobrandi: ahl-doh-BRAHN-dee
Amidei: ah-mee-DAY-ee
Amphiaraus: am-fee-uh-RAY-us
Amyclas: uh-MIGH-klus
Anaxagoras: an-ak-SAG-oh-rus
Anchises: ang-KIGH-seez
Antaeus: an-TEE-us
Arachne: uh-RAK-nee
Argenti; Filippo: ar-JEN-tee, fih-LEE-poh, fih-LIP-oh
Arles: ARL
Athamas: ATH-uh-mus
Averroës: uh-VEH-roh-eez
Avicenna: av-ih-SEN-uh
Azzolino da Romano: ah-tsoh-LEE-noh dah-roh-MAH-noh
Bachiglione: bah-kee-LYOH-nee, -lee-OH-nee
Beatrice: BEE-uh-tris, bay-ah-TREE-chay
Bolgia: BOLE-jee-uh
Boniface VIII: BAH-nih-fus
Borsiere, Guglielmo: bore-SYAY-ray, goo-LYEL-moh, bore-see-AY-ray, goo-lee-EL-moh
Buondelmonte: bwone-del-MONE-tay
Cacciaguida: kah-chah-GWEE-duh
Cacus: KAY-kus
Caïna: kah-EE-nuh
Capaneus: KAP-uh-noos

Casalodi: kah-sah-LOH-dee
Catiline: KAT-ih-line
Ceperano: chay-peh-RAH-noh
Ciacco: CHAH-koh
Cocytus: koh-SIGH-tus
contra passo: KAHN-truh PAH-soh
Dante Alighieri: DAHN-tay ah-lih-GYEH-ree
Dejanira: dej-uh-NIGH-ruh
Diogenes: digh-AH-jih-neez
Dioscorides: digh-us-KORE-ih-deez
Divina Commedia: dih-VEE-nuh kah-MED-ee-uh
Empyrean: em-PEE-ree-un
Erinyes: eh-RIN-ee-eez
Euryalus: yoo-RIGH-uh-lus
Fabricius: fuh-BREE-shus
Farinata degli Uberti: fah-ree-NAH-tah DEH-lyee oo-BEHR-tee
Feltro, Guido del Monte: FEL-troh, GWEE-doh del-MONE-tay
Fiesole: fyeh-SOH-lay, fee-eh-SOH-lay
Francesca: frahn-CHES-kah
Gallehaut: gah-LOH
Garisenda: gah-rih-SEN-duh
Geryon: JEE-ree-ahn, GEH-ree-ahn
Ghibelline: GIB-uh-leen
Glaucus: GLAW-kus
Gratian: GRAY-shun
Gualdrada: gwahl-DRAH-dah
Guelph: GWELF
Guerra, Guido: GWEH-ruh, GWEE-doh
Holofernes: hoh-loh-FUR-neez
Hyperion: high-PEE-ree-ahn, -un
Hypsipyle: hip-SIP-uh-lee
Judecca: joo-DEK-uh
Maccabaeus: mak-uh-BEE-us
Malebolge: mal-uh-BOWL-jay
Malebranche: mahl-uh-BRANK-eh
Maremma: muh-REM-uh
Monferrato: mawn-feh-RAH-toh
Montaperti: mawn-tah-PEHR-tee
Mosca dei Lamberti: MAW-skuh DAY-ee lahm-BEHR-tee
Mucius Scaevola: MYOO-shus SEE-voh-luh, SEV-uh-luh, SKIGH-voh-luh
Obizzo da Este: oh-BIT-soh dah-ES-tay
Orosius, Paulus: uh-ROO-zhee-us, PAW-lus, POW-loos
Paolo: POW-loh
Penthesilea: pen-thu-sih-LEE-uh
Pettignana, Pier: pet-in-YAH-nuh, pee-EHR
Phlegyas: FLEG-ee-us
Pier delle Vigne: pee-EHR deh-lah-VEEN-yay
Pistoia: pis-TOH-yah
Priscian: PRISH-un
Quarnero: kwar-NAY-roh
Rascia: RAH-shuh
Rinier da Corneto: reen-YEHR dah-kohr-NAY-toh
Rinier Pazzo: reen-YEHR PAHT-soh
Romagna: roh-MAHN-yah

Ruggieri: roo-JEH-ree
Rusticucci; Jacopo: roo-stih-KOO-chee, JAH-koh-poh
Santafiora: sahn-tah-FYOH-rah
Scipio: SKIP-ee-oh, SIP-ee-oh
Semiramis: seh-MEE-ruh-mis
Ser Brunetto Latino: sehr broo-NET-oh lah-TEE-noh
Sercho: SEHR-koh
Sichaeus: sih-KEE-us
Strophades: STRAH-fuh-deez
Tagliacozza: tahl-yah-KAWT-suh
Tityos: TIT-ee-us
Typhoeus: tigh-FEE-us
Ubaldino: oo-bahl-DEE-noh
Ugolino: oo-goh-LEE-no

ꙮ Inferno

Translated by Robert and Jean Hollander

CANTO I

Midway in the journey of our life[1]
I came to myself in a dark wood,
3 for the straight way was lost.

[handwritten: He's lost — disruption to start story]

Ah, how hard it is to tell
the nature of that wood, savage, dense and harsh—
6 the very thought of it renews my fear!

It is so bitter death is hardly more so.
But to set forth the good I found
9 I will recount the other things I saw.

Inferno. The Divine Comedy is rather simple to describe from a distance: a middle-aged man named Dante has lost his way in life. In order to regain the path of virtue and faith leading to his own ultimate salvation, he is first guided miraculously by the ancient poet Virgil through the two worlds of Hell and Purgatory so that he might gain knowledge of his own sins and at some point be cleansed of them. Finally, with the aid of the beatific Beatrice, Dante enters Paradise, where he experiences a vision of the Holy Trinity. The complexity comes when one is closer to the text, with its many allusions to works of theology, philosophy, mythology, and history. If one reads the *Comedy* as allegory, one could say that Dante stands for the ordinary Christian layman; Virgil stands for reason; the three beasts for lust, pride, and avarice; Beatrice for divine love, and so forth. Rather than viewing the text in such simplistic terms, however, it is perhaps better to see allegorical

---

[1] **Midway . . . life:** Dante was thirty-five at the time, 1300 C.E. This is a reference to Psalm 90, verse 10: "The days of our years are three score years and ten," meaning seventy years.

How I came there I cannot really tell,
I was so full of sleep
12 when I forsook the one true way.

But when I reached the foot of a hill,
there where the valley ended
15 that had pierced my heart with fear,

looking up, I saw its shoulders
arrayed in the first light of the planet[2]
18 that leads men straight, no matter what their road.

Then the fear that had endured
in the lake of my heart, all the night
21 I spent in such distress, was calmed.

And as one who, with laboring breath,
has escaped from the deep to the shore
24 turns and looks back at the perilous waters,

so my mind, still in flight,
turned back to look once more upon the pass
27 no mortal being ever left alive.

After I rested my wearied flesh a while,
I took my way again along the desert slope,
30 my firm foot always lower than the other.

But now, near the beginning of the steep,
a leopard light and swift
33 and covered with a spotted pelt

---

meanings as clustered around certain characters, and not to force allegory on everything in this multifaceted, profoundly soulful work.

In the *Inferno*'s intricate underworld geography and morality, poignant individuals manage to detach themselves from their coconspirators long enough to tell their stories, which Dante in his narrative genius somehow captures in but a few lines.

A note on the translation: The notes used in this selection are the editors'. They have been intentionally kept to a minimum and do not represent all possible meanings or explanations. Every third line is numbered in the following Hollander translation. Readers with more background in classical studies and Dante's *Comedy* might want to supplement our notes with more detailed commentaries available in the translations by Charles S. Singleton, Robert M. Durling, and Robert and Jean Hollander.

---

[2] **first light . . . planet:** The sun, symbolizing God.

refused to back away from me
but so impeded, barred the way,
36 that many times I turned to go back down.

It was the hour of morning,
when the sun mounts with those stars
39 that shone with it when God's own love

first set in motion those fair things,[3]
so that, despite that beast with gaudy fur,
42 I still could hope for good, encouraged

by the hour of the day and the sweet season,
only to be struck by fear
45 when I beheld a lion in my way.

He seemed about to pounce —
his head held high and furious with hunger —
48 so that the air appeared to tremble at him.

And then a she-wolf who, all hide and bones,
seemed charged with all the appetites
51 that have made many live in wretchedness

so weighed my spirits down with terror,
which welled up at the sight of her,
54 that I lost hope of making the ascent.

And like one who rejoices in his gains
but when the time comes and he loses,
57 turns all his thought to sadness and lament,

such did the restless beast make me —
coming against me, step by step,
60 it drove me down to where the sun is silent.

While I was fleeing to a lower place,
before my eyes a figure showed,
63 faint, in the wide silence.

---

[3] **first set . . . fair things:** In Christian mythology, the stars were set in motion during Creation in the spring of the year, on the same date as the Crucifixion. This is the morning of Good Friday.

When I saw him in that vast desert,
'Have mercy on me, whatever you are,'
66 I cried, 'whether shade or living man!'

He answered: 'Not a man, though once I was.
My parents were from Lombardy—
69 Mantua was their homeland.

'I was born *sub Julio*,[4] though late in his time,
and lived at Rome, under good Augustus
72 in an age of false and lying gods.

'I was a poet and I sang
the just son of Anchises[5] come from Troy
75 after proud Ilium[6] was put to flame.

'But you, why are you turning back to misery?
Why do you not climb the peak that gives delight,
78 origin and cause of every joy?'

'Are you then Virgil, the fountainhead
that pours so full a stream of speech?'
81 I answered him, my head bent low in shame.

'O glory and light of all other poets,
let my long study and great love avail
84 that made me delve so deep into your volume.

'You are my teacher and my author.
You are the one from whom alone I took
87 the noble style that has brought me honor.

'See the beast that forced me to turn back.
Save me from her, famous sage—
90 she makes my veins and pulses tremble.'

'It is another path that you must follow,'
he answered, when he saw me weeping,
93 'if you would flee this wild and savage place.

---

[4] ***sub Julio:*** Meaning "under Julius Caesar"; Virgil was born in 70 B.C.E.

[5] **son of Anchises:** Aeneas, the hero of Virgil's *Aeneid*.

[6] **Ilium:** Troy or the citadel of Troy.

'For the beast that moves you to cry out
lets no man pass her way,
96   but so besets him that she slays him.

'Her nature is so vicious and malign
her greedy appetite is never sated—
99   after she feeds she is hungrier than ever.

'Many are the creatures that she mates with,
and there will yet be more, until the hound
102   shall come who'll make her die in pain.[7]

'He shall not feed on lands or lucre
but on wisdom, love, and power.
105   Between felt and felt[8] shall be his birth.

'He shall be the salvation of low-lying Italy,
for which maiden Camilla, Euryalus,
108   Turnus, and Nisus died of their wounds.[9]

'He shall hunt the beast through every town
till he has sent her back to Hell
111   whence primal envy set her loose.

'Therefore, for your sake, I think it wise
you follow me: I will be your guide,
114   leading you, from here, through an eternal place

'where you shall hear despairing cries
and see those ancient souls in pain
117   as they bewail their second death.[10]

'Then you will see the ones who are content
to burn[11] because they hope to come,
120   whenever it may be, among the blessed.

---

[7] **the hound shall come . . . pain:** A prophecy by Dante possibly referring to Can Grande della Scala, the lord of Verona and Dante's benefactor during his exile from Florence.

[8] **Between felt and felt:** Often translated as between Feltro and Feltro, referring to Verona, which is in between the towns of Feltro and Montefeltro.

[9] **Camilla . . . wounds:** Four who die in Aeneas's conquest of Italy in *The Aeneid*.

[10] **second death:** The second death is the suffering of the damned in Hell.

[11] **to burn:** The burning in Purgatory.

'Should you desire to ascend to these,
you'll find a soul more fit to lead than I:
123 I'll leave you in her care when I depart.

'For the Emperor who has his seat on high
wills not, because I was a rebel to His law,
126 that I should make my way into His city.

'In every part He reigns and there He rules.
There is His city and His lofty seat.
129 Happy the one whom He elects to be there!'

And I answered: 'Poet, I entreat you
by the God you did not know,
132 so that I may escape this harm and worse,

'lead me to the realms you've just described
that I may see Saint Peter's gate[12]
and those you tell me are so sorrowful.'
136 Then he set out and I came on behind him.

CANTO II

Day was departing and the darkened air
released the creatures of the earth
3 from their labor, and I, alone,

prepared to face the struggle —
of the way and of the pity of it —
6 which memory, unerring, shall retrace.

O Muses, O lofty genius, aid me now!
O memory, that set down what I saw,
9 here shall your worth be shown.

I began: 'Poet, you who guide me,
consider if my powers will suffice
12 before you trust me to this arduous passage.

'You tell of the father of Sylvius
that he, still subject to corruption, went
15 to the eternal world while in the flesh.[13]

---

[12] **Saint Peter's gate:** The gate of penitence that leads into Purgatory.

[13] **went to . . . flesh:** The visit of Aeneas to the underworld (*Aeneid* VI).

'But that the adversary of all evil showed
such favor to him, considering who and what he was,
18 and the high sequel that would spring from him,[14]

'seems not unfitting to a man who understands.
For in the Empyrean[15] he was chosen
21 to father holy Rome and her dominion,

'both of these established—if we would speak
the truth—to be the sacred precinct where
24 successors of great Peter have their throne.

'On this journey, for which you grant him glory,
he heard the words that prompted him
27 to victory and prepared the Papal mantle.[16]

'Later, the Chosen Vessel° went there   St. Paul
to bring back confirmation of our faith,
30 the first step in our journey to salvation.

'But why should I go there? who allows it?
I am not Aeneas, nor am I Paul.
33 Neither I nor any think me fit for this.

'And so, if I commit myself to come,
I fear it may be madness. You are wise,
36 you understand what I cannot express.'

And as one who unwills what he has willed,
changing his intent on second thought
39 so that he quite gives over what he has begun,

such a man was I on that dark slope.
With too much thinking I had undone
42 the enterprise so quick in its inception.

'If I have rightly understood your words,'
replied the shade of that great soul,
45 'your spirit is assailed by cowardice,

---

[14] **the high sequel . . . from him:** Aeneas as the ancestor of later emperors.

[15] **the Empyrean:** The highest domain of Heaven, where one is in the presence of God.

[16] **prepared the Papal mantle:** The founding of Rome by Aeneas prefigures the founding of the Vatican in Rome and the Papacy.

'which many a time so weighs upon a man
it turns him back from noble enterprise,
48 the way a beast shies from a shadow.

'To free you from this fear
I'll tell you why I came and what I heard
51 when first I felt compassion for you.

'I was among the ones who are suspended[17]
when a lady called me, so blessèd and so fair
54 that I implored her to command me.

'Her eyes shone brighter than the stars.
Gentle and clear, the words she spoke to me —
57 an angel's voice was in her speech:

'"O courteous Mantuan spirit,
whose fame continues in the world
60 and shall continue while the world endures,

'"my friend, who is no friend of Fortune,
is so hindered on his way upon the desert slope
63 that, in his terror, he has turned back,

'"and, from what I hear of him in Heaven,
I fear he has gone so far astray
66 that I arose too late to help him.

'"Set out, and with your polished words
and whatever else is needed for his safety,
69 go to his aid, that I may be consoled.

'"I who bid you go am Beatrice.
I come from where I most desire to return.
72 The love that moved me makes me speak.

'"And when I am before my Lord
often will I offer praise of you to Him."
75 Then she fell silent. And I began:

---

[17] **ones who are suspended:** The virtuous heathen in limbo are suspended between punishment and bliss.

' "O lady of such virtue that by it alone
   the human race surpasses all that lies
78 within the smallest compass of the heavens,[18]

' "so pleased am I at your command that my consent,
   were it already given, would be given late.
81 You have but to make your desire known.

' "But tell me why you do not hesitate
   to descend into the center of the earth
84 from the unbounded space you long for."

' "Since you are so eager to know more,"
   she answered, "I shall be brief in telling you
87 why I am not afraid to enter here.

' "We should fear those things alone
   that have the power to harm.
90 Nothing else is frightening.

' "I am made such by God's grace
   that your affliction does not touch,
93 nor can these fires assail me.

' "There is a gracious lady[19] in Heaven so moved
   by pity at his peril, she breaks stern judgment
96 there above and lets me send you to him.

' "She summoned Lucy[20] and made this request:
   «Your faithful one is now in need of you
99 and I commend him to your care.»

' "Lucy, the enemy of every cruelty,
   arose and came to where I sat
102 at venerable Rachel's side,[21]

' "and said: «Beatrice, true praise of God,
   why do you not help the one who loved you so
105 that for your sake he left the vulgar herd?

---

[18] **smallest compass . . . heavens:** The cycle of the moon.

[19] **a gracious lady:** The Virgin Mary.

[20] **Lucy:** St. Lucy of Syracuse (third century), a martyr.

[21] **Rachel's side:** Rachel is mother of Joseph and Benjamin in the Hebrew Scriptures (Genesis 29–35).

'"«Do you not hear the anguish in his tears?
Do you not see the death besetting him
108   on the swollen river where the sea cannot prevail?»

'"Never were men on earth so swift to seek
their good or to escape their harm as I,
111   after these words were spoken.

'"to descend here from my blessèd seat,
trusting to the noble speech that honors you
114   and those who have paid it heed."

'After she had said these things to me,
she turned away her eyes, now bright with tears,
117   making me more eager to set out.

'And so I came to you just as she wished.
I saved you from the beast denying you
120   the short way to the mountain of delight.

'What then? Why, why do you delay?
Why do you let such cowardice rule your heart?
123   Why are you not more spirited and sure,

'when three such blessèd ladies
care for you in Heaven's court
126   and my words promise so much good?'

As little flowers, bent and closed
with chill of night, when the sun
129   lights them, stand all open on their stems,

such, in my failing strength, did I become.
And so much courage poured into my heart
132   that I began, as one made resolute:

'O how compassionate was she to help me,
how courteous were you, so ready to obey
135   the truthful words she spoke to you!

'Your words have made my heart
so eager for the journey
138   that I've returned to my first intent.

'Set out then, for one will prompts us both.
You are my leader, you my lord and master,'
I said to him, and when he moved ahead
142 I entered on the deep and savage way.

Canto III

THROUGH ME THE WAY TO THE CITY OF WOE,
THROUGH ME THE WAY TO ETERNAL PAIN,
3 THROUGH ME THE WAY AMONG THE LOST.

JUSTICE MOVED MY MAKER ON HIGH.
DIVINE POWER MADE ME,
6 WISDOM SUPREME, AND PRIMAL LOVE.

BEFORE ME NOTHING WAS BUT THINGS ETERNAL,[22]
AND I ENDURE ETERNALLY.
9 ABANDON ALL HOPE, YOU WHO ENTER HERE.

These words, dark in hue, I saw inscribed
over an archway. And then I said:
12 'Master, for me their meaning is hard.'

And he, as one who understood:
'Here you must banish all distrust,
15 here must all cowardice be slain.

'We have come to where I said
you would see the miserable sinners
18 who have lost the good of the intellect.'[23]

And after he had put his hand on mine
with a reassuring look that gave me comfort,
21 he led me toward things unknown to man.

Now sighs, loud wailing, lamentation
resounded through the starless air,
24 so that I too began to weep.

---

[22] THINGS ETERNAL: Primal matter, such as the heavens and divinities.

[23] the good . . . intellect: Knowledge of God.

Unfamiliar tongues, horrendous accents,
words of suffering, cries of rage, voices
27 loud and faint, the sound of slapping hands—

all these made a tumult, always whirling
in that black and timeless air,
30 as sand is swirled in a whirlwind.

And I, my head encircled by error, said:
'Master, what is this I hear, and what people
33 are these so overcome by pain?'

And he to me: 'This miserable state is borne
by the wretched souls of those who lived
36 without disgrace yet without praise.

'They intermingle with that wicked band
of angels, not rebellious and not faithful
39 to God, who held themselves apart.

'Loath to impair its beauty, Heaven casts them out,
and depth of Hell does not receive them[24]
42 lest on their account the evil angels gloat.'

And I: 'Master, what is so grievous to them,
that they lament so bitterly?'
45 He replied: 'I can tell you in few words.

'They have no hope of death,
and their blind life is so abject
48 that they are envious of every other lot.

'The world does not permit report of them.
Mercy and justice hold them in contempt.
51 Let us not speak of them—look and pass by.'

And I, all eyes, saw a whirling banner
that ran so fast it seemed as though
54 it never could find rest.

Behind it came so long a file of people
that I could not believe
57 death had undone so many.

---

[24] them: Those who choose neither good nor evil but in the words of Revelation 3:16 "art lukewarm."

After I recognized a few of these,
I saw and knew the shade of him
60 who, through cowardice, made the great refusal.[25]

At once with certainty I understood
this was that worthless crew
63 hateful alike to God and to His foes.

These wretches, who never were alive,
were naked and beset
66 by stinging flies and wasps

that made their faces stream with blood,
which, mingled with their tears,
69 was gathered at their feet by loathsome worms.

And then, fixing my gaze farther on,
I saw souls standing on the shore of a wide river,
72 and so I said: 'Master, permit me first

'to know who they are and then what inner law
makes them so eager for the crossing,
75 or so it seems in this dim light.'

And he to me: 'You shall know these things,
but not before we stay our steps
78 on the mournful shore of Acheron.'[26]

Then, my eyes cast down with shame,
fearing my words displeased him,
81 I did not speak until we reached that stream.

And now, coming toward us in a boat,
an old man, his hair white with age, cried out:
84 'Woe unto you, you wicked souls,

'give up all hope of ever seeing heaven.
I come to take you to the other shore,
87 into eternal darkness, into heat and chill.

---

[25] **him who . . . refusal:** Pope Celestine V, who at the age of eighty was elected pope in 1294 and resigned five months later.

[26] **Acheron:** River of death in Greek mythology.

'And you there, you living soul,
move aside from these now dead.'
90 But when he saw I did not move,

he said: 'By another way, another port,
not here, you'll come to shore and cross.
93 A lighter ship must carry you.'

And my leader: 'Charon,[27] do not torment yourself.
It is so willed where will and power are one,
96 and ask no more.'

That stilled the shaggy jowls
of the pilot of the livid marsh,
99 about whose eyes burned wheels of flame.

But those souls, naked and desolate,
lost their color. With chattering teeth
102 they heard his brutal words.

They blasphemed God, their parents,
the human race, the place, the time, the seed
105 of their begetting and their birth.

Then, weeping bitterly, they drew together
to the accursèd shore that waits
108 for every man who fears not God.

Charon the demon, with eyes of glowing coals,
beckons to them, herds them all aboard,
111 striking anyone who slackens with his oar.

Just as in autumn the leaves fall away,
one, and then another, until the bough
114 sees all its spoil upon the ground,

so the wicked seed of Adam fling themselves
one by one from shore, at his signal,
117 as does a falcon at its summons.

---

[27] **Charon:** The boatman in Greek mythology who ferries souls across the river Styx to Hades.

Thus they depart over dark water,
and before they have landed on the other side
120 another crowd has gathered on this shore.

'My son,' said the courteous master,
'all those who die in the wrath of God
123 assemble here from every land.

'And they are eager to cross the river,
for the justice of God so spurs them on
126 their very fear is turned to longing.

'No good soul ever crosses at this place.
Thus, if Charon complains on your account,
129 now you can grasp the meaning of his words.'

When he had ended, the gloomy plain shook
with such force, the memory of my terror
132 makes me again break out in sweat.

From the weeping ground there sprang a wind,
flaming with vermilion light,
which overmastered all my senses,
136 and I dropped like a man pulled down by sleep.

CANTO IV

A heavy thunderclap broke my deep sleep
so that I started up like one
3 shaken awake by force.

With rested eyes, I stood
and looked about me, then fixed my gaze
6 to make out where I was.

I found myself upon the brink
of an abyss of suffering
9 filled with the roar of endless woe.

It was full of vapor, dark and deep.
Straining my eyes toward the bottom,
12 I could see nothing.

'Now let us descend into the blind world
down there,' began the poet, gone pale.
15 'I will be first and you come after.'

And I, noting his pallor, said:
'How shall I come if you're afraid,
18 you, who give me comfort when I falter?'

And he to me: 'The anguish of the souls
below us paints my face
21 with pity you mistake for fear.

'Let us go, for the long road calls us.'
Thus he went first and had me enter
24 the first circle girding the abyss.

Here, as far as I could tell by listening,
was no lamentation other than the sighs
27 that kept the air forever trembling.

These came from grief without torment
borne by vast crowds
30 of men, and women, and little children.

My master began: 'You do not ask about
the souls you see? I want you to know,
33 before you venture farther,

'they did not sin. Though they have merit,
that is not enough, for they were unbaptized,
36 denied the gateway to the faith that you profess.

'And if they lived before the Christians lived,
they did not worship God aright.
39 And among these I am one.

'For such defects, and for no other fault,
we are lost, and afflicted but in this,
42 that without hope we live in longing.'

When I understood, great sadness seized my heart,
for then I knew that beings of great worth
45 were here suspended in this Limbo.[28]

---

[28] **Limbo:** The place for unbaptized infants and virtuous pagans who, living before Jesus' time, could not have
known him.

'Tell me, master, tell me, sir,' I began,
seeking assurance in the faith
48   that conquers every doubt,

'did ever anyone, either by his own
or by another's merit, go forth from here
51   and rise to blessedness?'

And he, who understood my covert speech:
'I was new to this condition when I saw
54   a mighty one descend, crowned, with the sign of victory.[29]

'Out of our midst he plucked the shade
of our first parent, of Abel his son, of Noah,
57   and of Moses, obedient in giving laws,

'the patriarch Abraham, and King David,
Israel with his father and his sons,
60   and with Rachel, for whom he served so long,

'as well as many others, and he made them blessed.
And, I would have you know, before these
63   no human souls were saved.'

We did not halt our movement as he spoke,
but all the while were passing through a wood —
66   I mean a wood of thronging spirits.

We had not yet gone far from where I'd slept
when I beheld a blaze of light
69   that overcame a hemisphere of darkness,

though still a good way from it,
yet not so far but I discerned
72   an honorable company was gathered there.

'O you who honor art and knowledge,
why are these so honored they are set
75   apart from the condition of the rest?'

---

[29] **victory:** A victory over Hell, referring to the belief that Jesus descended into Hell — after the Crucifixion and before the Resurrection — and rescued certain heroes of the Hebrew Scriptures. The event is called the Harrowing of Hell. (See the Gospel of Nicodemus.)

And he answered: 'Their honorable fame,
which echoes in your life above,
78 gains favor in Heaven, which thus advances them.'

Just then I heard a voice that said:
'Honor the loftiest of poets!
81 His shade returns that had gone forth.'

When the voice had paused and there was silence,
I saw four worthy shades approach,
84 their countenances neither sad nor joyful.

The good master spoke: 'Take note
of him who holds that sword in hand[30]
87 and comes as lord before the three:

'He is Homer, sovereign poet.
Next comes Horace the satirist,
90 Ovid is third, the last is Lucan.[31]

'Since each is joined to me
in the name the one voice uttered,
93 they do me honor and, doing so, do well.'

There I saw assembled the fair school
of the lord of loftiest song,
96 soaring like an eagle far above the rest.

After they conversed a while,
they turned to me with signs of greeting,
99 and my master smiled at this.

And then they showed me greater honor still,
for they made me one of their company,
102 so that I became the sixth amidst such wisdom.

Thus we went onward to the light,
speaking of things that here are best unsaid,
105 just as there it was fitting to express them.

---

[30] him who . . . sword in hand: Homer is the supreme poet of war in the *Iliad*.

[31] Horace . . . Lucan: Horace (65–8 B.C.E.), Ovid (43 B.C.E.–17? C.E.), and Lucan (39–65 C.E.) are Roman poets.

We came to the foot of a noble castle,
encircled seven times by towering walls,
108 defended round about by a fair stream.

Over this stream we moved as on dry land.
Through seven gates I entered with these sages
111 until we came to a fresh, green meadow.[32]

People were there with grave, slow-moving eyes
and visages of great authority.
114 They seldom spoke, and then in gentle tones.

When we withdrew over to one side
into an open space, high in the light,
117 we could observe them all.

There before me on the enameled green
the great spirits were revealed.
120 In my heart I exult at what I saw.

I saw Electra with many of her line,
of whom I recognized Hector, Aeneas,
123 and Caesar,[33] in arms, with his falcon eyes.

I saw Camilla and Penthesilea.
Seated apart I saw King Latinus,
126 and next to him Lavinia,[34] his daughter.

I saw that Brutus who drove out Tarquinius,
Lucretia, Julia, Marcia, and Cornelia.
129 And Saladin[35] I saw, alone, apart.

---

[32] green meadow: The setting is reminiscent of the Elysian Fields in Greek mythology, but the symbolism of the castle is disputed. Seven is an important number in medieval symbolism; perhaps the castle is a citadel of learning surrounded by the seven liberal arts (ethics, metaphysics, etc.).

[33] Electra . . . Caesar: Like Julius Caesar (d. 44 B.C.E.), these are prominent figures in Roman legend and history: Electra, the mother of Dardanus, the founder of Troy; Hector, a Trojan hero; and Aeneas, the hero of *The Aeneid*.

[34] Camilla . . . Lavinia: Lavinia is Aeneas's wife. Camilla is a warrior in *The Aeneid*, Penthesilea is a Trojan who fought the Greeks, and Latinus is king of Latium (in Italy).

[35] Brutus . . . Saladin: Sultan (d. 1193) of Egypt and Syria, Saladin was famed for his chivalrous fighting against Crusaders. Brutus (not the Brutus involved with assassinating Julius Caesar, but an earlier Roman who defeated Tarquin) founded the Roman Republic and was its first consul. The four women mentioned here were models of Roman virtue.

When I raised my eyes a little higher,
I saw the master° of those who know,   Aristotle
132 sitting among his philosophic kindred.

Eyes trained on him, all show him honor.
In front of all the rest and nearest him
135 I saw Socrates and Plato.

I saw Democritus, who ascribes the world
to chance, Diogenes, Anaxagoras, and Thales,
138 Empedocles, Heraclitus, and Zeno.[36]

I saw the skilled collector of the qualities
of things — I mean Dioscorides — and I saw
141 Orpheus, Cicero, Linus, and moral Seneca,[37]

Euclid the geometer, and Ptolemy,
Hippocrates, Avicenna, Galen,
144 and Averroes,[38] who wrote the weighty glosses.

I cannot give account of all of them,
for the length of my theme so drives me on
147 that often the telling comes short of the fact.

The company of six falls off to two
and my wise leader brings me by another way
out of the still, into the trembling, air.
151 And I come to a place where nothing shines.

Canto V

Thus I descended from the first circle
down into the second, which girds a smaller space
3 but greater agony to goad lament.

---

[36] **Democritus . . . Zeno:** Famous Greek philosophers from the seventh to fourth century B.C.E.

[37] **Dioscorides . . . Seneca:** Seneca was a Roman playwright and philosopher (d. 65 C.E.); Dioscorides (first century C.E.) was a Greek physician; Orpheus and Linus were mythical poets; Cicero (d. 43 B.C.E.) was a Roman orator.

[38] **Euclid . . . Averroes:** Averroes (d. 1298) was an Islamic scholar from north Africa and Spain whose commentary on Aristotle Dante respected; Euclid (fourth century B.C.E.) was a Greek mathematician; Ptolemy (second century C.E.) was an Alexandrian astronomer who devised the "Ptolemaic universe" in which the earth is a fixed center around which the heavenly bodies circle — a concept believed in by Dante. Hippocrates and Galen were Greek physicians (fourth and second centuries B.C.E.), and Avicenna (d. 1037) was an Arab physician whose writings on medicine influenced Europeans for several hundred years.

There stands Minos,[39] snarling, terrible.
He examines each offender at the entrance,
6 judges and dispatches as he encoils himself.

I mean that when the ill-begotten soul
stands there before him it confesses all,
9 and that accomplished judge of sins

decides what place in Hell is fit for it,
then coils his tail around himself to count
12 how many circles down the soul must go.

Always before him stands a crowd of them,
going to judgment each in turn.
15 They tell, they hear, and then are hurled down.

'O you who come to this abode of pain,'
said Minos when he saw me, pausing
18 in the exercise of his high office,

'beware how you come in and whom you trust.
Don't let the easy entrance fool you.'
21 And my leader to him: 'Why all this shouting?

'Hinder not his destined journey.
It is so willed where will and power are one,
24 and ask no more.'

Now I can hear the screams
of agony. Now I have come
27 where a great wailing beats upon me.

I reached a place mute of all light,
which bellows as the sea in tempest
30 tossed by conflicting winds.

The hellish squall, which never rests,
sweeps spirits in its headlong rush,
33 tormenting, whirls and strikes them.

Caught in that path of violence,
they shriek, weep, and lament.
36 Then how they curse the power of God!

---

[39] **Minos:** In classical mythology, the judge of the underworld.

I understood that to such torment
the carnal sinners are condemned,
39   they who make reason subject to desire.

As, in cold weather, the wings of starlings
bear them up in wide, dense flocks,
42   so does that blast propel the wicked spirits.

Here and there, down and up, it drives them.
Never are they comforted by hope
45   of rest or even lesser punishment.

Just as cranes chant their mournful songs,
making a long line in the air,
48   thus I saw approach, heaving plaintive sighs,

shades lifted on that turbulence,
so that I said: 'Master, who are these
51   whom the black air lashes?'

'The first of them about whom
you would hear,' he then replied,
54   'was empress over many tongues.

'She was so given to the vice of lechery
she made lust licit in her law
57   to take away the blame she had incurred.

'She is Semiramis, of whom we read
that she, once Ninus' wife, succeeded him.
60   She held sway in the land the Sultan rules.[40]

'Here is she who broke faith with the ashes
of Sichaeus and slew herself for love.
63   The next is wanton Cleopatra.[41]

---

[40] **Semiramis . . . the Sultan rules:** Semiramis was the legendary queen of Assyria; her capital, Babylon, is here confused with Babylon, Egypt, which was ruled by the sultan.

[41] **Cleopatra:** Queen of Egypt, mistress of Julius Caesar and of Marc Antony; Cleopatra committed suicide after Antony's death, in 30 B.C.E. Dido broke faith with the memory of her husband Sichaeus by having an affair with Aeneas.

'See Helen, for whose sake so many years
of ill rolled past. And see the great Achilles,
66 who battled, at the last, with love.[42]

'See Paris, Tristan,'[43] and he showed me more
than a thousand shades, naming as he pointed,
69 whom love had parted from our life.

When I heard my teacher name the ladies
and the knights of old, pity overcame me
72 and I almost lost my senses.

I began: 'Poet, gladly would I speak
with these two[44] that move together
75 and seem to be so light upon the wind.'

And he: 'Once they are nearer, you will see:
if you entreat them by the love
78 that leads them, they will come.'

As soon as the wind had bent them to us,
I raised my voice: 'O wearied souls,
81 if it is not forbidden, come speak with us.'

As doves, summoned by desire, their wings
outstretched and motionless, move on the air,
84 borne by their will to the sweet nest,

so did these leave the troop where Dido is,
coming to us through the malignant air,
87 such force had my affectionate call.

'O living creature, gracious and kind,
that come through somber air to visit us
90 who stained the world with blood,

'if the King of the universe were our friend
we would pray that He might give you peace,
93 since you show pity for our grievous plight.

---

[42] **Helen . . . with love:** In the medieval version of the Trojan War, Achilles is killed by Paris because of his love for the Trojan Polyxena. Helen's love affair with Paris was supposedly the cause of the Trojan War.

[43] **Tristan:** The lover of Iseult who was killed by King Mark.

[44] **these two:** Paolo and Francesca of Rimini.

'We long to hear and speak of that
which you desire to speak and know,
96   here, while the wind has calmed.

'On that shore where the river Po
with all its tributaries slows
99   to peaceful flow, there I was born.[45]

'Love, quick to kindle in the gentle heart,
seized this man with the fair form taken from me.
102 The way of it afflicts me still.

'Love, which absolves no one beloved from loving,
seized me so strongly with his charm that,
105 as you see, it has not left me yet.

'Love brought us to one death.
Caïna waits for him[46] who quenched our lives.'
108 These words were borne from them to us.

And when I'd heard those two afflicted souls
I bowed my head and held it low until at last
111 the poet said: 'What are your thoughts?'

In answer I replied: 'Oh,
how many sweet thoughts, what great desire,
114 have brought them to this woeful pass!'

Then I turned to them again to speak
and I began: 'Francesca, your torments
117 make me weep for grief and pity,

'but tell me, in that season of sweet sighs,
how and by what signs did Love
120 acquaint you with your hesitant desires?'

And she to me: 'There is no greater sorrow
than to recall our time of joy
123 in wretchedness—and this your teacher knows.

---

[45] **there . . . born:** Ravenna, in northern Italy.

[46] **Caïna waits for him:** Francesca's husband and Paolo's brother, Gianciotto Malatesta. Caïna is the circle of Cain, the deepest circle of Hell (Canto XXXII).

'But if you feel such longing
to know the first root of our love,
126   I shall tell as one who weeps in telling.

'One day, to pass the time in pleasure,
we read of Lancelot,[47] how love enthralled him.
129   We were alone, without the least misgiving.

'More than once that reading made our eyes meet
and drained the color from our faces.
132   Still, it was a single instant overcame us:

'When we read how the longed-for smile
was kissed by so renowned a lover, this man,
135   who never shall be parted from me,

'all trembling, kissed me on my mouth.
A Galeotto was the book and he[48] that wrote it.
138   That day we read in it no further.'

While the one spirit said this
the other wept, so that for pity
I swooned as if in death.
142   And down I fell as a dead body falls.

Canto VI

With my returning senses that had failed
at the piteous state of those two kindred,
3   which had confounded me with grief,

new torments and new souls in torment
I see about me, wherever I may move,
6   or turn, or set my gaze.

I am in the third circle, of eternal,
hateful rain, cold and leaden,
9   changeless in its monotony.

---

[47] **Lancelot:** The lover of King Arthur's wife, Guinevere.

[48] **he:** Galeotto, the intermediary between Guinevere and Lancelot.

Heavy hailstones, filthy water, and snow
pour down through gloomy air.
12 The ground it falls on reeks.

Cerberus,[49] fierce and monstrous beast,
barks from three gullets like a dog
15 over the people underneath that muck.

His eyes are red, his beard a greasy black,
his belly swollen. With his taloned hands
18 he claws the spirits, flays and quarters them.

The rain makes them howl like dogs.
The unholy wretches often turn their bodies,
21 making of one side a shield for the other.

When Cerberus — that huge worm — noticed us,
he opened up his jaws and showed his fangs.
24 There was no part of him he held in check.

But then my leader opened up his hands,
picked up some earth, and with full fists
27 tossed soil into the ravenous gullets.

As the dog that yelps with craving
grows quiet while it chews its food,
30 absorbed in trying to devour it,

the foul heads of that demon Cerberus were stilled,
who otherwise so thunders on the souls
33 they would as soon be deaf.

We were passing over shades sprawled
under heavy rain, setting our feet
36 upon their emptiness, which seems real bodies.

All of them were lying on the ground,
except for one who sat bolt upright
39 when he saw us pass before him.

'O you who come escorted through this Hell,'
he said, 'if you can, bring me back to mind.
42 You were made before I was undone.'

---

[49] **Cerberus:** Guardian of Hades in Greek mythology.

And I to him: 'The punishment you suffer
may be blotting you from memory:
45 it doesn't seem to me I've ever seen you.

'But tell me who you are to have been put
into this misery with such a penalty
48 that none, though harsher, is more loathsome.'

And he to me: 'Your city, so full of envy
that now the sack spills over,
51 held me in its confines in the sunlit life.

'You and my townsmen called me Ciacco.[50]
For the pernicious fault of gluttony,
54 as you can see, I'm prostrate in this rain.

'And in my misery I am not alone.
All those here share a single penalty
57 for the same fault.' He said no more.

I answered him: 'Ciacco, your distress so weighs
on me it bids me weep. But tell me,
60 if you can, what shall be the fate

'of the citizens within the riven city.
Are any in it just? And tell me why
63 such discord has assailed it.'

And he to me: 'After long feuding
they shall come to blood. The rustic faction,[51]
66 having done great harm, will drive the others out.

'But it in turn shall fall to them,
within three years, by power of him
69 who now just plays for time.

'These in their arrogance will long subject
the other faction to their heavy yoke,
72 despite its weeping and its shame.

---

[50] **Ciacco:** A Florentine whose name means "hog."

[51] **rustic faction:** The Whites will drive the "others," or the Blacks, out, but the Blacks aided by Pope Boniface
will ultimately triumph.

'Two men are just[52] and are not heeded there.
Pride, envy, and avarice are the sparks
75 that have set the hearts of all on fire.'

With that he ended his distressing words.
And I to him: 'I wish you would instruct me more,
78 granting me the gift of further speech.

'Farinata and Tegghiaio, who were so worthy,
Jacopo Rusticucci, Arrigo, and Mosca,[53]
81 and the rest whose minds were bent on doing good,

'tell me where they are and how they fare.
For great desire presses me to learn
84 whether Heaven sweetens or Hell embitters them.'

And he: 'They are among the blacker souls.
Different vices weigh them toward the bottom,
87 as you shall see if you descend that far.

'But when you have returned to the sweet world
I pray you bring me to men's memory.
90 I say no more nor answer you again.'

With that his clear eyes lost their focus.
He gazed at me until his head drooped down.
93 Then he fell back among his blind companions.

And my leader said to me: 'He wakes no more
until angelic trumpets sound
96 the advent of the hostile Power.

'Then each shall find again his miserable tomb,
shall take again his flesh and form,
99 and hear the judgment[54] that eternally resounds.'

So we passed on through the foul mix
of shades and rain with lagging steps,
102 touching a little on the life to come.

---

[52] **Two men . . . just:** The identity of the "two men" is unknown.

[53] **Farinata . . . Mosca:** Recent Florentines. Except for Arrigo, who does not appear again, the others are mentioned in Cantos X, XVI, and XXVIII.

[54] **the judgment:** The Last Judgment by Christ when the dead will be joined again to their bodies.

'Master,' I asked, 'after the great Judgment
will these torments be greater, less,
105 or will they stay as harsh as they are now?'

And he replied: 'Return to your science,[55]
which has it that, in measure of a thing's perfection,
108 it feels both more of pleasure and of pain.

'Although these accursèd people
will never come to true perfection,
111 they will be nearer it than they are now.'

We went along that curving road,
with much more talk than I repeat,
and reached the point of our descent.
115 And there we came on Plutus,[56] our great foe.

CANTO VII

'*Pape Satàn, Pape Satàn, aleppe!*'[57]
burst out Plutus in his raucous voice.
3 And the courteous, all-discerning sage,

to comfort me, said: 'Do not be overcome
by fear. However powerful he may be,
6 he'll not prevent our climbing down this cliff.'

Then he turned to that bloated face
and said: 'Silence, accursèd wolf!
9 Let your fury feed itself inside you.

'Not without sanction is this journey down the pit.
It is willed on high, where Michael
12 did avenge the proud rebellion.'[58]

As sails, swollen by the wind,
fall in a tangle when the mainmast snaps,
15 so fell that cruel beast to the ground.

---

[55] **your science:** Aristotle's teaching.

[56] **Plutus:** The classical god of wealth, possibly combined here with Pluto, the king of Hades.

[57] *Pape Satàn . . . aleppe!*: Apparently, a threat to Satan; its meaning is unknown. In their notes, the Hollanders provide a possible rendering: "O Pope Satan, my god."

[58] **the proud rebellion:** The rebel angels in Heaven, who were cast out by Michael and his angels.

Into the fourth hollow we made our way,
descending the dismal slope
18 that crams in all the evil of the universe.

Ah, Justice of God, who heaps up
such strange punishment and pain as I saw there?
21 And why do our sins so waste us?

Just as the waves clash above Charybdis,[59]
one breaking on the other when they meet,
24 so here the souls move in their necessary dance.

Here the sinners were more numerous than elsewhere,
and they, with great shouts, from opposite sides
27 were shoving burdens forward with their chests.

They crashed into each other, turned
and beat retreat, shoving their loads and shouting:
30 'Why do you hoard?' or 'Why do you squander?'

Thus they proceeded in their dismal round
on both sides toward the opposite point,
33 taunting each other with the same refrain.

Once at that point, each group turned back
along its semi-circle to the next encounter.
36 And I, my heart pierced almost through,

said: 'Master, now explain to me
who these people are. Were those with tonsured heads,
39 the ones there to our left, all clerics?'

'All of them had such squinting minds
in their first lives,' he said,
42 'they kept no measure in their spending.

'Their voices howl this clear enough
just as they reach the twin points on the circle
45 where opposing sins divide them.

'These were clerics who have no lid of hair
upon their heads, and popes and cardinals,
48 in whom avarice achieves its excess.'

---

[59] **Charybdis:** The whirlpool in the Italian Straits of Messina made famous in Homer's *Odyssey*.

And I: 'Master, in such a crew as this
I ought to recognize at least a few
51 who were befouled with these offenses.'

And he to me: 'You muster an empty thought.
The undiscerning life that made them foul
54 now makes them hard to recognize.

'The two groups will collide forever.
These will rise from the grave
57 with fists tight, these with hair cropped.[60]

'Ill-giving and ill-keeping have stolen
the fair world from them and set them to this scuffle.
60 As for that, I prettify no words for it.

'Now you see, my son, what brief mockery
Fortune makes of goods we trust her with,
63 for which the race of men embroil themselves.

'All the gold that lies beneath the moon,
or ever did, could never give a moment's rest
66 to any of these wearied souls.'

'Master,' I said, 'tell me more: this Fortune
whom you mention, who is she that holds
69 the world's possessions tightly in her clutches?'

And he to me: 'O foolish creatures,
what great ignorance besets you!
72 I'll have you feed upon my judgment of her:

'He whose wisdom transcends all
made the heavens and gave them guides,[61]
75 so that all parts reflect on every part

'in equal distribution of the light. Just so,
He ordained for worldly splendors
78 a general minister and guide

---

[60] **these with hair cropped:** Refers to the tonsure, or shaven crown, of the clergy.
[61] **guides:** Angelic orders that serve as guides in all areas of life.

'who shifts those worthless goods, from time to time,
from race to race, from one blood to another
81   beyond the intervention of human wit.

'One people comes to rule, another languishes,
in keeping with her judgment,
84   as secret as a serpent hidden in the grass.

'Your wisdom cannot stand against her.
She foresees, she judges, she maintains her reign,
87   as do the other heavenly powers.

'Her mutability admits no rest.
Necessity compels her to be swift,
90   and frequent are the changes in men's state.

'She is reviled by the very ones
who most should praise her,
93   blaming and defaming her unjustly.

'But she is blessed and does not hear them.
Happy with the other primal creatures,
96   she turns her sphere, rejoicing in her bliss.[62]

'Now we must descend to greater anguish.
For every star that rose when I set out[63]
99   is sinking now, and we must not linger here.'

We crossed the circle to the other bank,
beside a spring that bubbles up and flows
102   into a channel it has hewn itself.

The water was darker than the deepest purple.
Accompanied by its murky waves
105   we began our strange descent.

This dreary stream, once it has reached
these malignant, ashen slopes,
108   drains out into the swamp called Styx.[64]

---

[62] **her bliss:** Dame Fortune thought to be the instrument of God.

[63] **set out:** After midnight of Good Friday, it is now early Saturday morning.

[64] **Styx:** Another river in the classical Hades.

And I, my gaze transfixed, could see
people with angry faces in that bog,
111　naked, their bodies smeared with mud.

They struck each other with their hands,
their heads, their chests and feet,
114　and tore each other with their teeth.

The good master said: 'Son, now you see
the souls of those whom anger overcame.
117　And I would have you know for certain

'that plunged beneath these waters,
as your eyes will tell you, are souls whose sighs
120　with bubbles make the water's surface seethe.

'Fixed in the slime they say: "We were sullen
in the sweet air that in the sun rejoices,
123　filled as we were with slothful fumes.

'"Now we are sullen in black mire."
This hymn they gurgle in their gullets,
126　for they cannot get a word out whole.'

Thus we made our circle round that filthy bog,
keeping between the bank and swamp,
fixing our gaze on those who swallow mud.
130　And we came to the foot of a tower at last.

CANTO VIII

To continue, let me say that long before
we reached the foot of that high tower[65]
3　our eyes had noted at its top

two flaming lights displayed up there
to which another, so far off the eye
6　could hardly make it out, sent back a signal.

And turning to that sea of wisdom, I asked:
'What does this mean? And that other fire,
9　what does it answer? And who made it?'

---

[65] **tower:** The tower that guards the entrance to lower Hell.

And he to me: 'Over the filthy waves
you may already glimpse what is to come,
12 if the marsh-fumes do not hide it from you.'

Never did a bowstring loose an arrow
that whipped away more swiftly through the air
15 than, even as I watched, a skiff came skimming

toward us on the water,
under the guidance of a single helmsman,
18 crying: 'Now you are caught, damned spirit!'

'Phlegyas, Phlegyas,[66] this time you shout in vain,'
replied my lord. 'You will have us no longer
21 than it takes to cross this bog.'

Like one who learns of a deceitful plot
hatched against him and begins to fret,
24 Phlegyas became in his stifled wrath.

My leader stepped into the boat,
and had me follow after.
27 And only then did it seem laden.

As soon as he and I were in the bark
the ancient prow moves off, cutting deeper
30 through the water than when it carries souls.

While we crossed the stagnant swamp
one cloaked in mud rose up to say:
33 'Who are you that come before your time?'

And I to him: 'If I come, I do not stay.
But you, who are you, now become so foul?'
36 He answered: 'As you can see, I am one who weeps.'

And I to him: 'In weeping and in misery,
accursèd spirit, may you stay.
39 I know you, for all your filth.'

When he stretched both his hands toward the boat,
the wary master thrust him off, saying
42 'Away there with the other dogs!'

---

[66] **Phlegyas:** In his anger at Apollo for seducing his daughter, Phlegyas set fire to one of Apollo's temples.

Then my master put his arms around my neck,
kissed my face and said: 'Indignant soul,
45 blessed is she that bore you in her womb!

'In the world this man was full of arrogance.
Not one good deed adorns his memory.
48 That is why his shade is so enraged.

'How many now above who think themselves
great kings will lie here in the mud, like swine,
51 leaving behind nothing but ill repute!'

And I: 'Master, I would be most eager
to see him pushed deep down into this soup
54 before we leave the lake.'

And he to me: 'Before the shore
comes into view you'll have your satisfaction.
57 Your wish deserves to be fulfilled.'

Soon I watched him get so torn to pieces
by the muddy crew, I still give praise
60 and thanks to God for it.

All cried: 'Get Filippo Argenti!'⁶⁷
And that spiteful Florentine spirit
63 gnawed at himself with his own teeth.

Of him I say no more. Then we moved on,
when such a sound of mourning struck my ears
66 I opened my eyes wide to look ahead.

The good master said: 'Now, my son,
we approach the city known as Dis,⁶⁸
69 with its vast army and its burdened citizens.'

And I: 'Master, I can clearly see its mosques
within the ramparts, glowing red
72 as if they'd just been taken from the fire.'

---

⁶⁷ **Filippo Argenti:** A wealthy Florentine contemporary of Dante.

⁶⁸ **Dis:** In Roman mythology, the name Pluto, used by Dante to mean Satan and his fortified city in lower Hell.

And he to me: 'The eternal fire
that burns inside them here in nether Hell
75 makes them show red, as you can see.'

At last we reached the moats
dug deep around the dismal city.
78 Its walls seemed made of iron.

Not until we'd made a wide approach
did we come to a place where the boatman bellowed:
81 'Out with you here, this is the entrance.'

At the threshold I saw more than a thousand angels[69]
fallen from Heaven. Angrily they shouted:
84 'Who is this, who is not dead,

'yet passes through the kingdom of the dead?'
At this my prudent master made a sign
87 that he would speak with them apart.

Then they reined in their great disdain
enough to say: 'You come — alone. Let him be gone,
90 who has so boldly made his way into this kingdom.

'Let him retrace his reckless path alone —
let him see if he can, for you shall stay,
93 you who have led him through this gloomy realm.'

Reader, how could I not lose heart
at the sound of these accursèd words,
96 for I thought I would never make it back.

'O my dear leader, who seven times and more
have braced my confidence and saved me
99 from the dangers that assailed me,

'do not leave me,' I cried, 'helpless now!
If going farther is denied us,
102 let us at once retrace our steps.'

But the mentor who had brought me there replied:
'Have no fear. None can prevent our passage,
105 so great a power granted it to us.

---

[69] **angels:** The rebel angels (Revelation 12:9).

'Wait for me here. Comfort your weary spirit
and feed it with good hope.
108 I will not forsake you in the nether world.'

He goes away and leaves me there,
my gentle father, and I remain in doubt,
111 'yes' and 'no' at war within my mind.

I could not hear what he proposed,
but it was not long he stayed with them
114 before they pushed and scrambled back inside.

Then our adversaries slammed shut the gates
against my master, who, left outside,
117 came back to me with halting steps.

He had his eyes upon the ground, his brows
shorn of all confidence. Sighing, he muttered:
120 'Who dares deny me access to the realm of pain?'

To me he said: 'Be not dismayed
at my vexation. In this contest I'll prevail,
123 whatever they contrive to keep us out.

'This insolence of theirs is nothing new:
they showed it once before, at another gate.
126 It still stands open without lock or bolt.[70]

'Over it you saw the deadly writing.
Even now, making his unescorted way
down through the circles, one descends
130 by whom the city shall be opened.'

Canto IX

The pallor cowardice painted on my face
when I saw my leader turning back
3 made him hasten to compose his features.

He stopped, like a man intent on listening,
for the eye could not probe far
6 through that dim air and murky fog.

---

[70] **without . . . bolt:** In the legend of the Harrowing of Hell, Jesus burst through the gates and bolts of Hell.

'Yet we must win this fight,' he began,
'or else. . . . Such help was promised us.[71]
9 How long it seems to me till someone comes!'

I clearly saw that he had covered up
his first words with the others that came after,
12 words so different in meaning.

Still, I was filled with fear by what he said.
Perhaps I understood his broken phrase
15 to hold worse meaning than it did.

'Does ever anyone from the first circle,
where the only penalty is hope cut off,
18 descend so deep into this dismal pit?'

I put this question and he answered:
'It seldom happens that a soul from Limbo
21 undertakes the journey I am on.

'It is true I came here once before,
conjured by pitiless Erichtho,[72]
24 who could call shades back into their bodies.

'I had not long been naked of my flesh
when she compelled me to go inside this wall
27 to fetch a spirit from the circle of Judas.

'That is the lowest place, the darkest,[73]
and farthest from the heaven that encircles all.
30 Well do I know the way—so have no fear.

'This swamp, which belches forth such noxious stench,
hems in the woeful city, circles it.
33 Now we cannot enter without wrath.'

And he said more, but I do not remember,
for my eyes and thoughts were drawn
36 to the high tower's blazing peak

---

[71] **promised us:** By Beatrice.

[72] **Erichtho:** A Greek sorceress; it is possible that the story of Virgil's descent was invented by Dante or was the product of medieval legends.

[73] **the lowest . . . darkest:** Judecca, the lowest region of Hell.

where all at once, erect, had risen
three hellish, blood-stained Furies:[74]
39 they had the limbs and shape of women,

their waists encircled by green hydras.
Thin serpents and horned snakes entwined,
42 in place of hair, their savage brows.

And he, who knew full well the handmaids
to the queen[75] of endless lamentation,
45 said to me: 'See the fierce Erinyes.

'That is Megaera on the left. On the right
Alecto wails. In the middle
48 is Tisiphone.' And with that he fell silent.

Each rent her breast with her own nails.
And with their palms they struck themselves, shrieking.
51 In fear I pressed close to the poet.

'Let Medusa[76] come and we'll turn him to stone,'
they cried, looking down. 'To our cost,
54 we failed to avenge the assault of Theseus.'[77]

'Turn your back and keep your eyes shut,
for if the Gorgon head appears and should you see it,
57 all chance for your return above is lost.'

While my master spoke he turned me round
and, still not trusting to my hands,
60 covered my face with his hands also.

O you who have sound intellects,
consider the teaching that is hidden
63 behind the veil of these strange verses.

---

[74] **Furies:** Three avenging female spirits from Greek mythology, also called the Erinyes.

[75] **the queen:** Proserpine, wife of Pluto and queen of Hell; the Greek Persephone.

[76] **Medusa:** One of the Gorgons from Greek mythology; her appearance turned men to stone.

[77] **Theseus:** A legendary king of Athens who attempted to rescue Persephone (Proserpine) from Hades. He gained fame by killing the Minotaur on Crete.

And now there came, over the turbid waves,
a dreadful, crashing sound
66   that set both shores to trembling.

It sounded like a mighty wind,
made violent by waves of heat,
69   that strikes the forest and with unchecked force

shatters the branches, hurls them away, and,
magnificent in its roiling cloud of dust, drives on,
72   putting beast and shepherd to flight.

He freed my eyes and said: 'Now look
across the scum of that primeval swamp
75   to where the vapor is most dense and harsh.'

As frogs, before their enemy the snake,
all scatter through the water
78   till each sits huddled on the bank,

I saw more than a thousand lost souls flee
before one who so lightly passed across the Styx
81   he did not touch the water with his feet.

He cleared the thick air from his face,
his left hand moving it away,
84   as if that murky air alone had wearied him.

It was clear that he was sent from Heaven,°   an angel
and I turned to the master, who signaled me
87   to keep silent and bow down before him.

Ah, how full of high disdain he seemed to me!
He came up to the gate and with a wand
90   opened it, and there was no resistance.

'O outcasts of Heaven, race despised,'
he began on the terrible threshold, 'whence
93   comes this insolence you harbor in your souls?

'Why do you kick against that will
which never can be severed from its purpose,
96   and has so many times increased your pain?

'What profits it to fight against the fates?
Remember your own Cerberus still bears
99 the wounds of that around his chin and neck.'[78]

Then he turned back along the wretched way
without a word for us, and he seemed pressed,
102 spurred on by greater cares

than those of the man who stands before him.
We turned our steps toward the city,
105 emboldened by his holy words.

We entered without further struggle.
And I, in my great need to see
108 what such a guarded fortress holds,

as soon as I had entered eagerly surveyed
the wide plain stretching on all sides,
111 so filled with bitter torment and despair.

Just as at Arles where the Rhone goes shallow,
just as at Pola, near Quarnero's gulf,
114 which hems in Italy and bathes her borders,[79]

the sepulchers make the land uneven,
so all around me in this landscape
117 the many tombs held even greater sorrow.

For here the graves were strewn with flames
that made them glow with heat
120 hotter than iron is before it's worked.

All their covers were propped open and from them
issued such dire lamentation it was clear
123 it came from wretches in despair and pain.

---

[78] **Cerberus . . . neck:** Heracles dragged Cerberus from Hades with a chain. The meaning of this episode is unclear.

[79] **Just as at Arles . . . borders:** Arles, in Provence, and Pola, in Istri, both located near water, were ancient cemeteries.

And I: 'Master, who are these souls
entombed within these chests and who make known
126 their plight with sighs of sorrow?'

And he: 'Here, with all their followers,
are the arch-heretics of every sect.
129 The tombs are far more laden than you think.

'Like is buried here with like,
though the graves burn with an unlike heat.'
Then, after he turned to the right,
133 we passed between the torments and the lofty ramparts.

Canto X

Now my master takes a hidden path
between the city's ramparts and the torments,
3 and I come close behind him.

'O lofty virtue,' I began, 'who lead me
as you will around these impious circles,
6 speak to me and satisfy my wishes.

'The souls that lie within the sepulchres,
may they be seen? For all the lids are raised
9 and there is no one standing guard.'

And he to me: 'All will be shut and sealed
when the souls return from Jehosaphat[80]
12 with the bodies they have left above.

'Here Epicurus[81] and all his followers,
who hold the soul dies with the body,
15 have their sepulchres.

'But soon your need to have an answer
will be satisfied right here,
18 as will the wish you hide from me.'

---

[80] Jehosaphat: According to Hebrew Scriptures, the Last Judgment will take place in the Valley of Jehosaphat near Jerusalem (Joel 3:2, 12).

[81] Epicurus: A Greek philosopher (341?–270 B.C.E.) known for his advocacy of pleasure and his denial of immortality.

And I: 'Good leader, from you I do not keep
my heart concealed except to speak few words—
21 as you've from time to time advised.'

'O Tuscan, passing through the city of fire,
alive, and with such courtesy of speech,
24 if it would please you, stay your steps awhile.

'Your way of speaking makes it clear
that you are native to that noble city
27 to which I was perhaps too cruel.'

This voice came suddenly
from one sarcophagus, so that, startled,
30 I drew closer to my leader.

And he to me: 'Turn back! What are you doing?
Look, there Farinata stands erect[82]—
33 you can see all of him from the waist up.'

Already I had fixed my gaze on his.
And he was rising, lifting chest and brow
36 as though he held all Hell in utter scorn.

At which my leader: 'Choose your words with care,'
and his hands, ready, encouraging,
39 thrust me toward him among the tombs.

When I stood at the foot of his tomb
he looked at me a moment. Then he asked,
42 almost in disdain: 'Who were your ancestors?'

And I, eager to obey, held nothing back,
but told him who they were,
45 at which he barely raised his eyebrows

and said: 'They were most bitter enemies
to me, my forebears, and my party—
48 not once, but twice, I had to drive them out.'

---

[82] **Farinata stands erect:** Farinata degli Uberti, head of the Florentine Ghibellines when they twice expelled
the Guelphs from Florence.

'If they were banished,' I responded, 'they returned
from every quarter both the first and second time,
51   a skill that Yours have failed to learn as well.'[83]

Then, beside him, in the open tomb, up came
a shade, visible to the chin: I think
54   he had raised himself upon his knees.

He looked around me as though he wished to see
if someone else were with me,
57   and when his hesitant hopes were crushed,

weeping, he said: 'If you pass through this dark
prison by virtue of your lofty genius,
60   where is my son and why is he not with you?'

And I to him: 'I come not on my own:
he who stands there waiting leads me through,
63   perhaps to one° Your Guido held in scorn.'   ° Beatrice

His words and the manner of his punishment
already had revealed his name[84] to me,
66   and thus was my reply so to the point.

Suddenly erect, he cried: 'What?
Did you say "he held"? Lives he not still?
69   Does not the sweet light strike upon his eyes?'

When he perceived that I made some delay
before I answered, he fell backward
72   and showed himself no more.

But the other, that great soul at whose wish
I had stopped, did not change countenance,
75   nor bend his neck, nor move his chest.

And he, continuing from where he'd paused:
'That they have badly learned this skill
78   torments me more than does this bed.

---

[83] Yours . . . well: The Ghibellines were expelled in 1280 and became permanent exiles.

[84] his name: Cavalcante, a leading Guelph; his son Guido, who married Farinata's daughter, was a prominent
poet in Florence who died in exile of malaria.

'But the face of the lady reigning here
will be rekindled not fifty times[85] before you too
shall know how difficult a skill that is to learn.[86]

'And, so may you return to the sweet world,
tell me, why are your people,
in every edict, so pitiless against my kin?'

Then I to him: 'The havoc and great slaughter
that dyed the Arbia red caused them to raise
such prayers in our temple.'[87]

He sighed and shook his head, then spoke:
'I was not alone, nor surely without cause
would I have acted with the rest.

'But it was I alone, when all agreed
to make an end of Florence, I alone
who dared speak out in her defense.'[88]

'So may Your seed sometime find peace,
pray untie for me this knot,' I begged him,
'which has entangled and confused my judgment.

'From what I hear, it seems
you see beforehand that which time will bring,
but cannot know what happens in the present.'

'We see, like those with faulty vision,
things at a distance,' he replied. 'That much,
for us, the mighty Ruler's light still shines.

'When things draw near or happen now,
our minds are useless. Without the words of others
we can know nothing of your human state.

---

[85] **the lady . . . times:** The lady is Proserpine as goddess of the moon; fifty months later in 1304, an attempt to restore exiles to Florence—including Dante—failed.

[86] **a skill . . . learn:** Farinata predicts Dante's exile.

[87] **our temple:** Probably the Church of St. John; the Arbia is a stream near Montaperti, a mound where the Ghibellines defeated the Guelphs in 1260.

[88] **when all agreed . . . her defense:** At Montaperti the Ghibellines proposed the destruction of Florence.

'Thus it follows that all our knowledge
will perish at the very moment
108 the portals of the future close.'[89]

Then, remorseful for my fault, I said:
'Will You tell him who fell back down
111 his son is still among the living?

'And let him know, if I was slow to answer,
it was because I was preoccupied
114 with doubts You have resolved for me.'

And now my master summoned me,
so that I begged the spirit to reveal,
117 at once, who else was down there with him.

His answer was: 'More than a thousand lie
here with me: both the second Frederick
120 and the Cardinal.[90] Of the rest I do not speak.'

With that he dropped from sight. I turned my steps
to the venerable poet, mulling
123 those words that seemed to augur ill.

He started out, and then, as we were going,
asked: 'Why are you so bewildered?'
126 And I answered fully what he asked.

'Keep in mind what you have heard against you,
but also now give heed to this,'
129 the sage insisted—and he raised one finger.

'When you shall stand before the radiance
of her whose fair eyes see and understand,
132 from her you'll learn the journey of your life.'

Then he turned his footsteps to the left.
Leaving the wall, we headed toward the center
along a path that leads into a pit.
136 Its stench offended even at that height.

---

[89] **the portals . . . close:** Time itself ends on Judgment Day.

[90] **the second Frederick . . . Cardinal:** Cardinal Ottaviano degli Ubaldini was from a leading Ghibelline family. Frederick II, Holy Roman Emperor from 1215 to 1250, was known for his materialism; he denied the immortality of the soul.

Canto XI

At the brink of a high bank formed
by broken boulders in a circle
3 we stopped above a still more grievous throng.

Here, the unbearable foul stench
belched from that bottomless abyss
6 made us draw back behind the slab

of an imposing tomb, on which I saw inscribed
the words: 'I hold Pope Anastasius:
9 Photinus drew him from the right and proper path.'[91]

'We must delay descending so our sense,
inured to that vile stench,
12 no longer heeds it.'

So spoke the master. I replied: 'I know
you'll find a useful way to pass this time.'
15 And he: 'You'll see that is my plan.'

'My son,' he then began, 'beneath these rocks
there are three circles, smaller, one below the other,
18 but otherwise like those you leave behind.

'All these are filled with souls condemned.
So that the sight alone may later be enough,
21 know how and why they are confined this way.

'Every evil deed despised in Heaven
has as its end injustice. Each such end
24 harms someone else through either force or fraud.

'But since the vice of fraud is man's alone,
it more displeases God, and thus the fraudulent
27 are lower down, assailed by greater pain.

'The first circle holds the violent
but is divided and constructed in three rings,
30 since violence takes three different forms.

---

[91] **drew him . . . proper path:** Pope Anastasius (fifth century) was thought to have been persuaded by the theologian Photinus to deny the divinity of Jesus.

'Violence may be aimed at God, oneself,
or at one's neighbor — thus against all three
33 or their possessions — as I shall now explain.

'Violent death and grievous wounds may be inflicted
upon a neighbor or, upon his goods,
36 pillage, arson, and violent theft.

'And so murderers and everyone who wounds
unjustly, spoilers and plunderers — the first ring
39 punishes all these in separate groups.

'A man may lay injurious hands upon himself
or on his goods, and for that reason
42 in the second ring must he repent in vain

'who robs himself of the world above
or gambles away and wastes his substance,
45 lamenting when he should rejoice.

'Violence may be committed against God
when we deny and curse Him in our hearts,
48 or when we scorn nature and her bounty.

'And so the smallest ring stamps with its seal
both Sodom and Cahors[92] and those
51 who scorn Him with their tongues and hearts.

'Fraud gnaws at every conscience,
whether used on him who trusted
54 or on one who lacked such faith.

'Fraud against the latter only severs
the bond of love that nature makes.
57 Thus in the second circle nest

'hypocrisy, flatteries, and sorcerers;
lies, theft, and simony;
60 panders, barrators, and all such filth.

---

[92] **Sodom and Cahors:** Cahors, France, was identified with the sin of usury (charging interest on loans);
Sodom was identified with sodomy.

'Fraud against the trusting fails to heed
not only natural love but the added bond
63 of faith, which forms a special kind of trust.

'Therefore, in the tightest circle,
the center of the universe and seat of Dis,
66 all traitors are consumed eternally.'

And I: 'Master, your account is clear
and clearly designates the nature
69 of this abyss and its inhabitants.

'But tell me, those spirits in the viscous marsh,
those the wind drives, those the rain beats down on,
72 those clashing with such bitter tongues,

'why are they not punished inside the fiery city
if God's anger is upon them?
75 And if not, why are they so afflicted?'

And he: 'Not often do your wits stray
far afield, as they do now — or is your mind
78 bent on pursuing other thoughts?

'Do you not recall the words
your *Ethics*[93] uses to expound
81 the three dispositions Heaven opposes,

'incontinence, malice, and mad brutishness,
and how incontinence offends God less
84 and incurs a lesser blame?

'If you consider well this judgment
and consider who they are
87 that suffer punishment above, outside the wall,

'you'll understand why they are set apart
from these wicked spirits and why God's vengeance
90 smites them with a lesser wrath.'

'O sun that heals all troubled sight,
you so content me by resolving doubts
93 it pleases me no less to question than to know.

---

[93] *Ethics:* Aristotle's *Nicomachean Ethics.*

'But go back a little way,' I said,
    'to where you told me usury offends
96 God's goodness, and untie that knot for me.'

'Philosophy, for one who understands her,
    observes,' he said, 'and not in one place only,
99 how nature takes her course

'from heavenly intellect and its operation.
    And, if you study well your *Physics*,[94]
102 you will find, after not too many pages,

'that human toil, as far as it is able,
    follows nature, as the pupil does his master,
105 so that it is God's grandchild,[95] as it were.

'By toil and nature, if you remember Genesis,
    near the beginning, it is man's lot
108 to earn his bread and prosper.

'The usurer, who takes another path,
    scorns nature in herself and in her follower,
111 and elsewhere sets his hopes.

'But follow me now, for it is time to go.
    The Fishes are flickering at the horizon
    and all the Wain lies over Caurus.[96] And here,
115 a short way off, is the descent.'

CANTO XII

Steep was the cliff we had to clamber down,
    rocky and steep, but — even worse — it held
3 a sight that every eye would shun.

As on the rockslide that still marks the flank
    of the Àdige, this side of Trent,[97]
6 whether by earthquake or erosion at the base,

---

[94] *Physics*: Aristotle's *Physics*.

[95] God's grandchild: Nature is God's "art." If the poet's art follows nature, then it becomes God's grandchild.

[96] Fishes . . . Caurus: The Wain is the constellation of the Great Bear; Caurus is the northwest wind in classical mythology. The Fishes (Pisces) are just appearing on the horizon. In other words, the stars indicate it is 4:00 A.M. on Holy Saturday.

[97] the flank . . . Trent: The flank of a mountain on the Àdige River near Trent in northern Italy.

from the mountain-top they slid away from,
the shattered boulders strew the precipice
9 and thus give footing to one coming down —

just so was the descent down that ravine.
And at the chasm's jagged edge
12 was sprawled the infamy of Crete,

conceived in that false cow.[98]
When he caught sight of us, he gnawed himself
15 like someone ruled by wrath.

My sage cried out to him: 'You think,
perhaps, this is the Duke of Athens,[99]
18 who in the world above put you to death.

'Get away, you beast, for this man
does not come tutored by your sister,[100]
21 he comes to view your punishments.'

Like the bull that breaks its tether
just as it receives the mortal blow
24 and cannot run, but lunges here and there,

so raged the Minotaur. My artful guide
called out: 'Run to the passage:
27 hurry down while he is in his fury.'

And so we made our way down the steep landslide
on scree that often shifted
30 under my feet with unexpected weight.

I went on lost in thought. And he said:
'Perhaps you're wondering about this rockslide
33 guarded by that bestial rage I quelled just now.

'I want you to know, the other time
I came down into nether Hell
36 this rock had not yet fallen.

---

[98] **false cow:** Pasiphae, wife of King Minos of Crete, hid in a false cow and mated with a bull; she bore the Minotaur, with the head of a bull and the body of a man.

[99] **Duke of Athens:** Theseus, who sailed to Crete and killed the Minotaur in the labyrinth.

[100] **your sister:** Ariadne, daughter of Pasiphae, who taught Theseus the secret of the labyrinth.

'But surely, if memory does not fail,
it was just before He came who carried off
39 from Dis the great spoil of the highest circle[101]

'when the deep and foul abyss shook on every side,
so that I thought the universe felt love,
42 by which, as some believe,

'the world has many times been turned to chaos.[102]
And at that moment this ancient rock,
45 here and elsewhere, fell broken into pieces.

'But fix your eyes below, for we draw near
the river of blood that scalds
48 those who by violence do injury to others.'

O blind covetousness, insensate wrath,
which in this brief life goad us on and then,
51 in the eternal, steep us in such misery!

I saw a broad moat curving in its arc
that seemed to circle all the plain,
54 just as my guide had said.

Between the edge of moat and precipice
ran centaurs[103] in a file and armed with arrows,
57 as when they went off hunting in our world.

They saw us coming, stopped, and three
departed from the troop with bows
60 and shafts they had selected with great care.

One cried from afar: 'To what torment
do you come, you two approaching down the slope?
63 Tell us from there. If not, I draw my bow.'

---

[101] **carried off . . . circle:** The Harrowing of Hell; a description of the earthquake accompanying the Crucifixion of Jesus follows.

[102] **turned to chaos:** The Greek philosopher Empedocles (fifth century B.C.E.) taught that the world is balanced between love and hate; if one predominates over the other, chaos results.

[103] **centaurs:** Mythological creatures that are half man and half horse.

My master said: 'We will give our answer
to Chiron[104] once we have come closer.
66 Your will was always hasty, to your hurt.'

Then he nudged me, saying: 'That is Nessus,
who died for lovely Deianira[105]
69 and fashioned of himself his own revenge.

'The middle one, his gaze fixed on his chest,
is the great Chiron, he who raised Achilles.
72 The other one is Pholus,[106] who was so filled with wrath.

'Around the moat they go in thousands,
shooting arrows at any soul that rises
75 higher from the blood than guilt allows.'

As we drew near those swift wild beasts,
Chiron took an arrow and with its nock
78 pulled back his beard along his jaw.

When he had uncovered his enormous mouth
he said to his companions: 'Have you observed
81 the one behind dislodges what he touches?

'That is not what the feet of dead men do.'
And my good leader, now at Chiron's breast
84 where his two natures join, replied:

'He is indeed alive, and so alone,
it is my task to show him this dark valley.
87 Necessity compels us, not delight.

'One briefly left her song of hallelujah
and came to charge me with this novel task.
90 He is no robber, nor am I a thief.

'But, by that power by which I move my steps
on this wild road, lend us a guide,
93 one of your band to whom we may stay close,

---

[104] **Chiron:** A wise centaur; teacher of heroes such as Achilles.

[105] **Nessus . . . Deianira:** Nessus fell in love with Deianira, Heracles' wife; Heracles shot Nessus with a poisoned arrow, and while dying Nessus contaminated a robe that killed Heracles when he put it on.

[106] **Pholus:** A centaur who died from one of Heracles' poisoned arrows.

'one who will show us to the ford
and carry this man over on his back,
96   for he is not a spirit that can fly through air.'

Chiron bent his torso to the right, then said
to Nessus: 'Go back and guide them.
99   If you meet another troop, have it give way.'

And with this trusty escort we went on,
skirting the edge of the vermilion boil
102   from which the boiled cried out with piercing shrieks.

There I saw some sunken to the eyebrows,
and the great centaur said: 'They are tyrants
105   who took to blood and plunder.

'Here they lament their ruthless crimes.
Here is Alexander, here cruel Dionysius,
108   who gave to Sicily its years of woe.[107]

'And that brow with such jet-black hair
is Ezzelino, while the other blond one there
111   is Obizzo d'Este,[108] who was indeed

'slain by his stepson in the world above.'
Then I turned to the poet, and he said:
114   'Now let Nessus be your guide and I will follow.'

A little farther on the centaur stopped
above a crowd whose heads, down to their necks,
117   seemed to issue from that boiling stream.

He pointed out a shade apart, alone:
'In God's bosom that one clove in two
120   the heart that on the Thames still drips with blood.'[109]

---

[107] **Alexander . . . years of woe:** Alexander the Great of Macedon (356–323 B.C.E.) and Dionysius of Syracuse in
Sicily (fourth century B.C.E.), both presented here as tyrants.

[108] **Ezzelino . . . d'Este:** d'Este and Ezzelino were two tyrannical rulers in northern Italy in the thirteenth
century.

[109] **the heart . . . blood:** In order to avenge the death of his father, Guy de Montfort of England in 1272 stabbed
his cousin in a church in Viterbo, Italy, during a church service. The victim's heart was thought to be in a casket
in Westminster Abbey.

Then I saw some who had their heads,
even their whole chests, out of the river,
123 and of these I recognized a number,

as the blood became even more shallow
until it cooked nothing but their feet.
126 And here was our place to cross the moat.

'Just as on this side you can see
the boiling stream always diminishing,'
129 said the centaur, 'so, I'll have you know,

'on the other side the bottom falls away
until it plumbs the depths
132 where tyranny must groan.

'There divine justice stings Attila,
who was a scourge on earth, and Pyrrhus,
135 and Sextus,[110] and eternally wrings

'tears, loosed by the boiling,
from Rinier of Corneto and Rinier Pazzo,[111]
who on the highways made such strife.'
139 Then he turned back and crossed the ford again.

Canto XIII

Nessus had not yet reached the other side
when we made our way into a forest
3 not marked by any path.

No green leaves, but those of dusky hue —
not a straight branch, but knotted and contorted —
6 no fruit of any kind, but poisonous thorns.

No rougher, denser thickets make a refuge
for the wild beasts that hate tilled lands
9 between the Cècina and Corneto.[112]

---

[110] **Attila . . . Sextus:** Sextus was a first-century Roman pirate; Attila the Hun, the "Scourge of God," invaded Italy in the fifth century; Pyrrhus, the fourth-century B.C.E. king who fought against Rome, or Pyrrhus, the son of Achilles who killed Priam, the ruler of Troy.

[111] **Rinier . . . Pazzo:** Both Riniers were thirteenth-century robbers.

[112] **between the Cècina and Corneto:** The district between the river Cècina and the town of Corneto.

Here the filthy Harpies nest,[113]
who drove the Trojans from the Strophades
12 with doleful prophecies of woe to come.

They have broad wings, human necks and faces,
taloned feet, and feathers on their bulging bellies.
15 Their wailing fills the eerie trees.

And my good master then began to speak:
'Before you go in deeper you should know,
18 you are, and will be, in the second ring

'until you reach the dreadful sand. Look well—
you will see things that, in my telling,
21 would seem to strip my words of truth.'

Lamentations I heard on every side
but I saw no one who might be crying out
24 so that, confused, I stopped.

I think he thought that I thought
all these voices in among the branches
27 came from people hiding there.

And so the master said: 'If you break off
a twig among these brambles,
30 your present thoughts will be cut short.'

Then I stretched out my hand
and plucked a twig from a tall thorn-bush,
33 and its stem cried out: 'Why do you break me?'

When it ran dark with blood
it cried again: 'Why do you tear me?
36 Have you no pity in you?

'We once were men that now are turned to thorns.
Your hand might well have been more merciful
39 had we been souls of snakes.'

---

[113] **Here . . . nest:** Harpies were birds with women's faces and bird's bodies that drove Aeneas from the Strophades Islands in the Ionian Sea.

As from a green log, burning at one end,
that blisters and hisses at the other
42 with the rush of sap and air,

so from the broken splinter oozed
blood and words together, and I let drop
45 the twig and stood like one afraid.

'Could he have believed it otherwise,
O wounded soul,' my sage spoke up,
48 'what he had seen only in my verses,[114]

'he would not have raised his hand against you.
But your plight, being incredible, made me
51 goad him to this deed that weighs on me.

'Now tell him who you were, so that, by way
of recompense, he may revive your fame
54 up in the world, where he's permitted to return.'

And the stem said: 'With your pleasing words
you so allure me I cannot keep silent.
57 May it not offend if I am now enticed to speak.

'I am the one who held both keys
to Frederick's heart, and I could turn them,
60 locking and unlocking, so discreetly

'I kept his secrets safe from almost everyone.
So faithful was I to that glorious office
63 that first I lost my sleep and then my life.[115]

'The slut who never took her whoring eyes
from Caesar's household, the common bane
66 and special vice of courts,°   envy

'inflamed all minds against me.
And they, inflamed, did so inflame Augustus°   Frederick
69 that welcome honors turned to dismal woe.

---

[114] **in my verses:** In *The Aeneid.*

[115] **I am the one . . . my life:** Piero delle Vigne, chief advisor to the emperor Frederick II, was accused of treason. Blinded and imprisoned, he committed suicide in 1249. He held "both keys," that is, mercy and judgment.

'My mind, in scornful temper,
hoping by dying to escape from scorn,
72 made me, though just, against myself unjust.

'By this tree's new-sprung roots I give my oath:
not once did I break faith
75 with my true lord, a man so worthy of honor.

'If one of you goes back into the world,
let him restore my memory, which still lies helpless
78 beneath the blow that envy dealt it.'

The poet waited, then he said to me:
'Since he is silent now do not waste time
81 but speak if you would ask him more.'

And I replied: 'Please question him
about the things you think I need to know.
84 For I cannot, such pity fills my heart.'

Thus he began again: 'So that this man may,
with ready will, do as your words entreat,
87 may it please you, imprisoned spirit,

'to tell us further how the souls are bound
inside such gnarled wood, and tell us, if you can,
90 if from such limbs one ever is set free.'

Then the tree forced out harsh breath, and soon
that wind was turned into a voice:
93 'My answer shall be brief.

'When the ferocious soul deserts the body
after it has wrenched up its own roots,
96 Minos condemns it to the seventh gulch.

'It falls into the forest, in a spot not chosen,
but flung by fortune, helter-skelter,
99 it fastens like a seed.

'It spreads into a shoot, then a wild thicket.
The Harpies, feeding on its leaves,
102 give pain and to that pain a mouth.

'We will come to claim our cast-off bodies
like the others. But it would not be just if we again
105 put on the flesh we robbed from our own souls.

'Here shall we drag it, and in this dismal wood
our bodies will be hung, each one
108 upon the thorn-bush of its painful shade.'

Our attention was still fixed upon the tree,
thinking it had more to tell us,
111 when we were startled by a noise,

as a man, when he hears
the dogs, and branches snapping,
114 knows the boar and hunters near.

Now, from the left, two souls came running,
naked and torn, and so intent on flight
117 they broke straight through the tangled thicket.

The one in front cried: 'Come, come quickly, death!'
And the other, who thought his own pace slow:
120 'Lano, your legs were not so nimble

'at the tournament near the Toppo.'[116]
Then, almost out of breath, he pressed himself
123 into a single tangle with a bush.

Behind them now the woods were thick
with bitches, black and ravenous and swift
126 as hounds loosed from the leash.

On him who had hidden in the tangle
they set their teeth, tore him to pieces,
129 and carried off those miserable limbs.

And then my leader took me by the hand.
He led me to the bush,
132 which wept in vain lament from bleeding wounds.

---

[116] **two souls came running . . . near the Toppo:** The two souls are spendthrift thirteenth-century nobles, Giacomo of Padua and Lano of Siena; the latter was killed at the river Toppo in 1288.

'O Jacopo da Sant' Andrea,' it said,
'what use was it to make a screen of me?
135 Why must I suffer for your guilty life?'

When the master stopped beside it, he said:
'Who were you, that through so many wounds
138 pour out with blood your doleful words?'

And he to us: 'O souls who have arrived
to see the shameless carnage
141 that has torn from me my leaves,

'gather them here at the foot of this wretched bush.
I was of the city that traded patrons—
144 Mars for John the Baptist.[117] On that account

'Mars with his craft will make her grieve forever.
And were it not that at the crossing of the Arno
147 some vestige of him still remains,

'those citizens who afterwards rebuilt it
upon the ashes that Attila left behind[118]
would have done their work in vain.
151 I made my house into my gallows.'

CANTO XIV

Urged by the love I bore my place of birth,
I gathered up the scattered leaves and gave them back
3 to him, who had by this time spent his breath.

Then we came to the boundary that divides
the second circling from the third.
6 And here the dreadful work of justice is revealed.

To tell how strange the new place was,
I say we reached a barren plain
9 that lets no plant set root into its soil.

---

[117] **Mars for John the Baptist:** According to legend, Mars plagued Florence with wars when he was replaced as city patron by John the Baptist and was only partially appeased when his statue was preserved on a bridge—the Ponte Vecchio—over the Arno.

[118] **the ashes . . . Attila left behind:** A mistaken notion that Florence was destroyed by Attila.

The gloomy forest rings it like a garland
and is in turn encircled by the moat.
12 Here, at the very edge, we stayed our steps

at an expanse of deep and arid sand,
much like the sand pressed long ago
15 beneath the feet of Cato.[119]

O vengeance of God, how much
should you be feared by all who read
18 what now I saw revealed before my eyes!

I saw many a herd of naked souls,
all crying out in equal misery,
21 though each seemed subject to a different law:

some lay face up upon the ground,
some sat, their bodies hunched,
24 and others roamed about in constant motion.

Most numerous were those who roamed about,
those lying there in torment fewer,
27 though theirs the tongues crying out the most.

Above the stretching sand, in slow descent,
broad flakes of fire showered down
30 as snow falls in the hills on windless days.

If Alexander, on India's torrid plains,
seeing undiminished flakes of fire fall
33 upon the ground and on his troops,

ordered his men to trample down the soil
so that the flaming shower was put out
36 before the fire caught and spread,[120]

here untrammeled the eternal flames
came down, and the sand took fire
39 like tinder under flint, doubling the torment.

---

[119] **Cato:** Roman general (first century B.C.E.) in north Africa who fought against Caesar in the civil war.

[120] **put out . . . spread:** A medieval legend concerning Alexander the Great's conquest of India.

Ever without repose was the rude dance
of wretched hands, now here, now there,
42 slapping at each new scorching cinder.

I began: 'Master, you who overcome all things—
all but the obstinate fiends who sallied forth
45 against us at the threshold of the gate,

'who is that hero[121] who seems to scorn the fire
and lies there grim and scowling
48 so that the rain seems not to torture him?'

And he himself, who had discerned
that I had asked my guide about him,
51 cried: 'What I was alive, I am in death.

'Let Jove wear out his blacksmith[122]
from whom in rage he seized the shining bolt
54 he struck me with on that my final day.

'And though he weary all the others, one by one,
at their black forge in Mongibello,[123]
57 shouting "Help, good Vulcan, help!"

'as once he did on the battlefield of Phlegra,[124]
and though he hurl his shafts at me with all his might,
60 he still would have no joy in his revenge.'

Then my leader spoke with a vehemence
I had not heard him use before: 'O, Capaneus,
63 because your pride remains unquenched

'you suffer greater punishment.
In your own anger lies your agony,
66 a fitting torment for your rage.'

Then, with a calmer look, he said to me:
'He was among the seven kings who once laid siege
69 to Thebes and held—and he still seems to hold—

---

[121] **that hero:** In Greek legend, Capaneus is one of the seven kings who besieged Thebes; he boasted that he would burn the city even if Zeus opposed it, and he was killed by a thunderbolt for his presumption.

[122] **his blacksmith:** Vulcan; the Greek Hephaestus.

[123] **Mongibello:** A name for Mt. Etna, the interior of which served as Vulcan's forge.

[124] **battlefield of Phlegra:** At Phlegra, Jove defeated the Giants (Titans).

'God in disdain and to esteem Him lightly.
But his own spiteful ranting, as I made clear,
72 most fittingly adorns his breast.

'Now come along behind me, and be sure
you do not set your feet upon the burning sand
75 but keep your steps close to the forest's edge.'

In silence we went on until we came
to where a little stream spurts from the wood.
78 The redness of it makes me shudder still.

As from the Bulicame[125] flows out a rivulet
the sinful women then divide among them,
81 so this ran down across the sand.

Its bed and both its banks were made of stone,
as was the boundary on either side:
84 I saw our passage lay that way.

'In all else I have shown you
since we entered through the gate
87 whose threshold is denied to none,

'your eyes have yet seen nothing of such note
as is this stream before us:
90 its vapor quenches every flame above it.'

These were my leader's words. Hearing them,
I asked him to supply the food
93 for which he had provoked the appetite.

'In the middle of the sea there lies a land,'
he said, 'a wasteland known as Crete.
96 Under its king the world was innocent.[126]

'A mountain rises there, once glad
with leaves and streams, called Ida.
99 Now it is barren like a thing outworn.

---

[125] **the Bulicame:** A sulphurous spring near Viterbo, whose water fed the houses of prostitution.

[126] **Under its king . . . innocent:** The mythical reign of Saturn on Crete was the world's Golden Age.

'Once Rhea chose it as the trusted cradle
for her child, and there, the better to conceal him
102   when he cried, she had her people raise an uproar.[127]

'Within the mountain stands a huge old man.
He keeps his back turned on Damietta,[128]
105   gazing on Rome as in his mirror.

'His head is fashioned of fine gold,
his breast and arms of purest silver,
108   then to the fork he's made of brass,

'and from there down he is all iron,
but for his right foot of baked clay,
111   and he rests more on this than on the other.

'Every part except the gold is rent
by a crack that drips with tears, which, running down,
114   collect to force a passage through that cavern,

'taking their course from rock to rock into this depth,
where they form Acheron, Styx, and Phlegethon,[129]
117   then, going down this narrow channel,

'down to where there is no more descent,
they form Cocytus:[130] what kind of pond that is
120   you shall see in time—here I say no more.'

Then I asked: 'If that stream flows
down from our world, why do we see it
123   only at this boundary?'

And he answered: 'You know this place is round,
and though you have come far,
126   descending toward the bottom on the left,

---

[127] **Rhea . . . an uproar:** Saturn swallowed his own children to prevent one of his sons from overthrowing him;
Rhea preserved Jupiter, however, by substituting a stone for him that Saturn swallowed, and hid the baby
Jupiter in a cave on Mt. Ida. Mountain spirits hid his crying by clashing their swords and shields.

[128] **Damietta:** A city in Egypt. Made of different metals, the old man seems to represent the ages of humanity,
which have degenerated from gold to iron to clay.

[129] **Acheron, Styx, and Phlegethon:** Rivers of the classical underworld.

[130] **Cocytus:** The lowest part of Hell.

'you have not come full circle.
Should some new thing confront us,
129   it need not bring such wonder to your face.'

And I again: 'Master, where are Phlegethon and Lethe?[131]
About the one you're silent, and you say the other
132   is made into a river by this rain.'

'In all your questions you do please me,'
he replied, 'but the red and seething water
135   might well have answered one of those you ask.

'Lethe you shall see: not in this abyss
but where the spirits go to cleanse themselves
138   once their repented guilt has been removed.'

And then: 'Now it is time to leave this forest.
See you stay close behind me.
The borders, which are not on fire, form a path
142   and over both of them all flames are quenched.'

Canto XV

Now one of the stony borders bears us on
and vapor from the stream arose as mist
3   protecting banks and water from the flames.

As the Flemings between Wissant and Bruges,[132]
fearing the tide that rushes in upon them,
6   erect a bulwark to repel the sea,

and as the Paduans build dikes along the Brenta,[133]
to protect their towns and castles
9   before the heat brings floods to Carentana —

in just that way these banks were formed,
except the architect, whoever he was,
12   had made them not as lofty nor as thick.

---

[131] **Lethe:** The river of forgetfulness; Dante places it on the summit of Purgatory, as a passage into Paradise.

[132] **Wissant and Bruges:** Two cities that mark the ends of the dike for Dante.

[133] **the Brenta:** A river flowing through Padua fed by the melting snows from the mountains of Carentana in Austria.

By now we were so distant from the wood
that I could not have made it out,
15   even had I turned in its direction.

Here we met a troop of souls
coming up along the bank, and each
18   gazed at us as men at dusk will sometimes do,

eyeing one another under the new moon.
They peered at us with knitted brows
21   like an old tailor at his needle's eye.

Thus scrutinized by such a company,
I was known to one of them who caught me
24   by the hem and then cried out, 'What a wonder!'

And while he held his arm outstretched to me,
I fixed my eyes on his scorched face
27   until beneath the charred disfigurement

I could discern the features that I knew
and, lowering my hand toward his face,
30   asked: 'Are You here, Ser Brunetto?'[134]

And he: 'O my son, let it not displease you
if Brunetto Latini for a while turns back
33   with you and lets the troop go on.'

I said to him: 'With all my heart, I pray You,
and if You would have me sit with You, I will,
36   if he who leads me through allows.'

'O son,' he said, 'whoever of this flock stops
even for an instant has to lie a hundred years,
39   unable to fend off the fire when it strikes.

'Therefore, go on. I shall follow at your hem
and later will rejoin my band,
42   who go lamenting their eternal pain.'

---

[134] **Ser Brunetto:** Brunetto Latini (c. 1210–1294), active in Guelph politics, was the author of *Treasure,* a work about civil duty, and *Little Treasure,* a verse poem about an allegorical journey. Dante addresses Brunetto with the polite form *voi* ("you"), showing respect. *Voi* is used in the *Inferno* only twice — for Brunetto Latini and for Farinata (Canto X). Moreover, *Ser,* short for *messer,* is an honorific title used for a notary.

I did not dare to leave the higher path
to walk the lower with him, but I kept
45   my head bowed, like one who walks in reverence.

He began: 'What chance or fate is it
that brings you here before your final hour,
48   and who is this that shows the way?'

'In the sunlit life above,' I answered,
'in a valley there, I lost my way
51   before I reached the zenith of my days.

'Only yesterday morning did I leave it,
but had turned back when he appeared,
54   and now along this road he leads me home.'

And he to me: 'By following your star
you cannot fail to reach a glorious port,
57   if I saw clearly in the happy life.

'Had I not died too soon,
seeing that Heaven so favors you,
60   I would have lent you comfort in your work.

'But that malignant, thankless rabble
that came down from Fiesole[135] long ago
63   and still smacks of the mountain and the rock

'rightly shall become, because of your good deeds,
your enemy: among the bitter sorbs
66   it is not fit the sweet fig[136] come to fruit.

'The world has long believed them to be blind,
a people greedy, envious and proud.
69   Be sure you stay untainted by their habits.

'Your destiny reserves for you such honor
both parties shall be hungry to devour you,
72   but the grass shall be far from the goat.

---

[135] **Fiesole:** According to tradition, Florence was founded by a mixture of Romans and Fiesolans after Caesar destroyed the hill town of Fiesole, where stone was quarried for Florence.

[136] **bitter sorbs . . . sweet fig:** The fig refers to Dante. The sorb is a kind of sour apple.

'Let the Fiesolan beasts make forage
of themselves but spare the plant,
75   if on their dung-heap any still springs up,

'the plant in which lives on the holy seed
of those few Romans who remained
78   when it became the home of so much malice.'

'If all my prayers were answered,'
I said to him, 'You would not yet
81   be banished from mankind.

'For I remember well and now lament
the cherished, kind, paternal image of You
84   when, there in the world, from time to time,

'You taught me how man makes himself immortal.
And how much gratitude I owe for that
87   my tongue, while I still live, must give report.

'What You tell of my future I record
and keep for glossing, along with other texts,
90   by a lady of discernment,° should I reach her.   Beatrice

'This much I would have You know:
as long as conscience does not chide,
93   I am prepared for Fortune as she wills.

'Such prophecy is not unknown to me.
Let Fortune spin her wheel just as she pleases,
96   and let the loutish peasant ply his hoe.'

At that I saw the right side of my master's face
turned back in my direction. And he said:
99   'He listens well who takes in what he hears.'

Nonetheless, I go on speaking
with ser Brunetto, asking who, of his companions,
102   are most eminent, most worthy to be known.

And he: "Some of them it is good to know.
Others it is better not to mention,
105   for the time would be too short for so much talk.

'In sum, note that all of them were clerics
or great and famous scholars, befouled
108 in the world above by a single sin.°   sodomy

'Priscian goes with that wretched crowd,
and Francesco d'Accorso[137] too. And, had you had
111 a hankering for such filth, you might have seen

the one transferred[138] by the Servant of Servants
from the Arno to the Bacchiglione,
114 where he left his sin-stretched sinews.

'I would say more, but I cannot stay,
cannot continue talking, for over there I see
117 new smoke rising from the sand.

'People are coming with whom I must not be.
Let my *Treasure,* in which I still live on,
120 be in your mind—I ask for nothing more.'

After he turned back he seemed like one
who races for the green cloth on the plain
beyond Verona.[139] And he looked more the winner
124 than the one who trails the field.

CANTO XVI

I had arrived where I could hear the distant roar
of water falling to the lower circle,
3 like the rumbling hum of bees around a hive,

when three shades at a run
broke from a passing crowd
6 under that rain of bitter torment.

---

[137] **Priscian . . . d'Accorso:** d'Accorso was a thirteenth-century law professor, Priscian a sixth-century grammarian.

[138] **the one transferred:** Andrea de'Mozzi, bishop of Florence (1287–95), was transferred because of his scandalous life to Vicenza on the Bacchiglione by Pope Boniface VIII, the "Servant of Servants."

[139] **like one who races . . . beyond Verona:** It was traditional to hold a footrace on the first Sunday in Lent in which the runners were naked; the winner received a piece of green cloth and the loser a rooster.

Together they came toward us, each calling:
'Stop, you, who by your garb appear to be
9   a man from our degenerate city.'

Oh, what sores I noticed on their limbs,
both old and new ones, branded by the flames!
12   It pains me still, when I remember them.

My teacher was attentive to their cries,
then turned his face to me and said:
15   'Now wait: to these one must show courtesy.

'And were it not for the fire that the nature
of this place draws down, I would say
18   haste befits you more than it does them.'

When we stopped, they took up again
their old refrain, but once they reached us
21   all three[140] had joined into a single wheel.

As combatants, oiled and naked, are wont to do,
watching for their hold and their advantage,
24   before the exchange of thrusts and blows,

wheeling, each fixed his eyes on me,
so that their feet moved forward
27   while their necks were straining back.

One began: 'If the squalor of this shifting sand
and our blackened, hairless faces
30   put us and our petitions in contempt,

'let our fame prevail on you
to tell us who you are, who fearless
33   move on living feet through Hell.

'He in whose steps you see me tread,
though he go naked, peeled hairless by the fire,
36   was of a higher rank than you imagine.

---

[140] **all three:** The three Guelph leaders from Florence form a circle and are compared to wrestlers.

'He was grandson of the good Gualdrada.
Guido Guerra[141] was his name. In his life
39 he did much with good sense, much with the sword.

'This other, squinching sand behind me,
is Tegghiaio Aldobrandi,[142] whose voice
42 deserved a better welcome in the world.

'And I, who am put to torment with them,
was Jacopo Rusticucci.[143] It was my bestial wife,
45 more than all else, who brought me to this pass.'

Had I been sheltered from the fire
I would have thrown myself among them,
48 and I believe my teacher would have let me.

But because I would have burned and baked,
fright overcame the good intentions
51 that made me hunger to embrace them.

Then I began: 'Not contempt, but sadness,
fixed your condition in my heart so deep—
54 it will be long before it leaves me—

'the moment that my master's words
made me consider that such worthy men
57 as you were coming near.

'I am of your city. How many times
I've heard your deeds, your honored names resound!
60 And I, too, named you with affection.

'I leave bitterness behind for the sweet fruits
promised by my truthful leader.
63 But first I must go down into the very core.'

'That your spirit may long quicken
your limbs,' he replied once more,
66 'and your renown shine after you,

---

[141] **He was . . . Guerra:** Guido Guerra was a political leader in Florence; Gualdrada, his grandmother, was famous for her beauty.

[142] **Aldobrandi:** Like Guido Guerra, Aldobrandi advised Florence not to invade Siena in 1260 when the Florentines were defeated at Montaperti.

[143] **Rusticucci:** A political activist who blames his wife for his sodomy.

'tell us if valor and courtesy still live
there in our city, as once they used to do,
69   or have they utterly forsaken her?'

'Guglielmo Borsiere,[144] grieving with us here
so short a time, goes yonder with our company
72   and makes us worry with his words.'

'The new crowd with their sudden profits
have begot in you, Florence, such excess
75   and arrogance that you already weep.'

This, my face uplifted, I cried out. And the three,
taking it for answer, looked at one another
78   as men do when they face the truth.

'If at other times it costs so little
for you to give clear answers,' they replied in turn,
81   'happy are you to speak so free.

'Therefore, so may you escape from these dark regions
to see again the beauty of the stars,
84   when you shall rejoice in saying "I was there,"

'see that you speak of us to others.'
Then they broke their circle and as they fled
87   their nimble legs seemed wings.

'Amen' could not have been said as quickly
as they vanished. And then my master
90   thought it time to leave.

I followed him, and we had not gone far
before the roar of water was so close
93   we hardly could have heard each other speak.

As the river[145] that is the first to hold
its course from Monte Viso eastward
96   on the left slope of the Apennines,

---

[144] **Borsiere:** A Florentine pursemaker (*borsière* is Italian for pursemaker) and a man of peace.

[145] **the river:** Montone River.

and up there is called the Acquacheta,
before it pours into its lower bed
99 and, having lost that name at Forli,

reverberates above San Benedetto
dell'Alpe, falling in one cataract
102 where there might well have been a thousand,

so, down from a precipitous bank, the flood
of that dark water coming down resounded
105 in our ears and almost stunned us.

I had a cord[146] around my waist
with which I once had meant to take
108 the leopard with the painted pelt.

After I had undone it,
as my leader had commanded,
111 I gave it to him coiled and knotted.

Then, swinging round on his right side,
he flung it out some distance from the edge,
114 down into the depth of that abyss.

'Surely,' I said to myself, 'something new
and strange will answer this strange signal
117 the master follows with his eye.'

Ah, how cautious we should be with those
who do not see our actions only,
120 but with their wisdom peer into our thoughts!

He said to me: 'Soon what I expect
and your mind only dreams of will appear.
123 Soon it shall appear before your eyes.'

To a truth that bears the face of falsehood
a man should seal his lips if he is able,
126 for it might shame him, through no fault of his,

---

[146] **a cord:** The meaning of this cord is uncertain; some suggest it is the cord worn by Franciscans and that Dante may have been connected to them thereby. The leopard represents fraud (Canto I).

but here I can't be silent. And by the strains
of this Comedy — so may they soon succeed
129   in finding favor — I swear to you, reader,

that I saw come swimming up
through that dense and murky air a shape
132   to cause amazement in the stoutest heart,

a shape most like a man's who, having plunged
to loose the anchor caught fast in a reef
or something other hidden in the sea, now rises,
136   reaching upward and drawing in his feet.

Canto XVII

'Behold the beast with pointed tail, that leaps
past mountains, shatters walls and weapons!
3   Behold the one whose stench afflicts the world!'

was how my guide began.
Then he signaled to the beast to come ashore
6   close to the border of our stony pathway.

And that foul effigy of fraud came forward,
beached its head and chest
9   but did not draw its tail up on the bank.

It had the features of a righteous man,
benevolent in countenance,
12   but all the rest of it was serpent.

It had forepaws, hairy to the armpits,
and back and chest and both its flanks
15   were painted and inscribed with rings and curlicues.

So many vivid colors Turk or Tartar never wove
in warp and woof or in embroidery on top,
18   nor were such colors patterned on Arachne's loom.[147]

---

[147] **Arachne's loom:** Arachne challenged Minerva (Athena) to a weaving contest; she lost and was changed into a spider.

As sometimes barges lie ashore,
partly in water, partly on the land,
21 and as among the guzzling Germans

the beaver sets itself to catch its prey,[148]
so lay this worst of brutes upon the stony rim
24 that makes a boundary for the sandy soil.

Its length of tail lashed in the void;
twisting up its forked, envenomed tip,
27 armed like a scorpion's tail.

My leader said: 'Now we must change
direction for a moment till we reach
30 that evil beast stretched out down there.'

We descended, therefore, to our right,
and took ten steps along the edge to keep
33 our distance from the sand and flames.

And, when we reached the beast,
I see some people sitting on the sand
36 a short way off, near where it falls away.

Then the master said to me: 'So that nothing
in this circle escape your understanding,
39 go over and examine their condition.

'Let your talk be brief.
While you are gone, I'll ask the beast
42 to lend us its strong shoulders.'

Thus, on the seventh circle's edge,
still farther out, I went alone
45 to where the downcast souls were seated.

Their grief came bursting from their eyes.
With restless hands they sought relief,
48 now from the flame and now from burning sand.

Not otherwise do dogs in summer gnaw and scratch,
now with muzzle, now with paw,
51 when flies or fleas or horseflies bite them.

---

[148] **the beaver . . . prey:** Beavers were thought to catch fish by dangling their tails in the water.

Although I searched some of the faces
of those on whom the painful fire descends,
54 I knew not one, but I could see

the pouches hanging from their necks
were different colors, each with its coat of arms.
57 On these they seemed to feast their eyes.

And when I came among them and looked closer,
on a yellow purse I could make out
60 a lion's countenance and form in blue.

Then, farther on, my wandering gaze
made out another crest, blood-red
63 marked by a goose more white than butter.

And one, who had a pregnant sow, in azure,
embossed on his white wallet,[149] said to me:
66 'What are you doing in this ditch?

'Get out of here. Wait, since you're still alive,
know that my neighbor Vitaliano[150]
69 shall soon be seated to my left.

'Among these Florentines, I come from Padua.
Many a time they deafen me with shouting:
72 "May the sovereign knight come soon,

'"who brings the pouch with three goats on it!"'[151]
Then he twisted his mouth and stuck out his tongue
75 like an ox that licks its nose.

And I, fearing my delay might anger him
who had warned me to keep my stay brief,
78 turned back and left those weary souls.

I found my leader mounted
on the shoulders of the savage beast.
81 He said to me: 'Now be strong and resolute.

---

[149] the pouches hanging . . . white wallet: Various coats of arms on the purses of Italian usurers.

[150] Vitaliano: From Padua, but otherwise unknown.

[151] who brings ... goats on it: Biamonte, a prominent Florentine moneylender.

'From here on we descend such stairs as these.
You mount in front and I will take the middle
84 so that the tail may do no harm.'

As a man in a shivering-fit of quartan fever,
so ill his nails have lost all color,
87 trembles all over at the sight of shade,

so was I stricken at his words.
Rebuked by shame, which, in the presence
90 of a worthy master, makes a servant bold,

I mounted on those huge and ugly shoulders.
I wanted to say—though my voice did not come out
93 as I intended—'Make sure you hold me fast!'

But he who had helped me many times before,
in other perils, clasped me in his arms
96 and steadied me as soon as I was mounted,

then said: 'Geryon,[152] move on now. Let your circles
be wide and your descending slow.
99 Keep in mind your unaccustomed burden.'

As a bark backs slowly from its mooring,
so the beast backed off the ledge,
102 and when it felt itself adrift,

turned its tail to where its chest had been and,
extending it, made it wriggle like an eel's,
105 while with its paws it gathered in the air.

Phaeton,[153] I think, felt no greater fear
when he released the reins and the whole sky
108 was scorched, as we still see,

nor wretched Icarus[154] when he felt the melting wax
unfeathering the wings along his back
111 and heard his father shout: 'Not that way!'

---

[152] **Geryon:** A winged, three-headed monster killed by Hercules.

[153] **Phaeton:** Borrowed the chariot of the sun from his father, Apollo, and lost control of it. He scorched the earth and the heavens, creating the Milky Way.

[154] **Icarus:** The son of Daedalus, who attached wings to his son with wax; when Icarus flew too near the sun, the wax melted and Icarus fell into the sea.

than was my terror when I saw
air everywhere around
114 and all things gone from sight except the beast.

On it goes, swimming slowly, slowly
wheeling, descending, but I feel only
117 the wind in my face and blowing from below.

Now on our right I heard the torrent's hideous roar
below us, so that I thrust my head forward
120 and dared to look down the abyss.

Then I was even more afraid of being dropped,
for I saw fire and heard wailing,
123 and so, trembling, I hold on tighter with my legs.

And for the first time I became aware
of our descent and wheeling when I saw
126 the torments drawing closer all around me.

As the falcon that has long been on the wing—
and, without sight of lure or bird
129 makes the falconer cry out: 'Oh, you're coming down!'—

descends, weary, with many a wheeling,
to where it set out swiftly, and alights,
132 angry and sullen, far from its master,

so Geryon set us down at the bottom,
at the very foot of the jagged cliff,
and, disburdened of our persons,
136 vanished like an arrow from the string.

Canto XVIII

There is a place in Hell called Malebolge,[155]
fashioned entirely of iron-colored rock,
3 as is the escarpment that encircles it.

At the very center of this malignant space
there yawns a pit, extremely wide and deep.[156]
6 I will describe its plan all in due time.

---

[155] **Malebolge:** Italian for "evil pouches."

[156] **a pit . . . deep:** The ninth and last circle of Hell, seen in Cantos XXI through XXXIV.

A path that circles like a belt around the base
  of that high rock runs round the pit,
9   its sides descending in ten ditches.

As where concentric moats surround a castle
  to guard its walls, their patterns clear
12   and governed by a meaningful design,

in such a pattern were these ditches shaped.
  And, just as narrow bridges issue from the gates
15   of fortresses to reach the farthest bank,

so ridges stretched from the escarpment
  down across the banks and ditches
18   into the pit at which they end and join.

Dropped from Geryon's back, this was the place
  in which we found ourselves. The poet kept
21   to the left and I came on behind him.

To our right I saw a suffering new to me,
  new torments, and new scourgers,
24   with whom the first ditch was replete.

The sinners in its depth were naked,
  those on our side of the center coming toward us,
27   the others moving with us, but with longer strides,

just as, because the throngs were vast the year
  of Jubilee, the Romans had to find a way
30   to let the people pass across the bridge,

so that all those on one side face the castle,
  heading over to Saint Peter's,
33   these, on the other, heading toward the mount.[157]

Here and there on the dark rock above them
  I watched horned demons armed with heavy scourges
36   lashing them cruelly from behind.

---

[157] **so that all those . . . toward the mount:** The Jubilee of the church was instituted by Boniface VIII in 1300;
one end of the bridge from the city to St. Peter's pointed toward the Castle of St. Angelo, the other end pointed
to Mount Giordano.

Ah, how they made them pick their heels up
at the first stroke! You may be certain
39 no one waited for a second or a third.

While I went on my eye was caught
by one of them, and quickly I brought out:
42 'It seems to me I've seen that man before.'

And so I paused to make him out.
My gentle leader stopped with me,
45 and then allowed me to retrace my steps.

The scourged soul thought that he could hide
by lowering his face — to no avail.
48 I said: 'You there, with your eyes cast down,

'if I'm not mistaken in your features,
you're Venèdico Caccianemico.[158]
51 What has brought you to such stinging torture?'

And he replied: 'Unwillingly I tell it,
moved only by the truth of what you've said,
54 which brings to mind the world that once I knew.

'It was I who urged Ghisolabella
to do the will of that marquis,
57 no matter how the foul tale goes around.

'I'm not the only Bolognese here lamenting.
This place is so crammed with them
60 that not so many tongues have learned to say

'"sipa" between the Sàvena and the Reno.[159]
And if you'd like some confirmation,
63 bring our greedy dispositions back to mind.'

While he was speaking a demon struck him
with his lash and said: 'Away, pimp!
66 there are no women here to trick.'

---

[158] Caccianemico: From a leading family of Bologna; he betrayed his sister Ghisolabella to the marquis of Este.

[159] Sàvena . . . Reno: Two rivers bordering Bologna. *Sipa* is Bolognese for "yes."

Then I rejoined my escort. A few steps farther
and we came upon a place
69 where a ridge jutted from the bank.

This we ascended easily and,
turning to the right upon its jagged ledge,
72 we left behind their endless circling.

When we came to the point above the hollow
that makes a passage for the scourged,
75 my leader said: 'Stop, let them look at you,

'those other ill-born souls whose faces
you have not yet seen, since we have all
78 been moving in the same direction.'

From the ancient bridge we eyed the band
advancing toward us on the other side,
81 driven with whips just like the first.

And the good master, without my asking, said:
'See that imposing figure drawing near.
84 He seems to shed no tears despite his pain.

'What regal aspect he still bears!
He is Jason, who by courage and by craft
87 deprived the men of Colchis of the ram.[160]

'Then he ventured to the isle of Lemnos,
after those pitiless, bold women
90 put all the males among them to their death.

'There with signs of love and polished words
he deceived the young Hypsipyle,
93 who had herself deceived the other women.

'There he left her, pregnant and forlorn.
Such guilt condemns him to this torment,
96 and Medea too is thus avenged.

---

[160]Jason . . . the ram: Leader of the Argonauts' campaign to steal the Golden Fleece; he seduced and abandoned Hypsipyle, princess of Lemnos, after saving her father from Lemnos's women. He also seduced Medea,
princess of Colchis, and then abandoned her.

'With him go all who practice such deceit.
Let that be all we know of this first ditch
99   and of the ones it clenches in its jaws.'

Now we had come to where the narrow causeway
intersects the second ridge to form
102   a buttress for another arch.

From here we heard the whimpering of people
one ditch away, snuffling with their snouts
105   and beating on themselves with their own palms.

The banks, made slimy by a sticky vapor
from below, were coated with a mould
108   offending eyes and nose.

The bottom is so deep we could see nothing
unless we climbed to the crown of the arch,
111   just where the ridge is highest.

We went up, and from there I could see,
in a ditch below, people plunged in excrement
114   that could have come from human privies.

Searching the bottom with my eyes I saw
a man, his head so smeared with shit
117   one could not tell if he were priest or layman.

He railed: 'What whets your appetite to stare at me
more than all the others in their filth?'
120   And I answered: 'The fact, if I remember right,

'that once I saw you when your hair was dry —
and you are Alessio Interminei of Lucca.[161]
123   That's why I eye you more than all the rest.'

Then he, beating on his pate:
'I am immersed down here for the flattery
126   with which my tongue was never cloyed.'

And then my leader said to me: 'Try to thrust
your face a little farther forward,
129   to get a better picture of the features

---

[161] Alessio . . . of Lucca: His story is not known.

'of that foul, disheveled wench down there,
scratching herself with her filthy nails.
132 Now she squats and now she's standing up.

'She is Thaïs, the whore who, when her lover asked:
"Have I found favor with you?"
answered, "Oh, beyond all measure!"[162]
136 And let our eyes be satisfied with that.'

CANTO XIX

O Simon Magus![163] O wretches of his kind,
greedy for gold and silver,
3 who prostitute the things of God

that should be brides of goodness!
Now must the trumpet sound for you,
6 because your place is there in that third ditch.

We had come to where the next tomb lay,
having climbed to the point upon the ridge
9 that overlooks the middle of the trench.

O Supreme Wisdom, what great art you show
in Heaven, on earth, and in the evil world,
12 and what true justice does your power dispense!

Along the sides and bottom I could see
the livid stone was pierced with holes,
15 all round and of a single size.

They seemed to me as wide and deep
as those in my beautiful Saint John[164]
18 made for the priests to baptize in,

one of which, not many years ago,
I broke to save one nearly drowned in it—
21 and let this be my seal, to undeceive all men.

---

[162] when her lover asked . . . all measure!: An incident in a play by the Roman playwright Terence (190?–150? B.C.E.).

[163] Simon Magus: In the Bible, Simon Magus offered to buy spiritual powers from the Apostles (Acts 8:9–24). The selling of any spiritual good, like a church position, is known as simony.

[164] Saint John: The baptistery of Florence had several fonts; Dante was apparently baptized in one of them, although the drowning incident has not been explained.

From the mouth of each stuck out
a sinner's feet and legs up to the thighs
24 while all the rest stayed in the hole.

They all had both their soles on fire.
It made their knee-joints writhe so hard
27 they would have severed twisted vines or ropes.

As flames move only on the surface
of oily matter caught on fire,
30 so these flames flickered heel to toe.

'Who is that, master, who in his torment
wriggles more than any of his fellows
33 and is licked by redder flames?'

And he: 'If you like, I'll take you down
along the lower bank[165] and you will learn,
36 from him, his life and his misdeeds.'

And I: 'Whatever pleases you is my desire.
You are my lord and know I do your will.
39 You know, too, what I leave unsaid.'

Then we came to the fourth embankment,
turned and descended on our left
42 into a narrow bottom pierced with holes.

The good master clasped me to his side
and did not set me down until we came
45 to the pit of one lamenting with his shanks.

'Whoever you are, with your upper parts below,[166]
planted like a post, you wretched soul,'
48 said I, 'come out with something, if you can.'

I stood there like a friar who confesses
a treacherous assassin. Once done,
51 he calls the friar back to stay his death.

---

[165] **the lower bank:** The Malebolge slants toward the center, so that the inner edge of the ditch has an easier slope than the outer edge.

[166] **with your upper parts below:** Assassins were buried alive with their heads downward.

And he cried out: 'Is that you already,
are you here already, Boniface?
54 By several years the writing lied to me.

'Are you so swiftly sated with those profits
for which you did not fear to take by guile
57 the beautiful Lady and to do her outrage?'[167]

I became like those who stand there mocked,
not comprehending what is said to them,
60 and thus not knowing what to say in turn.

Then Virgil said: 'Tell him right away,
"I'm not the one, I'm not the one you think."'
63 I gave the answer I was told to give.

At that the spirits feet began to writhe.
Then, sighing, with a plaintive voice, he said:
66 'What is it then you want from me?

'If you are so keen to learn my name
that you descended from the bank for it,
69 know that I was cloaked in the great mantle.

'But in truth I was a son of the she-bear[168]
and so avid was I to advance my cubs
72 I filled my purse as now I fill this hole.

'Beneath my head are crushed the others
who practiced simony before me,
75 now flattened into fissures in the rock.

'In turn I, too, shall be thrust lower down
as soon as he arrives whom I mistook you for
78 when I called out my hasty question.

'But the time I have already roasted my feet,
standing here upside down, is already longer
81 than he'll be planted with his feet on fire.

---

[167] **the beautiful Lady . . . her outrage:** The speaker, Pope Nicholas III (r. 1277–80), in 1300 had been in Hell for twenty years; with his foreknowledge, he mistakes Dante for Boniface VIII, who did not die until 1303. The Lady is the church.

[168] **son of the she-bear:** Nicholas was an Orsini, whose crest was a she-bear.

'For after him shall come a lawless shepherd[169]
from the west, one even fouler in his deeds,
84   fit to be the cover over him and me.

'A new Jason shall he be, the one of whom
we read in Maccabees,[170] and even as the king indulged
87   Jason, so the king of France shall deal with him.'

I do not know if then I was too bold
when I answered him in just this strain:
90   'Please tell me, how much treasure

'did our Lord insist on from Saint Peter
before He gave the keys into his keeping?
93   Surely He asked no more than "Follow me,"

'nor did Peter, or the others, take gold or silver
from Matthias when he was picked by lot
96   to fill the place lost by the guilty soul.[171]

'Stay there then, for you are justly punished,
guarding well those gains, ill-gotten,
99   that made you boldly take your stand against King Charles.[172]

'And were it not that I am still restrained
by the reverence I owe the keys supreme,
102   which once you held in the happy life above,

'I would resort to even harsher words
because your avarice afflicts the world,
105   trampling down the good and raising up the wicked.

'Shepherds like you the Evangelist had in mind
when he saw the one that sits upon the waters
108   committing fornication with the kings,

---

[169] **a lawless shepherd:** Pope Clement V (r. 1305–14); he received support from King Philip of France because he agreed to move the Papacy from Rome to Avignon, France.

[170] **A new Jason . . . Maccabees:** Jason became the High Priest of the Jews by bribing the king with silver (2 Maccabees 4:7).

[171] **Matthias . . . soul:** Matthias was picked to replace Judas among the Apostles (Acts 1:15–26).

[172] **your stand . . . King Charles:** Nicholas was supposed to have been bribed to join a conspiracy against Charles of Anjoy (1226–1285), king of Sicily.

'she that was born with seven heads
and from ten horns derived her strength
111 so long as virtue pleased her bridegroom.[173]

'You have wrought yourselves a god of gold and silver.
How then do you differ from those who worship idols
114 except they worship one and you a hundred?

'Ah, Constantine, to what evil you gave birth,
not by your conversion, but by the dowry
117 that the first rich Father had from you!'[174]

And while I sang such notes to him,
whether gnawed by anger or by conscience,
120 he kicked out hard with both his feet.

Truly I believe this pleased my leader,
he listened with a look of such contentment
123 to the sound of the truthful words I spoke.

Therefore, he caught me in his arms
and, when he had me all upon his breast,
126 remounted by the path he had descended,

nor did he tire of holding me so close
but bore me to the summit of the arch
129 that crosses from the fourth dike to the fifth.

Here gently he set down his burden,
gently on account of the steep, rough ridge
that would have made hard going for a goat.
133 And there, before me, another valley opened.

CANTO XX

Of strange new pain I now must make my verse,
giving matter to the canto numbered twenty
3 of this first *canzone,* which tells of those submerged.

---

[173] **bridegroom:** Here, imagery from the Book of Revelation (17:1–3) is applied to the Papacy: The bridegroom is the pope, the seven heads are the sacraments, and the ten horns are the commandments.

[174] **the dowry . . . from you:** Based on a forgery called the Donation of Constantine, it was believed in Dante's time that the Roman emperor Constantine, when he removed his government to Byzantium (fourth century), endowed the Roman Church under Pope Sylvester I ("the first rich Father") with temporal power in the West, and therefore the mandate for acquiring wealth.

By now I was all eagerness to see
what sights the chasm, bathed in tears
6   of anguish, would disclose.

I saw people come along that curving canyon
in silence, weeping, their pace the pace of slow
9   processions chanting litanies in the world.

As my gaze moved down along their shapes,
I saw into what strange contortions
12   their chins and chests were twisted.

Their faces were reversed upon their shoulders
so that they came on walking backward,
15   since seeing forward was denied them.

Perhaps some time by stroke of palsy
a person could be twisted in that way,
18   but I've not seen it nor do I think it likely.

Reader, so may God let you gather fruit
from reading this, imagine, if you can,
21   how I could have kept from weeping

when I saw, up close, our human likeness
so contorted that tears from their eyes
24   ran down their buttocks, down into the cleft.

Yes, I wept, leaning against a spur
of the rough crag, so that my escort said:
27   'Are you still witless as the rest?

'Here piety lives when pity is quite dead.[175]
Who is more impious than one who thinks
30   that God brings passion to His judgment?

'Raise your head! Raise it and look on him
under whose feet the earth gaped open
33   in sight of all the shouting Thebans:

---

[175] **Here piety . . . quite dead:** This complex line suggests that there should be no sympathy or pity for the damned; the next two lines state that God's judgment is to be trusted. The irony here is that the damned are Dante's creation.

'"Where are you rushing, Amphiaraus?[176] Why
do you leave the war?" Nor did he stop his plunge
36 until he fell to Minos, who lays hold on all.

'See how his shoulder-blades are now his chest.
Because he aspired to see too far ahead
39 he looks behind and treads a backward path.

'See Tiresias,[177] who changed his likeness
when he was turned from male to female,
42 transformed in every member.

'Later on he had to touch once more
the two twined serpents with his rod
45 before he could regain his manly plumes.

'He who puts his back to that one's belly is Aruns.[178]
In the hills of Luni—where the Carraresi,
48 who shelter in the valley, work the earth—

'he lived inside a cave in that white marble,
from which he could observe the sea and stars
51 in a wide and boundless prospect.

'And that female whose backward-flowing tresses
fall upon her breasts so they are hidden,
54 and has her hairy parts on that same side,

'was Manto,[179] who searched through many lands
before she settled in the place where I was born—
57 for just a moment hear me out on this.

'After her father had parted from this life
and the city of Bacchus° was enslaved,   Thebes
60 she wandered for a time about the world.

---

[176] **Amphiaraus:** A Greek priest who hid himself in the battle of the Seven against Thebes and was swallowed up by the earth.

[177] **Tiresias:** The famous oracle from Thebes. Once he was transformed into a woman when he saw two snakes coupling; seven years later he was changed into a man again when he saw the same scene. Because he had experienced both sexes, he was asked to settle an argument between Zeus and Hera about whether males or females have more sexual pleasure. He was blinded by Hera when he said women, but was rewarded with prophetic powers by Zeus.

[178] **Aruns:** An Etruscan soothsayer who predicted Caesar's victory in the civil war.

[179] **Manto:** Daughter of Tiresias, a Theban soothsayer.

'High in fair Italy, at the foot of the alps
that form a border with Germany near Tyrol,
63 lies a lake they call Benàco.[180]

'By a thousand springs and more, I think,
the region between Garda, Val Camonica, and Pennino[181]
66 is bathed by waters settling in that lake.

'There is an island in its middle
that the pastors of Trent, Brescia, and Verona,
69 should they pass that way, would bless.[182]

'Peschiera, a strong and splendid fortress
against the Brescians and the Bergamese,
72 sits on the lowest point of land around.

'There all the water Benàco's bosom cannot hold
flows over and descends into a river
75 running through green pastures.

'This river, as it leaves the lake
and all the way to Govérnolo, is called
78 the Mincio until it falls into the Po.

'Before that, after but the briefest run,
it levels off and spreads to make a swamp
81 sometimes scarce of water in the summer.

'When she passed that way, the cruel virgin
saw dry land in the middle of the marsh
84 where no one lived and no one tilled the soil.

'There, to avoid all company, she stopped,
with only servants, to ply her magic arts.
87 There she lived and left her empty body.

'Later on, the people scattered round about
collected there because it was protected
90 by the marsh on every side.

---

[180] Benàco: The present Lake Garda.

[181] Garda . . . Pennino: Two towns and a valley (Val Camonica) below the lake.

[182] an island . . . would bless: A chapel on the island was under the jurisdiction of three bishops.

'They built the city over those dead bones
and, after her who first had claimed the spot,
93 named it Mantua, with no spells or incantations.

'Once, its population was more plentiful,
before the foolishness of Casalodi
96 bore the brunt of Pinamonte's guile.[183]

'I charge you, therefore, should you ever hear
my city's origin described another way,
99 allow no lie to falsify the truth.'

And I: 'Master, to me your explanation
is so convincing and so takes my trust
102 that any other tale would seem spent embers.

'But tell me, among these people who are passing,
if you see any worthy of my notice,
105 for my thoughts keep going back to them alone.'

Then he replied: 'The one whose beard
falls from his jowls onto his swarthy shoulders
108 was — when Greece was so deprived of males

'that scarcely one was left, even in the cradle —
a soothsayer. At Aulis, along with Calchas,
111 he told the favoring time for setting sail.[184]

'Eurypylus was his name, and thus he is sung
in certain verses of my lofty tragedy,[185]
114 as you know very well, who know it all.

'That other, with the skinny shanks,
was Michael Scot,[186] who truly understood
117 the way to play the game of magic tricks.

---

[183] **Pinamonte's guile:** Pinamonte, a Ghibelline, persuaded Count Casalodi, a Guelph, to exile the nobles of Mantua; Pinamonte then seized Casalodi's power in 1272.

[184] **told . . . setting sail:** The Greeks used two oracles, Calchas and Eurypylus, to determine when they should set sail for Troy and the Trojan War.

[185] **my lofty tragedy:** Here Virgil calls his *Aeneid* a tragedy, an epic told in a refined style.

[186] **Michael Scot:** A thirteenth-century Scottish scholar who spent time in Frederick II's court in Italy.

'See Guido Bonatti. See Asdente,[187] who now regrets
not having worked his leather and his thread—
120 but he repents too late.

'See the wretched women who gave up needle,
spool, and spindle to take up fortune-telling,
123 casting spells with images[188] and herbs.

'But come now, for Cain, with his thorns,
already stands above the border of both hemispheres
126 and touches the waves below Seville,[189]

'and last night was the moon already round.
Surely you recall it did not harm you
the other night in the deep wood.'
130 These were his words while we were moving on.

Canto XXI

Thus from one bridge to the next we came
until we reached its highest point, speaking
3 of things my Comedy does not care to sing.

We stopped to look into the next crevasse
of Malebolge and heard more useless weeping.
6 All I could see was an astounding darkness.

As in the arsenal of the Venetians[190]
in wintertime they boil the viscous pitch
9 to caulk their unsound ships

because they cannot sail—one rebuilds
his ship, while still another plugs
12 the seams of his, weathered by many a voyage:

---

[187] Bonatti . . . Asdente: A shoemaker from Parma, Asdente was noted for his soothsaying; Bonatti was the private astrologer to Guido of Montefeltro (Canto XXVII).

[188] casting spells with images: The piercing of dolls, for example.

[189] Cain . . . below Seville: In Christian folklore, Cain was placed in the moon after murdering his brother, Abel. Cain with his thorns is like the man in the moon, which is setting on the western horizon beyond Spain. It is early Saturday morning in Jerusalem.

[190] arsenal of the Venetians: The Venetian arsenal, one of the largest in Europe, was also a shipyard where weapons were made and stored.

one hammers at the stem, another at the stern,
this one makes the oars, that one twists the ropes
15 for rigging, another patches jib and mainsail—

so, not with fire, but by the art of God,
a thick pitch boiled there,
18 sticking to the banks on either side.

I saw the pitch but still saw nothing in it
except the bubbles raised up by the boiling,
21 the whole mass swelling and then settling back.

While I stared fixedly upon the seething pitch,
my leader cried: 'Look out, look out!'
24 and drew me to him, away from where I stood.

Then I turned like a man intent
on making out what he must run from,
27 undone by sudden fear,

who does not slow his flight for all his looking back:
just so I caught a glimpse of some dark devil
30 running toward us up the ledge.

Ah, how ferocious were his looks
and fierce his gesturing,
33 with wings spread wide and nimble feet!

One of his shoulders, which were high and pointed,
was laden with the haunches of a sinner
36 he held hooked by the tendons of his heels.

From our bridge he said: 'O Malebranche,[191]
here is one of Santa Zita's Elders.[192]
39 Thrust him under, while I head back for more

'to that city, where there's such a fine supply.
Every man there—except Bonturo[193]—is a swindler.
42 There money turns a No into an Ay.'

---

[191] **Malebranche:** Italian for "evil-claws," the name for devils.

[192] **Elders:** Elders from Lucca, here named after Lucca's patron saint, who died in 1275.

[193] **Bonturo:** A notorious swindler in Lucca, still living in 1300.

He flung him down and turned back up
the stony ridge. Never did a mastiff
45   set loose to chase a thief make greater haste.

The sinner sank, then rose again, his face all pitch.
Then demons, under cover of the bridge, cried out:
48   'This is no place for the Holy Visage!'[194]

'Here you swim a different stroke than in the Serchio!'[195]
Unless you'd like to feel our hooks,
51   don't let yourself stick out above the pitch.'

Then, with a hundred hooks and more,
they ripped him, crying: 'Here you must do your dance
54   in secret and pilfer—can you?—in the dark.'

In just the same way cooks command their scullions
to take their skewers and prod the meat down
57   in the cauldron, lest it float back up.

Then my good master said: 'Squat down
behind that rock and find some cover
60   so that they do not see that you are here.

'As for any outrage they may do me,
have no fear. I know this place and had
63   exactly such a scuffle here before.'[196]

After he had crossed the bridge
and reached the other bank,
66   he had to show how resolute he was:

With all the rage and uproar
of dogs that rush upon a beggar—
69   who quickly starts to beg where he has stopped—

they swarmed on him from underneath the bridge
with threatening hooks. But he cried out:
72   'Wait! Let none of you do harm!

---

[194] the Holy Visage: Refers to an ancient Byzantine crucifix in the Cathedral of Lucca.

[195] Serchio: A river near Lucca.

[196] such a scuffle . . . before: In Canto VIII, Virgil and Dante had trouble with fallen angels when trying to enter Dis.

'Before you grapple at me with your hooks
let one of you come forth to hear me out.
75 Then take counsel, whether to use your claws.'

All cried: 'Let Malacoda[197] go.' One moved—
the rest stood still—and he came forward,
78 grumbling: 'This won't do him any good.'

'Consider, Malacoda,' said my master,
'whether you would see me come this far
81 unstopped by all your hindering

'without the will of God and favoring fate?
Let us proceed, for it is willed in Heaven
84 that I guide another down this savage way.'

Then his pride was so abashed that he let drop
the billhook to his feet, saying to the others:
87 'Enough, let no one touch him.'

And my leader said to me: 'You there, cowering
among the broken boulders of the bridge,
90 now you may come back to me in safety.'

At that I stirred and hastened to him.
Then the devils all came surging forward
93 so that I feared they might not keep the truce.

Just so do I recall the troops
afraid to leave Caprona[198] with safe-conduct,
96 finding themselves among so many enemies.

I drew my body up against my leader
but kept my eyes fixed on their faces,
99 which were far from friendly.

They aimed their hooks, and one said to another:
'How about I nick him on the rump?'
102 And the other answered: 'Sure, let him have one.'

---

[197] **Malacoda:** Italian for "evil-tail."

[198] **Caprona:** A castle near Pisa that was seized by Florentine and Luccan troops in 1298.

But the demon who was speaking with my leader
turned round at once and said:
105   'Easy does it, Scarmiglione!'

And then to us: 'You can't continue farther
down this ridge, for the sixth arch
108   lies broken into pieces at the bottom.

'If you desire to continue on,
then make your way along this rocky ledge.
111   Nearby's another crag that yields a passage.

'Yesterday, at a time five hours from now,
it was a thousand two hundred sixty-six years
114   since the road down here was broken.[199]

'I'm sending some men of mine along that way
to see if anyone is out to take the air.
117   Go with them—they won't hurt you.'

'Step forward, Alichino, Calcabrina,'
he continued, 'and you Cagnazzo,
120   and let Barbariccia lead the squad.

'Let Libicocco come too, and Draghignazzo,
Ciriatto with his tusks, and Graffiacane,
123   Farfarello, and madcap Rubicante.[200]

'Have a good look around the boiling glue.
Keep these two safe as far as the next crag
126   that runs all of a piece above the dens.'

'Oh, master,' I said, 'I don't like what I see.
Please, let us find our way without an escort,
129   if you know how. As for me, I do not want one.

'If you are as vigilant as ever,
don't you see they grind their teeth
132   while with their furrowed brows they threaten harm?'

---

[199] Yesterday . . . broken: Dante dates the earthquake accompanying the Crucifixion at noon on Good Friday, 34 C.E., 1,266 years before 1300. It is now 7 A.M. on Holy Saturday.

[200] Libicocco . . . Rubicante: Insulting names for demons; Graffiacane, for instance, means "dog-scratcher."

And he to me: 'Don't be afraid.
Let them grind on to their hearts' content—
135   they do it for the stewing wretches.'

Off they set along the left-hand bank,
but first each pressed his tongue between his teeth
to blow a signal to their leader,
139   and he had made a trumpet of his asshole.

CANTO XXII

I have seen the cavalry break camp,
prepare for an attack, make their muster
3   and at times fall back to save themselves.

I have seen outriders in your land,
O Aretines.[201] I have seen raiding-parties,
6   tournaments of teams, hand-to-hand jousts

begun with bells, trumpets, or drums,
with signals from the castle,
9   with summons of our own and those from foreign lands.

But truly never to such outlandish fanfare
have I seen horsemen move, or infantry,
12   or ship set sail at sign from land or star.

On we went, escorted by ten demons.
What savage company! But, as they say,
15   'in church with saints, with guzzlers in the tavern.'

My attention was fixed upon the pitch
to note each detail of this gulch
18   and of the people poaching in it.

Like dolphins, when they arch their backs
above the water, giving sailors warning
21   to prepare to save their ship,[202]

---

[201] **outriders . . . land, O Aretines:** A reference to Arezzo's defeat by Florence in 1298.

[202] **Like dolphins . . . ship:** Dolphins were believed to warn ships about approaching storms.

so from time to time, to ease his pain,
one of the sinners would show his back
24   and, quick as lightning, hide it once again.

And just as in a ditch at water's edge
frogs squat with but their snouts in sight,
27   their bodies and their legs all hidden,

so were the sinners scattered everywhere.
But they, at the approach of Barbariccia,
30   withdrew back down beneath the boiling.

There I saw—and my heart still shudders at it—
one who lingered, as it can happen
33   that one frog stays while yet another plunges,

and Graffiacane, who was nearest him,
caught a billhook in his pitchy locks
36   and hauled him out, looking like an otter.

By now I knew their names,
since I had noted these when they were chosen
39   and when they called to one another.

'Set your claws to work, Rubicante,
see you rip his skin off,'
42   shouted all the accursèd crew together.

And I: 'Master, if you can do it,
find out the name of this poor wretch
45   caught in the clutches of his enemies.'

My leader got up close beside him
and asked him where he came from. He replied:
48   'I was born in the kingdom of Navarre.[203]

'My mother, who had conceived me by a wastrel—
destroyer of himself and all his goods—
51   put me in service with a man of rank.

---

[203] **I was born . . . Navarre:** This speaker's identity is unknown; Navarre is the Basque territory in Spain.

'Then I joined the retinue of worthy Thibaut:[204]
there first I set myself to taking bribes,
54 for which I pay the reckoning in this heat.'

And Ciriatto, from whose jaw curved up
on either side a tusk, like the wild boar's,
57 made him feel how one of these could rip.

The mouse had fallen in with wicked cats.
But Barbariccia blocked them with his arms
60 and said: 'Stand back and let me jab him,'

then turned to face my master:
'Speak up, if you are eager to learn more,
63 before I let him have a mangling.'

And my leader: 'Of the other sinners in the pitch,
tell me, is anyone Italian?'
66 And he: 'I just now came from one

'who hailed from near those parts. I wish
I still were with him in the pitch—
69 then I'd have no fear of hook or claw!'

Then Libicocco said: 'This is just too much,'
caught him with his grapple by the arm
72 and, ripping, gouged out a hunk of flesh.

Draghignazzo, too, wanted to catch him up,
by the legs, at which their captain
75 wheeled round on them with an ugly look.

After their fury had subsided,
my leader seized this chance to ask
78 the one still staring at his wound:

'Who is the one you spoke of, from whom
you parted so unwisely when you came ashore?'
81 And he replied: 'It was Fra Gomìta

---

[204]**Thibaut:** Thibaut II of Navarre (r. 1253–1270).

'of Gallura, a vessel full of fraud,[205]
who had his master's enemies in hand
84 but dealt with them so each one sings his praises.

'He took their money and discreetly let them off,
as he himself admits. And in his other actions
87 he was no small-time swindler but a king.

'Don Michel Zanche of Logudoro[206]
keeps company with him and, when speaking
90 of Sardegna, their tongues are never weary.

'Oh, look at that one there, gnashing his teeth!—
I would say more, but I'm afraid that demon's
93 getting set to give my mange a scratching.'

And the great marshal, turning to Farfarello,
who was rolling his eyes, ready to strike,
96 said: 'Back off, you filthy bird!'

'If you would care to see or hear,'
the frightened spirit then began again,
99 'Tuscans or Lombards, I can make some come.

'But let the Malebranche stand away
so that the sinners have no fear of vengeance,
102 and, keeping to my place right here,

'for one of me, I will make seven come
if I whistle, as is our custom
105 when one of us pulls free out of the pitch.'

At this Cagnazzo lifted up his snout and said,
shaking his head: 'Hear the cunning stunt
108 he has contrived to throw himself back in!'

And he, with artifice in store, replied:
'I must indeed be cunning if I procure
111 still greater anguish for my friends.'

---

[205] **Fra Gomìta . . . fraud:** A friar who was judge of Gallura, a division of Sardinia; he was hanged for selling freedom to prisoners.
[206] **Don Michel . . . Logudoro:** Judge of Logudoro, a division of Sardinia.

Alichino couldn't stand this any more and said,
in opposition to the others: 'If you dive
114 back in I won't pursue you on the run—

'oh no! I'll beat my wings above the pitch.
Let's leave the ridge and hide behind the bank.
117 We'll see if you alone can take us on.'[207]

Now, reader, you shall hear strange sport.
All turned their backs to where the sinner stood,
120 he first who'd most opposed the plan.

The Navarrese chose his moment well,
planted his feet and in a second
123 leaped and escaped from their designs.

At this they all were angry at their blunder,
but most of all the one whose fault it was,
126 so that he darted up and cried: 'Now you are caught!'

It did him little good, for even wings
could not catch up with terror: the sinner dove
129 and the devil turned up his breast in flight,

just as the wild duck, when the falcon nears,
dives for the bottom, and the bird of prey
132 must fly back up, angry and outsmarted.

Calcabrina, furious at this trick,
was winging close behind him, eager for the sinner
135 to break away as an excuse to scuffle,

and, since the barrator had vanished,
he turned his claws against his fellow
138 and came to grips with him above the ditch.

But the other was indeed a full-fledged hawk,
fierce with his talons, and the pair of them
141 went tumbling down into the scalding pond.

---

[207] **Let's leave . . . us on:** Using the embankment as a screen, they are attempting to cross to the inside edge of the dike that overlooks the next bolgia.

The heat unclutched them in a moment,
but they had so beglued their wings
144 there was no way to rise above the pitch.

Barbariccia, lamenting with the rest,
had four of them fly to the other bank,
147 each with his hook in hand, and in no time

on this side and on that they clambered down
to their posts, reaching out their grapples
to the pitch-trapped pair, already cooked to a crust.
151 And that is how we left them in that broil.

Canto XXIII

Silent, alone, and unescorted
we went on, one in front, the other following,
3 as Friars Minor walk along the roads.

The brawl played out before our eyes
put me in mind of Aesop's fable
6 in which he told the tale of frog and mouse,[208]

for 'issa' and 'mo'[209] are not more like in meaning
than one case and the other, if we compare
9 with circumspection their beginnings and their ends.

Just as one thought issues from another,
so, from the first, another now was born
12 that made me twice as fearful as before.

I thought, 'It's our fault they have been cheated,
and with such hurt and shame
15 I'm sure it must enrage them.

'If rage is added to their malice,
they will pursue us still more cruelly
18 than the hound that sets his fangs into a hare.'

---

[208] the tale of frog and mouse: A fable wrongly ascribed to Aesop (sixth century? B.C.E.) about a frog who gives a ride across a stream to a mouse, tries to drown the mouse, but is seized by a kite (a hawk-like bird) while the mouse goes free.

[209] 'issa' and 'mo': In Italian dialects, both words mean "now."

I could feel my scalp go taut with fear
and kept my thoughts fixed just behind me
21 as I spoke: 'Master, can't you quickly

'hide yourself and me? I am in terror
of the Malebranche; I sense them there behind us,
24 imagine them so clear I almost hear them.'

And he: 'If I were made of leaded glass°   a mirror
I could not reflect your outward likeness
27 in less time than I grasp the one inside you.

'Just now your thought commingled with my own,
alike in attitude and aspect,
30 so that of both I've formed a single plan.

'If the slope there to the right allows us
to make our way into the other ditch,
33 we shall escape the chase we both envision.'

Before he finished telling me his plan
I saw them coming, wings outspread,
36 closing in to catch us.

My leader in a moment snatched me up,
like a mother who, awakened by the hubbub
39 before she sees the flames that burn right near her,

snatches up her child and flees,
and, more concerned for him than for herself,
42 does not delay to put a shift on.

Down from the rim of that stony bank,
supine, he slid along the sloping rock
45 that forms one border of the next crevasse.

Never did water, as it nears the paddles,
rush down along the sluices
48 cut through earth to turn a millwheel

more swiftly than my master down that bank,
bearing me along clasped to his breast
51 as if I were his child, not his companion.

No sooner had he touched the bottom with his feet
than the devils were above us on the ridge.
54 Yet now we had no cause for feeling fear,

for high Providence, which made them
wardens of the fifth crevasse,
57 deprives them of the power to leave it.

Down there we came upon a lacquered people
who made their round, in tears, with listless steps.
60 They seemed both weary and defeated.

The cloaks they wore had cowls that fell
over their eyes, cut like the capes
63 made for the monks at Cluny.[210]

Gilded and dazzling on the outside,
within they are of lead, so ponderous
66 that those imposed by Frederick would seem but straw.[211]

Oh what a toilsome cloak to wear forever!
Once more we turned to the left, then went along
69 beside them, intent upon their wretched wailing.

Their burden made that weary people
move so slowly we had new companions
72 each time we put one foot before the other.

And I said to my leader: 'Cast your eyes
this way and that as we walk on.
75 See if you know the names or deeds of any.'

And one of them, hearing my Tuscan speech,
cried out behind us: 'Stay your feet,
78 you who race through this sullen air.

'I perhaps can answer what you asked.'
At that my leader turned around to say:
81 'Wait a moment,' then continue at his pace.

---

[210] **monks at Cluny:** A large monastery in France whose monks were known for their luxurious wear.

[211] **those imposed . . . straw:** A story attributed to Frederick II (Canto X) that he had traitors wrapped in lead coats that were then melted on them.

I stopped and noticed two whose looks
showed haste of mind to reach me,
84 but their load and the narrow way detained them.

When they came near they looked at me askance
for a while, without a word,
87 until they turned to one another, saying:

'The way his throat moves, this one must be alive.
And if they are dead, what gives them the right
90 to go uncovered by the heavy stole?'

and then to me: 'O Tuscan, who have come
to this assembly of sad hypocrites,
93 do not disdain to tell us who you are.'

'In the great city, by the fair river Arno,'
I said to them, 'I was born and raised,
96 and I am here in the body that was always mine.

'But who are you in whom I see distilled
the misery running down your cheeks in tears?
99 And what is the grief you bear that glitters so?'

And one of them answered: 'Our golden cloaks
are made of lead, and they're so dense,
102 like scales we creak beneath their weight.

'We were Jovial Friars,[212] born in Bologna.
My name was Catalano, his, Loderingo.[213]
105 Your city made the two of us a pair,

'where usually a single man was chosen,
to keep the peace within, and we were such
108 that all around Gardingo the ruins can be seen.'

I began: 'O Friars, your evil deeds . . .'
but said no more, for one there caught my eye,
111 fixed cross-wise to the ground by three short stakes.

---

[212] **Jovial Friars:** Knights of the Blessed Virgin Mary, a military order founded in 1261 to protect the weak; it was known for its easy life.

[213] **Catalano . . . Loderingo:** Two men who helped found the friars and who were appointed joint governors in Florence in 1266; they were later charged with corruption. The quarter of Florence called the Gardingo was destroyed by a civil war caused by the friars.

Seeing me, he writhed all over,
blowing sighs into his beard,
114 and Fra Catalano, observing this, said:

'That man you see nailed down[214]
advised the Pharisees it was the better course
117 that one man should be martyred for the people.

'He is stretched out naked, as you see,
across the path and he must feel
120 the weight of each who passes.

'Just so his father-in-law is racked with us
down here and with the others of the council[215]
123 that was a seed of evil for the Jews.'

I saw that Virgil marveled at the sight
of this shape stretched as on a cross,
126 so ignoble in his eternal exile.

Then he addressed the friar with these words:
'May it please you, if it is permitted,
129 to say if on our right there is a passage

'by which we two might leave this place
without requiring help from some black angels
132 to pluck us from these depths.'

And he replied: 'Nearer than you hope there lies
a rocky ridge that crosses all the savage valleys
135 from the farthest circle inward.

'It has fallen only here and fails to reach across.
You can clamber up the sloping rubble
138 that lies upon the bottom and piles up along the side.'

My leader stood a while, his head bent down, then said:
'He who rips the sinners in the other ditch
141 misled us in his picture of this place.'

---

[214] **That man . . . nailed down:** Caiaphas, the high priest under Pontius Pilate; he advised that Jesus be crucified (John 11:49–50).

[215] **his father-in-law . . . others of the council:** Annas, "father-in-law" to Caiaphas, along with the Jewish San-
hedrin, the supreme council of the Jews in Palestine.

And the friar: 'At one time in Bologna I heard tell
of the Devil's many vices, and I heard
144   he is a liar and the father of all lies.'

At that my leader stalked off with long strides,
a moment's look of anger on his face.
And so I left those overburdened souls
148   to follow in the imprints of his cherished feet.

Canto XXIV

In that season of the youthful year[216]
when the sun cools his locks beneath Aquarius
3   and the dark already nears but half the day,

and when the hoarfrost copies out upon the fields
the very image of her snowy sister —
6   although her pen-point is not sharp for long —

the peasant, short of fodder, rises,
looks out, and sees the countryside
9   turned white, at which he slaps his thigh,

goes back indoors, grumbling here and there
like a wretch who knows not what to do,
12   then goes outside again and is restored to hope,

and, seeing that the world has changed its face
in that brief time, he now picks up his crook
15   and drives his sheep to pasture.

Thus the master caused me to lose heart
when I saw how troubled was his brow
18   and just as quickly came the poultice to the wound,

for no sooner had we reached the broken bridge
than he turned to me with that gentle glance
21   I first saw at the mountain's foot.

He looked with care upon the ruin,
took thought, chose a plan of action,
24   then opened out his arms and took me in them.

---

[216] **In that season of the youthful year:** About January 20.

And like one who reckons as he works,
always planning beforehand what comes next,
27   thus, while raising me to a boulder's top,

he searched for yet another crag
and said: 'Take hold of that one next
30   but test to see if it will bear your weight.'

This was no climb for people wearing leaden cloaks.
Though he was weightless and I was being pushed,
33   how hard a climb it was from one crag to the other!

Were it not that on this side of the dike
the slope was shorter—I cannot speak for him—
36   I would have given up.

But since all Malebolge inclines
down to the mouth of the lowest pit,
39   it follows that each valley is constructed

with one side higher than the other.
At last we made it to the point
42   where the outermost stone had broken off.

And there I felt my lungs so sucked of breath
that I could go no farther,
45   but sat down as quickly as I could.

'Now must you cast off sloth,' my master said.
'Sitting on feather cushions or stretched out
48   under comforters, no one comes to fame.

'Without fame, he who spends his time on earth
leaves only such a mark upon the world
51   as smoke does on the air or foam on water.

'Get to your feet! Conquer this laboring breath
with strength of mind, which wins the battle
54   if not dragged down by body's weight.

'There is a longer stair that must be climbed.[217]
It's not enough to leave these souls behind.
57   If you take my meaning, let it be of use.'

---

[217] **a longer stair . . . climbed:** The distance from the earth's center to the summit of Purgatory.

At that I rose, pretending to more breath
than I had in me, and said:
60 'Go on then, for I am strong and resolute.'

We labored up a ridge,
rugged, narrow, difficult,
63 and steeper far than was the last.

Not to seem so spent, I talked as I climbed up.
Then, from the next ditch, came a voice
66 that seemed unfit for forming words.

I could not make out what it said,
though I was at the crown that arches over,
69 but he who spoke seemed to be moving.

Hard as I strained to see, it was too dark
for living eyes to plumb the depths.
72 And so I said: 'Master, take your way

'to the next encircling bank where we can leave
this bridge. From here I make out nothing
75 with my ears nor see a thing down there.'

'I give no other answer than to take you,'
he said, 'for a just request
78 should be followed by the act, in silence.'

We left the bridge at the abutment
where it comes to rest on that eighth bank.
81 From there the contents of the ditch came into view.

In it I saw a dreadful swarm of serpents,
of so strange a kind that even now
84 when I remember them it chills my blood.

Let Libya with all her sands no longer boast,
for though she fosters chelydri, jaculi,
87 phareae, cenchres, and amphisbaena,[218]

she never reared so many venomous pests,
nor so appalling—not with all of Ethiopia
90 and the lands that lie along the Red Sea coast.

---

[218] **chelydri . . . amphisbaena:** Venomous snakes mentioned by the Roman poet Lucan (39–65 C.E.).

Amid this fearsome and most awful plenty,
people, naked and in terror, were running
93 without hope of refuge or of heliotrope.[219]

Their hands were tied behind their backs with snakes
that thrust their heads and tails between the legs
96 and joined, knotting themselves in front.

And behold, one of these souls was near our ridge
when a serpent launched and pierced him through
99 right where the neck and shoulders join.

Never has 'o' nor even 'i' been writ so quick[220]
as he caught fire and burned, turned,
102 in the very act of falling, into ashes.

And as he lay unmade upon the ground,
the dust gathered itself of its own accord
105 and suddenly he was himself again.

Just, as is attested by great sages,[221]
the phoenix perishes and is reborn
108 when it approaches its five-hundredth year —

lifelong it feeds on neither grain nor grasses,
but thrives on drops of frankincense and cardamom,
111 while nard and myrrh make up its winding sheet —

and just as one who faints, and knows not why —
whether possessed by devils that pull him down
114 or seized by the sickness that causes men to fall —

rises to his feet, and gazes round,
wholly bewildered by the breathless anguish
117 he has undergone, and as he looks, he sighs,

such did that sinner seem when he had risen.
O how stern it is, the power of God,
120 hurling such blows as it takes vengeance!

---

[219] **heliotrope:** A kind of stone thought to make its wearer invisible.

[220] **'o' . . . writ so quick:** Letters that can be made with a single stroke.

[221] **attested by . . . sages:** The story about a phoenix that dies and is reborn out of its own ashes is told by Ovid and Lucan, among others; medieval writers linked the phoenix to Jesus.

When my leader asked him who he was:
'From Tuscany I rained down,' was his answer,
123 'not long ago, into this savage gorge.

'I loved the life of beasts and not of men,
just like the mule I was. I am Vanni Fucci,[222]
126 animal. Pistoia was my fitting den.'

And I to my leader: 'Tell him not to slip away,
then ask what sin has thrust him to this depth,
129 for I knew him as a man of blood and rages.'

And the sinner, listening, did not dissemble,
but set his mind and eyes on me,
132 then colored with a wrathful shame

and said: 'For you to catch me
in this misery pains me more
135 than when I was taken from the other life.

'I can't refuse to answer what you ask.
I am thrust so far below because I stole
138 its lovely ornaments from the sacristy

'and the blame was wrongly laid upon another.[223]
But, so you take no joy in seeing me this low,
141 if ever you escape from these dark regions,

'open your ears to my prophecy and hear:
First, Pistoia strips herself of Blacks,
144 then Florence changes families and fashions.[224]

'Next Mars draws up a bolt from Val di Magra,
engulfed by torn and threatening clouds,
147 and, with violent and stinging storms,

---

[222] **Vanni Fucci:** Fucci was the illegitimate son ("mule") of a noble from Pistoia, north of Florence, and violent leader of the Blacks, a division of the Guelphs.

[223] **blame . . . upon another:** The sacristy in the Pistoia Cathedral contained treasures, some of which were stolen in 1293. An innocent man was hung for the theft.

[224] **Florence changes . . . fashions:** The division of the Guelphs into Blacks and Whites spread from Pistoia to Florence; in Pistoia the Blacks were expelled by the Whites, but in Florence the dominance of the Blacks in 1302 led to Dante's exile. The "headlong bolt" (l. 149) was the leader of the Blacks from the Malaspina family.

'on Campo Piceno the battle shall be joined.
The headlong bolt shall rend the clouds,
striking and wounding every White.
151   And this I have told that it may make you grieve.'

Canto XXV

Then, making the figs with both his thumbs,[225]
the thief raised up his fists and cried:
3   'Take that, God! It's aimed at you!'

From that time on the serpents were my friends,
for one of them coiled itself around his neck
6   as if to say, 'Now you shall speak no more,'

while another enmeshed his arms and held him fast,
knotting itself so tight around his front
9   he could not even twitch his arms.

Ah, Pistoia, Pistoia, why won't you resolve
to burn yourself to ashes, cease to be,
12   since you exceed your ancestors in evil?[226]

Through all the gloomy rounds of Hell
I saw no soul so prideful against God,
15   not even him who toppled from the walls at Thebes.[227]

He ran away without another word.
And then I saw a centaur full of rage
18   come shouting: 'Where, where is that unripe soul?'

Maremma does not have as many snakes,
I think, as he had on his back,
21   from where the human part begins down to the rump.

On his shoulders, just at the nape of the neck,
crouched a dragon with its wings spread wide
24   that sets on fire whatever it encounters.

---

[225] **making the figs . . . thumbs:** An obscene gesture.

[226] **Pistoia . . . evil:** Pistoia was founded by Cataline, a conspirator against the Roman Republic in the first century B.C.E.

[227] **him who toppled . . . Thebes:** Capaneus (Canto XIV).

My master said: 'That is Cacus,[228]
who in the cave beneath the Aventine
27 many times over has made a lake of blood.

'His road is different from his brothers'
because he stole, with wicked cunning,
30 the herd of cattle he found near at hand.

'For that his wily ways were ended
beneath the club of Hercules, who struck perhaps
33 a hundred blows, though he felt not the tenth.'

While my master spoke the centaur had run past.
Below where we were standing, three new souls
36 had neared, although we did not see them

until we heard their shouts: 'You,
who are you?' At that he stopped his tale
39 and we gave heed to them alone.

I knew none of them, and yet it happened—
as often happens by some chance—
42 that one had cause to speak another's name,

asking: 'What's become of Cianfa?'[229]
And then, to catch my guide's attention,
45 I held my finger up from chin to nose.

If, reader, you are slow to credit
what I'm about to tell you, it's no wonder:
48 I saw it, and I myself can scarce believe it.

While I stood staring, with raised brows,
a reptile with six legs propelled itself
51 at one of them, and fastened itself to him.

It grabbed his belly with its middle claws,
then with its forepaws held his arms
54 and bit him on both cheeks.

---

[228] **Cacus:** A monster who stole cattle from Hercules and dragged them backwards into his cave. His brothers are the Centaurs (Canto XII).

[229] **Cianfa:** A thief from a noble Florentine family.

It stretched its hind feet down the other's thighs,
thrusting its tail between them
57   and curled it up behind, above the buttocks.

Never did clinging ivy fix itself
so tight upon a tree as did that fearsome beast
60   entwine itself around the other's limbs.

Then they fused together, as if made
of molten wax, mixing their colors
63   so that neither seemed what it had been before,

as over the surface of a scrap of parchment,
before the flame, a brownish color comes
66   that is not black, yet makes the white die out.

The other two were looking on and each
was shouting: 'Oh my, Agnello,[230] how you change!
69   Look, now you are neither two nor one!'

Already the two heads had been united,
two sets of features blending,
72   both lost in a single face.

Four separate limbs combined to form two arms.
The thighs and calves, the stomach and the chest
75   turned into members never seen before.

All trace of their first aspect was erased
and the unnatural figure seemed both two
78   and none; and off it went, at its slow pace.

As the green lizard beneath the scorching lash
of dog-day heat, between one hedge and the next,
81   seems lightning as it streaks across the road,

just so appeared—darting toward the bellies
of the other two—a little fiery reptile,
84   black and livid as a peppercorn.

That part where first we are nourished°   the navel
it transfixed in one of them
87   and then fell prone before him.

---

[230] **Agnello:** Another thief.

The one transfixed just stared, said nothing.
Indeed, with his feet stock-still, he yawned,
90 as if deep sleep or fever had assailed him.

He and the reptile stared at one another.
Both gave out dense smoke, one from its wound,
93 the other from its mouth. Then their smoke merged.

Let Lucan now fall silent where he tells
of poor Sabellus and Nasidius,[231]
96 and let him wait to hear what comes forth now!

Let Ovid not speak of Cadmus or Arethusa,[232]
for if his poem turns him into a serpent
99 and her into a fountain, I grudge it not,

for never did he change two natures, face to face,
in such a way that both their forms
102 were quite so quick exchanging substance.

Their corresponding changes went like this:
the reptile split its tail into a fork
105 and he that was wounded drew his feet together.

First his calves and then his thighs began
to knit so that in but a moment
108 no sign of a division could be seen.

The cloven tail assumed the shapes
the other one was losing, and his skin
111 was turning soft while the other's hardened.

I saw the man's arms shrinking toward the armpits
and the brute's forepaws, which had been short,
114 lengthen, precisely as the other's dwindled.

Then the hind-paws, twisting together,
became the member that a man conceals,
117 and from his own the wretch had grown two paws.

---

[231] **Sabellus and Nasidius:** Two soldiers in Cato's army (in Lucan's *Pharsalia*) bitten by serpents.

[232] **Cadmus or Arethusa:** Pursued by a river god, the nymph Arethusa asked Artemis to change her into a fountain; Cadmus, founder of Thebes, was changed into a serpent after killing a sacred dragon.

While the smoke veils one and now the other
with new color and grows hair here
120 and elsewhere strips it off,

one of them rose to his feet, the other fell,
but neither turned aside his baleful glare
123 under which each muzzle changed its shape.

In the one erect it shrank in to the temples,
and, from the excess flesh absorbed,
126 two ears extruded from smooth cheeks.

Whatever did not recede, left over
from that excess, made a nose for the face
129 and gave the lips a proper thickness.

The one prone on the ground shoves out his snout
and draws his ears into his head
132 as a snail draws in its horns,

and his tongue, till now a single thing
and fit for speech, divides, and the other's
135 forked tongue joins, and the smoke stops.

The soul just now become a brute takes flight,
hissing through the hollow, and the other,
138 by way of speaking, spits after him.[233]

Then he turned his new-made shoulders and he said
to the third: 'I want Buoso[234] to run, as I have done,
141 down on all fours along this road.'

Thus I saw the seventh rabble[235] change
and change again, and let the newness of it
144 be my excuse if my pen has gone astray.

And though my eyes were dazed
and my mind somewhat bewildered,
147 these sinners could not flee so stealthily

---

[233] **spits after him:** It was thought that human spit was poisonous to snakes.

[234] **Buoso:** The identity of this Buoso is not known.

[235] **rabble:** The sinners in this ditch.

but I with ease discerned that Puccio Lameshanks,[236]
and he alone, of the three companions
in that group, remained unchanged.

151   The other,[237] Gaville, was the one whom you lament.

Canto XXVI

Take joy, oh Florence, for you are so great
your wings beat over land and sea,
3   your fame resounds through Hell!

Among the thieves, I found five citizens of yours
who make me feel ashamed, and you
6   are raised by them to no great praise.

But if as morning nears we dream the truth,
it won't be long before you feel the pain
9   that Prato,[238] to name but one, desires for you.

Were it already come, it would not be too soon.
But let it come, since come indeed it must,
12   and it will weigh the more on me the more I age.

We left that place and, on those stairs
that turned us pale when we came down,
15   my leader now climbed back and drew me up.

As we took our solitary way
among the juts and crags of the escarpment,
18   our feet could not advance without our hands.

I grieved then and now I grieve again
as my thoughts turn to what I saw,
21   and more than is my way, I curb my powers

lest they run on where virtue fails to guide them,
so that, if friendly star or something better still
24   has granted me its boon, I don't refuse the gift.

---

[236] **Puccio Lameshanks:** A third thief from a Florentine family.

[237] **The other:** Francesco Cavalcanti, a Florentine living in Gaville, was killed for his oppressions by the towns-people; his family avenged him.

[238] **Prato:** Perhaps a reference to the rebellion of Prato, north of Florence, against Florence.

As when a peasant, resting on a hillside—
in the season when he who lights the world
27   least hides his face from us,

at the hour when the fly gives way to the mosquito[239]—
sees fireflies that glimmer in the valley
30   where he perhaps ploughs fields and harvests grapes,

with just so many flames the eighth crevasse
was everywhere aglow, as I became aware
33   once I arrived where I could see the bottom.

And as the one who was avenged by bears
could see Elijah's chariot taking flight,
36   when the horses reared and rose to Heaven,[240]

but made out nothing with his eyes
except the flame alone
39   ascending like a cloud into the sky,

so each flame moves along the gullet
of the trench and—though none reveals the theft—
42   each flame conceals a sinner.

Rising to my feet to look, I stood up
on the bridge. Had I not grasped a jutting crag,
45   I would have fallen in without a shove.

My leader, when he saw me so intent, said:
'These spirits stand within the flames.
48   Each one is wrapped in that in which he burns.'

'Master,' I replied, 'I am the more convinced
to hear you say it. That is what I thought,
51   and had it in my mind to ask you this:

'Who is in the flame so riven at the tip
it could be rising from the pyre
54   on which Etèocles was laid out with his brother?'[241]

---

[239] in the season . . . mosquito: A midsummer evening.

[240] the one who . . . Heaven: Elisha saw Elijah's ascension in a chariot (2 Kings 11:23–24).

[241] laid out . . . brother: Etèocles and his brother, Polynices, sons of Oedipus, killed each other.

He replied: 'Within this flame find torment
Ulysses and Diomed.[242] They are paired
57 in God's revenge as once they earned his wrath.

'In their flame they mourn the stratagem
of the horse that made a gateway
60 through which the noble seed of Rome came forth.

'There they lament the wiles for which, in death,
Deidamìa mourns Achilles still,[243]
63 and there they make amends for the Palladium.'

'If they can speak within those flames,'
I said, 'I pray you, master, and I pray again—
66 and may my prayer be a thousand strong—

'do not forbid my lingering awhile
until the twin-forked flame arrives.
69 You see how eagerly I lean in its direction.'

And he to me: 'Your prayer deserves
much praise. Therefore, I grant it,
72 but on condition that you hold your tongue.

'Leave speech to me, for I have understood
just what you want. And, since they were Greeks,
75 they might disdain your words.'

Once the flame had neared, when he thought
the time and moment right,
78 I heard my leader speaking in this way:

'O you who are twinned within a single fire,
if I have earned your favor while I lived
81 if I have earned your favor—in whatever measure—

'when, in the world, I wrote my lofty verses,
then do not move away. Let one of you relate
84 just where, having lost his way, he went to die.'

---

[242] **Ulysses and Diomed:** Two Greek leaders in the Trojan War; they stole the sacred image of Pallas Athene, the "Palladium," which protected Troy, and they devised the trick of the wooden horse that led to Troy's downfall.

[243] **mourns Achilles still:** Ulysses and Diomed persuaded Achilles to leave his lover Deidamìa and go to Troy, where Achilles died.

And the larger horn of that ancient flame
began to murmur and to tremble,
87　like a flame that is worried by the wind.

Then, brandishing its tip this way and that,
as if it were the tongue of fire that spoke,
90　it brought forth a voice and said: 'When I

'took leave of Circe,[244] who for a year and more
beguiled me there, not far from Gaëta,
93　before Aeneas gave that name to it,

'not tenderness for a son, nor filial duty
toward my agèd father, nor the love I owed
96　Penelope[245] that would have made her glad,

'could overcome the fervor that was mine
to gain experience of the world
99　and learn about man's vices, and his worth.

'And so I set forth on the open deep
with but a single ship, with that handful
102　of shipmates who had not deserted me.

'One shore and the other I saw as far as Spain,
Morocco — the island of Sardegna,
105　and other islands set into that sea.

'I and my shipmates had grown old and slow
by the time we reached the narrow strait
108　where Hercules marked off the limits,

'warning all men to go no farther.[246]
On the right-hand side I left Seville behind,
111　on the other I had left Ceüta.

'"O brothers," I said, "who, in the course
of a hundred thousand perils, at last
114　have reached the west, to such brief wakefulness

---

[244] **Circe:** A goddess and enchantress who turned men into beasts.　[245] **Penelope:** The wife of Ulysses.
[246] **the narrow strait . . . no farther:** The Pillars of Hercules, thought to be the edge of the habitable world.

'"of our senses as remains to us,
do not deny yourselves the chance to know—
117 following the sun—the world where no one lives.

'"Consider how your souls were sown:
you were not made to live like brutes or beasts,
120 but to pursue virtue and knowledge."

'With this brief speech I had my companions
so ardent for the journey
123 I could scarce have held them back.

'And, having set our stern to sunrise,
in our mad flight we turned our oars to wings,
126 always gaining on the left.

'Now night was gazing on the stars that light
the other pole, the stars of our own so low
129 they did not rise above the ocean floor.

'Five times the light beneath the moon
had been rekindled and as often been put out
132 since we began our voyage on the deep,

'when we could see a mountain, distant,
dark and dim. In my sight it seemed
135 higher than any I had ever seen.

'We rejoiced, but joy soon turned to grief:
for from that unknown land there came
138 a whirlwind that struck the ship head-on.

'Three times it turned her and all the waters
with her. At the fourth our stern reared up,
the prow went down—as pleased Another°—   god
142 until the sea closed over us.'

Canto XXVII

The flame now stood erect and still,
meaning to speak no more, and was departing
3 with the gentle poet's leave,

when another flame, coming close behind,
caused our eyes to fix upon its tip,
6 drawn by the gibberish that came from it.

As the Sicilian bull that bellowed first
with the cries of him whose instrument[247]
9 had fashioned it—and that was only just—

used to bellow with the victim's voice
so that, although the bull was made of brass,
12 it seemed transfixed by pain,

thus, having first no course or outlet
through the flame, the mournful words
15 were changed into a language all their own.

But once the words had made their way
up to the tip, making it flicker
18 as the voice had done when it had formed them,

we heard it say: 'O you at whom I aim my voice
and who, just now, said in the Lombard tongue:[248]
21 "Now go your way, I ask you nothing more,"

'though I've arrived, perhaps, a little late,
let it not trouble you to stay and speak with me.
24 Though I am in the flame, as you can see, it irks me not.

'If you are only a short while fallen
into this blind world from that sweet land
27 of Italy, from which I bring down all my sins,

'tell me if Romagna lives in peace or war.
I came from where the mountains stand between
30 Urbino and the ridge from which the Tiber springs.'[249]

I still stood bending down to hear,
when my leader nudged my side and said:
33 'It's up to you to speak—this one is Italian.'

---

[247] **him whose instrument:** Perillus fashioned for Phalaris, tyrant of Sicily, a brass bull for roasting victims and was himself the first victim.

[248] **in the Lombard tongue:** Virgil spoke the Lombard dialect.

[249] **I came from . . . Tiber springs:** Guido, count of Montefeltro, head of the Ghibellines in Romagna and a soldier, died in 1298.

And I, who had my answer ready,
without delay began to speak:
36 'O soul that is hidden from my sight down there,

'your Romagna is not, and never was,
free of warfare in her rulers' hearts.
39 Still, no open warfare have I left behind.

'Ravenna[250] remains as it has been for years.
The eagle of Polenta broods over it
42 so that he covers Cervia with his wings.

'The town that once withstood the lengthy siege,
making of the French a bloody heap,
45 is now again beneath the green claws of the lion.[251]

'The elder mastiff of Verrucchio and the younger,
who between them had harsh dealing with Montagna,
48 sharpen their teeth to augers in the customary place.

'The young lion on a field of white,
who rules Lamone's and Santerno's cities,
51 changes sides between the summer and the snows.

'And the city whose flank the Savio bathes:
as she lives between tyranny and freedom,
54 so she lies between the mountain and the plain.[252]

'But now, I beg you, tell us who you are.
Be no more grudging than another's been to you,
57 so may your name continue in the world.'

When the fire had done its roaring for a while,
after its fashion, the point began to quiver
60 this way and that, and then gave breath to this:

'If I but thought that my response were made
to one perhaps returning to the world,
63 this tongue of flame would cease to flicker.

---

[250] **Ravenna:** The major city in Romagna ruled then, along with Cervia, by the Polenta family.

[251] **The town . . . of the lion:** Forlì defeated the French but later was seized by the Ordelaffi family, whose coat of arms had green claws.

[252] **The elder mastiff . . . and the plain:** This list includes cities of Romagna, their rulers, and descriptions of their coats of arms.

'But since, up from these depths, no one has yet
returned alive, if what I hear is true,
66 I answer without fear of being shamed.

'A warrior was I, and then a corded friar,[253]
thinking, cinctured so, to make amends.
69 And surely would my hopes have come to pass

'but for the Great Priest[254]—the devil take him!—
who drew me back to my old ways.
72 And I would like to tell you how and why.

'While I still kept the form in flesh and bones
my mother gave me, my deeds were not
75 a lion's but the actions of a fox.

'Cunning stratagems and covert schemes,
I knew them all, and was so skilled in them
78 my fame rang out to the far confines of the earth.

'When I saw I had reached that stage of life
when all men ought to think
81 of lowering sail and coiling up the ropes,

'I grew displeased with what had pleased before.
Repentant and shriven, I became a friar.
84 And woe is me! it would have served.

'But he, Prince of the latter-day Pharisees,
engaged in battle near the Lateran
87 and not with either Saracen or Jew,

'for all his enemies were Christian[255]—
not one of them had gone to conquer Acre
90 or traffic in the Sultan's lands[256]—

---

[253] a corded friar: A Franciscan.

[254] the Great Priest: Pope Boniface VIII.

[255] enemies were Christian: On Guido's advice, Boniface broke faith with the Colonna, who had surrendered to the papal forces, and destroyed Palestrina, the Colonna's stronghold.

[256] to conquer Acre . . . Sultan's lands: Acre, the last stronghold of the Christians in Palestine, surrendered to the Muslims in 1291. An earlier pope forbade commerce with Muslims.

'paid no heed, for his part, to the highest office
or his holy orders, nor, for mine,
93 to the cord that used to keep its wearers lean.

'As Constantine once had Sylvester summoned
from Soracte to cure his leprous sores,²⁵⁷
96 so this man called on me to be his doctor

'and cure him of the fever of his pride.
He asked me for advice, but I kept silent
99 because his words were like a drunkard's words.

'And then he spoke again: "Let not your heart mistrust:
I absolve you here and now if you will teach me
102 how I can bring Praeneste to the ground.

'"I have the power, as well you know, to lock
and unlock Heaven, because the keys are two
105 for which the pope before me had no care."²⁵⁸

'His threatening tactics brought me to the point
at which the worse course seemed the one of silence.
108 And so I said: "Father, since you cleanse me

'"of the sin that I must even now commit:
Promising much with scant observance
111 will seal your triumph on the lofty throne."

'The moment I was dead, Francis came for me.
But one of the dark Cherubim cried out:
114 "No, wrong me not by bearing that one off.

'"He must come down to serve among my minions
because he gave that fraudulent advice.
117 From then till now I've dogged his footsteps.

'"One may not be absolved without repentance,
nor repent and wish to sin concurrently—
120 a simple contradiction not allowed."

---

²⁵⁷ **to cure . . . sores:** Prior to his conversion, Emperor Constantine contracted leprosy while persecuting Christians. Instructed to do so in a dream, he summoned Pope Sylvester from Mount Soracte, was converted, and was healed.

²⁵⁸ **the keys . . . no care:** Pope Celestine V, who resigned the Papacy after five months, had given up the keys of damnation and absolution.

'Oh, wretch that I am, how I shuddered
when he seized me and said: "Perhaps
123 you didn't reckon I'd be versed in logic."

'He carried me to Minos, who coiled his tail
eight times around his scaly back
126 and, having gnawed it in his awful rage,

'said: "Here comes a sinner for the thieving fire."
And so, just as you see me, I am damned,
129 cloaked as I am. And as I go, I grieve.'

Once he had brought his words to this conclusion,
the weeping flame departed,
132 twisting and tossing its pointed horn.

We continued on our way, my guide and I,
over the ridge and up the arch that spans
the ditch where those are paid their due
136 who, for disjoining, gather up their load.

Canto XXVIII

Who, even in words not bound by meter,
and having told the tale many times over,
3 could tell the blood and wounds that I saw now?

Surely every tongue would fail,
for neither thought nor speech
6 has the capacity to hold so much.

Could all the wounded troops again assemble:
first from Apulia, land laid low by war,
9 who grieved for their lost blood

shed by the Trojans,[259] then all those
of the long war,[260] whose corpses were despoiled
12 of piles of rings—as Livy[261] writes, who does not err—

---

[259] **blood shed . . . Trojans:** Losses by the Trojans under Aeneas when they fought battles in south Italy.
[260] **the long war:** The Second Punic War between Rome and Carthage (218–201 B.C.E.), in which Hannibal gathered three bushels of rings from dead Romans.
[261] **Livy:** First-century C.E. Roman historian.

together with the ones who felt the agony of blows
fighting in the fields against Guiscard,[262]
15 and those whose bones still lie in heaps

at Ceprano, where each Apulian played it false,
and those near Tagliacozzo,[263]
18 where old Alardo conquered without force of arms:

and should one show his limb pierced through,
another his, where it has been cut off,
21 it would be nothing to the ninth pit's filth.

No cask ever gapes so wide for loss
of mid- or side-stave as the soul I saw
24 cleft from the chin right down to where men fart.

Between the legs the entrails dangled. I saw
the innards and the loathsome sack
27 that turns what one has swallowed into shit.

While I was caught up in the sight of him,
he looked at me and, with his hands, ripped open
30 his chest, saying: 'See how I rend myself,

'see how mangled is Mohammed![264]
Ahead of me proceeds Alì, in tears,
33 his face split open from his chin to forelock.

'And all the others whom you see
sowed scandal and schism while they lived,
36 and that is why they here are hacked asunder.

'A devil's posted there behind us
who dresses us so cruelly,
39 putting each of this crew again to the sword

---

[262] **fighting . . . against Guiscard:** The Norman war under Guiscard (1015–1085) fought against Greeks and Saracens.

[263] **at Ceprano . . . and . . . near Tagliacozzo:** The town of Ceprano was betrayed by the barons of Apulia; men at Tagliacozzo were defeated by a trick by Alardo rather than by military might.

[264] **how mangled . . . Mohammed:** Muhammad (570–632), the founder of Islam, was thought to be a Christian convert and then a schismatic. Ali is Muhammad's son-in-law; the dispute over Ali's succession to leadership resulted in the division of Islam into the Sunni and Shi'ite sects.

'as soon as we have done our doleful round.
For all our wounds have closed
42   when we appear again before him.

'But who are you to linger on the ridge?—
perhaps you put off going to the torment
45   pronounced on your own accusation.'

'Death does not have him yet nor does his guilt
lead him to torment,' replied my master,
48   'but to give him greater knowledge

'I, who am dead indeed, must shepherd him
from circle to circle, through this Hell down here.
51   And this is as true as that I speak to you.'

On hearing this, more than a hundred souls
halted in the ditch to stare at me
54   in wonder, each forgetful of his pain.

'You, who perhaps will shortly see the sun,
warn Fra Dolcino[265] to provide himself—
57   unless he'd like to join me here quite soon—

'with stocks of victuals, lest the siege of snow
hand the Novarese the victory
60   not otherwise so easy to attain.'

One foot raised, halted in mid-stride,
Mohammed spoke these words,
63   then setting down that foot, went on his way.

Another, with his throat pierced through
and nose hacked off just where the brows begin,
66   and only one ear left upon his head,

stopped with the rest of them to gape in wonder
and, before the others did, opened his windpipe,
69   scarlet on the skin side as it was,

---

[265] **Fra Dolcino:** Head of the Apostolic Brothers, a communal sect whose members escaped into the hills near Novara only to be starved out by papal forces. Some were executed; Dolcino was burned alive with his mistress in 1307.

to say: 'O you whom guilt does not condemn
and whom I saw above in Italy,
72 if in your likeness I am not deceived,

'should you ever see that gentle plain again
that slopes from Vercelli down to Marcabò,
75 for Pier da Medicina[266] spare a thought.

'And let the two chief men of Fano know,
both messer Guido and Angiolello,
78 that, unless our foresight here is vain,

'through a brutal tyrant's treachery[267]
near La Cattolica they shall be heaved
81 out of their ship with weights to sink them down.

'Between the islands of Cyprus and Majorca
Neptune never witnessed so terrible a crime,
84 whether one committed by pirates or by Greeks.

'That traitor, who sees through one eye only
and rules the city that another down here with me
87 would take delight in never having seen,

'will have the men of Fano come to parley
and he will so deal with them that, to control
90 Focara's wind, they'll need no vows or prayers.'[268]

And I: 'Point out to me and make him known,
if you would have me carry news of you above,
93 the one to whom that city's sight was bitter.'

Then he laid his hand upon the jaw
of one of his companions, pried his lips apart,
96 and cried: 'This is he, but he does not speak.

'Banished, he quenched the doubt in Caesar,
affirming that, to a man prepared,
99 delay was always harmful.'

---

[266] **Pier da Medicina:** Of uncertain identity.

[267] **tyrant's treachery:** It is thought the tyrant Malestino, the one-eyed lord of Rimini, murdered two leaders of the opposite party in order to gain control of Fano, a town on the Adriatic coast.

[268] **the men of Fano . . . or prayers:** After being invited for a parley, the men were drowned before reaching the coast.

Ah, how distressed he seemed to me,
his tongue sliced off deep in his throat,
102   Curio, who'd been so bold in speech![269]

And then another whose hands had been chopped off,
raising his stumps up in the murky air
105   so that the blood from them befouled his face,

cried out: 'Surely you'll remember Mosca[270] also,
who said, alas: "A done deed finds its purpose."
108   For Tuscany, that was an evil seed.'

'And death to your own stock,' I added then.
At that, one sorrow piled upon another,
111   he made off, like a man berserk with grief.

But I stayed on to watch the troop
and saw a thing I would be loath
114   to mention without further proof,

were I not comforted by conscience,
the bosom friend that fortifies a man
117   beneath the armor of an honest heart.

I truly saw, and seem to see it still,
a headless body make its way
120   like all the others in that dismal flock.

And by its hair he held his severed head
swinging in his hand as if it were a lantern.
123   The head stared at us and said: 'Oh, woe!'

Of himself he made himself a lamp,
and they were two in one and one in two.
126   How this can be He knows who so ordains it.

When he was just at the foot of the bridge
he raised his arm high and, with it, that head,
129   so as to make his words sound more distinct:

---

[269] **Curio . . . speech:** Curio, a first-century B.C.E. Roman tribune, advised Julius Caesar to cross the Rubicon and invade the Roman Republic, which started the civil war.

[270] **Mosca:** Mosca is blamed for initiating civil strife in Florence; he advised the Amidei family to avenge their daughter who had been jilted by a Buondelmonte. Buondelmonte was murdered, and sixty years later Mosca's own family was either killed or exiled.

'You, who view the dead with breath yet in your body,
look upon my grievous punishment.
132 Is any other terrible as this?

'So you may carry back the news of me,
know I am Bertran de Born, the one
135 who urged the young king on with bad advice.[271]

'Father and son I set to enmity.
Ahithophel stirred no worse ill between
138 Absalom and David[272] with his wicked goading.

'Because I severed persons thus conjoined,
severed, alas, I carry my own brain
from its starting-point here in my body.
142 In me you may observe fit punishment.'

Canto XXIX

The many people and their ghastly wounds
did so intoxicate my eyes
3 that I was moved to linger there and weep.

But Virgil said: 'What are you staring at?
Why is your gaze so fixed upon the depths
6 that hold those mournful, mutilated shades?

'You have not done so at the other pits.
In case you plan to count the sinners one by one,
9 think: this hollow circles twenty-two miles round.

'The moon already lies beneath our feet.[273]
The time we are allotted soon expires
12 and there is more to see than you see here.'

'Had you understood,' I was quick to answer,
'the reason for my close inspection,
15 perhaps you would have let me stay there longer.'

---

[271] **bad advice:** Bertran de Born, lord of Hautefort in Provence and a twelfth-century noble and poet, advised
Prince Henry to revolt against his father, Henry II of England.

[272] **Absalom and David:** Ahithophel was Absalom's advisor in his rebellion against King David. (2 Samuel 15:12;
16:20–17:4).

[273] **The moon . . . feet:** The sun, unseen, is overhead; it is about 2 P.M. and only four hours remain of Dante's
journey through Hell.

All the while my guide was moving on,
with me, intent on my reply, behind him.
18   And then I added: 'Within that hole

'where I had fixed my gaze, I think I saw
someone of my own blood lament
21   the sin that costs so dear down there.'

Then the master said: 'Trouble your mind
no more because of him.
24   Turn it to other things and let him be,

'for I saw him there below the bridge,
pointing his finger at you, fierce with threats,
27   and I heard him called Geri del Bello.[274]

'Just then you were so thoroughly engrossed
in him who once was lord of Hautefort
30   you didn't glance that way before your kinsman left.'

'O my leader, the violent death he died,
for which no vengeance has been taken yet,'
33   I said, 'by any person partner to his shame,

'made him indignant. That is why he went away
without addressing me — or so I think —
36   and why he has made me pity him the more.'

Thus we continued talking till we reached
the first point on the ridge that could have shown
39   the next pit's bottom, had there been more light.

When we stood above the final cloister
of Malebolge and all of its lay brothers
42   became discernible to us,

strange arrows of lament, their shafts,
with pity at their tips, pierced me,
45   so that I pressed my hands against my ears.

---

[274]**Geri del Bello:** A cousin of Dante's father; a member of the Sachetti family murdered him after he had caused some trouble, which led to a feud between the families.

If the contagion of every hospital
in Valdichiana, from July until September,
48 and in the Maremma and Sardegna,[275] were amassed

in one malarial ditch, such suffering
was in that place. And from it rose
51 the stench of festering limbs.

We came down, always to our left, and reached
the last bank of the lengthy crag.
54 And then my eyes could have a better view

into the pit, there where the minister
of God on high, unerring justice, punishes
57 the counterfeiters whom she here records.

I think it could have been no greater sorrow
to see the people of Aegina stricken,
60 with such corruption in the very air

that every animal, even the smallest worm,
perished, and, later, as the poets hold for certain,
63 these ancient people were restored to life,

hatched from the eggs of ants[276] —
no greater sorrow, than in that somber valley
66 to see those spirits, heaped on one another, languishing.

Some lay upon the bellies or the backs
of others, still others dragged themselves
69 on hands and knees along that gloomy path.

Step by step we went ahead in silence,
looking and listening to the stricken spirits,
72 who could not raise their bodies from the ground.

Two I saw seated, propped against each other
as pans are propped to warm before the fire,
75 each of them blotched with scabs from head to foot.

---

[275] **Maremma and Sardegna:** The island of Sardinia and the region of Maremma, both plagued by malaria.

[276] **from the eggs of ants:** Depopulated by pestilence, the island of Aegina was repopulated when Jupiter transformed ants into humans.

And never did I see a stable-boy,
with his master waiting, nor youth whose chore
78 keeps him from sleep, ply his curry-comb

more hurriedly than each one clawed his nails
across his skin because of that mad itch,
81 which knows no other remedy,

and their nails tore off scabs
as a knife strips scales from bream
84 or other fish with even larger scales.

'You there, stripping off your coat of mail,'
began my leader, addressing one of them,
87 'and sometimes making pincers of your fingers,

'tell us whether, among those gathered here,
any are Italian, so may your nails
90 last you in this task for all eternity.'

'We whom you see so blasted are Italian,'
answered one of them, through his tears,
93 'but who are you, that you inquire of us?'

And my leader: 'I am one who makes his way
down with this living man from ledge to ledge.
96 And my intention is to show him Hell.'

They stopped propping one another up
and each one, trembling, turned in my direction,
99 as others did who'd overheard those words.

The good master drew up close to me,
saying, 'Ask them what you will.'
102 And I began, since this had been his wish:

'So that your memory may not fade away
from minds of men in the world above
105 but live on yet for many suns to come,

'tell me who you are, and where you hail from.
Do not let your foul and sickening torment
108 keep you from telling me your names.'

And one of them replied: 'I was of Arezzo.
Albero of Siena had me burned alive.
111 But what I died for does not bring me here.

'It is true I said to him in jest:
"I do know how to rise into the air and fly!"
114 And he, who had the will but not the wit,

'asked me to show him how. And just because
I failed to make him Daedalus, he had me set
117 on fire by one who took him as his son.[277]

'But Minos, incapable of error,
damned me to the last of these ten ditches
120 for the alchemy I practiced in the world.'

And I said to the poet: 'Was ever a people
quite so fatuous as the Sienese?
123 Why, not even the French can match them!'

Whereupon the other leper,[278] hearing me,
replied: 'Except, of course for Stricca—
126 he knew how to moderate his spending—

'and for Niccolò—the first one to devise
a costly use for cloves,
129 there in the garden where such seeds take root—

'and for that band in whose company
Caccia d'Asciano squandered his vineyards
132 and his fields, and Abbagliato showed his wit.[279]

'But, to let you know who's in your camp
against the Sienese, look close at me
135 so that my face itself may answer you.

---

[277] **I was of Arezzo . . . as his son:** Griffolino of Arezzo told slow-witted Albero that he could teach Albero how to fly. When Griffolino failed at flight, Albero, the natural son of the bishop—the Inquisitor of Siena—had his father burn Griffolino as a magician. Daedalus invented wings for human flight (Canto XVII).

[278] **the other leper:** Capocchio, who was burned for alchemy in Siena in 1293.

[279] **Stricca . . . Abbagliato . . . :** Stricca, Niccolò, Caccia, and Abbagliato were members of the Spendthrift Club in Siena (see Lano in Canto XIII). Cloves were used in cooking.

'You will see I am the shade of Capocchio,
who altered metal by means of alchemy.
And, if you are the man I take you for,
139   you will recall how good an ape I was of nature.'

Canto XXX

Once when Juno, furious with Semele,[280]
vented her rage against the house of Thebes,
3   as she had done on more than one occasion,

Athamas went so raving mad that when he saw
his wife come near with both their children,
6   holding one on this arm, one on that,

he shouted: "Let's spread the nets so I can trap
the lioness with her cubs as they go past!"
9   Then he reached out and with pitiless claws

he seized the one who was called Learchus,
whirled him round and dashed him on a rock.
12   At that she drowned herself with her other burden.

And when Fortune had subdued the haughty,
all-daring spirit of the Trojans,
15   so that both king and kingdom were brought down,

Hecuba — wretched, sorrowing, a captive —
when she saw Polyxena slaughtered and,
18   grieving woman, when she saw

Polydorus lying dead upon the shore,
went mad and started barking like a dog,
21   so greatly had her grief[281] deranged her mind.

But no Theban crazed with rage —
or Trojan — did ever seem as cruel
24   in rending beasts, much less human parts,

---

[280] **Semele:** The daughter of King Cadmus of Thebes who was loved by Jupiter, whose wife, Juno, took revenge on the Theban household by driving Athamas insane. Athamas was the husband of Ino, Semele's sister.

[281] **her grief:** Hecuba's family was destroyed when the Greeks conquered Troy: She was enslaved; her husband, Priam, was killed; her daughter, Polyxena, was sacrificed; and her son, Polydorus, was murdered by Polymnestor.

as did two pallid, naked shades I saw,
snapping their jaws as they rushed up
27 like swine charging from an opened sty.

The one came at Capocchio, set its tusks
into his neck, then dragged him
30 so his belly scraped the rock-hard ground.

And the Aretine,[282] who stood there, trembling,
said to me: 'That demon's Gianni Schicchi,
33 and in his rabid rage he mauls the others.'

'Oh,' I said to him, 'so may that other not fix
its teeth in you, be kind enough to tell me
36 just who it is before it runs away.'

And he answered: 'That is the ancient soul
of wicked Myrrha,[283] who became enamored
39 of her father with more than lawful love.

'She contrived to sin with him
by taking on another person's shape,
42 as did that other, eager to decamp,

'to gain the queen mule of the herd,
take on the shape of Buoso Donati,
45 drawing up a will and giving it due form.'[284]

When those two frenzied shades, on whom
I'd fixed my eyes, had hurried off,
48 I turned to look at others born for sorrow.

One I saw, fashioned like a lute—
had he been sundered at the groin
51 from the joining where a man goes forked.

The heavy dropsy, which afflicts the body
with its ill-digesting humor
54 so that the face and belly do not match,

---

[282] **the Aretine:** Griffolino (Canto XXIX).

[283] **Myrrha:** Daughter of the king of Cyprus.

[284] **due form:** When Buoso Donati died, the mimic Schicchi conspired with Buoso's nephew and imitated the dead man in his bed; he dictated a new will to a lawyer, giving himself a mare called "the lady of the stud."

forced his lips to draw apart
as a person parched with hectic fever curls
57 one lip to his chin and twists the other up.

'O you who go unpunished here—I know not why—
through this world of misery,'
60 he said, 'behold and then consider

'the suffering of Master Adam.[285]
Alive, I had in plenty all I wanted.
63 And now I crave a single drop of water!

'The streams that, in the Casentino,[286]
run down along green hillsides to the Arno,
66 keeping their channels cool and moist,

'flow before my eyes forever, and not in vain,
because their image makes me thirst still more
69 than does the malady that wastes my features.

'The rigid justice that torments me
employs the landscape where I sinned
72 to make my sighs come faster.

'In those parts lies Romena, where I forged
the coinage stamped with John the Baptist.
75 For that I left my body burned above.

'If I could only see down here the wretched souls
of Guido, Alessandro, or their brother,
78 I'd not give up that sight for Fonte Branda.[287]

'One of them is here with us already,
if the furious shades who move about don't lie.
81 What good is that to me whose limbs are bound?

'If I were only light enough to budge
a single inch each hundred years,
84 I would by now have started on my way

---

[285] **Master Adam:** Served the counts of Romena (see line 77) by counterfeiting coins with the figure of John the Baptist on them, for which he was burned in 1281.

[286] **in the Casentino:** Romena is a town in Casentino, a region on the upper Arno.

[287] **Fonte Branda:** A fountain near Romena.

'to seek him out in this pit's bloated shapes,
even though it runs eleven miles around
87 and spreads not less than half a mile across.

'It is their fault that I have such companions,
for it was they who made me strike the florins
90 that held three carats' worth of dross.'

And I to him: 'Who are these two wretches
who steam as wet hands do in winter
93 and lie so very near you on your right?'

'I found them when I rained into this trough,'
he said, 'and even then they did not move about,
96 nor do I think they will for all eternity.

'One is the woman[288] who lied accusing Joseph,
the other is false Sinon,[289] the lying Greek from Troy.
99 Putrid fever makes them reek with such a stench.'

And one of them, who took offense, perhaps
at being named so vilely, hit him
102 with a fist right on his rigid paunch.

It boomed out like a drum. Then Master Adam,
whose arm seemed just as sturdy,
105 used it, striking Sinon in the face,

saying: 'Although I cannot move about
because my legs are heavy,
108 my arm is loose enough for such a task.'

To which the other answered: 'When they put you
to the fire, your arm was not so nimble,[290]
111 though it was quick enough when you were coining.'

And the dropsied one: 'Well, that is true,
but you were hardly such a truthful witness
114 when you were asked to tell the truth at Troy.'

---

[288] **the woman:** Potiphar's wife (Gen. 39:6–20).

[289] **false Sinon:** Sinon fooled the Trojans by pretending that he was a deserter from the Greek forces; he persuaded them to accept the gift of a wooden horse containing Greek warriors as a compensation for the stolen Palladium, the sacred statue of Athena.

[290] **not so nimble:** Master Adam had been tied up when he was burned.

'If I spoke falsely, you falsified the coin,'
said Sinon, 'and I am here for one offense alone,
117   but you for more than any other devil!'

'You perjurer, keep the horse in mind,'
replied the sinner with the swollen paunch,
120   'and may it pain you that the whole world knows.'

'And may you suffer from the thirst,' the Greek replied,
'that cracks your tongue, and from the fetid humor
123   that turns your belly to a hedge before your eyes!'

Then the forger: 'And so, as usual,
your mouth gapes open from your fever.
126   If I am thirsty, and swollen by this humor,

'you have your hot spells and your aching head.
For you to lick the mirror of Narcissus[291]
129   would not take much by way of invitation.'

I was all intent in listening to them,
when the master said: 'Go right on looking
132   and it is I who'll quarrel with you.'

When I heard him speak to me in anger
I turned and faced him with a shame
135   that circles in my memory even now.

As a man who dreams that he is being harmed
and, even as he dreams, hopes he is dreaming,
138   longing for what is, as though it weren't—

so it was with me, deprived of speech:
I longed to seek his pardon—and all the while
141   I did so without knowing that I did.

'Less shame would cleanse a greater fault than yours,'
my master said, 'and that is why
144   you may set down the load of such remorse.

'Do not forget I'm always at your side
should it fall out again that fortune take you
where people are in wrangles such as this.
148   For the wish to hear such things is base.'

---

[291] **the mirror of Narcissus:** Narcissus fell in love with his own image reflected in the water of a spring.

Canto XXXI

The same tongue that had stung me
so that both my cheeks turned red,
3   had also brought my cure,

just as the spear of Achilles and his father —
so I have heard it told — would be the cause
6   first of a painful, then a welcome, gift.[292]

We turned our backs upon that dismal valley,
first climbing up the bank that circles it,
9   then crossing over, while speaking not a word.

Here it was less than night and less than day —
I could not see too far ahead.
12   But I heard a horn-blast that would have made

the loudest thunderclap seem faint.
To find its source I turned my eyes
15   back to the place from which the din had come.

After the woeful rout when Charlemagne
had lost his holy band of knights,
18   Roland did not sound so terrible a blast.[293]

I had not looked that way for long
when I saw what seemed a range of lofty towers,
21   and I said: 'Master, tell me, what city is this?'

And he to me: 'Because you try to pierce
the darkness from too far away,
24   it follows that you err in your perception.

'When you are nearer, you will understand
how much your eyesight is deceived by distance.
27   Therefore, push yourself a little harder.'

Then with affection he took me by the hand
and said: 'Before we travel farther,
30   and so the fact may seem to you less strange,

---

[292] **the spear . . . gift:** Peleus, the father of Achilles, had a spear that could heal the wound it caused.

[293] **Roland . . . blast:** In *The Song of Roland* (see p. 540), about the Crusade against the Saracens in Spain, Roland blows his horn to tell Charlemagne that his men are about to be defeated.

'you should be told: these are not towers,
but giants and, from the navel down,
33 each stands behind the bank that rings the pit.'

As, when the mist is lifting,
little by little we discern things
36 hidden in the air made thick by fog,

so, when my eyes saw through the heavy dark
and I got nearer to the brink,
39 error left me and fear came in its place.

For, as all around her ring of walls
Monteriggioni[294] is crowned with towers,
42 so at the cliff-edge that surrounds the pit

loomed up like towers half the body bulk
of horrifying giants, those whom Jove
45 still threatens from the heavens when he thunders.[295]

Now I could discern the face of one,
his chest and shoulders, a portion of his paunch,
48 and, hanging at his sides, his arms.

Surely nature did well when she renounced
the craft of making creatures such as these,
51 depriving Mars of such practitioners.

If she does not repent her elephants
and whales, if one reviews the matter closely,
54 she will be found more cautious and more just.

For when the power of thought
is coupled with ill will and naked force
57 there is no refuge from it for mankind.

His face appeared to me as long and broad
as is, in Rome, the pine cone[296] at St. Peter's,
60 his other parts as large in like degree,

---

[294] **Monteriggioni:** A castle built to protect Siena from Florence.

[295] **Jove . . . thunders:** In classical mythology, the giants attacked Olympus, home of the gods, and were overthrown by Jove (Zeus).

[296] **the pine cone:** In Dante's day, a bronze pine cone about eight feet high was in front of St. Peter's Cathedral, now in the Vatican.

so that the bank, which hid him like an apron
from his middle downwards, still showed
63 so much of him above that quite in vain

three Frieslanders[297] might boast of having reached
his hair. For I saw thirty spans[298] of him
66 beneath the place where men make fast their cloaks.

'Raphèl maì amècche zabì almi,'[299]
the savage mouth, for which no sweeter
69 psalms were fit, began to shout.

And, in response, my leader: 'You muddled soul,
stick to your horn! Vent yourself with that
72 when rage or other passion takes you.

'Search at your neck, you creature of confusion,
and you will find the rope that holds the horn
75 aslant your mammoth chest.'

Then he to me: 'He is his own accuser.
This is Nimrod,[300] because of whose vile plan
78 the world no longer speaks a single tongue.

'Let us leave him and not waste our speech,
for every language is to him as his
81 to others, and his is understood by none.'

Then, turning to our left, we continued
with our journey. A bowshot farther on
84 we found the next one, bigger and more savage.

Now who had plied his craft to bind him so
I cannot say, but his right arm
87 was bound behind him, the other one in front,

by chains that from the neck down held him fixed.
They wound five times around his bulk
90 on the part of him that we could see.

---

[297] **Frieslanders:** Inhabitants of present-day Netherlands, famous for their height.

[298] **thirty spans:** About fifteen feet.

[299] *Raphèl . . . almi:* Nonsense sounds.

[300] **Nimrod:** In Hebrew mythology, a giant who designed the Tower of Babel, the cause of multiple languages; as a hunter, Nimrod carries a horn (Gen. 10:8–10, 11:1–9).

'This prideful spirit chose to test his strength
against almighty Jove,' my leader said,
93   'and this is his reward.

'He is Ephialtes.[301] He joined the great assault
when giants put the gods in fear.
96   Those arms he brandished he can move no more.'

And I to him: 'If it is allowed,
I'd like to see with my own eyes
99   Briareus[302] and his immeasurable bulk.'

He replied: 'It is Antaeus[303] you shall see.
He is close by, he speaks, he is not fettered.
102   And he shall set us down into the very depth of sin.

'The one you want to see is farther on,
in fetters also, just like this one here,
105   except that from his looks he'd seem more fierce.'

Never did mighty earthquake shake a tower
with such great speed and force
108   as Ephialtes shook himself at that.

Then more than ever I was afraid of dying:
my fear alone would have sufficed to bring it on,
111   had I not noted how tightly he was bound.

Going farther on, we came upon Antaeus.
Without the added measure of his head,
114   he stood a full five ells above the pit.

'O you, who — in the fateful valley
that made Scipio an heir to glory,
117   when Hannibal with all his men displayed their backs[304] —

---

[301] **Ephialtes:** The giant Ephialtes and his brother tried to reach Olympus by piling Mt. Pelion on top of Mt. Ossa.

[302] **Briareus:** A giant with a hundred arms and fifty heads.

[303] **Antaeus:** A giant who did not participate in the war against the gods; he was known for eating lions. He kept his strength through contact with the earth, so Hercules defeated him in a wrestling match by lifting him off the ground.

[304] **Scipio . . . their backs:** Scipio saved the Roman Republic in 202 B.C.E. when he defeated Hannibal's army in a valley in Tunisia.

'you, who took as prey a thousand lions,
and by whose strength, it seems some do believe,
120 had you been at the war on Heaven with your brethren,

'the sons of earth would have prevailed—
pray set us down, do not disdain to do so,
123 upon Cocytus, shackled by the cold.

'Don't make us go to Tityus or Typhon.[305]
This man can give what everyone here longs for.
126 Therefore bend down and do not curl your lip.

'He still can make you famous in the world,
because he lives, and hopes for years of living,
129 if Grace does not recall him sooner than his time.'

Thus spoke the master. The other was quick
to reach out with his hands—the mighty grip
132 once felt by Hercules—and seized my guide.

Virgil, when he felt himself secured, said:
'Here, let me take hold of you!'
135 Then he made a single bundle of himself and me.

As when one sees the tower called Garisenda[306]
from underneath its leaning side, and then a cloud
138 passes over and it seems to lean the more,

thus did Antaeus seem to my fixed gaze
as I watched him bend—that was indeed a time
141 I wished that I had gone another road.

Even so, he set us gently on the bottom
that swallows Lucifer with Judas.[307]
Nor in stooping did he linger
145 but, like a ship's mast rising, so he rose.

---

[305] **Tityus or Typhon:** Two giants who were cast into Tartarus for offending Jove.

[306] **Garisenda:** A leaning tower in Bologna that sometimes appears to be falling when a cloud passes over it.

[307] **Lucifer with Judas:** Inhabitants of Cocytus.

Canto **XXXII**

If I had verses harsh enough and rasping
as would befit this dismal hole
3 upon which all the other rocks weigh down,

more fully would I press out the juice
of my conception. But, since I lack them,
6 with misgiving do I bring myself to speak.

It is no enterprise undertaken lightly—
describing the center of the universe—
9 nor for a tongue that cries 'mommy' and 'daddy.'

But may those ladies[308] who aided Amphion
to build the walls of Thebes now aid my verse,
12 that the telling be no different from the fact.

O you misgotten rabble, worse than all the rest,
who fill that place so hard to speak of,
15 better had you here been sheep or goats!

When we were down in that ditch's darkness,
below the ridge where the giants set their feet,
18 my gaze still drawn by the wall above us,

I heard a voice say: 'Watch where you walk.
Step so as not to tread upon our heads,
21 the heads of wretched, weary brothers.'

At that I turned to look about.
Under my feet I saw a lake
24 so frozen that it seemed more glass than water.

Never in winter did the Austrian Danube
nor the far-off Don, under its frigid sky,
27 cover their currents with so thick a veil

as I saw there. For had Tambernic fallen on it,
or Pietrapana,[309] the ice would not
30 have creaked, not even at the edge.

---

[308] **those ladies:** Muses who assisted the musician Amphion by charming the mountain rocks used to build the walls of Thebes.

[309] **Tambernic . . . Pietrapana:** Tambernic may be a mountain in the Alps; Mt. Pietrapana is in Tuscany.

And as frogs squat and croak,
their snouts out of the water, in the season
33   when peasant women often dream of gleaning,

so shades, ashen with cold, were grieving, trapped
in ice up to the place the hue of shame appears,
36   their teeth a-clatter like the bills of storks.[310]

Downturned were all their faces, their mouths
gave witness to the cold, while from their eyes
39   came testimony of their woeful hearts.

I gazed around a while; then I looked down
and saw two shades so shackled to each other
42   their two heads' hair made but a single skein.

'Tell me, you with chests pressed close,' I said,
'who are you?' They strained their necks,
45   and, when they had raised their faces,

their eyes, till then moist only to the rims,
dripped tears down to their lips, and icy air
48   then froze those tears — and them to one another.

Clamp never gripped together board to board
so tight, at which such anger overcame them
51   they butted at each other like two rams.

And one of the other shades, who'd lost both ears
to the cold, and kept his face averted, said:
54   'Why do you reflect yourself so long in us?

'If you would like to know who these two are,
the valley out of which Bisenzio flows
57   belonged once to their father, Albert, and to them.[311]

'From a single womb they sprang, and though you seek
throughout Caïna,[312] you will find no shade
60   more fit to be fixed in aspic,

---

[310] **a-clatter . . . storks:** A clacking sound made by storks with their bills.

[311] **belonged . . . to them:** Upon the death of Count Albert degli Alberti, c. 1280, his two sons fought over their inheritance and killed each other.

[312] **Caïna:** The outermost subdivision of Cocytus named for Cain, where traitors to their kin are punished.

'not him whose breast and shadow were pierced
by a single blow from Arthur's hand,[313]
63 nor Focaccia,[314] nor the one whose head so blocks

'my view that I cannot see past him
and whose name was Sassol Mascheroni[315] —
66 if you are Tuscan you know well who he was.

'And, so you coax no further words from me,
know that I was Camiscion de' Pazzi,[316]
69 and I await Carlino[317] for my exculpation.'

After that I saw a thousand faces purple
with the cold, so that I shudder still —
72 and always will — when I come to a frozen ford.

Then, while we made our way toward the center,
where all things that have weight converge,
75 and I was shivering in the eternal chill,

if it was will or fate or chance
I do not know, but, walking among the heads,
78 I struck my foot hard in the face of one.

Wailing, he cried out: 'Why trample me?
Unless you come to add to the revenge
81 for Montaperti,[318] why pick on me?'

And I: 'Master, would you wait for just a moment
so that I may resolve a doubt about this person.
84 And then I'll make what haste you like.'

---

[313] single blow from Arthur's hand: King Arthur lanced his nephew Mordred with such force that daylight was seen through the body.

[314] Focaccia: A noble from Pistoia who murdered his uncle.

[315] Sassol Mascheroni: A Florentine who murdered his nephew.

[316] Camiscion de' Pazzi: An unknown Florentine who murdered a relative.

[317] Carlino: Was to defend a castle belonging to the Florentine Whites in 1302, but he was bribed by the Blacks to surrender the castle. His guilt will absolve Camiscion's.

[318] revenge for Montaperti: At the battle of Montaperti in 1260, Bocca degli Abati, who was supposedly fighting for the Guelphs against the Ghibellines, betrayed them by cutting off the hand of the Guelph standard-bearer, causing confusion among the horse soldiers.

My leader stopped, and I said to the shade,
who was still shouting bitter curses:
87 'And who are you, so to reproach another?'

'No, who are you to go through Antenora,'[319]
he answered, 'buffeting another's cheeks?
90 Were I alive, this still would be an outrage.'

'Well, I'm alive,' I said, 'and if it's fame you seek,
it might turn out to your advantage
93 if I put your name among the others I have noted.'

And he: 'I long for just the opposite.
Take yourself off and trouble me no more—
96 you ill know how to flatter at this depth.'

Then I grabbed him by the scruff of the neck
and said: 'Either you name yourself
99 or I'll leave you without a single hair.'

And he: 'You can peel me bald and I
won't tell you who I am, nor lift my face,
102 even if you jump upon my head a thousand times.'

I now had his hair twisted in my hand
and had already plucked a tuft or two,
105 while he howled on, keeping his eyes cast down,

when another cried: 'What ails you, Bocca?
Isn't it enough, making noise with your jaws,
108 without that howling too? What devil's at you?'

'Now you no longer need to say a word,
vile traitor,' said I, 'to your shame
111 shall I bring back true news of you.'

'Be off,' he answered, 'and tell what tale you will.
But don't be silent, if you escape from here,
114 about the one whose tongue was now so nimble.

---

[319] **Antenora:** The second subdivision of Cocytus, for traitors to their country, named for Antenor, the Trojan who betrayed his city to the Greeks.

'Here he laments the Frenchmen's silver.
"I saw him of Duera,"[320] you can say,
117   "there where they set the sinners out to cool."

'And if someone were to ask you: "Who else was there?"
beside you is the one from Beccherìa[321] —
120   Florence sawed his throat in two.

'I think Gianni de' Soldanier[322] is farther on,
with Ganelon and Tebaldello,[323]
123   who opened up Faenza while it slept.'

We had left him behind when I took note
of two souls so frozen in a single hole
126   the head of one served as the other's hat.

As a famished man will bite into his bread,
the one above had set his teeth into the other
129   just where the brain's stem leaves the spinal cord.

Tydeus gnawed the temples of Melanippus[324]
with bitter hatred just as he was doing
132   to the skull and to the other parts.

'O you, who by so bestial a sign
show loathing for the one whom you devour,
135   tell me why,' I said, 'and let the pact be this:

'if you can give just cause for your complaint,
then I, knowing who you are and what his sin is,
may yet requite you in the world above,
139   if that with which I speak does not go dry.'

---

[320] **him of Duera:** Buoso of Duera, a Ghibelline, who betrayed the ruler of Naples in 1265 by accepting a bribe from French invaders, giving them free passage.

[321] **the one from Beccherìa:** A papal representative in Florence who was executed in 1258 for treason: He plotted with the exiled Ghibellines.

[322] **Gianni de' Soldanier:** A Florentine noble who switched to the Guelphs when the Ghibellines were exiled.

[323] **Ganelon and Tebaldello:** Tebaldello of Faenza, east of Florence, betrayed Ghibelline refugees to Guelphs; Ganelon betrayed Roland in *The Song of Roland*.

[324] **Tydeus gnawed . . . Melanippus:** In the war against Thebes, Tydeus was mortally wounded by Melanippus, whom he killed.

Canto XXXIII

He raised his mouth from his atrocious meal,
that sinner, and wiped it on the hair
3 of the very head he had been ravaging.

Then he began: 'You ask me to revive
the desperate grief that racks my heart
6 even in thought, before I tell it.

'But if my words shall be the seeds that bear
infamous fruit to the traitor I am gnawing,
9 then you will see me speak and weep together.

'I don't know who you are, nor by what means
you have come down here, but when I listen to you speak,
12 it seems to me you are indeed from Florence.

'Take note that I was Count Ugolino,[325]
and he Archbishop Ruggieri. Let me
15 tell you why I'm such a neighbor to him.

'How, as the consummation of his malicious schemes,
after I'd lodged my trust in him, he had me seized
18 and put to death, there is no need to tell.

'But when you learn what you cannot have heard—
that is to say, the cruelty of my death—
21 then you shall know if he has wronged me.

'A little spyhole in the Mew,° which now   prison
on my account is called the Tower of Hunger,
24 where others yet shall be imprisoned,

'had through its opening shown me several moons,
when, in a dreadful dream,
27 the veil was rent, and I foresaw the future.

'This man appeared to be the lord and master,
hunting the wolf and wolfcubs[326] on the mountain
30 that hides Lucca from the sight of Pisans.

---

[325] **Count Ugolino:** The Guelph governor of Pisa, betrayed by Archbishop Ruggieri, leader of the Ghibellines, in 1289.

[326] **the wolf and wolfcubs:** Ugolino and his four sons.

'Along with well-trained hounds, lean and eager,
he had ranged in his front rank
33 Gualandi, Sismondi, and Lanfranchi.[327]

'Father and sons, after a brief pursuit,
seemed to be flagging, and it seemed to me I saw
36 the flesh torn from their flanks by sharp incisors.

'When I awoke before the dawn of day
I heard my children, in that prison with me,
39 weep in their sleep and ask for bread.

'You are cruel indeed, thinking what my heart
foretold, if you remain untouched by grief,
42 and if you weep not, what can make you weep?

'Now they were awake, and the hour drew near
at which our food was brought to us.
45 Each of us was troubled by his dream.

'Down below I heard them nailing shut
the entry to the dreadful tower. I looked
48 my children in the face, without a word.

'I was so turned to stone inside I did not weep.
But they were weeping, and my little Anselm
51 said: "You look so strange, father, what's wrong?"

'Even then I shed no tear, and made no answer
all that day, and all the night that followed
54 until the next day's sun came forth upon the world.

'As soon as some few rays had made their way
into the woeful prison, and I discerned
57 four other faces stamped with my expression,

'the sorrow of it made me gnaw my hands.
And they, imagining I was doing this
60 from hunger, rose at once, saying:

'"Father, we would suffer less
if you would feed on us: you clothed us
63 in this wretched flesh — now strip it off."

---

[327] **Gualandi . . . Lanfranchi:** Pisan families opposed to Ugolino.

'Then, not to increase their grief, I calmed myself.
That day and the next we did not speak a word.
66 O hard earth, why did you not engulf us?

'When we had come as far as the fourth day
my Gaddo threw himself on the ground before me,
69 crying, "O father, why won't you help me?"

'There he died; and even as you see me now
I watched the other three die, one by one,
72 on the fifth day and the sixth. And I began,

'already blind, to grope over their bodies,
and for two days called to them, though they were dead.
75 Then fasting had more power than grief.'

Having said this, with maddened eyes he seized
that wretched skull again between his teeth
78 and clenched them on the bone just like a dog.

Ah Pisa, how you shame the people
of that fair land where 'sì'[328] is heard!
81 Since your neighbors are so slow to punish you,

may the islands of Capraia and Gorgona[329]
move in to block the Arno at its mouth
84 and so drown every living soul in you!

Even if Count Ugolino bore the name
of traitor to your castles, you still
87 should not have put his children to such torture.

Their tender years, you modern Thebes,[330]
declared Uguiccione and Brigata innocent,
90 and the other two this canto names above.

We went on farther, to where the ice-crust
rudely wraps another sort of souls,
93 their faces not turned down but up.

---

[328] **"sì"**: In Italian, *sì* means "yes."

[329] **Capraia and Gorgona:** Two islands in the mouth of the Arno, in view of Pisa.

[330] **modern Thebes:** Ancient Thebes was known for its atrocities.

The very weeping there prevents their weeping,
for the grief that meets a barrier at the eyelids
96 turns inward to augment their anguish,

since their first tears become a crust
that like a crystal visor fills
99 the cups beneath the eyebrows.

Although the cold had made
all feeling leave my face
102 as though it were a callus,

I still could feel a breath of wind.
And I said: 'Master, who sets this in motion?
105 Are not all winds banished here below?'[331]

Thus he to me: 'You will come soon enough
to where your eyes will give an answer,
108 seeing the source that puts out such a blast.'

And one of the wretches in the icy crust
cried out: 'O souls, so hard of heart
111 you are assigned the lowest station,

'lift from my face these rigid veils
so I can vent a while the grief that swells
114 my heart, until my tears freeze up again.'

'If you want my help, let me know your name,'
I answered. 'Then, if I do not relieve you,
117 may I have to travel to the bottom of the ice.'

He spoke: 'I am Fra Alberigo.[332] I am he
who harvested the evil orchard,
120 and here, for figs, I am repaid in dates.'

'Oh,' said I to him, 'are you already dead?'
And he to me: 'I have no knowledge
123 how my body fares in the world above.

---

[331] **winds banished here below:** Since it was believed that the heat of the sun caused winds, Dante wonders how he feels wind in the depths of Hell.

[332] **Fra Alberigo:** A Jovial Friar (Canto XXIII), who in order to get revenge for an injury, invited his brother and son to a banquet. They were assassinated when the Alberigo said, "Bring the fruit." Since a date is worth more than a fig, to get dates for figs meant getting more than one bargained for.

'Such privilege has this Ptolomea,[333]
that many times a soul may fall down here
126 before Atropos[334] has cut it loose.

'So that you may be all the more inclined
to scrape these tear-drops glazed upon my face,
129 know that the moment a soul betrays

'as I did, its body is taken by a devil,
who has it then in his control
132 until the time allotted it has run.

'The soul falls headlong to this cesspool.
Perhaps the body of this shade, who spends
135 the winter with me here, still walks the earth,

'as you must know, if you've come down just now.
He is Branca d'Oria.[335] Quite some years
138 have passed since he was thus confined.'

'I think,' I said to him, 'you're fooling me.
For Branca d'Oria is not yet dead: he eats
141 and drinks and sleeps and puts on clothes.'

'In the ditch above, of the Malebranche,'
he said, 'where the clingy pitch is at the boil,
144 Michel Zanche had not yet arrived

'when this man left a devil in his stead
to own his body, as did his kinsman,
147 his partner in the treacherous act.

'But now extend your hand and open
my eyes for me.' I did not open them.
150 And to be rude to him was courtesy.

O, men of Genoa, race estranged
from every virtue, crammed with every vice,
153 why have you not been driven from the earth?

---

[333] **Ptolomea:** The third division of Cocytus is for treachery to guests, named for Ptolemy, who murdered his father-in-law, Simon Maccabeaus, at a banquet.

[334] **Atropos:** One of the four Fates; Atropos determines the time of death.

[335] **Branca d'Oria:** A Ghibelline from Genoa who murdered his father-in-law, Michel Zanche (Canto XXII), at a banquet around 1290.

With the most heinous spirit of Romagna
I found a son of yours who, for his evil deeds,
even now in Cocytus bathes his soul

157 while yet his body moves among the living.

Canto XXXIV

'The banners of the King of Hell[336] advance
on us. Look straight before you

3 and see if you can make him out,' my master said.

As when a thick mist rises, or when our hemisphere
darkens to night, one may discern

6 a distant windmill by its turning sails,

it seemed to me I saw such a contrivance.
And, to avoid the wind, I drew in close

9 behind my leader: there was nowhere else to hide.

Now—and I shudder as I write it out in verse—
I was where the shades were wholly covered,

12 showing through like bits of straw in glass.

Some are lying down, still others stand erect:
some with heads, some with footsoles up,

15 some bent like bows, their faces to their toes.

When we had gotten far enough along
that my master was pleased to let me see

18 the creature who was once so fair of face,[337]

he took a step aside, then brought me to a halt:
'Look there at Dis! And see the place

21 where you must arm yourself with fortitude.'

Then how faint and frozen I became,
reader, do not ask, for I do not write it,

24 since any words would fail to be enough.

---

[336]**The banners . . . Hell:** In the original, this first phrase is written in Latin: *Vexilla regis prodeunt inferni*, which is a parody of a sixth-century Latin hymn used during Holy Week.

[337]**the creature . . . fair of face:** Lucifer, from the Latin for "light bearer," was the brightest of the angels before the rebellion in Heaven. Dante also calls him Satan, Dis, and Beelzebub.

I did not die, nor did I stay alive.
Imagine, if you have the wit,
27 what I became, deprived of both.

The emperor of the woeful kingdom
rose from the ice below his breast,
30 and I in size am closer to a giant

than giants are when measured to his arms.
Judge, then, what the whole must be
33 that is proportional to such a part.

If he was fair as he is hideous now,
and raised his brow in scorn of his creator,
36 he is fit to be the source of every sorrow.

Oh, what a wonder it appeared to me
when I perceived three faces on his head.
39 The first, in front, was red in color.

Another two he had, each joined with this,
above the midpoint of each shoulder,
42 and all the three united at the crest.

The one on the right was a whitish yellow,
while the left-hand one was tinted like the people
45 living at the sources of the Nile.[338]

Beneath each face two mighty wings emerged,
such as befit so vast a bird:
48 I never saw such massive sails at sea.

They were featherless and fashioned
like a bat's wings. When he flapped them,
51 he sent forth three separate winds,

the sources of the ice upon Cocytus.
Out of six eyes he wept and his three chins
54 dripped tears and drooled blood-red saliva.

---

[338] **the people . . . of the Nile:** Ethiopians. The three faces parody the Trinity, but the symbolism of the three colors is unclear. These colors might represent races, or qualities such as hatred, ignorance, and impotence.

With his teeth, just like a hackle
pounding flax, he champed a sinner
57   in each mouth, tormenting three at once.

For the one in front the gnawing was a trifle
to the clawing, for from time to time
60   his back was left with not a shred of skin.

'That soul up there who bears the greatest pain,'
said the master, 'is Judas Iscariot, who has
63   his head within and outside flails his legs.

'As for the other two, whose heads are dangling down,
Brutus is hanging from the swarthy snout—
66   see how he writhes and utters not a word!—

'and from the other, Cassius,[339] so large of limb.
But night is rising in the sky. It is time
69   for us to leave, for we have seen it all.'

At his request I clasped him round the neck.
When the wings had opened wide enough
72   he chose the proper time and place

and took a handhold on those hairy flanks.
Then from hank to hank he clambered down
75   between the thick pelt and the crusted ice.

When we had come to where the thighbone
swivels, at the broad part of the hips,
78   my leader, with much strain of limb and breath,

turned his head where Satan had his shanks
and clung to the hair like a man climbing upward,
81   so that I thought we were heading back to Hell.

'Hold on tight, for by such rungs as these,'
said my master, panting like a man exhausted,
84   'must we depart from so much evil.'

Then out through an opening in the rock he went,
setting me down upon its edge to rest.
87   And then, with quick and cautious steps, he joined me.

---

[339] **Cassius:** Along with Brutus and others, an assassin of Julius Caesar in 44 B.C.E.; since Dante regarded Caesar
as the founder of an empire, his betrayal rivals Jesus'.

I raised my eyes, thinking I would see
Lucifer still the same as I had left him,
90 but saw him with his legs held upward.

And if I became confused, let those dull minds
who fail to see what point I'd passed[340]
93 comprehend what I felt then.

The master said to me: 'Get to your feet,
for the way is long and the road not easy,
96 and the sun returns to middle tierce.'[341]

It was not the great hall of a palace,
where we were, but a natural dungeon,
99 rough underfoot and wanting light.

'Master, before I tear myself from the abyss,'
I said once I had risen,
102 'say a few words to rid me of my doubt.

'Where is the ice? Why is this one fixed now
upside down? And how in so few hours
105 has the sun moved from evening into morning?'

And he to me: 'You imagine you are still
beyond the center, where I grasped the hair
108 of the guilty worm by whom the world is pierced.

'So you were, as long as I descended,
but, when I turned around, you passed the point
111 to which all weights are drawn from every side.

'You are now beneath the hemisphere[342]
opposite the one that canopies the landmass—
114 and underneath its zenith that Man was slain

'who without sin was born and sinless lived.
You have your feet upon a little sphere
117 that forms Judecca's other face.

---

[340] **what point I'd passed:** Dante passed through the center of the earth, from the Northern to the Southern Hemisphere.

[341] **tierce:** A name given to the religious divisions of the day after sunrise; "middle tierce" is about 7:30 A.M.

[342] **beneath the hemisphere:** They are under the Southern Hemisphere, opposite to the Northern Hemisphere, at the center of which is Jerusalem (Ezek. 5:5).

'Here it is morning when it is evening there,
and the one whose hair provided us a ladder
120 is fixed exactly as he was before.

'It was on this side that he fell from Heaven.
And the dry land that used to stand, above,
123 in fear of him immersed itself in water

'and fled into our hemisphere. And perhaps
to escape from him the land we'll find above
126 created this lacuna[343] when it rushed back up.'

As far as one can get from Beelzebub,
in the remotest corner of this cavern,
129 there is a place one cannot find by sight,

but by the sound of a narrow stream that trickles
through a channel it has cut into the rock
132 in its meanderings, making a gentle slope.

Into that hidden passage my guide and I
entered, to find again the world of light,
135 and, without thinking of a moment's rest,

we climbed up, he first and I behind him,
far enough to see, through a round opening,
a few of those fair things the heavens bear.
139 Then we came forth, to see again the stars.[344]

---

[343] **created this lacuna:** To escape from Satan falling from Heaven, land from the Southern Hemisphere went to the Northern Hemisphere, and the ocean filled the depression. The interior of the earth, also reeling from Satan, moved upwards, forming Mt. Purgatory and creating a "lacuna."

[344] **the stars:** *Purgatorio* and *Paradiso* also end with stars, emblems of God's universe for the believer.

⚙ GIOVANNI BOCCACCIO
1313–1375

Like Chaucer's *Canterbury Tales,* **Boccaccio**'s *Decameron* (1353) is a collection of stories enclosed within a frame narrative, but unlike Chaucer's religious pilgrims, Boccaccio's storytellers are sophisticated young adults who have retreated to the countryside to escape the plague, which is sweeping through Florence. Also unlike Chaucer's tales, written mainly in verse, Boccaccio's is a prose work, the most important work of prose fiction of its time and the beginning of vernacular fiction in Europe. Boccaccio, often called "the father of the short story," in *The Decameron,* as Erich Auerbach points out, brought "Italian art prose, the first literary prose of post-classical Europe, into existence at a single stroke." In the vernacular Italian of his day, Boccaccio told earthy and realistic stories about love in all its aspects.

A Medieval or a Renaissance Man? Boccaccio's realism, use of prose, and secular frame narrative have led some commentators to describe him as a Renaissance writer who broke away from the spiritual preoccupations of the Middle Ages. But such a view may exaggerate the spirituality of the medieval mind. Boccaccio lived during an age of transition, and he is in many ways much like his friend and contemporary, Petrarch (1304–1374), among the defining figures of the Renaissance. Both men and their work are reminders that the divisions between historical periods are arbitrary and that life has a continuity that historical distinctions sometimes misrepresent.

Boccaccio was born in Paris in 1313, the illegitimate son of a Florentine businessman and a French woman. Although he spent much of his childhood in Florence, he went to Naples at the urging of his father when he was about fourteen to study commerce. Business, however, bored him and he turned for a time to canon law before becoming what he really wanted to be—a poet. Later in life he remarked, "If only my father had been indulgent to my wishes, I might have been one of the world's famous poets." Instead he became one of the world's great prose writers.

He began writing poetry in Naples, where he also may have met Maria d'Aquino, the woman he calls Fiametta ("little flame") in his writing and who, like Dante's Beatrice and Petrarch's Laura, inspired his adoration and his art. Although their affair was short-lived or perhaps even imaginary, Maria was the source of Boccaccio's experimentation in a number of genres: romance, pastoral, allegory, and the novel. She appears most significantly in *Fiametta* (*Elegia de Madonna Fiametta,* c. 1344), a psychological novel about an adulterous affair between a Neapolitan noblewoman and a Florentine businessman.

After Boccaccio returned to Florence in 1340, his work took a more realistic turn, culminating in his masterwork, *The Decameron,* which he completed in 1353. In the 1350s he also met Petrarch, with whom he became a close friend. Under Petrarch's influence, Boccaccio turned from

boh-KAH-choh

fee-ah-MET-ah

The First Day, 1467

An illuminated manuscript of Boccaccio's Decameron *shows the seven ladies welcoming the three men on day one of the tales. (Bodleian Library, University of Oxford)*

the vernacular prose fiction of *The Decameron* to more scholarly works written in Latin. In his later years he compiled classical myths, composed short biographies of famous men and women, and wrote a biography of Dante and a commentary on *The Divine Comedy*. In 1373 he was appointed to the Dante Chair in Florence. He died in 1375.

The Decameron.   The title of Boccaccio's masterwork literally translates as "the work of ten days." In it, seven women and three men who have retreated from Florence to the country to escape the ravages of a plague in the city tell stories. Altogether, they tell one hundred tales during their retreat, all generally concerned with the theme of love. On each day one of the ten is the "queen" or "king" for that day, and she or he may set a more specific thematic agenda. On the Third Day, for example, **Neifile**, a virginal young woman, decides that the tales will be "of those who by their wits obtained something they greatly desired or regained something they had lost." On the Fourth Day, Filostrato orders the others to tell tales "of those whose love had an unhappy ending."

nay-ee-FEE-lay

The frame narrative in *The Decameron,* though less developed than in Chaucer's Canterbury pilgrimage, does more than simply establish an excuse for the tale-telling. The plague from which the young people are fleeing is described in vivid detail in the opening to the first day, and the account is historical. Boccaccio lived through the BLACK DEATH that ravaged Florence in the spring of 1348. The frame thus establishes a measure of truth against which to judge the fiction of the storytelling. It reminds the reader of the transience of life and raises questions about the spiritual dimension of the human condition. The prologue implicitly asks whether the storytellers represent one or another of the reactions to the plague that the narrator describes and even the most frivolous tales are told against this contrasting historical backdrop. Insofar as the stories can make one forget their menacing context, they become celebrations of the power of imagination over mortal limitation.

Boccaccio took most of his stories from others, reworking traditional tales, jokes, historical anecdotes, and earlier literature. The power of his work is not in the originality of the stories, but in the telling of them. His use of realistic detail, dialogue, and quick strokes of characterization give the individual tales a life of their own. If Chaucer is memorable for his frame narrative and for his diverse cast of storytellers and their interactions, Boccaccio is memorable for the way he tells a story. Indeed, his name has become a by-word for a prolific and inventive storyteller; for example, Tirso de Molina called Cervantes "the Castilian Boccaccio."

Alibech and Rustico.

Alibech and Rustico.   Boccaccio is also famous — perhaps notorious — as a teller of bawdy tales. In this regard, he is clearly a man of his time: For Boccaccio, Chaucer, and their contemporaries, the division between body and spirit and between sexual ecstasy and spiritual rapture was not as marked as it later became. But Boccaccio's comments in the epilogue to *The Decameron* suggest that some of his stories offended even medieval readers. The tale of Alibech and Rustico (the Third Day, Tenth Tale) is a wonderful example of the medieval *fabliau*[1] and of Boccaccio's ability to turn a bawdy joke with blasphemous possibilities into a study of character and a celebration of human vitality. The story begins as a racy parody of the narratives known as saints' lives, such as that of Saint Anthony,

> The rhetorical tradition . . . in Boccaccio's hands suddenly becomes a miraculous tool which brings Italian art prose, the first literary prose of post-classical Europe, into existence at a single stroke.
>
> – ERICH AUERBACH, *Mimesis*, Scholar, 1953

---

[1] *fabliau:* Although the *fabliau* originated in France as comic or satiric tales in verse, by the time of Boccaccio and Chaucer the term also described bawdy and ribald prose tales like "The Miller's Tale" in Chaucer's *Canterbury Tales* or Boccaccio's story of Rustico and Alibech.

which tells of his going into the wilderness and overcoming temptations of the flesh. Boccaccio does not simply turn such stories on their head: Even though Rustico hypocritically breaks his vows by "putting the devil in hell," he does not do so without struggle; and Alibech's innocence blesses her unusual "service to God" and her later marriage.

gees-MAWN-duh;
gwees-KAR-doh

The third tale excerpted here, the tragic story of Prince Tancred, who "murders" his daughter, reveals a very different dimension of Boccaccio's storytelling genius. An unusual love triangle centers the story, linking the two lovers — the young widow **Ghismonda** and the page **Guiscardo** — and Ghismonda's father, the jealous ruler Tancred. With brief strokes, Boccaccio brings each of the characters to life, especially the independent Ghismonda, whose eloquent defense of her love challenges Tancred's patriarchal assumptions. In his presentation of the doomed relationships among these characters, Boccaccio unsettles conventional notions about the role of fathers, about independent and assertive women, and about love across class lines.

■ **CONNECTIONS**

Sophocles, *Antigone* (Book 1); Aristotle, *Poetics*, (Book 1). Both Sophocles' *Antigone* and Boccaccio's tale of Tancred and Ghismonda are about young women who disobey the commandments of an older man. Are Creon and Tancred justified in the demands they make on Antigone and Ghismonda, respectively? Who are the tragic heroes in these works? Does Sophocles' play and Boccaccio's tale fit Aristotle's model tragedy?

Aristophanes, *Lysistrata* (Book 1). Boccaccio's story of Alibech and Rustico participates in a long tradition that began with comic satyr plays in ancient Greece — dramas that employed sexual ribaldry for comic and satiric effect. Who is the comic hero of Boccaccio's story? What does the tale satirize?

***In the Tradition:* Marguerite de Navarre, *The Heptameron* (Book 3).** Boccaccio's romance of Ghismonda and Guiscardo presents an interesting contrast to the tale of Florida and Amadour in de Navarre's *Heptameron*. De Navarre's tale follows the conventions of courtly love and celebrates platonic love while Boccaccio's story challenges those very ideas. How in particular do these two stories treat the courtly love tradition?

***The Thousand and One Nights*, p. 43.** Like *The Thousand and One Nights*, *The Decameron* frames its tales within a larger narrative. Consider the frame narratives in these two collections. Is it important that in both works the storytellers face the threat of death? How do the particular stories in each collection relate to the frame narrative?

www For links to
more information
about Boccaccio,
a quiz on *The
Decameron,* and a
discussion of the
twenty-first-century
relevance of
Boccaccio, see *World
Literature Online* at
bedfordstmartins
.com/worldlit.

■ **FURTHER RESEARCH**

Almansi, Guido. *The Writer as Liar: Narrative Technique in the Decameron.* 1975.
Auerbach, Erich. "Frate Alberto." In *Mimesis: The Representation of Reality in Western
    Literature.* Trans. Willard Trask. 1953.
Bergin, Thomas. *Boccaccio.* 1982.
Branca, Vittore. *Boccaccio: The Man and His Works.* 1976.
Mazzotta, Giuseppe. *The World at Play in Boccaccio's "Decameron."* 1986.
Rodax, Yvonne. *The Real and the Ideal in the Novella of Italy, France, and England.* Ch. 2.
    1968.
Serafini-Sauli, Judith Powers. *Giovanni Boccaccio.* 1982.

■ **PRONUNCIATION**

Boccaccio: boh-KAH-choh, boh-KAH-chee-oh
Dioneo: dee-oh-NAY-oh
Fiametta: fee-ah-MET-uh
Ghismonda: gees-MAWN-duh
Guiscardo: gwees-KAR-doh
Neifile: nay-ee-FEE-lay
Pampinea: pahm-pee-NAY-uh

⤫ The Decameron

Translated by Richard Aldington

FIRST DAY

[Here begins the first day of *The Decameron,* wherein, after the author has showed the reasons why certain persons gathered to tell tales, they treat of any subject pleasing to them, under the rule of Pampinea.]

Most gracious ladies, knowing that you are all by nature pitiful, I know that in your judgment this work will seem to have a painful and sad origin. For it brings to mind the unhappy recollection of that late dreadful plague, so pernicious to all who saw or heard of it. But I would not have this frighten you from reading further, as though you were to pass through nothing but sighs and tears in your reading. This dreary opening will be like climbing a steep mountainside to a most beautiful and

---

The Decameron. Boccaccio's masterpiece was written between 1348 and 1350, in the two years after the plague had ravaged Florence, killing half its 100,000 citizens, including Maria d'Aquino, Boccaccio's Fiametta. The frame narrative tells of the ravages of the disease and a group of ten young people—seven women and three men—who go off to the country to escape the despair and contagion in the city. The realism in Boccaccio's description of the plague indicates that he wrote from direct observation and contrasts with the fictitious tales that the young people tell for diversion.

In their country retreat, these young women and men spend ten days in storytelling, with all the participants telling a tale each day, the theme of which is set by that day's leader. The "king" or "queen" for the day chooses a particular topic within the broad theme of love, the subject of all one hundred stories. The third day, which is devoted to tales "of those who by their wits obtained something they greatly desired or regained something they had lost," includes the story of Rustico and Alibech. The fourth day's tales are "of those whose love had an unhappy ending," including the tale of Tancred and his daughter, Ghismonda. Besides its thematic position, each tale reflects the character of its particular teller.

The story of Rustico and Alibech, a famous Boccaccio tale, is told by Dioneo, who is described in the General Prologue as "a most amusing young man and full of witticisms." He seems on a mission to shock the seven young women who make up the bulk of his audience. His tale on Day One, similar to that of Rustico and Alibech, brings "chaste blushes" to the listening ladies who react with

delightful valley, which appears the more pleasant in proportion to the difficulty of the ascent. The end of happiness is pain, and in like manner misery ends in unexpected happiness.

This brief fatigue (I say brief, because it occupies only a few words) is quickly followed by pleasantness and delight, as I promised you above; which, if I had not promised, you would not expect perhaps from this opening. Indeed, if I could have taken you by any other way than this, which I know to be rough, I would gladly have done so; but since I cannot otherwise tell you how the tales you are about to read came to be told, I am forced by necessity to write in this manner.

In the year 1348 after the fruitful incarnation of the Son of God, that most beautiful of Italian cities, noble Florence, was attacked by deadly plague. It started in the East either through the influence of the heavenly bodies or because God's just anger with our wicked deeds sent it as a punishment to mortal men; and in a few years killed an innumerable quantity of people. Ceaselessly passing from place to place, it extended its miserable length over the West. Against this plague all human wisdom and foresight were vain. Orders had been given to cleanse the city of filth, the entry of any sick person was forbidden, much advice was given for keeping healthy; at the same time humble supplications were made to God by pious persons in processions and otherwise. And yet, in the beginning of the spring of the year mentioned, its horrible results began to appear, and in a miraculous manner. The symptoms were not the same as in the East, where a gush of blood from the nose was the plain sign of inevitable death; but it began both in men and women with certain swellings in the groin or under the armpit. They grew to the size of a small apple or an egg, more or less, and were vulgarly called tumours. In a short space of time these tumours spread from the two parts named all over the body. Soon after this the symptoms changed and black or purple spots appeared on the arms or thighs or any other part of the body, sometimes a few large ones, sometimes many little ones. These spots were a certain sign of death, just as the original tumour had been and still remained.

"modest shame." By the third day the young women know what to expect from Dioneo and they "respond with laughter hundreds of times." Although the story of Rustico and Alibech could be understood as an attack on the hypocrisy of the clergy and the naivete of Alibech, or on the absurdity of attempting to suppress nature, above all it is—as the young women seem to recognize—a very amusing story adeptly told.

The verbal wit and double entendres in Rustico and Alibech's story serve comic purposes; in the story of Tancred and Ghismonda, Boccaccio adds a symbolic dimension that turns the fatal melodrama into a commentary on the relations of parents and children, class distinctions, and suppression of women. Fiametta, who earlier told a tale to show that "in men it is always wise to love women of better families than themselves; and in women it is prudent to know how to preserve themselves from the love of men of higher station," here again tells a tale about social inequality in love.

In the conclusion to *The Decameron,* Boccaccio defends his stories against charges that they are objectionable. Since his expected audience was to consist primarily of women of leisure, he makes it a point to argue that his tales are not inappropriate for "virtuous ladies."

No doctor's advice, no medicine could overcome or alleviate this disease. An enormous number of ignorant men and women set up as doctors in addition to those who were trained. Either the disease was such that no treatment was possible or the doctors were so ignorant that they did not know what caused it, and consequently could not administer the proper remedy. In any case very few recovered; most people died within about three days of the appearance of the tumours described above, most of them without any fever or other symptoms.

The violence of this disease was such that the sick communicated it to the healthy who came near them, just as a fire catches anything dry or oily near it. And it even went further. To speak to or go near the sick brought infection and a common death to the living; and moreover, to touch the clothes or anything else the sick had touched or worn gave the disease to the person touching.

What I am about to tell now is a marvelous thing to hear; and if I and others had not seen it with our own eyes I would not dare to write it, however much I was willing to believe and whatever the good faith of the person from whom I heard it. So violent was the malignancy of this plague that it was communicated, not only from one man to another, but from the garments of a sick or dead man to animals of another species, which caught the disease in that way and very quickly died of it. One day among other occasions I saw with my own eyes (as I said just now) the rags left lying in the street of a poor man who had died of the plague; two pigs came along and, as their habit is, turned the clothes over with their snouts and then munched at them, with the result that they both fell dead almost at once on the rags, as if they had been poisoned.

From these and similar or greater occurrences, such fear and fanciful notions took possession of the living that almost all of them adopted the same cruel policy, which was entirely to avoid the sick and everything belonging to them. By so doing, each one thought he would secure his own safety.

Some thought that moderate living and the avoidance of all superfluity would preserve them from the epidemic. They formed small communities, living entirely separate from everybody else. They shut themselves up in houses where there were no sick, eating the finest food and drinking the best wine very temperately, avoiding all excess, allowing no news or discussion of death and sickness, and passing the time in music and suchlike pleasures. Others thought just the opposite. They thought the sure cure for the plague was to drink and be merry, to go about singing and amusing themselves, satisfying every appetite they could, laughing and jesting at what happened. They put their words into practice, spent day and night going from tavern to tavern, drinking immoderately, or went into other people's houses, doing only those things which pleased them. This they could easily do because everyone felt doomed and had abandoned his property, so that most houses became common property and any stranger who went in made use of them as if he had owned them. And with all this bestial behaviour, they avoided the sick as much as possible.

In this suffering and misery of our city, the authority of human and divine laws almost disappeared, for, like other men, the ministers and the executors of the laws were all dead or sick or shut up with their families, so that no duties were carried out. Every man was therefore able to do as he pleased.

Many others adopted a course of life midway between the two just described. They did not restrict their victuals so much as the former, nor allow themselves to be drunken and dissolute like the latter, but satisfied their appetites moderately. They did not shut themselves up, but went about, carrying flowers or scented herbs or perfumes in their hands, in the belief that it was an excellent thing to comfort the brain with such odours; for the whole air was infected with the smell of dead bodies, of sick persons and medicines.

Others again held a still more cruel opinion, which they thought would keep them safe. They said that the only medicine against the plague-stricken was to go right away from them. Men and women, convinced of this and caring about nothing but themselves, abandoned their own city, their own houses, their dwellings, their relatives, their property, and went abroad or at least to the country round Florence, as if God's wrath in punishing men's wickedness with this plague would not follow them but strike only those who remained within the walls of the city, or as if they thought nobody in the city would remain alive and that its last hour had come.

Not everyone who adopted any of these various opinions died, nor did all escape. Some when they were still healthy had set the example of avoiding the sick, and, falling ill themselves, died untended.

One citizen avoided another, hardly any neighbour troubled about others, relatives never or hardly ever visited each other. Moreover, such terror was struck into the hearts of men and women by this calamity, that brother abandoned brother, and the uncle his nephew, and the sister her brother, and very often the wife her husband. What is even worse and nearly incredible is that fathers and mothers refused to see and tend their children, as if they had not been theirs.

Thus, a multitude of sick men and women were left without any care except from the charity of friends (but these were few), or the greed of servants, though not many of these could be had even for high wages. Moreover, most of them were coarse-minded men and women, who did little more than bring the sick what they asked for or watch over them when they were dying. And very often these servants lost their lives and their earnings. Since the sick were thus abandoned by neighbours, relatives and friends, while servants were scarce, a habit sprang up which had never been heard of before. Beautiful and noble women, when they fell sick, did not scruple to take a young or old manservant, whoever he might be, and with no sort of shame, expose every part of their bodies to these men as if they had been women, for they were compelled by the necessity of their sickness to do so. This, perhaps, was a cause of looser morals in those women who survived.

In this way many people died who might have been saved if they had been looked after. Owing to the lack of attendants for the sick and the violence of the plague, such a multitude of people in the city died day and night that it was stupefying to hear of, let alone to see. From sheer necessity, then, several ancient customs were quite altered among the survivors.

The custom had been (as we still see it today), that women relatives and neighbours should gather at the house of the deceased, and there lament with the family. At the same time the men would gather at the door with the male neighbours and other citizens. Then came the clergy, few or many according to the dead person's rank; the coffin was placed on the shoulders of his friends and carried with funeral pomp of lighted candles and dirges to the church which the deceased had chosen before dying. But as the fury of the plague increased, this custom wholly or nearly disappeared, and new customs arose. Thus, people died, not only without having a number of women near them, but without a single witness. Very few indeed were honoured with the piteous laments and bitter tears of their relatives, who, on the contrary, spent their time in mirth, feasting and jesting. Even the women abandoned womanly pity and adopted this custom for their own safety. Few were they whose bodies were accompanied to church by more than ten or a dozen neighbours. Nor were these grave and honourable citizens but grave-diggers from the lowest of the people who got themselves called sextons, and performed the task for money. They took up the bier and hurried it off, not to the church chosen by the deceased but to the church nearest, preceded by four or six of the clergy with few candles and often none at all. With the aid of the grave-diggers, the clergy huddled the bodies away in any grave they could find, without giving themselves the trouble of a long or solemn burial service.

The plight of the lower and most of the middle classes was even more pitiful to behold. Most of them remained in their houses, either through poverty or in hopes of safety, and fell sick by thousands. Since they received no care and attention, almost all of them died. Many ended their lives in the streets both at night and during the day; and many others who died in their houses were only known to be dead because the neighbours smelled their decaying bodies. Dead bodies filled every corner. Most of them were treated in the same manner by the survivors, who were more concerned to get rid of their rotting bodies than moved by charity towards the dead. With the aid of porters, if they could get them, they carried the bodies out of the houses and laid them at the doors, where every morning quantities of the dead might be seen. They then were laid on biers, or, as these were often lacking, on tables.

Often a single bier carried two or three bodies, and it happened frequently that a husband and wife, two or three brothers, or father and son were taken off on the same bier. It frequently happened that two priests, each carrying a cross, would go out followed by three or four biers carried by porters; and where the priests thought there was one person to bury, there would be six or eight, and often, even more. Nor were these dead honoured by tears and lighted candles and mourners, for things had reached such a pass that people cared no more for dead men than we care for dead goats. Thus it plainly appeared that what the wise had not learned to endure with patience through the few calamities of ordinary life, became a matter of indifference even to the most ignorant people through the greatness of this misfortune.

Such was the multitude of corpses brought to the churches every day and almost every hour that there was not enough consecrated ground to give them burial, especially since they wanted to bury each person in the family grave, according to the old custom. Although the cemeteries were full they were forced to dig huge trenches, where they buried the bodies by hundreds. Here they stowed them away like bales in the hold of a ship and covered them with a little earth, until the whole trench was full.

Not to pry any further into all the details of the miseries which afflicted our city, I shall add that the surrounding country was spared nothing of what befell Florence.

The villages on a smaller scale were like the city; in the fields and isolated farms the poor wretched peasants and their families were without doctors and any assistance, and perished in the highways, in their fields and houses, night and day, more like beasts than men. Just as the townsmen became dissolute and indifferent to their work and property, so the peasants, when they saw that death was upon them, entirely neglected the future fruits of their past labours both from the earth and from cattle, and thought only of enjoying what they had. Thus it happened that cows, asses, sheep, goats, pigs, fowls and even dogs, those faithful companions of man, left the farms and wandered at their will through the fields, where the wheat crops stood abandoned, unreaped and ungarnered. Many of these animals seemed endowed with reason, for, after they had pastured all day, they returned to the farms for the night of their own free will, without being driven.

Returning from the country to the city, it may be said that such was the cruelty of Heaven, and perhaps in part of men, that between March and July more than one hundred thousand persons died within the walls of Florence, what between the violence of the plague and the abandonment in which the sick were left by the cowardice of the healthy. And before the plague it was not thought that the whole city held so many people.

Oh, what great palaces, how many fair houses and noble dwellings, once filled with attendants and nobles and ladies, were emptied to the meanest servant! How many famous names and vast possessions and renowned estates were left without an heir! How many gallant men, and fair ladies and handsome youths, whom Galen, Hippocrates and Æsculapius[1] themselves would have said were in perfect health, at noon dined with their relatives and friends, and at night supped with their ancestors in the next world!

But it fills me with sorrow to go over so many miseries. Therefore, since I want to pass over all I can leave out, I shall go on to say that when our city was in this condition and almost emptied of inhabitants, one Tuesday morning the venerable church of Santa Maria Novella had scarcely any congregation for divine service except (as I have heard from a person worthy of belief) seven young women in the mourning garments suitable to the times, who were all related by ties of blood, friendship or neighbourship. None of them was older than twenty-eight or younger than eighteen; all were educated and of noble blood, fair to look upon, well-mannered and of graceful modesty.

I should tell you their real names if I had not a good reason for not doing so, which is that I would not have any of them blush in the future for the things they say and hearken to in the following pages. The laws are now strict again, whereas then, for the reasons already shown, they were very lax, not only for persons of their age but for those much older. Nor would I give an opportunity to the envious (always ready to sneer at every praiseworthy life) to attack the virtue of these modest ladies with vulgar speech. But so that you may understand without confusion what each one says, I intend to give them names wholly or partly suitable to the qualities of each.

---

[1] **Galen . . . Æsculapius:** Galen (130?–201? c.e.) was a Greek physician and anatomist, Hippocrates (460?–377? b.c.e.) a Greek physician, and Aesculapius a Roman god of medicine and healing.

The first and eldest I shall call Pampinea, the second Fiametta, the third Filomena, the fourth Emilia, the fifth Lauretta, the sixth Neifile, and the last Elisa (or "the virgin") for a very good reason. They met, not by arrangement, but by chance, in the same part of the church, and sat down in a circle. After many sighs they ceased to pray and began to talk about the state of affairs and other things. After a short space of silence, Pampinea said:

"Dear ladies, you must often have heard, as I have, that to make a sensible use of one's reason harms nobody. It is natural for everybody to aid, preserve and defend his life as far as possible. And this is so far admitted that to save their own lives men often kill others who have done no harm. If this is permitted by the laws which are concerned with the general good, it must certainly be lawful for us to take any reasonable means for the preservation of our lives. When I think of what we have been doing this morning and still more on former days, when I remember what we have been saying, I perceive and you must perceive that each of us goes in fear of her life. I do not wonder at this, but, since each of us has a woman's judgment, I do wonder that we do not seek some remedy against what we dread.

"In my opinion we remain here for no other purpose than to witness how many bodies are buried, or listen whether the friars here (themselves reduced almost to nothing) sing their offices at the canonical hours, or to display by our clothes the quantity and quality of our miseries to anyone who comes here. If we leave this church we see the bodies of the dead and the sick being carried about. Or we see those who had been exiled from the city by the authority of the laws for their crimes, deriding this authority because they know the guardians of the law are sick or dead, and running loose about the place. Or we see the dregs of the city battening on our blood and calling themselves sextons, riding about on horseback in every direction and insulting our calamities with vile songs. On every side we hear nothing but "So-and-so is dead" or "So-and-so is dying." And if there were anyone left to weep we should hear nothing but piteous lamentations. I do not know if it is the same in your homes as in mine. But if I go home there is nobody left there but one of my maids, which fills me with such horror that the hair stands upon my head. Wherever I go or sit at home I seem to see the ghosts of the departed, not with the faces as I knew them but with dreadful looks which terrify me.

"I am ill at ease here and outside of here and at home; the more so since nobody who has the strength and ability to go away (as we have) now remains here, except ourselves. The few that remain (if there are any), according to what I see and hear, do anything which gives them pleasure or pleases their appetites, both by day and night, whether they are alone or in company, making no distinction between right and wrong. Not only laymen, but those cloistered in convents have broken their oaths and given themselves up to the delights of the flesh, and thus in trying to escape the plague by doing what they please, they have become lascivious and dissolute.

"If this is so (and we may plainly see it is) what are we doing here? What are we waiting for? What are we dreaming about? Are we less eager and active than other citizens in saving our lives? Are they less dear to us than to others? Or do we think that our lives are bound to our bodies with stronger chains than other people's, and so believe that we need fear nothing which might harm us? We were and are deceived. How stupid we should be to believe such a thing! We may see the plainest proofs from the number of young men and women who have died of this cruel plague.

"I do not know if you think as I do, but in my opinion if we, through carelessness, do not want to fall into this calamity when we can escape it, I think we should do well to leave this town, just as many others have done and are doing. Let us avoid the wicked examples of others like death itself, and go and live virtuously in our country houses, of which each of us possesses several. There let us take what happiness and pleasure we can, without ever breaking the rules of reason in any manner.

"There we shall hear the birds sing, we shall see the green hills and valleys, the wheat-fields rolling like a sea, and all kinds of trees. We shall see the open Heavens which, although now angered against man, do not withhold from us their eternal beauties that are so much fairer to look upon than the empty walls of our city. The air will be fresher there, we shall find a greater plenty of those things necessary to life at this time, and fewer troubles. Although the peasants are dying like the townsmen, still, since the houses and inhabitants are fewer, we shall see less of them and feel less misery. On the other hand I believe we are not abandoning anybody here. Indeed we can truthfully say that we are abandoned, since our relatives have either died or fled from death and have left us alone in this calamity as if we were nothing to them.

"If we do what I suggest, no blame can fall upon us; if we fail to do it, the result may be pain, trouble and perhaps death. Therefore I think that we should do well to take our servants and all things necessary, and go from one house to another, enjoying whatever merriment and pleasure these times allow. Let us live in this way (unless death comes upon us) until we see what end Heaven decrees to this plague. And remember that going away virtuously will not harm us so much as staying here in wickedness will harm others."

The other ladies listened to what Pampinea said, praised her advice, and in their eagerness to follow it began to discuss details, as if they were going to leave at once. But Filomena, who was a most prudent young woman, said:

"Ladies, although what Pampinea says is excellent advice, we must not rush off at once, as you seem to wish. Remember we are all women; and any girl can tell you how women behave together and conduct themselves without the direction of some man. We are fickle, wayward, suspicious, faint-hearted and cowardly. So if we have no guide but ourselves I greatly suspect that this company will very soon break up, without much honour to ourselves. Let us settle this matter before we start."

Elisa then broke in:

"Indeed men are a woman's head and we can rarely succeed in anything without their help; but how can we find any men? Each of us knows that most of her menfolk are dead, while the others are away, we know not where, flying with their companions from the end we wish to escape. To ask strangers would be unbecoming; for, if we mean to go away to save our lives we must take care that scandal and annoyance do not follow us where we are seeking rest and amusement."

While the ladies were thus arguing, three young men came into the church, the youngest of whom was not less than twenty-five. They were lovers whose love could

not be quenched or even cooled by the horror of the times, the loss
friends, or even fear for themselves. The first was named Pam
Filostrato, the third Dioneo. They were pleasant, well-mannered
public calamity they sought the consolation of looking upon the
These ladies happened to be among our seven, while some of the ot.
to one or other of the three men. They no sooner came into sight than the lau.
them; whereupon Pampinea said with a smile:

"See how Fortune favours our plan at once by sending us these valiant and discreet young men, who will gladly act as our guides and servants if we do not refuse to
accept them for such duties."

Neifile then became crimson, for she was one of the ladies beloved by one of the
young men, and said:

"For God's sake, Pampinea, be careful what you are saying. I know quite well
that nothing but good can be said of any of them and I am sure they could achieve
greater things than this. I also think that their company would be fitting and pleasant, not only to us, but to ladies far more beautiful and charming than we are. But it
is known to everyone that they are in love with some of us women here; and so, if we
take them with us, I am afraid that blame and infamy will fall upon us, through no
fault of ours or theirs."

Then said Filomena:

"What does that matter? If I live virtuously, my conscience never pricks me,
whatever people may say. God and the truth will fight for me. If these men would
come with us, then indeed, as Pampinea said, fortune would be favourable to our
plan of going away."

The others not only refrained from censuring what she said, but agreed by common consent that the men should be spoken to, told their plan, and asked if they
would accompany the ladies on their expedition. Without more ado, Pampinea, who
was related to one of them, arose and went towards them where they stood looking
at the ladies, saluted them cheerfully, told them the plan, and begged them in the
name of all the ladies to accompany them out of pure and fraternal affection.

At first the young men thought this was a jest. But when they saw the lady was
speaking seriously, they said they were willing to go. And in order to start without
delay they at once gave the orders necessary for departure. Everything necessary was
made ready, and word was sent on ahead to the place they were going. At dawn next
morning, which was Wednesday, the ladies with some of their servants, and the
young men with a man servant each, left the city and set out. They had not gone
more than two miles when they came to the first place where they were to stay.

This estate was on slightly raised ground, at some distance from any main road,
with many trees and plants, fair to look upon. At the top of the rise was a country
mansion with a large inner courtyard. It had open colonnades, galleries and rooms,
all beautiful in themselves and ornamented with gay paintings. Round about were
lawns and marvelous gardens and wells of cool water. There were cellars of fine wines,
more suitable to wine connoisseurs than to sober and virtuous ladies. The whole
house had been cleaned, the beds were prepared in the rooms, and every corner was

strewn with the flowers of the season and fresh rushes. All of which the company beheld with no little pleasure.

They all sat down to discuss plans, and Dioneo, who was a most amusing young man and full of witticisms, remarked:

"Ladies, your good sense, rather than our foresight, has brought us here. I do not know what you are thinking of doing with your troubles here, but I dropped mine inside the gates of the city when I left it with you a little time ago. Therefore, either you must make up your minds to laugh and sing and amuse yourselves with me (that is, to the extent your dignity allows), or you must let me go back to my troubles and stay in the afflicted city."

Pampinea, who had driven away her woes in the same way, cheerfully replied:

"Dioneo, you speak well, let us amuse ourselves, for that was the reason why we fled from our sorrows. But when things are not organised they cannot long continue. And, since I began the discussion which brought this fair company together and since I wish our happiness to continue, I think it necessary that one of us should be made chief, whom the others will honour and obey, and whose duty shall be to regulate our pleasures. Now, so that everyone — both man and woman — may experience the cares as well as the pleasures of ruling and no one feel any envy at not sharing them, I think the weight and honour should be given to each of us in turn for one day. The first shall be elected by all of us. At vespers he or she shall choose the ruler for the next day, and so on. While their reigns last these rulers shall arrange where and how we are to spend our time."

These words pleased them all and they unanimously elected her for the first day. Filomena ran to a laurel bush, whose leaves she had always heard were most honourable in themselves and did great honour to anyone crowned with them, plucked off a few small branches and wove them into a fair garland of honour. When this was placed on the head of any one of them, it was a symbol of rule and authority over the rest so long as the party remained together.

Pampinea, thus elected queen, ordered silence. She then sent for the three servants of the young men and the four women servants the ladies had brought, and said:

"To set a first example to you all which may be bettered and thus allow our gathering to live pleasantly and orderly and without shame and to last as long as we desire, I appoint Dioneo's servant Parmeno as my steward, and hand over to him the care of the whole family and of everything connected with the dining hall. Pamfilo's servant Sirisco shall be our treasurer and buyer, and carry out Parmeno's instructions. Tindaro shall wait on Filostrato and Dioneo and Pamfilo in their rooms, when the other two servants are occupied with their new duties. Filomena's servant Licisca and my own servant Misia shall remain permanently in the kitchen and carefully prepare the food which Parmeno sends them. Lauretta's Chimera and Fiametta's Stratilia shall take care of the ladies' rooms and see that the whole house is clean. Moreover we will and command that everyone who values our good grace shall bring back only cheerful news, wherever he may go or return from, and whatever he may hear or see."

Having given these orders, which were approved by everyone, she jumped gaily to her feet and said:

"Here are gardens and lawns and other delicious places, where each of us can wander and enjoy them at will. But let everyone be here at the hour of Tierce[2] so that we can eat together while it is still cool."

The company of gay young men and women, thus given the queen's permission, went off together slowly through the gardens, talking of pleasant matters, weaving garlands of different leaves, and singing love songs. After the time allotted by the queen had elapsed they returned to the house and found that Parmeno had carefully carried out the duties of his office. Entering a ground floor room decorated everywhere with broom blossoms, they found tables covered with white cloths and set with glasses which shone like silver. They washed their hands and, at the queen's command, all sat down in the places allotted them by Parmeno. Delicately cooked food was brought, exquisite wines were at hand, and the three men servants waited at table. Everyone was delighted to see things so handsome and well arranged, and they ate merrily with much happy talk.

All the ladies and young men could dance and many of them could play and sing; so, when the tables were cleared, the queen called for musical instruments. At her command Dioneo took a lute and Fiammetta a viol, and began to play a dance tune. The queen sent the servants to their meal, and then with slow steps danced with the two young men and the other ladies. After that, they began to sing gay and charming songs.

In this way they amused themselves until the queen thought it was time for the siesta. So, at the queen's bidding, the three young men went off to their rooms (which were separated from the ladies') and found them filled with flowers as the dining hall had been. And similarly with the women. So they all undressed and went to sleep.

Not long after the hour of Nones[3] the queen arose and made the other women and the young men also get up, saying that it was harmful to sleep too long during the daytime. Then they went out to a lawn of thick green grass entirely shaded from the sun. A soft breeze came to them there. The queen made them sit down in a circle on the grass, and said:

"As you see, the sun is high and the heat great, and nothing can be heard but the cicadas in the olive trees. To walk about at this hour would be foolish. Here it is cool and lovely, and, as you see, there are games of chess and draughts which everyone can amuse himself with, as he chooses. But, if my opinion is followed, we shall not play games, because in games the mind of one of the players must necessarily be distressed without any great pleasure to the other player or the onlookers. Let us rather spend this hot part of the day in telling tales, for thus one person can give pleasure to the whole company. When each of us has told a story, the sun will be going down and the heat less, and we can then go walking anywhere we choose for our amusement. If this pleases you (for here I am ready to follow your pleasure) let us do it. If it does not please you, let everyone do as he likes until evening."

The women and men all favoured the telling of stories.

---

[2] **Tierce:** The third hour after sunrise.   [3] **Nones:** The ninth hour after sunrise.

"Then if it pleases you," said the queen, "on this first day I order that everyone shall tell his tale about any subject he likes."

She then turned to Pamfilo, who was seated on her right, and ordered him to begin with a tale. Hearing this command, Pamfilo at once began as follows, while all listened.

. . .

Third Day
Tenth Tale

[Alibech becomes a hermit, and the monk Rustico teaches her how to put the devil in hell. She is afterwards taken away and becomes the wife of Neerbale.]

Dioneo had listened closely to the queen's story, and, when it was over and only he remained to tell a story, he did not wait to be commanded, but smilingly began as follows:

Most gracious ladies, perhaps you have never heard how the devil is put into hell; and so, without departing far from the theme upon which you have all spoken today, I shall tell you about it. Perhaps when you have learned it, you also will be able to save your souls, and you may also discover that although love prefers to dwell in gay palaces and lovely rooms rather than in poor huts, yet he sometimes makes his power felt among thick woods and rugged mountains and desert caves. Whereby we may well perceive that all of us are subject to his power.

Now, to come to my story—in the city of Capsa in Barbery[4] there lived a very rich man who possessed among other children a pretty and charming daughter, named Alibech. She was not a Christian, but she heard many Christians in her native town crying up the Christian Faith and service to God, and one day she asked one of them how a person could most effectively serve God. The reply was that those best serve God who fly furthest from the things of this world, like the hermits who had departed to the solitudes of the Thebaid Desert.[5]

The girl was about fourteen and very simple-minded. Urged by a mere childish enthusiasm and not by a well-ordered desire, she secretly set out next morning quite alone, without saying a word to anyone, to find the Thebaid Desert. Her enthusiasm lasted several days and enabled her with great fatigue to reach those solitudes. In the distance she saw a little hut with a holy man standing at its entrance. He was amazed to see her there, and asked her what she was seeking. She replied that by God's inspiration she was seeking to serve Him, and begged the hermit to show her the right way to do so. But the holy man saw she was young and pretty, and feared that if he kept her with him he might be tempted of the devil. So he praised her good intentions, gave her some roots and wild apples to eat and some water to drink, and said:

---

[4] **Capsa in Barbery:** Now Gafsa in southern Tunisia.

[5] **Thebaid Desert:** An Egyptian desert notable for the many Christian ascetics, including St. Anthony, who retreated to its isolation to commune with God.

"Daughter, not far from here dwells a holy man who is a far greater master of what you are seeking than I am, go to him."

And so he put her on the way. When she reached him, she was received with much the same words, and passing further on came to the cell of a young hermit named Rustico, to whom she made the same request as to the others. To test his spiritual strength, Rustico did not send her away, but took her into his cell. And when night came, he made her a bed of palm leaves and told her to sleep there.

Almost immediately after this, temptation began the struggle with his spiritual strength, and the hermit found that he had greatly over-estimated his powers of resistance. After a few assaults of the demon he shrugged his shoulders and surrendered. Putting aside holy thoughts and prayers and macerations, he began to think of her beauty and youth, and then pondered how he should proceed with her so that she should not perceive that he obtained what he wanted from her like a dissolute man. First of all he sounded her by certain questions, and discovered that she had never lain with a man and appeared to be very simple minded. He then saw how he could bring her to his desire under pretext of serving God. He began by eloquently showing how the devil is the enemy of the Lord God, and then gave her to understand that the service most pleasing to God is to put the devil back into hell, to which the Lord God has condemned him. The girl asked how this was done, and Rustico replied:

"You shall soon know. Do what you see me do."

He then threw off the few clothes he had and remained stark naked, and the girl imitated him. He kneeled down as if to pray and made her kneel exactly opposite him. As he gazed at her beauty, Rustico's desire became so great that the resurrection of the flesh occurred. Alibech looked at it with amazement, and said:

"Rustico, what is that thing I see sticking out in front of you which I haven't got?"

"My daughter," said Rustico, "that is the devil I spoke of. Do you see? He gives me so much trouble at this moment that I can scarcely endure him."

Said the girl:

"Praised be God! I see I am better off than you are, since I haven't such a devil."

"You speak truly," said Rustico, "but instead of this devil you have something else which I haven't."

"What's that?" said Alibech.

"You've got hell," replied Rustico, "and I believe God sent you here for the salvation of my soul, because this devil gives me great trouble, and if you will take pity upon me and let me put him into hell, you will give me the greatest comfort and at the same time will serve God and please Him, since, as you say, you came here for that purpose."

In all good faith the girl replied: "Father, since I have hell in me, let it be whenever you please."

Said Rustico: "Blessings upon you, my daughter. Let us put him in now so that he will afterwards depart from me."

So saying, he took the girl to one of their beds, and showed her how to lie so as to imprison the thing accursed of God. The girl had never before put any devil into her hell and at first felt a little pain, and exclaimed to Rustico:

"O father! This devil must certainly be wicked and the enemy of God, for even when he is put back into hell he hurts it."

"Daughter," said Rustico, "it will not always be so."

To prevent this from happening, Rustico put it into hell six times, before he got off the bed, and so purged the devil's pride that he was glad to rest a little. Thereafter he returned often and the obedient girl was always glad to take him in; and then the game began to give her pleasure, and she said to Rustico:

"I see that the good men of Capsa spoke the truth when they told me how sweet a thing is the service of God. I certainly do not remember that I ever did anything which gave me so much delight and pleasure as I get from putting the devil into hell. I think that everyone is a fool who does anything but serve God."

Thus it happened that she would often go to Rustico, and say:

"Father, I came here to serve God and not to remain in idleness. Let us put the devil in hell."

And once as they were doing it, she said:

"Rustico, I don't know why the devil ever goes out of hell. If he liked to remain there as much as hell likes to receive and hold him, he would never leave it."

The girl's frequent invitations to Rustico and their mutual pleasures in the service of God so took the stuffing out of his doublet that he now felt chilly where another man would have been in a sweat. So he told the girl that the devil must not be chastened or put into hell except when pride made him lift his head. "And we," he said, "have so quelled his rage that he prays God to be left in peace." And in this way he silenced the girl for a time. But when she found that Rustico no longer asked her to put the devil in hell, she said one day:

"Rustico, your devil may be chastened and give you no more trouble, but my hell is not. You should therefore quench the raging of my hell with your devil, as I helped you to quell the pride of your devil with my hell."

Rustico, who lived on nothing but roots and water, made a poor response to this invitation. He told her that many devils would be needed to soothe her hell, but that he would do what he could. In this way he satisfied her hell a few times, but so seldom that it was like throwing a bean in a lion's mouth. And the girl, who thought they were not serving God as much as she wanted, kept murmuring.

Now, while there was this debate between the excess of desire in Alibech's hell and the lack of potency in Rustico's devil, a fire broke out in Capsa, and burned Alibech's father with all his children and servants. So Alibech became heir to all his property. A young man named Neerbale, who had spent all his money in riotous living, heard that she was still alive and set out to find her, which he succeeded in doing before the Court took over her father's property as that of a man who had died without heirs. To Rustico's great relief, but against her will, Neerbale brought her back to Capsa and married her, and together they inherited her large patrimony. But before Neerbale had lain with her, certain ladies one day asked her how she had served God in the desert. She replied that her service was to put the devil in hell, and that Neerbale had committed a great sin by taking her away from such service. The ladies asked:

"And how do you put the devil in hell?"

Partly in words and partly by gestures, the girl told them. At this they laughed so much that they are still laughing, and said:

"Be not cast down, my child, they know how to do that here, and Neerbale will serve the Lord God with you in that way."

As they told it up and down the city, it passed into a proverb that the service most pleasing to God is to put the devil into hell. And this proverb crossed the seas and remains until this day.

Therefore, young ladies, when you seek God's favour, learn to put the devil in hell, because this is most pleasing to God and to all parties concerned, and much good may come of it.

Dioneo's tale moved the chaste ladies to laughter hundreds of times, so apt and amusing did they find his words. When he had finished, the queen knew that the end of her reign had come, and therefore took the laurel wreath from her head and placed it upon Filostrato's, saying pleasantly:

"We shall soon find out if the wolf can guide the flock, as well as the flock has guided the wolves."

Filostrato laughingly replied:

"If my advice were followed, the wolves would have showed the flock how to put the devil in hell, as Rustico taught Alibech; and so they would not be called wolves, where you would not be the flock. However, since the rule now falls to me, I shall begin my reign."

Said Neifile:

"Filostrato, in trying to teach us, you might have learned wisdom, as Masetto da Lamporecchio[6] learned it from the nuns, and you might have regained your speech when your bones were rattling together from exhaustion!"

Filostrato, finding the ladies' sickles were as good as his shafts, ceased jesting, and occupied himself with the government of his kingdom. Calling the steward, he made enquiries into everything, and gave orders to ensure the well being and satisfaction of the band during his kingship. He then turned to the ladies and said:

"Amorous ladies, to my own misfortune — although I was quite aware of my disease — I have always been one of Love's subjects owing to the beauty of one of you. To be humble and obedient to her and to follow all her whims as closely as I could, was all of no avail to me, and I was soon abandoned for another. Thus I go from bad to worse, and believe I shall until I die. Tomorrow then it is my pleasure that we tell tales on a theme in conformity with my own fate — that is, about those persons whose love ended unhappily. In the long run I expect a most unhappy end for myself, and the person who gave me the nickname of Filostrato, or the Victim of Love, knew what she was doing."

So saying, he rose to his feet, and gave them all leave to depart until supper time.

---

[6] **Masetto da Lamporecchio:** In the first tale told on the third day of *The Decameron*, da Lamporecchio, pretending to be a deaf mute, secures a job as a gardener in a convent. His presumed disability makes him especially appealing to the nuns, who seek him out to have sex with him. In the end Masetto suffers from exhaustion from his attempts to satisfy so many women.

The garden was so delightful and so beautiful that they all chose to remain there, since no greater pleasure could be found elsewhere. The sun was now not so hot, and therefore some of them began to chase the deer and rabbits and other animals which had annoyed them scores of times by leaping in among them while they were seated. Dioneo and Fiammetta began to sing the song of Messer Guglielmo and the Lady of Vergiu. Filomena and Pamfilo played chess. Thus, with one thing and another, time passed so quickly that supper time arrived long before they expected. The tables were set round the fountain, and there they ate their evening meal with the utmost pleasure.

When they rose from table, Filostrato would not depart from the path followed by the preceding queens, and so ordered Lauretta to dance and sing a song. And she said:

"My lord, I do not know any songs of other persons, and I do not remember any of my own which are fitting for this merry band. But if you wish to have one of those I remember, I will gladly sing it."

"Nothing of yours could be anything but fair and pleasing," said the king, "so sing it just as it is."

Then to the accompaniment of the others, Lauretta sang as follows in a sweet but rather plaintive voice:

No helpless lady has such cause to weep as I, who vainly sigh, alas, for love.

He who moves the heavens and all the stars made me for His delight so fair, so sweet, so gracious and so lovely that I might show to every lofty mind some trace of that high Beauty which ever dwells within His presence. But a weak man, who knew not Beauty, found me undelightful and scorned me.

Once there was one who held me dear, and in my early years took me into his arms and to his thoughts, being quite conquered by my eyes. And time, that flies so swiftly, he spent in serving me; and I in courtesy made him worthy of me. But now, alas, he is taken from me.

Then came a proud presumptuous man, who thought himself both noble and valorous, and made me his, but through false belief became most jealous of me. And then, alas, I came near to despair, for I saw that I, who came into the world to pleasure many, was possessed by one alone.

I curse my luckless fate that ever I said "yes" to man, and changed to a wife's garb. I was so gay in my old plain maiden's dress! Now in these finer clothes I lead so sad a life, reputed less than chaste. O hapless wedding feast! Would I had died before I knew the fate it held for me!

O my first love, with whom I was so happy, who now in Heaven do stand before Him who created it, have pity on me. I cannot forget you for another. Let me feel that the flame wherewith you burned for me is not extinct, and pray that I may soon return to you.

Here ended Lauretta's song, which was noted carefully by them all, but interpreted differently. Some understood it in the Milanese sense—that it is better to be a good pig than a pretty girl. Others were of a better, more sublime and truer under-standing, but of this I shall not now speak.

After this the king had many torches brought and made them sing other songs as they sat on the grass and flowers, until the rising stars began to turn towards the west. Then, thinking it time for sleep, he said good night and sent each one to his room.

[End of the Third Day]

Fourth Day
First Tale

[Tancred, Prince of Salerno, murders his daughter's lover and sends her the heart in a gold cup. She pours poison on it, which she drinks; and so dies.]

> [. . .] Already the sun had driven every star from heaven and the damp shadow of night from the earth, when Filostrato arose and with him all his company. They went into the fair garden, and there took their delight. When the time to eat came, they dined in the place where they had supped the evening before. They took their siesta when the sun was at its highest, and then arose and, in their wonted manner, went and sat down by the fountain.
> Filostrato then ordered Fiametta to tell the first tale, and she, without waiting to be told again, in womanly fashion began as follows.

Our king [Filostrato] has given us a sad theme for tale-telling today, thinking that as we came here to enjoy ourselves it is befitting to speak of the tears of others, which cannot be heard without pity either by the teller or the listeners. Perhaps he did this to temper the happiness we have had in the past few days. But, whatever his motive, it is not for me to change his good pleasure, and so I shall tell you a piteous story of misadventure, worthy of your tears.

Tancred, Prince of Salerno, was a humane and kindly man, except that in his old age he stained his hands with the blood of lovers. In the whole of his life he had no child but one daughter, and it would have been happier for him if he had not had her. This girl was as much beloved by her father as any daughter ever was, and long after she had reached marriageable age this tender love of his prevented him from marrying her to anyone. At length he gave her to a son of the Duke of Capua, who died soon after the marriage; and she returned home a widow. In face and body she was most beautiful, and young and merry and perhaps cleverer than a woman should be. She lived with her father in great luxury like a great lady, and, when she saw that her father loved her so much that he cared little about marrying her again, while she thought it immodest to ask him to do so, she determined that if she could she would secretly have a valiant lover.

Many men, both nobles and others, frequented her father's Court. She observed the manners and behaviour of many of these men, among them a young servant of her father's named Guiscardo, a man of humble birth but whose virtues and noble bearing pleased her so much that she fell secretly in love with him, and the more she saw him the more she admired him. The young man, who was no novice, soon perceived this and took her so deep into his heart that he could think of scarcely anything but his love for her.

Since they both were secretly in love with each other, the young widow desired nothing so much as to be alone with him, and, as she would trust nobody in this love affair, she thought of a new device for telling him where to meet her. She wrote him a letter telling him what he had to do the next day in order to be with her, and then put it into a hollow stick, which she laughingly gave him, saying:

"Make a bellows of this tonight for your servant to blow the fire."

Guiscardo took it, and realised that she would not have given it to him and have spoken these words without some reason. When he got to his lodging he looked at the stick, saw it was hollow and found her letter, which he read. When he discovered what he was to do, he was the happiest man alive, and prepared to meet her in the way she had arranged.

Near the Prince's palace was a cave, hollowed out of a hill in the remote past, and dimly lighted by a small opening cut in the hill-side. The cave had been so long abandoned that this opening was almost covered over with brambles and other plants. A secret stairway, secured by a very strong door, led to the cave from one of the rooms in the palace where the lady had her apartments. This stairway had been disused so long that scarcely anyone remembered its existence. But Love, from whose eyes nothing secret can be hidden, brought it to the remembrance of this enamoured lady.

To avoid anyone's knowing about all this, she exerted her wits for many days until she had succeeded in opening the door. Having opened it, she entered the cave alone and saw the outer entrance, and afterwards told Guiscardo to find some means of entering it, telling him about how far it was from the ground. Guiscardo immediately prepared a rope with knots and loops so that he could climb up and descend. The next night he wrapped himself in a leather skin as protection against the brambles and, without allowing anyone to know about it, went to the cave entrance. There he fitted one of the rope loops round a strong tree stump which had grown up in the mouth of the cave entrance, and so let himself down into the cave, and waited for the lady.

Next day, under pretence of taking a siesta, she sent away her women and shut herself up alone in her room. Then, opening the door, she got into the cave where she found Guiscardo; and together they made much of one another. They afterwards went to her room and remained together with the greatest delight for a large portion of that day. They made the necessary arrangements to keep their love secret; Guiscardo returned to the cave, she locked the door, and returned to her waiting women. When night came Guiscardo climbed up his rope and got out by the same opening he had come in, and returned home. Having thus learned this way, he returned often in the course of time.

But Fortune, envious of this prolonged and deep delight, changed the lovers' joy into piteous lament by a grievous happening.

Tancred was sometimes accustomed to go alone to his daughter's room to talk to her for a time, and then depart. One day he went there while his daughter (whose name was Ghismonda) was in a garden with all her women. Unwilling to disturb her pleasure he went into the room unseen and unheard, and finding the windows of the room shut and the bed-curtains drawn, sat down at the foot of the bed on a low stool. He leaned his head on the bed, drew the curtain round him, as if he had been hiding himself, and went to sleep. As misfortune would have it, Ghismonda had bidden Guiscardo come that day, and therefore left her women in the garden and softly entered the room where Tancred was asleep. She locked the door without noticing that he was there, and opened the other door for Guiscardo, who was waiting for her. They went to bed together, as usual, and while they were playing together and taking their delight, Tancred awoke and saw and heard what his daughter and Guiscardo were doing. In his distress he nearly made an outcry, but then determined to remain silent and hidden if he could, so that he could carry out with less shame what he had already determined to do.

The two lovers remained a long time together, as they were accustomed to do, without noticing Tancred; and when they thought it was time they got out of bed, Guiscardo returned to the cave, and she went out of the room. Tancred, although he was an old man, climbed out of a window into the garden, and returned to his own apartment almost dead with grief.

That night, by Tancred's orders, Guiscardo was arrested by two men as he came out of the cave opening still wrapped in the leather skin, and was secretly taken to Tancred. And when Tancred saw him, he said almost in tears:

"Guiscardo, my kindness to you has not merited the outrage and shame you have done me, as this day I saw with my own eyes."

But to this the only reply Guiscardo made was:

"Love is more powerful than either you or I."

Tancred then ordered that he should be closely guarded in a neighbouring room; which was done. The next day, while Ghismonda was still ignorant of what had happened, Tancred went to his daughter's room as usual after dinner, having turned over all kinds of thoughts in his mind. He had her called, locked himself in with her, and said to her in tears:

"Ghismonda, I thought I knew your virtue and modesty so well that, whatever had been said to me, it would never have come into my mind (if I had not seen it with my own eyes) that you would have yielded to any man who was not your husband, or even have thought of doing so. Whenever I think of it I shall always grieve during that short space of life left me in my old age.

"Since you had to come to this disgrace, would to God that you had taken a man who was worthy of your noble blood. But among all the men in my Court you chose Guiscardo, a young man of the basest extraction, bred in my Court from childhood, almost out of charity. You have plunged my mind in the greatest perplexity, and I do not know what to do. Last night I had Guiscardo arrested when he came out of the cave opening, and I have him in prison; and I know what I shall do with him. But God knows what I am to do with you. On the one hand, I am urged by the love I feel for you, which is greater than any father ever felt for a daughter. On the other hand, I am urged by my indignation at your folly. The one urges me to forgive you, the other to punish you against my natural feeling. But before I make up my mind, I should like to hear what you have to say."

So saying he bowed his head, and wept like a beaten child. As Ghismonda listened to her father, she saw that her secret love was discovered, and that Guiscardo was in prison. This caused her inexpressible grief, which she was very near to show-ing by tears and shrieks, as most women do. But her lofty love conquered this weak feeling, she kept her countenance with marvellous strength of mind, and made up her mind that before she made any prayer for herself, she would not remain alive since she saw Guiscardo was already as good as dead. So she faced her father, not like a weeping woman detected in a fault, but like a brave and unconcerned one, and replied to him unperturbed, with a clear and open visage:

"Tancred, I am not prepared either to deny or to supplicate, because the former would not avail me and I do not want to avail myself of the latter. Moreover, I do not mean to make your love and gentleness of service to me, but to confess the truth, to defend my fame with good reasons and then with deeds to follow boldly the great-ness of my soul. It is true that I have loved and do love Guiscardo. As long as I live — which will not be long — I shall love him. And if there is love after death, I shall con-tinue to love him then. I was not drawn to this love so much by my womanish weak-ness as by your neglecting to marry me and by his virtues.

"Since you are flesh and blood, Tancred, you should know that you begot a daughter of flesh and blood, not of stone or iron. You should have remembered now and earlier, although you are now an old man, what and how powerful are the laws of youth. Although you spent the best years of your manhood in warfare, yet you should know the power of idleness and luxury upon the old as well as upon the young.

"Now, I was begotten by you and so am of flesh and blood, and I have not lived so long that I am yet old. My youth and my flesh are the reasons why I am filled with amorous desires; and they have been greatly increased by my marriage, which showed what pleasure there is in satisfying these desires. I could not resist them, but yielded to them, as a young woman would do; and fell in love. As far as I could, I endeavoured to avoid shame to you and to me in doing what I was drawn to do by natural sin. Compassionate Love and kindly Fortune found and showed me a secret way to reach my desires, without anyone else knowing. Nor do I make any denial of all this, however you may have learned it or whoever told you.

"I did not take Guiscardo at a venture, as many women would have done, but I chose him above all others deliberately and with forethought, and he and I have long enjoyed our desires. Whereby it appears from your bitter reproof that, in addition to my sin of loving, you think (following, in this, rather common opinion than the truth) that I have erred in addition by choosing a man of low birth, as if you thought you need not be angry if I had chosen a nobleman. Here you should not reprove my error but that of Fortune, who often lifts the unworthy on high and casts down the most worthy.

"But let us leave all this, and look at the principles of things. You will see that we all have the same flesh, and that all souls were created by the same Creator with equal powers, equal strength and equal virtues. It was virtue which first introduced differ-ences among us who were born and are born equal. Those who were most virtuous and most devoted themselves to virtue were called noble, and the others remained commoners. And although this law has been glossed over by contrary custom, yet it is neither repealed nor broken by Nature and good manners. Therefore, he who lives

virtuously manifests himself noble; and if such a man is called other than noble, the fault rests not with him but with those who call him ignoble.

"Consider all your nobles, examine their virtues, their manners, their behaviour; and then look upon Guiscardo. If you will pass judgment without prejudice, you will see that Guiscardo is most noble, and that all your nobles are peasants. Concerning the virtue and valour of Guiscardo I shall trust nobody's judgment save that of your words and my own eyes. Whoever praised him so much as you have praised him for all worthy deeds befitting a valiant man? And certainly you were not wrong. If my eyes did not deceive me, you never praised him for anything which I did not see him perform better than your words could express. If I was deceived here, I was deceived by you.

"Will you now say that I chose a man of base condition? You would speak falsely. You may say he is a poor man, and that is granted—to your shame, since you left one of your bravest servants in such a state. Poverty takes away nobleness from no man, but wealth does.

"Many Kings, many great Princes, were once poor. Many of those who plough and watch herds were once rich.

"Now, concerning your doubt as to what you should do to me—hesitate no further, if you are determined to be cruel, to do in your old age what you did not do in your youth. Wreak your cruelty upon me, for I will use no supplication to you, and it was I who was the real cause of this sin, if sin there is. And I tell you that if you do not do to me what you have done or may do to Guiscardo, my own hands shall perform it upon myself.

"Go, weep with women, and if you must be cruel and think we have deserved death, kill him and me with the same stroke."

The Prince saw his daughter's greatness of soul, but he did not believe she was as resolute as her words sounded. So he departed from her, and determined to use no cruelty upon her person but to cool her hot love with other punishment. He therefore commanded the two men who were guarding Guiscardo to strangle him the next night without any noise, to cut out his heart and send it to him. And they did as they were ordered.

Next day, the Prince sent for a large handsome gold cup and put Guiscardo's heart into it. This he sent to his daughter by a trusted servant, with orders to give it to her and to say: "Your father sends you this to console you for what you most loved, even as you consoled him for what he loved most."

When her father left her, Ghismonda did not abandon her desperate resolution, but sent for poisonous herbs and roots and distilled them with water, to have poison ready in case what she feared should happen. When the servant came with the Prince's present, and repeated his words, she took the cup with a firm countenance, opened it, saw the heart, and knew for certain that it was Guiscardo's heart. She turned her face to the servant, and said:

"Gold alone is a fitting burial place for such a heart. Herein my father has done wisely."

So saying, she carried it to her mouth and kissed it and then said:

"Always, in every respect my father's love has been most tender towards me, and herein more than ever. For this princely present I render him the highest thanks, as I ought to do."

And then, holding the cup tightly, she gazed upon the heart, and said:

"Ah! Thou most sweet dwelling-place of all my delight, cursed be the cruelty of him who has made me look upon you with the eyes of my head! It was enough for me to gaze upon you hourly with the eyes of my spirit. You have run your race, you are now free from all that Fortune imposed upon you. You have reached that bourn to which all men run. You have left the labours and miseries of the world, and from your enemy have you received that burial your valour deserved. Nothing is lacking to your funeral rites, save only the tears of her you loved so dearly in your life. That you might have them, God inspired my pitiless father to send you to me. Those tears I shall give you, although I had determined to die dry-eyed and with a calm face. And when I have wept for you, I shall straightway act in such a way that my soul shall be joined with yours, and do you accept that soul which of old was so dear to you. In what company could I go more gladly or more securely to an unknown land than with your soul? I am certain that it is yet here, and looks upon the place of its delight and mine. And since I am certain your soul loves me, let it wait for mine by which it is so deeply beloved."

So saying, she bowed weeping over the cup, and with no womanish outcries shed as many tears as if she had had a fountain of water in her head, kissing the dead heart an infinite number of times, so that it was a marvel to behold. Her women did not know whose heart it was, and did not understand her words, but all were filled with pity and began to weep, and pityingly but in vain asked her the cause of her lamentations, and strove to comfort her as best they could. But when she felt she had lamented long enough, she raised her head and dried her eyes, and said:

"O most beloved heart, I have performed all my duties to you; nothing now remains for me to do, save to come with my soul to bear company with yours."

So saying, she took the phial containing the poison she had made, and poured it into the cup where the heart was wet with her tears. Fearlessly she lifted it to her mouth and drank; and having drunk, she lay down on her bed and arranged her body as modestly as she could, and placed the heart of her dead lover upon her heart, and thus awaited death without uttering a word.

Her women, having heard and seen these things, sent word of them to Tancred, although they did not know that she had drunk poison. Dreading what might happen, Tancred came at once to his daughter's room, and reached it just as she had laid herself down upon the bed. He tried to comfort her with sweet words too late; and seeing to what extremity she was come, he began piteously to weep. And the lady said:

"Tancred, spare your tears for a fate less longed for than this of mine; give them not to me, for I do not want them. Whoever saw anyone but you weep over what he willed should happen. And yet, if any of the love you once felt for me is still alive, grant me one last gift—although it displeased you that I lived secretly and silently with Guiscardo, let my body lie openly with his in the place where you have cast it."

The agony of his weeping prevented the Prince from replying. Then she felt her end was come, and holding the dead heart to her bosom, she said:

"God be with you, and let me go."

She veiled her eyes and all sense left her and she departed this sad life.

Such, as you have heard, was the sad end of the love of Guiscardo and Ghismonda. Tancred wept much and repented too late of his cruelty; and, amid the general grief of all Salerno, buried them both honourably in the same grave.

. . .

CONCLUSION

Most noble ladies, for whose delight I have given myself over to this long task, I believe that with the aid of divine grace it is more through your pious prayers than any merit of mine that I have carried out what I promised to do at the beginning of this work. So now, after giving thanks, first to God and then to you, I shall rest my pen and weary hand. I know that these tales can expect no more immunity than any others, as I think I showed in the beginning of the Fourth Day; and so before I rest, I mean to reply to certain objections which might be made by you or others.

Some of you may say that in writing these tales I have taken too much license, by making ladies sometimes say and often listen to matters which are not proper to be said or heard by virtuous ladies. This I deny, for there is nothing so unchaste but may be said chastely if modest words are used; and this I think I have done.

But suppose it to be true — and I shall not strive with you, for you are certain to win — I reply that I have many arguments ready. First, if there is any license in some of them, the nature of the stories demanded it; and if any understanding person looks at them with a reasonable eye he will see that they could not be related otherwise, unless I had altered them entirely. And if there are a few words rather freer than suits the prudes, who weigh words more than deeds and take more pains to appear than to be good, I say that I should no more be reproved for having written them than other men and women are reproved for daily saying "hole," "peg," "mortar," "pestle," "sausage," "Bologna sausage," and the like things. My pen should be allowed no less power than is permitted the painter's brush; the painters are not censured for allowing Saint Michele to slay the serpent with a sword or lance and Saint Giorgio to kill the dragon as he pleases. They make Christ male and Eve female, and they fasten sometimes with one nail, sometimes with two, the feet of Him who died for the human race on the Cross.

In addition, anyone can see that these things were not told in church, where everything should be treated with reverent words and minds (although you will find plenty of license in the stories of the church); nor were they told in a school of philosophers, where virtue is as much required as anywhere else; nor among churchmen or other philosophers in any place; but they were told in gardens, in pleasure places, by young people who were old enough not to be led astray by stories, and at a time when everyone threw his cap over the mill and the most virtuous were not reproved for it.

But, such as they are, they may be amusing or harmful, like everything else, according to the persons who listen to them. Who does not know that wine is a most excellent thing, if we may believe Cinciglione and Scolaio,[7] while it is harmful to a man with a fever? Are we to say wine is wicked because it is bad for those who are feverish? Who does not know that fire is most useful and even necessary to mankind? And because it sometimes destroys houses, villages and towns, shall we say it is bad? Weapons defend the safety of those who wish to live in peace, but they also kill men, not through any wrong in them but through the wickedness of those who use them ill.

No corrupt mind ever understands words healthily. And just as such people do not enjoy virtuous words, so the well-disposed cannot be harmed by words which are somewhat less than virtuous, any more than mud can sully sunlight or earthy filth the beauty of the skies.

What books, what words, what letters are more holy, more worthy, more to be revered than those of the divine Scripture? Yet many people by perversely interpreting them have sent themselves and others to perdition. Everything in itself is good for something, and if wrongly used may be harmful in many ways; and I say the same of my tales. Whoever wants to turn them to bad counsel or bad ends will not be forbidden by the tales themselves, if by any chance they contain such things and are twisted and turned to produce them. Those who want utility and good fruits from them, will not find them denied; nor will the tales ever be thought anything but useful and virtuous if they are read at the times and to the persons for which they are intended.

Those who have to say paternosters and play the hypocrite to their confessor can leave them alone; my tales will run after nobody asking to be read. And yet bigots say and even do such little trifles from time to time!

There will also be people to say that if some of the tales here were absent it would be all the better. Granted. But I could only write down the tales which were related; if they had told better ones, I should have written them down better. But suppose that I was both the inventor and the scribe (which I was not), I say that I am not ashamed that they are not all good, because there is no one, save God alone, who can do everything well and perfectly. Charlemagne, who first devised the Paladins,[8] could not make enough of them to form an army. In a multitude of things we must be prepared to find diverse qualities. No field was ever so well cultivated that it contained no nettles, briars and thorns mingled with better plants.

Moreover, since I was speaking to simple young women such as most of you are, it would have been folly for me to go seeking and striving to find such exquisite things and to take pains to speak with great measure. However, those who read these tales can leave those they dislike and read those they like. I do not want to deceive anybody, and so all these tales bear written at the head a title explaining what they contain.

---

[7] **Cinciglione and Scolaio:** Proverbial drunkards.

[8] **Charlemagne . . . Paladins:** Charlemagne (742–814), king of the Franks, became the first emperor of the West in 800 C.E. The Paladins were the legendary group of knights who surrounded Charlemagne, serving as his personal retinue, much as the legendary Knights of the Round Table served King Arthur.

I suppose some people will say that some of the tales are too long. I reply that for those who have something else to do it is folly to read the tales, even when they are short. A long time has passed between the day when I began to write and now when I have come to the end of my labours; but I have not forgotten that I said my work is offered to those ladies who are unoccupied, and not to others. To those who read for pastime, no tale can be too long if it succeeds in its object. Brevity befits students, who labour to spend time usefully, not to make it pass; but not you, ladies, who have unoccupied all that time you do not spend in love pleasures. None of you has studied at Athens, Bologna or Paris; and so one must chatter a little more volubly for you than for those who have sharpened their wits by study.

I have no doubt that others will say that the things related are too full of jests and jokes, and that it ill befits a grave and weighty man to write such things. To them I must offer thanks and do thank them that they are so zealously tender of my good fame. But I shall reply to their objection. I confess I am weighty, and have often weighed myself. But, speaking to those who have not weighed me, I must observe that I am not grave but so light that I float in water. Considering that the friars' sermons, which are made to censure men's sins, are full of jokes and jests and railleries, I think that such things do not go ill in my tales, which are written to drive away ladies' melancholy. However, if the tales make them laugh too much, they can easily cure that by reading the lamentations of Jeremiah, the passion of the Saviour and the penitence of Mary Magdalene.[9]

Who can doubt that there will be others who will say that I have a wicked poisonous tongue, because in some places I have written the truth about the friars? I mean to pardon those who say that, because it cannot be believed but that they are moved except by just cause, since the friars are good men who avoid poverty for the love of God, and do good service to the ladies and say nothing about it. And if they did not all smell a little of the goat, their company would be most pleasant.

Yet I confess that there is no stability in the things of this world and that everything changes. So may it have chanced with my tongue. I do not trust my own judgment, which I always avoid in matters concerning myself, but one of my women neighbours the other day told me I have the best and sweetest tongue in the world. But, to speak the truth, when that happened there were not many of my tales left to finish. And so let what I have said suffice as a reply to those who make these objections.

I leave it to every lady to say and think what she pleases; for me it is time to end my words, giving thanks humbly to Him who by His aid and after so much labour has brought me to the desired end.

And you, fair ladies, rest in peace in His grace; and if in reading any of these tales you find any pleasure, remember me.

---

[9] **Jeremiah . . . Mary Magdalene:** Jeremiah (c. 628–586 B.C.E.) was a Hebrew prophet who pessimistically viewed the moral shortcomings of the Hebrew people and prophesied doom. Mary Magdalene was a follower of Jesus who attended his burial. Tradition describes her as a repentant prostitute who anointed Jesus' feet (Luke 7:36–50).

❧ GEOFFREY CHAUCER
C. 1340–1400

www For links to more information about Chaucer, a quiz on "The Wife of Bath's Tale," and a discussion of the twenty-first-century relevance of Chaucer, see *World Literature Online* at bedfordstmartins .com/worldlit.

For giving readers a vivid, lively, and delightful panorama of life in medieval England, no writer has exceeded Geoffrey Chaucer, one of the great English poets. Drawing on his wide reading in English, French, and Italian literature as well as his extensive experience as a statesman, Chaucer crafted his most important work, *The Canterbury Tales,* which he left unfinished at his death. Like Boccaccio's *Decameron* and the Arabic *Thousand and One Nights, The Canterbury Tales* is a collection of tales told within an overarching frame story. From ribald and bawdy to pious and chaste, this succession of stories told by a group of English pilgrims on their way from London to Canterbury merits its reputation as a *TOUR DE FORCE* that displays the variety of human character. In the individual portraits of each traveler — from the noble Knight to the base Miller, the lanky Clerk to the robust Franklin, the delicate Prioress to the earthy Wife of Bath — Chaucer creates unique and complex characters with all their vices and virtues as well as a picture of fourteenth-century England and its moral, social, philosophical, and spiritual concerns.

A Writer in the Service of the King. Geoffrey Chaucer was born in London about 1340 into a family of French descent who had made their fortune in trade. The poet's father, John Chaucer, was a property owner, wine merchant, and deputy to the king's butler who had served with Edward III at Antwerp. The young Geoffrey was most likely educated in London, where he learned Latin, French, and Italian; whether he studied with a tutor or at a school is not known. By 1357, when he was in his teens, Chaucer had entered into the service of Lionel, the third son of Edward III.[1] Soon he found himself serving in Edward's army in France, where he was captured in battle at Rheims. He was held captive for nearly six months, then ransomed in March 1360, after which he returned to England and served as a messenger between England and France.

Not long thereafter, Chaucer married Philippa Pan, who had been in the service of John of Gaunt's second wife, Constance of Castile. Sometime during this decade Chaucer began his first major literary project, the translation of *The Romance of the Rose* by Guillaume de Lorris, a work completed by Jean de Meun.[2] Although most of it is lost, this translation is important, for many of Chaucer's early works borrow plots, motifs, and form — such as the dream vision — from this and other French romances. In 1367 Chaucer was a king's yeoman, then esquire, engaged in diplomatic missions that took him to Spain, France, Flanders, and Italy.

---

[1] **Edward III** (1312–1377): King of England from 1327 to 1377, a period that included the Hundred Years' War, the rise of the Commons in Parliament, and The Plague.

[2] **Jean de Meun:** (d. 1305?) French author of the second part of *Romance of the Rose,* an epic-length allegorical poem that gives a broad overview of medieval life and thought.

The Wife of Bath, 1400–1410

The Ellesmere manuscript of The Canterbury Tales, *from which this illustration is taken, is thought to be Chaucer's most complete text, copied shortly after his death. In it, each pilgrim is shown astride a horse in the margin near where his or her tale begins. (Art Resource, NY)*

On his first mission to Italy, in 1372, Chaucer is thought to have met Petrarch, although no definitive evidence exists for such a meeting. On this and a later mission to Italy in 1378, Chaucer acquired Italian books and had the opportunity to familiarize himself with important Italian works, including Dante's *Divine Comedy,* Petrarch's poetry, and possibly the works of Boccaccio.[3]

---

[3] **Dante . . . Boccaccio:** Three great Italian writers of the medieval period. Dante Alighieri (1265–1321) is the poet responsible for *The Divine Comedy,* a monumental work allegorizing the journey the soul takes to reach or know paradise; Francesco Petrarch (1304–1374), the author of *Canzoniere,* wrote some of the greatest love lyrics in European literature; and Giovanni Boccaccio (1313–1375) authored *The Decameron,* a collection of brilliant and sometimes bawdy prose tales.

Revolutions of Favor and Fortune.   In June 1374, Chaucer was appointed controller of the Custom and Subsidy, in charge of keeping records of the wool trade. Ten years later he was appointed controller of the Petty Customs, an office he held for two years before resigning to serve as justice of the peace in Kent, where he also was elected as one of the knights of the shire. By this time, the young Richard II's court was being challenged by an opposition party under the leadership of the duke of Gloucester,[4] and Chaucer's fortunes took a brief but painful turn for the worse. Gloucester executed some of Chaucer's friends at court; Chaucer's wife died in 1387; and in May 1388, he was forced to sell his annuities. A grand decade of increasing personal prosperity had come to an abrupt end. In May 1389, however, Richard recovered his power, and in July Chaucer was appointed Clerk of the Works, responsible for the maintenance of various properties of the crown, including those at Westminster and the Tower of London.

All this time Chaucer had kept his property at Kent, and as far as is known, moved back and forth from London as duty called. When Richard II was removed from power and replaced by Henry IV, Chaucer, pressed for money, wrote a brief lyric called the "Complaint to His Purse," asking for more financial support and a "butt of wine." The new king promptly honored this request for patronage, enabling Chaucer to live out his final years in relative security and comfort. About a year before his death, Chaucer leased a home near Westminster Abbey; he died on October 25, 1400.

Early Poetry.   Throughout his adult life, Chaucer cultivated his literary interests while performing the duties of the various public offices he held. His diplomatic missions helped to broaden the scope of his poetry, influenced as it was by Latin, French, and Italian literature. Chaucer's early poems, *The Book of the Duchess* and *The Parliament of the Fowls,* adopt familiar motifs from continental models, though even early on Chaucer demonstrated a genius for innovation. His first long poem, *The Book of the Duchess,* is an elegy, written on the occasion of the death of John of Gaunt's first wife, Blanche, Duchess of Lancaster, in 1369. The poem takes the form of a dream, suggested by the narrator's reading of "A romaunce." As in other early poems, the influence of Ovid[5] is evident in the mythic apparatus of the poem involving the intervention of Juno and Morpheus. *The House of Fame* (c. 1374–1386), a second and unfinished long poem, uses the dream convention for comic purposes; it is a vision of love in which a series of parties petition the goddess Fame, whose blessing will confer upon them a good name. As in the classical journey

---

[4] **Richard . . . duke of Gloucester:** Richard II (1367–1400) ruled England from 1377 to 1399. During his reign, opposition nobles, including Thomas of Woodstock, the duke of Gloucester, challenged his authority. Richard ordered the duke assassinated in 1397.

[5] **Ovid:** Publius Ovidius Naso (43 B.C.E.–18 C.E.) is the Latin poet known for his love poems, including *Amores* and *The Art of Love,* and especially for his masterwork, *The Metamorphoses.* (See Book 1.)

to the underworld in Virgil's *Aeneid*[6] or Dante's *Divine Comedy,* to which the poem often alludes, the poet requires a guide, in this case a very noisy eagle, to lead him to the house of Fame and to explain to him the nature of the celestial journey and other spiritual matters.

Parliament of Fowls.   Birds play an even more important role in *The Parliament of Fowls,* written sometime between 1375 and 1385. The poem invokes the popular tradition that birds choose their mates on St. Valentine's Day. The speaker falls asleep lamenting his ill fate at love, has a vision of a garden similar to that in *Romance of the Rose,* and witnesses the competition among three eagles who vie for the love of a "formel," or female. The poem may have been written for an actual marriage—that of Richard II and Anne of Bohemia has been proposed, among others. Such bird fables are found not only in medieval and Latin literature but in Islamic literature as well; the most famous of such Islamic tales is *Conference of the Birds* by Farid ud-Din Attar.[7]

Troilus and Criseyde.   Chaucer's greatest love poem, *Troilus and Criseyde* (c. 1385), tells the story of the romance between Troilus, a hero from the Trojan War, and Cressida, who does not appear in classical literature but derives from medieval stories. Boccaccio's *Il Filostrato* was Chaucer's most immediate source for the love story, which tells how Troilus, hoping to win out over his rival Diomedes (also of *Iliad* fame), engages the services of the older matchmaker Pandarus to win the love of Cressida. Like *The Parliament of Fowls, Troilus and Criseyde* reviews the conventions of courtly love but treats them more seriously.

The Canterbury Tales.   Chaucer planned two other long poems: *The Legend of Good Women,* for which he completed in the late 1380s a prologue and nine stories, including the story of Cleopatra; and what became his greatest poem, *The Canterbury Tales,* begun in 1386 and left unfinished at his death. Though incomplete, this delightful set of tales consists of a prologue and twenty-four stories in more than 170,000 lines of verse, which begins as a socially diverse group of travelers set out on a pilgrimage to Canterbury, "the hooly blesful martir for to seke." Every year groups of pilgrims made the journey from London to Canterbury, to the shrine of Saint Thomas à Becket, the former archbishop of Canterbury who was murdered in the cathedral in 1170. To entertain one another along the way, Harry Bailly, the host of the journey and the proprietor of the Tabard Inn, where the journey begins, proposes that each of the twenty-nine pilgrims tell four stories, two on the way to Canterbury and two on the return home. Chaucer's actual intention was most likely

> I read Chaucer still with as much pleasure as any of our poets. He is a master of manners and of description and the first tale-teller in the true enlivened, natural way.
>
> – ALEXANDER POPE, Poet, eighteenth century

p. 406

---

[6] **Virgil's Aeneid:** Publius Vergilius Maro (70–19 B.C.E.), the greatest of Roman poets, is the author of *The Eclogues, The Georgics,* and the epic poem *The Aeneid.* (See Book 1.)

[7] **Farid ud-Din Attar** (1145–1221): Persian mystic poet known for *The Conference of the Birds,* a set of tales told by birds that have set out on a journey to find their god.

Chaucer is himself
then [a] great poetic
observer of men,
who in every age is
born to record and
eternalize its acts.
This he does as a
master, as a father,
and superior, who
looks down on their
little follies, from
the emperor to the
miller — sometimes
with severity, oftener
with joke and sport.

— WILLIAM BLAKE,
Poet, 1809

to complete only the stories on the way to the shrine, in itself a prodigious task. Whatever the author's plan, what Chaucer produced is a compendium of remarkably varied tales in a number of literary genres that brings to life the social, philosophical, and religious world of fourteenth-century England.

The framing story of the meeting of the pilgrims at the Tabard Inn provides structural unity to the successive tales told by each traveler. Along the way the travelers engage in friendly banter, prankish jesting, and downright disputes sometimes motivated by occupational rivalry, jealousy, or gender differences. The Miller, for example, tells a bawdy story about Nicolaus the clerk who tricks John the carpenter and sleeps with his wife. Offended, the Reeve, a carpenter, replies with an equally salacious story about Symkyn the greedy miller, who cheats two clerks out of some grain they've brought to be ground; they take revenge on him by sleeping with his wife and daughter, and to top it off, his wife clubs him over the head at the end of the tale.

Among the travelers is Chaucer the pilgrim, an innocent observer through whose eyes and ears the travelers are perceived. Chaucer the author, however, is anything but naive, and through the combined perspectives of the General Prologue, each teller's prologue, and the tales each tells, a multifaceted portrait of each character emerges. Although some characters — such as the Knight, the Parson, and the Nun's Priest — display values consistent with their occupations and thus command respect, others — such as the Pardoner, the Summoner, and the Friar — vacillate between their professed values and their real actions and intentions. The Monk, for example, loves to hunt, and the Friar is overly fond of riches; worst of all is the Pardoner, an outright hypocrite. The "portrait gallery of pilgrims," as the General Prologue is sometimes called, is actually a picture of English society in all its diversity.

Often an important ironic connection exists between each pilgrim and the tale he or she tells; even the form in which the pilgrims frame their tales indicates something about their character, taste, social position, and education. Thus the knight, for example, tells the tale of two heroes, Palamon and Arcite, who compete for the love of a beautiful, idealized woman, Emelye. In perfect compatibility with his position and interests, the Knight's tale is told in the form of a romance. The Second Nun retells the legend of St. Cecilia in the form of a saint's life, a type of narrative well suited to her. Most interesting are those tales that fall in ironic relation to their teller, discussed below. Other literary forms used by the pilgrims include the fabliau, or popular tale, the beast fable, and even a sermon.

The Wife of Bath: Prologue.   The Wife of Bath tells a story completely compatible with her character. Many readers see the Wife of Bath, with her worldly ways, self-assured contentiousness, and resolute independence, as the most colorful, vital, and engaging character in *The Canterbury Tales*. In her prologue, she single-handedly takes up the offensive against the doctrine of celibacy and those who would appeal to church doctrine to legitimate their abuse of, and contempt for, women. The Wife of Bath's prologue argues that women deserve to be respected and declares their independence from male tyranny. This argument is enhanced by the Wife's vital and earthy celebration of love and sexuality. She proudly boasts that "Housbondes at chirche dore I have had fyve," and that she is ruled by both Venus and Mars:

> For certes, I am al Venerien
> In feelynge, and myn herte is marcien.
> Venus me yaf my lust, my likerousnesse,
> And mars yaf me my sturdy hardynesse.

Her boldness and tenacity derive in part from her experience of the world, which she claims provides a more powerful authority on which to base judgment than do books, with their false doctrines and wrong-headed assumptions about women. As she puts it: "Experience, though noon auctoritee / Were in this world, is right ynogh for me / To speke of wo that is in marriage."

The Wife of Bath: Tale.   The Wife's tale is one of a series sometimes called the "marriage group" that show marriage in a variety of forms. The story the Wife tells takes the form of a popular romance about a handsome knight and a loathsome lady. The knight, who commits rape, will be pardoned for his act if he can discover what it is that women most desire. The loathsome lady promises to tell him provided that he marry her. What the knight learns is that women above all want "sovereynetee / As wel over hir housbond as hir love / And for to been in maistrie hym above"; that is, sovereignty over their husbands and lovers, and to be above them in mastery. When the knight finally submits to love the old woman, she transforms into a beautiful young woman and the story ends well for both parties.

Chaucer's Language.   Although the language of Chaucer's day may be recognizable to the modern reader as English, changes in sound, meaning, spelling, and grammar between the fourteenth and seventeenth centuries render Chaucer's English difficult today without careful study. The final "e" sounds in the original text, for example, though gradually phased out of the spoken language in Chaucer's time, were still pronounced to capture rhyme and meter. Initial consonants such as the "k" in "knight" also are pronounced, and the "gh" in "knight" or "drought" is pronounced as "ch," as in the German *nach.* Most other consonant sounds in Chaucer's English are similar to modern English, but long vowel sounds are not. As a general rule, these long vowels sound as they do in Spanish, French, and German today.

The following example, the opening of the General Prologue, should be compared with Theodore Morrison's translation beginning on page 884. Unfortunately, even the best translations cannot fully capture the delightful rhythm and melody of Chaucer's verse:

> Whan that Aprill with his shoures soote
> The droghte of March hath perced to the roote,
> And bathed every veyne in swich licour

Of which vertu engendred is the flour;
Whan Zephirus eek with his sweete breeth
Inspired hath in every holt and heeth
The tendre croppes, and the yonge sonne
Hath in the Ram his halve cours yronne,
And smale fowele maken melodye,
That slepen al the nyght with open yë
(So priketh hem nature in hir corages),—
Thanne longen folk to goon on pilgrimages,
And palmeres for to seken straunge strondes,
To ferne halwes, kowthe in sondry londes;
And specially from every shires ende
Of Engelond to Caunterbury they wende,
The hooly blisful martir for to seke,
That ham hath holpen whan that they were seeke.

■ **CONNECTIONS**

Giovanni Boccaccio, *The Decameron,* **p. 853;** *Arabian Nights,* **p. 441.** The frame story, an outer narrative that comprises several, sometimes otherwise unrelated, stories, has appeared throughout the history of literature. *The Canterbury Tales,* Boccaccio's *Decameron,* and *The Thousand and One Nights* all employ frame narratives. How do the frame stories in these three works serve to link and unify the stories they contain?

Margery Kempe, *The Book of Margery Kempe,* **p. 995.** The role of women in the Middle Ages has generated considerable interest among critics and scholars. Kempe's autobiographical narrative offers an important glimpse into the life of an extraordinary woman, a tenacious and spirited individual who challenged the patriarchal world of her time and struggled with her own spiritual and secular values. Chaucer's Wife of Bath, Alisoun, is another such woman, though she is a fictional character created by a male writer. Compare Kempe with the Wife of Bath. What are their strengths and weaknesses? Who seems more real to you?

Wu Chengen, *Monkey* **(Book 3).** Pilgrimage is an important motif in medieval literature. Chaucer modeled his *Canterbury Tales* on the travels to Canterbury undertaken by many Londoners in his time; Wu Ch'eng En based his novel *Monkey* on the Buddhist monk Xuanzang's pilgrimage to India. Consider the difference between fictional accounts of travel and pilgrimage and actual travel narratives. How do travel narratives employ the techniques of fiction?

■ **FURTHER RESEARCH**

Editions
Benson, Larry D. *The Riverside Chaucer.* 3d ed. 1987.

Biography
Howard, Donald R. *Chaucer: His Life, His Works, His World.* 1987.
Kane, George. *Chaucer.* 1984.
Pearsall, Derek. *The Life of Geoffrey Chaucer: A Critical Biography.* 1992.

Criticism
Aers, David. *Chaucer.* 1986.
Benson, C. David. *Chaucer's Drama of Style: Poetic Variety and Contrast in* The Canterbury Tales. 1986.
Crane, Susan. *Gender and Romance in Chaucer's* Canterbury Tales. 1994.
Hanson, Elaine Tuttle. *Chaucer and the Fictions of Gender.* 1992.

Howard, Donald R. *The Idea of* The Canterbury Tales. 1976.
Patterson, Lee. *Chaucer and the Subject of History.* 1991.
Pearsall, Derek A. *The Canterbury Tales.* 1985.
Ruggiers, Paul G. *The Art of the Canterbury Tales.* 1965.
———. *Editing Chaucer: The Great Tradition.* 1984.
Weatherbee, Winthrop. *Geoffrey Chaucer:* The Canterbury Tales. 1989.

ᵔ The Canterbury Tales

Translated by Theodore Morrison

FROM

GENERAL PROLOGUE

As soon as April pierces to the root
The drought of March, and bathes each bud and shoot
Through every vein of sap with gentle showers
From whose engendering liquor spring the flowers;
When zephyrs have breathed softly all about
Inspiring every wood and field to sprout,
And in the zodiac the youthful sun
His journey halfway through the Ram has run;[1]

The Canterbury Tales. Considered by most critics to be Chaucer's greatest work, this long poem consists of a General Prologue, included in the selections here, and twenty-four stories told by pilgrims making their way as a group to Canterbury. Chaucer began writing *Canterbury Tales* in 1386, leaving it unfinished at his death in 1400. Because he left behind no directions for the ordering of the tales, their sequence has been left up to editors working from the copied manuscripts arranged and left behind by copyists and scribes. Some modern editors follow the sequence established by the famous Ellesmere manuscript, a beautiful illuminated version of Chaucer's work assembled in the fifteenth century; other editors follow, with some modifications, the grouping established by the scholar and editor Frederick James Furnivall (1825–1910) for the 1868 Chaucer Society edition. Working from textual evidence—clues about place and time, hints in the Prologue, and thematic links among the tales—Furnivall assigned the tales to groups A through I. The excerpts presented here from the General Prologue and "The Wife of Bath's Tale" belong to groups A and D. In group A are the tales told by the Knight, the Miller, and the Reeve; Group D includes the stories told by the Wife of Bath, the Friar, and the Summoner. As the speaker recounts in the General Prologue, a group of pilgrims have assembled at the Tabard Inn preparing to embark for Canterbury and he is to join them, thus setting up the frame story of the pilgrimage. He introduces the other pilgrims, noting potential discrepancies between who and what they profess to be and who they really are.

---

[1] **the youthful sun . . . Ram has run:** The sun is in Aries, the Ram, from mid March to early April.

When little birds are busy with their song
10 Who sleep with open eyes the whole night long
Life stirs their hearts and tingles in them so,
Then off as pilgrims people long to go,
And palmers° to set out for distant strands   *pilgrims*
And foreign shrines renowned in many lands.
And specially in England people ride
To Canterbury[2] from every countryside
To visit there the blessed martyred saint
Who gave them strength when they were sick and faint.
    In Southwark at the Tabard one spring day
20 It happened, as I stopped there on my way,
Myself a pilgrim with a heart devout
Ready for Canterbury to set out,
At night came all of twenty-nine assorted
Travelers, and to that same inn resorted,
Who by a turn of fortune chanced to fall
In fellowship together, and they were all
Pilgrims who had it in their minds to ride
Toward Canterbury. The stable doors were wide,
The rooms were large, and we enjoyed the best,
30 And shortly, when the sun had gone to rest,
I had so talked with each that presently
I was a member of their company

Furthermore, Chaucer's economical but rich descriptions of these pilgrims—their costume, appearance, experience, and character—invites a comparison between their appearance and their true character. "The Wife of Bath's Tale," which includes a prologue and a tale, centers on the question of sovereignty in marriage and sets off a debate about marriage that emerges in several subsequent tales, including the Clerk's, the Merchant's, and the Franklin's. In contrast to the Wife of Bath, who argues for the sovereignty of the wife over the husband, the Franklin's tale suggests a compromise, arguing for the mutual respect and cooperation of both wife and husband. Although she portrays herself as having been a tough-minded, pragmatic, resilient, and even domineering partner to her past husbands, the Wife shows some tenderness when she speaks of her joy in finding true love and kindness with her last husband. The tale she tells centers on a cruel knight who undergoes a change of character as an old woman leads him to a more judicious and humane understanding of women and the world. Forced into marrying her, the knight learns from the woman that nobility of birth is not a guarantee of virtue, and that money, appearance, and age are not reliable indicators of character. When he finally submits to being governed by his wife, whose wisdom has enlightened him, he is rewarded with her transformation into a beautiful and faithful young lady.

---

[2] **Canterbury:** A city sixty miles southeast of London; site of Canterbury Cathedral, the shrine of St. Thomas à Becket ("the blessed martyred saint"), who was murdered there in 1170.

And promised to rise early the next day
To start, as I shall show, upon our way.
     But none the less, while I have time and space,
Before this tale has gone a further pace,
I should in reason tell you the condition
Of each of them, his rank and his position,
40 And also what array they all were in;
And so then, with a knight I will begin.
     A Knight was with us, and an excellent man,
Who from the earliest moment he began
To follow his career loved chivalry,
Truth, openhandedness, and courtesy.
He was a stout man in the king's campaigns
And in that cause had gripped his horse's reins
In Christian lands and pagan through the earth,
None farther, and always honored for his worth.
50 He was on hand at Alexandria's fall.
He had often sat in precedence to all
The nations at the banquet board in Prussia.
He had fought in Lithuania and in Russia,
No Christian knight more often; he had been
In Moorish Africa at Benmarin,
At the siege of Algeciras in Granada,
And sailed in many a glorious armada
In the Mediterranean, and fought as well
At Ayas and Attalia when they fell
60 In Armenia and on Asia Minor's coast.
Of fifteen deadly battles he could boast,
And in Algeria, at Tremessen,
Fought for the faith and killed three separate men
In single combat. He had done good work
Joining against another pagan Turk
With the king of Palathia. And he was wise,
Despite his prowess, honored in men's eyes,
Meek as a girl and gentle in his ways.
He had never spoken ignobly all his days
70 To any man by even a rude inflection.
He was a knight in all things to perfection.
He rode a good horse, but his gear was plain,
For he had lately served on a campaign.
His tunic was still spattered by the rust
Left by his coat of mail, for he had just
Returned and set out on his pilgrimage.
     His son was with him, a young Squire, in age
Some twenty years as near as I could guess.

His hair curled as if taken from a press.
He was a lover and would become a knight.
80 In stature he was of a moderate height
But powerful and wonderfully quick.
He had been in Flanders, riding in the thick
Of forays in Artois and Picardy,
And bore up well for one so young as he,
Still hoping by his exploits in such places
To stand the better in his lady's graces.
He wore embroidered flowers, red and white,
And blazed like a spring meadow to the sight.
He sang or played his flute the livelong day.
90 He was as lusty as the month of May.
His coat was short, its sleeves were long and wide.
He sat his horse well, and knew how to ride,
And how to make a song and use his lance,
And he could write and draw well, too, and dance.
So hot his love that when the moon rose pale
He got no more sleep than a nightingale.
He was modest, and helped whomever he was able,
And carved as his father's squire at the table.
      But one more servant had the Knight beside,
100 Choosing thus simply for the time to ride:
A Yeoman, in a coat and hood of green.
His peacock-feathered arrows, bright and keen,
He carried under his belt in tidy fashion.
For well-kept gear he had a yeoman's passion.
No draggled feather might his arrows show,
And in his hand he held a mighty bow.
He kept his hair close-cropped, his face was brown.
He knew the lore of woodcraft up and down.
His arm was guarded from the bowstring's whip
110 By a bracer, gaily trimmed. He had at hip
A sword and buckler, and at his other side
A dagger whose fine mounting was his pride,
Sharp-pointed as a spear. His horn he bore
In a sling of green, and on his chest he wore
A silver image of St. Christopher,
His patron, since he was a forester.
      There was also a Nun, a Prioress,
Whose smile was gentle and full of guilelessness.
"By St. Loy!" was the worst oath she would say.
120 She sang mass well, in a becoming way,
Intoning through her nose the words divine,
And she was known as Madame Eglantine.

She spoke good French, as taught at Stratford-Bow,[3]
For the Parisian French she did not know.
She was schooled to eat so primly and so well
That from her lips no morsel ever fell.
She wet her fingers lightly in the dish
Of sauce, for courtesy was her first wish.
With every bite she did her skillful best
130 To see that no drop fell upon her breast.
She always wiped her upper lip so clean
That in her cup was never to be seen
A hint of grease when she had drunk her share.
She reached out for her meat with comely air.
She was a great delight, and always tried
To imitate court ways, and had her pride,
Both amiable and gracious in her dealings.
As for her charity and tender feelings,
She melted at whatever was piteous.
140 She would weep if she but came upon a mouse
Caught in a trap, if it were dead or bleeding.
Some little dogs that she took pleasure feeding
On roasted meat or milk or good wheat bread
She had, but how she wept to find one dead
Or yelping from a blow that made it smart,
And all was sympathy and loving heart.
Neat was her wimple in its every plait,
Her nose well formed, her eyes as gray as slate.
Her mouth was very small and soft and red.
150 She had so wide a brow I think her head
Was nearly a span broad, for certainly
She was not undergrown, as all could see.
She wore her cloak with dignity and charm,
And had her rosary about her arm,
The small beads coral and the larger green,
And from them hung a brooch of golden sheen,
On it a large A and a crown above;
Beneath, "All things are subject unto love."
     A Priest accompanied her toward Canterbury,
160 And an attendant Nun, her secretary.
     There was a Monk, and nowhere was his peer,
A hunter, and a roving overseer.
He was a manly man, and fully able
To be an abbot. He kept a hunting stable,

---

[3] **Stratford-Bow:** A convent in Middlesex, near London.

And when he rode the neighborbood could hear
His bridle jingling in the wind as clear
And loud as if it were a chapel bell.
Wherever he was master of a cell
The principles of good St. Benedict,
170 For being a little old and somewhat strict,
Were honored in the breach, as past their prime.
He lived by the fashion of a newer time.
He would have swapped that text for a plucked hen
Which says that hunters are not holy men,
Or a monk outside his discipline and rule
Is too much like a fish outside his pool;
That is to say, a monk outside his cloister.
But such a text he deemed not worth an oyster.
I told him his opinion made me glad.
180 Why should he study always and go mad,
Mewed in his cell with only a book for neighbor?
Or why, as Augustine commanded, labor
And sweat his hands? How shall the world be served?
To Augustine be all such toil reserved!
And so he hunted, as was only right.
He had greyhounds as swift as birds in flight.
His taste was all for tracking down the hare,
And what his sport might cost he did not care.
His sleeves I noticed, where they met his hand,
190 Trimmed with gray fur, the finest in the land.
His hood was fastened with a curious pin
Made of wrought gold and clasped beneath his chin,
A love knot at the tip. His head might pass,
Bald as it was, for a lump of shining glass,
And his face was glistening as if anointed.
Fat as a lord he was, and well appointed.
His eyes were large, and rolled inside his head
As if they gleamed from a furnace of hot lead.
His boots were supple, his horse superbly kept.
200 He was a prelate to dream of while you slept.
He was not pale nor peaked like a ghost.
He relished a plump swan as his favorite roast.
He rode a palfrey brown as a ripe berry.
    A Friar was with us, a gay dog and a merry,
Who begged his district with a jolly air.
No friar in all four orders[4] could compare

[4] **all four orders:** The monastic orders: Franciscan, Dominican, Carmelite, and Augustinian.

With him for gallantry; his tongue was wooing.
Many a girl was married by his doing,
And at his own cost it was often done.
210 He was a pillar, and a noble one,
To his whole order. In his neighborhood
Rich franklins⁵ knew him well, who served good food,
And worthy women welcomed him to town;
For the license that his order handed down,
He said himself, conferred on him possession
Of more than a curate's power of confession.
Sweetly the list of frailties he heard,
Assigning penance with a pleasant word.
He was an easy man for absolution
220 Where he looked forward to a contribution,
For if to a poor order a man has given
It signifies that he has been well shriven,
And if a sinner let his purse be dented
The Friar would stake his oath he had repented.
For many men become so hard of heart
They cannot weep, though conscience makes them smart.
Instead of tears and prayers, then, let the sinner
Supply the poor friars with the price of dinner.
For pretty women he had more than shrift.
230 His cape was stuffed with many a little gift,
As knives and pins and suchlike. He could sing
A merry note, and pluck a tender string,
And had no rival at all in balladry.
His neck was whiter than a fleur-de-lis°   lily
And yet he could have knocked a strong man down.
He knew the taverns well in every town.
The barmaids and innkeepers pleased his mind
Better than beggars and lepers and their kind.
In his position it was unbecoming
240 Among the wretched lepers to go slumming.
It mocks all decency, it sews no stitch
To deal with such riffraff; but with the rich,
With sellers of victuals, that's another thing.
Wherever he saw some hope of profiting,
None so polite, so humble. He was good,
The champion beggar of his brotherhood.
Should a woman have no shoes against the snow,

---

⁵ **Rich franklins:** Landowners or country gentlemen who were not noblemen.

So pleasant was his *"In principio"*[6]
He would have her widow's mite before he went.
250 He took in far more than he paid in rent
For his right of begging within certain bounds.
None of his brethren trespassed on his grounds!
He loved as freely as a half-grown whelp.
On arbitration-days[7] he gave great help,
For his cloak was never shiny nor threadbare
Like a poor cloistered scholar's. He had an air
As if he were a doctor or a pope.
It took stout wool to make his semicope[8]
That plumped out like a bell for portliness.
260 He lisped a little in his rakishness
To make his English sweeter on his tongue,
And twanging his harp to end some song he'd sung
His eyes would twinkle in his head as bright
As the stars twinkle on a frosty night.
Hubert this gallant Friar was by name.
        Among the rest a Merchant also came.
He wore a forked beard and a beaver hat
From Flanders. High up in the saddle he sat,
In figured cloth, his boots clasped handsomely,
270 Delivering his opinions pompously,
Always on how his gains might be increased.
At all costs he desired the sea policed
From Middleburg in Holland to Orwell.
He knew the exchange rates, and the time to sell
French currency, and there was never yet
A man who could have told he was in debt
So grave he seemed and hid so well his feelings
With all his shrewd engagements and close dealings.
You'd find no better man at any turn;
280 But what his name was I could never learn.
        There was an Oxford Student too, it chanced,
Already in his logic well advanced.
He rode a mount as skinny as a rake,
And he was hardly fat. For learning's sake
He let himself look hollow and sober enough.
He wore an outer coat of threadbare stuff,
For he had no benefice for his enjoyment

---

[6] *"In principio"*: "In the beginning"—the opening phrase of the Gospel of St. John; the friar uses Latin ostentatiously to puff up his authority.   [7] **arbitration-days**: Special days for settling disputes.   [8] **semicope**: A cape or jacket.

And was too unworldly for some lay employment.
He much preferred to have beside his bed
290 His twenty volumes bound in black or red
All packed with Aristotle from end to middle
Than a sumptuous wardrobe or a merry fiddle.
For though he knew what learning had to offer
There was little coin to jingle in his coffer.
Whatever he got by touching up a friend
On books and learning he would promptly spend
And busily pray for the soul of anybody
Who furnished him the wherewithal for study.
His scholarship was what he truly heeded.
300 He never spoke a word more than was needed,
And that was said with dignity and force,
And quick and brief. He was of grave discourse,
Giving new weight to virtue by his speech,
And gladly would he learn and gladly teach.

  There was a Lawyer, cunning and discreet,
Who had often been to St. Paul's porch to meet
His clients. He was a Sergeant of the Law,
A man deserving to be held in awe,
Or so he seemed, his manner was so wise.
310 He had often served as Justice of Assize
By the king's appointment, with a broad commission,
For his knowledge and his eminent position.
He had many a handsome gift by way of fee.
There was no buyer of land as shrewd as he.
All ownership to him became fee simple.[9]
His titles were never faulty by a pimple.
None was so busy as he with case and cause,
And yet he seemed much busier than he was.
In all cases and decisions he was schooled
320 That were of record since King William[10] ruled.
No one could pick a loophole or a flaw
In any lease or contract he might draw.
Each statute on the books he knew by rote.
He traveled in a plain, silk-belted coat.

  A Franklin traveled in his company.
Whiter could never daisy petal be
Than was his beard. His ruddy face gave sign
He liked his morning sop of toast in wine.

---

[9] **fee simple:** Ownership without legal restrictions.   [10] **King William:** William the Conqueror (ruled 1066–1087 C.E.).

He lived in comfort, as he would assure us,
330 For he was a true son of Epicurus[11]
Who held the opinion that the only measure
Of perfect happiness was simply pleasure.
Such hospitality did he provide,
He was St. Julian[12] to his countryside
His bread and ale were always up to scratch.
He had a cellar none on earth could match.
There was no lack of pasties in his house,
Both fish and flesh, and that so plenteous
That where he lived it snowed of meat and drink.
340 With every dish of which a man can think,
After the various seasons of the year,
He changed his diet for his better cheer.
He had coops of partridges as fat as cream,
He had a fishpond stocked with pike and bream.
Woe to his cook for an unready pot
Or a sauce that wasn't seasoned and spiced hot!
A table in his hall stood on display
Prepared and covered through the livelong day.
He presided at court sessions for his bounty
350 And sat in Parliament often for his county.
A well-wrought dagger and a purse of silk
Hung at his belt, as white as morning milk.
He had been a sheriff and county auditor.
On earth was no such rich proprietor!
. . .

With us came also an astute Physician.
400 There was none like him for a disquisition
On the art of medicine or surgery,
For he was grounded in astrology.
He kept his patient long in observation,
Choosing the proper hour for application
Of charms and images by intuition
Of magic, and the planets' best position.
For he was one who understood the laws
That rule the humors, and could tell the cause
That brought on every human malady,
410 Whether of hot or cold, or moist or dry.
He was a perfect medico, for sure.

---

[11] **Epicurus:** Greek philosopher (341–270 B.C.E.); taught that refined pleasure was the greatest good.
[12] **St. Julian:** Patron saint of hospitality.

The cause once known, he would prescribe the cure,
For he had his druggists ready at a motion
To provide the sick man with some pill or potion—
A game of mutual aid, with each one winning.
Their partnership was hardly just beginning!
He was well versed in his authorities,
Old Aesculapius, Dioscorides,
Rufus, and old Hippocrates, and Galen,
420 Haly, and Rhazes, and Serapion,
Averroës, Bernard, Johannes Damascenus,
Avicenna, Gilbert, Gaddesden, Constantinus.[13]
He urged a moderate fare on principle,
But rich in nourishment, digestible;
Of nothing in excess would he admit.
He gave but little heed to Holy Writ.
His clothes were lined with taffeta; their hue
Was all of blood red and of Persian blue,
Yet he was far from careless of expense.
430 He saved his fees from times of pestilence,
For gold is a cordial, as physicians hold,
And so he had a special love for gold.

    A worthy woman there was from near the city
Of Bath, but somewhat deaf, and more's the pity.
For weaving she possessed so great a bent
She outdid the people of Ypres and of Ghent.[14]
No other woman dreamed of such a thing
As to precede her at the offering,
Or if any did, she fell in such a wrath
440 She dried up all the charity in Bath.
She wore fine kerchiefs of old-fashioned air,
And on a Sunday morning, I could swear,
She had ten pounds of linen on her head.
Her stockings were of finest scarlet-red,
Laced tightly, and her shoes were soft and new.
Bold was her face, and fair, and red in hue.
She had been an excellent woman all her life.
Five men in turn had taken her to wife,
Omitting other youthful company—
450 But let that pass for now! Over the sea
She had traveled freely; many a distant stream
She crossed, and visited Jerusalem

---

[13] **Aesculapius . . . Constantinus:** Ancient and medieval medical authorities from Greece, Arabia, and England.
[14] **Ypres . . . Ghent:** Cities in Flanders renowned for their textiles.

Three times. She had been at Rome and at Boulogne,
At the shrine of Compostella, and at Cologne.[15]
She had wandered by the way through many a scene.
Her teeth were set with little gaps between.
Easily on her ambling horse she sat.
She was well wimpled, and she wore a hat
As wide in circuit as a shield or targe.[16]
460 A skirt swathed up her hips, and they were large.
Upon her feet she wore sharp-roweled spurs.
She was a good fellow; a ready tongue was hers.
All remedies of love she knew by name,
For she had all the tricks of that old game.

     There was a good man of the priest's vocation,
A poor town Parson of true consecration,
But he was rich in holy thought and work.
Learned he was, in the truest sense a clerk
Who meant Christ's gospel faithfully to preach
470 And truly his parishioners to teach.
He was a kind man, full of industry,
Many times tested by adversity
And always patient. If tithes[17] were in arrears,
He was loth to threaten any man with fears
Of excommunication; past a doubt
He would rather spread his offering about
To his poor flock, or spend his property.
To him a little meant sufficiency.
Wide was his parish, with houses far asunder,
480 But he would not be kept by rain or thunder,
If any had suffered a sickness or a blow,
From visiting the farthest, high or low,
Plodding his way on foot, his staff in hand.
He was a model his flock could understand,
For first he did and afterward he taught.
That precept from the Gospel he had caught,
And he added as a metaphor thereto,
"If the gold rusts, what will the iron do?"
For if a priest is foul, in whom we trust,
490 No wonder a layman shows a little rust.
A priest should take to heart the shameful scene
Of shepherds filthy while the sheep are clean.
By his own purity a priest should give
The example to his sheep, how they should live.

---

[15] Compostella . . . Cologne: Shrines famous during the Middle Ages.   [16] targe: A small shield.   [17] tithes: Regular offerings to the church.

He did not rent his benefice[18] for hire,
Leaving his flock to flounder in the mire,
And run to London, happiest of goals,
To sing paid masses in St. Paul's for souls,
Or as chaplain from some rich guild take his keep,
500 But dwelt at home and guarded well his sheep
So that no wolf should make his flock miscarry.
He was a shepherd, and not a mercenary.
And though himself a man of strict vocation
He was not harsh to weak souls in temptation,
Not overbearing nor haughty in his speech,
But wise and kind in all he tried to teach.
By good example and just words to turn
Sinners to heaven was his whole concern.
But should a man in truth prove obstinate,
510 Whoever he was, of rich or mean estate,
The Parson would give him a snub to meet the case.
I doubt there was a priest in any place
His better. He did not stand on dignity
Nor affect in conscience too much nicety,
But Christ's and his disciples' word he sought
To teach, and first he followed what he taught.

    There was a Plowman with him on the road,
His brother, who had forked up many a load
Of good manure. A hearty worker he,
520 Living in peace and perfect charity.
Whether his fortune made him smart or smile,
He loved God with his whole heart all the while
And his neighbor as himself. He would undertake,
For every luckless poor man, for the sake
Of Christ to thresh and ditch and dig by the hour
And with no wage, if it was in his power.
His tithes on goods and earnings he paid fair.
He wore a coarse, rough coat and rode a mare.

    There also were a Manciple, a Miller,
530 A Reeve, a Summoner, and a Pardoner,
And I — this makes our company complete.

    As tough a yokel as you care to meet
The Miller was. His big-beefed arms and thighs
Took many a ram put up as wrestling prize.
He was a thick, squat-shouldered lump of sins.
No door but he could heave it off its pins

---

[18] **benefice:** His appointment as pastor.

Or break it running at it with his head.
His beard was broader than a shovel, and red
As a fat sow or fox. A wart stood clear
540 Atop his nose, and red as a pig's ear
A tuft of bristles on it. Black and wide
His nostrils were. He carried at his side
A sword and buckler. His mouth would open out
Like a great furnace, and he would sing and shout
His ballads and jokes of harlotries and crimes.
He could steal corn and charge for it three times,
And yet was honest enough, as millers come,
For a miller, as they say, has a golden thumb.
In white coat and blue hood this lusty clown,
550 Blowing his bagpipes, brought us out of town.
     The Manciple was of a lawyers' college,
And other buyers might have used his knowledge
How to be shrewd provisioners, for whether
He bought on cash or credit, altogether
He managed that the end should be the same:
He came out more than even with the game.
Now isn't it an instance of God's grace
How a man of little knowledge can keep pace
In wit with a whole school of learned men?
560 He had masters to the number of three times ten
Who knew each twist of equity and tort;
A dozen in that very Inn of Court
Were worthy to be steward of the estate
To any of England's lords, however great,
And keep him to his income well confined
And free from debt, unless he lost his mind
Or let him scrimp, if he were mean in bounty;
They could have given help to a whole county
In any sort of case that might befall;
570 And yet this Manciple could cheat them all!
     The Reeve was a slender, fiery-tempered man.
He shaved as closely as a razor can.
His hair was cropped about his ears, and shorn
Above his forehead as a priest's is worn.
His legs were very long and very lean.
No calf on his lank spindles could be seen.
But he knew how to keep a barn or bin,
He could play the game with auditors and win.
He knew well how to judge by drought and rain
580 The harvest of his seed and of his grain.
His master's cattle, swine, and poultry flock,

Horses and sheep and dairy, all his stock,
Were altogether in this Reeve's control.
And by agreement, he had given the sole
Accounting since his lord reached twenty years.
No man could ever catch him in arrears.
There wasn't a bailiff, shepherd, or farmer working
But the Reeve knew all his tricks of cheating and shirking.
He would not let him draw an easy breath.
590   They feared him as they feared the very death.
He lived in a good house on an open space,
Well shaded by green trees, a pleasant place.
He was shrewder in acquisition than his lord.
With private riches he was amply stored.
He had learned a good trade young by work and will.
He was a carpenter of first-rate skill.
On a fine mount, a stallion, dappled gray,
Whose name was Scot, he rode along the way.
He wore a long blue coat hitched up and tied
600   As if it were a friar's, and at his side
A sword with rusty blade was hanging down.
He came from Norfolk, from nearby the town
That men call Bawdswell. As we rode the while,
The Reeve kept always hindmost in our file.

　　A Summoner in our company had his place.
Red as the fiery cherubim his face.
He was pocked and pimpled, and his eyes were narrow.
He was lecherous and hot as a cock sparrow.
His brows were scabby and black, and thin his beard.
610   His was a face that little children feared.
Brimstone or litharge bought in any quarter,
Quicksilver, ceruse, borax, oil of tartar,
No salve nor ointment that will cleanse or bite
Could cure him of his blotches, livid white,
Or the nobs and nubbins sitting on his cheeks.
He loved his garlic, his onions, and his leeks.
He loved to drink the strong wine down blood-red.
Then would he bellow as if he had lost his head,
And when he had drunk enough to parch his drouth,
620   Nothing but Latin issued from his mouth.
He had smattered up a few terms, two or three,
That he had gathered out of some decree —
No wonder; he heard law Latin all the day,
And everyone knows a parrot or a jay
Can cry out "Wat" or "Poll" as well as the pope;
But give him a strange term, he began to grope.

His little store of learning was paid out,
So *"Questio quod juris"*[19] he would shout.
He was a goodhearted bastard and a kind one.
630 If there were better, it was hard to find one.
He would let a good fellow, for a quart of wine,
The whole year round enjoy his concubine
Scot-free from summons, hearing, fine; or bail,
And on the sly he too could flush a quail.
If he liked a scoundrel, no matter for church law.
He would teach him that he need not stand in awe
If the archdeacon threatened with his curse —
That is, unless his soul was in his purse,
For in his purse he would be punished well.
640 "The purse," he said, "is the archdeacon's hell."
Of course I know he lied in what he said.
There is nothing a guilty man should so much dread
As the curse that damns his soul, when, without fail,
The church can save him, or send him off to jail.
He had the young men and girls in his control
Throughout the diocese; he knew the soul
Of youth, and heard their every last design.
A garland big enough to be the sign
Above an alehouse balanced on his head,
650 And he made a shield of a great round loaf of bread.
      There was a Pardoner of Rouncivalle[20]
With him, of the blessed Mary's hospital,
But now come straight from Rome (or so said he).
Loudly he sang, "Come hither, love, to me,"
While the Summoner's counterbass trolled out profound —
No trumpet blew with half so vast a sound.
This Pardoner had hair as yellow as wax,
But it hung as smoothly as a hank of flax.
His locks trailed down in bunches from his head,
660 And he let the ends about his shoulders spread,
But in thin clusters, lying one by one.
Of hood, for rakishness, he would have none,
For in his wallet he kept it safely stowed.
He traveled, as he thought, in the latest mode,
Disheveled. Save for his cap, his head was bare,
And in his eyes he glittered like a hare.
A Veronica[21] was stitched upon his cap,

---

[19] *"Questio quod juris"*: "The question is, what law?," i.e., what law applies? [20] **Rouncivalle**: A religious house and hospital outside of London. [21] **A Veronica**: A copy of the veil of St. Veronica, said to have imprinted the image of Christ's face when Veronica used it to wipe Jesus' face on his way to the Crucifixion.

His wallet lay before him in his lap
Brimful of pardons from the very seat
670 In Rome. He had a voice like a goat's bleat.
He was beardless and would never have a beard.
His cheek was always smooth as if just sheared.
I think he was a gelding or a mare;
But in his trade, from Berwick down to Ware,
No pardoner could beat him in the race,
For in his wallet he had a pillow case
Which he represented as Our Lady's veil;
He said he had a piece of the very sail
St. Peter, when he fished in Galilee
680 Before Christ caught him, used upon the sea.
He had a latten[22] cross embossed with stones
And in a glass he carried some pig's bones,
And with these holy relics, when he found
Some village parson grubbing his poor ground,
He would get more money in a single day
Than in two months would come the parson's way.
Thus with his flattery and his trumped-up stock
He made dupes of the parson and his flock.
But though his conscience was a little plastic
690 He was in church a noble ecclesiastic.
Well could he read the Scripture or saint's story,
But best of all he sang the offertory,
For he understood that when this song was sung,
Then he must preach, and sharpen up his tongue
To rake in cash, as well he knew the art,
And so he sang out gaily, with full heart.
        Now I have set down briefly, as it was,
Our rank, our dress, our number, and the cause
That made our sundry fellowship begin
700 In Southwark, at this hospitable inn
Known as the Tabard, not far from the Bell.
But what we did that night I ought to tell,
And after that our journey, stage by stage,
And the whole story of our pilgrimage.
But first, in justice, do not look askance
I plead, nor lay it to my ignorance
If in this matter I should use plain speech
And tell you just the words and style of each
Reporting all their language faithfully.

---

[22] **latten**: A metal alloy.

710 For it must be known to you as well as me
That whoever tells a story after a man
Must follow him as closely as he can.
If he takes the tale in charge, he must be true
To every word, unless he would find new
Or else invent a thing or falsify.
Better some breadth of language than a lie!
He may not spare the truth to save his brother.
He might as well use one word as another.
In Holy Writ Christ spoke in a broad sense,
720 And surely his word is without offense.
Plato, if his are pages you can read,
Says let the word be cousin to the deed.
So I petition your indulgence for it
If I have cut the cloth just as men wore it,
Here in this tale, and shown its very weave.
My wits are none too sharp, you must believe.
        Our Host gave each of us a cheerful greeting
And promptly of our supper had us eating.
The victuals that he served us were his best.
730 The wine was potent, and we drank with zest.
Our Host cut such a figure, all in all,
He might have been a marshal in a hall.
He was a big man, and his eyes bulged wide,
No sturdier citizen lived in all Cheapside.[23]
Lacking no trace of manhood, bold in speech,
Prudent, and well versed in what life can teach,
And with all this he was a jovial man.
And so when supper ended he began
To jolly us, when all our debts were clear.
740 "Welcome," he said. "I have not seen this year
So merry a company in this tavern as now,
And I would give you pleasure if I knew how.
And just this very minute a plan has crossed
My mind that might amuse you at no cost.
        "You go to Canterbury — may the Lord
Speed you, and may the martyred saint reward
Your journey! And to while the time away
You mean to talk and pass the time of day,
For you would be as cheerful all alone
750 As riding on your journey dumb as stone.
Therefore, if you'll abide by what I say,

---

[23] **Cheapside:** A commercial street in London.

Tomorrow, when you ride off on your way,
Now, by my father's soul, and he is dead,
If you don't enjoy yourselves, cut off my head!
Hold up your hands, if you accept my speech."
    Our counsel did not take us long to reach.
We bade him give his orders at his will.
"Well, sirs," he said, "then do not take it ill,
But hear me in good part, and for your sport,
760 Each one of you, to make our journey short,
Shall tell two stories, as we ride, I mean,
Toward Canterbury; and coming home again
Shall tell two other tales he may have heard
Of happenings that some time have occurred.
And the one of you whose stories please us most,
Here in this tavern, sitting by this post
Shall sup at our expense while we make merry
When we come riding home from Canterbury.
And to cheer you still the more, I too will ride
770 With you at my own cost, and be your guide.
And if anyone my judgment shall gainsay
He must pay for all we spend along the way.
If you agree, no need to stand and reason
Tell me, and I'll be stirring in good season."
    This thing was granted, and we swore our pledge
To take his judgment on our pilgrimage,
His verdict on our tales, and his advice.
He was to plan a supper at a price
Agreed upon; and so we all assented
780 To this command, and we were well contented.
The wine was fetched; we drank, and went to rest.
    Next morning, when the dawn was in the east,
Up sprang our Host, who acted as our cock,
And gathered us together in a flock,
And off we rode, till presently our pace
Had brought us to St. Thomas' watering place.
And there our host began to check his horse.
"Good sirs," he said, "you know your promise, of course.
Shall I remind you what it was about?
790 If evensong and matins don't fall out,
We'll soon find who shall tell us the first tale.
But as I hope to drink my wine and ale,
Whoever won't accept what I decide
Pays everything we spend along the ride.
Draw lots, before we're farther from the Inn.
Whoever draws the shortest shall begin.

Sir Knight," said he, "my master, choose your straw.
Come here, my lady Prioress, and draw,
And you, Sir Scholar, don't look thoughtful, man!
800 Pitch in now, everyone!" So all began
To draw the lots, and as the luck would fall
The draw went to the Knight, which pleased us all.
And when this excellent man saw how it stood,
Ready to keep his promise, he said, "Good!
Since it appears that I must start the game,
Why then, the draw is welcome, in God's name.
Now let's ride on, and listen, what I say."
And with that word we rode forth on our way,
And he, with his courteous manner and good cheer,
810 Began to tell his tale, as you shall hear.
. . .

Prologue to the Wife of Bath's Tale

"Experience, though all authority
Was lacking in the world, confers on me
The right to speak of marriage, and unfold
Its woes. For, lords, since I was twelve years old
— Thanks to eternal God in heaven alive —
I have married at church door no less than five
Husbands, provided that I can have been
So often wed, and all were worthy men.
But I was told, indeed, and not long since,
10   That Christ went to a wedding only once
At Cana, in the land of Galilee.
By this example he instructed me
To wed once only — that's what I have heard!
Again, consider now what a sharp word,
Beside a well, Jesus, both God and man,
Spoke in reproving the Samaritan:
'Thou hast had five husbands' — this for a certainty
He said to her — and the man that now hath thee
Is not thy husband.' True, he spoke this way,
20   But what he meant is more than I can say
Except that I would ask why the fifth man
Was not a husband to the Samaritan?
To just how many could she be a wife?
I have never heard this number all my life
Determined up to now. For round and round
Scholars may gloze, interpret, and expound,

But plainly, this I know without a lie,
God told us to increase and multiply.
That noble text I can well understand.
30 My husband—this too I have well in hand—
Should leave both father and mother and cleave to me.
Number God never mentioned, bigamy,
No, nor even octogamy; why do men
Talk of it as a sin and scandal, then?
    "Think of that monarch, wise King Solomon.[24]
It strikes me that *he* had more wives than one!
To be refreshed, God willing, would please me
If I got it half as many times as he!
What a gift he had, a gift of God's own giving,
40 For all his wives! There isn't a man now living
Who·has the like. By all that I make out
This king had many a merry first-night bout
With each, he was so thoroughly alive.
Blessed be God that I have married five,
And always, for the money in his chest
And for his nether purse, I picked the best.
In divers schools ripe scholarship is made,
And various practice in all kinds of trade
Makes perfect workmen, as the world can see.
50 Five husbands have had turns at schooling me.
Welcome the sixth, whenever I am faced
With yet another. I don't mean to be chaste
At all costs. When a spouse of mine is gone,
Some other Christian man shall take me on,
For then, says the Apostle,[25] I'll be free
To wed, in God's name, where it pleases me.
To marry is no sin, as we can learn
From him; better to marry than to burn,
He says. Why should I care what obloquy
60 Men heap on Lamech[26] and his bigamy?
Abraham was, by all that I can tell,
A holy man; so Jacob was as well,
And each of them took more than two as brides,
And many another holy man besides.
Where, may I ask, in any period,
Can you show in plain words that Almighty God

---

[24] **King Solomon:** Solomon had 700 wives and 300 concubines (1 Kings 2:3).   [25] **the Apostle:** St. Paul, who recommends in 1 Corinthians 7:8–9 that celibacy is preferable to marriage, marriage to promiscuity.   [26] **Lamech:** A man with two wives (Genesis 4:19–24).

Forbade us marriage? Point it out to me!
Or where did he command virginity?
The Apostle, when he speaks of maidenhood,
70 Lays down no law. This I have understood
As well as you, milords, for it is plain.
Men may advise a woman to abstain
From marriage, but mere counsels aren't commands.
He left it to our judgment, where it stands.
Had God enjoined us all to maidenhood
Then marriage would have been condemned for good.
But truth is, if no seed were ever sown,
In what soil could virginity be grown?
Paul did not dare command a thing at best
80 On which his Master left us no behest.
          "But now the prize goes to virginity.
Seize it whoever can, and let us see
What manner of man shall run best in the race!
But not all men receive this form of grace
Except where God bestows it by his will.
The Apostle was a maid, I know; but still,
Although he wished all men were such as he,
It was only *counsel* toward virginity.
To be a wife he gave me his permission,
90 And so it is no blot on my condition
Nor slander of bigamy upon my state
If when my husband dies I take a mate.
A man does virtuously, St. Paul has said,
To touch no woman — meaning in his bed.
For fire and fat are dangerous friends at best.
You know what this example should suggest.
Here is the nub: he held virginity
Superior to wedded frailty,
And frailty I call it unless man
100 And woman both are chaste for their whole span.
          "I am not jealous if maidenhood outweighs
My marriages; I grant it all the praise.
It pleases them, these virgins, flesh and soul
To be immaculate. I won't extol
My own condition. In a lord's household
You know that every vessel can't be gold.
Some are of wood, and serve their master still.
God calls us variously to do his will.
Each has his proper gift, of all who live,
110 Some this, some that, as it pleases God to give.
          "To be virgin is a high and perfect course,

And continence is holy. But the source
Of all perfection, Jesus, never bade
Each one of us to go sell all he had
And give it to the poor; he did not say
That all should follow him in this one way.
He spoke to those who would live perfectly,
And by your leave, lords, that is not for me!
The flower of my best years I find it suits
120 To spend on the acts of marriage and its fruits.
   "Tell me this also: why at our creation
Were organs given us for generation,
And for what profit were we creatures made?
Believe me, not for nothing! Ply his trade
Of twisting texts who will, and let him urge
That they were only given us to purge
Our urine; say without them we should fail
To tell a female rightly from a male
And that's their only object—say you so?
130 It won't work, as experience will show.
Without offense to scholars, I say this,
They were given us for both these purposes,
That we may both be cleansed, I mean, and eased
Through intercourse, where God is not displeased.
Why else in books is this opinion met,
That every man should pay his wife his debt?
Tell me with what a man should hope to pay
Unless he put his instrument in play?
They were supplied us, then, for our purgation,
140 But they were also meant for generation.
   "But none the less I do not mean to say
That all those who are furnished in this way
Are bound to go and practice intercourse.
The world would then grant chastity no force.
Christ was a maid, yet he was formed a man,
And many a saint, too, since the world began,
And yet they lived in perfect chastity.
I am not spiteful toward virginity.
Let virgins be white bread of pure wheat-seed.
150 Barley we wives are called, and yet I read
In Mark, and tell the tale in truth he can,
That Christ with barley bread cheered many a man.[27]

---

[27] **That Christ . . . a man:** The miracle of feeding some five thousand people with five loaves and two fishes
(Mark 8:1–21; John 6:9).

In the state that God assigned to each of us
I'll persevere. I'm not fastidious.
In wifehood I will use my instrument
As freely by my Maker it was lent.
If I hold back with it, God give me sorrow!
My husband shall enjoy it night and morrow
When it pleases him to come and pay his debt.
160   But a husband, and I've not been thwarted yet,
Shall always be my debtor and my slave.
From tribulation he shall never save
His flesh, not for as long as I'm his wife!
I have the power, during all my life,
Over his very body, and not he.
For so the Apostle has instructed me,
Who bade men love their wives for better or worse.
It pleases me from end to end, that verse!"
      The Pardoner, before she could go on,
170   Jumped up and cried, "By God and by St. John,
Upon this topic you preach nobly, Dame!
I was about to wed, but now, for shame,
Why should my body pay a price so dear?
I'd rather not be married all this year!"
      "Hold on," she said. "I haven't yet begun.
You'll drink a keg of this before I'm done,
I promise you, and it won't taste like ale!
And after I have told you my whole tale
Of marriage, with its fund of tribulation—
180   And I'm the expert of my generation,
For I myself, I mean, have been the whip—
You can decide then if you want a sip
Out of the barrel that I mean to broach.
Before you come too close in your approach,
Think twice. I have examples, more than ten!
'The man who won't be warned by other men,
To other men a warning he shall be.'
These are the words we find in Ptolemy.
You can read them right there in his *Almagest*."[28]
190   "Now, Madame, if you're willing, I suggest,"
Answered the Pardoner, "as you began,
Continue with your tale, and spare no man.
Teach us your practice—we young men need a guide."
      "Gladly, if it will please you," she replied.

---

[28] *Almagest:* This aphorism appears not in the *Almagest* but in a collection of Ptolemy's writings.

"But first I ask you, if I speak my mind,
That all this company may be well inclined,
And will not take offense at what I say.
I only mean it, after all, in play.
　　"Now, sirs, I will get onward with my tale.
200　If ever I hope to drink good wine or ale,
I'm speaking truth: the husbands I have had,
Three of them have been good, and two were bad.
The three were kindly men, and rich, and old.
But they were hardly able to uphold
The statute which had made them fast to me.
You know well what I mean by this, I see!
So help me God, I can't help laughing yet
When I think of how at night I made them sweat,
And I thought nothing of it, on my word!
210　Their land and wealth they had by then conferred
On me, and so I safely could neglect
Tending their love or showing them respect.
So well they loved me that by God above
I hardly set a value on their love.
A woman who is wise is never done
Busily winning love when she has none,
But since I had them wholly in my hand
And they had given me their wealth and land,
Why task myself to spoil them or to please
220　Unless for my own profit and my ease?
I set them working so that many a night
They sang a dirge, so grievous was their plight!
They never got the bacon, well I know,
Offered as prize to couples at Dunmow[29]
Who live a year in peace without repentance!
So well I ruled them, by my law and sentence,
They were glad to bring me fine things from the fair
And happy when I spoke with a mild air,
For God knows I could chide outrageously.
230　　"Now judge if I could do it properly!
You wives who understand and who are wise,
This is the way to throw dust in their eyes.
There isn't on the earth so bold a man
He can swear false or lie as a woman can.
I do not urge this course in every case,

---

[29] **the bacon . . . at Dunmow:** A town in southeastern England that awarded such a prize to couples who had
no quarrels or doubts about marriage for a year after their wedding.

Just when a prudent wife is caught off base;
Then she should swear the parrot's mad who tattled
Her indiscretions, and when she's once embattled
Should call her maid as witness, by collusion.
240 But listen, how I threw them in confusion:
      "'Sir dotard, this is how you live?' I'd say.
'How can my neighbor's wife be dressed so gay?
She carries off the honors everywhere.
I sit at home. I've nothing fit to wear.
What were you doing at my neighbor's house?
Is she so handsome? Are you so amorous?
What do you whisper to our maid? God bless me,
Give up your jokes, old lecher. They depress me.
When I have a harmless friend myself, you balk
250 And scold me like a devil if I walk
For innocent amusement to his house.
You drink and come home reeling like a souse
And sit down on your bench, worse luck, and preach.
Taking a wife who's poor — this is the speech
That you regale me with — costs grievously,
And if she's rich and of good family,
It is a constant torment, you decide,
To suffer her ill humor and her pride.
And if she's fair, you scoundrel, you destroy her
260 By saying that every lecher will enjoy her;
For chastity at best has frail protections
If a woman is assailed from all directions.
      "'Some want us for our wealth, so you declare,
Some for our figure, some think we are fair,
Some want a woman who can dance or sing,
Some want kindness, and some philandering,
Some look for hands and arms well turned and small.
Thus, by your tale, the devil may take us all!
Men cannot keep a castle or redoubt
270 Longer, you tell me, than it can hold out.
Or if a woman's plain, you say that she
Is one who covets each man she may see,
For at him like a spaniel she will fly
Until she finds some man that she can buy.
Down to the lake goes never a goose so gray
But it will have a mate, I've heard you say.
It's hard to fasten — this too I've been told —
A thing that no man willingly will hold.
Wise men, you tell me as you go to bed,
280 And those who hope for heaven should never wed.

I hope wild lightning and a thunderstroke
Will break your wizened neck! You say that smoke
And falling timbers and a railing wife
Drive a man from his house. Lord bless my life!
What ails an old man, so to make him chide?
We cover our vices till the knot is tied,
We wives, you say, and then we trot them out.
Here's a fit proverb for a doddering lout!
An ox or ass, you say, a hound or horse,
290 These we examine as a matter of course.
Basins and also bowls, before we buy them,
Spoons, spools, and such utensils, first we try them,
And so with pots and clothes, beyond denial;
But of their wives men never make a trial
Until they are married. After that, you say,
Old fool, we put our vices on display.
    "'I am in a pique if you forget your duty
And fail, you tell me, to praise me for my beauty,
Or unless you are always doting on my face
300 And calling me "fair dame" in every place,
Or unless you give a feast on my birthday
To keep me in good spirits, fresh and gay,
Or unless all proper courtesies are paid
To my nurse and also to my chambermaid,
And my father's kin with all their family ties—
You say so, you old barrelful of lies!
    "'Yet just because he has a head of hair
Like shining gold, and squires me everywhere,
You have a false suspicion in your heart
310 Of Jenkin, our apprentice. For my part
I wouldn't have him if you died tomorrow!
But tell me this, or go and live in sorrow:
That chest of yours, why do you hide the keys
Away from me? It's my wealth, if you please,
As much as yours. Will you make a fool of me,
The mistress of our house? You shall not be
Lord of my body and my wealth at once!
No, by St. James himself, you must renounce
One or the other, if it drives you mad!
320 Does it help to spy on me? You would be glad
To lock me up, I think, inside your chest.
"Enjoy yourself, and go where you think best,"
You ought to say; "I won't hear tales of malice.
I know you for a faithful wife, Dame Alice."
A woman loves no man who keeps close charge

Of where she goes. We want to be at large.
Blessed above all other men was he,
The wise astrologer, Don Ptolemy,
Who has this proverb in his *Almagest:*
330   "Of all wise men his wisdom is the best
Who does not care who has the world in hand."
Now by this proverb you should understand,
Since you have plenty, it isn't yours to care
Or fret how richly other people fare,
For by your leave, old dotard, you for one
Can have all you can take when day is done.
The man's a niggard to the point of scandal
Who will not lend his lamp to light a candle;
His lamp won't lose although the candle gain.
340   If you have enough, you ought not to complain.
     "'You say, too, if we make ourselves look smart,
Put on expensive clothes and dress the part,
We lay our virtue open to disgrace.
And then you try to reinforce your case
By saying these words in the Apostle's name:
"In chaste apparel, with modesty and shame,
So shall you women clothe yourselves," said he,
"And not in rich coiffure or jewelry,
Pearls or the like, or gold, or costly wear."[30]
350   Now both your text and rubric, I declare,
I will not follow as I would a gnat!
     "'You told me once that I was like a cat,
For singe her skin and she will stay at home,
But if her skin is smooth, the cat will roam.
No dawn but finds her on the neighbors calling
To show her skin, and go off caterwauling.
If I am looking smart, you mean to say,
I'm off to put my finery on display.
     "'What do you gain, old fool, by setting spies?
360   Though you beg Argus[31] with his hundred eyes
To be my bodyguard, for all his skill
He'll keep me only by my own free will.
I know enough to blind him, as I live!
     "'There are three things, you also say, that give
Vexation to this world both south and north,

---

[30] **"In chaste apparel . . . costly wear":** Timothy 2:9.   [31] **Argus:** In Greek mythology, a giant with a hundred eyes; the goddess Hera had him spy on her husband, Zeus, who had amorous designs on the beautiful Io.

And you add that no one can endure the fourth.
Of these catastrophes a hateful wife—
You precious wretch, may Christ cut short your life!—
Is always reckoned, as you say, for one.
370   Is this your whole stock of comparison,
And why in all your parables of contempt
Can a luckless helpmate never be exempt?
You also liken woman's love to hell,
To barren land where water will not dwell.
I've heard you call it an unruly fire;
The more it burns, the hotter its desire
To burn up everything that burned will be.
You say that just as worms destroy a tree
A wife destroys her spouse, as they have found
380   Who get themselves in holy wedlock bound.'
       "By these devices, lords, as you perceive,
I got my three old husbands to believe
That in their cups they said things of this sort,
And all of it was false; but for support
Jenkin bore witness, and my niece did too.
These innocents, Lord, what I put them through!
God's precious pains! And they had no recourse,
For I could bite and whinny like a horse.
Though in the wrong, I kept them well annoyed,
390   Or oftentimes I would have been destroyed!
First to the mill is first to grind his grain.
I was always the first one to complain,
And so our peace was made; they gladly bid
For terms to settle things they never did!
       "For wenching I would scold them out of hand
When they were hardly well enough to stand.
But this would tickle a man; it would restore him
To think I had so great a fondness for him!
I'd vow when darkness came and out I stepped,
400   It was to see the girls with whom he slept.
Under this pretext I had plenty of mirth!
Such wit as this is given us at our birth.
Lies, tears, and needlework the Lord will give
In kindness to us women while we live.
And thus in one point I can take just pride:
In the end I showed myself the stronger side.
By sleight or strength I kept them in restraint,
And chiefly by continual complaint.
In bed they met their grief in fullest measure.

410 There I would scold; I would not do their pleasure.
Bed was a place where I would not abide
If I felt my husband's arm across my side
Till he agreed to square accounts and pay,
And after that I'd let him have his way.
To every man, therefore, I tell this tale:
Win where you're able, all is up for sale.
No falcon by an empty hand is lured.
For victory their cravings I endured
And even feigned a show of appetite.
420 And yet in old meat I have no delight;
It made me always rail at them and chide them,
For though the pope himself sat down beside them
I would not give them peace at their own board.
No, on my honor, I paid them word for word.
Almighty God so help me, if right now
I had to make my last will, I can vow
For every word they said to me, we're quits.
For I so handled the contest by my wits
That they gave up, and took it for the best,
430 Or otherwise we should have had no rest.
Like a mad lion let my husband glare,
In the end he got the worst of the affair.

   "Then I would say, 'My dear, you ought to keep
In mind how gentle Wilkin looks, our sheep.
Come here, my husband, let me kiss your cheek!
You should be patient, too; you should be meek.
Of Job and of his patience when you prate
Your conscience ought to show a cleaner slate.
He should be patient who so well can preach.
440 If not, then it will fall on me to teach
The beauty of a peaceful wedded life.
For one of us must give in, man or wife,
And since men are more reasonable creatures
Than women are, it follows that *your* features
Ought to exhibit patience. Why do you groan?
You want my body yours, and yours alone?
Why, take it all! Welcome to every bit!
But curse you, Peter, unless you cherish it!
Were I inclined to peddle my *belle chose,*[32]
450 I could go about dressed freshly as a rose.
But I will keep it for your own sweet tooth.

---

[32] *belle chose:* "Beautiful thing" in French.

It's your fault if we fight. By God, that's truth!'
    "This was the way I talked when I had need.
But now to my fourth husband I'll proceed.
    "This fourth I married was a roisterer.
He had a mistress, and my passions were,
Although I say it, strong; and altogether
I was young and stubborn, pert in every feather.
If anyone took up his harp to play,
460 How I could dance! I sang as merry a lay
As any nightingale when of sweet wine
I had drunk my draft. Metellius, the foul swine,
Who beat his spouse until he took her life
For drinking wine, had I only been his wife,
He'd never have frightened me away from drinking!
But after a drink, Venus gets in my thinking,
For just as true as cold engenders hail
A thirsty mouth goes with a thirsty tail.
Drinking destroys a woman's last defense
470 As lechers well know by experience.
    "But, Lord Christ, when it all comes back to me,
Remembering my youth and jollity,
It tickles me to the roots. It does me good
Down to this very day that while I could
I took my world, my time, and had my fling.
But age, alas, that poisons everything
Has robbed me of my beauty and my pith.
Well, let it go! Good-by! The devil with
What cannot last! There's only this to tell:
480 The flour is gone, I've only chaff to sell.
Yet I'll contrive to keep a merry cheek!
But now of my fourth husband I will speak.
    "My heart was, I can tell you, full of spite
That in another he should find delight.
I paid him for this debt; I made it good.
I furnished him a cross of the same wood,
By God and by St. Joce — in no foul fashion,
Not with my flesh; but I put on such passion
And rendered him so jealous, I'll engage
490 I made him fry in his own grease for rage!
On earth, God knows, I was his purgatory;
I only hope his soul is now in glory.
God knows it was a sad song that he sung
When the shoe pinched him; sorely was he wrung!
Only he knew, and God, the devious system
By which outrageously I used to twist him.

He died when I came home from Jerusalem.
He is buried near the chancel, under the beam
That holds the cross. His tomb is less ornate
500　Than the sepulcher where Darius[33] lies in state
And which the paintings of Appelles graced
With subtle work. It would have been a waste
To bury him lavishly. Farewell! God save
His soul and give him rest! He's in his grave.
　　　"And now of my fifth husband let me tell.
God never let his soul go down to hell
Though he of all five was my scourge and flail!
I feel it on my ribs, right down the scale,
And ever shall until my dying day.
510　And yet he was so full of life and gay
In bed, and could so melt me and cajole me
When on my back he had a mind to roll me,
What matter if on every bone he'd beaten me!
He'd have my love, so quickly he could sweeten me.
I loved him best, in fact; for as you see,
His love was a more arduous prize for me.
We women, if I'm not to tell a lie,
Are quaint in this regard. Put in our eye
A thing we cannot easily obtain,
520　All day we'll cry about it and complain.
Forbid a thing, we want it bitterly,
But urge it on us, then we turn and flee.
We are chary of what we hope that men will buy.
A throng at market makes the prices high;
Men set no value on cheap merchandise,
A truth all women know if they are wise.
　　　"My fifth, may God forgive his every sin,
I took for love, not money. He had been
An Oxford student once, but in our town
530　Was boarding with my good friend, Alison.
She knew each secret that I had to give
More than our parish priest did, as I live!
I told her my full mind, I shared it all.
For if my husband pissed against a wall
Or did a thing that might have cost his life,
To her, and to another neighbor's wife,
And to my niece, a girl whom I loved well,
His every thought I wouldn't blush to tell.

---

[33] **Darius:** Legendary king of Persia (c. 521–486 B.C.E.), notorious for his wealth.

And often enough I told them, be it said.
540 God knows I made his face turn hot and red
For secrets he confided to his shame.
He knew he only had himself to blame.
    "And so it happened once that during Lent,
As I often did, to Alison's I went,
For I have loved my life long to be gay
And to walk out in April or in May
To hear the talk and seek a favorite haunt.
Jenkin the student, Alice, my confidante,
And I myself into the country went.
550 My husband was in London all that Lent.
I had the greater liberty to see
And to be seen by jolly company.
How could I tell beforehand in what place
Luck might be waiting with a stroke of grace?
And so I went to every merrymaking.
No pilgrimage was past my undertaking.
I was at festivals, and marriages,
Processions, preachings, and at miracle plays,
And in my scarlet clothes I made a sight.
560 Upon that costume neither moth nor mite
Nor any worm with ravening hunger fell.
And why, you ask? It was kept in use too well.
    "Now for what happened. In the fields we walked,
The three of us, and gallantly we talked,
The student and I, until I told him he,
If I became a widow, should marry me.
For I can say, and not with empty pride,
I have never failed for marriage to provide
Or other things as well. Let mice be meek;
570 A mouse's heart I hold not worth a leek.
He has one hole to scurry to, just one,
And if that fails him, he is quite undone.
    "I let this student think he had bewitched me.
(My mother with this piece of guile enriched me!)
All night I dreamed of him—this too I said;
He was killing me as I lay flat in bed;
My very bed in fact was full of blood;
But still I hoped it would result in good,
For blood betokens gold, as I have heard.
580 It was a fiction, dream and every word,
But I was following my mother's lore
In all this matter, as in many more.
    "Sirs—let me see; what did I mean to say?

Aha! By God, I have it! When he lay,
My fourth, of whom I've spoken, on his bier,
I wept of course; I showed but little cheer,
As wives must do, since custom has its place,
And with my kerchief covered up my face.
But since I had provided for a mate,
590 I did not cry for long, I'll freely state.
And so to church my husband on the morrow
Was borne away by neighbors in their sorrow.
Jenkin, the student, was among the crowd,
And when I saw him walk, so help me God,
Behind the bier, I thought he had a pair
Of legs and feet so cleanly turned and fair
I put my heart completely in his hold.
He was in fact some twenty winters old
And I was forty, to confess the truth;
600 But all my life I've still had a colt's tooth.
My teeth were spaced apart; that was the seal
St. Venus printed, and became me well.
So help me God, I was a lusty one,
Pretty and young and rich, and full of fun.
And truly, as my husbands have all said,
I was the best thing there could be in bed.
For I belong to Venus in my feelings,
Though I bring the heart of Mars to all my dealings.
From Venus come my lust and appetite,
610 From Mars I get my courage and my might,
Born under Taurus, while Mars stood therein.
Alas, alas, that ever love was sin!
I yielded to my every inclination
Through the predominance of my constellation;
This made me so I never could withhold
My chamber of Venus, if the truth be told,
From a good fellow; yet upon my face
Mars left his mark, and in another place.
For never, so may Christ grant me intercession,
620 Have I yet loved a fellow with discretion,
But always I have followed appetite,
Let him be long or short or dark or light.
I never cared, as long as he liked me,
What his rank was or how poor he might be.
    "What should I say, but when the month ran out,
This jolly student, always much about,
This Jenkin married me in solemn state.
To him I gave land, titles, the whole slate

Of goods that had been given me before;
630 But my repentance afterward was sore!
He wouldn't endure the pleasures I held dear.
By God, he gave me a lick once on the ear,
When from a book of his I tore a leaf,
So hard that from the blow my ear grew deaf.
I was stubborn as a lioness with young,
And by the truth I had a rattling tongue,
And I would visit, as I'd done before,
No matter what forbidding oath he swore.
Against this habit he would sit and preach me
640 Sermons enough, and he would try to teach me
Old Roman stories, how for his whole life
The man Sulpicius Gallus left his wife
Only because he saw her look one day
Bareheaded down the street from his doorway.

    "Another Roman he told me of by name
Who, since his wife was at a summer's game
Without his knowledge, thereupon forsook
The woman. In his Bible he would look
And find that proverb of the Ecclesiast
650 Where he enjoins and makes the stricture fast
That men forbid their wives to rove about.
Then he would quote me this, you needn't doubt:
'Build a foundation over sands or shallows,
Or gallop a blind horse across the fallows,
Let a wife traipse to shrines that some saint hallows,
And you are fit to swing upon the gallows.'
Talk as he would, I didn't care two haws
For his proverbs or his venerable saws.
Set right by him I never meant to be.
660 I hate the man who tells my faults to me,
And more of us than I do, by your pleasure.
This made him mad with me beyond all measure.
Under his yoke in no case would I go.

    "Now, by St. Thomas, I will let you know
Why from that book of his I tore a leaf,
For which I got the blow that made me deaf.

    "He had a book, *Valerius*, he called it,
And *Theophrastus*,[34] and he always hauled it
From where it lay to read both day and night

---

[34] *Valerius . . . Theophrastus:* Walter Map's *Letter of Valerius Concerning Not Marrying* and Theophrastus's *Book Concerning Marriage* are two misogynist treatises in Jenkin's library.

670 And laughed hard at it, such was his delight.
There was another scholar, too, at Rome
A cardinal, whose name was St. Jerome;
He wrote a book against Jovinian.
In the same book also were Tertullian,
Chrysippus, Trotula, Abbess Héloïse
Who lived near Paris; it contained all these,
Bound in a single volume, and many a one
Besides; the Parables of Solomon
And Ovid's *Art of Love.*[35] On such vacation
680 As he could snatch from worldly occupation
He dredged this book for tales of wicked wives.
He knew more stories of their wretched lives
Than are told about good women in the Bible.
No scholar ever lived who did not libel
Women, believe me; to speak well of wives
Is quite beyond them, unless it be in lives
Of holy saints; no woman else will do.
Who was it painted the lion,[36] tell me who?
By God, if women had only written stories
690 Like wits and scholars in their oratories,
They would have pinned on men more wickedness
Than the whole breed of Adam can redress.
Venus's children clash with Mercury's;
The two work evermore by contraries.
Knowledge and wisdom are of Mercury's giving,
Venus loves revelry and riotous living,
And with these clashing dispositions gifted
Each of them sinks when the other is uplifted.
Thus Mercury falls, God knows, in desolation
700 In the sign of Pisces, Venus's exaltation,
And Venus falls when Mercury is raised.
Thus by a scholar no woman can be praised.
The scholar, when he's old and cannot do
The work of Venus more than his old shoe,
Then sits he down, and in his dotage fond
Writes that no woman keeps her marriage bond!
        "But now for the story that I undertook—

---

[35] **St. Jerome . . . Art of Love**: St Jerome's *Reply to Jovinian* accused women of licentiousness; Tertullian wrote treatises on modesty; Chrysippus is a misogynist mentioned in Jerome. Trotula was a female doctor, and Héloïse (Eloise) is the infamous lover of Abelard. Ovid's *Art of Love* and the Parables of Solomon are two other scandalous texts.

[36] **Who . . . the lion**: Aesop tells of a lion who, when shown a picture of a man killing a lion, remarks that lions would draw a picture of the reverse.

To tell how I was beaten for a book.
    "Jenkin, one night, who never seemed to tire
710 Of reading in his book, sat by the fire
And first he read of Eve, whose wickedness
Delivered all mankind to wretchedness
For which in his own person Christ was slain
Who with his heart's blood bought us all again.
'By this,' he said, 'expressly you may find
That woman was the loss of all mankind.'
    "He read me next how Samson lost his hair.
Sleeping, his mistress clipped it off for fair;
Through this betrayal he lost both his eyes.
720 He read me then—and I'm not telling lies—
How Deianeira, wife of Hercules,
Caused him to set himself on fire. With these
He did not overlook the sad to-do
Of Socrates with *his* wives—he had two.
Xantippe emptied the pisspot on his head.
This good man sat as patient as if dead.
He wiped his scalp; he did not dare complain
Except to say 'With thunder must come rain.'
    "Pasiphaë,[37] who was the queen of Crete,
730 For wickedness he thought her story sweet.
Ugh! That's enough, it was a grisly thing,
About her lust and filthy hankering!
And Clytemnestra[38] in her lechery
Who took her husband's life feloniously,
He grew devout in reading of her treason.
And then he told me also for what reason
Unhappy Amphiaraus[39] lost his life.
My husband had the story of *his* wife,
Eriphyle, who for a clasp of gold
740 Went to his Grecian enemies and told
The secret of her husband's hiding place,
For which at Thebes he met an evil grace.
Livia and Lucilia,[40] he went through

---

[37] **Pasiphaë:** Wife of Minos, king of Crete; angered at Minos, Poseidon caused Pasiphaë to fall in love with a bull, after which she gave birth to the Minotaur, part human and part beast.

[38] **Clytemnestra:** Clytemnestra killed her husband, King Agamemnon, on his return from the Trojan War.

[39] **Unhappy Amphiaraus:** Knowing that only her brother Adrastus would survive the war against Thebes, Eriphyle, the wife of Argive warrior Amphiaraus, forced him to go into that battle.

[40] **Livia and Lucilia:** Notorious Roman women who killed their husbands; Lucilia's husband was the poet Lucretius.

Their tale as well, they killed their husbands, too.
One killed for love, the other killed for hate.
At evening Livia, when the hour was late,
Poisoned her husband, for she was his foe.
Lucilia doted on her husband so
That in her lust, hoping to make him think
750   Ever of her, she gave him a love-drink
Of such a sort he died before the morrow.
And so at all turns husbands come to sorrow!
   "He told me then how one Latumius,
Complaining to a friend named Arrius,
Told him that in his garden grew a tree
On which his wives had hanged themselves, all three,
Merely for spite against their partnership.
'Brother,' said Arrius, 'let me have a slip
From this miraculous tree, for, begging pardon,
760   I want to go and plant it in my garden.'
   "Then about wives in recent times he read,
How some had murdered husbands lying abed
And all night long had let a paramour
Enjoy them with the corpse flat on the floor;
Or driven a nail into a husband's brain
While he was sleeping, and thus he had been slain;
And some had given them poison in their drink.
He told more harm than anyone can think,
And seasoned his wretched stories with proverbs
770   Outnumbering all the blades of grass and herbs
On earth. 'Better a dragon for a mate,
Better,' he said, 'on a lion's whims to wait
Than on a wife whose way it is to chide.
Better,' he said, 'high in the loft to bide
Than with a railing wife down in the house.
They always, they are so contrarious,
Hate what their husbands like,' so he would say.
'A woman,' he said, 'throws all her shame away
When she takes off her smock.' And on he'd go:
780   'A pretty woman, unless she's chaste also,
Is like a gold ring stuck in a sow's nose.'
Who could imagine, who would half suppose
The gall my heart drank, raging at each drop?
   "And when I saw that he would never stop
Reading all night from his accursed book,
Suddenly, in the midst of it, I took
Three leaves and tore them out in a great pique,
And with my fist I caught him on the cheek

So hard he tumbled backward in the fire.
790 And up he jumped, he was as mad for ire
As a mad lion, and caught me on the head
With such a blow I fell down as if dead.
And seeing me on the floor, how still I lay,
He was aghast, and would have fled away,
Till I came to at length, and gave a cry.
'Have you killed me for my lands? Before I die,
False thief,' I said, 'I'll give you a last kiss!'
    "He came to me and knelt down close at this,
And said, 'So help me God, dear Alison,
800 I'll never strike you. For this thing I have done
You are to blame. Forgive me, I implore.'
So then I hit him on the cheek once more
And said, 'Thus far I am avenged, you thief.
I cannot speak. Now I shall die for grief.'
But finally, with much care and ado,
We reconciled our differences, we two.
He let me have the bridle in my hand
For management of both our house and land.
To curb his tongue he also undertook,
810 And on the spot I made him burn his book.
And when I had secured in full degree
By right of triumph the whole sovereignty,
And he had said, 'My dear, my own true wife,
Do as you will as long as you have life;
Preserve your honor and keep my estate,'
From that day on we had settled our debate.
I was as kind, God help me, day and dark
As any wife from India to Denmark,
And also true, and so he was to me.
820 I pray the Lord who sits in majesty
To bless his soul for Christ's own mercy dear.
And now I'll tell my tale, if you will hear."
    "Dame," laughed the Friar, "as I hope for bliss,
It was a long preamble to a tale, all this!"
    "God's arms!" the Summoner said, "it is a sin,
Good people, how friars are always butting in!
A fly and a friar will fall in every dish
And every question, whatever people wish.
What do you know, with your talk about 'preambling'?
830 Amble or trot or keep still or go scrambling,
You interrupt our pleasure."
                       "You think so,
Sir Summoner?" said the Friar. "Before I go,

I'll give the people here a chance or two
For a laugh at summoners, I promise you."
    "Curse on your face," the Summoner said, "curse me,
If I don't tell some stories, two or three,
On friars, before I get to Sittingborne,[41]
With which I'll twist your heart and make it mourn,
840   For you have lost your temper, I can see."
    "Be quiet," cried our Host, "immediately,"
And ordered, "Let the woman tell her tale.
You act like people who've got drunk on ale.
Do, Madame, tell us. That is the best measure."
    "All ready, sir," she answered "at your pleasure,
With the license of this worthy Friar here."
    "Madame, tell on," he said. "You have my ear."

THE WIFE OF BATH'S TALE

In the old days when King Arthur ruled the nation,
Whom Welshmen speak of with such veneration,
This realm we live in was a fairy land.
The fairy queen danced with her jolly band
On the green meadows where they held dominion.
This was, as I have read, the old opinion;
I speak of many hundred years ago.
But no one sees an elf now, as you know,
For in our time the charity and prayers
10   And all the begging of these holy friars
Who swarm through every nook and every stream
Thicker than motes of dust in a sunbeam,
Blessing our chambers, kitchens, halls, and bowers,
Our cities, towns, and castles, our high towers,
Our villages, our stables, barns, and dairies,
They keep us all from seeing any fairies,
For where you might have come upon an elf
There now you find the holy friar himself
Working his district on industrious legs
20   And saying his devotions while he begs.
Women are safe now under every tree.
No incubus is there unless it's he,
And all they have to fear from him is shame.
    It chanced that Arthur had a knight who came
Lustily riding home one day from hawking,

---

[41] **Sittingborne:** A town forty miles north of London.

And in his path he saw a maiden walking
Before him, stark alone, right in his course.
This young knight took her maidenhead by force,
A crime at which the outcry was so keen
30 It would have cost his neck, but that the queen,
With other ladies, begged the king so long
That Arthur spared his life, for right or wrong,
And gave him to the queen, at her own will,
According to her choice, to save or kill.

She thanked the king, and later told this knight,
Choosing her time, "You are still in such a plight
Your very life has no security.
I grant your life, if you can answer me
This question: what is the thing that most of all
40 Women desire? Think, or your neck will fall
Under the ax! If you cannot let me know
Immediately, I give you leave to go
A twelvemonth and a day, no more, in quest
Of such an answer as will meet the test.
But you must pledge your honor to return
And yield your body, whatever you may learn."

The knight sighed; he was rueful beyond measure.
But what! He could not follow his own pleasure.
He chose at last upon his way to ride
50 And with such answer as God might provide
To come back when the year was at the close.
And so he takes his leave, and off he goes.

He seeks out every house and every place
Where he has any hope, by luck or grace,
Of learning what thing women covet most.
But it seemed he could not light on any coast
Where on this point two people would agree,
For some said wealth and some said jollity,
Some said position, some said sport in bed
60 And often to be widowed, often wed.
Some said that to a woman's heart what mattered
Above all else was to be pleased and flattered.
That shaft, to tell the truth, was a close hit.
Men win us best by flattery, I admit,
And by attention. Some say our greatest ease
Is to be free and do just as we please,
And not to have our faults thrown in our eyes,
But always to be praised for being wise.
And true enough, there's not one of us all
70 Who will not kick if you rub us on a gall.

Whatever vices we may have within,
We won't be taxed with any fault or sin.
      Some say that women are delighted well
If it is thought that they will never tell
A secret they are trusted with, or scandal.
But that tale isn't worth an old rake handle!
We women, for a fact, can never hold
A secret. Will you hear a story told?
Then witness Midas! For it can be read
80   In Ovid that he had upon his head
Two ass's ears that he kept out of sight
Beneath his long hair with such skill and sleight
That no one else besides his wife could guess.
He loved her well, and trusted her no less.
He begged her not to make his blemish known,
But keep her knowledge to herself alone.
She swore that never, though to save her skin,
Would she be guilty of so mean a sin,
And yet it seemed to her she nearly died
90   Keeping a secret locked so long inside.
It swelled about her heart so hard and deep
She was afraid some word was bound to leap
Out of her mouth, and since there was no man
She dared to tell, down to a swamp she ran—
Her heart, until she got there, all agog—
And like a bittern booming in the bog
She put her mouth close to the watery ground:
"Water, do not betray me with your sound!
I speak to you, and you alone," she said.
100 "Two ass's ears grow on my husband's head!
And now my heart is whole, now it is out.
I'd burst if I held it longer, past all doubt."
Safely, you see, awhile you may confide
In us, but it will out; we cannot hide
A secret. Look in Ovid if you care
To learn what followed; the whole tale is there.
      This knight, when he perceived he could not find
What women covet most, was low in mind;
But the day had come when homeward he must ride,
110 And as he crossed a wooded countryside
Some four and twenty ladies there by chance
He saw, all circling in a woodland dance,
And toward this dance he eagerly drew near
In hope of any counsel he might hear.
But the truth was, he had not reached the place

When dance and all, they vanished into space.
No living soul remained there to be seen
Save an old woman sitting on the green,
As ugly a witch as fancy could devise.
120 As he approached her she began to rise
And said, "Sir knight, here runs no thoroughfare.
What are you seeking with such anxious air?
Tell me! The better may your fortune be.
We old folk know a lot of things," said she.
　　"Good mother," said the knight, "my life's to pay,
That's all too certain, if I cannot say
What women covet most. If you could tell
That secret to me, I'd requite you well."
　　"Give me your hand," she answered. "Swear me true
130 That whatsoever I next ask of you,
You'll do it if it lies within your might
And I'll enlighten you before the night."
　　"Granted, upon my honor," he replied.
　　"Then I dare boast, and with no empty pride,
Your life is safe," she told him. "Let me die
If the queen herself won't say the same as I.
Let's learn if the haughtiest of all who wear
A net or coverchief upon their hair
Will be so forward as to answer 'no'
140 To what I'll teach you. No more; let us go."
With that she whispered something in his ear,
And told him to be glad and have no fear.
　　When they had reached the court, the knight declared
That he had kept his day, and was prepared
To give his answer, standing for his life.
Many the wise widow, many the wife,
Many the maid who rallied to the scene,
And at the head as justice sat the queen.
Then silence was enjoined; the knight was told
150 In open court to say what women hold
Precious above all else. He did not stand
Dumb like a beast, but spoke up at command
And plainly offered them his answering word
In manly voice, so that the whole court heard.
　　"My liege and lady, most of all," said he,
"Women desire to have the sovereignty
And sit in rule and government above
Their husbands, and to have their way in love.
That is what most you want. Spare me or kill
160 As you may like; I stand here by your will."

No widow, wife, or maid gave any token
Of contradicting what the knight had spoken.
He should not die; he should be spared instead;
He was worthy of his life, the whole court said.

The old woman whom the knight met on the green
Sprang up at this. "My sovereign lady queen,
Before your court has risen, do me right!
It was I who taught this answer to the knight,
For which he pledged his honor in my hand,
170   Solemnly, that the first thing I demand,
He would do it, if it lay within his might.
Before the court I ask you, then, sir knight,
To take me," said the woman, "as your wife,
For well you know that I have saved your life.
Deny me, on your honor, if you can."

"Alas," replied this miserable man,
"That was my promise, it must be confessed.
For the love of God, though, choose a new request!
Take all my wealth, and let my body be."

180   "If that's your tune, then curse both you and me,"
She said "Though I am ugly, old, and poor,
I'll have, for all the metal and the ore
That under earth is hidden or lies above,
Nothing, except to be your wife and love."

"My love? No, my damnation, if you can!
Alas," he said, "that any of my clan
Should be so miserably misallied!"

All to no good; force overruled his pride,
And in the end he is constrained to wed,
190   And marries his old wife and goes to bed.

Now some will charge me with an oversight
In failing to describe the day's delight,
The merriment, the food, the dress at least.
But I reply, there was no joy nor feast;
There was only sorrow and sharp misery.
He married her in private, secretly,
And all day after, such was his distress,
Hid like an owl from his wife's ugliness.

Great was the woe this knight had in his head
200   When in due time they both were brought to bed.
He shuddered, tossed, and turned, and all the while
His old wife lay and waited with a smile.

"Is every knight so backward with a spouse?
Is it," she said, "a law in Arthur's house?
I am your love, your own, your wedded wife,

I am the woman who has saved your life.
I have never done you anything but right.
Why do you treat me this way the first night?
You must be mad, the way that you behave!
210 Tell me my fault, and as God's love can save,
I will amend it, truly, if I can."
        "Amend it?" answered this unhappy man.
"It can never be amended, truth to tell.
You are so loathsome and so old as well,
And your low birth besides is such a cross
It is no wonder that I turn and toss.
God take my woeful spirit from my breast!"
        "Is this," she said, "the cause of your unrest?"
        "No wonder!" said the knight. "It truly is."
220   "Now sir," she said, "I could amend all this
Within three days, if it should please me to,
And if you deal with me as you should do.
        "But since you speak of that nobility
That comes from ancient wealth and pedigree,
As if *that* constituted gentlemen,
I hold such arrogance not worth a hen!
The man whose virtue is pre-eminent,
In public and alone, always intent
On doing every generous act he can,
230 Take him—he is the greatest gentleman!
Christ wills that we should claim nobility
From him, not from old wealth or family.
Our elders left us all that they were worth
And through their wealth and blood we claim high birth,
But never, since it was beyond their giving,
Could they bequeath to us their virtuous living;
Although it first conferred on them the name
Of gentlemen, they could not leave that claim!
        "Dante the Florentine on this was wise:
240 'Frail is the branch on which man's virtues rise' —
Thus runs his rhyme — 'God's goodness wills that we
Should claim from him alone nobility.'[42]
Thus from our elders we can only claim
Such temporal things as men may hurt and maim.
        "It is clear enough that true nobility
Is not bequeathed along with property,
For many a lord's son does a deed of shame

---

[42] 'God's goodness . . . nobility': *Purgatorio,* Canto VII.

And yet, God knows, enjoys his noble name.
But though descended from a noble house
250 And elders who were wise and virtuous,
If he will not follow his elders, who are dead,
But leads, himself, a shameful life instead,
He is not noble, be he duke or earl.
It is the churlish deed that makes the churl.
And therefore, my dear husband, I conclude
That though my ancestors were rough and rude,
Yet may Almighty God confer on me
The grace to live, as I hope, virtuously.
Call me of noble blood when I begin
260 To live in virtue and to cast out sin.
    "As for my poverty, at which you grieve,
Almighty God in whom we all believe
In willful poverty chose to lead his life,
And surely every man and maid and wife
Can understand that Jesus, heaven's king,
Would never choose a low or vicious thing.
A poor and cheerful life is nobly led;
So Seneca and others have well said.
The man so poor he doesn't have a stitch,
270 If he thinks himself repaid, I count him rich.
He that is covetous, he is the poor man,
Pining to have the things he never can.
It is of cheerful mind, true poverty.
Juvenal[43] says about it happily:
'The poor man as he goes along his way
And passes thieves is free to sing and play.'
Poverty is a good we loathe, a great
Reliever of our busy worldly state,
A great amender also of our minds
280 As he that patiently will bear it finds.
And poverty, for all it seems distressed,
Is a possession no one will contest.
Poverty, too, by bringing a man low,
Helps him the better both God and self to know.
Poverty is a glass where we can see
Which are our true friends, as it seems to me.
So, sir, I do not wrong you on this score;
Reproach me with my poverty no more.
    "Now, sir, you tax me with my age; but, sir,

---

[43]**Juvenal:** Roman satiric poet (c. 60–140 C.E.); see *Satires* X (Book 1) for the quote.

290 You gentlemen of breeding all aver
That men should not despise old age, but rather
Grant an old man respect, and call him 'father.'
    "If I am old and ugly, as you have said,
You have less fear of being cuckolded,
For ugliness and age, as all agree,
Are notable guardians of chastity.
But since I know in what you take delight,
I'll gratify your worldly appetite.
    "Choose now, which of two courses you will try:
300 To have me old and ugly till I die
But evermore your true and humble wife,
Never displeasing you in all my life,
Or will you have me rather young and fair
And take your chances on who may repair
Either to your house on account of me
Or to some other place, it well may be.
Now make your choice, whichever you prefer."
    The knight took thought, and sighed, and said to her
At last, "My love and lady, my dear wife,
310 In your wise government I put my life.
Choose for yourself which course will best agree
With pleasure and honor, both for you and me.
I do not care, choose either of the two;
I am content, whatever pleases you."
    "Then have I won from you the sovereignty,
Since I may choose and rule at will?" said she.
    He answered, "That is best, I think, dear wife."
    "Kiss me," she said. "Now we are done with strife,
For on my word, I will be both to you,
320 That is to say, fair, yes, and faithful too.
May I die mad unless I am as true
As ever wife was since the world was new.
Unless I am as lovely to be seen
By morning as an empress or a queen
Or any lady between east and west,
Do with my life or death as you think best.
Lift up the curtain, see what you may see."
    And when the knight saw what had come to be
And knew her as she was, so young, so fair,
330 His joy was such that it was past compare.
He took her in his arms and gave her kisses
A thousand times on end; he bathed in blisses.
And she obeyed him also in full measure
In everything that tended to his pleasure.

And so they lived in full joy to the end.
And now to all us women may Christ send
Submissive husbands, full of youth in bed,
And grace to outlive all the men we wed.
And I pray Jesus to cut short the lives
340   Of those who won't be governed by their wives;
And old, ill-tempered niggards who hate expense,
God promptly bring them down with pestilence!

Pilgrimage and Travel

Although travel during the Middle Ages was difficult, dangerous, and time-consuming, many people from Europe, the Arabic world, India, China, and elsewhere embarked on astonishingly long journeys for the purposes of trade, diplomacy, war, and pilgrimage. Some travelers wrote about their experiences, leaving behind fascinating accounts of their encounters with new cultures and places as well as records of their own wonder, adventure, and character. Like Chaucer's pilgrims in *The Canterbury Tales,* the narrators of these travelogues often reveal as much about themselves as they do about the places and peoples they describe. Also like Chaucer's pilgrims, these travelers often exaggerate the dangers and difficulties of their journeys, making themselves appear somewhat larger than life and often taxing the reader's trust. And, although travel writers often unwittingly impose their own cultural and personal preoccupations and prejudices on the worlds they encounter, early accounts of travel and pilgrimage offer a glimpse into the cross-cultural contacts of the Middle Period and are early examples of what would emerge as an important and popular genre in world literature, the TRAVEL NARRATIVE.

Because travels real or imaginary embody both a temporal and spatial structure, they lend themselves to narrative treatment. The movement toward a particular objective, the unexpected encounters along the way, and the inevitable setbacks and obstacles that must be overcome, follow deeply imbedded patterns of comic and tragic plots with their rising and falling actions, reversals, and denouements. Hence, travel tales provided convenient narrative frames and structures for many stories and became a popular form in the

Middle Ages, when much of the world was essentially unknown. For Christian writers and readers, pilgrimages were the contemporary parallel to both the journey that the ancient Hebrews undertook through the wilderness to the Promised Land and Christ's spiritual journey here on earth, his trials, temptation, agony, and Resurrection.

Ritual travel to sacred places was not unique to the Christian world. Indeed, stories about travel to strange locales or sacred sites date back to the ancient world, when those seeking knowledge, healing, or power would visit the shrines or sanctuaries of gods and goddesses. Ancient Greeks sought guidance from the oracle at Delphi while Jews looking for spiritual regeneration traveled to the Temple of the Mount, in Jerusalem. In the Middle Period, with the rise and spread of Christianity, Islam, and Buddhism, pilgrimages became more extensive and formalized. For Christians living in Europe, travel to the Holy Land, or Palestine, became a means to renew their faith and experience the spiritual presence of Jesus. For Muslims, the *HAJJ*, or pilgrimage to Mecca, was one of the five pillars of their faith and was supposed to be performed at least once in their lifetime. The Buddhist *Mahaparinibbana Sutta*, translated into several languages, including Chinese, recommends visits to sacred places associated with the life of Buddha. Thus, the sacred journey became an article of faith in the world's major religions, and those with the fortitude, courage, and means to do so set out to follow in the footsteps of their spiritual leaders or earlier pilgrims who already had marked the way.

PILGRIMAGE TO THE HOLY LAND

One of the earliest records of Christian pilgrimage is *Egeria's Travels*. Egeria, a woman from Gaul (France) or Spain, traveled to Jerusalem in the fourth century. In part because of the courage and the longing for God's grace demonstrated in her travels, Egeria was later canonized a saint, and her travels became a model for others. Through her writings and those of other early Christian pilgrims to Palestine, certain places in and around Jerusalem, Bethlehem, and Mount Sinai

p. 943

◀ **Women Shopping, thirteenth century**

Travel to distant lands bolstered commerce and trade. Here European women are shown examining luxury goods from the East. (Laura Platt Winfrey, Inc.)

Pilgrims, 1280

A diverse group of pilgrims, including one woman, are shown in this detail from a stained-glass window at Canterbury Cathedral, an important destination for religious pilgrimages. (The Art Archive / Canterbury Cathedral / Dagli Orti)

acquired new symbolic importance. Like later pilgrims to the Holy Land, Egeria sought out sites associated with the life of Jesus as well as churches and monasteries housing relics associated with biblical events or containing the tombs of martyrs. As early travels to the Holy Land increased, patterns and precedents were established for later pilgrims. Thus later Christian pilgrims tended to follow an established itinerary of sacred sites — a sacred tour of a storied landscape — in their own visits to the Holy Land. Although Jerusalem fell into Muslim hands in the seventh century, tolerance for Christians and Jews enabled pilgrimages to continue up to the period of the First Crusade (1095–99), when pilgrimages to Palestine became more perilous.

In the later Middle Ages, in part because the Holy Land had become an embattled region, Christians directed their attention to the sacred places of Europe — such as Rome and Santiago de Compostela, in Spain. After the tenth century, more and more European Christians traveled closer to home, as in the case of Chaucer's pilgrims, to lesser but nonetheless important shrines in cities such as Canterbury, Walsingham, Chartres, and other cathedral towns that housed holy relics or the tombs of martyrs. The increasing value and ubiquity of relics, many of them manufactured in order to attract visitors, promoted travel to local shrines. As seen in *The Canterbury Tales,* pilgrimages put in motion groups of people from different stratas of society in search of physical healing, spiritual renewal, and, to be sure, a good time.

ISLAMIC PILGRIMAGE—THE *HAJJ*

While Christians continued to visit Palestine even throughout the Crusades, Muslim pilgrims also visited the Holy Land to trace the steps of the prophets and visit the tombs of martyrs. Given the overlapping traditions of the Qur'an (Koran) and the Bible, Muslim pilgrims visited many of the same sites as Jews and Christians. The primary pilgrimage for Muslims, however, was to Mecca, the birthplace of Muhammad and the site of the great mosque housing the KA'BAH, the sacred Black Stone of Islam. The Qur'an enjoins every member of the Muslim faith to make a pilgrimage to Mecca at least once in his or her lifetime. This journey, known as the *hajj,* takes place in the twelfth month of the Islamic calendar. Because the *hajj* (and even the lesser pilgrimage to Mecca, known as the UMRAH) brought people from all over the Islamic world to a central holy site, it unified the Muslim population and spiritually empowered individual believers. Moreover, like the pilgrimage to Canterbury that Chaucer describes, the *hajj* and the *umrah* assembled people from all ranks of society and blurred or erased the worldly distinctions among them. In the selection from his *Travels,* Ibn Jubayr describes p. 947 Mecca's sacred mosque and the Black Stone with great detail, as well as the formal rituals that visitors to the mosque had to, and must still, follow.

BUDDHIST PILGRIMAGE

Buddhists too made sacred journeys to holy places during the Middle Period. Soon after Egeria made her journey to Jerusalem, in 399 a Buddhist monk from China named Faxian (Fa-hsien) traveled from China to India, where he spent fourteen years visiting sacred Buddhist sites in search of relics and teachings. Two hundred years later, Xuanzang (Hsuan Tsang), a Buddhist monk and one of China's p. 956

most celebrated travelers, crossed India from 629 to 645, also to gather relics and study with Buddhist masters. His observations of East Indian customs and descriptions of temples are recorded in *Records of Western Countries.* His travels as well as his biography, written by two of his students, inspired one of China's great novels, *Monkey,* written by Wu Chengen (c. 1506–1582).

MISSIONS, DIPLOMACY, AND TRADE

In addition to pilgrimage, many Middle Period travelers left home to pursue trade, diplomacy, missionary work, and war, as well as to simply satisfy their curiosity about other places. Land routes between European cities and trading centers, such as Constantinople and port towns along the Mediterranean, connected to ancient overland routes through Persia and India to China, one of which, the Silk Road, running from Chang'an in China to the Arabian Sea, dates to the second century B.C.E. By the tenth century, the Italian cities of Genoa, Pisa, and Venice had established a brisk trade with the Byzantine empire and port cities along the eastern Mediterranean. The overland trade routes linking Europe and China changed hands in concert with the shifting fortunes of the Arabic, Indian, Chinese, and Mongolian empires from the sixth through the fourteenth centuries. The consolidation of the Mongol empire beyond the Black Sea actually helped stabilize the region and promote trade and travel along the Silk Road, reaching from the Mediterranean through Central Asia and into China, then under Mongol rule. Thus travel across the continent, though still not without risks and danger, did not come to a standstill.

p. 961

In the mid-thirteenth century, the Holy See in Rome commissioned several Franciscan monks, including Giovanni da Pian di Carpine (Friar John) to gather information about the Mongols and to undertake missionary work in Central Asia. Friar John returned with a letter from the Great Khan, Guyuk, rejecting Pope Innocent IV's petition to recognize Christianity as the greatest religion and to vow suspending further attacks on Europe. Around this same time

p. 966
p. 972

the Venetian merchant Marco Polo, and the Moroccan traveler Ibn Battuta, the two greatest journeyers of the Middle Period, independently undertook extensive travels that took them as far east as China, where they found a cosmopolitan mix of Christians, Hindus, Buddhists, and Muslims. The written records of their travels fueled the imagination and the desires of many readers in Europe and in

Map of North Africa and Southern Spain, 1375
The Middle Period saw increasing contact between distant peoples. Whether on religious crusade, pilgrimages, or simple explorations, travelers, represented here by the figure riding on the camel, brought back tales from far away countries to the north, south, east and west, spurring cultural and intellectual exchange. (The Art Archive / John Webb)

the Arabic world for years to come. John Mandeville, p. 984, who wrote what was to become the most popular book of travels from the late Middle Ages in Europe, borrowed extensively from earlier travel accounts, including Marco Polo's, to produce his derivative but nonetheless fascinating *The Travels of Sir John Mandeville* in 1357. Overall, the period from 300 C.E. through the fourteenth century fostered an extensive network of pilgrimage, travel, and trade on the Eurasian continent and in Africa, and some of the era's eminent travelers, like Marco Polo, would visit regions in Mongolia and China that Westerners would not see again for more than nine hundred years.

■ CONNECTIONS

Homer, *The Odyssey* (Book 1); Virgil, *The Aeneid* (Book 1). In the epics of Homer and Virgil, the heroes Odysseus and Aeneas travel to many places known to them only through legend or prophecy. As in later travel narratives, these heroes exaggerate their experiences with unfamiliar places and peoples, perhaps reflective of the fear, curiosity, and in some cases bravery involved in their journeys. What are some of the other features that these heroic epics share with the travel narratives in this section?

Dante, *Inferno*, p. 689. Pilgrimage in the Christian Middle Ages operated on many levels. Literally, it meant travel to the Holy Land or sacred places, but allegorically it was a microcosm of life itself. Dante's *Divine Comedy* is perhaps the greatest literary expression of the many dimensions of the pilgrimage motif. Consider how Dante treats the soul's journey as a pilgrimage of life — a journey of the soul — and death. Does his work share any of the features of the pilgrimage narratives presented in the following pages?

Wu Chengen, *Monkey* (Book 3). Wu Chengen's *Monkey* is based on the travels of Xuanzang — who becomes Tripitaka in the novel. Compare excerpts from Xuanzang's travel writings with *Monkey*. How does the novel draw on and transform Xuanzang's actual account of his journey in order to heighten the drama and the importance of his trip to India?

EGERIA

LATE FOURTH CENTURY

All that is known about the pilgrim Egeria is what she wrote about her travels. A woman from either Gaul (France) or Spain, Egeria made a pilgrimage to Jerusalem between 381 and 384 C.E. Having traveled from a country a long distance from Palestine, she spent three years in the eastern region visiting sacred sites in and around Jerusalem, Constantinople, and Edessa. She writes that she spent "three full years" in Jerusalem, and she quotes Eulogios, the bishop of Edessa from 379 to 387, as saying to her: "My daughter, I can see what a long journey this is on which your faith has brought you—right from the other end of the earth." Interested in seeing and describing places associated with biblical stories, Egeria was also a keen observer and apparently an enthusiastic participant in the ritual ceremonies and services of the churches and monasteries she visited. Moreover, she sought advice and counsel from the priests, confessors, and bishops who met with her and who sometimes accompanied her on various legs of her journey.

Only a fragment preserved in an eleventh-century manuscript known as the Codex Aretinus remains of *Egeria's Travels (Itinerarium Egeriae)*, written in Latin, and various echoes of the work appear in later books on travel to the Holy Land. Egeria's text was one of the earliest Christian pilgrimage narratives, and her descriptions of the Holy Land served as a resource and model for later writers. Preserved by nuns—"the sisters" Egeria addresses in her work—the Latin manuscript of Egeria's travels also caught the notice of Valerius, a seventh-century Galician monk. Valerius's "Letter in Praise of the Life of the Most Blessed Egeria," still extant, praises her pilgrimage as a model of Christian devotion. Writing to the monks of Bierzo (El Vierzo, in northwestern Spain), Valerius holds up Egeria's knowledge of the Bible, her "courageous deeds," and her "longing for God's grace" as examples for devout Christians to emulate. In Valerius's words: "First with great industry she perused all the books of the Old and New Testaments, and discovered all its descriptions of the holy wonders of the world; and its regions, provinces, cities, mountains, and deserts. Then in eager haste (though it was to take many years,) she set out, with God's help, to explore them." For Valerius, Egeria was an "exemplary woman," who "by her own will and choice . . . accepted the labours of pilgrimage, that she might, in the choir of holy virgins with the glorious Queen of heaven, Mary, the Lord's mother, inherit a heavenly kingdom." In this letter Valerius captures one of the key aspects of pilgrimage: its significance as a devotional practice that prepares the worldly pilgrim for heaven.

Among the many holy sites on Egeria's tour was the monastery at Mount Sinai, where Moses is said to have received the Ten Commandments. As seen in the following excerpt, Egeria climbed the mountain, tracing with each step the story of Moses, making offerings, and celebrating church ritual at key points along the way.

A note on the translation. Egeria's Travels is translated by John Wilkinson; unless otherwise indicated, notes are adapted from the translator's.

FROM

❧ Egeria's Travels

Translated by John Wilkinson

[MT. SINAI]

In the meanwhile we were walking along between the mountains, and came to a spot where they opened out to form an endless valley[1]—a huge plain, and very beautiful—across which we could see Sinai, the holy Mount of God. Next to the spot where the mountains open out is the place of the "Graves of Craving."[2] When we arrived there our guides, the holy men who were with us, said, "It is usual for the people who come here to say a prayer when first they catch sight of the Mount of God," and we did as they suggested. The Mount of God is perhaps four miles away from where we were, directly across the huge valley I have mentioned.

The valley lies under the flank of the Mount of God, and it really is huge. From looking at it we guessed—and they told us—that it was maybe sixteen miles long and, they said, four miles wide, and we had to pass through this valley before we reached the mountain. This is the huge flat valley[3] in which the children of Israel were waiting while holy Moses[4] went up into the Mount of God and was there "forty days and forty nights." It is the valley where the calf was made, and the place is pointed out to this day, for a large stone stands there on the spot. Thus it was at the head of this very valley[5] that holy Moses pastured the cattle of his father-in-law and God spoke to him twice from the burning bush.[6] From here we were looking at the Mount of God; our way first took us up it, since the best ascent is from the direction by which we were approaching, and then we would descend again to the head of the valley (where the Bush was), since that is the better way down.

So this was our plan. When we had seen everything we wanted and come down from the Mount of God, we would come to the place of the Bush. Then from there we would return through the middle of the valley now ahead of us and so return to the road with the men of God, who would show us each one of the places mentioned in the Bible. And that is what we did.

So, coming in from Paran,[7] we said the prayer. Then, going on, we made our way across the head of the valley and approached the Mount of God. It looks like a single

---

[1] **an endless valley:** The Wadi er Raha, or Valley of Rest, leading to Jebel Musa, the traditional Mount Sinai.

[2] **"Graves of Craving":** The Hebrew "Kibroth-Hataava," the graves of the Israelites who had craved for the plenty of Egypt (Num. 11:34). Egeria was in the pass, and the graves stretched behind her for half a mile.

[3] **the huge flat valley:** The Wadi er Raha, or Valley of Rest.

[4] **Moses:** For the story of Moses and the Israelites at Mt. Sinai, see Exodus 19–32. [Editors' note.]

[5] **this very valley:** Wadi er Raha goes past the place where God is said to have spoken to Moses through a burning bush (the present Monastery of St. Katherine) and the view is closed by Jebel Muneija. Egeria is now proceeding to the right of the massif, up Wadi el Leja.

[6] **the burning bush:** See Exodus 3:1.

[7] **from Paran:** The modern Feiran, in Sinai; this is the site of Rafadim (Rephidim), the oasis where Joshua defeated the Amelecites. It is still a stopping point for travelers to Mount Sinai. [Editors' note.]

mountain as you are going round it, but when you actually go into it there are really several peaks, all of them known as "the Mount of God," and the principal one, the summit on which the Bible tells us that "God's glory came down,"[8] is in the middle of them. I never thought I had seen mountains as high as those which stood around it, but the one in the middle where God's glory came down was the highest of all, so much so that, when we were on top, all the other peaks we had seen and thought so high looked like little hillocks far below us. Another remarkable thing—it must have been planned by God—is that even though the central mountain, Sinai proper on which God's glory came down, is higher than all the others, you cannot see it until you arrive at the very foot of it to begin your ascent. After you have seen everything and come down, it can be seen facing you, but this cannot be done till you start your climb. I realized it was like this before we reached the Mount of God, since the brothers had already told me, and when we arrived there I saw very well what they meant.

Late on Saturday, then, we arrived at the mountain and came to some cells.[9] The monks who lived in them received us most hospitably, showing us every kindness. There is a church there with a presbyter;[10] that is where we spent the night, and, pretty early on Sunday, we set off with the presbyter and monks who lived there to climb each of the mountains.

They are hard to climb. You do not go round and round them, spiralling up gently, but straight at each one as if you were going up a wall, and then straight down to the foot, till you reach the foot of the central mountain, Sinai itself. Here then, impelled by Christ our God and assisted by the prayers of the holy men who accompanied us, we made the great effort of the climb. It was quite impossible to ride up, but though I had to go on foot I was not conscious of the effort—in fact I hardly noticed it because, by God's will, I was seeing my hopes coming true. So at ten o'clock we arrived on the summit of Sinai, the Mount of God where the Law was given, and the place where God's glory came down on the day when the mountain was smoking. The church which is now there is not impressive for its size (there is too little room on the summit), but it has a grace all its own. And when with God's help we had climbed right to the top and reached the door of this church, there was the presbyter, the one who is appointed to the church, coming to meet us from his cell. He was a healthy old man, a monk from his boyhood and an "ascetic" as they call it here—in fact just the man for the place. Several other presbyters met us too, and all the monks who lived near the mountain, or at least all who were not prevented from coming by their age or their health.

All there is on the actual summit of the central mountain is the church and the cave of holy Moses.[11] No one lives there. So when the whole passage had been read to

---

[8] **"God's glory came down":** See Exodus 19:18, 20.

[9] **some cells:** That is, *monasteria.* In Wadi Leja, possibly the Rephidim Valley, Egeria probably went to the convent now called El Arba'in (the Forty), which is nearest the ascent.

[10] **presbyter:** An elder of the early church. [Editors' note.]

[11] **the cave of holy Moses:** Cf. Exodus 33:22.

us from the Book of Moses (on the very spot!) we made the Offering in the usual way and received Communion. As we were coming out of church the presbyters of the place gave us "blessings," some fruits which grow on the mountain itself.

For although Sinai, the holy Mount, is too stony even for bushes to grow on it, there is a little soil round the foot of the mountains, the central one and those around it, and in this the holy monks are always busy planting shrubs, and setting out orchards or vegetable-beds round their cells. It may look as if they gather fruit which is growing in the mountain soil, but in fact everything is the result of their own hard work.

We had received Communion and the holy men had given us the "blessings." Now we were outside the church door, and at once I asked them if they would point out to us all the different places. The holy men willingly agreed. They showed us the cave where holy Moses was when for the second time he went up into the Mount of God and a second time received the tables of stone after breaking the first ones when the people sinned. They showed us all the other places we wanted to see, and also the ones they knew about themselves. I want you to be quite clear about these mountains, reverend ladies my sisters, which surrounded us as we stood beside the church looking down from the summit of the mountain in the middle. They had been almost too much for us to climb, and I really do not think I have ever seen any that were higher (apart from the central one which is higher still) even though they only looked like little hillocks to us as we stood on the central mountain. From there we were able to see Egypt and Palestine,[12] the Red Sea and the Parthenian Sea (the part that takes you to Alexandria), as well as the vast lands of the Saracens[13]—all unbelievably far below us. All this was pointed out to us by the holy men.

We had been looking forward to all this so much that we had been eager to make the climb. Now that we had done all we wanted and climbed to the summit of the Mount of God, we began the descent. We passed on to another mountain next to it which gives the church there its name "On Horeb."[14] This is the Horeb to which the holy Prophet Elijah fled from the presence of King Ahab, and it was there that God spoke to him with the words, "What doest thou here, Elijah?", as is written in the Books of the Kingdoms.[15] The cave where Elijah hid can be seen there to this day in front of the church door, and we were shown the stone altar which holy Elijah set up for offering sacrifice to God. Thus the holy men were kind enough to show us everything, and there too we made the Offering[16] and prayed very earnestly, and the passage was read from the Book of Kingdoms. Indeed, whenever we arrived anywhere, I myself always wanted the Bible passage to be read to us.

---

[12] **Egypt and Palestine:** In Egeria's time, Mount Sinai was part of Palaestina III, so everything around the mountain would be Palestine. The Gulf of Aqaba is sometimes visible. Beyond the Red Sea were the Egyptian mountains. Egeria may have seen all this from the summit of Jebel Musa, Mount Sinai, in the clear winter air.

[13] **lands of the Saracens:** (*Saracens* comes from the Arabic *sharqiyin,* meaning "easterners.") Refers to Arabia Felix and Arabia Petraea, today the Sinai Peninsula, Petra, and El Hisma.

[14] **Horeb:** Possibly Jebel ed Deir, or Sinai itself.

[15] **Books of the Kingdoms:** See I Kings 19:9.

[16] **the Offering:** This is the second Eucharist on the Sunday, in a different church from the first celebration.

When we had made the Offering, we set off again, with the presbyters and monks pointing things out to us, to another place not far away. It is where Aaron and the seventy elders stood[17] while holy Moses received from the Lord the Law for the children of Israel. There is no building there, but it is an enormous round rock with a flat place on top where the holy men are said to have stood, and a kind of altar in the middle made of stones. So there too we had a passage read from the Book of Moses and an appropriate psalm, and after a prayer we went on down. By then I suppose it must have been about two in the afternoon, and we still had three miles to go before emerging from the mountains which we entered on the previous evening. As I have already mentioned, we did not have to come out by the way we had gone in, because we had decided to visit all the holy places and cells in the mountains, and to come out at the head of the valley, of which I have spoken, below the Mount of God.

---

[17] **where Aaron . . . stood:** See Exodus 24:9–14.

❧ IBN JUBAYR

C. 1145–C. 1217

Abu 'l-Husayn Muhammad ibn Ahmad ibn Jubayr was born around 1145 in Valencia, Spain, then under Moorish rule. Eventually, Ibn Jubayr became secretary to the Muslim governor of Granada, who enticed his reluctant clerk to drink seven draughts of wine. Having up to that time observed the Islamic injunction against intoxicating drink, Ibn Jubayr decided to leave for a pilgrimage to Mecca to fulfill his duty to his faith and to atone for his violation of Islamic law. Thus in February 1183, Ibn Jubayr boarded a Genoese ship bound for Egypt. After visiting some of the ancient tombs there, he set out over the Red Sea on his way to Mecca. Before returning to Granada, he visited Medina, the site of Muhammad's tomb; Baghdad, the seat of the caliph; Nineveh, an ancient city along the Euphrates; and many other sites. On the journey home, Jubayr was shipwrecked off the coast of Sicily, where he spent time before finally making his way home in April of 1185.

Throughout his journey Ibn Jubayr had kept copious notes that he now fashioned into a book known as *The Travels (Rihlat-ul-Kinani)*. Since its publication, his travel account has been celebrated for its remarkably descriptive detail, clarity, and humanity. In the portion of Ibn Jubayr's account excerpted here, Jubayr visits Mecca in August and September of 1183. He vividly describes his preparations for visiting the holy KA'BAH, the sanctuary of the Black Stone of Islam, in the Grand Mosque. And in bounteous detail he depicts the mosque and shrine, giving special attention to such matters as the kissing of the Black Stone and the appearance of the *khatib*, or preacher, at prayer on Fridays.

Muslim Pilgrims, thirteenth century
Since the death of Muhammad in the seventh century, the hajj, or pilgrimage, to Mecca has been the sacred duty of every devout Muslim. (Giraudon / Art Resource, NY)

A note on the translation: The translation is Jubayr's *Travels* by R. J. C. Broadhurst; the notes are adapted from the translator's. Parentheses designate interpolations made by the translator to render the text in complete English sentences; brackets indicate explanatory words or phrases.

FROM

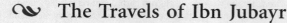 The Travels of Ibn Jubayr

Translated by R. J. C. Broadhurst

[THE GREAT MOSQUE AND THE KA'BAH AT MECCA]

FROM

THE MONTH OF RABI' AL-AKHIR (579)
[JULY 24–AUGUST 21, 1183]

May God let us know His favour

At eventide on Tuesday the 11th of the month, being the 2nd of August, we left Jiddah, after the pilgrims had guaranteed each other (for payment), and their names had been recorded in a register kept by the governor of the city. . . .

We passed on our way that night until we arrived at al-Qurayn, with the rising of the sun. This place is a staging post for pilgrims and a place of their encampment. There they put on the *ihram,*[1] and there they rest throughout the day of their arrival. . . . In this place is a well of sweet spring water, and by reason of it the pilgrims do not need to supply themselves with water save for the night on which they travel to it. Throughout the daylight hours of Wednesday we stayed resting at al-Qurayn, but when evening had come, we left it in the pilgrim garb to perform the '*Umra,*'[2] and marched throughout the night. With the dawn, we came near to the Haram, and descended as the light was about to spread.

We entered Mecca—God protect it—at the first hour of Thursday the 13th of Rabi', being the 4th of August, by the 'Umrah Gate. As we marched that night, the full moon had thrown its rays upon the earth, the night had lifted its veil, voices struck the ears with the *Talbiyat,*[3] from all sides, and tongues were loud in invocation, humbly beseeching God to grant them their requests, sometimes redoubling their *Talbiyat,* and sometimes imploring with prayers. Oh night most happy, the bride of all the nights of life, the virgin of the maidens of time.

And so, at the time and on the day we have mentioned, we came to God's venerable Haram, the place of sojourn of Abraham the Friend (of God), and found the Ka'bah, the Sacred House, the unveiled bride conducted (like a bride to her groom) to the supreme felicity of heaven, encompassed by the deputations of the All-Merciful. We performed the *tawaf*[4] of the new arrival, and then prayed at the revered Maqam.[5] We clung to the covering of the Ka'bah near the Multazam, which is between the Black Stone and the door, and is a place where prayers are answered. We entered the dome of Zamzam and drank of its waters which is 'to the purpose for which it is drunk,' as said the Prophet—may God bless and preserve him—and then performed the *sa'i*[6] between al-Safa and al-Marwah. After this we shaved and entered a state of *halal.*[7] Praise be to God for generously including us in the pilgrimage to Him and for making us to be of those on whose behalf the prayers of Abraham reach. Sufficient He is for us and the best Manager. We took lodging in Mecca at

---

[1] *ihram:* Prohibition. Several aspects of this ritual are the wearing of pilgrim garb denoting modesty before Allah, strict observation of chastity, and other prohibitions regarding such matters as covering the head and killing animals.

[2] the '*Umrah:* Lesser Pilgrimage, the journey to Mecca including the sevenfold circumambulation of the Ka'bah and the ritual run between al-Marwah and al-Safa; performed any time of the year except the three days of the *Hajj,* or Greater Pilgrimage.

[3] *Talbiyat:* "Waiting for orders," the cry pilgrims are supposed to utter as they approach Mecca. It begins, "Here I am, oh God, here I am."

[4] *tawaf:* The rite of the sevenfold circumambulation of the Ka'bah, an ancient practice preserved by Muhammad.

[5] the revered Maqam: *Maqam* can refer either to the sacred stone on which Abraham stood when he built the temple of Ka'bah, or the building that formerly housed this stone. In this text, the building is referred to by the word *Maqam,* the stone by the word *maqam.*

[6] the sa'i: The ritual run between al-Marwah and al-Safa, recalling the course run by Hagar, mother of Ishmael, until the angel Gabriel delivered water to her son who was dying of thirst. Pilgrims to Mecca must complete this course seven times.

[7] a state of *halal:* Release, here meaning release from the prohibitions of *ihram.*

a house called al-Halal near to the Haram and the Bab al-Suddah, one of its gates, in a room having many domestic conveniences and overlooking the Haram and the sacred Ka'bah.

FROM

THE MONTH OF JUMADA 'L-ULA (579)
[AUGUST 22–SEPTEMBER 20, 1183]

May God let us know His favour

The new moon rose on the night of Monday the 22nd of August, when we had been in Mecca—may God Most High exalt it—eighteen days. The new moon of this month was the most auspicious our eyes had seen in all that had passed of our life. It rose after we had already entered the seat of the venerable enclosure, the sacred Haram of God, the dome in which is the maqam of Abraham, the place from whence the Prophet's mission (was sent out), and the alighting place of the faithful spirit Gabriel with inspiration and revelation. May God with His power and strength inspire us to thanks for His favour and make us sensible of that amount of privilege He has made our portion, finally accepting us (into Paradise) and rewarding us with the accustomed generosity of His beneficent works, and giving us of His gracious help and support. There is no God but He.

A description of the Sacred Mosque and the Ancient House
May God bless and exalt it

[T]he venerable House has four corners and is almost square. . . . the custodians of the House . . . informed me that its height, on the side which faces the Bab [Gate] al-Safa and which extends from the Black Stone to the Rukn al-Yamani [Yemen Corner], is twenty-nine cubits. The remaining sides are twenty-eight cubits because of the slope of the roof towards the water-spout.

The principal corner is the one containing the Black Stone. There the circumambulation begins, the circumambulator drawing back (a little) from it so that all of his body might pass by it, the blessed House being on his left. The first thing that is met after that is the 'Iraq corner, which faces the north, then the Syrian corner which faces west, then the Yemen corner which faces south, and then back to the Black corner which faces east. That completes one *shaut* [single course]. The door of the blessed House is on the side between the 'Iraq corner and the Black Stone corner, and is close to the Stone at a distance of barely ten spans. That part of the side of the House which is between them is called the Multazam: a place where prayers are answered.

The venerable door is raised above the ground eleven and a half spans. It is of silver gilt and of exquisite workmanship and beautiful design, holding the eyes for its excellence and in emotion for the awe God has clothed His House in. After the same fashion are the two posts, and the upper lintel over which is a slab of pure gold about two spans long. The door has two large silver staples on which is hung the lock. It faces to the east, and is eight spans wide and thirteen high. The thickness of the wall in which it turns is five spans. The inside of the blessed House is overlaid with variegated marbles, and the walls are all variegated marbles. (The ceiling) is sustained by three teak pillars of great height, four paces apart, and punctuating the length of the House, and down its middle. One of these columns, the first, faces the centre of the side enclosed by the two Yemen corners, and is three paces distant from it. The third column, the last, faces the side enclosed by the 'Iraq and Syrian corners.

The whole circuit of the upper half of the House is plated with silver, thickly gilt, which the beholder would imagine, from its thickness, to be a sheet of gold. It encompasses the four sides and covers the upper half of the walls. The ceiling of the House is covered by a veil of coloured silk.

The outside of the Ka'bah, on all its four sides, is clothed in coverings of green silk with cotton warps; and on their upper parts is a band of red silk on which is written the verse, 'Verily the first House founded for mankind was that at Bakkah [Mecca]' [Qur'an III, 96]. The name of the Imam al-Nasir li dini Illa, in depth three cubits, encircles it all. On these coverings there has been shaped remarkable designs resembling handsome pulpits, and inscriptions entertaining the name of God Most High and calling blessings on Nasir, the aforementioned 'Abbaside (Caliph) who had ordered its instalment. With all this, there was no clash of colour. The number of covers on all four sides is thirty-four, there being eighteen on the two long sides, and sixteen on the two short sides.

The Ka'bah has five windows of 'Iraq glass, richly stained. One of them is in the middle of the ceiling, and at each corner is a window, one of which is not seen because it is beneath the vaulted passage described later. Between the pillars (hang) thirteen vessels, of silver save one that is gold.

The first thing which he who enters at the door will find to his left is the corner outside which is the Black Stone. Here are two chests containing Korans. Above them in the corner are two small silver doors like windows set in the angle of the corner, and more than a man's stature from the ground. In the angle which follows, the Yemen, it is the same, but the doors have been torn out and only the wood to which they were attached remains. In the Syrian corner it is the same and the small doors remain. It is the same in the 'Iraq corner, which is to the right of him who enters. In the 'Iraq corner is a door called the Bab al-Rahmah [Door of Mercy, usually called the Door of Repentance, Bab al-Taubah] from which ascent is made to the roof of the blessed House. It leads to a vaulted passage connecting with the roof of the House and having in it a stairway and, at its beginning, the vault containing the venerable maqam.[8] Because of this passage the Ancient House has five corners. The height of both its sides is two statures and it encloses the 'Iraq corner with the halves of each of those two sides. Two-thirds of the circuit of this passage is dressed with pieces of coloured silk, as if it had been previously wrapped in them and then set in place.

---

[8] **the venerable maqam:** The stone on which Abraham stood when, with the help of his son Ishmael, he built the *Ka'bah*; see note 5.

This venerable maqam that is inside the passage is the maqam of Abraham—God's blessings on our Prophet and on him—and is a stone covered with silver. Its height is three spans, its width two and its upper part is larger than the lower. If it is not frivolous to draw the comparison it is like a large potter's oven, its middle being narrower than its top or bottom. We gazed upon it and were blessed by touching and kissing it. The water of Zamzam[9] was poured on us into the imprints of the two blessed feet [of Abraham who stood on this stone when he built the Ka'bah], and we drank it—may God profit us by it. The traces of both feet are visible, as are the traces of the honoured and blessed big toes. Glory to God who softened the stone beneath the tread so that it left its trace as no trace of foot is left in the soft sand. Glory to God who made it a manifest sign. The contemplation of this maqam and the venerable House is an awful sight which distracts the senses in amazement, and ravishes the heart and mind. You will see only reverent gazes, flowing tears, eyes dissolved in weeping, and tongues in humble entreaty to Great and Glorious God.

Between the venerable door and the 'Iraq corner is a basin twelve spans long, five and a half spans wide, and about one in depth. It runs from opposite the door post, on the side of the 'Iraq corner, towards that corner, and is the mark of the place of the maqam at the time of Abraham—on whom be (eternal) happiness—until the Prophet—may God bless and preserve him—moved it to the place where now it is a *musalla* [place of worship]. The basin remained as a conduit for the water of the House when it is washed. It is a blessed spot [called al-Ma'jan] and is said to be one of the pools of Paradise, with men crowding to pray at it. Its bottom is spread with soft white sand.

The place of the venerated Maqam, behind which prayers are said, faces the space between the blessed door and the 'Iraq corner, well towards the side of the door. Over it is a wooden dome, a man's stature or more high, angulated and sharp-edged, of excellent modelling, and having four spans from one angle to another. It was erected on the place where once was the maqam, and around it is a stone projection built on the edge like an oblong basin about a span deep, five paces long, and three paces wide. The maqam was put into the place we have described in the blessed House as a measure of safety. Between the maqam and the side of the House opposite it lie seventeen paces, a pace being three spans. The place of the Maqam also has a dome made of steel and placed beside the dome of Zamzam. During the months of the pilgrimage, when many men have assembled and those from 'Iraq and Khurasan have arrived, the wooden dome is removed and the steel dome put in its place that it might better support the press of men.

From the corner containing the Black Stone to the 'Iraq corner is scarcely fifty-four spans. From the Black Stone to the ground is six spans, so that the tall man must bend to it and the short man raise himself (to kiss it). From the 'Iraq corner to the Syrian corner is scarcely forty-eight spans, and that is through the inside of the

---

[9] **water of Zamzam:** The Well of Zamzam was a central feature of Mecca whose waters drew nomadic tribes to the area long before the Ka'bah was built; according to Muslim tradition, the waters of the well disappeared under the sand until Muhammad's grandfather dreamed of the well. The angel Jibril (Gabriel) is said to have revealed the well to Hagar when she and her son Ishmael were suffering from thirst in the desert.

Hijr;[10] but around it from the one corner to the other is forty paces or almost one hundred and twenty spans. The *tawaf* [the circumabulator] moves outside. (The distance from) the Syrian corner to the Yemen corner is the same as that from the Black corner to the 'Iraq corner for they are opposite sides. From the Yemen to the Black is the same, inside the Hijr, as from the 'Iraq to the Syrian for they are opposite sides.

The place of circumambulation is paved with wide stones like marble and very beautiful, some black, some brown and some white. They are joined to each other, and reach nine paces from the House save in the part facing the Maqam where they reach out to embrace it. The remainder of the Haram, including the colonnades, is wholly spread with white sand. The place of circumambulation for the women is at the edge of the paved stones.

Between the 'Iraq corner and the beginning of the wall of the Hijr is the entrance to the Hijr; it is four paces wide, that is six cubits exactly, for we measured it by hand. . . . Opposite this entrance, at the Syrian corner, is another of the same size. Between that part of the wall of the House which is under the Mizab [waterspout] and the wall of the Hijr opposite, following the straight line which cuts through the middle of the aforementioned Hijr, lie forty spans. The distance from entrance to entrance is sixteen paces, which is forty-eight spans. This place, I mean the surroundings of the wall (of the Ka'bah, under the Mizab), is all tessellated marble, wonderfully joined . . . with bands of gilded copper worked into its surface like a chess-board, being interlaced with each other and with shapes of *mihrabs*.[11] When the sun strikes them, such light and brightness shine from them that the beholder conceives them to be gold, dazzling the eyes with their rays. The height of the marble wall of this Hijr is five and a half spans and its width four and a half. Inside the Hijr is a wide paving, round which the Hijr bends as it were in two-thirds of a circle. It is laid with tessellated marble, cut in discs the size of the palm of the hand, of a dinar and more minute than that, and joined with remarkable precision. It is composed with wonderful art, is of singular perfection, beautifully inlaid and checkered, and is superbly set and laid. The beholder will see bendings, inlays, mosaics of tiles, chessboard forms and the like, of various forms and attributes, such as will fix his gaze for their beauty. Or let his looks roam from the carpet of flowers of many colours to the mihrabs over which bend arches of marble, and in which are these forms we have described and the arts we have mentioned.

Beside it are two slabs of marble adjacent to the wall of the Hijr opposite the Mizab, on which art has worked such delicate leaves, branches, and trees as could not be done by skilled hands cutting with scissors from paper. It is a remarkable sight. . . . Facing the waterspout, in the middle of the Hijr and the centre of the

---

[10] **the Hijr:** A sanctuary in the Ka'bah said to be the burial place of Hagar and Ishmael; Hagar, a wife of Abraham, was Ishmael's mother. Although the biblical story of Ishmael, the half brother of Isaac, treats Ishmael as an outcast, the Qur'an sees him as a prophet and a founding father of the faith. (See Genesis 16 and the Qur'an, Suras 2, 6, 19, and 38.)

[11] **mihrabs:** Elaborately carved, highly ornate niches in every mosque that indicate the direction of Mecca and thus the direction Muslims face when they pray.

marble wall, is a marble slab of most excellent chiselling with a cornice round it bearing an inscription in striking black in which is written, '(This is) among the things ordered to be done by the servant and Caliph of God Abu 'l-'Abbas Ahmad al-Nasir li dini Ilah, Prince of the Faithful, in the year 576 [1180].'

The Mizab is on the top of the wall which overlooks the Hijr. It is of gilded copper and projects four cubits over the Hijr, its breadth being a span. This place under the waterspout is also considered as being a place where, by the favour of God Most High, prayers are answered. The Yemen corner is the same. The wall connecting this place with the Syrian corner is called al-Mustajar [The Place of Refuge]. Underneath the waterspout, and in the court of the Hijr near to the wall of the blessed House, is the tomb of Is'mail [Ishmael] — may God bless and preserve him. Its mark is a slab of green marble, almost oblong and in the form of a mihrab. Beside it is a round green slab of marble, and both are remarkable to look upon. There are spots on them both which turns them from their colour to something of yellow so that they are like a mosaic of colours, and I compare them to the spots that are left in the crucible after the gold has been melted in it. Beside this tomb, and on the side towards the 'Iraq corner, is the tomb of his mother Hagar — may God hold her in His favour — its mark being a green stone a span and a half wide. Men are blessed by praying in these two places in the Hijr, and men are right to do so, for they are part of the Ancient House and shelter the two holy and venerated bodies. May God cast His light upon them and advantage with their blessings all who pray over them. Seven spans lie between the two holy tombs.

The dome of the Well of Zamzam is opposite the Black Corner, and lies twenty-four paces from it. The Maqam, which we have already mentioned and behind which prayers are said, is to the right of this dome, from the corner of which to the other is ten paces. The inside of the dome is paved with pure white marble. The orifice of the blessed well is in the centre of the dome deviating towards the wall which faces the venerated House. Its depth is eleven statures of a man as we measured it, and the depth of the water is seven statures, as it is said. The door of this dome faces east, and the door of the dome of 'Abbas and that of the Jewish dome face north. The angle of that side of the dome named after the Jews, which faces the Ancient House, reaches the left corner of the back wall of the 'Abbaside corner which faces east. Between them lies that amount of deviation. Beside the dome of the Well of Zamzam and behind it stands the qabbat al-Sharab [the dome of drinking], which was erected by 'Abbas — may God hold him in His favour. Beside this 'Abbaside dome, obliquely to it, is the dome named after the Jews. These two domes are used as storerooms for pious endowments made to the blessed House, such as Korans, books, candlesticks, and the like. The 'Abbaside dome is still called al-Sharabiyyah because it was a place of drinking for the pilgrims; and there, until to-day, the water of Zamzam is put therein to cool in earthenware jars and brought forth at eventide for the pilgrims to drink. These jars are called *dawraq* and have one handle only. The orifice of the Well of Zamzam is of marble stones so well joined, with lead poured into the interstices, that time will not ravage them. The inside of the orifice is similar, and round it are lead props attached to it to reinforce the strength of the binding and the lead overlay. These props number thirty-two, and their tops protrude to hold the brim of the well round the whole of the orifice. The circumference of the orifice is forty spans, its depth four spans and a half, and its thickness a span and a half. Round the inside of the dome runs a trough of width one span, and depth about two spans and raised five spans from the ground, and it is filled with water for the ritual ablutions. Around it runs a stone block on which men mount to perform the ablutions.

The blessed Black Stone is enchased in the corner facing east. The depth to which it penetrates it is not known, but it is said to extend two cubits into the wall. Its breadth is two-thirds of a span, its length one span and a finger joint. It has four pieces, joined together, and it is said that it was the Qarmata[12] [Carmathians] — may God curse them — who broke it. Its edges have been braced with a sheet of silver whose white shines brightly against the black sheen and polished brilliance of the Stone, presenting the observer a striking spectacle which will hold his looks. The Stone, when kissed, has a softness and moistness which so enchants the mouth that he who puts his lips to it would wish them never to be removed. This is one of the special favours of Divine Providence, and it is enough that the Prophet — may God bless and preserve him — declare to be a covenant of God on earth. May God profit us by the kissing and touching of it. By His favour may all who yearn fervently for it be brought to it. In the sound piece of the stone, to the right of him who presents himself to kiss it, is a small white spot that shines and appears like a mole on the blessed surface. Concerning this white mole, there is a tradition that he who looks upon it clears his vision, and when kissing it one should direct one's lips as closely as one can to the place of the mole.

The sacred Mosque is encompassed by colonnades in three (horizontal) ranges on three rows of marble columns so arranged as to make it like a single colonnade. Its measurement in length is four hundred cubits, its width three hundred, and its area is exactly forty-eight *maraja*.[13] The area between the colonnades is great, but at the time of the Prophet — may God bless and preserve him — it was small and the dome of Zamzam was outside it. Facing the Syrian corner, wedged in the ground, is the capital of a column which at first was the limit of the Haram. Between this capital and the Syrian corner are twenty-two paces. The Ka'bah is in the centre (of the Haram) and its four sides run directly to the east, south, north and west. The number of the marble columns, which myself I counted, is four hundred and seventy-one, excluding the stuccoed column that is in the Dar al-Nadwah (House of Counsel), which was added to the Haram. This is within the colonnade which runs from the west to the north and is faced by the Maqam and the 'Iraq corner. It has a large court and is entered from the colonnade. Against the whole length of this

---

[12] **the Qarmata:** The Carmathians, a sect of Shi'ite Muslims founded by Hamdan Qarmat, dominated the peninsula for nearly one hundred years in the late ninth century. In 930 C.E. they captured Mecca, carrying the sacred Black Stone to Bahrain. The stone was returned to Mecca in 950 by order of the caliph al-Mansur.

[13] **forty-eight *maraja*:** A *maraj* equals fifty square cubits; a cubit is an ancient measure of about eighteen to twenty-two inches, the distance from the tip of the middle finger to the elbow.

colonnade are benches under vaulted arches where sit the copyists, the readers of the Koran, and some who ply the tailor's trade. [. . .]

On the door of the holy Ka'bah is engraved in gold, with graceful characters long and thick, that hold the eyes for their form and beauty, this writing: 'This is amongst those things erected by order of the servant and Caliph of God, the Imam Abu 'Abdullah Muhammad al-Muqtafi li Amri Ilah, Prince of the Faithful. May God bless him and the Imams his righteous ancestors, perpetuating for him the prophetic inheritance and making it an enduring word for his prosperity until the Day of Resurrection. In the year 550 [1155 C.E.].' In this wise (was it written) on the faces of the two door-leaves. These two noble door-leaves are enclosed by a thick band of silver gilt, excellently carved, which rises to the blessed lintel, passes over it and then goes round the sides of the two door-leaves. Between them, when they are closed together, is a sort of broad strip of silver gilt which runs the length of the doors and is attached to the door-leaf which is to the left of him who enters the House.

The *Kiswah*[14] of the sacred Ka'bah is of green silk as we have said. There are thirty-four pieces: nine on the side between the Yemen and Syrian corners, nine also on the opposite side between the Black corner and the 'Iraq corner, and eight on both the side between the 'Iraq and Syrian corners and on that between the Yemen and the Black. Together they come to appear as one single cover comprehending the four sides. The lower part of the Ka'bah is surrounded by a projecting border built of stucco, more than a span in depth and two spans or a little more in width, inside which is wood, not discernible. Into this are driven iron pegs which have at their ends iron rings that are visible. Through these is inserted a rope of hemp, thick and strongly made, which encircles the four sides, and which is sewn with strong, twisted, cotton, thread to a girdle, like that of the *sirwal* [the Arab cotton bloomers], fixed to the hems of the covers. At the juncture of the covers at the four corners, they are sewn together for more than a man's stature, and above that they are brought together by iron hooks engaged in each other. At the top, round the sides of the terrace, runs another projecting border to which the upper parts of the covers are attached with iron rings, after the fashion described. Thus the blessed *Kiswah* is sewn top and bottom, and firmly buttoned, being never removed save at its renewal year by year. Glory to God who perpetuates its honour until the Day of Resurrection. There is no God but He. [. . .]

---

[14] *Kiswah:* The "robe," or covering, of the *Ka'bah*.

Xuanzang (Hsuan Tsang), a Buddhist monk and one of China's most celebrated travelers, was born in Ch'in Liu, in Honan Province, sometime between the years 596 and 603. When he was twelve years old, Xuanzang entered the Pure Land Monastery, a Buddhist center located at the eastern capital city of Lo-yang, where he studied for the next five years. When the Tang dynasty formed in 618, Xuanzang moved to the new capital at Chang'an, but the hostility of the new dynasty toward Buddhism led him to move on to Chengdu (Ch'eng-tu), the capital of Szechuan Province and a sanctuary for Buddhist monks. He studied in Ch'eng-du from 620 until 622 before leaving on a circuitous journey of studying and lecturing that eventually led back to Chang'an. Having exhausted the Buddhist resources and teachers at home and feeling that his learning was still incomplete, Xuanzang decided to follow in the footsteps of the earlier Buddhist pilgrim Faxian, who had traveled to India in the early fifth century. Thus in the fall of 629 Xuanzang embarked on his great journey to the West—that is, to India—to study with Indian masters close to the geographical and spiritual fountainhead of Buddhism and to obtain texts and relics that would strengthen Buddhism in China. After having some trouble leaving China, Xuanzang traveled westward, over difficult mountain passes between Jinchang and Anxi, then following the Silk Road he skirted the northern edge of the plateau of Tibet (along the Kunlun Mountains and the Karakoram Range) to reach Samarkand. From there he went south, through what is now Afghanistan, across the Hindu Kush and into northern India. Once in India, Xuanzang visited nearly every major kingdom of that country, studying with monks and visiting holy sites. He did not return to his homeland until 645.

Xuanzang's account of his pilgrimage to and through India, *Records of the Western Countries (Si-Yu-Ki),* is a fascinating window into seventh-century India. While Xuanzang's primary interest in *Records* are Buddhist monasteries, relics, and the teachings of India as well as the places made sacred by events in the life of Buddha, he is also interested in the life and customs of the regions through which he travels. In the following excerpt, Xuanzang describes the kingdom of Magadha and his visit to the site of the sacred Bodhi tree under which the Buddha (whom Xuanzang calls Tathagata, "the Perfected One") received enlightenment. Typical of his writings, Xuanzang here not only describes a place but also recounts some of the stories surrounding the place, including the conversion of the Maurya emperor Asoka (Ashoka; r. c. 274–232 B.C.E.), whose pilgrimage through India to visit the holy sites of Buddha's life provided a model for Xuanzang's own journey.

❧ Records of Western Countries

Translated by Samuel Beal

FROM BOOK VIII
[THE KINGDOM OF MAGADHA
AND THE BODHI TREE]

The country of Magadha[1] (Mo-kie-t'o) is about 5,000 li[2] in circuit. The walled cities have but few inhabitants, but the towns are thickly populated. The soil is rich and fertile and the grain cultivation abundant. There is an unusual sort of rice grown here, the grains of which are large and scented and of an exquisite taste. It is specially remarkable for its shining colour. It is commonly called "the rice for the use of the great." As the ground is low and damp, the inhabited towns are built on the high uplands. After the first month of summer and before the second month of autumn, the level country is flooded, and communication can be kept up by boats. The manners of the people are simple and honest. The temperature is pleasantly hot; they esteem very much the pursuit of learning and profoundly respect the religion of Buddha. There are some fifty *sangharmas*,[3] with about 10,000 priests, of whom the greater number study the teaching of the Great Vehicle. There are ten Deva temples, occupied, by sectaries of different persuasions, who are very numerous.

To the south of the river Ganges there is an old city about 70 li round. Although it has been long deserted, its foundation walls still survive. Formerly, when men's lives were incalculably long, it was called Kusumapura (K'u-su-mo-pu-lo), so called because the palace of the king had many flowers. Afterwards, when men's age reached several thousands of years, then its name was changed to Pataliputra (Po-ch'a-li-tsu-ch'ing).

At the beginning there was a Brahman of high talent and singular learning. Many thousands flocked to him to receive instruction. One day all the students went out on a tour of observation; one of them betrayed a feeling of unquiet and distress. His fellow-students addressed him and said, "What troubles you, friend?" He said, "I am in my full maturity (*beauty*) with perfect strength, and yet I go on wandering about here like a lonely shadow till years and months have passed, and my duties (*manly duties*) not performed. Thinking of this, my words are sad and my heart is afflicted."

On this his companions in sport replied, "We must seek then for your good a bride and her friends." Then they supposed two persons to represent the father and mother of the bridegroom, and two persons the father and mother of the bride, and

---

[1] **Magadha:** A kingdom in the northeastern part of central India (now Bihar) intersected by the Ganges River; birthplace of the Buddhist movement in the sixth century B.C.E.

[2] **5,000 li:** About 1,700 miles; a *li* is a Chinese unit of measure equivalent to roughly one-third of a mile.

[3] **sangharmas:** Buddhist monasteries; from *sangha,* meaning "a community of followers."

as they were sitting under a *Patali (Po-ch'a-li)* tree, they called it the tree of the son-in-law. Then they gathered seasonable fruits and pure water, and followed all the nuptial customs, and requested a time to be fixed. Then the father of the supposed bride gathered a twig with flowers on it, gave it to the student and said, "This is your excellent partner; be graciously pleased to accept her." The student's heart was rejoiced as he took her to himself. And now, as the sun was setting, they proposed to return home; but the young student affected by love, preferred to remain.

Then the other said, 'All this was fun; pray come back with us; there are wild beasts in this forest; we are afraid they will kill you." But the student preferred to remain walking up and down by the side of the tree.

After sunset a strange light lit up the plain, the sound of pipes and lutes with their soft music (*was heard*), and the ground was covered with a sumptuous carpet. Suddenly an old man of gentle mien was seen coming, supporting himself by his staff, and there was also an old mother leading a young maiden. They were accompanied by a procession along the way, dressed in holiday attire and attended with music. The old man then pointed to the maiden and said, "This is your worship's wife (*lady*)." Seven days then passed in carousing and music, when the companions of the student, in doubt whether he had been destroyed by wild beasts, went forth and came to the place. They found him alone in the shade of the tree, sitting as if facing a superior guest. They asked him to return with them but he respectfully declined.

After this he entered of his own accord the city, to pay respect to his relatives, and told them of this adventure from beginning to end. Having heard it with wonder, he returned with all his relatives and friends to the middle of the forest, and there they saw the flowering tree become a great mansion; servants of all kinds were hurrying to and fro on every side, and the old man came forward and received them with politeness, and entertained them with all kinds of dainties served up amidst the sound of music. After the usual compliments, the guests returned to the city and told to all, far and near, what had happened.

After the year was accomplished the wife gave birth to a son, when the husband said to his spouse, "I wish now to return, but yet I cannot bear to be separated from you (*your bridal residence*); but if I rest here I fear the exposure to wind and weather."

The wife having heard this, told her father. The old man then addressed the student and said, "Whilst living contented and happy why must you go back? I will build you a house, let there be no thought of desertion." On this his servants applied themselves to the work, and in less than a day it was finished.

When the old capital of Kusumapura was changed, this town was chosen, and from the circumstance of the genii building the mansion of the youth the name henceforth of the country was Pataliputra pura (the city of the son of the Patali tree). [. . .]

Going south-west from Mount Pragbodhi about 14 or 15 li, we come to the Bodhi tree.[4] It is surrounded by a brick wall (*a wall of piled bricks*) of considerable

---

[4] **Bodhi tree:** The tree under which the Buddha sat and attained enlightenment. The site, commemorated by the Mahbodhi Stupa in what is now Bodhgaya, remains a major Buddhist shrine.

height, steep and strong. It is long from east to west, and short from north to south. It is about 500 paces round. Rare trees with their renowned flowers connect their shade and cast their shadows; the delicate *sha* herb and different shrubs carpet the soil. The principal gate opens to the east, opposite the Nairanjana river.[5] The southern gate adjoins a great flowery bank. The western side is blocked up and difficult of access (*steep and strong*). The northern gate opens into the great *sangharama*. Within the surrounding wall the sacred traces touch one another in all directions. Here there are *stupas*,[6] in another place *viharas*.[7] The kings, princes, and great personages throughout all Jambudvipa,[8] who have accepted the bequeathed teaching as handed down to them, have erected these monuments as memorials.

In the middle of the enclosure surrounding the *Bodhi* tree is the diamond throne (*Vajrasana*). In former days, when the Bhadra-kalpa[9] was arriving at the period of perfection (*vivartta*), when the great earth arose, this (*throne*) also appeared. It is in the middle of the great *chiliocosm;* it goes down to the limits of the golden wheel (*the gold circle*), and upwards it is flush with the ground. It is composed of diamond. In circuit it is 100 paces or so. On this the thousand Buddhas of the Bhadrakalpa have sat and entered the diamond *Samadhi;* hence the name of the diamond throne. It is the place where the Buddhas attain the holy path (*the sacred way of Buddhahood*). It is also called the *Bodhimanda*. When the great earth is shaken, this place alone is unmoved. Therefore when Tathagata was about to reach the condition of enlightenment, and he went successively to the four angles of this enclosure, the earth shook and quaked; but afterwards coming to this spot, all was still and at rest. From the time of entering on the concluding portion of the kalpa, when the true law dies out and disappears, the earth and dust begin to cover over this spot, and it will be no longer visible.

After the *Nirvana* of Buddha, the rulers of the different countries having learned by tradition the measurement of the diamond throne, decided the limits from north to south by two figures of Kwan-tsz'-tsai (Avalokitesvara) Bodhisattva, there seated and looking eastward.

The old people say that "as soon as the figures of this Bodhisattva sink in the ground and disappear, the law of Buddha will come to an end." The figure at the south angle is now buried up to its breast. The *Bodhi* tree above the diamond throne

---

[5] **Nairanjana river:** The river near today's Bodhgaya where Buddha spent six years seeking enlightenment before abandoning his practice of self-denial and engaging in meditation under the Bodhi tree.

[6] *stupas:* Originally, domed shrines built to house the tombs or relics of holy persons; Xuanzang refers here to shrines built to commemorate the Eight Great Deeds of the Buddha and to house relics associated with him. The *stupa* on the banks of the river Nairanjana commemorates the Buddha's enlightenment, one of the Eight Great Deeds.

[7] *viharas:* A Buddhist sanctuary or temple often connected to a monastery.

[8] **Jambudvipa:** A Sanskrit term used to define the geographical area of India; in the Buddhist cosmology, it also signifies the world of human beings and other living creatures.

[9] **Bhadra-kalpa:** Literally, the blessed age; a Buddhist epithet for the current age, which will last more than 236 million years, after one thousand Buddhas have appeared on earth.

is the same as the *Pippala* tree. In old days, when Buddha was alive, it was several hundred feet high. Although it has often been injured by cutting, it still is 40 or 50 feet in height. Buddha sitting under this tree reached perfect wisdom, and therefore it is called the (*Samyak sambodhi*) tree of knowledge (*Pu-ti-Bodhi*). The bark is of a yellowish-white colour, the leaves and twigs of a dark green. The leaves wither not either in winter or summer, but they remain shining and glistening all the year round without change. But at every successive *Nirvana*-day (*of the Buddhas*) the leaves wither and fall, and then in a moment revive as before. On this day (of the *Nirvana*?) the princes of different countries and the religious multitude from different quarters assemble by thousands and ten thousands unbidden, and bathe (*the roots*) with scented water and perfumed milk; whilst they raise the sounds of music and scatter flowers and perfumes, and whilst the light of day is continued by the burning torches, they offer their religious gifts.

After the Nirvana of Tathagata, when Asoka-raja[10] began to reign, he was an unbeliever (*a believer in heresy*), and he desired to destroy the bequeathed traces of Buddha, so he raised an army, and himself taking the lead, he came here for the purpose of destroying (*the tree*). He cut through the roots; the trunk, branches, and leaves were all divided into small bits and heaped up in a pile a few tens of paces to the west of the place. Then he ordered a Brahman who sacrificed to fire to burn them in the discharge of his religious worship. Scarcely had the smoke cleared away, when lo! a double tree burst forth from the flaming fire, and because the leaves and branches were shining like feathers, it was called the "ashes bodhi tree." Asoka-raja, seeing the miracle, repented of his crime. He bathed the roots (*of the old tree*) with perfumed milk to fertilise them, when lo! on the morning of the next day, the tree sprang up as before. The king, seeing the miraculous portent, was overpowered with deep emotion, and himself offered religious gifts, and was so overjoyed that he forgot to return (*to the palace*). The queen, who was an adherent of the heretics, sent secretly a messenger, who, after the first division of night, once more cut it down. Asoka-raja in the morning coming again to worship at the tree, seeing only the mutilated trunk, was filled with exceeding grief. With the utmost sincerity he prayed as he worshipped; he bathed the roots with perfumed milk, and in less than a day again the tree was restored. The king, moved by deep reverence at the prodigy, surrounded the tree with a stone (*brick)* wall above 10 feet, which still remains visible. In late times Sasanka-raja (She-shang-kia), being a believer in heresy, slandered the religion of Buddha, and through envy destroyed the convents and cut down the *Bodhi* tree, digging it up to the very springs of the earth; but yet he did not get to the bottom of the roots. Then he burnt it with fire and sprinkled it with the juice of the sugarcane, desiring to destroy it entirely, and not leave a trace of it behind.

---

[10] **Asoka-raja:** The Maurya emperor Ashoka (Asoka, third century B.C.E.), the greatest of the ancient Indian rulers, was known for uniting India and for his just laws and tolerance. Moved by the suffering his armies inflicted when he invaded Kalinga, Ashoka converted to Buddhism and traveled throughout India visiting sacred sites and building *stupas* to commemorate the life of Buddha. He attained legendary status through *Asokavadana*, a book about his life written in the second century.

Some months afterwards, the king of Magadha, called Purnavarma (Pu-la-na-fa-mo), the last of the race of Asoka-raja, hearing of it, sighed and said, "The sun of wisdom having set, nothing is left but the tree of Buddha, and this they now have destroyed, what source of spiritual life is there now?" He then cast his body on the ground overcome with pity; then with the milk of a thousand cows he again bathed the roots of the tree, and in a night it once more revived and grew to the height of some 10 feet. Fearing lest it should be again cut down, he surrounded it with a wall of stone 24 feet high. So the tree is now encircled with a wall about 20 feet high.

ଓ GIOVANNI DA PIAN DI CARPINE
c. 1185–1252

Born around 1185 at Pian di Carpine (now della Magione), a small town in Umbria, Giovanni da Pian di Carpine (John of Pian di Carpine) entered the Franciscan order as a young man, taking part in several missionary initiatives in Germany, Saxony, and Spain. In 1245, Pope Innocent IV (r. 1243–54) dispatched the at least sixty-year-old Friar John with Friar Stephen of Bohemia on a mission to meet with the Mongol leaders. The Pope feared that the Mongols, who recently had conquered parts of Hungary, Poland, and Russia and reached within a few miles of Vienna, were planning to invade more of central Europe. Passing through Poland, where he collected Friar Benedict, Carpine reached the Russian city of Kiev, on the Dnieper River, in the middle of winter. Nearly overcome by exhaustion and cold, the threesome nonetheless spent less than a month at Kiev before pushing on to meet the Mongols. Friar John met the first Mongol party in Cumans, in Mongol territory between Kiev and the Black Sea, in February 1246. Qurumshi, the territorial leader, sent Friar John to meet with Batu, the khan of Kipchak (later the Golden Horde), whose headquarters were on the Volga River south of Saratov. Batu in turn sent John to meet Guyuk, the preeminent Mongol leader, far to the east, at Karakorum. It took the monks almost five months to reach Karakorum, where they arrived in July after having crossed over the deserts and mountains of central Asia and Mongolia just as Guyuk was being elected to the khanate.

In the following selections taken from Carpine's *History of the Mongols* (*Ystoria Mongalorum*), written upon the friar's return to Italy in 1247 as an account of his travels to the pope, Carpine describes Guyuk's enthronement and his embassy to Guyuk's court. Also included is Guyuk's letter to Pope Innocent IV, which Friar John delivered upon his return from Mongolia. Friar John eventually was appointed the archbishop of Anativari in Dalmatia, a province along the Adriatic Sea in what is now Serbia and Croatia. He died only a few years later, in 1252.

FROM

❧ History of the Mongols

Translated by a nun of Stanbrook Abbey

[Embassy to the Guyuk, the Great Khan]

Next we entered the land of the Mongols, whom we call Tartars. We were, I think, journeying through this country for three weeks riding hard, and on the feast of St. Mary Magdalene [July 22nd] we reached Cuyuc, who is now Emperor.[1] We made the whole of this journey at great speed, for our Tartars had been ordered to take us quickly so that we could arrive in time for the solemn court which had been convened several years back for the election. And so we started at dawn and journeyed until night without a meal, and many a time we arrived so late that we did not eat that night but were given in the morning the food we should have eaten the previous evening. We went as fast as the horses could trot, for the horses were in no way spared since we had fresh ones several times a day, and those which fell out returned, as has already been described, and so we rode swiftly without a break.

On our arrival Cuyuc had us given a tent and provisions, such as it is the custom for the Tartars to give, but they treated us better than other envoys. Nevertheless we were not invited to visit him for he had not yet been elected, nor did he yet concern himself with the government. The translation of the Lord Pope's letter,[2] however and the things I had said had been sent to him by Bati.[3] After we had stayed there for five or six days he sent us to his mother[4] where the solemn court was assembling. By the time we got there a large pavilion had already been put up made of white velvet, and in my opinion it was so big that more than two thousand men could have got into it. Around it had been erected a wooden palisade, on which various designs were painted. On the second or third day we went with the Tartars who had been appointed to look after us and there all the chiefs were assembled and each one was riding with his followers among the hills and over the plains round about.

On the first day they were all clothed in white velvet, on the second in red—that day Cuyuc came to the tent—on the third day they were all in blue velvet and on the fourth in the finest brocade. In the palisade round the pavilion were two large gates,

---

[1] **Cuyuc . . . Emperor:** Guyuk (d. 1248), the son of the Great Khan, Ogodei (Ugedey; r. 1229–41), and his wife, Toregene (Turakina), had just been elected the new khan after a bitter power struggle following the death of his father in December 1241.

[2] **Lord Pope's letter:** Pope Innocent IV, the pope from 1243 to 1254, had sent Friar John on a papal embassy to the Mongols with a letter.

[3] **Bati:** Batu (d. 1255), the khan of Kipchak, the westernmost region of Mongol rule, which at the time of Friar John's mission included the newly occupied territories of southern Russia. Batu was a grandson of Chingis Khan and the cousin of Guyuk.

[4] **his mother:** Toregene (Turakina Khatun), the widow of the former khan Ogodei in Mongolia; she held power during the interregnum, the time when a throne is vacant.

through one of which the Emperor alone had the right to enter and there were no guards placed at it although it was open, for no one dare enter or leave by it; through the other gate all those who were granted admittance entered and there were guards there with swords and bows and arrows. If anyone approached the tent beyond the fixed limits, he was beaten if caught; if he ran away he was shot at, but with arrows however which had no heads. The horses were, I suppose, two arrow-flights away. The chiefs went about everywhere armed and accompanied by a number of their men, but none, unless their group of ten was complete, could go as far as the horses; indeed those who attempted to do so were severely beaten. There were many of them who had, as far as I could judge, about twenty marks' worth of gold on their bits, breastplates, saddles and cruppers. The chiefs held their conference inside the tent and, so I believe, conducted the election. All the other people however were a long way away outside the afore-mentioned palisade. There they remained until almost mid-day and then they began to drink mare's milk and they drank until the evening, so much that it was amazing to see. We were invited inside and they gave us mead as we would not take mare's milk. They did this to show us great honour, but they kept on plying us with drinks to such an extent that we could not possibly stand it, not being used to it, so we gave them to understand that it was disagreeable to us and they left off pressing us. [. . .]

Leaving there we rode all together for three or four leagues to another place, where on a pleasant plain near a river among the mountains another tent had been set up, which is called by them the Golden Orda;[5] it was here that Cuyuc was to be enthroned on the feast of the Assumption of Our Lady,[6] but owing to the hail which fell, as I have already related, the ceremony was put off. This tent was supported by columns covered with gold plates and fastened to other wooden beams with nails of gold, and the roof above and the sides on the interior were of brocade, but outside they were of other materials. We were there until the feast of St. Bartholomew,[7] on which day a vast crowd assembled. They stood facing south, so arranged that some of them were a stone's throw away from the others, and they kept moving forward, going further and further away, saying prayers and genuflecting towards the south. We however, not knowing whether they were uttering incantations or bending the knee to God or another, were unwilling to genuflect. After they had done this for a considerable time, they returned to the tent and placed Cuyuc on the imperial throne, and the chiefs knelt before him and after them all the people, with the exception of us who were not subject to them. Then they started drinking and, as is their custom, they drank without stopping until the evening. After that cooked meat was brought in carts without any salt and they gave one joint between four or five men. Inside however they gave meat with salted broth as sauce and they did this on all the days that they held a feast.

---

[5] **Golden Orda:** Altyn Orda, or the Golden Horde, which would eventually come to mean the western part of the empire.

[6] **the feast . . . Our Lady:** August 15.

[7] **feast of St. Bartholomew:** August 24.

At that place we were summoned into the presence of the Emperor, and Chingay[8] the protonotary wrote down our names and the names of those who had sent us, also the names of the chief of the Solangi and of others, and then calling out in a loud voice he recited them before the Emperor and all the chiefs. When this was finished each one of us genuflected four times on the left knee and they warned us not to touch the lower part of the threshold. After we had been most thoroughly searched for knives and they had found nothing at all, we entered by a door on the east side, for no one dare enter from the west with the sole exception of the Emperor or, if it is a chief's tent, the chief; those of lower rank do not pay much attention to such things. This was the first time since Cuyuc had been made Emperor that we had entered his tent in his presence. He also received all the envoys in that place, but very few entered his tent.

So many gifts were bestowed by the envoys there that it was marvellous to behold—gifts of silk, samite, velvet, brocade, girdles of silk threaded with gold, choice furs and other presents. The Emperor was also given a sunshade or little awning such as is carried over his head, and it was all decorated with precious stones. A certain governor of a province brought a number of camels for him, decked with brocade and with saddles on them having some kind of contrivance inside which men could sit, and there were, I should think, forty or fifty of them; he also brought many horses and mules covered with trappings or armour made of leather or of iron. We in our turn were asked if we wished to present any gifts, but we had by now used up practically everything, so had nothing to give him. There up on a hill a good distance away from the tents were stationed more than five hundred carts, which were all filled with gold and silver and silken garments and these things were shared out among the Emperor and the chiefs. Each chief divided his share among his men, but according to his own good pleasure.

Leaving there we went to another place where a wonderful tent had been set up all of red velvet, and this had been given by the Kitayans; there also we were taken inside. Whenever we went in we were given mead and wine to drink, and cooked meat was offered us if we wished to have it. A lofty platform of boards had been erected, on which the Emperor's throne was placed. The throne, which was of ivory, was wonderfully carved and there was also gold on it, and precious stones, if I remember rightly, and pearls. Steps led up to it and it was rounded behind. Benches were also placed round the throne, and here the ladies sat in their seats on the left; nobody, however, sat on the right, but the chiefs were on benches in the middle and the rest of the people sat beyond them. Every day a great crowd of ladies came.

The three tents of which I have spoken were very large. The Emperor's wives however had other tents of white felt, which were quite big and beautiful. At that place they separated, the Emperor's mother going in one direction and the Emperor in another to administer justice. The mistress of the Emperor had been arrested; she had murdered his father with poison at the time when their army was in Hungary

---

[8] Chingay: A Nestorian Christian who had also served under Ogodei. Nestorian Christianity, named after Nestorius, a fifth-century Syrian monk from Antioch, had taken hold in Mongolia and parts of Asia; the empress dowager Toregene was a Nestorian Christian.

and as a result the army in these parts retreated. Judgment was passed on her along with a number of others and they were put to death. [. . .]

Before the enthronement Cosmas[9] showed us the Emperor's throne which he himself had made and his seal which he had fashioned, and he also told us what the inscription was on the seal. We picked up many other bits of private information about the Emperor from men who had come with other chiefs, a number of Russians and Hungarians knowing Latin and French, and Russian clerics and others, who had been among the Tartars, some for thirty years, through wars and other happenings, and who knew all about them, for they knew the language and had lived with them continually some twenty years, others ten, some more, some less. With the help of these men we were able to gain a thorough knowledge of everything. They told us about everything willingly and sometimes without being asked, for they knew what we wanted. [. . .]

We then set out on the return journey.

---

[9] **Cosmas:** A Russian goldsmith in the service of Guyuk; both Friar John and William of Rubruck met with Russians, Hungarians, and other Europeans in the Mongolian court. Most were captives taken during the Mongol attacks on Europe in previous years.

Guyuk Khan's Letter to Pope Innocent IV

We, by the power of the eternal heaven,

> Khan of the great Ulus[1]

Our command: —

> This is a version sent to the great Pope, that he may know and understand in the [Muslim] tongue, what has been written. The petition of the assembly held in the lands of the Emperor [for our support], has been heard from your emissaries.

If he reaches [you] with his own report, Thou, who art the great Pope, together with all the Princes, come in person to serve us. At that time I shall make known all the commands of the *Yasa*.

You have also said that supplication and prayer have been offered by you, that I might find a good entry into baptism. This prayer of thine I have not understood. Other words which thou hast sent me: "I am surprised that thou hast seized all the lands of the Magyar and the Christians. Tell us what their fault is." These words of thine I have also not understood. The eternal God has slain and annihilated these lands and peoples, because they have neither adhered to Chingis Khan, nor to the Khagan,[2] both of whom have been sent to make known God's command, nor to

---

[1] **Ulus:** A social unit; here referring to all people under the rule of the khagan, or the supreme ruler.

[2] **Chingis Khan . . . Khagan:** Chingis Khan (r. 1206–27) and Ogodei (r. 1229–41), the "Supreme Ruler," were the two "Great Khans" who immediately preceded Guyuk. Ogodei, Chingis Khan's third son and his named successor, was the Guyuk's father.

the command of God. Like thy words, they also were impudent, they were proud and they slew our messenger-emissaries. How could anybody seize or kill by his own power contrary to the command of God?

Though thou likewise sayest that I should become a trembling Nestorian Christian, worship God and be an ascetic, how knowest thou whom God absolves, in truth to whom He shows mercy? How dost thou know that such words as thou speakest are with God's sanction? From the rising of the sun to its setting, all the lands have been made subject to me. Who could do this contrary to the command of God?

Now you should say with a sincere heart: "I will submit and serve you." Thou thyself, at the head of all the Princes, come at once to serve and wait upon us! At that time I shall recognize your submission.

If you do not observe God's command, and if you ignore my command, I shall know you as my enemy. Likewise I shall make you understand. If you do otherwise, God knows what I know.

At the end of Jumada the second in the year 644.[3]

THE SEAL

We, by the power of the eternal Tengri, universal Khan of the great Mongol Ulus—our command. If this reaches peoples who have made their submission, let them respect and stand in awe of it.

---

[3] **At the end . . . 644:** This date refers to the Muslim calendar, Jumada of the year 644 A.H., or early November 1246 C.E.

❧ MARCO POLO
1254–1324

Marco Polo was born in Venice, Italy, in 1254. When Marco was six years old, his father, Niccolo, a wealthy aristocrat with a vested interest in trade, and his uncle Maffeo Polo, embarked on a trading journey to Crimea that unexpectedly took them to the court of the Mongol emperor of China, Kublai Khan. The emperor dispatched the Polos back to Italy, asking them to return to his country with a hundred men well-versed in religion, science, and the arts so that he could assess the value of Christianity and the technology of the West. Thus, after an absence of nine years, Niccolo and his brother returned to Venice and were reunited with the fifteen-year-old Marco, whose mother had died. The Polos, eager to return to China, were delayed by the death of Pope Clement IV in 1268. In

**Kublai Khan
Receiving the Polos,
1413**
*Marco Polo recounted
his great adventures
in the East in his*
Travels, *which
appeared in several
translations that
captured the
imagination of
Western readers. The
Polos — Marco, his
father, and his
uncle — spent many
years at the courts of
the Mongol Chinese
leader Kublai Khan.
Here they are being
given a golden seal
while the khan looks
on in approval. (Art
Resource)*

1271, after receiving diplomatic authority from the newly elected pope Gregory X, the Polos, along with young Marco and two friars, began their long overland journey from Acre to Cathay. They traveled by way of Hormuz, on the Persian Gulf, then north-northwest across the deserts of Persia and the mountains of Pamir to the Silk Road, which they followed east around the Takla Makan and Gobi Deserts. After a journey of three and a half years, in May 1275 they arrived at what Marco Polo calls "Kemenfu." It appears that the Polos arrived first at Shangdu (Xanadu), where the Great Khan, as Kublai Khan was called, kept his summer palace, before going on to Khanbalik (now Beijing), the site of the winter palace. Marco Polo would remain in China for the next seventeen years, returning to Venice in 1295.

The Polos, particularly young Marco, received special favor from the emperor. Niccolo and Maffeo served as military advisors and helped to fashion artillery for the khan; Marco served as a government official and an ambassador for Kublai Khan, traveling as far as India and Burma on some missions. By his own account, Marco Polo traveled over most of China, learning about its climate, geography, and people — both Mongols and native Chinese — including their language, history, and customs. In 1292 the Polos left China as part of a cohort escorting a Mongol princess to Persia where she was to be married to the regional governor, the Ilkhan Arghun (r. 1284–91). They traveled by sea, reaching Sumatra and eventually Persia, but when they learned that Arghun had died, they then had to travel into Khurasan Province to deliver the princess to Arghun's son, Ghazan. From there they went on to Trebizond, on the Black Sea, where they were forced to leave behind a good deal of their treasured goods, then to Constantinople and, eventually, to Venice. In 1295, after an absence of twenty-four years, Marco Polo arrived home. Ironically, perhaps, this man who had traveled freely in China for so long ended up a prisoner of war in Genoa, which at the time was at war with Venice. During his detention, Marco Polo supposedly related the story of his magnificent travels to fellow prisoner Rustichello ("Rusticiaus") of Pisa, the author of a book of Arthurian romances. Released from prison in 1299, Marco moved back to Venice where he took up residence in a newly acquired estate, was married, and enjoyed the rise of his fame and glory as his book, *Description of the World,* or as it is better known, *The Travels of Marco Polo,* which was translated throughout Europe. He died in January 1324.

Polo's descriptions of paper money, the post, the canal system, the armies of the khan, his palace, the rise of Mongol power, the elaborate ceremonies of the court, and the vast wealth and extent of China fascinated readers of *The Travels,* which appeared shortly after Polo's release from the Genoese prison. Selections here include his famous description of the palace at Shangdu (Xanadu), which inspired the British Romantic poet Samuel Taylor Coleridge to write the lyric poem "Kubla Khan"; his description of paper currency; and the Great Khan's generosity toward his subjects.

FROM

℘ The Travels of Marco Polo

Translated by Ronald Latham

[KUBLAI KHAN'S PALACE AT SHANDU]

[. . .] If we leave this province and city and go on our way for three days, we shall find a city called Chagan-nor[1] where there is a large palace belonging to the Great Khan. He enjoys staying in this palace because there are lakes and rivers here in plenty, well stocked with swans. There are also fine plains, teeming with cranes, pheasants and partridges, and many other sorts of wild fowl; and that is a further attraction for the Great Khan, who is a keen sportsman and takes great delight in hawking for birds with falcons and gerfalcons. There are five sorts of crane, which I will describe to you. One is entirely black, like a raven, and very large. The second is pure white. Its wings are beautiful, with all the plumage studded with round eyes like those of a peacock but of the colour of burnished gold. It has a scarlet and black head and a black and white neck and is larger than any of the others. The third species is like the cranes we know. The fourth is small, with long plumes by its ears, scarlet and black in colour and very beautiful. The fifth is a very large bird, quite grey with shapely head coloured scarlet and black.

Beyond this city lies a valley in which the Great Khan keeps flocks of *cators,* which we call 'great partridges', in such quantities that they are a sight to behold. In order to feed them, he regularly has crops sown on the slopes in summer, consisting of millet and panic and other favourite foods of such fowl, and allows no one to reap them, so that they may eat their fill. And many guards are set to watch these birds, to prevent anyone from taking them. And in winter their keepers scatter millet for

---

[1] **Chagan-nor:** The name means "white pool"; the city was the site of an old Mongol fortress in the former Chahar Province in northern China.

them; and they are so used to this feeding that, if a man flings some of the grain on the ground, he has only to whistle and, wherever they may be, they flock to him. And the Great Khan has had many huts built, in which they spend the night. So, when he visits this country, he has a plentiful supply of these fowl, as many as he wants. And in winter, when they are nice and plump, since he does not stay there himself at this season because of the intense cold, he has camel-loads of them brought to him, wherever he may be.

When the traveller leaves this city and journeys north-northeast for three days, he comes to a city called Shang-tu,[2] which was built by the Great Khan now reigning, whose name is Kublai. In this city Kublai Khan built a huge palace of marble and other ornamental stones. Its halls and chambers are all gilded, and the whole building is marvellously embellished and richly adorned. At one end it extends into the middle of the city; at the other it abuts on the city wall. At this end another wall, running out from the city wall in the direction opposite to the palace, encloses and encircles fully sixteen miles of park-land well watered with springs and streams and diversified with lawns. Into this park there is no entry except by way of the palace. Here the Great Khan keeps game animals of all sorts, such as hart, stag, and roebuck, to provide food for the gerfalcons and other falcons which he has here in mew. The gerfalcons alone amount to more than 200. Once a week he comes in person to inspect them in the mew. Often, too, he enters the park with a leopard on the crupper of his horse; when he feels inclined, he lets it go and thus catches a hart or stag or roebuck to give to the gerfalcons that he keeps in mew. And this he does for recreation and sport.

In the midst of this enclosed park, where there is a beautiful grove, the Great Khan has built another large palace, constructed entirely of canes, but with the interior all gilt and decorated with beasts and birds of very skilful workmanship. It is reared on gilt and varnished pillars, on each of which stands a dragon, entwining the pillar with his tail and supporting the roof on his outstretched limbs. The roof is also made of canes, so well varnished that it is quite waterproof. Let me explain how it is constructed. You must know that these canes are more than three palms in girth and from ten to fifteen paces long. They are sliced down through the middle from one knot to the next, thus making two shingles. These shingles are thick and long enough not only for roofing but for every sort of construction. The palace, then, is built entirely of such canes. As a protection against the wind each shingle is fastened with nails. And the Great Khan has had it so designed that it can be moved whenever he fancies; for it is held in place by more than 200 cords of silk.

The Great Khan stays at Shang-tu for three months in the year, June, July, and August, to escape from the heat and for the sake of the recreation it affords. During these three months be keeps the palace of canes erected; for the rest of the year it is dismantled. And he has had it so constructed that he can erect or dismantle it at pleasure.

---

[2] **Shang-tu:** Shangdu (Xanadu), the summer palace of the Great Khan; near what is now Kalgan.

When it comes to the 28th day of August, the Great Khan takes his leave of this city and of this palace. Every year he leaves on this precise day; and I will tell you why. The fact is that he has a stud of snow-white stallions and snow-white mares, without a speck of any other colour. Their numbers are such that the mares alone amount to more than 10,000. The milk of these mares may not be drunk by anyone who is not of the imperial lineage, that is to say of the lineage of the Great Khan. To this rule there is one exception; the milk may be drunk by a race of men called Horiat, by virtue of a special privilege granted to them by Chinghiz Khan[3] because of a victory that they won with him in the old days. When these white steeds are grazing, such reverence is shown to them that if a great lord were going that way he could not pass through their midst, but would either wait till they had passed or go on until he had passed them. The astrologers and idolaters have told the Great Khan that he must make a libation of the milk of these mares every year on the 28th [of] August, flinging it into the air and on the earth, so that the spirits may have their share to drink. They must have this, it is said, in order that they may guard all his possessions, men and women, beasts, birds, crops, and everything besides. [. . .]

[THE GENEROSITY OF THE GREAT KHAN]

Now let me tell you something of the bounties that the Great Khan confers upon his subjects. For all his thoughts are directed towards helping the people who are subject to him, so that they may live and labour and increase their wealth. You may take it for a fact that he sends emissaries and inspectors throughout all his dominions and kingdoms and provinces to learn whether any of his people have suffered a failure of their crops either through weather or through locusts or other pests. And if he finds that any have lost their harvest, he exempts them for that year from their tribute and even gives them some of his own grain to sow and to eat—a magnificent act of royal bounty. This he does in the summer. And in winter he does likewise in the matter of cattle. If he finds any man whose cattle have been killed by an outbreak of plague, he gives him some of his own, derived from the tithes of other provinces, and to help him further he relieves him of tribute for the year.

Again, if it should happen that lightning strikes any flock of sheep or herd of other beasts, whether the herd belongs to one person or more and no matter how big it may be, the Great Khan will not take tithe of it for three years. And similarly if it chances to strike a ship laden with merchandise, he will not have any due or share of the cargo, because he accounts it an ill omen when lightning strikes any man's possessions. He reasons: 'God must have been angry with this man, since He launched a thunderbolt at him.' Therefore he does not wish that such possessions, struck by the wrath of God, should find their way into his treasury.

Here is another benefit that he confers.

---

[3] **Chinghiz Khan:** Chingis (Ghengis) Khan (r. 1206–27), one of the great Mongol emperors; establishing his capital at Karakorum, Chingis Khan united the Mongol tribes and spread Mongol rule throughout northern China, Turkestan, Afghanistan, and parts of Eastern Europe.

Along the main highways frequented by his messengers and by merchants and other folk, he has ordered trees to be planted on both sides, two paces distant from one another. They are so large that they can be seen from a long way off. And he has done this so that any wayfarer may recognize the roads and not lose his way. For you will find these wayside trees in the heart of the wilderness; and a great boon they are to travellers and traders. They extend throughout every province and every kingdom. Where the roads traverse sandy deserts or rocky mountain ranges, so that it is not possible to plant trees, he has other land-marks set up in the form of cairns or pillars to indicate the track. He has certain officials whose duty it is to ensure that these are always kept in order. Besides the reasons already mentioned, he is all the more willing to have these trees planted because his soothsayers and astrologers declare that he who causes trees to be planted lives long.

You must know that most of the inhabitants of the province of Cathay drink a wine such as I will describe to you. They make a drink of rice and an assortment of excellent spices, prepared in such a way that it is better to drink than any other wine. It is beautifully clear and it intoxicates more speedily than any other wine, because it is very heating.

Let me tell you next of stones that burn like logs. It is a fact that throughout the province of Cathay there is a sort of black stone, which is dug out of veins in the hillsides and burns like logs. These stones keep a fire going better than wood. I assure you that, if you put them on the fire in the evening and see that they are well alight, they will continue to burn all night, so that you will find them still glowing in the morning. They do not give off flames, except a little when they are first kindled, just as charcoal does, and once they have caught fire they give out great heat. And you must know that these stones are burnt throughout the province of Cathay. It is true that they also have plenty of firewood. But the population is so enormous and there are so many bath-houses and baths continually being heated, that the wood could not possibly suffice, since there is no one who does not go to a bath-house at least three times a week and take a bath, and in winter every day, if he can manage it. And every man of rank or means has his own bathroom in his house, where he takes a bath. So it is clear that there could never be enough wood to maintain such a conflagration. So these stones, being very plentiful and very cheap, effect a great saving of wood.

To return to the provision of grain, you may take it for a fact that the Great Khan, when he sees that the harvests are plentiful and corn is cheap, accumulates vast quantities of it and stores it in huge granaries, where it is so carefully preserved that it remains unspoilt for three or four years. So he builds up a stock of every sort of grain — wheat, barley, millet, rice, panic, and others — in great abundance. Then, when it happens that some crops fail and there is a dearth of grain, he draws on these stocks. If the price is running at a bezant for a measure of wheat, for instance, he supplies four measures for the same sum. And he releases enough for all, so that everyone has plenty of corn to meet his needs. In this way he sees to it that none of his subjects need ever go short. And this he does throughout all parts of his empire.

Let me now tell you how the Great Khan bestows charity on the poor people of Khan-balik. When he learns that some family of honest and respectable people have been impoverished by some misfortune or disabled from working by illness, so that they have no means of earning their daily bread, he sees to it that such families (which may consist of six to ten persons or more) are given enough to cover their expenses for the whole year. These families, at the time appointed, go to the officials whose task it is to superintend the Great Khan's expenditure and who live in a pala-tial building assigned to their office. And each one produces a certificate of the sum paid to him for his subsistence the year before, and provision is made for them at the same rate this year. This provision includes clothing inasmuch as the Great Khan receives a tithe of all the wool, silk, and hemp used for clothmaking. He has these materials woven into cloth in a specially appointed building in which they are stored. Since all the crafts are under obligation to devote one day a week to working on his behalf, he has this cloth made up into garments, which he gives to the poor families in accordance with their needs for winter and for summer wear. He also provides clothing for his armies by having woollen cloth woven in every city as a contribution towards the payment of its tithe.

You must understand that the Tartars according to their ancient customs, before they became familiar with the doctrines of the idolaters, never used to give any alms. Indeed, when a poor man came to them, they would drive him off with maledic-tions, saying: 'Go with God's curse upon you! If he had loved you as he loves me, he would have blessed you with prosperity!' But since the sages of the idolaters, in par-ticular the *Bakhshi* of whom I have spoken above, preached to the Great Khan that it was a good work to provide for the poor and that their idols would be greatly pleased by it, he was induced to make such provision as I have described. No one who cares to go to his court in quest of bread is ever turned away empty-handed. Everyone receives a portion. And not a day passes but twenty or thirty thousand bowls of rice, millet, and panic are doled out and given away by the officials appointed. And this goes on all the year round. For this amazing and stupendous munificence which the Great Khan exercises towards the poor, all the people hold him in such esteem that they revere him as a god. [. . .]

∾ IBN BATTUTA
1304–1377

Abu Abdallah ibn Battuta, known as the "Traveler of Islam," was one of the greatest travelers of the Middle Ages. Born in Tangier, Morocco, in 1304, Ibn Battuta first left home in 1325 to make the *hajj* to Mecca (in present-day Saudi Arabia). Spending more than eighteen months on this journey, he passed through North Africa, Egypt, Palestine, and Syria before reaching his goal. From Mecca, which acted as both a spiritual and a geographical center, Battuta took trips to Iraq, Persia, Africa, and parts of central Asia. Eventually, he settled for a time in India, where he served as an official, or *qadi*, for the sultan of Delhi.

Mecca Certificate,
1207
The recipient of this
thirteenth-century
certificate of
pilgrimage to Mecca
had successfully
completed the hajj,
one of the Five Pillars
of Islam, the duties
required of all devout
Muslims. (The Art
Archive / Turkish and
Islamic Art Museum,
Istanbul / Dagli Orti)

In 1341 Ibn Battuta set off on an ill-fated mission to China. Shipwrecked off the southwestern coast of India, Battuta spent two years there, visiting Ceylon and the Maldives, before heading to Canton, on the coast of China. En route he passed through Bengal, spending time in Burma and Sumatra. By 1347 he was back in Mecca, and two years later he returned to his homeland of Morocco. An experienced and devoted traveler by this time, Battuta left within a year to visit Granada, in what is now Spain. In 1353 Battuta undertook a perilous journey across the Sahara Desert to visit the West African nation of Mali. By the time of his final return to Morocco, he had traveled to the remotest peripheries of the Islamic world in virtually all directions, covering an estimated distance of seventy-three thousand miles altogether. At the request of the sultan Abu 'Inan of Morocco, in 1356 Battuta, assisted by Ibn Juzayy, a literary scholar, began writing his book of travels, a genre known as the *rihla* in Arabic. The result is one of the greatest travelogues of all time, equal in influence and reputation to *The Travels of Marco Polo.* Battuta died in 1368. His work lived on in the Muslim world and in the nineteenth and twentieth centuries was translated into many European languages. In the selections that follow, Ibn Battuta describes visiting Jerusalem, Mecca, and Constantinople.

A note on the translation: We are using the translation by H. A. R. Gibb, revised by C. Defrémery and B. R. Sanguinetti; notes are adapted from those of the translators. Parentheses and brackets indicate interpolations and explanatory notes by the translators.

FROM

∾ The Travels of Ibn Battuta in Bengal and China

Translated by H. A. R. Gibb; revised by C. Defrémery and B. R. Sanguinetti

[JERUSALEM: THE MOSQUE AND THE DOME OF THE ROCK]

We then arrived at Bait al-Muqaddas (Jerusalem) — God ennoble it — third in excellence after the two sacred Mosques [of Mecca and al-Madīna], and the place of ascension of the Apostle of God — God bless him and give him peace — whence he was caught up into heaven.[1] The town is large and imposing, and built of squared stones. The pious and noble king Ṣalāḥ al-Dīn b. Aiyūb[2] (God reward him with good on behalf of Islam) when he captured this city, destroyed a part of its wall, and subsequently al-Malik al-Ẓāhir [Baibars][3] completed its demolition, for fear lest the Christians of the East should occupy it and resist all assaults in it. There was no watercourse in this city in former times, and the water has been led into it in our own time by the amīr Saif al-Dīn Tankīz,[4] the governor of Damascus.

The Sacred Mosque.[5] This is one of those surpassingly beautiful mosques which excite wonder and admiration. It is said that there is not upon the face of the earth a mosque larger than it. Its length from east to west is seven hundred and fifty-two cubits, measuring in royal cubits, and its breadth from south to north four hundred and thirty-five cubits. It has many entrances on its three [outer] sides, but as for the southern side of it, I have no knowledge of more than one gateway in it, and that is the one from which the imām[6] enters. The entire mosque is an open court, unroofed except for the mosque al-Aqṣā;[7] this has a roof of the utmost perfection of architecture and skill in execution, and is embellished with gold and brilliant colours. There are other places as well in the mosque which are roofed over.

The Dome of the Rock. This is one of the most marvellous of buildings, of the most perfect in architecture and strangest in shape; it has been endowed with a plentiful share of loveliness, and has received a choice portion of every rare beauty. It

---

[1] **caught up into heaven:** Muhammad was said to have made an *isra,* or "night journey," during which he was transported to the Mosque at Jerusalem and ascended into heaven, where he was given a vision of paradise.

[2] **Aiyūb:** Saladin (1137–1193) was the Ayyubid sultan who gained control of Egypt, Syria, and the Levant, recapturing Jerusalem for the Muslims in 1187 and defeating the Crusaders. The wall, in fact, was not destroyed until 1219, during the Fifth Crusade, by Saladin's nephew, al-Malik al Mu'azzam, the prince of Damascus.

[3] **Baibars** (1223–1277): The fourth Mamluk sultan and ruler of Egypt and Syria from 1260 to 1277; during his rule, Baibars was occupied with fighting the Mongols and the Crusaders.

[4] **Tankīz:** (d. 1340) The governor of Damascus from 1312 and governor-general of Syria from 1315 until June 1341, the greatest Mamluk of al-Malik al-Nāṣir.

[5] *The Sacred Mosque:* The Ḥaram al-Sharīf, the revered Mosque at Jerusalem.

[6] **imām:** The leader of prayer in a mosque.

[7] **al-Aqṣā:** A composite building attached to the central part of the southern wall of the Dome of the Rock.

stands on an elevation in the centre of the mosque and is reached by ascending a flight of marble steps. It has four doors. The court around it is also paved with marble, of excellent workmanship, and its interior likewise. Both on its exterior and inside it is adorned with such a variety of decorations and such brilliance of execution as to defy description. The greater part of this decoration is surfaced with gold, so that it glows like a mass of light and flashes with the gleam of lightning; the eyes of him who would gaze on its splendours are dazzled and the tongue of the beholder finds no words to represent them. In the centre of the Dome is the blessed Rock of which mention is made in the Traditions, for the Prophet (God bless him and give him peace) ascended from it to heaven. It is a solid piece of rock, projecting about a man's height, and underneath it there is a cave the size of a small room and of about a man's height also, with steps leading down to it; in this there is the figure of a miḥrāb. Encircling the Rock are two grilles of excellent workmanship, completely enclosing it, one of them, that which is next to the Rock, being artistically constructed in iron, and the other of wood. Within the Dome there is also a great iron buckler, which is hanging up there, and the people assert that it is the buckler of Ḥamza b. 'Abd al-Muṭṭalib[8] (God be pleased with him).

[MECCA: THE GREAT MOSQUE AND THE KA'BAH]

We presented ourselves forthwith at the Sanctuary of God Most High within her, the place of abode of His Friend Ibrāhīm and scene of mission of His Chosen One, Muḥammad (God bless and give him peace). We entered the illustrious Holy House, wherein 'he who enters is secure', by the gate of the Banū Shaiba[9] and saw before our eyes the illustrious Ka'ba (God increase it in veneration), like a bride who is displayed upon the bridal-chair of majesty, and walks with proud step in the mantles of beauty, surrounded by the companies which had come to pay homage to the God of Mercy, and being conducted to the Garden of Eternal Bliss. We made around it the [seven-fold] circuit of arrival and kissed the holy Stone; we performed a prayer of two bowings at the Maqām Ibrāhīm[10] and clung to the curtains of the Ka'ba at the Multazam[11] between the door and the Black Stone, where prayer is answered; we drank of the water of Zamzam,[12] which, being drunk of, possesses the qualities which are related in the Tradition handed down from the Prophet (God bless and give him peace); then, having run between al-Ṣafā and al-Marwa, we took up our lodging there in a house near the Gate of Ibrāhīm. Praise be to God, Who hath honoured us by visitation to this holy House, and hath caused us to be numbered

---

[8] al-Muṭṭalib: One of Muhammad's uncles; he was killed by the Meccan forces at the battle of Uhud in 625.

[9] the gate of Banū Shaiba: The traditional entrance of pilgrims and visitors to the Ka'ba (Ka'bah).

[10] Maqām Ibrāhīm: The stone of Abraham, referring to a stone believed to have been used by Abraham when building the Ka'ba (Ka'bah).

[11] Multazam: A place between the Black Stone and the Iraq angle where it is said prayers are answered.

[12] the water of Zamzam: According to Muslim tradition, the angel Gabriel opened the well of Zamzam to quench the thirst of Hagar and Ishmael on their flight through the desert. After being filled in, the well was reopened by Muhammad's grandfather who had a vision of the waters while sleeping near the site of the Ka'ba (Ka'bah). Drinking from the well was said to have healing and restorative powers.

amongst those included in the prayer of al-Khalīl (blessing and peace upon him), and hath rejoiced our eyes by the vision of the illustrious Kaʿba and the honourable House, of the holy Stone, of Zamzam and the Ḥaṭīm.[13]

Of the wondrous doings of God Most High is this, that He has created the hearts of men with an instinctive desire to seek these sublime sanctuaries, and yearning to present themselves at their illustrious sites, and has given the love of them such power over men's hearts that none alights in them but they seize his whole heart, nor quits them but with grief at separation from them, sorrowing at his far journey away from them, filled with longing for them, and purposing to repeat his visitation to them. For their blessed soil is the focus of all eyes, and love of it the marrow of all hearts, in virtue of a wise disposition of God which achieves its sublime purpose, and in fulfilment of the prayer of His Friend [Abraham] (upon him be peace). Intensity of yearning brings them near while yet far off, presents them to the eye while yet unseen, and makes of little account to him who seeks them the fatigues which he meets and the distress which he endures. How many a weakling sees death before reaching them, and beholds destruction on their road, yet when God brings him safely to them he welcomes them with joy and gladness, as though he had not tasted bitterness, nor suffered torment and affliction for their sakes! Truly this is a divine thing and a God-given benefit, a proof uncontaminated by ambiguity, unobscured by dubiety, and inaccessible to deception, which is of compelling cogency in the perception of men of understanding, and shatters the rationalism of the intellectuals. He whose soul God Most High hath sustained [by granting him] to alight in those regions and to present himself in that court, upon him hath God bestowed the greatest of all favours and possession of the best of both abodes, that of his present world and the other of the world to come. It is meet for him, therefore, that he should abundantly give thanks for what He has bestowed upon him. May God Most High number us amongst those whose visitation is accepted, whose merchandise in seeking to perform it brings him gain [in the world to come], whose actions in the cause of God are written [in the Book of Life], and whose burdens of sin are effaced by the acceptance [of the merit earned by Pilgrimage], through His loving kindness and graciousness. [. . .]

The sacred mosque (God ennoble and sanctify it). The Sacred Mosque lies in the midst of the city and occupies an extensive area; its length from east to west is more than four hundred cubits (this figure is given by al-Azraqī)[14] and its breadth is approximately the same. The most venerable Kaʿba stands in the centre of it. The aspect of the mosque is [so] exquisite, its outward sight [so] beautiful [that] no tongue could presume to describe its attractions, and no voice of description do justice to the charm of its perfection. The height of its walls is about twenty cubits, and the roof [of its colonnades] is supported by tall pillars, arranged in a triple row, of most substantial and beautiful construction. Its three aisles are arranged on a marvellous plan, which makes them appear like a single aisle. The number of marble pil-

---

[13] Ḥaṭīm: Another name for the Hijr, or Enclosure, on the north side of the Kaʿba (Kaʿbah); it was part of a pre-Islamic temple.

[14] al-Azraqī: (d. 860) The author of *History of Mecca.*

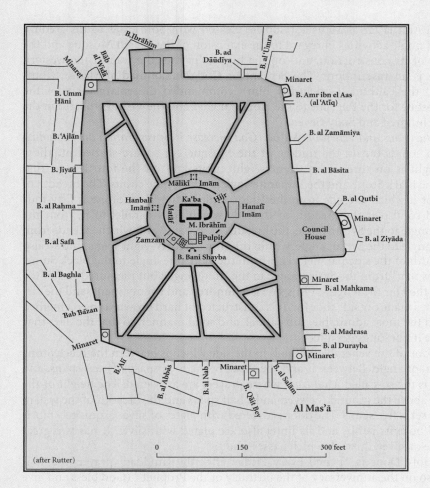

Plan of the Mosque
of Mecca.

*The positions and
the names of the gates
are shown as in the
present day. (After
Rutter)*

lars which it contains is 490, exclusive of the plaster pillars which are in the Dār al-Nadwa[15] annexed to the sanctuary. This building is incorporated in the colonnade running [from west] to north, and opposite it are the Maqām [of Ibrāhīm] and the 'Irāqī angle [of the Ka'ba]; its court is contiguous to and entered from the colonnade mentioned. Along the wall of this colonnade is a series of small platforms beneath vaulted arcades; these are occupied by teachers of the Qur'ān, copyists and tailors. On the wall of the parallel colonnade to this there are platforms resembling these; the other colonnades have at the foot of their walls platforms without arcades. By the Bāb Ibrāhīm there is [another] extension from the [south-] western colonnade, in which there are plaster columns. The Caliph al-Mahdī Muḥammad, son of

---

[15] **Dār al-Nadwa:** The ancient "Council House" of Mecca, which had fallen into ruin, was reconstructed as an annex to the northwest gallery of the sanctuary by the Abbasid caliph al-Mu'tadid in 894.

the Caliph Abū Jaʿfar al-Manṣūr (God be pleased with both), has to his credit a number of noble activities in regard to the extension of the Sacred Mosque and the perfection of its construction, and on the highest part of the wall of the western colonnade is an inscription: 'The Servant of God Muhammad al-Mahdī, Commander of the Faithful (God justify him), commanded the enlargement of the Sacred Mosque for the Pilgrims to the House of God and the Visitors thereto in the year One Hundred and Sixty-Seven.'[16]

The illustrious and venerable Kaʿba (God increase it in veneration and honour). The Kaʿba stands out in the middle of the Mosque—a square-shaped building, whose height is on three sides twenty-eight cubits and on the fourth side, that between the Black Stone and the Yamanite angle, twenty-nine cubits. The breadth of that side of it which extends from the ʿIrāqī angle to the Black Stone is fifty-four spans, and so also is the breadth of the side which runs parallel to it, from the Yamanite angle to the Syrian angle; the breadth of that side of it which extends from the ʿIrāqī angle to the Syrian angle, within the Ḥijr,[17] is forty-eight spans, and so also is the breadth of the side parallel to it, [from the Yamanite angle to the Black Stone, the same as that] from the Syrian angle to the ʿIrāqī angle; but measured round the outside of the Ḥijr the length of this side is a hundred and twenty spans, and the circuit is always made outside the Ḥijr. It is constructed of hard brown stones cemented together in the most admirable, substantial, and solid manner, so that the days may not change it nor long ages affect it.

The door of the venerable Kaʿba is in the side which is between the Black Stone and the ʿIrāqī angle. Between it and the Black Stone is [a space of] ten spans, and that place is the so-called *Multazam* where prayers are answered. The height of the door [sill] above the ground is eleven and a half spans and the breadth of the wall in which it is set is five spans. The door is covered with plates of silver exquisitely fabricated, and both its jambs and its lintel also are plated with silver. It has two great rings made of silver, through which passes a bolt.

The Holy Door is opened every Friday after the [midday] prayer and it is opened also on the anniversary of the birthday of the Prophet[18] (God bless and give him peace). The ceremony which they use in opening it is as follows. They bring up a bench resembling a mimbar, which has steps and wooden legs with four rollers upon which the bench runs, and place it against the wall of the illustrious Kaʿba so that its top step adjoins the holy threshold. When this is done, the chief of the Shaibīs[19] mounts the steps, carrying in his hand the holy key, and accompanied by the doorkeepers. The latter take hold of [and draw aside] the curtain which is hung over the door of the Kaʿba and is known by the name of the Veil [*al-Burquʿ*], while their chief opens the door. When he opens it, he kisses the illustrious threshold, enters the

---

[16] **year One Hundred and Sixty-Seven:** 167 A.H. is 783–84 C.E.; al-Mahdī was the third Abbasic caliph of Baghdad (r. 775–85).

[17] **Ḥijr:** See note 13.

[18] **birthday of the Prophet:** Observed on the twelfth of the month of First Rabi.

[19] **Shaibīs:** Muhammad conferred guardianship of the Kaʿba (Kaʿbah) on the family of Shaiba, from the Quraish clan of ʿAbd al-Dār.

House alone, closes the door, and remains there as long as he requires to make a prayer of two bowings. Then the rest of the Shaibīs enter, close the door also, and make their prayers. After this the door is opened, and the people rush to gain admission. During the preliminaries they stand facing the holy door with downcast eyes and hands outstretched to God Most High, and when it is opened they shout the *Takbīr*[20] and cry 'O God, open unto us the gates of Thy mercy and Thy forgiveness, O most Merciful of the merciful.'

The interior of the illustrious Ka'ba is paved with marble inlaid with arabesques and its walls have a similar facing. It has three tall pillars, exceedingly high and made of teak; between each pillar and the next is a distance of four paces, and they stand [lengthwise] in the middle of the space inside the illustrious Ka'ba, the central one being opposite to the midpoint of the side between the [Yamanite] and Syrian angles. The hangings of the illustrious Ka'ba are of black silk, with inscriptions in white; they gleam upon its walls with light and brilliance and clothe it entirely from the top to the ground.

One of the marvellous 'signs' in connexion with the holy Ka'ba is this: its door is opened at a time when the sanctuary is choked with a multitude of peoples whom none can number save God, who hath created them and sustained them; yet they enter it—the whole body of them—and it is not too narrow to contain them. Another of its marvels is that it is never at any time, whether by night or day, without some worshipper engaged in making the circuit, and none has ever reported that he has seen it at any time without worshippers. Yet another marvel is this: that the pigeons of Mecca, in spite of their number, and the other kinds of birds as well, do not alight upon it, nor do they pass over it in their flight. You can see the pigeons flying over the whole sanctuary, but when they come level with the illustrious Ka'ba they deflect their course from it to one side, and do not pass over it. It is said that no bird ever alights on it unless it be suffering from some disease, and in that case it either dies on the instant or is healed of its disease—magnified be He who hath distinguished it by nobility and holiness and hath clothed it with respect and veneration. [...]

The Black Stone. As for the Stone, its height above the ground is six spans, so that a tall man has to bend down in order to kiss it and a small man has to stretch himself up to reach it. It is set in the angle which points to the east, two-thirds of a span broad and a span in length, and is soldered in. No one knows the dimension of that side of it which is enclosed in the angle. It includes four fragments stuck together; the [usual] story is that the Qarmaṭī[21] (God curse him) broke it, but it has been said that the man who broke it was another person, who struck it with a club and smashed it. The people present at the time rushed up to kill him, and a number of Maghribines were killed on account of his action. The edges of the Stone are bound by a rim of silver, whose whiteness gleams against the black mass of the holy Stone,

---

[20] the *Takbīr*: *Allāhu akbar,* meaning "Allah (God) is great."

[21] Qarmaṭī: In 929 C.E., the Qarāmiṭa (Carmathians) seized Mecca and carried off the Black Stone; it was restored in 950 by order of the caliph al-Mansur.

so that all eyes see in it an overpowering beauty. The kissing of the Stone gives a [sensation of] pleasure which is peculiarly agreeable to the mouth, and as one places his lips against it he would fain not withdraw them from its embrace, by virtue of a special quality reposed in it and a divine favour accorded to it. What more is required [to prove its sublimity] than that the Apostle of God (God bless and give him peace) said that it is the Right Hand of God upon His earth?—God profit us by our kissing it and touching it, and bring to it all who yearn for it. In the unbroken portion of the Black Stone, near the edge of it which is to the right as one kisses it, is a small and glittering white spot, as if it were a mole on that glorious surface. You can see the pilgrims, as they make their circuits of the Ka'ba, falling one upon the other in the press to kiss it, and it is seldom that one succeeds in doing so except after vigorous jostling. They do just the same when they are entering the Holy House. | It is from beside the Black Stone that the beginning of the circuit is made and it is the first of the angles that the circuiter comes to. When he kisses the Stone, he steps back from it a little way, keeps the illustrious Ka'ba on his left side, and proceeds on his circuit. He comes next, after the Stone, to the 'Irāqī angle, which faces to the north; then he comes to the Syrian angle, which faces to the west; then to the Yamanite angle which faces to the south; and so returns to the Black Stone, which faces to the East.[22] [. . .]

[Constantinople: The Aya Sufiya (Hagia Sophia)]

Account of the City. It is enormous in magnitude and divided into two parts, between which there is a great river, in which there is a flow and ebb of tide, just as in the wādī of Salā in the country of the Maghrib. In former times there was a bridge over it, built [of stone], but the bridge has fallen into ruin and nowadays it is crossed in boats. The name of this river is Absumī. One of the two parts of the city is called Aṣṭanbūl, it is on the eastern bank of the river and includes the places of residence of the sultan, his officers of state, and the rest of the population. Its bazaars and streets are spacious and paved with flagstones, and the members of each craft have a separate place, no others sharing it with them. Each bazaar has gates which are closed upon it at night, and the majority of the artisans and sellers in them are women. The city is at the foot of a hill that projects about nine miles into the sea, and its breadth is the same or more. On top of the hill is a small citadel and the sultan's palace. This hill is surrounded by the city wall, which is a formidable one and cannot be taken by assault on the side of the sea. Within the wall are about thirteen inhabited villages. The principal church too is in the midst of this section of the city.

As for the other section of it, it is called al-Ghalaṭa, and lies on the western bank of the river, somewhat like Ribāṭ al-Fatḥ in its proximity to the river. This section is reserved for the Christians of the Franks dwelling there. They are of different kinds, including Genoese, Venetians, men of Rome and people of France, and they

---

[22] **It is from beside . . . faces to the East:** The circuit described here is the sevenfold circuit, or circumambulation (*ṭawāf*), of the Ka'ba (Ka'bah), part of the greater (*hajj*) and lesser (*umrah*) pilgrimages to Mecca. It is also observed as a separate rite by all visitors to Mecca.

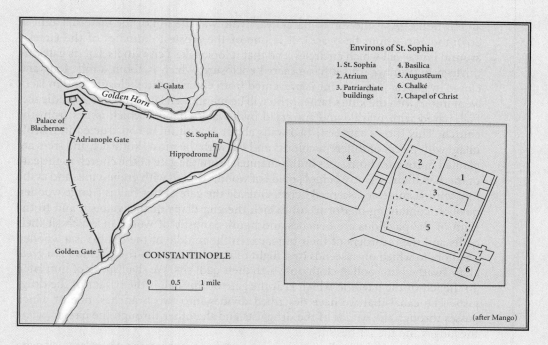

Environs of St. Sophia

1. St. Sophia
2. Atrium
3. Patriarchate buildings
4. Basilica
5. Augustēum
6. Chalké
7. Chapel of Christ

(after Mango)

Constantinople in the Time of Emperor Alexus (c. 1100).
He entertained the arriving Crusaders at the Palace of Blachernae, at the western edge of the walled city; later their descendants settled in al-Ghalata across the river and outside the city walls.

are under the government of the King of Constantinople, who appoints over them [as his lieutenant] one of their number whom they approve, and him they call the *Qumṣ*.[23] They are required to pay a tax every year to the king of Constantinople, but they often rebel against his authority and then he makes war on them until the Pope restores peace between them. They are all men of commerce, and their port is one of the greatest of ports; I saw in it about a hundred galleys, such as merchant vessels and other large ships, and as for the small ships they were too numerous to be counted. The bazaars in this section are good, but overlaid with all kinds of filth, and traversed by a small, dirty and filth-laden stream. Their churches too are dirty and mean.

Account of the Great Church. I can describe only its exterior; as for its interior I did not see it. It is called in their language *Ayā Ṣūfiyā*,[24] and the story goes that it was

---

[23] **Qumṣ:** That is, *comes* or *count;* the chief Genoese officer was, however, called Podestat, so Ibn Battuta may mean "consul."

[24] **Ayā Ṣūfiyā:** Originally a Christian church and then converted to a mosque after the Muslim conquest of Constantinople in 1453, the Hagia Sophia is one of the glories of Byzantine architecture. It was built for Justinian I in 532–37 C.E. by Anthemius of Tralles and Isidorus of Miletus.

an erection of Āṣaf the son of Barakhyā,[25] who was the son of the maternal aunt of Solomon (on whom be peace). It is one of the greatest churches of the Greeks; around it is a wall which encircles it so that it looks like a city [in itself]. Its gates are thirteen in number, and it has a sacred enclosure, which is about a mile long and closed by a great gate. No one is prevented from entering the enclosure, and in fact I went into it with the king's father, who will be mentioned later; it is like an audience-hall, paved with marble and traversed by a water-channel which issues from the church. This [flows between] two walls about a cubit high, constructed in marble inlaid with pieces of different colours and cut with the most skilful art, and trees are planted in rows on both sides of the channel. From the gate of the church to the gate of this hall there is a lofty pergola made of wood, covered with grape-vines and at the foot with jasmine and scented herbs. Outside the gate of this hall is a large wooden pavilion containing platforms, on which the guardians of this gate sit, and to the right of the pavilions are benches and booths, mostly of wood, in which sit their qāḍīs and the recorders of their bureaux. In the middle of the booths is a wooden pavilion, to which one ascends by a flight of wooden steps; in this pavilion is a great chair swathed in woollen cloth on which their qāḍī sits. We shall speak of him later. To the left of the pavilion which is at the gate of this hall is the bazaar of the drug-gists. The canal that we have described divides into two branches, one of which passes through the bazaar of the druggists and the other through the bazaar where the judges and the scribes sit.

At the door of the church there are porticoes where the attendants sit who sweep its paths, light its lamps and close its doors. They allow no person to enter it until he prostrates himself to the huge cross at their place, which they claim to be a relic of the wood on which the double of Jesus (on whom be peace) was crucified. This is over the door of the church, set in a golden frame about ten cubits in height, across which they have placed a similar golden frame so that it forms a cross. This door is covered with plaques of silver and gold, and its two rings are of pure gold. I was told that the number of monks and priests in this church runs into thousands, and that some of them are descendants of the Apostles, also that inside it is another church exclusively for women, containing more than a thousand virgins consecrated to religious devotions, and a still greater number of aged and widowed women. It is the custom of the king, his officers of state, and the rest of the inhabitants to come to visit this church every morning, and the Pope comes to it once in the year. When he is at a distance of four nights' journey from the town the king goes out to meet him and dismounts before him; when he enters the city, the king walks on foot in front of him, and comes to salute him every morning and evening during the whole period of his stay in Constantinople until he departs.

---

[25] **Āṣaf the son of Barakhyā:** In Jewish and Muslim legend, the vizier, or high executive officer, of Solomon.

JOHN MANDEVILLE

FOURTEENTH CENTURY

Proof of the identity of John Mandeville, the recorded author of *The Travels of Sir John Mandeville,* continues to elude scholars, though early biographers freely speculated about him. One tradition has it that he was a knight who, to avoid prosecution for a murder, fled in 1322 to Liège, Flanders, where he assumed the name of a physician, Jean de Bourgogne. Another suggests that "Mandeville" never existed at all, that the Liège physician was the author-compiler of *The Travels.* It now appears that neither is true, leaving the work to speak for itself; it appears to have been written in French at Liège in 1357 and translated into every major European language by the end of the fourteenth century. Whatever its origins and however spurious its accounts, *The Travels of Sir John Mandeville* was one of the most influential and widely read travel narratives in Europe before the age of discovery.

A charming compilation of stories about travel to the Holy Land and the Far East, *The Travels of Sir John Mandeville* combines the popular narrative of pilgrimage to Jerusalem with undoubtedly exaggerated tales of wider travel to Turkey, Persia, Egypt, Ethiopia, India, and China. Borrowing from earlier sources collected in a 1351 compendium of travels produced by Jean Le Long, a monk cloistered near Liège, Mandeville's *Travels* contains passages that parallel some in travelogues written by the Italian Odoric of Pordenone, William of Boldensele (William of Rubruck), and the Umbrian Giovanni da Pian di Carpine. Its debt to earlier written sources is so extensive, in fact, that some critics believe that its compiler-author never traveled at all. Certain descriptions, however, such as the one of a monastery near Mount Sinai or another of a tournament field in Constantinople, appear to be written from personal experience. Most important, the compiler-author, whoever he was, ever mindful of his audience's fascination with the religious, cultural, and material riches thought to exist in the remote regions he describes, recasts his original sources in such a way as to invoke a sense of wonder and discovery.

Included in the following selections are Mandeville's description of India and of Java and the surrounding islands, where the author gives free reign to his imagination in describing monsters and fabulous creatures. Here the native population is depicted as objects of curiosity, an attitude seen in as early a text as Homer's *Odyssey* and again in the exploration and travel narratives of later centuries. Mandeville also paints a picture of the palace of the Great Khan of Cathay, which demonstrates above all its debt to Marco Polo's *Travels.*

FROM

∾ The Travels of Sir John Mandeville

Translated by C. W. R. D. Moseley

[INDIA]

Of the customs in the isles around India;
of the distinction between idols and simulacres; [...]
and of the well that changes colour each hour of the day

In India there are very many different countries. It is called India because of a river that runs through that land, which is called Inde [Indus]. Eels of thirty feet long are found in that river. The people who dwell near the river are an ugly colour, yellow and green. In India there are more than five thousand good large isles that people live in, not counting those that are uninhabited. Each of these isles has many cities and towns, and many people. The people of India are not naturally disposed to travelling beyond their own country, for they live under [the influence of] the planet called Saturn. That planet performs his circle through the twelve signs [of the Zodiac] in thirty years; the moon, which is our planet, passes through the twelve signs in a month. Because Saturn is so slow-moving, men who live under him in that climate have no great desire to move about much, but stay in their own lands and desire no other. It is quite the opposite in our country. We are in a climate under the rule of the moon, which is a planet that moves quickly—the traveller's planet. So it gives us the desire to travel and visit different countries of the world, for it moves round the world more quickly than other planets.

Men travel through India by way of many countries to the Great Sea Ocean. Then they come to the isle of Chermes [Ormuz], whither merchants of Venice, Genoa and many other countries come to buy merchandise. But it is so hot there that the men have their testicles hanging down to their thighs because of the violent heat, which weakens their bodies. Men of that country who know what to do bind them up and use certain cooling astringent ointments to hold them up— otherwise they could not live. In this land and in Ethiopia and many other lands men and women frequently go to the rivers and lie in them all naked from undern [mid-morning] of the day until it be past noon, because of the great heat of the sun. They lie totally under water, except for their heads. Women there are not ashamed if men see them naked. Much ugliness can be seen there. In this isle there are ships made without nails or strappings of iron, because of the rocks of adamant in the sea, which would attract ships to themselves. There are so many of these rocks in those parts that if any ship in which there was any kind of iron passed that way, it would be drawn to the rocks by the power of the adamant, and would never get away again.

From this island men go by sea to the isle of Cana [Thana], where there is great plenty of wine and corn. Once it was a very big island, with a good harbour; but the largest part of it has been washed away by the sea. The King of that isle was once so great and powerful that he fought against Alexander the Great.[1] The people of that isle have a variety of religions: some worship the sun instead of God, some fire, some snakes, some trees, some the first thing they come across in the morning, and some worship simulacres and some idols. Now between simulacres and idols there is a great difference. For simulacres are images made in the likeness of something that occurs in nature, while idols are images made in the likeness of whatever a man wishes, that is not natural. Amongst all the varieties of animals you will not find one that has three heads—one a man's, one a horse's, another of an ox or of some other beast—as they make their idols. You must understand that those who worship simulacres honour them for the sake of worthy men, perhaps those who were doughty men in battle, like Hercules, Achilles and others like them, who performed many marvels in their lives. For they say they know well that they are not the God of nature, who made everything, but that they are beloved of God because of the marvels they performed. So they say of the sun; for it often alters the weather during the year, and gives heat to nourish the creatures of the earth. Because it is of such value, they say they are sure it performs God's will and that God loves it before any other thing; and therefore they worship it. They say the same about the other planets and about fire, because of the great good that comes from them. About idols, they say that the ox is the holiest animal, and most useful, on earth, for it does much good and no evil. They say they are sure that it cannot be without the special grace of God, and therefore they represent their God as half man and half ox, for man is the loveliest and best creature God made and the ox the holiest. They worship snakes too, and other beasts they meet first thing in the morning, especially those beasts which it is good luck to meet and after seeing which they are fortunate all the rest of the day, as they allege from long experience. So they say this lucky encounter comes from God, and therefore they have had images made like these creatures for their houses, so that they can worship them before they meet anything else. In this isle of Thana there are many wild beasts, like lions, leopards, bears, and others. There are rats there as big as dogs are here; the men catch them with great mastiffs, for cats are too small. In this country, as in many others, when men are dead, they do not bury them; for the heat is so great that immediately the flesh is consumed, even to the bone. [. . .]

[JAVA AND CEYLON]

Of the palace of the King of Java; of the trees
that bear flour, honey, wine and venom; and of other marvels
and customs in the environing isles

Near this isle of Lamory which I spoke of is another island, called Somober [Sumatra]. This is a great and good island with a noble and mighty King. The people of this

---

[1] **Alexander the Great** (356–323 B.C.E.): King of Macedon (r. 336–323) and student of Aristotle, Alexander was a brilliant military strategist who expanded the empire of Macedonia, overcoming Greece and the Persian empire of Darius III.

country mark themselves on the face with a hot iron, to be distinguished from other folk by this mark of their high rank; for they account themselves the noblest people in the world. They war unceasingly against the naked folk I spoke of before. Near there is another island, which is called Boteniga, a fertile island full of all kinds of riches. And round about this isle are many other, and different countries and different sorts of men, of which it would be too much to tell in full.

But passing thence a little way by sea, men come to a great isle called Iava [Java]. The King of this land is a great and mighty lord, and has seven other kings of seven isles nearby under him. There are a marvellous number of people in Java; they grow different kinds of spices in more abundance than in other places—ginger, cloves, nutmegs, mace, and many others. You should know that mace is the husk of the nutmeg. There is great plenty of everything in this isle. The King has a beautiful and costly palace. All the steps into his hall and his chambers are alternately of gold and silver. The walls inside are covered with plates of gold and silver, and on them are engraved stories of kings and knights and battles, with crowns and circlets of precious stones on their heads. No man would believe the grandeur and wealth of this palace if he had not seen it. The King is so great and powerful that he has often discomfited the Great Khan, the mightiest emperor in the world, in battle. For they have often been at war because the Great Khan wanted to make this King his vassal; but the King has always withstood him and put him off manfully. [. . .]

Thence men go across the Great Sea Ocean to another island called Caffilos. There they have a custom that when their friends are seriously ill, they hang them on trees, so that they can be chewed and eaten by the birds; for they say it is better for them to be eaten by birds, which are God's angels, than to be eaten by worms in the earth.

Thence one goes to another land, where the people are of evil customs. They train great dogs to worry men. And when their friends are getting near death and they believe they can live no longer, they make these dogs worry them; for they will not let them die naturally in their beds lest they suffer too much pain in dying. When they are dead, they eat their flesh instead of venison.

And from this country you go via many others in the sea to one called Melk [Malacca?]. There are wicked and cruel folk there too. For they have no delight or pleasure in anything except slaughtering people to drink their blood. And the man who can kill the greatest number of men is the mot respected and worthiest among them. There is no drink they like so much as man's blood, and they call it God. If there is any quarrel among them, no full agreement can be made until each has drunk the other's blood; and in the same way relationships are sealed between them. Agreement and relationships among them are not valid unless made in this way.

From here one goes to another isle, called Tracota, where the people are like animals lacking reason. They live in caves, for they do not have the intelligence to build houses; and when they see a stranger passing through the country, they run and hide in their caves. They eat snakes, and do not speak, but hiss to one another like adders. They care nothing for gold, silver, or other worldly goods, only for one precious stone which has sixty colours. It is called traconite after the country. They love this stone very much indeed, even though they do not know its properties; they desire it simply for its beauty.

Thence one travels by sea to another land, called Natumeran [Nicobar islands]. It is a large and fair island, whose circuit is nearly a thousand miles. Men and women of that isle have heads like dogs, and they are called Cynocephales. These people, despite their shape, are fully reasonable and intelligent. They worship an ox as their god. Each one of them carries an ox made of gold or silver on his brow, as a token that they love their god well. They go quite naked except for a little cloth round their privy parts. They are big in stature and good warriors; they carry a large shield, which covers all their body, and a long spear in their hand, and dressed in this way they go boldly against their enemies. If they capture any man in battle, they eat him. The King of that land is a great and mighty lord, rich, and very devout according to his creed. He has round his neck a cord of silk on which are three hundred precious stones [orient pearls], like our rosary of amber. And just as we say our *Pater Noster* and *Ave maria* by telling our beads, just so the King says each day on his beads three hundred prayers to his god, before he eats. He wears a splendid ruby round his neck, which is nearly a foot long and five fingers broad. They give him this ruby when they make him King, to carry in his hand, and so he rides round the city and they all make obeisance to him. After that he always wears it round his neck, for if he did not he would be King no longer. The Great Khan of Cathay has much coveted that ruby, but he could never win it in war or by any other means. This King is a very righteous man and just according to his law, for he punishes everyone who does another man wrong in his realm. Therefore men can travel safely and securely through his land, and no one is so bold as to annoy them, rob them, or take any kind of goods from them.

From here one goes to another isle called Silha [Ceylon]. The circumference of it is eight hundred miles. A great part of this country is waste and wilderness, and uninhabited; therefore there are great numbers of dragons, crocodiles and other kinds of reptiles, so that men cannot live there. The crocodile is a kind of snake, brown on top of the back, with four feet and short legs and two great eyes. The body is so long and so big that where it has travelled across the sand it is as if a great tree has been dragged there. In that wilderness there are also many other kinds of wild beast, especially elephants. And in that isle there is a high mountain, and on the very top of it is a great loch full of water. Men of that land say that Adam and Eve wept for a hundred years on that hill after they were expelled from Paradise, and that that water collected from their tears. In the bottom of that lake precious stones are found, and round it grow reeds in great profusion, among which there are crocodiles and other snakes living; in the lake there are horse eels [leeches?] of marvellous size. Once a year the King of that isle gives all the poor people leave to go into the lake and gather precious stones, out of charity and for love of Adam and Eve's God; each year enough of those precious stones are found. When these poor folk go into the lake to gather the stones, they anoint themselves all over with the juice of the fruit called lemons, and do not fear the crocodiles nor the other poisonous reptiles. The water of this lake empties down the side of the mountain. And by that river pearls and precious stones are found. Men say in that land that snakes and other venomous animals do no harm to strangers or pilgrims who pass through; they hurt only the natives and those who live there. There are also wild geese with two heads and white wolves with bodies as big as oxen, and many other kinds of animals. And understand that the sea which surrounds this island and other isles nearby seems so high above the land that it looks to men who see it as if it hung in the air on the point of falling and covering the earth; and that is a marvellous thing, as the prophet says, *Mirabiles elaciones maris*, that is, 'Wonderful are the risings of the sea.'[2] [. . .]

[THE GREAT KHAN OF CATHAY]

Of the Great Khan of Cathay;
of the royalty of his palace, and how he sits at meat;
and of the great number of servants who serve him

The land of Cathay is a great country, beautiful, rich, fertile, full of good merchandise. Every year merchants come there to get spices and other sorts of merchandise — they go there more frequently than they do elsewhere. You should understand that the merchants who come from Venice or Genoa or other places in Lombardy or the Greek Empire travel by land and sea for eleven or twelve months before they get to Cathay, the chief realm of the Great Khan. In the east there is an old city, near which the Tartarenes[3] have built another, called Gaydon [the great court of the Mongols, near Peking]. This city has twelve gates, and each gate is a mile from the next, so the circuit of the city is twenty-four miles [*sic*]. This city is the seat of the Great Khan; his throne is in a very fair palace, the boundary wall of which is two miles and more long. Within that wall there are other fine palaces too. In the garden of the great palace is a hill on which is another beautiful and rich palace — there is not another like it in all the world. And all round the palace and the hill are many trees, bearing many different sorts of fruit; beyond, there are deep broad dykes; beyond those again, there are many fishponds and pools, whereon there are many water fowl, like swans, cranes, herons, bitterns, mallards and others. Outside those again are all kinds of wild game — harts and hinds, bucks and does, and roe deer, and others. And whenever the Great Khan wants to have sport hawking or hunting, he can kill wild-fowl with hawks and kill deer with his hounds or other means without leaving his room. This palace, his seat, is wonderfully large and beautiful; and the hall of that palace is richly furnished. Within the hall are twenty-four pillars of gold; and all the walls are covered with the red skins of beasts, called *panters* [pandas?]. They are very fine animals, sweet smelling, and because of the good smell of the skins no harmful air can come therein. These skins are as red as any blood, and shine so in the sun that a man can hardly look at them because of their brightness. The folk of that country

[2] **'Wonderful are the risings of the sea':** From Psalms 92:4 of the Latin Vulgate Bible: *Mirabiles elationes maris; mirabilis in altis Dominus* (Wonderful are the risings of the sea; wonderful is the Lord on high).

[3] **Tartarenes:** The Tatars, whom the author confuses with the Mongols.

honour that beast, when they see it, on account of its good properties and the sweet smell that comes from it; they praise the skin of it as much as if it had been of fine gold. In the middle of the palace a dais has been made for the Great Khan, adorned with gold and precious stones. At its four corners there are four dragons made of gold. This dais has a canopy of silken cloth, barred across with gold and silver, and there are many large precious stones hanging on it. And below the dais are conduits full of drink, which the people of the Emperor's court drink from; beside the conduits are set vessels of gold which men can drink from when they wish. This hall is nobly and gloriously set out in every way. First, up on the top of the high dais, in the very middle, the throne for the Emperor is positioned, high up from the pavement, where he sits and eats his food. The table he eats on is made of jewels set in fine gold, and is bordered with gold set full of gems. The steps up which he goes to his throne are all of precious stone set in gold. At the left side of his throne is the seat of his chief wife, one step lower than his; it is of jasper, with sides of fine gold set with precious stones, and her table is of jasper bordered with gem-inlaid gold. The seat of his second wife is a step lower than the other's; and her seat and table are adorned as magnificently as the other wife's. The table and seat of the third wife is a step lower still. For he always has three wives with him, wherever he goes far or near. Next to his third wife on the same side sit other ladies of the Emperor's kin, each one a step lower than another according to how near they are in blood-relationship to the Emperor. The women of that country who are married have on their heads something like a man's foot, made of gold and gems and peacock feathers, beautifully made and glinting in the light; this is a token that they are under the rule of a man. Those who are not wedded do not have such hats. On the right hand of the Emperor sits his eldest son, who will rule after him, a step lower than his father. His seat and table are in every way exactly like the Empress's. Then there sit other lords of the Emperor's family, everyone according to his degree, like the ladies on the other side. Each has a table to himself, like the ladies; they are either of jasper or crystal or amethyst or *lignum aloes,* which comes out of Paradise, or of ivory. And all the tables are bordered with gold set full of precious stones, so that there is not one that is not worth a great treasure. Under the Emperor's table, at his feet, sit four clerks, who write down all the words he says while he is eating, whether they be good or ill. For everything that he says really must be done, for his word must not be gainsaid for anything.

On festival days great tables of gold are brought before the Emperor on which stand peacocks and other birds, cleverly and intricately made. Those birds are so wonderfully made by man's craft that it seems as if they leapt, and danced, and flapped their wings, and disported themselves in other ways; it is wonderful to see how such things are done. By what craft they do all this I cannot say; but I do know for sure that those people are marvellously clever in anything they want to do, more than any other people in the world. They surpass all other nations in cleverness, for good or ill, and they know it themselves. Therefore they say that they see with two eyes and Christian men with one; for after themselves they consider Christian men the most wise and clever. They say that people of other nations are blind, without eyes, as far as knowledge and craft are concerned. I busied myself greatly to know and understand by what means these things I mentioned were done; but the chief craftsman told me that he was so bound by a vow to his god that he could show the method to no man except his eldest son. Above the Emperor's table and round a great part of the hall is a great vine made of fine gold; it is wonderfully delicately wrought, with many branches and grapes like the grapes of a growing vine; some are white, some yellow, some red, some black, some green. All the red ones are made of rubies or garnets or alabandine, the white are made of crystal or beryl; the yellow are made of topazes or chrysolites; the green of emeralds; the black of onyx or garnets. This vine is made of precious stones so exactly and carefully that it looks like a growing vine.

And great lords and barons stand before the Emperor's table to serve the Emperor; and none of them is so bold as to speak a word unless the Emperor speak first to them—except for minstrels who sing him songs, or tell him tales, or crack jokes or jests to please the Emperor. All the vessels which are used for serving in his hall or chamber, especially at his own table or at those where great lords sit, are of jasper or crystal or amethyst or fine gold. And all their cups are of emeralds or sapphires, of topazes or other precious stones. They make no vessels of silver, for they set no store by silver. They will neither eat nor drink of vessels made of it; they use it for steps, pillars, pavements for halls and chambers. In front of the hall door stand certain lords and other knights to ensure that none enters that door except those the Emperor wishes, unless he be of the household or a minstrel; no others dare come near.

❧ MARGERY KEMPE
1373–1438

In Chaucer's *The Canterbury Tales* the Wife of Bath, deploring the misogynist literature her fifth husband collects, fervently wishes that "By Godde, wommen had writen stories." About fifty years after Chaucer created the fictional Wife, a woman did—a woman in her own way every bit as feisty, courageous, and devout as the Wife, albeit one who actively sought celibacy rather than toothsome young husbands. Margery Kempe was a young, illiterate, middle-class housewife in the prosperous fifteenth-century English town of Lynn when she began having the mystical experiences that turned her from worldly pride to fervent Christian belief. When she was more than sixty years old, "this creature," as she referred to herself, began to dictate the story of her life to a monkish scribe. Except for a collection of brief excerpts, *The Book of Margery Kempe* was lost until 1934, when a copy was discovered in a private library in England. Margery Kempe's associative, pungent narrative, noted for being the first autobiography written in English, is an invaluable document for several reasons. Because she chose not to join a religious order but lived out her spiritual adventures in the secular world, her memoirs are a record of everyday life in bustling ports and at pilgrimage sites across Europe and the Near East. Feminists and theologians value what she reveals about being a medieval woman mystic. Above all, *The Book of Margery Kempe* is a lively self-portrait of a bumbling, stubborn, and passionate fifteenth-century woman determined to live in the way she is convinced God wants her to, despite the pressures exerted on her by family, church, and society to lead a more conventional existence.

Her Life and Times.   Margery Kempe was born in 1373 into a prominent family at Lynn, in Norfolk, where her father, John Brunham, served several times as mayor. Her book begins with her marriage at twenty to John Kempe, a businessman who, Margery is quick to point out, is not as honored or as successful a citizen as her father. Her first pregnancy and childbirth were difficult, precipitating a mental and spiritual crisis that may well have been what we now call postpartum psychosis, a circumstance that once inclined some theologians to dismiss her mystical experiences as "hysterical." According to Margery Kempe, the illness resulted in part from her confessor scolding her too sharply before she had quite finished enumerating all her sins. Childbirth had made her aware of her mortality and, caught between her fear of the stern cleric and her fear of dying unconfessed and entering into eternal damnation, she was disturbed for some months.[1] She writes in her *Book* that she was rescued from her

www   For links to more information on Margery Kempe and a quiz on *The Book of Margery Kempe,* see *World Literature Online* at bedfordstmartins .com/worldlit.

---

[1] **disturbed for some months:** Recently, religious scholars have suggested that Margery Kempe underwent a "dark night of the soul," a state of terror at one's own spiritual sickness and a fear of dying a sinner. She seems to have been reprieved from this terror by her vision of Jesus.

If we are to read
Margery [Kempe]'s
work in a way that
does it and her
justice, we must
accept the realness of
her experience and
the realness of the
life she lived follow-
ing it, as strange or
unlikely or even
grotesque as
some details of
that life might
strike a modern sen-
sibility. . . . A clear,
vivid picture of an
immensely vital,
honest, and intense
human being
emerges, a woman
who is at times remi-
niscent of Saint Paul
and at others of the
Wife of Bath.

– WILLIAM PROVOST,
scholar

despair by Jesus, who appeared to her "clad in a mantle of purple silk." He sat down on her sickbed and gently rebuked her for forsaking him even though, as he assured her, he had never forsaken her.

Although this timely visitation healed Kempe of her madness, she describes herself as persisting for some time in an excessive attachment to the things of this world. She loved to flaunt her fashionable, brightly colored clothing, she prided herself on her distinguished family, and she valued above all the high opinion of her neighbors. In an attempt to make more money, she started her own brewing business and later tried her hand at running a grain mill. Both enterprises failed, somewhat mysteriously: Kempe's ale, though carefully prepared, would not ferment properly, and her ordinarily docile workhorses refused to turn her millstones. She interpreted these events as signs from God telling her to abandon worldly pride and ambition, and she dated her entrance into "the way of everlasting life" from that point.

During her first twenty years of marriage, while she bore John Kempe fourteen children, Margery Kempe's religious visions grew in frequency and intensity. After hearing heavenly melodies, she wrote, "Alas, that ever I did sin! It is full merry in heaven," and sought to sleep apart from her husband. He, however, doggedly insisted on his conjugal rights until, as Kempe records in Chapter 11, husband and wife sat down together in the shade of a wayside cross on a sweltering summer day in 1413 and after much wrangling and bargaining arrived at a compromise. They agreed that Margery might sleep alone if in return she would pay off John's debts and abandon her practice of fasting on Fridays in order to keep him company at meals. At some forty years of age, she at last became free to live the style of spiritual life she longed for.

Marks of Religious Devotion. Margery Kempe made her first and longest overseas pilgrimage to Jerusalem that same year, late in 1413. While on Mount Calvary, the site of Jesus' Crucifixion, she was visited by her first "crying." Weeping had previously played a part in her religious experiences, when she felt remorse and when she rejoiced in the sound of the heavenly music she sometimes was able to hear. But her tears in Jerusalem were of a new order—violent, copious, accompanied by loud screams, and clearly beyond her control. Indeed, her disruptive behavior often embarrassed her, especially when it caused her to be removed from churches where a priest was conducting a service. Even close friends were alienated by her prodigious weeping, some believing she was shamming, others that she had a disorder akin to epilepsy, whose victims were made outcasts in the European Middle Ages. More than once she sought help in dealing with these visitations of weeping, which were to endure for ten years. Perhaps she was comforted by the advice of the renowned English mystic and theologian Dame Julian of Norwich[2] before she departed on

---

[2] **Dame Julian of Norwich:** Born in 1342 in Norwich, about thirty years before Kempe, Julian suffered from a critical illness that was cured by spiritual visions in May 1373. She is best known for her book *The Revelations of Divine Love,* also titled *The Book of Showings,* completed after her visions of 1373 and expanded in 1393. Julian met Margery Kempe in 1413, before Kempe's first pilgrimage and shortly before her own death.

her first pilgrimage: "Set all your trust in God and fear not the language of the world," Julian had told her, "for the more despite, shame, and reproof that ye have in the world, the more is your merit in the sight of God." And Christ himself, Kempe writes, explained to her that her tears were to be understood as a mark of His love and a sign to other mortals of the sufferings of the Virgin Mary.

Margery Kempe continued to be a controversial figure among her contemporaries, disturbing to members of religious orders and the laity who did not deem her a holy woman touched by God's special grace. She was questioned, threatened, and even arrested on suspicion of heresy a number of times, but no accusation ever stuck. Dressed in bridal white and wearing a wedding ring inscribed in Latin *Jesus Christ Is My Love,* she wandered and wept and roared her way across Europe and the Middle East, telling people of her visions, such as the one in which she saw herself wed to Jesus, and of her attendance in turn at the births of both the Virgin Mary and Jesus. Fearlessly she preached to hostile crowds and confronted distinguished members of the clergy with their shortcomings and imperfections of faith. In about 1431 she went back to live with her husband, who was paralyzed in an accident, and nursed him until his death the same year. She died in Lynn sometime after 1438, the year of her last mention in public records.

Kempe's Spirituality and Worldly Affairs.   Modern feminist scholars point out that Margery Kempe's style of spirituality—her tears and the intensely domestic nature of her visions of the Holy Family, including scenes of marriage, childbirth, and the household at Nazareth—although most common among women, was not confined to the female gender. Monks and friars, especially Franciscans, also practiced the "affective piety" of compassionate tears and meditated on the everyday life of Jesus and his earthly parents. But her way of life does parallel in particular that of other holy women of Europe about whom she knew or might have known. Saint Bridget of Sweden, for example, also experienced conflict over sexual activity in her married life; and in the twelfth century, Hildegarde of Bingen,[3] a visionary like Kempe, had also dared to rebuke male clerics for their faults. The spiritual experiences of these medieval women were bolstered no doubt by the legends of female saints disseminated by the Catholic Church itself; a mystical tradition, however troubling at times for the church, lay behind Kempe's "feelings and revelations."

The Book of Margery Kempe exhibits certain features often found in women's writing. Kempe's narrative unfolds in an associative rather than a strictly chronological manner, with emotional connections, rather than

---

[3] **Saint Bridget . . . Hildegarde of Bingen:** St. Bridget (1303–1373), a member of the Swedish nobility, moved to Rome and was ordained after her husband's death in 1344. She was canonized despite serious controversy in 1391. Her biography was known to Kempe, who cites it in her book. Hildegarde of Bingen (1098–1179), a member of the German nobility, possessed powers of prophecy and experienced visions from an early age. She established a convent at Rupertsberg in 1150 and defended it against attacks by ecclesiastical authorities until her death. In addition to accounts of her mystical visions, Hildegarde wrote groundbreaking works on science, medicine, and philosophy, and was a brilliant poet and musical composer as well.

linear organization, often determining the order in which she narrates events. Her prose is also very personal and particular, sprinkled with gossipy anecdotes and homely details. She writes of the fabric and color of Christ's robe when he appears to her, and about how hot it was on the day that she and her husband reached a compromise concerning Margery's desired chastity. In Jerusalem she makes note that the slab on which Jesus' crucified body was said to have been laid out was made of marble, and that the cup in which she was given wine while visiting a poor household in Rome was stoneware. Kempe's relish for the physical world, with its weather, terrain, texture, and all its curious variety, shines through her narrative.

The fact that Kempe dictated her experiences in vernacular English and saw to their publication gives us a broader and deeper view of the world in which she lived. An appropriate form of praise for the secular part of Margery Kempe might be what the fictional Wife of Bath said about herself in Chaucer's *Canterbury Tales:* "For I have had my world as in my time."

■ CONNECTIONS

The New Testament, p. 23. The stories of the visions and miracles of Jesus recorded in the Gospels of Matthew and Luke in the New Testament are part of the context upon which Margery Kempe's visions are based. Medieval visions of Jesus often depicted him as a Redeemer appearing in this lifetime to bring hope to the Christian on earth. What do you think is "orthodox" and what, if anything, is "unorthodox" about Kempe's visions of Jesus?

St. Augustine, *Confessions,* p. 64. St. Augustine wrote the first and most influential spiritual autobiography of the Middle Ages. Augustine himself experienced his religious conversion in the form of a vision in his garden. How might St. Augustine have regarded Margery Kempe and her visions?

Geoffrey Chaucer, *The Canterbury Tales,* p. 884. Chaucer's fictional Wife of Bath as depicted in *The Canterbury Tales* is comparable to Margery Kempe in her worldly aspect. Trace similarities of speech and thought between these two women. Does this comparison shed any light on Kempe's popularity as a writer?

■ FURTHER RESEARCH

Editions
Butler-Bowden, William, ed. *The Book of Margery Kempe: A Modern Version.* 1944.
Meech, Sanford Brown, and Hope Family Allen, eds. *The Book of Margery Kempe.* 1940.

Related Works
Atkinson, Clarissa W. *Mystic and Pilgrim: The Book and the World of Margery Kempe.* 1983.
Colledge, Eric. *The Medieval Mystics of England.* 1961.
Knowles, Dom David. *The English Mystical Tradition.* 1961.
Power, Eileen. *Medieval Women.* Ed. M. M. Postan. 1975.
Provost, William. "The English Religious Enthusiast: Margery Kempe." In Katharina M. Wilson, ed. *Medieval Women Writers.* 1984.
Stone, Robert Carl. *Middle English Prose Style: Margery Kempe and Julian of Norwich.* 1970.

℘ The Book of Margery Kempe

Translated by W. Butler-Bowden

CHAPTER 1

Her marriage and illness after childbirth. She recovers.

When this creature was twenty years of age, or some deal more, she was married to a worshipful burgess (of Lynne) and was with child within a short time, as nature would. And after she had conceived, she was belaboured with great accesses[1] till the child was born and then, what with the labour she had in childing, and the sickness going before, she despaired of her life, weening she might not live. And then she sent for her ghostly father,[2] for she had a thing on her conscience which she had never shewn before that time in all her life. For she was ever hindered by her enemy, the devil, evermore saying to her that whilst she was in good health she needed no confession, but to do penance by herself alone and all should be forgiven, for God is merciful enough. And therefore this creature oftentimes did great penance in fasting on bread and water, and other deeds of alms with devout prayers, save she would not shew that in confession.

And when she was at any time sick or dis-eased, the devil said in her mind that she should be damned because she was not shriven of that default. Wherefore after her child was born, she, not trusting to live, sent for her ghostly father, as is said before, in full will to be shriven of all her lifetime, as near as she could. And when she came to the point for to say that thing which she had so long concealed, her confessor was a little too hasty and began sharply to reprove her, before she had fully said her intent, and so she would no more say for aught he might do. Anon, for the dread

---

The Book of Margery Kempe. Margery Kempe began dictating her autobiographical narrative in 1431, following the death of her husband. The first half of the two-part work was told to a scribe, an old friend who probably helped verify the accuracy of her memory on many occasions. His writing skills were somewhat limited, however, by his mixed-language background of English and German. This part of the work, comprising eighty-nine chapters, was corrected and rewritten by a second scribe, almost certainly a priest, in 1436, after the death of the first scribe. At this time Margery Kempe added ten more chapters, briefer and more cautiously edited, which she completed sometime before her own death around 1438. She reports that this second scribe feared that her visions and "cryings" might not be orthodox. Kempe had been accused more than once of heresy, and the scribe demanded textual proof that other women mystics had undergone similar experiences before he would finish work on the book.

Brief excerpts from *The Book of Margery Kempe* were printed in a pamphlet in 1501 and reprinted in 1521. These selections were confined to Kempe's relatively conventional visions of Jesus and the Virgin Mary, skirting her more sensation personal narrative. After four hundred years of obscurity, the *Book* was rediscovered in 1934 by Colonel William Butler-Bowden among a

---

[1] **accesses:** Attacks of pain.   [2] **ghostly father:** Spiritual advisor; a priest.

she had of damnation on the one side, and his sharp reproving of her on the other side, this creature went out of her mind and was wondrously vexed and laboured with spirits for half a year, eight weeks and odd days.

And in this time she saw, as she thought, devils opening their mouths all inflamed with burning waves of fire, as if they would have swallowed her in, sometimes ramping at her, sometimes threatening her, pulling her and hauling her, night and day during the aforesaid time. Also the devils cried upon her with great threatenings, and bade her that she should forsake Christendom, her faith, and deny her God, His Mother and all the Saints in Heaven, her good works and all good virtues, her father, her mother and all her friends. And so she did. She slandered her husband, her friends and her own self. She said many a wicked word, and many a cruel word; she knew no virtue nor goodness; she desired all wickedness; like as the spirits tempted her to say and do, so she said and did. She would have destroyed herself many a time at their stirrings and have been damned with them in Hell, and in witness thereof, she bit her own hand so violently, that the mark was seen all her life after.

And also she rived the skin on her body against her heart with her nails spitefully, for she had no other instruments, and worse she would have done, but that she was bound and kept with strength day and night so that she might not have her will. And when she had long been laboured in these and many other temptations, so that men weened she should never have escaped or lived, then on a time as she lay alone and her keepers were from her, Our Merciful Lord Jesus Christ, ever to be trusted, worshipped be His Name, never forsaking His servant in time of need, appeared to His creature who had forsaken Him, in the likeness of a man, most seemly, most beauteous and most amiable that ever might be seen with man's eye, clad in a mantle of purple silk, sitting upon her bedside, looking upon her with so blessed a face that she was strengthened in all her spirit, and said to her these words: —

'Daughter, why hast thou forsaken Me, and I forsook never thee?'

---

group of manuscripts at his estate in Lancashire, England. Identifying marks on the manuscript confirmed that it was a copy of the original made in the mid fifteenth century. A scholarly edition by Sanford Meech and Hope Emily Allen in 1940 was followed by Colonel Butler-Bowden's own editorial modernization of the text in 1944.

The following excerpts highlight crucial events in the personal and spiritual life of Margery Kempe. In chapter 1, Kempe describes her marriage, her emotional distress after the birth of her first child, her visions of torments by devils for her excessive sinfulness, and her redemptive vision of Jesus. In the next chapter, she treats her worldly pride and her failed attempts to succeed in business. In chapter 3, she reports having had a vision of Paradise that leads her to seek God through fasting, praying, and sexual abstention; in chapter 11 she tells of how she and her husband conclude that she should sleep alone. In later chapters she visits Dame Julian of Norwich, before she goes on a pilgrimage to Jerusalem. On the way, she falls out of favor with the other pilgrims. The beleaguered company finally arrives in Jerusalem, where she has many visions of Christ tormented and crucified. Her journey culminates in visits to the Holy Sepulchre, Mount Zion, and Bethlehem, where she receives "sweet speech and dalliance" from Jesus and his mother, Mary.

And anon, as He said these words, she saw verily how the air opened as bright as any lightning. And He rose up into the air, not right hastily and quickly, but fair and easily, so that she might well behold Him in the air till it was closed again.

And anon this creature became calmed in her wits and reason, as well as ever she was before, and prayed her husband as soon as he came to her, that she might have the keys of the buttery to take her meat and drink as she had done before. Her maidens and her keepers counselled him that he should deliver her no keys, as they said she would but give away such goods as there were, for she knew not what she said, as they weened.

Nevertheless, her husband ever having tenderness and compassion for her, commanded that they should deliver to her the keys; and she took her meat and drink as her bodily strength would serve her, and knew her friends and her household and all others that came to see how Our Lord Jesus Christ had wrought His grace in her, so blessed may He be, Who ever is near in tribulation. When men think He is far from them, He is full near by His grace. Afterwards, this creature did all other occupations as fell to her to do, wisely and soberly enough, save she knew not verily the call of Our Lord.

CHAPTER 2

Her worldly pride. Her attempt at brewing and
milling, and failure at both. She amends her ways.

When this creature had thus graciously come again to her mind, she thought that she was bound to God and that she would be His servant. Nevertheless, she would not leave her pride or her pompous array, which she had used beforetime, either for her husband, or for any other man's counsel. Yet she knew full well that men said of her full much villainy, for she wore gold pipes on her head, and her hoods, with the tippets, were slashed. Her cloaks also were slashed and laid with divers colours between the slashes, so that they should be the more staring to men's sight, and herself the more worshipped.

And when her husband spoke to her to leave her pride, she answered shrewdly and shortly, and said that she was come of worthy kindred—he should never have wedded her—for her father was sometime Mayor of the town of N . . . and afterwards he was alderman of the High Guild of the Trinity in N . . . And therefore she would keep the worship of her kindred whatever any man said.

She had full great envy of her neighbours, that they should be as well arrayed as she. All her desire was to be worshipped by the people. She would not take heed of any chastisement, nor be content with the goods that God had sent her, as her husband was, but ever desired more and more.

Then for pure covetousness, and to maintain her pride, she began to brew, and was one of the greatest brewers in the town of N . . . for three years or four, till she lost much money, for she had never been used thereto. For, though she had ever such good servants, cunning in brewing, yet it would never succeed with them. For when the ale was fair standing under barm[3] as any man might see, suddenly the barm would fall down, so that all the ale was lost, one brewing after another, so that her servants were ashamed and would not dwell with her.

Then this creature thought how God had punished her aforetime—and she could not take heed—and now again, by the loss of her goods. Then she left and brewed no more.

Then she asked her husband's mercy because she would not follow his counsel aforetime, and she said that her pride and sin were the cause of all her punishing, and that she would amend and that she had trespassed with good will.

Yet she left not the world altogether, for she now bethought herself of a new housewifery. She had a horse-mill. She got herself two good horses and a man to grind men's corn, and thus she trusted to get her living. This enterprise lasted not long, for in a short time after, on Corpus Christi Eve,[4] befell this marvel. This man, being in good health of body, and his two horses sturdy and gentle, had pulled well in the mill beforetime, and now he took one of these horses and put him in the mill as he had done before, and this horse would draw no draught in the mill for anything the man might do. The man was sorry and essayed with all his wits how he should make this horse pull. Sometimes he led him by the head, sometimes he beat him, sometimes he cherished him and all availed not, for he would rather go backward than forward. Then this man set a sharp pair of spurs on his heels and rode on the horse's back to make him pull, and it was never the better. When the man saw it would work in no way, he set up this horse again in the stable, and gave him corn, and he ate well and freshly. And later he took the other horse and put him in the mill, and like his fellow did, so did he, for he would not draw for anything the man might do. Then the man forsook his service and would no longer remain with the aforesaid creature. Anon, it was noised about the town of N . . . that neither man nor beast would serve the said creature.

Then some said she was accursed; some said God took open vengeance on her; some said one thing and some said another. Some wise men, whose minds were more grounded in the love of Our Lord, said that it was the high mercy of Our Lord Jesus Christ that called her from the pride and vanity of the wretched world.

Then this creature, seeing all these adversities coming on every side, thought they were the scourges of Our Lord that would chastise her for her sin. Then she asked God's mercy, and forsook her pride, her covetousness, and the desire that she had for the worship of the world, and did great bodily penance, and began to enter the way of everlasting life as shall be told hereafter.

---

[3] **barm:** The foam or head that forms on top of ale.

[4] **Corpus Christi Eve:** The night before the church feast of Corpus Christi, held in honor of the Eucharist and celebrated on the Thursday following Trinity Sunday, the eighth Sunday after Easter.

CHAPTER 3

Her vision of Paradise. She desires to live apart from
her husband. Does penance and wears a haircloth.

On a night, as this creature lay in her bed with her husband, she heard a sound of melody so sweet and delectable, that she thought she had been in Paradise, and therewith she started out of her bed and said: —

'Alas, that ever I did sin! It is full merry in Heaven.'

This melody was so sweet that it surpassed all melody that ever might be heard in this world, without any comparison, and caused her, when she heard any mirth or melody afterwards, to have full plenteous and abundant tears of high devotion, with great sobbings and sighings after the bliss of Heaven, not dreading the shames and the spites of this wretched world. Ever after this inspiration, she had in her mind the mirth and the melody that was in Heaven, so much, that she could not well restrain herself from speaking thereof, for wherever she was in any company she would say oftentimes: — 'It is full merry in Heaven.'

And they that knew her behaviour beforetime, and now heard her speaking so much of the bliss of Heaven, said to her: —

'Why speak ye so of the mirth that is in Heaven? Ye know it not, and ye have not been there, any more than we.' And were wroth with her, for she would not hear nor speak of worldly things as they did, and as she did beforetime.

And after this time she had never desired to commune fleshly with her husband, for the debt of matrimony was so abominable to her that she would rather, she thought, have eaten or drunk the ooze and the muck in the gutter than consent to any fleshly communing, save only for obedience.

So she said to her husband: — 'I may not deny you my body, but the love of my heart and my affections are withdrawn from all earthly creatures, and set only in God.'

He would have his will and she obeyed, with great weeping and sorrowing that she might not live chaste. And oftentimes this creature counselled her husband to live chaste, and said that they often, she knew well, had displeased God by their inordinate love, and the great delectation they each had in using the other, and now it was good that they should, by the common will and consent of them both, punish and chastise themselves wilfully by abstaining from the lust of their bodies. Her husband said it was good to do so, but he might not yet. He would when God willed. And so he used her as he had done before. He would not spare her. And ever she prayed to God that she might live chaste; and three or four years after, when it pleased Our Lord, he made a vow of chastity, as shall be written afterwards, by leave of Jesus.

And also, after this creature heard this heavenly melody, she did great bodily penance. She was shriven sometimes twice or thrice on a day, and specially of that sin she so long had [hid], concealed and covered, as is written in the beginning of the book.

She gave herself up to great fasting and great watching; she rose at two or three of the clock, and went to church, and was there at her prayers unto the time of noon and also all the afternoon. Then she was slandered and reproved by many people, because she kept so strict a life. She got a hair-cloth from a kiln, such as men dry malt on, and laid it in her kirtle as secretly and privily as she might, so that her husband should not espy it. Nor did he, and she lay by him every night in his bed and wore the hair-cloth every day, and bore children in the time.

Then she had three years of great labour with temptations which she bore as meekly as she could, thanking Our Lord for all His gifts, and was as merry when she was reproved, scorned and japed for Our Lord's love, and much more merry than she was beforetime in the worship of the world. For she knew right well she had sinned greatly against God and was worthy of more shame and sorrow than any man could cause her, and despite of the world was the right way Heavenwards, since Christ Himself had chosen that way. All His apostles, martyrs, confessors and virgins, and all that ever came to Heaven, passed by the way of tribulation, and she, desiring nothing so much as Heaven, then was glad in her conscience when she believed that she was entering the way that would lead her to the place she most desired.

And this creature had contrition and great compunction with plenteous tears and many boisterous sobbings for her sins and for her unkindness against her Maker. She repented from her childhood for unkindness, as Our Lord would put it in her mind, full many a time. Then, beholding her own wickedness, she could but sorrow and weep and ever pray for mercy and forgiveness. Her weeping was so plenteous and continuing that many people thought she could weep and leave off, as she liked. And therefore many men said she was a false hypocrite, and wept before the world for succour and worldly goods. Then full many forsook her that loved her before while she was in the world, and would not know her. And ever, she thanked God for all, desiring nothing but mercy and forgiveness of sin. [. . .]

Chapter 11

On the way back from York, she and her husband
argue as to their carnal relationship to each other.

It befell on a Friday on Midsummer Eve in right hot weather, as this creature was coming from York-ward carrying a bottle with beer in her hand, and her husband a cake in his bosom, that he asked his wife this question: —

'Margery, if there came a man with a sword, who would strike off my head, unless I should commune naturally with you as I have done before, tell me on your conscience — for ye say ye will not lie — whether ye would suffer my head to be smitten off, or whether ye would suffer me to meddle with you again, as I did at one time?'

'Alas, sir,' said she, 'why raise this matter, when we have been chaste these eight weeks?'

'For I will know the truth of your heart.'

And then she said with great sorrow:— 'Forsooth, I would rather see you being slain, than that we should turn again to our uncleanness.'

And he replied:— 'Ye are no good wife.'

She then asked her husband what was the cause that he had not meddled with her for eight weeks, since she lay with him every night in his bed. He said he was made so afraid when he would have touched her, that he dare do no more.

'Now, good sir, amend your ways, and ask God's mercy, for I told you nearly three years ago that ye should be slain suddenly, and now is this the third year, and so I hope I shall have my desire. Good sir, I pray you grant me what I ask, and I will pray for you that ye shall be saved through the mercy of Our Lord Jesus Christ, and ye shall have more reward in Heaven than if ye wore a hair-cloth or a habergeon.[5] I pray you, suffer me to make a vow of chastity at what bishop's hand God wills.'

'Nay,' he said, 'that I will not grant you, for now may I use you without deadly sin, and then might I not do so.'

Then she said to him:— 'If it be the will of the Holy Ghost to fulfil what I have said, I pray God that ye may consent thereto; and if it be not the will of the Holy Ghost, I pray God ye never consent to it.'

Then they went forth towards Bridlington in right hot weather, the creature having great sorrow and dread for her chastity. As they came by a cross, her husband sat down under the cross, calling his wife to him and saying these words unto her:— 'Margery, grant me my desire, and I shall grant you your desire. My first desire is that we shall lie together in bed as we have done before; the second, that ye shall pay my debts, ere ye go to Jerusalem; and the third, that ye shall eat and drink with me on the Friday as ye were wont to do.'

'Nay, sir,' said she, 'to break the Friday, I will never grant you whilst I live.'

'Well,' said he, 'then I shall meddle with you again.'

She prayed him that he would give her leave to say her prayers, and he granted it kindly. Then she knelt down beside a cross in the field and prayed in this manner, with a great abundance of tears:—

'Lord God, Thou knowest all things. Thou knowest what sorrow I have had to be chaste in my body to Thee all these three years, and now might I have my will, and dare not for love of Thee. For if I should break that manner of fasting which Thou commandest me to keep on the Friday, without meat or drink, I should now have my desire. But, Blessed Lord, Thou knowest that I will not contravene Thy will, and much now is my sorrow unless I find comfort in Thee. Now, Blessed Jesus, make Thy will known to me unworthy, that I may follow it thereafter and fulfil it with all my might.'

Then Our Lord Jesus Christ with great sweetness, spoke to her, commanding her to go again to her husband, and pray him to grant her what she desired, 'And he shall have what he desireth. For, my dearworthy daughter, this was the cause that I bade thee fast, so that thou shouldst the sooner obtain and get thy desire, and now it

---

[5] **a habergeon:** A coat of mail that could be worn for penance.

is granted to thee. I will no longer that thou fast. Therefore I bid thee in the Name of Jesus, eat and drink as thy husband doth.'

Then this creature thanked Our Lord Jesus Christ for His grace and goodness, and rose up and went to her husband, saying to him:—

"Sir, if it please you, ye shall grant me my desire, and ye shall have your desire. Grant me that ye will not come into my bed, and I grant you to requite your debts ere I go to Jerusalem. Make my body free to God so that ye never make challenge to me, by asking any debt of matrimony. After this day, whilst ye live, I will eat and drink on the Friday at your bidding.'

Then said her husband:—'As free may your body be to God, as it hath been to me.

This creature thanked God, greatly rejoicing that she had her desire, praying her husband that they should say three Paternosters in worship of the Trinity for the great grace that He had granted them. And so they did, kneeling under a cross, and afterwards they ate and drank together in great gladness of spirit. This was on a Friday on Midsummer's Eve. Then went they forth Bridlingtonward and also to many other countries and spoke with God's servants, both anchorites and recluses, and many others of Our Lord's lovers, with many worthy clerks, doctors of divinity and bachelors also, in divers places. And this creature, to many of them, shewed her feelings and her contemplations, as she was commanded to do, to find out if any deceit were in her feelings. [. . .]

CHAPTER 18

At Norwich she visits a White Friar, William
Sowthfeld, and an anchoress, Dame Jelyan.

This creature was charged and commanded in her soul that she should go to a White Friar, in the same city of Norwich, called William Sowthfeld, a good man and a holy liver, to shew him the grace that God wrought in her, as she had done to the good Vicar before. She did as she was commanded and came to the friar on a forenoon, and was with him in a chapel a long time, and shewed him her meditations, and what God had wrought in her soul, to find out if she were deceived by any illusion or not.

This good man, the White Friar, ever whilst she told him her feelings, holding up his hands, said:—'Jesu Mercy and gramercy.'

'Sister,' he said, 'dread not for your manner of living, for it is the Holy Ghost working plenteously His grace in your soul. Thank Him highly for His goodness, for we all be bound to thank Him for you, Who now in our days will inspire His grace in you, to the help and comfort of us all, who are supported by your prayers and by such others as ye be. And we are preserved from many mischiefs and diseases which we should suffer, and worthily, for our trespass. Never were such good creatures amongst us. Blessed be Almighty God for His goodness. And therefore, sister, I counsel you that ye dispose yourself to receive the gifts of God as lowly and meekly as ye can, and put no obstacle or objection against the goodness of the Holy Ghost, for He may give His gifts where He will, and of unworthy He maketh worthy, of sinful He maketh rightful. His mercy is ever ready unto us, unless the fault be in ourselves, for He dwelleth not in a body subject to sin. He flieth all false feigning and falsehood: He asketh of us a lowly, a meek and a contrite heart, with a good will. Our Lord sayeth Himself: — "My Spirit shall rest upon a meek man, a contrite man, and one dreading My words."

'Sister, I trust to Our Lord that ye have these conditions either in your will or your affection, or else in both, and I believe not that Our Lord suffereth them to be deceived endlessly, that set all their trust in Him, and seek and desire nothing but Him only, as I hope ye do. And therefore believe fully that Our Lord loveth you and worketh His grace in you. I pray God to increase it and continue it to His everlasting worship, for His mercy.'

The aforesaid creature was much comforted both in body and in soul by this good man's words, and greatly strengthened in her faith.

Then she was bidden by Our Lord to go to an anchoress in the same city, named Dame Jelyan,[6] and so she did, and showed her the grace that God put into her soul, of compunction, contrition, sweetness and devotion, compassion with holy meditation and high contemplation, and full many holy speeches and dalliance that Our Lord spake to her soul; and many wonderful revelations, which she shewed to the anchoress to find out if there were any deceit in them, for the anchoress was expert in such things, and good counsel could give.

The anchoress, hearing the marvellous goodness of Our Lord, highly thanked God with all her heart for His visitation, counselling this creature to be obedient to the will of Our Lord God and to fulfil with all her might whatever He put into her soul, if it were not against the worship of God, and profit of her fellow Christians, for if it were, then it were not the moving of a good spirit, but rather of an evil spirit. 'The Holy Ghost moveth ne'er a thing against charity, for if He did, He would be contrary to His own self for He is all charity. Also He moveth a soul to all chasteness, for chaste livers are called the Temple of the Holy Ghost, and the Holy Ghost maketh a soul stable and steadfast in the right faith, and the right belief.

'And a double man in soul is ever unstable and unsteadfast in all his ways. He that is ever doubting is like the flood of the sea which is moved and borne about with the wind, and that man is not likely to receive the gifts of God.

'Any creature that hath these tokens may steadfastly believe that the Holy Ghost dwelleth in his soul. And much more when God visiteth a creature with tears of contrition, devotion, and compassion, he may and ought to believe that the Holy Ghost is in his soul. Saint Paul saith that the Holy Ghost asketh for us with mourning and weeping unspeakable, that is to say, He maketh us to ask and pray with mourning and weeping so plenteously that the tears may not be numbered. No evil spirit may give these tokens, for Saint Jerome saith that tears torment more the devil than do

---

[6] **Dame Jelyan:** Julian of Norwich (1342–1413?), a Christian anchorite (one who lives apart for religious reasons) who recorded her visionary experiences, or "showings," in which she spoke of God as a maternal figure.

the pains of Hell. God and the devil are ever at odds and they shall never dwell together in one place, and the devil hath no power in a man's soul.

'Holy Writ saith that the soul of a rightful man is the seat of God, and so I trust, sister, that ye be. I pray God grant you perseverance. Set all your trust in God and fear not the language of the world, for the more despite, shame and reproof that ye have in the world, the more is your merit in the sight of God. Patience is necessary to you, for in that shall ye keep your soul.'

Much was the holy dalliance that the anchoress and this creature had by communing in the love of Our Lord Jesus Christ the many days that they were together. [...]

FROM

CHAPTER 26

*She starts from Yarmouth on her way to the Holy
Land. She has trouble with her companions owing
to her weeping and piety. She reaches Constance.*

When the time came that this creature should visit those holy places where Our Lord was quick and dead, as she had by revelation years before, she prayed the parish priest of the town where she was dwelling, to say for her in the pulpit, that, if any man or woman claimed any debt from her husband or herself, they should come and speak with her ere she went, and she, with the help of God would make a settlement with each of them, so that they should hold themselves content. And so she did.

Afterwards, she took her leave of her husband and of the holy anchorite, who had told her, before, the process of her going and the great dis-ease that she would suffer by the way, and when all her fellowship forsook her, how a broken-backed man would lead her forth in safety, through the help of Our Lord.

And so it befell indeed, as shall be written afterward.

Then she took her leave ... of other friends. Then she went forth to Norwich, and offered at the Trinity, and afterwards she went to Yarmouth and offered at an image of Our Lady, and there she took her ship.

And next day they came to a great town called Zierikzee, where Our Lord of His high goodness visited this creature with abundant tears of contrition for her own sins, and sometime for other men's sins also. And especially she had tears of compassion in mind of Our Lord's Passion. And she was housteled each Sunday where there was time and place convenient thereto, with great weeping and boisterous sobbing, so that many men marvelled and wondered at the great grace that God had wrought in His creature.

This creature had eaten no flesh and drunk no wine for four years ere she went out of England, and so now her ghostly father charged her, by virtue of obedience, that she should both eat flesh and drink wine. And so she did a little while; afterwards she prayed her confessor that he would hold her excused if she ate no flesh, and suffer her to do as she would for such time as pleased him.

And soon after, through the moving of some of her company, her confessor was displeased because she ate no flesh, and so were many of the company. And they were most displeased because she wept so much and spoke always of the love and goodness of Our Lord, as much at the table as in other places. And therefore shamefully they reproved her, and severely chid her, and said they would not put up with her as her husband did when she was at home and in England.

And she answered meekly to them: — 'Our Lord, Almighty God, is as great a Lord here as in England, and as good cause have I to love Him here as there, blessed may He be.'

At these words, her fellowship was angrier than before, and their wrath and unkindness to this creature was a matter of great grief, for they were held right good men and she desired greatly their love, if she might have it to the pleasure of God.

And then she said to one of them specially: — 'Ye cause me much shame and great grievance.'

He answered her anon: — 'I pray God that the devil's death may overcome thee soon and quickly,' and many more cruel words he said to her than she could repeat.

And soon after some of the company in whom she trusted best, and her own maiden also, said she could no longer go in their fellowship. And they said that they would take away her maiden from her, so that she should no strumpet be, in her company. And then one of them, who had her gold in keeping, left her a noble with great anger and vexation to go where she would and help herself as she might, for with them, they said, she should no longer abide; and they forsook her that night.

Then, on the next morning, there came to her one of their company, a man who loved her well, praying her that she would go to his fellows and meeken herself[7] to them, and pray them that she might go still in their company till she came to Constance.

And so she did, and went forth with them till she came to Constance with great discomfort and great trouble, for they did her much shame and much reproof as they went, in divers places. They cut her gown so short that it came but little beneath her knee, and made her put on a white canvas, in the manner of a sacken apron, so that she should be held a fool and the people should not make much of her or hold her in repute. They made her sit at the table's end, below all the others, so that she ill durst speak a word.

And, notwithstanding all their malice, she was held in more worship than they were, wherever they went.

And the good man of the house where they were hostelled, though she sat lowest at the table's end, would always help her before them all as well as he could, and sent her from his own table such service as he had, and that annoyed her fellowship full evil.

As they went by the way Constance-ward, it was told them that they would be robbed and have great discomfort unless they had great grace.

---

[7] **meeken herself:** Behave meekly, with humility.

Then this creature came to a church and went in to make her prayer, and she prayed with all her heart, with great weeping and many tears, for help and succour against their enemies.

Then Our Lord said to her mind: — 'Dread thee naught, daughter, thy fellowship shall come to no harm whilst thou art in their company.'

And so, blessed may Our Lord be in all His works, they went forth in safety to Constance.

[At Constance, Kempe is befriended by a papal legate and meets another supporter, William Wever of Devonshire. She travels alone with Wever to Bologna, where she rejoins the company of the pilgrimage. After the group's arrival in Venice, she has another falling out with them and they refuse to eat with her. She falls ill for six weeks but then recovers.]

Chapter 28

She sails from Venice and reaches Jerusalem.
Much trouble owing to her crying.

Also this company, which had put the aforesaid creature from their table, so that she should no longer eat amongst them, engaged a ship for themselves to sail in. They bought vessels for their wine, and obtained bedding for themselves, but nothing for her. Then she, seeing their unkindness, went to the same man where they had been, and bought herself bedding as they had done, and came where they were and shewed them what she had done, purposing to sail with them in that ship which they had chartered.

Afterwards, as this creature was in contemplation, Our Lord warned her in her mind that she should not sail in that ship, and He assigned her to another ship, a galley, that she should sail in. Then she told this to some of the company, and they told it forth to their fellowship, and then they durst not sail in the ship they had chartered. So they sold away their vessels which they had got for their wines, and were right fain to come to the galley where she was, and so, though it was against her will, she went forth with them in their company, for they durst not otherwise do.

When it was time to make their beds, they locked up her clothes, and a priest, who was in their company, took away a sheet from the aforesaid creature, and said it was his. She took God to witness that it was her sheet. Then the priest swore a great oath, by the book in his hand, that she was as false as she might be, and despised her and strongly rebuked her.

And so she had ever much tribulation till she came to Jerusalem. And ere she came there, she said to them that she supposed they were grieved with her.

'I pray you, Sirs, be in charity with me, for I am in charity with you, and forgive me that I have grieved you by the way. And if any of you have in anything trespassed against me, God forgive it you, and I do.'

So they went forth into the Holy Land till they could see Jerusalem. And when this creature saw Jerusalem, riding on an ass, she thanked God with all her heart, praying Him for His mercy that, as He had brought her to see His earthly city of Jerusalem, He would grant her grace to see the blissful city of Jerusalem above, the city of Heaven. Our Lord Jesus Christ, answering her thought, granted her to have her desire.

Then for the joy she had, and the sweetness she felt in the dalliance with Our Lord, she was on the point of falling off her ass, for she could not bear the sweetness and grace that God wrought in her soul. Then two pilgrims, Duchemen, went to her, and kept her from falling; one of whom was a priest, and he put spices in her mouth to comfort her, thinking she had been sick. And so they helped her on to Jerusalem, and when she came there, she said: —

'Sirs, I pray you be not displeased though I weep sore in this holy place where Our Lord Jesus Christ was quick and dead.'

Then went they to the temple in Jerusalem and they were let in on the same day at evensong time, and abode there till the next day at evensong time. Then the friars lifted up a cross and led the pilgrims about from one place to another where Our Lord suffered . . . His Passion, every man and woman bearing a wax candle in one hand. And the friars always, as they went about, told them what Our Lord suffered in every place. The aforesaid creature wept and sobbed as plenteously as though she had seen Our Lord with her bodily eye, suffering His Passion at that time. Before her in her soul she saw Him verily by contemplation, and that caused her to have compassion. And when they came up on to the Mount of Calvary, she fell down because she could not stand or kneel, and rolled and wrested with her body, spreading her arms abroad, and cried with a loud voice as though her heart would have burst asunder; for, in the city of her soul, she saw verily and clearly how Our Lord was crucified. Before her face, she heard and saw, in her ghostly sight, the mourning of Our Lady, of Saint John, and Mary Magdalene and of many others that loved Our Lord.

And she had such great compassion and such great pain, at seeing Our Lord's pain that she could not keep herself from crying and roaring though she should have died for it. And this was the first cry that ever she cried in any contemplation. And this manner of crying endured many years after this time, for aught any man might do, and therefore, suffered she much despite and much reproof. The crying was so loud and so wonderful that it made the people astounded unless they had heard it before, or unless they knew the cause of the crying. And she had them so often that they made her right weak in her bodily might, and especially if she heard of Our Lord's Passion.

And sometimes, when she saw the crucifix, or if she saw a man with a wound, or a beast, whichever it were, or if a man beat a child before her, or smote a horse or other beast with a whip, if she saw it or heard it, she thought she saw Our Lord being beaten or wounded, just as she saw it in the man or the beast either in the field or the town, and by herself alone as well as amongst the people.

First when she had her cryings in Jerusalem, she had them often, and in Rome also. And when she came home to England, first at her coming home, it came but seldom, as it were once a month, then once a week, afterwards daily, and once she had fourteen in one day, and another day she had seven, and so on, as God would visit her, sometimes in church, sometimes in the street, sometimes in her chamber, sometimes in the fields, whenever God would send them, for she never knew the time nor the hour when they would come. And they never came without passing great sweetness of devotion and high contemplation. And as soon as she perceived that she would cry, she would keep it in as much as she might that the people should not hear it, to their annoyance. For some said that a wicked spirit vexed her; some said it was a sickness; some said she had drunk too much wine; some banned her; some wished she was in the harbour; some wished she was on the sea in a bottomless boat; and thus each man as he thought. Other ghostly men loved her and favoured her the more. Some great clerks said Our Lady cried never so, nor any saint in Heaven, but they knew full little what she felt, nor would they believe that she could not stop crying if she wished.

And therefore when she knew that she would cry, she kept it in as long as she might, and did all she could to withstand it or put it away, till she waxed as livid as any lead, and ever it would labour in her mind more and more till the time it broke out. And when the body might no longer endure the ghostly labour, but was overcome with the unspeakable love that wrought so fervently in her soul, then she fell down and cried wondrous loud, and the more she laboured to keep it in or put it away, so much the more would she cry, and the louder. Thus she did on the Mount of Calvary, as is written before.

Thus she had as very contemplation in the sight of her soul, as if Christ had hung before her bodily eye in His Manhood. And when through the dispensation of the high mercy of Our Sovereign Saviour Christ Jesus, it was granted to this creature to behold so verily His precious tender body, all rent and torn with scourges, fuller of wounds than ever was a dove-house of holes, hanging on the Cross with the crown of thorns upon His head, His beautiful hands, His tender feet nailed to the hard tree, the rivers of blood flowing out plenteously from every member, the grisly and grievous wound in His precious side shedding blood and water for her love and her salvation, then she fell down and cried with a loud voice, wonderfully turning and wresting her body on every side, spreading her arms abroad as if she would have died, and could not keep herself from crying, and from these bodily movements for the fire of love that burnt so fervently in her soul with pure pity and compassion.

It is not to be marvelled at, if this creature cried and made wondrous faces and expressions, when we may see each day with the eye both men and women, some for the loss of worldly goods, some for affection of their kindred, or worldly friendships, through over much study and earthly affection, and most of all for inordinate love and fleshly affection, if their friends are parted from them, they will cry and roar and wring their hands as if they had no wits or senses, and yet know they well that they are displeasing God.

And, if a man counsel them to leave or cease their weeping and crying, they will say that they cannot; they loved their friend so much, and he was so gentle and so kind to them, that they may in no way forget him. How much more might they weep, cry, and roar, if their most beloved friends were with violence taken in their sight and with all manner of reproof, brought before the judge, wrongfully condemned to death, and especially so spiteful a death as Our Merciful Lord suffered for our sake. How would they suffer it? No doubt they would both cry and roar and avenge themselves if they might, or else men would say they were no friends.

Alas! Alas! for sorrow that the death of a creature, who hath often sinned and trespassed against their Maker, shall be so immeasurably mourned and sorrowed. And it is an offence to God, and a hindrance to the souls beside them.

And the compassionate death of Our Saviour by which we are all restored to life, is not kept in mind by us unworthy and unkind wretches, nor do we support Our Lord's own secretaries whom He hath endued with love, but rather detract and hinder them as much as we may.

CHAPTER 29

She visits the Holy Sepulchre, Mount Sion and Bethlehem.

When this creature with her fellowship came to the grave where Our Lord was buried, anon, as she entered that holy place, she fell down with her candle in her hand, as if she would have died for sorrow. And later she rose up again with great weeping and sobbing, as though she had seen Our Lord buried even before her.

Then she thought she saw Our Lady in her soul, how she mourned and how she wept for her Son's death, and then was Our Lady's sorrow her sorrow.

And so, wherever the friars led them in that holy place, she always wept and sobbed wonderfully, and especially when she came where Our Lord was nailed on the Cross. There cried she, and wept without measure, so that she could not restrain herself.

Also they came to a stone of marble that Our Lord was laid on when He was taken down from the Cross, and there she wept with great compassion, having mind of Our Lord's Passion.

Afterwards she was houselled on the Mount of Calvary, and then she wept, she sobbed, she cried so loud that it vas a wonder to hear it. She was so full of holy thoughts and meditations and holy contemplations on the Passion of Our Lord Jesus Christ, and holy dalliance that Our Lord Jesus Christ spoke to her soul, that she could never express them after, so high and so holy were they. Much was the grace that Our Lord shewed to this creature whilst she was three weeks in Jerusalem.

Another day, early in the morning, they went again amongst great hills, and their guides told her where Our Lord bore the Cross on His back, and where His Mother met with Him, and how she swooned and fell down and He fell down also. And so they went forth all the forenoon till they came to Mount Sion. And ever this creature wept abundantly, all the way that she went, for compassion of Our Lord's

Passion. On Mount Sion is a place where Our Lord washed His disciples' feet and, a little therefrom, He made His Maundy[8] with His disciples.

And therefore this creature had great desire to be housled in that holy place where Our Merciful Lord Christ Jesus first consecrated His precious Body in the form of bread, and gave it to His disciples. And so she was, with great devotion and plenteous tears and boisterous sobbings, for in this place is plenary remission,[9] and so there is in four other places in the Temple. One is on the Mount of Calvary; another at the grave where Our Lord was buried; the third is at the marble stone that His precious Body was laid on, when It was taken from the Cross; the fourth is where the Holy Cross was buried; and in many other places in Jerusalem.

And when this creature came to the place where the apostles received the Holy Ghost, Our Lord gave her great devotion. Afterwards she went to the place where Our Lady was buried, and as she knelt on her knees the time of two masses, Our Lord Jesus Christ said to her: —

'Thou comest not hither, daughter, for any need except merit and reward, for thy sins were forgiven thee ere thou came here and therefore thou comest here for the increasing of thy reward and thy merit. And I am well pleased with thee, daughter, for thou standest under obedience to Holy Church, and because thou wilt obey thy confessor and follow his counsel who, through authority of Holy Church, hath absolved thee of thy sins and dispensed thee so that thou shouldst not go to Rome and Saint James unless thou wilt thine own self. Notwithstanding all this, I command thee in the Name of Jesus, daughter, that thou go visit these holy places and do as I bid thee, for I am above Holy Church, and I shall go with thee and keep thee right well.'

Then Our Lady spoke to her soul in this manner, saying: —

'Daughter, well art thou blessed, for my Son Jesus shall flow so much grace into thee that all the world shall wonder at thee. Be not ashamed, my dearworthy daughter, to receive the gifts that my Son shall give thee, for I tell thee in truth, they shall be great gifts that He shall give thee. And therefore, my dearworthy daughter, be not ashamed of Him that is thy God, thy Lord and thy love, any more than I was, when I saw Him hanging on the Cross — my sweet Son, Jesus — to cry and to weep for the pain of my sweet Son Jesus Christ. Mary Magdalene was not ashamed to cry and weep for my Son's love. Therefore, daughter, if thou will be partaker in our love, thou must be partaker in our sorrow.'

This sweet speech and dalliance had this creature at Our Lady's grave, and much more than she could ever repeat.

Afterwards she rode on an ass to Bethlehem, and when she came to the temple and the crib where Our Lord was born, she had great devotion, much speech and dalliance in her soul, and high ghostly comfort with much weeping and sobbing, so that her fellows would not let her eat in their company, and therefore she ate her meat by herself alone.

---

[8] **Maundy:** The ceremony of washing the feet; see John 13:1–16.

[9] **plenary remission:** It was believed that visiting certain holy sites absolved one from previously committed sins.

And then the Grey Friars, who had led her from place to place, received her to them and set her with them at the meat so that she should not eat alone. And one of the friars asked one of her fellowship if she were the woman of England whom, they had heard said, spoke with God. And when this came to her knowledge, she knew well that it was the truth that Our Lord said to her, ere she went out of England:—

'Daughter, I will make all the world to wonder at thee, and many a man and many a woman shall speak of Me for love of thee, and worship Me in thee.'

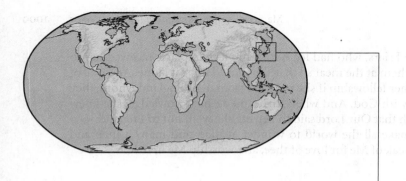

Early Japan, 600–800

By about 600, realizing their economy was not self-sufficient, Japanese merchants and traders set out from the island of Kyushu to trade with China. During the seventh and eighth centuries, Chinese culture heavily influenced Japanese social institutions, philosophy, religion, and art. The first permanent Japanese capital was established at Nara in 710; it was followed by Heian (modern-day Kyoto), built in 794.

JAPAN
Birth of a Culture

ᔕ Relations between Japanese tribal people and the late Han dynasty in China
are recorded in Chinese as early as the first century C.E. Anecdotal knowledge of
the Japanese dates from the third century C.E., when Chinese visitors attended a
funeral ceremony in the region of Fimiko (Wa in Chinese) and recorded purchases
of pottery, silk and woolens, and bronze objects. No written records appear in
Japan itself until *A Record of Ancient Matters,* written in Chinese characters in
712 C.E. In the five centuries in between, settlers had arrived in Japan from the
Asian mainland and the islands to the south, devoting themselves to the cultivation
of rice in the Japanese lowlands. This agricultural lifestyle, close to the wildness of
nature, seems to have influenced the early settlers to consider such matters as
natural beauty, the simplicity of their living arrangements, the impermanence of
life, and the virtue of working for the good of the majority. Already concerned with
sustaining themselves on the island, the Japanese settlers eventually realized their
economy was not self-sufficient, and they sought out their mainland neighbor,
China, for the knowledge necessary to manage their resources. In the seventh and
eighth centuries, Tang dynasty merchants traded freely with Japan, influencing not
only Japanese social institutions but Japan's philosophy, religion, culture, and art.
Nevertheless, from the beginning, the differences between China and Japan were
greater than the similarities. As soon as they achieved a measure of economic independence in the eighth century, the Japanese began to search for the roots of their
own national culture. As much as any nation in the world, Japan has learned to rely
on its own capacities, creating itself anew in the process.

One of the most important examples of the Japanese genius for reinvention
comes in religion. Buddhism was introduced into Japan from Korea in the sixth
century C.E. From it has come much of the Japanese fatalism about life and
death and a recurrent emphasis on the doctrine of reincarnation. Confucianism,

introduced from China largely in the eighth century, reinforces Japanese concern with ethical behavior, including the sacredness of family ties. Shinto, the original Japanese religion, focuses on nature worship and helps account for the scrupulous attention Japanese poetry pays to the seasons and the lives of plants and animals. Shinto also emphasizes emotional spontaneity, a strong feature of Japanese poetry and drama. Eventually, Shinto, Buddhism, and Confucianism adjusted to one another's presence on the island: Characters in Japanese literature hardly ever suffer from a conflict among religions because all religious beliefs in Japan tend to amalgamate.

THE NARA PERIOD: THE FIRST CIVILIZATION

After a heroic century of increasingly sharp struggles among warring family clans, the Japanese constructed their first permanent capital at Nara in 710. The building of the capital graphically reflected the Japanese absorption of Chinese architecture: Nara was a scaled-down version of the Chinese capital at Chang'an. Moreover, the Nara court adopted a Chinese-style legal code and bureaucracy and installed Chinese Buddhism as the state religion. Hoping to increase their political popularity, Nara rulers supported the arts and literary culture. They commissioned the *Record of Ancient Matters* (712) to preserve Japanese myths and legends and thus establish continuity with the past. The *Record* was followed by another historical collection, the *Chronicles of Japan* (720), some of which predates the *Record* by decades. But the most significant literary work of the Nara period is the *Man'yoshu* anthology (759), which includes the works of poets of ancient times as well as the revered seventh-century poet Kakinomoto Hitomaro (fl. 680–700).

The *Record of Ancient Matters* illustrates how Japan acquired its original system of writing from China. Borrowing Chinese written characters, the Japanese treated them in two distinct ways. Some were used as PHONOGRAMS, producing a monosyllable according to the Chinese sound of the character. Other characters were used as IDEOGRAMS, conveying the original idea but not the sound from the Chinese. Since Japanese words are polysyllabic, the use of Chinese characters as monosyllables in a chain to produce the sound of a Japanese word became unmanageable. On the other hand, it was difficult to use Chinese ideograms to signify Japanese words with no connection to the Chinese sound. It was most difficult of all to know which system of representation, phonograms or ideograms, was being employed at a given moment. Despite these problems, most writing of the Nara period (710–784) was done in the dual system of Chinese characters. When the dual system was abandoned in the next century, many of the early writings became unintelligible to the literate Japanese audience.

THE ERA OF THE HEIAN DYNASTY

In 784, the capital was removed from Nara under the direction of the Fujiwara family, the new power behind the throne. After a decade of turmoil, the new capital was established in 794 at Heian (modern Kyoto), strategically located with mountains on three sides and rivers on two sides. The Heian dynasty, which lasted continuously for four hundred years, witnessed the creation of great works of literature, many based on the activities of its own splendid court society, including the *Kokinshu* poetry anthology (c. 905), *The Pillow Book* (c. 1000) by Sei Shonagon, and the *Tale of Genji* (c. 1010) by Lady Murasaki. The Heian period came to a bitter end with the Gempei Wars of 1180–85, during which one of the great families of Japan, the Taira or Heike, was entirely wiped out and the other, the Minamoto or Genji, gradually ceded their authority to the military SHOGUNATE, the precursors of SAMURAI society.

THE END OF THE ARISTOCRACY

Following the Gempei Wars in 1185, Japanese society underwent fundamental changes. The days of the ruling families were gone. The capital was moved from Heian to Kamakura, the chief site of the military establishment, although bureaucratic functions soon reverted to the former capital. Therefore, the newly constituted Japanese political system consisted of the sharing of power by the military and civil authorities. In later eras, especially in the Kamakura period (1185–1333) and the Muromachi period (1338–1573), a formal balance of power was maintained, largely because neither the Heian (Kyoto) bureaucracy nor the Kamakura military elite could do without the other. Meanwhile the real leadership of the country slowly gravitated to the class of wealthy landowners who were also warriors. This group assumed actual authority in the Muromachi period.

During the Kamakura period, certain Buddhist sects in Japan began to adopt revolutionary doctrines. Following the twelfth-century crumbling of the aristocracy, there arose the concept of *mappo*, meaning "the Last Days of Buddha's Law," or the end of the world. The concept held that individual salvation had become impossible because people could no longer comprehend or practice the teachings of Buddha. At the end of the twelfth century the priest Honen (1133–1212) founded the Jodo or Pure Land sect in Japan, suggesting that Amida Buddha saves the souls of those who call upon him and transports them to a Pure Land in the west. While these two ideas were essentially in conflict, the first representing the fears of the collapsing aristocracy and the second representing the ambitions of the upper peasantry and some warriors, both gripped the public imagination, appearing in popular form in a newly created literature that focused on the tragedies of the past and the uncertainty of the future. In fact, the demise of the aristocracy had led to a new audience for literature and new concerns for it to address. In *The Tale of the Heike* (1371), the great literary epic of the Gempei Wars compiled during the Kamakura period and finally published in the Muromachi era, these new concerns finally were dramatized.

A LITERATURE FOR THE AGES

The power of medieval Japanese literature rests in its sense of the sorrowful or tragic and in its desire for an end of chaos and a restoration of harmony. Never straying far from its emotional core, this literature bypasses the apparent superficiality of court life to show real individuals struggling with defeat and despair and learning how to overcome them. The rich variety of Japanese writing — narrative poetry, lyric poetry, prose romances, historical tragedies, diaries and memoirs, and drama — points to both a love of literary forms and a cultivation of passion. Perhaps because of its freshness and immediacy, Japanese literature has a habit of staying modern.

THE EARLIEST LITERATURE: THE *MAN'YOSHU*.

The *Man'yoshu,* a wide-ranging poetic anthology produced in the eighth century, reflects early Japanese interest in the poetic tradition. The collection contains both long and short poems, CHOKA and TANKA, and an entire section of loosely constructed oral literature, testifying to some of this work's antiquity. Other poetry provides unique information about the dynasties and rulers of the seventh century. Chief among the collection's poets is Kakinomoto Hitomaro, who wrote in the last two decades of the seventh century. In his combination of public and private poetry, and particularly in his use of the *choka,* or ode, he conveys a rich emotional quality that has made him Japan's favorite poet. Other poets in the collection include the socially concerned author Yamanoue no Okura (c. 660–c. 733), and the last compiler of the *Man'yoshu* anthology, Otomo Yakamochi (718–785), who added many volumes to the work, including hundreds of his own poems.

WORKS OF THE HEIAN PERIOD

The *Kokinshu* anthology (c. 905), the largest single collection of Japanese poetry, exerted an important influence on subsequent Heian culture. For several hundred years members of the court memorized the five-line *tanka* lyrics of the *Kokinshu,* reciting them on appropriate occasions. Some *Kokinshu* poets, including Ariwara no Narihira and Ono no Komachi, the great male and female love poets respectively, as well as the work's chief editor, Ki no Tsurayuki, achieved lasting reputa-

Prince Genji, twelfth century
Written during the height of the Heian dynasty (784–1185), The Tale of Genji *is one of the most famous works of Japanese literature, and its author, Lady Murasaki, one of its most celebrated artists. The epic life and loves of Prince Genji and his family as told by Murasaki have inspired countless plays, poems, short stories, and films. (CORBIS)*

tions. Ono no Komachi also became a legendary figure, pictured as either a beautiful young courtesan or a frightening old woman in later *Nō* drama.

The Heian court at the beginning of the eleventh century was extremely dedicated to manners and proper conduct. The ladies-in-waiting of the noble families, designated as the keepers of the court's fashions, were subject to dangerous gossip and the temptations of court intrigues. Two of the most famous of these women served the court at about the same time: Sei Shonagon (c. 966–1017), author of *The Pillow Book,* a collection of brilliant reminiscences about court life, and Lady Murasaki Shikibu (c. 973–c. 1030), author of *The Tale of Genji,* a prose romance often called the first novel in world literature. Behind all the pomp and circumstance of court life, the rivalries and power struggles among the aristocratic families predicted a terrible outcome, which later materialized in the Gempei Wars.

Japan: The Nō *Drama (Fourteenth and Fifteenth Centuries)*

The *Nō* drama joins many elements, including theater design, music and dance, elaborate masks and costumes, and the stylized technique of the actors. The dramas, often performed in cycles, take place in a theater of prescribed design. The principal actor (the *shite*), his supporting actor (the *waki*), the announcer (the *kyogen*), and other actors play carefully determined roles, yet they also introduce spontaneity into their performances. To a Western observer, the demands upon the theater company appear paradoxical: freedom within constraint, movement within a fixed pattern, invention within tradition.

Nō theaters are open, raised spaces covered by a roof, even if the stage is indoors. The roof symbolizes both the sanctity of the stage and the unity of the theater space, since it overlaps a few rows of the seating area, physically including some of the audience in

Nō *Play, photograph, 1970.* A contemporary staging of a classical Nō *drama in Kyoto, Japan. (Morton Beebe / Corbis)*

THE HEROIC AFTERMATH

Two great literary works appeared in Japanese society at the end of the Middle Period. The first, *The Tale of the Heike,* was composed during the Kamakura period (1185–1333) in the thirteenth and fourteenth centuries and finally completed in 1371. It presents the story of the Gempei Wars in a vast panoramic setting, combining heroic action stories, highly charged narrative, and poetry to establish the nobility of the Heike warriors and portray their martyrdom to a lost cause. Significant to the action is a Buddhist interpretation that holds that while tragedy is inevitable,

Japan: The Nō Drama *continued*

the drama. The stage includes worship pavilions and dance platforms derived from earlier architecture, adding a rear section and a rear entrance bridge. No curtain separates the actors and the audience. The walls are plain except for a painted pine tree on the back wall and painted bamboo on the wall near the rear entrance. The pine tree may suggest oneness with nature, while the bamboo calls attention to the art of representation. The stage faces south; if it is outdoors, the sun lights it first from the east and later from the west, while the actors and dancers generally move in the opposite direction, from the western rear entrance to the south and then the east.

The music of *Nō* drama is provided by melodic vocal chants and several instruments: the flute, small drum, large drum, and lap drum. Singing or chanting, known as *utai,* is chiefly designed to move the action. The music, grounded in percussion, is called *hayashi:* It too propels the action while providing the dancers with rhythm. The tempo is determined by the *kurai,* the nature of the work. This includes the type of character represented, the contribution of the actors, and even the positioning of the play within a cycle of plays. The movements of all the characters are choreographed to have a defining rather than a decorative effect. Since the characters wear masks, their facial expressions are fixed; they reveal thought and emotion through gestures and voice. Japanese dramatic theory holds that pantomime is a truer vehicle of understanding than speech; *Nō* drama has been defined as "musical dance-drama, in which mime is a major element."

The masks used in *Nō* drama are beautiful and awe-inspiring. Though often works of art in themselves, they are not regarded as complete until an actor uses them. Three types of masks, depicting gods or demons, old men, and women, are traditional. Costumes—called *shozoku* or robes—are richly ornamented and distinguished by their weave, embroidery, and patterns. Even more than the masks, the costume reveals the personality of its wearer; it may include the outer kimono, a wig, a hat, a fan, and other accessories. The *shite,* or principal character, often wears a bright costume, while the *waki* wears darker colors. Women's costumes are especially symbolic, suggesting social rank, formality or informality, and even madness. Stage properties complete the artistic creations necessary for a *Nō* production. Movable sets are kept to a minimum.

the virtuous are certain to be transported to the Pure Land after death. *The Tale of the Heike* ends with the death of the sister of the former Heike warlord after she has retired from the world as a nun.

Another treatment of tragic and heroic themes followed in the Muromachi period (1338–1573), in the ritualistic *Nō* dramas, especially those of Zeami Motokiyo (1364–1443). Zeami's short, seemingly primitive plays, set on a spare stage with highly symbolic properties and accompanied by music and dance, capture the essence of tragedy in a few speeches and gestures. *Nō* dramas juxtapose two brief acts, one naturalistic and one symbolic, the second a response to the first. In Zeami's play *Atsumori,* based on a story in *The Tale of the Heike,* the ghost of a Heike warrior, a youthful member of the nobility who was murdered by a lesser Genji knight, meets his repentant killer at a crossroads. Through this dramatic encounter, justice is finally established and the concerns of the dead are set to rest.

www   For links to more information about the culture and context of Japan in the Middle Period, see *World Literature Online* at bedfordstmartins.com/worldlit.

❧ MAN'YOSHU

EIGHTH CENTURY

mahn-YOH-shoo

The *Man'yoshu* anthology, or *Gathering of Ten Thousand Leaves,* is the oldest and most revered book of Japanese poetry. An expression of Japanese national culture before it was heavily influenced by Chinese language and literature, the *Man'yoshu* brought together centuries of poetry, some of it naive and unsophisticated by eighth-century standards. More important, it features what became the enduring work of late-seventh- and -eighth-century Japanese poets, including **Kakinomoto Hitomaro** (fl. 680–700), **Yamanoue no Okura** (c. 660–c. 733), and **Otomo Yakamochi** (718–785). More than forty-five hundred poems are included in the twenty-volume collection, divided for the most part between five-line poems called TANKA and longer poems called CHOKA. The *chokas* of Kakinomoto Hitomaro, comprising both ceremonial and personal poems, are especially praised for their immediacy of feeling, beauty of imagery, and brilliance of composition. The poems collected in the *Man'yoshu* are regarded as quintessentially Japanese for their evocation of nature, their concern with the most important aspects of human existence, and their direct, richly emotional manner of expression.

kah-kee-noh-MOH-toh
hee-toh-MAH-roh
yah-mah-NOH-weh
noh-oh-KOO-rah
OH-toh-moh yah-kah-
MOH-chee
TAHN-kah

Despite its initial popularity, the *Man'yoshu* lost its readership within several centuries because of its peculiar writing system, which transposed the Japanese language into Chinese symbols with seemingly arbitrary rules for deciding their meaning and pronunciation. Later modified into a simplified system of Japanese characters, since the thirteenth century the *Man'yoshu* has been the subject of intensive literary study and cultural appreciation in Japan.

Contents of the Man'yoshu.   The *Man'yoshu* collection was conceived at the height of early Japanese civilization in the **Nara** period (710–784). The anthology, which includes written remnants of oral literature and folk songs, brought together poems on various themes, especially love

NAH-rah

Buddhist Goddess,
eighth century
*The Buddhist goddess
of beauty from a
Nara-era Japanese
painting. (The Art
Archive / Private
Collection, Paris /
Dagli Orti)*

Western literature
[. . .] reveals a faith
in action, in ideas,
and in moral respon-
sibility — these are
what matter. Japa-
nese literature
emphasizes human
feeling and reflection
in participation with
much that we think is
opposed to man —
especially nature and
the divine. The con-
trast, if simplified
more, is between
Western faith in per-
suasive ideas and
Japanese faith in cul-
tivated feeling.
    – EARL MINER, Critic,
        1968

relationships, reflections on the countryside, historical celebrations, and
elegies and laments. The arrangement of its twenty volumes suggests the
state of Japanese culture when the *Man'yoshu* was assembled. The first
Man'yoshu poets were drawn from the imperial family itself and from
among the courtiers who served the princes. Volumes one and two
apparently were compiled by imperial order and arranged chronologically. Succeeding volumes focus on the concerns of their editors, reflecting specific courts, regions, and periods of Japanese history. Some later
volumes focus on certain literary genres, such as folk songs, poems from
the provinces, sea chanties, legends, and humorous verse. The last four
volumes contain the work of their principal editor, Otomo Yakamochi,
and his circle of friends. Volume twenty also includes some poems of the
frontier guards from the eastern provinces as well as their imitators at
court.

   The traditional *tanka*, or short poem, consists of five lines of identical syllabic patterns (5-7-5-7-7) while the longer *choka* is made up of an
indefinite number of lines of five or seven syllables with a seven-syllable
line at its end. The *choka* is usually concluded by one or more additional
stanzas, an "envoy" in English, or what the Japanese call a **hanka**, a "verse
that repeats." The *choka* only remained in use for a hundred years after

HAHN-kah

www   For quizzes on the *Man'yoshu*, see *World Literature Online* at bedfordstmartins .com/worldlit.

the *Man'yoshu* appeared, whereas the *tanka* has endured to this day, suited as it is to the lyrical simplicity favored by the modern Japanese audience. The selections from the *Man'yoshu* in the following pages concentrate on the *chokas*, taking into account their unique contribution to Japanese expression in the eighth century.

Featured Works.   The famous courtier Kakinomoto Hitomaro (fl. 680–700) wrote about eighty poems, including twenty *chokas*, and inspired or contributed to hundreds of other poems in the *Man'yoshu* collection. Anyone encountering Japanese poetry will be moved by Hitomaro's elegy for his dead wife and his carefully restrained account of the discovery of a body lying in the rocks on an island beach. A poet from the provincial city of **Kyushu**, Yamanoue no Okura (c. 660–c. 733) must have studied Buddhism and Confucianism while serving as an emissary to China. His poems often center on questions of the suffering in this world and on a longing to escape from its sorrows, a tone characteristic of Buddhism. He also addresses family concerns, writing poems to his children, a topic more typical of Chinese than Japanese poetry. Probably the last major editor of the *Man'yoshu* as well as one of its principal poetic contributors, Otomo Yakamochi (718–785) became the head of his powerful family just as it was beginning its decline. The most appealing quality of his verse is his development of the theme of consolation, necessitated by the frustrations and sorrows of human existence.

KYOO-shoo

A Changing Legacy.   Critical reception of the *Man'yoshu* has varied for centuries. Originally, it was regarded as the epitome of "natural" Japanese poetry: Literature written before Chinese cultural influence reached its peak on the Japanese archipelago. Certainly both the form and the content of the *Man'yoshu* differ markedly from later imperial anthologies, beginning with the **Kokinshu** (c. 905), which despite its claims to the contrary has been seen by later Japanese scholars as derivative of Chinese culture. Part of the affection many have felt for the *Man'yoshu* is a kind of cultural nostalgia. Several times in more recent history Japanese poets have proclaimed the need for a "*Man'yoshu* revival," though one never has occurred on a significant scale. During the Meiji period (1868–1912), the *Man'yoshu* was viewed in two distinct ways: as the work of the most skilled Japanese poets in history and as an expression of the democratic impulse of the Japanese people. On the other hand, the introduction to the first major English translation of the *Man'yoshu*, published in Japan at the beginning of the Second World War, reflects the nationalist, militaristic ideology of the Japanese government of that period.

koh-KIN-shoo

The development of a literary canon—a group of writings believed essential to perpetuate the memory of the best in a given culture—takes place over centuries. Although the *Man'yoshu* has had to overcome formidable obstacles in order to win its place in the Japanese canon, its breadth of appeal, beauty of imagery, and genius of expression are likely to leave it in that charmed circle of literary works. The major reason for its seemingly unquenchable appeal is its apparent freshness of expression.

■ CONNECTIONS

The *Kokinshu*, p. 1044. Published more than a century after the *Man'yoshu*, the *Kokinshu* anthology was the first to be commissioned in its entirety by the imperial government. The *Kokinshu* attempted to revive native Japanese poetry at a time when the *Man'yoshu* had become impossible to study because of its antiquated writing system. Compare the lyrical poetry of the *Kokinshu* with the more celebratory, public poetry of the *Man'yoshu*. Which do you find more "authentic"?

Imru' al-Qays, The *Mu'allaqah*, p. 368. The *choka* form of public celebratory poetry functioned as a kind of ode, a poem invoking the memory of ancient times and heroic events. Compare the *choka* poems of Kakinomoto Hitomaro with the *Mu'allaqah*, the pre-Islamic Arabic ode of Imru' al-Qays. How would you define the two forms of "ode"?

Samuel Beckett, *Krapp's Last Tape* (Book 6). "Dialogue between Poverty and Destitution," a poem by Yamanoue no Okura, has a curiously modern ring. Compare it with Beckett's play *Krapp's Last Tape*, in which the sole character is suspended in a state of complaint, uncertain of his future and focused on the sufferings of the past. Do you find these works compatible?

■ FURTHER RESEARCH

Editions and Anthologies

Carter, Steven D., ed. *Traditional Japanese Poetry: An Anthology*. 1991.
Keene, Donald, ed. *Anthology of Japanese Literature*. 1955.
Levy, Ian Hideo, trans. *The Ten Thousand Leaves*. 1981.
Shinkokai, Nippon Gakujutsu, ed. *The Manyoshu*. 1965.

Literary History

Kato, Shuichi. *A History of Japanese Literature: The First Thousand Years*. 1979.
Keene, Donald. *Seeds in the Heart: Japanese Literature from the Earliest Times to the Late Sixteenth Century*. 1999.
Konishi, Jin'ichi. *A History of Japanese Literature: The Archaic and Ancient Ages*. 1984.

Literary Criticism

Brower, Robert H., and Earl Miner. *Japanese Court Poetry*. 1961.
Doe, Paula. *A Warbler's Song in the Dusk: The Life and Work of Otomo Yakamochi*. 1982.
Keene, Donald. *The Pleasures of Japanese Literature*. 1988.
Levy, Ian Hideo. *Hitomaro and the Birth of Japanese Lyricism*. 1984.
Miner, Earl. *An Introduction to Japanese Court Poetry*. 1968.

■ PRONUNCIATION

choka: CHOH-kah
Dazaifu: dah-ZIGH-foo
Etchu: EH-choo
Furuhi: foo-ROO-hee
Fujiwara Nakachiko: foo-jih-WAH-rah nah-kah-CHEE-koh
hanka: HAHN-kah
Iwami: ee-WAH-mee
Jinshin: JIN-shin
Jito: JEE-toh
Kakinomoto Hitomaro: kah-kee-noh-MOH-toh hee-toh-MAH-roh
Kinoe: kee-NOH-eh
Kokinshu: koh-KIN-shoo

Ironically, Hitomaro is so convincing in his poems on subjects that he could not have known from personal experience that doubts have been expressed about the truthfulness of poems that describe his own emotions [. . .] But reading Hitomaro's two great poems on the death of his wife [. . .] it is difficult to question their authenticity.

– DONALD KEENE, Translator and Critic, 1988

Kusakabe: koo-sah-KAH-beh
Kyushu: KYOO-shoo, kee-OO-shoo
Man'yoshu: mahn-YOH-shoo
Nara: NAH-rah
Otomo Tabito: OH-toh-moh tah-BEE-toh
Otomo Yakamochi: OH-toh-moh yah-kah-MOH-chee
tanka: TAHN-kah
Takechi: tah-KEH-chee
Temmu: TEM-oo
Tenji: TEN-jee
Yamanoue no Okura: yah-mah-NOH-weh noh-oh-KOO-rah

❧ KAKINOMOTO HITOMARO
FL. 680–700

koo-sah-KAH-beh

TEM-oo

ee-WAH-mee

All that is known about Kakinomoto Hitomaro, the poet responsible for some of the most esteemed Japanese verse, comes from the texts of his poems in the *Man'yoshu.* Though a courtier of low rank, he was undoubtedly a favorite of the court and greatly admired by the other poets. His first published poem was an elegy for Prince **Kusakabe**, son of Emperor **Temmu**, written in 689. His personal love poems were dedicated to at least two different wives. According to legend he died in the western province of **Iwami** around the age of fifty. Equally known for his earlier court compositions and his later personal poetry, he was called "the saint of poetry."

TEN-jee
JIN-shin

Were it not for changes in the practice of eulogizing the royal family of Japan, Hitomaro's early poetry and the direction of early Japanese poetry as a whole might have developed differently. After the death of Emperor **Tenji** in 671, his younger brother seized the throne following the **Jinshin** War in 673 and was installed as Emperor Temmu (r. 673–686). Extolled during his reign, Temmu was hailed as a god at the time of his death; elegies written to honor him include the formulation "our Lord, a very god." Three years later, Emperor Temmu's son, the crown prince Kusakabe, died before he could ascend to the throne. Hitomaro was commissioned to write an elegy for the prince, and following its success he became the leading court poet of his day. For a time, this ceremonial poetry took center stage, while the briefer, more personal *tanka* had to wait.

JEE-toh

Hitomaro's Court Poetry. After 689, Hitomaro wrote under the auspices of the emperor's court. His loyalty to Temmu's widow, Empress **Jito** (r. 690–697), was deeply expressed in his poetry. Hitomaro frequently expressed the sorrows of the world he lived in—and in some sense depended on. In "When He Passed the Ruined Capital at Ōmi," Hitomaro expresses in his own words the grief the court feels at having left the "hills of Nara, beautiful in blue earth." In one of the poem's envoys, while gazing at the castle ruins at Omi the poet addresses a broader theme: "but never again," he laments, "may I / meet the men of ancient times."

"At the Time of the Temporary Enshrinement of Prince Takechi at **Kinoe**" treats one of the deep themes of the court society of Hitomaro's day. Prince **Takechi** had been the champion of his father, Temmu, and stepmother, Jito, in the Jinshin War in 672. Passed over for emperor upon his father's death, Takechi died in 696 at the age of forty-three. Hitomaro's elegy written in his honor, comprising 151 phrases of "pure" Japanese (without any reliance on Chinese vocabulary), is the longest *choka* in the *Man'yoshu*. The poem recalls the majesty of Emperor Temmu and the valor of his son, Takechi, who upheld the family's cause in the Jinshin War. In the poem, the people who celebrated this victory remember Takechi at his funeral: "the courtiers who served him / now wear mourning clothes of white hemp." At the end of the poem, the same courtiers vow to retain an image of the prince in their minds, "preciously remembering, / awesome though it be." The envoy perfectly captures the dichotomy between heaven, where the god-prince has gone, and earth, which holds his subjects. This poem frequently has been called the nearest thing in Japanese poetry to an epic, due to its celebration of the past and its heroic description of battle. But the heart of the poem is elegiac, not epic: Hitomaro the public poet is mourning a death and celebrating a dynasty, personally committing his work about war to his empress and her courtly society.

Hitomaro's Personal Poetry.   The conventions of emotional expression that Hitomaro developed during his attachment to the court can be seen in his later personal poetry as well. As he grew older he expressed a sad and mournful view of existence in his work. His greatest poetry was never far from descriptions of death and its capacity to undo the human bond of love. His most memorable works lament a parting from his wife and the death of a later wife. In a poem of parting Hitomaro stirs the reader's sensual imagination with an image of his young wife, "who swayed to my side in sleep like sleek seaweed," while at the same time presenting her as a passing reality. The same imagery appears in his first poem on the death of his later wife, when a messenger comes to tell him "that my girl, / who swayed to me in sleep / like seaweed of the offing, / was gone. . . ." In the battle between life and death, death conquers, and the sensuous world is destroyed. As the second *choka* on his wife's death observes most bitterly, "My wife, whom I thought was of this world, is ash."

In "Upon Seeing a Dead Man Lying among the Rocks on the Island of Samine," Hitomaro turns from the discovery of an unidentified corpse to his own thoughts, reflecting in part on his own losses: "If your wife knew, / she would come and seek you out." Finally, in a last *tanka*, Hitomaro reflects on his own death: "my wife must still be waiting / for my return."

kee-NOH-eh

tah-KEH-chee

∽ When He Passed the Ruined Capital at Ōmi

Translated by Ian Hideo Levy

Since the reign of the Master of the Sun[1]
at Kashiwara by Unebi Mountain,
    where the maidens
        wear strands of jewels,
all gods who have been born
have ruled the realm under heaven,
each following each
like generations of the spruce,
       in Yamato[2]
that spreads to the sky.

What was in his mind
that he would leave it
and cross beyond the hills of Nara,
    beautiful in blue earth?
Though a barbarous place
at the far reach of the heavens,
here in the land of Ōmi
where the waters race on stone,
at the Ōtsu Palace
in Sasanami
    by the rippling waves,
the Emperor, divine Prince,
ruled the realm under heaven.

Though I hear
this was the great palace,
though they tell me
here were the mighty halls,
now it is rank with spring grasses.
Mist rises, and the spring sun is dimmed.
Gazing on the ruins of the great palace,
its walls once thick with wood and stone,
I am filled with sorrow.

10

20

30

---

[1] the Master of the Sun: Emperor Jimmu (660–585 B.C.E.), legendary founder of the Japanese state.
[2] Yamato: Traditional name for Japan.

ENVOYS

Cape Kara in Shiga
at Sasanami
   by the rippling waves,
you are as before, but I
wait for courtiers' boats in vain.

Waters, you are quiet
in deep bends of Shiga's lake
at Sasanami
   by the rippling waves,
but never again may I
meet the men of ancient times.

40

At the Time of the Temporary Enshrinement of Prince Takechi at Kinoe

Translated by Ian Hideo Levy

I hesitate to put it in words,
it is an awesome thing to speak.
Our Lord,
who, while we trembled,
fixed the far and heavenly
halls of his shrine
on the fields of Makami in Asuka
and, godlike, has secluded himself
     in the rocks there,
he,
who ruled the earth's eight corners,
crossed Fuwa Mountain,
lined with thick black pines,
in the northern land of his realm
and went down,
   as from heaven,
     to the provinces,
encamping on the plain of Wazami,
   Wazami
     of the Korean swords.
To hold sway over the realm under heaven
and bring his dominions to peace,
he gathered his soldiers

10

20

in the eastern country,
    where the cock cries,
and gave the task to his son,
he being an imperial prince:
to pacify the raging rebels
and subdue the defiant lands.

30   Then our Prince
girded his great body with his long sword
and took in his great hands his bow.
The sound of the drums,
calling the troops to ready,
boomed like the very voice of thunder,
and the echoing notes
of the signaller's flute
grew, to the terror of all,
like the roar of a tiger
40   with prey in its eyes.
The rippling of the high-held banners
was like the rippling of the fires
struck across every field
when spring comes, bursting winter's bonds,
and the roar of the bowstings they plucked
was so fearful, we thought it a hurricane
whirling through a snowfallen winter forest.
When the arrows they let loose
swarmed like a blinding swirl of snow,
50   the resisters, standing defiant,
also resolved to perish,
    if they must,
like the dew and frost.
As they struggled
    like zooming birds,
the divine wind
from the Shrine of our offerings
at Ise in Watarai
blew confusion upon them,
60   hiding the very light of day
as clouds blanketed the heavens
in eternal darkness.

Thus pacifying this land,
abundant in ears of rice,
our Lord, sovereign

of the earth's eight corners,
      a very god,
firmly drove his palace pillars
and proclaimed his rule
70   over the realm under heaven —
for ten thousand generations,
      we thought.
But just as his reign flourished
brilliant as the white bouquets
      of mulberry paper,
suddenly they deck his princely halls
to make a godly shrine,
and the courtiers who served him
now wear mourning clothes of white hemp.
80   On the fields
before the Haniyasu Palace gate
they crawl and stumble like deer
as long as the sun still streams its crimson,
and when pitch-black night descends
they crawl around like quail,
turning to look up at the great halls.
They wait upon him,
but they wait in vain,
and so they moan
90   like the plaintive birds of spring.
Before their cries can be stilled
or their mournful thoughts exhausted
the divine cortege
is borne from the Kudara Plain,
borne away.
Loftily he raises
the palace at Kinoe,
      good of hempen cloth,
as his eternal shrine.
100   A god, his soul is stilled there.
Yet could we even imagine
that his palace by Kagu Hill
      will pass away
in the ten thousand generations
he intended as he built?
I turn to gaze on it
as I would on the heavens,
bearing it in my heart
      like a strand of jewels,

110

preciously remembering,
awesome though it be.

ENVOYS

Although you rule
the far heavens now,
we go on longing for you,
unmindful of the passing
of sun and moon.

Not knowing where they will drift,
like the hidden puddles that run
on the banks of Haniyasu Pond,

120

the servingmen stand bewildered.

When He Parted from His Wife in the Land of Iwami: I

Translated by Ian Hideo Levy

I.

People may say that Tsuno Cove
in the land of Iwami
has no good inlets,
they may say it has no good lagoons,
but I don't care.
Though it has no good inlets,
I don't care.
Though it has no good lagoons,
the wind, with morning wings,

10

and the waves, with evening wings,
carry over those whale-hunted seas
to the desolate beach in Nikita harbor
green, sleek seaweed,
seaweed from the offing,
and the memory of my wife,
whom I left there
  as mist and frost
    are left on the ground,

who swayed to my side in sleep
 like sleek seaweed
swaying to and fro with the waves.

Though I look back ten thousand times
from each of this road's eighty bends,
my village has receded
farther and farther in the distance.
Higher and higher
are the mountains I have crossed.
That I might gaze on my wife's door
where she in her longing
wilts like the summer grass,
mountains, bend down!

ENVOYS

O does my wife
see the sleeves I wave
from between the trees
on Takatsuno Mountain in Iwami?

The whole mountain is a storm
of rustling leaves
of dwarf bamboo,
but I think of my wife,
having parted from her.

∾ On the Death of His Wife: I and II

Translated by Ian Hideo Levy

I.

On the Karu Road
is the village of my wife,
and I desired to meet her intimately,
but if I went there too much
the eyes of others would cluster around us,
and if I went there too often

others would find us out.
And so I hoped
that later we would meet
10   like tangling vines,
trusted that we would
as I would trust a great ship,
and hid my love:
faint as jewel's light,
a pool walled in by cliffs.

Then came the messenger,
    his letter tied
    to a jewelled catalpa twig,
to tell me,
20   in a voice
    like the sound
    of a catalpa bow,
that my girl,
who had swayed to me in sleep
like seaweed of the offing,
was gone
like the coursing sun
gliding into dusk,
like the radiant moon
30   secluding itself behind the clouds,
gone like the scarlet leaves of autumn.

I did not know what to say,
        what to do,
but simply could not listen
and so, perhaps to solace
a single thousandth
    of my thousand-folded longing,
I stood at the Karu market
where often she had gone,
40   and listened,
but could not even hear
the voices of the birds
that cry on Unebi Mountain,
    where the maidens
        wear strands of jewels,
and of the ones who passed me
on that road,
    straight as a jade spear,
not one resembled her.

50   I could do nothing
but call my wife's name
and wave my sleeves.

ENVOYS

Too dense the yellowed leaves
on the autumn mountain:
my wife is lost
and I do not know the path
to find her by.

With the falling away
of the yellowed leaves,
60   I see the messenger
with his jewelled catalpa staff,
and I recall the days I met her.

II.

She was my wife,
to whom my thoughts gathered
thick as the spring leaves,
like the myriad branches budding
on the zelkova tree
on the embankment (a short step
from her gate),
70   that we would bring
and look at together
while she was of this world.
She was my wife,
on whom I depended,
but now, unable to break
the course of this world,
she shrouds herself from me
in heavenly white raiments
on a withered, sun-simmered plain,
80   and rises away in the morning
like a bird,
and conceals herself
like the setting sun.

Each time our infant,
the memento she left,
cries out in hunger,

I, though a man,
having nothing to give it,
hug it to my breast.
90   Inside the wedding house
where the pillows we slept on
lie pushed together,
I live through the days
desolate and lonely
and sigh through the nights.
Lament as I may,
I know nothing I can do.
Long for her as I may,
I have no way to meet her.
100   And so when someone said,
"The wife you long for
dwells on Hagai Mountain,
          of the great bird,"
I struggled up here,
kicking the rocks apart,
but it did no good:
my wife, whom I thought
was of this world,
is ash.

Envoys

110   The autumn moon crosses the heavens
as it did when I watched last year,
but my wife, who watched with me—
the drift of the year has taken her.

Leaving my wife on Hikide Mountain
by the Fusuma Road,
I think of the path she has taken,
and I am hardly alive.

I come home
and gaze inside:
120   facing outward
on the haunted floor,
my wife's boxwood pillow.

Upon Seeing a Dead Man Lying among the Rocks on the Island of Samine

Translated by Ian Hideo Levy

The land of Sanuki,
    fine in sleek seaweed:
is it for the beauty of the land
that we do not tire
        to gaze upon it?
Is it for its divinity
that we deem it most noble?
Eternally flourishing,
    with the heavens
                and the earth,
    with the sun
                and the moon,
the very face of a god —
so it has come down
        through the ages.

Casting off
from Naka harbor,
we came rowing.
Then tide winds
blew through the clouds;
on the offing
we saw the rustled waves,
on the strand
we saw the roaring crests.
Fearing the whale-hunted seas,
our ship plunged through —
we bent those oars!
Many were the islands
near and far,
but we beached on Samine —
        beautiful its name —
and built a shelter
        on the rugged shore.

Looking around,
                we saw you
lying there
on a jagged bed of stones,

the beach
    for your finely woven pillow,
40 by the breakers' roar.
      If I knew your home,
I would go and tell them.
If your wife knew,
she would come and seek you out.
But she does not even know the road,
    straight as a jade spear.
Does she not wait for you,
    worrying and longing,
your beloved wife?

ENVOYS

50 If your wife were here,
she would gather and feed you
the starwort that grows
on the Sami hillsides,
but is its season not past?

Making a finely woven pillow
of the rocky shore
    where waves from the offing
      draw near,
you, who sleep there!

Written in His Own Sorrow as He Was about to Die in Iwami

Translated by Ian Hideo Levy

Not knowing I am pillowed
among the crags on Kamo Mountain,
my wife must still be waiting
    for my return.

❧ YAMANOUE NO OKURA

c. 660–c. 733

Apparently from modest origins, Yamanoue no Okura was sent to China on a diplomatic mission in 701 where he began to study the Chinese language, customs, and philosophy. He rose to the lower Japanese aristocracy in 714 and became a tutor to the crown prince in 721. Adept in both Confucian and Buddhist thought, he wrote prefaces in Chinese to several of his poems expounding one or the other of these doctrines. He also took from Chinese culture his preoccupation with social questions; in this he was unique among the poets of the *Man'yoshu* anthology. His personal detachment frequently produces irony or satire in his poetry, and he is not afraid to poke fun at himself.

    "A Lament on the Evanescence of Life" delineates the Buddhist Eight Great Hardships—birth, old age, sickness, death, separation, anger, greed, and the pain of consciousness. His complaint about old age, drawn from common sources, is not necessarily indebted to Buddhist philosophy. "Dialogue between Poverty and Destitution" is a vivid exchange about the hardships of life between a man who acknowledges that his worldly pride does him no good and another who sees his suffering as a pathway to eventual enlightenment. Both characters are hard put to find any relief in the present, which they describe in painful detail and unadorned speech. "Longing for His Son **Furuhi**" is an openly sentimen-   foo-ROO-hee
tal poem recalling the pleasures the poet and his wife had with their infant son, now dead, and questioning the reason for suffering in the world. Okura's unusual willingness to confront pain makes his work significant. (Footnotes in the following poems are amended from Steven D. Carter's *Traditional Japanese Poetry*, 1991.)

❧ A Lament on the Evanescence of Life

Translated by Steven D. Carter

What we must accept
    as we journey through the world
is that time will pass
    like the waters of a stream;
in countless numbers,
in relentless succession,
it will besiege us
    with assaults we must endure.
They could not detain
10   the period of their bloom,

when, as maidens will,
they who were then maidens
        encircled their wrists
                with gemmed bracelets from Cathay,
and took their pleasure
        frolicking hand in hand
                with their youthful friends.
So the months and years went by,
and when did it fall—
that sprinkling of wintry frost
        on glistening hair
                as black as leopard flower seeds?
And whence did they come—
those wrinkles that settled in,
marring the smoothness
        of blushing pink faces?
Was it forever,
the kind of life those others led—
those stalwart men,
who, as fine young men will do,
girded at their waists
        sharp swords, keen-bladed weapons,
took up hunting bows,
clasped them tight in their clenched fists,
placed on red horses
        saddles fashioned of striped hemp,
climbed onto their steeds,
and rode gaily here and there?
They were not many,
those nights when the fine young men
        pushed open the doors,
the plank doors of the chamber
        where the maidens slept,
groped their way close to their loves,
and slept with their arms
        intertwined with gemlike arms.
Yet already now
        those who were maidens and youths
                must use walking sticks,
and when they walk over there,
others avoid them,
and when they walk over here,
others show distaste.
Such is life, it seems, for the old.
Precious though life is,

it is beyond our power
    to stay the passing of time.

ENVOY

Would that I might stand
    a rock through eternity,
60   unchanged forever —
but life does not allow us
    to halt the passing of time.

∾ Dialogue between Poverty and Destitution

Translated by Steven D. Carter

[POOR MAN]

On nights when rain falls
    mingling with the blowing wind,
on nights when snow falls
    mingling with the pouring rain,
I have no choice
    but to endure the cold.
I eat lumpy salt,
keep nibbling away at it,
drink *sake* dregs,
10   keep sipping away at them,
keep clearing my throat,
snuffle the snot in my nose,
keep running my hand
    over my skimpy beard,
boast to myself,
"Where is there to be found
    a better man?"
But I'm cold all the same.
I pull over me
20   my bedding of coarse hemp,
pile on as clothing
    layers of sleeveless cloth coats —
every one I own —
and still the night is bitter.
The mother and father
    of someone whose lot

is worse than my own
    must be starving and freezing;
his wife and children
    must cry in weak voices.
At times like this,
how is it that you manage
    to keep going at all?

[DESTITUTE MAN]

Heaven and earth
    are said to be far-ranging,
yet they have become
    too narrow to fit me in.
The sun and the moon
    are said to be radiant,
yet they do not deign
    to cast their light upon me.
Is it like this
    for everyone, or just for me?
Although by good luck
    I have been born a human[1]
and though I till fields
    like any other human,
upon my shoulder
    I wear nothing but rags —
a sleeveless jacket
    not even stuffed with cotton,
hanging in tatters
    like strands of deep-pine seaweed.
Inside my crooked hut,
my hut with its leaning walls,
I lie on bare ground
    spread with a little loose straw.
My father and mother
    are beside my pillow,
my wife and children
    are at the foot of my bed;
all sit around me
    complaining and groaning;

---

[1] **by good luck . . . born a human:** According to Buddhist belief, one has to pass through the human stage to attain enlightenment and be released from the chain of death and rebirth.

at the cooking-place
　　nothing sends up any steam;
in the rice steamer
　　a spider has spun its web.
We have forgotten
　　how rice is supposed to be cooked.
70　And as we wail there,
voices thin as tiger thrushes,
to make matters worse
(cutting, as the saying goes,
the end of something
　　that is already too short),
the village headman
　　seeks me out, holding his whip,
comes with his summons
　　right up to my sleeping-place.
80　Must it be like this,
so utterly without hope—
a man's journey through the world?

ENVOY

Though we think of life
　　as a vale of misery,
a bitter trial,
it is not as if we were birds
　　who can simply fly away.

❧ Longing for His Son Furuhi

Translated by Steven D. Carter

What value to me
　　the seven kinds of treasures[1]
　　　　by which others set store—
the precious things coveted
　　by the run of men?
My son Furuhi,
the child fair as a white pearl,

---

[1] **the seven . . . treasures:** The seven treasures referred to in Buddhist texts: gold, silver, pearls, etc.

born of the union
    between his mother and me,
used to play with us
    when the morning star announced
        the dawn of each new day—
to stay close to the bedside
    where our sheets were spread,
to frolic with us
    standing and sitting.
And when evening
    came with the evening star,
he used to take us
    by the hand and say to us,
"Let's go to bed now,"
and then, in his pretty way,
"Father and Mother,
don't go where I can't see you.
I want to sleep
    right here in the middle."
And we thought, trusting
    as people trust a great ship,
"May the time come soon
    when he becomes an adult;
for good or for ill,
may we behold him a man."
But then suddenly
    a mighty storm wind blew up,
caught us from the side,
overwhelmed us with its blast.
Helpless, distraught,
not knowing what to do,
I tucked back my sleeves
    with paper-mulberry cords,
I took in my hand
    a clear, spotless mirror.[2]
With upturned face,
I beseeched the gods of the sky;
forehead to the ground,
I implored the gods of the earth.
"Whether he be cured
    or whether he die—

10

20

30

40

---

[2] **mirror:** Mirrors—representing the light of the sun goddess—were used in many Shinto religious rituals.

that is for the gods to say."
50 But though I begged them
in frantic supplication,
there resulted
not the briefest improvement.
His body wasted,
changing little by little;
he uttered no more
the words he had spoken
with each new morning;
and his life came to its end.
60 I reeled in agony,
stamped my feet, screamed aloud,
cast myself down,
looked up to heaven, beat my breast.
I have lost my son,
the child I loved so dearly.
Is this what life is about?

ENVOYS

He is still so young
that he won't know the way to go.
I will give you something —
70 only carry him on your back,
messenger from the netherworld![3]

Making offerings,
I utter this petition:
tempt him not afield,
but lead him straight ahead —
show him the way to heaven.

---

[3] **messenger from the netherworld:** A messenger was believed to guide souls on their way to the next world.

OTOMO YAKAMOCHI
718–785

OH-toh-moh
tah-BEE-toh
dah-ZIGH-foo

EH-choo

foo-jih-WAH-rah
nah-kah-CHEE-koh

Otomo Yakamochi, the son of the poet and public official **Otomo Tabito** (665–731), who had established a colony of poets in exile in **Dazaifu** in the province of Kyushu, may have attended a famous poetry banquet held by his father in Kyushu in 730. Inheriting his father's tendencies, Yakamochi developed an aversion to political affairs in the capital at Nara and often served as a provincial governor as far from the capital as possible. Appointed governor of **Etchu** in 745, he enjoyed five years of productivity as a writer while exchanging poetic letters with friends and receiving love poems—some of them rather demanding—from women at court. His poetry gradually acquired a depth of melancholy, perhaps associated with his recurrent periods of self-imposed exile. Later in his career, as his political fortunes gradually declined, he began to edit the last books of the *Man'yoshu*. Eventually he included nearly five hundred of his own poems in the anthology—too many, perhaps, for the good of his literary reputation. In 759 he published the last poem in the *Man'yoshu*. He wrote no more until his death in 785.

Yakamochi's elegy for the mother of his son-in-law, **Fujiwara Nakachiko**, was written near the end of his stay in Etchu in 750. This poem is the last funeral song in the *Man'yoshu*, combining traditional Japanese formality with signs of Chinese influence. It represents the work of this durable, productive poet at the height of his abilities.

Lament Addressed to His Son-in-Law, Fujiwara Nakachiko

Translated by Robert H. Brower and Earl Miner

Since that ancient time
When the heavens and earth began,
   It has been decreed
That of the eighty noble clans
   Each living man
Shall follow obediently the commands
   Of our great Sovereign.
So I, an official of the Court,
   Heard with veneration
10 The sacred words of our great Sovereign;
   And now I live
Governing this distant province
   Here in the wilds,

Cut off from home by hills and streams.
  Since my coming here
You and I have had but winds and clouds
  To bear our messages;
And as days have piled on days and still
  We have not met again,
20 I have longed to see you more and more,
  And sighed with yearning.

Straight as a courtier's spear
  Was the road he came on,
The traveler who has brought these tidings:
  He reports that you,
My amiable and noble friend,
  Are struck in grief
And lately spend your days in mourning.
  Truly the span of life
30 Is filled with sorrow and suffering:
  The very flowers open
Only to wither and fall with time,
  And we living men
Are creatures of like impermanence.
  Even that noble lady,
Your gracious and beloved mother,
  Shares the human lot,
And with it a fate for a certain hour.
  And now this news:
40 That in the full bloom of her womanhood,
  When one might still gaze
Upon her beauty with such rare delight
  As on a polished mirror,
Cherishing her like a string of precious jewels,
  Even she has faded away,
Vanished like the rising mists,
  Like dew on the grass;
That she lay listless as the gem-like seaweed
  Bending to the tide;
50 That like a running stream she ebbed away
  And could not be held back.
Can this be some fantastic tale I hear?
  Is not the message false,
Merely a rumor of a passing traveler?

   Though from afar—
Like the warning sound of bowstrings twanged

By palace guards at night—
I hear this news, my grief is freshened,
    And I cannot withhold
60 The tears from flowing down my cheeks
Like rivulets from a sudden shower.

ENVOYS

This news I hear,
That you, my friend, are plunged in grief,
    Comes from afar,
But still I must raise my voice in weeping:
Your distant sorrow weighs closely on my heart.

You know as I
The nature of this illusory world,
    How nothing stays—
70 Endeavor to be brave and stalwart,
Do not wear out that heart in grief.

❧ KOKINSHU
C. 905

koh-KIN-shoo

mann-YOH-shoo

kah-kee-noh-MOH-toh
hee-toh-MAH-roh

ah-ree-WAH-rah
noh-nah-ree-HEE-rah;
OH-noh
noh-koh-MAH-chee;
KEE noh-tsoo-rah-
YOO-kee

Hay-un

The **Kokinshu,** or *Collection of Ancient and Modern Times,* consisting of twenty volumes and more than a thousand poems, was the first anthology of Japanese poetry to be published at the command of the imperial dynasty. In the 150 years since the appearance of the earlier **Man'yoshu** collection, much had changed. While the *Kokinshu* honored the work of *Man'yoshu* poet **Kakinomoto Hitomaro** (fl. 680–700) and included some ancient Japanese poetry collected from court archives, it concentrated on the works of the major Japanese poets of the middle of the ninth century, including the celebrated **Ariwara no Narihira** (825–880) and **Ono no Komachi** (fl. 850), as well as the works of the anthology's principal compiler **Ki no Tsurayuki** (862–946) and his contemporaries. The *Kokinshu,* though much more sophisticated than the *Man'yoshu,* registering the effects of more than a hundred years of predominantly Chinese influence, still attempted to restore Japanese national culture to greatness. In this it was quite successful. Often cited in later works, with its poetry becoming habitual to the thinking of educated Japanese, it opened the way for the brilliant advances in Japanese literature during the next century of the **Heian** period (794–1185).

The Nature of the *Kokinshu*.   There are important differences between the *Kokinshu* and the *Man'yoshu*. The *Man'yoshu* was compiled over several hundred years by five to ten editors, of whom Otomo Yakamochi (d. 785) was the last. It made use of family archives and other private collections that included many ancient poems. Whereas the arrangement of separate books by topic and progression in subject matter (such as the cycle of the seasons or the stages of love) was applied imperfectly in the *Man'yoshu*, the *Kokinshu* was in every way a more deliberate anthology, put together over a shorter period of time by four editors jointly appointed by the imperial court. The chief editor, Ki no Tsurayuki, displayed his individual taste in his Japanese preface,[1] whether or not he consulted his coeditors before writing. The arrangement of the books by topic and the progression of themes was much more orderly in the *Kokinshu:* New books were not added after the major share of the work was completed, and the editorship did not change hands. Love and the passage of the seasons, the topics of choice, were the principal themes of regional poetry contests at the time, competitions that had assumed an important role in the development of the new poetic tradition. Poems of celebration, eulogies, and other forms of public poetry were not nearly as important in the Heian period as they had been in earlier times.

Critical attacks on the *Kokinshu* over the centuries have castigated its cultural "impurity," especially its use of Chinese elements in vocabulary, form, and expression. The anthology, however, did much to solidify the Japanese literary tradition, particularly its veneration of personal expression and its fascination with courtly society. Whatever remains unique in Japanese culture owes a great deal to the work of principal editor Ki no Tsurayuki and his fellow editors, who collected and produced 1,111 poems reflecting the nation's heritage. In particular, the Japanese poetic tradition is indebted to the anthology's preservation of the *TANKA* — a distant ancestor of the *HAIKU* — in this ambitious tenth-century collection.

A System of Writing and a Form of Composition.   Since the time of the *Man'yoshu*, in the eighth century, written Japanese had changed from a combination of Chinese and Japanese ideograms to simplified phonetic Japanese characters. For a time, however, most learned or "serious" poets composed their works in Chinese and wrote them down in Chinese ideograms; this lasted from the middle of the eighth to the middle of the ninth century, a period sometimes referred to as the "Dark Ages" of Japanese literature. Fortunately for Japanese writing, there was an exception to this practice. Because women were not ordinarily taught Chinese, the love poetry of the period, whether written by men for women or by women for men, customarily was written in Japanese. Since love poetry dominates the *Kokinshu*, and because a new generation of Japanese writers was seeking to break away from Chinese models in any case, the Japanese language reasserted itself for all subject matter in the *Kokinshu*.

www For quizzes on the *Kokinshu*, see *World Literature Online* at bedfordstmartins .com/worldlit.

TAHN-kah
HIGH-koo

---

[1]**Japanese preface:** Ki no Tsurayuki's introduction to the *Kokinshu* is called the Japanese preface to distinguish it from a Chinese preface designed to introduce the same poetry collection to a more cultured class of readers.

Ariwara no Narihira, twelfth to thirteenth century *The celebrated poet from the* Kokinshu *poetry anthology is shown here in a silk painting from the Kamakura period. (The Art Archive / Private Collection, Paris / Dagli Orti)*

CHOH-kah

In addition, the poetic forms of the *Man'yoshu* collection were simplified in the *Kokinshu*. The CHOKA, a long poem consisting of five- and seven-syllable lines in alternation, the favorite form of Kakinomoto Hitomaro, was effectively dead by the tenth century, and with it died most of the public ceremonial poetry that had been so important to the earlier volume. The other major poetic form used in the *Man'yoshu*, the five-line *tanka* of 5-7-5-7-7 syllables, became the predominant form of all new Japanese poetry. By now it was often called the WAKA, a term used simply to mean the poetry favored by the court as a whole. This brief lyrical form dominated the twenty books of the *Kokinshu*, with only a single book given to other kinds of verse, most of that of poor quality.

A New Editorial Direction. The principal editor of the new anthology and the author of its Japanese preface, Ki no Tsurayuki (862–946) took up his literary task at about the age of forty. The *Kokinshu* contains 102 of his poems, the most by any poet, and a generation after his death he was still regarded as a master poet. His Japanese preface, which expresses a love of lived experience and beautiful display—common to all later Japanese culture, not only literature—has been called the first work on aesthetics, or the theory of beauty, in Japanese literature. The best poetry in the collection is noteworthy for its connection to everyday life, its personal touches, and its thematic unity, none of which were distinguishing characteristics of the formal, allusive, and indirect Chinese poetry of the day. Tracing the origin of poetry back to "when heaven and earth first appeared," the Japanese preface states that poetry portrays the beauty that can be found in the everyday events of human life:

> Since then many poems have been composed when people were attracted by the blossoms or admired the birds, when they were moved by the haze or regretted the swift passage of the dew, and both inspiration and forms of expression have become diverse.

In the new collection, the great period of Japanese poetry is traced to the time of the *Man'yoshu,* and the great poet was acknowledged to be Kakinomoto Hitomaro, whose poems it reprinted. True poetry, however, is said to be timeless, for it resides in the human heart:

> Hitomaro is dead, but poetry is still with us. Times may change, joy and sorrow come and go, but the words of these poems are eternal, endless as the green willow threads, unchanging as the needles of the pine, long as the trailing vines, permanent as birds' tracks [*or* handwriting]. Those who know poetry and who understand the heart of things will look up to the old and admire the new as they look up to the moon in the broad sky. We have chosen poems on wearing garlands of plum blossoms, poems on hearing the nightingale, on breaking off branches of autumn leaves, on seeing the snow. We have chosen poems on wishing one's lord the life span of the crane and tortoise, on congratulating someone, on yearning for one's wife when one sees the autumn bush clover or the grasses of summer, on offering prayer strips on Osaka Hill, on seeing someone off on a journey, and on miscellaneous topics that cannot be catalogued by season. These thousand poems in twenty books are called the **Kokinwakashu** [*Kokinshu*].

A Textbook of Poetry. In addition to praising poetry's many virtues, the Japanese preface also analyzes some of the collection's poems and poets. Though Tsurayuki does not say so, this analytical practice comes from the Chinese academic tradition, which developed rhetorical approaches to the study of poetry. He names the "six poetic principles," persuasion, description, comparison, evocative imagery, elegance, and celebration, still recognized today as rhetorical modes of writing. The preface also includes examples of *tanka* written by Kakinomoto Hitomaro and **Yamabe no Akahito**, two poets of the eighth century. Following this, Tsurayuki criticizes the work of six poets of the ninth century, all of whom are included in the *Kokinshu*. Despite Tsurayuki's rather harsh criticism of some of these writers, they have been called "the Six Poetic Geniuses" for having been included in this discussion.

Thematic Arrangement of the Anthology. Books I and II of the *Kokinshu* treat spring, Book III summer, Books IV and V autumn, and Book VI winter. The poems, composed by different authors, are arranged so that a season begins at the start of a book, unfolds, and comes to a close as the book ends. Books VII through X treat occasional subjects and themes: ceremonial greetings, themes of parting, themes of travel, and

The seeds of Japanese poetry lie in the human heart and grow into leaves of ten thousand words. Many things happen to the people of this world, and all that they think and feel is given expression in the description of things they see and hear. When we hear the warbling of the mountain thrush in the blossoms or the voice of the frog in the water, we know every living being has its song.

– KI NO TSURAYUKI,
The Japanese
preface, Kokinshu

koh-kin-wah-KAH-shoo

yah-MAH-beh
noh-ah-kah-HEE-toh

loosely collected "wordplays" in which the clever use of language takes precedence over the content. Books XI through XV treat the subject of love, from unrequited love to love's expression to distress over love lost to sorrowful reflection. The books' internal development is supported by linking the tone and subject matter of each *tanka* to the next. Book XVI deals with grief, proceeding from death to burial ceremonies to the apprehension of one's own mortality. Books XVII and XVIII treat miscellaneous poems, Book XIX the few poems not written in the *tanka* pattern (*chokas* and folk materials). Book XX contains poems used at court for rituals and religious ceremonies.

The Principal Authors.   Some poets included in the *Kokinshu* were more highly regarded than others, with the editors themselves receiving the most prominent placement. The collection's principal editor, Ki no Tsurayuki, placed more poems of his own, 102 in all, than any other writer's in the collection. In one autumn poem (297), he praises the "rich brocade" of fallen leaves in a dark night, suggesting a beauty that remains unseen. In a poem of parting (381), he introduces a literary conceit: The fact of parting, though colorless, colors his feelings. In a love poem (804), he compares the first cries of the autumn geese to his own lover's lament. In poem 842, mourning a lost friend, he contemplates "this sad world's ephemerality" while climbing to a mountain temple. These poems demonstrate what one scholar has called Tsurayuki's insistence on "the naturalness of art, the spontaneity of song." While not the most personal of poets, Tsurayuki conveys ease in the most difficult endeavors. **Oshikochi no Mitsune** (fl. 900–920), another editor of the anthology, included sixty of his own poems in the collection; in an autumn poem (304), he portrays the conventional theme of leaves in the water in carefully balanced images. **Ki no Tomonori** (fl. 880–900), another of the anthologists, has forty-six poems in the collection; in one (565) he compares his lover to the unseen "jewel-weeds / swaying in the depths beneath / the river rapids."

One of the most famous authors in the collection, though not the most frequently represented, is Ono no Komachi (fl. 850). The *Kokinshu* contains eighteen of her poems. She was legendary throughout Japan for her physical beauty, her reputation for passionate relationships, her anger at mistreatment and rejection, her emotional and intellectual complexity, and her capacity for expressing vulnerability in defeat. The *Kokinshu* contains a number of her poems that speak to every aspect of passion: sleeplessness, yearning, missed words of love, pursuit, abandonment, despair. A final poem, curiously placed among some supposedly humorous works at the end of the collection, pronounces: "my blazing passion / wakens me   my pounding heart / shoots flame   then turns to cinders" (1030).

Despite her fame, Ono no Komachi was savagely attacked by Ki no Tsurayuki in his Japanese preface:

> Ono no Komachi is a modern Princess Sotori [a libertine]. She is full of sentiment but weak. Her poetry is like a noble lady who is suffering from a sickness, but the weakness is natural to a woman's poetry.

*oh-shee-KOH-chee
noh-mit-SOO-neh*

*KEE noh-toh-moh-
NOH-ree*

*OH-noh
noh-koh-MAH-chee*

Popular legends concerning Komachi after her death also drew a harsh moral. In folk stories and in a famous play by the Nō dramatist Zeami Motokiyo (1364–1443) she is depicted as a frightening old hag, despised by passers-by. History, however, has treated her with considerably more respect. Later generations of scholars have admired her poems' combination of emotional richness and pure skill. One critic has remarked, "What is especially individual about Komachi is that her strongest passions seem to bring forth her most complex techniques."

A contemporary of Ono no Komachi, Ariwara no Narihira (825–880) was in some respects her male counterpart on the subject of love. But whereas Komachi insists on love's passion and vulnerability, Narihira investigates its philosophical and psychological qualities. His probing of the mysteries of love rests in great part on his belief in the darkness of the human heart, an image Buddhists would have claimed proved that the passions of life are an unfathomable illusion. Narihira takes up the human side of the question by suggesting that one must somehow come to an understanding of one's torments in this life, no matter how difficult or contradictory they seem; he understands that the mind can tolerate only so much without falling into, or even seeking, confusion: In an exchange of poems with the Virgin of the Shrine of **Ise** he confesses, "I am lost in the/total darkness of my heart—/people of this world/you decide for me if love/was dream or reality" (646). As death approaches, he observes that a veil of illusion separates one even from the end of life's journey: "never did/I think I might set out on/it yesterday or today" (861). A poet of philosophy, Narihira brings the seemingly commonplace to the level of the mysterious. His life was depicted and many of his poems collected in *Tales of Ise,* a work of prose and poetry from the early tenth century. The *Kokinshu* contains thirty of his poems.

EE-seh

Lady Ise (fl. 900–920), a contemporary of Ki no Tsurayuki and one of the best women poets in the collection, has twenty-two poems in the anthology. In a memorable love poem (791) she compares her heart to a scorched winter field. Somewhat similarly, an anonymous folk song is included that recalls a flock of geese returning in the winter minus one of its members (412).

Place of the *Kokinshu*.   In Japanese poetry anthologies, the *Kokinshu* came between the heroic early poetry of the *Man'yoshu* and the increasingly mannered and sophisticated court poetry that followed. It reflected the attention given to poetry and other literature by the Heian imperial court. The greatest period of literary production in Japan saw the publication of the *Kokinshu* (c. 905), the related *Tales of Ise* (945), *The Pillow Book* of **Sei Shonagon** (c. 1000), *The Diary of* **Izumi Shikibu** (1004), and the epic narrative *The Tale of Genji* (c. 1010). This amazing achievement suggests that the poets and editors of the *Kokinshu* may indeed have reclaimed native Japanese poetry from the influence of the Chinese tradition, leading to a hundred years of magnificent literary production. For the poets Ono no Komachi and Ariwara no Narihira, the anthology provided recognition for literary work of the highest standards, work which has influenced readers to the present day.

SAY shoh-NAH-goon;
ee-ZOO-mee
shee-KEE-boo;
GEN-jee

■ CONNECTIONS

The *Man'yoshu*, p. 1018. The two great poetic collections of classical Japan invite comparison. The *Man'yoshu*, compiled in the eighth century, featured the work of native Japanese poets, the greatest of whom was Kakinomoto Hitomaro, whose style and poetic tradition favored the theme of public celebration and eulogies written in the long form of the *choka*. The *Kokinshu*, collected in the early tenth century, sought to reclaim Japanese poetry from its Chinese influences, chiefly through featuring the short lyric form of the *tanka*. Can you compare the two anthologies and illustrate their purposes?

***In the Tradition:* Courtly Love Lyrics, p. 628.** Two hundred years apart, the poets of the Heian court of Japan (fl. 850–1000) and the Muslim poets of Spain and Provençal poets of France (fl. 1000–1200) focused on similar themes and expressed like concerns on the subject of love. The poets of the *Kokinshu* (c. 905) treat love in Books XI–XV in its changing stages, from first infatuation to sorrow at love's loss. Similarly, Arabic scholar-poet Ibn Hazm (fl. 1020) and the monk Andreas Capellanus (fl. 1170) codified the stages of love and gave them contemporary expression. What parallels can be drawn between these poetic traditions of courtly love?

Matsuo Bashō (Book 4). Bashō (1644–1693) is the great seventeenth-century practitioner of the *haiku*, a poetic form derived from the *renga*, or linked verse, of the thirteenth century and ultimately from the *tanka*, the major verse form of the tenth-century *Kokinshu* anthology. How are the *tanka* and the *haiku* used and how do they reflect the times in which they were written?

■ FURTHER RESEARCH

Editions and Anthologies
Carter, Steven D., ed. *Traditional Japanese Poetry: An Anthology.* 1991.
Keene, Donald, ed. *Anthology of Japanese Literature.* 1955.
McCullough, Helen Craig, ed. and trans. *Kokin Wakashu: The First Imperial Anthology of Japanese Poetry.* 1985.
Rodd, Laura Rasplica, with Mary Catherine Henkenius, trans. *Kokinshu: A Collection of Poems Ancient and Modern.* 1984.

Literary History
Kato, Shuichi. *A History of Japanese Literature: The First Thousand Years.* 1979.
Keene, Donald. *Seeds in the Heart: Japanese Literature from the Earliest Times to the Late Sixteenth Century.* 1999.

Literary Criticism
Brower, Robert H., and Earl Miner. *Japanese Court Poetry.* 1961.
Keene, Donald. *The Pleasures of Japanese Literature.* 1988.
McCullough, Helen Craig. *Brocade by Night: Kokin Wakashu and the Court Style in Japanese Classical Poetry.* 1985.
Miner, Earl. *An Introduction to Japanese Court Poetry.* 1968.

■ PRONUNCIATION

Ariwara no Narihira: ah-ree-WAH-rah noh-nah-ree-HEE-rah
choka: CHOH-kah
Genji: GEN-jee
haiku: HIGH-koo
Heian: HAY-un
Ise: EE-seh
Izumi Shikibu: ee-ZOO-mee shee-KEE-boo

Kakinomoto Hitomaro: kah-kee-noh-MOH-toh hee-toh-MAH-roh
Ki no Tomonori: KEE noh-toh-moh-NOH-ree
Ki no Tsurayuki: KEE noh-tsoo-rah-YOO-kee
Kokinshu: koh-KIN-shoo
Kokinwakashu: koh-kin-wah-KAH-shoo
Man'yoshu: mahn-YOH-shoo
Ono no Komachi: OH-nohj noh-koh-MAH-chee
Oshikochi no Mitsune: oh-shee-KOH-chee noh-mit-SOO-neh
Sei Shonagon: SAY shoh-NAH-goon
Shuishu: shoo-EE-shoo
tanka: TAHN-kah
Yamabe no Akahito: yah-MAH-beh noh-ah-kah-HEE-toh

❧ *Kokinshu*

Translated by Laurel Rasplica Rodd with Mary Catherine Henkenius

FROM

BOOK I: SPRING

2   *Written on the first day of spring.*

> today   long-awaited
> day when spring begins   will
> the breeze melt icebound
> waters in which we once dipped
> cupped hands   drenching summer robes

Ki no Tsurayuki

Kokinshu. The poems selected here from the *Kokinshu* are numbered as they were in the original text. Each poem appears with its original descriptive title and any explanation that might have accompanied it.

Seven poems taken from Books I through VI address the seasons. A poem from Book VIII addresses the sorrow of parting and an anonymous poem from Book IX addresses travel. There follow thirteen love poems, including seven by Ono no Komachi, from Books XI through XV. Two poems from Book XVI treat the subject of grief; one "miscellaneous poem" comes from Book XVIII, and a final poem by Ono no Komachi comes from the collection of miscellaneous forms in Book XIX. In general, the intensity of the poems is heightened from the beginning to end of each book.

Two excellent modern English translations of the *Kokinshu* are available: those of Laurel Rasplica Rodd and Helen Craig McCullough. The Rodd translations are chosen here for their literal rendering of the originals, with a preference for plain language rather than poetic compression. Both translators offer good readings of the material in their notes, and both are recommended to the student. The footnotes that appear here are condensed from the Rodd edition.

43   *Plum trees blooming near the stream.*

    each spring   it seems   I
shall confuse reflections in
    the flowing stream   with
flowers   and again I'll drench
my sleeves seeking to pluck those boughs

Lady Ise

84   *Falling cherry blossoms.*

    the air is still and
sun-warmed on this day of spring—
    why then do cherry
blossoms cascade to the earth
with such restless changeful hearts

Ki no Tomonori

113   *Topic unknown.*

    the colors of the
blossoms have faded and passed
    as   heedlessly   I
squandered my days in pensive
gazing   and the long rains fell[1]

Ono no Komachi

FROM

BOOK III: SUMMER

162   *Hearing a nightingale singing in the mountains.*

    mountain nightingale
your cries sound as I await
    my love on Mount Pine
and suddenly my love has
grown heavy   weighting my heart

Ki no Tsurayuki

---

[1] **the colors of the / blossoms have faded . . . :** The complex rhetoric and the comparison of the beauty of the blossoms and of youth mark this as a poem by Komachi.

FROM

BOOK V: AUTUMN

297   On going to pick autumn leaves at Kitayama.

> deep in the mountains
they have fallen with no one
>   to see their splendor —
these autumn leaves are a rich
brocade spread in the dark night

Ki no Tsurayuki

304   On seeing the autumn leaves falling near a pond.

>   when the wind blows   the
falling leaves embroider the
>   limpid waters   where
even the leaves still clinging
>   are reflected in the depths

Ōshikōchi no Mitsune

FROM

BOOK VIII: POEMS OF PARTING

381   Parting from someone.

>   although the thing called
parting is devoid of all
>   color   somehow it
tortures me by dyeing my
heart through the sorrow's hue

Ki no Tsurayuki

FROM

BOOK IX: TRAVEL POEMS

412   Topic unknown.

>   hauntingly they cry
the northbound geese of the night —
>   one from their number

who flew this way in autumn
accompanies them not home

Anonymous
Some say this poem was composed by a woman who had gone with her husband to another province where he soon died. As she returned to the capital alone, she heard the wild geese cry and wrote this poem.

FROM

BOOK XII: LOVE POEMS

552   Topic unknown.

   in love-tormented
sleep I saw him beside me—
   had I known my love's
visit was but a dream   I
should never have awakened

Ono no Komachi

553   Topic unknown.

   since that brief sleep when
first I saw the one I love
   it is those fleeting
dreams   ephemera of the
night   on which I now rely

Ono no Komachi

554   Topic unknown.

   when my yearning grows
unendurable   all through
   the jet-black hours of
night   I sleep with my robes turned
inside out   awaiting him

Ono no Komachi

565

    like the jewel-weeds
swaying in the depths beneath
    the river rapids
unseen by human eyes   my
love lies hidden   all unknown

Ki no Tomonori

FROM

BOOK XIII: LOVE POEMS

635   *Topic unknown.*

    the autumn night was
long in name only   at last
    we met   but the blush
of dawn parted us before
the words of love were spoken

Ono no Komachi

644   *Sent to a lady on the morning after a tryst.*

    how fleeting the dream
of the night we two slept side
    by side   trying to
recapture it   I dozed   but
it only faded faster

Ariwara no Narihira

645   *Once when Narihira was in Ise Province, he had a secret tryst with
the Virgin of the Shrine.*[2] *The next morning, as he was worrying about
having no one to carry a message to her, this poem arrived from her.*

    did you come to me
or did I go to you   I
    cannot now recall
was it dream   reality
was I sleeping   or awake

Anonymous

---

[2] **Virgin of the Shrine:** Shrine virgins were unmarried princesses appointed to serve at the shrine of Ise.

646   In reply.

I am lost in the
total darkness of my heart—
　　people of this world
you decide for me if love
was dream or reality[3]

Ariwara no Narihira

658   Topic unknown.

though my feet never
cease running to him on the
　　byways of my dreams
such meetings do not equal
one waking glimpse of my love

Ono no Komachi

FROM

BOOK XV: LOVE POEMS

*791   Written when she saw fires in the fields as she traveled during a time
when she was longing for someone.*

my heart is like the
lonely winter-scorched fields that
　　lie before me   yet
even in burnt fields buds swell—
may I look forward to spring

Lady Ise

797   Topic unknown.

that which fades within
without changing its color
　　is the hidden bloom

---

[3] **I am lost in the / total darkness of my heart . . . dream or reality:** The vocabulary of this poem is laden with Buddhist overtones: "The darkness of the heart" refers to the blindness of the unenlightened; "lost" describes the lives of the unenlightened who live in darkness; and "dream" is the state from which one must awaken, achieving life in "reality."

of the heart of man   in
this world of disillusion

Ono no Komachi

804   *Topic unknown.*

    like the cries of the
first wild geese   my sobs echo
      through the skies   for how
sorrowful the autumn of
man's heart in the world of love

Ki no Tsurayuki

822   *Topic unknown.*

    lonely ears of grain
lie scattered on the field by
      chilly autumn winds
reminding me that I too
will remain unharvested

Ono no Komachi

FROM

Book XVI: Poems of Grief

842   *Composed on the way to a mountain temple in the autumn of a year
in which he was in mourning.*

    come to reap late rice
in mountain fields where morning
      dew gleams   my harvest
is the knowledge of this sad
world's emphemerality

Ki no Tsurayuki

861   *Composed when he was ill and weak.*

    although I've heard
there is a road we all must
      travel   never did

I think I might set out on
it yesterday or today

Ariwara no Narihira

Book XVIII: Miscellaneous Poems

*938   When Funya no Yasuhide was appointed Secretary of Mikawa, he
wrote, "Won't you come for a tour of the provinces?" and Komachi replied
with this poem.*

    I have sunk to the
bottom   and like the rootless
      shifting water weeds
should the currents summon me
I too would drift away

Ono no Komachi

Book XIX: Miscellaneous Forms

1030   Topic unknown.

    no moon lights the night
nor can I meet my lover
    my blazing passion
wakens me   my pounding heart
shoots flame   then turns to cinders

Ono no Komachi

❧ Sei Shonagon

c. 966–1017

The *Makura no Soshi*, known in English as *The Pillow Book*, brims with vignettes, stories, essays, and lists concerning court life in imperial Japan at the turn of the tenth century. Its author, **Sei Shonagon**, is usually counted among the greatest Japanese prose stylists. Her flights of lyricism, merciless descriptions, and compilations of "lists" of things to praise or condemn made her work popular as soon as it appeared; her candid and often revealing account of her career as a lady-in-waiting for **Teishi** (Empress **Sadako**) helps one understand this rich and sophisticated period of Japanese history. Often compared to Lady Murasaki's *The Tale of Genji*, written at about the same time, *The Pillow Book* treats the real lives of men and women at court while *Genji* transforms their stories into a highly stylized work of fiction. Both works are classics in their way, each a reflection of the other's world.

mah-KOO-rah
noh-SOH-shee
SAY shoh-NAH-goon

TAY-shee;
sah-DAH-koh

GEN-jee

The Author as We Know Her.   As is true of many Japanese writers who were not permanently attached to the court, Sei Shonagon's origins and her subsequent fate are partially obscured. Her father, **Kiyohara no Motosuke** (908–990), was a recognized poet and scholar as well as a minor public official. Sei Shonagon's real name is a mystery; *sei* is an alternate pronunciation of the first character of her family surname, Kiyohara, and *shonagon* means "minor counselor," a name commonly applied to those who served at court or to their dependents. Sei Shonagon served Empress Sadako (976–1000), the first consort of Emperor **Ichijo** (980–1011), as a lady-in-waiting from 993 to 1000, when the empress died following the birth of her second child. The end of Shonagon's life is unrecorded, though certain stories, possibly driven by jealousy, suggest that she died in poverty. She writes that she began to compose *The Pillow Book* while serving Empress Sadako and that her writing soon came to public attention despite her reluctance to show it. The work's title may suggest that Shonagon wrote it while lying on her pillow, though the author herself offers a more ingenious explanation. The book is an example of *ZUIHITSU*, or "following the brush" writing, that is, a collection of brief, informal essays containing observations about the author's life and circumstances. Technically it is not a diary, though other well-known women authors of Shonagon's day, such as **Izumi Shikibu** and Lady **Murasaki**, kept diaries.[1]

kee-yoh-HAH-rah
noh-moh-TOH-soo-keh

ee-chee-JOH

zoo-ee-HIT-soo

ee-ZOO-mee
shee-KEE-boo;
moo-rah-SAH-kee

---

[1]**women authors . . . kept diaries:** Izumi Shikibu (c. 976–1030) was the greatest poet of her time as well as a prolific and passionate lady of the court. Her diary contains the story of her love affair with Prince Atsumichi (aht-soo-MEH-chee), who took her into his palace in defiance of convention in 1003–1004. Lady Murasaki Shikibu (973–1014) wrote her diary between 1008 and 1010, after completing her masterpiece, *The Tale of Genji*, in 1007. Both Izumi Shikibu and Lady Murasaki served as ladies-in-waiting in the court of Shoshi, who was appointed consort to Emperor Ichijo in 1000 after Teishi fell from grace.

www For links to more information about Sei Shonagon and a quiz on *The Pillow Book,* see *World Literature Online* at bedfordstmartins .com/worldlit.

We know that Sei Shonagon had enemies. An attractive, energetic, and formidable woman whom men constantly attended, she was distinguished by her ingenuity, her sharp wit, and (some would say) her arrogance and snobbery. Her female cohorts, other ladies-in-waiting in the imperial court, undoubtedly competed with her for influential acquaintances, good standing in court, and literary repute. Lady Murasaki, who completed her masterpiece, *The Tale of Genji,* in about 1010, was particularly competitive with Shonagon, both as a writer and as a lady-in-waiting for a rival empress. Lady Murasaki wrote of Shonagon with crushing sarcasm:

> [She] has the most extraordinary air of self-satisfaction. Yet, if we stop to examine those Chinese writings of hers that she so presumptuously scatters about the place, we find that they are full of imperfections. Someone who makes such an effort to be different from others is bound to fall in people's esteem, and I can only think that her future will be a hard one. She is a gifted woman, to be sure. Yet, if one gives free rein to one's emotions even under the most inappropriate circumstances, if one has to sample each interesting thing that comes along, people are bound to regard one as frivolous. And how can things turn out well for such a woman?

Shonagon on Herself. With her cleverness, Sei Shonagon could have invented whatever persona she desired and thought appropriate. For this reason, it is misleading to think of *The Pillow Book* as merely a series of autobiographical sketches. Its author was likely far more interested in art than self-revelation. For the same reason, Shonagon's claims of transparency in her actions are also suspect. Still, the reader cannot help being charmed by the story the author tells of her work's conception:

koh-reh-CHEE-kah

> One day Lord **Korechika**, the Minister of the Centre, brought the Empress a bundle of notebooks. "What shall we do with them?" Her Majesty asked me. "The Emperor has already made arrangements for copying the *Records of the Historian.*"
> "Let me make them into a pillow," I said.
> "Very well," said Her Majesty. "You may have them."
> I now had a vast quantity of paper at my disposal, and I set about filling the notebooks with odd facts, stories from the past, and all sorts of other things, often including the most trivial material. On the whole I concentrated on things and people that I found charming and splendid; my notes are also full of poems and observations on trees and plants, birds and insects.

Her readers would have understood immediately that Shonagon never intended to use the paper as a pillow. Not only was it poorly designed for that purpose, but it was far too expensive. Beyond that, one need only read several pages of Shonagon's book to realize that her writing was not restricted to "things and people that I found charming and splendid," much less to "trees and plants, birds and insects," though she wrote about those things very well. Whatever merit one attaches to this passage, a closing anecdote in her book, it truly captures the writer's determination to make the best use of her materials. It also gives us a good idea of the somewhat subversive spirit that animated this gifted woman.

Stories of the Court. Scattered throughout *The Pillow Book* are accounts of the court, including encounters with men and the benevolence of Empress Sadako, which continued even after the empress encountered political problems. "When I First Went into Waiting" brilliantly captures the confusion of young Sei Shonagon arriving at court, her encounter with the teasing of Korechika, the major counselor, and her shyness before the young empress.[2] In "The Sliding Screen in the Back of the Hall" Shonagon participates in her first poetry competition, for which she is expected to know the entire ***Kokinshu***, the tenth-century Japanese anthology of more than a thousand poems. Here she is a beginner at court, painfully shy and trying to measure up to the standards expected of her.

Shonagon's stories about her friendships with men and about romance are of another order. Her mature attitude concerning her role as a woman at court first appears in the brilliant chapter "When I Make Myself Imagine," in which she defends women of the court from charges of wickedness and immodesty and celebrates their freedom and knowledge of etiquette. "It Is So Stiflingly Hot" describes sexual encounters between courtesans and their lovers, pausing over the rituals of rising early and writing a letter the morning after a lover has spent the night. "When a Court Lady Is on Leave" takes up the matter of sexual liaisons away from court in greater detail. "When a Woman Lives Alone" is a reflection on the later life of a single woman.

Shonagon frequently touches on her deep commitment to Empress Sadako. While stories such as "When I First Went into Waiting" emphasize the young empress' taste and her feelings for her ladies-in-waiting, the earlier story "When His Excellency, the Chancellor, Had Departed," tells of a time when the empress' increasing vulnerability was cause for concern. Though Shonagon alludes to intrigues at court in which she herself may have played a part, there is no reason to doubt her loyalty to the empress or her fervent admiration of court life in general. In fact, so amenable is she to the views of the court that she seems to have had an almost total lack of sympathy for commoners.

Topics of the Writer. Shonagon's love of writing and her devotion to its craft raise her work above the level of a diarist. Her lists, consisting of long or short entries on general themes, such as "Hateful Things," "Embarrassing Things," or "Pleasing Things," were much admired. Often her judgments add rich detail to her sketches, as when she describes the annoying habits of lovers or the offensive behavior of other ladies-in-waiting. Chapters devoted more purely to the writer's craft include astonishing physical and natural descriptions, such as one finds in "Wind Instruments," "Shortly after the Twentieth of the Ninth Month," and "Times When One Should Be on One's Guard." Throughout, the artist and craftswoman stands out. Shonagon's love of Chinese and Japanese

koh-KIN-shoo

As a writer she is incomparably the best poet of her time, a fact which is apparent only in her prose and not at all in the conventional *uta* [lyrics] for which she is also famous. Passages such as that about the stormy lake or the few lines about crossing a moonlit river show a beauty of phrasing that Murasaki, a much more deliberate writer, certainly never surpassed.

– ARTHUR WALEY, translator, 1928

---

[2] **the young empress:** When Sei Shonagon first began to serve at court, at twenty-seven, the empress was seventeen.

poetry served her well as a writer of beautiful prose, as one of her English translators, Arthur Waley, has pointed out.

It is not hard for the modern reader to view Sei Shonagon as a liberated woman. In "When I Make Myself Imagine," she not only defends the social status of ladies-in-waiting but also boldly argues that the freedom the court provides is more precious than the bonds of matrimony. Although it appears that Shonagon was married at least once and had a child, it remains true that she sought a life of independence and self-expression, things she may in fact have desperately needed. Her frequent departures from court suggest that she required time away from her participation in such a glittering society despite, or even because of, its many attractions. The image of Sei Shonagon, restless spirit of a brilliant milieu, tantalizes the reader to this day.

■ CONNECTIONS

Kokinshu, p. 1044. During the Heian period (794–1185), in which Sei Shonagon lived, the first imperial Japanese anthology of poetry, the *Kokinshu* (c. 905), was greatly revered. In "The Sliding Screen in the Back of the Hall," Shonagon shows the court's knowledge of the *Kokinshu*. What influence did these poems have on etiquette and manners, romantic affairs, and the relations between the empress and her ladies-in-waiting?

Lady Murasaki, *The Tale of Genji*, p. 1094. While *The Pillow Book* is an example of *zuihitsu* ("following the brush"), literary prose writing, *The Tale of Genji* is a courtly romance written in a sophisticated, elevated style designed to give its characters an almost otherworldly quality. Considering this and the personal and artistic differences between Sei Shonagon and Lady Murasaki, how can the two works be compared? Do their differences arise from the fact that one work is fiction and the other is nonfiction, or are the authors' personalities mostly responsible?

Virginia Woolf, *A Room of One's Own* (Book 6). Sei Shonagon's celebration of court life in "When I Make Myself Imagine" and her defense of individual freedom in several other writings invite comparison with Virginia Woolf's modern feminist essay, *A Room of One's Own*. It could be argued, however, that Shonagon was much more aware of the downside of independence than Woolf was when she wrote her essay. What concept of freedom does each writer develop?

■ FURTHER RESEARCH

Editions
Morris, Ivan, trans. *The Pillow Book of Sei Shonagon*. 2 vols. 1967. Also available in an abridged one-volume edition, 1967.
Waley, Arthur, trans. *The Pillow Book of Sei Shonagon*. 1928.

Anthologies
Keene, Donald, ed. *Anthology of Japanese Literature*. 1955.
McCullough, Helen Craig, ed. *Classical Japanese Prose: An Anthology*. 1990.

Literary Criticism and History
Brower, Robert, and Earl Miner. *Japanese Court Poetry*. 1961.
Keene, Donald. *Seeds in the Heart: Japanese Literature from the Earliest Times to the Late Sixteenth Century*. 1993, 1999.
Morris, Ivan. *The World of the Shining Prince: Court Life in Ancient Japan*. 1967.

■ PRONUNCIATION

Atsumichi: aht-soo-MEE-chee
Fujiwara no Korechika: foo-jee-WAH-rah-noh koh-reh-CHEE-kah, noh-koh-
RECH-ih-kah
Fujiwara no Michinaga: foo-jee-WAH-rah-noh mee-chee-NAH-gah
Fujiwara no Michitaka: foo-jee-WAH-rah-noh mee-chee-TAH-kah
Genji: GEN-jee
Ichijo: ee-chee-JOH
Izumi Shikibu: ee-ZOO-mee shee-KEE-boo
Kiyohara no Motosuke: kee-yoh-HAH-rah noh-moh-TOH-soo-keh, noh-moh-
TOH-skeh
Kokinshu: koh-KIN-shoo
Makura no Soshi: mah-KOO-rah noh-SOH-shee
Murasaki Shikibu (Lady Murasaki): moo-rah-SAH-kee shee-KEE-boo
Sei Shonagon: SAY shoh-NAH-goon
Shoshi (Empress Akiko): SHOH-shee, AH-kee-koh
Teishi (Empress Sadako): TAY-shee, sah-DAH-koh
zuihitsu: zoo-ee-HIT-soo

FROM

ॐ The Pillow Book

Translated by Ivan Morris

IN SPRING IT IS THE DAWN

In spring it is the dawn that is most beautiful. As the light creeps over the hills, their outlines are dyed a faint red and wisps of purplish cloud trail over them.

In summer the nights. Not only when the moon shines, but on dark nights too, as the fireflies flit to and fro, and even when it rains, how beautiful it is!

The Pillow Book. Sei Shonagon's sketches of life at court are the work of a writer of great wit and intelligence. She has often been called a snob for refusing to acknowledge the importance of the lower classes, including servants at court. Editors also have noted her obsessive devotion to the court itself. Yet many of her comments about court society are critical, and she is certainly a sharp-eyed observer with a penchant for satire. Her devastating criticism of manners, court intrigues, and the arrogance of male lovers inspires the work with a unique liveliness.

The book's sketches were not arranged according to the dates of their authorship but were ordered to give the work an aesthetic balance it would not have had if it had been assembled chronologically. The diverse orderings of surviving manuscripts make the job of pinpointing the author's final intentions as to arrangement difficult. This modern translation by Ivan Morris uses the original chapter headings for "lists," supplies other chapter headings not in the original, and attempts to convey the highly condensed effect of Shonagon's Japanese prose in modern English. As Morris remarks, readers are frequently surprised by the length of *The Pillow Book:* 326 chapters in all, it runs 268 pages in book format, with the notes and background material making up another volume. All footnotes have been adapted from the Morris translation.

In autumn the evenings, when the glittering sun sinks close to the edge of the hills and the crows fly back to their nests in threes and fours and twos; more charming still is a file of wild geese, like specks in the distant sky. When the sun has set, one's heart is moved by the sound of the wind and the hum of the insects.

In winter the early mornings. It is beautiful indeed when snow has fallen during the night, but splendid too when the ground is white with frost; or even when there is no snow or frost, but it is simply very cold and the attendants hurry from room to room stirring up the fires and bringing charcoal, how well this fits the season's mood! But as noon approaches and the cold wears off, no one bothers to keep the braziers alight, and soon nothing remains but piles of white ashes.

Especially Delightful Is the First Day

Especially delightful is the first day of the First Month,[1] when the mists so often shroud the sky. Everyone pays great attention to his appearance and dresses with the utmost care. What a pleasure it is to see them all offer their congratulations to the Emperor and celebrate their own new year![2]

I also enjoy the seventh day, when people pluck the young herbs that have sprouted fresh and green beneath the snow. It is amusing to see their excitement when they find such plants growing near the Palace, by no means a spot where one might expect them.

This is the day when members of the nobility who live outside the Palace arrive in their magnificently decorated carriages to admire the blue horses.[3] As the carriages are drawn over the ground-beam of the Central Gate, there is always a tremendous bump, and the heads of the women passengers are knocked together; the combs fall out of their hair, and may be smashed to pieces if the owners are not careful. I enjoy the way everyone laughs when this happens.

I remember one occasion when I visited the Palace to see the procession of blue horses. Several senior courtiers were standing outside the guard-house of the Left Division; they had borrowed bows from the escorts, and, with much laughter, were twanging them to make the blue horses prance. Looking through one of the gates of the Palace enclosure, I could dimly make out a garden fence, near which a number of ladies, several of them from the Office of Grounds, went to and fro. What lucky women, I thought, who could walk about the Nine-Fold Enclosure[4] as though they

---

[1] **the First Month:** In the Japanese lunar calendar, the moon is full on the fifteenth day of each month. The calendar is ahead of the Western calendar by about seventeen to forty-five days: on average, about a month.

[2] **new year:** New Year's Day is the time to pay respects to one's superiors and celebrate the passage of a year, corresponding in some ways to a Western birthday.

[3] **blue horses:** At the Festival of the Blue Horses, twenty-one horses, originally steel-gray, were paraded before the emperor to mark the beginning of an auspicious new year.

[4] **the Nine-Fold Enclosure:** A figure of speech denoting the enormous walled-in grounds of the Imperial Palace, a city in itself.

had lived there all their lives! Just then the escorts passed close to my carriage — remarkably close, in fact, considering the vastness of the Palace grounds — and I could actually see the texture of their faces. Some of them were not properly powdered; here and there their skin showed through unpleasantly like the dark patches of earth in a garden where the snow has begun to melt. When the horses in the procession reared wildly, I shrank into the back of my carriage and could no longer see what was happening.

On the eighth day there is great excitement in the Palace as people hurry to express their gratitude, and the clatter of carriages is louder than ever — all very fascinating.

The fifteenth day is the festival of the full-moon gruel, when a bowl of gruel is presented to His Majesty. On this day all the women of the house carry gruel-sticks, which they hide carefully from each other. It is most amusing to see them walking about, as they await an opportunity to hit their companions. Each one is careful not to be struck herself and is constantly looking over her shoulder to make sure that no one is stealing up on her. Yet the precautions are useless, for before long one of the women manages to score a hit. She is extremely pleased with herself and laughs merrily. Everyone finds this delightful — except, of course, the victim, who looks very put out.[5] [. . .]

Sometimes when the women are hitting each other the men also join in the fun. The strange thing is that, when a woman is hit by one of the men, she often gets angry and bursts into tears; then she will upbraid the man and say the most awful things about him — most amusing. Even in the Palace, where the atmosphere is usually so solemn, everything is in confusion on this day, and no one stands on ceremony.

It is fascinating to see what happens during the period of appointments. However snowy and icy it may be, candidates of the Fourth and Fifth Ranks come to the Palace with their official requests. Those who are still young and merry seem full of confidence. For the candidates who are old and white-haired things do not go so smoothly. Such men have to apply for help from people with influence at Court; some of them even visit ladies-in-waiting in their quarters and go to great lengths in pointing out their own merits. If young women happen to be present, they are greatly amused. As soon as the candidates have left, they mimic and deride them — something that the old men cannot possibly suspect as they scurry from one part of the Palace to another, begging everyone, 'Please present my petition favourably to the Emperor' and 'Pray inform Her Majesty about me.' It is not so bad if they finally succeed, but it really is rather pathetic when all their efforts prove in vain.

---

[5] **The fifteenth day . . . very put out:** Concerning the ceremony of the gruel at the first full moon, it was believed that if a woman was struck in the flanks with a gruel-stick she would produce a male child. It became a custom for the women to run about the house hitting each other playfully with these sticks.

The Sliding Screen in the Back of the Hall

The sliding screen in the back of the hall in the north-east corner of Seiryō Palace[6] is decorated with paintings of the stormy sea and of the terrifying creatures with long arms and long legs that live there. When the doors of the Empress's room were open, we could always see this screen. One day we were sitting in the room, laughing at the paintings and remarking how unpleasant they were. By the balustrade of the veranda stood a large celadon vase, full of magnificent cherry branches; some of them were as much as five foot long, and their blossoms overflowed to the very foot of the railing. Towards noon the Major Counsellor, Fujiwara no Korechika,[7] arrived. He was dressed in a cherry-coloured Court cloak, sufficiently worn to have lost its stiffness, a white under-robe, and loose trousers of dark purple; from beneath the cloak shone the pattern of another robe of dark red damask. Since His Majesty was present, Korechika knelt on the narrow wooden platform before the door and reported to him on official matters.

A group of ladies-in-waiting was seated behind the bamboo blinds. Their cherry-coloured Chinese jackets hung loosely over their shoulders with the collars pulled back; they wore robes of wistaria, golden yellow, and other colours, many of which showed beneath the blind covering the half-shutter. Presently the noise of the attendants' feet told us that dinner was about to be served in the Daytime Chamber, and we heard cries of 'Make way. Make way.'

The bright, serene day delighted me. When the Chamberlains had brought all the dishes into the Chamber, they came to announce that dinner was ready, and His Majesty left by the middle door. After accompanying the Emperor, Korechika returned to his previous place on the veranda beside the cherry blossoms. The Empress pushed aside her curtain of state and came forward as far as the threshold. We were overwhelmed by the whole delightful scene. It was then that Korechika slowly intoned the words of the old poem,

> The days and the months flow by,
> But Mount Mimoro lasts forever.[8]

Deeply impressed, I wished that all this might indeed continue for a thousand years.

As soon as the ladies serving in the Daytime Chamber had called for the gentlemen-in-waiting to remove the trays, His Majesty returned to the Empress's room. Then he told me to rub some ink on the inkstone. Dazzled, I felt that I should never be able to take my eyes off his radiant countenance. Next he folded a piece of white paper. 'I should like each of you,' he said, 'to copy down on this paper the first ancient poem that comes into your head.'

---

[6] **The sliding screen . . . of Seiryō Palace:** Seiryō Palace was the emperor's residence in the Imperial Palace. The sliding screen, with its terrifying Chinese figures, protected the emperor and empress from evil spirits when they met privately.

[7] **Fujiwara no Korechika:** The brother of Empress Teishi (Sadako) who was exiled in 966 because he was the principal rival of Fujiwara no Michinaga, the most powerful political figure in Japan after this date.

[8] **The days . . . lasts forever:** Wishing his sister prosperity, Korechika quotes from a poem from the *Man'yoshu*.

'How am I going to manage this?' I asked Korechika, who was still out on the veranda.

'Write your poem quickly,' he said, 'and show it to His Majesty. We men must not interfere in this.' Ordering an attendant to take the Emperor's inkstone to each of the women in the room, he told us to make haste. 'Write down any poem you happen to remember,' he said. 'The Naniwazu[9] or whatever else you can think of.'

For some reason I was overcome with timidity; I flushed and had no idea what to do. Some of the other women managed to put down poems about the spring, the blossoms, and such suitable subjects; then they handed me the paper and said, 'Now it's your turn.' Picking up the brush, I wrote the poem that goes,

> The years have passed
> And age has come my way.
> Yet I need only look at this fair flower
> For all my cares to melt away.

I altered the third line, however, to read, 'Yet I need only look upon my lord.'[10]

When he had finished reading, the Emperor said, 'I asked you to write these poems because I wanted to find out how quick you really were.

'A few years ago,' he continued, 'Emperor Enyū ordered all his courtiers to write poems in a notebook. Some excused themselves on the grounds that their handwriting was poor; but the Emperor insisted, saying that he did not care in the slightest about their handwriting or even whether their poems were suitable for the season. So they all had to swallow their embarrassment and produce something for the occasion. Among them was His Excellency, our present Chancellor,[11] who was then Middle Captain of the Third Rank. He wrote down the old poem,

> Like the sea that beats
> Upon the shores of Izumo
> As the tide sweeps in,
> Deeper it grows and deeper —
> The love I bear for you.

But he changed the last line to read, "The love I bear my lord!", and the Emperor was full of praise.'

When I heard His Majesty tell this story, I was so overcome that I felt myself perspiring. It occurred to me that no younger woman would have been able to use my poem[12] and I felt very lucky. This sort of test can be a terrible ordeal: it often happens

---

[9] **The Naniwazu:** A famous poem from the *Kokinshu,* supposedly the first poem composed by an emperor.

[10] **'Yet I need only look upon my lord':** Shonagon has altered this poem, from the *Kokinshu,* to praise Emperor Ichijo.

[11] **our present Chancellor:** Fujiwara no Michitaka (see note 7). The origin of this poem is unknown.

[12] **no younger woman . . . my poem:** Shonagon's choice of this poem, referring to herself in the line "And age has come my way," is appropriate. At the time she is thirty, while the empress and emperor are twenty and sixteen, respectively.

that people who usually write fluently are so overawed that they actually make mistakes in their characters.

Next the Empress placed a notebook of *Kokin Shū* poems before her and started reading out the first three lines of each one, asking us to supply the remainder. Among them were several famous poems that we had in our minds day and night; yet for some strange reason we were often unable to fill in the missing lines. Lady Saishō, for example, could manage only ten, which hardly qualified her as knowing her *Kokin Shū*. Some of the other women, even less successful, could remember only about half-a-dozen poems. They would have done better to tell the Empress quite simply that they had forgotten the lines; instead they came out with great lamentations like 'Oh dear, how could we have done so badly in answering the questions that Your Majesty was pleased to put to us?' — all of which I found rather absurd.

When no one could complete a particular poem, the Empress continued reading to the end. This produced further wails from the women: 'Oh, we all knew that one! How could we be so stupid?'

'Those of you,' said the Empress, 'who had taken the trouble to copy out the *Kokin Shū* several times would have been able to complete every single poem I have read. In the reign of Emperor Murakami there was a woman at Court known as the Imperial Lady of Senyō Palace. She was the daughter of the Minister of the Left who lived in the Smaller Palace of the First Ward, and of course you have all heard of her. When she was still a young girl, her father gave her this advice: "First you must study penmanship. Next you must learn to play the seven-string zither better than anyone else. And also you must memorize all the poems in the twenty volumes of the *Kokin Shū*."

'Emperor Murakami,' continued Her Majesty, 'had heard this story and remembered it years later when the girl had grown up and become an Imperial Concubine. Once, on a day of abstinence,[13] he came into her room, hiding a notebook of *Kokin Shū* poems in the folds of his robe. He surprised her by seating himself behind a curtain of state; then, opening the book, he asked, "Tell me the verse written by such-and-such a poet, in such-and-such a year and on such-and-such an occasion." The lady understood what was afoot and that it was all in fun, yet the possibility of making a mistake or forgetting one of the poems must have worried her greatly. Before beginning the test, the Emperor had summoned a couple of ladies-in-waiting who were particularly adept in poetry and told them to mark each incorrect reply by a *go* stone.[14] What a splendid scene it must have been! You know, I really envy anyone who attended that Emperor even as a lady-in-waiting.

'Well,' Her Majesty went on, 'he then began questioning her. She answered without any hesitation, just giving a few words or phrases to show that she knew each poem. And never once did she make a mistake. After a time the Emperor began to resent the lady's flawless memory and decided to stop as soon as he detected any

---

[13] **day of abstinence:** An inauspicious day when it was important to stay inside and abstain from all pleasurable activities.

[14] **a *go* stone:** A small black or white stone marker used in a Chinese boardgame.

error or vagueness in her replies. Yet, after he had gone through ten books of the *Kokin Shū,* he had still not caught her out. At this stage he declared that it would be useless to continue. Marking where he had left off, he went to bed. What a triumph for the lady!

'He slept for some time. On waking, he decided that he must have a final verdict and that if he waited until the following day to examine her on the other ten volumes, she might use the time to refresh her memory. So he would have to settle the matter that very night. Ordering his attendants to bring up the bedroom lamp, he resumed his questions. By the time he had finished all twenty volumes, the night was well advanced; and still the lady had not made a mistake.

'During all this time His Excellency, the lady's father, was in a state of great agitation. As soon as he was informed that the Emperor was testing his daughter, he sent his attendants to various temples to arrange for special recitations of the Scriptures. Then he turned in the direction of the Imperial Palace and spent a long time in prayer. Such enthusiasm for poetry is really rather moving.'

The Emperor, who had been listening to the whole story, was much impressed. 'How can he possibly have read so many poems?' he remarked when Her Majesty had finished. 'I doubt whether I could get through three or four volumes. But of course things have changed. In the old days even people of humble station had a taste for the arts and were interested in elegant pastimes. Such a story would hardly be possible nowadays, would it?'

The ladies in attendance on Her Majesty and the Emperor's own ladies-in-waiting who had been admitted into Her Majesty's presence began chatting eagerly, and as I listened I felt that my cares had really 'melted away.'

WHEN I MAKE MYSELF IMAGINE

When I make myself imagine what it is like to be one of those women who live at home, faithfully serving their husbands—women who have not a single exciting prospect in life yet who believe that they are perfectly happy—I am filled with scorn. Often they are of quite good birth, yet have had no opportunity to find out what the world is like. I wish they could live for a while in our society, even if it should mean taking service as Attendants,[15] so that they might come to know the delights it has to offer.

I cannot bear men who believe that women serving in the Palace are bound to be frivolous and wicked. Yet I suppose their prejudice is understandable. After all, women at Court do not spend their time hiding modestly behind fans and screens, but walk about, looking openly at people they chance to meet. Yes, they see everyone face to face, not only ladies-in-waiting like themselves, but even Their Imperial Majesties (whose august names I hardly dare mention), High Court Nobles, senior courtiers, and other gentlemen of high rank. In the presence of such exalted

---

[15] **Attendants:** Shonagon means palace attendants to the emperor. She is not implying that they have a sexual obligation.

personages the women in the Palace are all equally brazen, whether they be the maids of ladies-in-waiting, or the relations of Court ladies who have come to visit them, or housekeepers, or latrine-cleaners, or women who are of no more value than a roof-tile or a pebble. Small wonder that the young men regard them as immodest! Yet are the gentlemen themselves any less so? They are not exactly bashful when it comes to looking at the great people in the Palace. No, everyone at Court is much the same in this respect.

Women who have served in the Palace, but who later get married and live at home, are called Madam and receive the most respectful treatment. To be sure, people often consider that these women, who have displayed their faces to all and sundry during their years at Court, are lacking in feminine grace. How proud they must be, nevertheless, when they are styled Assistant Attendants, or summoned to the Palace for occasional duty, or ordered to serve as Imperial envoys during the Kamo Festival! Even those who stay at home lose nothing by having served at Court. In fact they make very good wives. For example, if they are married to a provincial governor and their daughter is chosen to take part in the Gosechi dances, they do not have to disgrace themselves by acting like provincials and asking other people about procedure. They themselves are well versed in the formalities, which is just as it should be.

Hateful Things

One is in a hurry to leave, but one's visitor keeps chattering away. If it is someone of no importance, one can get rid of him by saying, 'You must tell me all about it next time'; but, should it be the sort of visitor whose presence commands one's best behaviour, the situation is hateful indeed.

One finds that a hair has got caught in the stone on which one is rubbing one's inkstick, or again that gravel is lodged in the inkstick, making a nasty, grating sound.

Someone has suddenly fallen ill and one summons the exorcist. Since he is not at home, one has to send messengers to look for him. After one has had a long fretful wait, the exorcist finally arrives, and with a sigh of relief one asks him to start his incantations. But perhaps he has been exorcizing too many evil spirits recently; for hardly has he installed himself and begun praying when his voice becomes drowsy. Oh, how hateful!

A man who has nothing in particular to recommend him discusses all sorts of subjects at random as though he knew everything.

An elderly person warms the palms of his hands over a brazier and stretches out the wrinkles. No young man would dream of behaving in such a fashion; old people can really be quite shameless. I have seen some dreary old creatures actually resting their feet on the brazier and rubbing them against the edge while they speak. These are the kind of people who in visiting someone's house first use their fans to wipe away the dust from the mat and, when they finally sit on it, cannot stay still but are forever spreading out the front of their hunting costume or even tucking it up under their knees. One might suppose that such behaviour was restricted to people of humble station; but I have observed it in quite well-bred people, including a Senior

Secretary of the Fifth Rank in the Ministry of Ceremonial and a former Governor of Suruga.

I hate the sight of men in their cups who shout, poke their fingers in their mouths, stroke their beards, and pass on the wine to their neighbours with great cries of 'Have some more! Drink up!' They tremble, shake their heads, twist their faces, and gesticulate like children who are singing, 'We're off to see the Governor.' I have seen really well-bred people behave like this and I find it most distasteful.

To envy others and to complain about one's own lot; to speak badly about people; to be inquisitive about the most trivial matters and to resent and abuse people for not telling one, or, if one does manage to worm out some facts, to inform everyone in the most detailed fashion as if one had known all from the beginning—oh, how hateful!

One is just about to be told some interesting piece of news when a baby starts crying.

A flight of crows circle about with loud caws.

An admirer has come on a clandestine visit, but a dog catches sight of him and starts barking. One feels like killing the beast.

One has been foolish enough to invite a man to spend the night in an unsuitable place—and then he starts snoring.

A gentleman has visited one secretly. Though he is wearing a tall, lacquered hat, he nevertheless wants no one to see him. He is so flurried, in fact, that upon leaving he bangs into something with his hat. Most hateful! It is annoying too when he lifts up the Iyo blind that hangs at the entrance of the room, then lets it fall with a great rattle. If it is a head-blind, things are still worse, for being more solid it makes a terrible noise when it is dropped. There is no excuse for such carelessness. Even a head-blind does not make any noise if one lifts it up gently on entering and leaving the room; the same applies to sliding-doors. If one's movements are rough, even a paper door will bend and resonate when opened; but, if one lifts the door a little while pushing it, there need be no sound.

One has gone to bed and is about to doze off when a mosquito appears, announcing himself in a reedy voice. One can actually feel the wind made by his wings and, slight though it is, one finds it hateful in the extreme.

A carriage passes with a nasty, creaking noise. Annoying to think that the passengers may not even be aware of this! If I am travelling in someone's carriage and I hear it creaking, I dislike not only the noise but also the owner of the carriage.

One is in the middle of a story when someone butts in and tries to show that he is the only clever person in the room. Such a person is hateful, and so, indeed, is anyone, child or adult, who tries to push himself forward.

One is telling a story about old times when someone breaks in with a little detail that he happens to know, implying that one's own version is inaccurate—disgusting behaviour!

Very hateful is a mouse that scurries all over the place.

Some children have called at one's house. One makes a great fuss of them and gives them toys to play with. The children become accustomed to this treatment and start to come regularly, forcing their way into one's inner rooms and scattering one's furnishings and possessions. Hateful!

A certain gentleman whom one does not want to see visits one at home or in the Palace, and one pretends to be asleep. But a maid comes to tell one and shakes one awake, with a look on her face that says, 'What a sleepyhead!' Very hateful.

A newcomer pushes ahead of the other members in a group; with a knowing look, this person starts laying down the law and forcing advice upon everyone — most hateful.

A man with whom one is having an affair keeps singing the praises of some woman he used to know. Even if it is a thing of the past, this can be very annoying. How much more so if he is still seeing the woman! (Yet sometimes I find that it is not as unpleasant as all that.)

A person who recites a spell himself after sneezing. In fact I detest anyone who sneezes, except the master of the house.

Fleas, too, are very hateful. When they dance about under someone's clothes, they really seem to be lifting them up.

The sound of dogs when they bark for a long time in chorus is ominous and hateful.

I cannot stand people who leave without closing the panel behind them. [. . .]

A good lover will behave as elegantly at dawn as at any other time. He drags himself out of bed with a look of dismay on his face. The lady urges him on: 'Come, my friend, it's getting light. You don't want anyone to find you here.' He gives a deep sigh, as if to say that the night has not been nearly long enough and that it is agony to leave. Once up, he does not instantly pull on his trousers. Instead he comes close to the lady and whispers whatever was left unsaid during the night. Even when he is dressed, he still lingers, vaguely pretending to be fastening his sash.

Presently he raises the lattice, and the two lovers stand together by the side door while he tells her how he dreads the coming day, which will keep them apart; then he slips away. The lady watches him go, and this moment of parting will remain among her most charming memories.

Indeed, one's attachment to a man depends largely on the elegance of his leave-taking. When he jumps out of bed, scurries about the room, tightly fastens his trouser-sash, rolls up the sleeves of his Court cloak, over-robe, or hunting costume, stuffs his belongings into the breast of his robe and then briskly secures the outer sash — one really begins to hate him.

It Is So Stiflingly Hot

It is so stiflingly hot in the Seventh Month that even at night one keeps all the doors and lattices open. At such times it is delightful to wake up when the moon is shining and to look outside. I enjoy it even when there is no moon. But to wake up at dawn and see a pale sliver of a moon in the sky — well, I need hardly say how perfect that is.

I like to see a bright new straw mat that has just been spread out on a well-polished floor. The best place for one's three-foot curtain of state is in the front of the room near the veranda. It is pointless to put it in the rear of the room, as it is most unlikely that anyone will peer in from that direction.

It is dawn and a woman is lying in bed after her lover has taken his leave. She is covered up to her head with a light mauve robe that has a lining of dark violet; the colour of both the outside and the lining is fresh and glossy. The woman, who appears to be asleep, wears an unlined orange robe and a dark crimson skirt of stiff silk whose cords hang loosely by her side, as if they have been left untied. Her thick tresses tumble over each other in cascades, and one can imagine how long her hair must be when it falls freely down her back.

Nearby another woman's lover is making his way home in the misty dawn. He is wearing loose violet trousers, an orange hunting costume, so lightly coloured that one can hardly tell whether it has been dyed or not, a white robe of stiff silk, and a scarlet robe of glossy, beaten silk. His clothes, which are damp from the mist, hang loosely about him. From the dishevelment of his side locks one can tell how negligently he must have tucked his hair into his black lacquered head-dress when he got up. He wants to return and write his next-morning letter[16] before the dew on the morning glories has had time to vanish; but the path seems endless, and to divert himself he hums 'the sprouts in the flax fields.'[17]

As he walks along, he passes a house with an open lattice. He is on his way to report for official duty, but cannot help stopping to lift up the blind and peep into the room. It amuses him to think that a man has probably been spending the night here and has only recently got up to leave, just as happened to himself. Perhaps that man too had felt the charm of the dew.

Looking round the room, he notices near the woman's pillow an open fan with a magnolia frame and purple paper; and at the foot of her curtain of state he sees some narrow strips of Michinoku paper and also some other paper of a faded colour, either orange-red or maple.

The woman senses that someone is watching her and, looking up from under her bedclothes, sees a gentleman leaning against the wall by the threshold, a smile on his face. She can tell at once that he is the sort of man with whom she need feel no reserve. All the same, she does not want to enter into any familiar relations with him, and she is annoyed that he should have seen her asleep.

'Well, well, Madam,' says the man, leaning forward so that the upper part of his body comes behind her curtains, 'what a long nap you're having after your morning adieu! You really are a lie-abed!'

'You call me that, Sir,' she replied, 'only because you're annoyed at having had to get up before the dew had time to settle.'

Their conversation may be commonplace, yet I find there is something delightful about the scene.

---

[16] **next-morning letter:** It was proper etiquette for a man to write a love letter to a lady with whom he had spent the night; it usually included a poem and was attached to a spray of some appropriate flower. The letter had to be written as soon as the man returned home or arrived at work. The lady was expected to reply.

[17] **'the sprouts in the flax fields':** From a poem of the period that reassures a lady that her man will not leave her until the dew is gone from the fields. In reality, his duties and their mutual fear of detection might force him to leave sooner, and this was understood by both parties.

Now the gentleman leans further forward and, using his own fan, tries to get hold of the fan by the woman's pillow. Fearing his closeness, she moves further back into her curtain enclosure, her heart pounding. The gentleman picks up the magnolia fan and, while examining it, says in a slightly bitter tone, 'How standoffish you are!'

But now it is growing light; there is a sound of people's voices, and it looks as if the sun will soon be up. Only a short while ago this same man was hurrying home to write his next-morning letter before the mists had time to clear. Alas, how easily his intentions have been forgotten!

While all this is afoot, the woman's original lover has been busy with his own next-morning letter, and now, quite unexpectedly, the messenger arrives at her house. The letter is attached to a spray of clover, still damp with dew, and the paper gives off a delicious aroma of incense. Because of the new visitor, however, the woman's servants cannot deliver it to her.

Finally it becomes unseemly for the gentleman to stay any longer. As he goes, he is amused to think that a similar scene may be taking place in the house he left earlier that morning.

THINGS THAT CANNOT BE COMPARED

Summer and winter. Night and day. Rain and sunshine. Youth and age. A person's laughter and his anger. Black and white. Love and hatred. The little indigo plant and the great philodendron. Rain and mist.

When one has stopped loving somebody, one feels that he has become someone else, even though he is still the same person.

In a garden full of evergreens the crows are all asleep. Then, towards the middle of the night, the crows in one of the trees suddenly wake up in a great flurry and start flapping about. Their unrest spreads to the other trees, and soon all the birds have been startled from their sleep and are cawing in alarm. How different from the same crows in daytime!

EMBARRASSING THINGS

While entertaining a visitor, one hears some servants chatting without any restraint in one of the back rooms. It is embarrassing to know that one's visitor can overhear. But how to stop them?

A man whom one loves gets drunk and keeps repeating himself.

To have spoken about someone not knowing that he could overhear. This is embarrassing even if it be a servant or some other completely insignificant person.

To hear one's servants making merry. This is equally annoying if one is on a journey and staying in cramped quarters or at home and hears the servants in a neighbouring room.

Parents, convinced that their ugly child is adorable, pet him and repeat the things he has said, imitating his voice.

An ignoramus who in the presence of some learned person puts on a knowing air and converses about men of old.

A man recites his own poems (not especially good ones) and tells one about the praise they have received—most embarrassing.

Lying awake at night, one says something to one's companion, who simply goes on sleeping.

In the presence of a skilled musician, someone plays a zither just for his own pleasure and without tuning it.

An adopted son-in-law who has long since stopped visiting his wife runs into his father-in-law in a public place.

WHEN HIS EXCELLENCY,
THE CHANCELLOR, HAD DEPARTED

When His Excellency, the Chancellor, had departed from among us, there was much stir and movement in the world.[18] Her Majesty, who no longer came to the Imperial Palace, lived in the Smaller Palace of the Second Ward. Though I had done nothing to deserve it, things became very difficult for me and I spent a long time at home.[19] One day, when I was particularly concerned about Her Majesty and felt I could not allow our separation to continue, the Captain of the Left Guards Division came to see me. 'I called on Her Majesty today,' he said, 'and found it very moving. Her ladies were dressed as elegantly as ever, with their robes, skirts, and Chinese jackets perfectly matching the season. The blind was open at the side and, when I looked in, I saw a group of about eight ladies, elegantly seated next to each other. They wore Chinese jackets of tawny yellow, light violet skirts, and robes of purple and dark red. Noticing that the grass in the garden outside the palace had been allowed to grow very high and thick, I told them they should have it cut. "We've left it like this on purpose so that we might admire the dew when it settles on the blades." The voice was Lady Saishō's and I found her reply delightful.

'Several of the ladies spoke about you and said it was a shame you were staying at home. "Now that Her Majesty is living in a place like this," they told me, "she feels that Shōnagon should come back into waiting regardless of what business she may have at home. Why won't she return when Her Majesty wants her so much?" I definitely had the impression that they wanted me to pass this on to you. So please go. There's a charm about the place that will stir you deeply. The peonies in front of the terrace have a delightful Chinese air.'

'No,' I replied. 'Since they dislike me so much, I've come to dislike them.'

'You must try to be generous,' he said with a smile.

Shortly afterwards I visited the Empress. I had no way of telling what she thought about it all; but I did hear some of her ladies-in-waiting whisper, 'She is on

---

[18] **much . . . movement in the world:** After the death of Empress Sadako's father, Chancellor Fujiwara no Michitaka, in 995, and the exile of her elder brother, Fujiwara no Korechika, in 996, Fujiwara no Michinaga, the empress's uncle, became the leading political figure in Japan. Michinaga immediately removed Empress Sadako from the Imperial Palace, allegedly forcing her to become a nun.

[19] **a long time at home:** Shonagon, suspected by those close to Empress Sadako of siding with Michinaga, departed the court for a time, embittered and disillusioned.

close terms with people who are attached to the Minister of the Left.' I was coming from my room when I saw them all standing there muttering to each other. Noticing me, they became silent and each of them went about her own business. I was not used to being treated like this and found it most galling. Thereafter Her Majesty summoned me on several occasions, but I paid no attention, and a long time passed without my visiting her. No doubt the ladies-in-waiting made out that I belonged to the enemy camp and told all sorts of lies about me.

One day, when there had been an unaccustomed silence from the Empress and I was sitting at home sunk in gloomy thoughts, a housekeeper brought me a letter. 'Her Majesty ordered that this should be sent to you secretly by Lady Sakyō,' she told me. Yet there could be no reason for such secrecy when I was living at home. Examining the letter, I gathered that it was a personal message from Her Majesty and my heart was pounding as I opened it. There was nothing written on the paper. It had been used to wrap up a single petal of mountain rose, on which I read the words, 'He who does not speak his love.'[20] I was overjoyed; what a relief after the long, anxious days of silence! My eyes filled with 'the things that one knows first of all'.[21] 'The ladies-in-waiting are all wondering why you have stayed away so long,' said the housekeeper, who had been watching me. 'They consider it very strange, especially since you know how much Her Majesty is always thinking of you. Why don't you go?' Then she added, 'I have a short errand near by. I'll be back for your answer presently.'

But as I prepared to write my answer, I realized that I had completely forgotten the next line of the poem. 'Amazing!' I muttered. 'How can one possibly forget an old poem like that? I know it perfectly well and yet it just won't come.' Hearing this, a small page-boy who happened to be in the room said, " 'Yet feels its waters seething underneath"—those are the words, Madam.' Of course! How on earth could they have slipped my mind? To think that I should have to be taught by a mere child!

Shortly after sending my reply, I visited the Empress. Not knowing how she would receive me, I felt unusually nervous and remained half hidden behind a curtain of state. 'Are you a newcomer here?' asked Her Majesty with a laugh. 'I am afraid it was not much of a poem,' she went on, 'but I felt it was the sort of thing I should write. When I do not see you, Shōnagon, I am wretched all the time.'

Her Majesty had not changed. When I told her about the page-boy who had reminded me of the missing words, she was most amused. 'That's just the sort of thing that can happen,' she said, laughing, 'especially with old poems that one considers too familiar to take seriously.' [. . .]

---

[20] **'He who does not speak his love':** The text of the poem is:

> He who does not speak his love
> Yet feels its waters seething underneath
> Loves more than he who prates his every thought.

The empress is professing her love, pleading with Shonagon to return to court.

[21] **'the things that one knows first of all':** A figure of speech meaning "tears," from a poem in the *Kokinshu*.

WHEN A WOMAN LIVES ALONE

When a woman lives alone, her house should be extremely dilapidated, the mud wall should be falling to pieces, and if there is a pond, it should be overgrown with water-plants. It is not essential that the garden be covered with sage-brush; but weeds should be growing through the sand in patches, for this gives the place a poignantly desolate look.

I greatly dislike a woman's house when it is clear that she has scurried about with a knowing look on her face, arranging everything just as it should be, and when the gate is kept tightly shut.

WHEN A COURT LADY IS ON LEAVE

When a Court lady is on leave from the Palace, it is pleasant if she can stay with her parents. While she is there, people are always coming and going, there is a lot of noisy conversation in the back rooms, and the clatter of horses' hoofs resounds outside. Yet she is in no danger of being criticized.

Things are very different if she is staying in someone else's house. Let us suppose that a man comes to visit the lady, either openly or in secret. He stands by the front gate and says to her, 'I did not know you were at home, else I should certainly have called on you before. When will you return to Court?' If it is a man she has set her heart on, the lady cannot possibly leave him standing outside and she opens the front door for him.

Then, to her great annoyance, she hears the owner of the house, who has evidently decided that there is too much noise and that it is dangerous to leave the door unbolted so late at night. 'Has the outer gate been closed?' he asks the porter. 'No, Sir,' says the latter in a disgruntled tone. 'There's still a visitor in the house.' 'Well, be sure to close it as soon as he's left. There have been a lot of burglaries recently.' This is especially irking for the lady since the man who is with her can hear everything. Meanwhile the servants are constantly peeping in to see whether the guest is getting ready to leave — much to the amusement of the attendants who have accompanied him on his visit. Then the attendants start imitating the owner's voice. Oh, what a scolding there would be if he heard them!

Sometimes the lady will receive visits from a man who does not show any tender feelings for her in either his looks or his words. Presumably he must care for her; else why would he continue his visits night after night? Nevertheless the man may turn out to be quite heartless and will leave her saying, 'It's really getting late. And I suppose it *is* rather dangerous to keep the gate open at this hour.'

One can tell if a man really loves one, because he will insist on staying all night however much one may urge him to leave. Time after time the night watchman has made his rounds, and now he exclaims in a very audible voice, 'Good heavens! The dawn has come' (as if that were so surprising) 'and someone's gone and left the gate wide open all night. Such carelessness!' Then he securely bolts the gate, though it is now light and there is no need for such precautions. How unpleasant it all is!

Yes, things are a great deal better when one is staying with one's own parents. Parents-in-law, however, are the most awkward of all, since one is always worrying about what they are going to think. I imagine that it must also be difficult to stay with an elder brother.

What I really like is a house where no one cares about the gate either in the middle of the night or at dawn, and where one is free to meet one's visitor, whether he be an Imperial Prince or a gentleman from the Palace. In the winter one can stay awake together all night with the lattices wide open. When the time comes for him to leave, one has the pleasure of watching him playing upon his flute as he goes; if a bright moon is still hanging in the sky, it is a particular delight. After he has disappeared, one does not go to bed at once, but stays up, discussing the visitor with one's companions, and exchanging poems; then gradually one falls asleep.

It Is Delightful When There Has Been a Thin Fall of Snow

It is delightful when there has been a thin fall of snow; or again when it has piled up very high and in the evening we sit round a brazier at the edge of the veranda with a few congenial friends, chatting till darkness falls. There is no need for the lamp, since the snow itself reflects a clear light. Raking the ashes in the brazier with a pair of fire-tongs, we discuss all sorts of moving and amusing things.

It already seems to be quite late at night when we hear the sound of footsteps. We all look up, wondering who it may be. A man is approaching—the type of man that often visits us unannounced on such occasions. 'I was wondering how you ladies were enjoying today's snow,' he says. 'I had intended to come and see you earlier, but I was held up all day in some other place.'

'Ah!' says one of us and quotes the poem about 'the man who came today.'[22] Then, with a great deal of laughter, we begin talking about what has happened since the morning and about all sorts of other things. The visitor has been offered a round cushion, but he prefers to sit on the wooden veranda with one leg hanging over the edge.

The conversation goes on until the bell announces that dawn has come. The ladies sitting behind the blinds and the man in front feel that they still have many things to tell each other; but he has to be off before daylight. As he gets ready to leave, he charmingly recites, 'Snow lay upon such-and-such hills.' Then he is gone. If he had not been there, we should certainly not have stayed up all night like this; it was he who made the occasion so delightful, and now we start discussing what an elegant man he is.

---

[22] 'the man who came today': The whole poem reads:

> Here in my mountain home
> The snow is deep
> And the paths are buried [in white].
> Truly would he move my heart—
> The man who came today.

WHEN I FIRST WENT INTO WAITING

When I first went into waiting at Her Majesty's Court, so many different things embarrassed me that I could not even reckon them up and I was always on the verge of tears. As a result I tried to avoid appearing before the Empress except at night, and even then I stayed hidden behind a three-foot curtain of state.

On one occasion Her Majesty brought out some pictures and showed them to me, but I was so ill at ease that I could hardly stretch out my hand to take them. She pointed to one picture after another, explaining what each represented. Since the lamp had been put on a high stand, one could view the pictures even better than in the daytime, and every hair of the woman in one of them was clearly visible. I managed to control my embarrassment and had a proper look. It was a very cold time of the year and when Her Majesty gave me the paintings I could hardly see her hands; but, from what I made out, they were of a light pink hue that I found extraordinarily attractive. I gazed at the Empress with amazement. Simple as I was and unaccustomed to such wonderful sights, I did not understand how a being like this could possibly exist in our world.

At dawn I was about to hurry back to my room when Her Majesty said, 'Even the God of Kazuraki would stay a little longer.' So I sat down again, but I leant forward sideways in such a way that Her Majesty could not see me directly, and kept the lattice shut. One of the ladies who came into the room noticed this and said that it should be opened. A servant heard her and started towards it, but Her Majesty said, 'Wait. Leave the lattice as it is.' The two women went out, laughing to each other.

Her Majesty then asked me various questions and finally said, 'I am sure you want to return to your room. So off you go! But be sure to come again this evening—and early too.'

As soon as I had crept out of Her Majesty's presence and was back in my room, I threw open all the lattices and looked out at the magnificent snow.

During the day I received several notes from Her Majesty telling me to come while it was still light. 'The sky is clouded with snow,' she wrote, 'and no one will be able to see you clearly.'

Noticing my hesitation, the lady in charge of my room urged me, saying, 'I don't know how you can stay shut up like this all day long. Her Majesty has granted you the extraordinary good fortune of being admitted into her presence, and she must certainly have her reasons. To be unresponsive to another person's kindness is a most hateful way to behave.' This was enough to make me hurry back to the Empress; but I was overcome with embarrassment, and it was not easy for me.

On my way I was delighted to see the snow beautifully piled on top of the fire huts. When I entered Her Majesty's room, I noticed that the usual square brazier was full to the brim with burning charcoal and that no one was sitting next to it. The Empress herself was seated in front of a round brazier made of Shen wood and decorated with pear-skin lacquer. She was surrounded by a group of high-ranking ladies who were in constant attendance upon her. In the next part of the room a tightly packed row of ladies-in-waiting sat in front of a long, rectangular brazier, with their Chinese jackets worn in such a way that they trailed on the floor. Observing how experienced they were in their duties and how easily they carried them out, I could not help feeling envious. There was not a trace of awkwardness in any of their movements as they got up to deliver notes to Her Majesty from the outside and sat down again by the brazier, talking and laughing to each other. When would I ever be able to manage like that, I wondered nervously. Still further in the back of the room sat a small group of ladies who were looking at pictures together.

After a while I heard the voices of outrunners loudly ordering people to make way. 'His Excellency, the Chancellor, is coming,' said one of the ladies, and they all cleared away their scattered belongings. I retired to the back of the room; but despite my modesty, I was curious to see the great man in person and I peeped through a crack at the bottom of the curtain of state where I was sitting. It turned out that it was not Michitaka, but his son, Korechika, the Major Counsellor. The purple of his Court cloak and trousers looked magnificent against the white snow. 'I should not have come,' he said, standing next to one of the pillars, 'because both yesterday and today are days of abstinence. But it has been snowing so hard that I felt bound to call and find out whether all was well with you.'

'How did you manage?' said Her Majesty. 'I thought that all the paths were buried.'

'Well,' replied Korechika, 'it occurred to me that I might move your heart.'

Could anything surpass this conversation between the Empress and her brother? This was the sort of exchange that is so eloquently described in romances; and the Empress herself, arrayed in a white dress, a robe of white Chinese damask, and two more layers of scarlet damask over which her hair hung down loosely at the back, had a beauty that I had seen in paintings but never in real life: it was all like a dream.

Korechika joked with the ladies-in-waiting, and they replied without the slightest embarrassment, freely arguing with him and contradicting his remarks when they disagreed. I was absolutely dazzled by it all and found myself blushing without any particular reason. Korechika ate a few fruits and told one of the servants to offer some to the Empress. He must have asked who was behind the curtain of state and one of the ladies must have told him that it was I; for he stood up and walked to the back of the room. At first I thought he was leaving, but instead he came and sat very close to me; he began to talk about various things he had heard about me before I came into waiting and asked whether they were true. I had been embarrassed enough when I had been looking at him from a distance with the curtain of state between us; now that we were actually facing each other I felt extremely stupid and could hardly believe that this was really happening to me.

In the past, when I had gone to watch Imperial Processions and the like, Korechika had sometimes glanced in the direction of my carriage; but I had always pulled the inner blinds close together, and hidden my face behind a fan for fear that he might see my silhouette through the blinds. I wondered how I could ever have chosen to embark on a career for which I was so ill-suited by nature. What on earth should I say to him? I was bathed in sweat and altogether in a terrible state. To make matters worse, Korechika now seized the fan behind which I had prudently hidden myself, and I realized that my hair must be scattered all over my forehead in a terrible mess; no doubt everything about my appearance bespoke the embarrassment I felt at that moment.

I had hoped Korechika would leave quickly, but he showed no sign of doing so; instead he sat there, toying with my fan and asking who had done the paintings on it. I kept my head lowered and pressed the sleeve of my Chinese jacket to my face — so tightly indeed, that bits of powder must have stuck to it, making my complexion all mottled.

The Empress, who no doubt realized how desperately I wanted Korechika to leave, turned to him and said, 'Look at this notebook. Whose writing do you suppose it is?' I was relieved to think that now he would finally go; but instead he asked her to have the book brought to him so that he could examine it. 'Really,' she said. 'You can perfectly well come here yourself and have a look.' 'No I can't,' he replied. 'Shonagon has got hold of me and won't let go.' It was a very fashionable sort of joke but hardly suited to my rank or age, and I felt terribly ill at ease. Her Majesty held up the book, in which something had been written in a cursive script, and looked at it. 'Well indeed,' said Korechika, 'whose can it be? Let's show it to Shonagon. I am sure she can recognize the handwriting of anyone in the world.' The aim of all these absurd remarks, of course, was to draw me out.

As if a single gentleman were not enough to embarrass me, another one now arrived, preceded by outrunners who cleared the way for him. This gentleman too was wearing a Court cloak, and he looked even more splendid than Korechika. He sat down and started telling some amusing stories, which delighted the ladies-in-waiting. 'Oh yes,' they said, laughing, 'we saw Lord So-and-so when he was——.' As I heard them mention the names of one senior courtier after another, I felt they must be talking about spirits or heavenly beings who had descended to earth. Yet, after some time had passed and I had grown accustomed to Court service, I realized that there had been nothing very impressive about their conversation. No doubt these same ladies, who talked so casually to Lord Korechika, had been just as embarrassed as I when they first came into waiting, but had little by little become used to Court society until their shyness had naturally disappeared.

The Empress spoke to me for a while and then asked, 'Are you really fond of me?' 'But Your Majesty,' I replied, 'how could I possibly not be fond of you?' Just then someone sneezed loudly in the Table Room. 'Oh dear!' said the Empress. 'So you're telling a lie. Well, so be it.' And she retired into the back of the room.[23]

To think that Her Majesty believed I was lying! If I had said that I was *fairly* fond of her, that would have been untrue. The real liar, I thought, was the sneezer's nose. Who could have done such a terrible thing? I dislike sneezes at the best of times, and whenever I feel like sneezing myself I deliberately smother it. All the more hateful was it that someone should have sneezed at this moment. But I was still far too inexperienced to say anything that might have repaired the damage; and, since the day was dawning, I retired to my room. As soon as I arrived, a servant brought me an

---

[23] **And she retired . . . room:** There was a Japanese superstition that a sneeze signified someone was lying.

elegant-looking letter, written on fine, smooth paper of light green. 'This is what Her Majesty feels,' I read.

> How, if there were no God Tadasu in the sky,
> And none to judge what is the truth and what a lie,
> How should I know which words were falsely said?

My emotions were a jumble of delight and dismay, and once again I wished I could find out who had sneezed on the previous night. 'Please give Her Majesty the following reply,' I said, 'and help me to make up for the harm that has been done.

> "A simple sneeze might give the lie
> To one whose love is small,
> But sad indeed that she who truly loves,
> Should suffer from so slight a thing!

The curse of God Shiki is of course very terrible.' "[24]

Even after I had sent my reply I still felt most unhappy and wondered why someone should have had to sneeze at such an inopportune moment.

Wind Instruments

I love the sound of the flute: it is beautiful when one hears it gradually approaching from the distance, and also when it is played nearby and then moves far away until it becomes very faint.

There is nothing so charming as a man who always carries a flute when he goes out on horseback or on foot. Though he keeps the flute tucked in his robe and one cannot actually see it, one enjoys knowing it is there.

I particularly like hearing familiar tunes played on a flute. It is also very pleasant at dawn to find that a flute has been left next to one's pillow by a gentleman who has been visiting one; presently he sends a messenger to fetch the instrument and, when one gives it to him carefully wrapped up, it looks like an elegant next-morning letter.

A thirteen-pipe flute is delightful when one hears it in a carriage on a bright, moonlit night. True, it is bulky and rather awkward to play—and what a face people make when they blow it! But they can look ungraceful with ordinary flutes also.

The flageolet is a very shrill instrument, the autumn insect it most resembles being the long cricket. It makes a terrible noise, especially when it is played badly, and it is not something one wants to hear nearby. I remember one of the Special Festivals at Kamo, when the musicians had not yet come into His Majesty's presence. One could hear the sound of their flutes from behind the trees, and I was just thinking how delightful it was when suddenly the flageolets joined in. They became shriller and shriller, until all the ladies, even those who were most beautifully

---

[24] **'The curse of gold Shiki . . . terrible':** Shiki was the name of a demon invoked by magicians to put a curse on someone. Shonagon implies that the ill-timed sneeze was due to a power of this kind.

groomed, felt their hair standing on end.[25] Then the procession came before the Emperor with all the string and wind instruments playing in splendid unison.

SHORTLY AFTER THE TWENTIETH OF THE NINTH MONTH

Shortly after the twentieth of the Ninth Month I went on a pilgrimage to Hase Temple and spent the night in a very simple lodging. Being exhausted, I fell at once into a sound sleep.

When I woke up late at night, the moonlight was pouring in through the window and shining on the bed-clothes of all the other people in the room. Its clear white brilliance moved me greatly. It is on such occasions that people write poems.

PLEASING THINGS

Finding a large number of tales that one has not read before. Or acquiring the second volume of a tale whose first volume one has enjoyed. But often it is a disappointment.

Someone has torn up a letter and thrown it away. Picking up the pieces, one finds that many of them can be fitted together.

One has had an upsetting dream and wonders what it can mean. In great anxiety one consults a dream-interpreter, who informs one that it has no special significance.

A person of quality is holding forth about something in the past or about a recent event that is being widely discussed. Several people are gathered round him, but it is oneself that he keeps looking at as he talks.

A person who is very dear to one has fallen ill. One is miserably worried about him even if he lives in the capital and far more so if he is in some remote part of the country. What a pleasure to be told that he has recovered!

I am most pleased when I hear someone I love being praised or being mentioned approvingly by an important person.

A poem that someone has composed for a special occasion or written to another person in reply is widely praised and copied by people in their notebooks. Though this is something that has never yet happened to me, I can imagine how pleasing it must be.

A person with whom one is not especially intimate refers to an old poem or story that is unfamiliar. Then one hears it being mentioned by someone else and one has the pleasure of recognizing it. Still later, when one comes across it in a book, one thinks, 'Ah, this is it!' and feels delighted with the person who first brought it up.

I feel very pleased when I have acquired some Michinoku paper, or some white, decorated paper, or even plain paper if it is nice and white.

---

[25] **hair standing on end:** In Heian times, people's hair was said to stand on end when they were deeply impressed by something.

A person in whose company one feels awkward asks one to supply the opening or closing line of a poem. If one happens to recall it, one is very pleased. Yet often on such occasions one completely forgets something that one would normally know.

I look for an object that I need at once, and I find it. Or again, there is a book that I must see immediately; I turn everything upside down, and there it is. What a joy!

When one is competing in an object match (it does not matter what kind), how can one help being pleased at winning?

I greatly enjoy taking in someone who is pleased with himself and who has a self-confident look, especially if he is a man. It is amusing to observe him as he alertly waits for my next repartee; but it is also interesting if he tries to put me off my guard by adopting an air of calm indifference as if there were not a thought in his head.

I realize that it is very sinful of me, but I cannot help being pleased when someone I dislike has a bad experience.

It is a great pleasure when the ornamental comb that one has ordered turns out to be pretty.

I am more pleased when something nice happens to a person I love than when it happens to myself.

Entering the Empress's room and finding that ladies-in-waiting are crowded round her in a tight group, I go next to a pillar which is some distance from where she is sitting. What a delight it is when Her Majesty summons me to her side so that all the others have to make way!

Times When One Should Be on One's Guard

When one meets people who have a bad reputation. Such people often give a more sincere impression than those of good repute.

When one travels by boat. I remember one such excursion. It was a beautiful clear day and the sea was so calm that its surface looked like a sheet of light green, glossy silk. I was travelling with a group of young women, and none of us had the slightest sense of danger. Dressed in our short jackets, we helped the boatmen at the oars, singing song after song as we rowed. It was a most delightful trip, and I only wished that someone of high rank were there to see us gliding across the water.

Then all of a sudden a violent wind blew up and the sea became terribly rough. We were beside ourselves with fear. As we rowed back to the shore, the waves leapt over the boat, and I could not believe that this was the same sea that a little while ago had been so smooth.

When one thinks of it, sailors are the bravest people in the world. Even in reasonably shallow water their vessels are far too flimsy to be safe. Yet they do not hesitate to embark on a sea of any depth—perhaps even a thousand fathoms—entrusting their lives to a boat so heavily loaded that the water comes up almost to the edge. The common people who man the boat run up and down, never giving a thought to the danger; and, though it looks as if the slightest rocking would capsize it, one sees them banging down into the hold half a dozen great pine logs two or three feet in circumference. Amazing!

People of quality travel in boats with cabins. These, of course, seem far safer, especially if one is in the rear; but if one is near the side one gets very dizzy. The ropes that keep the oars in place — the 'fast cords' as they are called — look extraordinarily weak. What if one of them were to snap? Surely the rower would be plunged into the sea. Yet I have never seen anyone using heavy ropes.

I remember one journey on such a boat. We had a charming cabin, fitted with head-blinds, double doors, and lattices. Though the boat did not seem quite as sturdy as most of its kind, I felt as if I were in a snug little house. But when I looked out and saw the other boats, I was really frightened. Those in the distance looked as frail as bamboo leaves that have been made into toy boats and scattered across the water. When we finally returned to the harbour, lights were shining in all the boats, which was a delightful sight. On the following morning I was very moved to observe people rowing out to sea in those tiny vessels known as sampans; as they moved slowly into the distance, the white waves behind the boats did in fact 'disappear without a trace.'[26]

When all is said and done, only common people should go in boats. There are dangers enough when one travels by land, but then at least one has the firm ground under one's feet and that is a great comfort.

The sea is a frightening thing at the best of times. How much more terrifying must it be for those poor women divers who have to plunge into its depths for their livelihood! One wonders what would happen to them if the cord round their waist were to break. I can imagine men doing this sort of work, but for a woman it must take remarkable courage. After the woman has been lowered into the water, the men sit comfortably in their boats, heartily singing songs as they keep an eye on the mulberry-bark cord that floats on the surface. It is an amazing sight, for they do not show the slightest concern about the risks the woman is taking. When finally she wants to come up, she gives a tug on her cord and the men haul her out of the water with a speed that I can well understand. Soon she is clinging to the side of the boat, her breath coming in painful gasps. The sight is enough to make even an outsider feel the brine dripping. I can hardly imagine this is a job that anyone would covet.

IT IS GETTING SO DARK

It is getting so dark that I can scarcely go on writing; and my brush is all worn out. Yet I should like to add a few things before I end.

I wrote these notes at home, when I had a good deal of time to myself and thought no one would notice what I was doing. Everything that I have seen and felt

---

[26] **'disappear without a trace':** Shonagon is referring to a poem by the priest Mansei, from the *Man'yoshu*:

This world of ours —
To what shall I compare it?
To the white waves behind a boat
That disappear without a trace
As it rows away at dawn.

is included. Since much of it might appear malicious and even harmful to other people, I was careful to keep my book hidden. But now it has become public, which is the last thing I expected.

One day Lord Korechika, the Minister of the Centre, brought the Empress a bundle of notebooks. 'What shall we do with them?' Her Majesty asked me. 'The Emperor has already made arrangements for copying the "Records of the Historian".'

'Let me make them into a pillow,' I said.

'Very well,' said Her Majesty. 'You may have them.'

I now had a vast quantity of paper at my disposal, and I set about filling the notebooks with odd facts, stories from the past, and all sorts of other things, often including the most trivial material. On the whole I concentrated on things and people that I found charming and splendid; my notes are also full of poems and observations on trees and plants, birds and insects. I was sure that when people saw my book they would say, 'It's even worse than I expected. Now one can really tell what she is like.' After all, it is written entirely for my own amusement and I put things down exactly as they came to me. How could my casual jottings possibly bear comparison with the many impressive books that exist in our time? Readers have declared, however, that I can be proud of my work. This has surprised me greatly; yet I suppose it is not so strange that people should like it, for, as will be gathered from these notes of mine, I am the sort of person who approves of what others abhor and detests the things they like.

Whatever people may think of my book, I still regret that it ever came to light.

❧ MURASAKI SHIKIBU, LADY MURASAKI
C. 973–C. 1030

GEN-jee

The Tale of Genji (*Genji Monogatari*) (c. 1022), often considered Japan's greatest classic and a masterpiece of prose fiction, has been called the world's first psychological novel, remarkable for its subtle and dramatic evocation of character as well as its complex and elegant style. All Japanese recognize Genji, much as English readers know King Arthur and Sir Lancelot,[1] or Indian readers are familiar with Prince Rama.[2] Indeed, throughout the nearly one thousand years since *The Tale of Genji* first appeared, literary echoes and images of Lady Murasaki and the shining prince Genji have appeared in later novels and poems as well as on screen paintings and porcelains. Moreover, the story of **Genji** has been retold in

---

[1] **King Arthur and Sir Lancelot:** The heroes of the Arthurian legends and romances.

[2] **Prince Rama:** The hero of the great Indian epic the *Ramayana,* composed and revised from about 550 B.C.E. to 400 C.E.

countless forms, from *Nō* plays and the Japanese puppet theater known as Bunraku to short stories and film. In the early twentieth century, Yosamo Akiko (1878–1942) made the original *Tale of Genji* accessible to modern Japanese readers in her full translation completed in 1914. Other modern translations followed, including those by the great fiction writers Tanazaki Junichiro (1886–1964) and Enchi Fumiko (1905–1986), and most recently by contemporary writer and Buddhist nun Setouchi Jakucho (b. 1922). As *Genji*'s earliest translator into English noted, even European readers may recognize Lady Murasaki from the familiar motif in Japanese art of a woman seated at a writing desk, pen in hand, with the moon reflected on a lake in the background.

www   For links to more information about Lady Murasaki and quizzes on *The Tale of Genji*, see *World Literature Online* at bedfordstmartins .com/worldlit.

Early Life and Education.   Murasaki Shikibu is a nickname, derived from her father's title "Shikibu," meaning Bureau of Ceremony, and the name of her novel's main female character Murasaki. Murasaki Shikibu was destined for a life at court, for her father, Fujiwara no Tametoki, was a minor court official and a member of a branch of the ruling Fujiwara clan. She was born around 973 in the capital city of Heian (now Kyoto). Like that of many European women before the nineteenth century, Murasaki's education focused on abilities thought to increase a woman's value in men's eyes, skills such as fine handwriting, the rote memorization of classical poetry, and playing the *koto* and *biwa,* both stringed instruments. Like some of her European counterparts, Lady Murasaki managed to acquire a broader education, in part by eavesdropping on her brother's Chinese lessons. By her own account she excelled at Chinese, more so than her brother, but propriety led her to conceal her proficiency. Because Japanese women ordinarily did not receive training in writing Chinese characters—the official literary language, excellence in which earned men distinction and rank—women wrote in Japanese characters called KANA, which expressed the language as it was spoken. The great NIKKI (diaries) and MONOGATARI (tales)[3] written by Heian[4] women thus established a native literary tradition.

When she was in her early twenties, Lady Murasaki experienced two tragedies: the death of her older sister, with whom she was close, and the death of her husband of only two years, Fujiwara Nobutaka. After briefly joining her father, who had accepted a governorship in the northern province of Echizen, Lady Murasaki returned with her only child to

---

[3] *nikki . . . monogatari*: *Nikki* refers to an important genre of Japanese literature, the prose diary, which flourished among women writers in the Heian period; these diaries were written primarily in *kana*, the woman's form of writing, which formed the basis of the vernacular literary tradition in Japan and, like *The Tale of Genji*, contained poetic passages in the form of *waka*. *Monogatari*, loosely translated as "tale" or "telling of things," refers to fiction; as in the case of *nikki*, *monogatari* were written in *kana* and often contained poetic passages in the form of *waka*. *The Tale of Genji* is perhaps the greatest example of the *monogatari* in Japanese literature.

[4] **Heian:** From the Heian era (794–1185), a period in Japan dating from the removal of the imperial family from the old capital of Nara to Heian, or what is now Kyoto. It was a time dominated by the powerful Fujiwara family, and while court intrigue and rivalry were not uncommon, it was mostly a time of peace, prosperity, and isolation, characterized by refinement of manners and a flourishing of the arts.

**Lady Murasaki,
seventeenth or
eighteenth century**
*The famous author
of the classic* Tale of
Genji *is shown here
quietly reading. (The
Art Archive/Private
Collection, Paris/
Dagli Orti)*

Heian, where she began writing *The Tale of Genji*. At the capital she served as attendant to Empress Akiko Shoshi, whose residence at the imperial palace gave the writer firsthand experience of the complex rivalries and the sometimes comic, other times tragic, consequences of her mistress's naivete and strict standards of moral conduct. Critics have noted many parallels between Murasaki's recorded accounts of her years with Shoshi in *Murasaki Shikibu Nikki* (*Lady Murasaki's Diary*) and the incidents that occur in *The Tale of Genji*. With Shoshi, Lady Murasaki was able to put her extraordinary knowledge of Chinese to good use, for the princess wanted to learn the language, forbidden to women under Confucian tenets that relegated women to a low level of the intellectual hierarchy.

Although the court, including the emperor, apparently admired *The Tale of Genji*, Lady Murasaki noted in her diary that after hearing some passages of her tale the emperor announced that "this lady has been reading the *Annals of Japan*," giving rise to rumors that she prided herself on her learning and earning her the nickname, "Dame Annals." Little is known of Lady Murasaki's life after 1010, the year her *Diary* ends. *The Tale of Genji* was completed by 1022, and a Lady Murasaki participated in ceremonies at the birth of the Emperor Go-Ryozen in 1025. It is thought that Lady Murasaki died around 1030.

Refinement and Taste.   During the Heian era (794–1186), when Lady Murasaki lived, the Japanese aristocracy fostered a way of life characterized by elegance, luxury, and refinement. The aristocracy itself was divided into three groups, at the center of which was the imperial court at Heian (Kyoto), the "City of Peace." The "cloud dwellers" of the court lived in virtual exclusion from members of the lower aristocracy, the provincial governors, and the ordinary people of Japan. Their life was governed by a complex system of distinctions that involved intricate attention to detail and style in everything from performing ceremonies, such as the Chrysanthemum Festival,[5] to composing highly elevated and conventional poems (*WAKA*)[6] in Chinese. Dominated by the ruling Fujiwara clan, the court nobles cultivated a refined set of manners and ritual practices in accordance with the courtly tradition known as *MIYABI*.[7] An aesthetic sensibility permeated the speech, dress, and deportment of these courtiers, who transformed the business of governance into a subtle art of indirection and suggestion. This "rule of taste," as one historian of the era has called it, laid the groundwork for much of the subtlety found in later Japanese culture.

As in so much of court life, what was emphasized in romantic affairs — especially in *The Tale of Genji* — was not sexual conquest but a sensibility that stems from what the Japanese call *mono no aware*, a delicate but profound feeling for, and nuanced sensitivity to, things in the world. Lady Murasaki's novel masterfully evokes this complex feeling, which is often most fully realized at moments of untimely death or when tragic circumstances heighten the melancholy in Genji's romantic tale.

The Tale of Genji.   This work is a poetic study of the psychology of longing and love among elite members of the court in medieval Japan; it is also an extended meditation on the passing of time, the mutability of life, and the inevitability of disappointment and death. Tragic in tone and

> *The Tale of Genji* presents us with the emotional state of people who are aware that they live only once: "Life is not long, but make the most of it even if only one or two days remain." What is expressed here is human mortality — but also eternity caught in "one or two days."
>
> – SHUICHI KATO, critic, 1997

---

[5] **Chrysanthemum Festival:** The *Choyo no sekku* was one of the five sacred *gosekku* festivals of ancient Japan, held to honor the gods at the change of the seasons. Held in autumn, the Chrysanthemum Festival celebrates health and longevity, stemming from the belief that flowers have the power to prolong life and preserve youth.

[6] *waka:* A traditional form of Japanese poetry based on Chinese models and consisting of five lines a total of thirty-one syllables following a strict pattern (5-7-5-7-7). Writing *waka* was an important activity among the Heian aristocracy; it was a vehicle for the expression of refined feelings as well as a regular means of communicating messages of all kinds. Excellence at composing *waka* was a sign of accomplishment and refined sensibility.

[7] *miyabi:* A term denoting the concept of refined beauty; *miyabi* became a way of life in the court culture of the Heian period (794–1186 C.E.), governing taste, manners, and the arts.

The Tale of Genji is not only the quintessence of the aristocratic culture of Heian Japan, but has affected the aesthetic and emotional life of the entire Japanese people for a millennium.

– DONALD KEENE, critic, 1999

plot, the novel views the lives of its characters from a Buddhist perspective, which holds that one's fate in the present is tied to actions performed in the past (the doctrine of *KARMA*)[8]. In its insistence on the fleeting, even illusory nature of human existence, as well as the impurity or disorder of human relationships, the novel suggests that happiness must be found elsewhere, in the Pure Land beyond the cycle of death and rebirth, which one attains through right practices and through the grace of Buddha. Yet *The Tale of Genji* contains some of the most moving and sensitive depictions of nature in all of world literature, its characters' moods associated with such intricate details of the natural world as the subtle fragrance of a particular flower or a perfumed robe, the array of colors in the sky at sunset, the slant of moonlight in a passageway on a cold night, or the sound of raindrops gently troubling the surface of a pool. Murasaki, like many Japanese artists, pays great attention to the seasons, reflecting the natural cycle of change and the impermanence of things.

The fifty-four chapters of *The Tale of Genji* consist of a series of overlapping episodes centered primarily on the romantic adventures of the eponymous hero, Genji, the "shining one," the son of the emperor and his wife, Kiritsubo, an aristocratic woman of low rank. Covering a period of seventy-five years and involving hundreds of characters, the story of Genji's quest divides into two main parts, beginning with his birth and following his life to his death at the age of fifty-two; these are followed by a story that begins nine years after Genji's death and focuses on the lives of Niou, Genji's grandson, and Kaoru, Genji's nominal son, really the son of his wife, Nyosan, known as the Third Princess, and her lover, Kashiwagi.

Genji in Love.   Recent scholarship identifies three major parts to *Genji*. The first, chapters 1 through 33, recounts Genji's complicated succession of marriages and romances up to age thirty-nine. The precocious and charmingly handsome son of the emperor, the "shining" Genji is kept in subordinate positions at court because of a prophecy warning that disaster would befall the state should he take the throne. Genji enjoys great popularity within aristocratic circles, and his beauty and elegance draw many women to him, including his father's new consort, Lady Fujitsubo, a woman who resembles his mother, who died when Genji was only three. After his marriage to Aoi, with whom he has a son named Yugiri, Genji finds himself more attracted to Lady Fujitsubo than to his new wife. In the meantime, Genji enters into romantic affairs with several other women, including the lower-class Evening Faces (**Yugao**) and the proud and jealous Lady **Rokujo**. Even as Genji pursues these various love interests, his passion for Fujitsubo remains strong, and eventually Fuji-

yoo-GOW
ROH-koo-joh

---

[8] *karma:* In the Buddhism of Lady Murasaki's time, *karma* was a doctrine of moral causation within a scheme of reincarnation. According to *karma*, which means "action" in Sanskrit, actions are linked in a moral chain of cause and effect. Acts in a previous life can affect action as well as one's very being in the present, and present actions can shape events and one's being in future lives; one can escape the cycle of death and rebirth by attaining *nirvana*, liberation from incarnation.

tsubo bears Genji a son, who is thought to be the emperor's. After the emperor's death, the remorseful and guilt-ridden Fujitsubo renounces court life and takes vows as a Buddhist nun, a direction that other of Genji's lovers will take as well: Of the ten major female characters with whom Genji becomes involved, five become nuns, two die at a young age, and three manage to go on with their lives. Thus, *The Tale of Genji* presents the reader with its protagonist's many love affairs, all tinged with transgression and sadness, romantic impossibility, and unhappy consequences.

After the birth of his son by Fujitsubo, Genji eventually becomes involved with other women, including Oborozukiyo, Murasaki (Fujitsubo's niece whom he marries as a second wife), and the Lady of Akashi. His affair with Oborozukiyo, the sister of his mother's former rival Kokiden, leads to his being exiled from the court for eight years, during which time he meets the Lady of Akashi with whom he has a daughter. After Genji's return to court, his son by Fujitsubo succeeds to the throne as Emperor Reizei, under whom Genji serves as a minister. When Reizei learns that Genji is really his father, he is inspired by filial piety to give him the throne. Genji dissuades his son from abdicating and receives royal favors. Now prospering, Genji builds the Rokujo Palace, where he is joined by, among others, the Lady of Akashi and his favorite love, Murasaki, who receives the most prestigious quarters. Now in his midthirties, Genji finally seems to have found peace, though he now falls in love anew with Tamakazura. In "Fireflies," the third chapter presented in the following *Genji* selections, Genji manipulates events so that Prince Hotaru, his brother, will fall in love with Tamakazura. This chapter contains the famous passage in which Genji and Tamakazura discuss the value of reading romances, which many critics see as Lady Murasaki's justification for her art.

Although Genji's many romances and marriages may bring to mind the European Don Juan, we must remember that polygamy was an accepted, even essential, practice among the aristocracy in Lady Murasaki's time. A wealthy nobleman with only one or two wives might be subject to reproach from his peers or thought to be antisocial or indelicate for not having more. It was common for aristocratic men to have a primary wife and two or three secondary wives. While early marriages, such as Genji's to the Princess Aoi, often were arranged for political purposes, later marriages by mutual consent were for love. Moreover, as seen in *The Pillow Book* by Lady Murasaki's contemporary Sei Shonagon[9] (c. 966–1017), amorous affairs at court were commonplace, despite the era's Confucianist restrictions. Thus, having many lovers was not frowned on for men, though, as seen in *Genji* and *The Pillow Book,* this tacit acceptance did not prevent sometimes extreme jealousy and rivalry among both men and women.

> *The Tale of Genji* does not dwell on [Genji's] iniquitous and immoral acts, but rather recites over and over again his awareness of the sorrow of existence, and represents him as a good man who combines in himself all good things in men.
>
> – MOTOORI NORINAGA, eighteenth century, poet and scholar

---

[9] **Sei Shonagon** (c. 966–1017): Like Lady Murasaki, Sei Shonagon was a lady-in-waiting at the Heian court; Shonagon is the author of *The Pillow Book (Makura Soshi),* a series of short prose pieces on aristocratic life written with great poetic sensitivity. (See p. 1063.)

Disappointment and Death.   The second major part of the novel begins with chapter 34, New Herbs: Part 1. At forty years old, Genji agrees somewhat reluctantly to marry Nyosan, the Third Princess, the daughter of retired emperor Suzaku. Genji's fortunes take a turn for the worse from then on, and the mood of the novel as a whole becomes progressively more somber. Murasaki, for whom he has developed an even greater affection and respect, takes ill because of her jealousy of Genji's new wife. Taking advantage of Genji's preoccupation with the failing Murasaki, Kashiwagi, the son of Genji's friend **To no Chujo**, seduces the Third Princess, who eventually gives birth to a son, Kaoru. Kaoru, the hero of the third part of the novel, generally is thought to be Genji's. While Genji, mindful of his own past adulterous affair with Lady Fujitsubo, remains resigned to the news, Kashiwagi dies from shame, and the Third Princess renounces the world to become a nun; shortly after, Murasaki dies. Finally, the grief-stricken Genji also renounces the world, disposes of his property, and goes away to die.

toh-noh-CHOO-joh

The final twelve chapters focus on the life of Kaoru, whose story begins eight years after Genji's death, which is never described. Though Kaoru's adventures in some ways mirror Genji's own, this illegitimate son lacks the taste, refinement, and chivalry of his supposed father. Some critics see this third section as a sign that Lady Murasaki had come to believe that her society was in decline, that the era of fine taste and cultivation embodied in Genji, "the shining one," was a thing of the past. Thus, the great novel ends on a note of nostalgia, added to the feelings of sadness and regret already invoked throughout the story.

As Earl Miner has suggested, Genji's heroism derives from his "artistic command of life." He is much closer to the unrequited knights of European courtly romances, whose code of conduct and display of honor count more to their credit, than he is to such heroes as Achilles, Beowulf, and Bhima,[10] who earn their glory in physical combat. Genji does not engage in martial competition, nor does he act in accordance with any doctrine of chivalry. That kind of hero would arise in the next generation of Japanese literature, in works such as *The Tale of the Heike*, which celebrates the heroic deeds of the Heike[11] clan in the age of the SAMURAI.

p. 1148

While only a reading of the complete novel allows one to appreciate fully the richness and complexity of this great novel, the episodic structure of *The Tale of Genji* enables the reader to appreciate its poetic style and the complexity of its characters even in a few chapters. The chapters we have selected here demonstrate the way the novel anticipates events and characters and circles back to previous incidents, as Genji seeks the ideal woman. "The Broom Tree" sets the tone of the novel and in the famous discussion about the various types of women anticipates many

---

[10] **Achilles . . . Bhima:** Warrior heroes of the Greek epic *The Iliad,* by Homer; the Anglo-Saxon epic *Beowulf;* and the Indian epic *Ramayana,* attributed to Valmiki.

[11] **Heike:** Heike is another name for the Taira clan, who waged war against the Minamotos. One of the great heroic tales of early Japan, *The Tale of the Heike* (1371) chronicles the rise and fall of the Taira family in the twelfth century and the war with the Minamoto clan, also known as the Genji, fought between 1180 and 1185 C.E.

of the women Genji will encounter in his amours. "Evening Faces" captures the subtlety of Genji's romantic dealings, the intensity of his passion, and the hapless fate of some of his heroines. It characterizes too the tone of sadness and regret that ensues when misfortune befalls one of Genji's ill-fated lovers. In tandem with "Fireflies," "Evening Faces" also shows how earlier events and relationships are entangled with later ones, as Genji falls in love with the young Tamakazura, the daughter of Yugao and Genji's best friend, brother-in-law, and sometime rival To no Chujo. In the fine translation by Edward G. Seidensticker, these chapters amply show Lady Murasaki's poetic sensitivity to nature and her superb skill in evoking character.

■ **CONNECTIONS**

The *Man'yoshu*, p. 1018; The *Kokinshu*, p. 1044. Reading and composing poetry, as seen in *The Tale of Genji*, was an important aspect of court life in medieval Japan. As the mixture of poetry and prose in that novel demonstrates, Lady Murasaki was herself an accomplished poet as well as prose stylist, and her poems, which deepen the significance of events and often enhance the atmosphere or sustain a particular tone of a scene, are integral to the novel. Compare Lady Murasaki's poetry with that in the *Man'yoshu* and the *Kokinshu*. How does Murasaki draw on motifs and themes from earlier poetry and to what effect?

Andreas Capellanus, *The Art of Courtly Love*, p. 617; *In the Tradition*: The Courtly Love Lyrics of Muslim Spain and the South of France, p. 628. The courtly love traditions of the Middle Period vary according to the attitudes toward love, marriage, sexuality, and gender relations in Europe, Japan, and the Islamic world at the time. Compare Capellanus's ideal view of love with that in *The Tale of Genji*. Despite the obvious differences, what similarities are there between the two?

Cao Xueqin, *The Story of the Stone* (Book 4). Throughout their rich cultural histories, Japan and China have enjoyed an active and reciprocal exchange of ideas, styles, and literary forms. Cao Xueqin's *The Story of the Stone* presents the story of an amorous hero, Li Bao-yu, who in many ways resembles Genji. Cao Xueqin's novel also is infused with the sense of mutability found in *The Tale of Genji*, in part stemming from the Buddhist thought that informs both novels. What is historically and culturally distinctive about each of these works?

■ **FURTHER RESEARCH**

Biography
Bowring, Richard. *Murasaki Shikibu: Her Diary and Poetic Memoirs*. 1982.

Background/History
Kato, Shuichi. *A History of Japanese Literature: From the* Man'yoshu *to Modern Times*. 1997.
Keene, Donald. *Seeds in the Heart: Japanese Literature from the Earliest Times to the Late Sixteenth Century*. 1993, 1999.
Morris, Ivan. *The World of the Shining Prince*. 1964. Reprint, 1994.

Criticism
Bowring, Richard. *The Tale of Genji*. 1988.
Field, Norma. *The Splendor of Longing in* The Tale of Genji. 1987.
Miner, Earl. "The Heroine: Identity, Recurrence, Destiny." In *Ukifune: Love in* The Tale of Genji, ed. by Andrew Pekarik. 1982.
Shirane, Haruo. *The Bridge of Dreams: A Poetics of* The Tale of Genji. 1987.

■ **PRONUNCIATION**

To no Chujo: toh-noh-CHOO-joh
Genji: GEN-jee
Kiyomizu: kee-yoh-MEE-zoo
Koremitsu: koh-reh-MIT-soo
Nijo: NEE-joh
Rokujo: ROH-koo-joh
Ukon: OO-kone
Yugao: yoo-GOW

 # The Tale of Genji

Translated by Edward G. Seidensticker

[Chapter 1, "The Paulownia Court" (*Kiritsubo*), tells of the circumstances of Genji's birth to Kiritsubo, a low-ranking wife of the emperor. Subjected to the jealousy and ridicule of the emperor's higher-ranking consorts, particularly the jealous Kokiden, Genji's mother dies when Genji is just three years old. The emperor dotes on his beautiful and precocious son, and eventually invites a new lady, Fujitsubo, who bears a striking resemblance to Genji's mother, to be his new consort. But when it is predicted that should Genji ascend the throne, disaster would befall the court, the emperor assigns his son to commoner's status, giving him the name Genji.

The Tale of Genji.   According to Lady Murasaki's diary, a draft of at least part of her masterwork was completed in 1008. The manuscript circulated among friends and members of the court. Written in a difficult and archaic form of Japanese, the original novel, like *Beowulf* for readers of English, is inaccessible without special training. Several modern translations, however, do exist in Japanese and in English as well as in other languages. The translation used here, by Edward G. Seidensticker, offers a clear and poetic rendering of the novel in English.

Three interlinked chapters have been selected to represent the work as a whole. Chapter 2, "The Broom Tree," introduces the romantic theme of the novel with its famous discussion between Genji and his friends about various types of women — the jealous, the coy, the overly learned, the flirtatious, and the poor lover. The young men then describe the perfect woman — refined, deferent, and loyal — which becomes the ideal Genji sets out to find over the course of his life. In chapter 4, "Evening Faces," Genji embarks on a romantic but tragic affair with one of the women described in "The Broom Tree" — the lover of To no Chujo. In chapter 4, the seventeen-year-old prince, accompanied by his loyal servant, Koremitsu, goes to see Genji's old nurse. While visiting the dying nursemaid, Genji is attracted to a beautiful visitor in the neighbor's house. Genji calls this woman Evening Faces, or Yugao, after the white flowers of the yugao; like those flowers, she is "hapless" but beautiful, somewhat out of place in the shabby surroundings of the neighborhood. The gift of a suggestive poem on a scented fan that ultimately leads to the meeting of Genji and Yugao captures the spirit of the elaborate indirection on which Lady Murasaki's culture prided itself. Although the mysterious young woman ranks far beneath Genji socially, the amorous prince determines to meet her and eventually wins her affection. As he begins this brief affair with Yugao, the spirit of Lady Rokujo, a jilted lover, haunts him and appears to take the life of his new love.

When Genji turns twelve, he is married to Aoi, four years his senior and the daughter of a powerful official, the Minister of the Left. Neither Genji nor his new bride are especially enamored of each other, and Genji finds himself drawn to his father's new consort Fujitsubo. Because of his beauty, his taste, and his fine sensibility, Genji comes to be called *Hikaru*, "the shining one."

In chapter 2, "The Broom Tree," which follows, Genji and his friends gather at the palace, where they find themselves discussing the relative merits of different types of relationships with various kinds of women. The next day Genji sets out to visit Aoi but is detained at the house of the governor of Kii, who is the son of the vice-governor of Iyo, now married to Utsusemi, the Lady of the Locust Shell. Here Genji makes a secret visit to the bedroom of the governor's wife.]

CHAPTER 2

The Broom Tree

"The shining Genji": it was almost too grand a name. Yet he did not escape criticism for numerous little adventures. It seemed indeed that his indiscretions might give him a name for frivolity, and he did what he could to hide them. But his most secret affairs (such is the malicious work of the gossips) became common talk. If, on the other hand, he were to go through life concerned only for his name and avoid all these interesting and amusing little affairs, then he would be laughed to shame by the likes of the lieutenant of Katano.[1]

Murasaki's interest is really in Genji's response to the young woman's death, which he sees as the consequence of some action in a previous life. This instance of the doctrine of *karma* and Genji's allusion to an afterlife among the "highest summits of the Pure Land" allude to the Tendai Buddhism that permeates the religious dimensions of the novel. A complex and syncretic system, Tendai Buddhism teaches that all things of this world are fleeting, that human beings are caught up in a cycle of death and reincarnation from which, through right practice and the grace of Amida Buddha, they can escape into a land of purity and bliss. In the "Evening Faces" chapter, Genji begins to grasp the transience and fragility of life and reflects on the promise of a life beyond; his tragic, if problematic, response to death demonstrates both his aesthetic sensibility and his deep feeling. The chapter suggests that the joy of love — especially secret love, as here — like life, mixes melancholy with its joy, and is given only to be taken away.

In the last chapter presented here, "Fireflies," Genji, now thirty-six, finds himself involved in the life of Yugao's daughter by To no Chujo, Tamakazura. Tamakazura resembles her mother just as Murasaki resembled Fujitsubo, and just as Fujitsubo resembled Genji's mother, Kiritsubo. Not surprisingly, Genji falls in love with the twenty-one-year-old girl, who spurns his amorous advances, giving Genji occasion to reconsider his proper relation to her. To keep up the appearance of paternal duty toward Tamakazura, Genji resolves to marry her to one of three suitors, including his brother, Prince Hotaru. This chapter also contains Lady Murasaki's famous discussion of the value and importance of fiction.

A note on the translation: We are using the highly regarded translation by Edward G. Seiden-sticker, first published by Alfred A. Knopf in 1976 and now by the Charles E. Tuttle Company. The notes, unless otherwise indicated, are adapted from the translator's notes.

---

[1] **Katano:** Likely the hero of a romance that has been lost.

Still a guards captain, Genji spent most of his time at the palace, going infrequently to the Sanjō mansion of his father-in-law. The people there feared that he might have been stained by the lavender of Kasugano.[2] Though in fact he had an instinctive dislike for the promiscuity he saw all around him, he had a way of sometimes turning against his own better inclinations and causing unhappiness.

The summer rains came, the court was in retreat, and an even longer interval than usual had passed since his last visit to Sanjō. Though the minister and his family were much put out, they spared no effort to make him feel welcome. The minister's sons were more attentive than to the emperor himself. Genji was on particularly good terms with Tō no Chūjō.[3] They enjoyed music together and more frivolous diversions as well. Tō no Chūjō was of an amorous nature and not at all comfortable in the apartments which his father-in-law, the Minister of the Right,[4] had at great expense provided for him. At Sanjō with his own family, on the other hand, he took very good care of his rooms, and when Genji came and went the two of them were always together. They were a good match for each other in study and at play. Reserve quite disappeared between them.

It had been raining all day. There were fewer courtiers than usual in the royal presence. Back in his own palace quarters, also unusually quiet, Genji pulled a lamp near and sought to while away the time with his books. He had Tō no Chūjō with him. Numerous pieces of colored paper, obviously letters, lay on a shelf. Tō no Chūjō made no attempt to hide his curiosity.

"Well," said Genji, "there are some I might let you see. But there are some I think it better not to."

"You miss the point. The ones I want to see are precisely the ones you want to hide. The ordinary ones—I'm not much of a hand at the game, you know, but even I am up to the ordinary give and take. But the ones from ladies who think you are not doing right by them, who sit alone through an evening and wait for you to come—those are the ones I want to see."

It was not likely that really delicate letters would be left scattered on a shelf, and it may be assumed that the papers treated so carelessly were the less important ones.

"You do have a variety of them," said Tō no Chūjō, reading the correspondence through piece by piece. This will be from her, and this will be from *her,* he would say. Sometimes he guessed correctly and sometimes he was far afield, to Genji's great amusement. Genji was brief with his replies and let out no secrets.

"It is I who should be asking to see *your* collection. No doubt it is huge. When I have seen it I shall be happy to throw my files open to you."

"I fear there is nothing that would interest you." Tō no Chūjō was in a contemplative mood. "It is with women as it is with everything else: the flawless ones are

---

[2] **lavender of Kasugano:** This is one of many allusions in the novel to previous tales, in this case *Tales of Ise,* which contains the following poem: "Kasugano lavender stains my robe, / In deep disorder, like my secret loves." In Japanese, the word for lavender is *murasaki,* a term associated throughout the novel with positive feelings of connection or affinity.

[3] **Tō no Chūjō:** Genji's best friend and sometime rival; brother of Genji's wife, Lady Aoi.

[4] **Minister of the Right:** A high-ranking officer in the imperial court, fifth in rank from the emperor.

very few indeed. This is a sad fact which I have learned over the years. All manner of women seem presentable enough at first. Little notes, replies to this and that, they all suggest sensibility and cultivation. But when you begin sorting out the really superior ones you find that there are not many who have to be on your list. Each has her little tricks and she makes the most of them, getting in her slights at rivals, so broad sometimes that you almost have to blush. Hidden away by loving parents who build brilliant futures for them, they let word get out of this little talent and that little accomplishment and you are all in a stir. They are young and pretty and amiable and carefree, and in their boredom they begin to pick up a little from their elders, and in the natural course of things they begin to concentrate on one particular hobby and make something of it. A woman tells you all about it and hides the weak points and brings out the strong ones as if they were everything, and you can't very well call her a liar. So you begin keeping company, and it is always the same. The fact is not up to the advance notices."

Tō no Chūjō sighed, a sigh clearly based on experience. Some of what he had said, though not all, accorded with Genji's own experience. "And have you come upon any," said Genji, smiling, "who would seem to have nothing at all to recommend them?"

"Who would be fool enough to notice such a woman? And in any case, I should imagine that women with no merits are as rare as women with no faults. If a woman is of good family and well taken care of, then the things she is less than proud of are hidden and she gets by well enough. When you come to the middle ranks, each woman has her own little inclinations and there are thousands of ways to separate one from another. And when you come to the lowest — well, who really pays much attention?"

He appeared to know everything. Genji was by now deeply interested.

"You speak of three ranks," he said, "but is it so easy to make the division? There are well-born ladies who fall in the world and there are people of no background who rise to the higher ranks and build themselves fine houses as if intended for them all along. How would you fit such people into your system?"

At this point two young courtiers, a guards officer and a functionary in the ministry of rites, appeared on the scene, to attend the emperor in his retreat. Both were devotees of the way of love and both were good talkers. Tō no Chūjō, as if he had been waiting for them, invited their views on the question that had just been asked. The discussion progressed, and included a number of rather unconvincing points.

"Those who have just arrived at high position," said one of the newcomers, "do not attract the same sort of notice as those who were born to it. And those who were born to the highest rank but somehow do not have the right backing — in spirit they may be as proud and noble as ever, but they cannot hide their deficiencies. And so I think that they should both be put in your middle rank.

"There are those whose families are not quite of the highest rank but who go off and work hard in the provinces. They have their place in the world, though there are all sorts of little differences among them. Some of them would belong on anyone's list. So it is these days. Myself, I would take a woman from a middling family over one who has rank and nothing else. Let us say someone whose father is almost but not quite a councillor. Someone who has a decent enough reputation and comes from a decent enough family and can live in some luxury. Such people can be very pleasant. There is nothing wrong with the household arrangements, and indeed a daughter can sometimes be set out in a way that dazzles you. I can think of several such women it would be hard to find fault with. When they go into court service, they are the ones the unexpected favors have a way of falling on. I have seen cases enough of it, I can tell you."

Genji smiled. "And so a person should limit himself to girls with money?"

"That does not sound like you," said Tō no Chūjō.

"When a woman has the highest rank and a spotless reputation," continued the other, "but something has gone wrong with her upbringing, something is wrong in the way she puts herself forward, you wonder how it can possibly have been allowed to happen. But when all the conditions are right and the girl herself is pretty enough, she is taken for granted. There is no cause for the least surprise. Such ladies are beyond the likes of me, and so I leave them where they are, the highest of the high. There are surprisingly pretty ladies wasting away behind tangles of weeds, and hardly anyone even knows of their existence. The first surprise is hard to forget. There she is, a girl with a fat, sloppy old father and boorish brothers and a house that seems common at best. Off in the women's rooms is a proud lady who has acquired bits and snatches of this and that. You get wind of them, however small the accomplishments may be, and they take hold of your imagination. She is not the equal of the one who has everything, of course, but she has her charm. She is not easy to pass by."

He looked at his companion, the young man from the ministry of rites. The latter was silent, wondering if the reference might be to his sisters, just then coming into their own as subjects for conversation. Genji, it would seem, was thinking that on the highest levels there were sadly few ladies to bestow much thought upon. He was wearing several soft white singlets with an informal court robe thrown loosely over them. As he sat in the lamplight leaning against an armrest, his companions almost wished that he were a woman. Even the "highest of the high" might seem an inadequate match for him.

They talked on, of the varieties of women.

"A man sees women, all manner of them, who seem beyond reproach," said the guards officer, "but when it comes to picking the wife who must be everything, matters are not simple. The emperor has trouble, after all, finding the minister who has all the qualifications. A man may be very wise, but no man can govern by himself. Superior is helped by subordinate, subordinate defers to superior, and so affairs proceed by agreement and concession. But when it comes to choosing the woman who is to be in charge of your house, the qualifications are altogether too many. A merit is balanced by a defect, there is this good point and that bad point, and even women who though not perfect can be made to do are not easy to find. I would not like to have you think me a profligate who has to try them all. But it is a question of the woman who must be everything, and it seems best, other things being equal, to find someone who does not require shaping and training, someone who has most of the qualifications from the start. The man who begins his search with all this in mind must be reconciled to searching for a very long time.

"He comes upon a woman not completely and in every way to his liking but he makes certain promises and finds her hard to give up. The world praises him for his honest heart and begins to note good points in the woman too; and why not? But I have seen them all, and I doubt that there are any genuinely superior specimens among them. What about you gentlemen so far above us? How is it with you when you set out to choose your ladies?

"There are those who are young enough and pretty enough and who take care of themselves as if no particle of dust were allowed to fall upon them. When they write letters they choose the most inoffensive words, and the ink is so faint a man can scarcely read them. He goes to visit, hoping for a real answer. She keeps him waiting and finally lets him have a word or two in an almost inaudible whisper. They are clever, I can tell you, at hiding their defects.

"The soft, feminine ones are likely to assume a great deal. The man seeks to please, and the result is that the woman is presently looking elsewhere. That is the first difficulty in a woman.

"In the most important matter, the matter of running his household, a man can find that his wife has too much sensibility, an elegant word and device for every occasion. But what of the too domestic sort, the wife who bustles around the house the whole day long, her hair tucked up behind her ears, no attention to her appearance, making sure that everything is in order? There are things on his mind, things he has seen and heard in his comings and goings, the private and public demeanor of his colleagues, happy things and sad things. Is he to talk of them to an outsider? Of course not. He would much prefer someone near at hand, someone who will immediately understand. A smile passes over his face, tears well up. Or some event at court has angered him, things are too much for him. What good is it to talk to such a woman? He turns his back on her, and smiles, and sighs, and murmurs something to himself. 'I beg your pardon?' she says, finally noticing. Her blank expression is hardly what he is looking for.

"When a man picks a gentle, childlike wife, he of course must see to training her and making up for her inadequacies. Even if at times she seems a bit unsteady, he may feel that his efforts have not been wasted. When she is there beside him her gentle charm makes him forget her defects. But when he is away and sends asking her to perform various services, it becomes clear, however small the service, that she has no thoughts of her own in the matter. Her uselessness can be trying.

"I wonder if a woman who is a bit chilly and unfeeling cannot at times seem preferable."

His manner said that he had known them all; and he sighed at his inability to hand down a firm decision.

"No, let us not worry too much about rank and beauty. Let us be satisfied if a woman is not too demanding and eccentric. It is best to settle on a quiet, steady girl. If she proves to have unusual talent and discrimination — well, count them an unexpected premium. Do not, on the other hand, worry too much about remedying her defects. If she seems steady and not given to tantrums, then the charms will emerge of their own accord.

"There are those who display a womanly reticence to the world, as if they had never heard of complaining. They seem utterly calm. And then when their thoughts are too much for them they leave behind the most horrendous notes, the most flamboyant poems, the sort of keepsakes certain to call up dreadful memories, and off they go into the mountains or to some remote seashore. When I was a child I would hear the women reading romantic stories, and I would join them in their sniffling and think it all very sad, all very profound and moving. Now I am afraid that it suggests certain pretenses.

"It is very stupid really, to run off and leave a perfectly kind and sympathetic man. He may have been guilty of some minor dereliction, but to run off with no understanding at all of his true feelings, with no purpose other than to attract attention and hope to upset him—it is an unpleasant sort of memory to have to live with. She gets drunk with admiration for herself and there she is, a nun. When she enters her convent she is sure that she has found enlightenment and has no regrets for the vulgar world.

"Her women come to see her. 'How very touching,' they say. 'How brave of you.'

"But she no longer feels quite as pleased with herself. The man, who has not lost his affection for her, hears of what has happened and weeps, and certain of her old attendants pass this intelligence on to her. 'He is a man of great feeling, you see. What a pity that it should have come to this.' The woman can only brush aside her newly cropped hair to reveal a face on the edge of tears. She tries to hold them back and cannot, such are her regrets for the life she has left behind; and the Buddha is not likely to think her one who has cleansed her heart of passion. Probably she is in more danger of brimstone now in this fragile vocation than if she had stayed with us in our sullied world.

"The bond between husband and wife is a strong one. Suppose the man had hunted her out and brought her back. The memory of her acts would still be there, and inevitably, sooner or later, it would be cause for rancor. When there are crises, incidents, a woman should try to overlook them, for better or for worse, and make the bond into something durable. The wounds will remain, with the woman and with the man, when there are crises such as I have described. It is very foolish for a woman to let a little dalliance upset her so much that she shows her resentment openly. He has his adventures—but if he has fond memories of their early days together, his and hers, she may be sure that she matters. A commotion means the end of everything. She should be quiet and generous, and when something comes up that quite properly arouses her resentment she should make it known by delicate hints. The man will feel guilty and with tactful guidance he will mend his ways. Too much lenience can make a woman seem charmingly docile and trusting, but it can also make her seem somewhat wanting in substance. We have had instances enough of boats abandoned to the winds and waves. Do you not agree?"

Tō no Chūjō nodded. "It may be difficult when someone you are especially fond of, someone beautiful and charming, has been guilty of an indiscretion, but magnanimity produces wonders. They may not always work, but generosity and reasonableness and patience do on the whole seem best."

His own sister was a case in point, he was thinking, and he was somewhat annoyed to note that Genji was silent because he had fallen asleep. Meanwhile the young guards officer talked on, a dedicated student of his subject. Tō no Chūjō was determined to hear him out.

"Let us make some comparisons," said the guardsman. "Let us think of the cabinetmaker. He shapes pieces as he feels like shaping them. They may be only playthings, with no real plan or pattern. They may all the same have a certain style for what they are—they may take on a certain novelty as times change and be very interesting. But when it comes to the genuine object, something of such undeniable value that a man wants to have it always with him—the perfection of the form announces that it is from the hand of a master.

"Or let us look at painting. There are any number of masters in the academy. It is not easy to separate the good from the bad among those who work on the basic sketches. But let color be added. The painter of things no one ever sees, of paradises, of fish in angry seas, raging beasts in foreign lands, devils and demons—the painter abandons himself to his fancies and paints to terrify and astonish. What does it matter if the results seem somewhat remote from real life? It is not so with the things we know, mountains, streams, houses near and like our own. The soft, unspoiled, wooded hills must be painted layer on layer, the details added gently, quietly, to give a sense of affectionate familiarity. And the foreground too, the garden inside the walls, the arrangement of the stones and grasses and waters. It is here that the master has his own power. There are details a lesser painter cannot imitate.

"Or let us look at calligraphy. A man without any great skill can stretch out this line and that in the cursive style and give an appearance of boldness and distinction. The man who has mastered the principles and writes with concentration may, on the other hand, have none of the eyecatching tricks; but when you take the trouble to compare the two the real thing is the real thing.

"So it is with trivialities like painting and calligraphy. How much more so with matters of the heart! I put no trust in the showy sort of affection that is quick to come forth when a suitable occasion presents itself. Let me tell you of something that happened to me a long time ago. You may find the story a touch wanton, but hear me through all the same."

He drew close to Genji, who awoke from his slumber. Tō no Chūjō, chin in hand, sat opposite, listening with the greatest admiration and attention. There was in the young man's manner something slightly comical, as if he were a sage expostulating upon the deepest truths of the universe, but at such times a young man is not inclined to conceal his most intimate secrets.

"It happened when I was very young, hardly more than a page. I was attracted to a woman. She was of a sort I have mentioned before, not the most beautiful in the world. In my youthful frivolity, I did not at first think of making her my wife. She was someone to visit, not someone who deserved my full attention. Other places interested me more. She was violently jealous. If only she could be a little more understanding, I thought, wanting to be away from the interminable quarreling. And on the other hand it sometimes struck me as a little sad that she should be so worried about a man of so little account as myself. In the course of time I began to mend my ways.

"For my sake, she would try to do things for which her talent and nature did not suit her, and she was determined not to seem inferior even in matters for which she had no great aptitude. She served me diligently in everything. She did not want to be guilty of the smallest thing that might go against my wishes. I had at first thought her rather strong-willed, but she proved to be docile and pliant. She thought constantly about hiding her less favorable qualities, afraid that they might put me off, and she did what she could to avoid displaying herself and causing me embarrassment. She was a model of devotion. In a word, there was nothing wrong with her — save the one thing I found so trying.

"I told myself that she was devoted to the point of fear, and that if I led her to think I might be giving her up she might be a little less suspicious and given to nagging. I had had almost all I could stand. If she really wanted to be with me and I suggested that a break was near, then she might reform. I behaved with studied coldness, and when, as always, her resentment exploded, I said to her: 'Not even the strongest bond between husband and wife can stand an unlimited amount of this sort of thing. It will eventually break, and he will not see her again. If you want to bring matters to such a pass, then go on doubting me as you have. If you would like to be with me for the years that lie ahead of us, then bear the trials as they come, difficult though they may be, and think them the way of the world. If you manage to overcome your jealousy, my affection is certain to grow. It seems likely that I will move ahead into an office of some distinction, and you will go with me and have no one you need think of as a rival.' I was very pleased with myself. I had performed brilliantly as a preceptor.

"But she only smiled. 'Oh, it won't be all that much trouble to put up with your want of consequence and wait till you are important. It will be much harder to pass the months and the years in the barely discernible hope that you will settle down and mend your fickle ways. Maybe you are right. Maybe this is the time to part.'

"I was furious, and I said so, and she answered in kind. Then, suddenly, she took my hand and bit my finger.

"I reproved her somewhat extravagantly. 'You insult me, and now you have wounded me. Do you think I can go to court like this? I am, as you say, a person of no consequence, and now, mutilated as I am, what is to help me get ahead in the world? There is nothing left for me but to become a monk.' That meeting must be our last, I said, and departed, flexing my wounded finger.

"'I count them over, the many things between us.
One finger does not, alas, count the sum of your failures.'

"I left the verse behind, adding that now she had nothing to complain about.
"She had a verse of her own. There were tears in her eyes.

"'I have counted them up myself, be assured, my failures.
For one bitten finger must all be bitten away?'

"I did not really mean to leave her, but my days were occupied in wanderings here and there, and I sent her no message. Then, late one evening toward the end of the year—it was an evening of rehearsals for the Kamo festival—a sleet was falling as we all started for home. Home. It came to me that I really had nowhere to go but her house. It would be no pleasure to sleep alone at the palace, and if I visited a woman of sensibility I would be kept freezing while she admired the snow. I would go look in upon *her,* and see what sort of mood she might be in. And so, brushing away the sleet, I made my way to her house. I felt just a little shy, but told myself that the sleet melting from my coat should melt her resentment. There was a dim light turned toward the wall, and a comfortable old robe of thick silk lay spread out to warm. The curtains were raised, everything suggested that she was waiting for me. I felt that I had done rather well.

"But she was nowhere in sight. She had gone that evening to stay with her parents, said the women who had been left behind. I had been feeling somewhat unhappy that she had maintained such a chilly silence, sending no amorous poems or queries. I wondered, though not very seriously, whether her shrillness and her jealousy might not have been intended for the precise purpose of disposing of me; but now I found clothes laid out with more attention to color and pattern than usual, exactly as she knew I liked them. She was seeing to my needs even now that I had apparently discarded her.

"And so, despite this strange state of affairs, I was convinced that she did not mean to do without me. I continued to send messages, and she neither protested nor gave an impression of wanting to annoy me by staying out of sight, and in her answers she was always careful not to anger or hurt me. Yet she went on saying that she could not forgive the behavior I had been guilty of in the past. If I would settle down she would be very happy to keep company with me. Sure that we would not part, I thought I would give her another lesson or two. I told her I had no intention of reforming, and made a great show of independence. She was sad, I gathered, and then without warning she died. And the game I had been playing came to seem rather inappropriate.

"She was a woman of such accomplishments that I could leave everything to her. I continue to regret what I had done. I could discuss trivial things with her and important things. For her skills in dyeing she might have been compared to Princess Tatsuta and the comparison would not have seemed ridiculous, and in sewing she could have held her own with Princess Tanabata."[5]

The young man sighed and sighed again.

Tō no Chūjō nodded. "Leaving her accomplishments as a seamstress aside, I should imagine you were looking for someone as faithful as Princess Tanabata. And if she could embroider like Princess Tatsuta, well, it does not seem likely that you will come on her equal again. When the colors of a robe do not match the seasons, the flowers of spring and the autumn tints, when they are somehow vague and muddy,

---

[5] **Tatsuta . . . Tanabata:** Princesses Tatsuta and Tanabata were goddesses of autumn and patrons of dyeing, weaving, and sewing. Tanabata met her lover, the Herdsman (the stars Altair and Vega), annually on the seventh of the Seventh Month, hence Tō no Chūjō's remark about her fidelity, which follows.

then the whole effort is as futile as the dew. So it is with women. It is not easy in this world to find a perfect wife. We are all pursuing the ideal and failing to find it."

The guards officer talked on. "There was another one. I was seeing her at about the same time. She was more amiable than the one I have just described to you. Everything about her told of refinement. Her poems, her handwriting when she dashed off a letter, the koto[6] she plucked a note on—everything seemed right. She was clever with her hands and clever with words. And her looks were adequate. The jealous woman's house had come to seem the place I could really call mine, and I went in secret to the other woman from time to time and became very fond of her. The jealous one died, I wondered what to do next. I was sad, of course, but a man cannot go on being sad forever. I visited the other more often. But there was something a little too aggressive, a little too sensuous about her. As I came to know her well and to think her a not very dependable sort, I called less often. And I learned that I was not her only secret visitor.

"One bright moonlit autumn night I chanced to leave court with a friend. He got in with me as I started for my father's. He was much concerned, he said, about a house where he was sure someone would be waiting. It happened to be on my way.

"Through gaps in a neglected wall I could see the moon shining on a pond. It seemed a pity not to linger a moment at a spot where the moon seemed so much at home, and so I climbed out after my friend. It would appear that this was not his first visit. He proceeded briskly to the veranda and took a seat near the gate and looked up at the moon for a time. The chrysanthemums were at their best, very slightly touched by the frost, and the red leaves were beautiful in the autumn wind. He took out a flute and played a tune on it, and sang 'The Well of Asuka'[7] and several other songs. Blending nicely with the flute came the mellow tones of a Japanese koto.[8] It had been tuned in advance, apparently, and was waiting. The *ritsu* scale[9] had a pleasant modern sound to it, right for a soft, womanly touch from behind blinds, and right for the clear moonlight too. I can assure you that the effect was not at all unpleasant.

"Delighted, my friend went up to the blinds.

"'I see that no one has yet broken a path through your fallen leaves,' he said, somewhat sarcastically. He broke off a chrysanthemum and pushed it under the blinds.

"'Uncommonly fine this house, for moon, for koto.
Does it bring to itself indifferent callers as well?

---

[6] **koto:** A stringed instrument similar to a zither with thirteen silk strings, originating in China. Genji plays a seven-stringed version of the instrument. Mastery of the koto was considered a sign of high refinement, and playing it in *The Tale of Genji* serves as a means for lovers to communicate their feelings; individuals could be recognized by the stylistic signature of the playing.

[7] **'The Well of Asuka':** A type of folk song known as the *Saibara:* "It is good to rest beside the well of Asuka./ Deep the shade, cool the water, sweet the grasses."

[8] **Japanese koto:** A variety of the koto (see note 6) with six strings, sometimes called the *yamata koto* or the *azuma koto,* known as an instrument that facilitated creative improvisation.

[9] *ritsu* **scale:** A pentatonic scale, or a scale of five notes, similar to the Western minor scale but without half steps.

"'Excuse me for asking. You must not be parsimonious with your music. You have a by no means indifferent listener.'

"He was very playful indeed. The woman's voice, when she offered a verse of her own, was suggestive and equally playful.

> "'No match the leaves for the angry winter winds.
> Am I to detain the flute that joins those winds?'

"Naturally unaware of resentment so near at hand, she changed to a Chinese koto in an elegant *banjiki*.[10] Though I had to admit that she had talent, I was very annoyed. It is amusing enough, if you let things go no further, to exchange jokes from time to time with fickle and frivolous ladies; but as a place to take seriously, even for an occasional visit, matters here seemed to have gone too far. I made the events of that evening my excuse for leaving her.

"I see, as I look back on the two affairs, that young though I was the second of the two women did not seem the kind to put my trust in. I have no doubt that the wariness will grow as the years go by. The dear, uncertain ones—the dew that will fall when the *hagi*[11] branch is bent, the speck of frost that will melt when it is lifted from the bamboo leaf—no doubt they can be interesting for a time. You have seven years to go before you are my age," he said to Genji. "Just wait and you will understand. Perhaps you can take the advice of a person of no importance, and avoid the uncertain ones. They stumble sooner or later, and do a man's name no good when they do."

Tō no Chūjō nodded, as always. Genji, though he only smiled, seemed to agree.

"Neither of the tales you have given us has been a very happy one," he said.

"Let me tell you a story about a foolish woman I once knew," said Tō no Chūjō. "I was seeing her in secret, and I did not think that the affair was likely to last very long. But she was very beautiful, and as time passed I came to think that I must go on seeing her, if only infrequently. I sensed that she had come to depend on me. I expected signs of jealousy. There were none. She did not seem to feel the resentment a man expects from a woman he visits so seldom. She waited quietly, morning and night. My affection grew, and I let it be known that she did indeed have a man she could depend on. There was something very appealing about her (she was an orphan), letting me know that I was all she had.

"She seemed content. Untroubled, I stayed away for rather a long time. Then— I heard of it only later—my wife found a roundabout way to be objectionable. I did not know that I had become a cause of pain. I had not forgotten, but I let a long time pass without writing. The woman was desperately lonely and worried for the child she had borne. One day she sent me a letter attached to a wild carnation." His voice trembled.

"And what did it say?" Genji urged him on.

---

[10] *banjiki:* A harmonic mode often used in fourteenth-century romantic dramas and associated with passion.

[11] *hagi: Lespedeza japonica,* a Japanese bush clover.

"Nothing very remarkable. I do remember her poem, though:

> "'The fence of the mountain rustic may fall to the ground.
> Rest gently, O dew, upon the wild carnation.'

"I went to see her again. The talk was open and easy, as always, but she seemed pensive as she looked out at the dewy garden from the neglected house. She seemed to be weeping, joining her laments to the songs of the autumn insects. It could have been a scene from an old romance. I whispered a verse:

> "'No bloom in this wild array would I wish to slight.
> But dearest of all to me is the wild carnation.'

"Her carnation had been the child. I made it clear that my own was the lady herself, the wild carnation no dust falls upon.[12]

"She answered:

> "'Dew wets the sleeve that brushes the wild carnation.
> The tempest rages. Now comes autumn too.'

"She spoke quietly all the same, and she did not seem really angry. She did shed a tear from time to time, but she seemed ashamed of herself, and anxious to avoid difficult moments. I went away feeling much relieved. It was clear that she did not want to show any sign of anger at my neglect. And so once more I stayed away for rather a long time.

"And when I looked in on her again she had disappeared.

"If she is still living, it must be in very unhappy circumstances. She need not have suffered so if she had asserted herself a little more in the days when we were together. She need not have put up with my absences, and I would have seen to her needs over the years. The child was a very pretty little girl. I was fond of her, and I have not been able to find any trace of her.

"She must be listed among your reticent ones, I suppose? She let me have no hint of jealousy. Unaware of what was going on, I had no intention of giving her up. But the result was hopeless yearning, quite as if I had given her up. I am beginning to forget; and how is it with her? She must remember me sometimes, I should think, with regret, because she must remember too that it was not I who abandoned her. She was, I fear, not the sort of woman one finds it possible to keep for very long.

"Your jealous woman must be interesting enough to remember, but she must have been a bit wearying. And the other one, all her skill on the koto cannot have been much compensation for the undependability. And the one I have described to you—her very lack of jealousy might have brought a suspicion that there was another man in her life. Well, such is the way with the world—you cannot give your unqualified approval to any of them. Where are you to go for the woman who has no

---

[12] **Her carnation . . . falls upon:** An allusion to a poem from the *Kokinshu* (167): "Let no dust fall upon the wild carnation, / Upon the couch where lie my love and I." In her poetic reply, the woman uses a word for a wild carnation that commonly connotes "child"; and the man chooses a word whose first two syllables mean "bed."

defects and who combines the virtues of all three? You might choose Our Lady of Felicity[13] — and find yourself married to unspeakable holiness."

The others laughed.

Tō no Chūjō turned to the young man from the ministry of rites. "You must have interesting stories too."

"Oh, please. How could the lowest of the low hope to hold your attention?"

"You must not keep us waiting."

"Let me think a minute." He seemed to be sorting out memories. "When I was still a student I knew a remarkably wise woman. She was the sort worth consulting about public affairs, and she had a good mind too for the little tangles that come into your private life. Her erudition would have put any ordinary sage to shame. In a word, I was awed into silence.

"I was studying under a learned scholar. I had heard that he had many daughters, and on some occasion or other I had made the acquaintance of this one. The father learned of the affair. Taking out wedding cups, he made reference, among other things, to a Chinese poem about the merits of an impoverished wife.[14] Although not exactly enamored of the woman, I had developed a certain fondness for her, and felt somewhat deferential toward the father. She was most attentive to my needs. I learned many estimable things from her, to add to my store of erudition and help me with my work. Her letters were lucidity itself, in the purest Chinese. None of this Japanese nonsense for her. I found it hard to think of giving her up, and under her tutelage I managed to turn out a few things in passable Chinese myself. And yet — though I would not wish to seem wanting in gratitude, it is undeniable that a man of no learning is somewhat daunted at the thought of being forever his wife's inferior. So it is in any case with an ignorant one like me; and what possible use could you gentlemen have for so formidable a wife? A stupid, senseless affair, a man tells himself, and yet he is dragged on against his will, as if there might have been a bond in some other life."

"She seems a most unusual woman." Genji and Tō no Chūjō were eager to hear more.

Quite aware that the great gentlemen were amusing themselves at his expense, he smiled somewhat impishly. "One day when I had not seen her for rather a long time I had some reason or other for calling. She was not in the room where we had been in the habit of meeting. She insisted on talking to me through a very obtrusive screen. I thought she might be sulking, and it all seemed very silly. And then again — if she was going to be so petty, I might have my excuse for leaving her. But no. She was not a person to let her jealousy show. She knew too much of the world. Her explanation of what was happening poured forth at great length, all of it very well reasoned.

---

[13] **Our Lady of Felicity:** Kichijoten, or Srimahadevi, a Buddhist goddess of beauty and happiness.

[14] **Chinese poem . . . wife:** An allusion to Bo Juyi's "On Marriage," the first verse in *Ten Poems Composed at Chang'an.*

"'I have been indisposed with a malady known as coryza.[15] Discommoded to an uncommon degree, I have been imbibing of a steeped potion made from bulbaceous herbs. Because of the noisome odor, I will not find it possible to admit of greater propinquity. If you have certain random matters for my attention, perhaps you can deposit the relevant materials where you are.'

"'Is that so?' I said. I could think of nothing else to say.

"I started to leave. Perhaps feeling a little lonely, she called after me, somewhat shrilly. 'When I have disencumbered myself of this aroma, we can meet once more.'

"It seemed cruel to rush off, but the time was not right for a quiet visit. And it was as she said: her odor was rather high. Again I started out, pausing long enough to compose a verse:

> "'The spider must have told you I would come.[16]
> Then why am I asked to keep company with garlic?'

"I did not take time to accuse her of deliberately putting me off. "She was quicker than I. She chased after me with an answer.

> "'Were we two who kept company every night,
> What would be wrong with garlic in the daytime?'[17]

"You must admit she was quick with her answers." He had quietly finished his story.

The two gentlemen, Genji and his friend, would have none of it. "A complete fabrication, from start to finish. Where could you find such a woman? Better to have a quiet evening with a witch." They thought it an outrageous story, and asked if he could come up with nothing more acceptable.

"Surely you would not wish for a more unusual sort of story?"

The guards officer took up again. "In women as in men, there is no one worse than the one who tries to display her scanty knowledge in full. It is among the least endearing of accomplishments for a woman to have delved into the Three Histories and the Five Classics;[18] and who, on the other hand, can go through life without absorbing something of public affairs and private? A reasonably alert woman does not need to be a scholar to see and hear a great many things. The very worst are the ones who scribble off Chinese characters at such a rate that they fill a good half of letters where they are most out of place, letters to other women. 'What a bore,' you say. 'If only she had mastered a few of the feminine things.' She cannot of course intend it to be so, but the words read aloud seem muscular and unyielding, and in the end hopelessly mannered. I fear that even our highest of the high are too often guilty of the fault.

"Then there is the one who fancies herself a poetess. She immerses herself in the

---

[15] **coryza:** A mild flu or cold. [Editors' note.]

[16] **The spider . . . would come:** A folk belief from China held that a busy spider portended a visit from a lover.

[17] **garlic in the daytime:** The word *hiru* means both "garlic" and "daytime."

[18] **the Three Histories . . . Five Classics:** These works, grounded in Confucian teachings, made up the standard canon of Chinese learning valued in Heian Japan. The Five Classics are *The Book of Poetry, The Book of History, The I Ching,* the *Spring and Autumn Annals,* and *The Book of Rites.* [Editors' note.]

anthologies, and brings antique references into her very first line, interesting enough in themselves but inappropriate. A man has had enough with that first line, but he is called heartless if he does not answer, and cannot claim the honors if he does not answer in a similar vein. On the Day of the Iris he is frantic to get off to court and has no eye for irises, and there she is with subtle references to iris roots. On the Day of the Chrysanthemum,[19] his mind has no room for anything but the Chinese poem he must come up with in the course of the day, and there she is with something about the dew upon the chrysanthemum. A poem that might have been amusing and even moving on a less frantic day has been badly timed and must therefore be rejected. A woman who dashes off a poem at an unpoetic moment cannot be called a woman of taste.

"For someone who is not alive to the particular quality of each moment and each occasion, it is safer not to make a great show of taste and elegance; and from someone who is alive to it all, a man wants restraint. She should feign a certain ignorance, she should keep back a little of what she is prepared to say."

Through all the talk Genji's thoughts were on a single lady. His heart was filled with her. She answered every requirement, he thought. She had none of the defects, was guilty of none of the excesses, that had emerged from the discussion.

The talk went on and came to no conclusion, and as the rainy night gave way to dawn the stories became more and more improbable.

It appeared that the weather would be fine. Fearing that his father-in-law might resent his secluding himself in the palace, Genji set off for Sanjō. The mansion itself, his wife — every detail was admirable and in the best of taste. Nowhere did he find a trace of disorder. Here was a lady whom his friends must count among the truly dependable ones, the indispensable ones. And yet — she was too finished in her perfection, she was so cool and self-possessed that she made him uncomfortable. He turned to playful conversation with Chūnagon and Nakatsukasa and other pretty young women among her attendants. Because it was very warm, he loosened his dress, and they thought him even handsomer.

The minister came to pay his respects. Seeing Genji thus in dishabille, he made his greetings from behind a conveniently placed curtain. Though somewhat annoyed at having to receive such a distinguished visitor on such a warm day, Genji made it clear to the women that they were not to smile at his discomfort. He was a very calm, self-possessed young gentleman.

As evening approached, the women reminded him that his route from the palace had transgressed upon the domain of the Lord of the Center.[20] He must not spend the night here.

"To be sure. But my own house lies in the same direction. And I am very tired." He lay down as if he meant in spite of everything to stay the night.

---

[19] **Day of the Iris . . . Chrysanthemum:** The Day of the Iris fell on the fifth day of the Fifth Month, and the Day of the Chrysanthemum on the ninth day of the Ninth Month.

[20] **Lord of the Center:** A god associated with the planet Saturn who changed his place of dwelling periodically and did not permit trespassers.

"It simply will not do, my Lord."

"The governor of Kii here," said one of Genji's men, pointing to another. "He has dammed the Inner River and brought it into his garden, and the waters are very cool, very pleasant."

"An excellent idea. I really am very tired, and perhaps we can send ahead to see whether we might drive into the garden."

There were no doubt all sorts of secret places to which he could have gone to avoid the taboo. He had come to Sanjō, and after a considerable absence. The minister might suspect that he had purposely chosen a night on which he must leave early.

The governor of Kii was cordial enough with his invitation, but when he withdrew he mentioned certain misgivings to Genji's men. Ritual purification, he said, had required all the women to be away from his father's house, and unfortunately they were all crowded into his own, a cramped enough place at best. He feared that Genji would be inconvenienced.

"Nothing of the sort," said Genji, who had overheard. "It is good to have people around. There is nothing worse than a night away from home with no ladies about. Just let me have a little corner behind their curtains."

"If that is what you want," said his men, "then the governor's place should be perfect."

And so they sent runners ahead. Genji set off immediately, though in secret, thinking that no great ceremony was called for. He did not tell the minister where he was going, and took only his nearest retainers. The governor grumbled that they were in rather too much of a hurry. No one listened.

The east rooms of the main hall had been cleaned and made presentable. The waters were as they had been described, a most pleasing arrangement. A fence of wattles, of a deliberately rustic appearance, enclosed the garden, and much care had gone into the plantings. The wind was cool. Insects were humming, one scarcely knew where, fireflies drew innumerable lines of light, and all in all the time and the place could not have been more to his liking. His men were already tippling, out where they could admire a brook flowing under a gallery. The governor seemed to have "hurried off for viands."[21] Gazing calmly about him, Genji concluded that the house would be of the young guardsman's favored in-between category. Having heard that his host's stepmother, who would be in residence, was a high-spirited lady, he listened for signs of her presence. There were signs of someone's presence immediately to the west. He heard a swishing of silk and young voices that were not at all displeasing. Young ladies seemed to be giggling self-consciously and trying to contain themselves. The shutters were raised, it seemed, but upon a word from the governor they were lowered. There was a faint light over the sliding doors. Genji went for a look, but could find no opening large enough to see through. Listening for a time, he concluded that the women had gathered in the main room, next to his.

---

[21] **"hurried off for viands"**: An allusion to a folk song: "The little jeweled flask is here, / but where is our host, what of our host? / He has hurried off for viands, / Off to the beach for viands, / To Koyurugi for seaweed."

The whispered discussion seemed to be about Genji himself.

"He is dreadfully serious, they say, and has made a fine match for himself. And still so young. Don't you imagine he might be a little lonely? But they say he finds time for a quiet little adventure now and then."

Genji was startled. There was but one lady on his mind, day after day. So this was what the gossips were saying; and what if, in it all, there was evidence that rumors of his real love had spread abroad? But the talk seemed harmless enough, and after a time he wearied of it. Someone misquoted a poem he had sent to his cousin Asagao,[22] attached to a morning glory. Their standards seemed not of the most rigorous. A misquoted poem for every occasion. He feared he might be disappointed when he saw the woman.

The governor had more lights set out at the eaves, and turned up those in the room. He had refreshments brought.

"And are the curtains all hung?"[23] asked Genji. "You hardly qualify as a host if they are not."

"And what will you feast upon?" rejoined the governor, somewhat stiffly. "Nothing so very elaborate, I fear."

Genji found a cool place out near the veranda and lay down. His men were quiet. Several young boys were present, all very sprucely dressed, sons of the host and of his father, the governor of Iyo. There was one particularly attractive lad of perhaps twelve or thirteen. Asking who were the sons of whom, Genji learned that the boy was the younger brother of the host's stepmother, son of a guards officer no longer living. His father had had great hopes for the boy and had died while he was still very young. He had come to this house upon his sister's marriage to the governor of Iyo. He seemed to have some aptitude for the classics, said the host, and was of a quiet, pleasant disposition; but he was young and without backing, and his prospects at court were not good.

"A pity. The sister, then, is your stepmother?"

"Yes."

"A very young stepmother. My father had thought of inviting her to court. He was asking just the other day what might have happened to her. Life," he added with a solemnity rather beyond his years, "is uncertain."

"It happened almost by accident. Yes, you are right: it is a very uncertain world, and it always has been, particularly for women. They are like bits of driftwood."

"Your father is no doubt very alert to her needs. Perhaps, indeed, one has trouble knowing who is the master?"

"He quite worships her. The rest of us are not entirely happy with the arrangements he has made."

---

[22] **Asagao:** Asagao is Genji's cousin, the daughter of Prince Momozono, Genji's uncle; her name is associated with several morning flowers, including the morning glory.

[23] **"And are . . . curtains all hung":** An allusion to a folk song: "The curtains are all hung. / Come and be my bridegroom. / And what will you feast upon? / Abalone, *sazae*, / And sea urchins too."

"But you cannot expect him to let you young gallants have everything. He has a name in that regard himself, you know. And where might the lady be?"

"They have all been told to spend the night in the porter's lodge, but they don't seem in a hurry to go."

The wine was having its effect, and his men were falling asleep on the veranda.

Genji lay wide awake, not pleased at the prospect of sleeping alone. He sensed that there was someone in the room to the north. It would be the lady of whom they had spoken. Holding his breath, he went to the door and listened.

"Where are you?" The pleasantly husky voice was that of the boy who had caught his eye.

"Over here." It would be the sister. The two voices, very sleepy, resembled each other. "And where is our guest? I had thought he might be somewhere near, but he seems to have gone away."

"He's in the east room." The boy's voice was low. "I saw him. He is every bit as handsome as everyone says."

"If it were daylight I might have a look at him myself." The sister yawned, and seemed to draw the bedclothes over her face.

Genji was a little annoyed. She might have questioned her brother more energetically.

"I'll sleep out toward the veranda. But we should have more light." The boy turned up the lamp. The lady apparently lay at a diagonal remove from Genji. "And where is Chūjō?[24] I don't like being left alone."

"She went to have a bath. She said she'd be right back." He spoke from out near the veranda.

All was quiet again. Genji slipped the latch open and tried the doors. They had not been bolted. A curtain had been set up just inside, and in the dim light he could make out Chinese chests and other furniture scattered in some disorder. He made his way through to her side. She lay by herself, a slight little figure. Though vaguely annoyed at being disturbed, she evidently took him for the woman Chūjō until he pulled back the covers.

"I heard you summoning a captain," he said, "and I thought my prayers over the months had been answered."

She gave a little gasp. It was muffled by the bedclothes and no one else heard.

"You are perfectly correct if you think me unable to control myself. But I wish you to know that I have been thinking of you for a very long time. And the fact that I have finally found my opportunity and am taking advantage of it should show that my feelings are by no means shallow."

His manner was so gently persuasive that devils and demons could not have gainsaid him. The lady would have liked to announce to the world that a strange man had invaded her boudoir.

---

[24] **Chūjō:** The lady, the wife of the vice-governor of Iyo and the object of Genji's immediate desire, refers here to her female attendant, who goes by the name Chūjō, which means "captain." Genji, who holds the rank of captain, hopes to turn her query to his advantage in the dialogue that follows.

"I think you have mistaken me for someone else," she said, outraged, though the remark was under her breath.

The little figure, pathetically fragile and as if on the point of expiring from the shock, seemed to him very beautiful.

"I am driven by thoughts so powerful that a mistake is completely out of the question. It is cruel of you to pretend otherwise. I promise you that I will do nothing unseemly. I must ask you to listen to a little of what is on my mind."

She was so small that he lifted her easily. As he passed through the doors to his own room, he came upon the Chūjō who had been summoned earlier. He called out in surprise. Surprised in turn, Chūjō peered into the darkness. The perfume that came from his robes like a cloud of smoke told her who he was. She stood in confusion, unable to speak. Had he been a more ordinary intruder she might have ripped her mistress away by main force. But she would not have wished to raise an alarm all through the house.

She followed after, but Genji was quite unmoved by her pleas.

"Come for her in the morning," he said, sliding the doors closed.

The lady was bathed in perspiration and quite beside herself at the thought of what Chūjō, and the others too, would be thinking. Genji had to feel sorry for her. Yet the sweet words poured forth, the whole gamut of pretty devices for making a woman surrender.

She was not to be placated. "Can it be true? Can I be asked to believe that you are not making fun of me? Women of low estate should have husbands of low estate."

He was sorry for her and somewhat ashamed of himself, but his answer was careful and sober. "You take me for one of the young profligates you see around? I must protest. I am very young and know nothing of the estates which concern you so. You have heard of me, surely, and you must know that I do not go in for adventures. I must ask what unhappy entanglement imposes this upon me. You are making a fool of me, and nothing should surprise me, not even the tumultuous emotions that do in fact surprise me."

But now his very splendor made her resist. He might think her obstinate and insensitive, but her unfriendliness must make him dismiss her from further consideration. Naturally soft and pliant, she was suddenly firm. It was as with the young bamboo: she bent but was not to be broken. She was weeping. He had his hands full but would not for the world have missed the experience.

"Why must you so dislike me?" he asked with a sigh, unable to stop the weeping. "Don't you know that the unexpected encounters are the ones we were fated for? Really, my dear, you do seem to know altogether too little of the world."

"If I had met you before I came to this," she replied, and he had to admit the truth of it, "then I might have consoled myself with the thought—it might have been no more than self-deception, of course—that you would someday come to think fondly of me. But this is hopeless, worse than I can tell you. Well, it has happened. Say no to those who ask if you have seen me."[25]

---

[25] **Say no . . . if you have seen me:** An allusion to the *Kokinshu* (811): "As one small mark of your love, if such there be, / Say no to those who ask if you have seen me."

One may imagine that he found many kind promises with which to comfort her. The first cock was crowing and Genji's men were awake.

"Did you sleep well? I certainly did."

"Let's get the carriage ready."

Some of the women were heard asking whether people who were avoiding taboos were expected to leave again in the middle of the night.

Genji was very unhappy. He feared he could not find an excuse for another meeting. He did not see how he could visit her, and he did not see how they could write. Chūjō came out, also very unhappy. He let the lady go and then took her back again.

"How shall I write to you? Your feelings and my own—they are not shallow, and we may expect deep memories. Has anything ever been so strange?" He was in tears, which made him yet handsomer. The cocks were now crowing insistently. He was feeling somewhat harried as he composed his farewell verse:

> "Why must they startle with their dawn alarums
> When hours are yet required to thaw the ice?"

The lady was ashamed of herself that she had caught the eye of a man so far above her. His kind words had little effect. She was thinking of her husband, whom for the most part she considered a clown and a dolt. She trembled to think that a dream might have told him of the night's happenings.

This was the verse with which she replied:

> "Day has broken without an end to my tears.
> To my cries of sorrow are added the calls of the cocks."

It was lighter by the moment. He saw her to her door, for the house was coming to life. A barrier had fallen between them. In casual court dress, he leaned for a time against the south railing and looked out at the garden. Shutters were being raised along the west side of the house. Women seemed to be looking out at him, beyond a low screen at the veranda. He no doubt brought shivers of delight. The moon still bright in the dawn sky added to the beauty of the morning. The sky, without heart itself, can at these times be friendly or sad, as the beholder sees it. Genji was in anguish. He knew that there would be no way even to exchange notes. He cast many a glance backward as he left.

At Sanjō once more, he was unable to sleep. If the thought that they would not meet again so pained him, what must it do to the lady? She was no beauty, but she had seemed pretty and cultivated. Of the middling rank, he said to himself. The guards officer who had seen them all knew what he was talking about.

Spending most of his time now at Sanjō, he thought sadly of the unapproachable lady. At last he summoned her stepson, the governor of Kii.

"The boy I saw the other night, your foster uncle. He seemed a promising lad. I think I might have a place for him. I might even introduce him to my father."

"Your gracious words quite overpower me. Perhaps I should take the matter up with his sister."

Genji's heart leaped at the mention of the lady. "Does she have children?"

"No. She and my father have been married for two years now, but I gather that she is not happy. Her father meant to send her to court."

"How sad for her. Rumor has it that she is a beauty. Might rumor be correct?"

"Mistaken, I fear. But of course stepsons do not see a great deal of stepmothers."

Several days later he brought the boy to Genji. Examined in detail the boy was not perfect, but he had considerable charm and grace. Genji addressed him in a most friendly manner, which both confused and pleased him. Questioning him about his sister, Genji did not learn a great deal. The answers were ready enough while they were on safe ground, but the boy's self-possession was a little disconcerting. Genji hinted rather broadly at what had taken place. The boy was startled. He guessed the truth but was not old enough to pursue the matter.

Genji gave him a letter for his sister. Tears came to her eyes. How much had her brother been told? she wondered, spreading the letter to hide her flushed cheeks.

It was very long, and concluded with a poem:

> "I yearn to dream again the dream of that night.
> The nights go by in lonely wakefulness.

"There are no nights of sleep."[26]

The hand was splendid, but she could only weep at the yet stranger turn her life had taken.

The next day Genji sent for the boy.

Where was her answer? the boy asked his sister.

"Tell him you found no one to give his letter to."

"Oh, please." The boy smiled knowingly. "How can I tell him that? I have learned enough to be sure there is no mistake."

She was horrified. It was clear that Genji had told everything.

"I don't know why you must always be so clever. Perhaps it would be better if you didn't go at all."

"But he sent for me." And the boy departed.

The governor of Kii was beginning to take an interest in his pretty young stepmother, and paying insistent court. His attention turned to the brother, who became his frequent companion.

"I waited for you all day yesterday," said Genji. "Clearly I am not as much on your mind as you are on mine."

The boy flushed.

"Where is her answer?" And when the boy told him: "A fine messenger. I had hoped for something better."

There were other letters.

"But didn't you know?" he said to the boy. "I knew her before that old man she married. She thought me feeble and useless, it seems, and looked for a stouter

---

[26] **nights of sleep:** An allusion to a poem by Minamoto Shitago (911–983): "Where shall I find comfort in my longing? / There are no dreams, for there are no nights of sleep."

support. Well, she may spurn me, but you needn't. You will be my son. The gentleman you are looking to for help won't be with us long."

The boy seemed to be thinking what a nuisance his sister's husband was. Genji was amused.

He treated the boy like a son, making him a constant companion, giving him clothes from his own wardrobe, taking him to court. He continued to write to the lady. She feared that with so inexperienced a messenger the secret might leak out and add suspicions of promiscuity to her other worries. These were very grand messages, but something more in keeping with her station seemed called for. Her answers were stiff and formal when she answered at all. She could not forget his extraordinary good looks and elegance, so dimly seen that night. But she belonged to another, and nothing was to be gained by trying to interest him. His longing was undiminished. He could not forget how touchingly fragile and confused she had been. With so many people around, another invasion of her boudoir was not likely to go unnoticed, and the results would be sad.

One evening after he had been at court for some days he found an excuse: his mansion again lay in a forbidden direction. Pretending to set off for Sanjō, he went instead to the house of the governor of Kii. The governor was delighted, thinking that those well-designed brooks and lakes had made an impression. Genji had consulted with the boy, always in earnest attendance. The lady had been informed of the visit. She must admit that they seemed powerful, the urges that forced him to such machinations. But if she were to receive him and display herself openly, what could she expect save the anguish of the other night, a repetition of that nightmare? No, the shame would be too much.

The brother having gone off upon a summons from Genji, she called several of her women. "I think it might be in bad taste to stay too near. I am not feeling at all well, and perhaps a massage might help, somewhere far enough away that we won't disturb him."

The woman Chūjō had rooms on a secluded gallery. They would be her refuge.

It was as she had feared. Genji sent his men to bed early and dispatched his messenger. The boy could not find her. He looked everywhere and finally, at the end of his wits, came upon her in the gallery.

He was almost in tears. "But he will think me completely useless."

"And what do you propose to be doing? You are a child, and it is quite improper for you to be carrying such messages. Tell him I have not been feeling well and have kept some of my women to massage me. You should not be here. They will think it very odd."

She spoke with great firmness, but her thoughts were far from firm. How happy she might have been if she had not made this unfortunate marriage, and were still in the house filled with memories of her dead parents. Then she could have awaited his visits, however infrequent. And the coldness she must force herself to display — he must think her quite unaware of her place in the world. She had done what she thought best, and she was in anguish. Well, it all was hard fact, about which she had no choice. She must continue to play the cold and insensitive woman.

Genji lay wondering what blandishments the boy might be using. He was not sanguine, for the boy was very young. Presently he came back to report his mission a failure. What an uncommonly strong woman! Genji feared he must seem a bit feckless beside her. He heaved a deep sigh. This evidence of despondency had the boy on the point of tears.

Genji sent the lady a poem:

> "I wander lost in the Sonohara moorlands,
> For I did not know the deceiving ways of the broom tree.[27]

"How am I to describe my sorrow?" She too lay sleepless. This was her answer:

> "Here and not here, I lie in my shabby hut.
> Would that I might like the broom tree vanish away."

The boy traveled back and forth with messages, a wish to be helpful driving sleep from his thoughts. His sister beseeched him to consider what the others might think.

Genji's men were snoring away. He lay alone with his discontent. This unique stubbornness was no broom tree. It refused to vanish away. The stubbornness was what interested him. But he had had enough. Let her do as she wished. And yet— not even this simple decision was easy.

"At least take me to her."

"She is shut up in a very dirty room and there are all sorts of women with her. I do not think it would be wise." The boy would have liked to be more helpful.

"Well, you at least must not abandon me." Genji pulled the boy down beside him.

The boy was delighted, such were Genji's youthful charms. Genji, for his part, or so one is informed, found the boy more attractive than his chilly sister.

[In Chapter 3, "The Shell of the Locust" (*Utsusemi*), Genji makes further advances on the governor's wife. Her resistance leads Genji to write a poem in which he compares her scarf to the dainty shell of the cicada. Overcome with the tenderness of the message and the feelings Genji has awakened, Utsusemi tearfully writes a poem in exchange and resigns herself to her marriage to Iyo no Kami. Chapter 4, "Evening Faces," finds Genji returning to court from a visit to Rokujo, where one of his most jealous lovers, the Rokujo Lady, lives. When he stops to visit his old nurse, the aging mother of his servant Koremitsu, Genji meets the young woman he calls Evening Faces, named after the face-like features of the white *yugao* flowers.]

---

[27] **"I wander lost . . . broom tree":** An allusion to a poem from Sakanoe Korenori in the *Shinkokinshu* (997): "O broom tree of Fuseya in Sonohara / You seem to be there, and yet I cannot find you." The broom tree of Sonohara in the province of Shinano disappeared or changed shape when one approached it. Fuseya means "hut"; hence the hut of the lady's answer.

CHAPTER 4

Evening Faces

On his way from court to pay one of his calls at Rokujō,[28] Genji stopped to inquire after his old nurse, Koremitsu's mother, at her house in Gojō.[29] Gravely ill, she had become a nun. The carriage entrance was closed. He sent for Koremitsu and while he was waiting looked up and down the dirty, cluttered street. Beside the nurse's house was a new fence of plaited cypress. The four or five narrow shutters above had been raised, and new blinds, white and clean, hung in the apertures. He caught outlines of pretty foreheads beyond. He would have judged, as they moved about, that they belonged to rather tall women. What sort of women might they be? His carriage was simple and unadorned and he had no outrunners. Quite certain that he would not be recognized, he leaned out for a closer look. The hanging gate, of something like trelliswork, was propped on a pole, and he could see that the house was tiny and flimsy. He felt a little sorry for the occupants of such a place—and then asked himself who in this world had more than a temporary shelter.[30] A hut, a jeweled pavilion, they were the same. A pleasantly green vine was climbing a board wall. The white flowers, he thought, had a rather self-satisfied look about them.

"'I needs must ask the lady far off yonder,'"[31] he said, as if to himself.

An attendant came up, bowing deeply. "The white flowers far off yonder are known as 'evening faces,'"[32] he said. "A very human sort of name—and what a shabby place they have picked to bloom in."

It was as the man said. The neighborhood was a poor one, chiefly of small houses. Some were leaning precariously, and there were "evening faces" at the sagging eaves.

"A hapless sort of flower. Pick one off for me, would you?"

The man went inside the raised gate and broke off a flower. A pretty little girl in long, unlined yellow trousers of raw silk came out through a sliding door that seemed too good for the surroundings. Beckoning to the man, she handed him a heavily scented white fan.

"Put it on this. It isn't much of a fan, but then it isn't much of a flower either."

Koremitsu, coming out of the gate, passed it on to Genji.

"They lost the key, and I have had to keep you waiting. You aren't likely to be recognized in such a neighborhood, but it's not a very nice neighborhood to keep you waiting in."

Genji's carriage was pulled in and he dismounted. Besides Koremitsu, a son and

---

[28] **Rokujō:** Genji is on his way to meet Lady Rokujo, who is highly jealous of Genji's other lovers. Rokujō is the site where Genji builds a fabulous mansion.

[29] **Gojō:** A town southwest of Osaka.

[30] **who . . . a temporary shelter:** An allusion to a poem from the *Kokinshu* (987): "Where in all this world shall I call home? / A temporary shelter is my home."

[31] **'I needs . . . far off yonder':** An allusion to a poem from the *Kokinshu* (1007): "I needs must ask the lady far off yonder / What flower it is off there that blooms so white."

[32] **evening faces:** The Japanese name for this flowering gourd is *yugao.*

a daughter, the former an eminent cleric, and the daughter's husband, the governor of Mikawa, were in attendance upon the old woman. They thanked him profusely for his visit.

The old woman got up to receive him. "I did not at all mind leaving the world, except for the thought that I would no longer be able to see you as I am seeing you now. My vows seem to have given me a new lease on life, and this visit makes me certain that I shall receive the radiance of Lord Amitābha[33] with a serene and tranquil heart." And she collapsed in tears.

Genji was near tears himself. "It has worried me enormously that you should be taking so long to recover, and I was very sad to learn that you have withdrawn from the world. You must live a long life and see the career I make for myself. I am sure that if you do you will be reborn upon the highest summits of the Pure Land. I am told that it is important to rid oneself of the smallest regret for this world."

Fond of the child she has reared, a nurse tends to look upon him as a paragon even if he is a half-wit. How much prouder was the old woman, who somehow gained stature, who thought of herself as eminent in her own right for having been permitted to serve him. The tears flowed on.

Her children were ashamed for her. They exchanged glances. It would not do to have these contortions taken as signs of a lingering affection for the world.

Genji was deeply touched. "The people who were fond of me left me when I was very young. Others have come along, it is true, to take care of me, but you are the only one I am really attached to. In recent years there have been restrictions upon my movements, and I have not been able to look in upon you morning and evening as I would have wished, or indeed to have a good visit with you. Yet I become very depressed when the days go by and I do not see you. 'Would that there were on this earth no final partings.'"[34] He spoke with great solemnity, and the scent of his sleeve, as he brushed away a tear, quite flooded the room.

Yes, thought the children, who had been silently reproaching their mother for her want of control, the fates had been kind to her. They too were now in tears.

Genji left orders that prayers and services be resumed. As he went out he asked for a torch, and in its light examined the fan on which the "evening face" had rested. It was permeated with a lady's perfume, elegant and alluring. On it was a poem in a disguised cursive hand that suggested breeding and taste. He was interested.

> "I think I need not ask whose face it is,
>   So bright, this evening face, in the shining dew."

"Who is living in the house to the west?" he asked Koremitsu. "Have you perhaps had occasion to inquire?"

---

[33] **Lord Amitābha:** The Buddha of Infinite Life and Light described in the Amitābha Sutra, who, taking compassion on the suffering of sentient beings in the world, vowed to create a Pure Land where through his grace the faithful would find refuge.

[34] **'Would that . . . no final partings':** An allusion to a poem by Ariwara no Narihira in the *Kokinshu* (901): "Would that my mother might live a thousand years. / Would there were on this earth no final partings."

At it again, thought Koremitsu. He spoke somewhat tartly. "I must confess that these last few days I have been too busy with my mother to think about her neighbors."

"You are annoyed with me. But this fan has the appearance of something it might be interesting to look into. Make inquiries, if you will, please, of someone who knows the neighborhood."

Koremitsu went in to ask his mother's steward, and emerged with the information that the house belonged to a certain honorary vice-governor. "The husband is away in the country, and the wife seems to be a young woman of taste. Her sisters are out in service here and there. They often come visiting. I suspect the fellow is too poorly placed to know the details."

His poetess would be one of the sisters, thought Genji. A rather practiced and forward young person, and, were he to meet her, perhaps vulgar as well—but the easy familiarity of the poem had not been at all unpleasant, not something to be pushed away in disdain. His amative propensities, it will be seen, were having their way once more.

Carefully disguising his hand, he jotted down a reply on a piece of notepaper and sent it in by the attendant who had earlier been of service.

> "Come a bit nearer, please. Then might you know
> Whose was the evening face so dim in the twilight."

Thinking it a familiar profile, the lady had not lost the opportunity to surprise him with a letter, and when time passed and there was no answer she was left feeling somewhat embarrassed and disconsolate. Now came a poem by special messenger. Her women became quite giddy as they turned their minds to the problem of replying. Rather bored with it all, the messenger returned empty-handed. Genji made a quiet departure, lighted by very few torches. The shutters next door had been lowered. There was something sad about the light, dimmer than fireflies, that came through the cracks.

At the Rokujō house, the trees and the plantings had a quiet dignity. The lady herself was strangely cold and withdrawn. Thoughts of the "evening faces" quite left him. He overslept, and the sun was rising when he took his leave. He presented such a fine figure in the morning light that the women of the place understood well enough why he should be so universally admired. On his way he again passed those shutters, as he had no doubt done many times before. Because of that small incident he now looked at the house carefully, wondering who might be within.

"My mother is not doing at all well, and I have been with her," said Koremitsu some days later. And, coming nearer: "Because you seemed so interested, I called someone who knows about the house next door and had him questioned. His story was not completely clear. He said that in the Fifth Month or so someone came very quietly to live in the house, but that not even the domestics had been told who she might be. I have looked through the fence from time to time myself and had glimpses through blinds of several young women. Something about their dress suggests that they are in the service of someone of higher rank. Yesterday, when the evening light was coming directly through, I saw the lady herself writing a letter. She is very beautiful. She seemed lost in thought, and the women around her were weeping."

Genji had suspected something of the sort. He must find out more.

Koremitsu's view was that while Genji was undeniably someone the whole world took seriously, his youth and the fact that women found him attractive meant that to refrain from these little affairs would be less than human. It was not realistic to hold that certain people were beyond temptation.

"Looking for a chance to do a bit of exploring, I found a small pretext for writing to her. She answered immediately, in a good, practiced hand. Some of her women do not seem at all beneath contempt."

"Explore very thoroughly, if you will. I will not be satisfied until you do."

The house was what the guardsman would have described as the lowest of the low, but Genji was interested. What hidden charms might he not come upon!

He had thought the coldness of the governor's wife, the lady of "the locust shell," quite unique. Yet if she had proved amenable to his persuasions the affair would no doubt have been dropped as a sad mistake after that one encounter. As matters were, the resentment and the distinct possibility of final defeat never left his mind. The discussion that rainy night would seem to have made him curious about the several ranks. There had been a time when such a lady would not have been worth his notice. Yes, it had been broadening, that discussion! He had not found the willing and available one, the governor of Iyo's daughter, entirely uninteresting, but the thought that the stepmother must have been listening coolly to the interview was excruciating. He must await some sign of her real intentions.

The governor of Iyo returned to the city. He came immediately to Genji's mansion. Somewhat sunburned, his travel robes rumpled from the sea voyage, he was a rather heavy and displeasing sort of person. He was of good lineage, however, and, though aging, he still had good manners. As they spoke of his province, Genji wanted to ask the full count of those hot springs,[35] but he was somewhat confused to find memories chasing one another through his head. How foolish that he should be so uncomfortable before the honest old man! He remembered the guardsman's warning that such affairs are unwise, and he felt sorry for the governor. Though he resented the wife's coldness, he could see that from the husband's point of view it was admirable. He was upset to learn that the governor meant to find a suitable husband for his daughter and take his wife to the provinces. He consulted the lady's young brother upon the possibility of another meeting. It would have been difficult even with the lady's cooperation, however, and she was of the view that to receive a gentleman so far above her would be extremely unwise.

Yet she did not want him to forget her entirely. Her answers to his notes on this and that occasion were pleasant enough, and contained casual little touches that made him pause in admiration. He resented her chilliness, but she interested him. As for the stepdaughter, he was certain that she would receive him hospitably enough

---

[35] **hot springs:** The province of Iyo was known for its hot springs.

however formidable a husband she might acquire. Reports upon her arrangements disturbed him not at all.

Autumn came. He was kept busy and unhappy by affairs of his own making, and he visited Sanjō infrequently. There was resentment.

As for the affair at Rokujō, he had overcome the lady's resistance and had his way, and, alas, he had cooled toward her. People thought it worthy of comment that his passions should seem so much more governable than before he had made her his. She was subject to fits of despondency, more intense on sleepless nights when she awaited him in vain. She feared that if rumors were to spread the gossips would make much of the difference in their ages.

On a morning of heavy mists, insistently roused by the lady, who was determined that he be on his way, Genji emerged yawning and sighing and looking very sleepy. Chūjō, one of her women, raised a shutter and pulled a curtain aside as if urging her lady to come forward and see him off. The lady lifted her head from her pillow. He was an incomparably handsome figure as he paused to admire the profusion of flowers below the veranda. Chūjō followed him down a gallery. In an aster robe that matched the season pleasantly and a gossamer train worn with clean elegance, she was a pretty, graceful woman. Glancing back, he asked her to sit with him for a time at the corner railing. The ceremonious precision of the seated figure and the hair flowing over her robes were very fine.

He took her hand.

> "Though loath to be taxed with seeking fresher blooms,
> I feel impelled to pluck this morning glory."

"Why should it be?"

She answered with practiced alacrity, making it seem that she was speaking not for herself but for her lady:

> "In haste to plunge into the morning mists,
> You seem to have no heart for the blossoms here."

A pretty little page boy, especially decked out for the occasion, it would seem, walked out among the flowers. His trousers wet with dew, he broke off a morning glory for Genji. He made a picture that called out to be painted.

Even persons to whom Genji was nothing were drawn to him. No doubt even rough mountain men wanted to pause for a time in the shade of the flowering tree, and those who had basked even briefly in his radiance had thoughts, each in accordance with his rank, of a daughter who might be taken into his service, a not ill-formed sister who might perform some humble service for him. One need not be surprised, then, that people with a measure of sensibility among those who had on some occasion received a little poem from him or been treated to some little kindness found him much on their minds. No doubt it distressed them not to be always with him.

I had forgotten: Koremitsu gave a good account of the fence peeping to which he had been assigned. "I am unable to identify her. She seems determined to hide herself from the world. In their boredom her women and girls go out to the long gallery at the street, the one with the shutters, and watch for carriages. Sometimes the lady who seems to be their mistress comes quietly out to join them. I've not had a good look at her, but she seems very pretty indeed. One day a carriage with outrunners went by. The little girls shouted to a person named Ukon that she must come in a hurry. The captain[36] was going by, they said. An older woman came out and motioned to them to be quiet. How did they know? she asked, coming out toward the gallery. The passage from the main house is by a sort of makeshift bridge. She was hurrying and her skirt caught on something, and she stumbled and almost fell off. 'The sort of thing the god of Katsuragi[37] might do,' she said, and seems to have lost interest in sightseeing. They told her that the man in the carriage was wearing casual court dress and that he had a retinue. They mentioned several names, and all of them were undeniably Lord Tō no Chūjō's guards and pages."

"I wish you had made positive identification." Might she be the lady of whom Tō no Chūjō had spoken so regretfully that rainy night?

Koremitsu went on, smiling at this open curiosity. "I have as a matter of fact made the proper overtures and learned all about the place. I come and go as if I did not know that they are not all equals. They think they are hiding the truth and try to insist that there is no one there but themselves when one of the little girls makes a slip."

"Let me have a peep for myself when I call on your mother."

Even if she was only in temporary lodgings, the woman would seem to be of the lower class for which his friend had indicated such contempt that rainy evening. Yet something might come of it all. Determined not to go against his master's wishes in the smallest detail and himself driven by very considerable excitement, Koremitsu searched diligently for a chance to let Genji into the house. But the details are tiresome, and I shall not go into them.

Genji did not know who the lady was and he did not want her to know who he was. In very shabby disguise, he set out to visit her on foot. He must be taking her very seriously, thought Koremitsu, who offered his horse and himself went on foot.

"Though I do not think that our gentleman will look very good with tramps for servants."

To make quite certain that the expedition remained secret, Genji took with him only the man who had been his intermediary in the matter of the "evening faces" and a page whom no one was likely to recognize. Lest he be found out even so, he did not stop to see his nurse.

The lady had his messengers followed to see how he made his way home and tried by every means to learn where he lived; but her efforts came to nothing. For all his secretiveness, Genji had grown fond of her and felt that he must go on seeing her.

---

[36]**The captain:** Tō no Chūjō, the head of the Fujiwara clan and Genji's brother-in-law, is a friend and rival whose actions in the novel both parallel and contrast with Genji's; in this case, he is a former lover of Evening Faces.

[37] **the god of Katsuragi:** This god was so ugly that he would come out only at night to work on a bridge he had been ordered to build.

They were of such different ranks, he tried to tell himself, and it was altogether too frivolous. Yet his visits were frequent. In affairs of this sort, which can muddle the senses of the most serious and honest of men, he had always kept himself under tight control and avoided any occasion for censure. Now, to a most astonishing degree, he would be asking himself as he returned in the morning from a visit how he could wait through the day for the next. And then he would rebuke himself. It was madness, it was not an affair he should let disturb him. She was of an extraordinarily gentle and quiet nature. Though there was a certain vagueness about her, and indeed an almost childlike quality, it was clear that she knew something about men. She did not appear to be of very good family. What was there about her, he asked himself over and over again, that so drew him to her?

He took great pains to hide his rank and always wore travel dress, and he did not allow her to see his face. He came late at night when everyone was asleep. She was frightened, as if he were an apparition from an old story. She did not need to see his face to know that he was a fine gentleman. But who might he be? Her suspicions turned to Koremitsu. It was that young gallant, surely, who had brought the strange visitor. But Koremitsu pursued his own little affairs unremittingly, careful to feign indifference to and ignorance of this other affair. What could it all mean? The lady was lost in unfamiliar speculations.

Genji had his own worries. If, having lowered his guard with an appearance of complete unreserve, she were to slip away and hide, where would he seek her? This seemed to be but a temporary residence, and he could not be sure when she would choose to change it, and for what other. He hoped that he might reconcile himself to what must be and forget the affair as just another dalliance; but he was not confident.

On days when, to avoid attracting notice, he refrained from visiting her, his fretfulness came near anguish. Suppose he were to move her in secret to Nijō. If troublesome rumors were to arise, well, he could say that they had been fated from the start. He wondered what bond in a former life might have produced an infatuation such as he had not known before.

"Let's have a good talk," he said to her, "where we can be quite at our ease."

"It's all so strange. What you say is reasonable enough, but what you do is so strange. And rather frightening."

Yes, she might well be frightened. Something childlike in her fright brought a smile to his lips. "Which of us is the mischievous fox spirit?[38] I wonder. Just be quiet and give yourself up to its persuasions."

Won over by his gentle warmth, she was indeed inclined to let him have his way. She seemed such a pliant little creature, likely to submit absolutely to the most outrageous demands. He thought again of Tō no Chūjō's "wild carnation," of the equable nature his friend had described that rainy night. Fearing that it would be

---

[38] **fox spirit:** Foxes disguised as humans were said to seduce or otherwise harass unsuspecting people. [Editors' note.]

useless, he did not try very hard to question her. She did not seem likely to indulge in dramatics and suddenly run off and hide herself, and so the fault must have been Tō no Chūjō's. Genji himself would not be guilty of such negligence—though it did occur to him that a bit of infidelity might make her more interesting.

The bright full moon of the Eighth Month came flooding in through chinks in the roof. It was not the sort of dwelling he was used to, and he was fascinated. Toward dawn he was awakened by plebeian voices in the shabby houses down the street.

"Freezing, that's what it is, freezing. There's not much business this year, and when you can't get out into the country you feel like giving up. Do you hear me, neighbor?"

He could make out every word. It embarrassed the woman that, so near at hand, there should be this clamor of preparation as people set forth on their sad little enterprises. Had she been one of the stylish ladies of the world, she would have wanted to shrivel up and disappear. She was a placid sort, however, and she seemed to take nothing, painful or embarrassing or unpleasant, too seriously. Her manner elegant and yet girlish, she did not seem to know what the rather awful clamor up and down the street might mean. He much preferred this easygoing bewilderment to a show of consternation, a face scarlet with embarrassment. As if at his very pillow, there came the booming of a foot pestle, more fearsome than the stamping of the thunder god, genuinely earsplitting. He did not know what device the sound came from, but he did know that it was enough to awaken the dead. From this direction and that there came the faint thump of fulling hammers against coarse cloth; and mingled with it—these were sounds to call forth the deepest emotions—were the calls of geese flying overhead. He slid a door open and they looked out. They had been lying near the veranda. There were tasteful clumps of black bamboo just outside and the dew shone as in more familiar places. Autumn insects sang busily, as if only inches from an ear used to wall crickets at considerable distances. It was all very clamorous, and also rather wonderful. Countless details could be overlooked in the singleness of his affection for the girl. She was pretty and fragile in a soft, modest cloak of lavender and a lined white robe. She had no single feature that struck him as especially beautiful, and yet, slender and fragile, she seemed so delicately beautiful that he was almost afraid to hear her voice. He might have wished her to be a little more assertive, but he wanted only to be near her, and yet nearer.

"Let's go off somewhere and enjoy the rest of the night. This is too much."

"But how is that possible?" She spoke very quietly. "You keep taking me by surprise."

There was a newly confiding response to his offer of his services as guardian in this world and the next. She was a strange little thing. He found it hard to believe that she had had much experience of men. He no longer cared what people might think. He asked Ukon to summon his man, who got the carriage ready. The women of the house, though uneasy, sensed the depth of his feelings and were inclined to put their trust in him.

Dawn approached. No cocks were crowing. There was only the voice of an old man making deep obeisance to a Buddha, in preparation, it would seem, for a pilgrimage to Mitake.[39] He seemed to be prostrating himself repeatedly and with much difficulty. All very sad. In a life itself like the morning dew, what could he desire so earnestly?

"Praise to the Messiah to come," intoned the voice.

"Listen," said Genji. "He is thinking of another world.

> "This pious one shall lead us on our way
> As we plight our troth for all the lives to come."

The vow exchanged by the Chinese emperor and Yang Kuei-fei[40] seemed to bode ill, and so he preferred to invoke Lord Maitreya, the Buddha of the Future; but such promises are rash.

> "So heavy the burden I bring with me from the past,
> I doubt that I should make these vows for the future."

It was a reply that suggested doubts about his "lives to come."

The moon was low over the western hills. She was reluctant to go with him. As he sought to persuade her, the moon suddenly disappeared behind clouds in a lovely dawn sky. Always in a hurry to be off before daylight exposed him, he lifted her easily into his carriage and took her to a nearby villa. Ukon was with them. Waiting for the caretaker to be summoned, Genji looked up at the rotting gate and the ferns that trailed thickly down over it. The groves beyond were still dark, and the mist and the dews were heavy. Genji's sleeve was soaking, for he had raised the blinds of the carriage.

"This is a novel adventure, and I must say that it seems like a lot of trouble.

> "And did it confuse them too, the men of old,
> This road through the dawn, for me so new and strange?

"How does it seem to you?" She turned shyly away.

> "And is the moon, unsure of the hills it approaches,
> Foredoomed to lose its way in the empty skies?"

"I am afraid."

She did seem frightened, and bewildered. She was so used to all those swarms of people, he thought with a smile.

The carriage was brought in and its traces propped against the veranda while a room was made ready in the west wing. Much excited, Ukon was thinking about earlier adventures. The furious energy with which the caretaker saw to preparations made her suspect who Genji was. It was almost daylight when they alighted from the carriage. The room was clean and pleasant, for all the haste with which it had been readied.

---

[39] **Mitake:** A shrine south of Nara in the Yoshino Mountains.

[40] **Yang Kuei-fei:** The concubine of a Chinese emperor noted for her extraordinary beauty; their love affair, like that of the Trojan prince Paris and Helen, led to the downfall of an empire as well as to Yang Kuei-fei's execution.

"There are unfortunately no women here to wait upon His Lordship." The man, who addressed him through Ukon, was a lesser steward who had served in the Sanjō mansion of Genji's father-in-law. "Shall I send for someone?"

"The last thing I want. I came here because I wanted to be in complete solitude, away from all possible visitors. You are not to tell a soul."

The man put together a hurried breakfast, but he was, as he had said, without serving women to help him.

Genji told the girl that he meant to show her a love as dependable as "the patient river of the loons."[41] He could do little else in these strange lodgings.

The sun was high when he arose. He opened the shutters. All through the badly neglected grounds not a person was to be seen. The groves were rank and overgrown. The flowers and grasses in the foreground were a drab monotone, an autumn moor. The pond was choked with weeds, and all in all it was a forbidding place. An outbuilding seemed to be fitted with rooms for the caretaker, but it was some distance away.

"It is a forbidding place," said Genji. "But I am sure that whatever devils emerge will pass me by."

He was still in disguise. She thought it unkind of him to be so secretive, and he had to agree that their relationship had gone beyond such furtiveness.

> "Because of one chance meeting by the wayside
> The flower now opens in the evening dew.

"And how does it look to you?"

> "The face seemed quite to shine in the evening dew,
> But I was dazzled by the evening light."

Her eyes turned away. She spoke in a whisper.

To him it may have seemed an interesting poem.

As a matter of fact, she found him handsomer than her poem suggested, indeed frighteningly handsome, given the setting.

"I hid my name from you because I thought it altogether too unkind of you to be keeping your name from me. Do please tell me now. This silence makes me feel that something awful might be coming."

"Call me the fisherman's daughter."[42] Still hiding her name, she was like a little child.

"I see. I brought it all on myself? A case of *warekara*?"[43]

And so, sometimes affectionately, sometimes reproachfully, they talked the hours away.

---

[41] **"the patient . . . loons"**: An allusion to a poem in the *Man'yoshu* (4458): "The patient river of the patient loons / Will not run dry. My love will outlast it."

[42] **"Call me the fisherman's daughter"**: An allusion to a classic poem: "A fisherman's daughter, I spend my life by the waves, / The waves that tell us nothing. I have no home."

[43] *warekara*: Genji's phrase contains an allusion to a classic poem from the *Kokinshu*: "The grass the fishermen take, the *warekara*: / 'I did it myself.' I shall weep but I shall not hate you."

Koremitsu had found them out and brought provisions. Feeling a little guilty about the way he had treated Ukon, he did not come near. He thought it amusing that Genji should thus be wandering the streets, and concluded that the girl must provide sufficient cause. And he could have had her himself, had he not been so generous.

Genji and the girl looked out at an evening sky of the utmost calm. Because she found the darkness in the recesses of the house frightening, he raised the blinds at the veranda and they lay side by side. As they gazed at each other in the gathering dusk, it all seemed very strange to her, unbelievably strange. Memories of past wrongs quite left her. She was more at ease with him now, and he thought her charming. Beside him all through the day, starting up in fright at each little noise, she seemed delightfully childlike. He lowered the shutters early and had lights brought.

"You seem comfortable enough with me, and yet you raise difficulties."

At court everyone would be frantic. Where would the search be directed? He thought what a strange love it was, and he thought of the turmoil the Rokujō lady was certain to be in. She had every right to be resentful, and yet her jealous ways were not pleasant. It was that sad lady to whom his thoughts first turned. Here was the girl beside him, so simple and undemanding; and the other was so impossibly forceful in her demands. How he wished he might in some measure have his freedom.

It was past midnight. He had been asleep for a time when an exceedingly beautiful woman appeared by his pillow.

"You do not even think of visiting me, when you are so much on my mind. Instead you go running off with someone who has nothing to recommend her, and raise a great stir over her. It is cruel, intolerable." She seemed about to shake the girl from her sleep. He awoke, feeling as if he were in the power of some malign being. The light had gone out. In great alarm, he pulled his sword to his pillow and awakened Ukon. She too seemed frightened.

"Go out to the gallery and wake the guard. Have him bring a light."

"It's much too dark."

He forced a smile. "You're behaving like a child."

He clapped his hands and a hollow echo answered. No one seemed to hear. The girl was trembling violently. She was bathed in sweat and as if in a trance, quite bereft of her senses.

"She is such a timid little thing," said Ukon, "frightened when there is nothing at all to be frightened of. This must be dreadful for her."

Yes, poor thing, thought Genji. She did seem so fragile, and she had spent the whole day gazing up at the sky.

"I'll go get someone. What a frightful echo. You stay here with her." He pulled Ukon to the girl's side.

The lights in the west gallery had gone out. There was a gentle wind. He had few people with him, and they were asleep. They were three in number: a young man who was one of his intimates and who was the son of the steward here, a court page, and the man who had been his intermediary in the matter of the "evening faces." He called out. Someone answered and came up to him.

"Bring a light. Wake the other, and shout and twang your bowstrings. What do you mean, going to sleep in a deserted house? I believe Lord Koremitsu was here."

"He was. But he said he had no orders and would come again at dawn."

An elite guardsman, the man was very adept at bow twanging. He went off with a shouting as of a fire watch. At court, thought Genji, the courtiers on night duty would have announced themselves, and the guard would be changing. It was not so very late.

He felt his way back inside. The girl was as before, and Ukon lay face down at her side.

"What is this? You're a fool to let yourself be so frightened. Are you worried about the fox spirits that come out and play tricks in deserted houses? But you needn't worry. They won't come near me." He pulled her to her knees.

"I'm not feeling at all well. That's why I was lying down. My poor lady must be terrified."

"She is indeed. And I can't think why."

He reached for the girl. She was not breathing. He lifted her and she was limp in his arms. There was no sign of life. She had seemed as defenseless as a child, and no doubt some evil power had taken possession of her. He could think of nothing to do. A man came with a torch. Ukon was not prepared to move, and Genji himself pulled up curtain frames to hide the girl.

"Bring the light closer."

It was a most unusual order. Not ordinarily permitted at Genji's side, the man hesitated to cross the threshold.

"Come, come, bring it here! There is a time and place for ceremony."

In the torchlight he had a fleeting glimpse of a figure by the girl's pillow. It was the woman in his dream. It faded away like an apparition in an old romance. In all the fright and horror, his confused thoughts centered upon the girl. There was no room for thoughts of himself.

He knelt over her and called out to her, but she was cold and had stopped breathing. It was too horrible. He had no confidant to whom he could turn for advice. It was the clergy one thought of first on such occasions. He had been so brave and confident, but he was young, and this was too much for him. He clung to the lifeless body.

"Come back, my dear, my dear. Don't do this awful thing to me." But she was cold and no longer seemed human.

The first paralyzing terror had left Ukon. Now she was writhing and wailing. Genji remembered a devil a certain minister had encountered in the Grand Hall.[44]

"She can't possibly be dead." He found the strength to speak sharply. "All this noise in the middle of the night—you must try to be a little quieter." But it had been too sudden.

---

[44] **a devil . . . in the Grand Hall:** The *Okagami* tells how Fujiwara Tadahira met a devil in the Shishinden. It withdrew when informed that he was on the emperor's business.

He turned again to the torchbearer. "There is someone here who seems to have had a very strange seizure. Tell your friend to find out where Lord Koremitsu is spending the night and have him come immediately. If the holy man is still at his mother's house, give him word, very quietly, that he is to come too. His mother and the people with her are not to hear. She does not approve of this sort of adventure."

He spoke calmly enough, but his mind was in a turmoil. Added to grief at the loss of the girl was horror, quite beyond describing, at this desolate place. It would be past midnight. The wind was higher and whistled more dolefully in the pines. There came a strange, hollow call of a bird. Might it be an owl? All was silence, terrifying solitude. He should not have chosen such a place — but it was too late now. Trembling violently, Ukon clung to him. He held her in his arms, wondering if she might be about to follow her lady. He was the only rational one present, and he could think of nothing to do. The flickering light wandered here and there. The upper parts of the screens behind them were in darkness, the lower parts fitfully in the light. There was a persistent creaking, as of someone coming up behind them. If only Koremitsu would come. But Koremitsu was a nocturnal wanderer without a fixed abode, and the man had to search for him in numerous places. The wait for dawn was like the passage of a thousand nights. Finally he heard a distant crowing. What legacy from a former life could have brought him to this mortal peril? He was being punished for a guilty love, his fault and no one else's, and his story would be remembered in infamy through all the ages to come. There were no secrets, strive though one might to have them. Soon everyone would know, from his royal father down, and the lowest court pages would be talking; and he would gain immortality as the model of the complete fool.

Finally Lord Koremitsu came. He was the perfect servant who did not go against his master's wishes in anything at any time; and Genji was angry that on this night of all nights he should have been away, and slow in answering the summons. Calling him inside even so, he could not immediately find the strength to say what must be said. Ukon burst into tears, the full horror of it all coming back to her at the sight of Koremitsu. Genji too lost control of himself. The only sane and rational one present, he had held Ukon in his arms, but now he gave himself up to his grief.

"Something very strange has happened," he said after a time. "Strange — 'unbelievable' would not be too strong a word. I wanted a priest — one does when these things happen — and asked your reverend brother to come."

"He went back up the mountain yesterday. Yes, it is very strange indeed. Had there been anything wrong with her?"

"Nothing."

He was so handsome in his grief that Koremitsu wanted to weep. An older man who has had everything happen to him and knows what to expect can be depended upon in a crisis; but they were both young, and neither had anything to suggest.

Koremitsu finally spoke. "We must not let the caretaker know. He may be dependable enough himself, but he is sure to have relatives who will talk. We must get away from this place."

"You aren't suggesting that we could find a place where we would be less likely to be seen?"

"No, I suppose not. And the women at her house will scream and wail when they hear about it, and they live in a crowded neighborhood, and all the mob around will hear, and that will be that. But mountain temples are used to this sort of thing. There would not be much danger of attracting attention." He reflected on the problem for a time. "There is a woman I used to know. She has gone into a nunnery up in the eastern hills. She is very old, my father's nurse, as a matter of fact. The district seems to be rather heavily populated, but the nunnery is off by itself."

It was not yet full daylight. Koremitsu had the carriage brought up. Since Genji seemed incapable of the task, he wrapped the body in a covering and lifted it into the carriage. It was very tiny and very pretty, and not at all repellent. The wrapping was loose and the hair streamed forth, as if to darken the world before Genji's eyes.

He wanted to see the last rites through to the end, but Koremitsu would not hear of it. "Take my horse and go back to Nijō, now while the streets are still quiet."

He helped Ukon into the carriage and himself proceeded on foot, the skirts of his robe hitched up. It was a strange, bedraggled sort of funeral procession, he thought, but in the face of such anguish he was prepared to risk his life. Barely conscious, Genji made his way back to Nijō.

"Where have you been?" asked the women. "You are not looking at all well."

He did not answer. Alone in his room, he pressed a hand to his heart. Why had he not gone with the others? What would she think if she were to come back to life? She would think that he had abandoned her. Self-reproach filled his heart to breaking. He had a headache and feared he had a fever. Might he too be dying? The sun was high and still he did not emerge. Thinking it all very strange, the women pressed breakfast upon him. He could not eat. A messenger reported that the emperor had been troubled by his failure to appear the day before.

His brothers-in-law came calling.

"Come in, please, just for a moment." He received only Tō no Chūjō and kept a blind between them. "My old nurse fell seriously ill and took her vows in the Fifth Month or so. Perhaps because of them, she seemed to recover. But recently she had a relapse. Someone came to ask if I would not call on her at least once more. I thought I really must go and see an old and dear servant who was on her deathbed, and so I went. One of her servants was ailing, and quite suddenly, before he had time to leave, he died. Out of deference to me they waited until night to take the body away. All this I learned later. It would be very improper of me to go to court with all these festivities coming up,[45] I thought, and so I stayed away. I have had a headache since early this morning—perhaps I have caught cold. I must apologize."

"I see. I shall so inform your father. He sent out a search party during the concert last night, and really seemed very upset." Tō no Chūjō turned to go, and abruptly turned back. "Come now. What sort of brush did you really have? I don't believe a word of it."

Genji was startled, but managed a show of nonchalance. "You needn't go into the details. Just say that I suffered an unexpected defilement. Very unexpected, really."

---

[45] **festivities coming up:** There were many Shinto rites during the Ninth Month.

Despite his cool manner, he was not up to facing people. He asked a younger brother-in-law to explain in detail his reasons for not going to court. He got off a note to Sanjō with a similar explanation.

Koremitsu came in the evening. Having announced that he had suffered a defilement, Genji had callers remain outside, and there were few people in the house. He received Koremitsu immediately.

"Are you sure she is dead?" He pressed a sleeve to his eyes.

Koremitsu too was in tears. "Yes, I fear she is most certainly dead. I could not stay shut up in a temple indefinitely, and so I have made arrangements with a venerable priest whom I happen to know rather well. Tomorrow is a good day for funerals."

"And the other woman?"

"She has seemed on the point of death herself. She does not want to be left behind by her lady. I was afraid this morning that she might throw herself over a cliff. She wanted to tell the people at Gojō, but I persuaded her to let us have a little more time."

"I am feeling rather awful myself and almost fear the worst."

"Come, now. There is nothing to be done and no point in torturing yourself. You must tell yourself that what must be must be. I shall let absolutely no one know, and I am personally taking care of everything."

"Yes, to be sure. Everything is fated. So I tell myself. But it is terrible to think that I have sent a lady to her death. You are not to tell your sister, and you must be very sure that your mother does not hear. I would not survive the scolding I would get from her."

"And the priests too: I have told them a plausible story." Koremitsu exuded confidence.

The women had caught a hint of what was going on and were more puzzled than ever. He had said that he had suffered a defilement, and he was staying away from court; but why these muffled lamentations?

Genji gave instructions for the funeral. "You must make sure that nothing goes wrong."

"Of course. No great ceremony seems called for."

Koremitsu turned to leave.

"I know you won't approve," said Genji, a fresh wave of grief sweeping over him, "but I will regret it forever if I don't see her again. I'll go on horseback."

"Very well, if you must." In fact Koremitsu thought the proposal very ill advised. "Go immediately and be back while it is still early."

Genji set out in the travel robes he had kept ready for his recent amorous excursions. He was in the bleakest despair. He was on a strange mission and the terrors of the night before made him consider turning back. Grief urged him on. If he did not see her once more, when, in another world, might he hope to see her as she had been? He had with him only Koremitsu and the attendant of that first encounter. The road seemed a long one.

The moon came out, two nights past full. They reached the river. In the dim torchlight, the darkness off towards Mount Toribe was ominous and forbidding; but Genji was too dazed with grief to be frightened. And so they reached the temple.

It was a harsh, unfriendly region at best. The board hut and chapel where the nun pursued her austerities were lonely beyond description. The light at the altar came dimly through cracks. Inside the hut a woman was weeping. In the outer chamber two or three priests were conversing and invoking the holy name in low voices. Vespers seemed to have ended in several temples nearby. Everything was quiet. There were lights and there seemed to be clusters of people in the direction of Kiyomizu. The grand tones in which the worthy monk, the son of the nun, was reading a sutra brought on what Genji thought must be the full flood tide of his tears.

He went inside. The light was turned away from the corpse. Ukon lay behind a screen. It must be very terrible for her, thought Genji. The girl's face was unchanged and very pretty.

"Won't you let me hear your voice again?" He took her hand. "What was it that made me give you all my love, for so short a time, and then made you leave me to this misery?" He was weeping uncontrollably.

The priests did not know who he was. They sensed something remarkable, however, and felt their eyes mist over.

"Come with me to Nijō," he said to Ukon.

"We have been together since I was very young. I never left her side, not for a single moment. Where am I to go now? I will have to tell the others what has happened. As if this weren't enough, I will have to put up with their accusations." She was sobbing. "I want to go with her."

"That is only natural. But it is the way of the world. Parting is always sad. Our lives must end, early or late. Try to put your trust in me." He comforted her with the usual homilies, but presently his real feelings came out. "Put your trust in me — when I fear I have not long to live myself." He did not after all seem likely to be much help.

"It will soon be light," said Koremitsu. "We must be on our way."

Looking back and looking back again, his heart near breaking, Genji went out. The way was heavy with dew and the morning mists were thick. He scarcely knew where he was. The girl was exactly as she had been that night. They had exchanged robes and she had on a red singlet of his. What might it have been in other lives that had brought them together? He managed only with great difficulty to stay in his saddle. Koremitsu was at the reins. As they came to the river Genji fell from his horse and was unable to remount.

"So I am to die by the wayside? I doubt that I can go on."

Koremitsu was in a panic. He should not have permitted this expedition, however strong Genji's wishes. Dipping his hands in the river, he turned and made supplication to Kiyomizu. Genji somehow pulled himself together. Silently invoking the holy name, he was seen back to Nijō.

The women were much upset by these untimely wanderings. "Very bad, very bad. He has been so restless lately. And why should he have gone out again when he was not feeling well?"

Now genuinely ill, he took to his bed. Two or three days passed and he was visibly thinner. The emperor heard of the illness and was much alarmed. Continuous prayers were ordered in this shrine and that temple. The varied rites, Shinto and

Confucian and Buddhist, were beyond counting. Genji's good looks had been such as to arouse forebodings. All through the court it was feared that he would not live much longer. Despite his illness, he summoned Ukon to Nijō and assigned her rooms near his own. Koremitsu composed himself sufficiently to be of service to her, for he could see that she had no one else to turn to. Choosing times when he was feeling better, Genji would summon her for a talk, and she soon was accustomed to life at Nijō. Dressed in deep mourning, she was a somewhat stern and forbidding young woman, but not without her good points.

"It lasted such a very little while. I fear that I will be taken too. It must be dreadful for you, losing your only support. I had thought that as long as I lived I would see to all your needs, and it seems sad and ironical that I should be on the point of following her." He spoke softly and there were tears in his eyes. For Ukon the old grief had been hard enough to bear, and now she feared that a new grief might be added to it.

All through the Nijō mansion there was a sense of helplessness. Emissaries from court were thicker than raindrops. Not wanting to worry his father, Genji fought to control himself. His father-in-law was extremely solicitous and came to Nijō every day. Perhaps because of all the prayers and rites the crisis passed—it had lasted some twenty days—and left no ill effects. Genji's full recovery coincided with the final cleansing of the defilement. With the unhappiness he had caused his father much on his mind, he set off for his apartments at court. For a time he felt out of things, as if he had come back to a strange new world.

By the end of the Ninth Month he was his old self once more. He had lost weight, but emaciation only made him handsomer. He spent a great deal of time gazing into space, and sometimes he would weep aloud. He must be in the clutches of some malign spirit, thought the women. It was all most peculiar.

He would summon Ukon on quiet evenings. "I don't understand it at all. Why did she so insist on keeping her name from me? Even if she *was* a fisherman's daughter it was cruel of her to be so uncommunicative. It was as if she did not know how much I loved her."

"There was no reason for keeping it secret. But why should she tell you about her insignificant self? Your attitude seemed so strange from the beginning. She used to say that she hardly knew whether she was waking or dreaming. Your refusal to identify yourself, you know, helped her guess who you were. It hurt her that you should belittle her by keeping your name from her."

"An unfortunate contest of wills. I did not want anything to stand between us; but I must always be worrying about what people will say. I must refrain from things my father and all the rest of them might take me to task for. I am not permitted the smallest indiscretion. Everything is exaggerated so. The little incident of the 'evening faces' affected me strangely and I went to very great trouble to see her. There must have been a bond between us. A love doomed from the start to be fleeting—why should it have taken such complete possession of me and made me find her so precious? You must tell me everything. What point is there in keeping secrets now? I mean to make offerings every week, and I want to know in whose name I am making them."

"Yes, of course—why have secrets now? It is only that I do not want to slight what she made so much of. Her parents are dead. Her father was a guards captain. She was his special pet, but his career did not go well and his life came to an early and disappointing end. She somehow got to know Lord Tō no Chūjō—it was when he was still a lieutenant. He was very attentive for three years or so, and then about last autumn there was a rather awful threat from his father-in-law's house. She was ridiculously timid and it frightened her beyond all reason. She ran off and hid herself at her nurse's in the western part of the city. It was a wretched little hovel of a place. She wanted to go off into the hills, but the direction she had in mind has been taboo since New Year's. So she moved to the odd place where she was so upset to have you find her. She was more reserved and withdrawn than most people, and I fear that her unwillingness to show her emotions may have seemed cold."

So it was true. Affection and pity welled up yet more strongly.

"He once told me of a lost child. Was there such a one?"

"Yes, a very pretty little girl, born two years ago last spring."

"Where is she? Bring her to me without letting anyone know. It would be such a comfort. I should tell my friend Tō no Chūjō, I suppose, but why invite criticism? I doubt that anyone could reprove me for taking in the child. You must think up a way to get around the nurse."

"It would make me very happy if you were to take the child. I would hate to have her left where she is. She is there because we had no competent nurses in the house where you found us."

The evening sky was serenely beautiful. The flowers below the veranda were withered, the songs of the insects were dying too, and autumn tints were coming over the maples. Looking out upon the scene, which might have been a painting, Ukon thought what a lovely asylum she had found herself. She wanted to avert her eyes at the thought of the house of the "evening faces." A pigeon called, somewhat discordantly, from a bamboo thicket. Remembering how the same call had frightened the girl in that deserted villa, Genji could see the little figure as if an apparition were there before him.

"How old was she? She seemed so delicate, because she was not long for this world, I suppose."

"Nineteen, perhaps? My mother, who was her nurse, died and left me behind. Her father took a fancy to me, and so we grew up together, and I never once left her side. I wonder how I can go on without her. I am almost sorry that we were so close. She seemed so weak, but I can see now that she was a source of strength."

"The weak ones do have a power over us. The clear, forceful ones I can do without. I am weak and indecisive by nature myself, and a woman who is quiet and withdrawn and follows the wishes of a man even to the point of letting herself be used has much the greater appeal. A man can shape and mold her as he wishes, and becomes fonder of her all the while."

"She was exactly what you would have wished, sir." Ukon was in tears. "That thought makes the loss seem greater."

The sky had clouded over and a chilly wind had come up. Gazing off into the distance, Genji said softly:

> "One sees the clouds as smoke that rose from the pyre,
> And suddenly the evening sky seems nearer."

Ukon was unable to answer. If only her lady were here! For Genji even the memory of those fulling blocks was sweet.

"In the Eighth Month, the Ninth Month, the nights are long,"[46] he whispered, and lay down.

The young page, brother of the lady of the locust shell, came to Nijō from time to time, but Genji no longer sent messages for his sister. She was sorry that he seemed angry with her and sorry to hear of his illness. The prospect of accompanying her husband to his distant province was a dreary one. She sent off a note to see whether Genji had forgotten her.

"They tell me you have not been well."

> "Time goes by, you ask not why I ask not.
> Think if you will how lonely a life is mine.

"I might make reference to Masuda Pond."[47]

This was a surprise; and indeed he had not forgotten her. The uncertain hand in which he set down his reply had its own beauty.

"Who, I wonder, lives the more aimless life.

> "Hollow though it was, the shell of the locust
> Gave me strength to face a gloomy world.

"But only precariously."

So he still remembered "the shell of the locust." She was sad and at the same time amused. It was good that they could correspond without rancor. She wished no further intimacy, and she did not want him to despise her.

As for the other, her stepdaughter, Genji heard that she had married a guards lieutenant. He thought it a strange marriage and he felt a certain pity for the lieutenant. Curious to know something of her feelings, he sent a note by his young messenger.

"Did you know that thoughts of you had brought me to the point of expiring?

> "I bound them loosely, the reeds beneath the eaves,[48]
> And reprove them now for having come undone."

He attached it to a long reed.

The boy was to deliver it in secret, he said. But he thought that the lieutenant

---

[46] **"In the Eighth . . . nights are long"**: Genji quotes from "The Fulling Blocks at Night" by the Tang-dynasty Chinese poet Bo Juyi.

[47] **Masuda Pond**: An allusion to the following lines from the *Shūishū*: "Long the roots of the Masuda water shield, / Longer still the aimless, sleepless nights."

[48] **"reeds . . . eaves"**: "Reeds beneath the eaves," *Nokiba no ogi,* is the girl's name.

would be forgiving if he were to see it, for he would guess who the sender was. One may detect here a note of self-satisfaction.

Her husband was away. She was confused, but delighted that he should have remembered her. She sent off in reply a poem the only excuse for which was the alacrity with which it was composed:

> "The wind brings words, all softly, to the reed,
> And the under leaves are nipped again by the frost."

It might have been cleverer and in better taste not to have disguised the clumsy handwriting. He thought of the face he had seen by lamplight. He could forget neither of them, the governor's wife, seated so primly before him, or the younger woman, chattering on so contentedly, without the smallest suggestion of reserve. The stirrings of a susceptible heart suggested that he still had important lessons to learn.

Quietly, forty-ninth-day services[49] were held for the dead lady in the Lotus Hall on Mount Hiei. There was careful attention to all the details, the priestly robes and the scrolls and the altar decorations. Koremitsu's older brother was a priest of considerable renown, and his conduct of the services was beyond reproach. Genji summoned a doctor of letters with whom he was friendly and who was his tutor in Chinese poetry and asked him to prepare a final version of the memorial petition. Genji had prepared a draft. In moving language he committed the one he had loved and lost, though he did not mention her name, to the mercy of Amitābha.

"It is perfect, just as it is. Not a word needs to be changed." Noting the tears that refused to be held back, the doctor wondered who might be the subject of these prayers. That Genji should not reveal the name, and that he should be in such open grief—someone, no doubt, who had brought a very large bounty of grace from earlier lives.

Genji attached a poem to a pair of lady's trousers which were among his secret offerings:

> "I weep and weep as today I tie this cord.
> It will be untied in an unknown world to come."

He invoked the holy name with great feeling. Her spirit had wandered uncertainly these last weeks. Today it would set off down one of the ways of the future.

His heart raced each time he saw Tō no Chūjō. He longed to tell his friend that "the wild carnation" was alive and well; but there was no point in calling forth reproaches.

In the house of the "evening faces," the women were at a loss to know what had happened to their lady. They had no way of inquiring. And Ukon too had disappeared. They whispered among themselves that they had been right about that gentleman, and they hinted at their suspicions to Koremitsu. He feigned complete ignorance, however, and continued to pursue his little affairs. For the poor women it was all like a nightmare. Perhaps the wanton son of some governor, fearing Tō no

---

[49] **forty-ninth-day services:** According to Buddhist tradition, a dead spirit exists in a sort of limbo for forty-nine days before being reincarnated.

Chūjō, had spirited her off to the country? The owner of the house was her nurse's daughter. She was one of three children and related to Ukon. She could only long for her lady and lament that Ukon had not chosen to enlighten them. Ukon for her part was loath to raise a stir, and Genji did not want gossip at this late date. Ukon could not even inquire after the child. And so the days went by bringing no light on the terrible mystery.

Genji longed for a glimpse of the dead girl, if only in a dream. On the day after the services he did have a fleeting dream of the woman who had appeared that fatal night. He concluded, and the thought filled him with horror, that he had attracted the attention of an evil spirit haunting the neglected villa.

Early in the Tenth Month the governor of Iyo left for his post, taking the lady of the locust shell with him. Genji chose his farewell presents with great care. For the lady there were numerous fans,[50] and combs of beautiful workmanship, and pieces of cloth (she could see that he had had them dyed specially) for the wayside gods. He also returned her robe, "the shell of the locust."

> "A keepsake till we meet again, I had hoped,
> And see, my tears have rotted the sleeves away."

There were other things too, but it would be tedious to describe them. His messenger returned empty-handed. It was through her brother that she answered his poem.

> "Autumn comes, the wings of the locust are shed.
> A summer robe returns, and I weep aloud."

She had remarkable singleness of purpose, whatever else she might have. It was the first day of winter. There were chilly showers, as if to mark the occasion, and the skies were dark. He spent the day lost in thought.

> "The one has gone, to the other I say farewell.
> They go their unknown ways. The end of autumn."

I had hoped, out of deference to him, to conceal these difficult matters; but I have been accused of romancing, of pretending that because he was the son of an emperor he had no faults. Now perhaps, I shall be accused of having revealed too much.

[In Chapters 5 through 24, Genji continues his amorous exploits, which include romantic relationships with Fujitsubo; the Lady Rokujo; Murasaki, the niece of Lady Fujitsubo; and Oborozukiyo, the younger sister of his mother's archrival, Kokiden. Lady Aoi gives birth to Genji's son, Yugiri, and dies a few days later, possessed by the avenging spirit of the Lady Rokujo. Not long after his wife's death, Genji marries Murasaki, whom he had adopted as a child. Not long after he takes up with Princess Asagao. Lady Rokujo and Fujitsubo soon renounce court life to become nuns. Meanwhile Genji's father, the emperor, has passed the throne to Genji's half brother, Suzaku, the son of Lady Kokiden. When Genji's father dies, Suzaku and Lady Kokiden secure power at

---

[50] **numerous fans:** Because the sound of the Japanese word for "fan," *ogi,* bodes well for a reunion, fans were often given as farewell presents.

court. Because of his entanglements with Kokiden's sister, Genji goes into self-exile at Suma. While in exile, fate takes Genji overseas to Akashi, where he becomes romantically involved with Lady Akashi, the ex-governor's daughter. Within two years, Emperor Suzaku hands the throne over to Reizei, the son of Genji and Fujitsubo, supposed to be the son of the deceased emperor. Now back at court, Genji's life takes a turn for the better. He is appointed imperial advisor to the young emperor, Reizei, his son, and helps to arrange a marriage between Reizei and Akikonomu, the daughter of the Lady Rokujo. Reizei learns that Genji is his real father and bestows favor on him. Meanwhile, Genji's other son, Yugiri, a student, begins to act like a chip off the old block.

In Chapter 22, "The Jeweled Chaplet" ("*Tamakazura*"), Genji, now thirty-four, discovers Tamakazura, the twenty-one-year-old daughter of his friend To no Chujo and Evening Faces. Genji takes Tamakazura into his care at the Rokujo mansion he has recently built. As might be expected, Genji falls in love with Tamakazura, who resembles her mother — another instance of the chain of resemblances Genji follows in his quest for the ideal woman. But keeping his affection in check, Genji tries to help find a suitable marriage partner for Tamakazura, narrowing the choices to three possibilities: Kashiwagi, the son of To no Chujo; Higekuro, a high-ranking official; and Prince Hotaru, Genji's brother, whose name means "firefly." Here the final selection picks up the story.]

CHAPTER 25

Fireflies

Genji was famous and life was secure and peaceful. His ladies had in their several ways made their own lives and were happy. There was an exception, Tamakazura, who faced a new crisis and was wondering what to do next. She was not as genuinely frightened of him, of course, as she had been of the Higo man;[51] but since few people could possibly know what had happened, she must keep her disquiet to herself, and her growing sense of isolation. Old enough to know a little of the world, she saw more than ever what a handicap it was not to have a mother.

Genji had made his confession. The result was that his longing increased. Fearful of being overheard, however, he found the subject a difficult one to approach, even gingerly. His visits were very frequent. Choosing times when she was likely to have few people with her, he would hint at his feelings, and she would be in an agony of embarrassment. Since she was not in a position to turn him away, she could only pretend that she did not know what was happening.

She was of a cheerful, affectionate disposition. Though she was also of a cautious and conservative nature, the chief impression she gave was of a delicate, winsome girlishness.

Prince Hotaru continued to pay energetic court. His labors had not yet gone on for very long when he had the early-summer rains to be resentful of.

"Admit me a little nearer, please," he wrote. "I will feel better if I can unburden myself of even part of what is in my heart."

Genji saw the letter. "Princes," he said, "should be listened to. Aloofness is not permitted. You must let him have an occasional answer." He even told her what to say.

---

[51] **the Higo man:** A powerful but unpolished official from the province of Higo, where in Chapter 22 Tamakazura was taken after her mother's death. The official aggressively sought to form an attachment with Tamakazura before she was taken into Genji's protection. [Editors' note.]

But he only made things worse. She said that she was not feeling well and did not answer.

There were few really highborn women in her household. She did have a cousin called Saishō, daughter of a maternal uncle who had held a seat on the council. Genji had heard that she had been having a difficult time since her father's death, and had put her in Tamakazura's service. She wrote a passable hand and seemed generally capable and well informed. He assigned her the task of composing replies to gentlemen who deserved them. It was she whom he summoned today. One may imagine that he was curious to see all of his brother's letters. Tamakazura herself had been reading them with more interest since that shocking evening. It must not be thought that she had fallen in love with Hotaru, but he did seem to offer a way of evading Genji. She was learning rapidly.

Unaware that Genji himself was eagerly awaiting him, Hotaru was delighted at what seemed a positive invitation and quietly came calling. A seat was put out for him near the corner doors, where she received him with only a curtain between them. Genji had given close attention to the incense, which was mysterious and seductive—rather more attention, indeed, than a guardian might have felt that his duty demanded. One had to admire the results, whatever the motive. Saishō was at a loss to reply to Hotaru's overtures. Genji pinched her gently to remind her that her mistress must not behave like an unfeeling lump, and only added to her discomfiture. The dark nights of the new moon were over and there was a bland quartermoon in the cloudy sky. Calm and dignified, the prince was very handsome indeed. Genji's own very special perfume mixed with the incense that drifted through the room as people moved about. More interesting than he would have expected, thought the prince. In calm control of himself all the while (and in pleasant contrast to certain other people), he made his avowals.

Tamakazura withdrew to the east penthouse and lay down. Genji followed Saishō as she brought a new message from the prince.

"You are not being kind," he said to Tamakazura. "A person should behave as the occasion demands. You are unnecessarily coy. You should not be sending a messenger back and forth over such distances. If you do not wish him to hear your voice, very well, but at least you should move a little nearer."

She was in despair. She suspected that his real motive was to impose himself upon her, and each course open to her seemed worse than all the others. She slipped away and lay down at a curtain between the penthouse and the main hall.

She was sunk in thought, unable to answer the prince's outpourings. Genji came up beside her and lifted the curtain back over its frame. There was a flash of light. She looked up startled. Had someone lighted a torch? No—Genji had earlier in the evening put a large number of fireflies in a cloth bag. Now, letting no one guess what he was about, he released them. Tamakazura brought a fan to her face. Her profile was very beautiful.

Genji had worked everything out very carefully. Prince Hotaru was certain to look in her direction. He was making a show of passion, Genji suspected, because he thought her Genji's daughter, and not because he had guessed what a beauty she was. Now he would see, and be genuinely excited. Genji would not have gone to such trouble if she had in fact been his daughter. It all seems rather perverse of him.

He slipped out through another door and returned to his part of the house.

The prince had guessed where the lady would be. Now he sensed that she was perhaps a little nearer. His heart racing, he looked through an opening in the rich gossamer curtains. Suddenly, some six or seven feet away, there was a flash of light — and such beauty as was revealed in it! Darkness was quickly restored, but for the brief glimpse he had had was the sort of thing that makes for romance. The figure at the curtains may have been indistinct but it most certainly was slim and tall and graceful. Genji would not have been disappointed at the interest it had inspired.

> "You put out this silent fire to no avail.
> Can you extinguish the fire in the human heart?

"I hope I make myself understood." Speed was the important thing in answering such a poem.

> "The firefly but burns and makes no comment.
> Silence sometimes tells of deeper thoughts."

It was a brisk sort of reply, and having made it, she was gone. His lament about this chilly treatment was rather wordy, but he would not have wished to overdo it by staying the night. It was late when he braved the dripping eaves (and tears as well) and went out. I have no doubt that a cuckoo sent him on his way, but did not trouble myself to learn all the details.

So handsome, so poised, said the women — so very much like Genji. Not knowing their lady's secret, they were filled with gratitude for Genji's attentions. Why, not even her mother could have done more for her.

Unwelcome attentions, the lady was thinking. If she had been recognized by her father and her situation were nearer the ordinary, then they need not be entirely unwelcome. She had had wretched luck, and she lived in dread of rumors.

Genji too was determined to avoid rumors. Yet he continued to have his ways. Can one really be sure, for instance, that he no longer had designs upon Akikonomu?[52] There was something different about his manner when he was with her, something especially charming and seductive. But she was beyond the reach of direct overtures. Tamakazura was a modern sort of girl, and approachable. Sometimes dangerously near losing control of himself, he would do things which, had they been noticed, might have aroused suspicions. It was a difficult and complicated relationship indeed, and he must be given credit for the fact that he held back from the final line.

On the fifth day of the Fifth Month, the Day of the Iris, he stopped by her apartments on his way to the equestrian grounds.

---

[52] **Akikonomu:** The daughter of the Rokujo lady, who is now married to the emperor Reizei, Genji's son by Fujitsubo. [Editors' note.]

"What happened? Did he stay late? You must be careful with him. He is not to be trusted — not that there are very many men these days a girl really can trust."

He praised his brother and blamed him. He seemed very young and was very handsome as he offered this word of caution. As for his clothes, the singlets and the robe thrown casually over them glowed in such rich and pleasing colors that they seemed to brim over and seek more space. One wondered whether a supernatural hand might not have had some part in the dyeing. The colors themselves were familiar enough, but the woven patterns were as if everything had pointed to this day of flowers.[53] The lady was sure she would have been quite intoxicated with the perfumes burned into them had she not had these worries.

A letter came from Prince Hotaru, on white tissue paper in a fine, aristocratic hand. At first sight the contents seemed very interesting, but somehow they became ordinary upon repeating.

> "Even today the iris is neglected.
> Its roots, my cries, are lost among the waters."[54]

It was attached to an iris root certain to be much talked of.
"You must get off an answer," said Genji, preparing to leave.
Her women argued that she had no choice.
Whatever she may have meant to suggest by it, this was her answer, a simple one set down in a faint, delicate hand:

> "It might have flourished better in concealment,
> The iris root washed purposelessly away.

"Exposure seems rather unwise."
A connoisseur, the prince thought that the hand could just possibly be improved.
Gifts of medicinal herbs[55] in decorative packets came from this and that well-wisher. The festive brightness did much to make her forget earlier unhappiness and hope that she might come uninjured through this new trial.

Genji also called on the lady of the orange blossoms, in the east wing of the same northeast quarter.

"Yūgiri is to bring some friends around after the archery meet. I should imagine it will still be daylight. I have never understood why our efforts to avoid attention always end in failure. The princes and the rest of them hear that something is up and come around to see, and so we have a much noisier party than we had planned on. We must in any event be ready."

The equestrian stands were very near the galleries of the northeast quarter.

---

[53] **day of flowers:** *Ayame,* translated here as flowers, means both "iris" and "patterns"; the pun is repeated several times in the following passage, such as in Hotaru's poem where *ayame* suggests something like "discernment."

[54] **Its roots . . . among the waters:** There is a pun here on *ne,* which means both "root" and "cry," or "sob."

[55] **medicinal herbs:** Conventional gifts on the Day of the Iris.

"Come, girls," he said. "Open all the doors and enjoy yourselves. Have a look at all the handsome officers. The ones in the Left Guards are especially handsome, several cuts above the common run at court."

They had a delightful time. Tamakazura joined them. There were fresh green blinds all along the galleries, and new curtains too, the rich colors at the hems fading, as is the fashion these days, to white above. Women and little girls clustered at all the doors. The girls in green robes and trains of purple gossamer seemed to be from Tamakazura's wing. There were four of them, all very pretty and well behaved. Her women too were in festive dress, trains blending from lavender at the waist down to deeper purple and formal jackets the color of carnation shoots.

The lady of the orange blossoms had her little girls in very dignified dress, singlets of deep pink and trains of red lined with green. It was very amusing to see all the women striking new poses as they draped their finery about them. The young courtiers noticed and seemed to be striking poses of their own.

Genji went out to the stands toward midafternoon. All the princes were there, as he had predicted. The equestrian archery was freer and more varied than at the palace. The officers of the guard joined in, and everyone sat entranced through the afternoon. The women may not have understood all the finer points, but the uniforms of even the common guardsmen were magnificent and the horsemanship was complicated and exciting. The grounds were very wide, fronting also on Murasaki's southeast quarter, where young women were watching. There was music and dancing, Chinese polo music and the Korean dragon dance. As night came on, the triumphal music rang out high and wild. The guardsmen were richly rewarded according to their several ranks. It was very late when the assembly dispersed.

Genji spent the night with the lady of the orange blossoms.

"Prince Hotaru is a man of parts," he said. "He may not be the handsomest man in the world, but everything about him tells of breeding and cultivation, and he is excellent company. Did you chance to catch a glimpse of him? He has many good points, as I have said, but it may be that in the final analysis there is something just a bit lacking in him."

"He is younger than you but I thought he looked older. I have heard that he never misses a chance to come calling. I saw him once long ago at court and had not really seen him again until today. He has improved. Prince Sochi[56] is a very fine gentleman too, but somehow he does not quite look like royalty."

Genji smiled. Her judgment was quick and sure. But he kept his own counsel. This sort of open appraisal of people still living was not to his taste. He could not understand why the world had such a high opinion of Higekuro and would not have been pleased to receive him into the family, but these views too he kept to himself.

They were good friends, he and she, and no more, and they went to separate beds. Genji wondered when they had begun to drift apart. She never let fall the

---

[56] **Prince Sochi:** A brother of Genji and Prince Hotaru who does not appear elsewhere in the novel.

tiniest hint of jealousy. It had been the usual thing over the years for reports of such festivities to come to her through others. The events of the day seemed to bring new recognition to her and her household.

She said softly:

> "You honor the iris on the bank to which
> No pony comes to taste of withered grasses?"[57]

One could scarcely have called it a masterpiece, but he was touched:

> "This pony, like the love grebe, wants a comrade.
> Shall it forget the iris on the bank?"

Nor was his a very exciting poem.

"I do not see as much of you as I would wish, but I do enjoy you." There was a certain irony in the words, from his bed to hers, but also affection. She was a dear, gentle lady. She had let him have her bed and spread quilts for herself outside the curtains. She had in the course of time come to accept such arrangements as proper, and he did not suggest changing them.

The rains of early summer continued without a break, even gloomier than in most years. The ladies at Rokujō amused themselves with illustrated romances. The Akashi Lady, a talented painter, sent pictures to her daughter.

Tamakazura was the most avid reader of all. She quite lost herself in pictures and stories and would spend whole days with them. Several of her young women were well informed in literary matters. She came upon all sorts of interesting and shocking incidents (she could not be sure whether they were true or not), but she found little that resembled her own unfortunate career. There was *The Tale of Sumiyoshi*,[58] popular in its day, of course, and still well thought of. She compared the plight of the heroine, within a hairbreadth of being taken by the chief accountant, with her own escape from the Higo person.

Genji could not help noticing the clutter of pictures and manuscripts. "What a nuisance this all is," he said one day. "Women seem to have been born to be cheerfully deceived. They know perfectly well that in all these old stories there is scarcely a shred of truth, and yet they are captured and made sport of by the whole range of trivialities and go on scribbling them down, quite unaware that in these warm rains their hair is all dank and knotted."

He smiled. "What would we do if there were not these old romances to relieve our boredom? But amid all the fabrication I must admit that I do find real emotions and plausible chains of events. We can be quite aware of the frivolity and the idleness and still be moved. We have to feel a little sorry for a charming princess in the depths of gloom. Sometimes a series of absurd and grotesque incidents which we know to

---

[57] **"You honor . . . withered grasses":** This poem alludes to a verse in the *Kokinshu* (892): "Withered is the grass of Oaraki, / No pony comes for it, no harvester."

[58] ***The Tale of Sumiyoshi*:** The incident Tamakazura refers to is not found in the surviving version of this tale, which describes the narrow escape of a young woman from the clutches of a man she does not like.

be quite improbable holds our interest, and afterwards we must blush that it was so. Yet even then we can see what it was that held us. Sometimes I stand and listen to the stories they read to my daughter, and I think to myself that there certainly are good talkers in the world. I think that these yarns must come from people much practiced in lying. But perhaps that is not the whole of the story?"

She pushed away her inkstone. "I can see that that would be the view of someone much given to lying himself. For my part, I am convinced of their truthfulness."

He laughed. "I have been rude and unfair to your romances, haven't I. They have set down and preserved happenings from the age of the gods to our own. *The Chronicles of Japan*[59] and the rest are a mere fragment of the whole truth. It is your romances that fill in the details.

"We are not told of things that happened to specific people exactly as they happened; but the beginning is when there are good things and bad things, things that happen in this life which one never tires of seeing and hearing about, things which one cannot bear not to tell of and must pass on for all generations. If the storyteller wishes to speak well, then he chooses the good things; and if he wishes to hold the reader's attention he chooses bad things, extraordinarily bad things. Good things and bad things alike, they are things of this world and no other.

"Writers in other countries approach the matter differently. Old stories in our own are different from new. There are differences in the degree of seriousness. But to dismiss them as lies is itself to depart from the truth. Even in the writ which the Buddha drew from his noble heart are parables, devices for pointing obliquely at the truth. To the ignorant they may seem to operate at cross purposes. The Greater Vehicle[60] is full of them, but the general burden is always the same. The difference between enlightenment and confusion is of about the same order as the difference between the good and the bad in a romance. If one takes the generous view, then nothing is empty and useless."

He now seemed bent on establishing the uses of fiction.

"But tell me: is there in any of your old stories a proper, upright fool like myself?" He came closer. "I doubt that even among the most unworldly of your heroines there is one who manages to be as distant and unnoticing as you are. Suppose the two of us set down our story and give the world a really interesting one."

"I think it very likely that the world will take notice of our curious story even if we do not go to the trouble." She hid her face in her sleeves.

"Our curious story? Yes, incomparably curious, I should think." Smiling and playful, he pressed nearer.

> "Beside myself, I search through all the books,
> And come upon no daughter so unfilial."

---

[59] *The Chronicles of Japan:* An early history of Japan.

[60] **The Greater Vehicle:** Mahayana Buddhism, as opposed to Hinayana Buddhism, or "The Lesser Vehicle." Mahayana Buddhism, the form prevalent in Japan, China, and Tibet, emphasizes the divinity of Buddha, the possibility of salvation through grace, and the idea that material reality is illusion; it is more socially oriented and egalitarian than Hinayana Buddhism, which focuses on asceticism and psychological discipline.

"You are breaking one of the commandments."

He stroked her hair as he spoke, but she refused to look up. Presently, however, she managed a reply:

> "So too it is with me. I too have searched,
> And found no cases quite so unparental."

Somewhat chastened, he pursued the matter no further. Yet one worried. What was to become of her?

Murasaki too had become addicted to romances. Her excuse was that Genji's little daughter[61] insisted on being read to.

"Just see what a fine one this is," she said, showing Genji an illustration for *The Tale of Kumano*.[62] The young girl in tranquil and confident slumber made her think of her own younger self. "How precocious even very little children seem to have been. I suppose I might have set myself up as a specimen of the slow, plodding variety. I would have won that competition easily."

Genji might have been the hero of some rather more eccentric stories.

"You must not read love stories to her. I doubt that clandestine affairs would arouse her unduly, but we would not want her to think them commonplace."

What would Tamakazura have made of the difference between his remarks to her and these remarks to Murasaki?

"I would not of course offer the wanton ones as a model," replied Murasaki, "but I would have doubts too about the other sort. Lady Atemiya in *The Tale of the Hollow Tree*,[63] for instance. She is always very brisk and efficient and in control of things, and she never makes mistakes; but there is something unwomanly about her cool manner and clipped speech."

"I should imagine that it is in real life as in fiction. We are all human and we all have our ways. It is not easy to be unerringly right. Proper, well-educated parents go to great trouble over a daughter's education and tell themselves that they have done well if something quiet and demure emerges. It seems a pity when defects come to light one after another and people start asking what her good parents can possibly have been up to. Yet the rewards are very great when a girl's manner and behavior seem just right for her station. Even then empty praise is not satisfying. One knows that the girl is not perfect and looks at her more critically than before. I would not wish my own daughter to be praised by people who have no standards."

He was genuinely concerned that she acquit herself well in the tests that lay before her.

Wicked stepmothers are of course standard fare for the romancers, and he did not want them poisoning relations between Murasaki and the child. He spent a great deal of time selecting romances he thought suitable, and ordered them copied and illustrated.

He kept Yūgiri from Murasaki but encouraged him to be friends with the girl.

---

[61] **Genji's little daughter:** The daughter of Genji and Lady Akashi.

[62] ***The Tale of Kumano:*** Also called *The Tale of Komano;* it no longer survives.

[63] ***The Tale of the Hollow Tree:*** A tenth-century work of fiction.

While he himself was alive it might not matter a great deal one way or the other, but if they were good friends now their affection was likely to deepen after he was dead. He permitted Yūgiri inside the front room, though the inner rooms were forbidden. Having so few children, he had ample time for Yūgiri, who was a sober lad and seemed completely dependable. The girl was still devoted to her dolls. They made Yūgiri think of his own childhood games with Kumoinokari.[64] Sometimes as he waited in earnest attendance upon a doll princess, tears would come to his eyes. He sometimes joked with ladies of a certain standing, but he was careful not to lead them too far. Even those who might have expected more had to make do with a joke. The thing that really concerned him and never left his mind was getting back at the nurse who had sneered at his blue sleeves. He was fairly sure that he could better Tō no Chūjō at a contest of wills, but sometimes the old anger and chagrin came back and he wanted more. He wanted to make Tō no Chūjō genuinely regretful for what he had done. He revealed these feelings only to Kumoinokari. Before everyone else he was a model of cool composure.

Her brothers sometimes thought him rather conceited. Kashiwagi, the oldest, was greatly interested these days in Tamakazura. Lacking a better intermediary, he came sighing to Yūgiri. The friendship of the first generation was being repeated in the second.

"One does not undertake to plead another's case," replied Yūgiri quietly.

Tō no Chūjō was a very important man, and his many sons were embarked upon promising careers, as became their several pedigrees and inclinations. He had only two daughters. The one who had gone to court had been a disappointment. The prospect of having the other do poorly did not of course please him. He had not forgotten the lady of the evening faces. He often spoke of her, and he went on wondering what had happened to the child. The lady had put him off guard with her gentleness and appearance of helplessness, and so he had lost a daughter. A man must not under any circumstances let a woman out of his sight. Suppose the girl were to turn up now in some outlandish guise and stridently announce herself as his daughter—well, he would take her in.

"Do not dismiss anyone who says she is my daughter," he told his sons. "In my younger days I did many things I ought not to have done. There was a lady of not entirely contemptible birth who lost patience with me over some triviality or other, and so I lost a daughter, and I have so few."

There had been a time when he had almost forgotten the lady. Then he began to see what great things his friends were doing for their daughters, and to feel resentful that he had been granted so few.

One night he had a dream. He called in a famous seer and asked for an interpretation.

"Might it be that you will hear of a long-lost child who has been taken in by someone else?"

This was very puzzling. He could think of no daughters whom he had put out for adoption. He began to wonder about Tamakazura.

---

[64] **Kumoinokari:** Tō no Chūjō's daughter, who eventually becomes Yugiri's wife.

THE TALE OF THE HEIKE
1371

kah-mah-KOO-rah

Whether viewed as a national epic or a tragic drama of universal significance, the *Heike monogatari* or *The Tale of the Heike*, composed for the most part during the **Kamakura** period (1186–1336) and completed nearly two hundred years after the events it describes, is one of the monuments of Japanese literature. On one hand, its subject is eternal: It mourns the demise of an ill-fated dynasty and teaches a lesson about the general impermanence of the world. On the other hand, it is the story of the fratricidal war between two powerful clans that spelled the end of Japan's ancient aristocratic system of rule.[1] It is often called the second greatest national literary work after *The Tale of Genji*.[2] It has also been compared to such works of European literature as the medieval epics *Beowulf* and *The Song of Roland*[3] and Leo Tolstoy's great nineteenth-century novel, *War and Peace*.[4]

The Historical Background. When *The Tale of the Heike* was completed in 1371, the Japanese had had nearly two hundred years to reflect on the **Gempei** Wars (1180–1185), which decisively ended the **Heian** period (793–1185) and the culture it represented and which initiated the **SHOGUNATE**, named for the generals who led the new military government. In the Gempei Wars two embattled family clans, the **Minamoto** (Genji) and the **Taira** (Heike),[5] threw tens of thousands of combatants against one another in the most sustained military action in early Japanese history, ending with the catastrophic defeat of the Taira at the battle of **Dannoura** in 1185. As a result, the seat of government was removed from Heian (now **Kyoto**) to the military base at Kamakura, and the dictator **Minamoto no Yoritomo** supplanted the former chancellor **Taira no Kiyomori** (1118–1181), who had died during the war. Although nominally

GEM-pay
HAY-ahn
SHOH-gun-ut
mee-nah-MOH-toh
TIGH-rah
dah-noh-OO-rah
kee-OH-toh
mee-nah-MOH-toh-
noh yoh-rih-TOH-moh
TIGH-rah-noh
kee-yoh-MOH-ree

---

[1] **the end . . . aristocratic system of rule:** The system of family dynasties had mixed with the traditional imperial succession for centuries, so that the leading families in effect took over the functions of emperors. The fratricidal battle between the Taira and Minamoto clans in the twelfth century helped bring about the rise of a disciplined Japanese military body, the samurai, which soon overshadowed the family clans in authority and importance.

[2] *The Tale of Genji:* While *The Tale of Genji* is primarily a court romance, *The Tale of the Heike* is the classic example of *gunki monogatari*, or "martial tales," a collection of stories of warfare existing with or without other elements such as scenes at court and love plots.

[3] *Beowulf . . . The Song of Roland:* In the Old English *Beowulf* (tenth century), the death of the hero signals the passing of an age. (See p. 489.) In the French martial epic *The Song of Roland* (c. 1100), the ideal of chivalry is embodied in Count Roland, who leads his entire fighting force to disaster in the name of Christianity and the royal crown. (See p. 546.)

[4] *War and Peace:* This account of Russia's role in the Napoleonic Wars, written between 1865 and 1869, is considered by many Westerners the greatest epic war novel.

[5] **the Minamoto (Genji) and the Taira (Heike):** The Japanese names of the two clans are given first; the Chinese (and more "literary") names follow in parentheses. Here the names are used interchangeably.

Minamoto no Yoritomo represented the Minamoto, or Genji, clan, in actuality the military took control. The basis of the law changed from imperial decree to the SAMURAI code, a form of martial law, and the ethical framework of the government changed from aristocratic piety to military discipline.

SAH-moo-righ

Although the decline of the imperial court had begun long before the Gempei Wars, the new Minamoto government, which profited greatly from its confiscation of the landed estates of the Taira families, eventually saw the wisdom of returning many administrative tasks to the former bureaucratic seat in Heian. Thus there began a new system of shared governance, military and civil, that lasted until the modern Japanese period. This compromise also created a political atmosphere in which the traditional songs and ballads about the great struggle between the Minamoto and Taira families could be compiled, written down, and performed before audiences composed of a broader section of the Japanese public, no longer restricted to imperial court society.

The Song and Ballad Tradition.   The two great cultural traditions of the Kamakura period were the ballads based on the Heike legend and the sermons of Buddhist priests. The ballads were collected in the fourteenth century to make up part of *The Tale of the Heike,* while the content of the story was heavily influenced by the Buddhist morality found in the sermons. The final text, completed in 1371 and attributed to a blind storyteller named Kakuichi,[6] combines the original ballads with more "literary" features, such as a swiftly running narrative, the use of contrasting scenes and ironic commentary, an emphasis on visual effect, and the use of conventional nature descriptions as well as the shorter stories, letters, and lyric poetry (*TANKA*) imbedded in the text. A number of linking devices are also employed, such as omens that foretell fate, repetition of language to introduce characters and scenes, and recapitulation of past stories. At its best, *The Tale of the Heike* is a reader's wonderland of story, artful composition, and astute commentary.

TAHNG-kah

Interpretations of the Story.   Scholars have interpreted *The Tale of the Heike* in a variety of ways, reflecting their own preoccupations and values. At different periods of Japanese history, the work has been seen as a Buddhist religious allegory, a historical chronicle of the times, a battle epic, an artistic representation of human tragedy, and a fable of the opposition of the common people to the aristocratic government. The most suspect of these interpretations are those that carry patriotic overtones acquired during later periods of Japanese militarism. Those who interpret *The Tale of the Heike* as a national patriotic epic must account for its tone of grief and sorrow, which appears to overwhelm any celebration of military glory.

www   For a quiz on *The Tale of the Heike,* see *World Literature Online* at bedfordstmartins .com/worldlit.

---

[6] **Kakuichi:** According to available information, Kakuichi was active in a writers' guild patronized by a noble house in 1340. He is also said to have been a member of the *biwa hoshi,* a group of blind itinerant musicians and storytellers who had performed versions of the Heike story for many years.

One important aspect of *The Tale of the Heike* is its appeal to the idea of *mappo*, the so-called end of the Buddhist law, or decline of the world. (Similar ideas or images in Western culture include the German *Götterdämmerung*, or twilight of the gods, and the biblical APOCALYPSE.) As scholar Paul Varley comments, the idea had acquired both religious and practical meaning for the audience of *The Tale of the Heike*:

> To the courtier class, it seemed that not only the Buddhist Law but the "Imperial Law" — rule by the Emperor with the assistance of his courtiers in Kyoto — was in sharp, perhaps irreversible decline. Under such circumstances, it appeared that only warriors, with their coercive powers, might be able to restore order to the country.

One need not look far to find the theme of decay in *Heike*. At the beginning of the work, chapel bells toll for the impermanence of the world; in the final chapter, the daughter of the former Taira chancellor takes refuge in a nunnery amid visible evidence of the collapse of the old order in the devastation of the countryside.

But the tragedy of *The Tale of the Heike* also has to do with the actions of the individuals involved, some of whom even appear to choreograph their own fates. Two of the most romantic characters in the story, the poet **Taira no Tadanori** and the young knight Atsumori, virtually dictate their means of obtaining martyrdom to their respective enemies. The nobility of character exemplified by these and other members of the doomed Taira clan suggests that the sympathies of the compiler rest with them rather than the victorious Minamoto. One is expected to mourn for the passing of the virtues embodied by these young aristocratic warriors, especially their sense of honor and dignity, which it seems will die with them.

The Story of Taira no Kiyomori. The central character of the first part of *The Tale of Heike* is Taira no Kiyomori, the ruthless and ignoble leader of the Taira (Heike) clan who ruled from 1167 until his death in 1181. Just as Kiyomori accumulates power by clawing his way to the position of chancellor, his equally tempestuous decline anticipates the end of the clan system as the source of national authority, giving way to the rise of the shogunate. Kiyomori's disastrous rule, failing in part because of his lack of moral character, contrasts sharply with the nobility of his fellow clansmen. Despite the excesses of Kiyomori, the loss of so many virtuous fighters among the doomed Heike is the subject of mourning.

The story of Kiyomori, the cruel leader of a virtuous people, is full of ironies. His swift rise to power is foretold in the story "The Sea Bass," in chapter 1. When he is a young man a great sea bass leaps into his boat, and Kiyomori immediately eats it to take on its power. In doing so, he violates the prescribed seasonal fast. While power is his, one is led to believe retribution will follow. Later in the chapter, **Gio**, Kiyomori's consort who previously was a popular dancer, prevails on him to admit a younger dancer, **Hotoke**, for an unscheduled performance at court. Kiyomori is so attracted to Hotoke that he expels the unfortunate Gio from his palace. Gio, her sister **Ginyo**, and her mother **Toji** finally seek refuge at

Margin pronunciation guides:

TIGH-rah-noh
tah-dah-NOH-ree

GEE-oh

hoh-TOH-kay

GIN-yoh; TOH-jee

a Buddhist nunnery. Later they are joined by Hotoke, who protests that she never sought Kiyomori's favor. Together, the narrator reveals, they will be reborn after death through **Amida Buddha** in the Pure Land.[7] This story moved audiences greatly at a time when the treatment of women had become a significant theme in the literature of the court.

ah-MEE-dah BOO-duh

The death of Kiyomori is told in chapter 6. Incapacitated by illness, Kiyomori contracts a terrible fever so that "people could hardly bear to remain within twenty-five or thirty feet of the bed. His only words were 'Hot! Hot!'" In his dying words he seeks as a public memorial of his rule the display of the severed head of his rival when he is finally caught. Thus even as death approaches, Kiyomori imagines vile deeds and expresses revolting sentiments. As his life has been marked by cruelty, so his death is terrible. The narrator comments, "Most sadly, his only escorts must have been the evil deeds he had committed so often, come to greet him in the form of horse-headed and ox-headed torturers."

Death of Two Young Heike Noblemen.   As the fortunes of the Heike decline into calamity, the great lords and their dependents depart from the capital. In the midst of the general route, the young Heike nobleman Tadanori visits the home of **Fujiwara Shunzei**, his former tutor and a member of the Genji clan. Tadanori leaves his mentor a scroll containing the best poems he has written over the years. The romantic Tadanori then cries out, "Now I shall not mind sinking beneath the western waves or leaving my bones to bleach in the wilds. Nothing remains to bind me to this transient world. Farewell!" Shunzei later publishes one of his former pupil's poems in an anthology he is ordered to compile, but because of Tadanori's affiliation with the Heike he must say the work is anonymous. The poem itself seems to predict the Heike disaster:

foo-jee-WAH-rah
SHOON-zay

> It lies ruined now—
> the old Shiga capital
>   at Sazanami—
> yet the Nagara cherry trees
> bloom as in days gone by.

In a later chapter, the young Heike nobleman **Atsumori**, hardly more than a boy, is killed in combat. The Genji warrior **Naozane** unhorses the boy but delays killing him when he sees his age, about that of his own son. First he thinks to spare the boy but decides that other warriors will certainly kill Atsumori if he does not, while at least he will offer prayers for him from that day onward. With defiance, the boy commands Naozane to kill him. Finally, beheading Atsumori, Naozane searches his clothing for a bag in which to place the head, and finds a flute in his waistband. "Ah, pitiful!" he cries. "There are tens of thousands of riders in our eastern armies, but I am sure none of them has brought a flute to

aht-soo-MOH-ree
nah-oh-ZAH-neh

---

[7] **Amida Buddha in the Pure Land:** The doctrine of Pure Land Buddhism, established in Japan in the final years of the twelfth century by the priest Honen, stated that the Amida Buddha would save all souls who beseeched him by removing them to a sacred land in the west.

zay-AH-mee
moh-toh-KEE-yoh

the battlefield. These court nobles are refined men." This story is later expanded on by the great dramatist of the *Nō* theater, **Zeami Motokiyo** (1364–1443).[8]

The Story of the Imperial Lady.   The last chapter of *The Tale of the Heike*, "The Initiates' Chapter," is believed to have been composed later than the rest of the work. Written in a more formal literary style, it

ken-ray-MOH-nin

focuses on Kiyomori's daughter in exile, **Kenreimon'in**, beginning with her taking Buddhist vows in 1185 and ending with her death in 1191. More than the rest of *The Tale of the Heike*, it sustains a mood of sorrow and longing for the past; it also offers a Buddhist reading of the transience of life and a retelling from Kenreimon'in's point of view of the dispersal of the Heike. The Imperial Lady's own story in this chapter provides a consummate conclusion to the work. Also, in its more formal, ritual use of language, this chapter confirms the importance of prayer, intended to set to rest the tormented ghosts of the dead and restore stability to the world.

The beginning of the chapter concerns the removal of the Imperial Lady from the capital, first to an abandoned cloister and later to the hermitage of **Jakkoin** high in the mountains. With dignity and resolve she

jahk-KOH-in

accepts the changes in her manner of living. For some time her only visitor is a stag that has wandered by her tiny house. Eventually, however, she is visited by retired emperor **Go-Shirakawa** and his distinguished party.

goh-shee-rah-
KAH-wah
AH-wah-noh
NIGH-shee

The emperor first encounters the attendant **Awa-no-naishi**, formerly known to him at court, and then the Imperial Lady herself. When he expresses his sorrow at seeing her in such reduced conditions, she retells the story of the rise and fall of the Heike court under siege from the approaching Genji. Her story ends with the drowning of her son, the young emperor **Antoku**, by his grandmother as the Genji drew near.

ahn-TOH-koo

After the retired emperor leaves her, the Imperial Lady prays for the recovery of the dead Heike in Amida Buddha's Pure Land. The narrator then ends with a short, matter-of-fact description of the death of the defeated Heike nobility—again ascribing blame for the whole disaster to Chancellor Kiyomori—and with the death of the Imperial Lady herself.

"The Initiates' Chapter" is thought to have been added to the main body of the text by Kakuichi in the fourteenth century. Distinguished by its tone of melancholy and longing for the past, it is also heavily flavored by Buddhist thought, so that it serves as a moral *coda* to the rest of the story. Above all, it memorializes the Taira dead. As translator Helen Craig McCullough remarks:

> The first twelve chapters narrate [the Tairas'] history in gratifying detail, and the Initiates' Chapter recapitulates the facts, reasserts the truths of transitoriness and karmic retribution, adds a strong assurance that prayer is the way to salvation, states that petitions on their behalf are being offered day and night by none other than the Im-

---

[8] **Zeami Motokiyo** (1364–1443): See Zeami Motokiyo's *Atsumori* on p. 1180. Zeami based the majority of his plays on stories from *The Tale of the Heike*.

perial Lady Kenreimon'in . . . and virtually promises them rebirth in the Pure Land.

Calling the Warriors Home. The tolling of bells at the beginning of *The Tale of the Heike* and the peals of the Jakkoin night bell at the start of its final chapter effectively frame this work in its literary, historical, and moral setting. Exhaustive in scope, noble in character, the tale captures the essence of the Japanese spirit and has remained popular to this day. Punctuated as it is by narrative, dramatic scenes, stories of courage and suffering, and short poems designed to create mood at important moments, *The Tale of the Heike* is also quintessentially Japanese in its prescription of duties and obligations, its sense of legacy, and its belief in obedience to destiny.

■ **CONNECTIONS**

The Tale of Genji, p. 1094. The court romance *The Tale of Genji* was composed during the flowering of Genji society in the early eleventh century. *The Tale of the Heike* addresses the defeat of the Heike by the Genji in the late twelfth century. How recognizable are the warriors and their attendants later depicted in *Heike* from the idealized pictures drawn by Lady Murasaki in *Genji*? How do the two works differ in literary form and subject matter?

Zeami Motokiyo, *Atsumori*, p. 1180. *The Tale of the Heike* was completed in the thirteenth century, with a final section added late in the next century. The *Nō* drama *Atsumori* was created in the early 1400s. What liberties does Zeami take with the original *Heike* story in this "sequel," and how has he adapted the story for the stage?

Beowulf, p. 489; *The Song of Roland*, p. 546. The elegiac ending of the second half of *Beowulf* and the terrible defeat of Roland and his entire company in *The Song of Roland* provide occasions for remembrance and lament for the past in these two medieval European texts. The destruction of the Heike clan in *The Tale of the Heike* provides another such occasion. How are these stories from different cultures presented, and with what lessons for the future?

■ **FURTHER RESEARCH**

Translation and Commentary
Kitagawa, Hiroshi, and Bruce Tsuchida. *The Tale of the Heike*. 2 vols. 1975.
McCullough, Helen Craig. *The Tale of the Heike*. 1988.

Literary History and Criticism
Bialock, David T. "Nation and Epic: *The Tale of the Heike* as Modern Classic." In Haruo Shirane and Tomi Suzuki, eds. *Inventing the Classics: Modernity, National Identity, and Japanese Literature*. 2000.
Kato, Shuichi. *A History of Japanese Literature: The First Thousand Years*. I. 1979.
Keene, Donald. *Seeds in the Heart: A History of Japanese Literature*. I. 1999.
Varley, Paul. "The Tale of the Heike." In William Theodore Du Bary and Irene Bloom, eds. *Approaches to the Asian Classics*. 1990.

■ **PRONUNCIATION**

Amida Buddha: ah-MEE-dah BOO-duh
Antoku: ahn-TOH-koo
Atsumori: aht-soo-MOH-ree

[. . .] No other work of fiction or history is comparable to the *Heike* as a source from which the Japanese over many centuries have derived their sense of the character and ethos of the samurai class. The stories of the *Heike* have been told and retold by countless generations and in countless forms, including the *Nō*, puppet, and Kabuki theaters, historical novels, the radio, cinema, and television. The appeal of these stories and the characters in them seems to be timeless.

– PAUL VARLEY, Critic, 1990

Important literary creations often defy categorization, especially in foreign terms. Our best course is simply to read and enjoy *Heike monogatari* for what it is — a masterly blend of many disparate elements, a multifaceted examination of the human condition, and above all a pious tribute to the Taira dead.

– HELEN CRAIG
MCCULLOUGH,
Scholar, 1988

Awa-no-naishi: AH-wah-noh NIGH-shee
biwa hoshi: BEE-wah HOH-shee
Dannoura: dah-noh-OO-rah
Fujiwara Shunzei: foo-jee-WAH-rah SHOON-zay
Gempei: GEM-pay
Ginyo: GIN-yoh
Gio: GEE-oh
Go-Shirakawa: goh-shee-rah-KAH-wah
Heian: HAY-ahn
Heike: HAY-keh
Hotoke: hoh-TOH-kay
Jakkoin: jahk-KOH-in
Kamakura: kah-mah-KOO-rah
Kenreimon'in: ken-ray-MOH-nin
Kyoto: kee-OH-toh
Minamoto: mee-nah-MOH-toh
Minamoto no Yoritomo: mee-nah-MOH-toh-noh yoh-rih-TOH-moh
Naozane: nah-oh-ZAH-neh, now-
samurai: SAH-moo-righ
shogunate: SHOH-gun-ut, -ate
Taira: TIGH-rah
Taira no Kiyomori: (Chancellor Kiyomori) TIGH-rah-noh kee-yoh-MOH-ree
Taira no Tadanori: TIGH-rah-noh tah-dah-NOH-ree
tanka: TAHNG-kah
Toji: TOH-jee
Zeami Motokiyo: zay-AH-mee moh-toh-KEE-yoh

∿ The Tale of the Heike

Translated by Helen Craig McCullough

CHAPTER I

FROM

Gion Sho⁻ja

The sound of the Gion Shōja bells echoes the impermanence of all things; the color of the *śāla* flowers reveals the truth that the prosperous must decline. The proud do not endure, they are like a dream on a spring night; the mighty fall at last, they are as dust before the wind.

In a distant land, there are the examples set by Zhao Gao of Qin, Wang Mang of

---

The Tale of the Heike. Three strands of this story are followed in the selections: some incidents in the life of the Heike chancellor, Taira no Kiyomori; one battle scene and two vignettes of romantic young heroes of the Heike nobility, Tadanori and Atsumori; and the fate of the Imperial Lady

Han, Zhu Yi of Liang, and Lushan of Tang, all of them men who prospered after refusing to be governed by their former lords and sovereigns, but who met swift destruction because they disregarded admonitions, failed to recognize approaching turmoil, and ignored the nation's distress. Closer to home, there have been Masakado of Shōhei, Sumitomo of Tengyō, Yoshichika of Kōwa, and Nobuyori of Heiji, every one of them proud and mighty. But closest of all, and utterly beyond the power of mind to comprehend or tongue to relate, is the tale of Taira no Ason Kiyomori, the Rokuhara Buddhist Novice and Former Chancellor.

Kiyomori was the oldest son and heir of Punishments Minister Tadamori. [. . .]

FROM

The Sea Bass

Tadamori died at the age of fifty-eight, on the Fifteenth of the First Month in the third year of Ninpei,[1] after having attained the office of Punishments Minister. His heir, Kiyomori, succeeded him. [. . .]

People said the Heike prosperity was due to the divine favor of the Kumano gods. Once long ago, it seems, while Kiyomori was still Governor of Aki Province, a huge sea bass leaped into his boat while he was making a pilgrimage from Ise Bay to Kumano. "That is a sign of favor from our gods. Eat it at once," said the ascetic who was accompanying the party. "I have heard that a white fish jumped into King Wu of Zhou's boat in ancient days," Kiyomori said. "This is an auspicious event." Although it was a time for dietary abstinence and strict observance of the Ten Prohibitions,[2] he prepared the fish and fed parts of it to all his kinsmen and samurai. Perhaps that is why he was blessed by one stroke of luck after another, until he finally attained the lofty status of Chancellor. His sons and grandsons also rose in office faster than a dragon mounts the clouds. It was indeed cause for congratulation that he should have outstripped all of his kinsmen in the clan's nine generations. [. . .]

Kenreimon'in in the last chapter of the work, "The Initiates' Chapter." Although it is sometimes challenged as a late continuation of the text, this chapter has had its own ardent following since the fourteenth century.

There are two important modern translations of *The Tale of the Heike* in English. The first is a two-volume translation by Hiroshi Kitagawa and Bruce Tsuchida, published in Tokyo in 1975, recommended for its extremely clear text and good footnotes. The second is a single-volume translation with excellent apparatus and notes by Helen Craig McCullough in 1988. McCullough's tendency to condense the text in an approximation of the effect of the original Japanese and her strong literary tastes make this translation preferred for use here. All footnotes are based on the McCullough edition. Minor figures and dates are identified only if they directly affect the meaning of the story.

---

[1] **third year of Ninpei:** 1153.

[2] **the Ten Prohibitions:** Murder, theft, sexual misconduct, lying, use of immoral language, slander, evocation, greed, anger, and holding false views.

Giō

With the whole country in the palm of his hand, Kiyomori indulged in one freakish caprice after another, unabashed by the censure of society or the scorn of individuals. For example, in those days there lived in the capital two famous and accomplished *shirabyōshi* performers,[3] sisters called Giō and Ginyo. They were the daughters of another *shirabyōshi*, Toji. Kiyomori took an extravagant fancy to the older one, Giō; and the younger, Ginyo, found herself a popular favorite as a result. He also built a fine house for the mother, Toji, installed her in it, and sent her five hundred bushels of rice and a hundred thousand coins every month. The family was thus exceedingly prosperous and fortunate.

(Now, the first *shirabyōshi* dances in our country were performed during the reign of Emperor Toba by two women called Shima-no-senzai and Waka-no-mai. In the beginning, the dancers dressed in men's *suikan* overshirts and high caps and wore daggers with silver-decorated hilts and scabbards: their performances were thus called "male dancing." In more recent times, they have worn only the overshirts, dispensing with the cap and dagger. The name *shirabyōshi* [white rhythm] comes from the color of the overshirts.)

News of Giō's good fortune made some of the *shirabyōshi* in the capital envious and others spiteful. The envious ones said, "Lucky Giō! What entertainer wouldn't want to be exactly like her? It must be because she has used 'Gi' in her name; I'll do that, too." One called herself Giichi, another Gini, another Gifuku, another Gitoku, and so forth. The many spiteful ones kept their own names. "What difference could a name or part of a name make?" they sniffed. "Good fortune is something a person is born with from a previous existence."

After things had gone on in that way for three years, another renowned *shirabyōshi* appeared in the capital from Kaga Province. Her name was Hotoke, her age sixteen. High and low in the city praised her to the skies. "There have been many *shirabyōshi* from the old days on, but never have we witnessed such dancing," people said.

"However well known I may be, it is disappointing that I have received no summons from the Taira Chancellor-Novice, the greatest man of the day," Hotoke thought. "What is to keep me from offering my services according to the usual custom of entertainers?" She went to Kiyomori's Nishihachijō house one day.

"Hotoke, the dancer the capital is talking about nowadays, has come here," one of the household reported.

"What is this? Entertainers like her are not supposed to present themselves without being summoned. What makes her think she can simply show up like this? Besides, god or Buddha,[4] she has no business coming to a place where Giō is staying. Throw her out at once," Kiyomori said.

As Hotoke was about to leave after that harsh dismissal, Giō spoke to Kiyomori. "It is quite the usual thing for an entertainer to present herself without an invitation.

---

[3] *shirabyōshi* **performers:** These dancers are discussed in the next paragraph.

[4] **god or Buddha:** A play on Hotoke's name, which can mean "Buddha."

Then, too, they say Hotoke is still very young. It would be cruel to send her home with that harsh dismissal, now that she has ventured to come here. As a dancer myself, I cannot help feeling involved: I would be uncomfortable and sad, too. You would be doing her a great kindness by at least receiving her before sending her away, even if you don't watch her dance or listen to her sing. Won't you please be a little lenient and call her back to be received?"

"Well, my dear, since you make a point of it, I'll see her before she goes," Kiyomori said. He sent a messenger to summon Hotoke.

Hotoke had entered her carriage after that harsh dismissal and was just leaving, but she returned in obedience to the summons. Kiyomori came out to meet her. "I ought not to have received you today; I am doing it because Giō chose to make a point of it. But I may as well listen to you sing, as long as you are here. Give me an *imayō*,"[5] he said. Hotoke made respectful assent and sang an *imayō*:

> Now that it has encountered
>   this lord for the first time,
> it will live a thousand years —
>   the seedling pine tree.
> Cranes seem to have come flocking
>   to disport themselves
> where Turtle Island rises
>   from the garden lake.

She chanted the song three times, and the beauty of her voice astonished all who watched and listened. Kiyomori's interest was piqued. "You sing *imayō* nicely, my dear; I suspect you are a good dancer, too," he said. "I'll watch you perform a number. Call the drummer." The drummer was set to his instrument and Hotoke danced.

Hotoke was a beautiful girl with magnificent hair, a sweet voice, and flawless intonation. How could she have been a clumsy dancer? Kiyomori was dazzled and swept off his feet by the brilliance of her performance, which revealed a skill quite beyond imagination.

"What is this?" Hotoke said. "I came here on my own and was thrown out, but then I was recalled through Giō's intercession. If I were to be kept here, it would embarrass me to know what Giō's thoughts would be. Please let me go home right away."[6]

"That is out of the question. Are you hanging back because of Giō? If so, I'll dismiss her," Kiyomori said.

"How could such a thing be? I would feel terribly distressed even if the two of us were kept here together, but it would shame me deeply before Giō if you sent her away and kept me alone. I will answer any summons if you should happen to remember me later; please let me go today."

---

[5] *imayō*: Popular song.

[6] **"Please let me go home right away"**: Here the text is corrupt, but it appears that Kiyomori has decided to keep Hotoke as a mistress.

"What! What! That's out of the question. Tell Giō to leave the house at once." He sent Giō three separate messengers.

Although Giō had long ago resigned herself to the possibility, she had not dreamed that it might happen "so very soon as today."[7] But with Kiyomori insisting that she leave immediately, she resolved to go as soon as the room was swept and tidied.

Every parting brings sadness, even when two people have merely sheltered under the same tree or scooped water from the same stream. With what regret and grief did Giō prepare to bid farewell to her home of three years, her eyes brimming with futile tears! But she could not linger; the end had come. Weeping, she scribbled a poem on a sliding door as she set out — perhaps to serve as a reminder of one who had gone:

> Since both are grasses
> of the field, how may either
> be spared by autumn —
> the young shoot blossoming forth
> and the herb fading from view?

Giō entered her carriage, rode home, and fell prostrate inside the sliding doors, sobbing wildly.

"What is it? What is it?" her mother and sister asked.

She could not answer. They learned the truth only when they questioned the maid who had accompanied her.

The monthly rice and coin deliveries ceased thereafter, and it was the turn of Hotoke's connections to prosper. Men of every class sent Giō letters and messengers. "People say Kiyomori has dismissed her. Why not see her and have some fun?" they thought. But she could not shrug off her experience, mingle with others, and lead a gay life. She refused to accept their letters, much less receive the messengers, and spent more and more time weeping, her melancholy deepened by their importunities.

So the year ended. In the following spring, Kiyomori sent a messenger to Giō's house. "How have you been since we parted? Hotoke seems bored nowadays; come and amuse her with some *imayō* and dances." Giō made no response.

"Why don't you answer? Do you refuse to come? Say so, if you do. There are steps I can take," Kiyomori said.

Giō's mother, Toji, was greatly distressed. "Come, now, Giō, give him some kind of answer," she urged, weeping. "That would be better than having him scold you like this."

Giō still refused to answer. "I would say, 'I'll come at once,' if I thought I might go, but I don't intend to go, so I don't know how to answer. He says he will take steps unless I obey him when he summons me, but he can do no more than banish me from the city or kill me. Banishment would be no cause for sorrow, nor would I mind dying. I can't face him again after he has treated me with such contempt," she said.

---

[7] **"so very soon as today"**: Phrase from a death poem of Ariwara no Narihira (825–880) in the *Kokinshu* (861). (See p. 1057.)

The mother offered more advice. "Anyone who lives in this country had better not disobey Kiyomori. The bonds linking a man and a woman are fashioned before this life begins. Sometimes a couple part early after having sworn to stay together forever; sometimes a relationship that had seemed temporary lasts a lifetime. A sexual liaison is the most uncertain thing in the world. That you enjoyed Kiyomori's favor for three years was an unusual show of affection on his part. Of course he is not going to kill you if you refuse to answer his summons; he will simply expel you from the capital. You and your sister are young; you will probably survive very nicely, even among rocks and trees. But your weak old mother will be banished, too, and my heart sinks at the prospect of living in some strange country place. Won't you please let me finish out my life in the capital? I will think of it as a filial act in this world and the next."

Giō told herself that she must obey her mother, hard though it was. How pitiful were her emotions as she set out in tears! Unable to bring herself to go alone, she traveled to Nishihachijō in a single carriage with her sister, Ginyo, and two other *shirabyōshi*.

Giō was not directed to her old place, but to a much inferior seat. "What can this mean?" she thought. "It was misery enough to be discarded through no fault of my own; now I must even accept an inferior seat. What shall I do?" She pressed her sleeve to her face to hide her tears, but they came trickling through.

Hotoke was overcome with pity. "Ah, what is this?" she said. "It might be different if she were not accustomed to being called up here. Please have her come here, or else please excuse me. I would like to go and greet her."

"That is entirely out of the question." Hotoke had to stay where she was.

After that, Kiyomori spoke up, quite insensitive to Giō's feelings. "Well, how have you been since we parted? Hotoke seems bored; sing her an *imayō*."

Now that she had come, she could not refuse, Giō thought. She restrained her tears and sang an *imayō*:

> In days of old, the Buddha
>   was but a mortal;
> in the end, we ourselves
>   will be Buddhas, too.
> How grievous that distinctions
>   must separate those
> who are alike in sharing
>   the Buddha-nature.[8]

She repeated the words twice, weeping, and tears of sympathy flowed from the eyes of all the many Taira senior nobles, courtiers, Fifth-Rank gentlemen, and samurai who sat in rows looking on.

Kiyomori had found the performance diverting. "An excellent entertainment for the occasion," he said. "I'd like to watch you dance, but some urgent business has

---

[8] **In days of old . . . the Buddha-nature:** This song, an adaptation of a Buddhist chant, puns on Hotoke's name.

come up today. Keep presenting yourself from now on, even if I don't summon you; you must amuse Hotoke with your *imayō* and dances." Giō suppressed her tears and departed in silence.

"Alas! I forced myself to go to that detestable place out of reluctance to disobey my mother, and now I have suffered another humiliation. The same thing will happen again if I remain in society. I am going to drown myself," Giō said.

"If you do, I'll drown with you," said her sister, Ginyo.

The mother, Toji, was greatly distressed. Weeping, she offered more advice. "Your bitterness is all too natural. It grieves me that I urged you to go, with no suspicion of what might happen. But your sister says she will drown if you do. What would become of your weak old mother even if she managed to linger on after the deaths of her two daughters? I'll drown with you. I suppose it must be accounted one of the Five Deadly Sins[9] to make a parent drown before her time. The world is but a transient shelter. It matters not whether we suffer humiliation here; what is truly hard is the darkness of the long afterlife. This life is inconsequential; I am merely concerned about your facing the Evil Paths in the next one."

After listening to her mother's tearful plea, Giō suppressed her tears and spoke. "You are right. I would undoubtedly be committing one of the Five Deadly Sins if we all killed ourselves. I will abandon the idea of suicide. But it would mean additional suffering if I were to stay in the capital, so I will go elsewhere."

Thus Giō became a Buddhist nun at the age of twenty-one. She built a brush-thatched hermitage deep in the Saga mountains, and there she dwelt, murmuring Buddha-invocations.

"I vowed to drown myself with my older sister," Ginyo said. "Why would I hang behind when it came to renouncing the world?" Most pitifully, that nineteen-year-old girl also altered her appearance and secluded herself with Giō to pray for rebirth in paradise.

"Why should a weak old mother keep her gray hair in a world where even young girls alter their appearance?" the mother, Toji, said. She shaved her head at the age of forty-five and, like her daughters, performed Buddha-invocations in earnest prayer for rebirth in paradise.

Spring passed, summer waned, and the first autumn winds blew. It was the season when human beings gaze at the star-meeting skies and write of love on leaves of the paper-mulberry, the tree reminiscent of an oar crossing the heavenly stream. One afternoon, the mother and daughters watched the evening sun disappear behind the rim of the western hills. "People say the Western Paradise is situated in the place where the sun sets. We will be born there some day, to live free of all trouble,"[10] they said. The thought evoked a succession of painful memories, and they shed floods of tears.

---

[9] **the Five Deadly Sins:** These are killing one's father, mother, or a saint; injuring the body of Buddha; and creating disharmony among monks.

[10] **the Western Paradise . . . free of all trouble:** This is a reiteration of the doctrine of Pure Land Buddhism, a major theme throughout the work.

After the twilight hours had ended, they fastened their plaited bamboo door, lit the dim lamp, and settled down to intoning Buddha-invocations together. While they were thus employed, they heard a knocking at the door. They were terrified. "It must be a malevolent spirit, come to interfere with our humble invocations. What mortal would wait until late at night to visit a brush-thatched mountain hermitage where nobody ever calls, even in the daytime? The door is mere plaited bamboo; it would be the easiest thing in the world to smash it if we refused to open it. We had better let him in. If he is a merciless creature bent on our destruction, we must rely firmly on the Original Vow of Amida, in whom we have always placed our trust; we must maintain a constant stream of invocations. Since the heavenly host comes to meet believers, led by the sound of their voices, it will assuredly take us to the Pure Land. We must simply be careful not to falter in our invocations." Reassuring one another in that manner, they opened the plaited bamboo door.

The visitor was not a malevolent spirit but Hotoke.

"What is this?" Giō said. "Can it really be Hotoke? Am I awake or dreaming?"

Hotoke tried to restrain her tears. "What I say will sound self-serving, but I would seem callous if I remained silent, so I want to go over the whole story from the beginning. I went to Kiyomori's mansion on my own initiative and was turned away, but then I was called back, thanks entirely to Giō's intervention. A woman is a poor, weak thing, incapable of controlling her destiny. I was miserable about being kept there. When you were summoned again to sing the *imayō*, it brought home my own position. I was not in the least happy, because I knew my turn would come some day. I also recognized the truth of the lines you left on the sliding door, 'How may either be spared by autumn?' Later, I did not know where you had gone, but I heard that the three of you were living together as nuns. I envied you after that. I kept asking for my freedom, but Kiyomori would not grant it.

"When we stop to consider, flowering fortunes in this world are a dream within a dream; happiness and prosperity mean nothing. It is difficult to achieve birth in human form, difficult to gain access to the Buddha's teachings. If I sink into hell this time, it will be hard to rise again, no matter how many eons may pass. We cannot count on our youth; the old may outlive the young in this world. Death refuses to wait for the space of a breath; life is more evanescent than a mayfly or a lightning flash. I could not bear to live preening myself on my temporary good fortune and ignoring the life to come, so I stole away this morning, assumed this guise, and made my way here." She removed the robe covering her head, and they saw that she had become a nun.

"Now that I have come to you in this altered guise, please forgive my past offenses," Hotoke pleaded, with tears streaming from her eyes. "If you say you forgive me, I want to recite Buddha-invocations with you and be reborn on the same lotus pedestal. But if you cannot bring yourself to agree, I will wander away from here—it matters not where—to fall prostrate on a bed of moss or on the roots of a pine tree, there to recite Buddha-invocations as long as my life endures, so that I may attain my goal of rebirth in the Pure Land."

Giō tried to restrain her tears. "I never dreamed that you felt that way. I ought to have been able to accept my unhappiness here at Saga, for sorrow is the common lot in this world, but I was always jealous of you. I fear there would have been no rebirth in the Pure Land for me. I seemed stranded halfway between this world and the next. The change in your appearance has made my old resentment vanish like scattering dewdrops; there is no longer any doubt that I will be reborn in the Pure Land. That I may now attain my goal is the greatest of all possible joys. People have talked about our becoming nuns as though it were unprecedented, and I myself have had somewhat the same thoughts, but it was only natural for me to alter my appearance when I hated society and resented my fate. What I did is unworthy of mention in comparison with the vows you have just taken. You felt no resentment and knew no sorrow. Only true piety could instill such revulsion against the unclean world, such longing for the Pure Land, in the heart of one who has barely turned seventeen. I look on you as a great teacher. Let us seek salvation together."

Secluded in a single dwelling, the four women offered flowers and incense before the sacred images morning and evening; and their prayers never flagged. I have heard that all of those nuns achieved their goal of rebirth in the Pure Land, each in her turn. And so it was that the four names, "the spirits of Giō, Ginyo, Hotoke, and Toji," were inscribed together on the memorial register at Retired Emperor Go-Shirakawa's Chōgodō Temple. Theirs were touching histories.

CHAPTER VI

FROM

The Death of Kiyomori

[. . .] It became known that the Chancellor-Novice's condition was critical. "Ah! His deeds have come home to roost," people whispered in the city and at Rokuhara.

Kiyomori could swallow nothing, not even a sip of water, after the disease took hold. His body was fiery hot; people could hardly bear to remain within twenty-five or thirty feet of the bed. His only words were, "Hot! Hot!" It seemed no ordinary ailment.

The mansion's people filled a stone tub with water drawn from the Thousand-Armed Well on Mount Hiei,[11] but the water boiled up and turned to steam as soon as Kiyomori got in to cool off. Desperate to bring him some relief, they directed a stream of water onto his body from a bamboo pipe, but the liquid spattered away without reaching him, as though from red-hot stone or iron. The few drops that struck him burst into flame, so that black smoke filled the hall and tongues of fire swirled toward the ceiling. Now, for the first time, the onlookers understood what Bishop Hōzō must have experienced when he asked about the place of his mother's rebirth while he was visiting King Enma's court at the King's invitation: the compassionate King sent him to the Tapana Hot Hell with an escort of torturer-guards, and

---

[11] **Thousand-Armed Well on Mount Hiei:** A place of healing sacred to the Buddhist and Taoist traditions. The name of the well was sometimes written with ideographs meaning "thousand years," so it was probably believed to contain magic as well.

inside the iron gate he beheld flames like shooting stars, which ascended into the heavens for hundreds of yojanas.

Kiyomori's wife, the Nun of Second Rank, had a frightful dream. A flaming carriage was brought inside the gate, attended at the front and rear by horse-faced and ox-faced creatures, and bearing on its head an iron tablet inscribed with the single graph *mu* [without].

"Where has that carriage come from?" the Nun asked in the dream.

"From Enma's tribunal; it is here to fetch the Taira Chancellor-Novice," a voice answered.

"What is the meaning of the tablet?"

"It has been decided at the tribunal that the Chancellor-Novice will fall to the bottom of [the Hell of Punishment] Without Intermission [Mugen] for the crime of burning the one-hundred-sixty-foot gilt bronze Vairocana in the world of men. Enma has written the *mu* of Mugen, but he has not put in the *gen* [intermission] yet."

The Nun started awake, bathed in perspiration, and the hair of all whom she told about it stood on end. The family showered wonder-working shrines and temples with gold, silver, and the Seven Treasures; they even sent off horses, saddles, armor helmets, bows, arrows, swords, and daggers—but there was no indication of divine response. The sons and daughters gathered at the head and foot of their father's bed, grieving and racking their brains for something to do, but there seemed little likelihood that matters would turn out as they wished.

On the Second of the intercalary Second Month, the Nun of Second Rank braved the intolerable heat to approach her husband's pillow. "As I watch you, I cannot help feeling that things seem more hopeless every day," she said in tears. "If there is anything in this world you crave, tell me when your mind is clear."

The man who had been so formidable a figure spoke in a painful whisper. "Since Hōgen and Heiji, I have subdued court enemies more than once; I have received rewards beyond my deserts; I have become an Emperor's grandfather and a Chancellor; I have seen my prosperity extend to my offspring. There is nothing left for me to desire in this life. My sole concern is that I have not seen the severed head of the Izu Exile Yoritomo. Build no halls or pagodas after I die; dedicate no pious works. Dispatch the punitive force immediately, decapitate Yoritomo, and hang the head in front of my grave. That will be all the dedication I require." Those were deeply sinful words indeed.

On the Fourth, they tried to alleviate Kiyomori's suffering by laying him on a water-soaked board, but it did no good. Writhing in agony, he fell to the floor unconscious and died in convulsions. The sound of horses and carriages galloping in every direction was enough to set the heavens echoing and the earth trembling: it seemed there could have been no greater agitation if death had claimed the imperial master of all the realm, the Lord of a Myriad Chariots.

Kiyomori had turned sixty-four that year. It was not an age at which death was necessarily to have been expected, but karma had decreed that he should live no longer: the large rituals and the secret rituals lacked efficacy, the power of the gods and the Buddhas vanished, the heavenly spirits offered no protection. What could mere mortals do? There were tens of thousands of loyal warriors seated in rows high and low at the hall, each ready to exchange his life for his lord's, but none of them could hold off the unseen, invincible messenger from the land of the dead for even an instant. Kiyomori must have been quite alone when he set out on his journey through the nether regions, over the Shide Mountains from which no man returns, and past the River of Three Crossings.[12] Most sadly, his only escorts must have been the evil deeds he had committed so often, come to greet him in the form of horse-headed and ox-headed torturers.

Since matters could not go on like that forever, they cremated the body at Otagi on the Seventh. Dharma Eye Enjitsu hung the bones around his neck, took them down to Settsu Province, and buried them at Kyō-no-shima Island. Kiyomori's fame and power had extended the length and breadth of Japan, yet his flesh rose into the skies over the capital as a transitory plume of smoke, and his bones survived only briefly before becoming one with the earth, indistinguishable from the sands of the beach.

Chapter VII

Tadanori's Flight from the Capital

Somewhere along the way, the Satsuma Governor Tadanori turned back to Shunzei's Gojō house, accompanied by five samurai and a page. The gate was locked. "It is Tadanori," he announced.

There was an agitated stir inside. "One of the fugitives has come back!"

Tadanori dismounted. "It is nothing special, Shunzei," he called out himself in a loud voice. "I have just come back to speak to you. Come here if you would rather not open the gate."

"Ah, yes," Shunzei said. "I think I know what he wants. He won't make any trouble. Let him in." His people opened the gate and he received the visitor. It was a moving scene.

"I have not meant to be neglectful since you accepted me as a pupil some years ago, but my clan has had to bear the brunt of the unrest in the city and the rebellions in the provinces; I have been unable to call regularly during the last two or three years, even though poetry has remained very important to me. His Majesty has already left the capital; my clan's good fortune has already ended. I had heard that an imperial poetic anthology was to be commissioned, and had thought it would be the greatest honor of my life for you to include even one poem by me. Now, alas, this turmoil has arisen and there has been no commission, but there is sure to be one after the restoration of peace. If this scroll contains a single suitable poem, and if you should see fit to include it, I would rejoice in my grave and become your guardian spirit."

---

[12] **River of Three Crossings:** It was believed the dead had to cross this river after seven days; each ford was deeper than the last, and evil souls had to cross at the deepest ford.

On the point of departure, Tadanori had picked up a scroll in which he had inscribed more than a hundred poems, to his mind the best of the many he had composed and saved over the years. Now he withdrew it from the armhole in his armor and gave it to Shunzei.

Shunzei opened the scroll and looked at it. "I could not possibly treat this keepsake lightly. Please have no fears on that score. Your coming here at this time shows how much the art of poetry means to you: I am moved to tears."

Tadanori was overjoyed. "Now I shall not mind sinking beneath the western waves or leaving my bones to bleach in the wilds. Nothing remains to bind me to this transient world. Farewell!" He mounted his horse, tied the cords of his helmet, and went off toward the west. Shunzei watched until he had receded far into the distance. Someone was chanting a *rōei* in a resonant voice that sounded like his:

> Distant lies the way ahead;
> My thoughts run on to the Yanshan evening clouds.

Shunzei tried to restrain his tears as he went inside, moved anew by the sorrow of parting. Later, when he was compiling the *Collection for a Thousand Years* after the restoration of peace, he remembered Tadanori's appearance and speech with deep emotion. The scroll contained many suitable poems, but the author was a man who had suffered imperial censure, and thus he chose only one, on the topic "Blossoms at the Old Capital." He labeled it "Anonymous":

> It lies ruined now —
> the old Shiga capital
> at Sazanami —
> yet the Nagara cherry trees
> bloom as in days gone by.

Tadanori was an enemy of the throne, so there is nothing more to be said. Still, it is a pathetic tale.

CHAPTER IX

The Death of Atsumori

Kumagae no Jirō Naozane walked his horse toward the beach after the defeat of the Heike. "The Taira nobles will be fleeing to the water's edge in the hope of boarding rescue vessels," he thought. "Ah, how I would like to grapple with a high-ranking Commander-in-Chief!" Just then, he saw a lone rider splash into the sea, headed toward a vessel in the offing. The other was attired in a crane-embroidered *nerinuki* silk *hitatare*, a suit of armor with shaded green lacing, and a horned helmet. At his waist, he wore a sword with gilt bronze fittings; on his back, there rode a quiver containing arrows fledged with black-banded white eagle feathers. He grasped a rattan-wrapped bow and bestrode a white-dappled reddish horse with a gold-edged saddle. When his mount had swum out about a hundred and fifty or two hundred feet, Naozane beckoned him with his fan.

"I see that you are a Commander-in-Chief. It is dishonorable to show your back to an enemy. Return!"

The warrior came back. As he was leaving the water, Naozane rode up alongside him, gripped him with all his strength, crashed with him to the ground, held him motionless, and pushed aside his helmet to cut off his head. He was sixteen or seventeen years old, with a lightly powdered face and blackened teeth—a boy just the age of Naozane's own son Kojirō Naoie, and so handsome that Naozane could not find a place to strike.

"Who are you? Announce your name. I will spare you," Naozane said.

"Who are you?" the youth asked.

"Nobody of any importance: Kumagae no Jirō Naozane, a resident of Musashi Province."

"Then it is unnecessary to give you my name. I am a desirable opponent for you. Ask about me after you take my head. Someone will recognize me, even if I don't tell you."

"Indeed, he must be a Commander-in-Chief," Naozane thought. "Killing this one person will not change defeat into victory, nor will sparing him change victory into defeat. When I think of how I grieved when Kojirō suffered a minor wound, it is easy to imagine the sorrow of this young lord's father if he were to hear that the boy had been slain. Ah, I would like to spare him!" Casting a swift glance to the rear, he discovered Sanehira and Kagetoki coming along behind him with fifty riders.

"I would like to spare you," he said, restraining his tears, "but there are Genji warriors everywhere. You cannot possibly escape. It will be better if I kill you than if someone else does it, because I will offer prayers on your behalf."

"Just take my head and be quick about it."

Overwhelmed by compassion, Naozane could not find a place to strike. His senses reeled, his wits forsook him, and he was scarcely conscious of his surroundings. But matters could not go on like that forever: in tears, he took the head.

"Alas! No lot is as hard as a warrior's. I would never have suffered such a dreadful experience if I had not been born into a military house. How cruel I was to kill him!" He pressed his sleeve to his face and shed floods of tears.

Presently, since matters could not go on like that forever, he started to remove the youth's armor *hitatare* so that he might wrap it around the head. A brocade bag containing a flute was tucked in at the waist. "Ah, how pitiful! He must have been one of the people I heard making music inside the stronghold just before dawn. There are tens of thousands of riders in our eastern armies, but I am sure none of them has brought a flute to the battlefield. Those court nobles are refined men!"

When Naozane's trophies were presented for Yoshitsune's inspection, they drew tears from the eyes of all the beholders. It was learned later that the slain youth was Tayū Atsumori, aged seventeen, a son of Tsunemori, the Master of the Palace Repairs Office.

After that, Naozane thought increasingly of becoming a monk.

The flute in question is said to have been given by Retired Emperor Toba to Atsumori's grandfather Tadamori, who was a skilled musician. I believe I have heard that Tsunemori, who inherited it, turned it over to Atsumori because of his son's proficiency as a flautist. Saeda [Little Branch] was its name. It is deeply moving that music, a profane entertainment, should have led a warrior to the religious life.

THE INITIATES' CHAPTER

[The Imperial Lady Kenreimon'in, Chancellor Taira no Kyromori's daughter, has gone to live in exile in an abandoned cloister. Surrounded by ruins, deep in melancholy, she becomes a nun. She presents the priest who administers the holy precepts to her with a robe worn by Emperor Antoku, to whom she has been the royal consort and given birth to a son. After her decision to become a nun, her dilapidated cloister is struck by an earthquake, rendering it uninhabitable. She resolves to leave for the mountains, where she will build a sanctuary at Ohara.]

The Imperial Lady Goes to Ōhara

Although the Imperial Lady's plight was thus, her younger sisters, the wives of the Reizei Major Counselor Takafusa and the Shichijō Master of the Palace Repairs Office Nobutaka, found discreet ways of expressing their sympathy. "In the old days, it never occurred to me that I might have to depend on those two for a livelihood," she said, with tears streaming down her face. The ladies in attendance all drenched their sleeves.

Her present abode was close to the capital, near a road where there were many inquisitive passersby. She longed to move to some place in the innermost recesses of the deep mountains—a refuge too remote for distressing news to reach her ears, where she might remain while the dew of her life awaited the wind—but no suitable opportunity arose. Then a certain lady caller said, "The Jakkōin, far back in the mountains at Ōhara, is a very quiet place," and she resolved to go there. "It is true enough that a mountain hermitage is lonely, yet life is far better there than in the vexatious world,"[13] she said. I believe I have heard that Takafusa's wife made the arrangements for the palanquin and other necessities.

The Imperial Lady proceeded to the Jakkōin late in the Ninth Month of the first year of Bunji. Perhaps because the road led through mountains, the twilight shadows began to gather as she journeyed, her eyes lingering on the colored foliage of the surrounding trees. A lonely sunset bell boomed from a temple in the fields, the thick dew on the wayside plants added fresh moisture to her tear-dampened sleeves, a violent wind sent leaves scurrying in every direction, and a sudden shower descended from the cloud-blackened sky, accompanied by the faint belling of a deer and the almost inaudible plaints of insect voices. The melancholy effect of so many depressing sights and sounds was quite beyond comparison. "Even when we were going from bay to bay and island to island, nothing was as bad as this," she thought piteously.

With its mossy rocks and its atmosphere of tranquil antiquity, the Jakkōin seemed a place where she could settle down willingly. Might she have thought of her

---

[13] **"It is true . . . the vexatious world":** From the *Kokinshu* (944); anonymous.

own self when she saw the frost-stricken clumps of dewy bush clover in the court-yard, or gazed at the withering, fading chrysanthemums by the rough-woven fence? She went before the Buddha to pray: "May the Son of Heaven's holy spirit achieve perfect wisdom; may prompt enlightenment be assured." The face of the Former Emperor was before her as she spoke. Would she ever forget it in all the lives to come?

Next to the Jakkōin she built a ten-foot-square hermitage, with one bay as a bedroom and the other as a chapel, and there she spent the days in diligent performance of the six diurnal services and the perpetual Buddha-recitations.

Toward evening on the Fifteenth of the Tenth Month, the Imperial Lady heard footsteps in the scattered oak leaves blanketing the courtyard. "Who can have come to this recluse's dwelling? Look and see. If it is someone from whom I should hide, I will hurry and hide."

The intruder proved to be a passing stag. When the lady asked, "Well?" Dainagon-no-suke replied in verse, suppressing her tears:

> Who might be coming,
> treading on rocks, to call here?
> The visitor whose step
> rustles through fallen oak leaves
> is but a passing stag.

With a full heart, the lady wrote the poem on the small sliding door near her window.

Despite all its hardships, the Imperial Lady's tedious existence suggested many interesting comparisons: she likened the rows of native trees at her eaves to the seven tree circles surrounding the Pure Land, and she thought of the water collecting between the rocks as the Waters of Eight Virtues.

The ephemerality of worldly things is like springtime blossoms scattering in the breeze, the brevity of man's existence is like the autumn moon disappearing behind a cloud. On mornings when the lady had enjoyed blossoms at the Chengyang Hall, the wind had come and scattered their beauty; on evenings when she had composed poems about the moon at the Zhangqiu Palace, clouds had covered the moon's face and hidden its radiance. Once she had dwelt in a magnificent abode with jeweled towers, golden halls, and brocade cushions; now her brushwood hermitage drew tears even from the eyes of strangers.

The Imperial Journey to Ōhara

Meanwhile, around the spring of the second year of Bunji, Retired Emperor Go-Shirakawa conceived a desire to see Kenreimon'in's secluded abode at Ōhara, but fierce winds blew during the Second and Third months, and the cold weather dragged on. The white snows on the peaks had not melted completely, nor had the icicles in the valleys thawed. Spring passed, summer arrived, and the Kamo Festival took place. Then, one night while it was still dark, the former sovereign set out for the recesses of Ōhara. Although he traveled without ceremony, his entourage included Tokudaiji no Sanesada, Kazan'in no Kanemasa, Tsuchimikado no Michichika, and three other senior nobles, as well as eight courtiers and a few North Guards. The party took the Kurama highroad: His Majesty viewed Kiyowara no Fukayabu's Fuda-rakuji Temple and the place where the Ono Grand Empress had lived. At Ono, he changed to a palanquin. The white clouds on the distant hills recalled the now-scattered cherry blossoms; the green leaves on the trees served as poignant remind-ers of spring's departure. It was past the Twentieth of the Fourth Month, a season of lush summer growth, and the Retired Emperor, who had never gone that way before, beheld no familiar sight as his equipage parted the tips of the dense foliage. Most movingly, he recognized that he had come to a place unfrequented by men.

A lone Buddhist structure, situated at the foot of the western hills, proved to be the Jakkōin. The venerable aspect of the garden pond and the ancient groves made it seem a place with a noble history. Might it have been of just such a one that the poet wrote these lines?

> The roof tiles are broken, the fog burns perpetual incense;
> The doors have fallen, the moonbeams light eternal lamps.

Young grasses burgeoned in the courtyard, green willow branches tangled in the wind, and the duckweed on the pond, drifting with the waves, might have been mis-taken for brocade set out to be washed. The wisteria clinging to the islet pines had put forth purple flowers; the late-blooming cherries, interspersed among the green leaves, seemed a novelty more delightful than the season's first blossoms. The kerria on the banks was in full bloom, and a mountain cuckoo's song descended from a rift in the many-layered clouds, as though to welcome the awaited imperial guest. The Retired Emperor composed a poem:

> Wave-flowers in full bloom:
> on the surface of the pond,
>   blossoms have scattered
> from the cherry trees
> along the water's edge.

It was a place where everything seemed endowed with a special charm, even to the sound of the stream gushing from a cleft in the time-worn rocks. The fences were overgrown with green ivy; the mountains appeared etched with eyebrow pencil. No painter could have done justice to the scene.

When the Retired Emperor's eyes turned to the Imperial Lady's hermitage, he saw ivy and morning-glory vines climbing the eaves, and "forgetting-grass" day lilies mingled with "remembering-grass" ferns. It was an abode of which someone might have said, "The gourd and the rice tub are often empty, the grasses riot as in Yuan Xian's alley. Pigweed grows rampant, rain wets the doors as at Yan Yuan's house."[14] The crudely thatched cryptomeria roof seemed scarcely capable of excluding the rain, frost, and dew that vied with the infiltrating moonbeams for admittance. Be-hind, there were mountains; in front, barren fields where the wind whistled through low bamboo grass. The bamboo pillars, with their many joints, recalled the manifold

---

[14] **"The gourd . . . Yan Yuan's house"**: Adapted from a scholar's complaint about his poverty and failure to advance professionally.

sorrows of those who dwell apart from society; the brushwood fence, with its loose weave, brought to mind the long intervals between tidings from the capital. By way of visitors, there were only the cries of monkeys, swinging from tree to tree on the peaks, and the sounds of woodcutters' axes, felling timber to be used as firewood. For the rest, those who came were rare, unless we might count the curling tendrils of wild vines.

"Is anybody there? Is anybody there?" the Retired Emperor asked. There was no answer. Then, after a long delay, an aged, feeble nun made her appearance.

"Where has the Imperial Lady gone?" the Retired Emperor asked.

"To the mountain up there, to gather flowers."

"Was there no one she could have sent on such an errand? Nun though she may have become, it is pitiful that she must do it herself."

"She suffers her present hardships because there has been an end to the good karma she earned by observing the Five Commandments and the Ten Good Precepts," said the nun. "Why should she mind performing austerities that mortify the flesh? The *Cause and Effect Sutra* instructs us, 'If you want to know past causes, look at present effects; if you want to know future effects, look at present causes.' If Your Majesty understands past and future causes and effects, you will feel no grief at all. Prince Siddhārtha left Gayā at the age of nineteen, covered his nudity with garments of leaves at the foot of Mount Daṇḍaka, climbed to the peaks for firewood, descended to the valleys for water, and finally achieved perfect enlightenment through the merit of his difficult and painful austerities."

The Retired Emperor could not determine whether the ancient scraps of cloth in the nun's patchwork robe were silk or some other material. It was odd, he thought, that one thus attired should have spoken so. "Tell me who you are," he said.

Tears streamed down the nun's face: for a moment, she was unable to reply. She restrained her tears after a time. "It pains me to confess it, but I am the late Lesser Counselor-Novice Shinzei's daughter, the one who used to be called Awa-no-naishi. My mother was the Kii Lady of Second Rank. You used to be so very kind, but now I am such an old crone that you don't even recognize me! Oh, I can't bear it!" She pressed her sleeve to her face, unable to control her feelings any longer. It was a sight too pathetic to watch.

"So you are Awa-no-naishi! I did not know you. How like a dream this is!" The Retired Emperor could not suppress his tears.

"No wonder she seemed an unusual nun," the senior nobles and courtiers in the entourage said to one another.

The Retired Emperor inspected the surroundings. Heavy with dew, the bushes in the courtyard leaned against the brushwood fence; on the flooded rice paddy outside, there was not even space for a longbill to alight. He entered the hermitage and pulled the sliding door open. The first room contained the Welcoming Triad, with a five-colored cord attached to the central deity's hand. To the left, there was a painting of Fugen; to the right, there were pictures of the Teacher Shandao and the Former Emperor. There were also the eight scrolls of the *Lotus Sutra*[15] and the nine

---

[15] *Lotus Sutra:* Conversations with the Buddha; a principal book of Mahayana Buddhism (200 C.E.).

scrolls of Shandao's writings. Instead of orchid and musk fragrance, smoke ascended from offering-incense. Even thus, it seemed, must have been the ten-foot-square cell where Vimalakīrti aligned thirty-two thousand seats for the Buddhas of the ten directions. Noteworthy sutra passages, inscribed on bits of colored paper, were pasted to sliding doors here and there. There were also some lines of Chinese verse, the ones said to have been composed at Mount Qingliang by the monk whose lay name was Ōe no Sadamoto:

> From a lone cloud, mouth organs and singing resound in the distance;
> In front of the setting sun, the divine host approaches to bid me welcome.

Somewhat apart, there was a poem, seemingly from the Imperial Lady's brush:

> Did I ever think
> to find myself dwelling
>   deep in the mountains,
> gazing at the moon on high,
> far from the royal palace?

Off to the side, the Retired Emperor saw what appeared to be the Imperial Lady's bedchamber. A hemp robe, a paper quilt, and similar articles hung from bamboo rods. It seemed only a dream that the lady had once worn damask, gauze, brocade, and embroidery—the choicest stuffs of Japan and China. The senior nobles and courtiers, all of whom had witnessed her former splendor, recalled those earlier scenes as though they had just taken place; and they wept until their sleeves were drenched.

Presently, two nuns in deep black robes came picking their painful way down the steep, rocky path from the mountain above.

"Who are they?" the Retired Emperor asked.

The old nun tried not to weep. "The one carrying a basket of rock azaleas on her arm is the Imperial Lady. The one with the firewood and bracken is the Former Empress's nurse, Dainagon-no-suke, the daughter of the Torikai Middle Counselor Korezane and the adopted daughter of the Gojō Major Counselor Kunitsuna." She burst into tears as she spoke. Profoundly moved, the Retired Emperor also shed tears in spite of himself.

The Imperial Lady longed in vain to disappear: nun or not, it was too embarrassing to let him see her in her present garb. She stood helpless, choked with tears, neither returning to the mountain nor entering the hermitage. Perhaps she despaired of drying her sleeves, which she had soaked during the nightly holy-water drawing, and drenched again after rising before dawn to tread the dewy mountain path. Awa-no-naishi went up to her and took the flower basket.

The Matter of the Six Paths

"Yours is the customary garb of one who has renounced the world," Awa-no-naishi said. "It is quite all right to appear in it. Hurry and meet His Majesty: let him begin the return journey." Her mistress entered the hermitage.

In tears, the Imperial Lady met the Retired Emperor. "I have expected the radiance of the saving Buddha to shine before the window whenever I have pronounced a single invocation; I have awaited the divine host's appearance at the brushwood door whenever I have pronounced ten invocations. But never did I anticipate so remarkable an event as this visit."

"Even those who dwell in the Bhavāgra Heaven, where the lifespan is eighty thousand kalpas, must face the affliction of inevitable death; not even those who dwell in the six heavens of the world of desire can evade the sorrow of the Five Signs of Decay. The wondrous pleasures of the Joyful-to-See Palace, the delights of Bonten's Lofty Palace — all are but the good fortune of a dream, the happiness of a phantasm, subject to eternal change. They are like the turning wheels of a carriage. Alas! The grief of the heavenly beings' Five Signs of Decay has visited the world of men as well," the Retired Emperor said. "But tell me," he continued, "who comes to see you? There must be many things to remind you of the past."

"No visitors come from anywhere. I do hear occasionally from the wives of Takafusa and Nobutaka. In the old days, I never dreamed I might have to depend on those two for a livelihood," the Imperial Lady said, with tears streaming down her countenance. The ladies in attendance all drenched their sleeves.

The Imperial Lady restrained her tears. "Of course, this present state causes me temporary distress, but I look on it as a blessing when I think about my future enlightenment. I have hastened to become Śākyamuni's disciple and have reverently placed my faith in Amida's vow; thus, I escape the sorrows of the Five Obstacles and the Three Subordinations, I purify my six senses during each of the six divisions of the day, and I pray with all my heart for rebirth in the Pure Land of Nine Grades. There is no time when I do not await the Welcoming Triad, offering fervent prayers for my family's enlightenment. But never, in all the lives to come, shall I forget the Former Emperor's face. I try to forget, but forgetting is impossible; I try to control my grief, but that is also impossible. Nothing causes such sorrow as parental affection: that is why I pray faithfully for the Former Emperor's enlightenment, morning and evening. I believe my love for him will guide me to enlightenment, too."

"Although these remote islands are as tiny as scattered millet grains," the Retired Emperor said, "the merit remaining from observance of the Ten Good Precepts has conferred on me the awesome title of Lord of a Myriad Chariots; and, as befits my status, there is nothing that is not as I would have it. In particular, there can be no doubt that I will enter paradise in the next life, for I have been born in a land where men disseminate the Buddhist teachings, and my desire to follow the Way is fervent. There is no reason why evidence of this world's evanescence should come as a shock to me now. And yet I find it unbearable to see you as you are."

[The Imperial Lady tells the Retired Emperor the story of her flight from the capital at Heian with the rest of the Heike. After describing the military defeats the Heike suffered and their final battle in which all was lost, she relates how her mother seized her son, the little Emperor, and jumped with him in her arms into the sea. Her mother's last words to the Emperor were "Your good fortune has come to an end. Turn to the east and say goodbye to the Grand Shrine of Ise, then turn to the west and repeat the sacred name of Amida Buddha, so that he and his host may come to escort you to the Pure Land. This country is a land of sorrow; I am taking you to a happy realm called Paradise." The Imperial Lady consoles herself only by praying for the salvation of her dead son and the others who perished in the final battle.]

"We are told that Tripiṭika Xuanzhuang of China saw the Six Paths before he achieved enlightenment, and that the holy Nichizō of our land saw them through the power of Zaō Gongen. But it is rare indeed to behold them before one's very eyes, as you have done." The Retired Emperor choked with tears, and all the senior nobles and courtiers in his retinue wrung their sleeves. The Imperial Lady also shed tears, and her attendants drenched their sleeves.

The Death of the Imperial Lady

Presently, the boom of the Jakkōin bell announced nightfall, and the evening sun sank in the west. Hard though it was to say goodbye, the Retired Emperor set out for home, restraining his tears. The Imperial Lady flooded her sleeve with irrepressible tears, her memories more poignant than ever. After watching the procession recede gradually into the distance, the lady faced the sacred image. "May the holy spirit of the Son of Heaven and the dead spirits of the Heike clan achieve perfect wisdom and prompt enlightenment," she prayed, weeping. In the past, she had faced eastward and said, "May the Grand Shrine of Ise and the Bodhisattva Hachiman grant the Son of Heaven a thousand autumns and a myriad years of life"; now, most pathetically, she faced westward and prayed with joined hands, "May the holy spirit of the dead be reborn in Amida's Pure Land." She wrote two poems on the sliding door in her bedroom:

> How has it happened
> that suddenly of late
> my heart grows heavy
> with nostalgia for those
> who serve the imperial court?

> Since the past has become
> only a fleeting dream,
> surely this sojourn
> behind a woven-wood door
> will prove no more permanent.

I believe I have heard that this poem was inscribed on one of the hermitage pillars by the Tokudaiji Minister of the Left Sanesada, who was a member of the Retired Emperor's entourage:

> This is the Empress
> whom we compared to the moon
> in earlier days,
> but no radiance brightens
> the lonely mountain dwelling.

A hill cuckoo flew by, singing, just at a time when the Imperial Lady happened to be choked with tears, her mind full of the past and the future. She composed this verse:

> If we are to meet,
> cuckoo, in this way—come, then,

> let us compare tears,
> for I, also, like yourself,
> cry constantly in this cruel world.

The men captured at Dan-no-ura had either been paraded through the avenues and beheaded or else sent into distant exile, far from their wives and children. With the exception of the Ike Major Counselor Yorimori, not one had been allowed to remain alive in the capital. The forty or more women, to whom no punishments had been meted out, had turned to relatives for assistance or gone to stay with other connections. But there was no house free of disquieting winds, even inside jade blinds; there was no dwelling where the dust never rose, even beyond brushwood doors. Husbands and wives who had slept on adjoining pillows were as remote from one another as the sky; nurturing parents and their children were set apart, neither knowing the whereabouts of the other. Tormented by ceaseless longing, they managed somehow to struggle through the melancholy days. It was all the fault of the Chancellor-Novice Kiyomori, the man who had held the whole country in the palm of his hand and executed and banished as he pleased, unawed by the Emperor above and heedless of the myriad folk below, with no concern either for society or for individuals. There seemed no room for doubt that the evil deeds of a father must be visited on his offspring.

With the passing of time, the Imperial Lady fell ill. She recited Buddha invocations, clasping the five-colored cord attached to the hand of the central image. "Hail, Amitābha Tathāgata, Teaching Lord of the Western Paradise! Please admit me to the Pure Land." On her left and right, Dainagon-no-suke and Awa-no-naishi wailed and shrieked at the top of their lungs, overcome with sorrow as the end approached. After her chanting voice had gradually weakened, a purple cloud trailed in the west, a marvelous fragrance permeated the chamber, and the sound of music was heard in the heavens. Man's time on earth is finite, and thus the lady's life drew to a close at last, midway through the Second Month in the second year of Kenkyū. The parting brought agonies of inconsolable grief to the two attendants who had never left her side since her days as Empress. They had nowhere to turn for help, the grasses of old ties having long withered; nonetheless, they contrived most touchingly to perform the periodic memorial services. People said both of them attained the Nāga Girl's wisdom, emulated King Bimbisāra's wife, and achieved their goal of rebirth in the Pure Land.

◌ ZEAMI MOTOKIYO
1364–1443

The *Nō* drama is a Japanese artistic creation originally composed of elements of sacred ritual and festival performances. It reached its full development during the late thirteenth and early fourteenth centuries, adding story material to older performance spectacles. The first great master of *Nō* drama, **Kannami Motokiyo** (1333–1384), created realistic plays out of ritual drama, favoring in his simplicity of plot and themes the mood and tastes of the countryside. Following a more sophisticated Japanese literary tradition, his son **Zeami Motokiyo** developed plays based on the great stories of the Heian and **Muromachi** periods, from *The Tale of Genji* (c. 1000) to *The Tale of the Heike* (1371). But *Nō* drama consists of much more than embellished ritual performances of plays based on familiar stories. It embodies a philosophy of beauty, a deep understanding of theater design, music, dance, the fine arts, and stagecraft, and an impulse toward the mysterious that can only be called religious. All *Nō* drama provides a richer combination of artistic forms than that found in postclassical European theater. In fact, the only comparable European drama is either very early or very modern. The *Nō* plays of Zeami Motokiyo remind one of the Greek tragedies of **Aeschylus**, **Sophocles**, and **Euripides**.[1] Like Greek tragedies, *Nō* drama developed a formal artistic tradition of its own, a tradition Zeami substantially enlarged with his plays and his writings on the theater.[2] At the same time, its attention to brevity, gesture, the unseen, and the unspoken gives *Nō* drama a modern aspect. One might say it has been courted by thespians worldwide in the last hundred years or so, asked to give up its secrets, even abducted from time to time by the West.[3]

The Origins of *Nō* Drama. A valuable introduction to *Nō* drama is the *Okina*, a work that often precedes *Nō* plays at festivals and at special times of the year. The *Okina* is closer to a fertility ritual than it is to drama, and actors must undergo days of purification before performing it. The lead dancer, the actor playing Okina, must become a god in the middle of the performance. The performance consists of three dances: the spirited invocation of the god by the young man, **Senzai**; the dance of

NOH

kah-NAH-mee
moh-toh-KEE-yoh

zay-AH-mee
moh-toh KEE-yoh
moo-roh-MAH-chee
GEN-jee; HAY-keh

ES-kuh-lus;
SAH-fuh-kleez
yoo-RIP-ih-deez

oh-KEE-nah

SEN-zigh

---

[1] **Aeschylus . . . Euripides:** Aeschylus (525?–456 B.C.E.) was the author of *The Oresteia*, a trilogy of plays; Sophocles (496–406 B.C.E.) was the author of *Antigone* and *Oedipus Rex*, part of the Oedipus cycle; and Euripides (480–406 B.C.E.) was the author of *Medea*. The Greek theater underwent considerable development during the several generations in which these playwrights flourished, and each Greek playwright, like Zeami, was identified with a theater in transition.

[2] **writings on the theater:** In his writings on the theater, Zeami is comparable to the Greek philosopher Aristotle (384–322 B.C.E.), the author of the *Poetics*, a discussion of Greek tragedy.

[3] **even abducted . . . by the West:** Translations of and commentaries on *Nō* drama by W. B. Yeats (1865–1939), Ezra Pound (1885–1972), and Arthur Waley (1889–1966) have influenced a variety of modern playwrights.

sahm-BAH-soh

Okina, a performer who dons the mask of the deity and dances with great deliberation; and the dance of **Sambaso**, a down-to-earth figure who stamps, rings bells, and mimes the driving away of demons and the beginning of farming activities. The dance takes place in a specially marked space reminiscent of the time when religious festivals were performed in the fields. One part invocation to the gods, one part human magic, and one part an appeal to the tastes of the unsophisticated peasantry, the dance comprises many of the elements natural to *Nō* drama.

SHEE-teh

Even today, *Nō* plays are broken down according to a few themes: those of the god, warrior, woman, lunatic, and ghost. Five plays are often performed in a cycle in this order. The lead actor, or *SHITE*, is supposed to play a variety of roles, sometimes two in the same play. For each role he employs a separate mask and prepares himself spiritually and psychologically for his art. He confronts a *WAKI*, or supporting actor, who provides the impetus to the drama by identifying the lead actor's character

KYOH-gen

and often setting the time and place of the story. A third actor, or *KYOGEN*, comes before the audience and recites the background of the story between the two main acts. This character actually comes from a competing form of drama called *kyogen*, a kind of low comedy. Other actors in the *Nō* drama, supporters of either the *shite* or *waki*, represent the voices of ordinary people and sometimes function as a chorus, as in Greek plays.

Evolution of the *Nō* Drama. Kannami Motokiyo and his son Zeami enlarged the concept of *Nō* theater from its early association with ritual drama by concentrating on the human dimension. In order to do this,

YOO-gen

they invoked the notion of *YUGEN*, or sublimity, which is said to exist in all characters. *Yugen* is a quality of being, an inner elegance always worthy of respect, which Zeami associates with the life of an aristocrat as well as with *Nō* drama. Related to *yugen* is *HANA*, literally meaning "blossom," or

HAH-nah

more generally, "aesthetic beauty." The term is intended to denote both the beauty of the acting and the beauty of the masks, the costumes, the stage settings, and the theater itself. *Hana*, however, is not rigidly defined: Part of its reality is in the eye of the beholder. Though these terms may seem overly abstract to Westerners (in fact, the *yu* in *yugen* means "hazy, otherworldly"), they suggest the ambition of the dramatist to produce work pleasing to the higher sensibilities of the audience.

Many ideas connected with *Nō* theater depend on what might be called a doctrine of correspondences. In particular, the theater is indebted to the **FIVE-ELEMENT THEORY**, corresponding to the five senses. The five elements of the theater are said to be music, dance, acting, gesture, and emotion, all of which are integrated into a complex whole, each regarded as essential to the performance. Actors must make judgments at the point of performance; part of the "logic" of the drama is that anything might happen at any moment. As for the actors themselves, the drama is distinguished by its five themes, mentioned above, played by five principal characters. The skilled actor, or *shite,* is supposed to be able to play any two of these parts during a given play.

www   For links to more information about Zeami Motokiyo and a quiz on *Atsumori,* see *World Literature Online* at bedfordstmartins .com/worldlit.

A Writer of His Time.   There is little documentation concerning the development of *Nō* drama before the fourteenth century. Zeami Motokiyo was a child performer in the troupe of his father, Kannami. The young actor's talents were first noticed when he was only twelve by **Shogun Ashikaga Yoshimitsu,** and Zeami enjoyed the patronage of the SHOGUN until his death in 1408. Succeeding shoguns, however, treated Zeami first with indifference and later with outright hostility, particularly when the time came to name his successor as head of the theater company. In 1432 Zeami's eldest son died under mysterious circumstances, and in 1434 the elderly playwright was exiled to the island of **Sago** in the Sea of Japan. He managed to pass his writings on to his son-in-law, **Komparu Zenchiku** (1405–1468), who carried on the work of Zeami's theater company in his tradition.

Zeami's brilliance as an actor and playwright was matched by his intelligence as a writer on the theater. He apparently intended his writings only for his fellow actors, as they contain methods of performance cultivated by his father and perfected by himself. Incomplete versions of his treatises surfaced after his death, but the definitive text of his writings on the theater was not made public until 1909. His treatises grew in content and complexity from his first, entitled *Teachings on Style and the Flower,* to his last, *Reflections on Art.* As these two titles suggest, what began as directions for actors took on a more philosophical tone as Zeami grew older. He conceived of a "Way" of the *Nō,* a path of dedication and practice that would lead to excellence. In this context he explained the concept of the blossom (*hana*), beauty in both performance and staging, and *yugen,* the sublimity of the characters. He also provided the best existing description of many *Nō* plays, some of which are now lost. About fifty to sixty of Zeami's own plays are known to have existed.

Atsumori.   The subject matter of Zeami's plays was taken from a variety of sources, including legends, history, and popular stories. He was adept at writing plays concerning all five principal *Nō* characters, though his best-regarded works tended to center on the warrior, specifically a doomed hero who joins the tribe of restless ghosts after his death. He also focused on the love of beauty, even in the warriors he depicted. As Zeami remarked in one of his treatises, "If you take a famous character from the *Genji* or *Heike* and bring out the connection between him and poetry or music, then—so long as the play itself is well written—it will be more interesting than anything else." The character of Atsumori, the doomed knight in *Tale of the Heike,* apparently attracted Zeami's interest partly because of the flute he carried beneath his armor into battle, partly because of the misfortune of his death at the hands of a lesser knight.

In the first act of *Atsumori,* a priest named **Rensei** meets a mysterious villager who appears among farmers reaping grain. Rensei hears a flute playing in the distance and asks the villager who is playing it. The farmers fade away, among them the villager, who is the *shite,* or lead actor, in this oblique opening. At the intermission, a *kyogen* comes forward to recount the tale of Atsumori, a knight of the Heike clan killed by **Kuma-**

> Never forget the
> beginner's mind.
>
> – ZEAMI MOTOKIYO

SHOH-gun

ah-shee-KAH-gah
yoh-shee-MIT-so

SAH-goh
kohm-PAH-ro
zen-CHEE-koo

aht-soo-MOH-ree

REN-say

koo-mah-GIGH

Noh is a tight form, but it is nevertheless a liberating one. It allows the dramatist to use the powerful shorthand of symbols, to dramatize the inner world of the dreaming dead, and to go beyond prose into verse, and beyond words into the sounds of music, the concreteness and physicality of dance.

— ANDREW PARKIN, critic, 1993

gai, a Genji knight. In the second act Atsumori himself appears as the *shite*, a knight returned to the world as a troubled spirit. He narrates the story of his death to **Rensei**, recognizing that the priest is actually the former Kumagai, retired from the world to pray for Atsumori's spirit after returning victorious from the war against the Heike. Raising his sword as if to strike the priest, Atsumori is reminded that the priest's prayers have granted him salvation. Harmony is established as the two men reconcile.

Zeami's Legacy.   Zeami borrowed from the best of the past to create a new form that delighted his audiences. Much of the writing in his treatises, on the other hand, was intended not only to instruct actors on their craft but also to encourage their spiritual and intellectual commitment to their profession. Perfection became Zeami's major theme in these writings, while acting was viewed as a kind of spiritual exercise. At the same time, he saw the actor's highest goal as the satisfaction of the audience. Though his methods may appear idiosyncratic at times, Zeami also possessed a great understanding of his audience and a fierce desire to protect their interests — to entertain them in the best sense. His uncompromising nature and his dedication to others' pleasure no doubt contributed to the success of his plays, and does so even today.

■ CONNECTIONS

The Tale of the Heike, p. 1154. The *Nō* drama *Atsumori* follows the story of the noble young warrior Atsumori in *Tale of the Heike*. One might even say it "completes" that story. Compare the hero in the two versions: Does the end of the play satisfactorily conclude the tragic story told in the epic?

Aeschylus, Sophocles, and Euripides (Book 1); Aristotle, *Poetics* (Book 1). In the plays of Aeschylus, Sophocles, and Euripides, the scope of Greek drama is continually expanded. Aristotle comments on the growth of form and substance in these works, and on the overall activity in Greek drama in his *Poetics*. Since Zeami is both playwright and theorist, one can trace his development in both his dramas and his writings about them. How does his development compare with that of the Greek playwrights?

Samuel Beckett, *Krapp's Last Tape* (Book 6). Modern dramatists "discovered" the *Nō* drama about the same time they were challenging European assumptions about the uses of time and place as well as the representation of reality on the stage. Modern playwright Beckett defies ordinary logic and expectations about reality in his plays in order to create a powerful emotional impact. What is the effect of Zeami's *Atsumori* compared to Beckett's *Krapp's Last Tape*?

■ FURTHER RESEARCH

Texts

Rimer, J. Thomas, and Yamazaki Masakazu, trans. *On the Art of the* Nō *Drama: The Major Treatises of Zeami*. 1984.

Waley, Arthur, ed. *The* Nō *Plays of Japan: An Anthology*. 1922.

Critical Studies

Hare, Thomas Blenman. *Zeami's Style: The Noh Plays of Zeami Motokiyo*. 1986.

Keene, Donald. Nō: *The Classical Theater of Japan*. 1973.

Komparu, Kunio. *The Noh Theater: Principles and Perspectives.* 1983.
Sekine, Masaru. *Ze-Ami and His Theories of Noh Drama.* 1985.

Anthology
Keene, Donald, ed. *Twenty Plays of the Nō Theatre.* 1970.

■ **PRONUNCIATION**

Aeschylus: ES-kuh-lus
Atsumori: aht-soo-MOH-ree
Euripides: yoo-RIP-ih-deez
Genji: GEN-jee
hana: HAH-nah
Heike: HAY-keh
Kannami Motokiyo: kah-NAH-mee moh-toh-KEE-yoh
Kokinshu: koh-KIN-shoo
Komparu Zenchiku: kohm-PAH-roo zen-CHEE-koo, ZEN-chih-koo
Kumagai: koo-mah-GIGH
kyogen: KYOH-gen, kee-YOH-gen
Muromachi: moo-roh-MAH-chee
Nō: NOH
Okina: oh-KEE-nah
Rensei: REN-say
Sago: SAH-goh
Sambaso: sahm-BAH-soh
Senzai: SEN-zigh
shite: SHEE-teh
Shogun Ashikaga Yoshimitsu: SHOH-gun ah-shee-KAH-gah yoh-shee-MIT-soo
Sophocles: SAH-fuh-kleez
yugen: YOO-gen
Zeami Motokiyo: zay-AH-mee moh-toh-KEE-yoh

 Atsumori

Translated by Arthur Waley

PERSONS

THE PRIEST RENSEI *(formerly the warrior Kumagai).*
A YOUNG REAPER, *who turns out to be the ghost of Atsumori.*
HIS COMPANION.
CHORUS.

PRIEST:

Life is a lying dream, he only wakes
Who casts the World aside.
I am Kumagai no Naozane, a man of the country of Musashi. I have left my home and call myself the priest Rensei; this I have done because of my grief at the death of Atsumori, who fell in battle by my hand. Hence it comes that I am dressed in priestly guise.

And now I am going down to Ichi-no-Tani to pray for the salvation of Atsumori's soul.

[*He walks slowly across the stage, singing a song descriptive of his journey.*]

I have come so fast that here I am already at Ichi-no-Tani, in the country of Tsu.

Truly the past returns to my mind as though it were a thing of to-day.

But listen! I hear the sound of a flute coming from a knoll of rising ground. I will wait here till the flute-player passes, and ask him to tell me the story of this place.

Atsumori. Many of the finest dramatic moments in this play occur between the lines, so to speak. This type of theater is dependent on stage design, costume, dance, music, and acting as well as on the dialogue. There is also room for improvisation. The eerie sound of the flute at the play's beginning, the reaper who "stays loitering" to speak to the priest at the end of the first act, Atsumori's ghost at the beginning of the second act, Atsumori's dance and his miming of his own death, and the chilling line, "Pray for me again, oh pray for me again," at the end of the play—all these are moments of the highest drama that must be seen, heard, and felt in order to become completely real. In this way the Japanese *Nō* drama keeps the sense of theater intact, almost in spite of the literary beauty of the play's written language.

Arthur Waley's translations of *Nō* dramas reflected both his relationship to the period of literary modernism (roughly 1900–1920) and his aversion to some of its excesses. In his introduction to the translations published in 1922, he called for a modern theater aiming "boldly at stylization and simplification," but cautioned that translations of *Nō* drama should emphasize the work's "literary value" and embody "cautious scholarship." His ability to produce popular, readable, but accurate work has ensured its survival for nearly a century; generally speaking, his translations are not superceded even today. All footnotes are adapted from the Waley text.

REAPERS *(together):*
> To the music of the reaper's flute
> No song is sung
> But the sighing of wind in the fields.

YOUNG REAPER:
> They that were reaping,
> Reaping on that hill,
> Walk now through the fields
> Homeward, for it is dusk.

REAPERS *(together):*
> Short is the way that leads
> From the sea of Suma back to my home.
> This little journey, up to the hill
> And down to the shore again, and up to the hill, —
> This is my life, and the sum of hateful tasks.
> If one should ask me
> I too would answer
> That on the shores of Suma
> I live in sadness.
> Yet if any guessed my name,
> Then might I too have friends.
> But now from my deep misery
> Even those that were dearest
> Are grown estranged. Here must I dwell abandoned
> To one thought's anguish:
> That I must dwell here.

PRIEST:
> Hey, you reapers! I have a question to ask you.

YOUNG REAPER:
> Is it to us you are speaking? What do you wish to know?

PRIEST:
> Was it one of you who was playing on the flute just now?

YOUNG REAPER:
> Yes, it was we who were playing.

PRIEST:
> It was a pleasant sound, and all the pleasanter because one does not look for such music from men of your condition.

YOUNG REAPER:
> Unlooked for from men of our condition, you say!
> Have you not read: —
> "Do not envy what is above you
> Nor despise what is below you"?
> Moreover the songs of woodmen and the flute-playing of herdsmen,
> Flute-playing even of reapers and songs of wood-fellers
> Through poets' verses are known to all the world.

Wonder not to hear among us
The sound of a bamboo-flute.

PRIEST:

You are right. Indeed it is as you have told me.
Songs of woodmen and flute-playing of herdsmen . . .

REAPER:

Flute-playing of reapers . . .

PRIEST:

Songs of wood-fellers . . .

REAPERS:

Guide us on our passage through this sad world.

PRIEST:

Song . . .

REAPER:

And dance . . .

PRIEST:

And the flute . . .

REAPER:

And music of many instruments . . .

CHORUS:

These are the pastimes that each chooses to his taste.
Of floating bamboo-wood
Many are the famous flutes that have been made;
Little-Branch and Cicada-Cage,
And as for the reaper's flute,
Its name is Green-leaf;
On the shore of Sumiyoshi
The Corean flute they play.
And here on the shore of Suma
On Stick of the Salt-kilns
The fishers blow their tune.

PRIEST:

How strange it is! The other reapers have all gone home, but you alone stay loitering here. How is that?

REAPER:

How is it, you ask? I am seeking for a prayer in the voice of the evening waves. Perhaps *you* will pray the Ten Prayers for me?

PRIEST:

I can easily pray the Ten Prayers for you, if you will tell me who you are.

REAPER:

To tell you the truth—I am one of the family of Lord Atsumori.

PRIEST:

One of Atsumori's family? How glad I am!
Then the priest joined his hands *(he kneels down)* and prayed:—

NAMU AMIDABU.

Praise to Amida Buddha!
"If I attain to Buddhahood,
In the whole world and its ten spheres
Of all that dwell here none shall call on my name
And be rejected or cast aside."

CHORUS:

"Oh, reject me not!
One cry suffices for salvation,
Yet day and night
Your prayers will rise for me.
Happy am I, for though you know not my name,
Yet for my soul's deliverance
At dawn and dusk henceforward I know that you will pray."
So he spoke. Then vanished and was seen no more.

[*Here follows the Interlude between the two Acts, in which a recitation concerning Atsumori's death takes place. These interludes are subject to variation and are not considered part of the literary text of the play.*]

PRIEST:

Since this is so, I will perform all night the rites of prayer for the dead, and calling upon Amida's name will pray again for the salvation of Atsumori.

[*The ghost of* ATSUMORI *appears, dressed as a young warrior.*]

ATSUMORI:

Would you know who I am
That like the watchmen at Suma Pass
Have wakened at the cry of sea-birds roaming
Upon Awaji shore?
Listen, Rensei. I am Atsumori.

PRIEST:

How strange! All this while I have never stopped beating my gong and performing the rites of the Law. I cannot for a moment have dozed, yet I thought that Atsumori was standing before me. Surely it was a dream.

ATSUMORI:

Why need it be a dream? It is to clear the karma of my waking life that I am come here in visible form before you.

PRIEST:

Is it not written that one prayer will wipe away ten thousand sins? Ceaselessly I have performed the ritual of the Holy Name that clears all sin away. After such prayers, what evil can be left? Though you should be sunk in sin as deep . . .

ATSUMORI:

As the sea by a rocky shore,
Yet should I be salved by prayer.

PRIEST:

And that my prayers should save you . . .

ATSUMORI:

This too must spring
From kindness of a former life.[1]

PRIEST:

Once enemies . . .

ATSUMORI:

But now . . .

PRIEST:

In truth may we be named . . .

ATSUMORI:

Friends in Buddha's Law.

CHORUS:

There is a saying, "Put away from you a wicked friend; summon to your side a
virtuous enemy." For you it was said, and you have proven it true.

And now come tell with us the tale of your confession, while the night is still
dark.

CHORUS:

He[2] bids the flowers of Spring
Mount the tree-top that men may raise their eyes
And walk on upward paths;
He bids the moon in autumn waves be drowned
In token that he visits laggard men
And leads them out from valleys of despair.

ATSUMORI:

Now the clan of Taira, building wall to wall,
Spread over the earth like the leafy branches of a great tree:

CHORUS:

Yet their prosperity lasted but for a day;
It was like the flower of the convolvulus.
There was none to tell them
That glory flashes like sparks from flint-stone,
And after, — darkness.
Oh wretched, the life of men!

ATSUMORI:

When they were on high they afflicted the humble;
When they were rich they were reckless in pride.
And so for twenty years and more
They ruled this land.

---

[1] kindness of a former life: Atsumori must have done Kumagai some kindness in a former incarnation. This
would account for Kumagai's remorse.

[2] He: Buddha.

But truly a generation passes like the space of a dream.
The leaves of the autumn of Juyei[3]
Were tossed by the four winds;
Scattered, scattered (like leaves too) floated their ships.
And they, asleep on the heaving sea, not even in dreams
Went back to home.
Caged birds longing for the clouds, —
Wild geese were they rather, whose ranks are broken
As they fly to southward on their doubtful journey.
So days and months went by; Spring came again
And for a little while
Here dwelt they on the shore of Suma
At the first valley.
From the mountain behind us the winds blew down
Till the fields grew wintry again.
Our ships lay by the shore, where night and day
The sea-gulls cried and salt waves washed on our sleeves.
We slept with fishers in their huts
On pillows of sand.
We knew none but the people of Suma.
And when among the pine-trees
The evening smoke was rising,
Brushwood, as they call it,
Brushwood we gathered
And spread for carpet.
Sorrowful we lived
On the wild shore of Suma,
Till the clan Taira and all its princes
Were but villagers of Suma.
But on the night of the sixth day of the second month
My father Tsunemori gathered us together.
"To-morrow," he said, "we shall fight our last fight.
To-night is all that is left us."
We sang songs together, and danced.

PRIEST:

Yes, I remember; we in our siege-camp
Heard the sound of music
Echoing from your tents that night;
There was the music of a flute . . .

ATSUMORI:

The bamboo-flute! I wore it when I died.

PRIEST:

We heard the singing . . .

---

[3] **the autumn of Juyei:** The Taira evacuated the capital in the second year of Juyei, 1188.

ATSUMORI:
>   Songs and ballads . . .

PRIEST:
>   Many voices

ATSUMORI:
>   Singing to one measure.

[ATSUMORI *dances.*]
>   First comes the Royal Boat.

CHORUS:
>   The whole clan has put its boats to sea.
>   He[4] will not be left behind;
>   He runs to the shore.
>   But the Royal Boat and the soldiers' boats
>   Have sailed far away.

ATSUMORI:
>   What can he do?
>   He spurs his horse into the waves.
>   He is full of perplexity.
>   And then

CHORUS:
>   He looks behind him and sees
>   That Kumagai pursues him;
>   He cannot escape.
>   Then Atsumori turns his horse
>   Knee-deep in the lashing waves,
>   And draws his sword.
>   Twice, three times he strikes; then, still saddled,
>   In close fight they twine; roll headlong together
>   Among the surf of the shore.
>   So Atsumori fell and was slain, but now the Wheel of Fate
>   Has turned and brought him back.

[ATSUMORI *rises from the ground and advances toward the* PRIEST *with uplifted sword.*]
>   "There is my enemy," he cries, and would strike,
>   But the other is grown gentle
>   And calling on Buddha's name
>   Has obtained salvation for his foe;
>   So that they shall be re-born together
>   On one lotus-seat.
>   "No, Rensei is not my enemy.
>   Pray for me again, oh pray for me again."

---

[4] **He:** Atsumori. This passage is mimed throughout.

GLOSSARY OF LITERARY AND CRITICAL TERMS

Accent The emphasis given to a syllable or word, especially in poetry, that stresses a particular word in a line and may be used to define a poetic foot.

Acropolis The most fortified part of a Greek city, located on a hill; the most famous acropolis is in Athens, the site of the Parthenon.

Act A major division in the action of a play. In many full-length plays, acts are further divided into SCENES, which often mark a point in the action when the location changes or when a new character enters.

Adab An Islamic literary genre distinguished by its humanistic concerns on a variety of subjects that highlights the sensibilities and interests of authors and flourished throughout the tenth and eleventh centuries.

Aeneas The hero of Virgil's *Aeneid*, the Trojan Aeneas wanders for years after the Greek destruction of Troy before reaching the shores of Italy, where his descendants would later found the city of Rome.

The Aeneid The great epic poem of Virgil that tells of the adventures of its hero, Aeneas, after the Trojan War and provides illustrious historical background for the Roman Empire.

Age of Pericles The golden age of Athens in the fifth century B.C.E. when Pericles (c. 495–429 B.C.E.) was the head of the Athenian govern-ment. During this period, Athenian democracy was at its apex; the Parthenon was constructed and drama and music flourished.

Ahimsa The Buddhist belief that all life is one and sacred, resulting in the principle of non-violence toward all living things.

Akam In Indian Tamil poetry, *akam* are "inner" poems, chiefly concerning passion and personal emotions.

Allegory A narrative in which the characters, settings, and episodes stand for something else. Traditionally, most allegories come in the form of stories that correlate to spiritual concepts; examples of these can be found in Dante's *Divine Comedy* (1321). Some later allegories allude to political, historical, and sociological ideas.

Alliteration The repetition of the same consonant sound or sounds in a sequence of words, usually at the beginning of a word or stressed syllable: "*descending dew drops*"; "*luscious lemons.*" Alliteration derives from the sounds, not the spelling of words; for example, "*keen*" and "*car*" alliterate, but "*car*" and "*cite*" do not. Used sparingly, alliteration can intensify ideas by emphasizing key words.

Allusion A brief reference, sometimes direct, sometimes indirect, to a person, place, thing, event, or idea in history or literature. Such references could be to a scene in one of Shakespeare's plays, a historic figure, a war, a great love story, a biblical authority, or anything else that might enrich an author's work. Allusions, which function as a kind of shorthand, imply that the writer and the reader share similar knowledge.

Ambiguity Allows for two or more simultaneous interpretations of a word, phrase, action, or situation, all of whose meanings are supported by the work. Deliberate ambiguity can contribute to the effectiveness and richness of a piece of writing; unintentional ambiguity obscures meaning and may confuse readers.

Amor imperii Latin for love of power.

Anagnorisis The discovery or recognition that takes place in a tragedy, resulting in the protagonist's PERIPETEIA, or reversal of fortune.

Anagram A word or phrase made up of the same letters as another word or phrase; *heart* is an anagram of *earth*. Often considered merely an exercise of one's ingenuity, anagrams are sometimes used by writers to conceal proper names, veil messages, or suggest an important connection between words, such as that between *hated* and *death.*

Antagonist The character, force, or collection of forces in fiction or drama that opposes the PROTAGONIST and gives rise to the conflict in the story; an opponent of the protagonist, such as Caliban in Shakespeare's play *The Tempest.*

Anthropocentric Human-centered. A point of view that considers everything in the world or universe in terms of its relation to or value for human beings.

Apocalypse A prophetic revelation, particularly one that predicts the destruction of the world, as in the final battle between good and evil foreseen in Zoroastrianism and in the Revelation of St. John the Divine; the time when God conquers the powers of evil.

Apostrophe A statement or address made to an implied interlocutor, sometimes a nonhuman figure, or PERSONIFICATION. Apostrophes often provide a speaker with the opportunity to reveal his or her thoughts.

Archetype A universal symbol that evokes deep and sometimes unconscious responses in a reader. In literature, characters, images, and themes that symbolize universal meanings and basic human experiences are considered archetypes. Common literary archetypes include quests, initiations, scapegoats, descents to the underworld, and ascents to heaven.

Archon The chief ruler of Athens during the classical era.

Aryans A people who settled in Iran (Persia) and northern India in prehistoric times. Gradually, they spread through India in the first millennium B.C.E., extending their influence to southern India in the first three centuries C.E. Through their early writings in the Sanskrit language, the VEDAS, they established the basis of Hinduism and Indian culture.

Aside In drama, a speech directed to the audience that supposedly is not audible to the other characters onstage.

Assonance The repetition of vowel sounds in nearby words, as in "asl*ee*p under a tr*ee*" or "*ea*ch *e*vening." When words also share similar endings, as in "asl*eep* in the d*eep*," RHYME occurs. Assonance is an effective means of emphasizing important words.

Autobiography A narrative form of biography in which an author accounts for his or her own life and character to a public audience. As a literary genre, autobiography developed differently in several cultures: the *Confessions* of St. Augustine, written in Latin in the fifth century, served as a model in Europe; Ibn Ishaq's biography of Muhammad, written in Arabic in the eighth century, served as the model for both biographies and autobiographies by later Arabic writers.

Ballad A narrative verse form originally meant to be sung; it generally tells a dramatic tale or a simple story. Ballads are associated with the oral traditions or folklore of common people. The folk ballad stanza usually consists of four lines of alternating tetrameter (four accented syllables) and trimeter (three accented syllables) and follows a rhyme scheme of *abab* or *abcb.*

Ballad stanza A four-line stanza, known as a QUATRAIN, consisting of alternating eight- and six-syllable lines. Usually, only the second and fourth lines rhyme (an *abcb* pattern). Samuel Taylor Coleridge adapted the ballad stanza in *The Rime of the Ancient Mariner* (1798).

Baroque A style found in architecture, art, and literature from the late sixteenth century through the early eighteenth century, characterized by extravagance of theme, language, and form; striking and abrupt turns of line and logic; and ingenious and dynamic imagery. The English poet John Donne (1572–1631) and the Spanish-American poet Sor Juana Inés de la Cruz (c. 1648–1695) often employ what may be considered baroque styles.

Bhagavad Gita An ancient text of Hindu wisdom from the first century B.C.E. or first century C.E. inserted into the epic poem *Mahabharata.*

Bhakti From the Sanskrit for *devotion,* refers to the popular mystical movement stemming from Hinduism. In contrast to forms of Hinduism that stress knowledge, ritual, and good works, Bhakti cults emphasize that personal salvation may be achieved through the loving devotion and ecstatic surrender of an individual to a chosen deity, such as Shiva, Vishnu, and their consorts, often worshiped as a child, parent, beloved, or master.

Bible A collection of writings sacred to Christianity made up of the Hebrew Scriptures (also known as the Old Testament), containing the history, teachings, and literature of the ancient Hebrews and Jews, and the New Testament, the history, teachings, and literature associated with Jesus of Nazareth and his followers.

Biography A nonfiction literary genre that provides the history of an individual's life, detailing not only the facts of that life but also insights into the individual's personality and character. Biography is distinguished from autobiography in that it is written by someone other than the person who is the subject of the work. Biography became popular as a form beginning in the Renaissance.

Black Death The bubonic plague, a devastating disease that swept through Europe in the fourteenth century, leaving a trail of death in its wake.

Blank verse Unrhymed IAMBIC PENTAMETER. Blank verse is often considered the form closest to the natural rhythms of English speech and is therefore the most common pattern found in traditional English narrative and dramatic poetry, from Shakespeare to the writers of the early twentieth century.

Blazon A catalog of similes or metaphors drawn from nature wherein the fair parts of the lover's body are compared to what eventually came to be a stock set of images drawn from nature, seen in the Song of Songs, and earlier love poems. Shakespeare's "My mistress's eyes are nothing like the sun" parodies this convention.

Bodhisattva In Buddhism, a person who temporarily puts off nirvana in order to assist others on earth; one who has achieved great moral and spiritual enlightenment and is en route to becoming a Buddha.

Book of History An ancient collection of documents on Chinese history and politics written in prose dating back to the early years of the Zhou dynasty (c. 1027–221 B.C.E.), if not earlier. It is one of the oldest works of history and was a foundation for Confucian ideas; among other things it describes history as a process of change, and delineates the important "Mandate of Heaven," which said that emperors ruled by divine right, but if or when an emperor violated his office, the mandate would pass to another.

Book of Songs Also known as the *Poetry Classic, Book of Poems,* or *Book of Odes,* this is the oldest Chinese anthology of poems, dating from the ninth through the sixth centuries B.C.E. Written primarily in four-character verse, these poems treat a variety of subjects and form the foundation of later Chinese verse.

Brahman In the UPANISHADS—sacred Hindu texts—Brahman is the ultimate reality, the single unifying essence of the universe that transcends all names and descriptions. A Brahman, or Brahmin, is also a Hindu priest and thus of the highest caste in the traditional Hindu caste system.

Brahmanic period The period in ancient India (c. 1000–600 B.C.E.), in which VEDIC society was dominated by the Brahmins and every aspect of Aryan life was under the control of religious rituals. Both heroic epics of Indian culture, the *Mahabharata* and the *Ramayana,* were originally formulated and told in this period, though transcribed to written form much later, between 400 B.C.E. and 400 C.E.

Brahmin The priestly caste, the highest in the traditional Hindu caste system; a Hindu priest. Also spelled *BRAHMAN.*

Buddhism A religion founded in India in the sixth century B.C.E. by Siddhartha Gautama, the Buddha. While Buddhism has taken different forms in the many areas of the world to which it has spread, its central tenet is that life is suffering caused by desire. In order to obtain salvation, or nirvana, one must transcend desire through following an eightfold path that includes the practice of right action and right mindfulness.

Bunraku New name for *joruri,* traditional Japanese puppet theater.

Bushido The code of honor and conduct of the Japanese SAMURAI class. *Bushido* emphasizes self-discipline and bravery.

Cacophony In literature, language that is discordant and difficult to pronounce. Cacophony (from the Greek for "bad sound") may be unintentional, or it may be used for deliberate dramatic effect; also refers to the combination of loud, jarring sounds.

Caesura A pause within a line of poetry that contributes to the line's RHYTHM. A caesura can occur anywhere within a line and need not be indicated by punctuation. In scansion, caesuras are indicated by two vertical lines.

Caliph The chief civil and religious leader of a Muslim state, as a successor of Muhammad.

Caliphate Both the reign or term of a caliph as well as the area over which he rules.

Calvinists A Protestant denomination whose adherents follow the beliefs originally outlined by French Protestant reformer, John Calvin (1509-1564), especially predestination and salvation of the elect through God's grace alone.

Canon The works generally considered by scholars, critics, and teachers to be the most important to read and study and that collectively constitute the masterpieces of literature. Since the 1960s, the traditional English and American literary canons, consisting mostly of works by white male writers, have been expanding to include many female writers and writers of varying ethnic backgrounds. At the same time the world literature canon, as constructed in the West, has been broadened to include many works from non-Western literatures, especially those of Asia and Africa.

Canzoniere Medieval Italian lyric poetry. Masters of the form included Petrarch, Dante, Tasso, and Cavalcanti.

Carpe diem Latin phrase meaning "seize the day." This is a common literary theme, especially in lyric poetry, conveying that life is short, time is fleeting, and one should make the most of present pleasures. Andrew Marvell's poem "To His Coy Mistress" is a good example.

Caste The hereditary class to which a member of Hindu society belongs; stemming from the teachings of the VEDAS, Hindu society observes a strict hierarchy with the Brahmins, or priests, at the top; followed by the KSHA-TRIYAS, or warriors and rulers; and the Vaishyas, or farmers, merchants, and artisans; and a fourth class, added later than the others, the Shudras, servants. Only members of the first three "twice-born" castes could study the VEDAS and take part in religious rituals. Outside of this system were the outcastes, known as Untouchables.

Catechumen In the early Christian church, an individual officially recognized as a Christian and admitted to religious instruction required for full membership in the church.

Catharsis Meaning "purgation," or the release of the emotions of pity and fear by the audience at the end of a tragedy. In *Poetics,* Aristotle discusses the importance of catharsis.

The audience faces the misfortunes of the PROTAGONIST, which elicit pity and compassion. Simultaneously, the audience confronts the protagonist's failure, thus receiving a frightening reminder of human limitations and frailties.

Character, characterization A character is a person presented in a dramatic or narrative work; characterization is the process by which a writer presents a character to the reader.

Chin-Shi Examinations First begun in the Sui dynasty in China (581–618 C.E.) under Yang Jian and formalized during the Tang era, the system of chin-shi examinations brought bright and talented men from all over China into the government bureaucracy.

Chivalric romances Idealized stories from the medieval period that espoused the values of a sophisticated courtly society. These tales centered around the lives of knights who were faithful to God, king, and country and willing to sacrifice themselves for these causes and for the love and protection of women. Chivalric romances were highly moral and fanciful, often pitting knights against dark or supernatural forces.

Choka A Japanese form of an ode associated with Kakinomoto Hitomaro (late seventh century); a long poem often inspired by public occasions but also full of personal sentiment.

Chorus In Greek tragedies, a group of people who serve mainly as commentators on the play's characters and events, adding to the audience's understanding of a play by expressing traditional moral, religious, and social attitudes. Choruses are occasionally used by modern playwrights.

Christianity A world religion founded in Palestine in the first millennium C.E. upon the teachings of Jesus Christ, whose followers believe he is the Messiah prophesied in the Hebrew Scriptures (Old Testament). The central teachings of Christianity are that Jesus of Nazareth was the son of God, that his crucifixion and resurrection from the dead provide atonement for the sins of humanity, and that through faith in Jesus individuals might attain eternal life. Christianity has played a central role in the history of Europe and the Americas.

Chthonic From the Greek *chthonios,* meaning "in the earth," *chthonic* refers to the underworld spirits and deities in ancient religion and mythology.

Cliché An idea or expression that has become tired and trite from overuse.

Closet drama A play that is to be read rather than performed onstage. In closet dramas, literary art outweighs all other considerations.

Colloquial Informal diction that reflects casual, conversational language and often includes slang expressions.

Comedy A work intended to interest, involve, and amuse readers or an audience, in which no terrible disaster occurs and which ends happily for the main characters.

Comic relief A humorous scene or incident that alleviates tension in an otherwise serious work. Often these moments enhance the thematic significance of a story in addition to providing humor.

Comitatus Arrangement whereby young warriors attached themselves to the leader of a group and defended him in return for his economic and legal protection. Also, the bond among warriors attached to such a leader.

Conceit A figure of speech elaborating a surprising parallel between two dissimilar things. It was a favorite poetic device of the Petrarchan sonneteers and the English metaphysical poets of the seventeenth century.

Conflict In a literary work, the struggle between opposing forces. The PROTAGONIST is engaged in a conflict with the antagonist.

Confucianism A religious philosophy that has influenced Chinese and East Asian spirituality and culture for more than two thousand years. Based on the writings of Confucius (Kongfuzi; 551–479 B.C.E.), Confucianism asserts that humans can improve and even perfect themselves through education and moral reform. In its various manifestations, Confucianism has affected the social and political evolution of China and East Asia while providing a spiritual and moral template.

Connotation Implications going beyond the literal meaning of a word that derive from how the word has been commonly used and from ideas or things associated with it. For example, the word *eagle* in the United States connotes ideas of liberty and freedom that have little to do with the term's literal meaning.

Consonance A common type of near-rhyme or half rhyme created when identical consonant sounds are preceded by different vowel sounds: *home, same; worth, breath.*

Convention A characteristic of a literary genre that is understood and accepted by readers and audiences because it has become familiar. For example, the division of a play into acts and scenes is a dramatic convention, as are SOLILOQUIES and ASIDES.

Cosmogony An explanation for the origins of the universe and how the functioning of the heavens is related to the religious, political, and social organization of life on earth. The primary function of creation myths, such as the Hebrew Book of Genesis and the Mesopotamian *Epic of Creation,* is to depict a cosmogonic model of the universe.

Cosmology The metaphysical study of the origin and nature of the universe.

Cosmopolis A large city inhabited by people from many different countries.

Counter-Reformation The period of Catholic revival and reform from the beginning of the pontificate of Pope Pius IV in 1560 to the end of the Thirty Years' War in 1648 in response to the Protestant Reformation. Spearheaded in great part by members of the Society of Jesus (the Jesuits), it was a period in which the Roman Catholic church reaffirmed the veneration of saints and the authority of the pope and initiated many institutional reforms.

Couplet A two-line stanza.

Creation myth A symbolic narrative of the beginning of the world as configured by a particular society or culture. Examples of creation myths range from the Mesopotamian classic *Epic of Creation* to the Book of Genesis

in Hebrew Scriptures to the creation myths of the Ancient Mexicans of the Americas.

Crisis The moment in a work of drama or fiction in which the elements of the conflict reach the point of maximum tension. The crisis is is not necessarily the emotional crescendo, or climax.

Cultural criticism An approach to literature that focuses on the historical, social, political, and economic contexts of a work. Cultural critics use widely eclectic strategies, such as anthropology, NEW HISTORICISM, psychology, gender studies, and DECONSTRUCTION, to analyze not only literary texts but everything from radio talk shows to comic strips, calendar art, advertising, travel guides, and baseball cards.

Cuneiform The wedge-shaped writing characters that stood for syllables or sounds and not letters in ancient Akkadian, Assyrian, Persian, and Babylonian inscriptions.

Daoism (Taoism) A religion/philosophy based on the Dao De Jing (Tao Te Ching) of Laozi (Lao Tzu) that emphasizes individual freedom, spontaneity, mystical experience, and self-transformation, and is the antithesis of CONFUCIANISM. In pursuit of the dao, or the Way—the eternal creative reality that is the essence of all things—practitioners embrace simplicity and reject learned wisdom. The Daoist tradition has flourished in China and East Asia for more than two thousand years.

Deconstructionism An approach to literature that suggests that literary works do not yield single, fixed meanings because language can never say exactly what one intends it to mean. Deconstructionism seeks to destabilize meaning by examining the gaps in and ambiguities of a text's language. Deconstructionists pay close attention to language in order to discover and describe how a variety of close readings of any given work can be generated.

Denouement French term meaning "unraveling" or "unknotting" used to describe the resolution of a PLOT following the action's climax.

Deus ex machina Latin for "god from the machine," a phrase originally applied to Greek plays, especially those by Euripides, in which resolution of the conflict was achieved by the intervention of a god who was lowered onto the stage mechanically. In its broader use, the phrase is applied to any plot that is resolved by an improbable or fortuitous device from outside the action.

Dharma Cosmic order or law in the Hindu tradition that includes the natural and moral laws that apply to all beings and things.

Dhimmi See THE PEOPLE OF THE BOOK.

Dialect A type of informal diction. Dialects are spoken by definable groups of people from a particular geographic region, economic group, or social class. Writers use dialect to express and contrast the education, class, and social and regional backgrounds of their characters.

Dialogue Verbal exchange between CHARACTERS. Dialogue reveals firsthand characters' thoughts, responses, and emotional states.

Diaspora From the Greek for "dispersion," this term was initially applied to the Jews exiled to Babylonia after the destruction of the Temple of Jerusalem in 586 B.C.E. and again forced into exile after the Romans defeated Jerusalem in 70 C.E. The term now refers to other peoples who have been forced from their homelands, such as the Africans uprooted by the slave trade.

Diction A writer's choice of words, phrases, sentence structure, and figurative language, which combine to help create meaning.

Didactic Literature intended to teach or convey instruction, especially of a moral, ethical, or religious nature, such as a didactic essay or poem.

Digressions In epics such as *Beowulf*, these are narratives imbedded in the story to illustrate a point or recall another situation. Digressions may consist of conventional wisdom; suggest how one is supposed to behave; or remind the audience of events occurring either before or after those treated in the story.

Dionysiac festival In Athens, plays were performed during two major festivals in honor of the god Dionysus: the Lenaea during January and February, and the Great Dionysia in March and April.

Dionysus The god of wine in Greek mythology whose cult originated in Thrace and Phrygia, north and east of the Greek peninsula. Dionysus was often blamed for people's irrational behavior and for chaotic situations. However, many Greeks also believed that Dionysus taught them good farming skills, especially those related to wine production. Greek tragedy evolved from a ceremony that honored Dionysus, and the theater in Athens was dedicated to him.

Dithyramb Originally a highly passionate, lyrical hymn sung during the rites of Dionysius in Greece, dithyramb now refers to any impassioned sequence of verse or prose, often characterized by irregular or unrestrained rhythms and extravagant imagery.

Divine Comedy Dante Alighieri's fourteenth-century narrative poem that deals with the poet's imaginary journey through hell, purgatory, and paradise.

Doggerel A derogatory term for poetry whose subject is trite and whose rhythm and sounds are monotonously heavy-handed.

Drama Derived from the Greek word *dram*, meaning "to do" or "to perform," *drama* may refer to a single play, a group of plays, or to plays in general. Drama is designed to be performed in a theater: Actors take on the roles of CHARACTERS, perform indicated actions, and deliver the script's DIALOGUE.

Dramatic monologue A type of lyric or narrative poem in which a speaker addresses an imagined and distinct audience in such a way as to reveal a dramatic situation and, often unintentionally, some aspect of his or her temperament or personality.

Dravidians A group of dark-skinned peoples of India who were either ancient occupants of the southern peninsula, refugees of earlier tribes pushed down from the north, or late arrivals to India from the Mediterranean seacoast.

Edo The ancient name for Tokyo. During the Tokugawa period (1600–1868), Edo became the imperial capital of Japan.

Elegiac couplets The conventional strophic form of Latin elegiac love poetry, consisting of one dactylic hexameter line followed by one dactylic pentameter line. A dactylic hexameter line is composed of six feet, each foot comprising one long, or accented, and two short, or unaccented, syllables; the sixth foot may be shortened by one or two syllables; a pentameter line consists of five such feet. The elegiac couplet is also known as a "distich."

Elegy A mournful, contemplative lyric poem often ending in consolation, written to commemorate someone who has died. *Elegy* may also refer to a serious, meditative poem that expresses a speaker's melancholy thoughts.

Elizabethan Of or characteristic of the time when Elizabeth I (1558–1603) was the queen of England. This era was perhaps the most splendid literary period in the history of English literature in that it encompassed the works of Sidney, Spenser, Marlowe, and Shakespeare, among many others, and saw the flourishing of such genres as poetry, especially the SONNET, and was a golden age of drama of all forms.

Elysian Fields In Greek mythology, some fortunate mortals spend their afterlife in the bliss of these Islands of the Blest, rather than in Hades, the underworld.

End-stopped line A line in a poem after which a pause occurs. End-stopped lines reflect normal speech patterns and are often marked by punctuation.

Enjambment In poetry, a line continuing without a pause into the next line for its meaning; also called a run-on line.

Ennead The group of nine primary deities in the religion of ancient Egypt.

Epic A long narrative poem told in a formal, elevated style that focuses on a serious subject and chronicles heroic deeds and events important to a culture or nation. It usually includes a supernatural dimension, like the gods in Homer. Most epics follow established conventions, such as beginning *in medias res* (in the middle of things); employing elaborate comparisons known as epic similes; and

identifying characters with repeated epithets, such as "wily Odysseus." Oral or folk epics, recited tales told for many generations before being written down, such as *The Iliad* and *Sunjata*, are sometimes distinguished from literary epics like *The Aeneid* or *Paradise Lost*, whose original creation was the work of a single poet.

Epicureanism The doctrines of Epicurus (341–270 B.C.E.), the Greek philosopher who espoused a life of pleasure and the avoidance of pain; commonly thought of as a license for indulgence, Epicureanism actually stipulates a life of simplicity and morality.

Essays A literary form that is an analytical, interpretive, or critical composition usually shorter and less formal than a dissertation or thesis and more personal in nature. The term was coined in the Renaissance by the master of the form, Montaigne (1533–1592), who chose it to underscore that his writings (from the French word *essai*, literally meaning "trial," or "test") were attempts toward understanding.

Euphony From the Greek for "good sound"; refers to language that is smooth and musically pleasant to the ear.

Exposition A narrative device often used at the beginning of a work to provide necessary background information about characters and their circumstances. Exposition explains such matters as what has gone on before; the relationships between characters; theme; and conflict.

Fabliau Although the *fabliau* originated in France as a comic or satiric tale in verse, by the time of Giovanni Boccaccio (1313–1375) and Geoffrey Chaucer (1340–1400) the term also stood for bawdy and ribald prose tales like "The Miller's Tale" in Chaucer's *Canterbury Tales* or Boccaccio's "Rustico and Alibech."

Farce A form of humor based on exaggerated, improbable incongruities. Farce involves rapid shifts in action and emotion as well as slapstick comedy and extravagant dialogue.

Feminist criticism An approach to literature that seeks to correct or supplement a predominantly male-dominated critical perspective with a feminist consciousness. Feminist criticism places literature in a social context and uses a broad range of disciplines, including history, sociology, psychology, and linguistics, to provide interpretations that are sensitive to feminist issues.

Feudal aristocracy, Feudalism A system of government that existed with some variations in Europe, China, and Japan in the Middle Period. The feudal system refers to a mode of agricultural production in which peasants worked for landowners, or lords, in return for debt forgiveness, food, and military protection.

Fiction Literature created from the imagination and not presented as fact, though it may be based on a true story or real-life situation. Genres of fiction include the short story, the novella, and the novel.

Figures of speech Ways of using language that deviate from the literal, denotative meanings of words, through comparison, exaggeration, or other verbal devices in order to suggest additional meanings or effects.

Fixed form A poem characterized by a fixed pattern of lines, syllables, or METER. A SONNET is a fixed form of poetry because it must have fourteen lines.

Flashback A literary or dramatic device that allows a past occurrence to be inserted into the chronological order of a narrative.

Flying Dutchman The legend of a ghostly ship doomed to sail for eternity. If a vision of it appears to sailors, it signals imminent disaster. Most versions of the story have the captain of the ill-fated ship playing dice or gambling with the devil.

Foil A character in a literary work or drama whose behavior or values contrast with those of another character, typically the PROTAGONIST.

Foot A poetic foot is a poem's unit of measurement, defined by an accented syllable and a varying number of unaccented syllables. In English, the iambic foot, an accented syllable followed by an unaccented syllable, is the most common.

Foreshadowing Providing hints of what is to happen in order to build suspense.

Formalism A type of criticism dominant in the early twentieth century that emphasizes the form of an artwork. Two of its prominent schools are Russian formalism, which favors the form of an artwork over its content and argues that it is necessary for literature to defamiliarize the ordinary objects of the world, and American NEW CRITICISM, which treats a work of art as an object and seeks to understand it through close, careful analysis.

Founding myth A story that explains how a particular nation or culture came to be, such as Virgil's *Aeneid,* which describes the founding of Rome. Many epic poems, sometimes called national epics, are founding myths.

Four classes In Hindu tradition, humans are created as one of four classes, or VARNA: in descending order, the BRAHMINS (priests), the *KSHATRIYA* (warriors), the *Vaisya* (merchants and farmers), and the *Shudra* (laborers and servants).

Framed narration Also called *framed tale.* A story within a story. In Chaucer's *Canterbury Tales,* each pilgrim's story is framed by the story of the pilgrimage itself. This device, used by writers from ancient times to the present, enjoyed particular popularity during the thirteenth, fourteenth, and fifteenth centuries and was most fully developed in *The Arabian Nights,* a work in which the framing is multilayered.

Free verse Highly irregular poetry, typically, free verse employs varying line patterns and rhythms and does not rhyme.

Freudian criticism A method of literary criticism associated with Freud's theories of psychoanalysis. Early Freudian critics sought to illustrate how literature is shaped by the unconscious desires of the author, but the term now more broadly encompasses many schools of thought that link psychoanalysis to the interpretation of literature.

Fu A mixed-genre Chinese literary form developed during the Han dynasty (206 B.C.E.– 220 C.E.) that combines elements of prose and poetry; it begins with a prose introduction followed by lines of poetry of various metrical lengths.

Gaia From the Greek *Ge* meaning "earth," Gaia or Gaea was an earth goddess, mother of the Titans in Greek mythology.

Gay and lesbian criticism School of literary criticism that focuses on the representation of homosexuality in literature; also interested in how homosexuals read literature and to what extent sexuality and gender is culturally constructed.

Gender criticism Literary school that analyzes how an author's or a reader's sex affects the writing and reading experiences.

Genre A category of artistic works or literary compositions that have a distinctive style or content. Poetry, fiction, and drama are genres. Different genres have dominated at various times and places. Traditional genres include tragedy, comedy, romance, novel, epic, and lyric.

Georgic poetry Poetry dealing with the practical aspects of agriculture and rural affairs as first seen in the work of the Greek poet Nicander of Colophon (second century B.C.E.) and practiced by later poets such as Virgil (70–19 B.C.E.).

Ghazal A form of lyric poetry composed of three to seven couplets, called *sh'ir,* that follow the strict rhyme scheme of *aa ba ca da,* and so on, known as the *qafiyah.* Strict adherence to the form requires the use of the *radif,* a word that is repeated in a pattern dictated by the first couplet, throughout the poem. Literally meaning "dialogue with the beloved," the *ghazal,* as practiced in Arabia, Persia, Turkey, and India beginning around 1200, became the predominant form for love poetry.

Gnostics Members of an ancient sect in the Middle East who believed that hidden knowledge held the key to the universe. Throughout history there have been Gnostics who have formed secret societies with secret scriptures and who have believed they understood the workings of the cosmos.

Golden Age of Arabic science The period of the Abbassid caliphs, between 750 and 945 C.E., particularly the reigns of Harun al-Rashid (786–809) and al-Ma'mun (813–833). Al-Ma'mun founded a scientific academy in Baghdad, collected and had translated many ancient Greek and Indian manuscripts upon which Arab scholars built, and encouraged scholarship of all kinds, resulting in major advances in mathematics, astronomy, medicine, and geography.

Golden Age of Spain The "Siglo de Oro" period from the early sixteenth century to the end of the seventeenth century that is considered the high point of Spain's literary history. The age began with the political unification of Spain around 1500 and extended through 1681, the year in which Pedro Calderon (1600–1681) died. In addition to Calderon, this period saw the flourishing of such writers as Cervantes (1547–1616) and Lope de Vega (1562–1635).

Gothic A style of literature (especially novels) in the late eighteenth and early nineteenth centuries that reacted against the mannered decorum of earlier literature. Gothic novels explore the darker side of human experience; they are often set in the past and in foreign countries, and they employ elements of horror, mystery, and the supernatural.

Gravitas Formality in bearing and appearance; a reserved dignity of behavior and speech, especially in a leader or a ruler.

Great Chain of Being A conception of the universal order of things derived from Greek philosophy that exerted considerable influence on the European understanding of nature and the universe from the Renaissance through the eighteenth century. The Great Chain of Being posits that God ordered the universe so as to create the greatest possible diversity, continuity, and order, and envisions a hierarchical structure whereby every being, according to its nature, occupies a designated place on a ladder reaching from the basest matter to the highest spiritual entity, or God. This metaphor offered the assurance that degree, proportion, and place would be, or should be, observed in the social and natural order. Human beings occupy the middle position on this ladder or chain, sharing the spiritual potentials of "higher" beings as well as the material limits of the "lower" beings.

Greater Dionysia In ancient Greece, dramas were performed at festivals that honored the god Dionysus: the Lenaea during January and February and the Greater Dionysia in March and April. The best tragedies and comedies were awarded prizes by an Athenian jury.

Griot A storyteller in West Africa who perpetuates the oral traditions of a family or village.

Gupta dynasty The time of the reign of the Gupta emperors (320–550), considered the golden age of classical Indian history. The dynasty, established by Chandragupta I (r. 320–35), disintegrated in the middle of the sixth century. It was during this period that the great poetry of Kalidasa was written.

Gushi In Chinese literature, a verse form that consists of even-numbered, alternately rhymed lines of five syllables each. Referred to as "old-style verse."

Hadith Islamic source of religious law and moral guidance. According to tradition, the Hadith were passed down orally to the prophet Muhammad, and today they are critical to the study of the early development of Islam.

Hajj The pilgrimage to Mecca, Saudi Arabia, one of the five pillars of Islam and the duty of every Muslim at least once in his or her lifetime.

Hamartia A tragic flaw or error that in ancient Greek tragedies leads to the hero's reversal of fortune, known as the *peripeteia*.

Hebrew Scriptures A collection of thirty-nine books sacred to Judaism sometimes called the Hebrew Bible, these writings contain the history, teachings, and literature of the ancient Hebrews and Jews; called the Old Testament by Christians.

Hellene The name for a Greek, dating from the inhabitants of ancient Greece, who took their name from Hellen, the son of the legendary Deucalion and Pyrrha.

Hellenism The language, thought, art, customs, and literature characteristic of classical Greece.

Heroic couplet A rhymed, iambic-pentameter stanza of two lines that completes its thought within the two-line form. Alexander Pope (1688–1744), the most accomplished practitioner of the form in English, included this couplet in his *Essay on Criticism*: "True wit is nature to advantage dressed, / What oft was thought, but ne'er so well expressed."

Heroic poetry Narrative verse that is elevated in mood and uses a dignified, dramatic, and formal style to describe the deeds of aristocratic warriors and rulers. Typically, it was transmitted orally over several generations and written down at a later date. Examples of the form include *The Iliad* and *The Odyssey*.

Hexameter couplets The conventional strophic form of Greek and Latin epic poetry consisting of two dactylic hexameter lines; each line is composed of six feet, and each foot comprises one long (accented) and two short (unaccented) syllables. The final foot is known as a catalectic foot, for it is generally shortened by one or two syllables.

Hieroglyphic writing A writing system using picture symbols to represent sounds, words, or images instead of alphabetical letters. It was used by the ancient Egyptians, Mexicans, and others.

Hieros gamos Literally, "sacred marriage"; a fertility ritual in which the god-king or priest-king is united with the goddess or priestess-queen in order to provide a model for the kingdom and establish the king's right to rule.

Hinduism The major religion of India based on the ancient doctrines found in the SANSKRIT texts known as the VEDAS and the UPANISHADS, dating from 1000 B.C.E.

Historical criticism An approach to literature that uses history as a means of understanding a literary work. Such criticism moves beyond both the facts of an author's life and the text itself to examine the social and intellectual contexts in which the author composed the work.

Homeric Hymns At one time attributed to Homer, the *Homeric Hymns* (seventh through sixth centuries B.C.E.) are now believed to have been created by poets from a Homeric school or simply in the style of Homer. Five of the longer hymns contain important stories about gods such as Demeter, DIONYSUS, Apollo, Aphrodite, and Hermes.

Homo viator Latin for "man the traveler," used by Augustine to signify man's pilgrimage through life toward God.

Hoplite The name used to designate the foot soldiers of ancient Greece.

Hubris Exaggerated pride or arrogance; in Greek tragedies, hubris causes fatal errors.

Huguenots French Protestant members of the Reformed Church established in France by John Calvin in about 1555. Due to religious persecution, many Huguenots fled to other countries in the sixteenth and seventeenth centuries.

Humanism The learning or cultural impulse that flourished during the European Renaissance characterized by a revival of classical letters, an individualistic and critical spirit, and a shift from religious to secular concerns.

Hundred Years' War A series of wars between the English and the French that lasted from 1337 to 1453 in which England lost all of its possessions in France except Calais, also eventually lost in 1565.

Hymn A form of lyric poetry, characterized by solemnity and high religious feeling, intended to be sung in praise of gods or heroic men and women.

Hyperbole A figure of speech; using overstatement or extravagant exaggeration.

Iambic pentameter A poetic line made up of five feet, or iambs, or a ten-syllable line.

Idealism Philosophical Idealism in its various forms holds that objects of perception are in reality mental constructs and not the material objects themselves.

Ideogram A pictorial symbol used in writing that stands for an idea or concept.

Image A verbal representation of a sensory phenomenon—visual, auditory, olfactory, etc. The two types of images are literal and figurative. Literal images are very detailed, almost photographic; figurative images are more abstract and often use symbols.

Imam The leader of prayer in a Muslim mosque; also a title indicating respect for a man of learning.

In medias res Literally, "in the midst of things"; a term used to characterize the beginning of epic poems, which typically start at a crucial point far along in the story. Earlier details are conveyed by means of flashbacks and digressions.

Inquisition A medieval institution established by the Fourth Lateran Council of the Roman Catholic Church, which met in 1215 and was presided over by Pope Innocent III. The Inquisition was formed largely to combat heresy in the aftermath of the Albigensian Crusade in Spain (1209–1229). Punishments included death by burning at the stake and long imprisonment as well as forfeiture of land and property. One of the late and most notorious results of the Inquisition was the trial and execution of Joan of Arc in France in 1456.

Irony A device used in writing and speech to deliberately express ideas so they can be understood in two ways. In drama, irony occurs when a character does not know something that the other characters or the audience knows.

Islam A world religion founded in the seventh century C.E. on the teachings of the prophet Muhammad, whose followers believe that the Qur'an (Koran), the holy book of Islam, contains the revelations of Allah. The Five Pillars of Islam are: to recite the creed, "There is no God but Allah, and Muhammad is his Prophet"; to acknowledge the oneness of Allah in prayer five times each day by reciting the opening verses of the Qur'an; to practice charity and help the needy; to fast in the month of Ramadan; and to make the *hajj*, or pilgrimage to Mecca, at least once in a lifetime if possible. Islam has played a major role in the history of the Middle East and Asia.

Jainism A religion founded in India by Mahavira (d. 469 B.C.E.), a contemporary of the Buddha. In reaction to the rigid and hierarchical structure of traditional Hinduism, Jainism teaches that divinity resides within each individual. Salvation is achieved through the ascetic renunciation of the world and through the practice of AHIMSA, nonviolence toward all living beings.

Jen (Ren) As a basic element of CONFUCIANISM, *jen* means "benevolence" or "love for fellow humans"; Mencius (fourth century B.C.E.) argued that all humans are endowed with *jen*; also spelled *ren*.

Jesuits A Roman Catholic religious order founded in 1540 by Ignatius Loyola (1491–1556) under the title the Society of Jesus as part of the wider Counter-Reformation.

Jewish mysticism Like all forms of mysticism, Jewish mysticism focuses on learning and practices that lead to unity with the creator; its teachings are contained in the Cabala (Kabala, Kabbalah).

Jihad From the Arabic *jahada,* meaning "striving," "struggle," or "exertion," this term came to mean a holy war conducted by Muslims against unbelievers or enemies of Islam carried out as a religious duty. After the death of Muhammad in 632, Muslim conquests extended beyond Arabia until early into the next century. *Jihad* also denotes a spiritual struggle for perfection and self-control by practicing Muslims, as well as a struggle for the faith conducted peacefully with unbelievers.

Judgment of Paris In Greek legend, Paris (Alexandros) was selected by the god Zeus to judge which of three goddesses was the most beautiful. He chose Aphrodite, who had bribed him by agreeing to help him seduce Helen, the most beautiful woman in the world. Paris' abduction of Helen and refusal to return her was the cause of the Trojan War.

Ka'ba (ka'bah) The sacred Muslim shrine at Mecca, toward which believers turn when praying.

Kana The portion of the Japanese writing system that represents syllables.

Karma In Hindu and Buddhist philosophy, the totality of a person's actions in any one of the successive states of that person's existence, thought to determine the fate of the next stage. More generally, fate or destiny.

Karma-yoga One of four types of yoga; the practitioner of karma-yoga strives to serve humanity selflessly and without ego, a practice that purifies the heart and prepares the heart and mind for the reception of divine light, or the attainment of knowledge of the self.

Kharja The short, two- or four-line tag ending of an Arabic *muwashshah,* a long, formal beginning to a poem consisting of five or six end-rhymed stanzas. The *Kharja* was often written in MOZARABIC, the spoken language of Andalusia (Spain) that included elements of Arabic, Spanish, and Hebrew. It was often conceived of as a direct, provocative remark made by a servant girl or other uneducated person.

Kshatriya The second highest of the four primary Hindu castes, the military or warrior caste just below the Brahmin class.

Lacunae Spaces where something has been left out; particularly, a gap or missing portion of a text.

Laisses In Medieval poetry, stanzas composed of a variable number of ten-syllable lines; the concluding line of the first stanza is repeated as a refrain at the end of subsequent stanzas.

Lay (Lai) A song or musical interlude; by extension, a poem accompanied by a musical instrument. Marie de France, a popular Anglo-Norman poet of the twelfth century, composed what she called "Breton Lais," short versions of courtly romances suitable for recitation.

Leitmotifs Themes, brief passages, or single words repeated within a work.

Line A sequence of words. In poetry, lines are typically measured by the number of feet they contain.

Lingam The phallic symbol through which Shiva is worshipped in his personification as the creative and reproductive power in the universe.

Literary epic A literary epic—as distinguished from folk epics such as the *Mahabharata* or *The Iliad,* which are made up of somewhat loosely linked episodes and closely follow oral conventions—is written with self-conscious artistry, has a tightly knit organic unity, and is stylistically rooted in a written, literate culture. In actuality, great epics often blur the distinction between the oral or folk epic and the literary epic.

Loa In Spanish and Spanish American drama, a prologue that sets the scene and adumbrates the themes of a play.

Logos In ancient Greece, philosophers such as Aristotle (384–322 B.C.E.) used *logos* to mean reason or thought as opposed to pathos or feeling and emotion. Logos was thought of as the controlling principle of the universe made manifest in speech or rhetoric.

Lushi A highly structured Chinese form of poetry consisting of eight lines of five or seven syllables each. Also referred to as "regulated verse."

Lyric Originally, poetry composed to the accompaniment of a lyre (a stringed musical instrument). By extension, lyric is any poetry that expresses intense personal emotion in a manner suggestive of a song, as opposed to narrative poetry that relates the events of a story. Short poems, often on the subject of love, exist in most of the world's cultures and can fall under the common designation of lyric.

Maat An ancient Egyptian word for the idea of "right order" or justice, the basis of both cosmic order and a civil society. *Maat* was associated with either the sun-god Re or the creator Ptah.

Maghazi Legendary accounts of "the raids of the Prophet" in Islamic literature, examples of which can be found in Ibn Ishaq's *The Biography of the Prophet,* which depicts events of Muhammad's embattled later life.

Mahabharata One of the two great epics of ancient India and the longest poem in world literature, consisting of nearly 100,000 stanzas—more than seven times longer than *The Iliad* and *The Odyssey* combined. Attributed to Vyasa, whose name means the "compiler" or "arranger," the *Mahabharata* was composed between the fifth century B.C.E. and the fourth century C.E.; written in Sanskrit, the epic appeared in its final written form sometime in the fourth century C.E.

Manicheanism A dualistic religion founded by Mani, a Persian philosopher, in the third century C.E. Combining Christian, Buddhist, and Zoroastrian elements, Mani taught that there were two gods, one good and one evil, a school of belief that affected such later church thinkers as Augustine of Hippo, as seen in his *Confessions.*

Manuscript illumination The elaborate illustration of manuscripts (handwritten and handmade books) in the Middle Ages with beautiful images, borders, and letters, embellished with luminous color, especially gold.

Marathi A Sanskritic language of western India spoken by the Marathas, known as the SAMURAI of western India for their defense of Hinduism against the onslaught of the Muslim invaders of India.

Marxist criticism Literary criticism that evolved from Karl Marx's political and economic theories. In the view of Marxist critics, texts must be understood in terms of the social class and the economic and political positions of their characters.

Masque Developed in the Renaissance, masques are highly stylized and structured performances with an often mythological or allegorical plot, combining drama, music, song, and dance in an elaborate display.

Materialism A worldview that explains the nature of reality in terms of physical matter and material conditions rather than by way of ideas, emotions, or the supernatural.

Mathnavi Persian poetic form used for romantic, epic, didactic, and other types of poems whose subjects demand a lengthy treatment;

its verse structure is similar to that of the Western heroic couplet, but with two rhyming halves in a single line.

Mauryan empire The Indian empire that existed between 322 and 185 B.C.E. Established by Chandragupta Maurya (r. 322–296 B.C.E.), the empire eventually united all of India except for the extreme south under one imperial power. During this period trade flourished, agriculture was regulated, weights and measures were standardized, and money first came into use.

Maya From the Sanskrit for "deception" or "illusion," *maya* is the veil drawn over the ultimate, eternal reality of BRAHMAN and therefore represents the phenomenal world of appearances that humans misinterpret as the only reality.

Me According to Sumerian philosophers, the *me* were the divine laws and rules that governed the universe as well as the cultural elements, like metalworking and the arts, that constituted urban life. In Sumerian mythology, the *me* are the gift of the goddess Inanna to humankind.

Medieval Romances See CHIVALRIC ROMANCES.

Menippian satire Named for its originator, the Greek Cynic philosopher Menippus (first half of the third century B.C.E.), Menippian satire uses a mixture of prose, dialogue, and verse to make ludicrous a whole social class or a broad spectrum of social types. The form is sometimes called an "anatomy" because it catalogs the many social and intellectual types who constitute the social group it satirizes.

Mestizos Peoples in the Americas of mixed ethnic or cultural heritage, usually a combination of Spanish and Native American.

Metaphor A comparison of two things that does not use the words *like* or *as*. For example, "love is a rose."

Metaphysical poetry Poetry written primarily in seventeenth-century England that has as its focus the analysis of feeling. Its chief characteristics are complexity and subtlety of thought, frequent use of paradox, often deliberate harshness or rigidity of expression, and the use of bold and ingenious conceits—sometimes forced comparisons of unlike ideas or things that startle the reader into a closer analysis of the argument of the poem. John Donne and Andrew Marvell are known as metaphysical poets; the term is sometimes also used with other poetry of this type.

Meter The RHYTHM of a poem based on the number of syllables in each line and which syllables are accented. See also FOOT.

Middle Ages A term applied specifically to Europe, dating from the decline of the Roman Empire in the fourth to sixth centuries to the revival of learning and the arts in the Early Modern or Renaissance period in the late fourteenth and fifteenth centuries.

Millenarianism A utopian belief that the end of time is imminent, after which there will be a thousand-year era of perfect peace on earth.

Ming dynasty (1368–1644) Founded by Zhu Yuan-zhang, who restored native Chinese rule from the Mongols who had ruled China during the previous Yuan dynasty (1271–1368) established by Kubla Khan. The Ming dynasty saw a flourishing of Chinese culture, the restoration of CONFUCIANISM, and the rise of the arts, including porcelain, architecture, drama, and the novel.

Miyabi A Japanese term denoting a delicate taste for the beautiful—a refined sensibility for subtle nuances of style and form in art, literature, and social conduct.

Moira In Greek mythology, the deity who assigns to every person his or her lot.

Moksha In the Hindu tradition, the *moksha* is the highest goal for all humans; it means the final liberation from all earthly, material existence and complete union with God or the ultimate reality.

Monism A unitary conception of the world in which everything that is—the whole of reality—constitutes an inseparable self-inclusive whole, as opposed to dualism, which sees reality as made up of opposing elements, such as mind and matter, and good and evil.

Monogatari Loosely translated from the Japanese as "tale" or the "telling of things," *monogatari* refers to the genre of fiction; as in the case of NIKKI, *monogatari* were written in KANA and often contained poetic passages in the form of WAKA. Lady Murasaki's *The Tale of Genji* is perhaps the greatest example of the *monogatari* in Japanese literature.

Monologue A speech of significant length delivered by one person; in drama, speech in which a CHARACTER talks to himself or herself or reveals personal secrets without addressing another character.

Monotheism The doctrine or belief that there is only one deity or God, such as Allah or Yaweh, as opposed to the polytheistic religions of ancient Greece and Rome that involved the worship of numerous gods.

Mozarabic Pertaining to Spanish Christians and Jews who were permitted to practice their religions during the period of Muslim rule in Andalusia. Also refers to the vernacular language spoken in Andalusia, a combination of Arabic, Christian, and Hebrew elements.

Mullah (Mulla) A Muslim teacher or interpreter of Muslim religious law; the more current usage is as a general title of respect for a learned person.

Muse In ancient Greek mythology, any of the nine daughters of Zeus who presided over the arts; current usage denotes a muse as the spirit that inspires a poet or artist to create.

Muwashshah A conventional Andalusian love poem, usually written in Arabic but occasionally in Hebrew, consisting of five or six end-rhymed stanzas followed by a brief "tag" ending called a KHARJA, usually written in MOZARABIC.

Mystery religions Mystery cults were very popular in ancient Greece and Rome for at least one thousand years, beginning around 1000 B.C.E. The details of each cult were kept a secret, but all cults shared a rigorous rite of initiation, a concern about death, and a hope for immortality centered on a deity who had personal knowledge of the afterlife. The most popular Greek versions were the Orphic and Eleusinian mysteries. The mysteries of Isis and Mithra were favored in the Roman world.

Mysticism The belief that communion with God can be achieved intuitively through contemplation and meditation on the divine spirit akin to an act of faith rather than through the intellect.

Mythological criticism A type of literary criticism that focuses on the archetypal stories common to all cultures. Initiated by Carl Jung in the early twentieth century, mythological criticism seeks to reveal how the psychological impulses and patterns lodged deep in human consciousness take the form of ARCHETYPAL stories and are the basis for literature.

Narrative poem A poem that tells a story. Ballads, epics, and romances are typically narrative poems.

Narrator The voice that in fiction describes the PLOT or action of a story. The narrator can speak in the first, second, or third person and, depending on the effect the author wishes to create, can be very visible or almost invisible (an explicit or an implicit narrator); he or she also can be involved in the action or be removed from it. See also POINT OF VIEW and SPEAKER.

Nasib The prelude or introductory stanzas of a *qasidah*, the Arabic lyric form comparable to the ode.

Nataka In Sanskrit drama, the heroic romance with an idealized warrior king as its central figure and a comic story concentrating on heroic and erotic themes.

Necropolis Literally meaning "city of the dead," *necropolis* was the name given to a cemetery in the ancient world.

Neo-Confucianism Refers generally to the philosophical tradition in China and Japan based on the thought of Confucius (Kongfuzi, 551–479 B.C.E.) and his commentators, particularly Mencius (Mengzi, 370–290 B.C.E.) and Zhu Xi (Chu Hi, 1130–1200). Neo-Confucianism, which arose during the Sung dynasty (960–1279), asserts that an understanding of things must be based on their underlying principles; in moral and political philosophy, it emphasizes the study of history, loyalty to family and nation, and order.

Neoplatonism Considered the last great Greek philosophy, Neoplatonism was developed by Plotnus (204–270 C.E.), based on his reading of the works of Plato. This school of philosophy espouses a single source from which all forms of existence emanate and with which the soul seeks a mystical union.

New Criticism A type of formalist literary criticism that disregards historical and biographical information to focus on the text. The New Critics perform a close reading of a work and give special attention to technical devices such as irony and ambiguity.

New Historicism A school of literary criticism developed in the 1980s in part as a reaction to NEW CRITICISM and other formalist methods of literary analysis. In contrast to formalism, which focuses strictly on internal relations of form and structure in a text, New Historicism emphasizes the relation of the text to its historical and cultural contexts. New Historicists make a self-conscious attempt to place their own critical practice within the political and historical framework of their own time, and align the language, rhetorical strategies, and other features of the texts they study with those of works not usually considered literary.

New Testament The sacred writings of Christianity, which tell the life of Jesus in the Gospels, the history of the establishment of the early church in Paul's Epistles, and the prophesy of the ultimate fulfillment of Christian history in the Revelation of St. John the Divine. From the Christian perspective, the New Testament fulfills the prophesies of the Hebrew Scriptures, known to Christians as the Old Testament.

Nikki An important genre of Japanese literature, the prose diary, which flourished among women writers in the Heian period; these diaries were written primarily in KANA, the woman's form of writing, which formed the basis of the vernacular literary tradition in Japan, and, like *The Tale of Genji*, contained poetic passages in the form of WAKA.

Nirgun In Indian devotional tradition, or *glakti*, the idea that God is transcendent, having no physical or material attributes.

Nirvana In Buddhism, the state of perfect blessedness achieved by the extinction of individual existence and absorption of the soul into the supreme spirit, or by the extinction of all earthly passions and desires.

Nō The highly elaborate and ritualistic classical theater of Japan, known for its minimalist approach to plot, scenery, and stage effects and the stately performance and Zen-like mastery of its actors; *Nō* means "talent" or "accomplishment."

Novel An extended work of fictional prose narrative. The novel is a modern outgrowth of earlier genres such as the romance. There is considerable debate as to the origins of the novel; some critics trace it to Cervantes' *Don Quixote* (1605), others to Lady Murasaki's *The Tale of Genji* (c. 1022).

Octave A STANZA of eight lines in poetry.

Ode An elevated form of LYRIC generally written on a single theme, using varied metric and rhyme patterns. With the ode, poets working within classical schemes can introduce considerable innovation. There are three major types of odes in English: the Pindaric, or Regular; the Horatian; and the Irregular. The Pindaric ode is structured by three-strophe divisions, modulating between the strophe, antistrophe, and epode, which vary in tone. The Horatian ode uses only one STANZA type; variation is introduced within each stanza. The Irregular ode, sometimes called the English ode, allows wide variety among stanza forms, rhyme schemes, and metrical patterns. Related forms adopted by particular cultures include the Arabic QASIDAH as practiced by the pre-Muslim poet Imru al-Qays, and the ancient Japanese CHOKA as practiced by Kakinomoto Hitomaro.

Oedipus complex Sigmund Freud's conception of the unconscious male desire to kill one's own father and sleep with one's own mother. The term derives from the Greek myth of Oedipus, who unknowingly murdered his father and married his mother; his self-inflicted punishment was to blind himself. FREUDIAN CRITICS do not take the complex or the story literally, but frequently use the concept to examine in literature the guilt associated with sexual desire and with competition with or hostility toward one's father.

Onomatopoeia The quality of a word that sounds like the thing it refers to: for example, the *buzz* of bees.

Open form Also known as *free verse*. A type of poetry that does not follow established conventions of METER, RHYME, and STANZA.

Opera A musical drama in which the dialogue is sung to orchestral accompaniment. As a form, it has its origins in the liturgical drama of the Middle Ages. In sixteenth-century Italy, opera rose to grand musical productions marked by elaborate costuming, scenery, and choreography.

Organic form The concept that the structure of a literary work develops according to an internal logic. The literary work grows and becomes an organic whole that follows the principles of nature, not mechanics. The created work of art is akin to a growing plant that relies on all of its parts working together.

Ottava rima Italian stanza form composed of eleven-syllable lines, rhyming *ab ab ab cc* that originated in the late thirteenth and early fourteenth centuries in Italy. The early master of the form was Giovanni Boccaccio (1313–1375), who established it as the standard form for epic and narrative verse in his time, but later poets continued to make use of it.

Oxymoron A rhetorical figure of speech in which contradictory terms are combined, such as *jumbo shrimp* and *deafening silence.*

Panegyric An oration or eulogy in praise of some person or achievement. Primarily associated with classical antiquity, panegyrics continued to be written through the Middle Ages and Renaissance, especially in Elizabethan England, the Spanish Golden Age, and in France under Louis XIV.

Pantheism Literally, "God everywhere," the belief that God is immanent throughout the universe—that God is manifest in all things.

Pantheon Generally, all the deities of a particular religion considered collectively; also, a temple dedicated to all the gods; specifically, the temple built in Rome by Agrippa in 27 C.E. and rebuilt by Hadrian in the second century C.E.

Paraphrase To rewrite or say the same thing using different words.

Parataxis Literally, "placing one thing after another." The term refers to linear narrative, often employed in storytelling, consisting of a series of sentences or clauses joined by a coordinator (that happened..., then this happened...).

Parody A humorous imitation of another, usually serious, work. Parody can be a form of literary criticism that exposes defects in a work, or it can function as an acknowledgement of a work's cultural and literary importance.

Pastoral poetry A poem or a play dealing with the lives of shepherds or rural life in general and usually depicting shepherds as representative of a simple life of innocence and serenity as opposed to the misery and corruption of city or court life. An early example of the form is Virgil's *Eclogues,* which greatly influenced the Renaissance work of such writers as Dante, Petrarch, Boccaccio, and Shakespeare.

Patois A regional dialect of a language.

Patrician Originally, the hereditary aristocracy and nobility of ancient Rome. Later the term referred to any person who by birth or special compensation belonged to the nobility. More current usage denotes a person of high birth or a person of refined upbringing and manners.

Pax Romana Literally meaning "Roman peace," this is the long period of comparative peace enforced on states in the Roman Empire between the years 27 B.C.E. and 180 C.E.

People of the Book (Dhimmi) The Muslim name for Jews and Christians, followers of the teachings of the prophets of Hebrew Scriptures and the New Testament. Under normal conditions Islamic authorities granted Jews and Christians religious tolerance.

Peloponnesian War (431–404 B.C.E.) War between the Athenian and Spartan alliance systems that encompassed most of the Greek world. The war set new standards for warfare—Athens used its navy to support the land offensive, for instance—but the new tactics also prolonged the fighting; instead of there being one decisive battle, the war dragged on for three decades. Eventually, Athens was defeated, and Sparta took over the defeated power's overseas empire.

Peripeteia (Peripety) A character's reversal of fortune in the denouement of a plot. In tragedy, it means the hero's destruction, in comedy his or her happy resolution.

Persian Wars A series of wars between a coalition of Greek city-states and the Persian empire fought between 500 and 449 B.C.E.; the Greek victory set the stage for the flourishing of Greek culture.

Persona Literally, persona means "mask." In literature, a persona is a speaker created by a writer to tell a story or to speak in a poem. A persona is not a character in a story or narrative, nor does it necessarily directly reflect the author's personal voice.

Personification A figure of speech in which abstractions or inanimate objects are given human qualities or form.

Petrarchan conceit From *concept* or *conception,* this was an originally novel form of metaphor in which the speaker of a poem compared his or her beloved to something else, such as a doe, a rose, a summer's day, or even a newly discovered land. Originating with the Italian poet Petrarch, the freshness of this device soon wore off and the Petrarchan conceit became a stale convention, revitalized by only the most ingenious poets.

Petrarchan sonnet A fourteen-line lyric poem. The Petrarchan SONNET was the first basic sonnet form. It is divided into an eight-line octet and a six-line sestet, each with a specific but varied pattern of rhymes, for example *ab ba cd ec de.*

Philistines A powerful non-Semitic tribe that in biblical times inhabited the tract of land between Judea and Egypt; in almost perpetual war with the Israelites, they were ultimately conquered by the Romans.

Phonogram A letter, character, or mark used to represent a sound.

Picaresque A novel loosely structured around an episodic succession of adventures of a rogue hero—a *picaro*—who is on an aimless journey. The picaresque tale often provides a sweeping and satiric view of society and its customs. Examples include Petronius's *The Satyricon* and Voltaire's *Candide.*

Pictograh A picture used to represent an idea; hieroglyphics are pictographs.

Pieta A representation in painting or sculpture of the Virgin Mary mourning over the dead body of Jesus after the Crucifixion.

Pietas In ancient Roman Stoic philosophy, *pietas* is respect for authority.

Platonic Characteristic of the philosophy of Plato, essentially connoting idealistic or visionary outlooks.

Platonic love A pure, spiritual love between a man and a woman that is based on intellectual appreciation of the other person and is unmixed with sexual desire.

Platonist One who adheres to the philosophy of Plato, especially the doctrine that holds that things exist only as ideas in the mind rather than as material objects independent of the mind.

Plebeians Members of the ancient Roman lower class or common people, as opposed to PATRICIANS.

Plot The pattern of events told in a narrative or drama. Plot has a causal sequence and a unifying theme, in contrast to story, which is the simple narrative of the action.

Point of view The perspective from which the author, SPEAKER, or NARRATOR presents a story. A point of view might be localized within a CHARACTER, in which case the story is told from a first-person point of view. There is a range of possibilities between first-person point of view and omniscience, wherein a story is told from a perspective unlimited by time, place, or character.

Polis Greek term meaning "city"; designates the Greek city-states, such as Athens and Sparta, that arose in the sixth century B.C.E.

Polytheism The belief in or worship of many gods as opposed to monotheism, which is the doctrine or worship of a single god.

Pragmatism A philosophical approach that evaluates ideas and beliefs in terms of their usefulness and applicability to practical action.

Prologue Text that typically is placed prior to an introduction or that replaces a traditional introduction; often discusses events of importance for the general understanding of the work. See also LOA.

Protagonist A leading figure or the main character in a drama or other literary work.

Protestant Reformation See REFORMATION.

Psychological criticism An approach to literature that draws on psychoanalytic theories, especially those of Sigmund Freud (1856–1939) and Jacques Lacan (1901–1981), to understand more fully a text, its writer, and readers.

Pun A play on words that relies on a word's having more than one meaning or sounding like another word.

Punic Wars The series of wars between Rome and Carthage during the third and second centuries B.C.E. — the first taking place between 264 and 241 B.C.E., the second between 218 and 201, and the third between 149 and 146 — which the Romans ultimately won.

Purdah Practice adopted by some Muslims and Hindus that obscures women from public sight by mandating that they wear concealing clothing, especially veils. The custom originated in the seventh century C.E. and is still common in Islamic countries, though it has largely disappeared in Hinduism.

Purim A Jewish holiday, also known as the Feast of Lots, celebrating the deliverance of the

Jews by Esther from the planned massacre plotted by Haman.

Qasidah An Arabic form of lyric poetry, comparable to the ode, originally composed orally and consisting of several dozen to some sixty rhymed couplets, expressing reflection and sentiment while evoking scenes of desert life, romantic memories, and a tone of despair or self-glorification. Later literary versions of the *qasidah* often lost their desert setting but retained their reflective, romantic character.

Quatrain A stanza of four lines in a poem.

Quetzalcoatl The most important god of Mesoamerica, whose name means Plumed Serpent or Precious Twin. As a god, he was instrumental in creating the four previous worlds; as a hero-ruler of Tollan, he assumed the mantle of the priesthood of Quetzalcoatl, fell from grace, and delivered a messianic promise to return home.

Quietism Scholars use this term to characterize thinkers in the fourth century B.C.E. who advocated withdrawal from the turbulence of society and concentration on inner peace and harmony.

Quixotic Like Don Quixote, or having the characteristics of being romantic in the extreme, absurdly chivalrous, or foolishly idealistic.

Qur'an The sacred writings of Islam revealed by Allah to the prophet Muhammad.

Rahil That part of a QASIDAH's (or ode's) structure in Persian poetry — the "disengagement" — that tells of a solitary journey on horseback or camelback, or more metaphorically, of the separation of the poet from the source of his sorrowful memory.

Rasa Indian dramatic theory identifies eight *rasa*s (aesthetic emotions) that can focus a drama: the erotic, the heroic, the disquieting, the furious, the comic, the marvelous, the horrible, and the pathetic. Only two are appropriate for the NATAKA form, the erotic and the heroic.

Reader-response criticism A critical approach to literature in which the primary focus falls on the reader or the process of reading, not on the author. Reader-response critics believe that a literary work does not possess a fixed idea or meaning; meaning is a function of the perspective of the reader.

Realism Most broadly defined, realism is the attempt to represent the world accurately in literature. As a literary movement, Realism flourished in Russia, France, England, and America in the latter half of the nineteenth century. It emphasized not only accurate representation but the "truth," usually expressed as the consequence of a moral choice. Realist writers deemphasized the shaping power of the imagination and concerned themselves with the experiences of ordinary, middle-class subjects and the dilemmas they faced.

Realpolitik Foreign policy based on practical political expediency rather than moral or ideological considerations.

Recognition Based on the Greek concept of tragedy, recognition, or ANAGNORISIS, is the point in a story when the PROTAGONIST discovers the truth about his or her situation. Usually this results in a drastic change in the course of the plot.

Reformation Also known as the Protestant Reformation, this sixteenth-century challenge to the authority of the Catholic Church caused a permanent rift in the Christian world, with those loyal to the pope remaining Catholic and those rejecting papal authority forming new Protestant faiths such as the Anglican, Lutheran, Calvinist, Anabaptist, and Presbyterian. The Reformation originated—and was most successful—in Northern Europe, especially Germany; its notable leaders include Martin Luther and John Calvin.

Renaissance The revival of art, literature, and learning in Europe in the fourteenth, fifteenth, and sixteenth centuries based on classical Greek and Roman sources. The movement began in Italy, spread throughout Europe, and marked the transition from the medieval to the modern Western world.

Renaissance man A term used to describe someone accomplished in many disciplines, especially in both science and the arts, like Leonardo da Vinci and other figures of the European Renaissance.

Resolution The point in the plot of a narrative work or drama that occurs after the climax and generally establishes a new understanding; also known as *falling action.*

Reversal The point in the plot of a story or drama when the fortunes of the PROTAGONIST change unexpectedly; also known as the *PERIPITEIA.*

Rhyme The repetition of identical or similar-sounding words or syllables, usually accented, in lines of poetry. Rhymes may occur within or at the end of lines.

Rhythm The pattern of stressed and unstressed syllables in prose and especially in poetry that can lend emphasis, reinforce a sound association, or suggest regularity or recurrence. The rhythm of a literary work can affect the emotional response of the reader or listener.

Rishi (Ṛṣi) Sanskrit for sage or holy man.

Romance A medieval tale based on heroic conduct, adventure, or chivalric love, sometimes in a supernatural setting. Medieval romances were composed in France in the twelfth century, spreading to Germany, Spain, England, and other countries in the next several centuries. Later, in the seventeenth century, the romance form was parodied in Miguel de Cervantes' literary masterpiece, *Don Quixote.*

Romantic hero The PROTAGONIST of a romance, novel, or poem who is shaped by experiences that frequently take the form of combat, love, or adventure. The Romantic hero is judged by his actions more than his thoughts, and he is often on a journey that will affect his moral development.

Ruba'i (plural, Ruba'iyat) Equivalent to the quatrain in Western poetry, a *ruba'i* is a very intricate Persian poetic line structure consisting of four lines of equal length, divided into half lines, with the first, second, and fourth lines rhyming.

St. Francis (c. 1181–1226) Founder of the Franciscan religious order, beloved for his gentleness and humility. An account of his life and teachings, *The Little Flowers of Saint Francis,* was published in the century after his death.

Samsara A Hindu term for the cycle of birth, life, death, and rebirth; many Hindu practices are aimed at obtaining release, or *moksha,* from the otherwise endless repetition of life and death.

Samurai Japanese feudal aristocrat and member of the hereditary warrior class. Denied recognition during the Meiji period (1867–1912).

Sangha The Sanskrit word for a fraternity or association often formed out of spiritual or learning communities.

Sanskrit The classical language of ancient India, in which many of the major Hindu religious and literary texts were written.

Satire A literary or dramatic genre whose works, such as Petronius's *Satyricon* and Jonathan Swift's (1667–1745) *Gulliver's Travels,* ridicule human behavior.

Satyr In classical mythology, a minor woodland deity represented as part man and part goat whose chief characteristics are riotous merriment and lasciviousness.

Scansion A system of poetic analysis that involves dividing lines into feet and examining patterns of stressed and unstressed syllables. Scansion is a mechanical way of breaking down verse in order to understand the regularities and irregularities of its METER.

Scene In drama, a subdivision of an ACT.

Scholasticism The dominant philosophical system of the twelfth to fourteenth centuries in Europe, based on the writings of Aristotle and his commentators, including Avicenna (Ibn Sina) and Averroes (Ibn Rushdi). The great Christian Scholastic philosopher, St. Thomas Aquinas, completed his *Summa Theologica* in 1273.

Script The written version or text of a play or movie that is used by the actors.

Sentimentality Extravagant emotion; T. S. Eliot defined this as "emotion in excess of the facts."

Septuagint A Greek version of the Hebrew Scriptures (Old Testament), so called because the ancient tradition was that it was completed in seventy or seventy-two days by seventy-two Palestinian Jews, for Ptolemy II of Egypt.

Sestet A STANZA of six lines; the last stanza of a Petrarchan SONNET is a sestet.

Setting The time, place, and social environment in a narrative or a drama.

Shastra A treatise for authoritative instruction among the Hindu, especially a treatise explaining the VEDAS.

Shi In China, the term used to designate poetry in general.

Shi'ite One of the two great branches of the Muslim faith. Shi'ites insisted on a strict line of family succession from Muhammad and rejected interpretations of Islam construed after the death of Muhammad. They soon were considered heretical by the majority branch, Sunnite (Sunna) Muslims. Present-day Shi'ites primarily occupy Iran and southern Iraq.

Shintoism The indigenous polytheistic religion of Japan, the beliefs of which stress the worship of nature, ancestors, and ancient heroes, and the divinity of the emperor.

Shite The PROTAGONIST or main character in a Japanese *Nō* play.

Shiva (Śiva) The Hindu god of destruction and creation and a member of the supreme Hindu trinity of Shiva, Brahma, and Vishnu.

Shogun A military ruler of feudal Japan between 1192 and 1867. The shogunate was an inherited position in the military that operated under the nominal control of the emperor.

Sikhism The beliefs of those who belong to the Hindu religious sect founded in northern India around 1500 C.E., based on a belief in one God and on a rejection of the caste system and idolatry.

Simile A figure of speech, introduced by *like* or *as,* in which two things are compared as equals.

Smirti (Smṛti) One of the two major classifications of Hindu sacred texts. *Smirti,* which means "memory," comprises Hindu texts other than the VEDAS, which are considered SRUTI, or revealed (heard) texts. *Smirti* may be thought of as a secondary category of sacred literature that includes the Sutras, the Puranas, and the Indian epics the *Ramayana* and the *Mahabharata*.

Sociological criticism School of literary criticism that seeks to place a work of art in its social context and define the relationship between the two. Like Marxist critics, sociological critics are oriented toward social class, political ideology, gender roles, and economic conditions in their analyses.

Soliloquy A dramatic speech in which a character speaks his or her inner thoughts aloud before the audience.

Sonnet A fourteen-line lyric poem. The first basic sonnet form is the Italian or Petrarchan sonnet, which is divided into an eight-line octet and a six-line SESTET (see PETRARCHAN SONNET). The English or Shakespearean sonnet is divided into three four-line QUATRAINS followed by a two-line couplet; the quatrains are rhymed *abab cdcd efef* and the couplet is also end-rhymed, *gg*.

Sophists Literally, "wise men." Greek teachers who provided instruction in logic and rhetoric to pupils who could afford their expensive fees. Rhetoric was a new discipline whose study was observed to provide an advantage in politics and in the courts. *Sophist* came to mean one who used argumentation to undermine traditional beliefs.

Speaker The person or PERSONA who speaks in a poem, often a created identity who cannot be equated with the poet.

Spiritual autobiography An autobiography that gives special importance to self-examination, interpretation of Scripture, and belief in predestination. St. Augustine's *Confessions* (c. 400), detailing a life of sin, conversion, and spiritual rebirth, is generally regarded as the archetypal spiritual autobiography.

Sprezzatura An Italian term that has no equivalent in English, *sprezzatura* suggests a quality of perfect composure and nonchalance, the ability to act with studied artifice while giving the appearance of effortless spontaneity.

Sruti One of the two major classifications of Hindu sacred texts. *Sruti*, which means "hearing," is reserved for the primary sacred texts of Hinduism, the VEDAS, including the Smahtas, the Brahmanas, and the Aranyakas, the most important of which is the UPANISHADS.

Stage directions Written directions explaining how actors are to move onstage. See also SCRIPT.

Stanza A poetic verse of two or more lines, sometimes characterized by a common pattern of RHYME and METER.

Stock responses Predictable responses to language and symbols. See also CLICHÉ.

Stoicism A school of thought founded by the Greek philosopher Zeno c. 308 B.C.E. Stoicism advocated the view that virtue is the ultimate goal of life and that the virtuous seek happiness within by overcoming their passions and emotions while remaining independent of the external natural world, which follows immutable laws.

Stress A syllable receiving emphasis in accordance with a metrical pattern.

Style The distinctive manner in which an author writes and thus makes his or her work unique. A style provides a kind of literary signature for the writer.

Subplot A PLOT subordinate to the main plot of a literary work or drama.

Sufism A devotional movement among certain Muslims emphasizing the union of the devotee with God through ritual and ascetic practices, who hold to a kind of PANTHEISM and practice extreme asceticism in their lives.

Suspense The anxious emotion of an audience or reader anticipating the outcome of a story or drama, typically having to do with the fate of the PROTAGONIST or another character with whom a sympathetic attachment has been formed.

Symbol A representative of something by association. Though a symbol is often confused with a metaphor, a metaphor compares two dissimilar things while a symbol associates two things. For example, the *word* "tree" is a symbol for an *actual* tree. Some symbols have values that are accepted by most people. A flag, for instance, is for many a symbol of national pride, just as a cross is widely seen as a symbol of Christianity. Knowledge of a symbol's cultural context is sometimes necessary to understand its meaning; an apple pie is an American symbol of innocence that a Japanese person, for example, would not necessarily recognize.

Syncretism Combining disparate philosophical or religious beliefs, such as the blending of Christianity or Islam with indigenous religions.

Synoptic Gospels The first three gospels of the New Testament, which give a similar account of the life, death, and Resurrection of Jesus.

Syntax The way parts of speech are arranged in a sentence.

TANAK An acronym used to describe three groupings in Hebrew Scriptures: the Torah (Pentateuch, or first five books), the Nebi'im, (the Prophets), and Ketubim (the Writings); also spelled TENACH.

Tanka A Japanese verse form of thirty-one syllables in five unrhymed lines, the first and third having five syllables each, the second, fourth, and fifth having seven. See also WAKA.

Tantrism A minor Hindu tradition written down in scriptures called Tantras. Tantrism holds the supreme deity to be feminine and teaches that spiritual liberation can be won through erotic practices.

Taoism See DAOISM.

Tathagata An epithet for the Buddha that means "thus gone," having attained enlightenment.

Tercets A unit or group of three lines of verse, usually rhymed.

Terza rima A verse form composed of iambic three-line stanzas, with lines of ten or eleven syllables. Terza rima employed most brilliantly in Dante's (1265–1321) *Divine Comedy.*

Tetragrammaton The four consonants of the Hebrew alphabet, YHWH, used to approximate God's secret name; this name and its

utterances are believed to contain special powers.

Tezcatlipoca In Aztec mythology, he was the warrior god of the north and the god of sin and misery with an obsidian knife. In Toltec mythology, he was also the brother and/or antithesis of Quetzalcoatl.

Thanatos "Death" in Greek. According to Sigmund Freud, our two primary drives are Eros (love) and Thanatos (death).

Theme A topic of discussion or a point of view embodied in a work of art.

Theocracy Government of the state by God or a god as represented by a person or persons claiming to have divine authority.

Tolkappiyam The formal grammar developed in literary assemblies in and around the Indian city of Madurai between 100 and 250 C.E. created to classify aspects of Tamil poetry.

Tone A manner of expression in writing that indicates a certain attitude toward the subject or the implied audience.

Tour de force A masterly or brilliant creation, production, or performance; the phrase translates literally from the original French as "feat of strength."

Tragedy A dramatic or literary form originating in Greece that deals with serious human actions and issues. The actions are meant to create feelings of fear and compassion in the spectator that are later released (CATHARSIS). Typically, the main character is of a high stature or rank, so his or her fall is substantial. Even though tragedies are sad, they seem both just and believable. The tragedy raises serious moral and philosophical questions about the meaning of life and fate.

Tragicomedy A drama that combines tragedy and comedy and in which moral values are particularly questioned or ridiculed.

Travel narratives Also known as travel literature, a form of narrative that recounts the incidents that occur and the people and things that the narrator meets and sees while visiting a place with which she or he is typically unfamiliar. Prose and poetic accounts about exploration and adventure in unfamiliar lands and places as well as in more or less familiar locations are considered travel narratives. Examples of the genre include the travels of Marco Polo and the travels of Ibn Battuta.

Triplet In poetry, a group of three rhyming lines of verse.

Trobairitz Female troubadours, both members of the nobility and independent artists. See TROUBADOURS.

Troubadours Lyric poets and composers, sometimes of aristocratic rank but more often artists attached to regional courts, who flourished in the south of France in the twelfth and thirteenth centuries. Their compositions in the Provencal language centered on the subject of love. Their work derived in part from Arabic sources in Andalusia, and their influence spread throughout Europe in the thirteenth and fourteenth centuries.

Umrah Known as the "lesser pilgrimage"; in contrast to the *hajj*, which must be performed in the last month of the Islamic calendar year, *umrah* is a pilgrimage to Mecca that can be undertaken at any time.

Understatement A figure of speech that says less than what is intended. In Anglo-Saxon poetry, a special form of understatement known as the litote is an ironic form of address in which the full importance of something is concealed in order to force the listener to discover it by paying close attention.

Upanishads A body of sacred texts dating from the ninth century B.C.E. that provide a mystical development of and commentary on earlier VEDIC texts.

Urdu An Indo-European language closely related to Hindi. Urdu is the official language of Pakistan and is also spoken in India and Bangladesh.

Utopia In literature, a romance or other work describing an ideal place whose inhabitants live under seemingly perfect conditions. Though the term did not exist until coined by Sir Thomas More in 1516, earlier works such as Plato's *Republic* and Bacon's *New Atlantis* can be termed utopias due to the societies they depict.

Vandals Fierce warriors from near the Russian steppes who invaded Roman Gaul (France) in the fifth century C.E. and advanced through Spain to North Africa. They were notorious for their destruction of cities.

Varna Sanskrit word for "color" used in the sense of "class" to indicate the four classes or castes of Hinduism in India.

Vedas The earliest Indian sacred texts, written in Sanskrit, dating from sometime between 1000 and 500 B.C.E.; they contain hymns and ritual lore considered to be revelation, or SRUTI.

Vedic The Old Indic language of the VEDAS, it was an early form of Sanskrit.

Vernacular fiction Fiction that attempts to capture accurately the typical speech, mannerisms, or dialect of a region. The *Satyricon* of the Roman author Petronius is often considered the first work of vernacular fiction.

Waka Traditional Japanese poetry based on Chinese models that rose to prominence in the Heian Period (794–1195). The *waka* is a short five-line lyric consisting of thirty-one syllables with 5-7-5-7-7 syllables to a line. Writing *waka* was an important activity of the Heian aristocracy as well as their court followers. The poetry anthology *Kokinshu* (c. 905) is the most celebrated collection of *waka*. Now generally called *tanka,* these poems are still written today.

Waki Refers to the secondary PROTAGONIST or antagonist in Japanese *Nō* plays; the primary character is known as the shite.

Xiaopin A Chinese form of autobiographical essay that became an important medium in China in the late sixteenth century.

Yahweh A form of the Hebrew name for God in the Hebrew Scriptures.

Yin and yang A pair of opposites derived from a dualistic system of ancient Chinese philosophy; symbolically representing the sun and the moon, *yang* is positive, active, and strong, while *yin* is negative, passive, and weak. All things in the universe are formed from the dynamic interaction of these forces.

Yoni A representation of the vulva, a symbol used in the worship of the goddess Shakti in Hiduism.

Yuefu Chinese folk ballads that, during the Han dynasty, evolved into literary ballads written in quatrains of five-word lines. The ballad typically presented a monologue of dialogue presenting, in dramatic form, some misfortune.

Yugen From the Japanese meaning mystery or profound beauty, *yugen* refers to the aura of spiritual depth and beauty that is the aim of *Nō* drama.

Zajal One of two poetic forms that came to dominate the performance of the GHAZAL, or love poem, which consisted of elaborately rhymed strophes or stanzas in MOZARABIC, without the KHARJA ending.

Zen prominent school of Buddhism that seeks to reveal the essence of the enlightened mind. Zen teaches that everyone has the potential to attain enlightenment but that most are unaware of this potential because they are ignorant. The way to attain enlightenment is through transcending the boundaries of common thought, and the method of study is most frequently the intense, personal instruction of a student by a Zen master.

Zhong Guo The translation of the Chinese characters for "Middle Kingdom," which denotes what today is translated as China.

Ziggurat A temple tower of the ancient Akkadians and Babylonians in the form of a terraced pyramid with each story smaller than the one below it.

Zoroastrianism A dualistic religion founded in ancient Persia by Zoroaster (c. 12th century–7th century B.C.E.). It teaches that two powerful forces—light and darkness, good and evil—are engaged in a struggle that will eventually erupt into a cataclysmic war in which good will prevail, leading to the destruction of the earth.

Zuihitsu Japanese for "following the brush" and translated as "occasional writing" or "essays," *zuihitsu* denotes a genre of Japanese writing mixing poetry and prose that arose primarily among women writers during the Heian Period. Sei Shonagon's *Pillow Book* is an example of *zuihitsu*.

Acknowledgments (continued from p. iv)

Anonymous, "The First Contact of the Crusaders and the Turks" from *The Portable Medieval Reader,* by James Bruce Ross and Mary Martin McLaughlin. Copyright © 1949 by Viking Penguin, Inc., renewed © 1976 by James Bruce Ross and Mary Martin McLaughlin. Reprinted with the permission of Viking Penguin, a division of Penguin Putnam Inc.

Anonymous, 412 ["Hauntingly They Cry/the Northbound Geese"], and 645 ["Did You Come to Me/Or Did I Go to You"] from *Kokinshu: A Collection of Poems Ancient and Modern,* translated and annotated by Laurel Rasplica Rodd with Mary Catherine Henkenius (Princeton: Princeton University Press, 1984). Reprinted Boston, MA: Cheng & Tsui, 1996. Reprinted with the permission of Laurel Rasplica Rodd.

Ariwara no Narihira, 644 ["How Fleeting the Dream/of the Night We Two"], 646 ["I Am Lost in the/Total Darkness of My Heart"], and 861 ["Composed When He Was Ill and Weak"] from *Kokinshu: A Collection of Poems Ancient and Modern,* translated and annotated by Laurel Rasplica Rodd with Mary Catherine Henkenius (Princeton: Princeton University Press, 1984). Reprinted Boston, MA: Cheng & Tsui, 1996. Reprinted with the permission of Laurel Rasplica Rodd.

Faridoddin Attar, "The Story of Sheikh Sam'an" from *The Conference of the Birds,* translated by Afkham Darbandi and Dick Davis. Copyright © 1984 by Afkham Darbandi and Dick Davis. Reprinted with the permission of Penguin Books, Ltd.

St. Augustine, excerpts from *The Confessions of St. Augustine,* edited by John K. Ryan. Copyright © 1960 by Doubleday, a division of Bantam Doubleday Dell Publishing Group, Inc. Reprinted with the permission of the publisher.

Ibn Battuta, "Jerusalem: The Mosque and the Dome of the Rock," "Mecca: The Great Mosque and the Ka'ba," and "Constantinople: The Aya Sufiya (Hagia Sophia)" from *The Travels of Ibn Battuta,* translated by H. A. R. Gibb, revised by C. Defrémery and B. R. Sanguinetti (London: Hakluyt Society, 1958). Reprinted with the permission of David Higham Associates, Ltd.

Beowulf, revised edition, translated by Michael Swanton. Copyright © 1997 by Michael Swanton. Reprinted with the permission of Manchester University Press, Manchester, UK.

Conon de Béthune, "Alas, love, what hard leave / I must take," translated by Frederick Goldin, from *The Lyrics of the Troubadour and Trouveres,* translated by Frederick Goldin. Copyright © 1973 by Frederick Goldin. Reprinted with the permission of Doubleday, a division of Random House, Inc.

Bible, excerpts from the New Testament, translated by Edgar Goodspeed. Reprinted with the permission of The University of Chicago Press.

Giovanni Boccaccio, "The First Day," "The Third Day, Tenth Tale," "The Fourth Day, First Tale," and "Conclusion" from *The Decameron,* translated by Richard Aldington. Copyright 1930 by Richard Aldington. Reprinted with the permission of Rosica Colin, Ltd.

Bo Juyi, "Passing T'ien-mén Street in Ch'ang-an and Seeing a Distant View of Chung-nan Mountains" and "Madly Singing in the Mountains," translated by Arthur Waley, from *170 Chinese Poems* (New York: Alfred A. Knopf, 1919). "Watching the Reapers," translated by Arthur Waley, from *Chinese Poems* (London: Allen & Unwin, 1946). All reprinted with the permission of the Estate of Arthur Waley. "An Old Charcoal Seller," "Buying Flowers," "Winter Night," "On the Boat, Reading Yüan Chen's Poems," "Idle Song," and "Autumn Pool," translated by David Hinton, from *The Selected Poems of Po Chü-I.* Copyright © 1999 by David Hinton. Reprinted with the permission of New Directions Publishing Corporation.

Andreas Capellanus, "Book I: Introduction to the Treatise on Love" and "Book II: How Love May Be Retained" from *The Art of Courtly Love,* translated by John J. Parry. Copyright 1941 by John J. Parry. Reprinted with the permission of Columbia University Press.

Giovanni da Pian di Carpine, "Embassy to the Guyuk, the Great Khan," and "Letter of the Great Khan Guyuk to Pope Innocent IV" from "History of the Mongols," from *The Mongol Mission: Narratives and Letters of Franciscan Missionaries in Mongolia and China in the Thirteenth and Fourteenth Centuries,* translated by a Nun of Stanbrook Abbey. Copyright © 1955. Reprinted with the permission of Continuum.

Castelloza, "My friend, if I found you welcoming," translated by Peter Dronke, from *Medieval Women Writers,* edited by Katharina M. Wilson. Copyright © 1984 by The University of Georgia Press. Reprinted with the permission of the publishers.

Maturai Eruttalan Centamputan, 25 [Kapilar, "What She Said"], 68 [Allur Nanmullai, "What She Said"], 131 [Orerulavanar, "What He Said"], and 325 [Nannakaiyar, "What She Said"] from "Kuruntokai"; from "Akananuru"; 60 [Kakkaipatiniyar Naccellaiyar, "A King's Double Nature"] from "Patirruppattu"; 74 [Ceraman Kanaikkai Irumporal, "A King's Last Words"], 86 [Kavarpentu, "Mothers"], 87 [Auvaiyar, "A Chariot Wheel"], 109 [Kapilar, "His Hill"], 255 [Vanparanar, "A Woman and Her Dying Warrior"], 271 [Veripatiya Kamakkanniyar, "A Leaf in Love and War"], and 278 [Kakkaipatiniyar Nacellaiyar, "Mothers"], translated by A. K. Ramanujan, from *The*

Interior Landscape: Love Poems from a Classical Tamil Anthology (Bloomington: Indiana University Press, 1967). Copyright © 1967 by A. K. Ramanujan. Reprinted with the permission of Molly A. Daniels-Ramanujan.

Geoffrey Chaucer, excerpt from "General Prologue"; "Prologue to the Wife of Bath's Tale," and "The Wife of Bath's Tale" from *The Canterbury Tales, Revised Edition,* translated by Theodore Morrison. Copyright 1949, renewed © 1977 by Theodore Morrison. Reprinted with the permission of Viking Penguin, a division of Penguin Putnam Inc.

Anna Comnena, excerpts from *The Alexiad of Anna Comnena,* translated by E. R. A. Sewter. Copyright © 1969 by the Estate of E. R. A. Sewter. Reprinted with the permission of Penguin Books, Ltd.

Countess of Dia, "I've lately been in great distress" and "Of things I'd rather keep in silence I must sing" from *The Woman Troubadours,* translated by Magda Bogin (London: Paddington, 1976). Reprinted with the permission of the translator.

Baha ad-Din, excerpts from "A Life of Saladin," from *Arab Historians of the Crusades,* selected and translated from the Arabic by Francesco Gabrieli, translated from the Italian by E. J. Costello. Copyright © 1957 by Giulio Einaudi Editore S.p.A., Turin. Copyright © 1969 by Routledge & Kegan Paul Limited. Reprinted with the permission of the University of California Press.

Du Fu, "Restless Night," translated by Burton Watson, from *Classical Chinese Literature,* edited by John Minford and Joseph S. M. Lau. Copyright © 2000 by Columbia University Press. Reprinted with the permission of the publisher. "To Li Po on a Winter Day," translated by Sam Hamill from *Crossing the Yellow River: Three Hundred Poems from the Chinese.* Copyright © 2000 by Sam Hamill. Reprinted with the permission of BOA Editions, Ltd., Rochester, New York. "P'eng-ya Song," "Moonlit Night," "Dreaming of Li Po," "Spring Night, Delighted by Rain," and "Thoughts, Traveling at Night," translated by David Hinton, from *The Selected Poems of Tu Fu.* Copyright © 1988, 1989 by David Hinton. Reprinted with the permission of New Directions Publishing Corporation.

Egeria, "Mt. Sinai" from *Egeria's Travels, Revised Edition,* translated by John Wilkinson. Copyright © 1971, 1999. Reprinted with the permission of Aris & Phillips, Ltd.

Einhard, *A Life of Charlemagne* (excerpts), from *Einhard and Notker the Stammerer: Two Lives of Charlemagne,* translated by Lewis Thorpe. Copyright © 1969 by Lewis Thorpe. Reprinted with the permission of Penguin Books, Ltd.

Ibn Faraj, "Chastity," translated by Cola Franzen, from *Poems from Arab Andalusia.* Copyright © 1989 by Cola Franzen. Reprinted with the permission of City Lights Books.

Abu al-Qasem Ferdowsi, "The First Battle," "The Interval," "The Second Day," "The Death of Sohrab," "Rostam Asks Kay Kavus for the Nushdaru," "Rostam Mourns Sohrab," and "Rostam Conveys His Son to Zabolestan" from "The Tragedy of Sohrab and Rostam," translated by Jerome W. Clinton, from *Shahnama: The Tragedy of Sohrab and Rostam,* translated by Jerome W. Clinton. Copyright © 1987 by The University of Washington Press. Reprinted with the permission of the publishers.

Marie de France, "The Lay of the Chevrefoil (The Honeysuckle)," translated by Robert Hanning and Joan Ferrante, from *The Lais of Marie de France.* Copyright © 1978 by Robert Hanning and Joan Ferrante. Reprinted with the permission of Labyrinth Press, a division of Baker Book House Company.

Frederick Goldin (trans.), excerpts from *The Song of Roland.* Copyright © 1978 by W. W. Norton & Company, Inc. Reprinted with the permission of the publishers.

Husain Haddaway (trans.), "Foreword," "Prologue: The Tale of King Shahrayar and Shahrazad, His Vizier's Daughter," "The Tale of the Ox and the Donkey," "The Tale of the Merchant and His Wife," "The Story of the Merchant and the Demon," "The First Old Man's Tale," and "The Second Old Man's Tale" from *The Thousand and One Nights.* Copyright © 1990 by Hussain Haddawy. Reprinted with the permission of W. W. Norton & Company, Inc.

Ibn al-Athir, excerpt from "The Franks Seize Antioch," from *Arab Historians of the Crusades,* selected and translated from the Arabic by Francesco Gabrieli, translated from the Italian by E. J. Costello. Copyright © 1957 by Giulio Einaudi Editore S.p.A., Turin. Copyright © 1969 by Routledge & Kegan Paul Limited. Reprinted with the permission of the University of California Press.

Lady Ise, 43 ["Plum Tree Blossoming Near a Stream"] and 791 ["Written When She Saw the Fires in the Fields . . ."] from *Kokinshu: A Collection of Poems Ancient and Modern,* translated and annotated by Laurel Rasplica Rodd with Mary Catherine Henkenius (Princeton: Princeton University Press, 1984). Reprinted Boston, MA: Cheng & Tsui, 1996. Reprinted with the permission of Laurel Rasplica Rodd.

Muhammad Ibn Ishaq, excerpts from *The Life of Muhammad: A Translation of Ishaq's Sirat Rasul Allah,* translated by Alfred Guillaume (Oxford: Oxford University Press, 1955). Copyright © 1955 by Alfred Guillaume. Reprinted with the permission of the estate of Alfred Guillaume.

Joan of Arc, excerpts from *Joan of Arc by Herself and Her Witnesses* by Regine Pernoud, translated by Edward

Hyams. Copyright © 1996. Reprinted with the permission of Scarborough House.

Ibn Jubayr, "The Great Mosque and the Ka'ba at Mecca" from *The Travels of Ibn Jubayr*, translated by R. J. C. Broadhurst. Reprinted with the permission of Jonathan Cape/Random House Group, Ltd.

Kakinomoto Hitomaro, "When He Passed the Ruined Capital at Ōmi," "At the Time of the Temporary Enshrinement of Prince Takechi at Kinoe," "When He Parted from His Wife in the Land of Iwami: I," "On the Death of His Wife: I and II," "Upon Seeing a Dead Man Lying among the Rocks on the Island of Samine in Sanuki," and "Written in His Own Sorrow as He Was about to Die in Iwami," translated by Ian Hideo Levy from *Ten Thousand Leaves: A Translation of the Man, Yoshu, Japan's Premier Anthology of Classical Poetry*. Copyright © 1980 by Princeton University Press. Reprinted with the permission of the publishers.

Kalidasa, "Shakuntala and the Ring of Recollection," from *Theater of Memory: The Plays of Kalidasa*, translated by Barbara Stoler Miller. Copyright © 1984 by Barbara Stoler Miller. Reprinted with the permission of Columbia University Press.

Margery Kempe, excerpts from *The Book of Margery Kempe*, translated by W. Butler-Bowdon. Copyright 1944 by Devin-Adair, Publishers, Inc., Old Greenwich, CT, 06870. Reprinted with the permission of the publishers.

Chingis Khan, excerpts from *The Secret History of the Mongols: The Origin of Chingis Khan, Expanded Edition* by Paul Kahn, based primarily on the English translation by Frances Woodman Cleaves (Boston: Cheng & Tsui, 1988). Copyright © 1984, 1988 by Paul Kahn. Reprinted with the permission of the Cheng & Tsui Company and the Harvard-Yenching Institute.

Ki no Tsurayuki, 2 ["Written on the First Day of Spring"], 84 ["Falling Cherry Blossoms"], 162 ["Hearing a Nightingale Singing in the Mountains"], 297 ["On Going to Pick Autumn Leaves at Kitayama"], 381 ["Parting from Someone"], 565 ["Like the jewel-weeds / swaying in the depths"], 804 ["Like the cries / of the first wild geese"], and 842 ["Composed on the Way to a Mountain Temple"] from *Kokinshu: A Collection of Poems Ancient and Modern*, translated and annotated by Laurel Rasplica Rodd with Mary Catherine Henkenius (Princeton: Princeton University Press, 1984). Reprinted Boston, MA: Cheng & Tsui, 1996. Reprinted with the permission of Laurel Rasplica Rodd.

The Koran, excerpts from *The Koran, Fifth Edition*, translated by N. J. Dawood. Copyright © 1956, 1959, 1966, 1968, 1974, 1990 by N. J. Dawood. Reprinted with the permission of Penguin Books, Ltd.

Ibn al-Labbana, "He who has charged the eyes," translated by Linda Fish Compton, from *Andalusian Lyrical Poetry and Old Spanish Love Songs: The Muwashshah and its Kharja*. Reprinted with the permission of New York University Press.

Li Bai, "Going to Visit Tai-T'ien Mountain's Master of the Way without Finding Him," "Ch'ang-kan Village Song," "Drinking Alone beneath the Moon," "Teasing Tu Fu," and "Drinking in the Mountains with a Recluse," translated by David Hinton, from *The Selected Poems of Li Po*. Copyright © 1996 by David Hinton. Reprinted with the permission of New Directions Publishing Corporation. "Searching for Master Yung" and "Seeing Off a Friend" from *Chinese Poetic Writing With an Anthology of Tang Poetry*, edited by François Cheng, translated from the French by Donald A. Riggs and Jerome P. Seaton (Bloomington: Indiana University Press, 1975). Copyright © 1977 by Editions du Seuil. English translation copyright © 1982 by Indiana University Press. Reprinted with the permission of Jerome P. Seaton. "Sent to My Two Little Children in the East of Lu" from *The Columbia Book of Chinese Poetry: From Early Times to the Thirteenth-Century*, translated by Burton Watson. Copyright © 1984 by Columbia University Press. Reprinted with the permission of the publisher.

Judah Ha-Levi, "The Apple," translated by David Goldstein, from *The Jewish Poets of Spain* (London: Penguin, 1965). Copyright © 1965 by David Goldstein. Reprinted with the permission of David Higham Associates, Ltd.

Ibn Hazm, "My Beloved Comes," translated by Cola Franzen, from *Poems from Arab Andalusia*. Copyright © 1989 by Cola Franzen. Reprinted with the permission of City Lights Books.

Sir John Mandeville, excerpts from *The Travels of Sir John Mandeville*, translated by C. W. R. D. Moseley. Copyright © 1983 by C. W. R. D. Moseley. Reprinted with the permission of Penguin Books, Ltd.

Marcabru, "By the fountain in the orchard," translated by Frederick Goldin from *The Lyrics of the Troubadour and Trouveres*, translated by Frederick Goldin. Copyright © 1973 by Frederick Goldin. Reprinted with the permission of Doubleday, a division of Random House, Inc.

E. Powys Mathers (trans.), "Conclusion" from *The Book of the Thousand Nights and One Night*. Reprinted with the permission of Routledge and Kegan Paul.

Helen Craig McCullough (trans.), excerpt from "Gion Shoja," excerpt from "The Sea Bass," and "Gio" from Chapter One; "The Death of Kiyomori" from Chapter Six; "Tadanori's Flight from the Capital" from Chapter Seven; "The Death of Atsumori" from Chapter Nine; and "The Initiates' Chapter" from *The Tale of the Heike*. Copyright © 1988 by Helen Craig

McCullough. Reprinted with the permission of Stanford University Press.

Usamah Ibn Munqidh, excerpt from "The Book of Reflections," translated by Philip K. Hitti, from *An Arab-Syrian Gentleman and Warrior in the Period of the Crusades.* Copyright 1929, © 2000 by Columbia University Press. Reprinted with the permission of the publishers.

Ono no Komachi, 113 ["The colors of the blossoms / have faded"], 552 ["In love-tormented sleep / I saw him"], 553 ["Since that brief sleep when / first I saw"], 554 ["When my yearning grows / unendurable"], 635 ["This autumn night was / long in name only"], 658 ["Though my feet never / cease running to him"], 797 ["That which fades within"], 822 ["Lonely ears of grain / lie scattered on the field"], 938 ["I have sunk to the / bottom"], and 1030 ["No moon lights the night"] from *Kokinshu: A Collection of Poems Ancient and Modern,* translated and annotated by Laurel Rasplica Rodd with Mary Catherine Henkenius (Princeton: Princeton University Press, 1984). Reprinted Boston, MA: Cheng & Tsui, 1996. Reprinted with the permission of Laurel Rasplica Rodd.

Oshikochi no Mitsune, 304 ["On Seeing the Autumn Leaves Falling Near a Pond"] from *Kokinshu: A Collection of Poems Ancient and Modern,* translated and annotated by Laurel Rasplica Rodd with Mary Catherine Henkenius (Princeton: Princeton University Press, 1984). Reprinted Boston, MA: Cheng & Tsui, 1996. Reprinted with the permission of Laurel Rasplica Rodd.

Otomo Yakamochi, "Lament Addressed to His Son-in-Law, Fujiwara Nakachiko," translated by Robert H. Brower and Earl Miner, from *Japanese Court Poetry.* Copyright © 1961 by the Board of Trustees of the Leland Stanford Junior University. Reprinted with the permission of Stanford University Press.

Raimbaut d'Orange, "Listen, lords . . . but I don't know what," translated by Frederick Goldin. Reprinted by permission.

Marco Polo, "Kublai Khan's Palace at Shandu," and "The Generosity of the Great Khan" from *The Travels of Marco Polo,* translated by Ronald Latham. Copyright © 1958 by Ronald Latham. Reprinted with the permission of Penguin Books, Ltd.

Imru' al-Quays, "The Mu'allaqah of Imru' al-Qays," translated by Suzanne Pinckney Stetkevych, from "Structuralist Analyses of Pre-Islamic Poetry: Critique and New Directions" from *Journal of Near Eastern Studies* 42, no. 2 (1983): 85–107. Copyright © 1983 by The University of Chicago. Reprinted with the permission of the translator and The University of Chicago Press.

Ibn Quzman, "I am madly in love," translated by James T.

Monroe, from *Hispano-Arabic Poetry.* Copyright © 1974 by The Regents of the University of California. Reprinted with the permission of the University of California Press.

Jalaloddin Rumi, "A Basket of Fresh Bread," "The Gift of Water," "I Come Before Dawn," "Checkmate," "When you are with everyone but me," "The Food Sack," "The Gift of Water," and "Only Breath" from *The Essential Rumi,* translated by Coleman Barks. Reprinted with the permission of the translator.

Murasaki Shikibu, Chapters 2, 4, and 25 from *The Tale of the Genji,* translated by Edward Seidensticker. Copyright © 1976 by Edward G. Seidensticker. Reprinted with the permission of Alfred A. Knopf, a division of Random House, Inc.

Sei Shonagon, excerpts from *The Pillow Book of Sei Shonagon,* translated by Ivan Morris. Copyright © 1967 by Ivan Morris. Reprinted with the permission of Columbia University Press.

T'ao Ch'ien, "Back Home Again Chant," "Home Again Among Gardens and Fields (Part 1)," "Reading the *Classic of Mountains and Seas*," and "Elegy for Myself," translated by David Hinton, from *The Selected Poems of Tao Ch'ien.* Copyright © 1993 by David Hinton. Reprinted with the permission of Copper Canyon Press, P.O. Box 271, Port Townsend, WA 98368-0271. "The Gentlemen of the Five Willow Trees," "Substance, Shadow and Spirit," excerpt from "A Reply to Secretary Kuo," "In the Sixth Month of 408, Fire," translated by James Robert Hightower, from *The Selected Poems of Tao Ch'ien* (Oxford: Clarendon Press, 1970). Reprinted with the permission of Oxford University Press, Ltd.

Bernart de Ventadorn, "My heart is so full of joy," translated by Frederick Goldin from *The Lyrics of the Troubadour and Trouveres,* translated by Frederick Goldin. Copyright © 1973 by Frederick Goldin. Reprinted with the permission of Doubleday, a division of Random House, Inc.

Wallada, "To Ibn Zaydun," translated by James T. Monroe and Deirdre Lashgari from *Lyrics of the Middle Ages,* edited by James J. Wilhelm (New York: Garland, 1990). Originally published in *Woman Poets of the World,* edited by Johanna Bankier, Deirdre Lashgari, and Doris Earnshaw (New York: Macmillan, 1983), page 98. Reprinted by permission.

Wang Wei, "To Subprefect Chang" and "Seeing Someone Off," translated by Irving Y. Lo, from from *Sunflower Splendor: Three Thousand Years of Chinese Poetry,* edited by Wu-chi Liu and Irving Yucheng Lo (Bloomington: Indiana University Press, 1975, 1983, 1990 with an updated bibliography), page 96. Reprinted with the permission of the translator. "Bamboo Mile Lodge," translated by Burton Watson, from *The Wang River*

Collection from *The Columbia Book of Chinese Poetry: From Early Times to the Thirteenth Century.* Copyright © 1984 by Columbia University Press. Reprinted with the permission of the publishers. "Huatzu Hill," translated by G. W. Robinson, from *The Wang River Collection,* from *Poems of Wang Wei,* translated by G. W. Robinson (Harmondsworth: Penguin, 1973). Copyright © 1973 by G. W. Robinson. Originally published in *Art & Literature.* Reprinted with permission. "Deer Park," "At Lake Yi," "Hermitage at Chung-nan Mountain," and "Crossing the Yellow River," translated by Sam Hamill from *Crossing the Yellow River: Three Hundred Poems from the Chinese.* Copyright © 2000 by Sam Hamill. Reprinted with the permission of BOA Editions, Ltd., Rochester, New York.

William of Aquitaine, "My companions, I am going to make a *vers* that is refined" and "Now when we see the meadows once again," translated by Frederick Goldin. Reprinted by permission.

Yamanoue no Okura, "A Lament on the Evanescence of Life," "Dialogue Between Poverty and Destitution," and "Longing for His Son Furuhi," translated by Steven D. Carter, from *Traditional Japanese Poetry.* Copyright © 1991 by the Board of Trustees of the Leland Stanford Junior University. Reprinted with the permission of Stanford University Press.

Ibn Zaydun, see p. 1215, "Written from Al-Zahra," translated by Cola Franzen, from *Poems from Arab Andalusia.* Copyright © 1989 by Cola Franzen. Reprinted with the permission of City Lights Books.

Zeami Motokiyo, "Atsumori," translated by Arthur Waley, from *The Nō Plays of Japan* (New York: Dover Publications, 1998). Reprinted with the permission of the Estate of Arthur Waley.

INDEX